# The Fifth Fighter Command in World War II
## Vol. 2

# The Fifth Fighter Command in World War II

## Volume II: The End in New Guinea, the Philippines, to V-J Day

William Wolf

**Schiffer Military History**
Atglen, PA

# Dedication

To the brave, unheralded men of the Fifth Fighter Command who gave up their youth and often their lives to win the relentless air war over New Guinea and the Philippines.

Book Design by Ian Robertson and Stephanie Daugherty.


Library of Congress Control Number: 2011937278



Printed in China.
ISBN: 978-0-7643-4251-6

We are interested in hearing from authors with book ideas on related topics.

Published by Schiffer Publishing Ltd.
4880 Lower Valley Road
Atglen, PA 19310
Phone: (610) 593-1777
FAX: (610) 593-2002
E-mail: Info@schifferbooks.com.
Visit our web site at: www.schifferbooks.com
Please write for a free catalog.
This book may be purchased from the publisher.
Try your bookstore first.

In Europe, Schiffer books are distributed by:
Bushwood Books
6 Marksbury Avenue
Kew Gardens
Surrey TW9 4JF, England
Phone: 44 (0) 20 8392-8585
FAX: 44 (0) 20 8392-9876
E-mail: Info@bushwoodbooks.co.uk.
Visit our website at: www.bushwoodbooks.co.uk
Try your bookstore first.

# Contents

# Preface

While authoring 12 WWII aviation books, I have come to admire Roger Freeman's gargantuan efforts in memorializing the "Mighty Eighth" Air Force in several definitive volumes. Over the years the Pacific air war has been largely overlooked as compared to the extensive number of works on the European air war. The Fifth Fighter and Bomber Command was as instrumental in winning the war in the Pacific skies as was the Eighth Fighter and Bomber Command over Europe; perhaps more so. After the defeats in the Philippines, the East Indies, and New Guinea in early to mid-1942 due to the lack of air superiority, MacArthur and Kenney realized that gaining air superiority, while not eliminating the use of ground troops to win the victory, was the key to winning the war in the SWPA. MacArthur's infantry, without the exposure to enemy air intervention, was able to secure advanced airbases from which Kenney's fighters and bombers could extend the bomb line to attack distant enemy airbases and destroy enemy aircraft in the air, and more importantly on the ground. The westward leapfrogging infantry operations along the northern New Guinea coast and on to the Philippines were predicated on gaining air superiority, and would not have been possible without it. I have previously written a comprehensive account of the 13th Fighter Command in the Pacific (*13th Fighter Command in World War II: Air Combat over Guadalcanal and the Solomons*, Schiffer, 2004), and now, after 65 years of neglect of the subject by others, I have had the time, inclination, and resources to offer the first comprehensive and definitive account of the Fifth Fighter Command and its predecessors and successors from 8 December 1941 until VJ-Day.

# Acknowledgments

My lifelong hobby has been WWII aerial combat, and over the past 40 years I have collected over 20,000 books and magazines, along with hundreds of reels of microfilm on the subject. I probably have nearly every book written on WWII aviation and complete collections of every combat aviation magazine published since 1939. Also included in my collection are hundreds of aviation unit histories; intelligence reports; pilot, crew, flight, and training manuals; and technical, structural, and maintenance manuals for aircraft ordnance, armament, engines, and equipment. My microfilm collection includes vintage intelligence reports; hundreds of USAF, USN, and USMC group and squadron histories; After Combat Reports (ACRs), Narrative Combat Reports (NCRs), and Individual Combat Reports (ICRs); complete Japanese Monograph series; and complete U.S. Strategic Bombing Surveys, as well as complete USAF Historical Studies. The author wishes to thank the hundreds of persons, museums, and libraries that contributed photos and materials to my collection during the past 40 years.

Thanks go to cover and profile illustrator Steve Ferguson, who has done the outstanding covers and profiles for my other books and continues his superb artistry on these volumes. Steve has become a friend over the years, and has been a pleasure to work with and to spend time talking about our passion of WWII aircraft and pilots. My appreciation also goes to my editor, Ian Robertson, who is responsible for the integration of the 100s of photos, drawings, and maps into the rather lengthy texts of my 12 books published by Schiffer. I would also like to thank meticulous researcher Dr. Frank Olynyk for compiling his invaluable *USAF (Pacific Theater) Credits for the Destruction of Enemy Aircraft in Air-to-Air Combat*, which I kept at my fingertips to check names, ranks, and dates.

Again, my thanks go to my persevering wife, Nancy, who allows me to spend many hours researching and writing, and patiently (mostly) waits while I browse bookstores and visit air museums in search of new material and photos. Also, I thank her because her car sits out in the hot Arizona sun as my library luxuriates in the remodeled, air-conditioned three-car garage.

The author in his study with Dick Bong and Eddie Rickenbacker autographs in the middle of photo and a piece of the Yamamoto bomber with autographs of the 339FS participants in the background behind his head.

# Foreword

Over the past several years I have met with Bill Wolf at various local American Fighter Aces Association and Confederate Air Force meetings. I also have visited his home library and den, where he talked about writing a history of the Fifth Fighter Command. At the time he had finished a history of the 13th Fighter Command, which was very well done. In our talks I told him that a history of the Fifth Air Force Fighter Command was really needed, as we had been forgotten over the years. Besides Dick Bong and Tom McGuire no one knows anything about us. I also warned him that it would be a big job, but to go at it. I wished him luck on the project and looked forward to seeing it in print.

86 year old Joe Forster visiting the author's library in 2005 (holding a McGuire nose art facsimile). 25 year old 1Lt. Joe Forster was a 9 victory World War II Ace.

(Author's note: Joe wrote this rough draft Foreword in 2005, but in the meantime I became side tracked with my Bomber and U.S. Aerial Armament in WWII "Ultimate Look" books. Over the past several years Joe has had health problems and was unable to expand on the above Foreword, which I found in my notes along with his photo taken while visiting my home.)

# Introduction

As I described in my Introduction to Volume 1, during my research on the history of the Fifth Fighter Command I used the usual bibliographic sources (books and magazines), but also utilized several singular sources that were invaluable and were described there to give the reader an appreciation as to the scope of my research. Among these unique sources were hundreds of RAAF Attack Reports (Form C.F.), thousands of Narrative Combat Reports (NCR), and nearly 10,000 Individual Combat Reports (ICR). Each of these reports was read on microfilm converted to CDs. The microfilm frames of these reports varied greatly in quality depending if it were a WWII original or a second or third carbon copy, and I often had to read them using a large magnifying glass while looking at the microfilm reader screen. I found a much easier method was to read the microfilm was to view them on CDs, as each frame is shown on a computer screen and can be magnified to show two or three sentences, which makes distinguishing e's and c's that look like o's etc. and also save the reader's eyesight. I read and organized each Form C.F., NCR and ICR for each mission which often concerned one or more Groups, comprised of a number of Squadrons for each Group with one to four or more Flights of four to 20 pilots flying in swirling and confused air battles.

Over the years I have been fortunate to meet many fighter aces, other pilots, and fellow aviation buffs who have shared stories, material, and photographs with me (I have over 5,000 photos of fighter aces alone). Over the years, before digital cameras and PhotoShop®, I made many multi-day expeditions to various military libraries, museums, and photo depositories with my copy machine, film camera and copy stand accumulating literally reams of information and 1,000s of photographs. The photos credited to the American Fighter Aces Association (AFAA) were mostly collected during 1985-88 when I researched WW-2 aces as a co-editor of the American Fighter Aces Association Album (which was finally published in 1996). During this time I was fortunate to be able to meet with or corresponded with 100's of aces, and copied 1,000s of photos from their personal albums and those in the extensive AFAA archives. At one time I had a photo darkroom where I developed 1,000s of rare photos from microfilm negatives. Also, many photos were copied from contemporary magazines and publications, and because of their age many were deteriorating and discolored and have been scanned to improve their quality. Many photos were taken from wartime group photos to obtain an individual pilot photo and were grainy, but because these photos were the only ones available of the individual pilot they were used, nonetheless, because they were the only photo(s) available of a pilot or ace mentioned in the text and will probably never see publication again. Over the years the origin of many of the 1,000s of photos I have been lent to copy or have copied and collected personally have become obscured. Most are from military and government sources, but many are from private individuals and I apologize in advance as most are uncredited and should be considered as part of the author's collection.

# Japanese Aircraft Code Designations

In order for the reader to differentiate the numerous Japanese aircraft encountered in the text I have again, as in Volume I, included a table of the Allied code names for Japanese aircraft in service with the Japanese Navy (JNAF: Japanese Naval Air Force) or the Army (JAAF: Japanese Army Air Force), manufacturer, Japanese designation, and a brief description.

In summer 1942, Australian Air Commodore J.E. Hewitt, Allied Director or Air Intelligence (SWPA) assigned U.S. Army officer Capt. Frank McCoy of the Technical Air Intelligence Unit (TAIU) to devise a system of nomenclature to help identify the expanding number of Japanese aircraft for intelligence and communication purposes (question: was A6M2 or Ki-32 any more difficult than Me 109 or FW 190?). The basic guideline for naming was:

1) Fighters and reconnaissance seaplanes were given men's Christian names or first names (Zeke, Tony)

2) Bombers, dive bombers, torpedo bombers, flying boats, and reconnaissance aircraft other than seaplanes received women's Christian names or first names (Betty, Kate)

3) Transport aircraft were given girls' names beginning with T (Tess, Tabby)

4) The names of trees were used for trainers (Willow, Oak)

5) Gliders were named after birds (Gander, Buzzard)

| Code Name | Service | Manufac-turer | Designation Type | Description |
|---|---|---|---|---|
| Ann | Army | Mitsubishi | Ki-30 Type 97 | 2 place SE light bomber |
| Betty | Navy | Mitsubishi | G4M | 7 place TE bomber |
| Claude | Navy | Mitsubishi | A5M Type 96 | 1 place SE carrier fighter |
| Dinah | Army | Mitsubishi | Ki-46 | 2 place TE night/recon fighter |
| Emily | Navy | Kawanishi | H8K | 9 place TE recon flying boat |
| Frances | Navy | Kugisho | P1Y | 2-3 place TE bomber/night |
| Frank | Army | Nakajima | Ki-84 Type 4 | 1 place SE fighter/FB |
| George | Navy | Kawanishi | N1K2-J | 1 place SE fighter |
| Grace | Navy | Aichi | B7A | 2 place carrier torpedo/DB |
| Helen | Army | Nakajima | Ki-49 | 8 place TE heavy bomber |
| Irving | Navy | Nakajima | J1N1 | 2-3 place SE recon/night |
| Jack | Navy | Mitsubishi | J2M3 | 1 place SE fighter (land) |
| Jake | Navy | Aichi | E13A | 2 place SE float recon |
| Jill | Navy | Nakajima | B6N | 2 place SE carrier bomber |
| Kate | Navy | Nakajima | B5N | 3 place SE carrier bomber |
| Lily | Army | Kawasaki | Ki-48 Type 99 | 4 place TE light bomber |
| Nate | Army | Nakajima | Ki-27 Type 97 | 1 place SE fighter/FB |

| Code Name | Service | Manufac-turer | Designation Type | Description |
|---|---|---|---|---|
| Nell | Navy | Mitsubishi | G3M | 5 place TE bomber |
| Nick | Army | Kawasaki | Ki-45 Type 2 | 2 place TE FB/night fighter |
| Oscar | Army | Nakajima | Ki-43 Type 2 | 1 place SE fighter |
| Peggy | Both | Mitsubishi | Ki-67 Type 4 | 6-8 place TE bomber |
| Pete | Army | Kawasaki | Ki-10 Type 95 | 2 place SE observation |
| Rufe | Navy | Nakajima | A6M2-N Type 2 | 2 place SE float fighter |
| Sally * | Army | Mitsubishi | Ki-21 Type 97 | 5 place TE bomber |
| Sonia | Army | Mitsubishi | Ki-51 Type 97 | 2 place SE light bomber |
| Tabby | Navy | Showa | L2D | 3-5 place TE transport |
| Tess | Army | Douglas | DC-2 | 3-5 place TE transport |
| Tojo | Army | Nakajima | Ki-44 Type 2 | 1 place SE fighter |
| Tony | Army | Kawasaki | Ki-61 Type 3 | 1 place SE fighter |
| Val | Navy | Aichi | D3A Type 99 | 2 place SE carrier DB |
| Zero ** | Navy | Mitsubishi | A6M Type 0 | 1 place SE carrier fighter |

*also Jane
** also Zeke, Hap, Hamp
SE=Single Engine and TE=Twin Engine

# Part Six
## The End of the New Guinea Campaign

# 1

## November 1943

**Mid-November 1943: Situation**
The situation for the Japanese on New Guinea had become critical in the interior valleys located just beyond the coastal mountain range. Gen. Vasey's Australian troops had pushed into Dumpu in early October, and even though the Japanese were holding the high ground in their retreat, there was the presence of P-40s and A-20s now at Gusap, and even more B-24s and P-38s at Nadzab to harass the Japanese sea, land, and air forces.

American ground forces in the SWPA were organizing for *Operation Dexterity*, which would land American troops on New Britain's Cape Gloucester and at Saidor, laying midway between Finschhafen and Alexishafen. MacArthur set the invasion date for early December, but the 5AF, based on the Huon Gulf and Markham Valley, had to be reinforced before this major operation. After 11 November, the end of the Rabaul missions, the Japanese put up little local air opposition to 5AF tactical missions against their positions in the Huon Peninsula and the Nadzab area. This, along with missions being limited by poor weather, was responsible for the few American losses. The only Japanese aerial threat was their fighter force at Wewak and bombers based at Hollandia and Wakde Island. In early November, Allied air recon found that there were about 90 fighters at Wewak, but a reconnaissance on 15 November found an increase to over 100. The Japanese Army Air Forces were now in position to counter the Allied air threat with wide-ranging attacks against the airfields in the Ramu Valley.

**November 1943: Air Action during the Beginning of *Operation Dexterity***
Although the attack of 11 November was the Fifth Air Force's last strike of importance against Rabaul, the Bismarck Archipelago continued to be the principal objective of the Allied forces under the strategic direction of Gen. MacArthur. Overall plans ordered the continued air neutralization of the main Japanese bases in the Bismarcks, culminating in landings at New Britain and New Ireland by forces of both the South and Southwest Pacific. Halsey's Bougainville landing on 1 November was the initial South Pacific phase of the operations, and its early successes had split the enemy garrisons in the South Pacific and threatened the supply route from Rabaul into the upper Solomons. In the meantime, American land forces in the Southwest Pacific were preparing for *Operation Dexterity*.

*Operation Dexterity*, part of *Cartwheel*, was the decision to land in West New Britain approved on 22 September 1943. It was to be directed by MacArthur, and was to include amphibious landings in western New Britain, at Arawe on 15 December 1943 and Cape Gloucester on 26 December 1943, the capture of the Imperial Japanese held Tuluvu Airdrome on 30 December 1943, and amphibious landings at Saidor on 2 January 1944. *Dexterity* was to end on 10 February 1944.

*Operation Dexterity* was to be conducted in four separate phases:

*Operation Lazaretto*: A planned landing in southern New Britain at the plantation of Lindenhafen, approximately three miles from Gasmata, on 14 November 1943, and the neutralization of Japanese base at Gasmata to guard the eastern flank for the subsequent operation. This *Operation* was never unimplemented and was replaced by *Operation Director*. Units involved: 126th Regimental Combat Team (RCT) and elements of the 32nd Infantry Division and the Sixth Army.

*Operation Director*: A landing in southwestern New Britain at Arawe as a diversion for *Operation Backhander*. Arawe was planned as a patrol boat base. Unit involved: 112th RCT.

*Operation Backhander*: A landing in northwestern New Britain at Cape Gloucester to capture local Japanese airfields and convert them into a major Allied airbase. Units involved: 1st Marine Division.

*Operation Michaelmas*: A landing in New Guinea at Saidor to prevent the withdrawal of Japanese troops retreating in the advance of the Australian Army from Finschhafen. Units involved: 32nd Infantry Division.

**The Japanese on Cape Gloucester**
The Japanese Imperial Army Eighth Area Army High Command, directed by Gen. Hitoshi Imamura, controlled the Solomon Islands, New Guinea, and the Bismarck Islands. In early 1943, the Japanese expected that the Allies would attempt to break the inner Japanese defensive line in the Pacific and attack the bases on New Guinea, the Mariana Islands, Palau, and the Philippines. Imamura anticipated an attack on New Britain, at the latest after the Allies had occupied New Ireland, which was expected in February or March 1944.

Because of Allied air superiority, the Eighth Area Army relied solely on barge and submarine transport from Rabaul to New Guinea. In September 1943, Maj.Gen. Iwao Matsuda assumed command of the 65th Brigade and a number of troops of the 51st Division, and established his headquarters near the airfield on Cape Gloucester. On 5 October 1943 Matsuda's units came under the command of the 17th Division, which was commanded

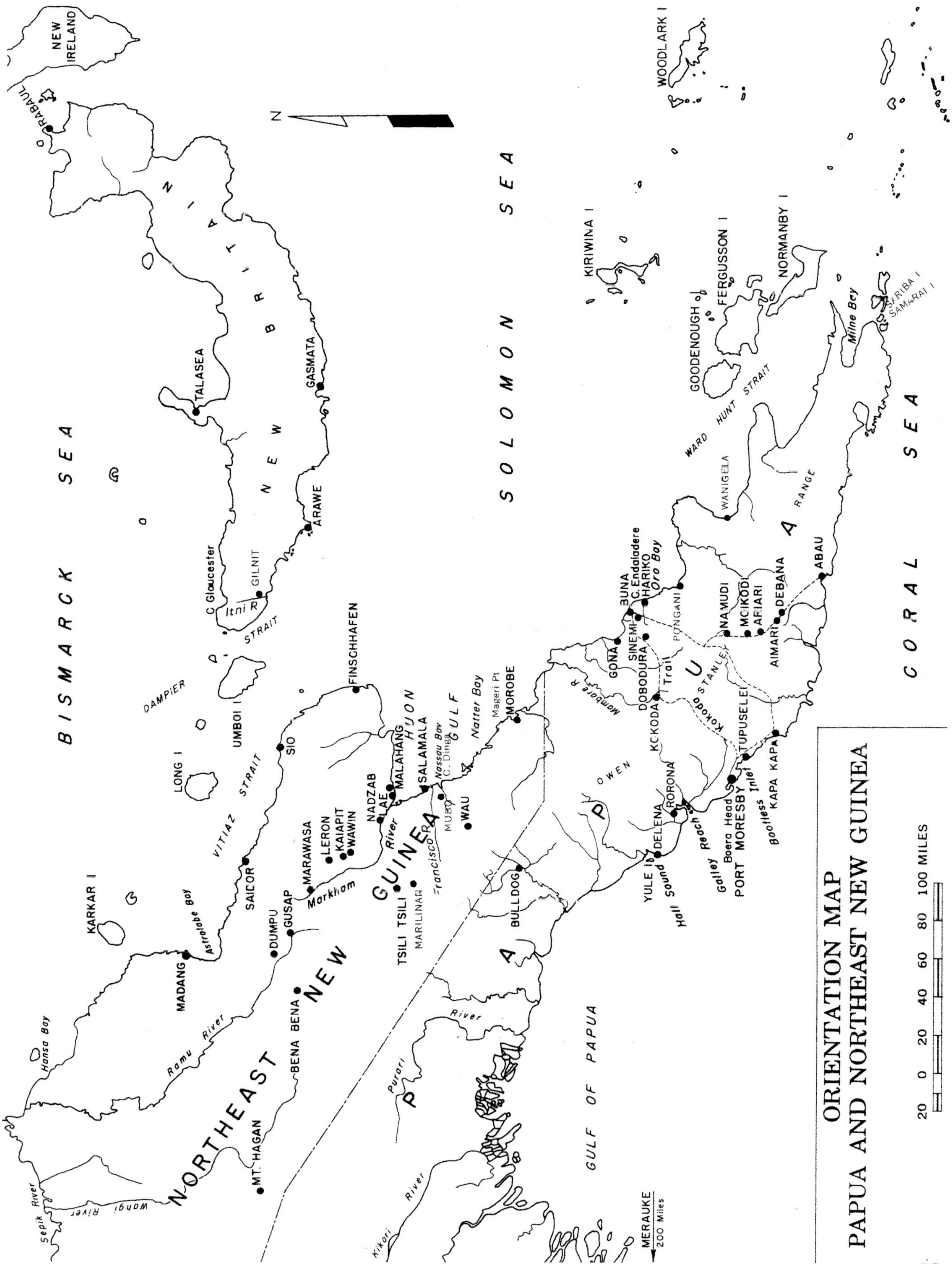
ORIENTATION MAP
PAPUA AND NORTHEAST NEW GUINEA
20 0 20 40 60 80 100 MILES
BISMARCK SEA
SOLOMON SEA
CORAL SEA
GULF OF PAPUA
NEW IRELAND
RABAUL
NEW BRITAIN
TALASEA
GASMATA
ARAWE
GILNIT
C Gloucester
Itni R
DAMPIER STRAIT
UMBOI I
LONG I
VITIAZ STRAIT
FINSCHHAFEN
SIO
SAIDOR
KARKAR I
MADANG
Astrolabe Bay
Hansa Bay
DUMPU
GUSAP
MARAWASA
LERON
KAIAPIT
WAWIN
NADZAB
LAE
MALAHANG
SALAMAUA
HUON GULF
Nassau Bay
C. Dinga
MUBO
WAU
Natter Bay
Mageri Pt
MOROBE
Markham River
Francisco R
TSILI TSILI
MARILINAN
BENA BENA
MT. HAGAN
Ramu River
Sepik River
Wahgi River
NORTHEAST NEW GUINEA
BULLDOG
PAPUA
Purari River
Kikori River
MERAUKE
200 Miles
WOODLARK I
KIRIWINA I
GOODENOUGH I
FERGUSSON I
NORMANBY I
Milne Bay
WARD HUNT STRAIT
WANIGELA
OWEN STANLEY RANGE
BUNA
C. Endaiadere
HARIKO
Oro Bay
GONA
SINEMI
DOBODURA
PONGANI
NAMUDI
MCIKODI
AFIARI
DEBANA
AIMARI
ABAU
KOKODA
Kokoda Trail
Mambare R
TUPUSELEI
KAPA KAPA
Bootless Inlet
PORT MORESBY
Boera Head
Galley Reach
RORONA
DELENA
YULE I
Hall Sound

by Lt.Gen. Yasushi Sakai, who had arrived in December 1943 from Japanese operations in China. Sakai established his HQ at Malalia, near Cape Hoskins on the East Williaumez Peninsula. Sakai immediately ordered the expansion of the defensive lines and located about half of all available Japanese troops in western New Britain in positions that could effectively defend Cape Gloucester. By mid-December 1943, the large number of Allied landing craft in New Guinea ports, the increased bombing of Rabaul and Wewak, and Allied air superiority caused the Japanese to realize that the invasion of New Britain was imminent.

**Gen. Hitoshi Imamura**. (AFHRC)

### *Dexterity* and the 5th Air Force

D-Day for *Dexterity* had been scheduled for early December and was to continue into February 1944. MacArthur wished to maintain this schedule, but his lower echelons were becoming more and more uncertain that preparations could be completed in time. The 5AF was adamant about building elaborate bases in the Markham Valley and on the Huon Peninsula which, while considered advantageous by GHQ, was not feasible due to excessive demand and inadequate shipping space for the equipment and materials for their construction.

*Dexterity* would have been a simple plan, if it had been the only mission of Allied air and land forces at the time, but it was only an essential diversion from the main drive along the New Guinea coast. Two Australian divisions and two Air Task Forces were committed to this drive and demanded their share of the supplies, which had to reach the north coast of New Guinea. To keep these widely separated forces supplied and reinforced was a logistical problem, but during November the situation was partially alleviated. During this time the 5AF flew only minor attacks, mainly low level attacks by B-25s or B-26s escorted by P-38 and P-47s, which met no meaningful enemy resistance and no Allied aircraft were lost.

### November 1943: 5AF Missions

Missions to Alexishafen/Madang

At this time the Japanese-held Alexishafen/Madang area was the greatest threat to the Allies on the Huon Peninsula, as it consisted of a series of tracks and roads that connected the harbor and airdromes around Hansa Bay with those near Alexishafen and Madang. Madang had an airfield that was not in use, but during November 79 P-38s and an equal number of P-47s were sent out on sweeps over the Madang/Bogadjim area, and along with medium low level bombers

**Alexishafen Airdrome**. (AAF)

(B-25s, B-26s, and A-20s) dropped 130 tons of bombs. No enemy aircraft were encountered on these missions. The two airfields near Alexishafen were suspected of being a staging area for hit-and-run raids on Nadzab and Gusap. Being only 150 miles from Allied advanced bases, these enemy airdromes were easy targets for 113 B-24, 78 B-25, and 21 A-20 bomber sorties, and even for 27 P-40 and 16 P-39 fighter sweeps that dropped 320 tons of bombs and parafrags. These bomber missions were escorted by 94 P-47s, 65 P-38s, 24 P-40s, and 16 P-39s. Only the 9 November mission met enemy interceptors when a mixed batch of 20 Zekes, Oscars, Tonys, Hamps, and Nicks lost 16 of their number without shooting down any Allied aircraft, while another 18 Japanese aircraft were destroyed on the ground. Only one B-25 and one P-40 were lost during the month-long Alexishafen raids.

Missions to Wewak

Wewak remained the strongest enemy base on New Guinea, as on 6 November 97 aircraft, mostly fighters, were based on the four Wewak airdromes, while enemy bombers were based in the rear at Hollandia and Wakde. Only 10 days later air recon photos showed 112 aircraft at Wewak and 82 twin-engine bombers based at Hollandia. The build up of aircraft on these bases indicated the Japanese intention to hold a defensive line east of Wewak. On 25 November, several large supply ships escorted by destroyers approached the Wewak anchorage. Small flights of no more than four fighters were frequently sent out to sweep Wewak to determine the degree of enemy reaction to these attacks; to report any "unusual activity" at Dagua, Boram, But, and Wewak; and to intercept, if possible, any reinforcing aircraft from Hollandia. The P-47, with its heavy firepower, speed, and diving ability, was the ideal fighter bomber, and although its short range was a handicap; Gusap was an ideal staging base, laying only 300 miles from Wewak. The 130 fighter sweeps were augmented by escorted B-24 and B-25 attacks during November. Weather again played a part in this air campaign, as several missions to Wewak had to be diverted to Alexishafen. Also, several medium bomber missions had to be aborted when Japanese attacks in the Nadzab and Gusap areas were reported and the fighter escort had to be sent there to intercept. AAF attacks on Wewak occurred 11 days in November, and were escorted by a total of 158 P-47s and 92 P-38s, but only on five occasions were enemy aircraft encountered, and rarely by more than 20 aircraft. During the month 17 Japanese fighters were shot down and 24 more destroyed on the ground for the cost of two P-38s and two B-25s. On the mission of 1 December eight enemy fighters and one bomber were destroyed on the ground and eight enemy fighters were shot down in air combat for the loss of two B-24s. These attacks on Alexishafen, Madang, and Wewak were not considered offensive but defensive, in that they were to cover the Australian infantry in the Huon Peninsula and Ramu Valley, and the American service units building advanced bases.

Missions to Western New Britain

Offensive missions were being sent to New Britain in preparation for the most extensive amphibious landings ever in the SWPA scheduled for mid-December. During November, the 5AF based on New Guinea flew 170 B-24, 100 B-25, and 10 B-26 sorties against the Gasmata, Lindenhafen, and the Cape Gloucester areas. More than 600 tons of bombs were dropped on airfields, supply points, and barge hiding

**Wewak Airdrome.** (AAF)

**Cape Gloucester Airdrome.** (AAF)

places. Neither the bombers nor the P-47 and P-38 escorts encountered any enemy interceptors, but one B-25 and one B-24 were lost, probably from anti-aircraft fire.

### November 1943: Japanese Air Missions

A conspicuous aspect about air operations during November was the Japanese ineptitude in the air, as shown by the rarity of fighter interception of Allied bombing attacks and their inability to mount sustained bombing attacks in spite of their having substantial numbers of available bombers. During November only a few Japanese offensive bombing attacks were particularly damaging. For example, on 6 November the fighter strip used by the 41FS at Nadzab was heavily bombed and strafed, and two enlisted men were killed, at least one P-39 was destroyed, and nine others damaged. On the following day the same squadron was attacked again, and three more fighters were destroyed and 10 were damaged. Despite the relative infrequency of these attacks, the fact that they could occur and cause some damage injured the morale of personnel, particularly units which had only recently been transferred to the advanced bases. Furthermore, the Allied aircraft warning system was found to be deficient, as alerts were not sounded properly and coordination between the warning units and the Fighter Controller was clearly lacking. On 6 November, for example, the Red Alert had been sounded four minutes after the attack started, and on 7 November the Fighter Sector was able to sound the warning, but not in time for an interception. Eight days later the warning system improved, and the pilots of two squadrons of intercepting P-40s had considerable success, particularly Lt. Richard West, who accounted for four of the 21 enemy planes shot down.

5AF fighters that actually encountered the enemy in combat, however, were the exceptions rather than the rule. During November, exclusive of bomber escort and offensive sweeps, Fifth Air Force fighters performed the following number of assigned flights: 2,155 P-39, 1,771 P-40, 736 P-47, and 535 P-38. The great majority of these flights consisted of escorting troop carrier aircraft, flying routine patrols over Allied territory, and scrambles under the direction of the Fighter Controller. On all these flights no more than 200 enemy aircraft were encountered, of which 53 were shot down for a loss of four P-38s, two P-40s, and two P-39s.

### New Air Bases and *Reno III*

While Finschhafen was to be captured and developed to meet current tactical requirements, MacArthur was considering the need for more bases to meet longer range strategic objectives of pressuring the Japanese. As originally envisaged in October 1943, *Reno III* called for occupation of bases in the Bismarck Archipelago and along the New Guinea coast northwestward of the Vitiaz Strait by SWPA forces for the isolation and neutralization of Rabaul during the end of 1944 and the early months of 1945. In *Reno III* the major offensive role was delegated to land based air power. The land based "Bomber Line" would be advanced northwestward along New Guinea towards the Philippines, with enemy forces bypassed and neutralized through air action wherever feasible to avoid costly and time consuming land operations. Ground forces would be moved forward by air and water to seize, hold, and develop an advancing line of bases. When these bases were developed to operational fighter requirements, the "Fighter Line" would be moved forward, adding to the destruction on the enemy caused by the bombers. Successive development of these bases would allow the staging or movement forward of bombers while ground forces and fighters leapfrogged ahead to repeat this pattern of advance. Any required naval bases would be established under the protection of land based aviation. Carrier aircraft would contribute by providing close support of landings beyond the reach of previously established land bases.

**November-December 1943: New Base Development**

In anticipation of the invasions into the Bismarck Archipelago, the air bases at Nadzab, Gusap, and Lae had been constructed or improved and expanded, while Finschhafen was to be captured and put into use. These bases were essential, not only for the advance in New Guinea, but for *Operation Dexterity*, as aircraft based at these airdromes would be stationed much closer to Cape Gloucester and Wewak than from previously constructed bases in New Guinea. Not only were existing bases too distant from the front lines; they had become overcrowded with new aircraft and units coming into the SWPA. For instance, at this point in the war Marilinan Airdrome had been taken over by the RAAF as a major supply depot for Australian troops who were to advance north to link up with the commando units in the Ramu River Valley. The base became so crowded that the 8FS Black Sheep had to take off across the flight path of the 35FG Lightnings and also had to evade approaching C-47s, which took off from the opposite end of the field.

Detailed requirements for airdrome construction in the Lae-Markham River Valley area as specified by Allied Air Forces were, in order of priority:

*Nadzab area:* three dry-weather airstrips for transport use and one all-weather airdrome of two parallel airstrips for heavy bombers, fighters, and troop carriers.

*Kaiapit area:* one all-weather airdrome of two parallel airstrips for medium bombers, fighters, troop carriers, and reconnaissance aircraft.

*Lae-Malahang area:* one all-weather airstrip for fighters and troop carriers and one all-weather road from Lae to Nadzab.

*Dumpu area:* one all-weather airdrome of two parallel airstrips for fighters.

*Wawin area:* one all-weather airdrome of two parallel airstrips for heavy and medium bombers, fighters, and troop carriers.

*Sawteeth Hills (near Wawin) area:* one all-weather airdrome of two parallel airstrips for medium bombers and fighters.

*Leron area:* one all-weather airdrome of two parallel airstrips for medium bombers and fighters.

*Marawasa area:* one all-weather airdrome of one airstrip for fighters and parallel taxiway capable of expansion to a second runway.

*Salamaua area:* no facilities required unless the Lae attack was seriously delayed, and in that event one airdrome for basing of a fighter group would be required.

Though much had been accomplished in the two months after the capture of Lae and Nadzab, the facilities at none of the new bases had developed much beyond a "primitive" stage. Construction at Gusap and Nadzab, even in late October and early November, necessitated the movement of between 750 and 900 tons of building material from Lae, which required the landing (and take offs) of more than 200 troop carriers per day. Thus, even at Lae, which was not primarily an air base, it was necessary to build extensive runways and hard stands, plus alert parking areas for two flights of fighters to intercept enemy attacks on the shipping in the harbor. At Nadzab, all-weather facilities for 75 fighters, 32 medium bombers, 18 light bombers, and 78 troop carriers; at Gusap for 75 fighters and 36 A-20s; and at Finschhafen for 75 fighters and possibly 26 troop carriers, were considered minimum requirements.

By the end of November there was a general movement to the improved advanced bases. The 7th and 8th Fighter Squadrons were flying out of Gusap, as were several troop carrier and service squadrons, and a nearby site was chosen for the 9FS. At the end of December Nadzab was ready for medium bombers and the 36th and 39th Fighter Squadrons. By 17 December the 348FG landed at Finschhafen, and on Christmas Day the 35th Fighter Squadron's P-40s flew in from Port Moresby. These bases placed 5AF fighter squadrons 200 miles nearer to Cape Gloucester and 150 miles closer to Wewak. Lae, Nadzab, and Gusap Airdromes were described in detail in Volume I (Part 5/Chapter 10).

**Finschhafen (Base F/Dreger Field)**

The Allied objective of driving Japanese forces from the Huon Peninsula was achieved by the capture and base development of Finschhafen. As early as mid-1943, Allied tactical plans were directed at driving the enemy out of this strategic area and establishing a forward base for aircraft and light surface vessels there, together with creating a staging area for future advances. Subsequent analysis by the Chief Engineer, GHQ, SWPA, indicated that the Finschhafen area, situated on the northeast coast of New Guinea, would be suitable for development of a forward supply base, as the Allies' previous tactical advances had left existing bases far behind the front lines. The Huon Peninsula generally consisted of mountainous, jungle-covered terrain, but the narrow, rolling coastal belt encompassing the eastern tip of the Peninsula in the vicinity of Finschhafen could be successfully cleared of its tropical undergrowth and the coconut plantations could be used to an advantage. Planners considered that a supply installation based here could support facilities for base service elements for 100,000 troops and could stage approximately 50,000 troops.

The Finschhafen Campaign had originally been scheduled for about a month after the fall of Lae. However, the unanticipated quick collapse of the Japanese resistance at Lae and Salamaua had exposed that the Japanese were not as formidable as believed. MacArthur decided to exploit this fact by accelerating his agenda, and organized a sudden amphibious assault on Finschhafen while the Japanese remained vulnerable from their recent heavy losses. On D minus 5 (17 September 1943) GHQ, SWPA, issued its first construction directive for Finschhafen: "The New Guinea Force was to establish advanced air base facilities for staging one fighter group and two light bombardment squadrons and Allied Naval Forces were to establish base facilities for the employment of light naval craft in the Vitiaz Strait."

**Finschhafen Airdrome**

On 22 September 1943, the 20th Australian Infantry Brigade made the initial landing at *Scarlet Beach*, seven miles north of Finschhafen. Light enemy resistance was quickly subdued and unloading was rapidly accomplished, but heavy fighting developed as the Australian troops moved south; however, by 2 October the Japanese were in retreat from the Finschhafen area. Before the arrival of the entire 808th Engineer Aviation Battalion, an advance party arrived at Dreger Harbor about 7 October (D plus 15) for a ground reconnaissance to locate a site for an airdrome using prior aerial recon photos as a guide. Poor landing approach situations eliminated several prospective sites, and the ground reconnaissance was continued until 10 October, when a suitable site was located approximately parallel with and a half mile inland from the inner shore of Schneider Harbor. Dense jungle covered the prospective site, which posed a problem for getting equipment to the site. The logical place

**Finschhafen Airdrome**

to unload the Battalion was Dreger Harbor, where equipment could be debarked in the immediate vicinity of the airdrome site. Immediately the advance party hacked another road through the jungle, but the day before the Battalion's scheduled arrival Allied Naval Forces decided that they would not risk their shipping in Dreger Harbor, and instead would land the Battalion at Langemak Bay. The advance party began hacking a road to Langemak Bay, where the Battalion landed on 23 October. The Battalion unloaded their bulldozers to cut a better road to their new campsite north of Buta Creek. First, a bridge needed to be built across Buta Creek, and a week later a 100 foot bridge spanned the creek. Soon it became evident that the new road would become impassable from overuse, and priorities had to be established. Trucks loaded with critical supplies and all the construction equipment needed in the early stages of the work were moved to the campsite first. As the 808th cleared the runway site, the 870th Battalion arrived at Langemak Bay with only a third of its equipment, but by this time the road was in such poor condition that the 870th could get only two D-7 dozers to the site. Then, on 3 November over 12 inches of rain fell in the area, turning it into a quagmire. Two days later the 60th Naval Construction Battalion arrived, but was able to use its LCMs (Landing Craft, Mechanized) to move its men and equipment by water to a beachhead nearer the camp. By 10 November the all-weather access road from Buta Creek to Dreger Harbor was completed, and construction could concentrate on earth moving at the runway. The soil at the airdrome site consisted of a top layer of black, mucky loam overlying clay and coral. The loam was stripped completely from the runway area and, because the terrain was rolling, a number of cuts and fills were necessary for a level runway. A compacted layer of coral was placed on the runway to an average thickness of eight inches, and pierced steel plank landing mat was then laid over the runway proper and the alert aprons. By 10 December 1943, the 6,000x100 foot runway was completed with a 500 foot overrun at each end, and with 100x800 foot alert areas at each corner of the strip. These facilities were considered adequate for accommodating two fighter squadrons in an emergency. But Kenney was anxious to move forward as quickly as possible, and the entire 348th Fighter Group was transferred to Finschhafen from Port Moresby on 17 December before the air warning and control systems were fully set up. By 25 December, the 35th Fighter Squadron also arrived from Port Moresby. By the end of 1943, 60 foot wide taxiways connecting to dispersal areas, a 200x1,500 foot transport unloading area, and 137 hardstands for fighters or medium bombers were completed. Most all scheduled construction deadlines had been met despite unfavorable conditions, and the airdrome was ready to accommodate the movement of four fighter squadrons 200 miles closer to Cape Gloucester in time for that operation and almost 150 miles closer to Wewak, which had been only temporarily neutralized.

The establishment of the airdromes at Lae, Nadzab, Gusap, and Finschhafen placed Allied aircraft much closer to the important Vitiaz Straits. The aircraft based at Finschhafen played a particularly significant role in gaining air superiority over these Straits. The landings in the Cape Gloucester area on New Britain and at Saidor, on the New Guinea coast, were significantly aided by the new base at Finschhafen, and further increased control over the Straits. With the establishment of Finschhafen as a base for fighter escorts, the 5AF was able to concentrate its efforts

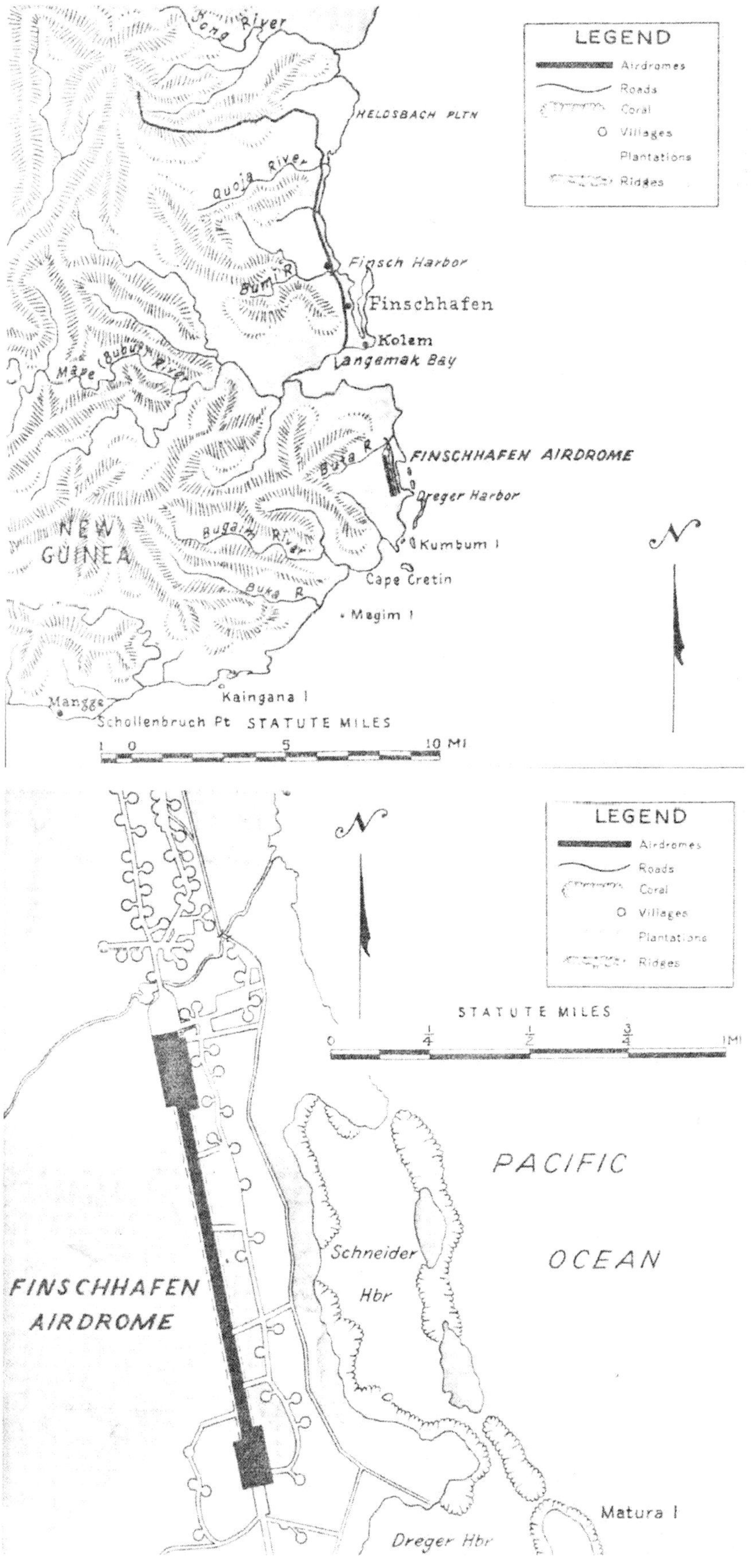


**Finschhafen Airdrome.** (AAF)

not only on the Cape Gloucester area, but subsequently against Kavieng, New Ireland; in support of landings by the South Pacific Force (SOPAC) on Nissan Island; as well as a Pacific Fleet carrier raid against Truk; and later SWPA operations in the Admiralties. Finschhafen was also strategically located for subsequent operations up the New Guinea coast. From Finschhafen ammunition and rations were flown into Hollandia, where the initial lack of suitable anchorages and swampy conditions threatened to slow the SWPA offensive. The establishment of a Navy Catalina squadron at Langemak Bay provided an air-sea rescue service which considerably lowered Allied aerial casualty rates and raised morale. Besides its logistic support to ground forces, Finschhafen also served a crucial supply role in Allied air operations.

5FC units based at Finschhafen included:

348FS: 340FS (P-47) from Port Moresby on 13 December 1943 to Saidor 13 March 1944
348FS: HQ from Port Moresby on 16 December 1943 to Saidor 29 March 1944
348FS: 341FS (P-47) from Port Moresby on 17 December 1943 to Saidor 27 March 1944
348FS: 342FS (P-47) from Port Moresby on 1 7 December 1943 to Saidor 27 March 1944
8FG: 36FS (P-47) from Nadzab 9 January 1944 to Nadzab 28 March 1944
8FG: 35FS (P-40) from ? on 19 February 1944 to ?
8FG: HQ from ? on 20 February 1944 to Cape Gloucester on ?
71 TRG: 82TRS (P-39) from Dobodura on 1 December 1943 to Saidor on 19 April 1944
49FG: HQ from Gusap on 19 April 1943 to Hollandia 17 May 1944
49FG: 7FS ((P-40) from Gusap on 27 April 1943 to Hollandia 3 May 1944
86FW: HQ from USA on 1 May 1944 to Toem Middelberg on 4 August 1944
418NFS from ? on 28 March 1944 to ? on 12 May 1944

Until the liberation of the Philippines, Finschhafen established itself as an invaluable base. But thereafter, Finschhafen gradually decreased in importance, and at the end the remaining troops were withdrawn and Base F was closed on 31 March 1946.

### Life on Airdromes

Living conditions at these bases naturally varied with the length of time that the base had been established. Life at the new bases at Tsili Tsili and Finschhafen was described as "rugged," but at the older base at Dobodura there had been numerous improvements. Tents which at first were on the ground had been raised at least three feet on wooden floors. Permanent mess halls with cement floors, dispensaries, and water facilities were constructed. Officers enlisted local native labor and their own devices to build stylish officers' clubs. At Dobodura the facility was known as "Club 38: 475 Dobodura Avenue" (referring to the P-38s of the 475FG). Enlisted men were supplied with their own recreation halls, with rooms for

**35FS/8FG Warhawk** at Finschhafen. (AAF)

relaxing, reading, and indoor games. The ever popular softball leagues were supplemented by volley and badminton facilities. Volleyball seemed to be a favorite outdoor game, as it required a minimum of equipment; a ball and net. Movies were usually shown three times a week, and USO shows occasionally arrived. The 49th Group Historian notes that in August the men enjoyed their third USO show in its "Zamboogie" Theater. Harry Ross, a former night club master of ceremonies, the Reese Brothers, and Hal Gustavison, an accordion player, entertained about 3,000 soldiers for an hour.

Health

By fall 1943, food and nutrition officers had organized mess management teams and succeeded in providing fresh meats and vegetables in increasing amounts transported by war weary B-25s and B-26s and C-47 transports, called "Fat Cats." But the detested bully beef, dehydrated foods, and C rations remained on the menu.

With more emphasis on control measures, the incidence of disease, which early in 1943 had been high, rapidly decreased during the summer. The 13th Malarial Control Unit, after its arrival at Dobodura in August, drained mosquito breeding areas, gave lectures and demonstrations, and formed anti-Malaria units within each organization.

The health of officers and enlisted men of the Fifth Air Force varied between the two extremes, generally depending on the length of time spent in New Guinea. Between 1 June and 31 August, an average of 16.24 patients per day were admitted to sick report per 1,000 officers and men in the Fifth Air Force. There was a daily average of 62.07 patients per 1,000 men in hospitals (vs. an average of 1.1 per 1,000 men in the entire Air Force), and an average of three men per day were evacuated to the United States for medical reasons. In spite of medical precautions and the general reduction of the incidence of Malaria, dengue, and diarrhea, the resistance of men to disease in

Tent bivouac at **Finschhafen**. (AAF)

some of the units was low due to extended service in the tropics, and the average weight loss was at least 10 pounds. The surgeon of the 46th Service Group stated:

> The health of this command is now encroaching problem stratus. On occasions I have noted lower blood pressure and anemia in about 21% and poor heart muscle tone in 30%. These symptoms are not due in my opinion to specific diseases but to living over a considerable period under adverse and difficult conditions. This in time leads to … the loss of a considerable number of man days. They simply do not care what happens, being in a state of mental fatigue.

This condition, generally known as "Combat or Battle Fatigue," was one of the most critical personnel problems in the SWPA, and was caused by a number of factors besides the stress of combat, such as poor equipment, poor living conditions, poor quality food, the lack of recreation facilities, and the lack of promotions. But more important, perhaps, than any of these factors was homesickness, together with the absence of a definite rotation policy. Pilots and crews who flew combat missions in a climate characterized by frequent rains and poor visibility did so without a set rotation goal, as the inconsistent replacement policy gave the men no choice but to fly until they burned out (no matter how many combat hours they had flown). Once Kenney set the 300 combat hours flown requirement for rotation home the men did have some hope, though unrealistic, of going home. However, the rotation situation was much better for air crews than for ground crews, who were informed that "personnel can be returned only under the most exceptional circumstances…and little hope is held out for an early improvement."

### Pay

The men were paid on time, although money was of such little importance in the forward areas that it was usually not drawn more than once every three or four months.

*Typical Flying Officer Pay Scales*

| Rank AAF | Col | LtCol | Maj | Capt | 1Lt | 2Lt/FO |
|---|---|---|---|---|---|---|
| Typical years of service | *12* | *9* | *6* | *>3* | *>3* | *>3* |
| Monthly base $ | 333.33 | 291.67 | 250.00 | 200.00 | 166.67 | 150.00 |
| Longevity $ (1) | 66.67 | 43.74 | 25.00 | 10.00 | 8.33 | 7.50 |
| Ration subsistence $ | 42.00 | 63.00 | 63.00 | 42.00 | 42.00 | 42.00 |
| Rental allowance $ | 120.00 | 120.00 | 105.00 | 90.00 | 75.00 | 60.00 |
| Flight pay $ (2) | 200.00 | 167.70 | 137.50 | 105.00 | 87.50 | 78.75 |
| Overseas pay $ (3) | 53.33 | 45.94 | 38.75 | 30.50 | 25.42 | 22.88 |
| Monthly pay $ | 815.33 | 732.05 | 619.05 | 477.50 | 404.92 | 361.13 |
| Annual pay $ | 9,784.00 | 8,785.00 | 7,431.00 | 5,730.00 | 4,859.00 | 4,334.00 |

(1) 5% for every 3 year service
(2) 50% of the sum of base pay + longevity pay
(3) 10% of the sum of base pay + flight pay

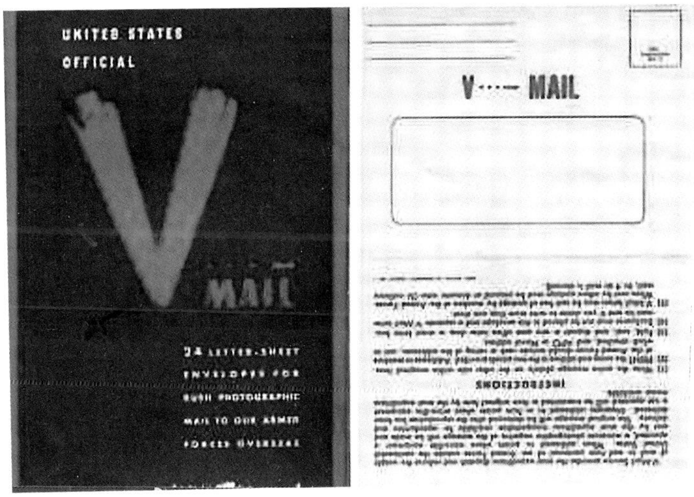


**V-mail.** (Author)

### Mail

Throughout the theater the delivery of mail was excellent, and V-mail was received by most units in New Guinea within 10 to 14 days after posting. V, or Victory mail, which originated in England, was the microfilming of specially designed letter sheets which were a combination of letter and envelope. The letter sheets were gummed to fold into a uniform and distinctively marked envelope. The writer composed the message in the limited space provided, added the name and address of the recipient, folded the form, affixed postage, if necessary, and mailed the letter. V-mail correspondence was then reduced to 3/8 x 1/4 inch size on microfilm rolls that were sent for developing at a receiving station in the area of the addressee. V-mail saved thousands of tons of valuable shipping space that could store war materials. One V-mail sack replaced 37 regular mail bags required to carry 150,000 one page letters, and the weight of that same amount of mail was reduced dramatically from 2,575 pounds to only 45. The microfilm rolls were developed near their destination and reproduced into individual facsimiles of the letter sheets; about one-quarter the original size.

### Furloughs and R&R

Officers had been allowed furloughs to Australia, but finally a plan was adopted to give enlisted men the same privilege. The plan varied, but generally it was seven days furlough, not including travel time, allowed for every six months served in New Guinea. However, the military "situation" and the availability of transport (the wounded and officers first) often interfered with fulfilling the furlough, and it was often nine months or more before ground crews or service personnel reached Australia. Once in Australia the enlisted man could go only to certain specified areas controlled by MPs. Sydney was a popular furlough area, but the city was a long distance from New Guinea and difficult to get transport, so Camp Mackey, in northern Queensland, had been purposely constructed to provide recreation; while being well stocked with food and beer it was not overly popular due to the lack of nearby women.

### November 1943 Air Operations Over New Guinea after the Rabaul Missions

### 11 November 1943: 35FG /41FS

Alexishafen was a major Japanese base just north of Astrolabe Bay and well north of the Huon Peninsula. Japanese had constructed roads and bridges in the Madang-Alexishafen area which they intended to use as a staging point for air raids against Allied advanced lines. MacArthur's plan was to bypass many of the enemy bases that would be too costly in men and time to capture, so he decided that Alexishafen would be bypassed. However, it would be neutralized as a threat by heavy air attacks.

After taking off at 0702, Maj. Fred Thompson led 16 Airacobras to strafe #2 Strip at Alexishafen. After a 30 minute flight he dropped to 500 feet and he saw a lone Val dive bomber taking off from the field. He dove and fired a short burst into its right wing tank and watched as his victim dove straight into the ground.

**15 November 1943: 8FG/35FS**

On the 15th Lily bombers of the 208th Sentai heavily escorted by Oscars of the 1st and 248th Sentai led the Japanese assault. For the day the Japanese would lose 23 aircraft, eight probables, and one damaged. The eight P-40s of the 35FS took off from Nadzab to fly a patrol over the Lae-Kaiapit area from 0900 until about 1030. At 1000, while flying 15 miles north of Kaiapit they contacted an enemy formation of 25 Sally bombers covered by about 30 Oscars over the upper Markham Valley. The Squadron had the initial advantage, since they were above the Japanese formation, and saw the enemy first. 1Lt. Robert Parker and his Wingman, 1Lt. Charles Rainville, attacked the large formation of enemy bombers and fighters; Parker shot one down, but then had three Zeros break off to attack him and his Wingman.

**1Lt. Richard West** scored four victories and two damaged to make him an ace with six victories. (AFAA)

**1Lt. Charles Rainville** downed his only enemy aircraft of the war. (AAF)

Only three 25 **Sallys** were lost, but for the loss of 19 protecting fighter escorts. (AAF)

Rainville turned into the first one and fired a long burst, getting hits, and then turned suddenly to get on the tail of one of the others. As he came in on this pass he saw the same fighter he had previously hit now smoking badly and going down. At this point Rainsville lost Parker, and as he turned for another pass on the Zeros he stalled and inverted but recovered quickly and dove away from the Zeros, which got on his tail in the stall.

1Lt. Richard West, flying as the #2 man in 1Lt. Bennett McCoy's White Flight, spotted the enemy bombers first, flying at 9 o'clock and 25 miles out headed for the Allied forward position at Kaiapit, north of Lae. When the Americans closed in a diving attack on the enemy formation, which was arced across the valley, turning toward the northwest. The P-40s overtook the bombers from 4 o'clock and their surprised fighter escorts were too late to intercept. West fired on the Sally furthest to the right and it erupted in flames, but flew along with its formation for a short time before it broke off and plunged into the ground. West then fired at the second Sally and got good hits, but it didn't smoke and flew on for a probable. Soon the Zero escorts arrived and a dogfight began. West chased a Zero from the tail of a P-40 by firing a quick burst, setting it on fire. West saw the P-40 he had rescued going into a climbing bank and then heading toward him with its guns firing. West looked back and saw that a Zero had gotten on his tail and the P-40 that he rescued was now rescuing him! West watched as the P-40 turned into a head on attack on another Oscar and the two fighters collided, clipping a wing off each fighter, and both spun into the sea. West followed the P-40 down, hoping its pilot would bail out, but he didn't. West learned later that the P-40 pilot was 1Lt. Robert Parker, who was credited with two victories that day. West turned toward the bomber formation and fired at several Zeros, with one crashing in the jungle. West attacked a Sally that was straggling from its formation and made a pass from astern and above; the bomber burst into flames and crashed. West climbed into the cloud base and then attempted to catch the enemy formation again. He saw a number of twin engine bombers not far below, and as he began firing he realized that they were B-25s; luckily he didn't cause any damage. He caught up to the enemy bombers to the north near Alexishafen. As he approached the bombers for a head on pass the Zero escorts engaged him. West turned into a head on pass on a bomber and fired and saw hits, but lost it when his P-40 took hits in the fuselage near the tail. West then decided to head to base with four victories and two probables to give him six victories, thus becoming the 35th Fighter Squadron's first ace.

McCoy's White Flight second element of 1Lt. Elliott Brogden and Wingman 2Lt. Dean Jacobson did not recognize the Sallys as enemy aircraft and did not fire, climbing back up with the first element. As they were climbing Brogden saw two Zeros peel off and head for McCoy. Brogden got behind the enemy fighter on the left and hit it with a full deflection shot. The enemy pilot dove away and Brogden lost sight of it for a damaged claim when he had to dive away as another Zero turned into him. The enemy pilot rolled his fighter over on its back and fired. Brogden turned into the attack and fired, getting hits on the Zero's engine and starting a fire just as it passed under him. Another Zero dove on Brogden as he pulled away, and he tried to reef around to meet the Zero head on but spun out instead. Brogden let his Warhawk spin for three to four thousand feet to evade his attacker and succeeded in pulling out and left for home. Meanwhile, Jacobson also did not fire on the Sallys during McCoy's first pass. He climbed and took over the #2 position behind McCoy when West and Brogden left. Jacobson followed McCoy and closed on the tail of a Sally from underneath and fired a long burst that hit the right wing root. The Sally dropped off on one wing and crashed into the mountains. Jacobson looked around and saw two Zeros on his tail, but lost them when he joined P-47s (348FG/342FS) escorting the B-25s. Jacobson flew with them to Gusap, where he saw a dogfight to the left and joined another flight to attack enemy bombers escorted by Zeros. Four Zeros made head on passes on the flight of American fighters. The Thunderbolt Flight Leader made a pass on the one on the right which dove away. Jacobson went after the left Zero which climbed straight up, and

Jacobson climbed after it firing into the cockpit, killing the pilot.

1Lt. Bacchus Crow's old P-40 could not keep up with the Squadron formation and he dropped behind and didn't get to the bombers, but "got a beautiful pass at two Zekes from above." The Japanese pilots didn't detect Crow's attack, as they took no evasive action. Crow fired on the rear Zero, getting hits in its fuselage, and as it started down the lead Zero got on his tail and Crow had to dive away to safety. The 35th had a very good day with 11 confirmed victories, four by West.

**15 November 1943: 49FG/8FS**

After rendezvousing at Madang, the Japanese flew south just over the haze shrouding Shaggy Ridge until they were due east of Gusap village. At 14,000 feet, just across the plain from the Gusap airdromes, the Lily bombers turned west on their bombing run. To meet the Japanese, the Black Sheep had posted a patrol of eight Warhawks stacked between 8,000 to 12,000 feet led by 1Lt. Bernard Makowski. Just as the enemy bombers made their turn over Gusap Village the Americans spotted the formation off in the distance to the east. Makowski requested confirmation of the approaching formation from the Air Controller, whose reply was uncertain, so Makowski turned his flights to the east to investigate first hand and met the Japanese escorts head on and at point blank range. Makowski's higher Yellow Flight wingmen were 1Lts. Joel Thorvaldson, Donald Meuten, and James Reynolds, while his lower level Blue Flight was led by 1Lt. Daniel Moore, with wingmen 1Lts. William Runey, Robert Aschenbrener, and William Drier.

Blue Flight dropped their tanks and climbed away from the threatening Oscars at full throttle and lost them. Five minutes later Blue Flight was at 13,000 and over the Lilys, and all four Warhawks dove together to get ahead of the enemy bomber V's right flank. Once in position the Flight broke and rolled headlong in perfect formation directly back to face the enemy. Flight Leader Moore and Wingman Runey fired on the two Lilys on the formation's starboard side, but broke off toward incoming Oscar and Zero escorts. Moore fired and downed a Zeke while Runey and Aschenbrener fired and downed Oscars. As Drier was about to fire at a Zero, Aschenbrener roared in and scored his second victory of the day.

Red Flight was just behind Moore's Blue Flight as they attacked the Lily V's right side. Mission Leader Makowski held his Red Flight back, but the Oscars began to turn toward his Warhawks and Makowski called for the break and dove on the Lilys on the left flank. Makowski, Wingman 1Lt. Donald Meuten, and Element Leader Thorvaldson went after the bombers while #4 man Reynolds trailed to watch for the escorts. After their initial unproductive firing pass Meuten returned to attack the bombers, while Makowski, Thorvaldson, and Reynolds met the intervening escorts. After executing a chandelle to exit the dogfight, Meuten dove on a Lily from astern and systematically shot away the canopy, then tore out the cockpit and finished off the bomber by tearing pieces out of the starboard engine. Makowski and Thorvaldson joined Blue Flight in their attack and each Red Flight pilot knocked down a Zero in flames.

**1Lt. Robert Aschenbrenner** scored his first two of 10 victories. (AFAA)

**2Lt. William Runey** claimed his last two of three wartime victories. (AAF)

**Capt. Donald Moore** had a probable and his second of two total victories. (AAF)

Squadron Leader Maj. Ernest Harris led another eight Warhawks from Gusap #3 and headed due south, but by the time they climbed to 15,000 feet the combat was over. He then split his two flights and took his Red Flight toward Madang to look for stragglers. While heading for the coast Harris met Blue Flight Leader Capt. Daniel Moore, and the five Black Sheep headed north in hope of catching the retreating Japanese. Finally, over Bogadjim, they saw the bombers, which were much too far ahead. The five Black Sheep dropped their tanks and quickly dove toward the trailing Oscars. The opponents separated as they got closer to the sea, and Harris caught his victim from dead astern and fired and the pilot bailed out. It was Harris' last victory of the war, but without a witness the double ace was not credited with his 11th kill. During the combat Moore caught up with a Zeke beyond the shoreline and was credited with a probable, then just made it back to Gusap running on fumes.

**15 November 1943: 348FG/342FS**

Fifteen P-47s of the 342FS were assigned to a B-25 escort, but were unable to rendezvous with the bombers and flew on to Wewak on a fighter sweep. They arrived over Wewak at 1110 at 20,000 feet when they saw a mixed group of 15 to 20 Zeros, Oscars, and Tonys taking off and others climbing from Wewak and Boram Strips.

Capt. Walter Benz dove on a Zeke at 6,000 feet from 6 o'clock and got hits on it, but its pilot Split-S'd and came back on Benz. 1Lt. Robert Martin, Benz' Wingman, was behind his leader and dove head on into the Zeke, getting some hits on its wings near the fuselage. Martin's ICR states that "I believe that Capt. Benz got many more hits on this Zeke than I did." When Martin climbed he saw a parachute in the vicinity of the combat with the Zeke. Despite this apparent confirmation Benz was credited with a probable, as Benz' ICR states that he did not see it crash and he claimed it as a probable. Benz then got hits on another Zeke that got away. He encountered a Hamp at 4,000 feet that had just taken off from Boram Strip and fired several bursts that exploded it. After Martin and Banks encountered their Zeke, Martin immediately saw an Oscar at 6,000 feet and dove on it from "4:30 o'clock" and closed from behind. He fired a long burst from 6 o'clock and observed many hits and pieces flying off. The Oscar did a "sloppy" half roll and began smoking and the pilot bailed out. Immediately Martin saw another Oscar that just came out of an Immelmann in front of

**Capt. Walter Benz** claimed a probable and his third victory. (AFAA)

**Capt. William Banks** (right center) scored his second and third victory. (AFAA)

**1Lt. Robert Sutcliffe** got his first victory and a probable on his way to becoming an ace. (AAF)

him and fired a short burst into its engine; its pilot half rolled away for a probable claim.

Capt. William Banks led his flight down and made a series of passes. Banks fired at an Oscar from the rear and above and observed hits just before the pilot bailed out and the fighter exploded. He then fired on a Zero from the rear and got a direct hit on its tail, then watched it dive into the ground, shedding pieces on the way down.

1Lt. Robert Sutcliffe saw a lone Oscar at 13,000 feet and dove in a tight turn, getting hits on the right wing, and the Oscar rolled over and down. Sutcliffe claimed a victory with "No witnesses, pending outcome of film." He climbed back to 20,000 feet and saw another Oscar and closed from the rear, firing a short burst, and it rolled over and burst into flames and its pilot bailed out.

**15 November 1943:475FG/432FS**

1Lt. Theodore Fostakowski took off just after noon on a scramble over Nadzab but experienced a mechanical problem and returned to base. While attempting to land on Strip #5 he overshot the runway, and as he tried to go around again he crashed 400 yards off one end of the field and was killed.

**15 November 1943: 418NFS Arrives**

The 418th Night Fighter Squadron arrived at Dobodura on 15 November. Detachment "A" Night Fighter Squadron was attached to the 418th shortly after their arrival. By the end of November Detachment "A" Night Fighter Squadron was disbanded. Some personnel were sent back to the States, while the remainder were scattered among the other organizations within the Fifth Air Force.

**16 November 1943: 475FG/431FS/432FS/433FS**

Early in the morning about 30 475FG Lightnings took off on a fighter sweep extending from Lae, to Finschhafen, to Madang, to Rubia, to Wewak. The three 475th Squadrons rendezvoused over the Gona wreck at 1000 and cruised along the coast at between 10,000 to 20,000 feet, and the final turn inland at Wewak was made on schedule. Ten P-38s of the 433FS were to fly top cover at 23,000 feet, while the 431st and 432nd attacked the airfields. Cloud cover made visibility poor between the stacked flights of the different squadrons, but the schedule was maintained; the 433rd lost contact with the other two Squadrons in the overcast.

431FS

Maj. Frank Nichols led 16 P-38s on a fighter sweep to Wewak at 0720. When they arrived over the Wewak area they saw no enemy aircraft over the airfields at Wewak, Boram, Dagua, or But. On their return they saw Clover Squadron making passes on Zeros near Dagua and provided top cover until the 432FS Clover P-38s became outnumbered. Nichols ordered tanks to be dropped, but as they were about to dive they were attacked from above by 30 Zeros and the Squadron had to dive away for their lives and head for home. In the battle 1Lt. Christopher Herman's fighter's port engine was shot out, its port wing filled with holes, and his left arm was bleeding profusely. Herman was escorted to Nadzab, where he crash landed successfully. Later that day Lt. Robert Smith was MIA during a non-combat flight.

432FS

Maj. Meryl Smith joined the 432FS from Group HQ to lead 10 P-38s (2Lt. Perry Dahl aborted) off Dobodura at 0730 on a sweep to Wewak via Alexishafen and Nubia. Red Flight Leader Smith had 2Lt. Joseph Forster (who had moved up into Dahl's #2 position from Blue flight) on his wing and 1Lt. Eugene McGuire as his Second Element Leader with 2Lt. Henry Condon on his wing. Alexishafen was closed in and the squadron proceeded to Nubia, where they saw only one fighter on the strip, and then flew on to Wewak at 19,000 feet. After arriving at Wewak at 0945, about five minutes later two formations of 11 enemy aircraft were spotted climbing toward them. Smith ordered the Squadron to drop their tanks at 15,000 feet and led the Clover Lightnings down on the first enemy flight, which was now only a few thousand feet below. Smith attacked the #2 Oscar in the lead formation when it left the flight. Smith's bullets hit the enemy's wing root and the flames soon spread over the entire aircraft. Smith flew on to attack several other enemy fighters and fired a quick 90 degree deflection shot that missed, but then he got heavy hits on another Oscar which turned under his P-38 and Smith was able to see

**Maj. Meryl Smith** scored his first two of nine career victories. (AFAA)

**1Lt. James Ince** claimed his sixth and last victory of the war. (AAF)

the pilot bail out of the spinning wreckage. After Smith shot down his second Zero Forster, who had made several unsuccessful previous passes, finally got a long burst at a Zero that was in a climb. The Zero slid off under Forster's wing in a spin but he was credited with a probable. Smith took several more unsuccessful shots before he flew to Nadzab to refuel at 1015 and landed back at Dobodura at 1420. Forster escorted Lt. Herman of the 431FS back to Nadzab. Meanwhile, the Second Element of McGuire and Condon broke off the fight and returned directly to Dobodura.

White Flight Leader 1Lt. James Ince and Wingman 2Lt. Ferdinand Hanson followed Smith's flight down to the attack, and after Ince attacked an Oscar that managed to roll away to safety they lost Red Flight in the background of the jungle below. They flew ahead, and both fired at an Oscar that also escaped by rolling away under the P-38s. Meanwhile, Smith's flight was approaching from the rear to rejoin Ince and Hanson to engage 15 enemy fighters that were climbing rapidly from 90 degrees. Using full power Ince climbed quickly to about 1,000 yards behind and 200 yards above the enemy. The 10 P-38s flying in string turned to fire at the first enemy flight, which turned sharply into the Americans. Ince fired a long burst at one nearly head on but lost sight of it as the Zero passed under his wing. 1Lt. Arthur Peregoy later confirmed Ince's sixth and last victory. White Second Element Leader 1Lt. Vivian Cloud and Wingman 2Lt. John Fogarty made "a couple of deflection shots" before Cloud's starboard engine cut out and Fogarty's hydraulic system failed. The two headed back to Nadzab, where Fogarty had to use his emergency hydraulic system to lower his landing gear while Cloud had mechanics check and correct his engine failure.

Peregoy, the Blue Flight Leader, and his Wingman, 2Lt. Edwin Christian, made several ineffective firing passes, but then were forced to leave the combat early, as Christian was unable to drop one of his wing tanks, and the two also headed back to Nadzab to refuel and then return to Dobodura.

433FS

Ten P-38s took off at 0745 as top cover on a fighter sweep from Finschhafen to Wewak, but two would abort the mission. The 433rd arrived over Wewak, but lost contact with the other Squadrons in the overcast. As the Squadron made its 90 degree turn over Wewak toward the Harbor they spotted a mixed batch of enemy fighters taking off from Wewak and Boram, and others approaching from But and Dagua. When they arrived directly over the Harbor they saw 20 to 25 Oscars and Tonys at 7,000 feet and climbing toward them at high speed. The Squadron dropped their tanks and dove toward the enemy fighters, but they Split-S'd away into the overcast. The Squadron climbed to regain altitude and speed and was confronted by "60 to 70" enemy fighters. Being outnumbered, the P-38s used hit-and-run tactics in twos and fours in the 30 minute combat. 2Lt. Richard Kimball and Wingman 2Lt. William Grady dove away in a turn from the enemy horde when a Zero came at them at 11 o'clock. Kimball turned into it, but the enemy pilot made a quick left turn that put him head on to Grady, who fired a long burst at 50 yards, turning the Zero belly up into ball of flames. 1Lt. William Jeakle and Wingman 1Lt. John Ehlinger had a Tony attack them at 2 o'clock, and Jeakle pulled up to meet its attack head on. He fired at 100 yards and saw a cannon shell hit its prop spinner and radiator, and the Tony went into a dive into the ground for his second victory.

**17 November 1943: 348FG Kearby Moves to HQ of the 5FC**

On 17 November 1943, Lt.Col. Neel Kearby was transferred to Headquarters and Headquarters Squadron of the 5th Fighter Command; Lt.Col. Robert Rowland would replace him, with Maj. Gallagher Raymond becoming his XO. Once at 5FC HQ Kearby realized that his administrative duties there would reduce his combat time. Kenney was known for his caution in protecting his top combat leaders by sending them home on furlough or assigning them to training or administrative jobs before they became "burnt out" and killed while flying one last mission to increase their victory total. Events occurring at the end of 1943 and early 1944 would affect Kenney profoundly. Kenney had restricted Kearby to two combat flights a week or less, and Kearby stated that, "The General put a lot of emphasis on that 'or less.'" When reporters asked him, Kearby insisted that he was not out to break any records: "I just like to hunt, it isn't that I like to kill anybody, but I do like to hunt. Since we are hunting in good, profitable ground, it makes each flight really a stimulant."

**19 November 1943: 475FG/432FS**

Capt. Frank Tomkins led six P-38s (1Lts. Campbell Wilson, Arthur Peregoy, Eugene McGuire, Billy Gresham, and 2Lt. Perry Dahl) on a patrol 30 to 35 miles southeast of the Finschhafen area. The Air Controller advised Tomkins of a plot "with friendly indications" headed toward the area and was not ordered to investigate. But Tomkins decided that he "would look into the matter," and as his flight approached Finschhafen at 1645 at 9,000 feet he saw AA bursts at their level, and then saw a dozen Betty bombers directly overhead at 15,000 feet escorted by 15 to 20 Zeros and Oscars. Tomkins ordered belly tanks dropped and led a climbing port turn into the sun. The Bettys had passed over Finschhafen and made a right turn to make another bombing run. The P-38s approached the bombers level head on, while the enemy fighters seemed to be oblivious until the Lightnings began to fire. The first three P-38s met heavy return fire from the bombers and were attacked by the escorts after this pass, making it impossible to make any more passes. Tomkins made a pass on a bomber that was somewhat out of formation and set its wing and engine on fire; he last saw it descending 500 feet from the main formation. Tomkins was credited with a probable because he lost sight of his victim when he went to the aid of the last man in his flight, who had lost an engine. 1Lt. Campbell Wilson didn't fire at his first target because he couldn't get sufficient lead. As Wilson broke away from his attack on the bombers a Zero attacked him from his port front quarter. Wilson turned into his attacker and fired a two second burst that hit the Zero and caused it to dive away towards cloud cover. Wilson claimed this Zero as a probable. McGuire and Peregoy both damaged Bettys on their first pass before having to break off when the enemy fighters arrived. Dahl had problems dropping his belly tank and then his starboard engine began to detonate. Dahl radioed Tomkins that he was returning to base, but as he left a cloud after finally dropping his tank three Zeros attacked him from 30 degrees high. One shot out his left coolant line and it began streaming Prestone, and then his engine began to smoke and McGuire escorted Dahl back to Dobodura. Gresham was also unable to drop his belly tank, but went to assist Dahl and fired a "fairly good" deflection shot that drove an Oscar off Dahl's tail. Gresham turned toward home, but after five minutes his belly tank jettisoned and he continued to patrol until he ran low on fuel. The enemy bombers and fighters broke off their mission, and four P-38s reformed and continued to patrol until they ran low on fuel. After the battle Wilson, Peregoy, and Gresham were forced to land at Lae to refuel, where they spent the night due to bad weather. The next day they took off for Dobodura at 1030, and 10 minutes later Wilson's port engine failed and he tried to head back to Lae, but continued to lose altitude and was forced to ditch in Huon Gulf, where he was quickly rescued by a launch and returned to Lae. This would be the last combat in which the 432FS would have any claims until 13 December. The Group continued flying patrols and sweeps for the next few days, but each mission met less and less opposition, and finally Allied planners considered Japanese airpower at Wewak was not a threat.

**19 November 1943: 58FG Arrives in Australia**

On 20 November 1940, the 58th Pursuit Group (Interceptor) was constituted to be one of the AAC's new combat groups. The 58th Pursuit was assigned to the GHQ Air Force. The Group, consisting of the 67th, 68th, and 69th Pursuit Squadrons (Interceptor), were all constituted on 20 November, and all were activated on 16 January 1941. The Group's first CO was Capt. John Sterling, and its first station was at Selfridge Field, MI. The 68th Pursuit Squadron would remain with the 58th Pursuit Group after the departure of the 67th and 68th, which were to become the nucleus of the new squadrons to be formed in early 1942. The 310PS and 311PS were constituted on 21 January 1942 and activated on 9 February 1942, then assigned to the 58FG the same day. The cadre for the 58th Pursuit Group, eight officers, and 150 enlisted men, was furnished by the transfer of personnel from the 1st Pursuit Group (the majority was from the 27PS) of the GHQ Air Force, and the initial authorized strength of the 58th Group was established by the Adjutant General.

During their time at Selfridge the 58FG performed the usual training in an assortment of training and pursuit aircraft, and garrison duties, while attached to the 1PG. By mid-September 1941 the 58PG roster had reached 20 officers and 528 enlisted men and had a full complement of pilots, and the Group was deemed capable of operating independently. On 1 October 1941 the Group left by truck for Harding Field, Baton Rouge, LA, where the Group was commanded by Lt.Col. Lee Wasser with 32 officers, none of whom would serve with the Group beyond October 1942. After Pearl Harbor it became necessary to reassign and redeploy Air Corps units, particularly to the islands along the ferry and sea routes to Australia. The 58PG (along with the 35PG and 50PG) were designated to give up their squadrons. The 67th was assigned to New Caledonia, the 68th to Canton, and the 69th to Palmyra. However, the three squadrons were not up to strength, especially in pilots, and the deficit was made up by personnel from the 69th; then the 67th and 68th were sent to their assignments, while the 69th was retained at Harding Field in mid-March 1942. Meanwhile, the 310th and 311th Pursuit Squadrons were constituted on 21 January 1942 and activated on 9 February 1942 at Harding Field, LA, and assigned them to the 58PG. At the end of February the 58FG was assigned to Dale Mabry Field, Tallahassee, FL, arriving by motor convoy. At Mabry the Group would function as a pilot replacement training unit until another unit could be created to take over that duty. By September the 338PG assumed the 58th's replacement function (until May 1944 when it was disbanded) and the 58th was now free to begin operational training to prepare for overseas assignment. However, to bring the 338th up to strength the 58FG had to transfer over 75% of its enlisted men and nearly all its officers to the 338th. On 18 September 1942, 58FG CO Lt.Col. Wasser was replaced by Lt.Col. Morley Slaght and retained only nine officers and 170 enlisted men.

On 14 October 1942 the 58th left Dale Mabry, relinquishing all its equipment to the 338PS for a brief two week reassignment stay at Richmond AAB, VA. Its 69th and 310th Fighter Squadrons were assigned to Philadelphia Municipal Airport and the 311FS went to Bolling Field, Washington, DC, to defend the Capitol and to train in P-40s. On 8 December 1942 Maj. Gwen Atkinson became Group Commander, and would be considered the heart and soul of the Group. After completing their operational training in late January 1943, 16 pilots were sent to the Buffalo, NY, Curtiss Factory to ferry new P-40Es intended to be used as replacements for fighters lost during the North African Campaign. To their surprise, pilots and enlisted men of the 311FS were to be transported with 75 P-40s on the carrier *Ranger* to Casablanca. Upon reaching North Africa, the 58th pilots made their first and only carrier take offs, and all landed safely at Casablanca to become replacement pilots, while after 22 days at sea the remainder of the 58th's men returned to America.

Meanwhile, the remaining 16 Group pilots and 265 enlisted men who had completed their training were assigned to training duties. During this period the 58th was to be deactivated, but now Lt. Colonel Atkinson persuaded the Fighter Branch to cancel a new fighter group that was to be activated and allow the 58FG to continue. On 2 March the Group moved to Bradley Field, Hartford, CT, without planes and only a few pilots. On 22 March Gen. Arnold informed Gen. Kenney that the 5FC would receive three new Fighter Groups equipped with the P-47, and eventually the 58FS would be one of these groups. On 1 May 1943 the 58th began its operational training in the P-47 at Green Field, Providence, RI. The 69FS was commanded by Capt. Milton Self; the 310FS by Capt. Joseph Klemovich; and the 311FS by Capt. Howard Tuman. After gunnery training at Suffolk County AAB the Group moved to Grenier Field, NH, for overseas staging on 15 September 1943. On 15 October they left by train for Camp Stoneman, CA, to be transported on the large liner *Nieu Amsterdam* to Sydney, Australia, via Wellington, New Zealand, on 19 November. From Sydney they were immediately transported by train to Brisbane for future shipment to New Guinea. However, when they arrived it seems that the 348FG had already received its Thunderbolts, and someone had convinced Kenney that the 35FG should receive the P-47s intended for the 58FG. Kenney did allow selected pilots from the 58th to fly on temporary duty with the 5FC HQ at Eagle Farm, and eventually more 58th pilots were allowed to fly. The problem for the 58th at the time was that it was split into four components, which would be reunited at Dobodura, New Guinea, in February 1944. The Advanced Echelon was already at Dobodura preparing for the arrival of the Group; the Ground Echelon would arrive by ship; the pilots were engaged in testing and ferrying aircraft in Australia and to New Guinea; and a number of the more experienced crews remained at Eagle Farms to prepare aircraft for combat.

By mid-January 1944, the entire 311FS and the 58FG had arrived at Dobodura, with the exception of the pilots and a small number of mechanics. About one half the pilots had been sent to New Guinea to gain combat experience with squadrons of the 348FG, while the others had been occupied by testing and ferrying duties. By the end of the month the pilots and their P-47s began to arrive, and the 311th had its full complement of 25 fighters.

**23 November 1943: 35FG/40FS**

Yellow Flight, under Capt. Jack Grimm, was assigned to escort Australian Boomerangs to Finschhafen, and on their arrival there saw nine bogies below that were identified by *Rex* Controller as B-25s. Soon *Rex* called approaching enemy aircraft, and the flight turned 180 degrees and spotted them at 18,000 feet. The flight started to climb, but both second element fighters temporarily dropped out with engine problems. Grimm and Wingman Lt. Sturgeon saw nine unescorted Nell bombers heading toward the 40FS base, but the bombers then made a 330 degree turn along the coast. Soon 10 Zero and Oscar escorts appeared to protect the bombers, and Grimm called for 40FS Red and White Flights to join at Saidor to make the interception. At 0955 Grimm and his flight caught the enemy at 22,000 feet about 35-40 miles from Saidor, and Grimm attacked the bombers while 1Lt. Francis Vetort's second element were to concentrate on the fighters. As Grimm looked back he saw Wingman Sturgeon following at 500 yards and then saw two Zeros 500 yards behind him. Grimm broke away and never saw Sturgeon again. Vetort made a pass through the Zeros and shot the empennage off one, then fired on the bombers with no observed results at his high speed. 1Lt. Carlos Dannagner of White Flight had seen a P-39 cartwheel into the water after being chased by an Oscar.

White and Yellow Flights, trailing Red Flight, came on to the scene after Red's initial contact. White Flight, led by Capt. Irvin Henze, followed Red Flight and saw action, but did not score before the bombers disappeared in the clouds. 1Lt. Billy Grey, Henze's Wingman, hit an Oscar that was on the tail of the #3 man and claimed a probable. Dannagner attacked the Oscar that was chasing Sturgeon's smoking fighter, but he approached too fast in his dive to get a good shot; he managed to chase it away, but he was too late to save Sturgeon. After Yellow #3 man Lt. Heins aborted with a bad engine, 1Lt. Carl Nelson, the #4 man, continued on with the other two P-39s. As he started down he saw three Oscars in trail closing from behind and above Grimm and Sturgeon, who were busy attacking the Nells. Nelson turned into the attackers and opened fire on an Oscar from 250 yards in a head on pass. When Nelson closed pieces came off the enemy fighter and hit his aircraft. As Nelson turned to chase the other bombers he saw the Oscar crash into the sea. By this time the bombers were too far away, and Nelson flew back toward Saidor and joined P-39s from the other 40FS flights.

**25 November 1943: 348FG/342FS**

Capt. William Banks of the 342FS led four P-47s on a fighter sweep to Wewak at 1010 at 21,000 feet. Banks saw a lone Dinah flying southeast at 18,000 feet and allowed the Dinah to pass under him. Banks dropped his belly tank and dove 3,000 feet, closing on a level astern attack. He fired two "medium" bursts; the first exploded the starboard engine and the second "caused the whole fuselage to burn" for his fourth victory.

**26 November 1943: 35FG/40FS/41FS**

40FS

26 November was the last combat of the month for the 5th Fighter Command when eight P-39s of the 40FS' Blue and Yellow Flights were on a patrol over the Lae-Kaiapit area. Yellow Flight Leader 1Lt. Francis Vetort led his flight over the shore while Blue Flight Leader Capt. Thomas Warrick led his Flight out 30 miles to sea. Enemy aircraft were first spotted in the far distance, 30 miles south of the mainland, just south of Long Island. At 1110, as the Americans closed they saw the bombers out in front in four flights of four, and then eight Oscars at 10 o'clock in loose formation.

Vetort's Flight closed on the eight Oscars which were formed in flights of four; one going right and the other left, so that either could get on the Airacobras' tails if they attacked either of the two enemy flights (Warrick's flight did not see them). Yellow Flight was above (21,000 feet) and between the two enemy formations. Vetort's first pass was too steep, and he was unable to fire at the first two Oscars and made a 90 degree deflection on the last, knocking pieces off the fuselage and canopy. Off to Vetort's side, 1Lt. Alvaro Hunter, Yellow #4, fired on the lower left Oscar, which went into a slow Split-S. Hunter followed and continually fired all the way through, but had gained so much speed that he had to either pull up or pass it, thus losing it from his sights and losing speed and altitude advantage. However, as he pulled around Hunter saw the Oscar in a spin and pieces falling off for his first victory. Hunter then saw a lone Oscar below and went into a high speed, 400 mph dive and caught the unaware enemy pilot with a long burst from behind and above. The Oscar turned into Hunter, who turned sharply and got on the enemy's tail again and fired, causing both landing gears to drop and the plane to go out of control. 2Lt. Henry Wilkes, Vetort's Wingman, got an Oscar probable. Capt. Thomas Warrick, Blue Flight Leader, claimed an Oscar probable and strafed several villages between Pommern and Sareauk Bays, then joined his Wingman, 2Lt. Robert Steffy, to strafe barges on the way home. 1Lt. David Pardy, Blue Flight Second Element Leader, got an Oscar probable. 1Lt. John Doordan, Second Element Leader in Yellow flight, claimed an Oscar probable, but his P-39 was hit by several bullets. For the day the 40FS claimed three Oscars and five Oscar probables, and would not score again until 4 March 1944, after they transitioned to P-47s and flew over the Wewak area.

**1Lt. Alvaro Hunter** claimed his first two of five victories. (AAF)

41FG

The 42FS sent out three P-39s (Flight Leader 1Lt. Roy Lawhorn, F/O Jamie Wallace, and Second Element Leader 1Lt. Walter Hymovitch – whose Wingman seems to have aborted) at 0922 to escort four RAAF Boomerangs to Finschhafen. When they arrived at 0955 at 18,000 feet they circled for about an hour when bomb explosions were seen off shore. The Airacobras were at 9,000 feet when they saw 20 to 25 Oscars at 15,000 feet escorting nine "single tail" bombers flying at 6,000. Lawhorn led his flight up above the escorting fighters, but as he was about to make a pass he was bounced by three Oscars and turned away to escape. Once clear, Lawhorn climbed back toward the Boomerangs and saw an Oscar below making a pass on a Boomerang and dove to fire at 300 yards until he passed under it. When Lawhorn looked around he saw the Oscar splash in the water, but also saw Oscars chasing him. He outdistanced them and climbed to 10,000 feet, where he saw another Oscar chasing a Boomerang. He dove on the Oscar and it turned away, but Lawhorn's diving speed was too great, and he was unable to turn with the nimble enemy. Lawhorn came out of his dive and saw Hymovitch shoot down an Oscar. Hymovitch had made the initial diving attack on an Oscar, but broke away when the three Oscars attacked. After he evaded them he climbed back toward the Boomerangs and also saw an Oscar at 100 feet over the water coming off an attack on a Boomerang. As Hymovitch approached he fired a two second burst and the Oscar rolled over and crashed for his only victory of the war. F/O Jamie Wallace flew toward the Oscar formation and saw one on Hymovitch's tail; he pulled off his pass to chase the Oscar away from Hymovitch. He then made a stern attack on an Oscar that then turned inside him, and he had to make a quick diving starboard turn to escape. As Wallace climbed for altitude he was bounced by an Oscar diving out of the sun. The Oscar pilot fired from far out of range and gave his position away, allowing Wallace to chandelle up into him. The Oscar passed within 100 feet and made a steep climbing turn, trying to get on the P-39's tail. The dogfight descended from 14,000 to 7,000 feet and lasted five minutes, with the Oscar getting four bursts, but all were low and behind, and the frustrated Japanese pilot finally turned back toward Cape Gloucester. Wallace climbed back up to close on the enemy fighters, and at 17,000 feet dove out of the sun and fired a short burst at one from 150 yards and sent it into the sea. Wallace climbed to 8,000 feet and made another pass from out of the sun on an Oscar and blew its canopy off, killing the pilot. Wallace pulled up and headed toward Madang, trying to catch the bombers. An Oscar dove on Wallace from 9,000 feet with a front quarter attack from out of range. Wallace pulled up in a turn, trying to get into position for a head on pass. The Oscar pilot went into a diving left turn, and Wallace countered with a right turn and closed to fire a short burst, getting some hits (for a probable), but had to break off when an Oscar closed dead astern to 150 yards and fired a three second burst at Wallace but missed. Wallace went into a steep dive and the Oscar followed, firing one more burst as he chased the P-39 into the clouds, where he lost contact. Wallace returned to base with the last two of his three career victories and a probable.

The 40th and 41st Fighter Squadrons of the 35th Fighter Group scored seven victories and six probables. After these aerial victories the 35FG would not score another aerial victory until 3 March 1944. Its principal operations during that time were uneventful patrols over the newly conquered northeastern New Guinea.

**26 November 1943: 8FG/35FS**

Four P-40s were sent up to patrol the Moresby to Nadzab area under 1Lt. Harold Souther and Wingman 1Lt. Roy Klandrud, with the second element of 1Lt. Elliott Brogden and Wingman Lt. Arthur Sullivan at 15,000 feet. The Nadzab Controller sent them to investigate two bandits near Saidor. Souther climbed his flight to 19,000 feet, where they spotted two bandits at 1 o'clock on the water. Souther ordered tanks to be jettisoned and a high speed dive to be initiated. Souther's first attack was inaccurate, and his next pass was interrupted by a P-40 firing at him. Brogden's first shot was inaccurate due to the high rate of diving speed, and he chandelled to meet the Zero head on. He was unable to reef the Warhawk around and Klandrud came after the Zero, which went into a shallow port turn. Klandrud's Warhawk became difficult to control in the dive and he had to pull out to lose some speed. He then went into a wingover to proceed after the enemy Wingman. Brogden pulled up as the enemy pilot turned slightly to the left and Klandrud fired a long burst from 400 yards at about 30 degrees and missed high, but nosed down and hit the fuel tank behind the cockpit, causing a tremendous explosion. Brogden got on the second Zero's tail but it was out of range. Sullivan, who also missed on his pass due to high diving speed, joined Souther as his Wingman dove on this Zero, flashing past Brogden. With his windscreen fogged over Sullivan closed for a high side pass but missed, then turned around for a second pass from 500 yards and put it into the sea. Sullivan then joined Brogden to fly home. After his second career victory Klandrud continued down the coast at 2,000 feet, where he was attacked from the rear by a Zero. Klandrud could hear bullets penetrating his aircraft and "pushed the nose down and everything forward" and got away from his pursuer. Klandrud turned his badly damaged fighter back toward base, ducking behind his armor plate and expecting another attack. He nursed his fighter back to base with his coolant system leaking and elevator shot up. When he landed he saw that three bullets had hit his seatback armor plate and glanced off through the canopy glass.

**November 1943: 475FG**

During November there were changes in the 475FG. Capt. Warren Lewis transferred from the 35FS and assumed command of the 433FS, while Col. George Prentice was replaced as Group CO by newly promoted to Lt. Colonel Charles MacDonald on 26 November. As opposed to Prentice, who was a very good administrator, MacDonald was a great air combat leader, and at war's end he would be the third ranking fighter ace in the 5FC with 27 victories. MacDonald wisely continued the administrative policies initiated by Prentice. MacDonald took command at a time when the Group's combat efficiency was gaining momentum, and with MacDonald leading it in combat by example and insisting on strict aerial discipline, the 475th became known as a superlative unit. By the end of the year the 475th Fighter Group would come to be known as "Satan's Angels." MacDonald would have to wait for several weeks before seeing any combat with the enemy, as the Group's missions were routine and uneventful during the mop up of Finschhafen and Wewak.

**Late November 1943: 49FG/9FS**

In late November the 9FS was training for their transition to P-47 Thunderbolts at Dobodura. Eager to get back into combat, 9FS CO Maj. Gerald Johnson asked that his remaining ex-Lightning pilots, as well as the newly arrived Thunderbolt pilots, qualify for attached combat duty with the veteran P-47-equipped 348FG as quickly as possible. The 39FS of the 35FG was also re-equipped with the P-47, and several times Johnson had flown with both groups. While on one of these forays, flying a fighter sweep to Finschhafen with Col. Kearby's 348FG, Johnson left the formation and bounced a radial engine aircraft flying on deck just above the trees. On his return to Dobodura, Johnson discovered his victim was a RAAF Wirraway artillery spotter whose pilot had survived. As compensation Johnson personally flew a case of gin to his Aussie victim. There are photos of Johnson standing under his cowling scoreboard with the Australian flag victory symbol displayed. During the first week in December, Johnson felt that his pilots had sufficient instruction in the Thunderbolt to resume combat and move to Gusap.

During the first week in December, 49er CO Lt.Col. James Selman began a complex reorganization and mobilization of the 49th Fighter Group. There was a change of command in two of his squadrons; the transition to a new type aircraft; and the transfer of all their ground echelon by air to their new Ramu Valley airdrome. The 49ers had senior Captains who had reached command grade, and Selman made many recommendations and advances in rank for men in his group. Several officers were assigned to the new 49ers' Headquarters unit at Gusap, while others continued to fly attached to whatever squadron required an experienced flight leader. Maj. Raymond Melikian of the 7FS, who had overseen the Demons' move from Dobodura in October, ended his tour and was replaced by Capt. Arland Stanton on 1 November. After his final combat on 15 November, Maj. Ernest Harris, who had flown 250 missions and was the highest scoring P-40 ace in the Pacific with 10 victories, was a contender for relieving Lt.Col. Selman as 49er Group Commander. But Harris was qualified to return to the States and passed command of the Black Sheep to Capt. Bernard Makowski on 22 November.

**1Lt. Arthur Sullivan** scored his only victory of the war. (AAF)

**1Lt. Roy Klandrud** (right) was credited with his second of three victories, but was lucky in landing safely in his badly damaged fighter. (AAF)

**Maj. Gerald Johnson** has an Australian Wirraway victory on his scoreboard. (AAF)

**Capt. Arland Stanton** replaced veteran 7FS CO Maj. Ray Melikian. (AAF)

# 2

# December 1943

### December 1943: Air Operations

During December, despite its preoccupation with New Britain, the Bogadjim-Madang-Alexishafen area was to receive increasing attention from the 5AF, all of whose advanced bases were all within easy reach of these targets. The last Japanese positions on the Huon Peninsula were attacked without enemy interception, while Madang and Alexishafen along the coast and Bogadjim inland received unprecedented bomb tonnage for the loss of only three bombers. On the ground, the Japanese were tenaciously holding on to hopeless positions and organized small counterattacks against the tired Australians. To counter this Japanese resistance, medium and heavy bombers attacked Japanese lines of supply and communication.

Original *Dexterity* plans called for the amphibious assault on Gasmata, followed by another on Cape Gloucester. But as the plan developed, a landing at Arawe was substituted for Gasmata and Arawe received a heavy preliminary softening up by air. After easy landings, the Allied forces met tenacious resistance over the next month and were aided by 5AF light bombers and fighters. The landings at Cape Gloucester were also preceded by heavy air bombardment operations with 972 heavy bomber, 742 medium, and 182 light bomber sorties. Japanese air reaction did not begin until the day of the landings, when over 100 Japanese aircraft attempted to penetrate the large American air cover. During the day P-38s flew 118 sorties, P-47s flew 117, P-39s flew 36, and P-40s flew 30 over the beachhead. Sixty-three Japanese aircraft were shot down for the loss of five AAF fighters. December was a significant month in the SWPA, as 5AF bombers dropped a record 7,000+ tons of bombs. The 5AF aided the amphibious forces at Cape Gloucester to establish and expand their beachhead, and prevented the Japanese from reinforcing the beleaguered Finschhafen area from New Britain and elsewhere in New Guinea.

**2Lt. George Della** scored his first of five victories. (AAF)

### December 1943: Group Movements

December 1943 saw the completion of a number of movements by units of the 5th Fighter Command as squadrons were transferred up the New Guinea coast to position them for the landings that would take place. The 49th Fighter Group completed its transfer to Gusap. In early November the advanced personnel of that Group left Moresby for Finschhafen by LST to establish a new base, while the remainder of the Group left in mid-December. The lull in air combat starting in mid-November continued until mid-December.

### 1 December 1943: 348FG/341FS

Nine P-47s in two flights; one of six and one of three from the 341FS took off from Nadzab at 1100 on a B-24 escort to Wewak. At 17,000 feet over Wewak at 1245 they saw "15 to 30" Tonys approaching from the northwest at 18,000 feet. Second flight Element Leader 1Lt. Wilburn Henderson and his Wingman, Lt. Craddock, saw two Tonys maneuvering to attack the bombers head on. These Tonys dived in front of the two P-47s and began a left turn when Henderson fired and hit the second Tony's fuselage; it crashed into a forest 10 miles inland. The two pilots climbed to 17,000 feet and formed a moving Lufbery over the bombers. The Tonys made concerted attacks on the bombers and Lufbery, but Henderson and Craddock drove them away, On one attack Henderson was flying about 2,000 yards away from Flight Leader 1Lt. Merle Zeine when a Tony made a head on pass at Zeine and then turned toward Henderson and flew through the American's sights, sustaining hits to the engine that froze the prop, and it went into a fatal dive. Henderson continued to fire short bursts at the Tonys without a chance to hit them, but only to drive them away. Henderson was climbing back into the Lufbery when a Tony coming out of a dive got on his tail and used his diving speed to gain on Henderson, who went into a Split-S straight down, ending in a 540 mph dive that lost the Tony at 2,000 feet. Henderson turned for home, but had forgotten to switch on his belly tank and used about 100 gallons of fuel from his main tank, landing with only 10 gallons of fuel remaining; a lucky pilot with his final two of three victories.

1Lt. Clarence Blend was the Element Leader for Zeine's flight and had 1Lt. George Della as his Wingman. Blend's radio antenna had broken off during the flight and he had no communications with the Squadron. Two Tonys attacked Blend and Della, and Blend turned into the attack but could not shoot, as his radius of turn was too short. However Della, behind

Blend, saw the Tony begin a dive and pulled his nose up and met the Tony head on, trying to scare it off. The Tony banked to his left and then right, and then went into a shallow dive. As the Tony completed the maneuver Della fired a long burst at full deflection, killing the pilot. Blend saw a Tony chasing a P-47 and fired from out of range, driving the enemy off. Blend made three passes on Tonys that had gotten on the P-47s' tails, and on his last pass flamed a Tony that crashed into the ground. Another Tony came up on Blend's blind spot and hit his aileron; Blend dove away and flew on instruments through the overcast, and then flew through broken clouds in the valleys and landed at Nadzab with his first of two victories.

**1 December 1943: 8FG/36FS**

The 36FS sent out 13 P-47s to fly top cover for B-24s over Wewak. The 36th did not pick up the bombers until they reached Wewak Harbor, as the Liberators left the rendezvous point 10 minutes early. At 1300 1Lt. Donald Campbell and his Wingman saw two Zeros near the B-24 formation three miles away at 2 o'clock and 2,000 feet below. Campbell dove as one of the Zeros made a head on pass on the bombers and passed under them, rolling on its back, and then climbed as it passed the last bomber. The enemy pilot did not see Campbell, who had closed behind him and fired a long burst at 200 yards. Campbell's shots fell behind the Zero and he had to throttle back, as he was closing too fast. Campbell fired again, and the Zero pilot finally made an evasive maneuver; half rolling to port, but to no avail, as Campbell's shots hit the cockpit and the Zero went into a steep dive.

Outstanding leader **Maj. Donald Campbell** scored his only victory of the war. (AAF)

**3 December 1943: 348FG/Kearby Special Flight**

On 3 December 1943 Kearby arrived at Nadzab early in the morning to organize another "special" four plane sweep over Wewak. He selected Col. Robert Rowland and Capt. Frank Oksala as one element and took Capt. Meade Brown of the 341FS as his Wingman.

The four P-47s took off at 0900 and arrived over Manchu Island at 27,000 feet at about 1100, where they saw 20 to 30 enemy fighters approaching from the northwest at 15,000 feet. Rowland developed engine trouble and Oksala followed him back, but before they were out of sight, Kearby called out a formation of 20 to 25 Tonys and Oscars just below, flying southeast along the coast. Oksala returned to the Flight while the disgruntled Rowland continued back to Nadzab.

Kearby maneuvered into the sun and began a high speed 180 degree dive that ended in the 7 o'clock position behind an Oscar. He opened fire from 300 yards at a closing speed of about 350 mph. The doomed Japanese fighter began to break up and trail fire from the port wing and fuselage. Kearby turned onto the tail of another Oscar, but two more were turning sharply to Kearby's left, so he turned his fighter even more sharply and met these enemy fighters head on. Both pilots opened fire at about the same time, but Kearby's eight heavy .50 caliber guns scored strikes on the fuselage near the cockpit. Kearby then quickly shifted his fire to the enemy Wingman and hit it hard, and as he passed over the two ill-fated Oscars, he almost collided with another enemy fighter flying behind the first two.

Oksala shot down a Tony for his third and last victory, while Brown had followed Kearby down in his 180 degree dive and got good hits on a Tony's wing roots and near the canopy for his first victory. As the enemy fighter plunged into the sea Brown rejoined Kearby to head for base, as the Japanese were massing to eradicate the Americans. As Kearby went into the landing pattern he pulled up and executed three victory rolls for his three victories that made him a triple ace with 15 victories.

**7 December 1943: 348FG/ Kearby Special Flight**

On 7 December Kearby again organized a special four plane flight flying to Wewak at 1200 with the same pilots as on the 3rd. The flight patrolled for a half hour at 27,000 feet when Kearby saw three Tonys in the landing pattern at Wewak. He led the flight in a north to south dive, but at 20,000 feet Brown saw 18 Tonys and Hamps at 9 o'clock at 23,000 feet flying northwest. Brown and the Rowland/Oksala element attacked this new opponent, leaving Kearby alone. The unaware Kearby headed down toward the Wewak strip and approached the field just after two Tonys had landed. His Thunderbolt was registering 500 mph when he came up behind the third Tony and opened fire at 5 o'clock, getting hits on its canopy, and the Tony rolled over on its back at about 200 feet. However, at this time Kearby's canopy frosted over due to rapid pressure change during his fighter's rapid dive and he could not see out of it. Kearby opened the side window and looked for the remains of his latest victim, but found neither the Tony nor his Wingman. Wewak AA fire cut his search short as he climbed back to 26,000 feet and had to settle for a probable claim, as there were no witnesses to his 16th victory. Of the other three special pilots, only Capt. Meade Brown made a Tony probable claim.

**Capt. Francis Oksala** (right), with **Max Wiecks** (center) and **Floyd Meyer** (left), shot down a Tony for his third and last victory. (AAF)

**Lt.Col. Neel Kearby** led another "Special Flight" and downed three Zeros to become a triple ace. (AAF)

**10 December 1943: 49FG/7FS/8FS/9FS**

By the second week in December Gusap Airstrip #5, a second shorter pierced steel matting runway stretching parallel to the south side of the 3rd Attack Squadron's Strip #10, had been completed for use by the 9 FS. 9FS CO Maj. Gerald Johnson and Wingman 2Lt. Raymond Swift, Element Leader Capt. Walter Markey, and Wingman 1Lt. Ralph Wandrey flew from Horanda, Dobodura, on their first official Thunderbolt sortie to their new Gusap base. Part of the transfer to Gusap was the squadron's oldest veteran, "Huckleberry Duck," a large white duck mascot who would travel in Ralph Wandrey's fighter, firmly wrapped in a sheet and stuffed under the seat. The Flight climbed due north to 9,000 feet for the hour flight.

On that day the Japanese at Wewak would fly a maximum effort against the Allied airdromes in the Ramu Valley. The Tony-equipped 68th Sentai had recently returned from Manila and, with the 78th Sentai, staged into Madang during the first week in December. Those veteran units were reinforced by the newly arrived Oscar-equipped 33rd and 63rd Sentais. The veteran Oscar 24th and 248th units also staged into Alexishafen during the following week, providing the 4th Air Army with over 80 fighter aircraft for the next air campaign against Gusap. The Japanese began the day's operations at daybreak when a large random formation of Tonys left Madang for the Ramu Valley, hiding their approach in the broken clouds above the Finistere Range. The first wave of Tonys descended to strafe the Gusap runways before the alert was given.

The eight fighters, led by new 8FS CO Capt. Bernard Makowski, had been airborne for only 30 minutes when an alert was radioed by *Nephew* Air Controller. Makowski's Red Flight turned due south at 9,500 feet over Dumpu and then headed up the Ramu Valley, followed by White Flight under 1Lt. Carl Lambert. The Flights turned through broken cloud formations when four Tonys were spotted at the same altitude, followed by a larger scattered formation of Oscars at 14,000 feet. Makowski decided to climb higher for a better position to attack, and as his Red Flight slowly began a climbing starboard turn, Makowski suddenly reversed his direction when they entered a cloud and the entire flight became completely separated. Lambert's White Flight entered their climbing turn and lost sight of the Red Flight. Red Flight's tail end P-40, flown by F/O Walter Linder, was ambushed and hit. Prestone coolant streamed from his Allison engine, and Linder could not escape and had to fight alone. He fired on the swirling enemy pilots and destroyed a Tony, but his Warhawk was being torn to pieces. As Linder tried to escape an explosive round detonated on the back of his headrest and shrapnel cut his left ankle. The desperate pilot continued on, but his engine fully seized eight miles north of the airfield; Linder though was able to make a skilful belly landing on the kunai plain with more than 100 holes in his fighter and lucky to survive to celebrate his second and last victory.

Meanwhile, veteran Red Element Leader 1Lt. William Runey was the only Black Sheep to climb and gain an altitude advantage over one of the Oscars. Runey attacked in a head on pass and hit it from wingtip to wingtip, but had to dive away, as more Oscars descended on him before he was able to finish off the enemy fighter and was awarded a damaged claim.

Maj. Johnson and his three 9FS wingmen were approaching Gusap from Dobodura and were descending for their landing at 0845 when *Nephew* alerted them of the Japanese attack. The flight climbed back up to 9,000 feet, and after 15 minutes of searching through scattered clouds the Thunderbolts encountered eight Tonys 20 miles beyond Gusap Village, heading for the coast at 5,000 feet. The flight dove their heavy P-47s into a head on attack, and Johnson and Element Leader Markey each opened fire, with Johnson damaging his target, but Markey's victim burned and crashed into the valley floor. The Thunderbolts then went into a high speed climb and turned into a frontal attack, in which Markey got his second victory of the day, but leaving him one short of becoming an ace before he went home. Johnson got into a turning dogfight with a Tony and flamed its engine with an outstanding deflection shot which made him a double ace.

**1Lt. Robert DeHaven** was lucky to be alive, but became an ace with his Tony victory. (AFAA)

**1Lt. Bobby Harrison** claimed his only victory of the war. (AAF)

**Maj. Gerald Johnson** became a double ace with 10 victories. (AFAA)

Swift and Wandrey had been in ideal firing position to attack several targets, but both had faulty gun switches. To make matters worse, Wandrey's passenger, Huckleberry Duck, had escaped from under the seat, and the pilot had to struggle with a terrified bird that covered the cockpit floor with feathers and excrement. All Flying Knights and one duck were able to land safely at Gusap #5.

As the Japanese fighters retreated to their bases on the coast, the Screamin' Demons were simultaneously flying inland from a fighter sweep to Hansa Bay. The Demon mission was led by recently appointed Assistant Ops Exec 1Lt. Robert Harrison. His Blue Flight Wingman was the new CO, Capt. Arland Stanton, who was accompanied by element leader Capt. Sheldon Brinson and his Wingman, 1Lt. Robert DeHaven. As the clouds closed in the other flight, led by Ops Exec Capt. Carl Aubry, separated.

At 0920, Blue Flight had just passed Madang a few miles inland at 12,000 feet when Flight Leader Harrison called out the mixed flight of Tonys and Oscars below headed for Alexishafen. Harrison immediately dove into the attack, with Stanton and

Element Leader Brinson and Wingman DeHaven following closely. Harrison's burst destroyed one of the Tonys, which crashed near Alexishafen (his only victory). Capt. Stanton shot down another Ki-43 which crashed into the missionary churchyard in Madang Village (his fourth victory). Capt. Brinson was about to fire at a Tony when DeHaven spotted another enemy Wingman who had in turn targeted Brinson. DeHaven fired a wide angle deflection to divert the attacker, but was forced to break away when yet another Tony came into firing range. Brinson continued in the pursuit of two other targets but was unable to rejoin DeHaven. The trailing veteran Sentai pilot hit DeHaven's fighter with his first burst of machine gun fire, and DeHaven's rudder controls were destroyed. DeHaven racked his damaged P-40 into a hard aileron roll and began a twisting descent, but the Tony pilot skillfully kept his position at DeHaven's 6 o'clock. Each time his Warhawk bottomed out in its rolling evasive maneuver, the Sentai pilot fired a devastating burst, destroying DeHaven's radio, hitting his cowling, and exploding his port ammunition bay. DeHaven was still minutes away from the Gusap airfields as the Japanese pilot closed again. DeHaven had lost altitude and could only skim the treetops in his last chance to lose his pursuer, who was closing for the kill. But when DeHaven anxiously looked back he saw the Tony suddenly snap upward into a chandelle to join four other Tonys who were flying in the opposite direction for their return to Madang. Once in the Gusap #7 landing pattern DeHaven found that his hydraulics had been shot out, so he had to land without landing gear or flaps and decided on a belly landing on the side of the strip. He throttled the Warhawk back to the edge of a stall and carefully swung back and forth with aileron control to lose air speed. Then, as he approached the field, a C-47 transport suddenly appeared head on from the west with its flaps down and landing gear extended. DeHaven advanced the throttle and dropped his port wing, using his engine torque to sneak past the transport by only a few feet. Now flying at only a hundred feet above the kunai grass, he had to re-approach the field, flying over the river, and then make a broad flat turn to try to land again from the west. DeHaven's shuttering P-40 drifted down to the edge of the runway and slid to a stop in a cloud of dust and debris. DeHaven quickly got out of the cockpit shaken but safe, and an ace with his fifth victory.

**Capt. Sheldon Brinson** scored a probable and his last of three victories. (AAF)

**2Lt. Louis Martin** shot down a Betty and claimed another damaged for his only claims of the war. (AAF)

**12 December 1943: 49FG/7FS**

Both sides flew sporadic fighter sweeps the day before, but no significant contacts were made in the marginal weather. On the 12th a large force of Oscars of the 24th and 63rd Sentais would escort Nakajima Ki-49 Helen heavy bombers to attack Gusap. At mid-morning Demon Blue Flight Leader Capt. Sheldon Brinson was on patrol with Lts. Russell Cash, Element Leader 1Lt. John Miller, and lucky but now composed 1Lt. Robert DeHaven in the #4 position. Red Flight was led by 1Lt. Joseph O'Conner with Wingman 2Lt. Fernley Damstrom, Element Leader 2Lt. Louis Martin, and Wingman 1Lt. Lewis Smith. At 1000 the Demons were flying over Gusap at 10,000 feet when a bomber formation of three Vs and a large Oscar escort were seen approaching from the east. O'Conner's Red Flight was closest, and he led his Warhawks in a climbing attack as the Japanese abandoned their bomb run at 11,000 feet. As the Red Flight jettisoned their tanks, O'Conner's engine briefly lost power and he fell out of formation in a flat spin; his Wingman Damstrom lost O'Conner and returned to Gusap. Element Leader Martin assumed the lead of Red Flight, and he and Smith overtook the Helens over the foothills and closed on the enemy formation's right flank. Both pilots targeted the same bomber, which was closest to the right, and fired until the bomber's starboard engine began to smoke, and Martin was credited with his only victory of the war. The two sped past, then turned around under the bomber formation and attacked the left flank, and Martin damaged another Betty. However, a tail gunner on one of the left flank Helens hit both Martin and Smith's radiators and put them out of action.

Red Flight Leader O'Conner's Allison regained power and he tried to overtake the bombers. O'Conner saw a Helen on the right flank falling behind with its engine on fire, and as he was about to get into firing range his Warhawk was hit by enemy bullets from behind. The Oscar moved into point blank range and poured a continuous volley of fire into O'Conner's fighter. Somehow O'Conner was not wounded and was able to safely land at Gusap #7, but his Warhawk was written off.

Meanwhile, Mission Leader Brinson's Blue Flight had climbed higher than the unfortunate Red Flight. Blue Flight closed in waiting to make a firing pass on the Helens after Red Flight's second pass on the bombers' left flank. But just as Brinson was about to fire on a Helen, its tail gunner fired and his shells exploded on Brinson's canopy, knocking him unconscious. He came to moments later partially blinded by the smoke and glass shards in his eyes, and burning shrapnel lacerations in his left arm and both legs. He jettisoned the shattered canopy, and when the slip stream cleared out the smoke, he found his instruments were operating and the engine functioning. Not wanting to bailout over the coastal mountains, Brinson turned his wounded P-40 for home. Once over Gusap #7 he attempted a belly landing, but his distorted vision and shrapnel wounds caused him to overshoot the runway, and the Warhawk slid 100 yards through the rough kunai grass. He was rescued from the smoldering wreck and immediately transported for surgery at Port Moresby. He survived the surgery and was sent back to America with three victories and two probables but never flew again. The Moresby surgeons reported that after the tough Brinson had one of his lacerated testicles removed he requested "Issue me one of them nurses and I'll test-hop your handy work, Doc."

Meanwhile, DeHaven got into a solo dogfight with the Oscars up the Valley as far as Alexishafen. He made turning attacks against several foes but was getting too close to the enemy base, and as he turned back for Gusap he came upon a pair of Oscar stragglers. DeHaven could not pass on the prospect of gaining more victories. As a P-47 zoomed by he rolled over through a Split-S turn to come directly head on to the trailing fighter. The Oscar pilot turned to starboard, giving DeHaven a deflection shot that set fire to the enemy's starboard wingroot. DeHaven and the P-47 circled over the stricken Oscar, which finally exploded on a hillside just southwest of Alexishafen Village (DeHaven's sixth victory).

The P-47 pilot was Maj. Gerald Johnson, 9FS CO, who had returned to Dobodura two days earlier and led another four Thunderbolts on a cross country transfer to Gusap, and had again arrived there as the enemy was leaving. The P-47s had reached Gusap at 8,000 feet and used most of their remaining fuel in their climbing pursuit of the higher Japanese formation, but Element Leader Capt. Wallace Jordan was able to overtake and damage an Oscar, which was not credited.

**13 December 1943: 475FG/432FS**

At 0915 Capt. John Loisel rendezvoused his 11 (two aborted) P-38s with B-24s headed for Cape Hoskins, which was weathered in. The alternative target was Lindenhaven Plantation at Gasmata, and as the Liberators finished their bombing run they were attacked by four single engine enemy fighters from above. Loisel saw two Zeros headed at the bombers at 10,000 feet and his flight dove on them. The Zero pilots split, and Loisel and his Wingman, 2Lt. Joseph Forster, went after one that pulled up into him. He fired "approximately 10 rounds of 20mm cannon and 200 rounds of .50 caliber" at the Zero, and Forster then came in and fired a short burst at it. Forster wrote in his ICR that "it was Capt. Loisel who started the Zeke smoking, which resulted in its final destruction" for his sixth victory.

**Capt. John Loisel** shot down a Zero over Gasmata for his sixth victory. (AFAA)

**13 December 1943: 8FG**

Twelve P-38s led by Maj. Edward Cragg took off at 0900 and rendezvoused with 18 B-24s over Gona for a strike on Cape Hoskins, located near the southern end of New Britain. When they reached the target only a few of the bombers dropped their bombs on the target because of the closing weather, while the others diverted to the secondary target at the Ring-Ring Plantation near Gasmata. All but six B-24s bombed the target, and while those six bombers circled again for another run, one P-38 flight led by Capt. John Jones stayed with them. When these bombers completed their bomb run four Japanese interceptors climbed from behind at 13,000 feet, which was the same altitude as the P-38 escort. 1Lt. Kenneth Ladd was flying in the tail end position of the flight when an enemy fighter attacked him from below before he could drop his tanks. The surprised Ladd dropped his tanks and turned into the Zeros, then got on the tail of one as it turned to attack the bombers. Ladd fired from out of range to discourage the enemy pilot's attack, but he continued to get quite close to the Liberator before he broke away. Ladd followed and fired two bursts that hit its wing and fuselage and sent it into a steep dive. Ladd had to roll out before he saw what happened to it, and in his ICR said "I can make no claims," but was nonetheless credited with a victory, his fourth.

2Lt. Howard Donaldson had a hair raising experience when he was following his Flight Leader Capt. Gordon Willetts in trail. Willets spotted enemy aircraft and quickly leveled off and dropped his tanks, but Donaldson did not have time to swing out of trail and one of Willetts' tanks hit his port engine, tearing off the prop and setting the engine on fire. Fortunately, Donaldson was able to immediately drop his tanks and the fire went out after five minutes; 1Lt. Robert Hanson escorted him safely back to base.

The other 80th Lightnings sighted eight enemy fighters in the area and turned after them, but the broken clouds allowed Japanese to break off combat at will and take immediate cover. Post mission interrogations determined that some of these enemy fighters were Ki-44 Tojos; one of the first sightings of this type in the SWPA. Capt. John Jones damaged one of the fighters later identified as a Tojo.

**14 December 1943: 35FG Arrives at Nadzab**

The ground echelon of the 39FG left Moresby for Nadzab by sea transportation in early November. They landed at Lae late in the month and

**1Lt. Kenneth Ladd** scored his fourth victory. (AFAA)

The Japanese sent up **Zeros** to defend targets in New Britian before the Arawe Landings. (AAF)

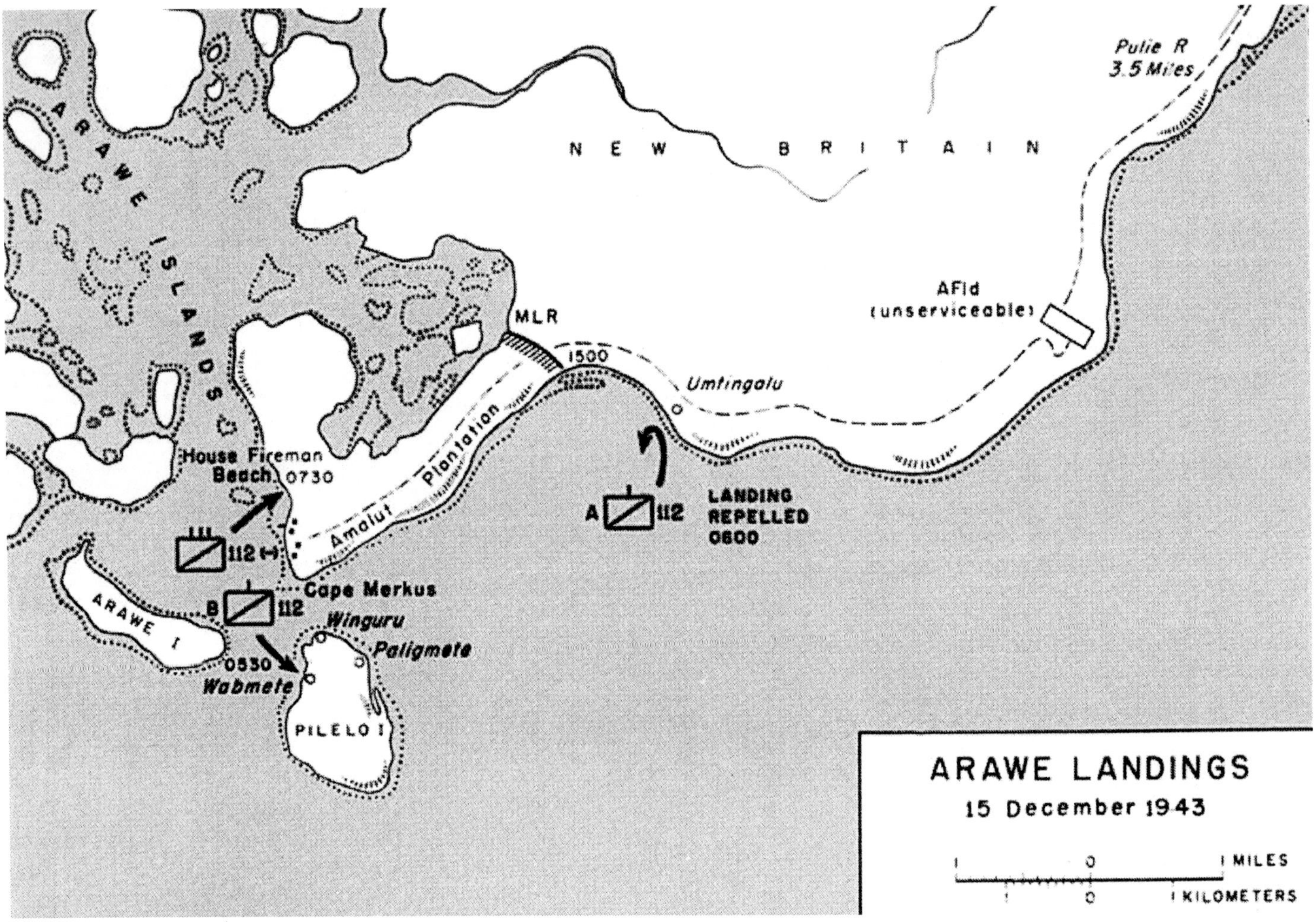


proceeded overland to Nadzab on the newly built road. Their movement there was delayed several times to wait for the finishing touches on the road and they finally arrived on 14 December. The Squadron's pilots and their new P-47 Thunderbolts arrived soon after and relieved the Group's other two squadrons of their monotonous patrol duties. This was the first time since the Group left training at Mt. Gambier, Australia, in April 1942 that all squadrons were together at one base, as their previous bases at Sydney, Moresby, and Tsili Tsili had been inadequate to base all three Squadrons.

**15 December 1943: Arawe Invasion (*Operation Director*)**

The Arawe Campaign (*Operation Director*) was part of *Operation Cartwheel*, and had the objective of isolating the key Japanese base at Rabaul. Arawe was invaded on 15 December 1943 by United States and Australian forces to secure an advanced base on the southern coast of New Britain and was secured after a month of fighting.

The Allied Air Forces began pre-invasion attacks on western New Britain on 13 November, but in order to achieve tactical surprise only a few attacks were made on the Arawe area. Instead, heavy attacks were made against Gasmata and the Ring Ring and Lindenhafen Plantations. The Arawe area was attacked for the first time on 6 December, and again on 8 December with little air or AA opposition. It was not until the day before the landings, 14 December, that heavy 5BC air attacks on Arawe were made when 273 sorties were conducted against targets on New Britain's south coast.

The *Director* Task Force was concentrated at Goodenough Island in early December 1943, and the Task Force proceeded to Buna to rendezvous with most of the escorting destroyers and made a feint towards Finschhafen before turning towards Arawe after dusk on 14 December. The convoy was detected by a Japanese aircraft shortly before it anchored off Arawe at 0330 on 15 December, and the Japanese 11th Air Fleet at Rabaul began to prepare aircraft to attack it. The Japanese air units at Rabaul had been greatly weakened in the months prior to the landing at Arawe by the protracted Allied attacks there and the transfer of the 7th Air Division to western New Guinea. Nevertheless, the Japanese 11th Air Fleet had 100 fighters and 50 bombers based at Rabaul at the time of the landing at Arawe.

Once ashore the 112th Cavalry rapidly secured the Arawe Peninsula with little resistance, and by the end of the day over 1,600 Allied troops were ashore. However, the Allied naval force off Arawe was subjected to a heavy air raid shortly after the landing. At 0900 eight Val dive bombers escorted by 56 Zero fighters evaded the AAF combat air patrol of 16 P-38 Lightnings. The Japanese air force attacked the recently-arrived first supply echelon, which comprised five LCTs and 14 LCMs, but these ships managed to evade the bombs dropped on them.

Eighty-two P-38s of the 8th, 49th, and 475th Fighter Groups, plus 46 P-47s of the 348th Group covered the landings during the day, but these fighters had little success against the two attacks that the Japanese mounted against the offshore invasion shipping, as only one Japanese aircraft was shot down by an American fighter of the 433FS.

**15 December 1943: 475FG/433FS/432FS**

433FS

At 1115 four P-38s led by Capt. Warren Lewis with Wingman 1Lt. Chase Brenizer were on patrol over central New Britain from Arawe to Telasea. While over Commodore Bay at 15,000 feet Lewis saw a lone enemy aircraft 3,000 feet below. Lewis dove first and fired without any result. Brenizer followed and fired a long burst at 200 yards as it rolled and Split-S'd to starboard. There were several flashes seen on its canopy, fuselage, and wing root, with large pieces of the cowling and canopy falling off for his second of three victories.

432FS
At 1730 two flights of eight P-38s were vectored by Finschhafen *Harvest* Controller to a plot heading from Lae to Aware, and 1Lt. William Ritter's flight made contact with two groups of enemy bombers escorted by Zeros 40 miles due east of Finschhafen. Ritter was at 8,000 feet, and the enemy Sally and Betty bombers about 1,000 feet above them. Ritter climbed "well above" the bomber formation when they were attacked by eight to 10 Zeros from above. Ritter ordered his flight to drop their tanks and dive away. The enemy pilots fired from out of range but did not follow the Americans. Ritter climbed back up to 18,000 feet in a weaving pattern that put him on the tail of the bomber formation. He made a number of passes, changing his lead several times, but saw no results. "Five or six" Zeros got on Ritter's tail and he was forced to escape into the clouds. When he exited he found that he was alone, and landed at Finschhafen for refueling. 1Lt. Elliott Summer, who had taken over the lead of the other flight, didn't see the enemy fighters until they were diving and he dove away from them. When Summer pulled out he saw two Lightnings climbing and decided to join them, but his engine began to overheat and smoke. Summer decided it was best to roll out and head home and landed at 1905. 1Lt. Vivian Cloud also escaped the diving Zero escort and made several ineffective passes at the "uneager" Zeros and then the bombers, which stayed in tight formation. The 432FS had missed a good opportunity to increase their victory total.

**1Lt. Francis Lent** claimed his ninth victory. (AAF)

**2Lt. John Tilley** got his first of five victories. (AFAA)

**16 December 1943: 475FG/431FS/432FS/433FS**
431FS
On the day following the Arawe Invasion, the 5FC had more success combating the Japanese attackers during a patrol over Arawe. At the 1130 take off 1Lt. David Allen led the 431FS, but soon his compass malfunctioned and he turned the lead over to 1Lt. Donno Bellows, and Allen followed Bellows as the Mission Leader of Green Flight. Bellows soon was forced to abort and passed the lead to Capt. Thomas McGuire, who had returned to combat status after his October leave. Hades Squadron was now reduced from 16 to nine P-38s as it arrived over the target at 21,000 feet. At 1345 the Controller at Arawe radioed McGuire the plot of a formation of 12 enemy bombers high over Baker Island. The Squadron flew out 35 miles toward the vector but, had to return to their assigned patrol area to protect against enemy bombers attacking from under the overcast. After circling for about 10 minutes the Squadron headed for Cape Gloucester, and at 1400 spotted seven Betty bombers at 18,000 feet in tight formation escorted by 15 to 20 Zeros. McGuire did not see the Bettys despite calls from his flights, and 1Lt. Carl Houseworth led his intact Green Flight with Wingman 1Lt. Franklin Monk and second element 1Lt. Francis Lent and Wingman 1Lt. Christopher Herman down from 21,000 feet. Lent attacked the third Betty on the right side of the formation and shot off pieces of canopy during his head on pass for his ninth victory. 1Lt. David Allen and 2Lt. John Tilley followed Green Flight into the attack, and Allen a made a pass on the lead Betty on the far side of the formation, which began to smoke and make evasive turns. The bomber's waist gunner was firing at Allen, but he "was too busy watching the waist gunner firing" at him that he did not see the fate of his Betty. However his Second Element Leader, 1Lt. William O'Brien, was following and saw Allen's victim burst into flames for Allen's eighth and last victory of the war. Allen and Tilley were attacked from above by Zeros and dove away; once safe the two climbed back to 20,000 feet to close on the Bettys. Allen got a "good shot" on the lead bomber and claimed it as a probable in his ICR but was never officially credited for the probable. The two pilots had to break off their attack when a Zero dove on them, and they again dove away to safety below the overcast at 12,000 feet. They entered the overcast, and when they emerged they saw a lone Betty. Tilley was in the better firing position, directly astern, and closed and fired from 500 yards until he was almost on its tail, starting a fire in its port engine to claim his first victory. The frustrated McGuire, who had scored his last (13th) victory on 17 October, was eager for more, as Bong now had 21. But he was much too late to engage any of the remaining Bettys before they escaped into the clouds. He chased a straggling Zero and fired a 90 degree deflection shot at it and saw "some smoke and red glow of fire near the engine, but the Zero made it to the clouds before I could see anything else."

432FS

The Squadron sent out 16 P-38s to escort the B-24s to Cape Gloucester when a plot was called in and Blue Flight, lead by 1Lt. Elliott Summer and Wingman 1Lt. Vivian Cloud and Second Element Leader, Capt. John Loisel and Wingman 2Lt. Ferdinand Hanson, took off to search for the enemy at 1400. As the Flight began to climb they spotted 30 Zeros and Tonys escorting seven Betty bombers but they were bounced by three enemy fighters before they could attack. Summer ordered the tanks dropped and the Flight peeled away to about 21,000 feet to lose their attackers who seemed intent on protecting the bombers. The Flight climbed to 25,000 feet, 2,000 feet above the escorts which were circling and weaving around the bombers at various altitudes. No matter what angle the P-38s tried to attack the bombers three or four escorts intervened but then Split-S'd away for about 1,000 feet before returning to cover their bomber formation. The bombers then entered the overcast at 20,000 feet but Blue Flight got a number of passes at the Zeros: Loisel and Summer scored several hits on Zeros that started smoking as they entered the overcast for damaged claims. The Flight returned to base, escorting the B-24s. Summer noted in his ICR that the "(enemy) pilots seemed very capable, not giving us many shots."

433FS

At 1400, 16 P-38s of the 433FS under Capt. Warren Lewis were on a patrol over Aware at 13,000 feet when a lone Zero was spotted in a clearing in the overcast at 15,000 feet above them south of Eleanora Bay. As Lewis led the Squadron in a climb to gain altitude for the attack, he saw two Bettys flying next to each other toward Talasea on the north coast. He closed and fired on the left bomber that became a ball of fire after he hit its right engine. Lewis' Wingman fired a short burst causing a white puff of smoke from its engine. Capt. John Babel who was leading the second flight with Wingman, 2Lt. Louis Longman, continued the attack on this Betty, firing a six second burst from dead astern and set both engines on fire for his third and last victory to go with three probables.

Lewis' Second Element Leader, 1Lt. William Jeakle, followed Lewis when he attacked the two Bettys and Jeakle saw a lone Zero make a pass on Lewis. Jeakle and Longman climbed toward the Zero and Jeakle and opened fire at 250 yards at 45 degrees. Jeakle realized his airspeed was getting too low and drew his fire through the Zero at 50 yards for his third and last victory.

1Lt. Charles Grice was leading the second flight and followed Lewis' first flight as it made its turn on the two Bettys. The Lightnings flew through the overcast and the Zeros dove on them and Grice had to lead his flight back into the clouds. As Grice left the clouds he saw a Lightning make a pass at a Betty and then break away without doing any damage. As the Betty turned slightly to port Grice pumped machine gun and cannon rounds into the rear gunner's position and then into the left wing root and the Betty caught fire immediately and did a wingover into the ground. 2Lt. Clarence Rieman, Grice's Wingman, followed Grice down when he attacked the Betty and saw a Tony make a pass on Grice at 10 o'clock and then fly through the P-38 formation. Rieman followed it in a diving turn to starboard and fired at it from 200 yards at 30 degrees deflection from above. Cannon shells hit

**1Lt. William Jeakle** scored his third and last victory, but he counted the probable of 9 November as a victory. (AAF)

**Capt. Warren Lewis** (with John Babel) claimed his third and fourth victories. (AAF)

**1Lt. Charles Grice**, being decorated by Gen. Wurtsmith, scored his fourth and last victory. (AAF)

**Capt. John Babel** was credited with his last of three victories. (AAF)

the Tony's canopy but he lost sight of it when he returned to his flight but was credited with his first of two victories. Grice hit his bomber in its wing root and it burst into flames and went down in a spiral with two crew men bailing out before it crashed for his fourth and final victory.

As Babel's flight dove away it was attacked by two enemy fighters but all escaped into the clouds. As they climbed up through the overcast they spotted three Bettys headed north toward Talasea which were chased by Lewis' flight. Lewis had led his flight above the overcast where he approached a Betty protected by three enemy fighters at 12,000 feet. Lewis ignored the enemy fighter escort and fired a rear quarter volley that hit its port engine for his second kill of the day and four so far for the war.

**16 December 1943: 348FG/342FS**

On the 16th the 342FS sent eight P-47s in two flights, Red and White, at 1445 and then sent nine P-47s in two flights, Yellow and White, at 1620 on a patrol over the Arawe invasion convoy.

Early 1445 Mission

The early mission left at 1445 on a patrol mission over Arawe. They flew at 16,000 feet and at about 1700 when they neared the target descended to about 5,000 feet. Soon, three enemy fighters at 16,000 feet and a Kate bomber at 2,000 feet were seen approaching from the northeast. White Element Leader, 1Lt. Marvin Grant, flew toward the enemy attackers, careful to stay out of range of the AA fire of the destroyers escorting the convoy. Grant saw the Kate heading for rain and thunder clouds immediately north of the convoy and he dove toward the cloud at 300 mph. Grant fired out of range at the Kate and after about two minutes he exited the cloud at 130 mph at 2,500 feet. When he looked down he saw the Kate below and 1,500 feet ahead on its back in a steep dive. Grant snapped off a quick burst as the Kate crashed into a mountain north of Arawe.

Capt. Edward Roddy was Red Flight Leader and dove on one Zero and fired a burst at maximum deflection but his tracers fell behind it. Roddy increased his lead and set the Zero on fire. Later Roddy was chasing a Zero when he saw another Zero sneaking onto the tail of another P-47. Roddy climbed and put a burst in front of the attacking Zero which rolled into a dive. Roddy dove after him and slowly closed to 50 yards and opened fire and decimated the enemy fighter. A piece flew off the Zero and hit Roddy's port wing but he was able to return to base safely.

Late 1620 Mission

At 1645 Capt. Lester Wolf, Operations Officer of the 310FS of the 58FG, joined a patrol over Arawe with the 342FS, leading a second element, with Wingman, 2Lt. Herman Bissonnette, also of the 310th. After the *Beach* Controller reported bombing and strafing by the Japanese, the Flight Leader, Capt. Edward Roddy, dove 2,000 feet on a Zero and shot it down. Flying at 2,000 feet Wolf saw 12 Zeros flying in a Lufbery Circle at about 8,000 feet and climbed to the attack with Bissonnette. One of the Zekes rolled out of the Circle in a turning dive, to engage the two 310th pilots. As the Zero made its attack Wolf was unable to get a deflection shot as the enemy plane passed. Wolf continued to follow the Zero and finally got a three second 90 degree deflection shot but did not observe any results. Another Zeke peeled out of the Circle and Wolf engaged at about 6,000 feet and immediately got on the enemy's tail at about 600 yards and closed rapidly and began to fire with only three guns working at about 500 yards. He continued to fire until he closed to about 250 yards when he ran out of ammunition. Bissonnette confirmed the kill when he saw pieces of the Zeke's canopy and fuselage near the cockpit splinter off. The Zero pulled up, rolled over, fell off on one wing and disappeared into a cloud layer at 1,500 feet. Wolf was credited with a probable because no one witnessed the final destruction of the enemy plane after it entered the cloud layer although it was apparent that it was not going to recover (his only witness, Bissonnette, was MIA on a ferry mission a few days later). Therefore, Wolf was the first pilot of the 58th Fighter Group to engage the enemy in air-to-air combat but not its first victor. (A side note on this mission: Capt. Edward Roddy who was credited with two victories would eventually become the CO of the 58FG in the Philippines in 1945.)

1Lt. Franklin Love was the Second Element Leader of Yellow Flight with 1Lt. Robert Gibb as his Wingman. The two climbed to engage the 12 Zeros milling in a Lufbery and Love fired at one possibly damaging it and then took a 90 degree deflection shot at 400 to 500 yards hitting both wings and the cockpit but had to break away with two Zeros on his tail. Gibb came in to rescue Love and one Zero turned into his attack, giving Gibb a head on shot and his Zero burst into flames and exploded. The second Zero continued after Love and hit his port wing with 20mm shells before Love's P-47 pulled away.

**1Lt. Marvin Grant** scored his first of seven victories. (AAF)

**Capt. Edward Roddy** shot down two Zeros to give him four victories. (AAF)

**1Lt. Robert Gibb** scored his first of five victories. (AAF)

**17 December 1943: 348FG/58FG First Aerial Victory**

Morning Mission

At 0715 the 341FS sent eight P-47s led by Capt. Samuel Blair in two flights to Arawe at 0715 and proceeded at 10,000 feet when one Thunderbolt had engine problems and was escorted back to base by another. They were patrolling at 8,000 feet over the Arawe, New Britain beachhead at 0900 when the Fighter Controller *Duckbutt* on a USN Destroyer reported an enemy formation at 14,000 feet consisting of 21 dive bombers flying in three ship Vs and 15 fighters. Blair's flight consisted of Wingman, 1Lt. Frank Morrison, and 2Lts. Harvey Chapman and 2Lt. Robert Ducharme. Accompanying the flight on their fourth combat missions were two members of the 69FS; 69th Operations Officer, Capt. Howard Tuman, and 2Lt. Francis Donar who had been selected to fly a few missions with the 348FG.

As the Vals began their dive on the convoy, the P-47s climbed in string and dove in line astern on the Vals but were turned back by the heavy friendly AA fire put up by the destroyers. The P-47s changed course to hit the Vals after their attack. Capt. Samuel Blair was the Flight Leader of the first flight with 1Lt. Frank Morrison as his Wingman. Blair dove through a flight of Vals at 400 mph and fired a short burst with no observable results. Blair chased two Vals but was unable to get into range. Blair then saw three more Vals and fired short bursts but they took violent evasive actions and Blair was unable to get a good lead on them. Blair climbed over them and descended and fired at 200 feet and one rolled over onto the trees. When he pulled up the others were gone and he headed back to Arawe. Blair saw three Oscars and made several hit and run firing passes on them which caused them to finally separate. He climbed and made one final pass starting to fire from out range and while closing the got some hits and the Oscar then flew into a hill. 1Lt. Frank Morrison was the Flight Leader of the second flight, which after the two aborts, now consisted of Morrison and Wingman 2Lt. Harvey Chapman. After diving on the retreating Vals, Morrison shot down a Val from dead astern while Chapman, unable to shed his belly tank got another which crashed inland. Morrison then took a two second deflection shot on a Val that burst into flames and crashed into the sea. Morrison made passes at three Oscars and joined Blair in attacking Oscars and shot one down for his third victory of the day (of four total). Meanwhile, Chapman made several ineffective passes on violently turning Vals but finally one flew into his line of fire and exploded and burst into flames. 2Lt. Robert Ducharme added the sixth Val victory for the 342nd that day (his only victory of the war).

**Gen. Frederick Smith** in an awards ceremony for Maj. Howard Tuman, 310FS/58FG CO, who scored the first victory for the 58FG while flying with the 341FS/348FG. (AAF)

**Capt. Samuel Blair** shot down an Oscar and Val to become an ace. (AAF)

**2Lt. Robert Ducharme** claimed his only victory of the war. (AAF)

**2Lt. Francis Donar** of the 69FS/58FG scored his only victory while flying with the 348FG. (AAF)

58FG Victory with the 348FG

Capt. Tuman followed his element and flight leader when they suddenly pulled up and dropped their belly tanks to engage a large formation of Val bombers ahead and below. The inexperienced Tuman lost the flight and suddenly the enemy scattered in all directions and one headed straight for him. He fired first from about 500 yards but as the two aircraft closed he hit the Val's engine and the it passed under him trailing smoke and then burst into flames and crashed into the ground. Blair and Morrison both witnessed Tuman's victim crash into a wooded area. Tuman then found he was alone and looked around to rejoin the flight and saw three P-47s with large round radial engine cowlings at 11 o'clock high. As he turned to rejoin the formation the aircraft started shooting at him and he discovered that the Vals had radial engined Oscars as top cover. Tuman did what he was taught to do to escape in the Thunderbolt; "drop the nose, firewall the throttle, and hit the deck." 2Lt. Francis Donar was on Tuman's right wing and slightly behind to meet the Vals when they saw two approaching from below one head on and the other from 2 o'clock which Donar went after. When he began firing, the guns in the starboard wing fired one round each and then stopped. The Val began a starboard turn directly in front of him giving him several good bursts with the port wing that started the Val burning and went into the sea near a small coral island just off the shore. On his way back to base Donar met a solid wall of weather and had to land at Lae. No member of the 58FG would score another aerial victory until 3 January 1945 as the Group would be almost exclusively and heavily engaged in escort and ground support missions.

**Capt. Edward Roddy** became an ace when he shot down a Dinah. (AFAA)

Afternoon Mission

The 342FS dispatched eight P47s to patrol Arawe in the afternoon. Capt. Edward Roddy, the Flight Leader of the second flight, arrived over Arawe at 1430 at 15,000 feet. Roddy spotted a Dinah recon bomber coming in toward the convoy and peeled off and shot it down to become an ace. Later the Squadron was flying at 20,000 feet when another bomber was spotted approaching the convoy. Roddy dove again and made a pass without firing and saw it was a B-17. The controller misidentified the 342nd and called for top cover to come down and get the "Little Bastards." Roddy *et al* made a swift retreat before being shot down by friendly AA fire and interceptors.

**1Lt. Kenneth Ladd** (left with CC Yale Saffro) became an ace when he shot down a Kate. (AFAA)

**17 December 1943: 8FG/80FS**

Maj. Edward Cragg led 16 P-38s, taking off at 1430 on a patrol over Arawe, from 1500 to 1640. At the end of the patrol, the Squadron was about to return to base after one last sweep towards Cape Gloucester. They were at 10,000 feet over the strip at Cape Gloucester when two fighters took off. Cragg and his Wingman dove first but built up too much speed in their dive and overran the enemy fighters. The second element of Capt. Jay Robbin's third flight, composed of 1Lt. Kenneth Ladd and Wingman, 2Lt. C.B. Ray, dropped their tanks and dove after the Zero that was flying at 100 feet over the coastline heading at top speed toward Rabaul. Ladd's first burst, a 90 degree deflection shot, hit the cockpit and started a fire. While, the Ladd and Ray swung around for another pass, three other P-38s all made firing passes that over led their targets. Ladd's second firing pass hit the Zero again and it went down in flame for his fifth victory to make him an ace. During the attack on the enemy airfield Cragg observed that, despite no AA fire, most Squadron pilots "had to[o] much speed in their attack and as a result of this lesson, corrective measures will be taken in the future."

**18 December 1943: 475FG/433FS**

Capt. Warren Lewis led four flights of 16 P-38s on a patrol over Arawe and at 1400 was ordered to investigate a plot southeast of Cape Raoult. Lewis led the Squadron to 25,000 feet over the designated area where they engaged a mixed formation of 10 to 15 Zero and Tony interceptors off Cape Raoult at 24,000 feet headed toward Arawe. The Squadron dropped their tanks and dove on the enemy who immediately Split-S'd and scattered. As the Squadron was coming out of its dive a similar size enemy formation bounced them from out of the clouds but evaded them by continuing their dive. Lewis led the flight back up to 22,000 feet and then dove on the Japanese fighters. The combat then developed into a series of individual dogfights. Since the Squadron was outnumbered two to one their only effective tactic was to gain altitude and then make diving passes, clear the area, and then climb again.

On his second pass Lewis fired a 30 degree head on deflection shot and observed his cannon shells hitting the Zero but only hit hard enough to file a damaged claim. Lewis' #4 man, 2Lt. Stanley Northrup, made several unsuccessful passes until he fired a three second burst from 50 yards on a lone Zero approaching head on. Northrup's cannon shells exploded between the engine and canopy and it began smoking and then flamed for Northrup's only victim of the war. Northrup then joined 1Lt. William Jeakle's Flight and watched as Jeakle made a sharp port turn with 1Lt. Austin Neely trying to cut under him. Neely's port prop grazed Jeakle's starboard boom; tearing off the tail of Jeakle's fighter. Jeakle went into a spiral but seemed to maintain control; losing altitude slowly while circling. Neely was able to regain control and returned safely to base. The squadron saw no parachute but believed that since he was not on fire and spiraling slowly at enough altitude that there was the chance that he could have ditched or bailed out. Jeakle bailed out and was fortunate as one of the few PBYs on rescue service was in the area and pulled him from the water. On 28 December a fatigued Jeakle returned to Dobodura.

**1Lt. Robert Tomberg** claimed the last of two total victories. (AAF)

**Capt. William Banks** shot down a Dinah to become an ace. (AAF)

Maj. Merle Smith was leading the second flight and first saw the enemy after they had scattered into groups of twos or threes and dropped their tanks to attack. Smith missed on his first pass on two Zeros and then saw a Zero on the tail of his #4 man, Lt. Knecht. Smith tried to pull his turn into the Zero but was unable to get around soon enough. Knecht's P-38 was leaking coolant from both engines and Smith led him to the southeast coast where Knecht bailed out just east of Aware where he was picked up by a corvette. Smith's Second Element Leader, 1Lt. Robert Tomberg, began combat by going after three Zeros on a P-38's tail and scared them off. He then saw three enemy fighters in trail ahead and above him. He pulled up and followed a Tony in a loop and fired a four second burst into its engine and cockpit from 100 yards. The Tony's canopy blew off and it trailed smoke and headed straight down. A Zero then made a 90 degree pass on Tomberg and his Wingman, 2Lt. William Grady, came to the rescue. Grady fired from 150 yards, getting hits on the canopy area and the flaming Zero started in a steep dive for his second victory.

The Narrative Combat Report of 1Lt. R.G. Hawley, S-2 stated: "The Japanese pilots were very aggressive and appeared more skilled than pilots recently encountered… They easily outmaneuvered us and evaded by Split-S'ing or making tight turns or loops in an effort to attack us from the rear… We were definitely outnumbered and on the defensive throughout."

1Lt. William Jeakle was able to open the canopy with some difficulty and bail out during his Lightning's spin and waited until he was on his back to pull the rip cord so he wouldn't lose his boots. On his descent four Zeros circled him and made passes but did not fire. Jeakle surveyed the terrain and oriented a route on his way down. He hit the tree tops and ripped his way through the branches and had a free fall of 60 feet to the ground; severely wrenching his right leg. Once on the ground Jeakle accessed his jungle kit and chose the most important items to carry with him. His jungle knife, compass, and heavy leather gloves were to be the best choices. He cut a three square foot section from his parachute to carrying the jungle kit items and to use as a cover at night. He buried the remainder of the chute and his goggles, flying helmet, and earphones. Jeakle hid when Japanese fighters buzzed the area and waded down a shallow stream for two hours to conceal his tracks. Jeakle checked his compass every 10 minutes as he found that he had the tendency to head for clear areas and go off course. For the next three days he walked through dense forest and torrential rains that fell every day from 1400 to 1700 hours. On the second day, while crawling up a steep embankment, he lost his parachute bag including a mosquito head net, mosquito repellant, fishing rig, and parachute cord. After that he slept on reeds or grass and covered himself with palm fronds and covered his face with a piece of cloth for protection against the insects that swarmed at night. He used part of his Mae West life jacket to carry water which he scooped out of puddles or streams. Jeakle subsisted almost entirely on the chocolate rations which he ate one square at a time in the evening. He also found numerous small snails which he sucked out of their shells; the white ones were edible but the black ones were bitter. For the next three days he used his jungle knife to force his way through sago swamps and on Christmas Day he arrived on the coast and made his way through the mangroves to the Omei River. He was unable to cross the river and followed it back inland and the next morning he found a 30 foot log that floated and poled his way along the coast on the log until he found a native canoe at the junction of two rivers. He paddled the canoe to a native village where he attracted the attention of a PBY that rescued him in the morning of 28 December.

**18 December 1943: 71TRG**

That day the 71[st] Tactical Recon Group scored its first victory when 2Lt. Delta Graham shot down a Val near Lepeula Point, Huon Peninsula at 1735.

**20 December 1943: 348FG/342FS**

Capt. William Banks was leading a four plane flight of the 342FS over Arawe at 20,000 feet. At 0800 the Controller called a vector at 23,000 feet 20 miles northwest of Arawe. When Banks arrived in the areas he spotted a lone roving Dinah five miles ahead at 25,000 feet. Banks chased the Dinah for 50 miles before getting astern for a long fatal burst to make him an ace.

**21 December 1943: Situation**

During the week before Christmas 1943 fighters from both the 5AF and 13AF began to put the pressure on the enemy. The Fifth still patrolled Arawe and escorted bombers to the Cape Gloucester area in preparation for the invasion there, which was scheduled for 26 December. To take pressure off the forthcoming landing at Cape Gloucester, the fighter aircraft of COMAIRSOLS (13AF and USMC) began to escort bombers striking the airfields and shipping in the Rabaul area. For the first time since 15 November the Japanese lost 20 or more aircraft in a day.

**21 December 1943: 475FG/432FS**

Col. Charles MacDonald was leading a squadron of 18 Clover P-38s patrolling over Arawe when the Arawe Controller reported a large flight of enemy aircraft coming in from the northeast and directed him to lead his flight to 23,000 feet. Soon the Controller reported that the base was under attack from the aircraft on the deck. MacDonald sighted the scattered enemy flying only 500 to 1,000 feet over the water and it took several minutes to descend to prevent their windshields from fogging. As the Lightnings arrived the Val dive bombers broke away to escape while the escorts came up to intercept. MacDonald took his Red Flight down after the bombers and just as he began to close on the bombers, a Zeke closed in on the rear man of the second flight. MacDonald turned and fired a 60 degree deflection shot into the Zero and as it turned away MacDonald got another momentary shot. The Zero seemed to go out of control but its pilot recovered just above the treetops in time to be hit again and finished off by two other P-38s. MacDonald closed from under a Val and fired a three second burst that blew off half its stabilizer and it crashed unto the jungle. The flight continued its chase in string to Cape Hoskins at minimum altitude and caught up with six Vals on the deck before they had a chance to take evasive action and their escort failed to sight the Lightnings over the jungle background before it was too late. MacDonald fired from a few hundred feet astern, hitting the wing roots and setting the Zero aflame to crash into the jungle for his eighth victory. MacDonald's Second Element Leader, 1Lt. Elliott Summer, and Wingman, 1Lt. Farris, followed their Flight Leader down and pursued three Vals. The two fired all tail shots, closing to 100 feet and Summer claimed two to make him an ace while Farris got his third and last victory. The two flew on to Finschhafen to refuel before returning home.

**1Lt. Elliot Summer** destroyed two Vals to make him an ace.

**Col. Charles MacDonald** downed two Vals to give him eight victories. (AAF)

While in string, Yellow Flight leader, 1Lt. William Ritter, who previously had his second element snafu, overtook the P-38 in front of him and while turning to lose speed, lost his Wingman (1Lt. John Michener). Ritter then spotted a Val flying on the tree tops and he and another P-38 flown by 2Lt. Edward Dickey took off after it. Dickey was flying alone as he had problems jettisoning his wing tanks but had finally succeeded. The Val turned tightly as both Americans closed and Ritter was able to circle faster and fired at only 20 feet tearing off a large piece of its right wing near the fuselage which almost hit Ritter's fighter. The Val's other wing folded as Ritter passed and Dickey saw the dive bomber crash. Ritter then followed three P-38s (White Flight's 1Lt. Arthur Peregoy, 2Lt. Robert Hadley, and an unnamed pilot) as the last man in string along the north coast and watched while one shot down a Val. The four plane string continued on and spotted another Val headed inland and Ritter cut out the third Lightning in the string and took advantage of the first and second P-38s' unsuccessful passes to get on the Val's tail to shoot it down at 30 feet away. After Peregoy watched Ritter shoot down his second Val, Peregoy was informed by Hadley, his Wingman, that he had been unable to drop his tank and escorted him from the battle. On the way home, Peregoy spotted a lone Val flying low and 10 miles from the beachhead. Peregoy fired from the left rear quarter and hit its wings and then saw a cannon shell explode in its cockpit for his second and last victory of the war.

After Michener could no longer follow Ritter he joined 2Lt. Edward Dickey and the two saw three P-38s chasing an enemy fighter. The duo had excess speed which they used to reef to starboard and to close on the enemy's tail. The Japanese pilot skidded back and forth before Michener fired but he made the mistake of cutting with the enemy pilot the first time and was left off balance to fire when the enemy cut back. The enemy pilot then slow rolled to starboard and Michener missed again. Michener was so close that the enemy pilot had no choice but to Split-S and was fortunate to find the overcast and escape. Michener headed back to Arawe in climbing turns and as he was turning right tracers zipped in front of his fighter. As he looked around he saw a Zero in flames behind him with Loisel firing on the tail of Michener's former attacker. Michener then climbed to 10,000 feet and saw two P-38s chasing an Oscar off the south Arawe coast. One of the P-38s pulled up as if it was out of ammunition and the Oscar turned a 180 to the left and Michener cut it off. This Oscar also skidded but as its pilot skidded left Michener didn't follow but when he cut back to the right Michener was in position to fire and he "nailed" the Oscar in the fuselage and wings for his only victory. Forster joined Michener and the two climbed and circled searching for more enemy fighters but the fight had moved inland and the two returned to base, low on fuel.

Capt. John Loisel was leading Blue Flight with 1Lt. Joseph Forster on his wing and followed MacDonald's flight into the fray. Loisel saw a Zero on the tail of a P-38 and turned to the rescue. Loisel's first shots hit the Zero's wing fuel tank and pieces flew off the wounded Zero; one of which Loisel's prop; slightly damaging it. Loisel fired another volley which finished off the Zero for his seventh victory. Loisel fired at several more enemy fighters but made no claims and headed to Finschhafen to refuel before returning to base.

Green Flight, led by Capt. Oliver McAfee, became separated from the rest of the Squadron and made several unsuccessful passes at "aggressive but cautious" enemy fighters.

During the morning the **432FS** shot down eight Vals, while in the afternoon the 342FS shot down eight more, with two probables and a damaged. (AFHRC)

**1Lt. Robert Gibb** shot down two Vals and damaged another to give him three victories. (AAF)

**Capt. William Dunham** shot down three Vals to make him an ace with seven victories. (AFAA)

**1Lt. Randall Hilbig** shot down two Vals and was credited with two probables for his only claims of the war. (AAF)

**21 December 1943: 348FG/342FS/340FS**

The 342FS was flying seven P-47s (one had aborted) in two flights in an afternoon convoy patrol over Arawe at 16,000 feet. There was cloud cover at 2,000 feet so the flights were split with three fighters at 2,000 feet under Capt. William Dunham and four to remain at 16,000 feet under Capt. William Banks and were to continue to patrol there. At 1630 approximately 25 to 30 enemy Val bombers were sighted in a scattered formation about 500 feet off the water.

1Lt. Robert Gibb, the Element Leader of the second flight made stern attacks on three different Vals and silenced the rear gunners of two of them while the pilot of the third was killed and his Val plunged into the water. 1Lt. Randall Hilbig shot at three Vals on his first pass and one burst into flames for a probable. Hilbig returned to attack another Val and got hits but lost him as he turned inland over the jungle for another probable. Hilbig then turned after another Val which headed inland over a river and was hit by his P-47's .50s and crashed into the jungle in a 30 degree dive for a confirmed victory. As Hilbig continued on he was jumped by a Zero that was quickly driven away by three P-47s with 2Lt. Willis Cooley claiming it as a probable. Hilbig then chased the Vals toward Gasmata and fired on three and got hits on one. 2Lt. Frank Russo, Hilbig's Wingman, dove with his leader and hits on the tail of a Val, killing its gunner and then raked the fuselage but over flew the Val and lost it and claimed it as a probable. Russo flew over to attack the next Val and fired a three second burst for a victory.

Capt. William Dunham downed a Val with a long burst and immediately swung over to another which took evasive action but Dunham kept firing and the Val crashed into the sea. Dunham turned to port and attacked another Val from astern and started firing from 300 yards down to 25 feet when the Val crashed into the jungle. He attacked another Val but had five of his eight guns jam and that Val got away. Dunham fired on two more but didn't have enough firepower to put them down and he finally ran out of ammunition. In his ICR Dunham notes: "It would have been a simple matter to knock down seven or eight if my guns and ammo would have held out." The three victories gave Dunham seven total and made him an ace.

340FS

The 340th scrambled four Thunderbolts over Arawe at 11,000 feet and at 1720 saw "15-20 Tonys and Hamps escorting 10 Nell bombers" at 7,000 feet, heading east in the opposite direction. 1Lt. Guy Roberts and Wingman, 2Lt. Stanley Souders, dove to attack the formation. Roberts fired a long burst at one which burst into flames and crashed into the ocean. Roberts then "easily" climbed away and made another pass at an enemy fighter that slow rolled away. Roberts looked back and saw five Zeros on his tail and dove away to safety. Meanwhile, Souders made a 45 degree deflection pass "slightly out of range" at the bombers but was driven away by Hamps. After pulling out of his dive Souders climbed to 10,000 feet to gain the height advantage over the bombers and as he made an attack two Hamps came into range head on. Souders fired a long burst at the lead fighter that hit its cockpit and the enemy fighter burst into flames and crashed into the sea. The two American pilots were outnumbered and at an altitude disadvantage and headed back to base.

**1Lt. Guy Roberts** scored his only victory of the war. (AAF)

**22 December 1943: 8FG/80FS**

Seventeen P-38s led by Maj. Carl Taylor took off from Dobodura at 0720 to act as top cover at 10,000 feet for two squadrons of B-25s on a low level attack to Wewak. The 432FS of the 475FG was assigned as close cover for the B-25s. The P-38s rendezvoused with the bombers at 0830 at 8,000 feet over Gusap and proceeded up the Ramu Valley toward Wewak. Over Wewak the weather was very poor but the target was open. At this the Japanese had sent a convoy of transports to resupply Wewak with Oscars of the 59[th] and 248[th] Sentais and Tonys of the 68[th] and 78[th] Sentais protecting the convoy.

During this time the 80[th]'s P-38s were able to remain together despite the bad weather and at 0930, just as the Squadron was approaching Wewak eight Tonys and Oscars came out of the dense cloud and up sun to bounce the last flight of P-38s and immediately damaged one. The third Lightning flight immediately returned to deal with the attack and two of their fighters covered the damaged P-38 while the others pursued the Japanese.

Cragg's flight was bounced by 20 or more diving Tonys and Oscars and turned into the attack and closed to get within 200 yards behind a Tony but his deflection shot missed as the Tony looped away from his line of fire. Cragg's Wingman, 2Lt. Delbert Furgason, fired at this Tony and the pilot bailed out just ahead of Cragg's P-38. Cragg could not evade and his starboard wing and propeller hit the parachute and the pilot plummeted to his death. #4 man 1Lt. Robert Hanson cut off a Tony and fired a deflection shot from the rear. His next burst hit the cockpit and wing and its pilot Immelmanned up and Hanson put a last burst into it at 50 yards and the pilot bailed out. 2Lt. Bertram Reed followed Cragg and the other P-38s in his flight in firing on the Tony that Hanson finally shot down. As Cragg's flight proceeded toward Sepik they met three Tonys and a lone Zero that made a head on pass from below. Cragg fired head on from 250 to 50 yards and set it on fire for his 14[th] victory. 1Lt. Paul Murphey, leading Cragg's second element, met the second Tony head on and saw it roll over out of control in flames. 1Lt. Robert Hanson, Murphey's Wingman heavily damaged the third Tony for a probable.

1Lt. Cornelius Smith was leading the last flight of five aircraft and dropped down to 7,000 feet to get under the heavy overcast and rain clouds when his flight was attacked by two Tonys from out of the rain directly above and behind. Smith turned into them as they hit his Wingman, 2Lt. John Stanifer, but when Smith completed his turn they broke away. Smith's tanks did not release due to an electrical failure and he dropped them manually. Stanifer managed to stay with Smith and the two joined a five or six P-38s flying in string and circled around the area. A Zero was spotted flying over the water southeast of Wewak and the string of Lightnings dove on it. Somehow the first six all undershot it and when the enemy pilot turned under them Smith cut his throttle, dropped his nose and cut it off. The Zero headed toward shore and Smith caught it just over Brandi Plantation at 500 feet and fired a long burst and Stanifer confirmed that it crashed offshore. 1Lt. Jennings Myers was flying in Smith's flight and shot down a Tony for his fifth victory to become an ace before he was shot down over the Sepik River. Myers was reported to have crash landed in the Karau Lagoon near the Sepik River and was seen to have swum ashore into the jungle but was never seen again. 1Lt. Jess Gidley, the #5 spare man in Smith's flight, came out of the rain clouds and was hit and the left side of his canopy was blown away and there was a hole in his windshield. The attacking Tony continued to follow Gidley but Smith came in and the Tony broke off its attack. The speed of Gidley's fighter was greatly reduced by the hole in his canopy and he lost the flight. He saw 2Lt. Howard Donaldson, the #4 man in Smith's flight, off by himself with his port engine smoking badly. Gidley and then Roberts and Schriber joined Donaldson, circling and instructing him. Soon Donaldson's engine went from smoking and into flames and they told

**2Lt. Bertram Reed** claimed his only victory of the war. (AAF)

**1Lt. Jennings Myers** became an ace by destroying a Tony. (AFAA)

**1Lt. Paul Murphey** scored his third career victory. (AAF)

80FS Victors (L-R): **2Lt. Louis Schriber** (1v.), **1Lt. Paul Murphey** (1v.), and **1Lt. Jennings Myers** (1v.). (AFAA)

**1Lt. Cornelius Smith** shot down a Zero for his sixth victory. (AFAA)

**2Lt. Delbert Furgason's** only victory of the war was over a Tony near Wewak. (AAF)

Donaldson to feather that engine and to turn back to base. For some reason it took some time for Donaldson to turn around. About five minutes later his right engine started to smoke and Donaldson's Lightning continued to descend until it burst into flames; plunging in to a marsh about 35 miles from Wewak. The trio circled the burning wreckage several times and saw no sign of life before returning home with Gidley's fighter vibrating and flying rather slowly. Upon landing Gidley had to pump his flaps and landing gear down by hand. There was a three foot hole in the left cockpit/canopy area, four or five holes in the back of the canopy, another in the hydraulic tank, one in the left wing and fuel tanks that cut the flap wire and oxygen line, four or five holes in the horizontal stabilizer that cut the rudder trim tab, four or five holes in the right vertical fin, and two or three holes in the horizontal fin. It was a bad day for the 80th with two P-38s lost and two others badly damaged for five Tonys and an Oscar destroyed and another Tony listed as probably destroyed.

**22 December 1943: 475FG/431FS/433GF**

Another B-25 mission was scheduled for Wewak on 22 December with its escort by both the 475FG and the 80FS which comprised nearly all the operational P-38s in New Guinea. Fighter cover was scheduled at altitudes between 4,000 feet and no higher than about 8,000 feet with the weather over the Wewak Complex reported as increasingly cloudy.

431FS

Maj. Merle Smith from 475FG/HQ led 17 P-38s from Dobodura at 0715 on a close cover escort of 18 B-25s to Boram Airstrip. They rendezvoused with the bombers over Gusap at 0830 and arrived over the Boram Strip at 0915 with 14 Lightnings (White #2 and #3 and Red #4 aborted) at 4,000 feet. White Flight Leader, 1Lt. William O'Brien and his #4 man joined Smith's first Red Flight. Smith led Red Flight on a diving pass on a Zero flying just above the water three miles off Cape Moem. O'Brien followed the Flight as they made a pass of the Zero and when they pulled away O'Brien fired but also missed as he did not have the proper lead. He continued after it and the Japanese pilot Split-S'd only about 100 feet above the sea and crashed before he could pull out for his first victory. Nearby, Maj. Smith saw enemy fighters at 1,000 feet breaking away from attacks on the Mitchells about three miles off Cape Moem. After taking several shots at a Tony it burst into flames and the pilot bailed out just before it crashed into the sea. Blue Flight Leader, 1Lt. Donno Bellows, confirmed Smith's victory in his ICR but official records do not credit Smith with this tenth victory which would have made him a double ace. After Bellows had seen both Smith's and O'Brien's victories he led his third flight down and as he made a turn a Zero crossed his path. Bellows fired and shot off pieces of its engine cowling and canopy and watched it crash into the water. As Bellows pulled away he saw tracers whiz by and looked back and saw two Tonys on his tail. Bellows fire walled his Lightning and went into a gentle climb and slowly pulled out of range. Capt. Thomas McGuire, leading Green Flight, made an unsuccessful pass at a pair of Oscars before he was forced to break away. 2Lt. Alvin Kidd, McGuire's Wingman, and 2Lt. Vincent Elliott damaged an Oscar and Tony, respectively, before the 431st left the area. The P-38 of 2Lt. Robert Donald, Bellows' Wingman, was hit from behind and his starboard engine began to smoke and he joined four P-38s in string but was hit again from behind and the engine was smoking worse and his hydraulic

**1Lt. Donno Bellows** scored his second and last victory. (AAF)

system and radio were out. Donald flew on both engines for 15 minutes and caught up with 1Lt. Perry Dahl of the 432FS and then feathered his engine. Dahl escorted him half way to Gusap where he continued on to Dobodura. On his approach Donald found that his landing gear would not descend but was able to make a successful wheels up landing. The Squadron saw a P-38 (80FS 1Lt. Jennings Myers) crash land in Murik Lagoon and get out of his fighter and head toward shore and reported his position.

432FS

Lt.Col. Charles MacDonald led 17 P-38s on a close escort for B-25s striking Wewak. When the Squadron approached Wewak Harbor, 30 enemy single engine fighters were seen about to attack the Mitchells from 8 and 12 o'clock. The enemy was spread out from ground level to 8,000 feet as if they had been scrambled on short notice. MacDonald ordered tanks to be dropped and realizing he was at a disadvantage started climbing into four of them. The enemy fighters that then abandoned their attack and tried to escape. MacDonald fired at one that was climbing but the Japanese pilot Immelmanned away to escape. MacDonald's Red Flight Second Element Leader, 1Lt. Elliott Summer, saw a Zero close and climb in an Immelmann putting Summer in position for a 2-3 second firing run at only 50 feet that flamed the Zero for his sixth victory. Summer's ICR reports that when he passed behind his flaming victim he could feel the intense heat. Summer and his Wingman, Farris circled the Harbor through "accurate and quite heavy ack-ack" and made several more passes at Zeros and Tonys but were unable to get good shots.

Green Flight, led by 1Lt. Zack Dean, followed MacDonald's Red Flight into the battle and also started to climb. Dean fired several short bursts at a Zero that was flying head on into Green Flight. As the Zero passed by, Dean saw flames erupt from the enemy's engine and then saw the pilot bail out. Dean fired at two more Zeros, missing both but Dahl came in a fired on the second Zero. Dean saw pieces flying off of it and confirmed Dahl's victory. Dean then saw three Zeros low on the water and dove and fired on the enemy leader as he was climbing at low speed and the Zero burst into flames and crashed into the sea. The two victories gave Dean his last of seven for the war.

Blue Flight led by 1Lt. Vivian Cloud approached Wewak at 1000 and dropped their tanks and dove to 2,000 feet and headed out to sea, climbing out to 7,000 feet and then headed inland in a dive. On their way in Cloud fired at a Tony and damaged it (after the mission Dahl reported that he saw it crash into the water). Blue Flight made four more passes back and forth from land to sea and back. On the second pass as his flight climbed out to sea, Cloud overran his flight when a Zero chandelled toward the formation. Cloud turned into it and cut it off and closed to 100 feet. Cloud's tracers hit the Zero's tail and canopy to become an ace. Blue Flight Second Element, 1Lt. Howard Hedrick and 2Lt. Perry Dahl approached Wewak when a Tony Split-S'd on Dahl's tail as Dahl was in a steep dive. The Tony cut inside Dahl who broke right and left Blue Flight. The Tony pilot also broke right and closed to within 150 feet. As the Tony pilot began to fire Dahl cut his inside right throttle and hit his right rudder and aileron. The Tony pilot broke left and as he did Cloud came in and fired a 90 degree deflection shot that sent the Tony into the sea. Dahl then saw a Zero and fired a long 60 to 90 degree deflection shot blew off the Zero's tail. As Dahl continued to fly over Wewak he saw an 80FS P-38 with its port engine out and it starboard engine streaming coolant and also saw a 431FS Lightning with its port engine out. Dahl tried to cover both but the 80th pilot headed toward the water and the 431st headed off to the east. Dahl found the 431st pilot (2Lt. Robert Donald) and escorted him back to the safety of the Dumpu area and then headed for Nadzab to refuel.

433FS

The only claim made by the 433rd was by 2Lt. James Malloy who was the Wingman to the Leader of the last flight of 14 P-38s. At 0950 the Squadron was flying at 4,000 feet and saw eight to ten Zeros, Tonys, and one Nate milling around between 5,000 feet and the deck. Malloy followed his Flight Leader down and saw the Nate at 400 yards ahead flying at 50 to 100 feet above the ground. Malloy fired along burst, starting at 300 yards to 50 yards and saw pieces of the tail and canopy coming off and the Nate fell off. At this point Malloy experienced violent buffeting of his fighter as both engines seemed to have gone out. Malloy concentrated on restarting his engines and did not see the Nate crash; however, Malloy's Wingman, 2Lt. Louis Longman, confirmed Malloy's third victory (plus two probables).

**22 December 1943: 348FG/341FS/Kearby Special**

Eager to get into combat Kearby formed another special flight on the 22nd for yet another sweep to Wewak. Kearby chose to fly with the 341FS and assigned 1Lt. Clarence Blend as his Wingman, while Capt. Samuel Blair led the second element with 1Lt. Charles Cronk as his Wingman.

**1Lt. Vivian Cloud** shot down a Tony and Zero to become an ace for his last victories of the war. (AFAA)

**1Lt. Zach Dean** got his last two of seven victories. (AFAA)

**Capt. Samuel Blair** is shown after scoring his sixth victory. (AFAA)

**Col. Neel Kearby** chose to fly with the 341FS and claimed his 16th victory. (AAF)

At 1320 the patrol was cruising at 18,000 feet when two Zeros were sighted at 6,000 feet over the Boram Airstrip. Kearby ordered tanks jettisoned and dove on the two Zeros which were widely separated in a loose line astern formation. Kearby attacked the surprised Zeros, who retained their belly tanks, from the 7 o'clock position and chased them over the end of the airstrip and opened fire on the rear fighter from 300 yards with a single three second burst which exploded the Zero but somehow its pilot parachuted from the devastation. Blair followed closely and flew under the parachuting enemy pilot and fired at a Zero that was making a turn out of range. The fighter emitted smoke but Blair claimed it as a probable. Blair chased a Zero out to sea and closed to 200 yards and fired but the enemy pilot banked to starboard and Blair chopped his throttle and hit the Zero hard with a two second burst and it was seen to crash just inland for his sixth victory. Meanwhile, Kearby made seven more passes with only one gun functioning as the others jammed during his first successful pass and he was forced to leave the area and to settle for his 16th victory.

**23 December 1943: 348FG/341FS Kearby Special**
The next day Kearby led another flight from the 341FS on a sweep to Wewak. Four Thunderbolts took off from Gusap at 0940 but one P-47 aborted (Capt. Samuel Blair) and three (Kearby, 1Lt. Charles Cronk, and 1Lt. Clarence Blend) arrived over the target at 1040 at 27,000 feet. They patrolled for no more than five minutes when a pair of Tonys was observed below at 3,000 feet over the Boram Airstrip. Kearby ordered the belly tanks to be dropped and dived to the attack. As the Tonys disappeared in the broken clouds a bomber was sighted approaching Dagua for a landing. But a Tony appeared at 8,000 feet and Kearby attacked him from 7 o'clock getting a four second burst from 1,500 to 500 feet closing rapidly at 350 mph. Kearby got hits on the wing roots and fuselage and as he pulled up he lost him but saw another Tony at 200 feet heading for Dagua. Kearby attacked from dead astern, opening a very long burst at 500 yards and the Tony banked to the left and crashed burning in the trees at the end of Dagua strip. As the three P-47s left Boram they were attacked by eight to ten Zeros and had to outrun them in the overcast up the Ramu Valley at 100 to 500 feet and landed at Finschhafen at 1200.

**Col. Neel Kearby** (with Gen. George Kenney) scored his 17th victory in four months and only trailed Bong, who had 21 victories. (AAF)

Kearby had scored his 17th victory in only four months and only Dick Bong, who was on a furlough in the U.S. since November, was ahead of Kearby with 21 victories. Tom Lynch was also in the States with 16 victories and Tom McGuire had just returned to operations after being wounded had a total of 13 victories but would quickly have 16 when he claimed three on 26 December.

**23 December 1943: 475FG/432FS/431FS**
While the beaches of Cape Gloucester were being subjected to intensive pre-invasion bombardment, the only other 5FC claim (Kearby's was the other) until the invasion D-Day on 26 December was made on 23 December by 2Lt. Charles Ratajski. The 432nd pilot was on an escort of a PBY on a search and rescue mission over Murik Lagoon with 431FS pilot Maj. Meryl Smith. The two pilots flying at 3,000 feet spotted a lone Sally at 2,000 feet at 90 degrees. They dropped their tanks and made two passes from each side but the Sally continued flying. Ratajski made a third pass from very little deflection, closing for a tail shot. The Sally pilot went into a steep climb and Ratajski fired and had to shove the wheel forward to avoid hitting the bomber. The Sally's two engines were on fire and it went into a dive and crashed into the sea for his second of four victories. The 432FS would not have another victory until 10 January 1944.

**25 December 1943: 8FG/35FS**
On Christmas Day Capt. Harold McClelland led eight P-40s of Red and White Flight on a patrol over the Arawe coast area at 4,000 feet. A lone bogie was called out and McClelland took his Red Flight to investigate, leaving White Flight to patrol. Instead of trying to outrun the Americans the enemy pilot skillfully evaded. Several times he would make a slight turn until he had the four P-40s inside him and then would turn in the other direction. To counter this maneuver McClelland sent his second element on the opposite side of the bogie, now identified as a Ki-46 Dinah, while he and Wingman, 1Lt. Glendi Holder remained on the other side. The Dinah pilot then decided to try to outrun the P-40s and made a slight diving turn toward McClelland who made

a stern pass but missed. Holder made a starboard pass from above and slightly ahead and but observed no hits. Holder then pulled up sharply to starboard and rolled over and fired from 400 to 150 yards and started its right engine and wing smoking and it plunged into the sea for Holder's first victory of three.

**26 December 1943: Cape Gloucester Invasion**
*(Operation Backhander)*
The invasion of Cape Gloucester, *Operation Backhander*, was a major part of *Operation Cartwheel*, the main Allied strategy in the SWPA and POA. The main objective of the Allies was the capture and expansion of the Japanese airfield at Cape Gloucester from which they would increase the isolation and attacks on Rabaul. The capture of the area would also ensure Allied sea passage through the Vitiaz Straits separating New Britain from New Guinea. *Backhander* was delayed throughout November and early December by logistical problems in the Huon Gulf and in the Markham Valley areas. The veteran Australian 7th and 9th Divisions had problems removing tenacious Japanese units from the muddy, Malaria-ridden ground above Finschhafen while roads connecting Lae and Nadzab were being completed very slowly. As a consequence of the delays it was not until 26 December that *Backhander* began.

Supporting operations for these landings had begun on 15 December when the U.S. 112th Cavalry Regiment landed at Arawe on the south-central coast to block the route of Japanese reinforcements and supplies from east to west and as a diversionary attack from the future Cape Gloucester landings. The main operation began on December 26 with a naval barrage by USN and RAN warships, followed by air attacks by the USAAF and the RAAF. B-24 bombers dropped 500 pound bombs inland of the beaches from high altitude, scoring a hit on a fuel dump at the Cape Gloucester airfield complex; after which B-25 medium bombers and A-20 light bombers, attacked from lower altitude. These attacks and an aerial smoke screen were followed by the landing of the U.S. Marine First Division under Maj. Gen. William Rupertus. The Marines landed in an area of swampy terrain and thick jungle but met only rear-echelon Japanese troops. The usual Japanese strategy was to meet the invasion on the beach, but instead, they pulled into the dense jungle to engage the Marines. The Marines were then opposed by the Japanese 17th Division, commanded by Maj.Gen. Iwao Matsuda. The Japanese Air Forces did not attempt to attack the task force that morning but between 1430 and 1510 Val dive bombers escorted by fighters arrived from Rabaul to engage in a furious air battle in which the 5th Fighter Command would have its best day in the war, so far, shooting down 61 enemy aircraft.

**26 December 1943: 475FG/431FS**
A formation of 15 431FS Lightnings took off at 1200 on a patrol of the Cape Gloucester beachhead scheduled from 1300 to 1500. Capt. Thomas McGuire was leading Hades Squadron with 1Lt. Franklin Monk on his wing when *Duckbutt* Controller on the destroyer *Shaw* (which had been heavily damaged during the Pearl Harbor attack) ordered Hades and Copper (80FS) Squadrons to send two flights to patrol over the Control Ship at 6,000 feet and two at 10,000 feet. At 1420 the Controller discovered enemy aircraft coming in about 65 miles from the northeast. The 80FS was sent out to intercept them while McGuire was ordered to lead his Squadron in a climb to 15,000 feet. At 1425 the Controller gave McGuire a plot of enemy aircraft coming in from 85 degrees, 50 miles out. As McGuire closed to 30 miles *Duckbutt* lost both plots. The Controller then ordered McGuire and the 80FS to move closer to each other at 18,000 feet and kept the 35FS and 36FS over the Control Ship. As the 475th and 80th reached 18,000 feet the 80th spotted the enemy heading in at 23,000 feet. Since their auxiliary tanks were almost empty McGuire ordered the tanks to be released and

**Capt. Thomas McGuire** shot down three Vals to make him a triple ace with 16 victories. (AAF)

**1Lt. Vincent Elliott** shot down an escorting Oscar and Zero to give him seven victories. (AFAA)

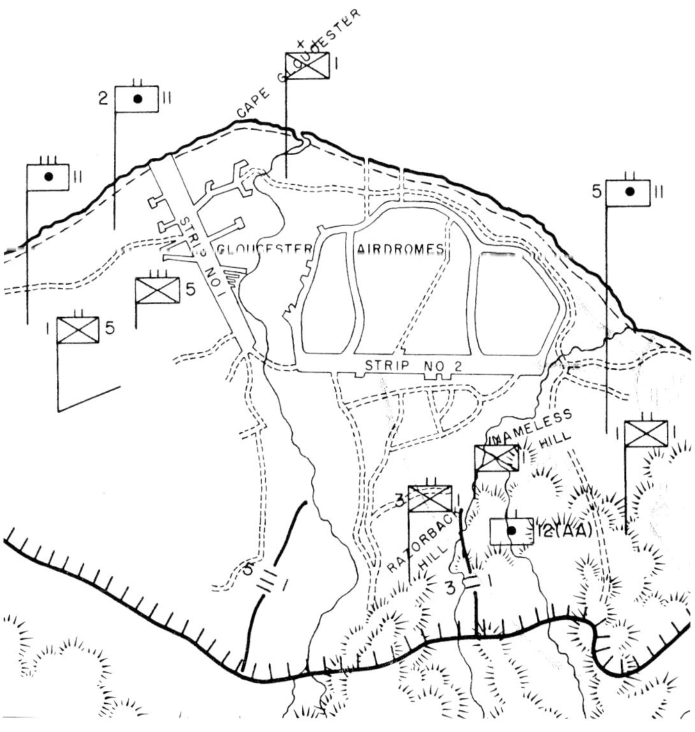


**Groucester Airdromes.**

**1Lt. Franklin Monk** scored his third victory during the battle. (AAF)

**Capt. Warren Danson** scored his only victory and second probable of the war. (AAF)

climbed to 23,000 feet where they contacted 30 to 40 Zeros and Oscars, 10 to 15 miles northeast of the Control Ship. As McGuire led the Squadron on a head on pass he saw 15 to 20 Zeros coming down from 8 to 10 o'clock high which forced McGuire to turn under them to port in a slight dive. As McGuire turned back into the fight he saw 25 to 30 Vals at 17,000 to 18,000 feet in two flights, a lead flight of 10 and a second flight of 15 to 20. The Vals were below just starting to dive at a 45 degree angle in string headed for the Allied shipping. Since the Squadron's primary mission was to protect the shipping McGuire led them down on the Vals. White Flight (Leader, Capt Verl Jett and Wingman, F/O William Gronemeyer, and second Element, 1Lt. Vincent Elliott and Wingman 1Lt. John Tilley) did not hear McGuire and did not come down until the Vals had completed their bombing run and were on the deck trying to escape. The Blue third flight (Leader Capt. Oliver McAfee and Wingman, 2Lt. Warren Cortner, and second element 2Lt. Herman Zehring and Wingman, 2Lt. Ormand Powell) had not climbed to altitude with the first two flights and caught the Vals just after they dropped their bombs. McGuire's Red Flight (Wingman 1Lt. John Cohn, and second element 1Lt. Franklin Monk and Wingman, 1Lt. Fredric Champlin) hit the Vals as they were on their dive bombing run and forced them to drop their bombs prematurely causing no damage except for one Val that hit a destroyer which sunk in minutes.

McGuire fired at a Val at 8,000 feet that started smoking and was seen to crash by Red #4, Champlin. McGuire lost his Second Element Leader Monk who ran low on fuel and joined the 80FS but continued to chase the Vals down to the water. Once on deck McGuire followed the Vals as they headed along the shore of Borgen Bay and then turned up the coast toward Cape Hoskins. McGuire made at least eight passes at different Vals flying above the water, mostly from astern. One Val was hit by several bursts and Red #3 Cohn witnessed it to explode. McGuire made a few more unsuccessful passes and then got behind a Val and fired from 90 degrees deflection to dead astern which Champlin witnessed to crash. McGuire lost his second element and fired on another Val which started smoking and headed inland. As McGuire followed it he was joined by a P-47 of the 36FS (Capt. Warren Danson) and the two attacked the smoking Val. McGuire's ICR: "I got directly behind the Val at minimum altitude and gave him a good burst. Pieces flew off and the Val blew up just as he hit a tree. He crashed directly below me and the explosion lifted me in the air and tore my horizontal fin… and the P-47 pilot who was off to one side saw the Val go down." Danson's ICR tersely reports: "I believe I was entirely responsible for the destruction of this aircraft." McGuire amended his 30 December ICR: "Although Capt. McGuire feels that his Combat Report was accurate of the description of the manner of which the Val attacked jointly by him and a pilot from the 36th Fighter Squadron was destroyed; a conversation with the other pilot revealed that his pilot also claimed the destruction of the Val. Rather than argue the matter, Capt. McGuire withdraws his claim." So McGuire had to settle for three Vals to give him 16 victories and he reclaimed the title of top scoring 475FG ace. Although he gave up the fourth Val (reluctantly, in the face overwhelming evidence) he had his Crew Chief paint another Rising Sun victory symbol for the disputed P-47 victory on his P-38's nose.

After Monk lost McGuire he joined another flight from the 80FS and made a diving pass at two Zeros and fired a long burst that sent one down smoking heavily and then crash straight into the ocean which was confirmed for his third victory. McGuire's Second Element Leader Cohn had problems dropping tanks and had to use the manual release. As the Red Flight dove, a Zero got on McGuire's tail and Cohn fired a short burst that chased it away but lost his flight and turned toward the destroyers and saw about 15 Vals heading for the warships. Three Vals turned toward the destroyer nearest Cohn who turned into them and got on the tails of two which caused them to drop their bombs before they reached their target. However, the lead Val continued on and its bomb hit the destroyer amidships and it blew up. Cohn continued after it to 100 feet above the water and made a 6 o'clock pass but overshot. Cohn turned for another pass and fired three short bursts with the last hitting its wing root causing the fuel tank to blow up. He met another Val heading toward Long Island and turned onto its tail as it took evasive action, making diving turns from 500 feet to the water. Cohn fired a shot that passed over the Val's wing and its pilot made a violent port turn and his port wing tip hit the water and cartwheeled into the sea (these two victories were never officially confirmed). Cohn joined a few other Lightnings that were headed to Dobodura. Red #4, Champlin lost the flight when he had to dive out of the way of fuel tanks being jettisoned by the diving enemy fighters. Champlin joined Elliott of White Flight and watched him shoot down a Zero. Champlin then joined McGuire and they dove on a Val and McGuire shot it down. Champlin dove to the deck and made four passes with the last one putting the flaming Val into the sea for his fourth victory.

White Flight led by Capt. Verl Jett encountered a large number of Oscars flying at their altitude and below the Zero top cover. Jett and Wingman, F/O William Gronemeyer, made several passes at enemy aircraft but made no claims. Element Leader 1Lt. Vincent Elliott with 1Lt. John Tilley as his Wingman anticipated that Jett would lead them in a shallow climbing turn but instead he turned and descended toward the Vals that were attacking the shipping. Elliott and Tilley had to break off their attack and climb away from four attacking Oscars and then made a fast climbing turn back toward the Vals. Two Oscars tried to make a steep turn into Elliott who had the firing advantage and opened fire inside the Oscar's turn. The Oscar rolled over and went down smoking and then caught fire. Elliott then joined the 80FS P-38s and 36FS P-47s which were engaging Oscars and Zeros. Elliott had the altitude advantage on a Zero that was chasing two Lightnings. He opened fire at close range at 45 degrees deflection and the Zero half rolled and caught fire for his seventh and last victory.

Blue Flight Leader Capt. McAfee and Wingman 2Lt. Warren Cortner made several ineffective passes on the Vals before returning home. 2Lt. Herman Zehring of Blue Flight had problems dropping his tanks and when he finally was able to drop them he had also lost his Wingman, 2Lt. Ormand Powell, and the flight. He descended directly toward the Control Ship and when he reached 1,000 feet he spotted a Val and slipped in behind and exploded it with a short burst. Zehring then chased after another Val that was flying just over the surface and fired another short burst and sent this Val cartwheeling into the sea for his first two of four victories. Zehring's Wingman, Powell, was unable to get completely serviced and took off with only 75 gallons in each wing tank and after patrolling for one and a half hours he had used all his auxiliary fuel and was down to two-thirds in his main tanks. In this situation Powell thought that he should remain behind to escort any distressed pilot home. When his flight leader Zehring had problems dropping his tanks Powell waited until Zehring had dropped them and joined four P-38s flying at 500 feet chasing a Val. Powell watched as each Lightning pilot made two passes at the Val but each P-38 was attacking at 350 mph while the Val was flying at 120 mph, making sharp turns just over the water and the Lightnings either overran or were unable to get a good shot. Powell cut his throttles and descended to 25 feet over the water and got behind the Val and continued firing from 600 yards to 100 feet and the Val hit the water. With only 40 gallons in each reserve tank Powell headed toward Finschhafen to refuel and landed there with only 15 gallons remaining after getting his only victory. 2Lts. Robert Herman, a spare, and Robert Donald, who took off late, joined McAfee's last Green Flight. 1Lt. Paul Morriss had to change fighters and took off late and also joined Green flight as its fifth man. When one of the Vals pulled up from its bombing attack at 1,500 feet, the first four Green Flight pilots made passes at it and overshot. Morriss pulled up behind the Val and fired until it started burning and crashed into the water for his second victory. The 11 victories for the day made the 431FS the first squadron of the 475FG to score more than 100 victories while the Group passed the 250 mark.

**Capt. Jay Robbins** got two victories to give him 13. He was named 80FS CO after Cragg's death. (AFAA)

**26 December 1943: 8FG/80FS**

Fighter patrols continued from early morning until sunset and the 80FS flew two extended patrols over the Cape Gloucester area beginning at 0600 and ending after 1600. Japanese aircraft were only encountered during the 1230 to 1530 afternoon patrol that took off at 1135 to patrol Yellow Beach. The 80[th] had covered the invasion shipping for about two hours at altitudes ranging from 10,000 to 18,000 feet when USN fighter controller, *Duckbutt*, sent the 80[th] off to a plot to the northeast at 1445. They flew about 60 miles and circled for five minutes before *Duckbutt* ordered them back. On their way back they heard *Duckbutt* give the 432FS a vector of 85 degrees and as they neared the patrol area they saw 40 to 50 fighters at 24,000 feet escorting about 30 dive bombers at about 8,000-10,000 feet below and about four miles west of Borgen Bay at 1445. Some Lightnings attempted to keep the fighter escorts engaged while the other P-38s went after the dive bombers but in the ensuing air battle many of the 80[th]'s P-38s were forced to break away and initiate individual attacks. Maj. Edward Cragg took his

Ladd's rookie Wingman, **2Lt. C.B. Ray**, scored his first victory on the way to becoming an ace. (AFAA)

**1Lt. Kenneth Ladd** shot down two Vals to give him eight victories. (AAF)

**Maj. Edward Cragg** shot down a Tojo to become a triple ace, but the excellent leader was lost in the combat. (AAF)

**1Lt. Cornelius Smith** was credited with his seventh victory. (AAF)

flight down to the altitude of the dive bombers while the P-38 flights of Capt. Jay Robbins and Maj. Carl Taylor stayed at altitude to attack enemy interceptors in that sector.

Flight Leader, Capt. Jay Robbins had lost two aircraft from his flight due to mechanical problems and he and his Wingman, 2Lt. Charles Ray climbed behind Maj. Carl Taylor's Flight to attack the Japanese flying above. Robbins fired a 90 degree deflection burst and got some hits on a Zero but he passed by so quickly that he had to claim it as a probable. When they turned back Robbins and Ray saw four Zeros on the tail of a P-38 that had its port engine shot out. Robbins took a 30 degree deflection shot that demolished the cockpit of the lead Zero which spiraled into the water. Another Zero got behind Robbins and as Ray looked around to clear his tail he saw three more closing in on him. Before diving to lose his own attackers, Ray fired a burst that drove off the Zero on Robbins' tail. By this time Ray's airspeed was low and he had to out dive his attackers in a tight spiral into a cloud base at 3,000 feet. When Ray came out the cloud he had lost the pursuers and saw a Val that was diving on one of the barges below coming almost head on at him. Ray dove after the Val and fired a long burst that the dive bomber flew into and crashed. As Ray climbed away he saw a P-47 pilot bail out abut four miles away. Meanwhile, Robbins saw a Zero climbing almost straight up after making a pass at American fighters below and set its starboard wing on fire. Robbins made at least two more 90 degree passes on other Japanese aircraft but was unable to observe the results since he was busy avoiding attacks. He finally left the battle at 1540 and landed at Finschhafen with his 12th and 13th victories.

Meanwhile, Maj. Carl Taylor's third flight was flying top cover at 19,000 feet and climbed to 24,000 feet into the large formation of Zeros and Oscars. Taylor made eight to ten passes but could not get close enough as the enemy fighters would Split-S away leaving the Americans with only difficult 90 degree deflection shots. However, on one of his passes Taylor got on the tail of an Oscar and shot it down for his third and last victory. As he turned away, Taylor's port engine started to smoke and saw two Oscars on his tail. He called for help and a P-38 arrived and shot one of the Oscars down and the last Taylor saw of his rescuer was with an Oscar turning into it. By this time Taylor decided to bail out and was picked up by a USN minesweeper shortly after landing in the water. 1Lt. Cornelius Smith was leading the second element of Taylor's flight and had the same problem with the enemy fighters Split-S'ing away to leaving the Americans only snap shots. After 25 minutes he left combat to head home but noticed a single Japanese fighter below to port and dove on it but lost it in a cloud. Smith then joined some P-47s and unsuccessfully shot at several targets until all but one persistent Oscar remained. A P-47 got on its tail and Smith followed. The P-47 gradually fell behind the speeding Oscar while Smith's Lightning gained on it. He chased the enemy fighter 50 miles up the New Britain coast and finally caught him and his cannon shells exploded it to give Smith his seventh victory.

Maj. Edward Cragg was leading a flight when *Duckbutt* called in a plot about 50 miles from the target and investigated the plot area but saw nothing and returned to the patrol area. Soon they saw large Japanese formations at 10 o'clock and 7,000 feet above and ordered the tanks to be dropped. Cragg and 1Lt. Burnell Adams made the first pass on the dive bombers. Cragg closed the tail of a Val but missed while Adams saw a Val off to the left and maneuvered for a deflection shot from the port and rear. He overshot and then throttled back and fired several bursts from the rear and put the Val into the water. Adams then pursued a Val across the coastline and inland and finally hit it hard enough to start it smoking and crash into a hillside for his fourth victory. Adams had lost Cragg after the first attack but saw a P-38 in the area attacking a Val near Borgen Bay but when Adams approached the Lightning he found it was a 475FG Lightning and not Cragg. Adams joined that P-38 and flew after some of the Vals skipping from cloud to cloud trying to get back to Rabaul. After the combat subsided Adams continued to search for Cragg and saw a P-38 in the distance firing at a Tojo but behind the P-38 was another Tojo firing at it. The first Tojo went down in flames but Adams was unable to close on the second Tojo as it hit the P-38 causing it to pull straight up into the clouds with its engine burning. The second Tojo saw Adams approaching at high speed and turned into a head on pass but didn't fire. Adams fired a burst when the Tojo came into range and hit its engine and but it then broke off into the clouds for a no claim. As Adams flew under the cloud formation he saw a P-38 spinning out of the clouds in flames and crash in a fiery explosion. Adams circled the crash area for a while, hoping to see the pilot in his parachute. When Adams returned to base he learned that Cragg had not returned it was obvious that Cragg was the pilot who died in the crash that Adams observed.

1Lt. Kenneth Ladd was leading Cragg's second element and followed him to the *Duckbutt* vector. When they returned to the patrol area they attacked the large enemy formation. Ladd closed directly on the tail of a Val and fired a long burst that sent it down into a flaming dive. Two Zeros forced Ladd to break away into a steep dive and he evaded successfully. Ladd lost Cragg and headed for some Lightnings in the distance and on his way to join them he saw another Val low on the water and shot at close range and Ladd had to pull up sharply to avoid hitting the Val as it hit the water to give him seven victories.

Jay Robbins became CO of the 80th Fighter Squadron as soon as 15 victory ace Cragg was listed MIA. Under Cragg's capable leadership the "Headhunters" of the 80th Squadron had downed over 160 planes in nine months. Robbins was now the leading active Headhunter ace with 13 victories and would continue Cragg's legacy.

**26 December 1943: 8FG/35FS/36FS**

35FS

The 35FS sent 16 of their new P-40Ns to patrol Cape Gloucester area and cover a convoy when at 1430 *Duckbutt* plotted bogies 30 miles away. The 35FS Warhawks also had to wait at lower altitude until the Japanese formations had been dispersed and were driven to lower levels. Sixteen P40Ns were orbiting at 12,000 feet when the first Japanese fighters were sighted coming down from the rear.

Maj. Emmett Davis was leading Blue Flight with wingman, Capt. Clifton Troxell at 9,000 feet at 1440 when an "undetermined number" of enemy fighters at all attitudes were seen covering enemy dive bombers attacking the Allied convoy. Davis dove on a fighter from astern firing two long bursts without observed results as the enemy pilots escaped into the clouds. Davis and Troxell went into a fast climb and at the top of the climb saw two Zeros below and straight in front and rolled into the attack. Both

**1Lt. Norman Reid** scored his second of three victories. (AAF)

Leading by example, **Maj. Emmett Davis** scored his last two of his three total victories. (AAF)

**Capt. Harold McClelland** shot down his second enemy aircraft, and would add his third and last the next day. (AAF)

**1Lt. George Goolsby** shot down two Zeros to give him three victories. (AAF)

**1Lt. Harold Souther** shot down three Zeros to give him four total victories for his career. (AAF)

**Capt. Clifton Troxell** (top) of the 8FGHQ scored his first P-40 victory to become an ace. He is shown here later with Charles Lindbergh. (AFAA)

**Maj. Carl Taylor** shot down his third and last enemy aircraft. (AAF)

Americans fired a long burst at the leader and both Zero pilots pulled up and the leader then went into a dive. Troxell followed but as he got into range he saw that it was on fire from Davis' bullets and diving toward the water. Davis went off and attacked a Zero on the tail of a P-40 and the Zero pilot turned away from his attack and pulled up hard to port and Davis followed to very close range and fired causing a stream of smoke as the two continued their turn. Davis was unable to turn with the Zero and half-rolled away as the Zero was about to get on his tail. Troxell rejoined Davis and soon they ran into two Zeros straight ahead and Troxell fired on the leader who pulled up. Troxell passed under the Zero and pulled into a tight right hand turn and saw that the Zero was smoking and as Troxell closed to finish off the Zero; it crashed into the water for his fifth and last victory to become an ace. Troxell lost Davis and despite having his engine sputter, continued to search for the enemy and came up on two Zeros. Troxell fired as the leader broke away in a tight starboard turn and flew directly into the stream of bullets but without result. Troxell then chased another Zero for several minutes and just as he got into firing range the enemy pilot pulled straight up and rolled on its back. Troxell started firing and continued firing until the enemy fighter passed under him. He then made a hard right turn after the fleeing enemy and attempted an out of range deflection shot when another P-40 came in and made a firing run forcing the enemy pilot to climb away. Troxell's engine was still missing badly and he returned to base. Meanwhile, Davis saw three Zeros roll onto a flight of P-40s and dove to get on the tail of one but the P-40 Flight Leader had turned into the Zero and shot down in front of Davis. Davis then attacked one of the other three Zeros and fired a long burst at 100 yards from dead astern. The enemy pilot went into a slow roll directly in front of Davis who held his fire until the Zero was "in point blank range" but had to pull away before firing in order to avoid a collision. As he was turning away Davis saw the Zero burst into flames. Davis fired on another Zero without observing any results. "Zooming back up into the fight" he saw a Zero firing on the tail of a Warhawk. Davis made a head on pass and the Zero pilot pulled up his fire to Davis' P-40 but his bullets passed 30 feet below. Davis fired head on for about two seconds before running out of ammunition and then had to pull sharply away to avoid another collision.

1Lt. George Goolsby was the Second Element Leader of Blue Flight with 1Lt. Robert Colgrove as his Wingman. When the enemy fighters were first sighted high to port, they dove and forced Goolsby away from his flight. Goolsby fired at three or four Zeros from long range and then caught one at his altitude and fired a long burst that caused it to smoke. A second burst hit the wing root and the Zero went into a "messy" half roll into the ocean. Goolsby lost Wingman Colgrove and joined White Flight Leader, 1Lt. Harold Souther. As Zero dove between them, Souther dove on it and set on fire. Goolsby then caught one coming out of a dive and fired .50 caliber bullets into its wing root and fuselage for his second victory of the day. He continued to patrol before returning to base. Colgrove initially followed Goolsby down on his attack on the Zeros but broke off when two Zeros came in from above. These Zeros did not press their attack but loitered in the area and Colgrove joined 1Lt. Roy Klandrud, Element Leader of White Flight, and climbed with him into a swirling dogfight. Klandrud had lost his Flight Leader and Wingman when he blacked out when he pulled up sharply as he fired a deflection shot on a Zero that his Flight Leader missed. The Colgrove and Klandrud had many firing opportunities during the next few minutes but they were mostly deflection shots because of the constant maneuvering of the enemy pilots. As Colgrove reentered the fight he saw a Zero smoking badly with 1Lt. Voy Winders chasing it and watching the enemy pilot finally bailing out. Colgrove closed and fired short of a Zero and Klandrud looped around and rejoined Colgrove who took the lead and climbed for altitude and dove on a Zero that was chasing a P-40. Colgrove continued his attack even though another enemy fighter fired a burst in front of him. Colgrove scored several hits before the target broke off and Klandrud would confirm the victory. Klandrud and Colgrove saw four Zeros and dove on them. Klandrud fired a burst at a Zero that was pulling up and saw explosions that sent it into a spin trailing smoke. Colgrove pulled from his unsuccessful pass and began another attack when he saw a Zero outrunning a P-40 about a mile below and dove. He held his fire until he closed to within 200 to 250 yards when enemy pilot began to turn sharply from side to side. Colgrove got a good leading shot as the Zero pilot turned sharply to port but the enemy pilot's turn was so tight that Colgrove could not stay with it to see the results. Klandrud made another quick firing pass on a Zero but did not claim it as it did not smoke or burn. Colgrove and Klandrud rejoined and circled *Duckbutt* for 10 more minutes before returning to base.

1Lt. Harold Souther and his White Flight were at 12,000 feet when the enemy fighters were first seen diving from seven o'clock high. Souther first peeled his flight off to the right and then banked to the left which caused the enemy pilots to pull up without completing their runs. A Zero passed under the flight and pulled up in front of Souther who fired a short burst, hitting it and then it rolled over, burst into flame, and dove into the sea. Souther became separated from his flight but continued to attack. He banked to port and caught another Zero trying to turn into him and shot it down in flames with two long bursts. Souther saw another Zero trying to outmaneuver a P-40 and fired from out of range and chased it away. Goolsby joined Souther and after one circle Souther saw a Zero below and dove on it sending it down in flames for his third victory of the day and fourth and last victory of the war. Goolsby followed Souther and hit another Zero from astern and it half rolled on fire into the water. The two victorious pilots rejoined and half rolled on another Zero that Goolsby hit and sent it into spiral into the water. 1Lt. Voy Winders, the White #4 man, called out four enemy aircraft diving on them at 7 o'clock but his flight didn't follow him as dove away. Winders saw a Zero to his right diving for a cloud with several P-40s chasing it. As the Zero left the cloud it was under Winders who wasted ammunition when he fired too far out of range and it escaped into another cloud. Winders then saw a number of "radial engine" fighters (Tojos) and saw one under him and it half rolled and dove. Winders dove after it and fired and got numerous hits on its tail, wings, and fuselage and the pilot bailed out and was confirmed by 1Lt. Robert Colgrove.

Souther's separated Wingman, 1Lt. Norman Reid, was flying at 11,000 feet and heard that another flight had contacted enemy fighters and bombers and watched in the reported direction for them to arrive but had became separated from his Flight Leader. Reid tried to rejoin his Flight at full throttle but as five enemy fighters dove onto the Flight's tails they concentrated on Reid as he still trailed and was vulnerable. Reid called out his attackers and dropped his tanks and dove without the Zeros following. Reid was alone again and climbed back to 8,000 feet where he saw a stubby enemy fighter and hit its tail and fuselage with full deflection shots and then with another burst from 20 to 30 degrees astern. Reid then saw tracers whiz past his canopy and broke off his attack to dive to safety. Reid rejoined some P-40s that were chasing a lone stubby enemy fighter that went into a right evasive turn that put it directly in front of Reid who opened fired with a very long burst at full deflection and didn't stop firing until all but one of his guns were firing and the enemy fighter was amass of flames for his second victory of the day and of three.

Meanwhile, 1Lt. Leo Everhart, leading Yellow Flight, saw P-38s and P-47s chasing bandits everywhere above him and ordered tanks dropped. When they climbed to 14,000 feet and started into a starboard turn, Yellow Element Leader, 1Lt. Lynn Witt called out a Zero diving from his portside and another Zero coming down directly on him. Witt had to break to escape in the opposite direction which split the flight. Everhart was unable to fire a shot and followed Witt down and found a Zero flying at 5,000 feet. As he was closing on the tail of the Zero he heard *Duckbutt* calling all flights to intercept Vals that were approaching the ships. Everhart had passed the Vals as he was almost in firing range and pressed his attack on the Zero and shot it down at 1,000 feet above the shoreline and then turned to engage the Vals. He fired at one but had to stop firing when a P-38 cut in front of him and when he chased another Val, a P-47 caused him to break away. He then saw two Vals heading inland and followed them into a cloud; shooting down one but overrunning the other. The two adversaries then maneuvered for 10 minutes with Everhart firing and missing until the Val dove as Everhart began to climb and Everhart got on its tail and followed into a rainy valley. Everhart continued taking shots but without getting any hits. The Val continued on until it came to the end of the valley where the mountains rose and as the low-flying Val tried to climb out; it crashed. Everhart turned back over Cape Gloucester and saw another Val and fired but only his port guns were firing and he ran out of ammunition as the Val flew on. Meanwhile, a Zero made a pass at Witt but its tracers passed just over his P-40's canopy and Witt half rolled away but his Wingman, 2Lt. William Dwyer, fell behind with his tanks still attached. Witt pulled up and saw Everhart shoot down a Zero and then made a pass on another Zero and then saw a P-40 (McClelland) shoot at the same Zero and send it down in flames. Witt flew near the convoy and saw Val dive bombers in a steep dive. Witt rolled over in a dive after a Val and fired a long burst into its canopy and it spiraled down in flames for his first victory. As he pulled away Witt saw a Zero on his tail and headed for some nearby clouds. When he emerged Witt joined another P-40 and continued to patrol for a half hour before returning to base.

Capt. Harold McClelland led the Red Flight and after patrolling for 45 minutes a lone bogie was spotted by McClelland's Wingman flying south of Arawe. McClelland had trouble approaching the bogie as its pilot skillfully turned until he got all four Red Flight P-40s inside him and then would turn in the opposite direction. Finally, when one Red element got on one side and the second element on the other side, the enemy pilot made a slight turn toward McClelland who got behind the Dinah which pulled away. McClelland's Wingman, 1Lt. Glendi Holder, then made a firing pass from astern and started a fire in its port engine. McClelland turned into another firing run and set the other engine on fire and the Dinah headed for the sea for McClelland's second victory.The 35th had scored 17 victories: 11 Zeros, three Vals, and three Tojos in their new P-40Ns.

36FS

Throughout December while the 35FS was having great success with its P-40s the 36FS claimed only six victories for two losses with five on 26 December. Part of the reason was that the 36th was engaged on operations that did not normally contact the enemy. Another reason was that the P-47 Thunderbolt required a lot of training for the pilot to become proficient. The most successful P-47 units had extended and rigorous training periods in which to learn the advantages of the fighter. The 36th did not have the benefit of such a period and as a result they were deprived of utilizing the Thunderbolt's celebrated performance characteristics.

Four Agate flights of 16 P-47s led by: Red: Capt. Warren Danson; White: 1Lt. James McLaughlin; Blue: 1Lt. Donald Campbell; and Yellow: 1Lt. Ralph Tuuri were patrolling the shipping lanes of Dampier Strait, Cape Gloucester at 1445 when the P-38s of the 80FS attacked the Japanese formations of Vals, Oscars and a few Zeros first. The 36FS waited below to attack when the Lightnings forced the Japanese down. Although the Japanese had the initial altitude advantage when they did come down to fight; it was not long before the 36th's Thunderbolts had won the day in air near Kokopo.

At 1440 Capt. Warren Danson's Red Flight was over Kokopo at 14,000 feet when they saw 12 to 15 Vals at the same altitude. The Vals immediately peeled off to attack the shipping and Red Flight followed. Danson missed on his first pass at 4,000 feet and got some hits on his second and third passes. He then made three passes on a third Val that was already damaged and heading down for a probable. He made five or six passes on another Val; killing its gunner on the second pass and causing "plenty of smoke." The Val dropped down to the tree tops and lowered its diving flaps and kept flying. On his last pass on this Val Danson had a P-38 (McGuire 431FS) following closely waiting to finish the Val off. Danson fired and when he pulled up he saw the Val crash (Danson ICR: "I believe I was entirely responsible for the destruction of this aircraft"). Danson's Wingman, 2Lt. Robert Cordell, had followed his Leader down in the first pass and fired at 60 degrees and saw his .50 calibers fall behind and moved his sights ahead and fired again but in doing so lost track of his speed and closed too fast and had to pull up to avoid a collision and claimed a probable (but was not awarded any claim) He then made several more passes on the dive bombers but overran on each. A Val flew directly in front of Cordell and he fired from 5 o'clock at very close range and it burst into flames and exploded on its way down. Cordell was at 2,000 feet and climbed to 4,000 feet when he saw a Val below and dove but the Val pilot saw Cordell and escaped into a cloud. Cordell climbed to 5,500 feet and headed out to sea where he saw a Zero at his altitude but way out of range. The Zero pilot saw the Thunderbolt closing and made a hard starboard turn toward a cloud. Cordell fired but his tracers passed in front of the Zero and he continued to fire until the Zero flew into the stream of bullets that hit the cockpit and wing roots. Cordell reported the Zero was last seen heading down out of control and claimed a victory but was awarded a damaged. Danson's Red Element Leader, 1Lt. Jack Ericsson, was unable to release his belly tank but after finally releasing it he had lost his flight but his Wingman, 2Lt. Arthur Heckerman, stayed him. The two saw two Oscars diving below at 7,000 feet along the coast heading for the clouds. Ericsson dove at full throttle and caught an Oscar and fired into its cockpit as it pulled up but Ericsson did not file a damaged claim. Heckerman tried to get into position to fire on this Oscar but stalled out. Ericsson followed and half rolled and turned around a cloud where he met a Val dive bomber headed directly toward him. He waited until the Val was very close and "let him have it," blowing off the canopy and killing the pilot. The Val nosed over and plunged into the sea for his only victory. After Heckerman recovered from his stall he came out of a cloud and lost Ericsson. He climbed and met an unknown P-47 and tried to join its wing when a Zero carrying a belly tank emerged from a cloud to the left. The P-47 fired and when the Zero crossed Heckerman's path he fired and hit the belly tank and the Oscar exploded. Heckerman was alone again and joined a P-38 when a Zero closed on them and dove away. Heckerman followed the Zero and as he closed on its tail and fired and saw white smoke streaming from its belly and as Heckerman pulled up at 1,000 feet and saw the Zero explode as it hit the water. Heckerman was officially credited with two probables for his only claims of the war. During his attack Heckerman thought he saw tracers whizzing past his wing from another friendly fighter firing on his Zero but afterward a P-47 joined Heckerman and its pilot waved at him, indicating that something Heckerman's fighter had been hit. Soon Heckerman saw heavy black smoke coming out of the right side of the cowling and it became so hot in his cockpit that he was forced to bail out. He opened the canopy, rolled the fighter over, and fell out of the cockpit. Heckerman was circled by another P-47 and several P-38s on the way down to protect him from strafing enemy fighters. About 10 minutes after he landed in the water, Heckerman was picked up by a sub-chaser six miles north of Cape Gloucester and returned to the 36FS three days later.

1Lt. James McLaughlin's White Flight did not make any claims during the day's combat as they first patrolled the area from Borgen Bay to Kokopo. As they next headed west they saw a large flight of approximately 25 aircraft at 20,000 feet heading south. The flight dropped their tanks and began to climb when they saw about a dozen more enemy aircraft approaching from the northeast. White Flight turned towards this second enemy formation which sent down decoy aircraft to lure the outnumbered Americans into an attack but with eight to ten more enemy aircraft above McLaughlin decided it was unwise to attack. McLaughlin got his Flight into position, remaining at 13,000 to 15,000 feet, and tried to keep the Zeros and Oscars engaged "as much as possible. There were too many to

**1Lt. Jack Ericsson** scored his only victory. (AAF)

**1Lt. John Perkins** also scored his only career victory. (AAF)

take much time in planning an attack." McLaughlin finally had to have the Flight Split-S away as the Japanese dove to attack. The P-40 of 1Lt. Alden Woodworth, McLaughlin's Wingman, was hit in the cowling just ahead of the cockpit by an explosive shell. Woodworth dove away from the combat to access the damage to his fighter and to himself and found his fighter flyable but he had been hit in his right arm and body by aircraft fragments. Nonetheless, he headed back alone to the fight but saw many Zeros about 1,000 feet above and hoped not to be seen. However, one peeled off to attack him. Woodworth dove, using violent skids, and barely escaped, his fighter receiving several bullets in his wing. Woodworth raced home and landed safely where the Medical Officer removed 20 to 25 pieces of metal fragments from him. McLaughlin's #4 man, 2Lt. Devin Gilchrist, bailed out of his damaged fighter and rescue vessels were unable to find him and he was listed as killed in action.

1Lt. Donald Campbell's Blue Flight was at 6,000 feet about five miles from the invasion landing area when he saw the Vals below as they were about to attack. Blue Flight split up and dove into the attack. Campbell and his Wingman dove on the enemy dive bombers but Campbell fired and missed a 60 degree deflection shot. Blue #3, 1Lt. John Perkins, saw an enemy fighter on the tail of his Wingman, 1Lt. Robert Cox, and the two Americans Split-S'd away. They then saw a dogfight at 10,000 feet and climbed above it to attack. Perkins got a short burst on a fighter that pulled up in front of him but did not see any damage and then fired on another Oscar, again without seeing any results. Wingman Cox closed on an Oscar from behind and slightly below and fired a short burst from 250 yards and saw his .50s go over the Oscar. Cox adjusted his attack and fired a long burst that caused a 10 foot flash of flame to erupt from the cowl, followed by black smoke as the Oscar turned upside down and crashed. Perkins saw an Oscar to his right and fired at it from 6 o'clock and observed hits near the wing root and continued to fire until the Oscar reached 3,000 feet and clearly was going to crash into the water.

Yellow Flight Leader 1Lt. Ralph Tuuri was leading his flight over Kokopo at 11,000 feet and peeled off after a passing Val but had to leave his Element Leader and his Wingman behind when the #4 man had engine problems. Tuuri got behind the Val but his guns failed to fire as he had not turned his gun switch on. Later, Tuuri and his Wingman, 2Lt. Darrel Spurlin, saw 15 enemy fighters about 4,000 feet above and began a wide climbing turn to get above them for a firing pass. As they approached a enemy fighter peeled down and hit Spurlin's vertical stabilizer with a cannon shell and put some machine gun bullet holes in his wing. The two Americans easily dove away and Tuuri escorted his Wingman back to base.

**26 December 1943: 348FG/342FS/Special Flight**
342FS
On 26 December the 5FC sent over 100 fighters over the Cape Gloucester beachhead to cover the convoy and landings. The 342FS, led by Squadron Commander, Maj. Raymond Gallagher, was assigned a late afternoon patrol slot and 20 P-47s took off at 1455 (with one soon aborting) to cover the withdrawal of the landing ships. As soon as the 342nd took off *Duckbutt* radioed that they should "give it the needle as there was a scrap going on" over Cape Gloucester. However, when they arrived at 1515 the "scrap" was apparently over and they patrolled over Umboi Island at 13,000 feet. At 1700 a V formation of Japanese bombers, identified as either Bettys or Helens, approached from the northwest at 16,000 feet.

As soon as they spotted the first bombers, Capt. Walter Benz and Wingman, 1Lt. Robert Gibb, immediately climbed about a 1,000 feet and dived to the attack from the rear. Benz closed to about 500 feet behind one of the bombers and fired a four second burst from 20 degrees deflection and Benz and Gibb watched the Japanese trail fire from its fuel tanks and crash into the water below for Benz' fourth victory. Squadron Commander, Maj. Raymond Gallagher, had a number of problems while shooting down

**Capt. Edward Roddy's** Crew Chief on his charge with another victory decal. (AFAA)

**1Lt. Lawrence O'Neill** shot down four Betty bombers to become the day's high scorer and an ace. (AFAA)

a Betty. Once Benz began his attack Gallagher turned right and started climbing but found that his drop tank had not released and continued to fly parallel to the Bettys while trying to get the tank to release while the Betty gunners began to take long range pot shots at him. One Betty broke out of the formation and Gallagher fired a five second burst at it, scoring hits on the fuselage and engines which started burning and crashed into the sea for his only victory.

Capt. Edward Roddy was leading Red Flight and opened the attack with a climbing front quarter attack from beneath the lead V formation of bombers. He hit two of the bombers and observed flames coming from one of them. A 7.7 mm bullet ricocheted off Roddy's canopy and cracked the windshield and the wind howled through the cockpit. His fighter was next hit in the belly by a 20mm shell fired by the tail cannon of an enemy bomber. 1Lt. Marvin Grant was following on Roddy's wing and moved to the left side of the enemy formation and made a long 45 degree pass and watched hits all over the bomber before it caught fire and fell into the sea. 1Lt. Edward Wyroba, Grant's Wingman, sprayed the bomber formation and saw several ineffective hits before going after the lead bomber which was diving away from the formation. He fired from astern and got hits on the port engine and the bomber began to burn. Wyroba made a second pass to finish it off for his only victory. Roddy's #4, 1Lt. Lawrence O'Neill, was the high scorer of the day with four victories to make him an ace. O'Neill's combat report was very concise:

My flight leader made a head on pass and the lead bomber fell out of the formation in flames. I followed with a 45 degree pass and hit the number two bomber. After this I pulled around and made three consecutive attacks from astern and each time a different one of the bombers fell out of formation in flames.

1Lt. Robert Sutcliffe was leading the Blue Flight with 1Lt. George Orr on his wing at 19,000 feet 30 miles northwest of Umboi Island when they sighted six Betty bombers in a V at 17,000 feet with an escort of two Tonys and a Zero. Sutcliffe and Orr circled at 1,500 to 2,000 feet above the bombers and dived to the attack at opposite ends of the bomber formation. Sutcliffe made a head on pass and set one enemy on fire while another left trailing smoke. Sutcliffe returned and sent this bomber down in an explosion and these two victories gave him three so far. Orr fired at one Betty but missed and dived away to make a stern attack on the bomber formation. Like Sutcliffe, Orr's volley started one on fire and another started to smoke. Orr attacked the smoker from the rear at close range it burst into flames and crashed into the sea. These two Bettys were Orr's first victories. Blue Second Element Leader, 1Lt. James Pratt, and his Wingman, 1Lt. Wynans Frankfort, were circling the bombers when the Tonys arrived and they both dove to attack. Frankfort fired a long range burst and his Tony went into a steep climb and Frankfort closed to 200 yards and tore pieces off the enemy which started on fire and half rolled into the water. A second Tony flashed past Frankfort who fired but four of his guns were jammed and he did not get any hits before he ran out of ammo. Pratt's Thunderbolt was later seen to be hit by friendly AA fire and he was killed in the crash of his aircraft after scoring two career victories.

*Special Flight*

For the mission, 348FG CO, Col. Robert Rowland, formed a Parry Special Flight of eight fighters. Just after they took off at 1545 *Duckbutt* told Rowland to rush to Cape Gloucester and intercept an incoming raid on shipping in the area. At 1700 Rowland's P-47s were at 15,000 feet over the beachhead ships and saw a dogfight to the south. As he headed in that direction the Fighter Director radioed that an enemy torpedo bomber was starting a run on an American warship in Borgen Bay. Rowland saw a dark brown Japanese bomber at 2,000 feet turning toward the American ships. Another P-47 attacked the bomber, missed, overran, and then climbed away from the area. Rowland dropped his belly tank and rolled over to attack with his Wingman following while the rest of the flight climbed toward the dogfight above. Rowland dove at 450 mph and made one pass getting hits on its fuselage and starboard engine. Despite the damage and Rowland's presence the Japanese continued to press its attack. Rowland drove home another attack to within 200 yards from astern and the Betty exploded, losing its left wing and falling in a ball of flames into the sea and Rowland became an ace.

**Lt.Col. Robert Rowland** scored his sixth career victory and would add his seventh the next day. (AFAA)

## 27 December 1943: 348FG/340FS/341FS

340FS

Just as the 341FS was about to encounter the enemy the 340FS was scrambled on a vector to the same enemy formation as met by the 341FS. Maj. Hervey Carpenter led 16 P-47s to Arawe and at 12,000 feet they sighted an enemy force of 15 to 20 fighters at about 15,000 and 12 dive bombers below at about 1,000 feet heading toward Rabaul after attacking the USN PT Boats.

Maj. Carpenter led his flight on the Vals and left his Wingman, 1Lt. Jerome Fischer, behind as he made a high head on pass on a Val which was seen to crash in the sea. Carpenter fired long deflection shots on two other Vals and observed hits but he made no damaged claims for these aircraft. When Fischer arrived to rejoin Carpenter he was jumped by Zeros and his fighter was hit in tail and he went into a steep dive to escape. A Zero which had made the pass on the Americans continued after them and dove in front of Fischer and then pulled back up and Fischer followed. Apparently the enemy pilot was unaware that Fischer was behind and did not try to evade until fired on and hit. The Zero rolled on its back and Split-S'd but burst into flames for Fischer's only victory.

Capt. Meade Brown led Blue Flight down on the Vals and fired and exploded the leading Val with an accurate burst from 100 yards astern. Meade's Wingman, 1Lt. Richard Fleischer, attacked another group of three Vals and fired on the last one which immediately caught fire and crashed and exploded. Fleischer then made a slight port turn and fired at a second Val which exploded and its pieces fell onto the sea. Then Brown and Fleischer saw another Zero carrying a bomb at their altitude and Fleischer dove but overran and Brown followed and claimed the victory. 1Lt. Myron Hnatio was leading the second element of Blue Flight when he noticed two Vals ready to attack shipping and closed in on the last one, fired and turned to starboard slightly and fired at the first one. When he looked back he saw the first crash into the sea and then the second hit beside it in flames. Hnatio turned sharply to the right and started to climb when four Zeros came in from above and about 2 o'clock. He turned into the fighters and closed on the second Zero in the formation. The Zero pulled up to the right and Hnatio followed, firing all the time and the Zero crashed into the sea. Meanwhile the other three Zeros broke away. Hnatio's P-47 had been hit and he returned to base with three victories toward becoming a five ace.

1Lt. Richard Lake, leading the White Flight with 2Lt. Stanley Souders on his wing, dropped his belly tank and dove on a Zero and fired a long burst at 20 degree deflection and it began to smoke. As Lake flew past his victim, a piece of the Zero's fuselage penetrated his wing. The damage did not affect the performance of Lake's Thunderbolt and he flew on and saw another P-47 in combat with six Zeros at about 1,000 feet above the jungle northeast of Arawe. As he dove to the rescue a Tony turned into him and Lake fired a long head on burst and the Tony half rolled and crashed into the jungle for his second of three victories. Meanwhile, Souders closed on a Zero and shot it down. On his second pass Souders hit another Zero that started to smoke and Lake followed and on his next pass, with only one gun firing, Souders shot the Zero's wing off for his last of three victories. 1Lt. Richard Frost, an Element Leader in White Flight saw a Zero in a right turn and fired and his victim was seen to crash for his first of three victories.

1Lt. Lloyd Zaage, an Element Leader in Yellow Flight, and his Wingman 2Lt. Joel Pitchford, made two passes on Vals flying at 500 feet at 9 o'clock. Zaage got hits on both passes and on the second the Val crashed into the water for Zaage's first of two victories. Pitchford dove on the Vals and hit one from 500 yards and followed it as it pulled up and then stalled long enough for two crewmen to bail out for Pitchford's only victory.

**Maj. Hervey Carpenter** led the 340FS and was credited with his first of three victories. (AAF)

**1Lt. Jerome Fisher** was credited with his only victory. (AAF)

**1Lt. Myron Hnatio** shot down two Vals and a Zero for his first victories of five total. (AAF)

**1Lt. Richard Fleischer** scored his first of two victories. (AAF)

**2Lt. Joel Pitchford** (right with Lt.Col. George Prentice) scored his only victory. (AAF)

341FS

The 341FS took off from Finschhafen at 0730 arrived over Arawe at about 0900 with 16 P-47s in four flights Parry Red, White, Blue, and Yellow. These flights patrolled at 5,000 to 7,000 feet over the water when about 40 single engine fighters were sighted dead ahead, above and below the American formation. USN PT boats, 20 miles off Arawe, were being bombed and strafed by 12 single-engine fighters.

Rowland

Col. Robert Rowland had trouble with his radio but led two flights, Parry Blue under Capt. Kenneth Briggs and Parry Yellow under Capt. Arthur Weeks, to the Cape Gloucester area but the weather was so bad there that they had to patrol Borgen Bay and Arawe area. Rowland saw the PT Boats under attack down to the attack and called Parry Red to dive with his flights but did not hear Rowland and he led Parry Blue and Yellow to rescue the PT Boats but only the Week's Yellow Flight followed. Rowland only found a Zero which was just climbing away from strafing run on a patrol boat. Rowland chased the fighter at less than 1,000 feet off the water and just west of Arawe the Zero suddenly pulled up into a chandelle. Rowland followed the Zero and put a burst into its belly and engine and the Zero exploded in the sea for Rowland's seventh victory.

Yellow Flight

1Lt. John Lolos was flying on Weeks' wing and dove to help a P-40 that was chasing two Zeros when one turned head on into him. Lolos fired until the Zero passed very close to starboard and during a sharp climbing turn he saw his flaming victim crash into the water. Another Zero flew in front of Lolos from the starboard and he fired a short burst and the enemy fighter rolled on its back and the pilot bailed out for Lolos' first two of four victories. In the meantime a Zero got onto Lolos' tail and he jinked and skidded until Capt. Weeks was able to come to his rescue. As Weeks closed the Zero half rolled and began to turn into Weeks who fired a long burst and it crashed into the water. A few minutes later, while flying at 1,500 feet, Weeks saw a Zero at 1,000 feet flying overland north of Arawe heading for a cloud bank. Weeks dove and opened fire at 200 yards at 90 degrees deflection and the Zero crashed in the jungle just inland for Weeks only two victories. 1Lt. James Rea, the Second Element Leader in Week's Yellow Flight fired a few short bursts but was unable to get into good position. Rea saw a P-47 being pursued and shot down and went after the victorious Zero that headed over the wave tops toward Rabaul and caught it and fired a long telling burst and the Zeke started to smoke. Rea began to turn back but the Zero continued to fly and Rea resumed the chase. Rea fired until he was out of ammunition and saw the Zero crash into a wooded area north of Sauren for his only victory. Rea found three Zeros on his tail with a P-47 chasing them. One closed and fired and Rea skidded and finally out ran him. When he landed there were 12 holes in his fighter but the small caliber 7.7 mm bullets did little damage. Rea's Wingman, 1Lt. Robert Anderson, dove and joined a P-40 that was chasing a Zero. Both American pilots fired but as the Zero was turning, Anderson hit the Zero's port wing with a long burst that tore off pieces that sent it into the sea for Anderson's only victory.

White Flight

While Capt. John Moore was patrolling with his Parry White Flight, the Controller vectored him to Zeros attacking a PT Boat. Moore flew at 500 feet to get through rain clouds but had to turn around and climb along the south coast. *Duckbutt* became even more urgent and finally someone in his flight spotted four Zeros at 3 o'clock high and low. The flight dove from 8,000 feet and attacked just after the Zeros broke off their attack on the PT Boats. One Zero broke away to the left and Moore was able to give him an accurate

**1Lt. Robert Anderson** scored his only victory. (AAF)

**Capt. John Moore** claimed two victories to become an ace, and would shoot down a Kate the next day. (AFAA)

**1Lt. William Foulis** got his first of six victories, but would not score again until December 1944, and would eventually become an ace. (AAF)

**Capt. Arthur Weeks** shot down two Zeros for his only victories of the war. (AAF)

two second burst that hit the Zero. Moore broke away and climbed to 6,000 where two Zeros half rolled from 8,000 feet on him and his Wingman, 1Lt. Wilbur Henderson. The P-47s ran for a cloudbank and lost the enemy and when he emerged Moore saw another Zero diving away and followed it into the overcast. Moore followed the Zero in and out of the clouds and overcast until he closed and fired a long burst into the cockpit and engine area. The Zero fell off on its wing and crashed into the jungle about 10 miles north of Arawe to make Moore an ace. When Moore emerged from the cloud after the Zeros rolled him and Henderson; his wingman did not follow.

Red Flight

1Lt. James Lynch led Red Flight at 8,000 feet about 15 miles southwest of Arawe when, at 0900, they spotted "30 radial engined fighters scattered from 2,000 to 20,000 feet with the lower ones bombing a couple of PT-Boats." The Flight dropped their belly tanks and climbed to 12,000 feet and went into a dive on the Oscars below. Lynch was unable to drop his belly tank but continued to lead the dive and fired on an Oscar from astern just over the water for his only victory. Lynch's Wingman, 1Lt. Frank Morrison, fired from large deflection through dead astern and then a small deflection to start it smoking as it dove away. Morrison checked his tail and saw three Zeros closing and shook them by going full throttle into the clouds.

Blue Flight

Capt. Kenneth Briggs, Blue Flight Leader, and Wingman, 1Lt. William Doyal, dove to protect the PT Boats. Doyal chased after a Zero that was strafing a PT-Boat and lost Briggs. Doyal then got a full deflection shot and the Hamp broke away to the right and Doyal circled and watched it go down: "I think the plane went into the water and I consider it probably destroyed." Brigg's Second Element Leader, 1Lt. Merle Zeine, and Wingman, 1Lt. William Foulis dropped their tanks and climbed to engage four Zeros that were separated from the others. Foulis made a steep climbing turn and while still climbing made a slight deflection shot that scored hits on the tail and on the canopy and engine. The canopy flew off and smoke and flame poured from the engine. and as Foulis flew over his victim he was amazed to see the pilot bail out just before the Zero crashed into the ground west of Arawe for his first of six victories. Foulis saw Zeine finish off another Zero which fled, smoking badly and crashed nearby into the jungle east of Arawe for his only victory.

At this time the Japanese had withdrawn from the fight after losing 13 aircraft in exchange for one P-47 whose pilot, 1Lt. Milburn Henderson (341FS), was reported to have parachuted and was captured. 1Lt. James Lynch was wounded in the arm and he ditched off Arawe and was picked up by a PT Boat that saw the marker dye in the water.

**27 December 1943: 8FG/35FS**

Morning Mission

Capt. Harold McClelland was leading a flight of 16 35FS Warhawks to Cape Gloucester but the weather prevented them from reaching the area and *Duckbutt* sent them to patrol the Sagsag area. At 0845 the Controller at Arawe called for help and McClelland climbed and 10 miles from Arawe spotted a number of aircraft at 12 o'clock high. The P-40s were able to climb above the bogies flying in tight formation of three ship Vs without being seen. McClelland and Wingman, 1Lt. Carl Weaver, (his second element snafued) attacked the last V and its aircraft began to spread out as McClelland fired at the one on the left of the enemy leader which spiraled down in flames. The enemy leader turned into McClelland and fired wide as McClelland dove away with his third and last victory of the war. Weaver went after the second "Nip" but had to break off when the aggressive enemy leader turned inside him and fired but Weaver tightened his turn and evaded. Weaver then saw a "Nip" on McClelland's tail and dove to scare it off to the left. Weaver zoomed and Split-S'd onto its tail and fired a long burst into its cockpit setting it on fire. As Weaver pulled up he saw a "Nip" below but a P-47 outraced him to the

**Capt. Harold McClelland** shot down a Zero for his third and last victory. (AAF)

**1Lt. Carl Weaver** shot down two Zeros to give him three career victories. (AAF)

target. Weaver climbed and saw another "Nip" below and dove and fired a long 10 degree deflection. The "Nip" pulled straight up and fell off on one wing and went into a spin. Weaver's ICR states that he could not identify the "Nip" fighters as Zeros or Oscars but they were probably Zeros.

Afternoon Patrol
Maj. Emmett Davis and another P-40 of the 35FS were on patrol over the water when they came across a flying boat that looked like a PBY Catalina. As they approached the flying boat did not respond with suitable identification; with the daily code either visually or by radio. Davis flew in for a visual check but as he closed the "enemy" fired a burst at him. It was standard policy that unidentified aircraft were to be shot down and Davis carefully aimed and fired to disable it and force it down on the water. When he returned to base Davis was informed that his victim was an USN Catalina whose anxious gunners also were unable to identify themselves to Davis. Fortunately, only one crewmember was wounded in the incident.

**28 December 1943: 348FG/341FS**
The 341FS sent 10 P-47s to Cape Gloucester at 0730. Capt. John Moore the Leader of the first flight flew to the patrol area at 7,000 feet and arrived at 0820. During the patrol Moore saw a lone Kate torpedo bomber heading east at 12,000 feet and started to climb to intercept. The Kate spotted the Thunderbolts and dove toward the overcast at 2,000 feet and Moore's flight followed but lost the Kate. The enemy bomber broke through the overcast at 5,000 feet and was seen by the Americans who climbed to intercept. As Moore closed the Kate dove to 1,500 feet where Moore fired and started a fore at the right wing root and the Kate crashed into the sea in a ball of flame for Moore's sixth victory and third in two days.

**31 December 1943: 8FG/35FS**
Maj. Philip Rasmussen, who shot down a Zero flying a P-36 as a Second Lieutenant with the 46FG over Pearl Harbor, led four P-40s on a patrol to Cape Gloucester. After flying for two and a half hours they had finished their patrol when, at 1300, the Arawe Controller sent them 60 miles up the coast to a plot. The flight made contact 15 minutes later with three bogies at 6 o'clock high in the thin overcast at 9,000 feet. Although the enemy fighters were in "excellent" position to attack Rasmussen led the flight in a 360 degree climbing turn, dropping their belly tanks. The enemy fighters dove at 60 degrees trying to escape toward Rabaul. The P-40s dove after them but were unable to gain any distance on them. Upon leveling out the enemy fighters split up; two along a cloud bank over low mountains and the other one into a cloud. Rasmussen and his Wingman followed the one into the clouds which were lying on the mountains and about 500 feet thick. Rasmussen stayed above the clouds and the enemy broke into a clear area twice and on the second time Rasmussen fired a three second burst that sent it into the mountains. Meanwhile, the second element led by 1Lt. Charles Rainville and his Wingman, 1Lt. Dean Jacobson, chased the other two enemy fighters into a low layer of clouds. Rainville fired from out of range as it was his only chance before it went into the clouds. He saw small pieces come off its tail but it never smoked and he claimed it as a probable. Jacobson had to throttle back to avoid overrunning his target and fired a short burst from 300 yards as the enemy pilot turned to port. Jacobson saw no visible results and closed again and fired a long burst from astern getting hits as the enemy turned to starboard. As Jacobson closed to 150 feet he fired a long burst from directly astern getting good hits on bandit's tail and fuselage. As he closed to 10 feet Jacobson turned away just in time to avoid a large explosion. Rasmussen identified the victim as resembling a P-43 and probably was a Tojo. However, Rainville and Jacobson identified their victims only as Oscars.

**31 December 1943: 348FG/340FS/342FS**
The 348FG celebrated the end of 1943 when Mission Leader, Maj. William Banks, led the Group to another 10 victories, two by the 340FS and eight by the 342FS to bring the Group's victory total to over 120.

340FS
While flying at 6,000 feet above Arawe, 1Lt. Richard Lake Wingman to White Flight Leader, 1Lt. Lyle Dowsett, spotted three Val dive bombers flying in loose formation heading northeast at 500 feet. Lake dove into a

**Maj. Philip Rasmussen** shown after his P-36 sortie over Pearl Harbor, where he shot down a Zero and would score his last victory over an Oscar. (AAF)

**1Lt. Dean Jacobson** got his third and last victory. (AAF)

stern attack, firing a very long burst while closing to 100 yards when the Val exploded for his third and last victory. Dowsett dove and came up under the Val and fired a short burst and then turned and fired another short burst and it crashed into the sea for his first of four victories.

342FS

The squadron took off with 16 Thunderbolts at 1230 but after 15 minutes the Arawe controller vectored them toward Japanese fighters coming in from the southwest again to attack PT Boats. To reach the vector area Green Flight Leader, 1Lt. Theodore Wood, had to lead his flight around friendly AA fire protecting the beachhead. Green Flight was flying to the rescue when enemy bombs were seen falling on the convoy about 10 miles away and changed course. As Wood approached he saw a Val heading north on deck and then dropping his bomb in the jungle to escape. Wood pursued the Val and fired a three second burst from 150 yards from 6 o'clock and the enemy bomber exploded in the jungle for his second and last victory. 2Lt. George Davis of Green Flight saw three Vals, just pulling up from their attack, escorted by a single Zero about 2,000 feet above them. Davis fired from 5 o'clock at 300 yards and the Val crashed off shore of Arawe for his first of seven victories.

Red Flight Leader, Maj. William Banks, and Wingman, 2Lt. Malcom Rand, saw six Vals and five Zeros on the deck and dropped their tanks. They dove on a Val that was accompanied by a Zero which were heading east out to sea from the Arawe Peninsula. Since the Zero had an altitude advantage the Americans broke off their attack. Meanwhile Banks saw another Zero at 1,000 feet below and when Banks dove, the Zero pulled up into a tight chandelle to the left into a cloud behind Banks and out of range. Rand closed into range of this Zero and fired bullets into its tail section. Rand corrected his sights and sprayed its wings and fuselage and soon the Zero was enveloped in flames for his first of two victories. 2Lt. Robert Knapp, Second Element Leader of Red Flight, saw three Zeros and four Vals below, heading north overland. He passed another P-47 chasing a pair of the Vals and went after the pair flying ahead. He fired on the first Val at 6 o'clock only 300 feet off the ground and started a fire in its port wing root. He passed this Val and fired a long burst on the second Val also from 6 o'clock and it spurted flames from both wing roots and spiraled off toward the ground. As he turned he saw the first Val still in the air with its prop wind milling and he came around and finished it off. A nearby Zero Split-S'd to get on Knapp's tail but Knapp headed into the clouds before the enemy pilot could fire.

At 1310 1Lt. Robert Gibb, the Second Element Leader of White Flight, saw three Zeros at 5,000 to 7,000 feet and five Vals, lower, near the water in front of them. White flight went after the Zeros first and Gibb fired a 45 to 90 degree deflection shot and scored some non-fatal hits. He then dove through the enemy fighters toward the Vals that had disappeared into the overcast. Gibb went under the overcast and spotted a Val dead ahead and fired a one second burst from 300 yards and another two second burst from 100 yards. The Val veered off to cross the shoreline and crashed into the trees. Gibb then cleared his tail and pulled up through the overcast and then went down through it again after the other Val. Gibb fired another two second burst from astern and became an ace.

1Lt. Edward Popek dropped his tanks and dove and fired a short burst with no observed hits and then came around to make a second pass firing at a 15 degree deflection which started the Val on fire and plunged into the trees. Five minutes later he saw another Zero flying over the trees and got hits on his first pass and finally ran out of ammunition after four more ineffective passes.

**1Lt. Robert Gibb** shot down two Vals to become an ace. (AFAA)

**1Lt. Edward Popek** scored his second victory. (AFAA)

**1Lt. Robert Knapp** shot down two Vals for his first victories toward becoming a five victory ace. (AFAA)

**Maj. David Campbell** of the 35FG was selected as the new 49FG CO. (AAF)

**Late December 1943: 49FG Inactivity and a New Group CO**

As 1943 ended, Lt.Col. James Selman and Col. Paul Wurtsmith chose a successor for the 49ers command. Popular veteran leader, Maj. David Campbell, of the 35FG was selected and by Christmas, he was visiting the pilots and crews of the Squadrons in his command as well flying missions attached to Warhawk and Thunderbolt squadrons. During the last two weeks of the year 49FG P-40s and P-47s rotated in the routine patrols over Ramu Valley, flew escort for bomber raids from Finschhafen to Wewak, and also flew search and destroy bombing sorties but met no enemy air opposition. The only notable event was Robert DeHaven's sinking of a freighter with a 500 pound bomb in Astrolabe Bay.

The number of ground support sorties increased as Vasey's 7th Australian Division closed in on Bogadjim. 49ers Intelligence units selected targets from daily recon photos and harassed enemy bivouacs and supply depots and coastal shipping lanes and docks from Bogadjim to Hansa Bay. Both the Demons and Black Sheep carried modified detonator-armed drop tanks filled with Napalm. Maj. Johnson's Flying Knight P-47s armed with eight .50 caliber machine guns became a fearsome strafing unit.

# 3

# January 1944

**2 January-10 February 1944: *Operation Michaelmas***

Background

Fighting in the South West Pacific Area in late 1943 and early 1944 was dominated by MacArthur's *Operation Cartwheel*, a series of operations directed at isolating and neutralizing Rabaul, the main base of the Japanese forces in the SWPA. MacArthur's original *Elkton III* plan called for Australian troops to first capture Lae, then Finschhafen, and finally Madang with a combination of airborne and amphibious assaults. However, the distance from Finschhafen to Madang at 178 miles was considerable and a shore-to-shore operation would be limited in radius of action to the distance that landing craft could travel in one night. With this in mind, in August 1943, Gen. Sir Thomas Blarney, the Commander of Allied Land Forces, recommended that an intermediate objective be seized first. Saidor was chosen as it had accessible landing beaches, a harbor, and a pre-war airstrip. It was recognized that the capture of Saidor might make that of Madang unnecessary, as both could cover the Dampier and Vitiaz Straits, and both would provide air bases close to the Japanese base at Wewak.

The battle for Finschhafen had prevented the early occupation of Saidor and the Japanese regained the initiative and threatened to disrupt MacArthur's strategy but ultimately failed to dislodge the Australian 9th Division or prevent the occupation of the Finschhafen area. Once Finschhafen was captured, the 9th Division initiated a pursuit of Lt.Gen. Hatazo Adachi's retreating Japanese 18th Army on 5 December 1943. Adachi was then placed into a difficult and insecure position, attempting to conduct a fighting withdrawal with his inland right flank vulnerable to attack from the Australian 7th Division in the Ramu Valley and his seaborne left flank open to amphibious assault. MacArthur lost the opportunity to destroy Adachi's army when he decided on 10 December that Saidor should be captured on or about 7 January; provided that *Operation Backhander* was proceeding satisfactorily (*Backhander* was the landing at Cape Gloucester, New Britain by the 1st Marines). On 17 December, Lt.Gen. Walter Krueger, the Commander of the Alamo Force, received orders setting a target date for Saidor of 2 January 1944. For the time being though, both were considered objectives. GHQ allocated the operation the codename *Michaelmas*.

The operations at Cape Gloucester and Arawe were only two phases of *Operation Dexterity*; the third and most important phase, code named *Operation Michaelmas*, was the amphibious landings at Saidor, Papua New Guinea, 2 January 1944. Saidor was located on Vitiaz Strait, midway between Blucher Point and Madang. Once captured by the Allies; Saidor would become a stepping stone towards Madang, which was the ultimate objective of MacArthur's Huon Peninsula Campaign. The capture of the airstrip at Saidor also allowed construction of an air base to assist Allied air forces to conduct operations against Japanese bases at Wewak and Hollandia. MacArthur's immediate objective was to cut off the 6,000 Japanese troops retreating from Sio as the Australians advanced from Finschhafen. Once the Allies landed at Saidor, the Japanese chose to retreat rather than fight and withdrew over the foothills of the rugged Finistere Range. For the enemy troops, the retreat was horrendous, as they struggled through the dense jungles, across the raging rivers, and over rugged mountains in the face of inclement weather. Nonetheless, the determined and resourceful Japanese were able to escape U.S. troops in large numbers. Despite extremely rainy weather and through great effort, the Allied air base was completed and put into use. While the base at Nadzab was surrounded by mountains; it was unsuited for nighttime missions but the Saidor base was suitable for nocturnal use. During March 1944, B-24 bombers staged through Saidor for night attacks on Hollandia.

Preparation

Krueger selected the 32nd Infantry Division for the Saidor operation as it was billeted at Goodenough Island and was no longer required for the New Britain Campaign. The Assistant Division Commander, Brig.Gen. Clarence Martin was appointed Commander of the *Michaelmas* Task Force, which was centered around the 126th Infantry Regimental Combat Team that had been re-established after the Battle of Buna-Gona and had received six weeks amphibious training in Australia and a further three weeks training at Milne Bay. Units assigned to the Task Force were at Goodenough Island, Milne Bay, Oro Bay, Lae, Finschhafen, Port Moresby, Kiriwina, Arawe, Cape Cretin, and Australia.

The objective of the *Michaelmas* Task Force was to:

1) Seize the Saidor area;
2) Establish facilities for a fighter group;
3) Assist in the establishment of air forces in the area;
4) Assist in the establishment of light naval forces in the area;
5) Construct minimal port and base facilities and
6) Secure the Allied hold on the Huon Peninsula by destroying enemy forces along the New Guinea coast in conjunction with the Australians advancing from Finschhafen.

Remarkably, it did not contain any explicit instructions on how to fight the Japanese! The rainy season occurred from the December to March period which would make both ground and air operations unpredictable. However, the advantages of the operation clearly outweighed the risks as the Japanese defenses were weak and the tactical surprise of another amphibious landing so soon after the New Britain landings at Arawe and Cape Gloucester would stun the Japanese. After the landings the land forces were to advance along the coast supported by the Allied Air Forces; destroying enemy forces isolated by the Saidor landings with the objective to drive toward the Bogadjim area. The Allied air Forces were to establish an airdrome in the Saidor area large enough for one fighter group and were to prevent any seaborne reinforcement and supply of the Madang-Alexishafen area.

Lt.Gen. Frank Berryman's Australian II Corps would cooperate by conducting operations along the coast, while the Australian 7th Division would contain Japanese forces in the Bogadjim area by fighting patrols. There was insufficient time and opportunity for ground reconnaissance, so three beaches, codenamed Red, White, and Blue, on the west shore of Dekays Bay were chosen from aerial photographs but these beaches were shown to be "narrow, rocky and exposed to heavy seas," Allied intelligence at Brisbane GHQ estimated that there were no more than 4,500 Japanese forward of Sio and only 1,500 more between Sio and the Madang area. They anticipated that if the Japanese decided to counterattack at Saidor, they would require a week to move 3,000 men. Consequently, Gen. Martin chose to eliminate the usual preliminary aerial bombardment which would then allow a sunrise landing. The assault troops and their supplies and equipment had to be loaded on board the invasion ships on 31 December 1943, only five days after the assault on Cape Gloucester. R.Adm. Daniel Barbey's VII Amphibious Force encountered a last minute problem on 30 December when it was revealed that there were not enough landing ships available requiring revised embarkation and landing time tables, and the transferring of personnel not required in the assault waves. The difficulty of simultaneously supplying operations at Saidor, Arawe, Long Island, and Cape Gloucester was so daunting that Gen. Krueger requested a postponement of the Saidor operation. But V.Adm. Thomas Kinkaid, the Commander of the Allied Naval Forces and the USN Seventh Fleet, assured MacArthur that enough supplies would be delivered, and MacArthur then rejected Krueger's appeal by stating "I am most anxious that if humanly possible this operation take place as scheduled… Its capture will have a vital strategic effect which will be lost if materially postponed."

**Lt.Gen. Walter Krueger**. (U.S. Army)

**V.Adm. Thomas Kinkaid**. (U.S. Navy)

Air Plan

The air plan for the operation stipulated the thorough bombardment of the Saidor area with strong fighter protection and additional bomber and fighter squadrons on alert in case of emergency. On D minus 1 nine heavy bomber squadrons, eight medium bomber squadrons, covered by the 475th Fighter Group were to attack the Saidor area. P-47s from the 348th Fighter Group and one squadron of P-40s were to patrol the Cape Gloucester area and an additional Fighter and Bomb Group were to be on ground alert. The heavy air and naval bombardment was not needed as the Japanese force at Saidor was small (only 11 enemy soldiers were killed during the landings). It was expected that the landings would provoke the Japanese Army Air Force to send 60 to 100 aircraft into the strong Allied fighter cover and AA defenses that were to be notified by an effective air warning unit. However, no enemy aircraft appeared during the first eight hours of D-Day when nine Helens escorted by 20 Zekes attacked the beachhead. As 12 P-40s approached, the Japanese bombers quickly jettisoned their bombs and the fighters and made a hasty retreat. The P-40s pursued and shot downed three Zekes and two Helens, losing one of their own. There were three more raids during the night and then 49 more during the next month.

Landings

The ships and landing craft arrived in Dekays Bay before dawn on 2 January 1944 to find the shore obscured by low hanging cloud and drizzling rain. Admiral Barbey postponed H-Hour from 0650 to 0705 to provide more light for the naval bombardment, and then to 0725 to allow the landing craft more time to from up. Destroyers fired 1,725 5 inch rounds, while rocket equipped LCIs fired 624 4.5 inch rockets. There was no simultaneous aerial bombardment but 5AF B-24s, B-25s, and A-20 bombed Saidor airstrip later that morning. The landing was a success as there was minimal opposition and the American suffered only one killed and five wounded. The Japanese could never mount an effective counterattack on Saidor and during the first week of the invasion they attempted small but ineffective night attacks. Japanese Lt.Gen. Hidemitsu Nakano ordered a holding action while the 51st Division made a difficult bypass of the Allied Saidor perimeter and withdrew across the rugged Finistere Mountains. Krueger's *Michaelmas* Task Force tried to block the enemy escape routes but the torrential rains, the rough countryside with its impenetrable rain forests and jungles and impassable rivers, along with the dogged enemy allowed about 8,000 semi-starved, ill-equipped, and disheartened Japanese to bypass Saidor. These troops would later fight the 32nd Infantry Division during the Battle of Driniumor River.

The defensive nature of Japanese plans for the SWPA centered on the air defense of Rabaul; so much so that they decided to abandon their remaining troops on the Huon Peninsula and New Britain. The Japanese would try to maintain their fighter force to provide "reasonable protection" for Rabaul and Wewak and would hold back their bomber forces until the Allies "seriously threatened" Rabaul and Wewak.

The victory at Saidor marked the end of the Huon Peninsula Campaign as it eliminated Japanese forces in that area and in conjunction with the Australian success in the Ramu Valley put pressure on the Japanese at Alexishafen and Madang and thus opened the New Guinea coast to further advances. *Operation Dexterity* officially ended on 10 February 1944 and was extremely successful as it drove enemy forces from western New Britain and established bases there that threatened Rabaul. South Pacific Forces were making slow but steady progress on Bougainville and air and sea forces there were hammering Rabaul's airdromes and supply depots. The forces in the Central Pacific had made successful landing in the Marshall and Gilbert Islands which encroached on the Japanese defensive perimeter.

After the capture of Saidor the Allies found the master code books for the Imperial Army communications network which the Japanese Army Staff at Saidor buried rather than destroyed. The Allies had deciphered the Imperial Navy and Merchant Marine codes since early in the war and with the Army codes the Allies now were well aware of the Japanese intentions in the Pacific throughout the last 16 months of the war. Using these codes, Intelligence deduced that the capture of the enemy held Admiralty Islands on the north flank of the Solomon Sea would deny their base at Wewak another source of reinforcements and the schedule for the invasion of the Philippines could be advanced by months. With the promise of the early invasion of the Philippines MacArthur enthusiastically approved of the Admiralties invasion while Kenney increased his attacks over the New Guinea coast from Finschhafen to Wewak with the Wewak Airfield Complex being a particular objective

**Saidor Landings**. (U.S. Army)

**2 January 1944: 49FG/7FS Air Operations**

On the day after New Year's, MacArthur again cut the northern escape route to Wewak for the ravaged Imperial 18th Army. Under a 5AF aerial armada, 7,000 troops of the 32nd Division made an amphibious landing a 100 miles north of Finschhafen at the coastal mining village of Saidor and the 200 man enemy garrison fled into the forest.

The Japanese Air Headquarters at Wewak learned of the surprise landing at Saidor from an early morning reconnaissance flight which found the Allied fleet of 18 destroyers and 30 transports located off the Huon coast. The Japanese attempted to send a morning fighter attack on the beach head but bad weather delayed that sortie. When the weather cleared, their only response was a rather paltry counterattack of 34 fighters and nine Helen bombers.

Meanwhile, 11 P-40s of the 7FS in three flights took off at 1445 on a fighter sweep on Alexishafen and Madang with Capt. Duncan Myers as Mission and White Flight Leader; 1Lt. Owen Schwartz was Blue Flight Leader; and 1Lt. George Allen was Green Flight Leader. Joining Myers in White was Maj. Selmon Wells, detached from the 312BG for the mission and Capt. William Lown attached from 49FG HQ with 1Lt. William Gaskill as his wingman.

At 1610 the Demons were over Astrolabe Bay at 15,000 feet Myers called out 13 enemy aircraft; four Oscars in close support of nine Helen bombers in three Vs approaching at 5,000 feet high. Myers did not see two flights of 11 Tonys in high cover at 15,000 feet. Initially, Myers thought the aircraft might be friendly but changed his mind when "three Jap radial engine fighters popped out in front of me." The Screamin' Demon Leader called the break, dropped his belly tank, and dove on the Sentai that broke and turned to fend off the Warhawks as their bomber crews continued on toward Saidor

Myers dove straight for the leading escort element of Oscars and fired and missed and continued through a circle to the left and hit the cockpit probably killing the pilot as the aircraft did not smoke of burn but plunged into the Bay. The enemy bombers headed for Pommern Bay and then turned toward Saidor and Myers attempted to head them off when he ran into a "very experienced" Hamp pilot that "every time I turned, he turned with me…and after several attempts, I gave it up as a bad job and dived out." Myers headed for Saidor where he got into a dogfight with the enemy fighter escorts that were "eager to play with me until I would pull my nose into them at which time they would scatter." Myers fired an almost full deflection side pass a Zeke, made some hits that did not slow it up. Myers tightened his turn on the Zero but spun out. Myers then climbed to get ahead of the bombers that were now leaving Saidor, He made a full head on pass at the center Helen of the V and got some hits but observed no damage. Myers came on two stragglers, one of which was being engaged by Wells. Myers followed one that was hugging the coastline and climbed ahead of the Helen three different times to make front quarter attacks but the Helen pilot turned into Myers each time; foiling his attacks. On his fourth attack Myers "took his time" and made a full tail attack and shot out its port engine and it crash landed in the water just off at Bau Plantation. Four enemy crewmen were seen to leave the sinking bomber which was Myers' fourth and last victory. Maj. Wells managed to

**1Lt. Duncan Myers** shot down a Zero and Helen for his last two of four career victories. (AAF)

stay with Myers despite having fuel transfer problems when he dropped his tank. Wells also had problems dispatching his straggling Helen. He shot out the left engine on the first pass but on the next passes the Helen pilot turned into his attacks and finally on his fifth pass the Helen finally went down over Bibi Village for his only victory of the war.

After Myers led his Flight down Green and Blue Flights stayed above. When enemy fighters climbed at them from Karkar Island the Flights dropped their belly tanks and dove on them. Green Flight Leader, 1Lt. George Allen, got on the tail of a Zero and followed it toward Madang at 14,000 feet. The Zero used steep climbing and diving turns as evasive actions but Allen was able to stay with him as the enemy pilot did not take any offensive action. He took six passes from the rear and above until only three of his guns were firing. As they approached Madang the Zero began to trail some smoke and the "inexperienced and very uneager" enemy pilot went down with his fighter for Allen's only victory. Allen's Element Leader, 1Lt. James O'Neill, led his wingman toward Tonys slightly above and when the Tony pilots responded by diving away, O'Neill followed. As he pulled out of his dive a Tony "whizzed" by and O'Neill went into a tight climbing turn after it. He closed to 100 yards and fired a long burst that hit the fuselage behind the canopy but the Tony continued to dive. O'Neill followed and fired another long burst that hit its right wing root near the canopy. O'Neill looked around and saw two Tonys stalking him and he continued his dive and these Tonys gave up the chase after five minutes and O'Neill had to settle for a damaged claim.

Blue Element Leader 1Lt. Robert DeHaven remained as top cover while Myers' White Flight attacked but when the Tonys approached he turned into them, head on, and fired a snap shot and then snap-rolled away. A Tony sped past him and he followed and fired and missed as another Tony attacked and he had to climb away. When he pulled out of his climb he saw a P-40 and a Tony in a circling dogfight and joined in. DeHaven fired and missed a two second deflection shot and withdrew and watched another P-40 try to interfere, again without result. DeHaven pulled into the "merry-go-round and banking him out fired a long four or five second burst." The right wing broke off about two feet from the fuselage and the pilot bailed out for his seventh victory.

With fuel and ammo exhausted, Myers called for his Flights to regroup but on the descent into Gusap airspace, Capt. Lown did not rejoin was listed as missing in action.

**1-9 January 1944: 475FG**

During this period the 475FG flew missions escorting B-24s and participated in some strafing against almost no enemy aerial opposition and moderate AA fire. On 1 January they flew to Saidor; on 4 January through flak that damaged several B-24s on an escort to Alexishafen; on 6 January another mission escorting B-24s to Alexishafen; and on 8 January a B-25 escort to Ulingan Harbor near Wewak.

During January there were rotations and command changes in the 475FG. The 432FS lost two experienced officers when Maj. Franklin Tomkins rotated home on 16 January and Capt. John Rundell followed him two days later. When Tomkins left, Capt. James Ince was assigned as the interim 432FS Commander until Capt. John Loisel was able come on board on 22 January. Five victory ace, outstanding pilot, and Operations Officer of the 431FS, 1Lt. Marion Kirby, also went home in January. His replacement was leading 475FG ace, Thomas McGuire who as Squadron Operations Officer could fulfill his aspirations of rising in rank and primarily of becoming America's top ace of the war.

**Early January 1944: 35FG**

Although most of the month would be devoted to transitional training flights in their new P-47s, the 35FG participated in the landing of the U.S. Sixth Army at Saidor on 2 January. After the initial landings the Group flew fighter sweeps over the Huon Peninsula as the infantry advanced toward Bogadjim and Madang.

**2 January 1944: 418NFS Arrives**

The 421st was not alone in experiencing a lack of adequate aircraft. When Maj. Carroll Smith arrived at Dobodura with the 418th Night fighter Squadron, he received five P-70s and two modified P-38Gs "night fighters" transferred from then Detachment "A" Night fighter Squadron. Four P-38Js were received from the 10th Service Squadron but these "Js" were taken away and replaced by war weary P-38Fs and Gs. By the end of January the unit's aircraft strength stood at ten P-70s and six P-38s, all of which were war-weary.

The 418th's mission was to consist of early morning P-38 missions, night alerts, and night patrols over Dobodura, Port Moresby, and Finschhafen on New Guinea and over Kiriwina Island. Four of the unit's P-38s were assigned to cover the convoy which landed the Allies at Saidor on 2 January 1944. The detachment of the 418th operated from the strip at Finschhafen and flew their patrols from 0600 to 0815 and proved uneventful for the 418th as the Allied landing was virtually faultless.

**3 January 1944: 348FG/Kearby Special Flight**

When Saidor was invaded and Wewak was neutralized, Col. Kearby knew that his P-47s would likely be relegated to ground attack missions to which the heavily armed Thunderbolt was well suited. At the turn of the year Kearby was pressing the gain the five victories which would make him the leading ace in the Pacific and continued to fly his usual fighter sweeps with the 348FG whenever he could get away from his desk. On 3 January, the day after Saidor was invaded; Kearby flew a morning and afternoon sweep with the 341FS from Gusap.

That morning while the rest of the 341st was escorting a bombing attack over Borgen Bay, Kearby selected three pilots to cover him while he hunted Japanese at Wewak. He led three P-47s from Gusap and arrived over Wewak just as a Sally was taking off to the west from Wewak and Kearby and his Wingman left the second element at 25,000 feet for cover. As there were six or so enemy fighters visible in the area. Despite the risk Kearby came in on the tail of the airborne enemy bomber and exploded both engines with a short burst.

On the second mission his flight left Gusap at 1330 but two fighters had to turn back and only Kearby and his Wingman arrived over Wewak at 1430 at 27,000 feet. Fifteen minutes later they spotted a lone Zero flying at 4,000 feet from But Airfield to Wewak. Kearby opened fire at 1,000 feet from dead astern at 350 mph. His first volley hit the Zero and his second set it on fire. Kearby turned to watch the Zero go down but saw the fire go out and continue on. Kearby made a 360 and fired a long six second burst from astern and the Zero caught on fire again but as Kearby flew by the fire

**Col. Neel Kearby** (shown with movie actor John Wayne) scored two victories to give him 19. (AAF)

went out again. As Kearby turned again the two opponents were at 1,000 feet and before he could get into firing position the Zero crashed into the sea for his 19th victory.

**3 January 1944: 8FG/36FS**

The 36FS was flying ground support missions on Japanese positions north of Lae at 1815. The mission was uneventful but 1Lt. George Ghramm's P-39 was probably hit by ground fire and went into a spin but recovered but then immediately stalled and descended into the 4,000 foot overcast. An Australian patrol found the still smoldering wreckage buried deep in the ground with its dead pilot still in the cockpit.

**4 January 1944: 421NFS Arrives and Languishes**

On 4 January 1944 the Fifth Air Force's night fighter strength was increased with the arrival of the 421st Night fighter Squadron at Milne Bay, New Guinea. The 438 enlisted men and 40 officers had completed their training and were ready for combat except they had no aircraft and it was almost three weeks later before they received their first aircraft, a single P-38.

In late January an advanced party of the 421NSF was sent to Nadzab, where their initial operations as a fighting unit were to begin. The rest of the Squadron, and their one plane, followed on 1 February 1944 but with only one fighter it was almost impossible to fly combat. The camp site was established and perimeter defenses were established to fend off any attacks by Japanese forces. Many ground classes were held to keep up their proficiency.

It was not until mid-February that the 421st received two additional aircraft, another P-38 and a tired P-70. The first mission flown by the 421st was a dawn weather reconnaissance flight on the morning of 25 February 1944. This was just the first of numerous weather reconnaissance sorties, many of which were in cooperation with Navy PT patrols.

It would not be until mid-April before the 421st had an inventory of four P-38s and four P-70s. A report issued by 421HQ in mid-July 1944 stated the unit's frustration: "The major difficulty in using the squadron effectively has been a lack of understanding on the part of higher headquarters as to the purpose and means of operation of night fighters, and assignments of airplanes to the squadron."

**6-12 January 1944: 49FG**

Kenney increased 49er escorts and sweeps which promised that they would continue their scoring tempo against Japanese aircraft. On 6 January, the 49ers flew their first mission to the Wewak airstrip with 475FG P-38s. The 8FS Black Sheep who were to attack the docks at Dallman Harbor while the 7FS Demon P-40s and 475FG flew mission CAP over the foothills from Borum to Wewak, protecting the Black Sheep as they swept in over the Harbor from seaward. The Black Sheep flew through sporadic and inaccurate AA fire as they sunk a small tanker and set fire to two barges. The mission met no enemy air resistance.

The 8FS tried to return to Wewak on the 8th but a weather front caused them to attack the secondary target, Alexishafen's Uligan Harbor, with only minimal damage done to the docks and jetty.

During the first week of January, the 9FS had intended to enter combat using their new P-47s but they were side tracked by an outbreak of Dengue Fever. The medical unit cleaned the water supply facilities and by 10 January, the Flying Knights were back on flying rotation. That day, 16 P-47s joined the escort to Alexishafen in the marginal weather with no enemy contacts. On 12 January, 15 P-47s strafed shipping at Karkar Island north of Alexishafen but the Japanese did not appear.

**8 January 1944: 35FG**

On 8 January Capt. Harris Denton was leading 16 new P-47s on a fighter sweep of Wewak and arrived at 1125 to circle the area at 24,000 feet. Enemy fighters were sighted and Col. Edwin Doss and 1Lt. Richard Tansing could not drop their tanks and dove away. However, an enemy fighter got behind Doss and 1Lt. Harvey Clymer turned in time to get a full deflection shot on the Zero which went into a diving turn, started smoking, and burst into flames but Clymer's claim was to be downgraded to a probable and the Squadron would not make any aerial claims until 6 November during the Philippines Campaign.

**9 January 1944: 348FG/5FC/Kearby Special Flight**

Kearby formed another special flight in hope of increasing his victory total and talked skilled veteran Capt. Walter Benz into leading his second element in case the situation became dicey. The four P-47s took off from Finschhafen at 1010 and were over Wewak about an hour and a half later among rain squalls and clouds up rising to 20,000 feet. After patrolling for about a half hour, 18 Tonys arrived from the south at 18,000 feet at 3 o'clock. Kearby and his Wingman, 1Lt. Charles Cronk, turned into the attack. Kearby opened fire at the leader when they were about 300 yards apart and the Tony was hit in its fuselage and began smoking when it flashed by Kearby. Meanwhile, Benz and his Wingman engaged the formation of Tonys that Kearby and Cronk had passed through only a moment before. Soon Kearby saw two Tonys diving after a P-47 at about the 10 o'clock position and Kearby and Cronk flew in to the rescue and caused the Tonys to break away. The three Thunderbolts then pursued the Tonys with Kearby in the lead, following one of the Japanese into a twisting climb and getting in one good, long burst. The other Tony was now coming in at Kearby from his port side causing him to shift his attention into his new attackers. The Japanese pilot, probably only wanting to rescue his companion, made a sudden port turn away from a head on confrontation with Kearby who quickly closed into range at about 800 feet and hit the Tony's belly with a precise 90 degree deflection shot. Kearby found that he was alone and at 6,000 feet with a crowd of Tonys waiting at 5,000 feet above him. Kearby realized his difficult situation and dove to the protection of the low clouds on the deck and headed for Gusap.

So on 9 January 1944 with these two Tonys victories Kearby was now tied with Dick Bong as top-scoring ace of the SWPA with 21 victories. Bong and Lynch were still back in America but would be back in action within the next few weeks to take part in the race to break Eddie Rickenbacker's WW-1 American record of 26 victories. If Kearby could keep up his recent pace it was possible he could break the record within days or weeks at the most. But Kearby was flying combat much more than Kenney had wanted and on 13 January Kearby was replaced as 5FC Commander by Gen. Paul Wurtsmith and was reassigned to HQ, 308th Bomb Wing where Kenney wished to use Kearby's substantial administrative ability to coordinate operations between the 5FC and 5BC.

**Col. Neel Kearby** became a quadruple ace with 21 victories to tie him with Richard Bong for top SWPA ace. (AAF)

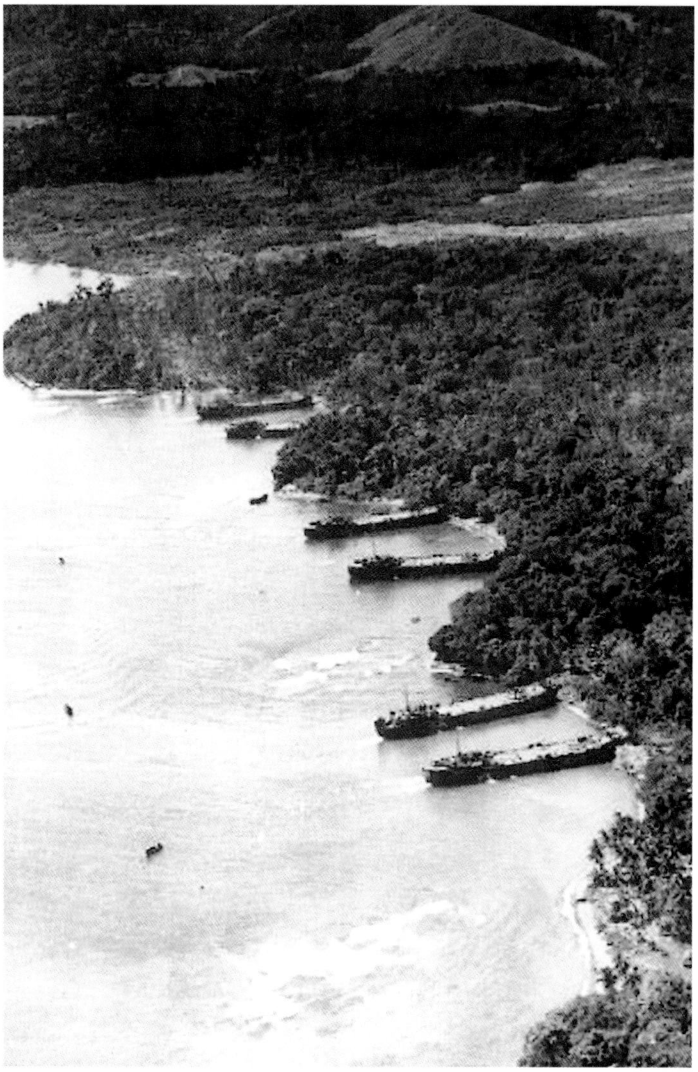

**Saidor Landings.** (U.S. Army)

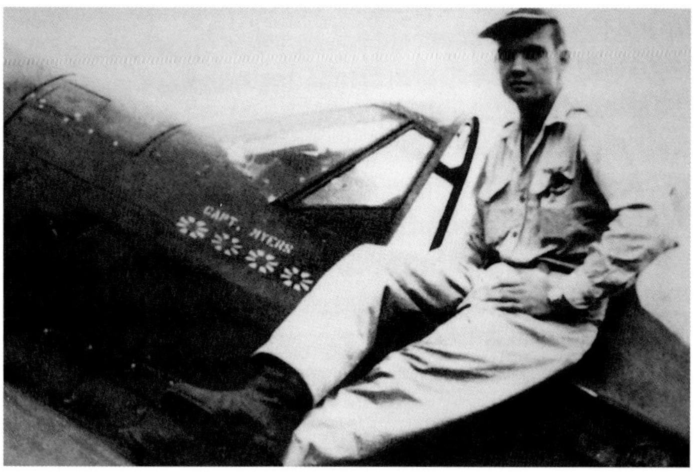

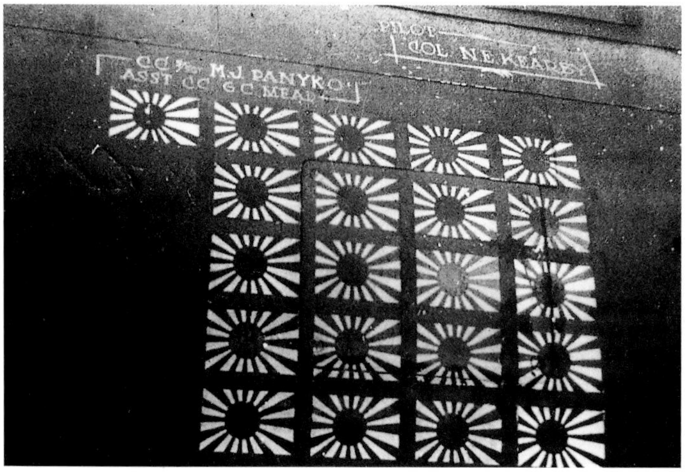

**10 January 1944: 475FG/432FS MacDonald Special Flight**

After Lt.Col. Charles MacDonald had been assigned to the 475FG HQ he chose to lead from the 432FS in combat. On this combat he led a six plane sweep to the Wewak area with two P-38s each from the 433FS (the second flight): Capt. Oliver McAfee and Wingman, 1Lt. Robert Tomberg, and the 431FS (the third flight): Capt. Verl Jett and 1Lt. William O'Brien comprising the rest of the formation. MacDonald chose 1Lt. William Ritter as his Wingman who had previously flown as MacDonald's Wingman on 21 December when he shot down two Vals over Arawe. At 1115 the six P-38s arrived over Wewak at 15,000 feet flying through light rain and overcast. After circling the Boram Strip for 10 minutes they flew to Wewak where they saw about 30 Japanese fighters on the Strip. MacDonald took his outnumbered flight out to sea and circled back toward Boram where they spotted scattered Zeros below and a formation of eight Tonys at his own altitude (15,000 feet) and climbing. The Tony formation seemed to be oblivious of MacDonald's P-38s as he was able to sneak in behind the last Japanese fighter in the formation and open fire with a three second burst within 500 feet from dead astern and flew on before it slowly rolled over and went down. Ritter confirmed the victory which gave MacDonald nine victories. MacDonald flew on behind the enemy leader who also was oblivious to the American's approach and took hits and but quickly rolled over and MacDonald was unable to follow it for a damaged claim. After the first attack the Tonys scattered for individual attacks but MacDonald's veteran flight remained together. Despite being greatly outnumbered, the P-38 pilots found that "in each case it was only necessary to turn into them to make them Split-S away." As MacDonald's formation approached the Sepik River about 15 Oscars dove out of the overcast onto the P-38's tails. MacDonald turned his flight into the enemy fighters, keeping his P-38s in string. MacDonald got in a few quick bursts at a pair of Oscars without observable results but found it impossible to remain in string. The P-38s finally broke away and headed for Gusap to refuel before returning to Dobodura.

**Lt.Col. Charles MacDonald** shot down a Tony and damaged another for his ninth victory. (AAF)

**13 January 1944:475/432FS**

1Lt. John Fogarty was flying a P-38 on a test flight in the late afternoon and could not pull out of a dive and crashed on the field.

**13 January 1944: 418NFS**

The 418NFS first air victory was claimed by their CO, Maj. Carroll Smith, while flying a dusk fighter sweep. Smith and Lt. Harold Wittern were flying P-38s in the Madang and Alexishafen area when Smith spotted a Val dive bomber approaching the Japanese air strip at Alexishafen. Smith closed in the waning light and fired three bursts, the third from point blank at around 400 feet altitude, sending the enemy into the water.

**Maj. Carroll Smith** shot down a Val for the 418NFS' first victory. (AFAA)

**14 January 1944: 418NFS**

Two 418NFS Squadron P-38s were sent out on a strafing mission to Alexishafen. While heading out they saw a 100 foot Japanese ship with two masts near Palos Point. The pilots scored direct hits, sinking the ship. On their way to the Japanese strips at Alexishafen they strafed an enemy encampment and a camouflaged native canoe. Upon their arrival at Alexishafen, they found a number of aircraft on Strip #2 and dove into a low level strafing attack scoring one Sally confirmed and eight or nine probables.

**15 January 1944: Enemy Attack on Gusap**

During the morning the Japanese attacked Ramu Valley with a fighter force from Wewak. The Tonys arrived low over Gusap #5 without an air raid warning and swept the flight line and strafed the dispersal area. A 3AG A-20 on the flight line was heavily damaged by a bomb blast, two 9FS Thunderbolts were set on fire and four 9FS enlisted men in a Jeep were bracketed by machine gun fire but were unhurt.

The 388BS sent up four White Flight P-40s at 0900 and two more in Red Flight at 0920 to patrol the Gusap-Dampu area but the two flights never joined each other. Red Flight climbed to 15,000 feet and about 25 miles out from Gusap were attacked from the rear by an unknown number of enemy fighters. Second Element Leader, Maj. William Kemble, was hit and dove away into a high speed spin and was fortunate to pull out. Kemble crash landed at Gusap with bullet holes in both wings, fuselage, tail, canopy, and cockpit. His vertical stabilizer, rudder, and radio were shot out. However, Kemble suffered only a minor arm injury. Kemble's Wingman, 2Lt. John Reisbig, was shot up from the rear and crash landed on Gusap without oxygen, oil pressure, electrical system, or hydraulics, but was wounded in his right leg by fragments. 2Lt. Billy Hollingshead, Flight Leader Wingman, was attacked from behind by two Hamps and warned his flight and tried to pull ahead to cover his Leader. The Hamps barrel rolled and came up on his rear and fired putting holes in the P-40's cockpit, wings, fuselage, and flaps. Hollingshead landed safely despite fragments in his left leg.

**15 January 1944: 35FG**

The 35FG began the New Year abandoning the last of their P-39s on 14 January when the 40th and 41st Squadrons joined the 39FS in transitioning to the P-47 Thunderbolt. The Group continued these transitional training flights and had seen no combat since the three Oscar victories on 26 November. In the early morning of the 15th, a fog veiled the arrival of eight Tonys which strafed Nadzab. Fortunately, there were no casualties except for damage to four of the Group's Thunderbolts. Soon afterward the 35th was informed that it was to move to Gusap. Nadzab had become too crowded with bomber groups and the 35th and several other fighter groups were transferred to other bases. On 25 January the ground echelon left to establish a bivouac at Gusap.

### Mid-January 1944: Air Situation

It was not until 16 January that the JAAF mounted a serious attack when a mixed formation of 35 to 40 Vals, Hamps, Tonys, and Oscars in three or four plane elements attacked an Allied convoy near Saidor. During this period bomber attacks on important Japanese bases were escorted by several squadrons of either P-39s or P-47s. However, enemy fighter interception was negligible, being even less than the previous month. During January 38 Japanese bombers and fighters were shot down, 10 in the Northwestern area. For the loss of three B-24s, two P-40s, and one P-38 with AA fire accounting for eight B-25s and U.S. Navy AA fire brought down one P-40. Five P-38s, two P-40s, one B-25, and one P-39 were lost to "unspecified causes." From 1-13 January there were 13 aerial combats in the SWPA which compared to 27 the previous 13 days. Japanese air reaction to Allied amphibious invasions also declined with only 20 attacks (14 at night). During the first 13 days of the Aware action there were 205 enemy air attacks; 160 during the Cape Gloucester invasion; and 83 during the first 13 days of the Saidor invasion.

**1Lt. Robert Colgrove** (right) shot down two Zeros to give him three total victories. (AAF)

### 16 January 1944: 8FG/35FS

During this time Allied commanders had expected the heaviest Japanese air resistance over New Britain instead of Saidor. On the morning of the 16th P-38s escorted B-25s to Arawe, New Britain, expecting strong opposition from Japanese interceptors. Meanwhile the 5FC sent 15 Warhawks of the 35FS over the Saidor to cover the convoys (*Sauce Pan*) at 11,000 feet moving in the landing area and would have their best day of the war with 19 victories. The Japanese would send its total operational strength of 60 aircraft to attack the Saidor landing area. The Squadron took off at 0830 and was to relieve another squadron and then patrol over the convoy for about two hours when 1Lt. Leo Everhart saw 30 Bogeys at 3 o'clock descending from Saidor at about 2,000 feet above the Americans. There were four flights with Red Flight taking the low position at 8,000 feet and White and Yellow were high at 12,000 feet while Blue Flight trailed the other three flights. The Flights were composed of:

1Lt. George Goolsby led the Squadron as head of Red Flight with 1Lt. Glendi Holder as his Wingman and 1Lt. William Gardner as Red #3 and rookie 2Lt. Lieutenant Kenneth Pool as his Wingman.

1Lt. Lynn Witt was leading White Flight when his Wingman reported that he had an oil leak and was turning back and 2Lt. Richard Neer, White #3, moved up as Witt's Wingman and 2Lt. Delmar King was the tail end man.

1Lt. Norman Reid led Yellow Flight with 2Lt. William Dwyer as his Wingman and 1Lt. Robert Colgrove as Yellow #3 with Wingman, 2Lt. Albert Winton.

1Lt. Roy Klandrud was Blue Leader with Wingman, 2Lt. Vernon Robbins, and 1Lt. Lee Everhart as Blue #3 Element Leader with Wingman, 2Lt. John Henry.

**1Lt. William Gardner** (right) scored three victories on his way to becoming an ace. (AFAA)

Goolsby was leading Red Flight at 8,000 feet when Bandits were called at 3 o'clock high and he ordered tanks to be dropped and turned his flight toward them "to take a look" and decided to climb for more altitude. The flight was attacked by a flight of Japanese aircraft and Goolsby warned Second Element Leader Gardner who turned into the attack with his Wingman Pool. Goolsby's Wingman Holder saw a Tony making a tight turn on Goolsby's tail and turned onto the attacker who went into a dive when he saw Holder. Holder fired a long burst from 60 degrees and set its starboard wing on fire. As he closed to finish off the Tony, its pilot bailed out. Goolsby and Holder dove away and then climbed for more altitude again and attacked two Hamps. Goolsby was to attack one while Holder was to take on the other. As Goolsby closed and was firing on his target, Holder's target made sharp turn away, so Holder would have to fire over Goolsby's wing at his target. But Holder did not fire so as not to hit his leader and Goolsby finished off the Hamp which cartwheeled into the water for his fourth and last victory. Goolsby then followed Holder in a climb after the second Hamp which Holder shot down from 30 degrees above with a long burst that the Hamp passed through. Before returning to base the two dove on two Hamps flying low over the water but two other diving P-40s beat them to the target and shot them down. Meanwhile, Gardner and Pool had turned into the Hamps diving out of the overcast. Gardner hit the #3 Hamp and shot off four feet of each wing tip causing it to go into a flat spin. Gardner then pulled up over the stricken enemy fighter and took another shot from above and the Hamp spun into the sea. As Gardner continued up Pool saw a Hamp get on Gardner's tail and fired into its cockpit, killing the pilot, after which it exploded. While pulling out Pool was inverted when he saw a Hamp below and dove. He fired a short accurate burst and this Hamp also exploded for the first two of five victories. Gardner climbed to join a P-40 Lufbery but was cut off by four Hamps. Gardner turned into them but they maintained a perfect formation as they went into a turn. Gardner immediately turned past the #3 enemy fighter and fired on #4 which began to smoke after a short burst and inverted straight into the sea. Gardner

**1Lt. Lynn Witt** shot down a Val and two Oscars to give him four victories. (AAF)

**1Lt. Glendi Holder** shot down a Tony and Zero to give him three total victories. (AAF)

**2Lt. William Dwyer** got his only victory of the war. (AAF)

**1Lt. Lee Everhart** shot down two Zeros to make him an ace. (AAF)

followed it down and used his diving speed to regain altitude as quickly possible to get back into the fight. Gardner met three Hamps at 7,000 feet and took several passes on them before two turned north. Gardner closed from the rear quarter and fired a 50 degree deflection shot at the leader and then let his lead fall on his Wingman getting hits on engine and cockpit for his third victory of the day. Gardner dove away and met a group of Oscars circling in a Lufbery near the deck. Gardner and another P-40 made a pass but both ran out of ammunition and left for home. Pool saw a P-40 being attacked by an Oscar but before he could help the Oscar had hit the P-40's right wing and then broke away. Pool escorted the damaged Warhawk out of danger and then returned to the fight but too late and returned to base. Red Flight had scored eight of the Squadron's victories.

Witt's White Flight was at northeast of Saidor at 12,000 feet and had been patrolling for an hour and a half when they spotted aircraft approaching and climbed to 13,000 feet where they identified them as Japanese. White Flight dropped their tanks and continued to climb to 14,500 feet when the leading enemy flight dove on them. Witt turned sharply into them and caught the #2 Oscar as it turned and sent it down rolling away in flames. As Witt attacked his Oscar, Wingman Neer was setting up to fire on an Oscar when four Oscars attacked from behind. Neer went into a sharp starboard dive and two Oscars followed. As he rolled out of his turn Witt saw an Oscar on the Neer's tail and hit the American fighter. Witt dove after them and set fire to the Oscar's port quarter with a long burst and drove the others away. Neer had one third of his port aileron shot away and Witt escorted him to safety. Witt returned to the fight where he saw Colgrove shoot down his second Hamp for his third and last victory. Witt joined a circle of battling P-40s and Hamps and only got a few snap shots before he was attacked from the rear and dove away. At the end of his dive he met a Val and made a high starboard pass and started it smoking and then burst into flames and crash for his fifth victory to become an ace. Witt climbed to 6 or 7,000 feet and joined four Warhawks and then saw six Hamps in formation on the water and dove only to find he was out of ammunition. During White Flight's battle 2Lt. King made several firing passes, using all his ammunition without seeing any results before he returned home with Dwyer of Yellow Flight.

Yellow Flight Leader Reid saw the bogeys that Everhart called out but at first believed them to be friendly because they were flying "our type of formation." While White Flight ahead of them dropped their tanks and then climbed and turned into the bogeys; Yellow Flight, dropped their tanks and continued climbing to make a diving head on attack. Reid forgot to switch on his guns during his first pass and climbed again to get another chance. He saw two Hamps racing below which quickly passed through his sights so that he got only a short burst that hit the cockpit of a Hamp that flew for a about 300 yards before slowly rolling over inverted and then headed straight into the water. Reid closed astern on another Hamp but before he could open fire the Hamp made a turn that put in it in his Wingman Dwyer's sights. Dwyer's burst hit the Hamp's wing root and it caught fire and crashed for his only victory. During the remainder of the combat Reid took "at least a half dozen" snap shots, mostly deflection, while Dwyer "fired on eight ships;" both pilots fired without observable results. Simultaneously, while Reid and Dwyer made their head on pass, Colgrove and his Wingman Winton climbed above them to make their pass. Colgrove chose a Hamp in the middle so that Winton could shoot at one behind. As they began to close the enemy flight broke away and Colgrove fired a long burst making definite hits on the wings and canopy. The Hamp pilot turned left but his nose fell and his fighter spiraled into the sea. As Colgrove was following the Hamp another flew 350 yards in front of him for an easy shot into its wings and fuselage; tearing off pieces. Afterward the Squadron went into a Lufbery and then reformed into four ship flights, Colgrove saw 12 Hamps and Tonys milling around at 1,000 feet and started after a brightly painted Tony but broke away when two other P-40s came and one shot it down (Holder, Red Flight #2). He then dove on an the last plane in a two ship element and made an overhead deflection firing pass; getting some hits but did not see any results and had to break away and dove on two Oscars near the water. As Colgrove approached them from behind, the Oscars turned right and he fired a long leading burst at the second Hamp making a turn. As Colgrove was pulling his turn his engine began to cut out and backfire and the enemy leader began to turn on him but then turned away. After his engine smoothed out Colgrove joined some other P-40s and returned to base with two victories to give him three total. After the combat Colgrove stated in his ICR: "Our coordination was the best we have done in combat." Meanwhile, Winton followed Colgrove and could only watch as two Tonys raced in front of him as his guns did not fire. He saw tracers whizzing over his canopy and when he looked around he saw a Japanese fighter on his tail and had to break away as a cannon shell exploded in his starboard wing. With a hole in his wing and his guns jammed Winton was escorted from combat by Red Flight #4 Pool.

At 1040 Blue Fight Leader, Klandrud, heard his #3 Everhart call out a large group of bandits at 2 o'clock high coming out of the cloud layer at 14,000 feet and began to maneuver to attack. The bandits were carrying underwing bombs and dropped them when Klandrud ordered his flight to jettison its tanks and climb toward the enemy. Second Element Leader, Everhart, broke away to engage a Hamp that dove on his Wingman and Klandrud and Wingman Robbins climbed and Split-S'd on Hamps below them and both fired without observable results. They then made a head on pass at two Oscars in string which initially were thought to be P-40s. As they closed they identified them as bandits and Klandrud fired at the trailing Oscar getting some hits but lost it for no claim. As Klandrud looked around he saw Gardner shooting at a Hamp causing its pilot to bail out. He also saw three other enemy pilots in parachutes in the area and counted 11 oil slicks in the area. Klandrud and Robbins were at 8,000 feet when they saw two Oscars on deck being attacked by a lone P-40 whose bullets were falling well behind their target. Klandrud saw the Oscar turn and get on the P-40's tail and he dove and closed to very close range for a 20 degree deflection shot that caused the Oscar to began go into a shallow smoking dive. Robbins continued his lead and fired the *coup d'grace* just as it exploded above the water to claim the victory away from Klandrud. Klandrud's ICR stated: "The Nip pilots were very cunning; using sharp turns and aerobatics" but didn't mention Robbins steal. Second Element Leader, Everhart, who first saw the large group of enemy fighters approaching, broke away from the flight when a Hamp dove on Wingman Henry. Everhart pulled up into the attack and the Hamps broke away with Everhart and Henry in pursuit. Everhart fired a few short bursts with some hits but tightened his turn which allowed him to get his lead and as he slacked up in his turn he got hits in the cockpit. As he pulled his turn a little more he fired again and his bullets hit again but Everhart's Warhawk snapped and spun in the tight turn and he lost the Hamp but Robbins saw it crash. As Everhart climbed back into the combat he lost Henry. He then saw a P-40 chasing an enemy fighter but it also had two enemy fighters on its tail. Everhart pulled up to save the P-40 and made a head on pass on the enemy and fired into its engines. However, Everhart's P-40 snapped away again and he lost sight of the Hamp. He then joined Holder (Red Flight #2) who reported that he saw Everhart's Hamp go down smoking. Holder left for home and Everhart joined a large Lufbery of about 10 P-40s. He saw three enemy fighters in the distance heading for Saidor but decided they were too far away to pursue. He then saw a Warhawk on the deck with two enemy fighters on its tail and dove to drive them off. The enemy fighters turned to attack Everhart instead but the American's diving speed was too high for them to follow and he easily pulled away and then headed home with two victories to make him an ace.

These were the last aerial victories scored by the 35FS while flying P-40s. The Squadron had claimed about 50 kills between October 1943 and the end of January 1944 which was more than any other 5FC P-40 unit during the period. The P-40s of the 35FS moved to Cape Gloucester by the middle of February and its P-38s arrived and would not score again until 16 June.

**16 January 1944: 475FG/433FS**

Capt. Warren Lewis led 16 P-38s on a B-25 escort on a bombing and strafing run from Cape Gourdon to Cape Croisilles. At 1105 the Squadron was at 3,000 feet and was met by eight Tonys coming from the sea west of Alexishafen. The Squadron turned into the attack and Lewis chased two Tonys and fired a long burst at one and its oil and smoke covered his windshield but this Tony escaped into the clouds over the mountain tops. Lewis' Wingman, 2Lt. William Hasty took after the second Tony and fired a two second burst that damaged it. Soon 20 to 25 more Tonys approached from 9 o'clock high at 10,000 Feet and 1Lt. John Howard, fourth Flight Leader, circled at 6,000 feet to protect Lewis' Flight 3,000 feet below. As the Tonys came down Howard took his flight under Lewis' flight which turned into the Japanese who broke off. Lewis and Hasty pulled up into four of the Tonys. Lewis fired a 45 degree deflection shot at one that missed while Hasty pulled over Lewis and closed at 90 degrees and saw some hits on its fuselage before he broke away. Three Tonys turned up in front of Howard who fired at the lead Tony; getting a good hit on its radiator; the Tony seemed to lose momentary control but then dove away for a damaged claim. 1Lt. John Ehlinger also got a quick head on shot on another Tony for no claim. Lewis realized that the Squadron was at an altitude disadvantage and low on fuel, and decided to take them home. 2Lt. Richard Hancock was listed MIA but was not part of this combat.

**18 January 1944: 5FC**

On this day the 5FC sent out four squadrons on a major fighter sweep mission to Wewak: 340FGS/348FG (lead); 431FS and 432FS/475FG (second and third); and the 80FS/8FG (last).

**18 January 1944: 348FG/340FS**

By the end of 1943 the 348th had one of the best victory-to-loss ratios in the theater. January was a period of general calm but the 348th would continue to score sporadically during the month. On the 18th the 340FS flew another "Kearby-style" four plane sweep over Wewak but while there were about 15 enemy fighters in the area only 1Lt. Myron Hnatio would score for the Squadron. The 340th took off from Finschhafen at 0705 and arrived over Wewak at 28,000 feet. After patrolling over the area until 1100 they spotted eight to ten Zeros were sighted below at 20,000 feet approaching Wewak from the south. The flight maneuvered into the sun and as soon as Hnatio started his dive on the lead Zero, the other three P-47s were sidetracked when they avoided a pass by a flight of P-38s. Not realizing he was alone Hnatio dove at high speed on the unsuspecting enemy fighters which did not evade. He quickly slipped into position on the tail of the Wingman of the flight leader and fired single savage burst that shot off the Zero's canopy and tore up the tail so that it detached itself from the fuselage. Hnatio came so close to his victim that his windshield became covered with its oil and he had to pull up to avoid colliding with another Zero. There were about

**1Lt. Myron Hnatio** scored his fourth victory, the only one for the 340FS during the day's combat. (AFAA)

15 other Japanese fighters now visible in the area and the three P-47s could see Hnatio's fighter struggle in the general direction of home but Hnatio was able to clear his canopy enough to see to get back to base.

**18 January 1944: 475FG/431FS/432FS/433FS**

Between 0835 and 0845 33 P-38s of the 475FG took off for a major fighter sweep to Wewak led by Lt.Col. Charles MacDonald, flying with 432nd Clover Squadron with 431st Hades Squadron following with Maj. Merle Smith at its head.

431FS

Maj. Merle Smith of 475FG/HQ led 18 P-38s from Dobodura at 0830. Smith headed the lead Red Flight; Capt. Verl Jett led the second Blue Flight; Capt. David Allen led the third White Flight; while1Lt. Vincent Elliott led the Green last Flight. During the trip to the target, six P-38s had to turn back, leaving that Squadron with 12 fighters to meet about 40 Tonys and Oscars at 1045. The 432nd was at 15,000 feet and slightly ahead of the 431st flying at 19,000 feet while the enemy fighters had a 2,000 to 3,000 foot altitude advantage over the 431st. The enemy pilots were Split-S'ing in front of the 431st which had dropped their tanks and was climbing to meet them head on. About 20 enemy fighters came down and the Squadron followed some of them down. There were enemy fighters remaining above which dove on the Smith's Flight. Jett fired a quick shot at a Zero and flamed it for his sixth victory. Jett was flying behind Smith's Wingman, 2Lt. John Weldon, who had a Zero on his tail. Jett was unable to catch the Zero as his supercharger was out but fired from long range and chased the Zero that turned away. However, Weldon's fighter was hit and he flew off. Jett was forced to shut down the bad engine and returned to base. Meanwhile, Capt. Allen and Wingman, 2Lt. John Tilley, went after the Zero that had hit Weldon's plane and followed it down to 500 feet. Allen fired first but Tilley fired a damaging shot and the Oscar pilot half rolled away toward Boram Strip. After the battle 2Lts. John Weldon and Joseph Robertson of the 431FS were listed as MIA. Robertson's P-38 was hit by a released belly tank from the 433FS and his fighter was seen to go down in a tight spin and he bailed out to an unknown outcome near Wewak. Weldon was last seen flying at 15,000 feet a few miles south of Boram by Jett and was never seen again.

432FS

Lt.Col. MacDonald led Clover Squadron and Green Flight at 15,000 feet below and to the right of Jett's formation at 19,000 feet when nearly 40 enemy fighters in the standard two ship formation dove on the rear of the Clover flights. MacDonald turned his 15 P-38s to the starboard to meet the enemy fighters and a gigantic dogfight developed. As he saw enemy fighters going down around him, MacDonald fired deflection shots on a Tony and at least two Oscars that all managed to get away. MacDonald then saw two P-38s, one of which had a damaged engine with heavy smoke pouring from it being chased by four Hamps at treetop level. MacDonald, followed by Wingman, 2Lt. John Hannan, led the five other P-38s remaining with him down to the rescue. MacDonald fired at two Hamps and started one smoking and heading down. MacDonald followed it down and fired hitting its engine but the Hamp flew on and MacDonald then turned to fire again. The Hamp was seen to roll over and crash by Dahl to make MacDonald a double ace with 10 victories. MacDonald went after two Zeros and fired without result and then circled Boram, Wewak, and Dagua for 15 minutes without seeing any enemy aircraft and returned to base. MacDonald's Second Element Leader, 1Lt. Billy Gresham, fired a snap 30 degree deflection shot at an Oscar that was chasing a P-38 and succeeded in making it give up its attack. Gresham then turned toward Wewak where he saw a Zero break away from four Lightnings 2,000 feet above. This Zero continued to dive toward Gresham who took a 60 degree, four second, deflection shot into its left side and canopy before it burst into flames. Gresham followed MacDonald in a gradual climbing port turn when two Zeros in trail made a pass on Hannan. At the time Gresham was turning left and the Zeros were attacking from the right rear quarter and Gresham was unable to fire. The Zeros did not see Gresham and one almost ran into him. Gresham managed to get in a short burst with his .50s hitting the fuselage and a few cannon shells hitting its rudders but Gresham did not see any apparent results and flew back to base with his sixth and last victory of the war. Gresham's Wingman, 1Lt. George Beatty, dutifully followed his leader and took a few ineffective shots before returning to base.

1Lt. Arthur Peregoy was leading Blue Flight with Wingman, 2Lt. Robert Hadley and Second Element Leader, 1Lt. Howard Hedrick, and his Wingman, 2Lt. Ferdinand Hanson. They followed MacDonald's flight down and saw two P-38s (Robertson and Weldon) from the 431FS go down; one in flames and one in a spin. Peregoy then saw a Zero on Dahl's tail which broke off when Peregoy made a long range pass starting from 1,000 down to the 700 yards. Blue Flight was then attacked by a large number of enemy fighters and Peregoy and Hadley attacked a Zero. Hadley's gunfire blew

**Lt.Col. Charles MacDonald** (right), with Col. Neel Kearby (center) and Gen. Frederick Smith, became a double ace with his 10th victory. (AAF)

**Capt. Verl Jett** scored his sixth of seven victories. (AFAA)

**1Lt. Billy Gresham** scored his sixth and last victory of the war. (AFAA)

off pieces that sent it into a spin and later Dahl confirmed Hadley's victory. They chased another Zero toward But Airdrome where it turned between the two pursuers and tried to ram them but missed when Hadley fired and knocked off pieces as it flew by for Hadley's third and last victory.

When Peregoy's Blue Flight was attacked by enemy fighters, the Element Leader Hedrick and Wingman, Hanson, joined up with Clover Green Flight and the remainder of MacDonald's Clover Red Flight and all went into a defensive Lufbery Circle. 1Lt. James Farris of White Flight had his intercooler damaged in the initial Japanese attack and moved to #3 in the Red Flight Lufbery for protection in the Circle and was joined by White Flight Leader, 2Lt. Henry Condon, and F/O Joe Barton. Enemy fighters would try to break into the Circle but would Split-S away when they failed. Hedrick drifted out of the Circle long enough to fire an ineffective head on shot from out of range at an Oscar. He then returned to the Circle behind 2Lt. Perry Dahl who was in the Circle with one belly tank still attached limiting his Lightning's performance. Two Oscars slipped into the Lufbery and got on Dahl's tail. Dahl weaved left and right while Hedrick closed and fired at the first Oscar which Split-S'd away but the second waited too long to Split-S and took hits in its right wing and fuselage. The Oscar smoked and then caught on fire but the Japanese pilot rolled his stricken fighter over and bailed out for Hedrick's fourth and last victory. (Note: Dahl's ICR describes the enemy fighters as Zekes while Hedrick's identifies them as Oscars.)

1Lt. William Ritter and his Wingman, 1Lt. John Michener, were at 18,000 feet when they first sighted 12 Tonys about 1,000 feet in front and above them. Both Ritter and Michener had problems dropping their belly tanks and were flying in very tight formation. For some reason one Tony pilot dropped out of formation and didn't see the two Lightnings until they fired at him at very close range. Michener swerved over Ritter to starboard and got the first shot before the Tony was directly in front of them. Michener pulled back over to port to avoid hitting Ritter and fired at the Tony who swerved to port. As he did, Ritter fired a short burst that set the Tony ablaze. When the Tony was hit it swung up to starboard and Ritter's left wingtip collided with the center of the Tony's right wing. Ritter's fighter immediately caught on fire and descended. Michener was then attacked by two Tonys as he was trying to see if Ritter was able to bail out. Michener outdistanced the Tonys and joined six Lightnings but had to return to base when his starboard engine quit and he had to feather it. Ritter was posthumously given credit for his third and last victory.

433FS

Capt. Warren Lewis took off at 0830 leading 17 Lightnings to fly top cover at 25,000 feet for the fighter sweep to Wewak. As they reached the target area at 1055 they saw about 30 fighters approaching at 10,000 to 20,000 feet and saw the 431st turn into them. Lewis ordered tanks to be dropped and dove to 17,000 feet where the Squadron made many passes on the enemy fighters whose pilots were "uneager" and dove away from contact. There were several enemy fighters hit for "no observable result" but only Lewis came out of the mission with claim which was only a probable. 2Lt. William Grady had an engine malfunction and had to be escorted home. 2Lt. John Knecht heard a loud explosion in his starboard engine and it immediately caught fire and he was unable to stay in formation. He dove 500 feet to try to put the fire out and feathered the engine but the fire continued to burn for about 20 minutes and damaged the right tire and Knecht made a successful wheels up landing at Dumpu.

475FG Losses

In addition to Ritter, the losses of Weldon and Robertson reflected a strong resurgence of Japanese air presence in the Wewak area as both the 63rd, 68th, and 78th Sentais were back in full operation to reinforce the area's defenses.

**18 January 1944: 8FG/80FS**

The 80FS flew a fighter sweep over Wewak and were over the target area at 1050 and at 1100 encountered a mixed group of Tonys, Zeros, and Oscars that were engaged by the 475FG's Clover and Hades Flights northwest of the Wewak Strip. When they arrived there was a large flash as an enemy fighter and a P-38 (475FG's 1Lt. William Ritter) collided with the enemy, exploding and the P-38 having its port wing and engine sheered off, causing the Lightning to spin into the water.

**1Lt. Cyril Homer** being decorated by Gen. Paul Wurtsmith, scored his sixth of 15 victories. (AAF)

**1Lt. Allen Hill** scored his sixth of nine victories. (AAF)

**1Lt. Cornelius Smith** shot down two Zeros for his eighth and ninth victories. (AAF)

After being credited with five probables **1Lt. Louis Schriber** was finally credited with his first victory. (AFAA)

**Maj. Gerald Johnson** (with Capt. James Watkins' fighter) scored his 11[th] and last victory until mid-October 1944. (AFAA)

1Lt. Cyril Homer was the Flight leader of the last flight (Yellow) and saw an Oscar to his left and turned into it. The Oscar pilot turned into and under Homer who fired a two second burst at 30 degrees from 300 to 200 yards hitting its engine and cockpit. The Oscar spiraled down into the water south of the Wewak Strip for Homer's sixth victory. Homer's flight then made a pass on the rear plane in a flight of five Oscars but they all half-rolled under the Lightnings for the tree tops toward Wewak Strip. The Americans broke off when they encountered heavy AA fire over Wewak Strip.

1Lt. Cornelius Smith was the Leader of the third (Red) flight and saw the 475[th] 432FS Clover Flight fighting about 20 enemy aircraft at 19,000 feet above the coast north of the Boram Strip. Smith made a 90 degree deflection pass at a Zero and hit its left wing and fuselage and it spun down in flames. Several minutes later Smith hit another Zero in the wing and fuselage with another 90 degree deflection shot. Pieces sheered off and hit the P-38 of Smith's Wingman but did no serious damage. The Zero plummeted several thousand feet before a parachute opened and the enemy pilot descended to earth for Smith's ninth victory. Unlike enemy pilots in previous combats who Split-S'd or rolled away, neither of these pilots made any evasive actions as if "they were inexperienced or else resigned to being shot down." 1Lt. Allen Hill was a member of Smith's flight and had a Tony make an overhead pass on him but overran putting it on the tail of Capt. William Hailey. But now Hill had a tail away shot and the Zero started smoking and it smoked until it crashed into a forest for Hill's sixth victory. 1Lt. Louis Schriber joined Smith and Hill after they had scored their victories and made a pass on two Tonys and shot one down with a 45 degree defection shot and the Tony trailed black smoke until it hit the ground north of the Wewak Strip as Schriber finally got his first victory after five discouraging probable awards.

1Lt. Leland Blair was the Leader of the White Flight and when they got into the target area they saw 475FG Clover Squadron dogfighting the enemy and went into a large Lufbery Circle and members of the Circle left to go after the scattered 20 to 30 Zeros in the area and then returned. While circling Blair saw two Tonys climbing toward the left side of his Flight and they went into a gentle climbing tight turn to intercept them. The second Tony broke down and to the right and the flight in front of Blair went after it. Blair continued after the lead Tony which climbed to 18,000 feet with no evasive tactics and Blair closed to 200 yards and fired a long 45 degree deflection shot into its cockpit and central fuselage for his first victory. 2Lts. Delbert Furgason and John Stanifer added a Zero probable each during the combat.

**18 January 1944: 49FG/7FS/8FS**

While the 7FS and 8FS flew an uneventful escort for B-24s, the 9FS flew high escort over the target for the 22BG. On the bomber withdrawal from Wewak, a brave lone Oscar made a pass through the 49er fighters and then broke away in a climbing port turn. When the Oscar pilot returned for another pass Flying Knight Mission Leader, Capt. Gerald Johnson was ready and turned into the Oscar and dove after it. There was no escape for the Japanese pilot trying to out dive the heavy Thunderbolt. Johnson claimed his 11[th] confirmed victory. During this time Johnson was assigned to 49FG HQ which cut down his combat flying time. Johnson flew a "food mission" in a P-40 to buy fresh fruit from the locals near Mt. Hagen. On his take off from Mt. Hagen his P-40's wing hit a tree and Johnson had to nurse his Warhawk that was minus three feet of wing and part of an aileron safely back to Gusap.

**22 January 1944: 475FG/431FS**

2Lt. Martin Hawthorne was testing a P-38 and listed as killed in an aircraft accident.

**17-22 January 1944: 49FG/7FS *Cutthroat Operation***

After the Saidor landings the Allied advance along the Huon Peninsula progressed rapidly but the Australians were thwarted in the Ramu Valley. To help break the stalemate a RAAF Boomerang led four 7FS P-40s armed with a 500 pound bomb to dive bomb Japanese positions. The Boomerang indicated the target on the top of a ridge by firing tracers and one P-40 scored a direct hit and the other three "close misses." The success of this mission led to a more involved mission later in the week on the so-called "Pimple" strongpoint on Shaggy Ridge. Two sections with two flights of 7FS P-40s were sent out and after a short artillery barrage the second section was to provide top cover while the first dive bomber, dropping a 500 pound bomb. After the first section completed its attacks the second section dived bombed the Japanese position while the first traded places and provided top cover. Then each first section strafed the target and returned to base while the second remained to patrol the area to strafe targets indicated by the Boomerang as the Australian infantry moved forward but battered Shaggy Ridge remained a Japanese strongpoint. A series of B-25 and P-40 coordinated attacks called the *Cutthroat Operation* were executed against Shaggy Ridge. For three days, from 17-20 January, B-25s from Nadzab and Port Moresby escorted by 49er P-40s "plastered" the Ridge with "amazing accuracy." On 21 January P-40s guided by a Boomerang, looked for white panels laid out by the infantry and smoke shells, accurately bombed the Japanese positions. The P-40s attacked again with great accuracy the next day and their attack was followed by an artillery barrage which aided the infantry in routing the enemy from their positions on Shaggy Ridge.

**23 January 1944**

During the third week of January, reconnaissance flights discovered a major enemy air force staging into to Wewak from the west. On 23 January, 5AF medium and heavy bombers were ordered to attack all four Wewak strips. Lightnings from the 80th and the 432nd and 433rd Fighter Squadrons and Warhawks and Thunderbolts of the 49FG would provide cover.

**23 January 1944: 8FG/80FS**

Sixteen P-38s, led by Capt. Albon Hailey, took off at 0845 to escort B-24s to Wewak and rendezvoused with the bombers over Gusap at 1045 and arrived over the target at 1100. Some 50 to 60 Japanese fighters were airborne but only 20 to 25 had sufficient altitude to be in a position to attack the bombers. The enemy attacks, unlike the enemy attacks on the 18th, were mostly very aggressive head on attacks pressed to close range.

1Lt. Kenneth Ladd was the Second Element Leader in 1Lt. Robert Siebenthal's flight and on their arrival saw a flight of enemy fighters 1,000 feet above flying across their flight path. As the P-38s dropped their tanks three of the enemy fighters made a pass on the bombers and Ladd started after them but a flight of P-40s came in first and he rejoined the formation. Several more enemy fighters left their formation to attack Siebenthal's flight and Ladd turned into them. He fired a 60 degree deflection shot on their Leader and started it smoking. He made another pass, waiting to fire a short burst at 75 feet and set it on fire and the pilot bailed out just as the plane exploded. As Ladd looked around he saw a Zero starting to dive on him from 3 o'clock above and he turned as tightly a possible and used full combat flaps to turn to get a head on pass. As he got it in his sights Ladd had to maneuver violently to avoid being rammed and returned to base with his eighth victory.

**1Lt. Cyril Homer** scored his seventh and eighth victories and added a probable. (AAF)

**1Lt. Jess Gidley** (decorated by General Paul Wartsmith) was killed in a collision with a Tony fighter. (AAF)

1Lt. Cyril Homer was flying somewhat behind his Flight as he was having problems with his right turbo. He saw P-40s diving ahead over the target but then saw 10 to 12 more enemy fighters coming down on his Flight from the rear. Homer called the Squadron Leader and then peeled off to the right into the enemy fighters and fired a few shots but he saw no results. As he tried to join his Flight he saw a lone P-38 was trying to make a pass at an Oscar that pulled away and Homer continued after it directly over Boram Strip at about 7,000 feet. Homer closed to 150 yards and shot it down and then flew through heavy AA fire getting away. Homer continued about four miles from Boram out over the water, climbing to about 16,000, and saw a Tony at the same altitude flying out to sea. Homer closed in on a 60 degree deflection shot and hit it around the engine. He then closed to about 200 yards into a "terrific" explosion which he just barely cleared and "flipped me over on my back." When Homer recovered, oil was on his windshield and nose and pieces had dented the leading edges of his wing. As he turned left he saw the elevator and rudder assembly of a P-38 spinning down intact along with a collection of wings and an engine. Homer had not seen the P-38 before but assumed it had been making a head on pass at the Tony and the two collided. Homer soon realized that a Tony was on his tail when shells hit his right wing. He immediately rolled over and the Tony skimmed over his canopy by not more than 10 feet. Homer climbed away and headed for home but found that his fighter was performing satisfactorily except for the aileron trim control. Homer turned back and tried to join three P-38s when a lone Oscar dove on the tail of the rear P-38. Homer called them out and dropped his flaps trying to turn around but the rear P-38 turned into Homer and dived with the Oscar about 200 feet behind him. Homer Split-S'd but could not catch them as he had to pull away when his fighter started buffeting. Homer gradually closed on the Oscar and caught him about a mile and a half from Boram at about 2,000 feet. The Oscar turned slowly left as Homer fired from about 250 yards and then rolled over burning and went straight into the water for his eighth victory. After he landed Homer learned that the victim of the collision was 1Lt. Jess Gidley who had three victories to his credit.

**23 January 1944: 475FG/432FS/433FS**

432FS

Lt.Col. Charles MacDonald led four flights of 16 Lightnings off at 0840 on a B-24 escort to Wewak. Soon MacDonald aborted after one of his drop tanks fell off in flight and was followed by four more P-38s that returned early. Capt. Loisel then assumed command of 11 Lightnings. The Squadron rendezvoused with the Liberators over Gusap at 1005 and reached the target area just over an hour later at about 2,000 feet above and to the left of the bombers. As the bombers turned out to sea before beginning their bomb run; Japanese fighters approached just off the deck and at the same time another flight of six or seven enemy planes closed to attack the lead bomber formation. Loisel ordered tanks dropped and tried to intercept the Japanese before they could attack the bombers head on. Meanwhile, 49FG Warhawks had gotten behind

**Capt. John Loisel** shot down his eighth enemy fighter over Brandi Plantation. (AAF)

**2Lt. Perry Dahl** claimed his third victory. (AFAA)

the attacking Japanese fighters and broke up the threat to the B-24s. Loisel and Wingman 2Lt. Perry Dahl found that they were alone at about 12,000 feet with the rest of Clover Squadron high above chasing other targets. Dahl followed Loisel closely as he descended on several Zeros all of which Split-S'd away before they could fire. Finally, Loisel closed on an Oscar, at 1,000 feet, heading inland a mile east of Cape Moem. He eventually caught up with the Oscar pilot who was making uncoordinated barrel rolls and fired his cannon and .50 caliber machine guns that caused the Oscar to erupt into flames and crash into the jungle near Brandi Plantation for Loisel's eighth victory. Loisel and Dahl then dove to the rescue of four P-38s flying below being closely pursued by Japanese fighters. Loisel was too late to save one of the P-38s which was smoking profusely before it rolled over at 500 feet and crashed into the water near the shore. Loisel broke quickly as his own P-38 was about to be bounced by Japanese fighters. As Dahl turned sharply to clear his own tail an Oscar zoomed past his P-38 trying to get at Loisel. Dahl warned Loisel over the radio and Loisel broke to port along the shoreline. Dahl pulled up at a 30 degree angle and fired continuously, trying to scare off the Oscar pilot who was closing in behind Loisel. The Oscar continued after Loisel but Dahl was able to close on its tail and hit in the fuselage and wings. The Oscar began to smoke and then glided downward until it hit the trees. After Dahl's third victory the two P-38s started home as there were no more Japanese in the area. On their way home Dahl checked his mirror and saw a Tony only 50 fifty yards behind. The alert Loisel immediately pulled out to the side and turned back into the Japanese and drove it away. The 432FS would not score another victory until 3 April when it would claim 11.

433FS
Capt. Richard Kimball was leading nine of the original 13 P-38s that were scheduled as starboard medium cover for B-24s attacking Wewak. As the Squadron neared the target area at 1110 at 22,000-24,000 feet, they saw 10 to 15 Tonys and Zeros approach the bombers from the direction of Manchu Island at 24,000-26,000 feet. P-40s of the 49FG were providing low cover at 20,000 feet and intercepted the enemy fighters. Kimball ordered tanks to be dropped and made a pass but returned to protect the bombers and cleared the area of enemy fighters. Soon a P-38 developed engine problems and returned to base escorted by another Lightning and then the second Flight Leader also had engine problems and left for home; taking his entire flight with him. This left Kimball with only his Wingman, 2Lt. Carl Danforth, and Element Leader, 1Lt. Donald Revenaugh, from the original 13 and the three joined P-38s of other Squadrons and headed home. At 12-15,000 feet over Brandi Plantation they saw two Tonys near a cloud layer at 8,000 feet which they used to escape. Then 10 to 12 Zeros and Tonys attacked from a cloud and Kimball saw a Tony on the tail of the last P-38 and fired a long burst damaging its cockpit causing it to break away from the P-38. Three Tonys got on Kimball's tail but he was able to pull away into a cloud after being chased for several minutes. Kimball reports that he saw a P-38 flying over Brandi Plantation with its engine on fire (Danforth) and he heard Revenaugh call that he was over the Sepik River heading home in damaged fighter. Neither pilot returned to Dobodura. The 433FS would not have another claim until 15 March.

**23 January 1944: 49FG/7FS/8FS**
The 49ers had flown more escort, armed reconnaissance, and patrols for the five previous days but no enemy contact was made. On the 23rd 49er Warhawks and Thunderbolts left from their respective Ramu Valley bases at 0940. They rendezvoused with the northbound bomber force immediately over the Finistere foothills and flew a direct route to the target and reached Bomm Village at 1100.

**1Lt. Elliott Dent** (right, with crew) shot down two Zeros to give him three victories. (AFAA)

7FS
Capt. Arland Stanton led 17 Demon P-40s stacked from 21,000 through 24,000 feet over the right flank of the B-24s. As the formation passed over Borum, Stanton's flights were located above the Liberators on the starboard and he saw the dogfight between the early-arriving P-38s and Oscars in the distance over the sea. Stanton held his escort position and after the Liberators salvoed their bombs on the Wewak airdrome. He then followed them five miles through their inland turn over Cape Noem but then the first enemy fighters began to approach the B-24s. Stanton directed White Flight to remain in high cover, while he ordered Blue, Green, and Red Flight elements to drop their tanks and engage the enemy fighters. The Japanese started attacking in groups of two or three and six different attacks were attempted but only two materialized.

Green Flight Leader 1Lt. John Haher was positioned at 21,000 feet as the lowest echelon in the Demon escort group. Haher had lost one Wingman due to engine trouble but took his remaining rookie 2Lts. Jay Rogers and Frederick Dick, into combat. Haher dove and made a firing pass on an Oscar from the front high quarter and when the enemy pilot straightened out Haher was dead astern and on his second pass it started smoking and spun into the water off Cape Noem. Haher lost his flight and headed home with the B-24s. Haher looked back and saw a P-40 climbing toward the bombers and turned back to join it but as he closed he saw the Warhawk was an Oscar. The enemy pilot never saw Haher who fired a four second burst from the left rear quarter from 200 feet into the Oscar that never tried to evade. Large pieces fell off as the Oscar dove 6,000 feet into the water northwest of Cape Terabu. A second Oscar dove on Haher who dove away and headed home with his first two of three victories. Rogers damaged another Oscar and then the flight climbed and headed south to rejoin the homeward bound Liberators.

Squadron and Blue Flight Leader Stanton took Wingman 2Lt. John Fenimore, Element Leader 1Lt. Elliot Dent and his Wingman 2Lt. Nicanor Zuniga were flying escort at 22,000 feet and saw "approximately 30 Tonys" flying somewhat higher. Dent and Zuniga dove on an Oscar that was making a pass on a Liberator and Dent shot it down. Dent then saw a lone "Nip" at about 2,000 feet and dove on it and fired "one good burst" and it half rolled trailing a light wisp of smoke and crashed into the water for his third victory. Zuniga continued with Dent and climbed to 10,000 feet and spotted another lone "Nip" to the left and slightly lower. DeHaven got on its tail and followed it when it started weaving and fired at it through these maneuvers and it half rolled toward the water for his eighth victory.

From their highest position in the escort, 1Lt. Robert DeHaven's Red Flight was the last to pass over the target. DeHaven had seen the earlier Demon flights engage and when he passed over Dallman Harbor and dropped their tanks and dove into the fray. As he descended DeHaven saw a lone Oscar make an attack on the bomber and saw another Oscar about a mile and a half behind. DeHaven led the Flight on the first Oscar that rolled away offering DeHaven a tail shot. He fired until he had to break away to avoid a collision. DeHaven used his diving speed to get back up to the bombers but as he looked back he saw the second element continuing after the Oscar with the second Oscar diving after them and a third coming in from the side. During the combat DeHaven's rookie Wingman 2Lt. Marion Hawke stayed with his Leader and climbed back toward the bombers but briefly blacked out at the top of the climb and lost DeHaven. Element Leader, 1Lt. John Crowley, and his Wingman, 1Lt. John Suggs, did not see the enemy attack on their rear and continued to dive with the Oscars on their tails. DeHaven quickly dove again just as the vulnerable Crowley and Suggs were overwhelmed at about 10,000 feet. But he was too late. Crowley pulled out of his dive much too low and was forced to escape just above the water where one of the Oscars dove on him and hit the P-40 which rolled over and crashed into the Bay. DeHaven, chased after Crowley's victor "who didn't gloat long" as DeHaven closed into point blank range and claimed his eighth Japanese aircraft. By the time Hawke recovered from his blackout, Suggs' fighter was heavily damaged with his port aileron controls shot out and his cockpit damaged by a round that hit the armor of his headrest. Hawke led Suggs down to the safety of a cloud in a frightening dive and then led him back to base. As Suggs entered the landing pattern at base his engine cut out and he crash landed safely.

8FS
Black Sheep CO Capt. Bernard Makowski and his 14 Warhawks took off at 0945 on an escort to Boram Drome and arrived over Wewak with the second wave of Liberators at 1130 at 20,000 feet. Blue Flight Leader 1Lt. James Hagerstrom had two wingmen abort but he decided to stay with the mission with Wingman 2Lt. John Bodak as both were flying new P-40N-5s and Hagerstrom had not scored for three months and had finally had recovered from the Malaria which plagued him. Hagerstrom saw 10 to 15 Zeros coming down on his flight and ordered tanks to be dropped. Hagerstrom and Bodak dove on four or five Zeros diving on a P-38 and caught them at 10,000 feet where Hagerstrom fired a high tail on pass at 100 yards closing to 50 yards and sent it down in flames. They continued diving and Hagerstrom made a pass on the last man of a two Hamp flight but as he pulled around to see the results the first Hamp "latched" onto Hagerstrom and Hagerstrom's supposed victim got on Bodak's tail. Bodak swung around and shot the Hamp off Hagerstrom's tail while enduring the fire from the Hamp on his tail. Hagerstrom then turned and shot the Hamp off Bodak's tail. Two Hamps came in from above and Hagerstrom pulled up and fired a burst and one turned into Hagerstrom who made a head on pass and fired into its engine and belly and was so close that the P-40 was rocked by its prop wash. Hagerstrom then fired a "good" burst at the other Hamp that also made a head on pass and Hagerstrom fired tracers into its cowling. The two Americans descended to 2,000 feet and attacked a lone Hamp and Hagerstrom fired a long burst from close astern and watched his burst hit along its wings and fuselage. The Hamp burst into flames and crashed into the sea for Hagerstrom's third Hamp victory of the day. Bodak went after two Hamps chasing a P-38 and fired a 30 degree deflection shot, hitting the engine and Hagerstrom saw its pilot bail out and the Hamp crash into the sea. Two or three more Zeros appeared out of the clouds from above and then a Tony was seen approaching two P-38s from astern. The two Blacksheep followed the Tony and Hagerstrom fired a short

**1Lt. James Hagerstrom** shot down three Zeros and a Tony to make him an ace with six victories. (AFAA)

**Maj. James Hagerstrom** scored 8½ victories over Korea flying F-86s for the 4FG. (AFAA)

**2Lt. John Bodak** claimed two of his three victories. (AAF)

burst that got some hits but the Tony went into a steep wingover and Hagerstrom followed through some turns and when it leveled out he fired a long burst from short range and it started smoking, caught fire, and rolled over and dove straight down 1,500 feet into the sea. Hagerstrom and Bodak continued on and made unsuccessful passes on two or three more lone Hamps and ran out of ammunition and turned for home with six victories between them. Hagerstrom's four victories would be his last of the war but made him an ace with six.

White Flight Leader 1Lt. Louis Graton with wingmen 2Lts. George Smerchek, Carl Lambert, and Merle Wolfe were over Boram at 21,000 feet when they saw "approximately 40 enemy aircraft…in two ship formation at about 30,000 feet." The enemy dived and Graton fired a burst into the engine and cockpit of a Zero and set it on fire and then Graton fired a short burst at it and finally Smerchek came in and finished it off with a long burst into its cockpit for his only victory. The flight climbed and saw another Zero at 300 feet and dove on it and as the enemy pilot turned Graton fired a short burst hitting its tail and then Smerchek came in and fired a long 90 degree deflection shot that started it on fire. Wolfe was credited with a probable and Lambert with a damaged Zeke.

### Late January 1944: 49ers

On 25 January 49er CO, Lt.Col. James Selman was promoted in rank and joined the 5FC operations staff at Nadzab. Selman had led the original 9th Pursuit Squadron from training Florida into combat in Australia; then helped plan the New Guinea air offensive; and as 49er CO had made the Group the highest scoring unit in the entire AAF. With these credentials Selman was an ideal choice for the new position. The command of the 49ers was assigned to newly promoted Lt.Col. David Campbell.

On 28 January, Maj. Gerald Johnson, 9FS' CO was furloughed to Command School in the States with 11 victories and would not score again until 14 October. Johnson's Deputy CO, Capt. Wallace Jordan, became the Flying Knight CO. Jordan, was an outstanding fighter pilot and tactician and was a top candidate for the 49er Group Ops Exec but both Johnson and Campbell wanted the veteran Jordan to guide the Squadron's rookie Thunderbolt pilots.

8FS CO, Capt. Bernard Makowski, moved to a new position on the Fighter Command Staff and senior officer, the newly promoted Maj. Robert McHale, was assigned as Black Sheep Commander with Capt. Carl Petersen as his Ops Exec.

### Late January 1944: 475FG

During the rest of January air action was routine except for a record breaking B-25 escort to Manus Island on the 24th which was the northernmost target for Clover Squadron to date. The first P-38J models had appeared in small number as early as the beginning of December, 1943 and by the end of January 1944 they were arriving in large numbers in their natural metal finish which was supposed to increase their speed by several miles per hour. Throughout February and the first weeks of March the ground crews used paint solvent and scraping tools to remove the camouflage from the older P-38s. Only a few camouflaged P-38s remained in operation as late as May 1944 but after midyear the natural metal Lightnings glistened on the 475th's runways.

# 4

## February 1944

**February 1944: Strategic and Air Situation**

MacArthur's future plans involved the continued western advances in New Guinea as components of the main drive in the SWPA and the Bismarck Campaign as thrusts against the flank. A change in plans was made, substituting operations in the Kavieng-Manus prior to landings at Hansa Bay in order to better coordinate with the increasingly successful operations in the Central Pacific.

MacArthur felt that Allies could continue to be successful and the Japanese would offer little effective resistance if the Allies carefully chose the point of attack as they had at Saidor. The Japanese naval and air forces in both New Guinea and the Bismarcks posed a genuine threat to any future Allied expansion and to their advanced air bases. On 1 February 1944 the Japanese had 188 aircraft on New Britain airfields and an additional 54 on New Ireland and the Admiralties. The Japanese were moving more aircraft into New Guinea, maintaining air strength at Wewak (78 aircraft) and increasing it at Hollandia (178 aircraft) and 47 at four other small New Guinea airstrips. Increased sea traffic, construction, and air reinforcement at Wewak, Hansa Bay, and Madang made it obvious that the Japanese were going to use these bases as defensive strong points.

While the Japanese Air Forces in the SWPA intended to remain on the defensive the 5AF planned an energetic air offensive with the objectives of advancing the bomb line and putting Japanese airdromes in range of single engine fighters. By February 1944 the victories in the Huon Peninsula and Ramu Valley placed even P-40s in range of Wewak. Although ADVON was headquartered there, Port Moresby was no longer a forward base and plans were being made to move it to Nadzab. The 5th Fighter Command had already moved there as well as the air echelon of the 5th Bomber Command. Dobodura no longer was included in 5AF plans as the construction of the 10,000 foot concrete runway was cancelled and the First Air task Force was ordered to move to Finschhafen. The 43rd and 90th Bomb groups and the 475th Fighter Group and the 415th Night fighter Squadron continued to be based at Dobodura. All other 5AF units were based either on the Huon Peninsula or Ramu Valley.

Allied Intelligence estimated Japanese air strength located from the Solomons and Philippines as 435 fighters, 288 bombers, and 195 other aircraft types. The 5AF had an overwhelming 1,981 operational aircraft including 745 fighters and 738 bombers. Of its 77,000 personnel there were 800 bomber crews and 750 fighter pilots. The RAAF possessed more than 500 tactical aircraft and the Dutch had 20. By February 1944, the obsolete P-39s and early P-40 models had been replaced and new fighter squadrons were arriving.

While the P-38 with its twin engines was preferred in the theater the P-47 served with distinction as 350 were involved in 37 air combats downing 162 enemy aircraft for the loss of only two Thunderbolts. In February 1944 there were nine fighter squadrons equipped with P-47s; four with P-38 F through J models; three with P-40Ns; two night fighter squadrons with P-70s and modified P-38s; three reconnaissance squadrons with P-38s and B-25s; and a photo recon squadron with F-5s and P-38s. These totals included the newly arrived 58th Fighter Group; 415th and 421st Night fighter Squadrons; and the 71st Reconnaissance Group.

The October and November 1943 attacks on Rabaul did destroy many enemy aircraft on the ground and in the air and the attacks on shipping decreased the delivery of supplies. However, they did not eradicate Rabaul as an enemy base as aircraft continued to fly off its four airdromes and shipping used its harbor.

By February 1944 the 5th Fighter Command had expanded its air superiority from over its bases to within the maximum range of the fighters based there. Enemy fighters were only rarely encountered and the threat to Allied aircraft was mainly to poor weather conditions and to a lesser extent enemy AA fire. During 1943 as study by the AAF Statistical Control determined that with 16% of the combat aircraft in all theaters the 5AF destroyed 29% of all enemy aircraft claimed; lost only one aircraft for every 7.7 aircraft it destroyed as compared to a 3.7 to 1 ratio in all other theaters.

**February 1944: Fifth Air Force Order of Battle**

The Fifth Air Force had the following combat units available for the coming operations:

5th Fighter Command

The 8th Fighter Group's 35FS and 36FS were based at Finschhafen and the 80FS was at Dobodura and were scheduled to move to a new field on Cape Gloucester on 20 February. The 35FS moved their P-38s into Cape Gloucester on 19 February and the 80FS moved there from Dobodura on 28 February. The field at Cape Gloucester never became suitable for the P-38s and by 25 March the entire 8FG would reassemble at Nadzab.

It had originally been the plan to move the 58FG into Cape Gloucester but the experience of the 8th precluded the use of the even heavier Thunderbolts there.

The 35th Fighter Group moved from Nadzab to Gusap on 7 February. Their 39FS, having been converted to P-47s at Brisbane, moved to Gusap on 27 January. The 35th's other two Squadrons, the 40FS and the 41FS, were converting from P-38s and P-39s to P-47s, and moved to Gusap on 5 and 15 February.

The 49th Fighter Group had been based at Gusap since November and December when it moved from Dobodura and was replaced there by the 58FG. Their 7FS and 8FS were still flying P-40s and the 9FS was flying a mixture of old P-38s and new P-47s.

The 348th Fighter Group, the original P-47 unit in the SWPA, and its 340FS, 341FS, and 342FS, was based at Finschhafen.

The 475th Fighter Group and its 431FS, 432FS, and 433FS, was located at Dobodura.

5th Bomber Command

The 3rd Bomb Group (Light), usually referred to in the SWPA as the 3rd Attack Group, with their A-20s and B-25s, had moved to Nadzab between 30 January and 3 February. The 417th Bomb Group (L) had completed its conversion to the A-20 and moved into Dobodura between 4 and 7 February, replacing the 3BG(L). The 38th Bomb Group (Medium), flying B-25s, 71st, 405th, 822nd, and 823rd Bomb Squadrons, remained based across the Owen Stanley Mountains at Port Moresby. The 345th Bomb Group (Medium), "Air Apaches," flying B-25s in four squadrons, the 498th, 499th, 500th, and 501st, were based at Dobodura but moved to Nadzab on 23 February. The 22nd Bomb Group (M), transitioned from B-26 Marauders in October and November 1943 to B-25s. Soon they began another change to the B-24 Liberator and was redesignated a heavy bomb group at the end of February. The 22nd's four squadrons, the 2nd, 19th, 33rd, and 408th were all based at Nadzab. The 43rd Bomb Group (Heavy), B-24s, consisting of the 63rd, 64th, 65th, and 403rd Squadrons, were located at Dobodura on the opposite end of the complex from the 58FG. The 90th Bomb Group (H), B-24s, operating the 319th, 320th, 321st, and 400th Squadrons, from Dobodura until 23 February when they completed a move up to Nadzab.

The 26th Photo Recon Squadron, converted to F-4 and F-5s (P-38s) and moved into Dobodura on 26 January and then moved on to Finschhafen on 19 February. They were assigned to the 6th Reconnaissance Group, which also had the 8th Recon at Port Moresby and Nadzab, the 20th Recon at Port Moresby, and the 25th Photo Recon at Nadzab. The 71st Reconnaissance Group headquarters was at Nadzab while their 17th Recon (Bomb) Group flying B 25s was based at Dobodura. The 82nd Tactical Recon Squadron, flying P-39s, was operating from Dobodura. The 110th Tactical Recon, flying P-39s and P-40s, was based at Gusap. The 25th Liaison Squadron was operating detachments at Port Moresby, Lae and Nadzab. Supporting these combat units were four Troop Carrier Groups, the 317th, 374th, 375th, and 433rd, comprised of 18 squadrons was located throughout the SWPA.

**February 1944: An All P-47 Fifth Fighter Command?**

From the end of November 1943 until the middle of March 1944 there were only four operational P-38 squadrons in 5th Fighter Command; the three squadrons of the 475FG and the 80FS of the 8FG. Attrition during the Rabaul operations had forced the conversion of the 9FS and 39FS to P-47 aircraft. So Kearby's expectation for an all P-47 equipped Fifth Air Force almost became a realization during January 1944. When the 58FG became operational in February there would be 19 Fighter Squadrons in the 5FC and 11 would be equipped with Thunderbolts with four other squadrons equipped with P-38s while three flew P-40s and one more attached to a bomb group that used available P-40s or P-39s. However, early 1944 would be the apogee of P-47 numbers and mark the phase out of the P-40 in the SWPA. Thus, when 58 P-38s were allocated to 5FC in February 1944 to re-equip the 35th and 36th Squadrons of the 8FG, there would be six P-38 squadrons available to escort the B-24s to Hollandia. By the end of the year P-51 fighters would mostly replace the P-47 and the P-40 would finally be relieved of its yeoman service.

Because of the slow arrival of P-38s in the SWPA, when the **58FG** (311FS/58FG P-47s shown) arrived in February there would be 11 P-47, four P-38, and three P-40 Squadrons available in the 5FC. (AAF)

**February 1944: Leave**

For much of the war the Fifth Air Force had no official rotation policy; and pilots and crews only could look forward to endless missions, dull routine, poor living conditions, and dreadful weather. The only relief was a short leave to Sydney, mostly for officers, as regular breaks were the privilege of officers, especially aircrew (bomber) officers. But as the general situation, combat and logistical, eased so did leave for enlisted men. But instead of leave to Sydney enlisted men were consigned to the officially sanctioned Camp Mackay, a small coastal town with little to recommend it. Meanwhile, officers' leave to Sydney or the temperate coastal resort of Brisbane was extended to two weeks. A typical leave for pilots would entail a shared rented apartment in Sydney or Brisbane. Australian women during the war were celebrated for their "friendliness" toward Americans and the apartments were utilized for entertaining by the officers who were flush with cash which could not be spent in the middle of the New Guinea jungles, but could especially be spent on Black Market beer and liquor available in Australia.

**Early February 1944: Bong Returns**

Bong had returned to fly combat but the AAF's leading ace did not rejoin the 9FS Flying Knights flying their new P-47s. He was to report to 5FC at Nadzab where he was to be attached to Fighter Command Headquarters. At first Bong thought that this posting would make him a "desk jockey" but Kenney put Bong (21 victories) and his good friend Lt.Col. Thomas Lynch (16 victories), on "special operations" where they would freelance as a team and remain in P-38s and fly attached to the unit of their choice. Kenney also stipulated that neither ace was to be "bothered with paper work as I didn't think that either of them would be very good at it." Kenney seems to ignore that Lynch had done a very good job as the CO of the 39FS. It has always been inferred that Bong was Kenney's "fair-haired boy" and that this posting was a show of favoritism. But there is the possibility that since Bong was the leading active AAF ace in both Europe and the Pacific and was closing in on the American Ace-of-Aces record of 26 and Kenney realized the publicity advantage of the posting. Plus Kenney hedged this bet by teaming Bong with Lynch and also having Neel Kearby who had accumulated 21 victories as of 9 January also stationed at Nadzab as possible record breakers. USMC Capts. Joseph Foss had tied Rickenbacker's record of 26 in January over Rabaul but Foss was back in the States receiving the Medal of Honor from FDR. It was a matter of time before Bong in his silver Lightning would become America's Ace of Aces.

**Late January and February 1944: 475FG**

During late January and February 475th operations were more effectively discouraged by weather clouds, rain, and wind than by the Japanese. On the 9th the 432nd Squadron was on alert all day but not one P-38 got into the air because of the continuous torrential rain. Several bomber escort missions did get through to Kavieng during the middle of February but many others were scrubbed because of the weather. In spite of the weather several 475th flights were dispersed to Cape Gloucester and Finschhafen. The last 475th combat claims until 15 March would be made on 3 February. The 475FG would continue with patrol and ground support missions mainly when it moved from Dobodura to Nadzab late in March.

**2 February 1944: 58FG/311FS First Combat Mission**

After bad weather on 1 February had kept the 311FS out of action; on the next day the Squadron conducted its first real combat mission of the war for the 58FG. Group Operations Officer, Maj. Joe Klemovich, led eight P-47s off Horanda Strip #7 to Finschhafen where they refueled and then escorted C-47 transports supplying the new base being constructed at Saidor. The other pilots on this first mission were John Brown, (leading the second flight) and Raymond Evans, Thomas Bullington, Max Itzkowitz, Arthur Marston, Leonard Erzen and George Taylor. Although the mission was a success as the transports returned safely to base after delivering their cargo without encountering any enemy; the 311FS had its problems. Only 15 minutes from Finschhafen on the way to Saidor, Erzen, Taylor, and Bullington all had engine problems and returned to Finschhafen, escorted by Marston. The remaining four P-47s continued on to Saidor where Evans experienced total engine failure. He dropped his belly fuel tank made an emergency dead stick landing on the 2,800 feet of Saidor runway that was serviceable. The remaining three escorts returned to Finschhafen, refueled, and along with the now repaired "mechanicals," returned to Dobodura at 1415 while Evans was able to return the next day.

**3-7 February 1944: 475FG Downed Fliers Rescued**

On 3 February 1944 the USN submarine *Gato* left New Guinea on a rescue mission of a number of shot down Allied airmen. During the day the *Gato* ran submerged and raced on the surface at night. At 2215 on 4 February, while the *Gato* was running on the surface a large enemy flying boat caused it to dive and it surfaced as soon as possible to clear the area and headed to the Gazelle Peninsula at top speed. It arrived submerged off the Gazelle coast in the predawn hours of 5 February and began to scan the shoreline by periscope. At 1100 a white marker was sighted on the shore which was a signal set by the Australian Coastwatcher, a Maj. Roberts, who was sheltering the airmen. The *Gato* waited for darkness and surfaced in a flooded down state to make a quick escape. At a prearranged flashlight signal two rubber boats were immediately launched and picked up Roberts who was bringing two Australian and two American airmen with him. While Roberts and his rescued airmen were heading toward the *Gato* some new and unexpected signals were coming from the beach. The *Gato's* radioman read the signal as "67 more aviators arriving for rescue." While a *Gato* class submarine was more spacious compared to other USN types, to house 72 more personnel was a problem. Once the two rubber boats returned to the *Gato* a second time they brought back only three more American pilots. Among those three taken aboard were 431FS pilots Edward Czarnecki and Owen Giertsen.

**1Lt. Edward Czarnecki** was shot down on 23 October 1943 and finally rescued by the submarine *Gato* on 7 February, but would later die of a jungle disease. (AAF)

Czarnecki had paddled to shore after he parachuted into the water on October 23 while Giertsen had crash landed about eight miles off Wide Bay. Both pilots, in company with Carl Planck of the 9th Fighter Squadron, had been picked up by friendly natives. The three had avoided the enemy patrols that captured other P-38 pilots shot down during the Rabaul raids. A native runner informed them of the submarine evacuation, and they made it across mountains and to the rendezvous with the *Gato* just in time. The *Gato* took them to Dreger Harbor in New Guinea, and they were transferred to the *USS Fortunas* during the afternoon of 7 February, where Giertsen and Czarnecki were evacuated to Australia; both Giertsen and the ill Czarnecki were sent home to the U.S., where Czarnecki died of a jungle disease he had contracted on New Britain.

**3 February 1944: 348FG/340FS/342FS**

The first large scale air battle for the 348th since the December 1943 battles over Wewak occurred on 3 February when the 342FS and 340FS were providing close air cover for a B-24 strike on Wewak.

340FS

The 340FS was the first 348th Squadron to met Japanese interceptors in providing close cover for B-24s when 16 P-47s met the initial Japanese attack at 1115. They were patrolling at 20,000 feet when Zeros and Tonys were detected at 16,000 feet. 1Lt. Richard Fleischer dove 10,000 feet to 1,000 feet and then zoomed up to 16,000 feet to get on the tail of a Zero. The enemy pilot made a sharp turn to starboard but Fleischer continued to fire and got hits on the fuselage and after the Zero made a 90 degree turn it crashed into the ground for Fleischer's third victory. 1Lt. Lyle Dowsett began an attack on a Tony but broke off and then reinitiated the attack and followed and fired at it in a fatal spiral dive for his second victory. 1Lt. Charles Allen saw a Tony making a pass on his first element and climbed to make a head on pass. Allen's bullets hit the cockpit, killing the pilot, and the enemy tumbled twice before crashing into the ground for his only victory. 2Lt. Michael Ditkovitsky was the 340th's high scorer when he dove on a Tony at 10 o'clock, Split-S'd, and fired and exploded the enemy fighter. He then fired on a Zero that rolled over on its back and crashed for his first victories of the war.

**2Lt. Michael Dikovitsky** claimed his first two victories of the war. (AFAA)

342FS

At about 1140 the 16 Thunderbolts of the 342FS were just leaving the Wewak area after the B-24s had bombed when three Oscars and four Tonys attacked from behind and above. However, the 16 P-47s outnumbered the seven Japanese who went on the defensive in a brief but fierce dogfight at 22,000 feet about five miles west of Wewak while the B-24s flew in peace toward home. 2Lt. George Davis was in a forward flight and had to turn back to help the rear flights under attack. When Davis arrived he looked above and to his right and saw a P-47 under attack by a Tony. Davis climbed to get on its tail but the Tony broke away and dove to the right. Davis followed him down to 10,000 feet and fired a long 25 degree deflection shot from 300 yards that caused smoke to pour from the cockpit and engine. The enemy pilot bailed out as Davis pulled away for his second victory. 2Lt. William Wallace and his Flight Leader turned into the attack and met the Japanese head on but when a Tony pilot tried to get on his tail Wallace tried to out turn him but stalled several times and went into a steep vertical dive to lose him. Wallace then pulled up in a climbing turn after the Tony and fired a long 45 degree burst from 300 yards but had to stop firing when another P-47 crossed his path and fired on Wallace's Tony and exploded it. Wallace saw another Tony below and dove vertically for about 6,000 feet only to overshoot and have to pull up behind the Tony that was flying inverted. Wallace began firing at 300 yards from astern, placing bullets in the left wing root and fuselage and as Wallace flew away the Tony exploded for his first of two victories. 1Lt. Malcolm Rand followed Flight Leader, Capt. William Dunham, into the dogfight when he spotted a Tony on Dunham's tail. Dunham was firing at an Oscar (later claimed as a probable because he was forced to break away with this Tony on his tail) when Wallace rolled and dived his fighter after the fleeing Tony; firing throughout the dive. He closed range and fired a burst striking the enemy in the fuselage and wings. It burst into flames and tried to break away but Rand fired another burst which tore off pieces and the Tony spiraled down and the pilot bailed out for Rand's second and last victory. Dunham suffered the only damage during the day's combat when his fighter showed minor hits in the wing and engine cowling.

**3 February 1944: 49FG/7FS**

The 49ers continued routine fighter sweeps and armed reconnaissance of the coast but the Japanese had once again had dispersed their decimated air force to the west. For the 10 days from their 23 January mission, the 49ers flew as far west as the satellite Wewak airfield at But, however, targets had become scarce. On 3 February, 17 P-40s in four flights took off at 1020 to escort B-25s to Dagua Airfield. The P-38s of the 432FS were to fly high cover on the mission and then drop down to the deck. As the Demons approached Wewak at 8,000 feet, two Oscars were seen to take off from Dagua, one to the north and the other to the south. The lead Red Flight under Capt. Arland Stanton dove first and got hits but mostly overran it. The Oscar continued to fly without any apparent damage and it was White Flight Leader, 1Lt. Roger Farrell's turn to down the Oscar. Farrell went into a diving port turn and fired a long burst from above and behind at 8 o'clock which set the Oscar on fire and rolled over on its right wing and crashed into the water off the Dagua Strip for Farrell's second victory. After Farrell's victory the Squadron strafed targets on Muschu Island just off Cape Moem.

**3 February 1944: 475FG/431FS**

Maj. Meryl Smith of the 475FG/HQ led 15 (one abort) on a B-25 escort to the Dagua Airstrip. They arrived over the target at 1145 at 10,000 feet and dropped down to the deck about 10 miles from the Strip. While starting down Smith saw an Oscar on the water heading for a cloud bank but the P-40 piloted by 1Lt. Roger Farrell of the 7FS beat Smith to the Oscar. Smith then saw six Lilies flying low on the water near But Airdrome and Smith dove on Lily #4 with a three quarter attack from the left rear and shot it down for his fourth victory. Smith then made passes on three other Lilies, all of which already had been attacked and were going down. Smith's #4, 1Lt. Wood Clodfelter, also made a three quarter attack from the rear and shot out Lily #2's port engine and it crashed into the ocean for his only victory. White Flight led by Capt. Verl Jett followed Smith's Red Flight down and Jett shot out both engines of a Lily that was seen to crash by 1Lt. Vincent Elliott (Green #3). Jett's Second Element Leader, 1Lt. John Cohn, watched Jett shoot down his Lily (for his seventh and last victory) and had to move further out to get into position to fire on the Lily behind it. He hit its left engine and its wheel dropped but another P-38 flight cut Cohn off before

**Capt. Verl Jett** shot down a Lilly for his seventh and last victory. (AFAA)

**2Lt. Wood Clodfelter** shot down his only enemy aircraft. (AAF)

One of six Lily bombers shot down by the **432FS** over But Airdrome. (AAF)

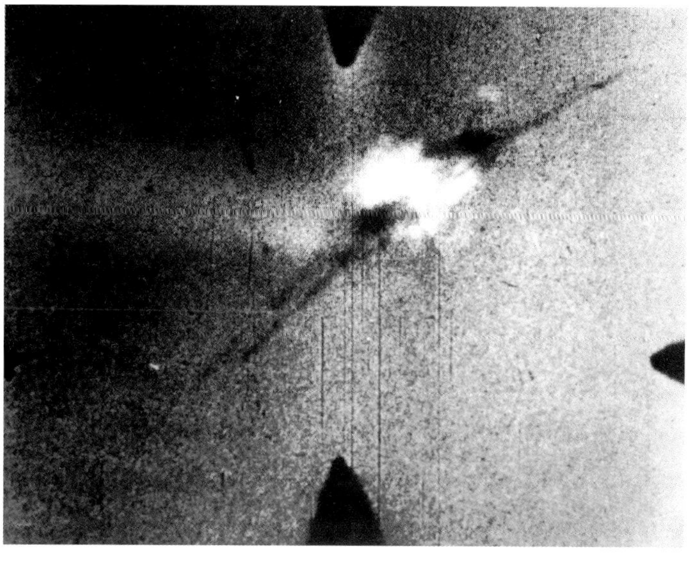

he could finish it off. Cohn then turned away and made a 6 o'clock attack on the lead Lily as it approached the shore. Two other Lightnings made an attack on this Lily but fired high and Cohn went under these P-38s and fired a short burst. His tracers and cannon shells hit the rear gunner position and cockpit, blowing the canopy off and he had to pull up to avoid a collision (for his third victory). Jett's #4, 2Lt. Fulkerson, closed on a Lily that was weaving back and forth trying to evade Jett and when his Leader pulled up Fulkerson fired and set its port engine on fire and watched it explode when it hit the water for his first victory. Fulkerson's ICR claims another Lily which does not appear in official records. 2Lt. William Gronemeyer the Second Element Leader of Capt. Thomas McGuire's Blue Flight, followed McGuire down on a Lily. When McGuire closed and fired, his guns jammed and then his Wingman, 1Lt. Robert Crosswait, closed, fired, and missed. Gronemeyer closed and hit its port engine and then kicked rudder and fired at its starboard engine to complete the annihilation of all six Lily bombers in the formation and claim his second victory.

**Capt. Edward Roddy** was credited with his eighth and last victory of the war. (AFAA)

**4 February 1944: 348FG/342FS**

Capt. Edward Roddy led a four plane late afternoon sweep over Wewak and arrived at 26,000 feet just as a Japanese fighter that had landed at Boram. A few minutes later a Helen bomber was seen almost directly below over the water heading for Boram. Roddy ordered belly tanks dropped and the four P-47s dove vertically into a stern attack. Roddy noticed that the Helen's usual tail cannon was not firing and decided that the bomber was a converted transport and pressed his attack. The enemy bomber was about 500 feet off the end of the Peninsula when Roddy opened fire and saw his bullets strike everywhere over the port wing and fuselage. When Roddy overshot the Helen he ran into a barrage of AA fire and retreated only to see another P-47 going after "his" Helen and made a quick 360 and weaved through the hail of AA fire and fired at the bomber again as it flew directly over Boram strip. The Helen caught fire, rolled over and crashed into the small hill near Boram strip for Roddy's eighth and last victory.

**6 February 1944: 49FG/8FS**

At 0740 17 P-40s in four flights took off on an escort of 3AG A-20s to strafe Muschu Island and the Japanese sent a small mixed flight of Oscars and Tonys to intercept. At 0925 Squadron and Blue Flight Leader, Capt. Arland Stanton, was orbiting at 8,000 feet above Muschu when the first enemy fighter was seen at 4,000 feet high. Two Warhawk flights dove to the attack while two stayed as top cover.

Stanton dove on the Zeke as it was turning and fired from 500 yards and the enemy pilot made a steep right 360 turn and Stanton stayed with the enemy pilot through a half roll and climb firing all the while and then overrunning him as he turned steeply left. Stanton pulled up to the right and turned into the Zeke and dropped down on its tail. Three other P-40s got behind the Zeke but were out of range. Another P-40 came in on its right and it and Stanton both had good firing passes but the Zeke continued on and started climbing to the right with five P-40s following. Stanton climbed above the Zeke and made a head on pass and both pilots fired as the Zeke, now on fire, passed under Stanton. The flaming Zeke continued to fly on with three Warhawks trailing him but not firing. The frustrated Stanton chased after the Zeke and fired a deflection shot from 4 or 5 o'clock high as the Zeke Split-S'd toward the water. The pilot bailed out at 200 feet but his chute did not open and his body splashed into the water next to his fighter. The hard won victory was Stanton's fifth to make him an ace.

**Capt. Arland Stanton** (center with crew) became an ace with his fifth victory. (AFAA)

Meanwhile, the close support escort was flown by three Black Sheep Lieutenants of Blue Flight and had finished strafing a pair of barges when the flights circling overhead called out the three enemy fighters about 400 feet over the water. Flight Leader 1Lt. Elferd Elofson, and Element Leader, 1Lt. Donald Meuten, and Wingman, 1Lt. Marion Felts were flying at only 200 feet over the water when the enemy crossed in front of them. Elofson pulled up to his left to get on the tail of a Tony and followed it through a 360 degree starboard turn; firing four good bursts through the turn getting hits on its wing roots and cockpit. His next burst went through the cockpit and cowling and the Tony burst into flames and crashed into the sea for Elofson's first of three victories. Meanwhile, Felts noticed a Zero and broke formation to go after it. As the enemy pilot made a slight turn away, Felts fired two bursts into its cockpit and engine and the Zero began to smoke profusely and rolled over and crashed 200 yards from the shore for Felts' first of five victories. Meuten climbed after the second Tony and made a 60 degree pass from the rear and then pulled around for a pass from 45 degrees from the rear and above. The Tony pilot made a steep turn to the left and both pilots were on a head on course. The Tony pilot was slightly higher and broke away first flying under Meuten's port wing. Meuten went into a 180 climbing turn to the left while the Tony turned right, Meuten made his last pass from between 80 and 90 degrees straight down and hit the Tony's engine and cockpit with a long burst and it exploded and burned. Meuten wrote in his ICR: "There was very poor marksmanship on both our parts." Meuten's victory was his second and the Squadron's 400th of the war.

**6 February 1944: 8FG/36FS: Last P-47 Victory**

In January, the 80FS scored only 10 victories and the 35FS had only one aerial combat (but with 19 victories). February was much the same, except for the added hindrance of a temporary move to Cape Gloucester from which the 8FG squadrons were even more liable to fly monotonous and uneventful missions. Also the impending landing near Talasea on the northwestern part of central New Britain also boded more uneventful patrols.

On 6 February four 36FS Thunderbolts of Flight Leader, Capt. Robert Smith, and Lieutenants Slingmeyer, Perkins, and Fox took off for the staging area at Gusap on a fighter sweep to Wewak. Fox experienced fuel system problems and aborted before reaching Gusap and the three P-47s took off from Gusap at 1500 and climbed to 21,000 feet toward Wewak in a three fighter V formation. Capt. Smith was a Headquarters pilot who occasionally flew with one of the squadrons on sweeps or patrols and had scored an Oscar victory while flying a P-400. Since the 36FS was scheduled to convert to the P-38 Smith wanted to fly at least one mission in the P-47. At 1220 about 20 minutes from Wewak they sighted a Dinah near Hansa Bay about six miles away at 15,000 feet, 3,000 feet below. As they dropped their tanks the Dinah dove and raced northeast for the clouds. Smith used his Thunderbolt's diving speed and caught the Dinah and fired a single long burst from high astern and set fire to the Dinah's port engine. The Dinah's wing burst into flame and the bomber went into a fatal flaming half roll into the clouds. The flight refueled at Gusap and then returned to Finschhafen. By 25 February the 36FS had 14 P-38s and its P-47s were transferred out.

**7 February 1944: 348FG**

At 0900 Maj. William Banks of the 348FG/HQ shot down a Tony east of Cape Gloucester for his sixth victory

**7 February 1944: 35FG arrives at Gusap**

On 7 February the 35FG was finally operating with all three squadrons in one place since the April training days in Australia. The Strip was established on the banks of the Ramu River that ran through a flat area that was cooled somewhat by gentle breezes. Gusap, like Tsisli Tsili, was isolated and could only be supported by air transport.

**10 February 1944: 71TRG/82TRS**

At 1100 2Lt. Claude Diffenderffer shot down a bomber near the Pantanga Village, Willaurez Peninsula, Philippines. It was the 82nd's second victory and first since 2Lt. Delta Graham shot down a Val on 18 December 1943.

**10 February 1944: 1st Flying Circus Victory**

On 10 February Maj. Thomas Lynch and Capt. Richard Bong took off for a sweep of Tadji Airdrome and when they arrived at 1555 at 15,000 feet they saw six enemy aircraft taking off from the strip. After these six took off a twin engine bomber took off in the opposite direction. Lynch overtook the Lily bomber when it was about a quarter mile from the end of the strip. Lynch dove to 800 feet and fired a short burst into the right wing, starting a fire, and the Lily crashed straight into ground for Lynch's 17th victory and his first since 16 September 1943.

This was the first victory scored by the self-named Lynch-Bong "Flying Circus" which was an ideal situation for the two aces. They could fly whenever and wherever they wanted. On some missions they tacked onto squadrons escorting bombers to Wewak, Kavieng, or Tadji. Sometimes they went out on two plane sweeps, morning weather recons, or dusk patrols hoping to meet enemy CAP or stragglers.

**Maj. Thomas Lynch** scored his 17th victory and the first for the Lynch/Bong "Flying Circus." (AAF)

**12 February 1944: 35FG Command Changes**

On 12 February, 35FG CO, Lt.Col. Edwin Doss left for temporary duty and leave in the U.S. and was succeeded by Deputy Group CO, Lt.Col. Furlo Wagner. Maj. William McDonough, Group Operations Officer became its Deputy CO. 40FS CO, Maj. Joseph Lamphere rotated home and was succeeded by Capt. John Davis.

**14 February 1944: 49FG/7FS/8FS**

The 7th and 8th Fighter Groups took off on a Valentine's Day escort of A-20s to Dagua Drome, Wewak. Four flights of 15 P-40s took off at 0930 and proceeded to Dagua at 6,000 feet while five flights of 19 P-40s of the 7FS took off at 0945 with one Warhawk returning to base due to electrical problems while the remainder flew on at 8,000 feet.

8FS

The 8FS arrived over Dagua at 1120 at 4,000 feet where Black Sheep Mission Leader 1Lt. Elferd Elofson led his 8FS Blue Flight elements on a pair of Zeros patrolling over Dallman Harbor at 4,000 feet at 8 o'clock. Elofson put his flight into a slight circling turn to make the enemy pilots believe that the P-40s had not seen them. When he got into range, Elofson made a sharp port turn; making it impossible for the enemy to turn into and get a lead on them. Element Leader 1Lt. Donald Meuten was the first to score; shooting down the #2 Zero (his third victory) but the other Zero escaped to the west. Blue Flight reformed over of the A-20s which were descending to strafe and bomb their target.

A lone Oscar was seen trailing the A-20s at 2 o'clock at the same altitude and the Flight turned into it. The Oscar dove away through Red Flight and finally seven or eight P-40s were chasing this Oscar. Elofson and Wingman, 1Lt. Marion Felts both fired nearly all their ammunition at the Oscar whose pilot skillfully and luckily evaded using a series if skids and jinks and flew through Red Flight.

While flying at 2,000 feet, 8FS Red Flight Leader 1Lt. Robert Aschenbrener with Wingman, 1Lts. Thomas Holstein and Element Leader 1Lt. David Winternitz, and Wingman, rookie 2Lt. Edward Glascock, saw the lone Oscar attacking the A-20s and watched Elofson's unsuccessful attack. Aschenbrener led his flight after the Oscar, whose expert pilot climbed and then went into an Immelmann. Aschenbrener fired until the Oscar pilot rolled out and fired at the second Red element. By this time seven or eight P-40s were after the Oscar. Two Warhawks fired short in the race to down the Oscar but Red Element Leader, 1Lt. David Winternitz, made a 180 turn and got on its tail and after a series of hard turns Winternitz's second volley set fire to an Oscar which finally and valiantly plunged into the sea. After Winternitz shot down the Oscar for his first and only victory, Glascock had a Tony make a firing pass on his fighter from high and slightly from the front and knock out its hydraulics, radio, sever several cables, and put a large hole in the port wing. Fortunately, the Tony unexpectedly disappeared into the western mist.

The Tony which had just shot up Glascock then had come under attack by 8FS Yellow Flight Leader, 1Lt. Nelson Flack, and his Wingman 1Lt. James Reynolds. The Tony pilot while under fire from other P-40s engaged Flack who turned into the Tony, nose-to-nose. The two pilots fired but Flack's heavier .50s prevailed and he pulled up over the speeding Ki-61, just as it nosed over and plunged into the sea for Flack's second victory but found that his fighter had been damaged but was still flying.

Mission leader Elofson called for the scattered Black Sheep to regroup but Glascock and Flack in their damaged fighters both struggled back over the foothills alone but only Glascock would reach Gusap. Flack's Warhawk just cleared the Alexander Mountain Range but the climb caused his Allison engine to overheat and it began to smoke and lost power and started to drift downward. Flack radioed his uncertain position and was descending into the Ramu River swamps over 60 miles from Gusap. Flack attempted to slide his P-40 in on the deep kunai grass of a small clearing but instead was abruptly stopped, splitting his forehead open on the gunsight. Flack crawled out of the P-40 and bandaged his head wound. He decided to burn his fighter so as not to let it fall into enemy hands and hoping the column of smoke would mark his location for pilots returning to Gusap. A Black Sheep pilot saw the smoke and charted its position. At Gusap, 7FS CO, Maj. Robert McHale, first sent an experienced guide in to evaluate the terrain after which an Australian commando, Sgt. Hector Henstridge, was to be parachuted into area. He was to find Flack and treat any wounds and prepare a landing strip, if possible. On the second day, Henstridge landed on the crash site but Flack had left alone on foot. Later that day, Australian L-5 pilot, Sgt. Eugene Saltirnik, attempted to land his Stinson in a clearing but wrecked his aircraft. Now two Aussies were also stranded but were surprised when Flack suddenly approached through the 10 foot high kunai grass. Flack was in poor condition, cut and bruised, badly sunburned, and bitten by hundreds of insects. After being treated Flack improved after a full day of rest and was able to join in on the construction of a rough hewn runway which became known as Flack Field. After six days, Sgt. James Nichols of the 25th Liaison Squadron was the next pilot to attempt to land at the isolated site. His L-5 caught on the kunai stubble, shattering its wooden prop and bending the landing gear struts but Nichols was not injured. L-5 pilot, Sgt. Thomas Stallone, was able to land safely the following morning but the field was much to dangerous to attempt a take off with two men on board, so Stallone had to leave the four behind and then was barely able to lift off from Flack Field alone in his Stinson. The next day, commando Henstridge led Flack, Saltirnik, and Nichols on a 60 mile trek to the nearest outpost. For the next 21 days, Henstridge led them through the swamps while food supplies were airdropped along the way. After reaching the forest where the airdrops ended, the commando rationed the last of the food until they were forced to live off the land. An assortment of raw fish, lizards, and birds plus a variety of fruits, nuts, and roots kept them from starving but caused severe dysentery. The normally thin Nichols' weight went to 100 pounds while the tall Saltirnik became weak and stumbling. The men's feet were raw and bleeding as their shoes rotted away. Henstridge temporarily lost vision in one of his eyes from an insect bite. After three weeks they encountered Australian camp and Flack was eventually transported back to Australia where he completely recuperated and returned to flight duty at Gusap by the end of April.

**1Lt. Nelson Flack** scored his third victory but was shot down and struggled through the jungle for three weeks before reaching safety. (AFAA)

**2Lt. James Keck** shot down an Oscar for his only victory of the war. (AAF)

**1Lt. Roger Farrell** scored his third and last victory. (AAF)

7FS

The trailing high cover Blue Flight of 7FS Screamin' Demons led by 1Lt. Roger Farrell and wingmen, 2Lt. Fenton Epling, Element Leader, 1Lt. Robert Croft, and Wingman, 2Lt. James Keck, on the leading Oscars and attacked the surprised enemy pilots from the rear and four quickly plummeted in flames. Croft and Keck dove on an Oscar in a rear quarter attack without results and continued the chase but their Oscar was attacked by another 7FS Element (1Lt. Lemuel Pollock and 1Lt. Russell Cash) who caused some damage but Croft finally prevailed to score his first and only victory. After Keck had made an ineffective pass on the Oscar, he and Croft went after an Oscar that had left its leader and headed for Dagua Strip. Keck fired from close range, astern and shot off its aileron and wing trailing edge. The Oscar burst into flames and crashed into the sea for Keck's only victory. Farrell fired a short burst at an Oscar that then out turned and escaped. Farrell, Epling, and Croft fired on another Oscar that went down. Farrell's ICR states: "One of the three of us shot this one down," At debriefing Flight Leader Farrell was given his third and last victory. Since Wingman Epling and the second element had been credited with Oscars in the battle perhaps it was Farrell's turn to get a victory credit? The Demons then zoomed back to their high cover while the other Oscars dispersed.

**14 February 1944: 475FG/431FS**

2Lt. Wood Clodfelter had reported mechanical problems with his P-38 several days before taking off on an uneventful mission before dying in a crash.

**14 February 1944: 5FC Bong/Lynch**

The Bong/Lynch "Flying Circus" would attach itself to an A-20 mission to Kavieng, New Ireland which were escorted by 18 P-38s of the 80FS. No enemy aircraft were seen until 1050 on the return trip home when Bong spotted a lone Tony flying at 12,000 feet over Cape Hoskins heading for Rabaul. Bong made a 180 turn to the left and caught it after a few minutes chase. He closed on its tail and fired at 75 yards and the Ki-61 exploded in mid-air and crashed into the water about 10 miles north of Cape Hoskins for his 22nd victory. Bong was so close to the explosion that he flew through the fireball and claimed that his cockpit was hot to the touch for several minutes afterward.

**14 February 1944: 35 FG**

At 1015 Maj. William McDonough of the 35FG shot down a Zeke and Oscar over Wewak in his P-47 to give him four victories.

**15 February 1944: 49FG/8FS**

At 0830 Blue Flight Leader, Maj. Robert McHale, led four 8FS flights stacked from 12,000 up through 15,000 feet over Cape Moem at 1030 where they came upon an estimated 15 Oscars and Tonys patrolling the harbor. McHale immediately ordered the tanks to be dropped and all his flights to attack. As the Eightballers climbed they saw only a few enemy fighters as the enemy had seen the P-40s and dove away out to sea with Yellow Flight after them. Blue Element Leader, 1Lt. Harold Sawyer, saw White Flight chasing a Zero on the water and he dove on it and closed behind 1Lt. Glascock who fired on the Zero. The Zero "mushed" into the water but bounced off back into the air and started a chandelle to the right. Sawyer closed and fired from 100 to 50 yards and hit the wing root and canopy and the Zero clipped a wing off on the water and crashed violently for his third and last victory.

White Flight Leader 1Lt. Robert Aschenbrener, Wingman 1Lt. Edward Glascock, Element Leader, 1Lt. Richard Polhamus, and Wingman, 1Lt. James Reynolds, were the lowest Black Sheep flight at 15,000 feet when they saw 15 Hamps, Zekes, and Tonys flying in loose formation about 4,000 feet overhead. Aschenbrener led them in a 360 degree turn in 5,000 foot climb but then the Zeros dove away. Aschenbrener dove after one that was doing a series of Split-S maneuvers and when he caught up he fired two different times from overhead and partly head on but the Zero flew on. A Tony then crossed his path and made four passes; the first two head on; the third from astern; and the last from above which got good hits from its prop to its cockpit for his third victory. Aschenbrener's ICR states: "He dipped a wing in the water then went in without burning." Reynolds saw four or five P-40s chasing an enemy aircraft and he Split-S'd and got on the enemy's 5 o'clock position low on the water. As the Oscar banked Reynolds fired and the enemy hit the water and Reynolds flew through the spray of the crash and his bullets for his only victory.

Yellow Flight #4 man, 1Lt. John Porteous' engine was running rough at the beginning of the flight and he could not report it to Lee as his radio was out and he continued on despite his better judgment to return to base. As the formation approached Wewak it was advised of enemy aircraft at 19,000 feet over Kairiru Island but Porteous was the last man in the formation and was just barely keeping up. He saw 10 to 13 Zeros or Hamps approaching from 5 to 6 o'clock high but could not call them out in due to his bad radio. He boosted his fighter to 3,000 rpm and tried to catch his Element Leader, 1Lt. Averette Lee, wagging his wings and pointing back to the approaching enemy fighters. Yellow Flight then turned sharply to the right into the enemy. Lee saw two Zeros at 3 o'clock and turned onto their tails and fired at the Wingman. The Wingman started on fire after the first burst and continued to smoke on the second pass and peeled away. Lee switched his attention to the other Zero as it climbed and hit it "square in the tail" from 6 o'clock and it smoked momentarily. Lee's second burst went

While flying with **Maj. Thomas Lynch**, Capt. Richard Bong scored his first victory since his November furlough to give him 22. (AAF)

**Maj. William McDonough** shot down a Zeke and Oscar to give him four victories. (AAF)

**1Lt. Averette Lee** had his best career day with a victory (one of two total), a probable, and a damaged claim. (AAF)

**1Lt. James Reynolds** got his only victory of the war. (AAF)

behind the Zero and as he zoomed up he saw where his first victim splashed and saw the second heading toward it for a probable as it was not smoking. He then engaged a Tony and fired four times hitting it twice for a damaged claim. Lee would limp back to base with a dead battery, his generator out, a rough right magneto with his first victory, a Zero probable, and a damaged Tony. Meanwhile, Porteous had slid under his Element Leader so as not to overrun the Flight and then turned sharply back into the enemy. By this time the other pilots in his flight were firing at the Zeros which were now diving away. Three Zeros followed Porteous and his Element Leader and two Split-S'd; one to the left and the other to the right. He fired on one, getting good hits but it did not smoke or burn. He then closed on a Zero on a P-40s tail (2Lt. John Bodak) and "made this ship my definite objective and without looking behind which was very careless" and he kept on firing until he almost collided with his foe. The Zero kept on flying but seemed out of control as Porteous followed at a 60 to 70 degree angle. Porteous closed to 250 yards and easily finished off the Zero at 2,000 feet. He then climbed back to 7,000 feet where he saw two Zeros and one pulled off and he took after the other. He fired a long burst, adjusting his angle of fire as they maneuvered. The Zero continued down and Porteous broke off his attack at 3,000 feet so as not to hit the water at a 60 degree angle. Sawyer confirmed Porteous second victory and final victory.

Red Flight finally got into the battle and made a few last firing passes on the Oscars they caught on the harbor surface but only Element Leader, 1Lt. Philip Kriechbaum, made a claim of a damaged an Oscar.

**15-21 February 1944: Situation**

The SOPAC landings in the Green Islands, about 100 miles from Rabaul and the constant attacks by the 5AF on New Ireland and the Admiralties caused a reaction from the Japanese forces. After USN carrier aircraft flew two destructive missions on Truk on 16 and 17 February, the Japanese withdrew nearly all their remaining aircraft at Rabaul back to Truk and their 11th Air Fleet was virtually non-existent. A 14 ship enemy convoy was discovered off New Hanover and was first attacked by 10 Navy Catalinas, and then by B-25s on 16 February. Other convoys of five to seven ships were sighted leaving Rabaul and Kavieng and B-25s continued to hit these targets, supported by A-20s of the 3AS on 19 February. The B-24s, which continued to batter Kavieng and Panapai on 19 February, joined in the anti-shipping strikes on 20 February and claimed two ships sunk. The final attack occurred on 21 February when 16 Mitchells of the 500th and 501st Squadrons attacked a convoy made up of the last large five ships to leave Rabaul and sank two. In these actions the Japanese lost 13 ships, totaling 16,465 tons including two which were evacuating ground personnel of the air units which had already flown to Truk. After the defeat and retreat of the Japanese there was a lull in air combat over New Britain and there would be no further successful combat activity until 2 March 1944.

On 15 February 1944 Adm. William "Bull" Halsey, Commander of the South Pacific (SOPAC) forces occupied Green Island, about 100 miles east of Rabaul and built a fighter base there. In support of Halsey's operations, the 5AF destroyed Japanese airfields at Kavieng, New Ireland while SOPAC aircraft would be assigned to take over the destruction of Rabaul from the 5AF. In preparation for the projected invasions of New Ireland and the Admiralty Islands, Japanese air fields along the New Guinea coast from Madang to Wewak were to continue to be "supervised and neutralized" while "constant pressure" was also to be applied against enemy installations and airfields in the Admiralties. New fighter bases at Saidor and Cape Gloucester were to cover these operations but construction was far behind schedule because of the heavy rains.

**17 February 1944: 58FG/69FS First "Combat"**

The 69FS pilots and crew chiefs remained in Brisbane until 7 February awaiting 25 new P-47s to arrive at Amberley Field, Townsville. After leaving Amberley the entire Squadron stopped at Cairns only 170 miles away for three days instead of flying the normal ferry route which was a direct flight from Townsville to Horn Island, a distance of 640 miles. Maj. Milton Self must have decided to keep the entire squadron at Cairns rather than leave one or more aircraft behind in Australia before proceeding to Dobodura.

As the 69th began combat operations the roster included Maj. Milton Self as the CO, Capt. Howard Tuman as the Ops Officer, while Capt. Harry McMullen led "A" Flight, 1Lt. Arthur Jackson led "B" Flight, 1Lt. Joseph Dover led "C" Flight, and 1Lt. George Bosenbark led "D" Flight. The 69FS flew its first mission of the war at 1405 on 17 February 1944 when the controller scrambled four 69th Thunderbolts to intercept an unidentified aircraft approaching Buna. Upon interception, the aircraft was identified as friendly.

**18 February 1944: 348FG/340FS**

Four P-47s of the 340FS were orbiting the Finschhafen area on a routine local patrol when veteran Lieutenants Donald Riley and Walter Monroe collided and spiraling wrecks fell five miles northeast of the Finschhafen strip. Patrol boats and PBY patrol planes immediately searched for any survivors but their bodies were never recovered.

Note: During the war the 348FG suffered 162 actual combat losses and only eight were definitely attributed to combat while 47 others were listed as KIA or MIA due to operational accidents. Presumably, the others were claimed by Japanese AA except for one that was shot down by friendly AA fire and another that was mistakenly shot down by a "friendly" fighter.

**19 February 1944: 8FG/80FS**

The 80FS would see no aerial combat during the month but saw some action on 19 February, when 18 P-38s took off in the afternoon to rendezvous with A-20 light bombers at Narage and then were to proceed with the bombers to intercept a Japanese convoy in the vicinity of Kavieng, New Ireland, just north of New Britain. At 1645 the convoy which had been previously attacked was sighted along the south coast of New Ireland. One destroyer was stationary in the water and the A-20s flocked over it and sunk it. Two large freighters were already burning when the A-20s and P-38s arrived and were strafed by the Havocs and Lightnings along with another destroyer or large corvette which was set on fire and exploded. When the P-38s got low on fuel they withdrew but the A-20s continued to strafe the many Japanese personnel in the water.

**24 February 1944: 58FG/310FS First Sorties**

At 1500 on 19 February a large contingent of 310FS pilots flew into Dobodura with 21 new P-47s. The 310th had departed Brisbane on 13 February, landed at MacKay and then went on to Townsville for the night. The next day they had continued on to Cairns, where they remained until the morning of the 18th. On 18 February they flew to Port Moresby, stopping to refuel at Horn Island. The ferry flight was completed 19 February when they crossed to Owen Stanley Mountains to Dobodura. They were the first 58FG Squadron to be equipped with a full complement of identical aircraft (P-47D-16s).

Once the 311FS was available to cover the movement of the 8FG the 310FS saw its first combat when it was assigned to ground cover on 24 February. Capt. Lester Wolf and 2Lt. Ellsworth Charlton were scrambled to intercept an unidentified aircraft but found nothing.

**25 February 1944: 58FG/310FS First Squadron Mission**

On the 25th, the 310th flew its first squadron-strength mission, sending 16 Thunderbolts in two sections of eight planes each on a patrol over New Britain. Capt. Lester Wolf led the first section and Group Operations Officer Capt. Joseph Klemovich led the second. Flying with Wolf were Lts. Charlton, Driscoll, and Chadwell. Capt. Charles Gracey led the second flight composed of Lts. Dugan, Harris and Stressing. Klemovich's flight included Lts. Reid, Harrington and Tully. The last flight, led by 1Lt. Donald Booty, consisted of Lts. Edwards, Peugeot and Totty. The assignment of the first section was to provide fighter cover for amphibious operations in the area between Yellow Beach, the initial Cape Gloucester invasion beach, and Rottack Bay, 25 miles to the east along the north coast of New Britain. Klemovich's eight P-47s covered the area from Rottack Bay to Rein Bay, another 30 miles to the east. All 16 Thunderbolts completed this long first mission which took almost four and a half hours; two and a half hours over the patrol area.

**Capt. Joseph Klemovitch** led a second of 310FS/58FG P-47s on their first mission. (AAF)

**25 February 1945: 8FG/36FS**

On 25 February 1Lt. Robert Cordell was testing an old P-38 when he lost an engine which he feathered. As he was coming around for an emergency landing his other engine quit and his fighter pancaked from 400 feet, killing its pilot.

**27 February 1944: 348FG**

By the end of February 1944 air combats around the Wewak area looked as though it was dissipating and Kearby was becoming impatient as Bong and Lynch had both returned to combat and were scoring victories while flying on any mission they chose as freelance pilots attached to the 5FC. Rickenbacker's magic 26 victories were almost hypnotically driving all contestants. Bong was slightly ahead with 22 confirmed victories, Lynch had 17, while Kearby still had 21 on 27 February.

On the 27th Kearby was flying with Wingman, 348FG CO Col. Robert Rowland, as part of a 340FS mission in a late afternoon patrol over Cape Hoskins at 22,000 feet. When a lone Sally bomber appeared far below, Kearby and Rowland dropped their tanks and dove more than 20,000 feet to position themselves behind the bomber. Dusk was approaching and shadows were forming which momentarily hid the Sally. Kearby closed and opened fire from about 300 yards astern and scored hits, setting fire to the wing and fuselage. Kearby pulled up and broke away to port. Meanwhile Rowland was following and decided to turn on his gun camera to record Kearby's victory. However, the fire appeared to go out and the smoke trail behind the Sally faded and Rowland automatically pressed his own gun trigger from dead astern at 250 yards and got further hits over the bomber's wings, engines, and fuselage. The Sally rolled to port and both wings erupted into flame before it crashed into the water northeast of Cape Hoskins strip. A few months later, Rowland's film was reviewed by HQ, Fifth Fighter Command Intelligence who decided that the Sally should be awarded to Rowland who submitted a new Individual Combat Report and his victory was confirmed.

**28 February 1944: Bong/Lynch Flying Circus**

Fifth Air Force Intelligence decoded an intercepted Japanese radio message that told of a transport aircraft that was to carry high ranking Japanese officers to Wewak. Bong and Lynch were hurriedly briefed and then scrambled to make the intercept. The two aces had to fly to Wewak at full throttle and on their arrival at 1810 found that the Betty was ahead of schedule and in the Wewak landing pattern. Lynch and Wingman Bong dove from 9,000 feet through "medium, intense, accurate AA." Lynch made the first pass on the taxiing Betty without observed results except for scattering the 60 to 70 persons in the greeting party. Bong strafed the transport after it came to a stop and it burst into flames with no occupants seen to escape. Subsequent decoded enemy radio intercepts revealed that a Major General and other staff officers were killed in the attack.

There is story, perhaps invented, that during the debriefing Kenney urged Bong to file a victory claim for the Betty as possibly the Betty could have been "an inch or so above the runway." Bong declined saying the Betty was on the ground and had even stopped rolling.

**28 February 1944: 58FG/310FS First Destruction of an Enemy Aircraft**

On 28 February 2Lts. James Driscoll and Ellsworth Charlton of the 310FS were flying an escort mission to Saidor and afterward flew an additional 60 miles to Madang where they strafed and destroyed a Sally bomber parked on the airstrip.

**Late February 1944: Air Situation**

After the costly air battles during the first half of the month the JAAF abandoned operations at Wewak to retreat 250 miles further west up the coast to their airdrome complex at Hollandia. In February, during their planning for amphibious landings in the Admiralties, Allied Intelligence downgraded enemy air capabilities throughout the New Guinea-Bismarck area as the bombing of enemy air bases and the destruction of his aircraft in the air had taken its toll. Enemy airdromes throughout the Bismarcks were generally inoperative and Japanese aircraft seldom were in the air, except in defense of Rabaul. Reports stated that within a week Japanese air strength in the Bismarcks had dropped from 536 to 322 planes and that "it is probable the estimate is not keeping pace with developments." An intelligence report of 27 February stated that the Japanese air forces in the Bismarcks were about to make a strategic air withdrawal from the area. During 22 and 23 February five USN destroyers sunk a 3,800 ton enemy vessel about a 100 miles due east of Lorengau and the survivors appeared to be 400 enemy aircraft personnel being transferred to bases farther north at Palau and Truk.

South of the Admiralties, the enemy airbase at Wewak remained a threat to a movement into the Bismarck Sea and toward the end of February the air strength there was estimated at 200 aircraft, including more than 80 fighters. However, these had not tried to intercept the two latest raids on

**Col. Robert Rowland**, 348FG CO, was awarded his eighth and final victory several months after the fact. (AAF)

Wewak. The most recent threat at interception had been on 15 February, when the defending force had merely escaped out to sea as soon as they sighted an equal number of Allied fighters.

The situation was such that enemy defense of the Admiralty Islands could count on little support, air or naval, from nearby bases. In the last week of February MacArthur changed his plans. In place of the assault scheduled for 1 April, an immediate reconnaissance in force would be made on the Admiralties, by a landing near Momote air strip on Los Negros Island with D-Day to be no later than 29 February. If the attacking troops, limited to 800 men, found the Momote area inadequately defended, they would hold on and await reinforcement; reconnaissance would then be transformed into invasion and the Momote airstrip would be prepared as soon as possible for fighter operations.

**29 February 1944: Admiralty Islands/Los Negros Campaign**

The Admiralty Islands Campaign (*Operation Brewer*) was a series of battles in the New Guinea Campaign in which the U.S. Army 1st Cavalry Division occupied the Japanese-held Admiralty Islands. Acting on aerial reconnaissance data that there were no signs of enemy activity and these Islands may have been evacuated, MacArthur decided to advance his timetable for capturing the Islands and ordered an immediate reconnaissance in force. The Campaign began on 29 February 1944 when a force landed on Los Negros, the third largest island in the group. By landing on a small, isolated beach where the Japanese had not anticipated an invasion, complete tactical surprise was realized but the Islands were definitely occupied by the enemy and a more difficult battle developed for control of the Admiralties but did not affect the development of the Manus' Airfields.

By 7 March, the Seabees had prepared Momote Airfield and on 9 March 25, twelve P-40 Kittyhawks of RAAF No. 76 Squadron, guided by a B-25 arrived from Kiriwina via Finschhafen and the remaining 12 aircraft of the squadron following the next day when air operations began and from this time on naval and ground units in the Admiralties had air support just minutes away. The initial runway was 3,600 feet which was sufficient for the Kittyhawks and Spitfires but the runway was increased to 7,800 feet by late April and B-24s of 5BG moved in on 18 April 1944 and flew their first mission, against Woleai two days later.

Eventually, air and naval superiority enabled the Allies to heavily reinforce their position on Los Negros and the 1st Cavalry Division was then able to take the islands. The Campaign officially ended on 18 May 1944 and the Allied victory completed the isolation of the major Japanese base at Rabaul that was the ultimate objective of the Allied during 1942 and 1943. A major air and naval base was developed in the Admiralty Islands that became an important launching point for the campaigns of 1944 in the Pacific.

**29 February 1944: 421NFS: First Combat Mission**

The 421st Night fighter Squadron was formed on 1 May 1943 at the U.S. Army Air Forces School of Applied Tactics (AAFSAT), Orlando, FL under the command of Capt. Walter Pharr. Over the next few months the Squadron's personnel roster was steadily increased but without pilots or aircraft Pharr instituted a training regimen emphasizing drills, discipline, and military subjects. It was not until 1 October that it received its first pilots and Radar Operators (R/Os) when 12 aircrews arrived and formed three flights. On 4 October the Squadron moved to Kissimmee, FL which would become the main Night fighter training base in the future. Seven well-worn P-70s were awaiting the air crews and an intensive operational training program was instituted.

On 3 November 1943 the Squadron was ordered to proceed to San Francisco by train for overseas embarkation. After a stay at Camp Stoneman the unit boarded the *USAT Sea Pike*, crossed the Equator, and landed at

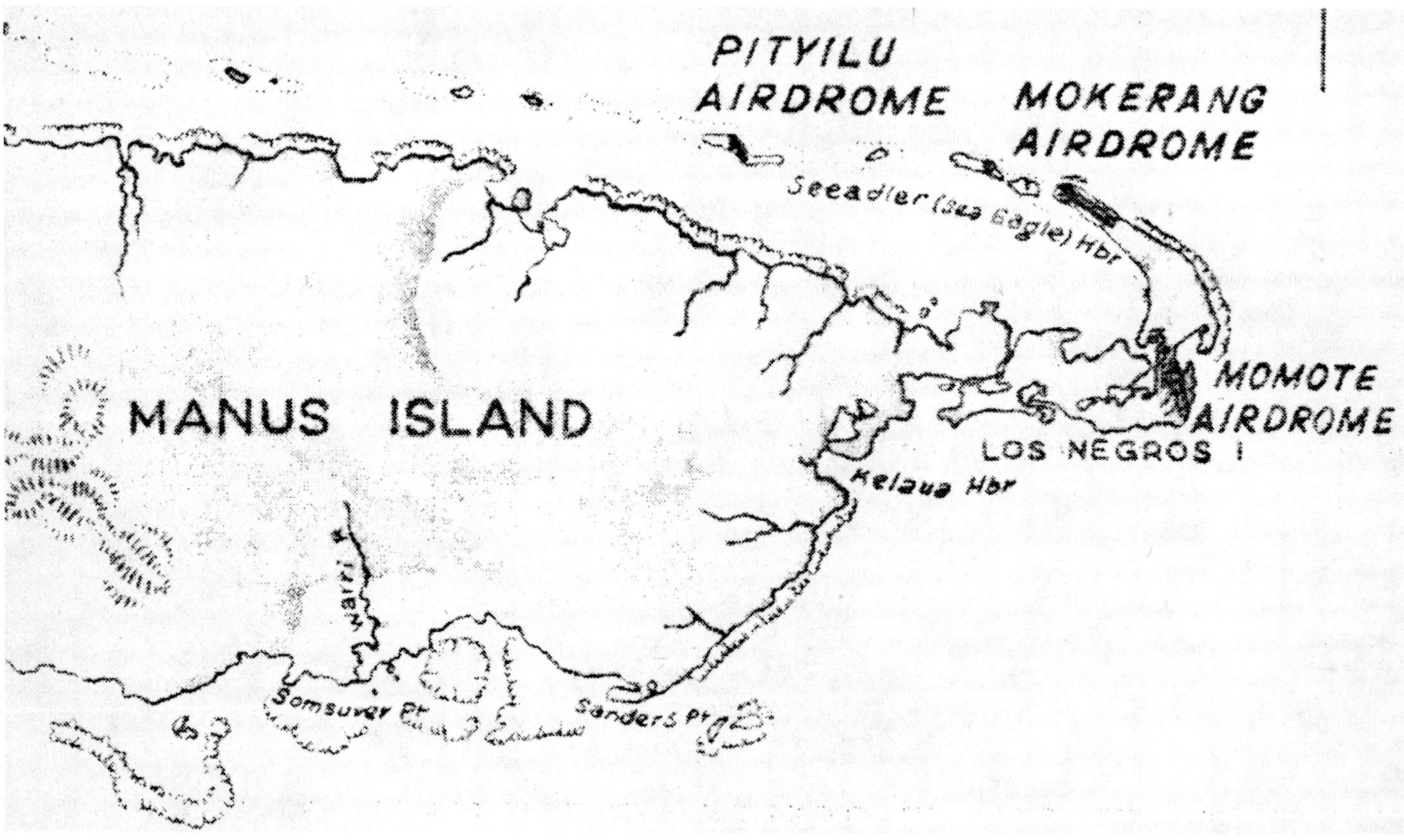


Manus' Airdromes

Townsville, Australia on Christmas Day, 1943. After a brief stay on board the ship the Squadron landed at Milne Bay, New Guinea on 3 January 1944. The 438 enlisted men and 40 officers had completed their training and were ready for combat except they had no aircraft and it was almost three weeks later before they received their first aircraft, a single P-38. By this time Milne Bay was far from the combat area but the P-61 night fighters projected for the 421st were not scheduled to arrive until April or May. On 27 January, the Squadron's advanced party was ordered to move to Nadzab to establish facilities there. The rest of the Squadron followed on 1 February 1944 but with their lone P-38 all they could do was establish perimeter defenses to fend off any attacks by the Japanese stragglers but many ground classes were held to keep up their proficiency.

During February the 5th Fighter Command began sending well-used P-38s to the Squadron. It was not until mid-February that the Squadron received two additional aircraft, another P-38 and a tired P-70. The first mission flown by the 421st was a dawn weather reconnaissance flight on the morning of 25 February 1944 which was to be just the first of such flights, many of which were in cooperation with Navy PT patrols. On 29 February the Squadron flew its first combat mission when three Lightnings took off from the secondary field at Finschhafen at 0540 to fly top cover for the Army invasion on Los Negros Island in the Admiralties. Two P-38s had to abort due to mechanical problems with one pilot forced to bail out. Only one 421st Lightning reached Los Negros but the overcast blocked the pilot's view and he returned to base.

It would not be until mid-April before the 421st had an inventory of four P-38s and four P-70s. A report issued by 421HQ in mid-July 1944 stated the unit's frustration: "The major difficulty in using the squadron effectively has been a lack of understanding on the part of higher headquarters as to the purpose and means of operation of night fighters, and assignments of airplanes to the squadron."

**Capt. Walter Pharr** was instrumental in the formation and training of the 421FG. (AAF)

**29 February 1944: 475FG/432FS**

432FS P-38s took off at 0720 and landed at Nadzab at 0915 for a scheduled ground support mission. The eight plane force took off at near noon and crossed New Britain to attack positions on the Los Negros, where American troops were in danger of being overrun. The mission ran into a heavy rainstorm about 20 miles from the target, and the eight P-38s turned around and headed home flying on the deck. The formation leader followed the New Britain coast to avoid becoming totally lost in the rapidly deteriorating weather but soon the ceiling and visibility were down to zero. Two P-38s were fortunate to break out of the weather and get back to Finschhafen but the others were in dire trouble. As the remainder of the formation followed on the wave tops, for some reason 1Lt. Harold Howard banked sharply and caught a wingtip on a wave and cartwheeled into the water. Two more P-38s in this flight, piloted by 2Lts. Edward Dickey and Clifford Mann, crash landed into the water near the Allied invasion beach where the pilots were later picked up. 2Lts. Perry Dahl and Jack Hannan spotted lights on the land and then an airstrip. They circled the strip until they got a green light and Dahl immediately put down landing gear and flaps and headed for the runway. Soon Dahl realized that the green light was not for him but for a B-24 about to take off. The strip's control tower had not even seen the two P-38s and when Dahl touched down on the runway the B-24 had just turned on its take off run from the opposite direction. Dahl instinctively pressed the right brake and swerved to miss the bomber's fuselage but this action only diverted his P-38 enough to skid directly between the bomber's port wing engines. The B-24's Hamilton Standard propellers were torn off by the sturdy P-38 which was spun around and thrown backward off the end of the runway into a gully. Dahl, in shock but uninjured, exited his torn plane while Hannan landed safely, despite a broken nosewheel.

# 5

# March 1944

**March 1944: Planning the Hollandia Invasion and Beyond**

The end for the Japanese in New Guinea was near as their major base at Wewak had been rendered useless by Allied airpower and most Japanese air and ground elements were scuttling to reach Tadji or Hollandia located far to the northwest of Wewak. With the conquest of Los Negros and Manus Islands in the Admiralties, the supply line between New Guinea and New Britain was cut and the isolation of Rabaul was complete. Allied plans for the move up the New Guinea coast and eventual invasion of the Philippines could go forward with absolute safety on the flank. The only Japanese option was a desperate but apparently futile defense of Hollandia.

After the Admiralties/Negros landings on 29 February MacArthur and Kenney discussed bypassing Hansa Bay to attack Hollandia, with a preliminary operation to seize Tadji to establish an advanced fighter base to cover the troops and the shipping as they landed at Hollandia. They agreed on Hollandia but only after Halsey completed his Kavieng operation. On 3 March Halsey met with MacArthur and Kenney to further discuss the next operations and everyone agreed on the substitution of Hollandia for Hansa Bay. When MacArthur asked Halsey to advance the date of the Kavieng invasion to 15 March; Halsey said that date was too soon but he could occupy Emirau Island on that date. MacArthur objected and wanted Halsey to proceed with the original plan as soon as possible. The date agreed on as feasible was between 15 and 24 April. Kenney's 5AF was to destroy enemy air power from Wewak to Hollandia and keep it subdued so that the Halsey's carriers escorting the invasion convoy could manage any attempted enemy air attack. The Joint Chiefs of Staff was informed that MacArthur and Halsey were in complete agreement on the substitution of Hollandia for Hansa Bay and asked for a directive confirming their agreement. The JCS had been surprised by the initial ease of the Admiralties invasion and on 12 March they decided that the best approach to the Luzon-Formosa-China area was by way of the Marianas-Carolines-Palau-Mindanao path. The JCS directed that the Kavieng Campaign was to be abandoned and the Rabaul-Kavieng area isolated with minimum forces and Halsey was to occupy Emirau, after all. The Admiralties Campaign was to be completed and developed as a base for the air forces in the SWPA from which the 5AF could complete the neutralization of Kavieng and Rabaul; assist Halsey's Naval air forces in neutralizing Truk and Palau; and base units of the USN there. Hollandia was to be captured with a target date of 15 April and, after that date the 5AF was to do whatever was practical to prepare for the support of Nimitz's capture of Palau on 15 September and for MacArthur's move into Mindanao on 15 November. Plans and routes were indefinite after that date, except for the Nimitz plan to invade Formosa on 15 February 1945 and for MacArthur to invade Luzon, also on that date. However, it was possible that either the Formosa or Luzon plans would be implemented at a later date. Nimitz was to occupy the southern Marianas about 15 June 1944 and build bases for the B-29s for air operations against the Japanese Home Islands. Nimitz was also to use his carriers to provide cover for our occupation of Hollandia and other operations in the Southwest Pacific Area.

Kenney was "dumbfounded" when he read the directive:

> I couldn't figure out why the Joint Chiefs had reversed a recommendation made by the three Commanders in the Pacific. The unanimity at the Pearl Harbor Conference evidently had not made much impression anywhere else. I had almost laughed at MacArthur when he suggested not getting too excited about that Conference until we got the Joint Chiefs' directive. He had certainly been right. The suggestion that we bypass the main

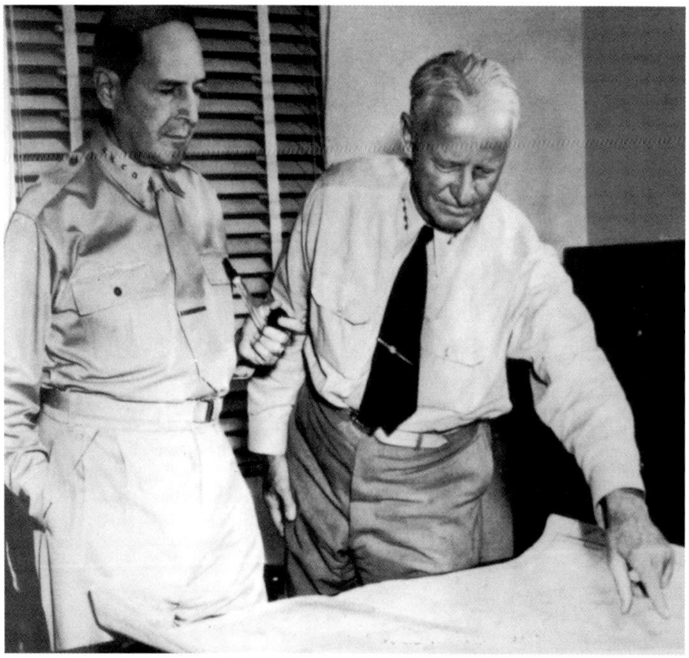

**MacArthur** and **Halsey** were in complete agreement on the substitution of an invasion at Hollandia for one at Hansa Bay. (AFHRC)

Philippine Island of Luzon and go to Formosa before liberating the Filipinos was unthinkable to me. That people belonged to us and had fought loyally on our side. If we blockaded them and left a half million or so Japs in their country to steal their food and subject them to misery and starvation, I felt we would not be keeping faith with them. The Japs certainly would live off the country and let the Filipinos starve rather than go hungry themselves. From a purely military view we would have a large landmass, with a lot of airfields and a lot of airplanes, right in our midst; it would offer much more of a problem than the bypassing of some small island or an isolated place like Wewak on the edge of a comparatively uninhabited place like New Guinea. However, as MacArthur observed, we had Hollandia to think about right now and could worry about the future later.

**Kenney** was "dumbfounded" when the JCS suggested that the main Philippine Island of Luzon be bypassed and Formosa be invaded before liberating the Filipinos. (AAF)

**March 1944: 475FG Situation**

Although combat in the air slowed during February and early March 1944 the pace of ground war accelerated in New Guinea. The hard won gains of the past months were consolidated and Fifth Air Force bases were advanced to reach the retreating enemy once again. On 20 February, 475FG construction units and their building materials were transported to Cape Gloucester but after only five days they were ordered to abandon all their supplies and were sent to build a new base at Finschhafen. Some 475FG P-38s and personnel from the 431FS and 432FS were flown into Finschhafen on 26 February and were joined by the Cape Gloucester construction units two days later. The choice of Finschhafen as an air base would prove to be a poor one as a bivouac and for air operations. The area was described as a "mixture of humid heat, torrential rains, violent electrical storms, mud, and numerous daytime-biting dengue-bearing mosquitoes." It was so obviously bad that three weeks later an order came for the move to Nadzab. The new base at Nadzab was likened to the prairie country of the American West. The 475th Fighter Group arrived there after other units had selected the choicest locations for bivouacs and the Group was relegated to the periphery where only "antiaircraft outposts dwelt." Obtaining fresh water proved to be one of the immediate problems after a 25 foot well was dug without success. The shallow, muddy Erap River flowed so swiftly through the camp area that several men were swept away and drown.

Capt. Dennis Cooper, who had semi-successfully suggested the 431FS' nickname to be the "Satan's Angels," was promoted to Group Headquarters Intelligence Officer in late February. In this position he pressed that the entire 475FG was to be known by that sobriquet. "We take Death into the Skies" was the motto of the 431FS and by the end of March the Squadron had over 115 confirmed kills (the 9FS led the 5FC with over 180 victories while the 80FS had 170, and the 39FS followed with about 130 victories before it transferred from the P-38 for P-47s in November 1943).

**Finschhafen Airdrome.** (AAF)

**2 March 1944: 348FG/341FS**

At 1100 eight P-47s of the 341FS, led by Maj. John Moore, took off from Finschhafen on a shipping patrol off Manus Island. While flying about five miles south of the eastern tip of Manus at 6,000 feet they encountered 10 Zeros and Hamps in loose formation at 2,000 feet, heading toward a formation of B-25s.

Moore led his two flights on the enemy formation that broke rank to fight off the Americans individually. Moore picked up a Zero making a port turn and fired at it from astern and as the Zero changed directions Moore saw explosions on the right wing root. He then saw a P-47 shoot down a Hamp on the deck but then saw another Zero start to dive on that P-47. Moore dove after the Zero and although it was out of range he fired a volley out ahead of it to try to scare him away. The Zero pilot broke off his attack and Moore chased him to the eastern end of Manus and started to fire at 500 feet as the enemy pilot went into a slow climbing turn which increased near the top so that Moore lost sight of the Zero under his nose as he broke to the right. Moore went into a Split-S and saw his Zero in a 60 degree dive straight into ground for Moore's seventh and last victory. Moore continued along Manus Island and saw a lone Zero on the deck, heading north toward the clouds covering the island. Moore nosed over into a dive and caught the Zero before it reached the clouds. The enemy pilot did not evade until Moore got into range when he went into a steep left chandelle and got on Moore's tail. Moore fire walled his Thunderbolt and used his water injection to pull away in a climb to get behind and 3,000 feet above the Zero. But the skilled enemy pilot went into a steep stall turn and got behind Moore again and Moore escaped again. This cat and mouse game continued for four or five passes as the Japanese pilot did not press his attack as it appeared he was trying to return to base. On the last two passes Moore was able to get a few hits but the Japanese finally got into the clouds and Moore lost him.

**Maj. John Moore** scored his seventh and last victory. (AFAA)

**3 March 1944: 35FG/41FS**

On this day the 41FS and the 35FG would score their first victory since 26 November 1943 and their first since transitioning to the P-47. Four Thunderbolts were sent out to rendezvous with rescue PBY *Guardiania I* over Vulcan Island. At 1010 while flying at 4,000 feet Element Leader, 1Lt. John Wallace, spotted a twin engine Dinah at 4,000 feet off the north tip of Vulcan heading back to Rabaul or Kavieng. Wallace turned and closed astern of the Dinah and fired a short deflection shot from 500 yards and hit it from nose to tail. Its right engine started on fire as the Dinah dropped its bombs and its gunner fired but missed. The Dinah turned into Wallace but he easily got on the Dinah's tail and fired a three second burst from 275 yards and the right engine became a ball of flame and the bomber glided out of control through a cloud front toward the sea for his only victory.

During this "Flying Circus" mission both pilots scored two victories: **Lynch** (#18 and #19) and **Bong** (#23 and #24). (AAF)

**3 March 1944: 5FC/HQ: Bong/Lynch Flying Circus**

During the afternoon of 3 March, Maj. Thomas Lynch and Capt. Richard Bong had another successful sweep to Tadji. Just as they approached the airstrip they spotted a Sally bomber taking off and Lynch dropped his auxiliary tanks and pulled up to get on its tail. The bomber's starboard engine began to smoke after taking hits from Lynch who overran and peeled off. Following right behind, Bong's bursts put the Sally into the jungle. As the two pilots returned to the Tadji area Bong sighted five fighters over the ocean just offshore and initiated an attack. The enemy turned back into Lynch and a fighter began a head on attack but instead of pressing the attack, the enemy pilot pulled up into a climbing turn to the right. With its belly exposed Lynch put a short burst into the enemy and pilot bailed out as his fighter began to burn. Lynch then dived and fired on a Tony and it started smoking, lost altitude, and crashed near the Tadji Airstrip. Another Tony half rolled over Lynch, who pulled up sharply and made a quick shot head on without results. As the Tony swung around to get on his tail, Lynch slammed the throttles forward and climbed away from him. Leveling out, Lynch sighted two Sally bombers under the clouds and radioed for Bong to follow him. Lynch made a tail on pass on one and observed a few hits on the fuselage and engine but then ran out of ammunition. Bong followed the escaping bomber put another burst into it and observed it to crash. The two victories gave Lynch #18 and #19 while Bong's two Sally victories were his #23 and #24.

**4 March 1944: 35FG/40FS/41FS/HQ**

40FS

The 40FS sent out 16 P-47s at 0950 on an escort of B-24s to Wewak. Red Flight Leader, 1Lt. John Young, and Wingman, 1Lt. Robert Furman, Second Element Leader, 1Lt. Jack Marvin, and Wingman, 2Lt. Anthony Faikus, were at 20,000 feet at 1115 over the east end of Manchu Island. Here they spotted three Tonys 5,000 feet below at 8 o'clock and called them to other 40FS flights. Young led the dive on them despite not having his belly tank release. He fired a long six second burst closing from 500 to 100 yards on the surprised enemy pilot whose fighter went into a gentle port turn before spiraling, trailing heavy smoke into the ground. Marvin called out another Tony at 9 o'clock and Young pulled up sharply into it. The Tony attempted to out climb the P-47 but couldn't even though Young still hadn't released his tank. The enemy pilot Split-S'd into Young who fired a long burst at 400 to 200 yards at which time the Tony passed under Young. The Tony was then picked up by Marvin and Faikus who dove and fired several long bursts but was unable to get a proper lead on the fast and evasive Tony. Marvin pulled out at 3,000 feet when the damaged Tony's aggressive pilot turned inside of him. During his pull out Marvin blacked out momentarily and strained his back but recovered and climbed back to 10,000 feet to join his flight. Marvin and Faikus spotted a straggling fighter southeast of Wewak, looking like it wanted to join their formation. The two Thunderbolt pilots went into a slow dive and then climbed behind the suspicious fighter which turned quickly away; showing itself to be a Zero. Marvin and Faikus dove and fired from out of range when the Zero turned into Faikus who fired getting a few hits and ran out of ammunition. The enemy pilot turned into Marvin who fired long bursts as he pulled his nose up as the Zero disappeared smoking into the low overcast. Three ship White Flight Leader 1Lt. David Pardy and Wingman 2Lt. Roger Howe Second Element Leader, 1Lt. William Strand followed Red Flight down and got several shots at the Oscars but only Strand made a claim, a damaged Oscar.

41FS

The Squadron sent out 16 P-47s to provide escort of two groups of B-24s over Wewak. At 1220 Element Leader 1Lt. Edward Park was escorting two P-47s with engine problems back to Gusap. Park's Wingman, 2Lt. Paul Lorick's P-47 had a bad oil leak and Park requested permission to make an emergency landing and while circling the field when Park spotted a Tony over Bogadjim Plantation at tree top level. Parks left his charges and dove almost vertically on the Tony at 350 mph and got on its tail undetected and fired a burst from 75 yards and raked it with hits everywhere. With pieces falling off and engine smoking, the Tony rolled on its back toward the ground. Park saw two more Tonys at 1,000 feet and a mile ahead on the tree tops and pulled over to the right Tony and fired a short burst but did not see any hits. As he chandelled right and turned 180 Parks saw the parachute from his victim and Lorick closing on a Tony from 150 yards dead astern on the tree tops. Lorick fired two burst which sent the Tony into the trees. Park made a pass on the parachuting Japanese pilot but did not shoot. Lorick chandelled and make two firing passes on the "parachuting Jap" who was killed by Lt. Lorick's first burst and "he hung in his chute like a side of beef on a butcher's rack. On the second pass the chute disintegrated." These were Lorick's and Park's only victories of the war.

35FG/HQ

During the late morning a special flight of three P-47s led by Maj. William McDonough with wingmen, Capt. Fred Harries, who had returned from furlough in the U.S. just a few days before, and Col. Furlo Wagner were returning to base ahead of the B-24s at 19,000 feet while the remainder of the P-47s were 20 to 30 miles behind the bombers. At 1130 they saw six to eight Zeros and Tonys diving on them from about 1,500 above. McDonough dove 9,000 feet to escape before the Zero broke off and headed for the clouds. McDonough continued his escort of the Liberators to their base and while approaching his strip saw AA fire. As he circled the strip he saw a Tony on his tail and pulled up quickly and got on the Tony's tail and fired his .50s into it in full view of hundreds of spectators down on his home field who saw him become an ace. Harries saw tracers coming from behind his cockpit and cleared his tail in a dive and zoomed up and after two 180 degree turns saw four Zeros 1,000 feet high, dead ahead at 15,000 feet. He climbed and closed and fired at 150 yards when the Zero chandelled to the right. Hits were seen on its canopy, wings, and engine. The Zero never completed its chandelle as Harries continued to fire and went into a stall; inverted on fire and went into a spin into the ground for his only victory.

**5 March 1944: 5FC/HQ: Bong/Lynch Flying Circus**

The two P-38s piloted by Maj. Thomas Lynch and Capt. Richard Bong took off from Gusap at 1115 to make a fighter sweep over Wewak and arrived there at 1245 and found no airborne enemy aircraft. They moved on to Dagua and Tadji again without any sightings. On the their return trip, flying at 17,000 feet Lynch spotted three Oscars flying toward Dagua from the Wewak area at 3,000 feet.

Lynch's ICR: "I dropped my tanks and made a tail attack on the rear plane in the enemy formation. The Oscar burst into flames and fell off flaming from my first burst. I made several more passes with nil results and then sighted six more enemy aircraft approaching. I called Captain Bong to break off and we headed for the overcast at 6,000 feet. We started to return to base and then decided to attack again. I made a head on pass at an Oscar and observed hits around the engine. A fairly large piece of metal came off his plane and hit behind my left prop, denting the engine cowling. I made more passes and then called Captain Bong to break off."

Meanwhile, Bong took a shot at the #1 Oscar but missed and then made two 90 degree deflection shots but also missed. He then followed an Oscar headed toward the coast and opened fire from 400 yards as the enemy pilot began to turn. He claimed to get several good hits on the tail section and the Oscar fell out of control and crashed and exploded about 1,000 yards off the Dagua Strip. Bong's ICR states: "This action took place under the cloud layer and Major Lynch was above it and was unable to witness the action." But Bong claimed it as destroyed. (Both Lightnings were equipped with gun cameras but Bong's had malfunctioned and the Victory Board had no choice but to award Bong with a probable.) Bong pulled up through the cloud layer and rejoined Lynch and fired a 45 degree deflection shot at an Oscar that "scored some hits but not enough to cause him to go down." Bong took a 90 degree shot at an Oscar but missed and the two super aces were approached by five more Oscars and wisely elected to return to base with Lynch claiming his 20th victory.

**Maj. William McDonough** became an ace when he shot down a Tony near Gusap. (AFAA)

**Lt.Col. Thomas Lynch** became a quadruple ace for the Flying Circus' only victory of the day. (AAF)

**5 March 1944: 348FG: Death of Kearby**

On 3 March both Bong with one victory and Lynch with two had scored and moved closer to Rickenbacker's record and Kearby's probability to break the record was rapidly dwindling. By mid-afternoon on 5 March the only claims in the 5FC were registered again by Lynch and Bong. Lynch scored his 20th victory over an Oscar and had a damaged claim while Bong claimed an Oscar probable and damaged. Lynch had scored his victory near Dagua, southeast of Wewak and Kearby scheduled a sweep there in hope of finding quarry there to increase his score. Kearby took off from Saidor at 1600 with his own special Flying Circus comprised of Capts. William Dunham and Samuel Blair. Kearby had flown into Saidor when his P-47, *Fiery Ginger IV*, developed a problem and Kearby flew the mission in another P-47. At 1710 they arrived at Wewak at 22,000 feet where they patrolled up the coast for about 10 minutes. Kearby was the first to see a Tony approaching the Dagua strip but did not attack as the enemy fighter would have landed before they could attack and they remained in orbit at 22,000 feet. About three to five minutes later the flight saw three bombers approaching the Dagua Strip from the sea at about 500 feet and parallel to the strip. The bombers were identified as G3M Nells but probably were Ki-48 Lily bombers of the 75th Sentai, as Nells had not operated over the area for some time and records show that the 75th Sentai 12 Lilys from Hollandia to the Wewak area on or about 5 March.

After dropping his tanks, Kearby led the way as the bombers started circling Dagua strip to the right but as the P-47s descended to 1,000 feet the Nells saw them and began a gradual descent to head west up the coast. Kearby fired at the lead bomber which was flying at about 200 feet and set it on fire. Dunham then attacked the left Nell and shot it down in flames. Dunham reported that he saw Kearby then fire at the right Nell without seeing any hits and then he made a pass on this Nell that Kearby had just unsuccessfully attacked but missed.

Almost simultaneously, Blair closed to 200 yards behind the bomber on the right and fired a two second, nearly no deflection burst, and flames poured back from the fuselage. The stricken bomber fell off on its port wing and exploded when it crashed into the ground. Blair pushed his Thunderbolt into a turning zoom climb to the left and looked around for Dunham and Kearby. He saw Kearby reversing his turn to port and break to starboard with an Oscar on his tail.

Dunham was completing a 180 degree turn when he saw Kearby with the Oscar on his tail and swung into firing position and met the Oscar head on hitting its engine and fuselage. The Oscar then turned into Dunham who held his fire until the Oscar was in point blank range where Dunham's eight .50s. The Oscar was set on fire and its canopy blew off and it crashed in the same area where the Nells crashed. Dunham passed very close to Kearby and looked around to see what he believed to be the P-47's canopy flying off but by the time he was able to level off he saw no sign of Kearby's plane.

Other Oscars were diving on Blair from behind and he escaped into the protection of clouds in a valley. To his relief, Blair found Dunham a few minutes later and the two headed for home after vainly trying to reach Kearby by radio. Blair was troubled by the fact that he saw a radial engine airplane crash into the ground at Dagua strip and Dunham reported that he saw a crash site on the opposite side of the runway from where the three Japanese bombers and Oscar had crashed.

After firing on the lead Nell, Kearby lost the momentum of his dive by making a 360 degree turn to attack the second bomber. It may have taken as much as five to ten seconds for him to complete the circle with a dangerous loss of speed and altitude. The Oscar flying above Kearby's P-47, that was climbing slowly to regain valuable speed and altitude, thus had the definite combat advantage of speed and altitude. It seems that Kearby was aware of the Oscar descending on him but had limited options for escape as he was too slow and too low to dive or find cloud cover. It has been speculated that the Oscar pilot was a veteran from the 77th Sentai (identified by the stylized 7s on their tails) which was still active in the area. Japanese records for 5 March only cite that an Oscar was engaged by enemy fighters and heavily damaged but managed to crashland at one of the Japanese strips. Kearby had scored his 22nd victory while Dunham's victory was his ninth and Blair scored his seventh and last victory of the war.

**Col. Neel Kearby** destroyed a Nell for his 22nd victory before being KIA. (AAF)

**Capt. Samuel Blair** shot down Nell for his seventh and last victory. (AFAA)

**Capt. William Dunham** claimed two victories to give him nine. (AFAA)

When the distressed Dunham returned to Saidor he demanded a fighter be readied so he could go back and search for Kearby and finally he had to be restrained from going back alone. Dunham and the 348th lost Colonel Neel Kearby who was a consummate pilot and leader who trained and then led them to unexpected great success. Kearby wanted to prove the P-47 and himself in combat and paid the ultimate price to accomplish his goal.

**8-24 March 1944: 58FG moves to Saidor**

On 8 March as the 58FG was ordered to move to Saidor, New Guinea, the most advanced air base controlled by U.S. forces. The advanced echelon was to leave by air at once on 26 C-47 transports. The echelon, headed by Maj. Matthew Hall, 58FG Group Executive Officer, comprised of seven other officers and 105 enlisted men; 33 from each squadron and 6 from Group Headquarters. The C-47s arrived at Saidor without mishap. The Liberty Ship, *SS Sharen,* was to carry the Group's heavy equipment and supplies and remaining men. The ship arrived on the 13th and 75 more men arrived by C-47 on the 24th.

**Saidor Airdrome**

With the new Allied air and naval facilities on the western tip of New Britain Island there was a need to establish corresponding facilities on the New Guinea side of the Vitiaz Strait to be incorporated into future operational plans. Air and ground reconnaissance showed that Saidor was not only strategically situated to cut off the Japanese retreat from the Huon Peninsula but was also adaptable to the early development of airdrome and light naval facilities. Saidor was village located between Blucher Point and Madang on the coast of Northeast New Guinea at the northern entrance to the Strait, about 100 miles northwest of Finschhafen. Reconnaissance found only minimal enemy activity in the area and the existing civil airstrip that was left inoperable by trenches dug across it by evacuating Australian troops in 1942 could be repaired and extended in a relatively short time. This 2,250x240 foot grass airstrip, located about a mile inland, was approximately 50 feet above sea level and the terrain sloped toward the coast providing natural drainage features which made it easy to develop. River gravel for runway construstion, although mixed with large water washed stones, was reported readily available. Heavy rainfall was the greatest problem, averaging 140 inches per year, often coming down in flooding downpours.

On 22 December 1943, the construction directive for the Saidor airdrome facilities was issued and specified the construction of one 6,000x100 foot all-weather runway; one all-weather parallel taxiway; all-weather dispersal facilities for 84 P-38 fighters or medium bombers; an alert area for 32 fighters; and one 3,500x100 foot transport runway. The directive also prescribed that the airdrome layout should be arranged, if possible, so that a second 6,000x100-foot runway could be constructed later on the opposite side of the taxiway paralleling the first runway. This second runway layout was to be prepared only if it would not increase construction time for facilities definitely specified.

The Task Force Engineer Section was organized on 24 December, only nine days prior to the scheduled D-Day, and consisted of personnel from various organizations that had not worked together: the 808th and 863rd Engineer Aviation Battalions, and elements from the 453rd Engineer Depot Company and the 8th Engineer Squadron. The Task Force Engineer and his staff landed at Saidor on D-Day, 2 January 1944 and since there was no enemy opposition, an immediate reconnaissance was made of the prewar civil airstrip. Since an immediate priority was to bring in C-47 air transports to supply the invasion it was decided that this strip could be easily reconditioned. On 3 January 1944 (D plus 1) the 8th Engineer Squadron survey detachment conducted a preliminary survey for the main drome which found a suitable location where construction was possible and the 808th Engineers, who had landed on D plus 3, began clearing the site. The 863rd Engineers landed on D plus 7, and first worked on improving the existing prewar grass runway for transport use before moving on to the main airdrome. Despite heavy rains, this grass field was sufficiently reconditioned to permit the landing of 12 C-47s loaded with ammunition two days later.

In mid-January 1944, Fifth Air Force inspected the site to determine its possibilities in view of their proposed changes in the distribution of aerial units. They requested that the GHQ, SWPA, revise the original specifications for airdrome construction. New plans called for the operation of 232 aircraft from Saidor which was twice as many as previously specified and also a proportionate increase in dispersal and alert area requirements. Two parallel, 6,000x100 foot, steel mat surfaced runways provided with minimum overruns of 500 feet were now required. The revisions were approved by GHQ and the revised construction requirements were forwarded by Alamo Force to the Task Force on 24 January 1944. Because of a 20 foot high terrace at one end and the sea at the other end of both runways it was impossible to provide the length of overruns and spacing of taxiways as specified. Proposed modifications were submitted through channels for GHQ approval. While the higher echelons were reviewing these plans, torrential rains were critically hampering progress on the airstrip already under construction. From 10 to 31 January there were only three days during which it did not rain and the total rainfall for this period was nearly 25 inches. Despite the rain and mud the engineers continued to work and the base of the runway was covered with nearby river gravel and then the entire runway, shoulders, and warm up aprons were covered with aggregate. The frequent rains and continuous rolling created a reasonable good water bound surface. At each end of the runway the first 750 feet were covered with bitumen and although sufficient bitumen was on hand, the urgency for an operational field, and the delays caused by the heavy rains did not permit bitumen treatment of the remainder of the runway prior to placement of pierced steel mat. The runway was made operable by 4 February (D plus 33) for emergency purposes but some of the surface gravel became loose and worked up through openings in the mat and the incessant rain and ensuing mud delayed the full use of the runway until 6 March (D plus 64). The almost uninterrupted rain and muddy living conditions and inadequate food supply resulted in an average weight loss of 30 pounds per man in one battalion. Under the prevailing poor conditions, the 860th Engineer Aviation Battalion began to arrive on 29 January (D plus 27) to augment the worn out 808th and 863rd. The driving of vehicles over the wet, partially constructed runway, taxiways, and hardstands necessitated redoing much of the work over again. The impact of landing aircraft on soft spots of unbonded bitumen caused damage and its repair contributed to further delays in construction.

In April, Allied Air Forces advised GHQ, SWPA, that recent changes in the deployment of air units would cause the cancellation of the second runway and that the number of required hardstands could be reduced from 232 to 148 consisting of 26 100 foot diameter keyhole type hardstands and 122 80 foot diameter slot-type hardstands. The old transport airstrip was absorbed into the completed airdrome as part of the transport unloading apron. Construction of the final taxiways and dispersals was expedited during April, and by 7 May (D plus 126) the airdrome, including control tower, operations buildings, and alert huts, was finally complete and in full operation.

The later development of this advanced base area significantly added to the Allied potential for subsequent operations in 1944. Even while work on the airdrome was still underway, operations were being flown against enemy airfields at Hollandia. Between 28 and 31 March, Fifth Air Force bombing of the Hollandia Dromes was limited to night attacks as a diversion while elements of the USN Fifth Fleet completed necessary refueling operations after making hydrographic surveys off Humboldt and Tanahmerah Bays. Since Nadzab was partially surrounded by mountains it was not suitable for staging missions that had to take off after dark but Saidor was. On the night

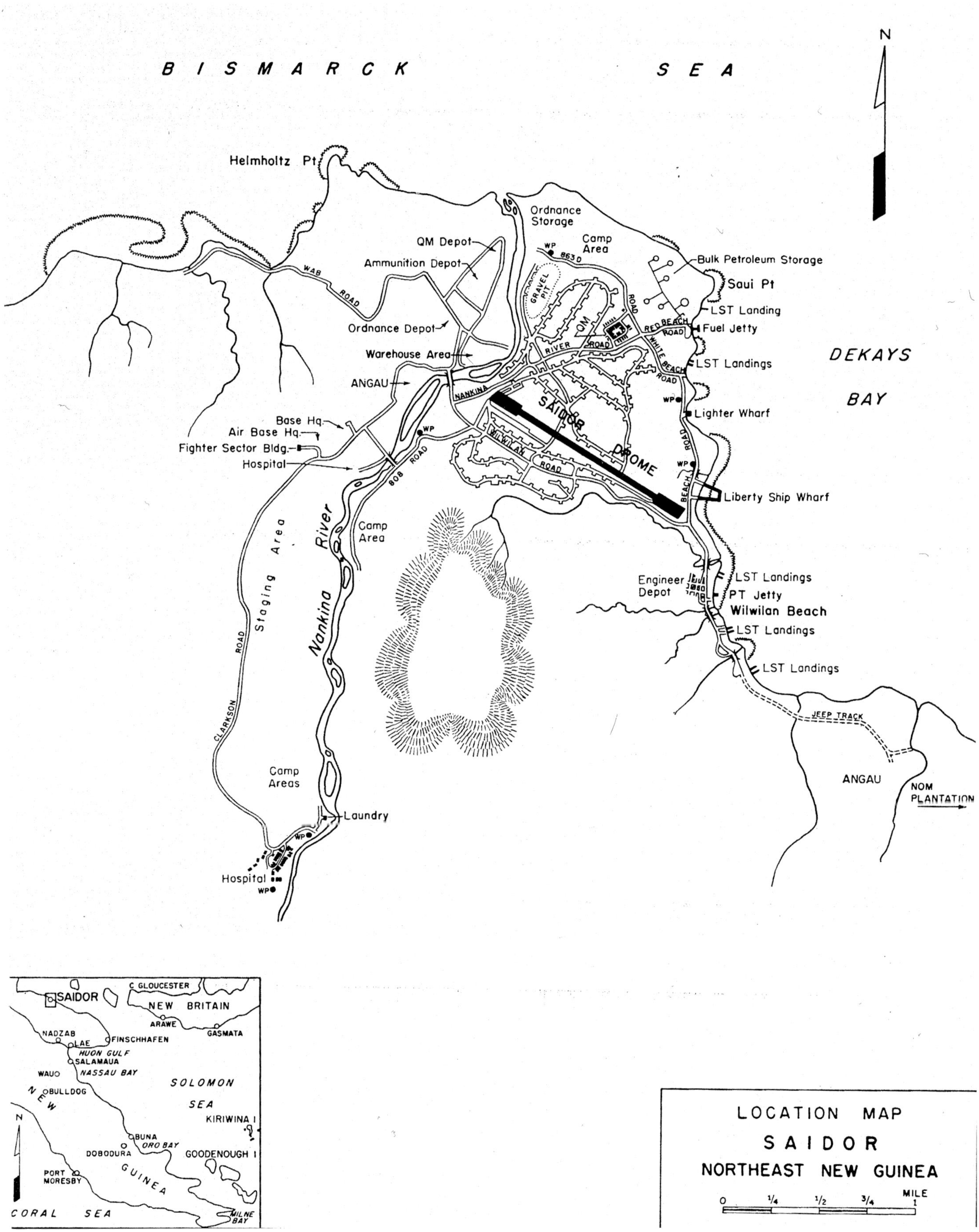
B I S M A R C K S E A
N
Helmholtz Pt
Ordnance Storage
Camp Area
QM Depot
Ammunition Depot
WAB ROAD
GRAVEL PIT
Bulk Petroleum Storage
Saui Pt
LST Landing
Fuel Jetty
RED BEACH
WHITE BEACH
Ordnance Depot
Warehouse Area
RIVER ROAD
LST Landings
DEKAYS BAY
ANGAU
NANKINA
SAIDOR DROME
Lighter Wharf
Base Hq.
Air Base Hq.
Fighter Sector Bldg.
Hospital
808 ROAD
WILWILAN ROAD
BEACH ROAD
Liberty Ship Wharf
Camp Area
Staging Area
Nankina River
Engineer Depot
LST Landings
PT Jetty
Wilwilan Beach
LST Landings
LST Landings
CLARKSON ROAD
JEEP TRACK
Camp Areas
ANGAU
NOM PLANTATION
Laundry
Hospital
SAIDOR
C GLOUCESTER
NEW BRITAIN
ARAWE
GASMATA
NADZAB
LAE
FINSCHHAFEN
HUON GULF
SALAMAUA
WAUO
NASSAU BAY
SOLOMON SEA
BULLDOG
NEW GUINEA
KIRIWINA I
BUNA
ORO BAY
DOBODURA
GOODENOUGH I
PORT MORESBY
CORAL SEA
MILNE BAY
LOCATION MAP
SAIDOR
NORTHEAST NEW GUINEA
0 1/4 1/2 3/4 MILE 1

of 29 March, B-24 staging through Saidor despite poor weather dropped 10 tons of fragmentation and delayed action bombs in the vicinity of the three Hollandia Dromes with good results.

A group of light bombers was transferred from Dobodura to the newly established Saidor Drome in April which put the entire 5BC medium and light bomber force within range of Hollandia from Nadzab, Gusap, and now Saidor. So, by April, despite bad flying weather which took its toll, the Fifth Air Force had gained air superiority over Hollandia and exercised it. Saidor proved the value of engineer construction units and their construction of advanced bases that steadily moved forward during a mission on 16 April. On that mission a coordinated formation of heavy, medium, and light bombers, escorted by fighters, made an attack which destroyed fixed defenses in the Humboldt Bay area. On the return trip, however, the formation ran into heavy low clouds and heavy rain and more than 30 of the aircraft headed for Saidor, which was the nearest airdrome. Flight patterns were ignored by the aircraft which had only enough gasoline for direct approaches as they converged over the runway. One P-38, landing on one end of the runway, met a B-24 coming in from the opposite end and literally leaped over it. However, an F-5 (Photo P-38) and a B-25 collided in the middle of the runway as did a P-38 and an F-7 (Photo B-24) but all the other aircraft seeking refuge at Saidor made safe landings and successfully reached their home bases later.

In addition to its strategic location, and the subsequent bombing operations launched from its airdrome, Saidor served as a staging and supply area for elements of the 32[nd] Division which had participated in its capture. However, by June 1945, succeeding bases had been established far forward of Saidor, and the sub-base located there was consolidated with Base F at Finschhafen.

5FC units based on Saidor included:

**348FG:** 340FS (P-47) from Finschhafen on 13 March 1944 to Wakde on 26 May 1944f
**348FG:** 341FS (P-47) from Finschhafen on 27 March 1944 to Wakde on 22 May 1944
**348FG:** 340FS (P-47) from Finschhafen on 13 March 1944 to Wakde on 26 May 1944
**348FG:** HQ from Finschhafen on 27 March 1944 to Wakde on ? May 1944
**348FG:** 342FS (P-47) from Finschhafen on 27 March 1944 to Wakde on 22 May 1944
**58FG:** 310FS (P-47) from Dobodura on 2 April 1944 to Noemfoor on 30 August 1944
**58FG:** HQ & 69FS from Dobodura on 3 April 1944 to Noemfoor on 20 August 1944
**71 TRG:** 82TRS (P-39) from Dobodura on 5 April 1944 to Biak/Owi on 12 June 1944
**58FG:** 311FS (P-47) from Dobodura on 5 April 1944 to Noemfoor on 30 August 1944

**8 March 1944: 49FG**

Once the Japanese moved to Hollandia, poor weather and the 800 mile round trip there made it difficult for 49er CO Campbell's short range Warhawks and Thunderbolts to find any enemy contact. Even the sweeps to the staging air strips at Tadji 100 miles west of Wewak were out 49er fighter range. So the Flying Knights bid their time consigned to high altitude escort where they could employ their great weight and horsepower to advantage. No fighter in the Pacific, not even the Lightnings, could outrun a Thunderbolt in a full power dive. Nonetheless, ex-Lightning pilots disliked their huge new fighter even though 348 FG CO, Col. Neel Kearby had accumulated 22 kills in his P-47 and had been challenging Bong and

**Capt. Arland Stanton** (right with Gerald Johnson) was credited with his sixth victory. (AAF)

Lynch to be the first to the magic 26 victory mark. The Flying Knight P-47s were predominantly production model D-4 types which weighed six and half tons when fully loaded and even after burning off fuel, they could not effectively maneuver in the heavy wet tropical air. The exhaust from their aft-mounted supercharger blew out directly on to the tail wheel which swelled and eventually shredded on the Marston mat. The main gear tires also blew out much too often in the oppressive 100F degree heat of Ramu Valley. One unhappy P-47 pilot lamented: "If the Army engineers built a runway all the way around the world, Republic would build an airplane that needed every foot of it to take off."

**8 March 1944: 49FG/7FS**

Finally, air reconnaissance found that enemy planes and shipping were again staging at Wewak despite the efforts of 5[th] Bomber Command. The Japanese merchant fleet was able to reach Wewak and land a substantial reinforcement of thousands of men and tens of thousands of tons of supplies and equipment to repulse the Allied invasion. At 1230 Squadron CO, Capt. Arland Stanton led 18 P-40s in four flights and escorted two A-20 Squadrons on a routine armed reconnaissance of the Wewak complex. They arrived at 1400 at 1,500 feet where Stanton found a lone Oscar flying over the foothills just south of Wewak village at 3,500 feet in 8/10s cloud. Stanton climbed at full throttle but lost speed on the way up and the Oscar went into a 90 degree diving turn behind a cloud. Stanton followed and exited the cloud unseen directly behind the Oscar and fired at 300 yards and hit the wings and canopy but continued to climb. Stanton and his Wingman both fired and got more hits and the Oscar pilot turned sharply right and down. Stanton followed and fired more short bursts that finally set it on fire and the Oscar crashed in flames in a steep dive for Stanton's sixth victory.

**8 March 1944: Death of Lynch**

Lynch was assigned to a unit under Gen. Paul Wurtsmith, who commanded the 49FG with Lynch as Wurtsmith's Operations Officer and Bong named as his Assistant. In his book, *Dick Bong,* Gen. Kenney suggested Lynch was determined to become the top ace. Lynch led the 39FS with 16 kills when Kenney sent him stateside on leave. When Lynch returned, he needed four kills to catch Kearby and five to catch Bong and all three were the "buzz" in the southwest Pacific in February 1944. Kenney wrote: "Tommy Lynch was anxious to go after the top score…I told him to take it easy, don't get in a race with anybody. He left for New Guinea promising to behave himself."

After celebrating Lynch's promotion to Lieutenant Colonel the night before, Lynch and Bong returned to the Tadji area and when they couldn't lure any Japanese aerial opposition they descended to Aitape Harbor where they strafed three Luggers cruising along the coast and carrying fuel drums. Lynch led Bong on the second firing pass and just as the two P-38s pulled up at only 20 feet, Bong saw Lynch's nose section was destroyed and the right engine began to smoke. Lynch pulled up to 2,500 feet and radioed Bong that he was alright and Bong told Lynch that his engine was now on fire and that he should bail out. Lynch immediately headed for the shore and as he approached it, his P-38 either exploded into a ball of fire and consumed Lynch or "Colonel Lynch was seen trying to get out of the left side of the cockpit. Finally at about 100 feet the whole canopy flew off and Colonel Lynch was seen to fall out of the plane. The plane exploded below Colonel Lynch. His parachute came out of the pack but did not have time to open." Bong flew around the area but did not see any sign of a parachute and returned to Gusap; having to feather his engine before landing. The latter parachute version is the "for the first time the official summary of what happened" according to Carl Bong in his book, *Ace of Aces: The Dick Story* while the former explosion version is taken from Bong's ICR.

Newly promoted **Lt. Col. Thomas Lynch** (20 victories) was KIA while strafing luggers in Aitape Harbor. (AAF)

The reason that Bong had to feather his engine is that there is speculation that the luggers may have been "Flak Ships" which were heavily armed and would lure unsuspecting fighters down to strafe the normally vulnerable targets. Bong's Crew Chief reported that his fighter had 87 holes with an oil line cut in one engine.

Kenney was worried about the affect that Lynch's death would have on Bong and to give him time to pull himself together he immediately sent him to Brisbane to ferry a new P-38 back to Nadzab. However, Bong did not go to Brisbane but instead flew eight more combat missions before going there on 20 March and then returned to Nadzab on the 31st to continue to chase Rickenbacker's record. Bong would shoot down 27 enemy aircraft before being sent stateside on a 15 state publicity tour. During the tour Bong flew into Pittsburgh on 12 May to visit Lynch's wife Rosemary and into the then Allentown-Bethlehem Airport to personally tell Lynch's mother Alice the details of her son's death.

**11-16 March 1944: Wewak**

From 9 to 16 March over 1,600 tons of bombs and nearly a million rounds of ammunition eliminated the But, Dagua, Wewak, and Borum airstrips so that on the 16th there were no targets left at these Dromes. The runways were full of deep craters and hundreds of wrecked and burned out aircraft littered these airdromes. During the six days of the attack 68 Japanese fighters were shot down while about a 100 destroyed on the ground. Hollandia now became the major enemy target.

**11 March 1944: 49FG**

When more enemy aircraft reached Wewak the 5AF heavy bombers attacked them for four successive days during which B-24s dropped 1,000 pound bombs that pocked the four Wewak airfields with immense craters and the American escorts decimated the outnumbered newcomers. Lt.Col. David Campbell led an uneventful early morning 49er escort and would miss the noontime dogfight over Wewak where the Thunderbolts of the newly refitted 35FG and the veteran 348 FG, scored almost two dozen kills.

**11 March 1944: 348FG/340FS**

On this day the 348th fought its last combat mission before the Group moved to Saidor and the 340FS would record its best day of combat in the war. The 340FS sent off 18 P-47s at 0845 under Maj. Hervey Carpenter for a late morning sweep of the Wewak area. They arrived at Wewak at 1015 and after patrolling at 25,000 to 27,000 feet for 25 minutes; White Flight Leader had mechanical problems and was escorted back to base by his Wingman. At 1045 the Japanese arrived in force and for the next 20 minutes the P-47s engaged in a savage dogfight with 30 to 35 Oscars, Tonys, and few of the new Ki-44 Tojos.

Carpenter made first sighting of two silver enemy fighters taking off from But (or Dagua) Airfields heading out to sea but they were too far out of range to attack. Then eight more enemy fighters were called out flying at about 1,000 feet over the sea but Carpenter couldn't see these fighters and sent his second flight after them and said he would follow. Carpenter's Wingman, 1Lt. Harry Quant, then called out six more enemy fighters that had been at 23,000 feet and followed Carpenter down to 8,000 feet. Carpenter saw three Oscars at 3,000 feet and decided to use his excess diving speed to attack them and then zoom back up at the higher enemy fighters. Carpenter dove and shot off pieces of the Oscar but was unable to press his attack as the Oscar disappeared (it was later confirmed to have crashed by 1Lt. Lloyd Zaage). Carpenter then turned into the second Oscar which had turned into him and got solid hits (it was confirmed to have exploded by 1Lt. Myron Hnatio). Carpenter climbed from 2,000 to 6,000 feet where he saw a P-47 being fired on by an enemy fighter and intervened and scared it off. As Carpenter continued his climb his fighter was shot at from behind and he dove to escape. His Element Leader, 1Lt. William Bennett came to the rescue and shot the attacking Tojo down. By this time Carpenter's flights had completely separated and he concentrated on returning back to base at 500 feet but was bounced by a Tony, head on from above. Carpenter pulled up and fired a short burst that drove off his attacker. As he passed between Manshu and Newak Islands he was followed by two Oscars and a Tony but as he was slowly pulling away from them his port wing was hit by an explosive 20mm shell and caught fire only two feet from his cockpit and was drawing flame from his exhaust into the hole, burning his tire. Once he was free from the Japanese he throttled back to keep the fire under control but meanwhile, his radio, airspeed, hydraulic, and water injection systems malfunctioned. Carpenter to make a successful wheels up crash landing with two Oscar victories to give him three total.

1Lt. William Bennett and Wingman, 1Lt. Floyd Meyer, saw what they at first believed to be two P-47s until they started an attack on 340FS CO, Carpenter. Bennett raced in to get the Tojo off his Leader's tail. As the Tojo pulled up, Bennett fired from 300 yards and Carpenter was greatly relieved when he saw his former attacker zoom up and then crash into the sea. Bennett then found three Oscars on his tail and ran for base.

1Lt. Lyle Dowsett was leading the White Flight at 22,000 feet over Wewak when he sighted about 15 Japanese fighters in two plane flights ranging in altitude from 25,000 feet to the deck. 1Lt. Andrew Lytle was flying as Dowsett's Wingman when he saw six Oscars about 2,000 feet below. Dowsett dove on one and fired a short burst and Oscar made a sharp turn to port when its wing burst into flame and tore off for Dowsett's third victory. Lytel and Dowsett rejoined and attacked two Tonys and Lytel shot one down with a long burst. After White Flight Leader Dowsett, made an

**1Lt. Myron Hnatio** (left with Crew Chief) became an ace with his Zero shoot down. (AFAA)

**1Lt. Richard Fleischer** shot down two Oscars to become an ace. (AFAA)

**1Lt. Michael Dikovitsky** claimed his third victory. (AFAA)

**1Lt. Lloyd Zaage** claimed his last of two total victories. (AAF)

**Maj. Hervey Carpenter** scored his second of three victories. (AAF)

**Capt. William Chase** got his only victory. (AAF)

initial attack on two Oscars, White Second Element Leader, 1Lt. Gerald Woodruff, and Wingman, 1Lt. Thomas Barber, followed Dowsett's attack in a steep diving port turn and Barber arrived in time to shoot down an Oscar closing on Dowsett's tail (for his second and last victory). Woodruff's Oscar broke to the right but another Oscar approached Woodruff head on and he fired a two second burst that hit the Oscar and Barber confirmed Woodruff's only victory. Woodruff spotted another Oscar on the deck but lost him overland and returned to base.

Blue Flight Leader, 1Lt. Richard Fleischer, saw an Oscar break out of formation and dive toward his flight just as they dropped their tanks. Fleischer turned to starboard to meet it head on and fired a long burst into its belly and engine. The Oscar broke left and plunged straight down but while its pilot was able to bail out; his chute did not open. Fleischer was then bounced by three Oscars but easily pulled away to safety. Fleischer's second attack of the combat was from astern on an Oscar flying about 1,000 feet off the water. He fired a long burst and the Oscar snapped a half roll and crashed into the water west of Kairiru Island. It was Fleischer's fifth victory to make him an ace.

1Lt. Myron Hnatio, with Wingman 1Lt. William Carter, was leading the second element of Blue Flight and saw six Zeros coming in from the west and circling north. Immediately the Americans dropped their tanks and made their first pass at the Zeros approaching head on. Hnatio made a sharp turn to get on a Zero's tail and fired a 30 degree deflection lead but missed low. He pulled his fighter into a tighter turn and hit the Zero's engine and then followed firing and getting hits from dead astern and Carter saw it fall into the sea two to three miles off But Airdrome and Hnatio became an ace.

1Lt. William Chase, Yellow Flight Leader, made a pass on an Oscar that made a climbing right turn and fired a long burst before it passed out of his sights. As Chase pulled up to 7,000 feet he saw the Oscar smoking heavily and then crash near a mall island off But Airdrome. After Chase had scored his only victory he made two more passes but their evasive tactics prevented him from getting a good shot on them. A Tony got on his tail and put a hole in his elevator and Chase, running low on fuel, ran for Saidor. 1Lt. Michael Ditkovitsky, Wingman to Capt. William Chase of Yellow Flight, had joined 1Lt. Fleischer on the return back to Saidor as they were low on fuel when they saw seven Oscars at 500 feet over Wewak. Ditkovitsky dove on one Oscar at 4 o'clock and when it turned sharply to the right he fired a 60 degree deflection shot and it crashed into the sea. He was attacked by three Oscars and fled for home with his third victory.

1Lt. Lloyd Zaage, Element Leader of Yellow Flight dove on a lone Oscar in the But Drome landing pattern and downed him before he landed with a burst from 1,000 feet astern. Zaage climbed to 6,000 feet where he saw another Oscar dive on a P-47 and dove and fired and exploded the Oscar and Zaage barely pulled up in time to avoid crashing into the sea but this victory was not witnessed and not confirmed. Zaage was running low on fuel and descended to 4,000 feet to head home. Suddenly he heard bullets hitting his fighter and his engine began to run so rough that he couldn't read his instrument panel through the vibration. He dove to get away and pulled out near the water and when he tried to trim his fighter he looked over to see a black Tony only a wing length away. The Japanese pilot "looked at me for a long time and probably saw that I was hurt and got on my tail and proceeded to put more holes in my plane." Zaage's P-47 was so badly damaged that he was unable to make any evasive maneuvers except to skid. After awhile the Tony stopped firing perhaps because he ran out of ammunition or supposed the American pilot wouldn't make it back to base. The enemy pilot joined two Oscars overhead and left Zaage to limp back to Saidor. He flew only a few feet off the water, and with only ten gallons of fuel remaining Zaage managed to make a wheels down landing at Sailor.

The 340FS had their best day of the war claiming 15 victories for three damaged P-47s all of which landed safely. Maj. Hervey Carpenter commented on the day's combat:

> "The Japanese pilots were very aggressive and determined. It seems that they had a patrol out to sea about 23,000 feet when we arrived over the target and were waiting for us to lose our advantage of altitude by attacking the fighters on the deck, whose primary mission was to draw us down. Their teamwork was excellent. I am of the opinion that we all mixed it up too much with the enemy, three of our ships being damaged as a consequence. However, after committing ourselves on the first attack it was impossible to do otherwise. Another point of interest was the fact that on several occasions the enemy fighters passed up our planes which had no white tails or white markings. This ties in with the statement of my Element Leader who saw two enemy planes with wings similar to a P-47, which he believed to be Tojos. The enemy might have mistaken our unmarked P-47s for friendly Tojos."

**11 March 1944: 35FG/40FS/41FS**

40FS

Capt. Edwin Schneider was leading 16 P-47s during a mid afternoon area top cover over Wewak at 23,000 feet. Just as they were about to head home at 1400 Schneider spotted two Tonys on the deck at 8 o'clock low and started to dive after them. When his tanks failed to release he ordered 1Lt. Robert Yaeger's Blue Flight to go after them. Yaeger caught them near But Airdrome about a mile out to sea. Yaeger exploded a Tony from the rear as its pilot bailed out. Yaeger was at only 100 feet over the water and making a starboard climbing turn when he saw a Tony at 4 o'clock low turning to the right and shot it down. Yaeger turned left and saw a P-47 (1Lt. John Garrity) chasing another Tony and followed. The Tony made a turn to the left and then a vertical reverse that Yaeger followed and fired and the Tony went into a high speed stall and crashed into the sea. Yaeger saw an Oscar heading for the shore and caught it over the tree tops but its skilled pilot made "excellent evasive maneuvers to the left and right, and flew so low that he was below the taller trees, flying around them. I had a hard time hitting him." But Yaeger did hit the Tony and became an ace. Yaeger's Second Element Leader, 1Lt. Robert Steffy, claimed a Tony probable. Yaeger's victories were to be the 40FS' last until 10 October 1944 when Capt. Charles Clark shot an Oscar over Borneo.

**Capt. Robert Yeager** scored three victories to become an ace. These victories would be the last for the 40FS until 10 October. (AFAA)

41FS

The 41FS was assigned the midday escort of B-24s and area cover over Wewak with 16 P-47s in four flights. At 1250 the Thunderbolts were at 16,000 feet when 12 bandits in two formations were spotted at 1 o'clock flying at 2,000 feet above, flying in the opposite direction. The 41FS flights dropped their tanks as the Japanese attacked the last two flights which were the highest but allowed the first two flights to gain altitude.

As the dozen Japanese fighters swooped down, Yellow Flight Leader, 1Lt. Emery Lischka, ordered tanks to be dropped but his tanks did not release. Wingman, 2Lt. James Scott, dropped his and turned toward a Zero at 11 o'clock and 3,000 feet below. Scott then saw an Oscar on Lischka's tail and turned into it and fired until it went down in flames. Scott saw tracers fly past his wing from an Oscar on his tail and dove out to sea at 7,000 feet "pushing everything to the firewall" but could not gain on his pursuer. Scott remembered a tip he had heard to increase speed and fired all his ammunition and his lighter fighter raced to 22,000 feet and 30 miles out to sea and lost the Oscar. Meanwhile, Lischka flew out to sea to work on releasing his tanks and was finally successful and returned to the battle at 12,000 feet. Lischka saw a P-47 on the tail of an Oscar and an Oscar on the tail of that P-47. He fired on the latter Oscar from far out of range and drove it away from the P-47. As he pulled up Lischka saw an Oscar in a gentle turn two miles from Manshu Island and dove on it from 4 o'clock. As he closed the Oscar went into a tight right turn and Lischka was able to fire a short burst into its cockpit. The enemy pilot rolled his fighter on its back and Split-S'd. As Lischka followed it down, the Oscar began to smoke heavily and headed for the water and crashed. As he leveled off Lischka saw an Oscar make head on pass toward him and before passing each other the enemy pilot broke left and Lischka right and both made a 360 to make another head on pass at each other. But as Lischka approached, the Japanese pilot lost his nerve; broke off and dove away. Lischka climbed to 10,000 feet and saw five P-47s about to return to base and as he started to follow them he saw two Oscars on the deck just south of Boram Airfield. One started to climb at him and Lischka fire a short burst from 400 yards and the Oscar broke off sharply to starboard and streaked away along the coast and Lischka headed for home with his only victory. 1Lt. Douglas Parsons, #4 man in Yellow Flight, saw four to six bogeys at 3 o'clock about 1,000 yards out. Several bogies turned up toward Parson but could not turn inside him as he turned down and picked up 350IAS and then chandelled up to 14,000 feet. As he leveled off he saw an Oscar closing on a P-47 and Parsons rushed to a front quarter attack from its 2 o'clock. He fired from 200 yards into the Oscar's line of flight and it rolled over and spiraled slowly down. Parsons rolled, climbing to port to clear his tail and headed south where he saw two Oscars completing a head on attack. Parsons headed for one that headed for him in a turn which put it at 90 degrees to him. Parsons fired a blind deflection shot at 300 yards as the Oscar rolled left and then he fired another blind deflection shot as the Oscar passed under his nose. The Oscar turned tightly and escaped. As he flew on, Parsons saw an Oscar chasing another P-47 and fired on it from very long range which was enough to scare it off and then Parsons left for Gusap with his first of three victories. F/O Albert Koen, Second Element Leader of Yellow Flight, saw four or six enemy fighters coming at him at 90 degrees to starboard but was unable to get a shot as he turned into them. He saw Lischka and Scott dive away and he dove toward Muschu Island and saw three Tonys trying to get on the tail of a Thunderbolt. He tried to fire two volleys from out of range but failed to drive them away. Koen continued his attack and fired a long burst at a Tony that still had its wing tanks attached. Koen started to fire and the Tony pilot dropped the tanks as the Tony was hit and its landing gear dropped and it trailed away for Koen's only victory.

Red Flight Leader, 1Lt. Edward Hoyt, made a climbing pass at an Oscar but had to break off because his air speed was too low after climbing. He continued climbing out to sea and returned after he had gained altitude and airspeed but had lost his Wingman. He returned to combat and made a pass at on Oscar at 10 o'clock and slightly lower but did not give enough lead and missed. Hoyt then spotted another Oscar lower and at 9 o'clock and lead it so that it flew through the stream of .50s and it broke down and away and finally crashed into an island. As he was watching his victim, Hoyt saw a P-47 approach but then it opened fire on him almost out of range at 1,000 yards. Hoyt hit the deck with a full throttle in a steep diving turn; trying not to turn too tightly so not to kill airspeed. Even though the P-47 reached 400 mph the Japanese fighter (Tojo?) gained and Hoyt went into a gradual climb to be able to bailout if necessary. When he looked back the enemy fighter was gone; perhaps out of ammunition.

1Lt. Lewis Barnes was the #3 man in Red Flight and followed Hoyt into the enemy fighters in a gradual climb after building up speed in a dive. The enemy fighters made a quick 180 degree turn which put them on the P-47's tails. The Americans dove to escape at 45 degrees to starboard. When Barnes looked around he saw an Oscar firing on Red #2 and then it turned to make another pass which allowed Barnes to get behind the Oscar. But then a Tony with its wing tank still attached fired on Barnes from 60-70 degrees lead but out of range. But Barnes continued his pass on the Oscar and fired a three second burst from dead astern seeing hits around the cockpit. The Oscar slowly rolled over onto its back and as it went into a steeper dive Barnes took one last short burst before pulling away from the closing Tony still on his tail. After escaping the Tony Barnes joined the lucky Red #2 and returned to base.

35FG Losses

The day was a costly one for the 35th as it lost three pilots, one from each squadron. 2Lt. John Garrity of the 40FS spun in over Wewak while in combat with a Tony. 2Lt. George Gaffney of the 41FS had engine problems over Wewak but landed at Saidor and after his fighter was repaired he took off but was never seen again. 1Lt. Gene Duncan of the 39FS crash landed in the water near the mouth of the Sepik River while returning from Wewak. His Wingman, 2Lt. Leroy Grosshuesch, although he was running low on fuel, circled the downed pilot in his life raft until nightfall. An intensive search the next day did not recover the pilot.

**Mid-March 1944: Air Battle over Hollandia**

As the campaign to secure the Admiralties was coming to a successful conclusion, MacArthur and Kenney focused on the next advance westward along the New Guinea coast. The Japanese had expected the next Allied advance to land at one of two of several places along the coast from west of Madang to the Hansa Bay area. MacArthur's earlier plans were to invade the Hansa Bay area but those plans had recently changed and he looked northwest to the Hollandia area of Dutch New Guinea. Hollandia was appealing because it offered the only combination of air and sea bases between Hansa and Geelvink Bays. Lying between Humboldt and Tanahmerah Bays, the immediate region was dominated by the 7,000 foot Cyclops Mountain, which paralleled the coast in steep cliffs but sloped off to a saddle-like basin surrounding Lake Sentani. In this basin the Japanese had built three airfields; Hollandia, Cyclops, and Sentani, which were joined to both Bays by an inadequate road system.

In close association with Hollandia Campaign, in both Japanese and Allied planning, was Aitape, situated 123 miles southeast of Hollandia, in Australian New Guinea. The Aitape Roads anchorage was sheltered by offshore islands and provided a fair weather anchorage. Eight miles southeast of Aitape, the Japanese had three airfields under construction at Tadji, of which one bomber strip had already become operational. Gen. Hatazo Adachi, Commander of the Japanese 18th Army was responsible for the defense of New Guinea and was certain that the next Allied move would be directed at the Hansa Bay-Wewak area and sent 70,000 troops to that (wrong) area. MacArthur estimated that Hollandia would be defended by about 13,500 troops but Adachi sent 6,000 more troops from Hollandia to Wewak at the last minute.

Air strength of the Japanese Navy had been greatly diminished by the fighting around Rabaul and Truk and all its carriers were now refitting in home waters or at Singapore. The Japanese Combined Fleet Headquarters had retreated from beleaguered Truk to Palau and future naval plans were to be centered on the super battleship *Musashi*. The only operational naval aircraft remaining on New Guinea were reconnaissance aircraft so the air defense of New Guinea was to be placed on the Fourth Air Army. On 8 March the strength of this force was 12 Flying Regiments (Groups), two separate squadrons, and an air transport unit. It was reported that 319 operational planes were in service on 3 March but by the time of the coming invasion of Hollandia on 15 April only 25% of these were still operational.

The main 5AF striking force was based at Nadzab with its six all-weather runways and one grass strip and 536 paved dispersal spaces. Since it was 515 miles from Nadzab to Hollandia; Gusap and Saidor were to be the chief fighter bases to cover the Hollandia operation which still were not within the normal 350 mile combat range of the P-38. To cover the Hollandia invasion there would be two possible solutions: to depend upon carrier-based air cover until an airfield was secured and/or to extend the range of 5AF fighters. Kenney's plans for attacking Hollandia were based upon deceiving the Japanese as to the range of his attacking aircraft. First, in mid-March, Wewak would be destroyed by a maximum effort by all available units. The deception involved the new longer-range J- model P-38s that carried up to 120 gallons of extra fuel internally in leading edge tanks in the wings. By 11 March 58 J-models had arrived and another 37 were scheduled to arrive in Brisbane. Meanwhile, 56 of the older P-38s already in New Guinea were sent back to Townsville to have tanks added from modification kits that had arrived there. Of the P-38s remaining in New Guinea only 37 could be converted and specially trained service crews were sent to Nadzab to convert them. Firm orders were given to all P-38 pilots with the new fuel tanks that under no circumstances were they to fly beyond Tadji and while at Tadji, even if engaged in combat, no P-38 was to remain there any more than 15 minutes before heading home. Kenney's intention was to have the Japanese believe that they were safe at Hollandia from the P-38 and they would then import all available aircraft. Allied reconnaissance indicated that the Japanese were so confident in their safety that they were dispersing new aircraft on the three Hollandia airfields.

The first phase of Kenney's attack was the eradication of Wewak's four airfields: Boram, Wewak, Dagua, and But. Wewak was the headquarters of the Japanese 18th Army and the 4th Air Army. By 11 March the weather over Wewak had entered the transitional interval between the northeast and the southeast monsoons that permitted the 5AF to begin a sustained attack four days earlier than had been predicted. The campaign began on 11 March and continued until 27 March with missions flown every day except 20 March when light and medium bombers needed a respite from their hectic schedule and on 24 March when bad weather prevented all missions. In this period the 5th Air Force flew 911 fighter sorties to cover the bombers and 500 sorties by B-24s, 488 by B-25s, and 555 by the A-20s. Bomber and fighter pilots found that by flying between 10,000 to 13,000 feet they were relatively safe from enemy AA batteries as Japanese heavy AA guns were too slow to track at this altitude range and the light batteries could not reach them.

**12 March 1944: 49FG/7FS/8FS/9FS**

After a 1010 take off two 49er Warhawk squadrons flew close escort for A-20s which bombed and strafed Japanese bivouacs at the Brandi Plantation. Lt.Col. David Campbell's 9FS Flying Knight P-47s flew top cover while Capt. Arland Stanton's 14 7FS Screamin' Demon Warhawks flew in spread formation from 8,000 to 12,000 feet on the A-20s right flank and Capt. Robert McHale's 16 8FS Black Sheep P-40s flew on the A-20's left flank at the same altitude.

The four Wewak area airfields (**Dagua** shown) came under attack from 11 to 27 March in a concentrated effort to finally eradicate these fields. (AAF)

7FS

At 1230 Mission and Blue Flight Leader, Capt. Arland Stanton and Wingman; 1Lt. Jack Langenberg, led 18 P-40s on an escort of A-20 two squadrons to Wewak and arrived over Brandi Plantation about one minute before the bombers. While flying under the clouds at 1,500 feet along the coastal mountains southwest of Wewak, Stanton's Wingman spotted a lone Oscar above at 3,500 feet. The enemy fighter was positioning itself to make a head on pass at the A-20s. Stanton called to drop tanks and climbed and as the P-40s gained altitude but lost speed and the Oscar turned 90 degrees and ducked into a cloud. Stanton and his Wingman followed through the cloud and when they emerged they found themselves only 300 yards behind the Oscar. Stanton fired and hit the wings and cockpit and continued to fire as the enemy pilot climbed slightly and then turned down to starboard. Stanton fired a few short bursts and had to break off at 800 feet above the water as the Oscar crashed into the water about 20 miles from Wewak. 1Lt. William Ferris was Blue Flight Second Element Leader with, 1Lt. Laurine Suggs as his Wingman. Suggs saw two Oscars and followed them down into the clouds but lost the first (Stanton's?) but caught the other on the other side of the cloud. The Oscar pilot dove toward the water where another P-40 made a pass on it in a tight climbing port turn. The P-40 was firing but missing badly as the Oscar was climbing off the water. Ferris made a head on pass on this Oscar as it continued turning left and as he turned Ferris was able to get behind the Oscar and fired a good burst as it leveled out. Suggs was inside Ferris and also shooting but the Oscar made a short port turn which Ferris was unable to follow. Suggs followed as the Oscar made a sharp left turn into a high speed stall and "dished out" of the stall and mushed into the water for Suggs' only victory. Ferris and Suggs then climbed to 4,000 feet where they fired on another Oscar as did three Warhawks from another squadron. The Oscar pilot outmaneuvered these P-40s by making a sharp left turn and then leveled off but directly in front of Ferris. As Ferris fired a long burst another P-40 flew directly in front of Ferris and fired a short burst. The enemy pilot pulled up and Ferris continued firing and the Oscar smoked heavily from its right side. Its engine quit and Ferris began to rapidly overrun and as he passed over the Oscar turned left and headed toward Nightingale Bay for Ferris' only victory which he capped off when he pulled up and "shot a Nip out of his parachute off Sand Beach just as he hit the water."

**1Lt. Laurine Suggs** was credited with his only victory of the war. (AAF)

White Flight led by 1Lt. Louis Martin with Wingman, 1Lt. William Minto, and Second Element Leader, 1Lt. Lemuel Pollack and distinguished HQ Wingman, Lt.Col. J.A. Wilson, were flying over Brandi Plantation when two Zeros crossed in front of Martin. Pollack took a 30 degree deflection shot and then pulled up and then back down to place him dead astern. He fired a burst that started it smoking and a large piece fell off. The enemy pilot pulled into a loop and bailed out and Pollack "put in another burst for good measure" to insure his only victory.

Red Flight led by 1Lt. James Chandler, with Wingman, 2Lt. Robert Decker, and Second Element Leader, 1Lt. James O'Neill, saw a lone Oscar below at 5,000 feet and Chandler fired a short burst first but the enemy pilot went into a vertical reverse and lost Chandler. O'Neill "jumped on the Nip's tail" and fired a short burst but the Oscar pilot went into a tight right turn which O'Neill could not follow and pulled up. He dove on the Oscar again and made another pass without apparent result and pulled up again while two other P-40s made passes at it. The Oscar pilot went into a sharp bank just above the water that put O'Neill on its tail. O'Neill fired and the enemy pilot began a left turn and O'Neill stayed inside him until his wingtip hit the water and the Oscar disintegrated as it catapulted over the waves and crashed and O'Neill's first victory was confirmed by Wingman, 2Lt. Nicanor Zuniga.

**Capt. Arland Stanton** claimed his seventh victory. (AFAA)

**1Lt. Lemuel Pollock** was also credited with his only victory of the war. (AAF)

8FS

At 1010 8FS Red Flight approached the target area at 8,000 feet and spotted enemy aircraft flying east at 7,500 feet and the Flight dropped their belly tanks and dove to the attack. Red Flight Leader, Capt. Robert McHale, got on an Oscar's tail and fired from very close range and saw explosions along its fuselage and in its right wing and the wing tank which hadn't been dropped began to smoke. But McHale had to settle for a probable as he pulled up to 4,000 feet and saw another Oscar below him. McHale dove astern and closed as the enemy pilot began a right turn when McHale fired and continued firing a long burst as the Oscar turned left to escape. McHale's bullets had found their mark and the Oscar started smoking, caught fire, and crashed into Dove Bay. 2Lt. Burton Hall was McHale's Wingman and followed him into his attack. McHale approached the Oscar from directly astern and Hall was to McHale's right. McHale fired and pulled up to the left and the Oscar then turned into Hall who made a pass from the rear right quarter to astern. Hall's volley caused smoke and flames from the Oscar's engine and hits on the cockpit. Hall followed the Oscar until it approached Boram Strip and turned away to avoid AA fire. 1Lt. William Runey saw the Oscar crash to confirm Hall's only victory. Hall confirmed 1Lt. Robert Sweeney's only victory of the war Oscar and then returned to base.

Red Element Leader, 1Lt. Averette Lee, saw a lone Oscar off his port wing 400 feet below and turned into it and fired but the Oscar pilot outmaneuvered Lee and he missed his shot. When Lee banked up he saw that McHale had fired on the Oscar and had it smoking. Lee turned to slow down and turned on the tail of a Zero and closed on the water and fired until the enemy pilot reached Cape Moem where he pulled up sharply trying to run Lee into the trees. Lee managed to pull up and fired until he reached the coast where he pulled up to avoid any AA fire and as he did a wing over he saw where the Zero had crashed in the middle of the Peninsula for his second and last victory.

At 1120 Blue Flight Leader, Capt. Elferd Elofson, was off Moran Point at 8,000 feet when he spotted 20 Oscars in a single formation at 6,000 feet high. Elofson ordered the tanks to be dropped and Elofson and Wingman, 1Lt. Marion Felts attacked two other Oscars coming in from above while his second element of 1Lt. Donald Meuten and Wingman 1Lt. Wayne Howard dove on two Oscars below. As they chased the two Oscars one broke away and Elofson and Felts took the one that chandelled into them. Elofson turned into it and fired without result. Felts fired and the Oscar pulled up into a loop on fire and soon the pilot bailed out for Felts' second victory. Elofson notes in his ICR that they did not strafe the parachuting pilot. They then saw two P-40s "working" an Oscar on deck and saw the Warhawks "seem" pull away. Elofson and Felts dove on the Oscar and Elofson fired a 90 degree deflection shot that entered the cockpit and engine. Felts came in and fired a short burst and Elofson had to maneuver to avoid hitting his Wingman. Elofson winged over and saw the Oscar flatten out and hit the water, bounce off, and then drag a wing in the water as two more P-40s came in and fired as the Oscar nosed into the sea. Elofson emphatically states in his ICR that he claimed he destroyed this Oscar and was given credit for his second victory.

Blue Flight Second Element Leader, 1Lts. Meuten and Wingman Howard, dove on the two Oscars below that were turning up into them. Meuten followed one in a 360 turn and fired a 45 degree shot from 100 feet and the Oscar immediately rolled over on its back and went down. Meuten pulled straight up and went into a vertical roll when he saw an Oscar in a turn. Meuten went into an Immelmann and took a short burst as the enemy pilot went into a 360. Meuten skidded up fast and did an aileron roll and took a 45 degree deflection shot at about 200 feet. The Oscar snap rolled and exploded for Meutens' second victory of the day which made him an ace. Meuten took a short shot at an Oscar pulling up and saw a piece of cowling come off. The Oscar flew on and did an Immelmann only to be shot down by another P-40. He then saw a Zero out turn two P-40s and come directly into Meuten's sights for a "perfect" 90 degree shot. And fired a long burst at 300 feet blowing up the cockpit and then flames enveloped the entire fuselage. While the Zero was burning another P-40 came in and fired but Meuten "claimed him as already destroyed and Lt. Felts will confirm it" for his third victory of the day and the sixth and last of the war.

Yellow Flight #4 Wingman 1Lt. Robert Sweeney was unsuccessful in releasing his tank but he had to engage an Oscar coming straight up at him and fired without result. He then rolled over and joined four P-40s who were chasing an Oscar. The enemy pilot turned back into Sweeney who fired at 90 degrees and then a head on 30 degree burst and saw "smoke and possible flame." Sweeney had to pull up quickly to avoid a collision and broke away when he saw an Oscar with P-40s on its tail. The Oscar pulled up and Sweeney chased it over the shoreline and fired until it hit the water and Sweeney's only victory was confirmed by 1Lt. Hall.

9FS

Lt.Col. David Campbell's 8FS Flying Knights were shut out while having to stay at high cover.

**12 March 1944: 35FG/41FS**

The 35FG sent 17 P-47s of the 41FS under, Squadron CO, Capt. Francis Dubisher, on a mid-morning escort of two B-24 formations to Wewak. Red Flight and White Flight, 500 feet below, were flying at 19,000 feet and saw five enemy fighters at 15,000 feet heading toward the Liberators.

2Lt. Richard Murr, Red #4, first spotted the enemy fighters heading toward the B-24s and Red Flight Leader, Edward Hoyt, followed Dubisher on the five bandits and picked out an Oscar and fired a long burst that caused smoke and the Oscar rolled on its back and crashed. Meanwhile, Murr saw a Tony get on Hoyt's tail as Hoyt was chasing his Oscar. Murr was in position to intervene and got on the Tony's tail and fired into its canopy and wing root. The Tony's wing dipped and then it rolled over on its back and crashed for Murr's only victory. White Flight Leader, 1Lt. Homer Dellinger, was unable to drop his tank and Second Element Leader, 1Lt. Robert Johnson, took over with #2, 2Lt. Thomas Schatzman as his Wingman (there was no #4 man) and dove to the attack but in different directions. Johnson climbed back to 14,000 feet where he saw a lone Tony below and to port and fired a 45 degree deflection two second burst on the unsuspecting Japanese pilot. The Tony was hit in the cockpit and tail and a slowly turn into the water 10 miles off Dagua for Johnson's first of four victories. When Schatzman broke left he fired a 60 degree deflection on a Tony but the enemy pilot pulled up sharply with Schatzman climbing after him and got into firing position and hit its engine. Schatzman then pulled up and climbed straight ahead and away placing his P-47's gunsight on the escaping Tony for a long burst that caused black smoke. Schatzman's last pass got "very good hits" but he had to dive away from another Tony on his tail and headed home with his only victory.

**12 March 1943: 8FG/36FS**

The old P-38s that the 36th inherited were a problem. F/O Robert Ritchie of the 36FS crashed after take off from Dreger Drome when an engine on his aged P-38 began missing and he circled to land but the fighter went into a sideslip and crashed and its two full drop tanks exploded, killing Ritchie.

**13 March 1944: 49FG/7FS/9FS**

Eighteen P-40s of the 7FS and 9FS left Gusap at 1020 on an A-20 escort to Brandi Plantation and an hour later were over the target when they encountered enemy interceptors.

7FS

49er CO Lt.Col. David Campbell chose to fly with the 7FS Warhawks who seemed to have all the success at the lower altitudes. Campbell led White Flight with 49er Staff Capt. Robert McDaris as his Wingman and 1Lt. Joel Paris as his #3 man and 1Lt. John Haher as his Wingman. Five Oscars were seen at 10 o'clock high and the Flight started to climb and the Oscars went into a series of turns that put the P-40s behind them. Campbell picked out the #2 Oscar and fired a short burst getting hits on the starboard wing and the enemy pilot made a steep port turn and McDaris shot it down for his second and last victory to go with a probable and damaged. Campbell continued on with a stern attack on the Leader and fired two bursts; one from 300 yards and the next at 150 yards; hitting the right wing and fuselage. The Oscar began to smoke and chandelled to the right and its pilot bailed out for Campbell's fourth and last victory and

**Lt.Col. David Campbell** shot down an Oscar for his fourth and final victory. (AAF)

**Capt. Robert McDaris** shot down an Oscar for his second and last victory. (AAF)

**1Lt. Joel Paris** scored his first victory on his way to becoming an ace. (AFAA)

his first since leaving the 8FG. Paris saw five Oscars and called them out but his radio was it was not transmitting and only he and Haher turned toward them. Paris attacked the third Oscar that went into a 180 degree turn and started a loop. Paris closed and fired and the Oscar caught fire at the top of the loop and went into an inverted flat spin and its pilot bailed out for Paris' first of nine victories.

**Capt. Ralph Wandrey** scored his sixth and last victory. (AFAA)

9FS

At 0935 newly promoted Capt. Ralph Wandrey led 16 Flying Knight Thunderbolts in four flights at 16,000 feet over Wewak. At 1115 the Squadron was at 19,000 feet when 30 mixed enemy fighters in loose four ship formations appeared 3,000 feet overhead. The P-47s dropped their tanks and climbed into the attack. Wandrey dove on a Zero that "turned tail and ran" diving at a 60 degree angle. Wandrey's heavy Thunderbolt easily followed and he scored hits on its fuselage and right wing root. The Zero fell off on its right wing and dove into the ocean in an explosion for Wandrey's sixth and last victory.

Yellow Flight Leader, 1Lt. Bernard Krankowitz, was flying at 21,000 feet north of Boram Drome when he saw eight enemy fighters at 15,000 feet high. Krankowitz made an attack at 6 o'clock on an Oscar in a vertical dive; holding his fire until he was 100 yards behind; getting hits but the damaged Oscar Split-S'd and escaped. Blue Flight Leader, 1Lt. Jacob Crowder, was credited with a damaged Oscar. 2Lt. Frederick Helterline, Wingman to Green Flight Leader, 1Lt. Raymond Swift, snap rolled to get a Tony off his tail and reversed positions and his .50s started the Tony smoking badly but it was not seen to crash for a probable.

The Oscars scored two holes in Krankowitz' fuselage while 2Lt. William Huisman had his hydraulic lines cut by a single explosive round but both returned safely to Gusap without further incident. Wandrey's assessment of the Japanese pilots was: "The enemy pilots appeared to be experienced but unwilling to engage in combat. Their evasive tactics consisted of Split-S, dives, and rolls. They favored turns to the right."

**13 March 1944: 35FG/41FS**

At 1140 Capt. Francis Dubisher, 41FS CO, was leading 16 P-47s on a late morning escort of B-25s to Wewak and to provide top cover over Wewak. At 1140 Yellow Flight Leader called out an enemy fight on the water about a mile and a half off shore. Dubisher, as CO took the first shot and fired a short burst that sent the Oscar burst that caused the port wing to snap over violently. While in this position Dubisher fired again and the enemy crashed spectacularly into the water northwest of Dagua Airstrip. Dubisher's ICR stated: "It was so easy that I was afraid I was going to miss." Dubisher became an ace when he shot down this Oscar.

**13 March 1944: 421NFS**

It would not be until 13 March 1944 that the Squadron began to fly actual combat missions from Nadzab. These missions consisted mostly of daily early morning weather recon flights as far as Tadji for the 5FC which would use these weather reports to plan attack missions later that morning.

**14 March 1944: 49FG/9FS**

At 0930 Capt. Wallace Jordan's 9th Squadron escorted B-24s that again attacked Boram Airstrip and Brandi Plantation. At 1045 they reached Boram at 12,500 feet when they saw six bandits in a haphazard formation at 13,000 feet high. The Squadron dropped their belly tanks and climbed to the attack. Jordan made a head on climbing pass on an Oscar that was starting to dive on him. The Oscar pilot steepened his dive and passed directly in front of Jordan who pushed over slowly and fired getting hits on its engine and cockpit. The Oscar plunged burning furiously into the sea for Jordan's second victory and first in seven and a half months. 2Lt. Edward Howes was flying as Jordan's Wingman and after following Jordan through his victory Howes made several ineffective passes on other enemy fighters. He saw a lone Oscar and fired a long burst that hit its wings and fuselage and this Oscar was seen to crash. Red Flight Element Leader, 1Lt. Richard Kirkland was credited with an Oscar probable.

**14 March 1944: 35FG/41FS**

At 1105 16 P-47s of the 41FS led by 1Lt. Edward Hoyt were flying another bomber escort over Wewak at 22,000 feet when two enemy fighters were spotted at 5,000 feet at 9 o'clock. Hoyt instructed Blue and Yellow Flights to remain as top cover (which they did during the entire battle) while he ordered Red and White Flights to drop their tanks and follow him. At 10,000 feet he lost sight of the two enemy fighters but saw four more 1,000 feet above, directly under the overcast.

Hoyt started to climb after two Oscars that were coming down toward him in a gradual descent. Hoyt turned into the leading Oscar and fired a long burst starting at 1,000 yards and closed to a matter of yards during which the enemy pilot did not break off and Hoyt just missed a collision. But Hoyt's P-47s eight .50s took their toll and the Oscar went into a steep dive and crashed. Hoyt reformed the Flight and circled Dagua several times and then flew up the coast at 7,000 feet and found two Oscars flying up the coast at tree top level. As Hoyt closed to 500 feet, the left Oscar turned sharply left and the right turned sharply right. Hoyt closed on the right Oscar to 250 yards and fired only a short burst but with his great airspeed (450IAS) he overran and had to pull up and turn to make another attack. He made two more passes at great deflection but saw no hits before he broke off to meet an Oscar in a head on pass only 100 feet off the water. This determined Oscar pilot did not break off and Hoyt hit the enemy fighter hard but had to roll his fighter violently to avoid a collision with the Oscar that plunged into the water. After scoring four victories in four days Hoyt would have to wait until the last day of the war to become an ace.

After losing the original two Oscars, White Flight Leader, 1Lt. Robert Johnson, and Wingman, F/O Denby Noble, climbed to 10,000 feet where Noble saw four more Oscars headed to make an attack on the first bombers over Wewak. Noble slipped in on the Oscar's tail and fired into its wings and fuselage but he was traveling too fast and overran just as the Oscar blossomed into a ball of orange fire. Johnson turned into the Oscars and before one was in range Johnson snapped a 180 that put him behind the Oscar. He fired at 200 yards getting telling hits despite his high speed which caused him to overrun. As Johnson turned to make another pass he saw his Oscar crash in the foothills near the coast for his second of four victories. 1Lt. John Wallace, was the Second Element Leader of White Flight with 2Lt. Philip Walcott as his Wingman. Wallace saw a Lily at 9 o'clock escorted by two Oscars and they chased the Lily but lost it into a cloud. They circled the area at 9,000 feet when Wallace saw a lone Oscar at 6,000 feet flying down the coast. The two P-47s slipped behind the Oscar and Wallace made a stern attack getting hits but saw no smoke. The Oscar pilot Split-S'd away directly toward the last bombers heading out to sea. During the attack the B-25 gunners fired at the Oscar and then the Thunderbolts. After making his head on pass on the Mitchells, the enemy pilot headed over the water to Cape Noem but had been so intent on his attack on the bombers he was surprised when Wallace fired on him as he was making landfall. The Oscar snap rolled right at 1,000 feet and then made a vertical reverse putting Wingman Walcott in position to fire a very long burst from very close range at 15 degrees deflection and the Oscar crashed into Cape Noem for Walcott's only victory.

**15 March 1944: 475FG/433FS**

Fourteen Possum P-38s were escorting B-25s to Wewak and at 1020 at 14,000 feet over Kairiru Island they saw two enemy fighters headed south on the deck over Victoria Bay. Capt. Richard Kimball, third Flight Leader, followed the first two flights down but broke away at 5,000 feet when saw the first two flights had the situation in hand. As Kimball's flight circled they were bounced by a Tony from above and starboard. Kimball turned under it but it broke away and second Flight Leader, Capt. John Ehlinger, made a 70 degree pass and the Tony turned away in a climb and Kimball followed and gained on the Tony to 14,000 feet. Kimball fired a short burst from out of effective range to get the Japanese pilot to commit himself and turn slightly to starboard. Kimball closed and fired again and the enemy pilot turned to port and pulled up and Kimball fired another short burst. The enemy pilot then leveled out then went into a high speed dive as Kimball closed to short range and fired into the Tony's wings and fuselage and it burst into flames and the pilot bailed out to give Kimball two victories.

2Lt. William Grady, the Second Element Leader of the first flight made several unsuccessful passes at a Tony and Zero on the deck. The Zero turned into Grady and made a 45 degree pass on Grady who fired a long burst and got several hits that sent it rolling several times into the water for Grady's third victory. Grady then fired at the Tony and got a few hits before another American fighter shot it down.

1Lt. Paul Peters was flying as the Second Element Leader of the second flight when he spotted a Tony headed for Muschu Island. Peters closed astern and fired a short burst from 300 yards and hit its starboard wing tearing out pieces and starting a vapor trail. The Tony pilot made right turn and Peters followed but a P-47 cut in front and the two Americans both fired and Peters claimed that "neither of us caused additional damage." Peters fired another short burst as the Tony turned right and hit its cockpit and the pilot bailed out as his fighter exploded. Capt. John Ehlinger, Peters' second Flight Leader stated in his ICR: "…I could not tell who actually shot it down. The Tony exploded while the P-47 was on its tail and I therefore assumed that the P-47 pilot nailed it." Peters was later officially credited with the first of his two victories.

**15 March 1944: 49FG/7FS/9FS**

7FS

1Lt. Robert DeHaven led 20 7FS Pinky Squadron P-40s from Gusap at 0910, escorting A-20s to Kairiru Island. At 1115 the A-20s had left the target when a lone Oscar was spotted heading toward the A-20s at 1,000 feet. DeHaven immediately rolled over and started down but had to do a half roll to dump some speed so that he would not overrun. The Oscar made a head on pass at an A-20 but missed and then turned on the tail of another. DeHaven dropped his tank and closed from dead astern, diving slightly, as the Oscar had closed to 200 yards from the A-20. DeHaven closed and needed to fire the most accurate burst of his career to save the A-20 and fired all the way in and got numerous hits on the Oscar's cockpit before its pilot could fire. The Oscar rolled over on its back and skipped off the water trailing smoke before finally settled under the waves for DeHaven's ninth victory.

9FS
On the 15th Capt. Wandrey was in the 9FS lead when he spotted three Oscars and led the flight into a steep dive. Several of the 9FS elements fired and 2Lt. William Huisman made a head on pass that nearly ended in a collision but then turned in behind a fleeing Tony and fired until it crashed in the sea. Huisman's first of three victories would be the last P-47 victory by the Flying Knights.

**15 March 1944: 35FG/41FS**

The 41FS sent 16 P-47s on a mid-morning B-25 escort to Wewak. 1Lt. Keith Brown, White Flight Leader, with F/O Milton Rowell, flying on Brown's wing saw three or four Oscars and Tonys headed toward the Mitchells that were headed inland across the Wewak Strip. Brown maneuvered to get on an Oscar's tail and pursued it inland across the Harbor at 9,000 feet and fired several short bursts. The Oscar pilot turned up quickly and Brown could not stay with him. Rowell was trailing about 400 yards behind and was able to turn with the Oscar which went into a stall. Rowell fired a 25 degree deflection shot getting numerous hits and the fighter "fell like a bird shot in the wing" for Rowell's first of two victories. 1Lt. John Bomar was leading the two man Red Flight as his second element had returned to base. Red Flight followed White Flight as it turned to make a stern attack. Bomar was on the left flank when a Tony turned directly in front of him and he chased it up the coast where the Tony made a turn south of Kairiru Island. As Bomar closed to fire eight P-38s came in and tried to claim the victory away from him but before they arrived the Oscar pilot bailed out. Bomar's only victory would be the last victories for the 41FS until 10 October during the Borneo missions.

**15 March 1944: 8FG/36FS**

March was more of the same for the 8FG with no successful air combats occurring except for the middle and last two days of the month. The 36FS was assigned to take off at 0835 for a high cover escort for a bomber strike over Wewak, patrolling over the target area from 1010 to 1025. Two P-38s never took off due to mechanical problems and one left the formation later leaving 13 Lightnings for the mission. The Flight leaders were: Yellow: Capt. James McLaughlin; Red: Capt. Donald Campbell; White: Captain Ralph Tuuri; and Blue: Capt. Warren Danson.

Tuuri's White Flight was at 26,000 feet when they were intercepted by eight Oscars from 1,000 feet below to starboard. The flight dropped their tanks and Tuuri chose the lead Oscar and fired a 90 degree deflection shot that sent it rolling over on its back with black smoke pouring out as it hit the water for his second and last victory. Tuuri's Wingman, 1Lt. William Giroux, took the #2 Oscar that had pulled up sharply and did a wingover that positioned it for a head on pass by Giroux who fired a three second burst. The Oscar pilot broke away above and then half rolled and dove straight down; smoking badly for Giroux' first victory after the three probables on 7 November 1943. As they continued their patrol they saw two large columns of smoke on the water to confirm the Squadron's first P-38 victories. Tuuri's Wingman, 1Lt. Thomas Huff, lost track of the other Oscars during the initial attack and then circled seeing an eight plane formation that turned out to be P-47s. They saw no further enemy aircraft and strafed barges (which were seen to be wrecks on closer examination) and camouflaged buildings at Alexishafen before refueling at Gusap and then returning to base.

**1Lt. William Giroux** got his first victory of 10 after being credited with three previous probables. (AFAA)

Capt. Donald Campbell's Red Flight sighted the first eight Oscars too late and did not engage. Campbell forgot to change his selector valves when dropping his tanks and dropped 8,000 feet while trying to restart his engines. Campbell's Wingman, 1Lt. John Perkins, was attacked by a Tony over Dallman Harbor and had his starboard engine shot out; starting a fire. At the same time another Tony crossed 300 yards in front of Perkins and turned and fired a short burst with one bullet hitting Perkin's engine. Perkins then dove and extinguished the engine fire and feathered the prop. While he was diving two enemy fighters closed on him from out of range but were chased off by Capt. Warren Lewis of the 433FS/475FG. Perkins landed safely at Gusap.

James McLaughlin was leading Yellow Flight and had two men abort; he was joined by Capt. Warren Danson's Blue Flight, which had lost a man. The combined flights were flying at 25,000 feet over Kairiru Island when they saw 10 or 12 enemy fighters flying below at 2,000 feet. Danson and his new Wingman McLaughlin dropped their tanks and dove on the top flight of four Oscars. Danson made two ineffective passes and then lost power either through a mechanical problem or from enemy fire and was last seen descending west of Kairiru Island. McLaughlin's engines were having power problems and his top speed was only 250-300 mph. He tried to follow Danson but at 10,000 feet his windshield started to fog when he lost sight of Danson. Now flying at 7,000 feet McLaughlin felt bullets hitting his fighter and he turned away but the Oscar pursuer pulled up and made another pass and hit McLaughlin's canopy covering him with splinters of Plexiglas. McLaughlin could no longer see outside and decided to bail out at 2,000 feet and 250 mph. He released the canopy and turned on the emergency IFF and as he released his seat belt was sucked out of the fighter but was able to grab the edge of the cockpit and hold on until he placed his feet on the wing. He then let go and passed only about a foot under the elevator and opened his chute. Two Oscars were circling and McLaughlin slipped his chute to get into the water as soon as possible to avoid being strafed. He was unable to unbuckle his chute and hit the water with his chute on. After he hit the water he struggled to get out of wet flying gloves which made removing his chute harness and the inflation of his Mae West impossible. Once he removed his gloves, unbuckled his chute harness, inflated life vest and raft he was exhausted and his legs were entangled in his chute shroud lines. He had to hang on to the raft to gather his strength to climb in which took him two or three attempts. After he gathered up his chute canopy and jungle kit, he cut the harness and chute cover and dumped them overboard to get more room on the small raft and tested everything else in the raft in case of rough seas. McLaughlin had landed in Kairiru Strait, two miles from Kairiru Island and a mile and a half from Manshu Island. He could not raise a sail in the daytime for fear that the Japanese would see him from the nearby Islands. After about an hour at sea he saw A-20s bombing and strafing nearby Kairiru Island, about a mile way and waved his chute at them but they left without indicating that they had seen him. Soon two P-38s passed nearby at 2,000 feet and McLaughlin waved his chute at them. At 1530 McLaughlin heard the noise of a plane approaching but did not recognize it and gathered up his chute and hid. But as it closed to a mile and half he recognized it as a PBY rescue amphibian which would have to land within range of Japanese guns and in six foot swells. He tried to light his smoke bomb but it was wet and he then billowed out his chute which was seen and he was picked up and returned to base. The PBY crew that rescued McLaughlin "showed great courage when they flew into Wewak Harbor directly under Japanese observation." McLaughlin "showed equal courage in diving under his Squadron Commander when he knew his own plane was failing mechanically. He remained very cool at all times and used his equipment skillfully to save himself."

The mission was a costly one for the 36th as Flight Leader Danson's P-38 went down over Kairiru Island and McLaughlin's P-38 was lost due to enemy fighters and mechanical problems. Perkins' P-38 had an engine shot by a 20mm shell but Perkins extinguished the fire by diving. After these victories enemy air activity disappeared over Gusap/Wewak but March had been the most active month since November 1943 with 27 victories in 1341 combat sorties. The 36FS would not have another claim for three months, on 16 June.

**Mid-March 1944: Situation and *Reno IV***

In March 1944 MacArthur's "reconnaissance-in-force" into Los Negros in the Admiralties and subsequent three day success surprised the Joint Chiefs of Staff (JCS). Lt.Gen. Richard Sutherland, MacArthur's Chief of Staff, went to Washington to appear before the JCS on 7 March to discuss revisions of Pacific strategy and brief an operation "remarkable in scope, daring in execution, and promising to cut months off the Southwest Pacific advance." Adm. Chester Nimitz and his Chief of Plans, Adm. Forrest Sherman, also were present at the meeting. On the agenda was the fourth revision of the SWPA *Reno Plan*, which charted the movement of MacArthur's forces northwestward in New Guinea, to the Halmahera Islands, to Mindanao and Luzon and on to Formosa and the China coast. *Reno IV* had to be coordinated with Nimitz's campaign in the Pacific Ocean Area (POA) by advancing through the Marianas, Palau, and on to Formosa. The success of these two campaigns would cut off the Japanese Home Islands from its captured resources in Southeast Asia and the Netherlands East Indies. *Reno IV* also gave MacArthur and Kenney a forward air base that extended the range of 5th FC fighters past Wewak.

In a closed session on 12 March, Gen. George Marshall, Chief of Staff, and Adm. Ernest King, Chief of the Navy, and the JCS, approved and sent a directive to MacArthur and Nimitz. MacArthur was directed to complete the isolation of Rabaul and Kavieng with a minimum of forces but not occupy them; to launch an attack on Hollandia on 15 April with the purpose of establishing heavy bombardment groups there to aid the New Guinea Campaign and to support the neutralization of the Palaus; conduct operations along the New Guinea coast and other such operations as were feasible in preparation for support of the Palaus and Mindanao operations; and to invade Mindanao on 15 November. Nimitz was to neutralize and bypass Truk; advance into the southern Marianas on 15 June; and into the Palaus on 15 September. Commander-in-Chiefs, Nimitz and MacArthur were to coordinate their planning, for the occupation of Formosa by CINCPOA and Luzon by CINCSWPA; with a target date of 15 February 1945. The JCS Directive also provided for the transfer of all SOPAC forces as the campaign in the South Pacific Area was considered to be ended. This part of the Directive would lead to the eventual establishment of the Far East Air Forces (FEAF) under the command of Kenney, which would include the 5AF in the SWPA and the entire 13AF in the South Pacific.

MacArthur's reconnaissance-in-force on Los Negros on 29 February was accomplished without air support as only a few aircraft from the many units sent out reached the target area because of very bad weather. Fortunately the weather improved on 1 March. Old B-17s, assigned to transport units for air drop of supplies, delivered emergency supplies and then strafed targets of opportunity on Los Negros. B-25s of the 38th and 345th Groups maintained air alerts and delivered support as requested by ground forces. 16 B-24s of the 43rd Group attacked Jap assembly areas with 1,000 pound bombs. The B-25s of the 345th flew a second mission in the afternoon, striking the two air fields at Hansa Bay in an effort to keep air support from reaching the Japanese defenders on Los Negros.

**16 March 1944: Wewak Resupply Convoy**

The Japanese evacuated what was left of their aircraft and pilots from Wewak to Hollandia on 16 March in an effort to cover an attempt to resupply Wewak. The Japanese sent the 21st Wewak Resupply Convoy from the Palaus, via Hollandia, to Wewak. However, when this convoy came within range it was discovered and attacked by 5AF reconnaissance bombers on 16 March. One transport was so badly damaged that the ship had to run for Hollandia and did not continue to Wewak. Although five USN Seventh Fleet destroyers shelled shore installations at Wewak a few hours before, two her transports were able to slip into Wewak on the night of 18/19 March and unloaded food, ammunition, and troops. Next morning B-24s, assigned to bomb Boram Airdrome, were diverted to the convoy and sank another transport. B-25s and A-20s of the 345BG, which had already attacked Wewak earlier that morning, were rearmed and refueled and returned with escorting fighters and sunk the remaining large ship and the escorting destroyers. The destruction of the Japanese convoy doomed the Japanese forces at, and east of, Wewak and marked the last enemy attempt to send reinforcements and supplies to the forces to Wewak.

**March 1944: Hollandia Campaign Begins**

After the Japanese abandoned Wewak because of the devastating air raids on 11-16 March, Hollandia became their major base in New Guinea which was beyond 5FC fighter range, even of the P-38s that operated from their closest airdrome at Gusap. The Japanese built three airdromes on the north side of Sentani Lake, about 15 miles inland from Humboldt Bay on which was located the port of Hollandia. Hollandia was a former Dutch trading post, which had a population of nearly 2,000 natives and a dozen whites and had a stone pier and several sizeable warehouses. A road adequate for light motor traffic led into the Sentani Lake area from Pim, a small village named located on Humboldt Bay and about five miles east of Hollandia. Pim was connected by another similar road leading to Sentani Lake and the three airdromes. Confident that they were safe from air attacks, the Japanese increased their air strength and parked aircraft almost wingtip to wingtip, with big fuel and ammunition dumps on the borders of the fields. Radio Tokyo was so secure that its broadcasts boasted of the large air force they were building up at Hollandia in preparation for an early offensive "that was to sweep the arrogant Americans out of the New Guinea skies."

During February, 58 new P-38s had arrived, with extra wing tanks that supplied them sufficient fuel to escort bombers all the way from Gusap to Hollandia and back with enough reserve to allow an hour of combat over the target. With over a 100 enemy fighters certain to intercept the bombers as soon as they flew anywhere near Hollandia, more than the 58 fighters were required to protect the bombers and strafers on a major mission intended to destroy enemy air opposition. Kenney ordered 75 extra wing tanks for the old P-38s ASAP which were to be installed by 25 March. Until then Kenney did not permit Whitehead to fly any of his P-38s, long range or not, any farther than Tadji. When reaching Tadji, no P-38 was to linger any more than 15 minutes, even if they were in combat, before returning to base. It was Kenney's intention to have the Japanese believe that the Lightnings were unable to reach Hollandia so that they would continue to concentrate aircraft there. Kenney wanted to have the Japanese believe that he wouldn't send a daylight attack with unescorted bombers, so he ordered Whitehead to make night attacks with single bombers on the Lake Sentani area, beginning about the middle of March. Usually the bomber crews were unable to see their targets because of clouds but hitting the target was not important as just being there. Radio Tokyo taunted the Americans for their futile nightly bombing; 5FC P-38 pilots were frustrated by their Tadji limit; but 5FC depots continued to build up their drop tank

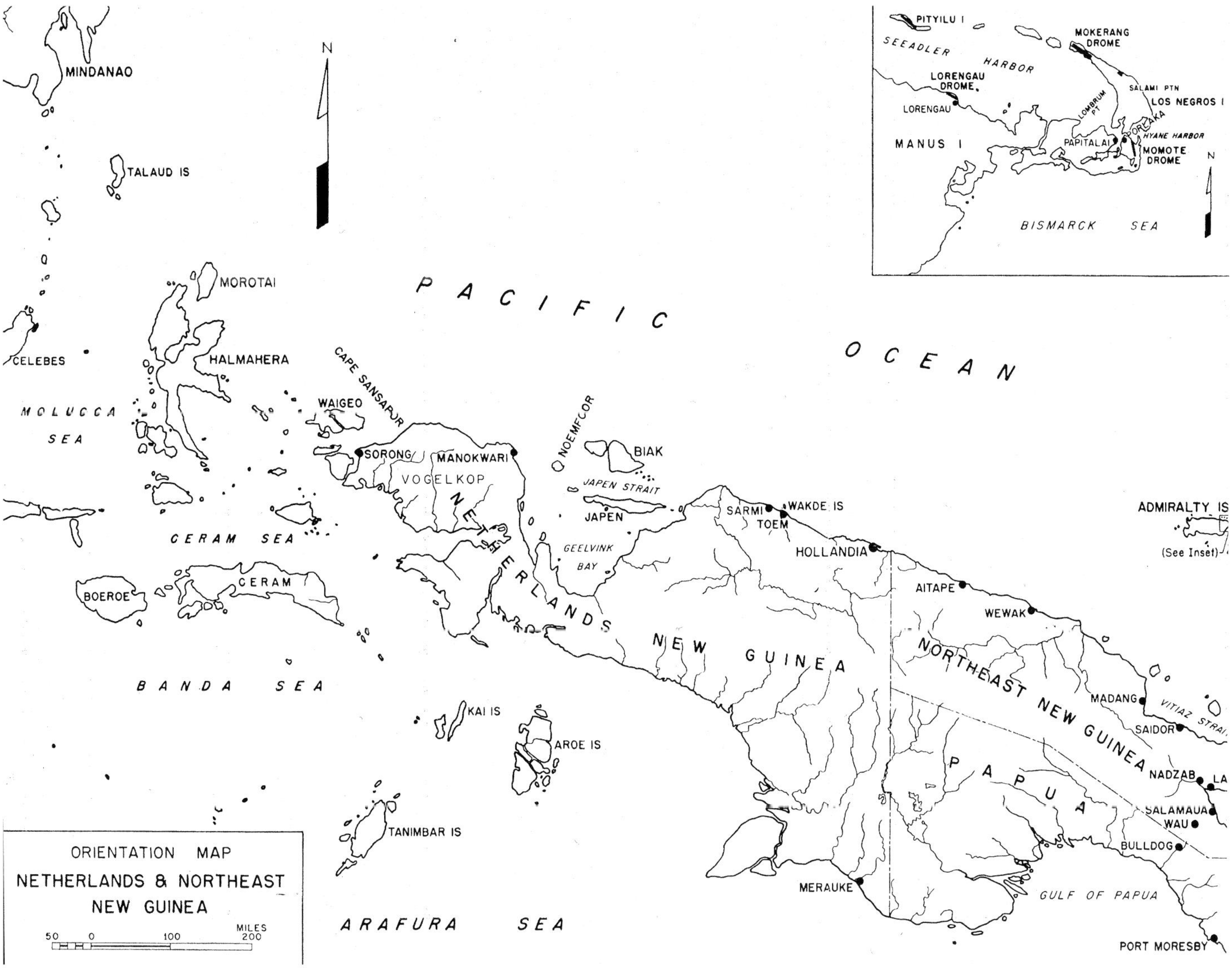


supply. Meanwhile, reconnaissance photographs showed the Japanese air force at Hollandia steadily growing with overconfidence as their aircraft continued to be parked wingtip to wingtip and sometimes in double lines alongside the runways.

While the battered Japanese air force had been withdrawn from the Wewak area, 100,000 Japanese troops remained there which had to be reinforced and supplied. Allied Intelligence determined that the Japanese would try to sneak a convoy of reinforcements and supplies from Hollandia to Wewak sometime around the 18th or 19th of March. On the night of 17/18 March nine enemy vessels were intercepted by two B-24s and two mornings later only two of the nine enemy vessels limped back to Hollandia.

Admirals Nimitz and Sherman arrived at Brisbane on the 25th for a final conference in MacArthur's office to arrange for the cooperation of their carrier force with the Hollandia invasion. Nimitz was worried about the danger to his carrier force if enemy air strength at Hollandia was not significantly reduced by the time he was to support the landing. His carriers were scheduled to conduct a series of raids on Palau, Yap, Ulithi, and Woleai, and then return to Hollandia to give air support to Krueger's landings. One division was to land in Humboldt Bay at Pim and drive west to the airdrome area, while the other was to land at Tannemerah Bay and advance east toward the same objective. Simultaneously, one regiment was scheduled to land near Aitape, seize Tadji, and repair the enemy airdrome there as quickly as possible to operate fighters. Halsey's troops landed unopposed on Emirau Island, 75 miles northwest of Kavieng, on March 20th.

Nimitz reported that he would start the Palau strikes between 1 and 3 April with 11 carriers which would arrive at Hollandia, less any losses, on the 20th. The carriers could remain until the afternoon of the second day following the landing. If an airdrome was not ready for fighters at Tadji or Hollandia by that time Kenney would be unable to cover the unloading of the supply vessels in Humboldt or Tannemerah Bays and he requested that some carriers remain a little longer. Adm. Kincaid was to secure some small carriers on loan to cover the Aitape invasion for eight days after the landing, to supplement on fighter cover at Hollandia in case Kenney's forward airdrome was not completed on time.

Nimitz continued to voice his concern over the threat of the "200 to 300" Japanese aircraft at Hollandia and said that he didn't want to send his carriers to Hollandia if they were still there by the time he arrived. Kenney again promised to destroy them by 5 April but Halsey remained skeptical as Kenny's long range P-38s would not be ready to attack Hollandia before March 30. In order that Kenney could utilize his entire bomber force on Hollandia; 13AF bombers flying out of Los Negros were assigned to any necessary operations in the Marianas or Carolines.

Nimitz left on the 27th and soon Kenney was asked by a Central Pacific liaison officer to start a four day bombing operation to Woleai but Kenney did not have the bombers available without jeopardizing his bombing attack on Hollandia.

The Joint Chiefs' plan concerning Formosa and the Philippines was mentioned during the discussion. Nimitz said he believed the occupation of Luzon was an essential preliminary to the movement against Formosa and that Formosa could not be attacked by any expedition from the Marianas-Palau line. MacArthur agreed and said that the idea of a direct attack on Formosa, bypassing the Philippines, was not only strategically unsound but basically immoral, because it would abandon all the American prisoners that the Japanese held in the Philippines and 17 million Filipinos.

**15 March 1944: Invasion of Manus**

As the second phase of *Operation Brewer*, the Admiralties Campaign, U.S. Infantry went ashore at Manus on 15 March against weak opposition and by 17 March they had occupied the airfield there and had broken the primary enemy resistance. Air opposition in that area was such that the Fifth Air Force was able to divert its attention elsewhere.

**Mid-March 1944: 348FG Moves to Saidor**

In March the 348th began its move from Finschhafen to Saidor. On 13 March the 340th Squadron aircraft and air echelon arrived at Saidor. The Squadron mess and showers were constructed and the proposed clubs and administration buildings scheduled due to be built relatively soon. The 341FS began arriving at Saidor by 27 March and the 342FS was to move by the end of the month. However, the move to Saidor took them out of the air action and caused it to fight the less glorious but nonetheless vital battles in the ground attack role of dive bombing and strafing in support of ground troops. The first missions from Saidor would include patrol, convoy cover and other missions that didn't include the prerequisite of long range. Only when the 348th moved its base to Insoemanai Island off Wakde in May would it have another opportunity for aerial combat.

**Mid-March 1944: 418NFS Moves to Finschhafen**

In mid-March the 418NFS was ordered to move to Finschhafen and spent most of the latter half of the month packing up their camp at Dobodura and by 28 March the Squadron was established at Finschhafen.

**17 March 1944: 35FG Command Changes**

Maj. William McDonough, Group Deputy CO, was transferred to the 5FC. Maj. Francis Dubisher, 41FS CO, was transferred to Group HQ Squadron as its Deputy Commander and was replaced by 1Lt. Douglas Parsons as 41FS CO. During this time a number of the leading pilots of the Group were rotated home: Capt. Paul Stanch, Group Operations Officer and a 10 victory ace with the 39FS; Capt. Richard Smith, Group Deputy Operations Officer and seven victory ace with the 39FS, and Capt. Edwin Schneider, a combat leader with the 40FS with four hard-earned victories.

**19 March 1944: 348FG/342FS**

On 19 March the 342FS flew a 16 plane sweep over Wewak and patrolled at 20,000 feet when 16 enemy fighters and one bomber was spotted by 1Lt. John Sutcliffe and his White Flight at 7,000 feet but Sutcliffe was unable to call the contract as his radio was out. Sutcliffe picked out a flight of enemy fighters (identified as Oscars) off by themselves at 3,000 feet. Sutcliffe dove and closed quickly from astern firing a three second burst on the lead Oscar down to 25 yards and set it on fire for his fourth victory. Sutcliffe used his diving speed to zoom back up and then dove on the other three Oscars but they saw him approaching and broke away out of range in a well executed maneuver. The leader pulled up in a tight loop and his two wingmen chandelled, one to the left and the other to the right. Had Sutcliffe fallen into this trap each of the three Oscars would have been in position to shoot at him.

**22 March 1944: 49FG/7FS**

The P-40s of the 7FS barely had the range to reach Tadji, 300 miles away, with a full belly tank and two 300 pound bombs. On 22 March, the Screamin' Demons encountered light but accurate flak over the target and Capt. Russell Cash, Group Operations Executive, was lost on the mission.

**24 March 1944: Bong Loses an Aircraft**

During mid-March 5FC 24 victory ace, Maj. Dick Bong, was sent to the 49FS to convey combat pointers and fly a few missions with them. On 24 March, 1Lt. Thomas Malone took Bong's famous P-38J up on a weather recon flight. The cowling on Bong's Lightning was adorned with the enlarged photo of his girlfriend, Marge (Vattendahl) and 24 Rising Sun victory symbols. After about an hour the fighter began to have engine problems and then the electrical system failed, and Malone was unable to feather the prop. When the fighter went into a spin Malone bailed out over the jungle. After nearly drowning in an attempt to float his dinghy down a rapid jungle river he met American soldiers and was returned to base to face an irritated Bong. After Bong calmed down he admitted that he, too, had problems with the Lightning.

**26 March 1944: 58FG/311FS**

On 25 March, 16 P-47s of the 311FS took off from Dobodura to spend the night at Nadzab to fly its most important mission thus far. After preparing for weeks the 311th had been chosen to supply middle cover for B-25s during a maximum effort on the Japanese air bases at But and Dagua. The 16 Thunderbolts left Nadzab at 0815 led by Capt. Donald Jander but on their arrival at the target area there was no enemy air interception. After 3:45 in the air the Squadron returned to Nadzab for refueling and returned to Dobodura the same day.

**26 March 1944: 475FG/433FS**

Four P-38s, led by 1Lt. Calvin Wire, were returning from Yakamul while flying a PBY escort to Wewak. At 1715 at 4,000 feet over Victoria Bay they saw 18 to 20 enemy fighters at 15,000 feet and two Tonys and two Zeros dove on the Lightnings from behind and out of the sun. Wire's Element Leader, 1Lt. Paul Peters looked around and saw a Zero on his tail and made a violent port turn which gave Wire a chance to came around and fire a two second burst. The Zero took some damaging hits which persuaded its pilot to break away. A Tony then got on #4 2Lt. Howard Stiles' tail and fired a long burst and in his effort to escape Stiles' fighter hit some prop wash and was flipped on its back. Wire turned into the Tony and his fire also made this enemy pilot turn away from his attack. Stiles righted his fighter and as he pulled up he saw a Tony in a climbing turn at 250 yards and fired a five second burst at 60 degrees, knocking a few pieces of its wing for a damaged claim. Peters heard a shouted radio warning and saw a Tony firing at only 100 yards behind and kicked hard rudder and pushed over and got behind the Tony as it pulled up to port. Peters fired a short burst but saw no damage. Fortunately, the other enemy fighters never came down to help; thinking that Wire's flight was decoys.

**March 1944: 58FG March Recap**

During March the 69FS flew 225 sorties, the 310FS flew 221, and the 311FS completed 55 combat missions and 256 combat sorties. Because the 58th's base at Dobodura was now so far from the front another 361 sorties were necessary to get the squadron to the front to fly the combat missions of which many were flights to Goodenough Island. No enemy aircraft had been encountered but the pilots had encountered anti-aircraft fire. The Group had 17 accidents and only one fatality; 1Lt. James Farmer of the 69FS.

**Late March to Early May 1944: 49FG**

For the 49er operations in April became routine for the pilots of Ramu Valley. Only the P-38 wing at Nadzab was able to keep up the chase of the JAAF at far off Hollandia. The 9FS pilots were disgruntled as they felt that they were burdened with their lumbering P-47s. Though they still led in the victories with 177 confirmed kills, they would claim only one enemy aircraft between 15 March and 7 May 1944.

**The Hollandia Campaign: *Operation Reckless and Persecution***

Now that Rabaul was isolated the *Reno IV Plan* gave the green light for an advance of an unprecedented 400 miles up the New Guinea coastline to capture the major Japanese air and supply base at Hollandia. Code named *Reckless* (Hollandia) and *Persecution* (Aitape) the Hollandia operation was a masterpiece of excellent planning that took full advantage of extremely accurate intelligence obtained from deciphering of Japanese codes which had facilitated the Yamamoto shoot down by the 339FS of the 13AF in April 1943. For MacArthur it proved the decisive operation on New Guinea and was the turning point in his war against the Japanese. The breaking of the Japanese codes revealed that MacArthur's next landing, scheduled for 26 April at Hansa Bay, midway between Madang and Wewak, could anticipate strong ground resistance. Furthermore, the Japanese were reinforcing their air bases at Hollandia from where they could support the defense of Madang. This intelligence also revealed that Hollandia's land defenses were minimal and vulnerable to an Allied landing.

The approval of *Reckless* by the JCS did not necessarily guarantee its success. MacArthur required carrier air support because Hollandia was beyond the range of Kenney's land-based fighter aircraft. However, the USN was preparing for its invasion of the Marianas and would be able to provide no more than three days of carrier support. Planners at General Headquarters then decided to capture Aitape (*Persecution*), about 140 miles east of Hollandia whose airstrips could provide land-based fighter support to the infantry at Hollandia after the carriers left. *Reckless* would involve 217 ships, which would transport 80,000 men, their equipment, and supplies over 1,000 miles, to carry out three separate amphibious landings deep in the enemy rear area. After the Japanese fleet had been withdrawn from Rabaul to the safety of the Philippines it was no longer a threat but air superiority along the invasion route was a requirement for success. Using deciphered Japanese communications Allied intelligence placed about 350 enemy aircraft concentrated near Hollandia in late March.

Although Kenney was probably MacArthur's closest advisor during the war, occasionally he ignored Kenney's recommendations as he did in the planning for the attack on Hollandia. Previously MacArthur's operations had always been protected by Kenney's 5AF. The invasion at Hollandia was designed to avoid the strong Japanese garrison at Hansa Bay but was too far from American air bases to provide air cover during the long hours of the landings, which forced MacArthur to rely on Navy carriers for protection. Kenney heartily disagreed with this plan, maintaining that carrier aircraft had limited range and could carry only small bomb loads, which made them ill equipped to support an amphibious invasion. Kenney also pointed out the limitations of the carriers *per se*, such as bad weather and the need to routinely stop flying operations in order to replenish fuel, food, and ammunition which limited operations and could cause them to leave the battle at a critical time.

However, MacArthur maintained that Kenney's position was offset by the outflanking of the largest concentration of Japanese forces in New Guinea and thus avoiding a long and costly ground battle; the capture of a supply base that could support the invasion of the Philippines; and the opportunity to accelerate the advance toward the Philippines. So while Kenney's aircraft would not cover the actual landing at Hollandia they would eradicate Japanese airpower in the area prior to the invasion. Using surprise and excellent timing achieved by excellent Intelligence, Kenney's 5AF attacked the Japanese after they had packed their airfields at Hollandia with aircraft and equipment and then did not evacuate these aircraft west to locations that would have allowed them to interdict the landing at Hollandia from a safe distance. Kenney's attack was characteristic of him; using long range fighters to escort a low level bombing force to produce impressive results so that the Japanese were able to offer only slight resistance to the invasion at Hollandia.

In order to gain air supremacy over Hollandia and provide long range escort against the bases there, a number of P-38s had been modified at the depots in Australia by installing 110-to-120 gallon tanks in the leading edges of the wings of the P-38Js already in New Guinea that could be modified in record time. As the modifications were completed and the new aircraft were moved up from Australia, it was decided to assign all the long range P-38s to the 8th and 475th Fighter Groups, while the 9th Fighter Squadron of the 49th Fighter Group exchanged its P-47s for the older P-38s. By employing these new longer-range P-38s, Kenney sent 60 B-24 heavy bombers against Hollandia on 30 March. Follow-up raids demolished nearly all the operational Japanese aircraft at Hollandia on the ground permanently gaining air superiority the enemy over New Guinea.

**Late March 1944: Wewak Abandoned**

On 25 March, Supreme Imperial Commander Gen. Hatazo Adachi ordered the 4th Air Army Headquarters Staff to abandon devastated Wewak airfield complex and to withdraw to Hollandia. His remaining troops dispersed into the Alexander Mountains where many would die of starvation and disease. The victory at Wewak was ultimately gained by the air power of the 5th Air Force and complemented by U.S. Navy carrier aircraft. Like the other enemy garrisons to the east, the destruction of Wewak was so complete that it could safely be bypassed. MacArthur was able to advance his New Guinea strategic schedule ahead by four months and by early April he was ready to attack Hollandia.

**Late March 1944: Air Attacks on Hollandia**

The original attack plan on Hollandia was for a large low level surprise attack, similar to that on Wewak in August 1943. But then the recon photos showed an increase of AA machine gun batteries at both ends of the valley where the three airdromes were located. On 29 March, a message from the Japanese Army High Command to Lt. Gen. Kumaichi Teramoto was intercepted by the Allies. This message ordered Teramoto to move the aircraft stationed at Hollandia because of the Fifth Air Force's planned attack, which made the timing of the B-24 assault urgent. The attacking force would have to climb over several low hills at each end of this valley several miles from the airdromes which could result in losing the first and maybe the second wave of strafers. Whitehead, and Colonels Merian Cooper and Jared Crabb of the Fifth Bomber Command, decided to send 60 B-24s carrying a maximum load of 200 fragmentation bombs apiece; dropping them from 10,000-12,000 feet to blanket the target with 12,000 frags. This first day's attack was to destroy the AA machine gun positions and the fuel dumps as the primary target and the enemy aircraft on the field secondarily. The second day's attack, also by the heavy bombers was to have the enemy aircraft as their primary target. The third and final "clean up" attack was to be opened by the heavy bombers and followed by all available strafers finishing off anything not already destroyed. Each mission was to be covered by all the long range fighters available.

In the meantime, the small night attacks were continued to lull the Japanese into the belief that unescorted daylight bomber missions were not presently possible. The recon photos of the three Hollandia airdromes taken on the morning of 30 March revealed nearly 300 aircraft on the ground and 16 others that had evidently been destroyed or badly damaged by previous night's attacks.

The first daylight attack on the **Hollandia Airfields** took place on 30 March. (AAF)

### 30 March 1944: Hollandia

A few night missions were flown by B-24s before the first big daylight strike was scheduled for 30 March. On the morning of 30[th] the first large daylight strike on Hollandia took place when 65 B-24s, dropped over 14,000 23 pound fragmentation bombs. The bombers were escorted by 59 long range P-38s with increased fuel capacity of the 8[th] and 475[th] Fighter Groups flying from Nadzab. The bombers destroyed 25 aircraft and badly damaged another 67 on the ground. Many fuel dumps were burned with heavy black smoke rising to 10,000 feet and visible 150 miles away. The post strike photos showed that the AA machine-gun positions were taken out and the heavy AA gunfire was described as light and inaccurate. The 80 P-38s intercepted the 40 enemy fighters and downed 10 definite and seven probable with no losses.

### 30 March 1944: 475FG/431FS/432FS

Col. Charles MacDonald led 22 P-38s of the 431[st] and 432[nd] Squadrons on the B-24 escort to Hollandia. The Lightnings were equipped with new fuel tanks with increased capacity but four of these Lightnings had to abort because of defects in the system. At least six enemy aircraft were sighted during the mission but only Macdonald and 2Lt. Alvin Kidd, the Second Element Leader, made a claim when they both got damaging hits on a Tony at 1030 and shared a damaged claim.

### 30 March 1944: 8FG/80FS

For this extremely long (for that time) flight to Hollandia; the P-38s were to take off from Nadzab and stage then through Gusap on the way back to refuel. At 0800 23 P-38s led by Capt. Jay Robbins took off to rendezvous with the bombers at 0930 and then fly an hour to the Hollandia. When they reached Hollandia at 18,000 feet seven Oscars and Tonys were seen off to the right. Robbins called in the enemy planes to the trailing 431FS and 432FS of the 475FG and ordered his flight to drop their tanks. The enemy fighters were starting to Split-S into the bomber formation when the P-38s arrived. Robbins got on the tail of an Oscar and got some hits before it rolled out of range for a probable. Robbins then dove through light AA fire and drove off several more enemy fighters from the Liberators. One dove away and then turned to port which gave Robbins a 30 degree deflection shot that hit the fuselage and it soon flamed and crashed. Robbins fired a few shots at an Oscar that rolled away without seeing any results. Robbins

**Capt. Jay Robbins** had two victories and a probable claim to make him a triple ace with 15 victories (shown with L to R: George Davis, Robbins, and Generals Whitehead and Wurtsmith). (AAF)

**1Lt. Cyril Homer** (left) tangled with Tonys and got his ninth victory and two damaged claims, while 1Lt. Cornelius Smith damaged an Oscar. (AAF)

**1Lt. Louis Schriber** collected his second victory, and would get his third the next day. (AFAA)

then led his flight in a climb to 12,000 feet where they found a large group of Japanese fighters. Robbins quickly maneuvered on three Oscars flying in trail and got on the tail of one that half rolled out of range and Robbins made a fast diving turn and got into firing position again. The Oscar pilot tried to Split-S away but was much too low and crashed when he tried to pull out of the dive. 2Lt. Bud Fletcher was flying on Robbins' wing and followed him through his first victory and accompanied him on his pass on the Oscars. He then dropped down under Robbins and when the Oscars started to roll away he got a four second burst on the center Oscar that started smoking for a probable. 1Lt. Louis Schriber of Robbins' Flight saw 12 Zeros and climbed into them "but they turned tail and we chased them." And while Robbins was shooting down his Oscar Schriber made several passes on Tonys that only wanted to escape by rolling away or heading for clouds. Finally, Schriber and his Wingman, 1Lt. Jesse Corallo, got on the tail of a Tony and followed it in a Split-S and Schriber set it afire with a burst from dead astern which crashed 30 miles north of Hollandia for his second victory. On the way home Corallo attacked an Oscar and start it smoking but dove away toward safety for a no claim.

The second flight of Headhunter P-38s, led by 1Lt. Kenneth Ladd, followed Robbins in a long string into the attack on the Oscars as they looked as though they to attack the bombers. The Oscars were not eager to fight and Split-S'd away. The two Headhunter flights became separated and Ladd ran into approximately 15 Japanese fighters but again these Japanese did not respond aggressively. Ladd made five passes before he got hits on an Oscar and saw pieces fly off it but did not see it go down for a probable. On another pass he saw flashes as his fire hit an Oscar but did not see any other results and claimed a damaged. Ladd's flight members separated and Ladd got an Oscar on his tail but Homer and his flight scared it away with Homer claiming a damaged. Ladd joined Homer's flight and watched Homer shoot down a Tony (his ninth victory). Before they returned to base, Homer and Ladd made a pass on a Tony, getting hits; with Homer credited with a damaged. 1Lt. Paul Murphey, leading Ladd's second element with 2Lt. Ardice Roberts as his Wingman, stayed with Ladd in the battle and made passes but did not take any shots until five Oscars dove on them and two of the Oscars rushed in on Ladd's tail. Murphey took a long burst at one of Oscars and hit the cockpit and the Oscar rolled over on its back and crashed for Murphey's fourth victory. Three Oscars got on Wingman Roberts' tail and Murphey dove on them but Roberts Split-S'd away and the two separated and returned to base.

The third flight led by 1Lt. Leland Blair engaged the enemy but did not make any claims. Blair started to close on an enemy fighter but his Wingman began to fire from too far out of range and the enemy pilot Split-S'd and Blair Split-S'd with enemy fighter and fired at it diving straight down but had to pull up and as he did he blacked out and did not observe the fate of the diving enemy fighter. 2Lt. Orin Anderson was Blair's Wingman who fired much too far out range and reported in his ICR: "The big thing I learned was not to fire when out of range. I spoiled good passes by my Flight Leader by doing so."

The fourth flight led by 1Lt. Burnell Adams also made no claims as the enemy fighters they encountered were reluctant to engage and he and Wingman 2Lt. Ralph Giel did not even fire their guns.

Capt. Cornelius Smith was leading the fifth flight at 20,000 feet over Hollandia when he saw two Zeros make their run on the lead B-24s and saw Robbins make an attack and ordered his flight to drop their tanks and dove with the other Headhunter flights on scattered Tonys and Zeros. They saw two Oscars close in on the flight ahead and dove on them as they tried to dive away. Smith followed for about 10,000 feet but broke off when he realized that the enemy pilots were trying to lure him to lower altitudes and began to climb back to altitude. As they climbed they saw four Zeros about a mile ahead at 15,000 feet. The Zeros climbed away to attack four P-38s above them. These P-38s turned into them and the four Zeros then turned into Smith's flight head on in line abreast. Smith and Wingman 1Lt. Charles Ray open fire. Smith fired at the left Zero from at 500 yards and saw pieces come off but it passed under Smith for a damaged claim. Ray fired a long burst at the right Zero that hit the cowling and the Zero was smoking as it passed under Ray for his second victory. He then fired on another Oscar and hit its cowling but there was no smoke or fire for a damaged claim. 1Lt. Vernon Jenner turned into one of the four Zeros and he and Element Leader, Mark Kaspar, fired at another but it was Jenner's burst that set it on fire and crash for his first of four victories.

1Lt. Cyril Homer led the sixth and last Headhunter flight and his flight dropped their tanks and about 10 minutes later he saw an Oscar close in behind 1Lt. Kenneth Ladd and drove the Oscar away but scored no visible hits. Homer then reversed his turn and got behind a Tony that evaded with vertical reverses during a 60 degree dive. Homer's cannon shells hit the Tony's port wing but it evaded underneath for a damaged claim. Homer pulled up and met another Tony in a head on pass but couldn't it in his sights soon enough as this unenthusiastic Tony pilot fired from far out of range and broke away. Homer saw another Tony with a bomb (fuel tank?) slung under its wing and followed from below and behind, and was able to close to within 100 yards. Homer fired a few bursts that missed low and then adjusted his sights and fired again hitting the fuselage and the damaged Tony rolled over on its back and headed down out of sight with its prop windmilling. Later Ladd hit this Tony with another burst before it dove into the clouds. Five minutes later Homer fired at another Tony whose pilot put it into a steep 45 degree dive and Homer followed at 480 mph before he caught up to the Tony at 6,000 feet and fired. As he pulled out of the dive he saw the Tony hit the water about a mile offshore. Homer claimed his ninth victory and two damaged and gave Ladd a victory credit for the Tony he damaged. 2Lt. Edwin DeGraffenreid had his port engine cut out and called Flight Leader Homer to reduce his speed so he could keep up but has call was not heard and he separated from the flight. DeGraffenreid saw Tony and fired getting some hits for a damaged claim before he returned to base early.

The 80th scored eight victories, one damaged, and seven probables. Twenty two P-38s landed at Nadzab between 1300 and 1330 while the other P-38 landed at Gusap but returned to Nadzab an hour after the others. Only one P-38 was very slightly damaged by a single large caliber bullet. The B-24s dropped their bombs successfully on the dispersal points of the airfields and returned to base without loss. Bomb damage to the target was difficult to assess as a large column of black smoke from an unidentified source obscured direct inspection of the target but as predicted many enemy aircraft were parked on the field of which many were probably destroyed or damaged.

### 31 March 1944: Hollandia

On the 31st 68 heavy bombers and 70 P-38s attacked Hollandia and the post strike photos showed that there were now 138 aircraft totally destroyed on the ground with another 42 damaged. The heavy smoke following the bombing indicated that the fuel dumps suffered further destruction. On this mission about half the bombers dropped heavy bombs which cratered all three runways and made them at least temporarily unserviceable. This mission was similar to the previous day's mission to Hollandia with the 80FS and two squadrons of the 475FG flying escort to B-24s. The Japanese sent up 30 fighters which briefly intercepted and then escaped heading west after losing 14 and probably losing eight others. One P-38 was lost.

### 31 March 1944: 8FG/80FS

Capt. Jay Robbins led six flights of 22 P-38s from Nadzab at 0800. Robbins led the first flight; 1Lt. Cyril Homer the second; 1Lt. Leland Blair the third; 1Lt. Burnell Adams the fourth; 1Lt. 1Lt. Cornelius Smith the fifth; and 1Lt. Kenneth Ladd the sixth. The Headhunters rendezvoused with the bombers 20 miles north of Buriu. The formation arrived over the target at 1030 in clear weather at 16,000 feet. Once more there were about two dozen disorganized Zeros and Oscars circling the target area.

**Capt. Cornelius Smith** shot down a Dinah over Hollandia to become a double ace. (AFAA)

**1Lt. Kenneth Ladd** scored his ninth victory. (AAF)

Robbins was leading the first Red Flight at 16,000 feet when he called out enemy fighters just above and to port. He climbed into them and got behind an Oscar for a deflection shot that hit the engine, port wing, and cockpit and he saw it peel off slowly and go straight in. Robbins' Wingman, 2Lt. Bud Fletcher, fired a four second burst at the second Oscar but got no hits. Robbins' fighter experienced fuel supply problems and he returned to base early with his 16th victory. 1Lt. Louis Schriber, Robbin's Second Element Leader, followed his leader and saw him attack another Oscar before he left the battle. Schriber and his Wingman, 1Lt. Jesse Corallo, chased after the Oscars that had Split-S'd down from Robbins' attack. An Oscar passed through Schriber's sights and he fired a 90 degree shot and followed it around in its turn to get on its tail and fired hitting it hard to put it into a vertical dive to crash for his third victory. Corallo saw another Oscar while he was following Schriber and fired a 40 degree deflection shot and Schriber confirmed Corallo's first victory. The two made several more ineffective attacks before going home.

1Lt. Cyril Homer's second flight made no claims. His flight lost its #4 man and was engaged nine "eager" Oscars. As Homer led his flight down through the Oscars, the enemy pilots would turn under Smith and as they would pull out there would always be an Oscar under the #3 man. Smith claims that "15 different times" he forced the Oscars to break away by doing a loop with combat flaps to get a firing lead but never was able to do so.

1Lt. Leland Blair's third flight also made no claims on the reluctant Oscars they encountered. Blair got several ineffective hits and observed P-38s from other flights get kills.

1Lt. Burnell Adam's fourth flight circled around outside the target until the bombers came out and then remained in the area for 15 minutes before heading home.

Capt. Cornelius Smith was leading the fifth flight at about 20,000 feet over Hollandia when he spotted Oscars a few thousand feet below. The flight dropped their tanks and descended on the enemy that would Split-S away before the P-38s got into range. Smith decided to search elsewhere and saw an aircraft flying about 5,000 or 6,000 feet above and climbed after it. As he closed he saw it was a lone Dinah whose pilot saw the Smith's flight approaching and went into a shallow climb to escape. After four minutes Smith caught up at 18,000 feet and as the speedy Dinah leveled off out of its climb and Smith then had problems catching it in level flight. Smith finally closed but his gunsight malfunctioned and he fired by adjusting his aim by following the line of tracers which hit the Dinah's engine that began to smoke heavily but it continued to fly. He fired again, scoring more hits but several Oscars appeared and forced him to turn away from the Dinah and to turn into his attackers. The Oscars immediately Split-S'd away and Smith took an ineffective snap shot with no sight. Smith turned back and saw the Dinah diving toward the water with its port side engulfed in flames and Smith's Wingman, 1Lt. Charles Ray, confirmed Smith's 10th victory to make him a double ace. 1Lt. John Stanifer saw six to eight Oscars at 3 o'clock low and with his height advantage dove, fired, and returned to altitude. For the next 15 minutes he was able to get in only a few snap shots as the enemy pilots "seemed to be very skilled, especially in evasive tactics, though not very aggressive." Finally an Oscar flew directly into Stanifer's sights and got hits in the engine and cowling and Stanifer's Element Leader, 1Lt. Paul Murphey, confirmed Stanifer's first of two victories. Murphey made "quite a few" passes on the Oscars and only got one "fairly good pass" on one flying under him and "got some hits and consider him as damaged."

1Lt. Kenneth Ladd led the sixth P-38 flight and arrived over the target just as the combat began and got onto the tail of a halfhearted Oscar pilot and fired a two second burst and overshot the Oscar but he got many hits that spattered oil on his windscreen. The Oscar went down in a steep dive near the water and crashed. Ladd then saw another Oscar low over the water and reduced his throttle and quickly got in behind him but overshot after only getting in a short burst. Ladd went into a steep turn but then saw the Oscar almost on top of him in a head on pass. Both pilots fired ineffective short bursts before they passed and this Oscar was picked up by two other P-38s after they passed and Ladd looked for other target but his fuel was running low and he returned to base with his ninth victory. 1Lt. William Caldwell saw two enemy fighters Split-S'ing and dove on them and got on its tail and started fired from 200 yards from 70 degrees to 40 degrees. It started smoking and went into a steep spiraling dive got his only victory.

The 80th pilots claimed seven victories for this combat and once again no 80th pilots were lost but fuel shortage required nine P-38s to land at forward bases to refuel. One P-38 suffered some damage and landed with a leaking hydraulic system. The Japanese pilots were clearly dispirited and did not forcefully confront the 5AF formations and the P-38s of the 80FS and 475FG scored virtually at will with minimal risk.

**31 March 1944: 475FG/431FS/432FS**

431FS

Lt.Col. Charles MacDonald led 21 Hades P-38s off at 0755 in five flights: Red: MacDonald; White: Maj. Verl Jett; Blue: 1Lt. Francis Lent; Green: Capt. Thomas McGuire; and Yellow: 1Lt. Franklin Monk. The Squadron led B-24s to Hollandia and rendezvoused with them at 0915 over Buriu. The Squadron was intercepted at 1015, flying at 17,000 feet, well above the 431FS, by 25 to 30 Oscars and Tonys coming in from the north about 30 miles south of Lake Sentani.

At the beginning of the combat McGuire's Second Element Leader, 1Lt. Alvin Kidd, had his port supercharger malfunction as the flight dove away from the first Japanese attack and pulled away to return to base. As he rolled away a Zero came in at 10 o'clock and fired a short burst that started a fire and Kidd put out the fire and then returned to base escorted by Wingman, 2Lt. Richard Roark.

1Lt. Franklin Monk was leading Yellow Flight at the rear of the formation and called for belly tanks to be dropped when 15 Oscars dove to attack McGuire's fourth, Green Flight from three o'clock, 1,000 feet above. Monk dove after Green Flight and chased the Zeros off and as the enemy pilots broke to starboard Monk was able to get on the third Zero's tail and fired a long burst that shattered its wing, canopy, and engine and it finally exploded for his fourth victory. Monk then led his flight into a steep climbing starboard turn and made a few turns to clear them of any pursuing Japanese fighters. Once clear Monk rejoined his Wingman, new pilot, 2Lt. Horace Reeves, his

**1Lt. Francis Lent** shot down two Zeros to give him 11 total victories. (AFAA)

**1Lt. Robert Crosswait** claimed his only victory of the war and would be KIA in June 1944. (AAF)

**1Lt. Franklin Monk** downed a Zero to put him one victory away from becoming an ace. (AAF)

element leader, 1Lt. Herman Zehring, but could not find his #4, 2Lt. Robert Donald, who was last seen by Zehring to Split-S away after a Hamp. As they were climbing Monk spotted five enemy planes climbing head on from the right but Reeves also saw enemy fighters low at 10 o'clock. Monk, who was unable to see them, radioed to Zehring to take over the flight. Just as Monk turned the flight over, Zehring sighted 10 to 15 enemy fighters below over Humboldt Bay. Zehring dove and got on the tail of an Oscar and sent in down shedding pieces as it crashed into the ocean. A dogfight ensued and Zehring fired at a few fleeting targets and then fired a long burst at another Oscar that crashed on the shore of Humboldt Bay for his fourth and last victory. Low on fuel, Yellow Flight withdrew and returned to Nadzab. In the debriefing witnesses reported seeing Donald's right engine smoking and a Zero shoot off his tail and then seeing the P-38 spiral into the ground.

Lent's Blue Flight arrived when the Japanese came in from the right and were disrupted by Monk's Yellow Flight. Lent's three flight members took evasive action but Lent saw White #3 and #4, ahead of him, 1Lt. Robert Herman and his Wingman, 1Lt. Robert Crosswait, being attacked by an Oscar that shot out Herman's Prestone reservoir. Lent dove ahead to the rescue and closed on the tail of the enemy fighter and fired off two quick bursts that hit its engine. The Japanese pilot tried to dive away but is fighter exploded. By this time Lent's Blue Flight was scattered and Lent joined a formation of three P-38s at a lower altitude and continued to cover the bombers. Near the target area Lent noticed the P-38 ahead (undoubtedly 2Lt. Robert Donald) begin to trail smoke from its starboard engine. Lent radioed to the pilot to head home but as the P-38 turned around; the white smoke turned to a dark black. Lent called to the pilot to feather the engine but without success and after several minutes the engine burst into flames and the Lightning went into a spin. As it was descending, an Oscar dove from above left to make a pass but Lent who was covering the crippled P-38 hit the Oscar with a burst that set it aflame and it was observed to crash for Lent's 11th and last victory. Lent watched as the P-38's tail boom disintegrated at 5,000 feet and then exploded in a fiery crash into the ground. Lent's Wingman, 2Lt. Merle Pearson rejoined Lent who was now circling higher over the crash site and they headed home.

After Herman's Lightning was hit Crosswait escorted him back to Nadzab. During their dive away from the fight Crosswait saw two Zeros about to make a pass at them. He pulled up and shot its cowling off and it went down trailing heavy smoke (1Lt. Alvin Kidd would confirm Crosswait's only victory). Crosswait fired a short burst at the second Zero which flew off without observable results.

432FS

The 432FS sent up 21 P-38s led by Capt. Arthur Peregoy at 0755 to escort another B-24 strike to Hollandia. At 0905 rendezvous was made with the three groups of bombers over Buriu which was just north of the Sepik River and southwest of Wewak. 2Lt. Warren Cortner's oxygen supply ran out a few minutes before reaching the target and he was forced to turn back. About 10 minutes before reaching the target area Tonys were sighted approaching the bombers at 9 o'clock high. The squadron dropped their tanks and dove on the Tonys that then turned away from their attack on the bombers while they were still far out of range. Three more Oscars came toward the bombers and were easily discouraged by the Lightning pilots who only had to turn into them to make them break off. Nine more attacks were turned away without firing a shot. The only Squadron pilot to score that day was Red Flight Element Leader, 1Lt. Billy Gresham, who got several hits on the fuselage and near the cockpit of an Oscar. Gresham didn't see the enemy fighter crash as he had to pull up out of his dive and had to claim a probable. Squadron Leader, Capt. Peregoy writes in his ICR: "The Nips were very 'uneager' and avoided contact with us even when they had the advantage. They were fair at evasive tactics but could have maneuvered to better advantage and gotten a shot or two at us."

# 6

## April 1944

**3 April 1944: Attack on Hollandia**
Fragmentation bombs dropped by the nocturnal B-24s had destroyed the enemy aircraft parked in their revetments and the two missions of 30 and 31 March against Hollandia, destroyed over 200 enemy aircraft in the area. Unable to prevent 5th Air Force from destroying their aircraft based a Hollandia the Japanese finally reacted by removing the majority of the bombers from their Hollandia bases leaving fighters to intercept the 5AF raids that were certain to come after the bad weather occurring during 1-2 April. The weather gave both the Americans and Japanese at Hollandia a brief respite. The 5FC used the opportunity for much needed maintenance on its P-38s while the Japanese tried to regroup and make major repairs to their base. On 3 April the weather cleared and the P-38s escorted the Liberators to the targets in the Hollandia area once more. The B-24s were followed by a second wave was composed of Douglas A-20 attack bombers which swept in at treetop level, strafing, and dropping parafrag bombs. To conclude what was one of the most successful missions ever flown by the Fifth Air Force, a third wave of B-25 Mitchells bombed and strafed targets of opportunity and when they left the remaining Japanese aerial strength at Hollandia was decimated.

**3 April 1944: 8FG/80FS**
There was no enemy interception over the target but as the 80FS Lead and Second Flights arrived over the Hollandia Airfields they saw enemy fighters overhead at 11 o'clock. The two flights dropped their tanks and the Lead Flight climbed toward the enemy fighters overhead while the Second Flight Leader turned into four enemy fighters closing from starboard.

Mission Leader, Capt. Cornelius Smith and Wingman, 1Lt. Charles Ray, of Red Flight had dropped their tanks and followed them from the target when they saw two Oscars make a pass at the bombers. The two American pilots pursued the enemy fighters down through the bomber formation. Ray closed rapidly and caught an Oscar and began firing from 300 yards and closed to about 150 yards hitting the wing root and canopy causing the fighter to explode for his third victory. During this mission Lt.Col. Emmett Davis of the 5FC HQ was a guest pilot leading the second element of the first flight when two Oscars got on his tail. 1Lt. Vernon Jenner was flying on Davis' wing and chased off the two enemy attackers.

1Lt. Leland Blair started the mission by leading a flight but due to various snafus ended up joining the second flight as its Element Leader. Blair and his Wingman climbed to port after the top two enemy planes, Blair took one on and fired a short burst at 60 degrees deflection sending it down smoking. Blair saw two enemy fighters firing on the last two P-38s in his flight and then saw one trailing coolant. Blair climbed to help the P-38s in trouble but two Oscars attacked his Wingman and Blair had to turn into to them to chase them away. Blair got a long 45 degree burst that set on fire and saw it crash north of Humboldt Bay for his third and last victory. Two Oscars maneuvered behind Blair and his Wingman and the two dove away to safety

The star of the day's battle was 1Lt. Cyril Homer who was credited with four victories; two over Oscars and two over Tonys. Homer recounts the air battle:

> One Oscar dove away while the other two started a gentle turn into me as I climbed under them. I fired a 10 degree deflection shot at the rear enemy fighter and hit him when he half rolled. I rolled down with him and got in a direct tail shot as he leveled off. Black smoke poured from the engine, and a few seconds later this Oscar caught fire and dove into the mountain north of the target. He carried a bomb under his right wing.
>
> I then saw two Tonys in range behind two P-38s firing. I called the P-38s but they continued in a gentle climb. As I was out of range, I could do no good. The first P-38 half rolled with his left engine smoking badly. The second P-38 followed with his right engine smoking. The Tonys continued level flight until they saw me. They began a gentle dive toward Cyclops Strip. My Wingman, Lieutenant Fletcher (2Lt. Bud Fletcher), and I followed, closing into range very gradually. Three thousand feet from the ground I caught the rear Tony, closing to 75 yards before firing. When I fired, the smoke from this Tony was so bad I could not see him and had to pull up as he fell off to the left. I continued and both Lieutenant Fletcher and I fired at the first Tony, which all this time had been trailing quite a bit of smoke. I caught him with a burst as he tried to enter a cloud, whereupon he fell to the left and dived straight into the ground.
>
> I made a 180 degree turn and dived over the other Tony, which had hit a small hill and created quite a fire. When I next looked back my Wingman was gone. As I turned back I saw an Oscar about 100 yards from his tail. I forced this Oscar to break away but scored no hits. More Oscars dived on us and I saw Lieutenant Fletcher set one aflame about 400 yards to the rear of me. [Author: Meanwhile, Fletcher then flew off alone and made two passes at an Oscar and shot it down with a four second 60 degree deflection shot. After Fletcher scored his victory another Oscar sneaked to 100 yards of Fletcher's tail but Homer saw it and chased it off. Ten more Oscars dove on the two pilots but six more P-38s arrived.] Six more P-38s joined us as about 10

Oscars dived on us. I caught one Oscar with a 60 degree deflection shot. This enemy fighter was about 300 yards behind a P-38. It started smoking and half rolled. As it recovered I put in a three second burst tail shot from about 300 yards. It rolled to the right, pulled up once, then dived into the water northwest of target area about 40 miles.

As I pulled off him I looked back to find a Tony directly behind firing at me. I pushed over and did vertical reverses, going straight down till I attained 400 miles per hour. I pulled out just over the water and flew due north, gradually outdistancing the Tony. After five minutes he turned back, so I turned and followed him until he joined about five enemy fighters.

Being alone and having two holes in my left wing, I turned for home, climbing to 20,000 feet and continuing to Buriu in a gentle letdown, where I picked up Lieutenant Dwinell, who had his right engine feathered. I escorted him back to Nadzab. All Oscars I observed were camouflaged brown and green. Red roundels with white outer rim. Some had two white stripes where tail joined fuselage. Some, about two I remember, had yellow rings on leading edge of engine cowling.

**1Lt. Kenneth Ladd** became a double ace when he shot down an Oscar. (AAF)

**1Lt. Cyril Homer** was the day's top scorer with four victories (two Tonys and two Oscars), to give him 13 victories. (AFAA)

The four victories gave Homer 13 victories.

1Lt. Kenneth Ladd was leading the fifth and last flight and after dropping tanks followed the flight ahead in a long string. The string made two passes at enemy fighters that were attacking the bombers and succeeded in scattering them. Ladd's Flight spotted a lone Oscar at 12 o'clock and he closed to 200 yards and his cannon shells hit the enemy's fuselage and sent it down for his 10th victory to become a double ace. 1Lt. Jesse Corallo was flying as Ladd's Wingman and went after an Oscar that began a Split-S and dropped below it and shot it down for his second and last victory.

The 80th P-38s did not break off the combat until the B-24s were safely on their way back to base. In this combat the Japanese were more determined but lost 10 fighters but three P-38s were damaged and rookie 2Lt. Stephen Endres was wounded in the hand and arm and landed at Gusap for medical treatment. Endres' Element Leader, 1Lt. William Dwinell, lost coolant in an engine and feathered it. Homer, who escorted Dwinell home, had two holes in his port wing. Thus far in the Hollandia bombing campaign the 80th had shot down 24 fighters and only five P-38s had been damaged and one 432FS Lightning and pilot had been lost.

**3 April 1944: 475FG/432FS/431FS/433FS**

432FS

On the 3rd the 475th was able to put up 55 Lightnings but it was the 432nd that did the heavy scoring. At 0910 Lt.Col. MacDonald led Clover Squadron and Red Flight with the 2Lt. John Hannan as his Wingman. 1Lt. Henry Condon (Wingman: 2Lt. John Temple) was leading Clover Green, 1Lt. John Loisel (Wingman: 2Lt. Jack Luddington) was Clover Blue Leader, and 1Lt. Elliot Summer (Wingman: 2Lt. Calvin Anderson) led Clover White Flight. The two plane spare flight was led by 1Lt. Clifford Mann with F/O Joseph Barton. The Squadron took off at 0900 to escort A-20s and B-25s to Hollandia and rendezvoused with the bombers north of Gusap at 0930. They arrived at the target area at 1135 at 8,000 feet where the bombers called enemy fighters in the area and they dropped their tanks and went into combat formation.

MacDonald's Clover Red Flight came upon six Oscars in loose string approaching the A-20s on the southeast side of Sentani Lake and led his P-38s down to break up the enemy attack. Wingman Hannan followed MacDonald in an attack on another Oscar that he had to break off to avoid crashing into the mountains. The two P-38s navigated between the mountain peaks until they came back toward the Hollandia Airstrips. Hannan took a long 45 degree deflection shot at an Oscar that flamed briefly and then its pilot turned so tightly that he almost rammed Hannan before crashing. MacDonald and Hannan made a few more passes in the area before flying over Humboldt Bay to rejoin the bombers and at 1210 they were heading back to base. Clover Red Second Element Leader, 1Lt. John Michener, and Wingman 2Lt. Alex Ilnicki, followed MacDonald and Michener made a pass on a Zero at close range but missed and overran it when the enemy pilot went into a violent turn.

1Lt. Elliot Summer led Clover White Flight down on this Zero attacking the A-20s dodging bursts of AA fire. Summer got into very close range and flamed the Oscar for his seventh victory. Summer then saw a P-38 with an Oscar on its tail directly above and pulled straight up and fired until he stalled and the surprised Oscar pilot broke off his attack. Summer and his Wingman, 2Lt. Calvin Anderson, made several more passes with Anderson hitting a Zero that was already smoking but did not see the ultimate result and made no claim. White Flight then joined the bombers after their run and escorted them home.

Red #3 and #4 continued to follow Red #1 and #2 in trail and saw two enemy fighters about 500 feet above them east along Sentani Lake. One began to dive on Michener who turned 90 degrees into a cloud while Ilnicki turned into the Zero and fired at 200 yards causing it to break away and Ilnicki did not have a chance to observe any results. When Michener

**Maj. Richard Bong** selected the 432FS as a means to score his 25th victory, and to move one victory closer to the American victory record. (AAF)

**Capt. John Loisel's** P-38 shows the two new victories to make him a double ace. (AAF)

**1Lt. Perry Dahl** poses in a fighter with four victories, which is unexplained, as Dahl scored two victories on 3 April to move from three immediately confirmed victories to five to make him an ace. (AFAA)

**1Lt. Joseph Forster** claimed his first three victories after two previous probables. (AFAA)

came out of the cloud he saw another Zero approaching and ducked back into the cloud. Michener then joined Loisel's Blue Flight and tagged along to Sentani Lake where he saw P-38s chasing a Zero just over the water. Michener closed to 100 yards and fired a long burst that only damaged the Zero which flew off as Michener passed over it. While heading for Humboldt Bay to rejoin his own flight Michener observed Loisel and his Wingman, 2Lt. John Luddington descending to strafe the enemy luggers in the water near shore.

When Loisel and Clover Blue Flight reached the southeast shore of Lake Sentani, he heard the A-20 crews call out Japanese fighters over the radio. The P-38s were at an altitude of 8,000 feet when Loisel sighted the group of Japanese fighters flying in a loose string heading west which were about to be intercepted by MacDonald's Red Flight. He then looked down and saw eight Oscars in two flights flying just off the deck. Loisel immediately dove on these lower Oscars and quickly closed on their tails. He opened fire on the leader from 300 yards with a short burst and then turned on the Wingman, pressing to only 50 yards, hitting its fuselage

**1Lt. Elliott Summer** (left) scored one victory to give him seven, while **1Lt. Henry Condon** (right) scored his third victory (1Lt. William Ritter is in the center). (AAF)

and wing roots and the enemy fighter broke sharply to port and fell off and crashed. Loisel and Wingman, Luddington, made numerous attacks, mostly short difficult deflection shots, at close range at the fleeing enemy fighters. Loisel got on the tail of a Hamp and fired a short burst and it "augured into the mountains" for his tenth victory to become a double ace. Meanwhile, the Clover Blue Flight second element of 1Lt. Perry Dahl and Wingman, 1Lt. Joseph Forster, met a four Oscar flight over Lake Sentai. They then spotted a two Tony element heading south preceding the Oscars and chased them. Forster was the first to score as he caught the first Tony with hits behind its engine and the Oscar was observed by Dahl to go down on the Lake's shore. Forster then continued his fire through to the second Tony which was hit and he watched it crash into a hillside. Forster and Dahl pulled back into string and made several more passes without result. Forster made a head on pass at another Oscar that started to smoke as he passed over it and then watched another P-38 finish it off. As he pulled back into the string, Forster saw an Oscar and made several passes at it getting some cannon hits. Loisel then led his Flight and trailed the enemy across Hollandia Drome and finally "cornered it against the mountains." Forster fired a head on pass and the Zero began to smoke and then go out of control. The enemy pilot climbed out on the wing and Forster gave him a short burst and both plane and pilot headed for the water for his third victory of the day and first on his way to becoming an ace. After Forster shot down the Oscar, Dahl saw that Temple had a Zero on his tail but evaded it by diving into a cloud. Dahl followed the Zero into the cloud and as it exited the cloud Dahl gave it a short burst in the starboard wing root and gasoline streamed out the tanks and the Zero crashed into the Lake. Dahl pulled up and immediately began to fire an Oscar hitting from nose to tail and starting its engine on fire and its pilot tried to make it to the strip but crashed and burned for Dahl's fifth victory to become an ace. On their way back to rejoin the bombers, Dahl and Forster strafed a twin bomber on the Hollandia Strip and set on fire and then a strafer lugger in the Harbor.

Condon's Clover Green Flight trailed Blue Flight behind the original six Oscars and after Condon watched Loisel score his victory, Condon turned his Flight back south away from the Lake and became separated from Wingman Temple and #4 man, 2Lt. Harrold Owen. As Temple emerged from the clouds alone he saw P-38s chasing an Oscar and joined the Lightnings and saw Loisel destroy the Oscar. Temple then joined Dahl and the two saw Zeros climbing toward them. But before the Zeros could attack, Temple was attacked by an Oscar and Temple escaped into a cloud. After pulling out of the cloud Temple saw a Zero flying into range 600 feet below and 400 feet to port. He fired a short 40 degree deflection shot and flashed past the enemy at high diving speed. (Dahl later confirmed this victory as he saw it splash into Sentani Lake.) Meanwhile, Owen went off and made several unsuccessful passes with undetermined results. After losing his #2 and #4, Condon found he only had 1Lt. Laurence LeBaron continuing with him. When he arrived over the south side of Sentani Lake, Condon saw an Oscar at about 500 feet being pursued by six P-38s. This skillful Oscar pilot was adeptly turning inside the fire of his attackers because they were consistently overshooting him while the enemy pilot skidded and turned at about 150 miles an hour. Condon cut his throttles to lower his airspeed to that of the Oscar and slipped in behind. As soon as he began firing the Oscar turned to the right, giving a Condon a better shot and the Oscar took hits in the wings and cockpit before it began to smoke slightly and plunged into the trees for Condon's third victory.

Capt. Richard Bong, the leading ace in the Pacific with 24 confirmed victories, could attach himself to any P-38 unit in action and joined the Clover Squadron for the day. He took off from Gusap at 0905 and joined the Squadron at Annenberg. On his arrival over the target at 1130 he spotted "four or five SSF over Sentani Lake…two were shot down immediately by the lead flight" (MacDonald's Red). Bong fired on an Oscar but missed and followed it down as its pilot Split-S'd away. Bong fired two 90 degree deflection shots with no result and then got on its tail and scored a few hits but the Oscar continued on. Another flight of P-38s came in and made passes with result. Bong got on its tail again and finally got enough hits and it gradually descended to port; its engine catching fire and crashing into the side of a hill 50 yards from the west side of the Lake for his 25th victory; one away from Rickenbacker and Foss.

The last Clover Squadron flight was the two ship spare flight of 1Lt. Clifford Mann and Wingman, F/O Joseph Barton which came in behind Clover Green during the combat. Mann spotted two Tonys closing quickly behind his Wingman and warned him to drop his tanks and dive away to starboard. Barton eluded these Tonys at 4,000 feet and rejoined Mann but the two lost Green Flight. Mann saw a string of P-38s below and started to join them when he saw that Barton was again being pursued by two Tonys. Mann turned to aid Barton but his Wingman flew into a cloud and Mann was unable to follow. Mann was unable to contact Barton by radio and was too low on fuel to search for him and Barton was listed as MIA as his fighter was seen to crash by an A-20 crew.

Loisel's ICR described the Japanese pilots "as on the whole as inexperienced and not aggressive." When the 432nd left Hollandia MacDonald's ICR reported that the "strips looked like junk yards." The 432FS would not have another aerial claim until 8 June.

431FS

Maj. Verl Jett led 20 P-38s off from Nadzab Strip #3 at 0910 to escort B-25 and A-20 strafers to Hollandia and rendezvoused with them at 1040 north of the Sepik River. When the Squadron arrived over the target area at 1140 they orbited the area while weaving at 9,000 feet for a half hour while the bomber strafers "did an excellent job on the strips at Hollandia, causing many fires of the burning aircraft and fuel variety." (Jett ICR) Only a lone Oscar was spotted flying on the deck and Red Leader, Maj. Jett, and his entire flight made several passes on an Oscar, appearing to score hits. The second flight dove after it but overran. 1Lt. John Cohn of the third flight then made a diving turn onto its tail and fired as it turned to port. There were explosions in its wing and fuselage and it then turned and crashed into the trees for the Squadron's only claim for the day; Cohn's second and last victory.

433FS

Capt. Richard Kimball was leading Green Flight with 1Lt. Clarence Ricman as his Wingman and Maj. Warren Lewis as his #4 man (Lewis snafued earlier and returned to fly with Green Flight). The Flight was part of 16 Possum Lightnings flying at 9,000 feet on a B-25 escort to Hollandia. At 1145 they saw a lone Zero flying at 1,000 feet and Lewis (probably using

**Capt. Warren Lewis** finally became an ace after five previous probables and two damaged claims. (AFAA)

his Major's rank) dove first and after a short chase out to sea on the deck he fired a long burst from the rear quarter from 100 yards into its cockpit and engine. The Zero cartwheeled onto the water and then skidded into the jungle and Lewis became an ace after five previous probable and two damaged claims. As Green Flight flew southeast at 3,000 feet along the Hollandia coast they saw a lone Oscar flying west on the deck. Kimball dove on it and the enemy pilot turned back toward land. Kimball cut his throttles and stayed behind the Oscar and fired two long bursts that hit its mid-fuselage. The Oscar turned sharply to port, hit the water, bounced off, and crashed into the trees without burning for his third and last victory.

**Capt. Richard Kimball** was credited with his third and last victory. (AAF)

### 3 April 1944: Hollandia Destroyed

On 3 April the destruction of all enemy aircraft based at Hollandia was completed. Recon photos revealed a total of 288 wrecked and burned out aircraft. Sixty-three B-24s had opened the attack, by dropping 492 1,000 pound bombs on the antiaircraft positions followed by 171 B-25 and A-20 strafers which attacked over the tree tops to finish off any remaining intact enemy aircraft. The heavy bombers were escorted by 76 P-38 which met 30 enemy fighters and downed 25 of them while bomber gunners claimed two more. One P-38 was lost (Barton/432FS). Kenney received congratulations from Admiral Nimitz and MacArthur who sent his message without encoding it so that the Japanese could read it.

Although engineers later discovered that the value of the Hollandia area to support air bases and supply depots was overestimated; 5AF airfields there would suppress the Japanese presence in New Guinea and support the remainder of the fighting in New Guinea. Ground forces would advance under air protection to capture another airfield which could then be used to support the next leap forward.

### April 1944: 348FG at Saidor

By the end of March the 348[th] endured constant rain and mud of Saidor that curtailed much operational flying. There were only a few clear days and the Owen Stanleys were chronically under heavy cloud cover. However, an improvement at Saidor was that the group's tents all had wood floors and were on raised platforms to avoid the muddy jungle floor. On 12 April a new A-20 attempted an emergency landing on the downhill, rain-soaked Saidor strip and slid into parked 348FG P-47s, destroying two P-47s including Capt. Benz' favorite, *Dirty Old Man*.

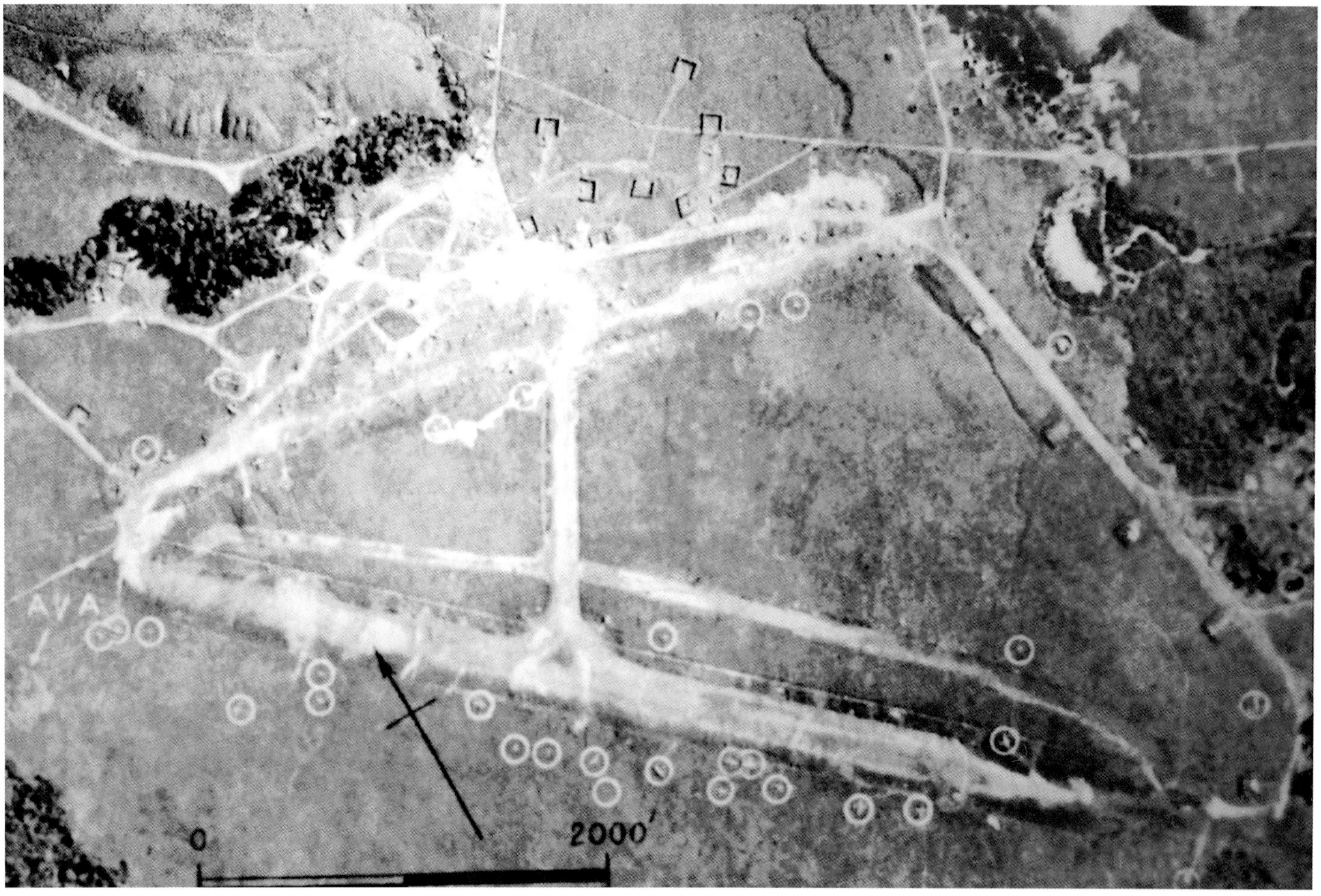


The 3 April raid on **Hollandia** was the most successful 5AF mission, as the bombers and fighters decimated Japanese aerial strength in the area. The circles on the photo show enemy aircraft destroyed on the ground (an additional 25 were destroyed in the air). (AAF)

**Lily** bombers as part of the 288 enemy aircraft destroyed on the ground during the 5th Air Force attacks on Hollandia. (AAF)

Thunderbolts of the **342FS/348FG** at Saidor. (AAF)

The Japanese would occasionally attack Saidor. Red alerts were usually only "Washing-machine Charlie," a badly tuned bomber, slipping under the radar to drop a bomb or two just to harass the sleeping troops. Tokyo Rose even claimed that Imperial Japanese bombers had bombed a secret underground hangar at Saidor which caused the men to chuckle as they had not seen a hangar since they left Australia.

**April 1944: 49FG**

MacArthur's decision to move his invasion plans for the Philippines forward excluded the 49FG from the frontline air forces for the first time in the war. With the 7th and 8th squadrons still equipped with the short range P-40 and the 9FS about to reequip with the P-38, Lt.Col. David Campbell's high scoring fighter group was relegated to a benign tactical and escort role over the north central New Guinea coast while the 80FS Headhunters of the 8FG battled over the new JAAF headquarters at Hollandia and replaced Maj. Wallace Jordan's Flying Knights as the top scoring squadron in the Pacific.

During this time, the Warhawks of Capt. Arland Stanton's 7FS and Capt. Robert McHale's 8FS flew tactical or escort missions; strafing and bombing targets along the coast or flying to Tadji to escort the returning B-24s and B-25s returning to Nadzab. In these slow times pilots from the three squadrons were scheduled for additional training in their aircraft. Other pilots were sent to Nadzab or Dobodura where they would fly familiarization flights in the P-38.

During the first week in April 7FS CO Stanton was ordered by 5FC CO Wurtsmith to mobilize to leave Gusap. No one was disappointed to leave the poor weather and monotony of the remote base and by mid April, the enlisted men from HQ and the 7FS were ready to board the C-47s. Maj. McHale had also been ordered to ready his 8th Squadron for a move and trucks transported men and equipment to the 49ers headquarters at Gusap for the imminent move. Operations were soon relegated to the target egress escorts.

Campbell's 49ers ground echelons eventually boarded air transports at Gusap and flew off to the Allied staging harbor at Finschhafen. In the interim, the air echelons awaited transports to the north but due to another change in MacArthur's plans their destination presented the 5AF with a logistical dilemma.

**April 1944: 421NFS: Night fighter Operations Begin**

During February and March the Squadron was being prepared for its designated night fighter duties. On 13 February the first Douglas P-70 had been transferred to the Squadron from the 419NFS at Dobodura. The 418th sent another Nighthawk on the 16th and three more on 10 March. A lone P-70 arrived from Brisbane a day later. All these aircraft required extensive maintenance before they could be considered operational at Saidor by the end of the month. Spare parts and aircraft equipment were virtually non-existent to service these stripped down P-70s, including most of the radio equipment. Squadron personnel cannibalized damaged and wrecked aircraft and conducted "midnight raids" on service depots. By the end of March Nadzab was becoming further away from the combat zone and the Squadron began to stage out of Saidor on the northeastern coast of New Guinea. On 5 April Maj. Walter Pharr led a detachment, "A" Flight, of all six P-70s to base at Saidor to fly patrols, and to bomb and strafe bridges, barges, and road traffic. Meanwhile, the major portion of the Squadron remained at Nadzab.

The **421NFS** flew the inferior P-70 Nighthawk until the first P-61 Black Widows arrived in early June. (AAF)

The Saidor detachment began flying combat missions against the Japanese in the area. "A" Flight benefited from the period of the full moon and began flying a series of night bombing and harassing attacks along with patrols. Japanese air activity was negligible and only one interception was attempted when Lt. Rolland Forrester, who was airborne during an enemy attack, was directed toward an enemy bomber. However, the bomber was too far away and Forrester returned to base after a short chase. During the remainder of the month the 421st "A" detachment at Saidor launched numerous successful bombing and strafing attacks on installations, bridges, barges.

Meanwhile, at Nadzab the main Squadron experienced its first casualty of the war when on 8 April 2Lt. Alexander Kusmack was killed during a landing accident at Nadzab. During the month the Nadzab contingent flew weather recon missions until they were finally closed down on the 25th. The Squadron's P-38s were withdrawn by the end of April but the P-70 operations continued their mostly routine missions when the weather permitted. The Squadron's pilots had no training in low level night bombing and the results were not usually observed.

On 21 April, 421 CO. Maj. Pharr received orders to proceed to Brisbane to examine the new Northrop P-61 Black Widow night fighters that had just arrived from the States. The Squadron personnel assembled four of the Black Widows and pilots test flew them before the Northrop factory techs and technical plans arrived to help them. However, while at Brisbane Maj. Pharr suffered a mental breakdown and had to be replaced by Squadron Operations Officer, Capt. William Bradley on 15 May. On 1 June the first three P-61s arrived at Nadzab (the fourth turned back after it was damaged landing on a grass field at Rock Hampton). On 8 June two more P-61s arrived at Nadzab and three were sent to Wakde to replace the P-70s. The pilots and R/Os immediately clocked as much flying time as possible in their new aircraft.

**April 1944: 35FG**

April was a quiet month for the Group as it participated in no aerial combat as the Japanese air forces had been so diminished that it could not mount even token resistance and the Group roamed at will; fearing only minimal AA fire. The Group's 1,612 combat sorties for the month included routine patrol and the escort of bombers and transports but fighter sweeps of the Wewak area provided a large part of its sorties and excitement. The sweeps attacked enemy personnel and bivouac areas; supply, ammunition, and fuel dumps, and targets of opportunity such as coastal shipping and barge traffic, road and personnel movement, etc. On 22 April, Maj. William McDonough, five victory ace and well-liked former Group Ops Officer and Deputy Commander was killed at Port Moresby just before he was to be rotated home. During a routine flight his engine failed and he was forced to bail out and died of a broken neck.

**April 1944: 58FG P-47 Tire Problems**

On 1 April, 2Lt. James Farmer of the 69FS was taking off in a P-47 D-4 from Dobodura when his tire blew out and landing gear collapsed. The fighter's 200 gallon belly tank burst into flames but Farmer escaped the inferno but died the next day from his burns. This incident was the beginning of a series of tire problems on the Thunderbolt. The 58FG reported seven blown tires in one day during take offs and landings and finally Goodrich Tire Company sent out a representative who worked with Squadron Engineering Departments who observed and tested the tires. The P-47's loaded weight was about 16,000 pounds and the pierced metal matting prevalent throughout the area ripped the knobby tire tread, especially if the tire pressure was low. The introduction of smooth contour tires later and careful monitoring and maintaining of tire pressure seemed to be of great help but the tire problem never was never completely eliminated during the war.

**11 April 1944: 49FG/7FS**

By April, the 5th Bomber Command missions to Wewak were considered a milk run and new bomber crews were often initiated to combat by attacking the once impressive enemy complex from low altitude against light, inaccurate AA fired by the few remaining troops. On 11 April the 312BG flying their new A-20s, were on an orientation mission, escorted by the 7FS Black Sheep. The P-40 pilots were surprised to see a lone Tony at 10,000 feet over the abandoned airdrome. Mission leader 1Lt. Robert Aschenbrener called the target and began a climbing attack. The outnumbered enemy pilot, rather than using his large altitude advantage to escape, plunged toward the shoreline and headed west and suddenly turned into the five Black Sheep. Aschenbrener fired over 700 rounds and the other pilots hit him as well. Finally, 1Lt. Edward Glascock administered the *coup d'grace* for his first victory.

**11 April 1944: 58FG/311FS**

During the morning of 11 April the 311FS was assigned a maximum effort sending 16 Thunderbolts to cover the B-25s on a bombing mission to Boram Airdrome at Wewak. Foster was scheduled to fly although he was already on leave orders. The Squadron took off from Saidor at 1010 with one aborting after 20 minutes with engine problems. The remaining fighters rendezvoused with the bombers at 10,000 feet over Annenberg at 1050. As the Mitchells turned northwestward, the 311th climbed to their assigned middle cover altitude of 12,000 feet. At 1125 the B-25s bombed Boram Airdrome with good results. Squadron pilots saw what appeared to be a twin engine A-20 bomber in the water off Boram and also saw a flight of P-47s from another squadron in combat with four Tonys just southeast of Wewak. Then looking up they observed seven Tonys and four Hamps at about 13,000 feet, coming toward them flying abreast, head on from the northwest. The enemy fighters had the altitude advantage when they made a pass from the north toward a 311th's three plane flight. The American flight dove away to the starboard, then climbed in a 360 degree turn to 20,000 feet. Once at 20,000 feet, 2Lt. Marvin Rothman, who had lost his Wingman earlier as an abort, was mysteriously missing. Other 311th pilots made

Five victory ace **Maj. William McDonough** (right) was killed during a routine non-combat flight just before he was to rotate home. (AAF)

short firing passes at the Japanese fighters but with no definite results. One Thunderbolt dove to the deck and then headed back to base. Several others climbed and circled at 10,000 feet where they sighted two Tonys below and dove but were unable to get within firing range. The Squadron rejoined on the deck and left the target area at 1150. During the initial encounter 2Lt. Thomas Bullington and his Wingman, 2Lt. William Graham, were last seen diving toward the clouds to evade the enemy fighters who had significant altitude advantage. A radio message from Bullington was received at the beginning of the action requesting directions but neither Bullington nor Graham returned to Saidor nor did Rothman.

**12 April 1944: 8FG/80FS Bong Becomes America's Ace-of-Aces**

Capt. Jay Robbins led 19 80FS P-38s in five flights on the two hour flight to Hollandia area on a B-24 escort mission. Maj. Richard Bong had scored his 25th victory with the 432FS on the 3 April Hollandia mission and since the 80FS was in the thick of the fighting Bong decided to fly with them on this mission. When the P-38s first saw the Oscars and Tonys, they were making diving passes at the Liberators in groups of two and three. Before the 80th could come to the rescue a B-24 was hit and dropped out of formation.

Robbins saw three Tonys at 9 o'clock on the tails of several P-38s and then he saw two others coming up behind him. He continued turning and fired a long burst that forced two of the Tonys off the rear of one P-38. He had hit the Tony but couldn't see the results. Second Flight Leader, Capt. Cornelius Smith, dropped his tanks when he saw two Oscars going after Robbins ("who seemed to pick him out as their special target"). Smith was flying in a wide circle and dropped his flaps to cut off the Oscars. Once in range he fired two long 90 degree deflection shots and hit one of the Oscars which crashed into Lake Sentani. The victory was Smith's 11th and last of the war.

After Smith freed Robbins from his attackers Robbins saw two Tonys at three o'clock low and dove after one toward the deck and the enemy pilot went into the standard Japanese defensive Split-S that was frequently effective in evading P-38s. But as the Tony pulled out very low and went into a gentle climb Robbins expertly went into a steep turn back under the tail of the Tony that was turning sharply to port. Robbins fired at very close range and shot it down in flames near Lake Sentani. Robbins then climbed and found himself in the middle of another dogfight. Robbins spotted a Tony and climbed on it; making a turn and a half and fired and got some damaging hits but it escaped. He saw three Tonys at 9 o'clock high and climbed to make a pass. One Tony pilot turned briefly into Robbins but then headed toward the clouds over the mountains. Robbins got two passes at the retreating Tony pilot but couldn't get a good shot and climbed over the Hollandia Strip at 3,000 feet. He then chased a diving and turning Tony down to the deck over the strip. Robbins shot the Tony down just over the airstrip as "friendly" bombs began exploding around him and he quickly climbed away from the bomb bursts. As he got above the clouds Robbins closed on another enemy fighter but found his gunsight was out he fired a long range shot, getting some hits before heading back to base with two Tony victories and two damaged claims which gave him 18 total victories.

2Lt. Russell Roth had an Oscar pilot flying barrel rolls make an overhead pass on him but Roth did not fire as these maneuvers made the Oscar hard to hit. Roth left his formation to go after another Oscar that made a pass from the side. He fired a short 90 degree deflection shot but under led it. Two more Oscars Split-S'd in trail from above as they were fired on by other P-38s. Roth turned head on into them and got hits on the cowling of one and it began to smoke for a probable as no witnesses saw it crash. Roth hit the second Oscar at close range and it exploded and the wreckage spiraled into the trees. The busy Roth made pass at another Oscar at 7,000 feet and followed it down without seeing any results. He then fired at yet another Oscar but it escaped into a cloud. Finally he chased an Oscar for 10 miles out to sea and when two more Oscars appeared they convinced Roth to turn around and find other Lightnings to follow back to base. Roth's Wingman, 1Lt. Vernon Jenner, attacked another Oscar that took many hits but did not burn or go out of control for a damaged claim. Capt. Edward Robertson, leading the third flight, was credited with a probable. For his busy day Roth was credited with his first of two victories and a probable.

Capt. Burnell Adams and Wingman 2Lt. Nicholas Zinni were flying in the rear element of the last six P-38s in the 80FS escort and were joined by top Pacific ace Capt. Richard Bong. The three P-38s were in the high flight at 14,000 feet and dropped tanks as soon as they saw five Oscars flying in two groups of two and three above them at 17,000-18,000 feet. They began climbing toward the two Oscars and Adams was able to close on one unsuspecting enemy pilot and fired until it burst into flame and crashed about two miles northwest of Hollandia. The other Oscar rolled over quickly and dove away with Bong and Zinni in pursuit. But that Oscar escaped while Zinni was having trouble releasing one of his drop tanks.

After Zinni jettisoned the tank he saw Bong trailing an Oscar that was descending with heavy smoke spilling behind it. Bong broke off the combat as the Oscar hit the water and soon was on the tail of another Oscar. He fired a short burst and it flew away smoking. Adams and Zinni rejoined and

Ex-6NFS night fighter pilot **Capt. Burnell Adams** shot down a Tony and Oscar to become an ace with six victories. (AFAA)

**Capt. Jay Robbins** was credited with two victories to give him 18. (AFAA)

**Capt. Cornelius Smith** and his CC celebrate next to a recently applied 11 victory symbol. (AFAA)

engaged two Oscars milling around at 5,000 feet in some clouds. Adams closed an Oscar that was partially obscured in a thin cloud and fired a long burst and the enemy pilot turned sharply. Adams wrote in his ICR: "the next thing I knew he was sitting on my tail firing at me. I don't know how in the hell he did it but he did it damn fast." Adams dove out of the cloud expecting his Wingman to "knock him off' but Zinni was not there and Adams had to dive away. Adams then saw Bong make a pass at another Oscar but did not witness the result as he saw an enemy fighter come out of a cloud to port and turned into it but couldn't get into range and lost it. Adams then attacked an Oscar and saw his gunfire hit it but it kept on flying. Bong made a head on pass on it but did not score. Adams then got on its tail and fired a long burst that exploded it; sending oil over his windshield causing him to dive away. Adams then saw Bong dive on the tail of an Oscar flying on the deck and fire a short burst that sent into the water. Adam's two victories gave him six to become an ace.

The highlight of the day's combat occurred when Bong finally scored his 26th and 27th victories but a third Oscar went unconfirmed due to lack of witnesses. Bong became the first American pilot to top Rickenbacker's legendary total of 26 aerial victories and Maj. Joseph Foss' WWII record. However, the record 28 victories would be matched in May by Thunderbolt pilot Capt. Robert Johnson of the 56 FG in England.

Bong describes his record breaking combat:

> "I shot at the second one (Oscar) with no apparent effect. He dove for the clouds and I followed. I shot at him from the stern and he started smoking; we both went through a cloud and the Oscar went into the sea in Tanermerah Bay. Lt. Zinne saw me shoot at this plane and the smoke, and the resultant splash in the water. At this time we were separated from the rest of the squadron. I pulled up and saw two more SSF in an element headed towards a cloud. I closed on their tails and started the Wingman smoking and he turned off to the left. I shot at the leader and he started smoking and then entered a cloud and I lost him. Saw an Oscar on a P-38's tail and took a 30 degree deflection shot at him. His engine conked out and I got some hits in his left wing. He spiraled down and crashed into Tanermerah Bay. No one observed this forced landing. Sighted one Oscar below me and dove on him. He Split-S'd and I missed, pulled around and dove after him. He went down right to the deck and I closed and started shooting, he tried to turn and caught his wing on the water and crashed. Lt. Adams also made a pass on this airplane and he saw it crash as I closed and fired. We pulled up and joined some more P-38s when I saw another Oscar being chased by P-38s. I turned to cut him off and he Split-S'd. Another P-38 shot at him and he started to turn and he Split-S'd again. He pulled out two feet above the ground and shot at me coming up. I never saw this one again. Sighted no more enemy so I left the target at 1220 and landed at 1420."

At the end of the day April Hollandia mission the 80th had claimed more than 175 aerial victories and was in a virtual dead heat with the 9FS as top ranking Fighter Squadron in Fifth Air Force. The Headhunters began advertising itself as the top scoring twin engine fighter squadron in the world. The 5th Fighter Command would not score a victory until 7 May.

**12 April 1944: Bong Breaks Rickenbacker's Record and is Grounded!**
That same day General Kenney promoted Bong to Major, told him he would investigate the 28th kill as soon as Hollandia was in American hands and pulled him out of combat! Congratulations came in. MacArthur wired his "highest admiration for Major Bong's aerial skill and gallantry." Arnold wrote that "the Army Air Forces are proud of you and your splendid record." Even, Eddie Rickenbacker sent a message: "Just received good news that you are the first to break my record in World War I, by bringing down those 27 planes in combat as well as your promotion, so justly deserved. I hasten to offer my sincere congratulations with the hope that you will double or triple this number. But in trying, use the same cool, calculating technique that has brought you the results to date for we will need your kind back home after this war is over."

Kenney's grounding of Bong was due, in part, to a radio message that Arnold sent Kenney expressing his concern over "the high rate of loss of pilots who have shot down many enemy aircraft (meaning Kearby and Lynch)." Arnold requested Kenney's opinion on the "desirability of restricting from action combat flying or return to the United States of this type of personnel. A case in point is Captain Bong, who is credited with 27 victories." Kenney had started cutting orders to send Bong home.

Although Bong was not credited with the third Oscar he maintained it had definitely crashed and could be located on "kind of a coral reef, not very deep." After the Hollandia area had been secured Kenney sent in a diver to locate the Oscar that Bong claimed he shot down but was not confirmed. The diver found the Japanese fighter in the area where Bong said it went in and he was credited with three victories for the day in a corrected ICR on 24 December 1944.

**Maj. Richard Bong** scored two victories to give him 27 to break Capt. Eddie Rickenbacker and Maj. Joseph Foss' American victory record of 26. (AAF)

**16 April 1944: Black Sunday**

Easter Sunday, 16 April 1944, will always be known as "Black Sunday" to the Fifth Air Force. Despite sketchy weather conditions enroute to Hollandia almost every available P-38 was assigned to escort 58 B-24s, 46 B-25s, and 118 A-20s that were to conduct one last major strike before the invasion of Hollandia on 22 April. The attack phase was nearly faultless as the Japanese sent up no interceptors and no AA fire was encountered while the bombers carried out another successful attack that all but wiped out the fixed defenses in the Humboldt Bay area. On their way back to base, however, the aircraft encountered a weather front that had very suddenly spread across the Markham Valley to blanket Nadzab and the other fields in the area with low clouds and rain. The fighter aircraft in particular were running low on fuel and they desperately tried to get to the field at Saidor. Flight patterns were ignored and soon there was confusion everywhere as the pilots attempted landings with their last few drops of gasoline. When the final total was added, 19 bombers had been lost and 11 P-38s had gone down, along with two reconnaissance aircraft. But according to diligent Australian researcher Michael Claringbould's book on the subject, *Black Sunday*, the Fifth Air Force lost 37 aircraft.

8FG

The 19 experienced P-38 pilots of the 80FS all safely landed by 1530 despite flying into solid overcast from the southwest of Madang to Nadzab. However, the 16 Lightnings of the 36FS became disoriented when they were caught in heavy rain and blinding overcast in which fighters could collide or crash into the valley or run out of gas searching for a place to land. Then as the 36th fighters turned toward the coast they found an opening in the clouds. Once in the clearing the fighters were to circle to the left so that the flight leaders could find their bearings to make the flight down the coast to safety. Most of the P-38s made an orderly turn but in the confusion one of the flights became separated when one element consisting of 1Lt. Lawrence Reeves and 2Lt. Robert Keown turned to the right rather than the left and was never seen again. 2Lt. Walter Mikucky was last seen circling near Yulu Point and then his Lightning plunged and exploded into the sea.

475FG

The 475FG was to send up a total of 48 P-38s at 1100 with the 432FS escorting A-20s, the 433FS covering the B-25s, and the 431FS was to stay with the B-24s. Despite closing weather, four 432FS P-38s left earlier to escort F-7 Liberator photo-reconnaissance bombers over the target area from 1320 to 1400 to photograph the bombing results. Meanwhile the overcast near Dobodura finally closed in and the mission was cancelled. However, once near the target, F-7 escort, 1Lt. Robert Hubner experienced mechanical problems and was forced to abort and 1Lt. John Luddington escorted him back home.

By midmorning the sun was shining again and the mission was back on with the B-24s, B-25s and A-20s to be met by the P-38s at 10,000 feet on the way to the target, south of Wewak. Capt. Richard Kimball was leading 16 Lightnings of the 433FS as Possum Red One, 1Lt. Calvin Cal Wire led Possum White Flight, and 1Lt. Robert Tomberg, on his 100th mission, was leading 433FS Blue Flight. Two Possum P-38s were forced to abort with fuel problems leaving 14 to cover the B-25s as they closed on Humboldt Bay. The B-24s and the 431st P-38s went in first followed by Blue Flight that stayed with the B-25s until they dropped their bombs and turned around to go home. There were no enemy fighters and only a few puffs of AA fire coming from batteries that escaped the B-24 attack. With the extra remaining fuel because of the lack of Japanese air opposition Kimball led the Squadron into a "rat race" in and around the bombers, demonstrating their agility to the bomber crews. One by one the P-38s would use up the fuel in their external tanks, jettison them, and switch to their main tanks.

For the two days preceding the 16 April mission the weather services had recommended cancellation of operations because of the possibility of severe conditions developing in the late morning or afternoon. While the P-38s were cavorting in the lingering pocket of calm weather, a massive storm front extending from the Admiralty Islands in the north to the Gulf of Papua in the south would be blocking their way home as far north as Saidor.

1Lt. Calvin Wire and his Wingman, rookie 2Lt. Morton Ryerson, had aborted the mission earlier with fuel problems. When the two pilots arrived south of Wewak and as they approached the Owen Stanley Mountains they met a solid cloud bank reaching from the ground to as high as they could see. The veteran Wire calmly led his Wingman up to 20,000 feet to avoid the highest peaks of the mountain range but the clouds still towered above them. Wire and Ryerson then flew to the north looking for an opening but found none and the two continued to fly back and forth looking for an opening. Wire and Ryerson met a B-24 and decided to follow as it had a navigator and radioman aboard and following it would increase their likelihood of reaching home. The two Lightnings tagged along into the front for 15 minutes, staying close behind the Liberator which suddenly turned away and lost the P-38s inside the front. Wire climbed and turned 180 degrees in order to get back to where they entered the front. Wire regained his bearings for home and then met a B-25 and they again followed the trailing bomber. However, after a few minutes these bombers flew off into the weather and Wire again had to reverse directions to take them out of the clouds. Wire then decided to fly along the coast as in this type of weather he knew that there should be a 50 foot area of relative clearing above the shoreline which would allow them to see well enough to find a landing area. It was raining so hard that they had to look of their side windows to maintain sight of each other. As they flew along keeping the shoreline on their starboard side; suddenly the shoreline jutted out to sea and Wire's starboard prop hit the top of a palm tree and that engine began to shake and vibrate. He feathered the propeller and shut down the engine. Ryerson became impatient and called Wire saying, since he had enough gas and instrument training, he was going to try climbing up and over the weather. Wire continued down the coast on single engine; hoping he was approaching Lae. Unexpectedly he saw a small landing field with a number of aircraft on it. He turned directly toward the field but had too much airspeed and overshot it and had to turn back toward the water and turned for a longer approach. However, the clouds began to descend, forcing Wire closer to the waves. One of the waves broke higher than the P-38 and Wire's lightning plowed through the top of it. The fighter immediately went out of control just over the water and Wire prepared for the crash by cutting the mixture control and jettisoning the canopy and then bracing himself. After the impact the dazed pilot found himself underwater and he loosened his seat belt and the innate floatation of his parachute and clothing helped him float the 25 feet to the surface. After some struggling he got his Mae West and life raft inflated in the churning waves about a half mile from shore. A dugout canoe was coming toward him and fortunately it was manned by two Americans. He was taken to a First Aid Station with a badly broken nose, serious facial cuts, and lower lip bitten through by his front teeth. Two B-24s and two B-25s crash landed on the strip while he waited for treatment. The next day he boarded an LST to Saidor and was eventually evacuated to a hospital in Sydney and would rejoin the 433rd at Biak.

Meanwhile, 14 Lightnings of the 433FS were approaching the weather front and heard the radio exchanges between Wire and Ryerson and also between the B-24 crews ahead that informed them of the "socked-in weather" over the Markham Valley and that the route to Nadzab was blocked. Possum Flight Leaders considered an alternate landing area but soon the Possum formation was breaking up into individual flights looking for the safest and fastest place to land and increasingly frantic calls to Gusap for directional homing. The pilots turned on their artificial horizon and gyro compass, and checked the fuel gauges before leaning out the mixture for maximum endurance. The weather ahead continued to worsen as Possum Blue Flight Leader, 1Lt. Robert Tomberg, entered weather at 12,000 feet southeast of Madang. Tomberg first tried to get under the front and then climbed to 25,000 feet without getting over it. He finally settled the flight at 15,000 feet which should be sufficient to get him over any mountains. But when Possum Blue entered a clear area that was as completely surrounded by clouds 2Lt. Pierre Schoener broke formation to try and make it on his own. Wingmen 2Lts. Andrew Anderson and Joseph Price continued with Tomberg who entered the foul weather again and he was not seen by his flight again. Eventually, Price landed at Saidor and Anderson flew all the way back to Nadzab almost out of fuel. As luck would have it, one of his drop tanks that he thought had been jettisoned had been hung up and dropped off on its own accord on the final approach and exploded near the tower! The remainder of the 433 Squadron landed at Saidor or Nadzab but 1Lts. Robert Tomberg, Louis Longman, Lewis Yarbrough and Austin Neely were all lost in the weather.

Capt. Loisel was able to keep the 432FS together for awhile but the pilots, fearing a collision, separated the flights but somehow all 16 P-38s of the main escort landed safely but the two aborting Clover Lightnings of 1Lts. Robert Hubner and John Luddington flying the F-7 escort ran into problems on their way home. When Loisel got into radio contact with Hubner he found that the shaken pilot was in no condition to fly on instruments into the weather and advised him to bail out. Hubner slipped out of communication and both he and Luddington disappeared into the weather front and were never heard from again. 1Lt. Milton MacDonald was the only 431FS casualty listed for the day.

After he lost his flight 1Lt. Robert Tomberg entered a small opening in the overcast and flew his fighter into it when his electrical system went out and he no longer had the use of his blind flying equipment and radio. His fighter went into a gentle spiral from 12,000 feet and he was able to pull it out at 9,000 feet; barely missing a mountain top. Tomberg joined four other Lightnings but as they climbed he was unable to keep up and the others had to break off to avoid stalling. At 1545 Tomberg was at 20,000 feet and decided to bail out. He released his canopy, stood up, and the slip stream drew him out. Tomberg drifted out of the clouds at 400 feet toward the trees and to break his fall he landed in the treetops on his back; uninjured. His parachute caught on a limb 100 feet above the ground and Tomberg slowly descended down the tree trunk. He tried to take bearings for the coast and walked for 45 minutes and found a native shelter and slept there and stayed out of the nightly rain. The next morning he found a native trail but soon lost it but came upon a native village. The only two native women there ran from him but slept there that night, out of the rain. He left early the next morning and after walking for 1½ hours he climbed a tall tree to get his bearings. While in the tree he heard voices which he determined were not Japanese, called out. Five natives appeared and led him to their village where they fed him, dried his clothes, and gave him a dry place to sleep. The next day they led him to another village and on the fourth day the party continued on the trail. At noon an L-5 Liaison aircraft flew over and Tomberg signaled it with a mirror while a native waved his Mae West. The L-5 pilot saw them and waggled its wings and headed toward Saidor. Tomberg was moved on by the natives to another village. The next day he continued to move on until on the sixth day they arrived at the U.S. Infantry station at Yamat where he boarded a barge to Saidor and returned to Nadzab the next day by aircraft. (Note: There are exaggerated Tomberg escape stories involving native handshaking ceremonies, 20 foot snakes being shot at, flying as a tail gunner on a B-26 to get back to Finschhafen from Saidor, and then being unable to board a C-47 to Nadzab because he had no official orders! The above version was taken from Tomberg's debriefing.)

58FG

The three squadrons of the 58FG were fortunate on this ominous day. The 310FS was assigned to provide a ground alert at Saidor with a four plane flight scrambled at 0945 to an unidentified plot in the area but no interception resulted and the flight returned at 1130. The pilots of the 69FS and the 311FS were not assigned a mission.

For the day 11 Lightnings had gone down:

**8FG:** 1Lt. Lawrence Reeves, 2Lt. Robert Keown, and 2Lt. Walter Mikucky.

**475FG/433FS:** 1Lts. Robert Tomberg, Calvin Wire, Louis Longman, Lewis Yarbrough and Austin Neely.

**475FG/432FS:** 1Lts. Robert Hubner and John Luddington.

**475FG/431FS:** 1Lt. Milton MacDonald

**April 1944: 421NFS**

The first half of April was very uneventful, and night patrols staging out of Saidor were flown in the Cape Croisilles and Karkas Island areas. By mid-April intruder missions were flown over the Hansa Bay and the Alexishafen area as this was the beginning of the full moon period. Intruder work was initiated in England and proved to be highly successful as night fighters would orbit over Luftwaffe airfields, waiting for the return of their bombers, also the strafing and harassing of the enemy troops at night. The 421NFS history states:

> "Being strafed in the daytime is quite a sensation in itself but being strafed at night is the most horrifying and nerve-wracking experience that could possibly happen to anyone. Were it not for the fact that we still remember the enemy at Pearl Harbor and his other treacherous deeds, one could have a sense of pity even for the Nip."

An unusual innovation for attacking enemy troops at night was developed by 1Lt. Gilbert Eissman who augmented his usual bomb load of four 250 pound bombs. His R/O Walter Fradin loaded the rear cockpit of the P-70 with six 20 pound fragmentation bombs which he fused by hand and passed to gunner S/Sgt. George DeHaven, who dropped them at Eissman's command. This technique became quite successful and was adopted by all crew members of the organization despite a HQ directive stating: "We do not advise this; however, for general practice, because fusing bombs by hand is not conducive to long life."

**April-May 1944: 418NFS Receives the B-25**

In April Squadron CO, Maj. Carroll Smith, was disappointed in the performance of their P-70s and P-38s and thought that the B-25 would be a better intruder. The only B-25 model available was the "H" model that had a large 75mm cannon mounted in the nose which necessitated deletion of the co-pilot's position. Smith tried to convince Brig.Gen. Whitehead to give him 12 B-25Hs but Whitehead balked until Kenney intervened. Once the Mitchells arrived Smith had all turrets and the 75mm cannon removed and mounted additional .50 caliber machine guns. In its final configuration the B-25 had 14 forward firing .50s plus two in the waist position. The Mitchells were to be used until the P-61 came into the theater.

In mid-May the 418th was ordered to move to Hollandia and the ground echelon transferred immediately, leaving the air echelon at Finschhafen to fly their few aircraft (mostly P-38s and P-70s) up later. The 5th Fighter Command HQ issued orders for the air echelon to move immediately to Port Moresby where their war-weary aircraft were turned in to the Replacement Pool and transition training was started in B-25Hs as "night intruders." To Smith's dismay the B-25s were to be used permanently instead of the coveted P-61s! This came about despite having 1Lt. Willard Hall,

Engineering Officer of the 418th and 20 enlisted men stationed at Brisbane in preparation to transition over to P-61s. The flight crews, 1Lt. Mervin Lyall, Ordnance Officer and 38 enlisted men, as well as the personnel that had been in Australia were all sent to Port Moresby for transition training into the B-25s. The B-25's crew would consist of pilot, navigator-observer (now the R/O), radio operator/gunner, and rear gunner.

**17 April 1944: 49FG Aircraft**

9FS Re-equips with Lightnings

On 17 April the Flying Knights were set to fly their first combat mission in a P-38 since November 1943. Seven old F and G reserve model Lightnings had been completely refitted and were approved for duty at Gusap #10. Capt. Ralph Wandrey remarked, "They're tired old tubs, but they're not those damned P-47s!" The first sortie was a routine escort to Tadji, with Campbell flying lead in the only J model formerly flown by the 80 FS, while Squadron CO Jordan and five senior Flight Leaders flew the old F and G models. By the end of April, the older P-38s were replaced by more of the refurbished, uncamouflaged J models which were handed down from the 80FS and 432FS who had received newer Lightnings. The P-38J was basically the same as the old model G but was easily distinguishable by the deeper radiators under the prop spinners and supercharger cooling radiators on the rear fuselages were enlarged.

7FS and 8FS modify their P-40s

Meanwhile, Seventh and Eighth Squadron line crew mechanics tried to extend the range of their Warhawks beyond their normal 400 mile combat radius to reach distant Hollandia. A temporary fuel line was plumbed to each underwing bomb shackle and a free swinging 75 gallon fuel tank was bolted on to each wing shackle in addition to another attached beneath the fuselage. The two wing tanks could not be dropped so their fuel was to be consumed first. In a test of the system a Demon pilot remained airborne over Ramu Valley for seven hours which was calculated as a range of 1,200 miles well within a round trip sortie to Hollandia. However, the modification came too late for the April campaign and was not approved for combat but would prove to be useful later.

**19 April 1944: 58FG**

On 19 April 58FG carried out the first of what was to become the principal mission of the Group for the remainder of the war. The 69th and 310th Squadrons flew the first of their fighter bomber missions of the war. The 69FS was assigned to bomb "Target No. 5" while 16 Thunderbolts of the 310FS armed with two 500 pound bombs each were to bomb Walog Plantation, about 10 miles northwest of Cape Croisilles. Pilots of the 310th began their dive bombing runs at 7,000 feet and put 28 bombs in the general target area with four exploding near four huts believed to be the radio station and other explosions observed near Megiar and Magiar Missions. Two other bombs hit west of Biranik and another bomb exploded within 50 feet of the bridge at Walog Plantation. From this date forward fighter bomber missions would be flown on a recurring basis by the Group.

**21 April 1944: USN**

Carrier aircraft from U.S. Navy Task Force 58 attacked the airfields at Hollandia on 21 April, the day before invasion but encountered little enemy air opposition and further air strikes were canceled due to lack of air resistance.

**April 1944: Planning *Operation Reckless*, the Invasion of Hollandia**

The Allied SWPA High Command were planning for an attack on Hollandia while the Japanese were busily attempting to augment their defenses in the Wewak-Hansa Bay-Madang area of New Guinea. Hollandia, located at the northeast corner of Netherlands New Guinea, was the logical point for the Allies' next attack as it was a major Japanese air and supply base located several hundred miles to the northwest along the New Guinea coast. An attack on Hollandia would not only bypass intermediate enemy held areas but was intended to surprise the Japanese and provide the Allies with a site for air and naval installations to support future tactical operations. The Hollandia landings were to be the largest operations conducted thus far by SWPA forces. Their intention was the capture and occupation of a 32 mile area between Tanahmerah Bay and Humboldt Bay and to establish a major air facility, an intermediate supply base, and minor naval facilities in the area.

Planning **Hollandia-Aitape** (L-R): Lt.Gen. Robert Eichelberger, R.Adm. Daniel Barbey, Maj.Gen. Stephen Chamberlin, and Lt.Gen. Walter Krueger. (U.S. Army)

The Japanese had occupied the Hollandia area on 20 April 1942 but its development had been delayed until Japanese planners finally recognized that Port Moresby would never be captured and that Hollandia was the best site to locate their most forward major supply base for operations in New Guinea. The Hollandia area possessed an attribute that was unique along the 450 miles of New Guinea coast between Wewak and Geelvink Bay which was a valley with a flat floor and nearby sheltered anchorages that made it a favorable location for the rapid development of air and supply bases. The valley is positioned between Tanahmerah and Humboldt Bays and between the Cyclops Mountains which paralleled the coast and Lake Sentani. There are two entrances to this valley: from Depapre on Tanahmerah Bay and from Humboldt Bay in the vicinity of Hollandia and Pim. They constructed three airfields on the flat plain between the Cyclops Mountains and Lake Sentani and began construction of a fourth at Tami, five miles east of Hollandia on the coast of Humboldt Bay.

In early 1944 the Allies decided to bypass Wewak and it was determined that Hollandia was the best site other than Geelvink Bay for developing a major base. The invasion at Hollandia would be the longest leap by the Allies along the New Guinea coast and was scheduled for 22 April 1944. For MacArthur to eradicate the Japanese 18th Army, it was essential that Lt.Gen. Hatazo Adachi continue to think that MacArthur's next attack would be on the Madang-Hansa area and he provided Adachi and his staff with a constant flow of bogus information about an Allied landing in Hansa Bay. Because of the long flying distances MacArthur requested carrier support from the Seventh Pacific Fleet but the Navy could only provide their carriers for the first few days of the landing. The nearest Allied airfield was at Nadzab, 500 miles away and MacArthur therefore ordered a simultaneous landing at lightly-held Aitape (*Operation Persecution*), on the coast 125 miles east of Hollandia. At Aitape they would capture the Tadji airstrip which would block any westward movement by the encircled Japanese army at Wewak.

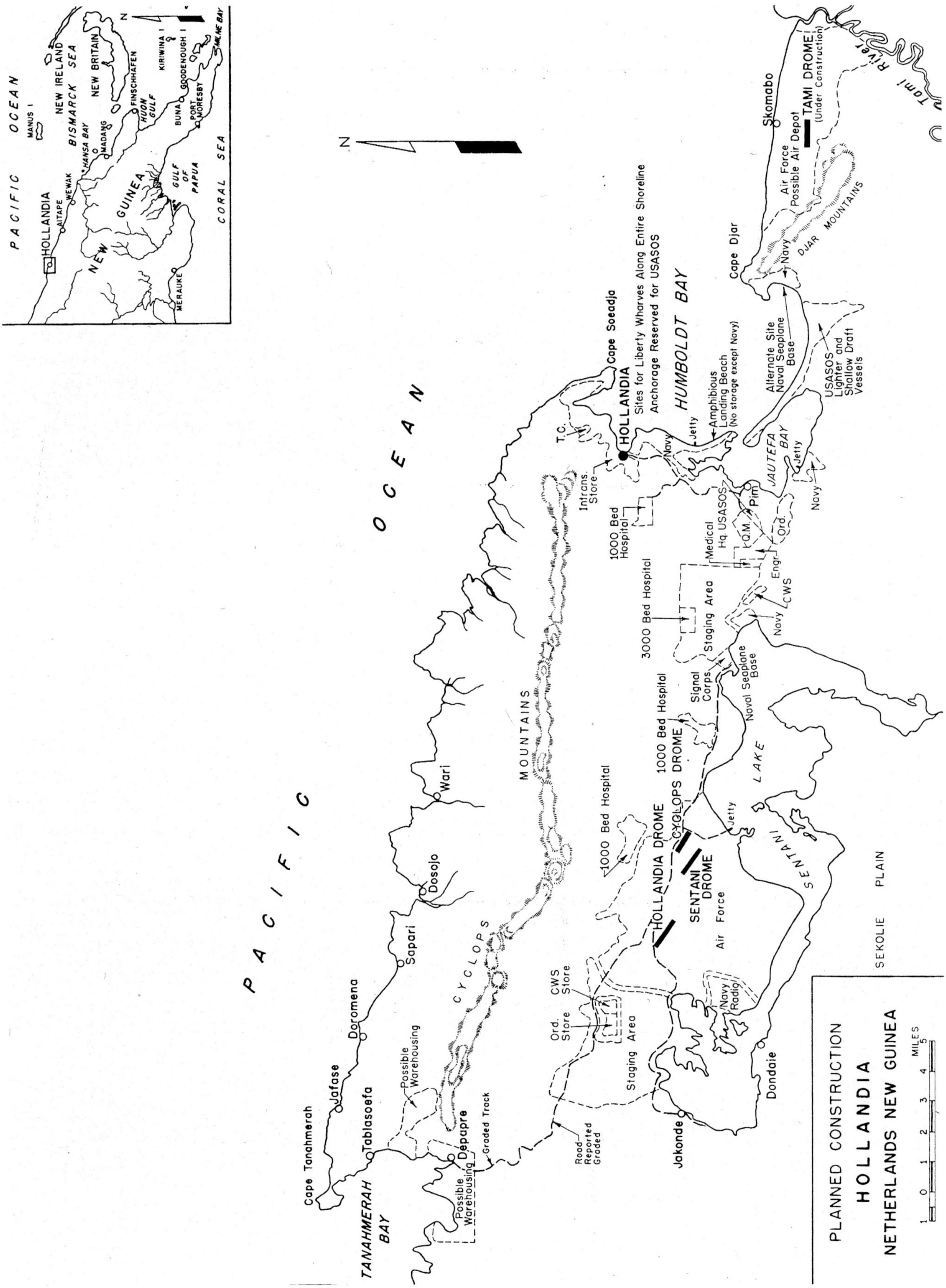
PLANNED CONSTRUCTION
HOLLANDIA
NETHERLANDS NEW GUINEA
MILES
PACIFIC OCEAN
HUMBOLDT BAY
HOLLANDIA
Cape Soeadja
Sites for Liberty Wharves Along Entire Shoreline
Anchorage Reserved for USASOS
Cape Djar
Skomabo
TAMI DROME
(Under Construction)
Tami River
Air Force
Possible Air Depot
DJAR MOUNTAINS
Navy
Alternate Site
Naval Seaplane
Base
USASOS
Lighter and
Shallow Draft
Vessels
Amphibious
Landing Beach
(No storage except Navy)
Jetty
JAUTEFA BAY
Pim
T.C.
Intrans. Store
1000 Bed Hospital
3000 Bed Hospital
Medical
Hq. USASOS
Q.M.
Ord.
Engr.
CWS
Staging Area
Signal Corps
Naval Seaplane Base
1000 Bed Hospital
CYCLOPS DROME
HOLLANDIA DROME
SENTANI DROME
Air Force
SENTANI LAKE
SEKOLIE PLAIN
CYCLOPS MOUNTAINS
Wari
Dosojo
Sapari
Doromena
Jafase
Tablasoefa
Cape Tanahmerah
TANAHMERAH BAY
Depapre
Possible Warehousing
Graded Track
Road Reported Graded
CWS Store
Ord. Store
Staging Area
Navy Radio
Jakonde
Dondaie
PACIFIC OCEAN
BISMARCK SEA
NEW GUINEA
CORAL SEA
MANUS I
NEW IRELAND
NEW BRITAIN
HANSA BAY
MADANG
WEWAK
AITAPE
FINSCHHAFEN
HUON GULF
BUNA
PORT MORESBY
GOODENOUGH I
KIRIWINA I
MILNE BAY
GULF OF PAPUA
MERAUKE

CHART 2—AIR ORGANIZATION FOR THE HOLLANDIA–AITAPE OPERATIONS (AMPHIBIOUS PHASE)

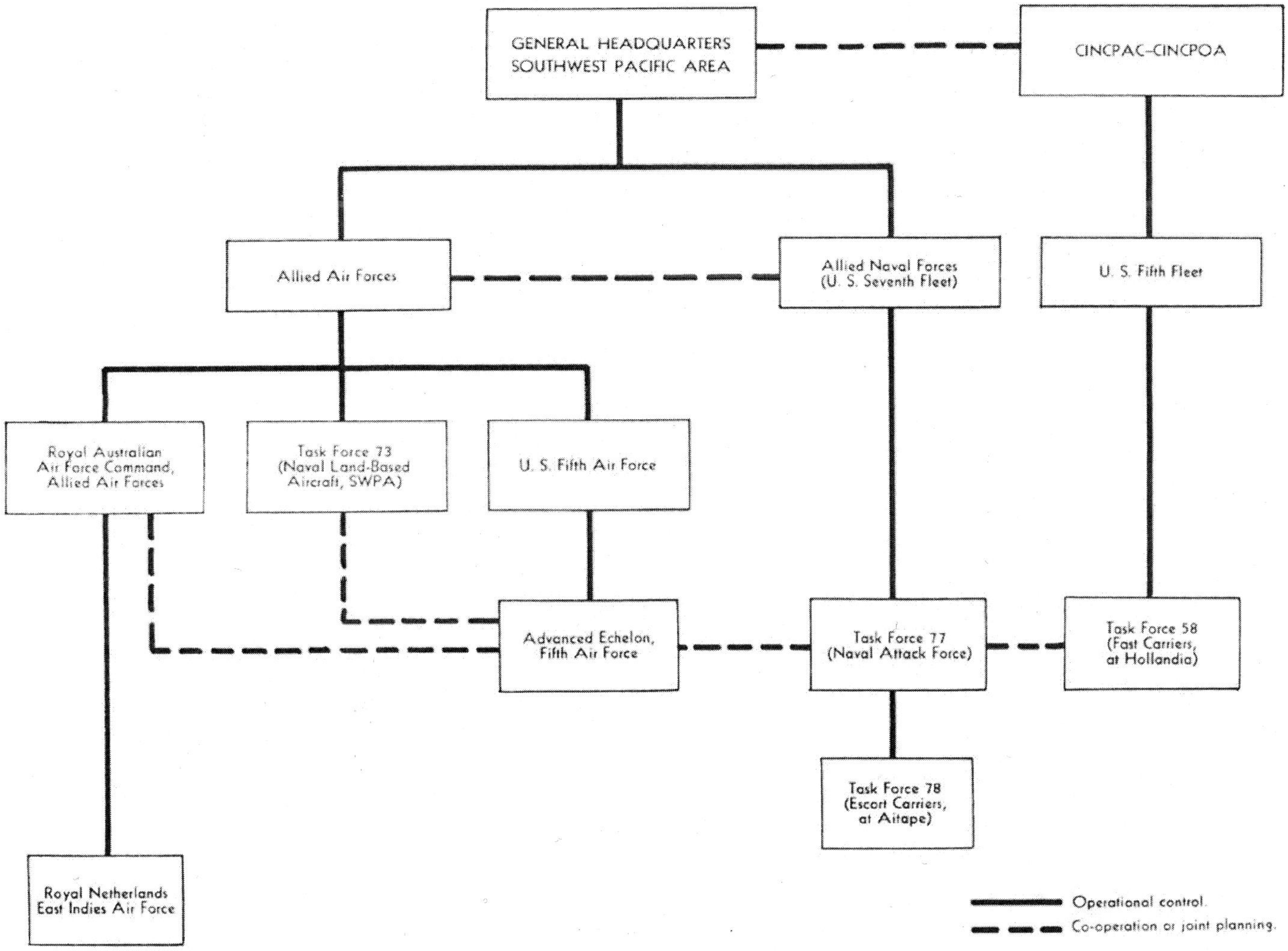


Western New Guinea was to be an important part of the Japanese inner defense perimeter and in October 1943 the 2nd Army in Manchuria (Manchukuo) and the 6th Air Division was assigned to the area. In March 1944 two more divisions were sent from China to the 2nd Army commanded by Lt.Gen. Fusataro Teshima. Lt.Gen. Hatazo Adachi's battered 18th Army in eastern New Guinea was put under Teshima's command at this time and Teshima ordered Adachi move west. Adachi ignored the order because he was convinced the Americans meant to land at Hansa Bay. The Americans conducted heavy bombing raids, naval bombardments, and patrols against Wewak in order to reinforce Adachi's notion. However, on 12 April Gen. Korechika Anami, who directed operations in western New Guinea and was senior to both Teshima and Adachi, sent his Chief of Staff to Wewak to prod the reluctant Adachi west and two regiments of 18th Army were headed toward Hollandia by 22 April.

Allied preparations for the landings at Hollandia began on 30 March to 2 April 1944 with an USN deep carrier raid against Palau where Japanese Combined Fleet posed a threat to any move against Hollandia. This raid was forced the Combined Fleet to retreat to bases further west. Simultaneously, the 5th Air Force struck Hollandia with over 80 B-24 Liberators escorted by P-38 Lightnings modified for greater range. By mid-April Hollandia was no longer an air base complex, as over 340 wrecked Japanese aircraft were later found on the runways, with an estimated additional 50 aircraft shot down over dense jungle. As a result of this debacle, the commander of the 6th Air Division, Gen. Masazumi Inada, was relieved in disgrace and sent to Thailand in a minor position.

The *Operation Reckless* Task Force, under Lt.Gen. Robert Eichelberger, the CG of I Corps, was composed of the 24th and 41st Divisions which were divided into two forces in order to land simultaneously at Tanahmerah Bay and Humboldt Bay. Staging from Finschhafen and Goodenough Island, the *Reckless* Task Force, together with the *Persecution* Task Force headed for Aitape, sailed north of and around the Admiralty Islands, then westward to about 100 miles seaward of New Guinea where they separated to approach their respective objectives on 22 April 1944.

**24 April 1944: *Operation Reckless*: Invasion of Hollandia**

On 21 April 1944, Hollandia was hit hard by strikes from the 12 carriers of Mitscher's Task Force 58 that also struck Wakde, Sawar, and Sarmi, located about 120 miles west of Hollandia. The operation met virtually no resistance in the air. The next day, elements of I Corps under Gen. Robert Eichelberger began their landings from Task Force 7 under V.Adm. Daniel Barbey. The 24th Division under Maj.Gen. Frederick Irving was assigned to land at Tanahmerah Bay while two regiments of 41st Division under Maj.Gen. Horace Fuller landed at Hollandia. Barbey personally supervised the landings at Tanahmerah Bay; the most

***Operation Reckless***, the Invasion of Hollandia under Lt.Gen. Robert Eichelberger, the CG of I Corps, was composed of the 24th and 41st Divisions, which were divided into two forces in order to land simultaneously at Tanahmerah Bay and Humboldt Bay (shown). (U.S. Army)

Hollandia landings at **Red Beach** at Tanahmerah Bay. (U.S. Army)

exposed of the three landings, and assigned Adm. William Fechteler to direct the Hollandia landings.

The Allies were fortunate that the two Japanese divisions that had been ordered to New Guinea from China in March 1944 lost nearly half of their number to submarine attacks while at sea and the survivors were diverted to Halmahera. Over 84,000 Americans landed opposed by just 11,000 defenders of whom only several thousand were combat troops while the remainder was service troops many of whom fled into the hills when the pre-invasion bombardment began. The Japanese were caught by surprise and rendered only minimal resistance. However, the landing at Tanahmerah Bay almost became a disaster as Allied intelligence had incorrectly concluded that there was a partially completed road to Lake Sentani built by the Dutch. Initial aerial photographs seemed to show two good landing beaches but later aerial photographs indicated the beaches were not as ideal as originally thought but Gen. Walter Krueger, over all Commander of *Reckless*, felt that planning had progressed to the point that it was too late to change. When the infantry came ashore, it found that *Red 2 Beach*, while almost ideal for beaching landing ships, had an impassable swamp located in front and the beach quickly became congested. The other beach, *Red 1*, was only a 100 yards wide and located in a cove full of coral heads that only allowed LVTs or LCMs and nothing larger from reaching the beach. However, the terrain behind *Red 1*, while tangled and steep was at least passable. Men and supplies began to be transferred by boat from *Red 2* to *Red 1* while a USN demolition team began blasting to a clear channel for larger landing ships to approach *Red 1* directly.

Meanwhile patrols had found that the former Dutch road from Tanahmerah Bay to Lake Sentani actually was a narrow trail winding up the slope behind the beaches and could not be used by any kind of vehicle. It was obvious that the main landing could not continue at Tanahmerah Bay and Eichelberger ordered the reserve regiment of 24th Division to relocate to Humboldt Bay, leaving two Regiments of 24th Division to continue up the trail to Lake Sentani. Despite difficulties in moving supplies up the trail and rearguard actions by small groups of Japanese; the Regiments arrived at the westernmost airfield at Sentani and established contact with 41st Division advancing from Humboldt Bay only two days later. It would then take three months for engineers to complete an adequate road from Tanahmerah Bay to Sentani.

However, the landings at Humboldt Bay proceeded better than expected as Allied planners had only two poor landing beaches, *White 1* and *White 2* and predicted that the Japanese would deploy most of their troops there. Despite these difficulties the landings were successful and any obstacles were quickly and efficiently cleared against little resistance. By that night 4,200 tons of supplies had been unloaded and 300 vehicles were ashore and by the end of the next day, the 186th Regiment was halfway to Sentani and 162nd Regiment had captured Hollandia and the surrounding area. The landings experienced a severe setback on the night of 23-24 April, when a lone Japanese aircraft dropped a string of bombs across *White 1* setting supplies on fire and hitting ammunition that exploded and devastated the area. Landing craft had to be used to evacuate troops from the beach but 24 were killed and 100 wounded, and over 60% of the supplies landed on the beach were destroyed. The fires did not subside enough to allow engineers to return until 27 April and for a time the 186th Regiment was put on half rations. But by noon on 24 April the Americans had reached Lake Sentani and encountered the first organized Japanese resistance but the old mining station of Hollandia Village had been captured. The 24th Division came ashore at Humboldt Bay and moved inland to the southwest through a low narrow pass in the coastal Cyclops Mountains to a broad valley containing the long, narrow Sentani Lake. By the end of the day on 26 April the Sentani airfields were in Allied hands and the 186th Regiment joined the 24th Division. The supply dilemma was alleviated when the airstrip at Tami was captured on 1 May and supplies could be flown in by transport.

The Japanese put up negligible resistance for the Sentani area until 6 June when the area was declared secure as the greatly outnumbered, demoralized, and ill equipped Japanese fled into the jungle hoping to reach Sarmi, about 150 miles to the northwest. Approximately, 3,300 Japanese were killed at a cost of 152 Americans killed or missing and 1,057 wounded. Inada attempted to reassemble his devastated forces west of Lake Sentani and retreated toward Wakde but of the 7,500 troops who began this march, only about a 1,000 survived. The Japanese 14th Air Brigade, the 33rd and 77th Sentais operating Oscars and the 68th and 78th Sentais operating Tonys had begun to evacuate the Hollandia area in April. Most of the aircraft of these units were either destroyed or abandoned when the remaining personnel in the brigade attempted to evacuate through the jungle to join other Japanese units. These units vanished when most of those on foot were either captured or died on the way out. After all the planning and the cost of the execution of *Persecution* and *Reckless* the Sentani airfield complex would be unable to support heavy bombers without extensive engineering work.

**24 April 1944: *Operation Persecution*: Invasion of Aitape**

Aitape was occupied by the Japanese on 1 April 1942 and the Japanese built Tadji Airfield a few miles southeast near the coast. SWPA Headquarters was advised by intelligence reports that Aitape was only lightly garrisoned, and MacArthur decided in March 1944 to invade Aitape in order to bypass the large Japanese garrisons at Hansa Bay and Wewak. The objective was to isolate the Japanese 18th Army at Wewak, to provide flank protection against any westward movement on of the Japanese 18th Army towards Hollandia, to secure Tadji Airfield to provide support to the more important Hollandia landings after the carriers of Task Force 58 departed and to establish light naval facilities at Aitape to support further operations. *Operation Persecution* and *Operation Reckless* were supported by 217 ships, to transport and protect the 80,000 men, their equipment, and supplies over 1,000 miles to conduct the separate amphibious landings at Aitape and Hollandia deep in enemy territory.

Bulldozers at **Humboldt Bay** ready to improve the road to the airdromes at Lake Sentani. (U.S. Army)

***Operation Persecution,*** the Invasion of Aitape. (U.S. Army)

The invasion force of the U.S. 163rd Infantry Regiment of the 41st Infantry Division was commanded by Brig.Gen. Jens Doe faced less than 1,000 Japanese defenders. Task Force 7 Commander, V.Adm. Daniel Barbey, sent his Chief of Staff, Capt. Alfred Noble, to direct operations at Aitape. The landings took place at Wapil on 22 April 1944 with most Japanese defenders fleeing into the hills and only one landing force transport was badly damaged by a Japanese torpedo bomber. MacArthur watched the landings from a light cruiser and went ashore afterwards in a landing boat. No. 62 Works Wing of the RAAF went ashore on the morning of 22 April to help secure and repair Tadji Airfield. The airfield was secured that day by 1300 and the fighter strip was made ready within two days when 25 P-40s from the No. 78 Wing of the RAAF landed on the field with the rest of the wing arriving the 25th to provide support to the Aitape and Hollandia landings.

**Hollandia-Aitape Captured**

With the Japanese disorganized and in full retreat MacArthur's strategy was to capture additional forward airfields from which to cover his advance into Geelvink Bay and then the Vogelkop Peninsula. Gen. Krueger's Sixth Army, the "Alamo Force," pressed the advance rapidly to the west to exploit the Japanese debacle at Hollandia but simultaneously had to prevent Adachi's 18th Army from breaking through to Hollandia. Only five days after the Hollandia/Aitape landings, MacArthur ordered the 41st Division to leapfrog to Wakde Island and the airstrips at Sarmi on the adjacent New Guinea coast by mid-May. (Note: In November 1943, Krueger formed a top secret ad hoc unit called the Alamo Scouts named for his association with San Antonio, Texas, and the Alamo. Krueger envisaged that the Alamo Scouts, comprised of small teams of highly trained volunteers, would operate deep behind enemy lines to provide intelligence gathering and tactical reconnaissance in advance of U.S. 6th Army landing operations.)

The easy and decisive victory at Hollandia allowed Krueger to have the Sixth Army's other ongoing operations proceed on or ahead of schedule and validated MacArthur's theory of bypassing enemy positions. Adachi's overwhelming defeat left the 18th Army trapped between the Americans in the west and the Australians in the east. In mid-December 1944 Australian forces began a slow, determined drive from the east toward Wewak which finally fell on 10 May 1945 but approximately 13,000 Japanese escaped into the jungle and only surrendered in September 1945.

The New Guinea Campaign has been referred to as "the story of two Allied armies fighting two kinds of war, one of grinding attrition and one of classic maneuver." The attrition stage, which was characteristic of eastern New Guinea land operations, lasted from January 1943 through the seizure of the Saidor in January 1944. During this period the Allies suffered more than 24,000 battle casualties; about 70% Australians; all to advance the front line 300 miles in 20 months. But during the maneuver stage beginning with the decisive Hollandia envelopment in April 1944, losses were 9,500 battle casualties, primarily American, to drive 1,300 miles in just 100 days and complete the re-conquest New Guinea without enemy interference from the air.

**The Hollandia and Aitape/Tadji Airfields**

The invasion of Aitape/Tadji and Hollandia had been a complete success but MacArthur's amphibious offensive had gotten too far ahead of the tactical air force. On the 23rd, newly promoted Brig.Gen. Paul Wurtsmith and his Air Task Force Coordinator, Col. Robert Morrissey, flew their P-38s to inspect the Tadji airstrip. Once there they found the primitive sandy strip unsuitable for bombers and even for the rugged Warhawks. So Hollandia was chosen as the center of 5AF operations.

On 26 April the 24th Division/186th Regiment pincers closed on the airdromes which were littered the wreckage of enemy aircraft. The JAAF 4th Air Army had hurriedly constructed three landing fields on Sentani's north shore. There was only one narrow dirt road through the pass which was inadequate to carrying the large number of men from the congested beachhead. The truck crews had to travel three miles on the muddy road over the pass and then descend inland another seven miles until they reached Cyclops Airfield and adjacent Sentani Strip and then travel another three

The Japanese had hurriedly built three airdromes on the north side of **Lake Sentani** that were improved once the area was captured. (AAF)

miles to Hollandia Airfield. Once they arrived the American engineers found that the April Fifth Air Force air attacks had totally ravaged the airfields. The Hollandia airfields were concentrated in the narrow valley and there were burned out buildings, vehicles, and over 400 aircraft everywhere on the valley floor. Despite bad weather the engineers were supplied by air drops and by 28 April they put the Hollandia Strip into operation. On 3 May, P-40s of the 49th Fighter Group arrived to begin combat air patrol. By 15 May the P-38s of the 9th Fighter Squadron of the 49th Group and the P-38s of the entire 475th Fighter Group were on the ground at Hollandia ready for further operations but not over New Guinea.

**Hollandia/Base G**

As early as April 1943 Allied aerial reconnaissance revealed a vacant Japanese airstrip located about halfway between Hollandia and Depapre, near Lake Sentani. By September, air recon reported that this airstrip, identified as Hollandia Drome, was now developed and serviceable. By November 1943 enemy construction was reported on two new airstrips, named Sentani and Cyclops, located east of Hollandia Drome. The Japanese had built a mediocre motor transport road to join these three airfields with the village of Pim on an indentation of Humboldt Bay. The Japanese then started construction on two other airstrips. Tami Drome was the farthest east, located on a coastal flat separated from Hollandia by Humboldt Bay, swamplands, and the Djar Mountains. Sekolie Drome was located on Sekolie Plain south of Lake Sentani and about 6.5 miles southeast of Hollandia Drome.

Original Allied plans for the development of a base at Hollandia considered supply facilities for 75,000 troops and airdrome facilities including two runways. But in January 1944, GHQ, SWPA, requested that its Chief Engineer, USASOS, Brig.Gen. Lewis Ross, determine the viability of locating a major supply base capable of supporting 200,000 troops in the Hollandia area. Ross' preliminary report, based on inadequate information, stated that a major supply base of the scale specified could be constructed at Hollandia but would require "considerable" effort. Subsequent studies by Chief Engineer Ross estimated that the required construction could be completed in seven months by the "expenditure of 138 battalion-months of engineer effort." The airdrome development plan was expanded from two runways to two Type E fighter/heavy bomber airfields, one Type G fighter airfield, and one emergency Type C fighter airfield. (Note: See Airdrome Construction Volume 1 for description of Airfield Types.)

After the landings a detailed study of the Hollandia area determined that there was inadequate acreage available to develop a base to provide logistic support for 200,000 troops. Maj.Gen. James Frink, the CG of the USASOS, recommended that Alamo Force concentrate only on the construction of airdrome and naval facilities while the Allied Air Forces request for an air depot in the Hollandia area was eliminated. The USASOS

**Hollandia** area with Airdrome (lower left), Jautefa Bay (middle left), Humboldt Bay (upper), and Cyclops Mountains (left). (AAF)

**Hollandia** area. (AAF)

supply base, Base G, was now to provide logistic support for only 140,000 men of which 60,000 were to be garrison troops, 40,000 troops staging at Hollandia, and 40,000 troops located in more forward areas.

The over all plan for the operation assigned Alamo Force (Sixth Army) the responsibility for capturing and holding the Hollandia area and for establishing airdrome facilities. The Task Force Commander was to be responsible for all base activities until the activation of the large USASOS intermediate base and transshipment depot. At the time of the activation of this installation, scheduled for D plus 45, USASOS was to assume all responsibility for base operation.

On 10 April 1944 (D minus 12) Alamo Force issued revised construction requirements and an area allocation plan. The new planned air facilities were to consist of three Type D airfields which were later to be expanded into Type E airfields, and one Type B airfield, later to be expanded into a Type C airfield. Highest priority was given to the construction of two Type D airfields with limited dispersal for three groups of fighters and one squadron of night fighters. Dispersed hardstands were to be constructed for 96 heavy bombers and 533 other aircraft, of which 225 were to be fighters that could be parked in pairs on medium bomber hardstands. Airdrome operations buildings, headquarters for major air units, an air depot to provide for the operation of two air depot groups and camps for air personnel, were also included. Immediate docking facilities were to be provided by four floating Liberty Ship docks and it was planned to eventually construct a total of 16 Liberty Ship wharves. Bulk petroleum storage was to be eventually provided for 218,000 barrels of aviation gasoline, motor transport gasoline, and automotive diesel fuel combined and 100,000 barrels of navy special fuel oil. A major supply base to handle all classes of supply for 200,000 troops and a staging area for 100,000 troops were to be prepared. The engineer troop strength was to total approximately 25,000 men. This was the first major SWPA operation for which detailed engineer planning was made and while unforeseen problems and delays occurred they were mostly surmounted quickly and efficiently because of this thorough advanced planning.

In June the required airdrome facilities were reduced to two Type D and one Type C airfields. Dispersal facilities for 150 fighters, 192 light bombers, and 104 transports were to be provided on either heavy bomber hardstands or transport unloading aprons with three fighters or two light bombers parked on each hardstand.

### The Hollandia Airfields

The airbase at Hollandia was considered scenically the most beautiful of any of the base locations in New Guinea. It was built along the slope of the dark and forbidding 6,000 foot Cyclops Mountain whose crest was perpetually covered with black rain clouds. A half mile to the north was Sentani Lake which separated the base from the Pacific Ocean. Sentani Lake is a narrow, winding lake over 20 miles long and varying in width from half a mile to only a 100 yards, and is surrounded by the deep green hills and backed by peaks, ravines, and jungle growth. Sprinkled over the Lake are small cone shaped green islands that had native houses on stilts in the water clinging to its shores. Two miles behind the camp was a 750 foot waterfall that seemed to spring out of the center of Cyclops Mountain. MacArthur arrived at Hollandia on 11 September to open up his advanced headquarters which was on the crest of a hill about a mile east of Kenney's HQ.

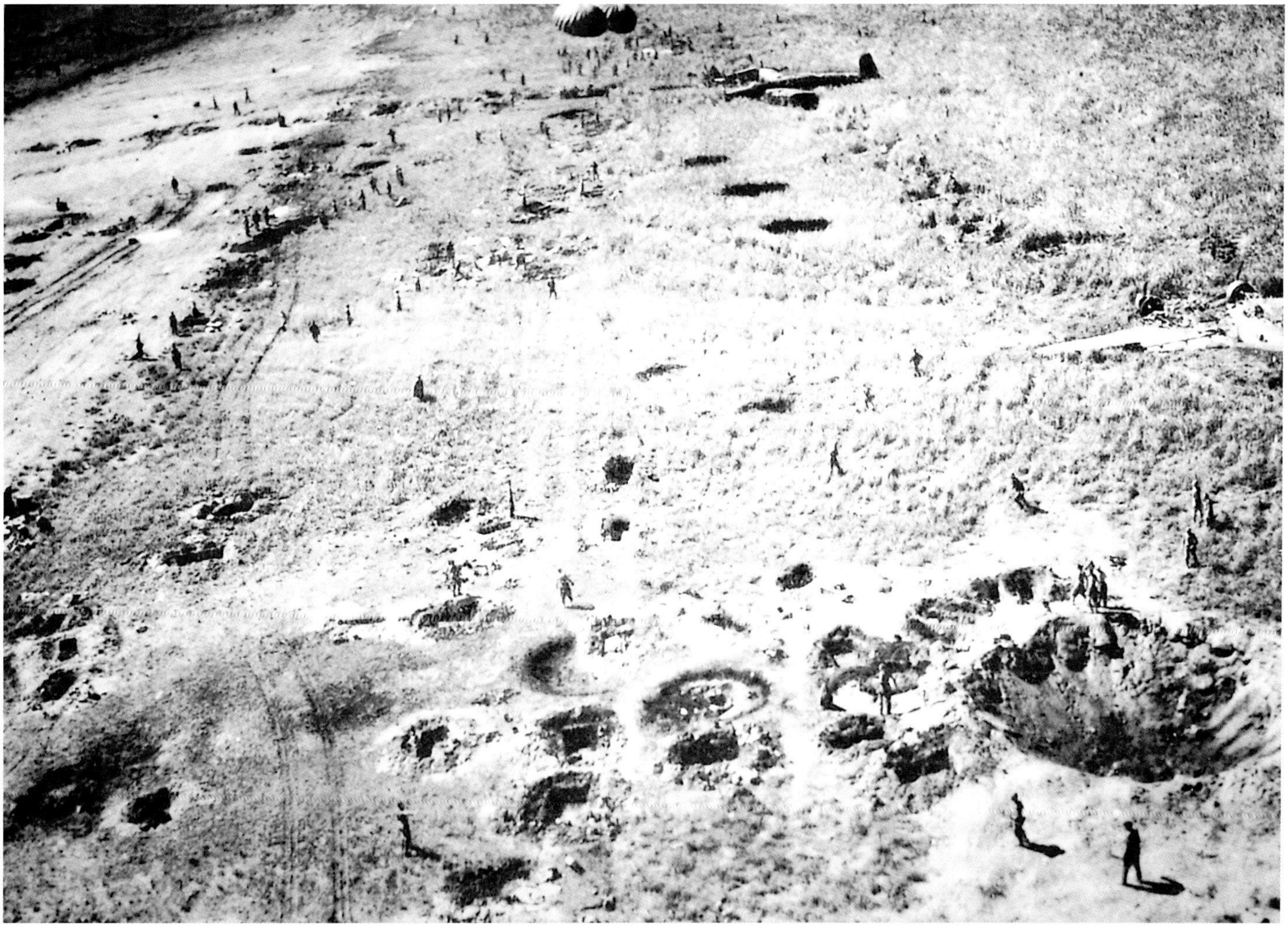

After its capture, the condition of **Hollandia Airdrome** made it inoperable. (AAF)

Due to the extensive area involved in both the tactical and base development phases of the operation and to the scale of the planned construction, the Task Force Engineer divided the territory into five sectors: Hollandia, Sentani, Tami, Tanahmerah, and Dock, and appointed Sector Engineers.

After their capture, a survey of the existing Japanese airstrips revealed that the Hollandia Drome was inoperable due to Allied bombing; Sentani Drome runway was surfaced with light gravel for a length of 3,200 feet but a 40 foot diameter bomb crater limited its operational length to 2,000 feet; Cyclops was found to have 2,800 feet of usable runway; while at Tami a 2,000 foot section of the eastern end of the runway was unserviceable due to poor drainage and the remaining 4,000 foot section was pocked by many small bomb craters. The engineers used captured Japanese equipment and a few light machines that they brought with them over the road from Pim to level and repair the Cyclops airstrip which then became the first of the Hollandia

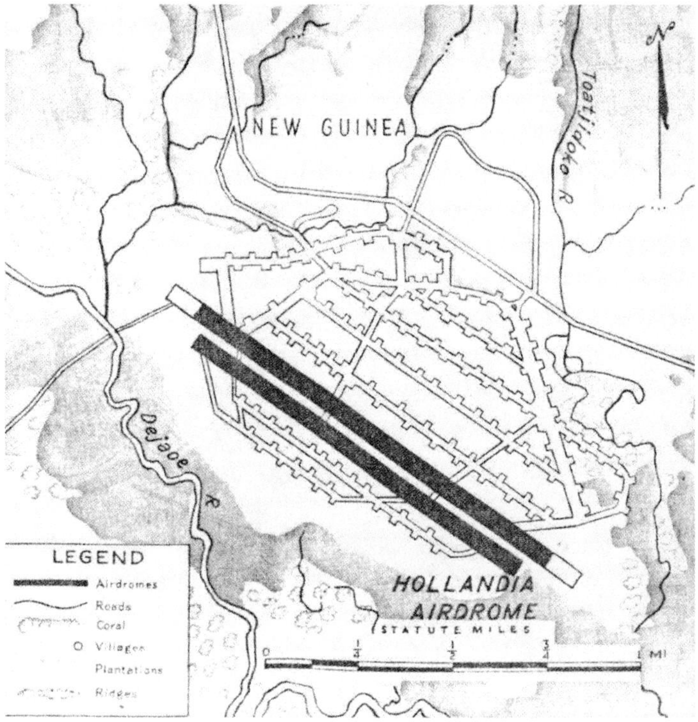


airstrips to be operable. On 27 April (D plus 5), a C-47 transport landed successfully at Cyclops Drome and by D plus 7 Cyclops was serviceable in dry weather for 4,000 feet by transport aircraft. Tami Drome was next slated for restoration for use by transport aircraft so that fuel, supplies, and personnel could be lightered from Humboldt Bay to Tami Drome, and then flown by air transport to Cyclops Drome in the Lake Sentani area. Tami was situated on a flat coastal plain that was cut off from the Hollandia area by the Djar Mountains and by large swamps around Hollekang. The engineers found the existing airstrip to be was just a bomb cratered grassy ridge in the middle of a swamp. The engineers built a 4,200x100 foot, dry weather runway and 12 hardstands and made it serviceable for C-47s on 3 May (D plus 11). During the decisive days in early May, C-47's carried almost 500 loads of supplies from Tami Drome inland to Cyclops to support the infantry. Nevertheless, Tami Drome was found unsuitable for further development and was abandoned by the end of the month. Meanwhile, Cyclops was improved to all-weather standards during May. Its 4,000x100 foot fighter runway was constructed of earth with a stabilized surface. Work continued on essential operations and to repair buildings and hardstands until August when all construction at Cyclops Drome was suspended in order to release engineer equipment for use at the Hollandia and Sentani Dromes. Thereafter, engineer work at the airdrome was limited to maintenance.

On 3 May, only one week after the capture of Hollandia Drome, a 5,000 foot section of the existing airstrip was usable and the first squadrons of fighters were stationed there. However, heavy rains kept this former Japanese air strip from continuous operation and in late in May it was abandoned. A second runway running parallel to the existing Japanese airstrip was planned for completion on 23 May (D plus 31). However, completion was delayed for a month due to unseasonably heavy rains, insufficient equipment, and inexperienced construction crews. The runway sub-base should have been carefully removed but was not, and numerous soft spots developed. Before construction began drainage was not considered and its consequent installation required additional labor and loss of time. The original surfacing specifications could not be met due the lack of proper equipment and it was necessary to lay a new surface over the previous surface in order to make it suitable for all-weather operations. When completed in October 1944, Hollandia Drome consisted of

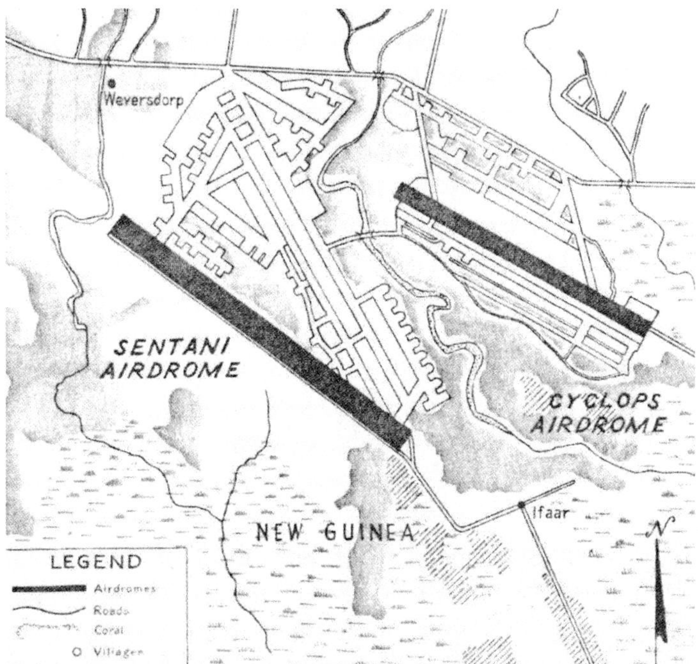


two parallel, all-weather runways constructed of hematite and sand with crushed rock surface treated with bitumen and limestone chips. One was 6,000x100 feet with 50 foot shoulders and 500 foot overruns while the second was 5,500 x100 feet. Parking for aircraft was provided by 154 all-weather hardstands and three all-weather surfaced alert aprons, each measuring 150x800 feet. Construction of Hollandia Airdrome required the clearing of 520 acres; stripped of 199,500 cubic yards of unsuitable material while 163,500 cubic yards of material was moved in grading. The base was composed of 43,000 cubic yards of hematite (a reddish-

**Sentani Drome** was the last Hollandia Airdrome to become operational, and work was concentrated on Hollandia after Cyclops was suspended. (AAF)

**Cyclops Airdrome** was improved to all weather standards during May and work continued until August, when all construction was suspended in order to release engineer equipment for use at the Hollandia and Sentani Dromes. (AAF)

On 3 May (D plus 11) **Tami Airdrome** became serviceable, and during the decisive days in early May, C-47s carried supplies to Cyclops to support the infantry. (AAF)

**Hollandia** bivouacs were shaded by tall coconut palm trees and cooled by gentle breezes. (AAF)

Only one week after the capture of **Hollandia Drome** the existing Japanese airstrip was usable, but heavy rains kept this strip from continuous operation, and in late May it was abandoned and a second runway running parallel was not completed until the end of June. (AAF)

brown iron oxide) over which 182,800 cubic yards of limestone schist (flakes) was laid. The surface coat consisted of 169,500 gallons of 30% cutback used in the prime coat and 200,500 gallons of bitumen which then was covered with 8,200 cubic yards of crushed gravel. Control tower, operations buildings, alert buildings, briefing huts, and 14 squadron areas with shop buildings provided the necessary facilities for operation of the airdromes.

At Sentani a 5,000x100 foot runway was constructed of limestone schist with a crushed rock surface. By late November 1944, 125 all-weather hardstands and a transport unloading area, 300x1,500 feet,

**Cyclops Airdrome's** 4,000x100 foot fighter runway was improved to all weather standards during May and occupied by 7FS Warhawks. (AAF)

Captured **Tadji Airdrome** under construction. (AAF)

were constructed to provide parking space for aircraft. This airdrome required the clearing of 170 acres, stripping of 94,500 cubic yards of material, grading of 95,600 yards, and addition of 118,400 cubic yards of selected material as a base course. The prime coat required 95,900 gallons of 30% cutback, while the surface course required 114,700 gallons of bitumen and 4,650 cubic yards of crushed gravel. Operations and repair shop buildings, together with service areas, were also provided at Sentani Drome.

The airfield construction agenda in the Hollandia area never achieved its planned development, mainly due to the emergence of more suitable sites opened by offensives after the occupation of Hollandia. Nevertheless, the availability of good-weather airstrips in the Lake Sentani area during early May permitted the forward movement of sufficient fighter and light bomber units to support landings in the Wakde Islands-Arara, New Guinea, area on 17-18 May. The all-weather strips and other essential construction projects in the Hollandia area, although only partially

**Tadji Airdrome** under 5BC B-25 parafrag attack. (AAF)

completed, were available to support of the landings on Biak Island on 27 May. Construction continued on facilities for the further buildup of air strength in the area and during June and early July the last tactical air elements were moved to Hollandia and were involved in the Noemfoor landings on 2 July.

As major construction projects at Hollandia progressed toward completion, the construction units were relieved, reequipped, and staged for movement to forward bases and only maintenance and utilities detachments remained at Hollandia while the aircraft on the base were fully engaged in the support of further offensive operations.

Hollandia bivouacs were shaded by tall coconut palm trees and cooled by gentle breezes. Unlike the raging Erap River at Nadzab; a cold, clear stream flowed near the camp and allowed the men to escape the New Guinea heat. However, gunfire could still be heard in the distance as the Army was mopping up enemy pockets of resistance. By the end of May the Biak Campaign had slowed and became evident that the stay at Hollandia was going to be extended. Consequently, logistics did not keep up in supplying the creature comforts such as beer and cigarettes which had to be supplied by the inferior captured Japanese stocks that had suffered from the wet, humid jungle climate.

When the war ended all Base G activities were concerned with the closing of the base and on 15 November 1945 the Netherlands Indies Government purchased most of the serviceable facilities. During January 1946 all movable supplies not sold to Australian or Netherlands Indies authorities were shipped out and the base closed.

### Aitape/Tadji Area

Concurrent with the Hollandia invasion, GHQ, SWPA planned an attack 120 miles to the southeast, on Aitape, Northeast New Guinea code named *Persecution*. Allied planners decided that the quick installation of air and naval facilities at Aitape would prevent bypassed Japanese forces in the Wewak-Hansa Bay-Madang area from moving north to attack the Allied forces and shipping at Hollandia. Securing local air superiority was crucial to supporting ground operations and depended on the immediate capture of runways in the Aitape area. The GHQ, SWPA operations instructions issued for this operation were for the Alamo Force, supported by Allied Air Forces and Allied Naval Forces to establish facilities for one fighter and one light bomber group at Aitape as soon as possible.

The Japanese occupied Aitape in 1942 and first used it as a staging and dispersal area for their airdromes at Wewak and Madang. In December 1943 the Japanese started construction on three airstrips at a site located about seven miles southeast of Aitape. By the end of January 1944, Allied air reconnaissance detected enemy fighters on one of the airstrips. The 163rd Regimental Combat Team of the 41st Division, with attached units, made up the initial infantry portion of the *Persecution* Task Force for the Aitape invasion. The Task Force staged from Cape Cretin in the Finschhafen area and, together with the *Reckless* Task Force headed for Hollandia, sailed north and westward. The landing was made on 22 April 1944 after a heavy naval and aerial bombardment, and met light resistance. By 0800 on 24 April (D plus 2), the 4,000x80 foot runway was operable for fighter aircraft and 25 RAAF P-40s arrived to support the ground troops at Hollandia and cover the shipping in that area. Due south of the newly improved fighter runway was a substandard kunai grass enemy airstrip but work on improving this strip was slow. The third enemy runway, located to the west of the other two, was found unsuitable for development and was utilized as an open storage area.

### Tadji Airdrome

Tadji Airdrome was located near its namesake, Tadji Village, and to the east of Aitape in a sago swamp area and immediately to the west was Waitanan Creek.

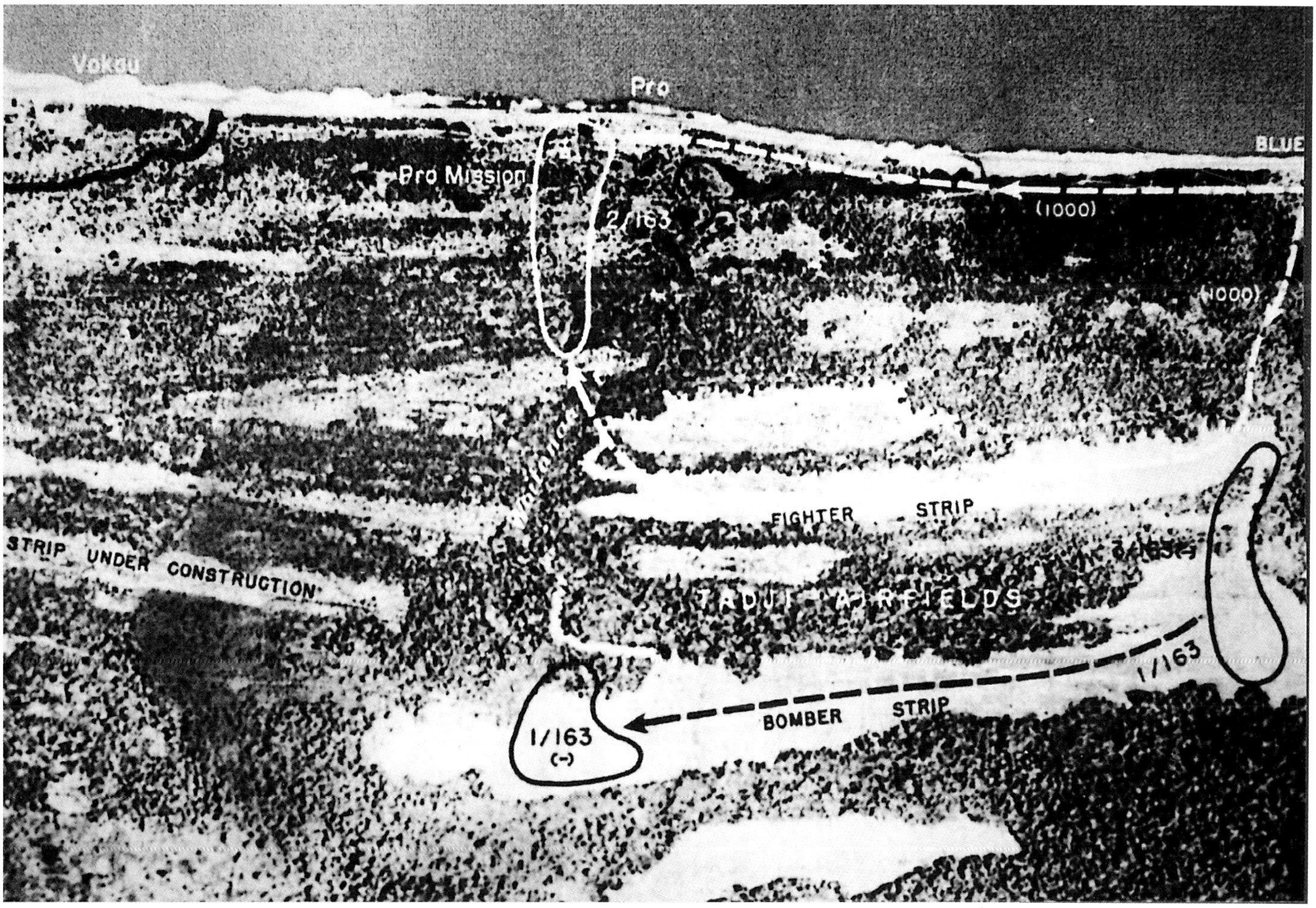


Aerial view of **Tadji Airdrome**. (AAF)

**Col. Robert Morrissey** and **Gen. Paul Wurtsmith** inspect Tadji. (AAF)

During early 1943, the Japanese Army built two parallel runways surfaced with crushed coral. To the north, a fighter strip was located nearest to the coastline and further inland was a bomber strip. The Japanese constructed Tadji primarily to serve as satellite field, staging and dispersal areas for Hollandia and Wewak airfields. It was used by Japanese Army Air Force fighter and bomber aircraft. From 17 August 1943 to 21 April 1944 Tadji was neutralized by air attacks by the 5AF during their campaign against Wewak and for the preparations for the landings at Hollandia and Aitape on 22 April 1944.

On 22 April 1944 in conjunction with the American landings at Hollandia, Tadji was also attacked and Australian engineers began an immediate repair of the north fighter strip and two days later it was operational and several P-40 Kittyhawks from RAAF 76 Squadron began using the strip for patrols over the Hollandia area. The airfield was used by American and Australian aircraft. The northern fighter runway was used as a crash strip while the southern bomber runway was used as the main runway.

American Units Based at Tadji:

433TCG, 65TCS (C-47 det) Nadzab 3 May to June 1944 Nadzab
433TCG, 66TCS (C-47 det) Nadzab 12 May to June 1944 Nadzab
433TCG, 68TCS (C-47 det) Nadzab 12 May to June 1944 Nadzab
71TRG, 110TRS (P-40, P-39) Gusap 25 May to 11 September 1944 Biak

Aitape fulfilled its purpose as an intermediate base between established New Guinea bases and newly secured Hollandia. During May 1944 three troop carrier squadrons flew out of Tadji Drome with ammunition and rations needed by Allied troops at Hollandia. During the same month, two RAAF P-40 squadrons moved from Aitape to Hollandia to support the Wakde and Biak landings. The next, missions flown from Tadji Drome effectively harassed Japanese troops during their drive along the coast from their base at Wewak westward toward Aitape and Hollandia and ultimately contributed to their utter defeat when they were isolated along the Drinumor River. During the critical phase of this battle in July, U.S. troops had 671 tons of supplies delivered by air drops from Tadji-based transports.

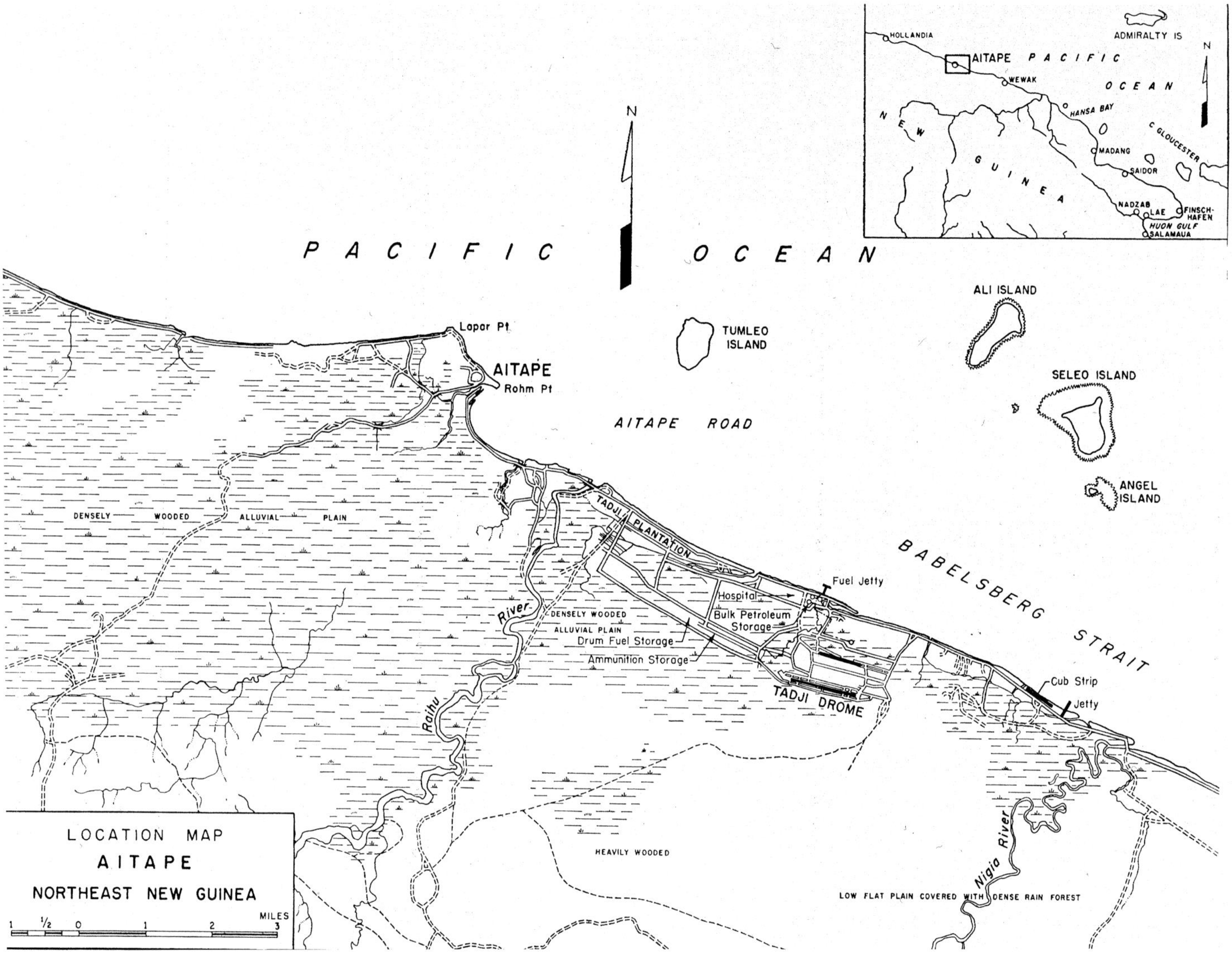


**27 April 1944: 58FG/311FG**

The 311FS flew its first fighter bomber mission on 27 April 1944. The 311th had a three week head start in combat for the 58FG because it was first equipped with an assortment of old P-47s that were not equipped with the new wing fuel tanks and bomb pylons of the forthcoming later models to be used by the 69th and the 310th Squadrons. At 0715, four Thunderbolts, led by Capt. Harry Odren, took off from Saidor carrying two 500 pound, nose and tail fused, demolition bombs to glide bomb a suspected Japanese personnel assembly area one mile northwest of Bunabum Harbor. The flight arrived over the target at 7,000 feet in clear weather where the pilots identified the target and descended into the attack. Two bombs were observed hitting near a heavy position at the mouth of the Bunabum River while six bombs struck along the shore line near Bibikom Point. The mission was considered a success with all the bombs hitting within the target area. All aircraft returned safely to Saidor at 0845.

**April 1944: 58FG Monthly Totals**

During April the 58FG flew 1,118 sorties, dropping 1,653 tons of bombs, and fired 6,385 rounds of .50 cal. ammunition, mainly against enemy bivouac areas. After moving up to Saidor on 5 April the necessity for extra flying time to get to the combat area was eliminated, reducing the number of non-combat sorties. The 311FS lost three aircraft and the three pilots: Bullington, Rothman, and Graham while the 310FS lost one pilot as MIA; 2Lt. Clement Theed.

**April 1944: 475FG Monthly Totals**

The previous raids had virtually destroyed the formerly large Japanese air base at Hollandia and air opposition was nonexistent. The Japanese were abandoning the defense of Hollandia and its air base and from April through August 1944 the Japanese would retreat to bases farther along the Dutch New Guinea coast. Many of these troops died during the 125 mile retreat north Sarmi along the coast from Hollandia. The last 475FG mission to Hollandia in which Japanese interceptors were encountered in any numbers was 12 April. On that day the 80th Fighter Squadron claimed nine Japanese fighters, three of which were eventually credited to Dick Bong to give him a record-breaking victory total of 28. The 475th would not make a claim until 16 May over Noemfoor.

# 7

# May 1944

**May 1944: SWPA Situation and Future**
MacArthur's forces in the SWPA, mainly American but with Australian Naval and Aviation Engineer contingents captured Hollandia in Dutch New Guinea on 22 April, to establish a new forward base and airdrome there. The capture of Hollandia would be followed by a succession of thoroughly thought out and then efficiently executed invasions that would capture Wakde, Biak, Noemfoor and Sansapor. MacArthur's final advance up the north coast of New Guinea and the landing at Hollandia finally ended Japanese resistance and also the end of air operations from that area.

During the period of the air attacks on Hollandia, the 475FG was the only 5FC fighter Group to fly the P-38 in New Guinea (at the time the 80FS was considered as operating attached to the 475FG rather than its parent 8FG). Between February and the end of April 1944, the 9FS reconverted from P-47s to P-38s and the remainder of the 8FG became P-38 equipped to from a second group flying only P-38s. After the Japanese retreated from the Hollandia area there were seven P-38 squadrons available to the 5AF. The USN in the Central Pacific and MacArthur in the Southwest Pacific were converging on the Philippines to surround Japan's secondary defense perimeter. In the advance toward the Philippines, MacArthur and Kenney would use these squadrons strategically in attacking airfield and oil targets and tactically in disposing of the remaining Japanese forces on New Guinea's Vogelkop Peninsula.

**May 1944: 475FG Situation**
During May 1944 the 475th's P-38s were moved to the newly captured and reconstructed air bases at Hollandia. Their stay there was supposed to be a short, lasting only until Biak, an island farther north in Geelvink Bay, was captured. However, the fight to take Biak proved to be more difficult than the nominal enemy resistance offered at Hollandia and the 475FG remained at Hollandia until the middle of July.

The 475th left Nadzab on 1 May 1944 with the equipment sent to the staging area at Lae, by the Liberty Ship, *SS Francis A. Wardwell*, and the ground echelon was moved to Lae by ground transport. The air echelon remained at the stripped Nadzab bivouac while the ground contingent at Lae enjoyed a day at the beach and movies or the Red Cross canteen at night. For once the enlisted men had it better than the officers. On the 15th the 432FS air echelon was ordered to Hollandia ahead of the Lae "boat" echelon. Despite their scenic surroundings, the Hollandia bases were austere at best and most initial descriptions noted that "it was possible to stand ankle deep in mud with dust blowing in your face." While the bases were not troubled by enemy air attacks vigilance was needed for the occasional starving Japanese straggler who ventured into the 475th camp from the nearby jungle. After the area was secured, MacArthur and his staff commandeered the very comfortable house of the Governor of Dutch New Guinea.

**May 1944: 58FG: Situation**
Despite the continued movement of the war away from them to the northwest putting them in the war's backwater morale remained high. When weather permitted, three or four daily missions were normal and consisted primarily of bombing. At this time the Japanese situation in New Guinea was becoming increasingly precarious. Australian ground forces were moving into the Hansa Bay area and the target area (bomb line) for the 58FG was moved beyond that area and their last mission to Hansa Bay was 7 June. Pilots of the 58FG were directed to desist from bombing and strafing there because it was impossible to distinguish Australian positions from those of the Japanese. At the end of May the strafing missions were discontinued because the losses incurred did not offset the damage inflicted on the Japanese.

This movement of the bomb line required a flying distance of about 500 miles to deliver the bombs on a target. To compensate for this long distance the 58th took off from Saidor, landed at Tadji, and then returned to Saidor, bombing the target in between, both ways. This shuttle-type mission gave close air support to Allied troops around Tadji, who were being harried by the thousands of Japanese ground troops that were being pushed into the area between the mouth of the Sepik River and Tadji.

During May the 58FG flew 1,378 sorties of all types, dropping 107 tons of bombs, and firing 337,975 rounds of ammunition which was a record month by far. The 69FS flew 340 combat sorties, dropping 47 tons of bombs; the 310FS flew 365 combat sorties, dropping 40 tons of bombs; while the 311FS flew 346 combat sorties; dropped over 20 tons of bombs. Two pilots were lost during the month: 2Lt. John Mars, after he hit the mast of a freighter anchored in the harbor just after take off on the 9th and 1Lt. George Wood (69FS) to AA fire over Wewak on the 29th.

**May 1944: 35FG Situation**
May operations for the 35FG were again uneventful with no enemy contacts. The sorties from Gusap were limited to patrol, escort, and strafing ground support over Wewak, But, and Dagua. On 4 May, after being gone for 84 days, Lt.Col. Edwin Doss returned to the Group and reassumed command with Lt.Col. Furlo Wagner as his Deputy Commander.

**Early May 1944: 49FG**
MacArthur's success stranded the 49FG ground echelon at Finschhafen with no tents and no transport to a better facility. At the same time, the

Group's air echelon remained in Ramu Valley ostensibly waiting to transfer to Tadji. 49er CO, Lt.Col. David Campbell was in Gusap in command of a unit whose ground personnel were stranded at Finschhafen while his pilots were scheduled to move to Hollandia.

On 3 May the 7FS ground echelon was transported from Finschhafen directly to Hollandia and then on the 5$^{th}$, the 8FS ground echelon left Finschhafen and the 9FS ground echelon followed on the 6$^{th}$. During the morning of 4 May Screamin' Demons' CO Arland Stanton led his Warhawks from Gusap carrying three auxiliary fuel tanks 450 miles north to Hollandia. Two days later, Black Sheep CO Robert McHale took his Warhawk squadron north also carrying three tanks and Wallace Jordan's Flying Knights followed on the 10$^{th}$ in their rebuilt P-38s.

**1Lt. Robert DeHaven** shot down a Judy to become a double ace. (AFAA)

**7 May 1944: 49FG**

At 1000, on 7 May, the 49ers would take off from Hollandia for their first real combat mission in a month when 49er CO, Lt.Col. David Campbell sent out 11 Black Sheep and 16 Demon Warhawks on B-24s escort to attack Biak.

**Maj. Arland Stanton** (2$^{nd}$ left with his ground crew) scored his eighth and last victory. (AAF)

7FS

At 1000 7FS CO Maj. Arland Stanton led 16 P-40s from Hollandia to provide escort for B-24s attacking Biak Airdromes. Stanton led Red Flight with Wingman, 1Lt. James Keck, Second Element Leader, Capt. Bobby Harrison, and Wingman, 1Lt. Fenton Epling. Green Flight was led by 1Lt. Robert DeHaven with Wingman, 1Lt. Jay Rogers, and Second Element Leader, 1Lt. Joel Paris, and Wingman, 1Lt. Frederick Dick. Blue Flight was led by Capt. Edward Peck with Wingman, 1Lt. Laurine Suggs, and Second Element Leader, 1Lt. James Menger, and Wingman, 1Lt. Jack Langenberg. White Flight was led by 1Lt. Robert Croft with Wingman, 1Lt. James O'Neill. This flight did not engage in the combat as it flew top cover.

At 1155 while flying at 16,000 feet about six miles from the Biak Drome Stanton's Red Flight saw two enemy fighters at 12 o'clock level. Maj. Arland Stanton ordered his other three flights to stay above as his flight dropped their tanks and dove to 14,000 feet. Red Flight made a head on pass at the Zeros but missed and they turned to make another pass when the Zeros pulled up. Red Flight made another pass which only resulted in Stanton getting a Zero on his tail. As Stanton rolled away he saw another P-40 firing at and chasing away the Zero on his tail. Other enemy fighters were seen coming in and Stanton then called down his other three flights from top cover. As they flew on Stanton saw a P-40 below firing at a Zero that pulled up in a loop toward Stanton who fired at the top of the enemy's loop and it caught on fire and as it fell out of its loop the pilot bailed out while his fighter disintegrated for his eighth and last victory. By this time Stanton had lost his altitude and escorted the bombers on their way home.

**1Lt. Joel Paris** poses with two new victory symbols after he shot down two Oscars to give him three victories. (AFAA)

On Stanton's call to attack, 1Lt. Robert DeHaven cautiously led his Green Flight on an unidentified fighter approaching the B-24s but it flew off without firing. Meanwhile, DeHaven's second element of 1Lts. Paris and Dick saw an Oscar make a head on pass at the bombers and then pull up under the flight. Paris rolled over and made an overhead pass and saw hits on its wings before he blacked out. When Paris came to he was on the Oscar's tail and fired another burst and it started to burn, inverted, and then crashed on the west end of Owi Island. Dick followed Paris down and also blacked out and when he recovered he saw an Oscar about 500 feet below and climbing at a low speed. Dick pushed his nose down and made a head on pass and fired a short burst into its propeller hub and the enemy pilot bailed out for his first of five victories. Dick lost Paris at 8,000 feet and Split-S'd to 11,000 feet where he saw a Tojo with about eight P-40s in string on its tail. The Tojo pilot was getting the best of the turning battle. As the opponents kept turning, Dick dove below them and pulled up inside to kill his speed and found the Tojo turning in front of him. Dick reefed in and fired a long burst that raked the enemy fighter from nose to tail. The Tojo rolled over in flames and Dick fired another burst from such close range that his right wing guns were hitting the engine and cockpit while his left guns were knocking pieces off its tail. The pilot bailed out and Dick turned around and fired at the descending pilot to punctuate his victory. For an unknown reason Dick was only given an official probable for this Tojo despite his ICR description. Meanwhile, Paris then joined Stanton's flight and started back with the bombers when he saw an Oscar at 11 o'clock low.

Paris rolled over behind the Oscar and fired and the Oscar burned and as it fell its wing came off for his second and third victories. While his second element of Paris and Dick had scored four (three?) victories, DeHaven and Wingman Rogers were never in position to join in the fight and were the last to return home escorting the bombers. When DeHaven approached the New Guinea coast, he spotted a lone Oscar in the distance flying parallel to the B-24s. DeHaven and Rogers slowly descended undetected behind and below the Ki-43. DeHaven closed to within 50 feet and killed the pilot and the Japanese fighter rolled and dropped inverted into the sea to make DeHaven a double ace with 10 victories.

While flying at 16,000 feet 10 miles south of Seride Strip on Biak Blue Flight Leader Capt. Peck led a diving attack on a lone Oscar flying in the opposite direction. Peck opened fired as the Oscar suddenly pulled up but had to break away as his #4, 1Lt. Jack Langenberg fired a long burst. Langenberg's ICR states: "...at the same instant that Peck broke away and I started firing the enemy plane started burning violently...I'm sure that I scored a few hits on the enemy airplane and I will verify it as Capt. Peck's victory." However, Peck's ICR makes no mention of Langenberg and states: "I began firing in range and as I came up on him I observed pieces coming off from the cockpit area and then flames appeared...and I broke off and saw him go down." (for his first of two victories)

8FS

Mission Leader Capt. Elferd Elofson had his three 8FS flights stacked between 12,000 to 15,000 feet over the bomber formation when they reached the target. Elofson led Red Flight with 1Lts. Robert Sweeney and Marion Felts on the high left flank in front of the formation. On Elofson's right was 1Lt. Nelson Flack's White Flight of 1Lts. William Runey, Howard Wayne, and John Davis. To the rear came three Green Flight P-40s remained in trailing high cover and would not engage in the combat.

The B-24s had completed their bombing run and had just turned southeast to return home when Elofson saw two Zeros closing in on the Liberator's starboard flank. As he was about to call for the break toward the two Zeros the 7FS Screamin' Demons located on the opposite side of the bomber formation called out more fighters in their area. Elofson could not locate the newly called fighters and turned toward the pair of Zeros that were about to attack the B-24s. Both Black Sheep Red and White Flights followed Elofson as he chased after the Zeros. Despite being fired on by seven Warhawks, the aggressive leading enemy pilot continued toward the bombers and fired on a Liberator on first pass. Instead of breaking away from uneven odds the enemy pilot climbed for another pass. As he climbed he passed in front of Elofson who fired and hit the Zero's engine for his third and last victory of the war. The Japanese pilot bailed out but White Flight Wingman Davis executed the enemy pilot before he reached the sea. Meanwhile, Red Wingman Felts overtook the other Zero and hit it on his first pass and then half rolled out and came back down to finish it off in a head on pass for his third victory.

**7 May 1944: 8FG**

Capt. Jay Robbins led a flight of P-38s from other units to cover a PBY Catalina on a search mission for a B-24 crew and two P-40 pilots over northwest Hollandia. Robbins had flown in from Nadzab to Hollandia and damaged the nosewheel of his P-38, *Jandina III*, on the muddy strip but took off again to lead the escort flight. On the way back to Hollandia rain squalls were developing in the direction of the Markham Valley and along the New Guinea north coast. Robbins' fuel supply was running low and then he found that his nosewheel would not come down. Since he could not reach Nadzab Robbins decided to land at Saidor but was informed that Saidor's traffic pattern was totally congested. It was getting to be late and the weather was closing while Robbins continued unsuccessfully to lower his nose wheel. As Robbins considered bailing out along the coast

**Maj. Jay Robbins** made a wheels up landing on a 1,000 foot light plane strip when his nose wheel would not drop. (AAF)

near Saidor he saw a dirt strip surrounded by high trees a few miles to the northwest. As he reconnoitered the strip he saw that it was occupied by Americans and he circled the strip to use up his remaining fuel in preparation for a wheels up landing. (The strip was Yemi Cub which was used for light observation aircraft and was less than a 1,000 feet long.) In increasing darkness and with rain beginning to fall harder the personnel below turned on their jeep lights to try to illuminate the strip. Robbins dropped full flaps to slow his fighter as much as possible and prepared for a full stall belly landing on the darkened strip. The Lightning skidded smoothly down the wet strip, dragging bent props, and slid past the end of the strip and into a small ditch. Robbins departed *Jandina* with a large cut on his forehead and spent the night there. The next day he was flown to Saidor where he waited several days for a C-47 ride back to Nadzab.

**9 May 1944: 348FG Leaves Saidor for Wakde**

After Hollandia fell in late April 1944 the nearest Japanese aircraft were based over 400 miles away on the Vogelkop Peninsula. From the beginning of May, the 348FG was engaged in glide bombing Japanese installations from Kar Island to the north and to the mouth of the Sepik River, 50 miles east of Wewak. On 3 April Capt. Max Wiecks and 1Lt. Andrew Lytle had been assigned to conduct the Group's first glide bombing tests. For the next few days Wiecks and Lytle dropped small bombs on a house on the southern end of Kar Island and the tests were judged successful. Over the next several months as air combat moved out of range, the Group morale suffered as it became engaged in important but very routine ground support mission as none of the Group's Squadron's had not scored any victories since the 340th's great day on 11 March.

On 9 May most of the 340th's personnel embarked by LST from Saidor to their new base on Wakde Island, northwest of Hollandia which had not been captured. While the LST was being loaded a furious thunder storm thoroughly soaked much of the equipment and personnel belongings causing a great deal of lost time before sailing. Meanwhile, 70 enlisted men with five ground officers, and 30 pilots remained behind to continue the bombing missions on areas near Hansa Bay, Bogia Harbor, Potsdam Harbor and Nubia until they also moved to the new base by the end of May. Like every other unit making the move to Wakde, after three nights and two days aboard the ships they landed at Hollandia. This base was suitable for some fighter units but others, especially groups equipped with the short range P-47s, had to use other fields located closer to the frontlines. The Hollandia airfields at Sentani and Cyclops had short runways that could not be used by the heavy Thunderbolts. As soon as the 348th got ashore at Hollandia a huge fire broke out destroying much of their food and ammunition. For the next nine days the unit reorganized and reboarded the LSTs for the Wakde Islands where a small adjacent island, Insomanai, was to be their new base while the ground echelon constructed the new facilities and were joined by the air echelon.

**Mid-May 1944: 8FG/35FS Dive Bombing Missions**

During May the Fifth Air Force began its attack on Biak. The 35FS participated in the routine dive bombing missions beginning during the middle of the month which continued until the squadron moved to Biak in June and began escort missions once more.

**14 May 1944: 58FG/310FS**

On 14 May the 58FG added strafing to their fighter bomber assignment. At 1425 the 310FS sent eight Thunderbolts to strafe Boram Airdrome in the Wewak complex. Once over the target area they systematically strafed targets of opportunity from Wewak Point to Cape Moem. Over the Boram Airdrome they set one enemy aircraft on fire in the dispersal area at the west end of the airdrome, another plane was seen smoking near the center of the airdrome, while columns of black smoke rose from the dispersal area northwest of the airdrome. Wewak Town and many buildings and stores were strafed along the shoreline near Cape Moem. Two of the P-47s were unable to release their drop tanks and did not participate but the other six expended 10,246 rounds of .50 caliber ammunition. During the following fighter bomber mission, the Group would suffer from small arms fire and AA fire.

**15 May 1944: 49FG/7FS**

At 1115, a pair of 71st Reconnaissance Squadron B-25 Photo Mitchells arrived over Biak escorted 16 7FS Warhawks in four flights led by Capt. Owen Swartz. Once over Biak Swartz found the area covered with heavy cumulus clouds and he stacked his flights from 15,000 to 20,000 feet. Swartz took his Red Flight and 1Lt. James Menger's White Flight under the cloud cover to remain with the B-25s that nonetheless soon vanished in the overcast. Swartz circled the area several times unsuccessfully for 10 minutes searching for the Mitchells and finally Swartz departed back to base with eight his Warhawks.

Meanwhile, Blue Flight Leader, 1Lt. John Haher, and Green Flight Leader, 1Lt. Lewis Smith, remained in high cover but had descended to 11,000 feet to keep the Swartz' eight Warhawks and the two Mitchells in sight. Smith's Green Flight was flying on the left flank when they saw eight Oscars and four Zeros approaching head on from 2,000 feet high. The four Zeros to Smith's left immediately began to dive and turned toward his flight. Smith quickly turned into the diving Zeros and soon the two were nose to nose and both opened fire. Smith hit the Zero's fuselage and its pilot snap rolled and bailed out. Smith comments that the enemy pilot's parachute must have been damaged as he was falling very quickly. Smith and Wingman 1Lt. Nicamor Zuniga then turned 270 to the port to re-engage four Zeros heading toward Blue Flight. In a head on pass, Smith's .50s tore off the port wing from the lead Zero, whose debris smashed into Zuniga's fighter, causing a five foot gash in the P-40's starboard wing's leading edge; Zuniga fell away in a spin. Smith was alone and chased by two Oscars and Smith was wounded in the arm by a round which exploded in his cockpit and he dove to safety in nearby clouds. Meanwhile Zuniga recovered from his spin, chopped his throttle and found a Zero in front of him. Zuniga fired and got hits and saw smoke coming from the cowling. Smith would confirm Zuniga's only victory while Zuniga confirmed Smith's only two victories.

After an ineffective first firing pass, Green second Element 1Lts. Jack Fenimore and Laurence Mclnnis were able to stay with Smith's lead Element. The 1st Lieutenants engage four Zeros and Fenimore fired at one with nil results and stalled out and when he recovered he was 180 from his flight where he met a Zero approaching head on. The two fired all the way in

**1Lt. Frederick Dick** shot down an Oscar for his second victory. (AFAA)

and Fenimore saw some hits for a damaged claim. Fenimore turned to find his flight and saw an Oscar at 2 o'clock with its belly exposed. Fenimore began firing when he got within range and followed it in a 180 turn; getting numerous hits but it did not smoke or flame. Fenimore, fixed on his target only stopped firing when he ran out of ammunition and almost collided with the Oscar whose pilot bailed out for his only victory. Fenimore saw the two B-25s below and joined them when an Oscar came down and fired on him from 7 o'clock. The impotent Fenimore could only watch but then Blue #4 1Lt. Warren Greczyn came in and shot it down.

After Fenimore dove away the trailing Mclnnis got hits on one of the turning Oscars. As Mclnnis' turned for another firing run, another Oscar closed from the right front quarter and opened fire hitting his cockpit with a large explosion. Mclnnis was hit in the right arm and legs and tried to roll back his canopy but it wouldn't jettison. The enemy rounds had shattered against the seat armor plate but most of the shrapnel had lodged in the oxygen equipment and parachute pack. Seeing that his instruments were functioning Mclnnis decided to remain with his fighter. Holding the control stick between his knees, he retrieved the first aid kit from his parachute pack with his left hand and cut the kit free with his knife. Using his good arm and teeth, he somehow applied a tourniquet to his wounded arm. He pressed another bandage against the wound in his right leg until the bleeding stopped. After two hours Mclnnis reached Cyclops and made a successful belly landing.

Blue Flight was flying a short distance behind Green Flight when the Zeros attacked. Blue Leader 1Lt. John Haher turned toward them in a flanking counterattack but was cut off by the veteran Oscar pilots. Haher and his rookie Wingman, 2Lt. Douglas Hart, became widely separated and both prudently dove away from the fight. Meanwhile, Blue Flight elements, 1Lts. Frederick Dick and Warren Greczyn, remained together at 12,000 feet and saw eight Oscars above when two Oscars got on their tails. Greczyn dove out and Dick reefed around and took a quick deflection shot at Greczyn's pursuer and got hits near the cockpit and engine and the Oscar broke off and Dick followed and started firing at 200 to 25 yards seeing explosions on its wing roots, canopy, engine, and fuselage. The Oscar burst into a sheet of flames as its pilot bailed out for Dick's second victory. Dick had lost Greczyn and was climbing for altitude when two Zeros got on his tail and then dove away in a high speed dive. He pulled out when he thought that he had lost them but when he looked back there was "a radial engine staring me right in the face about 100 yards behind…I'm sure he had six guns firing." Meanwhile, the other Zero closed on an over head pass and an Oscar, "I don't know where the hell he came from" was in a loop below him, firing all the way. Dick kicked left rudder and reefed and slid inside the circle and somehow evaded the fire from his three pursuers. Finally the Oscar stalled

**Capt. Arland Stanton** finished his tour as eight victory 7FS CO and Capt. Edward Peck took over the Demons. (AAF)

**Capt. Cornelius Smith** rotated home with eight victories and would remain in the Air Force. (AAF)

**1Lt. John Purdy** was credited with his first of seven victories. (AFAA)

**Maj. Warren Lewis** scored his sixth victory. (AAF)

out but the Zeros continued their pursuit and then another Oscar came into the fray. Dick went into another high seed dive and lost the Oscar but the Zeros continued after him toward Japen Island. Dick managed to skid and evade their fire and finally they ran out of ammunition but one frustrated enemy pilot tried to ram him but missed and Dick left for home.

Meanwhile, Greczyn spiraled down through the attacking Oscars and saw two Oscars I trail heading for some P-40s ahead. Greczyn pulled in front of the last one and started to fire and hit its tail and it started on fire and went down. Greczyn was then attacked by an Oscar head on and the two "kept firing until the props almost touched" but Greczyn lost it as passed him. Greczyn then headed toward the B-25s and saw three Oscars diving on a P-40 flown by Fenimore. He fired a deflection shot that exploded its right wing for his second of three victories. The other Oscars were coming toward Greczyn and he turned into then and turned away to draw them away from the Mitchells. The Oscars chased and fired at him but he pulled away and returned to base.

In the future the Demons and Black Sheep flew missions over coastal targets and islands of Geelvink Bay but would not encounter another enemy aircraft. Greczyn's victory was the Screamin' Demons' 112[th] victory while Black Sheep Felt's victory on 7 May was that squadron's 152[nd], the most for any Warhawk unit in the Pacific.

Blacksheep CO Robert McHale left the 8FS to join the 49ers HQ staff and newly promoted Major Charles Petersen became CO. Maj. Arland Stanton, Screamin' Demons' CO, completed his tour and returned to the States to attend Command School. Senior Capt. Edward Peck was scheduled for Squadron CO over double-ace DeHaven. Although Peck had only been in aerial combat once he was considered one of the best tacticians in the Group. DeHaven became 7FS Ops Exec. After 169 missions and eight victories Capt. Cornelius Smith rotated home and remained in the Air Force; retiring as a Colonel in 1968.

**15 May 1944: Japanese Attack Hollandia**

While the 49ers were over Biak the Japanese bombed Hollandia and a stick of bombs hit the ordnance stored on the beach which erupted in an enormous explosion, heard for miles. The fires burned for many hours, destroying a large portion of the ordnance stockpile.

**16 May 1944: 475FG/433FS**

The initial 475FG operations from Hollandia were to be bomber escorts to Biak in preparation for the scheduled 27 May invasion. The 475FG saw its first air combat since the very successful 3 April mission over Hollandia. Capt. Warren Lewis led Possum P-38s in on an armed photo-recon mission to Kamiri Airdrome on Noemfoor Island. Lewis' 16 P-38s were divided into two groups of eight, two flights flying at 15,000 feet and the other two at 18,000 as high cover. The P-38s rendezvoused with the F-7 Liberator photo bombers at 1315 and flew on to the airdrome. At 1415 the formation arrived at Kamiri Airdrome and saw three Oscars taking off 5,000 feet below. Lewis ordered auxiliary tanks to be dropped and dove to the attack with the lower two flights of P-38s; leaving the other eight as high cover. Red Flight Leader, Lewis and his Wingman, 2Lt. Howard Stiles, made a passes at two of the Oscars. Lewis made a head on 50 degree pass from above at the lead Oscar as it made a starboard turn. Lewis then fired a two second burst at the Oscar which exploded for his sixth victory. Stiles followed and fired long burst into the cockpit of his Oscar from the rear quarter and exploded it spinning into the water for his only victory. Lewis and Stiles made a pass at the third Oscar and Lewis got some hits before running out of ammunition and as they pulled up they saw it descending, smoking, with #3 man, 1Lt. John Purdy and Wingman, 2Lt. Ethelbert Roberts, after it from 3,000 feet. The Oscar was on the deck when Purdy closed to 75 yards and fired two short bursts from astern and it crashed into the water southwest of Noemfoor for his first of seven victories. After the F-7s dropped their bombs and took their photos the Lightnings broke escort and headed back to base.

**17 May 1943: Wakde Operations**

On 28 April Kenney flew to Port Moresby for a conference called by MacArthur and the GHQ Staff, about accelerating the schedule for the advance west along the New Guinea coast. Kenney wanted to capture Wakde and the coast opposite Wakde near Maffin Bay as soon as his fighter groups were established in the Hollandia area to cover the amphibious landings. However, GHQ argued that there was not enough shipping to advance any farther but Kenney countered that there were already too many troops in Hollandia and it would not be much more difficult to supply them at Wakde than Hollandia.

Kenney needed new airdromes as most of 5AF bases were out of range of the war. The Dobodura area and Port Moresby were abandoned as operating bases. The Kiriwina, Woodlark, and Goodenough Island airdromes and the fields around Milne Bay were of no value since the capture of the Admiralties while the area around Hollandia was limited by the accommodation of the

Sixth Army troops landed unopposed at **Toem**, near Sarmi on Maffin Bay, opposite Wakde Island. (U.S. Army)

Fifth and Thirteenth Air Forces. The area around Maffin Bay was a possibility for airdrome development but Kenney wanted to capture Biak where the Japanese had built three good coral runways. Since there was a large supply of coral there, the engineers could have additional fields ready in a few days whereas, ordinary sand-clay soil fields would require a month or even two.

MacArthur settled the debate by setting 15 May as a date for the invasion of Wakde and Sarmi on Maffin Bay and instructed Gen. Walter Krueger and Adm. Daniel Barbey to begin planning. MacArthur wouldn't commit himself on Biak until he saw how the Wakde-Maffin Bay invasion progressed. Kenney noted, "We were definitely on the move. The Philippines didn't look anywhere near as far away as they had just a few months before." MacArthur decided to move his advanced headquarters from Brisbane to Hollandia as soon as feasible and Kenney would follow. Kenney then instructed Whitehead to "Gloucesterize" Wakde and the Maffin Bay area with a concentrated air assault.

During the low altitude strafing and bombing attacks on the Maffin Bay area, air reconnaissance showed that it was "extremely doubtful if we would have any luck getting airdromes there without so much engineer effort that our movement toward the Philippines would be delayed for months. Biak looked better than ever as an objective to follow quickly after the Wakde show (Kenney)." MacArthur then set 27 May as the date to invade Biak when Kenney assured him that if Wakde was taken on the 17th the coral strip there would be ready to operate fighters to cover Biak if enough engineers and equipment were immediately put ashore. Kenney reminded the GHQ Staff when they questioned the shortage of shipping to haul supplies that "his Air Force had been hauling most of the food and ammunition up to now."

On 9 May MacArthur sent Sutherland and Kenney to Finschhafen for a conference at Krueger's Headquarters at which GHQ, the Sixth Army, the 7th Fleet, and the Allied Air Forces were represented to discuss the Biak operation. Supply again was the big issue due to the lack of shipping, insufficient time to load, and then having the means of getting the men and supplies ashore. Kenney remarked "that the Japs had put between eight and ten thousand troops in there, were operating aircraft from three airdromes on the island, and it seemed funny for us to confess that we were not as good as the Nip." Adm. William Fechteler, who was to be in charge of the amphibious landings, assured the conference that he would certainly be able to land men and supplies. Kenney settled the debate when he reminded Krueger that MacArthur had called the conference to decide how, not when, to capture Biak.

Whitehead's bombers "Gloucesterized" Wakde daily until the landings on the 17th; knocking out enemy bivouacs, supply and fuel dumps, shore defenses, and AA positions around Maffin Bay, and the airdromes on Biak. Meanwhile, 380th Heavy Bombardment Group attacked the enemy airdromes in Dutch New Guinea, west and south of Biak, near Nabire, Fakfak, Babo, and Manokwari. From 1 to 17 May over 1,500 tons of bombs and a half a million rounds of ammunition destroyed Wakde and Sarmi and also destroyed 27 enemy fighters and 25 bombers parked on the airdromes there. The Japanese were unable to send up interceptors over Wakde because of the 5BC heavy attacks on their bases at Biak and Noemfoor. During the first Biak attacks the Japanese sent up from 15 to 20 fighters but each encounter cost them heavily and by 10 May there was no further air opposition. The Japanese withdrew their air units to the new airdromes at Galela, Lolobata, Miti, and Kaoe in the Halmaheras, where Japanese intended to build another large base like Hollandia out of range of 5AF combined fighter and bomber strafer attacks.

On the 17th Sixth Army troops landed unopposed at Toem, near Sarmi on Maffin Bay, opposite Wakde Island. The next morning the 163rd Regiment went ashore unopposed at Wakde but then met stiff resistance by 800 recently landed veteran marines. Wakde's occupation was delayed until the afternoon of the 19th. Two days before the landings, the Japanese had evacuated their valuable service and air troops to Sarmi.

### Wakde Airstrip

Before the Hollandia-Aitape attack, *Operation Straight Line*, had started MacArthur was preparing to send troops for the next drive along the New Guinea coast. Ground space on the Hollandia Drome had become limited so three airfields were to be established in the vicinity of the Wakde Islands, located approximately 100 miles northwest of Hollandia. Tentatively, two of the airfields were to be located on the New Guinea mainland at Sarmi, approximately 17 miles west of the Wakde group and a third on Insoemoar Island, the main island of the two Wakde Islands. The airfields on the New Guinea mainland were planned to be constructed on a 25 mile long coastal strip situated between Sarmi and Toem villages. Swamps and dense jungles bounded the strip that extending two to six miles inland. The Japanese had occupied this coastal region since 1942 and by the end of 1943 had begun to reinforce their garrison in the Sarmi area and to construct airfields at nearby Sawar and Maffin and in early 1944 Sawar was the operational enemy field. Prior to the Allied landings, Intelligence indicated that the Sarmi area was not suitable for airfield construction and planning was then directed on the development of the air facilities only on the much smaller satellite island, Insoemoar Island, lying a few hundred yards to the south of Wakde but would be known to the Allies as Wakde Island.

Wakde Island is irregularly shaped; one and two thirds mile long at its greatest length and only 540 acres in area. It is made up of mainly flat raised coral with firm and well drained soil except for a few limestone hillocks on the west end near the coast and a mangrove swamp at the southwestern end. A coconut plantation covered all the cultivable land on the island and when the Japanese occupied the island in June 1942 they developed a military road network and a well water supply system. A sheltered anchorage was available for the safe unloading of small vessels. During 1943, the Japanese had cleared a portion of the coconut plantation to construct a 5,400x300 foot coral surfaced runway which could be extended at both ends to 6,900 feet. It had dispersal areas on the north side and a barracks area on the south side. By September the Japanese had added a radio station and barracks for 1,000 personnel.

After the establishment of the required air facilities at Hollandia and Aitape the Alamo Force (Sixth Army) was to invade, occupy, and defend the Wakde Islands and also establish control over adjacent areas on the New Guinea mainland. Facilities for one fighter group were to be provided immediately after capture of the islands and facilities for a second fighter group, a long range reconnaissance squadron, and a night fighter flight were to be added as soon thereafter as feasible. Only 10 days after the landing;

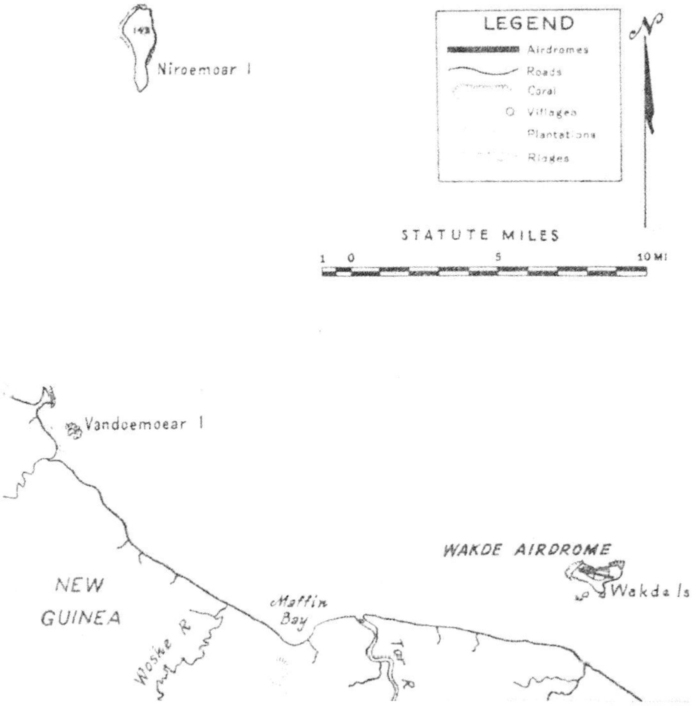


the Wakde airfield was to be able to support attacks against Biak Island and then they were to be used to support subsequent Allied operations further westward.

The fighter airfield was to be capable of expansion into a medium bombardment airfield with a 7,000 foot runway, 64 heavy bomber hardstands, and a surfaced parking area for staging 96 heavy bombers. It was estimated that the runway on Wakde would be operable for fighters on D plus 5 and for staging of bombers, with runway length of 6,000 feet, by D plus 10. Keeping these scheduled completion dates was absolutely necessary since the target date for the start of the Biak campaign was predicated upon the establishment of a fighter group on Wakde and two bomber squadrons at either Hollandia or Wakde. Because of the island's small size only one aviation battalion was assigned for the construction phase.

Alamo Force assigned the 163[rd] Regimental Combat Team of the 41[st] Division to capture Wakde and adjacent objectives on D Day, 17 May 1944 with H Hour at 0715. The initial landing was made on schedule at a point on the New Guinea coast between Arara and Toem and the Wakde Island landing was made against strong Japanese resistance at 0900 on D plus 1. The 836[th] Engineer Aviation Battalion landed the same day but the very small beachhead had been almost blocked by the pre-invasion bombardment and the bulldozing of the debris was necessary before equipment and supplies could be off-loaded. The beach access roads were open and equipment was moved to the existing Japanese airstrip by D plus 2, despite incessant enemy sniper fire. Task Force Engineers surveyed the airstrip

**Wakde Airdrome**

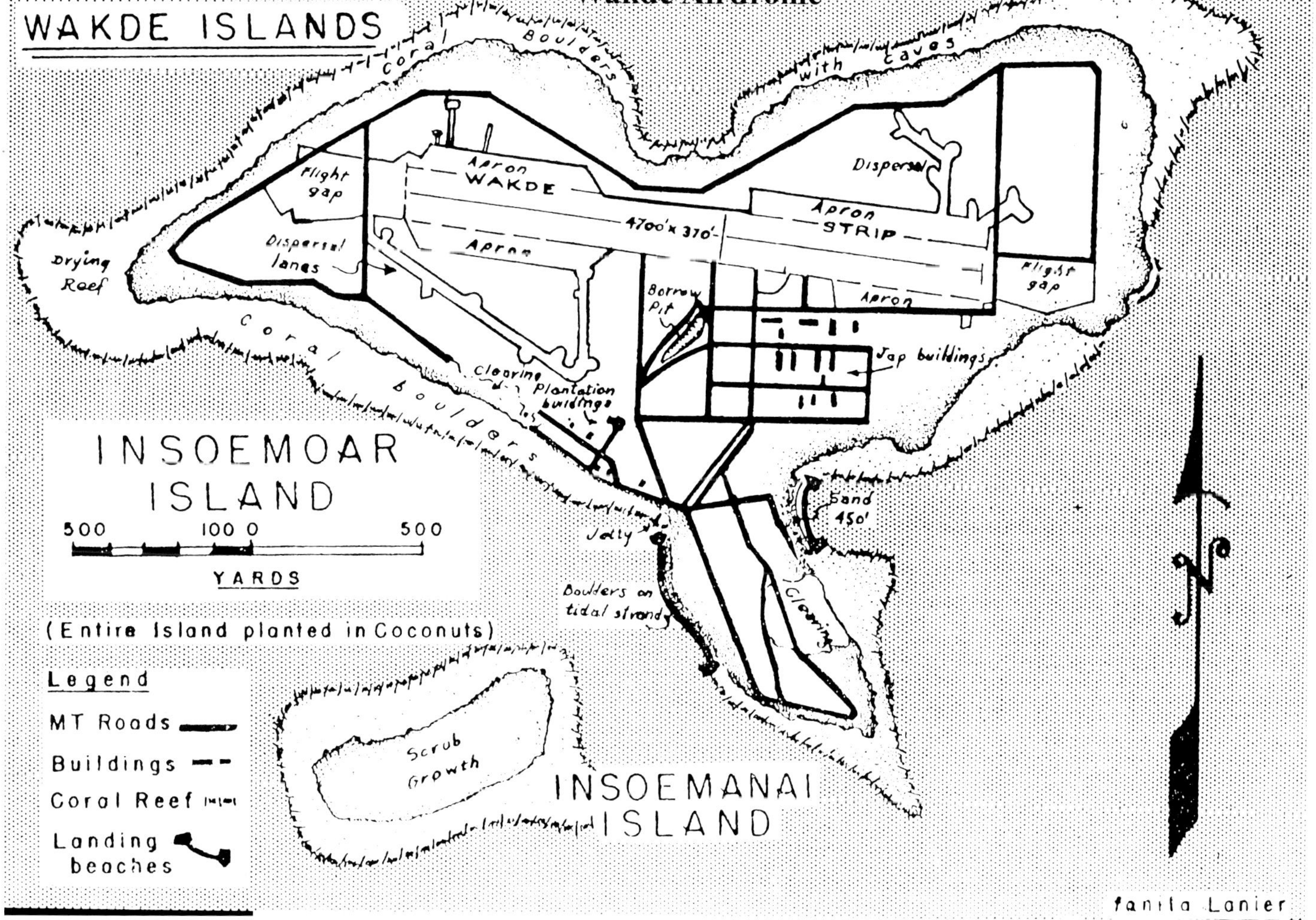

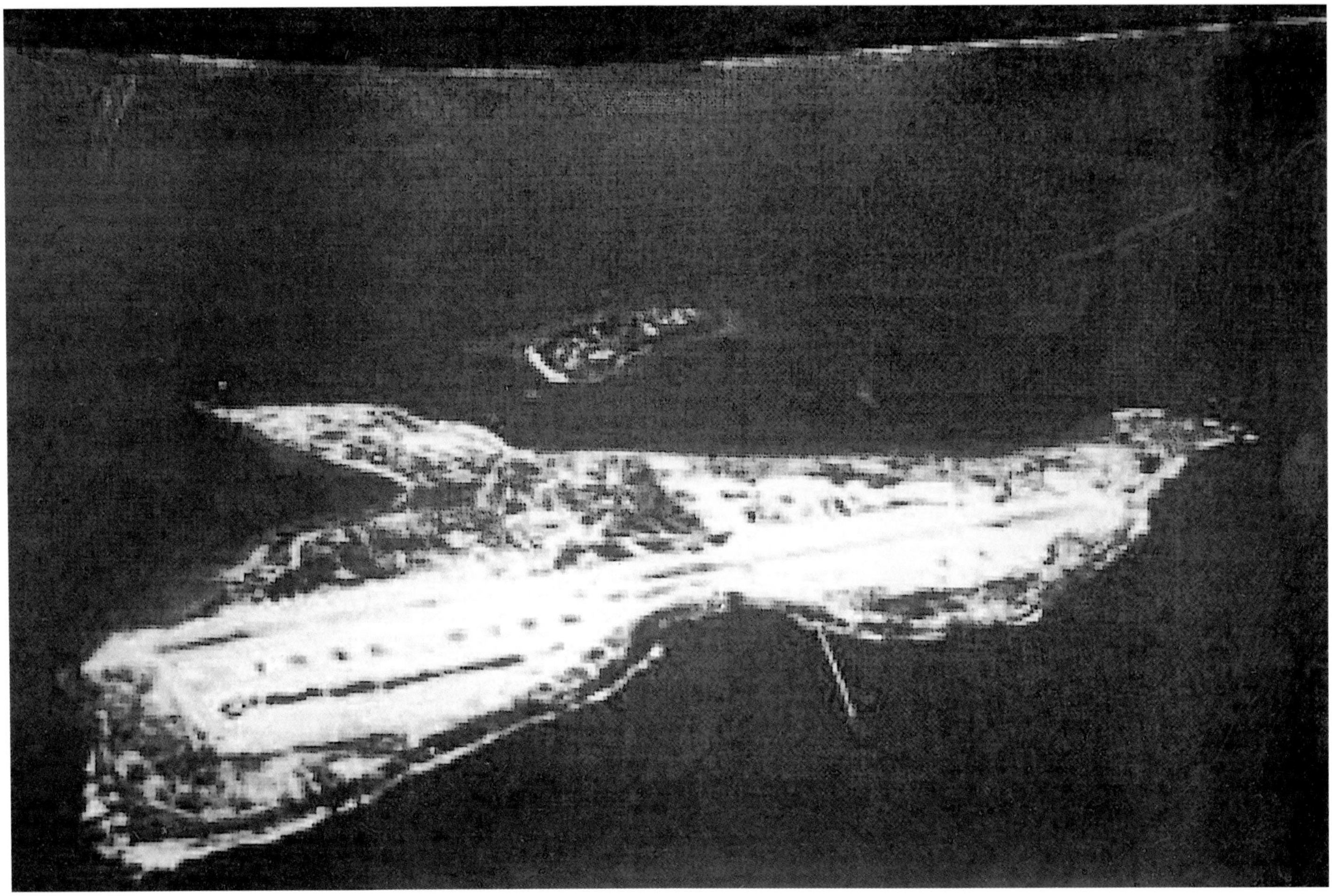

**Wakde Airdrome** utilized almost every square foot of the island. (AAF)

which was 4,700x300 feet and approximately half of the runway width was surfaced with material which precluded heavy bomber operations in wet weather. Also the entire area was covered with craters, unexploded bombs, debris from trees and wrecked aircraft, and oil drums. In order to expedite the completion of facilities for a fighter group, a 6,500x100 foot runway on the northeast side of the center line of the Japanese runway was to be constructed along with a temporary taxiway on the northwest side of the existing runway. The existing parking areas and taxiway were to be improved and a 200x750 foot alert area was to be constructed. The 35 existing Japanese hardstands were poorly constructed and surrounded by high revetments that had to be removed before an adequate dispersal area could be developed.

At sunrise on D plus 2, an enemy patrol slipped through the perimeter defenses; and before being eliminated, it had set fire to several vehicles and some equipment. Until D plus 5 it was necessary that all men and equipment work in one area within a tight defensive perimeter formed by a company of combat engineers. Despite the enemy disruption, a 6,000x100 foot fighter runway was operable by 21 May (D plus 4). The first elements of a fighter group moved to Wakde the following day and, by furnishing air support, materially assisted Allied ground units to expand their area of control east and west of Arara on the nearby New Guinea coast. However, the portion of the new runway width which overlaid the Japanese runway was unsatisfactory for use by heavy aircraft during periods of wet weather. Finally, in order to permit all-weather operating conditions for heavy bombers, the runway was widened until a full width of new runway construction was attained.

On 24 May (D plus 7), after a ground reconnaissance of the area, an Alamo Force directive provided more detailed airdrome requirements for Wakde; changing the initially specified Type C airfield with limited dispersals for one fighter group to a Type D airfield, with 7,000 foot runway by D plus 14; parking areas for staging 96 heavy bombers by D plus 16; and complete airdrome facilities, including alert areas and 64 heavy bomber hardstands, by D plus 30.

Within a week after its capture, the runway at Wakde was crowded with aircraft either based or refueling there. On 25 May (D plus 8) a reconnaissance squadron moved to Wakde with the mission of staging patrols over Biak during the operation there. The next day seven PB4Ys from Wakde made the first air reconnaissance of southern Mindanao since early 1942. The construction pace did not slow and by 27 May (D plus 10) the runway was extended to 6,500x200 feet; one week later, it had reached the required length of 7,000 feet. Airfield construction was significantly slowed by the early transfer of air service units onto the construction of essential air facilities. Nevertheless, by 28 June (D plus 42), the runway on Wakde had been widened to 350 feet while a 8,550x200-foot parking and alert area, 13,800 feet of 50 foot taxiway, and 64 hardstands had been completed.

When the airdrome facilities were completed in mid-July, Wakde Drome consisted of a 7,000x380 foot, coral surfaced runway, of which a section, 6,850x200 feet, was bitumen sealed. The taxiway had been widened to 85 feet and dispersal bays for 67 heavy bombers were available. There were also four alert areas, each averaging 200x1,600 feet. Essential operations buildings and a control tower, together with several small shops and warehouses, were completed.

All airfield construction had been completed on schedule to meet the main objective of the Wakde operation: to provide Allied air cover to the west of Hollandia and fighter support for the landing on Biak. Later, bomber aircraft based on Wakde played a significant part in the neutralization of Japanese airfields and bases in the Vogelkop Peninsula-Moluccas area in preparation for subsequent Allied landings on Noemfoor Island, Sansapor, and Morotai Island. By late 1944, as the battlefront moved rapidly far to the west and northwest of Wakde the use of air facilities and the need for bulk aviation gasoline storage on the island decreased. In January 1945, orders were issued for the two storage tanks to be dismantled and reconditioned for immediate shipment forward. By November 1945 the base was closed and the airdrome facilities were sold to the Netherlands Indies Government on 5 April 1946.

5FC units based at Wakde included:

**348FG**: HQ & 342FS (P-47) from Saidor on 22 May 1944 to Noemfoor on 24 August 1944
**348FG**: 340FS & 341FS (P-47) from Saidor on 26 May 1944 to Noemfoor on 24 August 1944
**5FC**: from Nadzab on 28 May 1944 to ? on 21 September 1944

**17 May 1944: 475FG/431FS**

During the Group's move from Nadzab to Hollandia Capt. Thomas McGuire was promoted to Major and was assigned as CO of the 431FS to the displeasure of many of those under his new command as he became even more driven and reckless in combat and reigned with a heavy hand.

McGuire led 16 P-38s from Hollandia on a B-24 escort to Biak and rendezvoused with the bombers over the target at 1120. The Squadron stayed with the bombers for 10 minutes after their run and returned over Noemfoor at 17,000 feet where McGuire saw two Oscars on the deck. McGuire instructed his first two flights to drop their tanks and attack. McGuire led the way but lost the Oscars and started climbing and at 3,000 feet he saw another flight of P-38s chasing two Oscars and "cut over to box them in." He got "several fair shots in deflection and astern" before he got an Oscar from 30 degrees deflection to full astern but as the range closed the enemy pilot started turning and McGuire fired several shots at slight deflection from 50 to 75 feet astern. Hits were made from the wing into the cockpit and pieces flew back and McGuire's windshield was covered with oil. Element Leader, 1Lt. Franklin Monk, witnessed McGuire's 17th victory.

In the meantime the other two flights spotted two more pairs of Oscars and dropped their tanks and dove on them.

Newly promoted **Maj. Thomas McGuire** (left) shot down an Oscar for his 17th victory to close on Maj. Jay Robbins (center) with 18 victories (13 victory ace Capt. Cyril Homer is on the right). (AFAA)

**1Lt. John Tilley** claimed his third victory. (AAF)

When McGuire led the first two flights down on the Oscars, Capt. William O'Brien's Blue Flight and Green Flight remained above at 15,000 feet. O'Brien's element leader, 1Lt. John Tilley, spotted two more enemy aircraft, and the two flights dropped their tanks. As they descended Blue Flight saw another P-38 flight chasing after the enemy fighters, but then saw two more Oscars above; as they started to climb toward them they dove and Blue and Green Flight pursued. O'Brien's ICR describes the combat as "quite complex because of the numerous passes made by the two flights but I eventually found an opening and flew right up an Oscar's tail." O'Brien fired a short burst that exploded the Oscar and sent it into the sea for his second victory. Meanwhile, Tilley and his Wingman, 2Lt. Louis DeMontier, turned to meet the Oscars head on after they had got on Green #4, 1Lt. Wilson Ekdahl's tail and fired but "did no harm" and the Oscars passed over them. Tilley looked for O'Brien but was unable to locate him and went into a climbing port turn for a 360 when they spotted the two Oscars below. Tilley "dove down and latched on the first one, shooting at every opportunity." As the enemy pilot turned to port Tilley chopped his throttles and reefed his fighter up to the stalling point and stayed with him for 360 degrees, firing all the way around at no deflection and the wounded Oscar spattered Tilley's windshield with oil before it crashed into the sea. Tilley's forward vision was completely obscured by the oil and he had to be escorted back to base where he managed a successful landing with his second victory.

**19 May 1944: 475FG/431FS**

Capt. McGuire led 12 P-38s off Hollandia at 1120 on another B-24 escort to Manokwari Island. At 1335 the Hades P-38s arrived over the target at 17,000 feet giving them an altitude advantage but having to remain with the Liberators put them in range of the unusually heavy and accurate enemy AA fire. While the bombers were approaching the target, McGuire was leading Red Flight when a flight of a Tojo and three "probable" Oscars was contacted just west of Manokwari. The P-38s dropped their tanks and dove after them as the enemy fighters were diving from above and in front. As the flight "slipped behind them," McGuire picked out the Element Leader and fired a short burst and followed him up until he stalled out and began to roll. McGuire fired another burst into the Tojo's cockpit and it exploded but the pilot was blown out and parachuted to safety and McGuire had his 18th victory. Bomber crews called in a flight of Tojos in the distance but McGuire had turned back to bomber escort. Later McGuire learned 9FS Lightnings had intercepted this enemy formation and claimed three victories and a probable and a damaged.

**Maj. Thomas McGuire** scored his 18th victory (at this point his aircraft carried one more victory symbol than his official count). (AAF)

**19 May 1944: 49FG/9FS**

Maj. Wallace Jordan's 9FS Flying Knights finally received a mixed batch of 24 P-38 J models and newer L models. After ridding themselves of their hated P-47s the Flying Knights were eager to get back into combat and regain their top scoring squadron lead from the rival 80FS Headhunters. With Biak scheduled for imminent invasion, more attacks were scheduled further west on the enemy air staging bases. Air recon had discovered enemy fighters dispersed at Manokwari on the western shore of Geelvink Bay and 5BC B-24s were deployed to destroy them so they wouldn't with the Allied landings at nearby Biak.

On the morning of the 19th, 11 Flying Knight Lightnings rendezvoused with Liberators over Hollandia to for the 475 mile flight to Manokwari. At 1230 Maj. Jordan led his Red Flight composed of 1Lts. Richard Kirkland, Charles Kamphausen, and Willis Treadway to 15,000 feet west of the target to protect the Liberators' starboard flank. Soon four Tojos appeared approaching from the southeast with one in high cover and the other three were together at 9,000 feet. Also spotted in the distance and out of sight of Red Flight were four other Ki-44s but they were seen by White and Blue Flights. Mission Leader Jordan climbed toward the single top cover Tojo to eliminate that threat from above but the Tojo rolled away as Jordan took a shot at it. Jordon then dove on a firing pass at the other three enemy fighters. The one in front chandelled away to the left; leaving the other two in front and slightly below Jordan who came in from directly behind the Element Leader. He fired a short burst at it and then swung over to the Wingman and it started burning furiously and exploded. Meanwhile, Jordan's Wingman, 1Lt. Richard Kirkland, fired on the Element Leader that Jordan missed and it slow rolled and its pilot bailed out. Red Flight #4 man, 1Lt. Willis Treadway, and Element Leader, 1Lt. Charles Kamphausen, dove on a Tojo that tried to loop and Treadway was waiting for him and scored several hits and the enemy pilot dove away. Treadway followed and made a head on pass knocking off pieces and the Tojo dove straight down and Treadway had to settle for his first of two victories.

Capt. Delman Moore was leading the White Flight in their top cover position at 20,000 feet when they saw the other four Tojos approaching from the northwest. Moore and Wingman, 2Lt. Edwin Cooper, Element Leader, 1Lt. William Maddox, and Wingman, 2Lt. Nile Lambert, dove to attack the Tojo formation. Moore shattered the canopy of his target but the fighter flew on for a probable claim. Element Leader Maddox followed Moore, making a rear quarter firing pass then chandelling back up for a second head on pass which left the enemy trailing smoke for a damaged claim.

Flying at 20,000 feet, Yellow Flight Leader, 1Lt. Charles McElroy, with wingmen 1Lts. William Baxter and Huard Norton were the last to attack the turning Tojos. Baxter saw a Tojo and in a 400 mph diving chase closed to 400 yards at 11,000 feet where he began to fire with machine guns and cannon until its fuselage started smoking and its port wing burst into flames to conclude Flying Knight scoring for the day and give Baxter his first of two victories.

**19 May 1944: 475FG/433FS**

At 1000 Capt. Warren Lewis was leading 14 Lightnings on a close cover escort for A-20s to Manokwari when they spotted a lone Pete recon biplane at 1,000 feet about 10 miles off the northwest coast of Noemfoor Island. Lewis descended to 3,000 feet and made a level astern four second pass for his seventh and last victory of the war along with an extraordinary five probables and three damaged.

**Maj. Wallace Jordan** scored his third victory. (AFAA)

**1Lt. Richard Kirkland** claimed his only victory. (AAF)

**1Lt. Willis Treadway** claimed his first of two victories. (AAF)

**24 May 1944: 348FG Command Changes**

On 24 May Maj. John Moore became the Deputy Group Commander while Maj. William Dunham assumed command of the 342FS from Maj. William Banks who moved up to Group HQ and would eventually commanded the Group late in the war.

**27 May 1944: Biak Invasion**

The JAAF Command had withdrawn from New Guinea to their new Headquarters at Manado in the Celebes Islands. The JAAF had only about a 100 serviceable aircraft and had abandoned irreplaceable ground crews in New Guinea. The major staging airfield between the Celebes and Hollandia was on Biak Island, located across the entrance to large Geelvink Bay on the New Guinea north coast. Biak runways were constructed on hard white coral that was ideal for 5[th] Bomber Command operations. Biak was MacArthur's next objective in his advance toward the Philippines but first Kenney's bombers and fighters would have to soften up the island's defenses. The 5BC continued to bomb Biak, with intermittent missions to Noemfoor, Manokwari, Babo, and Fakfak. On the 27[th], the day of the invasion, nearly 150 heavy bombers and strafers dropped 317 tons of bombs ten minutes before Maj.Gen. Horace Fuller's 41[st] Division went ashore at Bosnek, Biak.

**Maj. Warren Lewis** claimed his seventh and last victory of the war. (AFAA)

Biak is a triangular shaped island about 70 miles long from east to west. The terrain is hilly jungle that extended to the narrow sandy coastal beaches. On the southeastern coast just west of Mokmer Village the Japanese had carved out three runways from the rugged jungle. The 41[st] Division's amphibious forces came ashore at Bosnek Village 10 miles east of Mokmer against negligible opposition and swiftly secured the coastal road connecting the two villages as the enemy garrison retreated to fortified caves in the interior. The Americans advanced toward the three enemy airdromes about seven miles away. However, when the landing forces approached the closest airstrip at Mokmer they were met by 10,000 veteran heavily armed enemy troops waiting in caves in cliffs with light artillery and machine guns. Mokmer Strip was captured on 7 June but it was not until the 20[th] that the two old airdromes at Sorido and Borokoe, five miles to the west of Mokmer, were taken and several more weeks before the island was completely secured. The engineer units that had landed immediately after the infantry to restore the newly captured enemy airfields were immobilized by the stubborn Japanese resistance. About two miles south of Biak is uninhabited Owi Island which is flat, vegetated only with low shrub, well drained, and solid coral, except for about a foot of black topsoil. The engineer units were transferred to Owi and by the 21[st] the first troop carriers landed with personnel and equipment on which would soon became an important airbase.

MacArthur had argued that capturing Biak and the Japanese airfields there would provide valuable support to the Navy's offensive in the Marianas. Instead, the savage and fluctuating fighting led to the sacking of 41[st] Division's CO, Gen. Krueger, and the diversion of valuable resources to what essentially was a "sideshow." MacArthur's premature declarations of an easy and quick victory were a chronic embarrassment and he barred any mention of the Battle of Biak in his presence for the rest of his life.

**27 May 1944: 348FG/342FS**

During the Biak invasion on 27 May the 348[th] finally engaged in its first combat since 11 March as the Japanese surprised Allied planners with a strong reaction both on the ground and in the air and the Biak campaign stalled and developed into a fierce and protracted battle. Over the next week the 348[th] covered the Biak invasion beaches and three combats accounted for 14 Japanese aircraft for the loss of one P-47 and its pilot.

On 27 May 16 P-47s of the 342FS were patrolling at between 10,000 and 15,000 feet over the Biak beachhead at about 1500 looking for enemy bombers or low flying fighters looking to bomb, torpedo, or strafe the invasion convoy.

White Flight Leader, 1Lt. Robert Sutcliffe, saw a flight of four Oscars at 1,000 feet, 10 miles east of Bosneck at 1645. He took his flight down from 6,000 feet but lost sight of the enemy fighters for a moment when he saw one coming directly at him and fired a long burst from 300 yards and saw the Oscar burst into flames, roll over and Split-S into the trees without making any evasive action, indicating the unaware Oscar pilot did not see the P-47. The victory was Sutcliffe's fifth making him an ace. After patrolling for an hour and a half 1Lt. Marvin Grant, leading the second element of White Flight, saw four enemy fighters flying at 300 feet which were identified as three Oscars and a lead Tony. Grant dove on the Tony's Wingman at 475 mph but could not get a good shot at the Oscar as it made a violent port turn out of his gunsight. But the Tony leader was still ahead and Grant closed, "flying right up his tail" and fired a short burst

**1Lt. Robert Sutcliffe** became an ace when he shot down an Oscar over Biak. (AAF)

**1Lt. Marvin Grant** was credited with his third victory. (AAF)

from about 75 yards and the Tony rolled over and burst into flames before it crashed for Grant's third victory.

1Lt. George Burgess in Green Flight dropped his belly tank at the same time as Grant and followed him in the attack on the apparently oblivious Japanese formation. When Grant overshot the first Oscar, Burgess fired a long burst and it crashed into the trees and exploded. Burgess then made a climbing turn and closed behind another Oscar and fired a long burst which also sent it to crash into the trees and explode for his first two of three victories.

2Lt. Lieutenant Charles Nickell was flying as an element Wingman at 5-6,000 feet and followed the Flight down to 500 feet under a layer of overcast but lost his element leader but ran into a flight of three Oscars. Nickell fired a 90 degree deflection shot but missed and made a 180 turn and got behind another Oscar. He fired and got several hits before the Oscar broke to the left while Nickell turned to the right. Nickell then turned 270 degrees and saw an Oscar on the tail of a P-47 and got on the Oscar's tail and started firing. The Oscar pilot turned slightly to port and headed at treetop level toward the sea. Nickell closed to 100 yards and fired a long burst, getting some hits on the cockpit and wings before he had to swerve to avoid a patch of tall trees. As he recovered he saw the Oscar had crashed and was burning in the trees for hi only victory.

1Lt. Winans Frankfort who had been shot down over New Guinea on 22 October 1943 walked out of the jungle to return to the 342FS disappeared during this combat. 348FG Historian John Stanaway reports that around 1990 a construction crew working for a logging company found Frankfort's P-47 in the Biak area. A few months later, Dutch aircraft archaeologist, Max Ammer, found Frankfort's P-47 but also a nearby Zero that had .50 caliber bullet holes in what remained of the fuselage. Ammer concluded that the P-47 was chasing the Japanese fighter in a dive when both aircraft ran into the ground. Both wrecks were in very poor condition indicating that both had crashed in the pursuit. So perhaps Frankfort added one more victory, during his final mission, giving him three confirmed and one probable.

**29 May 1944: 348FG/342FS**

Sixteen P-47s of the 342FS were patrolling over the southern sector of the Biak beachhead covering the Fighter Director Ship. At 0830 1Lt. Robert Knapp was leading Green Flight when he heard several A-20s radioing that they were being attacked and at the same time Ground Control reported that Zeros were strafing the beachhead. Knapp saw the A-20s flying east on the deck followed by one unidentified Japanese fighter. Knapp was able to chase it off but lost it in the sun. He directed his flight to turn west where he spotted a Zero heading due west along the beach. Knapp chased and caught it after three miles and fired about a four second burst commencing at 300 yards and closing to 100 yards from dead astern and the plane burst into flames and hit the water for his third victory.

1Lt. Marvin Grant was again leading an element of White Flight with Wingman, 2Lt. Albert Newman, when he sighted three Zeros flying southwest, close to the ground. Grant called them out to the rest of the Squadron and made a diving turn to get on their tails. Two of the Zeros changed direction but Grant got on the tail of the third and after a four minute pursuit, Grant lost his anticipated victim. But Wingman Newman passed Grant in the chase and sighted Grant's Zero dead ahead and called out its position. Grant fired a long range shot intended to make the Oscar pilot to commit himself and the Japanese pilot executed a steep chandelle to port. Newman and Grant began to shoot at the same time, Newman from 50 degrees deflection and Grant from head on, and the Zero, trailing flame and smoke, plunged straight into the sea and Newman had his only victory of the war. Grant tried to maneuver to attack the other two Oscars but, instead, they got on his tail but he was able to out run them.

**1Lt. Robert Knapp** celebrates the destruction of a Zero for his third victory. (AFAA)

Capt. George Orr, flying at 8,000 feet, saw an Oscar that was just leaving after making a low level attack on an USN destroyer. His Thunderbolt drew to within 200 yards before he fired at the unaware Oscar that did not evade and crashed about 20 miles southwest of Mokmer strip for his third victory.

**Biak Island-Base H**

Scheduled for 10 days after initial landings in the Wakde Island-Arara area, the next Allied attack was to be on Biak Island, the largest in the Schouten Group laying about 180 miles to the northwest. Because the Hollandia airfields were unsuitable for heavy bomber operations and ground space at Wakde Island was too limited, the most forward 5FC heavy bomber bases remained at Nadzab, New Guinea, and the Admiralty Islands, more than 400 miles east of Hollandia. Aerial reconnaissance revealed that Biak was the nearest site suitable for the construction of heavy bomber runways that would put 5BC heavy bombers in range to attack the Japanese in the Philippines. After hurried planning and preparation the *Hurricane* Task Force, under Alamo Force (Sixth Army) command, was assigned to neutralize Japanese airstrips on Biak and to establish an advanced major permanent base for both tactical and service units and more importantly a base from which tactical air units could be staged just as soon as facilities could be constructed.

Biak, a roughly triangular island, approximately 50 by 25 miles in size, is located at the mouth of Geelvink Bay and is separated from other Schouten Islands by a narrow strait. The almost impenetrable mountainous northwest section of Biak rises to 2,400 feet while the southeast section is primarily a narrow coastal shelf. This shelf is a generally flat area of eroded coral and limestone with nearly parallel limestone ridges and cliffs rising in steps to an inland plateau. Within these ridges and cliffs are numerous caves, many of which are interconnected by fissures and tunnels. Biak's vegetation is primarily rain forest on the coast while scrub growth flourishes inland. The Allied assault was to be directed against the southern shore in the vicinity of the Japanese airstrips at Sorido, Borokoe, and Mokmer. Preliminary engineer intelligence prepared by the Office of the Chief Engineer, GHQ, SWPA, was used in planning the Biak attack and subsequent base construction. This data disclosed a number of unfavorable conditions, including: a six foot tide, a fringing reef along the south coast, a barrier reef outside the fringing reef, a lagoon inside the barrier reef that was so narrow it restricted large vessels from turning, 20 to 50 foot cliffs along the shore, and little water supply available. The Japanese had constructed small ship jetties to their main supply and bivouac area near Bosnek and a passable motor road along the shore line. Aerial recon photos also revealed that four Japanese airstrips were in varying degrees of construction and one was apparently in use.

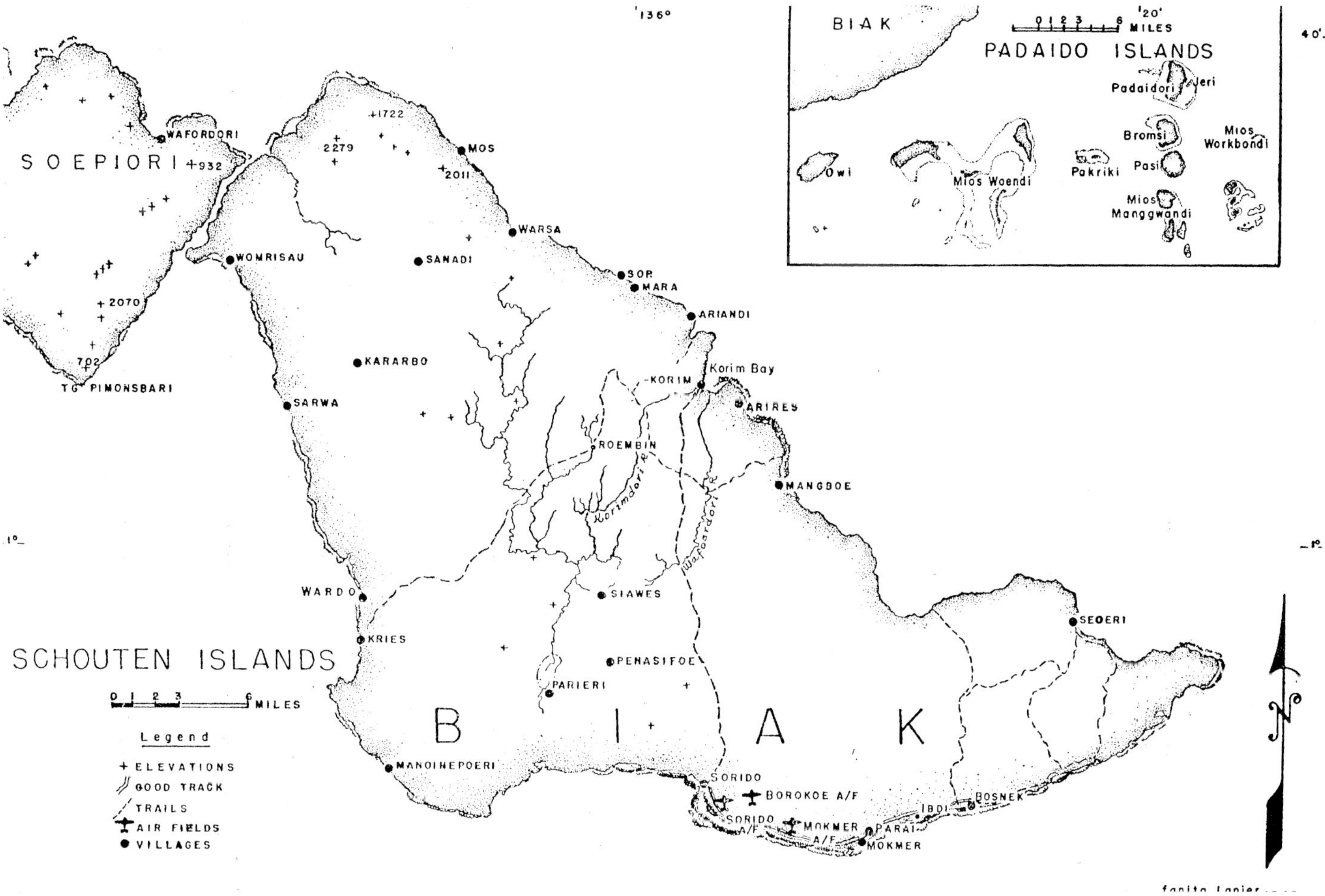


Biak is inhospitable with temperatures exceeding 100 degrees and oppressive humidity. The seaward side of Mokmer is swampy and generates a cloud of black flies and Malarial mosquitoes and made insect repellant and Atabrine anti-Malarial tablets as critical as food and aviation fuel for survival. Tents and flooring materials were in short supply. It was impossible to dig air raid slit trenches or foxholes and latrines in the hard packed brittle coral.

A major difficulty encountered by the engineers on Biak was the large number of changes in the scope of construction directives caused by the delays in securing the construction areas and poor planning. Each revision of the plans by the Task Force Engineer interfered with the efficiency of the construction units. However, unlike that at previous airdrome along the New Guinea coast, the weather was generally good and Biak had a good draining soil that relieved the drainage problem that arose at other bases. On Biak, as in previous airbase construction, the shortage of spare parts for the repair of equipment resulted in considerable delays and the reduction of construction efficiency. Nails for building construction were in very short supply while lumber production was behind schedule because timber was located in areas unsuitable for logging and often shrapnel had to be removed before cutting. Although, later when two sawmills were set up, production still did not meet the demand.

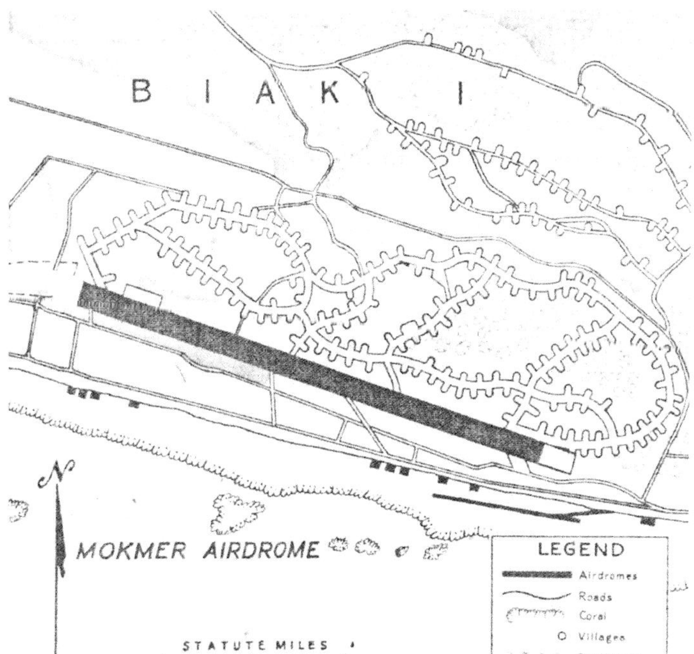


### Mokmer Airdrome

On 10 May 1944 (Z minus 17), GHQ, SWPA, issued the construction requirements for Biak: immediately after securing the island facilities for one fighter group were to be established at one of the three existing airstrips and, as soon as feasible, facilities for an additional

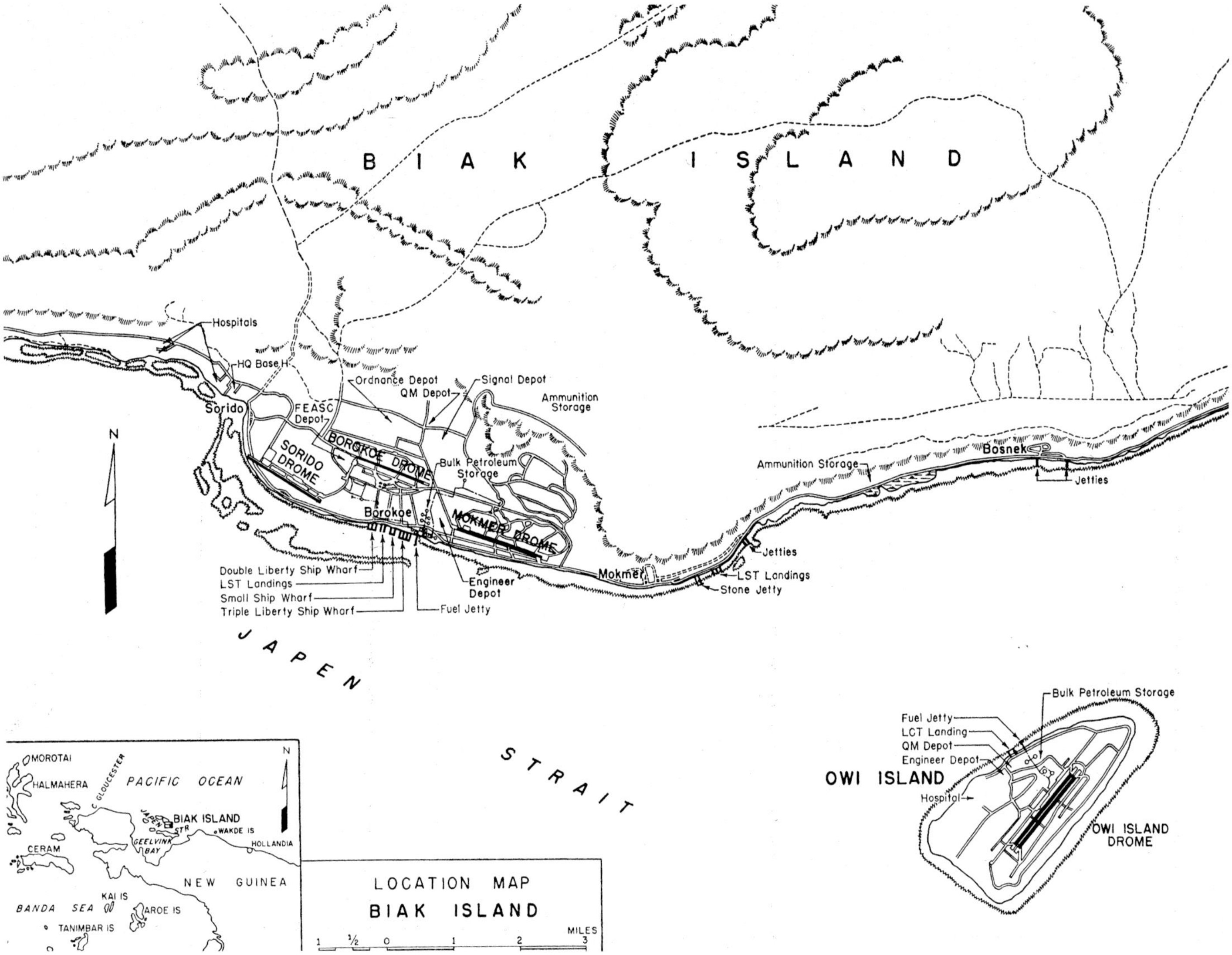

**Mokmer Airdrome**. (AAF)

fighter group, a heavy bomber group, a reconnaissance group, a night fighter squadron, and a photographic reconnaissance squadron were to be added. If local conditions were favorable Biak was then to be developed into a major air base to which units from rear bases would be transferred. This major air base was to consist of a fighter airfield, suitable for expansion to medium bomber specifications, with a 7,000 foot runway and 52 heavy bomber hardstands and a heavy bomber airfield with 73 heavy bomber hard stands. One runway with limited dispersals for a fighter group was to be usable by Z plus 2 and the fighter airfield with dispersal for two fighter groups to be operational by Z plus 10. One 7,000 foot runway at the heavy bomber airfield, together with limited dispersal for a heavy bomber group, was to be ready for use on Z plus 20 while all airdrome facilities would be completed by Z plus 60. Engineer troops assigned to the operation for combat included a combat battalion of approximately 2,400 engineer troops. The units assigned for construction operations consisted of three aviation battalions and auxiliary units of approximately 2,700 engineer troops.

The assault, capture, and development of Biak were delegated to the *Hurricane* Task Force; the 41st Division, less 163rd Regimental Combat Team. In the weeks prior to the invasion, numerous air attacks were made against the area by bombers based at Nadzab and fighters from Hollandia. Heavy bombers from bases in northwest Australia, with fighter cover from Hollandia, neutralized all Japanese airfields along the shores of Geelvink Bay and the Vogelkop Peninsula of New Guinea which were capable of reinforcing or supporting the defense of Biak. Also, during this pre-invasion phase, Admiralty based aircraft were flying missions against Japanese air bases at Truk and Woleai. Then, on Z Day, 27 May 1944, an intensive naval gunfire and aerial bombardment by two B-24 squadrons staging from the Admiralties was launched and at 0715 the troops landed near the village of Bosnek. Except for a short period of bad weather, fighter cover was continuously furnished by aircraft from Hollandia and Wakde. The initial landing forces found that the cliffs along the shore were not the anticipated single, relatively sheer climbs but were instead a succession of from three to seven precipitous knife back ridges covered by thick jungle.

The LSTs of the second wave, which landed on the Japanese jetties near Bosnek, carried bulldozers and other engineer equipment in order to expedite the repair and widening of these jetties. Access roads and storage areas were cleared of wreckage and opened by the shore battalion of the Engineer Boat and Shore Regiment.

The U.S. combat forces on Biak were soon to be found to be under strength and unable to make much progress against the well entrenched Japanese. The stubborn enemy defenses delayed the capture of Mokmer Airstrip at until 7 June (Z plus 11). Even after its capture the Allied situation there was so uncertain that the construction of the required facilities for one fighter group could not be begun. The Mokmer-Bosnek road which was to be a main supply route was not opened until Z plus 13 days because of the shortage of supplies, collective fatigue, and harassing enemy artillery fire. It was not until the night of 9/10 June (Z plus 13/14), that elements of the 863rd Engineer Aviation Battalion were landed near the airstrip to begin construction of the fighter runway. During unloading, the tide came in so rapidly that nearly all of the equipment, except bulldozers and carryalls, were submerged and had to be pulled ashore and dried out before they could be used. After 12 hours of intermittent work extending over a period of three days because of Japanese artillery fire, the 863rd Engineers had completed 4,000 feet of the runway to minimum operational standards for fighters and transports and a limited dispersal area. However, it was not until nine days later on 21 June (Z plus 25), when new combat units were finally able to overrun the enemy artillery positions and aircraft were able to land. The delay in reducing the Japanese defenses on Biak and the inadequate number of engineer units assigned to the Task Force made it totally impossible to complete construction on the island within the schedule specified in GHQ, SWPA, directives.

Despite the insufficient number of construction troops, work on further extending and improving the initial 4,000 foot Mokmer airstrip was started immediately after enemy opposition in this vicinity was finally overcome on 21 June (Z plus 25). The preceding day, GHQ, SWPA, had issued a revised airdrome construction plan for Mokmer which included a heavy bomber airdrome with 115 hard stands but without the parallel runway. Three days later (Z plus 28), the runway had been extended to 5,100 feet and was usable for transports and fighters and by 2 August (Z plus 67), the runway was completed to 7,000 feet. When completed in mid-September Mokmer Drome consisted of the compacted 7,000x100 foot coral runway with 500 foot overruns, two alert aprons, a 100 x5,500 foot apron, approximately 28,000 feet of 50 foot wide taxiway, and 165 hardstands, along with the essential operations buildings. Mokmer was primarily used for heavy bomber operations.

Borokoe Airdrome

The airstrip at Borokoe was under construction at the time of the Allied landing and was not captured until 20 June (Z plus 24) at which time the GHQ, SWPA issued a revised airdrome construction directive for Borokoe which was to be a fighter airdrome with 94 hardstands or equivalent parking aprons for two troop carrier groups. The first phase in runway improvement was removal of the hand-excavated coral which the Japanese placed in a thin layer directly upon the light topsoil and its replacement with new coral. By 15 August (Z plus 80), Borokoe Drome had been developed from a rough 3,500 foot runway without dispersals to a 5,500x100 foot runway with 500 foot overruns at each end, a 5,500 foot parallel taxiway, and 28 heavy bomber dispersals. The airdrome was later expanded until by early October there were approximately 14,250 feet of 50 foot wide taxi-way and 146 heavy bomber hardstands. The necessary facilities were provided for fighter and transport operations.

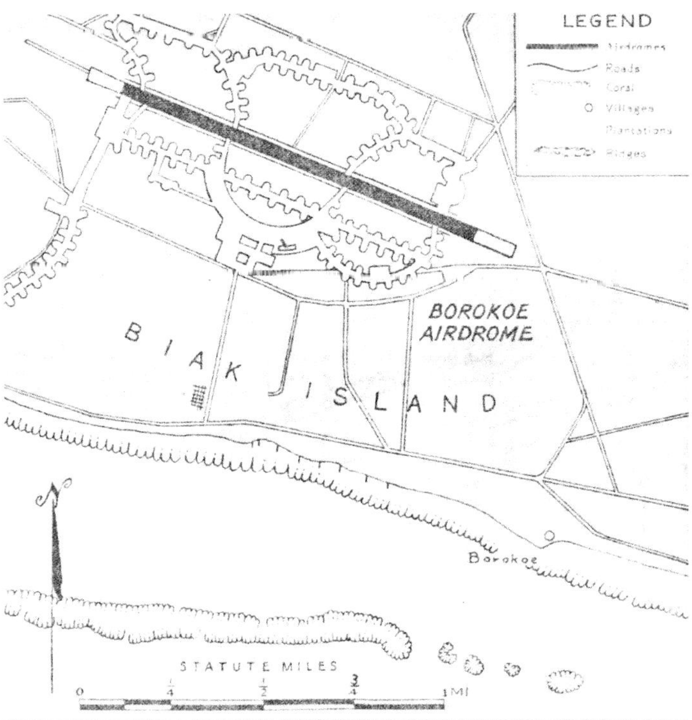

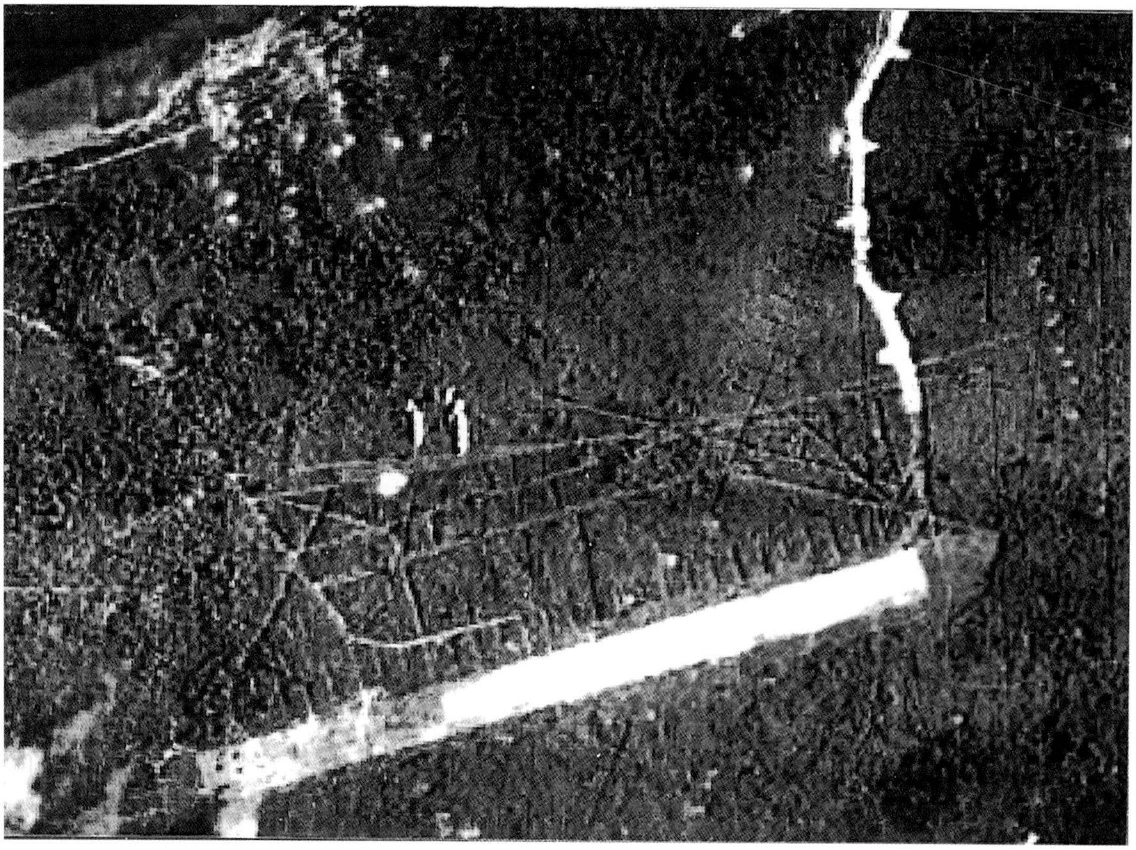

**Borokoe Airdrome.** (AAF)

Sorido Airstrip
The airstrip at Sorido had also been under construction by the Japanese but not completed. Like Borokoe, Sorido also had been captured on the 20[th] and the construction plan issued on 20 June by GHQ, SWPA, specified that it was to be a heavy bomber airdrome, less parallel taxiway, with 115 hardstands. Although it had been captured on 20 June, development of Sorido Drome was not started until early August because the available engineer units were assigned to higher priority construction at Owi and Mokmer Dromes and because shipping bottlenecks delayed the movement of additional engineer troops and equipment to Biak. By 12 August a rudimentary 4,000 foot runway was available for the operation of transport aircraft. A change in the total Biak airdrome requirements reduced the original construction plans for Sorido Drome to only the repairing of the existing 4,000 foot airstrip for use as a crash strip. Sorido Drome was abandoned and was to be used for the storage of aircraft, photographic laboratories, troop housing, and ammunition dumps. But in September plans were again changed and work began on the improvement and extension of the runway and by October the length of the runway reached 5,000 feet and during November an additional 1,700 feet were added. When completed in January 1945, Sorido Drome consisted of a compacted 6,700x100 foot coral runway, more than 9,000 feet of 60 foot wide taxiway, a 4,187x100 foot apron, and 67 heavy bomber hardstands. Facilities were provided for heavy transport operations. A taxiway was constructed from the Liberty ship wharves to Sorido and Borokoe Dromes to enable aircraft to be moved directly from ships to runways.

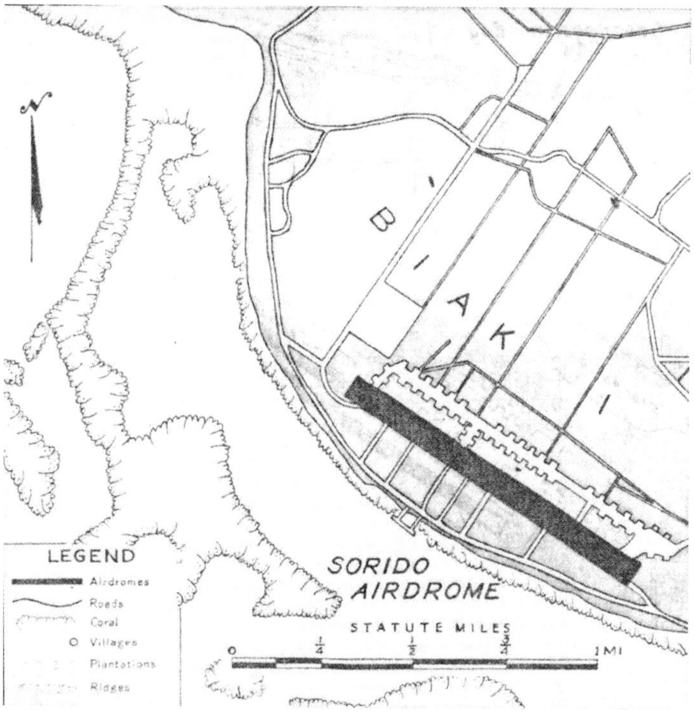


### Biak Airdrome Use

Heavy bomber aircraft from Fifth Air Force had been moved to the Biak area as soon as facilities were operational, and, using these advanced airfields, they made extensive long range attacks as part of the softening up operations in preparation for the liberation of the Philippines and Borneo.

Almost to the end of the war Biak/Base H remained an important in the supply chain in the advance toward Japan. In May 1945 Biak provided and protected "all facilities for the receipt, storage and supply (30 day level) for 35,000 air troops and 40,000 ground troops. To provide hospitalization for evacuated troops. To provide, protect and operate airfields for operational, troop transport and air freight purposes."

Upon completion of the major portion of the construction on Biak, most engineer construction units on the island were moved to forward bases. Nevertheless, even after July 1945, construction of miscellaneous small projects and maintenance of this large base still required the full time services of a General Service Regiment. Originally, it had been planned to close Base H in December 1945 but due to the large amount of supplies to be moved out and because most of the available shipping was being used for the return of troops to the United States, the base was not deactivated until March 1946.

**Owi Island**

Advance planning for the Biak Campaign had omitted unoccupied Owi Island, one of the Padaido Group, located about three miles off the south shore of Biak. The capture of this small island had not been considered primarily because of the added logistic problems involved in the simultaneous supply of it and Biak. However, when the tactical delay in securing and beginning construction on the Biak airdrome sites; aerial reconnaissance revealed that the terrain on Owi was suitable for the construction of a large airdrome. On 7 June (Z plus 11) the 860th Engineer Aviation Battalion immediately started work at Owi and, on 17 June (Z plus 21), 15 fighters and a B-25 were able to make emergency landings on the runway. On 20 June (Z plus 24), GHQ, SWPA, as part of a revised airdrome plan for Biak, specified construction of a standard heavy bomber airdrome with 180 hardstands on Owi Island. The following day the 4,000x100 foot runway was declared as usable for fighter operations and the first squadrons were moved forward. The runway was lengthened and improved until on 12 July (Z plus 46 a length of 7,000 feet. After the first runway was completed, a second parallel 7,000 foot runway was begun and by mid September both runways were operational for heavy bombers and fighters. In early September fully loaded bombers were sent on the first daylight raid against the Philippines since early 1942. The second runway was constructed jointly by the 864th Engineer Aviation Battalion and the 60th Naval Construction Battalion (Seabees or NCB). The NCB unit was detailed to this project because the runway was to be used by both naval and military air units. The Owi runways were compacted coral complete with 500 foot overruns at both ends and 50 foot shoulders. The Owi Drome also included approximately 730,000 square feet of paved apron, 37,000 feet of 50 foot wide taxiway, and 219 heavy bomber dispersals. This entire project was completed by early October 1944 despite the numerous cases of scrub typhus that were suffered by engineer personnel on the island.

5FC units based on Owi included:

**5AF HQ:** 10 August to 20 November 1944
**5FC HQ:** July to November 1944
**8FG:** HQ, 35FS, 36FS, 80FS, (P-38) from 17 June to 19 September 1944
**35FG:** HQ, 39FS, 41FS, (P-47) from 22 July 1944 to 27 September 1944
**418NFS:** (det) (P-61) from 16 September 1944 to 5 October 1944
**421NFS:** (P-61) from 28 June 1944 to 25 October 1944
**547NFS:** (P-61) from 6 October 1944 to 31 December 1944

**Mid-May to June 1944: Situation**

In the time frame 17-27 May: Wakde was captured on 17 May; followed only ten days later by the landing at Biak; Nimitz's carriers raided Marcus Island, 1,100 miles southeast of Tokyo on the 19th; on the 20th the Kuriles at Shimusku, about the same distance to the northeast of the Japanese capital were attacked; Marcus again on the 21st; and then Wake Island on the 23rd. 5BC bombers were raiding Yap and Palau almost daily and recon flights were beginning to appear over Mindanao in the Philippines. This increase in Allied air activity moved the Japanese high command to action; moving their bombers and fighters into Sorong, on the western tip of New Guinea;

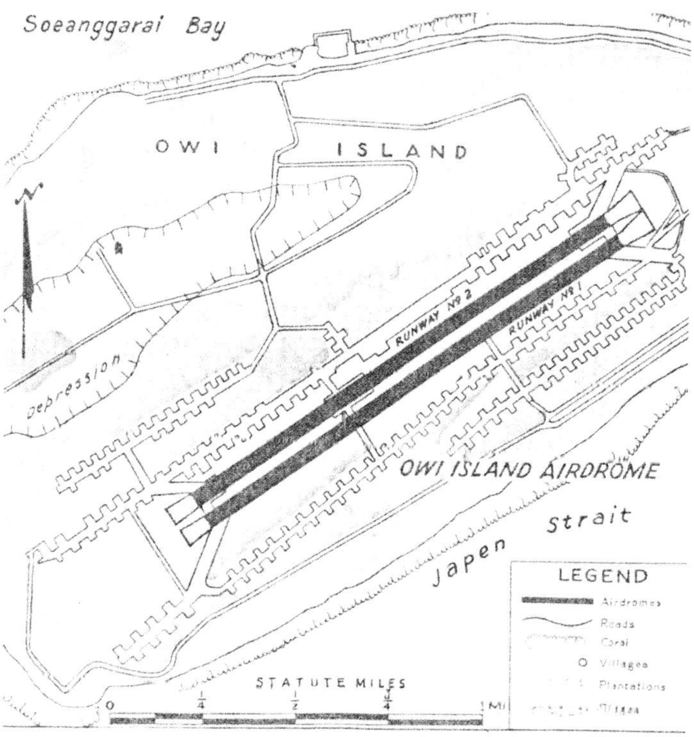


and Babo, on MacCluer Gulf, which had been abandoned after a week of bombing by the 380BG from Darwin and then became active again.

Meanwhile, Allied ground forces found themselves up against determined Japanese resistance and it was immediately apparent that the conquest of the forces on Biak would require reinforcements and close ground support from aircraft. To prevent enemy air raids, the P-38s of the 5th Fighter Command continued to escort the bombers to air bases in Netherlands New Guinea and against a Japanese base on Jefman Island off the coast of that area. Then almost daily from 1 to 5 June, Japanese fighters and bombers appeared over Biak, to give 5FC P-38s their first targets in awhile.

**Late May 1944: 348FG at Wakde Airstrip**

Aviation engineers began work on the Wakde strip at once and by 22 May the ground echelons of the 348th Fighter Group moved in but found the island so crowded with men and equipment that they set up their camp on the small island of Insoemanai, 300 yards offshore. Four days later the air echelon flew in its P-47s and began operations.

**May-July 1944: 421NFS on Wakde Island**

While operations were still being flown out of Nadzab orders were received that four P-70s would be transferred to Wakde Island at the end of May. The P-70s were to intercept Japanese bombers based at Noemfoor on Biak and at the Halmaheras that were attacking Allied bases in the Wakde area at night damaging or destroying a number of aircraft and killing many personnel. A detachment of four P-70s led by 1Lt. Dorrie Jones, left Nadzab on 28 May for an extended stay at Wakde where the detachment would continue routine patrols. Wakde was a very small island measuring 6,000 feet by 3,000 feet which was basically a coral reef with a runway stretching from the sea at one end to the sea at the other end and so targets were concentrated. Once the Americans were on the Island the Japanese flew nightly raids with Betty bombers flying at 17-20,000 feet driving the 421st personnel into foxholes and local caves and occasionally causing damage to tents, equipment, and aircraft. The foxholes were very difficult to dig out of the solid coral and explosives were used to construct them. On 10 July 1Lt. Owen Wolf took command of the Wakde detachment from 1Lt. Dorrie Jones who was going on leave. On the 25th Wolf

## Owi Airdrome Gallery

**Owi** under construction. (AAF)

**Owi** near completion with C-47s bringing in supplies. (AAF)

**Owi** completed. (AAF)

left to take over for Capt. Paul Zimmer at Owi who was also going on leave and 1Lt. William Robbins took over command of the Wakde detachment. The Wakde detachment continued uneventful patrols, weather recon missions, and occasional search and rescue missions but after a while there was a lack of targets and the war was moving further away. On 21 September 1Lt. Dorrie Jones and the personnel, equipment, and the four P-61s of the detachment returned to Owi and the squadron was together again for the first time in many months.

# 8

# June 1944

### June 1944: Japanese Situation

The Japanese had many of their combat units wiped out during the Hollandia operation and had to reorganize their defense to counter both the Allied thrusts from the Southwest and Central Pacific which were converging above New Guinea. The 5th Fighter Command P-38s and the Imperial Japanese Navy would clash more often during and after June 1944. The Japanese 23rd Air Flotilla had about 20 Zeros and a 12-15 land-based bombers around the Vogelkop area on 1 June which were soon reinforced by 70 Zeros and 16 Judy dive bombers. Japanese Army air units were so badly mauled and disorganized that they were able to make only random sorties.

### June 1944: 475FG Situation

Prior to the move to Hollandia many veterans were being rotated back to the States and there were a large number of new pilots arriving who needed training in theater operations. Consequently, accidents involving wheels up landings or hard landings damaging struts were frequent. To encourage the quick development of P-38 operational proficiency and preserve his irreplaceable Lightnings Lt.Col. MacDonald issued the so-called "Japanese Air Medal," an embarrassing award to any rookie pilot damaging a P-38 through negligence.

After the appalling losses on "Black Sunday," 16 April, the 475th had suffered virtually no air casualties until early June but accidents did damage or destroy some of the group's valuable P-38s (During May only three new P-38s were transferred to service squadrons). On 16 June, 2Lt. John Knecht (433FS) ran out of gas during an emergency landing at Hollandia and bailed out over an area of Lake Sentani that contained crocodiles. When the rescue team arrived it found him on the only piece of open land on the lake having cocoa with a refugee family. On 21 June, Capt. Billy Gresham took a P-38 up for a test hop and crash landed on Hollandia Strip totaling the fighter but sustaining only minor injuries.

During May 1944 the 475FG carried out its normal patrols between Hollandia and Sarmi and returned to escorting "Biscuit Bomber" transport aircraft to Wakde. The dull routine of this escort was occasionally broken by an opportunity to strafe enemy troops. While returning to base after a Biscuit Bomber mission, 1Lt. Paul Lucas made two strafing passes on a large number of Japanese soldiers crossing a small stream on the coast about midway between Hollandia and Wakde.

### June-August 1944: 35FG Situation

On 24 May the Group received orders to move to an undisclosed new base within 24 hours. The ground echelon was flown to Lae while the air echelon remained behind as usual until the new advanced base was ready. Minimal ground personnel remained behind at Gusap to continue administrative and maintenance functions. On 27 May U.S. forces landed on Biak on Geelvink Bay bringing the Allies 200 miles closer to the Philippines. The 35FG flew its last mission from Gusap on 2 June. From 3-8 June all squadrons were released for training and maintenance and on the 9th the air echelon left Gusap for Nadzab where it was quartered until the ground echelon readied its new base on Biak. On 26 May the ground echelon arrived at Lae and on the 30th embarked on the *USAT Frederick E. Eilers* and sailed for Finschhafen to rendezvous with a convoy. However, they were forced to return to Lae when one of the greatest tank battles fought in the Pacific and strong enemy counter attacks held up progress on Biak. It would not be until 19 June that the ground echelon again left for Biak but got only to Hollandia where they anchored for a month in Humboldt Bay. On 20 July the *Eilers* left Hollandia and landed on Owi Island two days later where the ground echelon unloaded and set up a temporary camp on the beach. During the night of 30 July a Japanese bomber flew in at low level and dropped six fragmentation bombs that killed one officer and four enlisted men of the HQ Squadron and one officer of the 40FS. Finally, after training at Nadzab since June, the 35FG air echelon received its orders to move to Noemfoor Island in early August. Noemfoor was a small island in Geelvink Bay located about 80 miles west of Owi. It had been captured without opposition on 2 July by an amphibious force which quickly captured Kamiri Airstrip in less than two hours. Konasoren Strip was captured two days later. On 3 August the 35FG air echelon less that of the 41FS left from Nadzab and flew 900 miles non-stop to Noemfoor.

### June 1944: 418NSF Missions

8 June 1944

On 8 June 1944, Maj. Carroll Smith and two other crews flew to Wakde Island to conduct night raids in the Geelvink Bay area. The crews would fly in shifts against the Japanese in an attempt to cause damage their installations but also to keep the enemy awake all night. Smith and his crew flew the first mission that night against the Babo Airdrome. They fired some 6,000 rounds of ammunition on strafing runs and dropped nine 100 pound bombs. 418th XO, Capt. Leo Gunn, and his crew flew the next shift but bad weather prevented them from their reaching their target and they returned to base with a full bomb load. 1Lt. Richard Day and his crew, flew the third and final shift of the night and bombed and strafed the target. Intelligence reports later estimated the 418th's attack on Babo to have destroyed about 14 enemy aircraft.

However, at 0400 the Japanese retaliated and dropped bombs on the Wakde strip. One bomb hit Capt. Gunn's fully bombed aircraft and when it exploded it in turn destroyed Smith's B-25 parked on one side and damaged a B-25 on the other side beyond repair. The Japanese attackers destroyed 18 aircraft on the raid on Wakde.

**19 June 1944**

The entire 418NFS took off in bad weather for a daylight raid on Wide Bay about 30 miles south of Rabaul. Because of the weather their escort was unable to accompany them but their mission to destroy field gun emplacements, bivouac areas, and radio towers was carried out successfully.

The other missions flown in June were as uneventful. Night harassment missions were flown against Wewak, Dagua, and But airfields as well as other installations in the surrounding area. They also flew cooperative missions with PT boats in which the B-25s would fly as "bait" in luring enemy AA to fire at them. When fired at, the PT boats that were moving stealthily along the shore would fire on the gun emplacement firing on the aircraft.

**3 June 1944: 348FG/340FS/342FS**

On 3 June, 12 P-47s of the 340FS joined four Thunderbolts from the 342FS over Biak but only the 340th would claim any victories although the 342nd did see combat. At 1120 Maj. Max Wiecks and his Wingman, 2Lt. William Daley, were flying at 3,000 feet and saw a Hamp at about 1,000 feet climbing over a cloud and when it turned left Wiecks was able to get on its tail. As Wiecks closed the Hamp pilot made another port turn trying to get back into the clouds but Wiecks fired at 10 to 20 degree deflection getting hits on the cockpit and engine. Wiecks pulled up to the right to avoid going into the clouds when he saw the Hamp crash for his fourth and last victory after scoring the Squadron's first victory in August 1943. After climbing to 8,000 feet they heard the Fighter Controller calling out bogeys to the southwest and headed for Mokmer Strip on the Channel coast between Biak and Dutch New Guinea. Twenty miles south of the Mokmer area Wiecks looked behind and saw two P-47s approaching out of the sun but then saw the non-retractable tail wheels that distinguished the Oscar and he and Daley broke to port and evaded as the Oscars drew into firing position.

At about the same time Capt. Richard Fleischer and his Wingman, F/O Roy Martin, saw four Oscars strafing USN barges and attacking a PBY. They dropped their tanks and got on the tails of two Oscars. However, the other two Japanese turned into the Americans head on and Fleischer got a burst at both fighters and they broke away and down. Fleischer then continued to pursue his original Oscar and fired a few shots before it entered the overcast. Fleischer followed it so closely that he was still able to see the Oscar's green tail and soon they broke into the clear sky and Fleischer fired a long burst which caused the Oscar's engine to catch on fire for his sixth and last victory. F/O Martin then shot down the second Oscar when it made a pass at him and then banked away to the right. Martin followed and fired a long fatal burst at a slight deflection for his only victory.

1Lts. Ralph Heiden and Noble Jones in Fleisher's second element saw two Zeros flying south from the invasion convoy with USN AA fire following them. The two 340th Lieutenants broke from their flight to pursue the Zeros which soon turned into them. The first Zero pilot turned off to port and Heiden followed him while Jones turned with the second and fired a long 90 degree deflection shot that caused its engine to smoke as the Zero crashed into the sea. Heiden fired at the other Zero on a head on pass and it immediately burst into flames and large pieces flew off as it went down for his only victory. The two Americans then rejoined and saw AA fire from a USN destroyer to the west and as they approached they saw a lone Zero heading southeast. Jones closed and fired three short burst that sent this Zero down for the first two of three career victories.

**Capt. Richard Fleischer** poses with his last victory decal. (AAF)

**Maj. Max Wiecks** (center with 1Lt. Floyd Meyer, right, and Capt. Francis Oksala) scored his last of four victories. (AAF)

**3 June 1944: 49FG/9FS**

Just after Biak's airdrome at Mokmer was captured the 49er ground echelons at Hollandia were mobilized to move to Biak. On 2 June the ground crews were loaded on two LSTs for the three day crossing of Humboldt Bay to Biak. A small number of ground crewmen remained at Cyclops to service the last of the sorties from Hollandia.

Remnants of the JAAF were harassing the Allied beachhead at Biak in nightly raids and 5AF air reconnaissance discovered their source at a large staging base near remote Babo Village on McCluer Gulf on the west coast of New Guinea, 500 miles due west of Hollandia. Babo needed to be eliminated and 5FC CO Wurtsmith assigned the job to Maj. Wallace Jordan's 9FS Flying Knights. However, 49er Group CO, Lt.Col. David Campbell, sensing that the mission was to be the last great air battle over New Guinea, bumped Jordan and opened the mission to the senior pilots at Hollandia. Maj. Robert McHale from HQ and the returned veteran Capt. Donald Lee volunteered. The mission's 20 Lightnings left at 0830, climbing to 15,000 feet on a direct route over the interior then on over Geelvink Bay. Nineteen pilots reached the narrow southern isthmus of Vogelcop Peninsula and beyond was McCluer Gulf, 50 miles to Babo which was obscured by clouds.

At 1130 Mission Leader Campbell headed Yellow Flight with Maj. McHale on his wing and Element Leader, 1Lt. Alfred Lewelling, and Wingman, 1Lt. Huard Norton, in trail. Yellow Flight descended through the cloud layer and flew over the coast at 8,000 feet where they met four Oscars heading east, maneuvering through the clouds. Simultaneously, Squadron Leader Lee with his White Flight rookie Wingman, 2Lt. Robert Hamburger, Element Leader, 1Lt. James Poston, and Wingman, 2Lt. Edwin Cooper, were on the left flank at the same altitude as Campbell when they sighted eight enemy fighters headed west. Following the Yellow and White Flights was the Green Flight of Capt. Edward Howes with wingmen 2Lts. Warren Curton and Frederick Helterline who also spotted the eight enemy fighters headed west. On Howes left flank and somewhat lower, was Red Flight's 1Lt. William Williams, leading wingmen 1Lts. Donald Fisher, Charles McElroy, and 2Lt. Alex Datzenko. Blue Flight flew high

**Maj. Robert McHale** claimed his last of three victories. (AAF)

49er Group CO **Lt.Col. David Campbell** vanished as he chased after an Oscar in a vain attempt to become an ace. (AAF)

**1Lt. Leslie Nelson** shot down his first of three enemy aircraft. (AAF)

**2Lt. Frederick Helterline** poses after his only victory of the war. (AAF)

cover at 11,000 feet a short distance in trail to the leading four flights. Blue Flight consisted of 1Lt. Jacob Chandler and his Wingman, 2Lt. Nile Lambert, Element Leader, 1Lt. Leslie Nelson, and rookie 2Lt. Carl Estes. Blue Flight was just entering a turn to starboard when Campbell's Flight came into sight within the haze.

Four Oscars passed under Campbell's Flight east bound and disappeared into the clouds below. Campbell had his entire P-38 group descend in a 360 to the right and spotted four more Oscars and as they dove they saw three of the four burst into flame and head down. Suddenly there were 16 or more P-38s and eight to ten enemy fighters turning in one small area. Beaten to a combat Campbell looked toward Babo Field where they saw enemy fighters taking off from one end of the field and then the other. At that time an Oscar flew up in front of McHale who fired and pulled away with his third and last victory and then chased another Oscar into one of the many clouds.

1Lt. Alfred Lewelling, Yellow #3, lost Campbell and spotted a lone Oscar still carrying its two drop tanks and closed to 300 yards and fired a short and then extra long burst that started the Oscar smoking violently but it half rolled and passed out of sight for a probable. Lewelling soon came upon another Oscar, carrying one tank, and closed as the enemy pilot dropped the tank and started turning to port in a 180. Lewelling stayed with the Oscar by doing a wing over and exploded it with his next burst and it crashed in the trees near the water for his second victory. Lewelling's Wingman, 1Lt. Huard Norton, chased an Oscar at 500 feet above the water and closed to 50 yards in a diving turn and blew it up with a three second burst. Norton climbed to 3,000 feet where he saw another Oscar about 1,000 feet above, ready to roll over to make a head on pass. Norton pulled straight up and both pilots fired but only Norton scored, getting hits in its engine. The Oscar dove past Norton in a half roll going straight down but Norton did not see it crash for a probable. Meanwhile, Campbell, who had had four career victories, took off after a lone Oscar that he hoped would make him an ace. The two raced to the east at tree top altitude but the Japanese pilot eluded him. Low on fuel, Campbell recalled his Yellow Flight to regroup at the predetermined rendezvous point over Osmoetoe Island on the eastern end of the Gulf.

1Lt. William Williams' Red Flight was the first to enter combat over Babo. The Flight saw six enemy fighters traveling in the same direction and Williams went after the fifth in the formation but was flying too fast and switched to the Flight Leader of the first flight. Williams fired three long burst and the Oscar burst into flames and was confirmed. At this time Williams discovered that his port tank did not release and it would be with him throughout the combat. Williams entered a cloud and when he came out he saw an Oscar that was just finishing a 180 and closed to 300 yards and fired. Flames came out from its engine just as Williams had to pull up to avoid a collision and he claimed it as a probable pending gun camera evaluation but it was later affirmed as his second victory of four total. Red Flight Element Leader, 1Lt. Charles McElroy opened fire on an Oscar from 10 degrees deflection and the Oscar slowed and turned to the right, flamed, and then crashed for his first victory of four. McElroy closed too fast on another Oscar and then gained an Oscar on his tail. McElroy's Wingman, 2Lt. Alex Datzenko turned into his Leader's pursuer and shot it down for his only victory.

Only seconds after Red Flight attacked, 1Lt. Donald Lee led his White Flight after the remaining three Oscars and as Red Flight shot down three, Lee went after one that went into a port turn, fired but missed. #3 man, 1Lt. James Poston, came in and "knocked big holes in its wings" and it dove burning into the ground for his first of three victories. Lee chased after another Zero that went into a cloud and as Lee came out the other side he saw his Wingman, 2Lt. Robert Hamburger, hit its canopy and fuselage and it started down: "This Zeke is at least a probable and my gun camera should make it a definite." Hamburger was awarded a probable.

Green Flight Leader Capt. Edward Howes and 2nd Lieutenant wingmen Warren Curton and Frederick Helterline saw 10 enemy fighters about 1,000 feet high. Howes was the first to attack a lone Oscar but it turned inside him and Curton then pulled up and fired a 30 degree deflection shot getting hits on its canopy and fuselage. The enemy pilot leveled out and Curton a no deflection shot and the Oscar's cockpit and wings burst into flames and crashed about five miles from Babo. Howes then caught an Oscar at 1,000 feet making a shallow port bank. He fired a short 20 degree deflection shot that hit a wing but the enemy pilot straightened out and Howes then fired a long burst at no deflection and its wheels dropped and it started smoking. By this time Howes was overrunning and pulled up, dropping a wing, to make another pass. When he looked down Howes saw the Oscar blazing fiercely and in a fatal 45 degree dive and he claimed a hard-earned third victory. Curton and Helterline lost Howes in a cloud and Helterline followed Curton in a chandelle after a Zero. After Curton broke off Helterline took a 90 to 10 degree deflection shot that hit the cockpit and wings and the Zero winged over and crashed for his only victory. Curton and Helterline started climbing and saw an enemy fighter at 6 o'clock that was in a dive on them. They made a tight turn and the enemy pilot overran and pulled up in a chandelle giving Helterline a quick shot that scored some hits but without any observable results and then ran out of ammunition and saw his intended victim being pursued by other P-38s.

1Lt. Jacob Chandler's Blue Flight soon arrived but too late and only made a few ineffective firing passes. 1Lt. Leslie Nelson had problems jettisoning his tanks and lost his Blue Flight and tried to join another flight. As he looked down he saw the P-38 Flight Leader and his Wingman making a pass on a Zero. Nelson was in position to make a head on pass as the Zero dove under him. Nelson winged over and got behind it but the Zero pilot looped but was unable to shake Nelson who fired until he stalled out, Nelson kicked over to the right and then rolled left while the Zero pilot kicked over to the left and down. Nelson dove 2,000 feet while gaining speed and the Zero leveled out and was about 3,000 yards ahead and started to turn into Nelson. Nelson began to shoot at 400 yards and kept firing until 100 yards when the Zero when into a vertical dive into the sea. In the combat Nelson's port boom was hit and he limped back to base; lucky to have the first of his four victories.

On the Group's rendezvous 17 Lightnings rejoined over Osmoetoe and two pilots were missing. Nelson made a solo return flight and was the last man to land at Hollandia. As he landed the badly damaged starboard boom fractured and the tail section fell to the ground. During the battle 49er Group CO David Campbell had vanished over McCluer Gulf and the area was too distant to organize an aerial search.

David Campbell, Neel Kearby and Thomas Lynch were being groomed as a new generation of young group commanders who were to lead the 5th Fighter Command into combat in the Philippines campaign and would difficult to replace. Senior 49FG HQ staff officer Lt.Col. Furlo Wagner was named to act as interim Group CO until another officer could be trained to be the permanent 49er CO. Lt.Col. George Walker, who had recently arrived from Command School in the US, was assigned as Wagner's assistant and probable successor.

**Capt. Marvin Grant** became an ace when he shot down two Kates. (AAF)

**3 June 1944: 475FG/432FS**

Maj. John Loisel was leading eight P-38s (Red and White Flights) on an A-20 escort to Manokwari but the weather was so bad that the A-20s bombed and strafed the alternate target at Mokmer Drome on Biak Island. As the 432nd was leaving the area at 1100 the Air Controller and Fighter Director destroyer reported "bogeys in the area." Loisel requested more information but received none. He saw some P-40s engaged in a dogfight above and climbed toward them. When they reached altitude these P-40s had left and were reforming. Loisel saw several enemy fighters on the deck at the edge of a cloud front and dropped tanks and dove. On the way down he lost sight of them but saw a Zero on the tail of two P-47s and fired a long burst which was only effective in that it drove off the enemy fighter. Loisel's ICR reflects his disappointment in the Controllers: "It appears to me that an interception of a more decisive nature could have been made had the Controller been more specific about the enemy airplanes with regard to their specific type, altitude, direction of their attack and retreat. This information was necessary as the combat area was 6/10 cloud cover."

**4 June 1944: 475FG/431FS**

During an escort of A-20s to Manokwari 475th Lightnings made their first contact with enemy aircraft since 19 May when McGuire got his last (18th) victory. McGuire led 15 Hades P-38s off Hollandia at 0645 on an A-20 escort mission to Manokwari. On this mission the contact was so fleeting that most of the 15 P-38s in the 431FS formation didn't have a chance to drop their tanks. McGuire was leading the Squadron during an uneventful bomb run and retirement from the target area. Since there seemed to be no imminent danger, McGuire left the A-20s on their own to return home. Soon Capt. Paul Morriss, leading the third flight, saw a lone Oscar flying on the deck along the east coast of Mois Neom Island, which was located between Manokwari and Japen Island. Morriss called out the enemy plane to McGuire who again was unable to locate the called out aircraft. Morriss decided to start down with his Element Leader, 1Lt. Robert Crosswait, who had moved onto Morriss' wing to cover him. The Oscar disappeared under a cloud for a brief time but Morriss continued down and rolled in to close on its tail. He fired a short burst and the Oscar rolled off and crashed into the sea for the Squadron's only victory for the day and his third.

**4 June 1944: 348FG/342FS**

On 4 June the 342FS sent four P-47s to patrol the Biak area northeast over Bosnek at 10,000 feet. Capt. Marvin Grant was leading the Flight with Wingman, 2Lt. Albert Newman, and as he turned south he heard bullets hitting his fighter. He could not see the enemy fighters coming out of the sun and frantically rolled and dove and then saw his Wingman heading down with black smoke trailing behind. As Grant pulled out of his dive he saw his Wingman crash into the sea. When he got back to 14,000 feet Grant looked down and saw four Zeros 4,000 feet below. He dove but three Zeros chandelled left and Grant followed and got a 90 degree deflection shot on the leader which burst into flames. Grant then fired on the Zeke leader's Wingman which went down smoking into the sea to make Grant an ace. He was unable to get a good shot at the third Zeke and the fourth had gotten on his tail and was firing at long range. The Zero chased Grant for five minutes before being outdistanced. After the battle Grant found that it was not his Wingman Newman who was seen going down and crash but was the same Japanese fighter that had attacked Grant and was subsequently shot off Grant's tail by second Element Leader, 1Lt. George Burgess. Burgess had seen the Zero on Grant's tail and closed and fired a three second burst getting numerous hits around the canopy. All the time another Zero was closing on Burgess and he had to break off to safety with his third and last victory.

#4 wingman 2Lt. William Overbey had seen the four Zeros coming down out of the sun but was not to be able to warn Grant because of a malfunctioning transmitter. While he was watching these four attackers another came in from behind and hit Overbey's tail section and he dove and skidded to 4,000 feet, shaking his pursuer. He climbed back up but had low manifold pressure and he decided to return to base alone. While flying at 4,000 feet about 20 miles north of Japen Island he saw a "Nip" several miles away astern at his altitude. Overbey began to climb to intercept but the Zero began a slight turn toward him but then decided to head away. Overbey started in a shallow dive, dropping slightly below, and throttled back so as not to overshoot. At about 100 yards he started firing and its mid section immediately burst into flames and the Zero crashed into the sea and Overbey returned to base with his first unexpected victory.

**5 June 1944: 6NFS**
The 6NSF was transferred to the 7th Fighter Command based on Saipan.

**6 June 1944: 475FG/433FS**
1Lt. Paul Peters took off at 0940, leading White Flight with a B-25 on a search mission for 1Lt. William Hasty who had bailed out six miles south of Babo Drome. Red Flight was to provide top cover but took off 15 minutes late. As they approached Babo they saw clouds of dust rising as if many aircraft were taking off. Meanwhile, the B-25 dropped to the deck and Peters stayed at 5,000 feet and they headed for the search area. Two Oscars climbed toward them at 3,000 feet and 3 o'clock. Peters turned to get into better position to protect the B-25 but the Oscars ducked into the clouds. Soon Peters' #4 man, 1Lt. Clarence Rieman, called out a Zero at 6 o'clock and White Flight dropped their tanks. The B-25 called that two Zeros were making passes but Peters could not see them at once as their camouflage blended with the jungle. Peters could see the enemy bullets hitting the water and led his flight in string in a high speed dive. As Peters approached the B-25 the Oscar pulled up in a climbing port turn. Peters chopped his throttles and held his fire until he was 100 yards astern and apparently the enemy pilot did not see him and Peters was able to close to 25 yards to fire a four second burst. The Oscar dove in flames toward a swamp and on its way down Peters' Wingman, 1Lt. John Knecht, took an unnecessary pass at it and Peters was awarded his second victory. Peters continued the search, escorting the B-25 for 20 minutes before the Mitchell headed home. On the way back to base, Knecht's P-38 lost both engines but he managed to get one restarted and landed safely.

**7-8 June 1944: The Battle of Waigeo Island**
Because the Japanese were encouraged by being able to hold off the Allies at Biak they rushed 2,500 reinforcing troops of the 2nd Amphibious Brigade from Mindanao to Biak during the first days of June. The enemy convoy moved cautiously after they were sighted by USN submarines and AAF recon aircraft and then were given false intelligence that a strong U.S. Naval force was stationed off Biak (In fact, the USN had only a single destroyer at Biak to oppose the Japanese landing and with their strong escort of warships the Japanese could land these troops and devastate the Allied beachhead). Nonetheless, the Japanese convoy did not turn around and continued on toward Biak still hoping to land its troops.

**7 June 1944: 475FG**
Meanwhile, the Fifth Air Force shuttled B-25s to Wakde Island hoping to intercept and destroy the convoy before it reached Biak. On 7 June, Col. MacDonald led 17 P-38s of the on an escort of B-25s on their anti-shipping strike to Waigeo. The mission was canceled and the Clover P-38s landed at Wakde where 1Lt. Elliot Summer successfully crash landed when his nosewheel collapsed.

**1Lt. Perry Dahl** shot down an Oscar and damaged another to give him six victories. (AAF)

**8 June 1944: 475FG/432FS/433FS**
Early on 8 June the Japanese convoy committed itself to reach Biak leaving it open to a noontime attack by 10 B-25s covered by 18 P-38s of Clover Squadron (and several from 433FS Possum Squadron). Col. Charles MacDonald led the P-38s off Wakde at 1030 but one P-38 aborted leaving 17 to continue. MacDonald led the P-38s through poor weather to the rendezvous point and then followed the B-25s about 60 miles northwest of Manokwari to find seven ships of the Japanese convoy sailing in clear weather near Amsterdam Island. Red and White Flights were to fly close cover while Blue and Green were to fly top cover at about 7,000 feet. When the Mitchells turned to port make their bombing and strafing runs on the ships, the P-38s climbed to starboard to draw off the convoy's AA fire from the bombers. MacDonald sighted two Zeros about 5,000 feet above and started climbing to meet them. Three more enemy aircraft came out of the clouds and passed 1,000 feet overhead but made no move to attack. As the Lightnings continued to climb, four Zeros were called out approaching the B-25s which were on their attack runs on the Japanese ships. It seemed as though these Zeros were trying to draw the P-38s into the AA fire above the escorting destroyers. MacDonald attacked the Zero Flight Leader from 9 o'clock; who hesitated on making a head on pass giving MacDonald a two second 30 degree deflection shot; setting fire to its engine for his 11th victory. The Japanese pilots broke away when the P-38s entered the AA zone above the enemy destroyers. MacDonald continued on the tail of an Oscar that led the P-38 down into the cloud cover at 3,000 feet, trying to lose him. MacDonald followed and fired a short burst that caused it to smoke and then peeled back its wing with a 20mm cannon shell. The frantic Oscar pilot maneuvered his damaged fighter in and out of the clouds until MacDonald came out of a cloud directly behind the Oscar and fired. The Oscar turned 180 and went back into the clouds. MacDonald followed and fired into the cloud and saw a bright orange flash inside the cloud. MacDonald circled the cloud but was unable to find the Oscar and made no claim.

Blue Flight consisted of Flight Leader, Maj. John Loisel, Wingman, 2Lt. Joseph Miller, Second Element Leader, 1Lt. Perry Dahl, and his Wingman, 1Lt. Laurence LeBaron. Dahl called out enemy fighters but Loisel could not see them and sent Dahl and LeBaron after them and said he would follow. Dahl and LeBaron rolled over to attack an Oscar which broke for the cover of the clouds but Dahl took a 90 to 30 degree deflection shot and saw some hits and the Oscar began to smoke as it entered a cloud for a damaged claim. Four more Japanese fighters came out of the same cloudbank, trying to dive on the B-25s below. Dahl had lost Loisel and Miller but still had LeBaron on his wing and the two broke up the enemy attack and chased the four Japanese back into the clouds. They then circled the cloud front waiting for enemy fighters to emerge. A lone Oscar arrived at 240 degrees and Dahl pursued and caught it just off the coast of Waigeo Island and fired a fatal no deflection dead astern shot for victory #6. As Dahl and LeBaron turned for home they crossed over the smoking convoy and saw four ships apparently on fire and sinking (the B-25s had actually sunk one ship and damaged three others but lost three of the 10 Mitchells and every bomber that survived returned to base badly damaged). While flying back to base Dahl had to fly through and around the same bad weather and when he was ready to land he found that his wheels would not lower with the normal hydraulic system so he pumped the wheels down by hand and the indicator light showed that the wheels were down and locked. As he made his landing the port gear collapsed and the P-38 veered off the runway and crashed into the trees, demolishing his fighter, but Dahl walked away uninjured.

Capt. Zack Dean was leading White Flight at 5,000 feet when he saw seven or eight enemy fighters at 8,000 feet and followed MacDonald in a climb toward them. Dean missed a head on pass at an Oscar that broke away in a sharp port turn and Split-S'd away. Dean's Wingman 1Lt. Clifford Mann was flying about 500 yards behind Dean and fired a three or four second burst as it Split-S'd and saw the Oscar dive straight into the water 40 miles west of Cape Waios for the last victory of the day and Mannings' only victory.

Despite the efforts of the courageous B-25 crews and P-38 pilots, the Japanese convoy did not turn around until a USN destroyer group appeared. The Mitchells sunk a destroyer and damaged three others but lost three bombers. The enemy ships withdrew, regrouped, and returned to Biak that night but were met by American destroyers which dispersed the enemy force which fled to the north. Later a larger enemy naval force, including two battleships, was gathered to reinforce Biak but the American invasion of the Marianas Islands ended any hope for the garrison at Biak being reinforced and they were abandoned.

The **342FS** shot down seven Nakajima B5N Kate Torpedo bombers, which would be the 348FG's last victories until December. (AFHRC)

**Capt. Stanley Popek** shot down three Kates to become an ace. (AFAA)

**8 June 1944: 421NFS: First Combat Mission**

On the night of 8 June 1Lt. Rolland Forrester and his R/O 2Lt. James McQuire flew the first P-61 combat mission which was a standard patrol mission that made no contacts.

**11 June 1944: 475/432FS**

Lt. Troy Martin was part of an A-20 escort to Biak and after he took off his wheels would not retract. As he circled Lake Sentani to drop his tanks his engines stopped and he crashed and was killed in a swamp.

**Early June 1944: Situation: Wakde**

Within a week after its capture, Wakde was crowded with aircraft based there or refueling on their way to or returning from distant missions. The majority of 5BC heavy bombers were still based at Nadzab, as the airfields at Hollandia were found to only be suitable for fighters and light bombers. The ground around Maffin Bay was too soft for quick airdrome construction and the development of Owi was progressing as quickly as possible so Wakde was packed to its limit with aircraft parked dangerously wingtip to wingtip tempting a Japanese attack. But the 5FC had to move their fighters forward to maintain cover over the shipping, continually unloading at Biak and using the "best offense is the best defense" mentality as it relied on attacking the enemy airdromes to keep the enemy from attacking 5AF airdromes. But beginning 5 June the Japanese began concerted night attacks and on that night exploded a bomb dump and destroyed three P-47s. Two nights later enemy night attacks destroyed 10 more aircraft on the ground while on the 11th the runways were deeply cratered and four more aircraft were destroyed. All the while the air and ground crews spent these nights in their foxholes. During this time night fighters arrived only once to drive off the Japanese attackers.

**12 June 1944: 348FG/342FS**

On 12 June the 342FS sent 12 P-47s on a morning patrol over Biak. Capt. Edward Popek was leading two P-47s (1Lt. Marvin Grant and 2Lt. William Overbey) of Blue Flight when he heard the Air Controller vector an incoming plot at 15,000 feet. Popek and his flight started climbing but when they reached 14,000 feet the Controller vectored them 90 degrees to the eastern end of Biak Island. As soon as they leveled out they saw five Kates directly in front and headed south, then diving on the American shipping below. Popek then saw two more Kates and ordered his flight to drop their wing tanks but he was unable to drop his right tank. The three Thunderbolts closed to 1,000 feet on the Kates but the enemy bombers were able to drop their bombs and closed up and headed south. Popek chose the left Kate, Grant the middle, and Overbey the right and all three Kates went down in flames. Popek turned to starboard and fired a 10 degree deflection shot that exploded this Kate. Popek made another starboard turn that put him onto another Kate out in front of him and after a five minute chase he fired and flamed this Kate for his third victory of the day and his fifth of the war to make him an ace. Overbey, with his belly tank still attached, attacked the right Kate that made a tight turn just as Overbey got into range but he adjusted his lead and hit the Kate's belly and wing and it started to burn and Overbey had to quickly pull up to avoid a collision for his second and last victory. Grant easily shot down the middle Kate that flew directly into his long burst and went down in flames and went on to shoot down another Kate for his seventh and last victory.

Capt. George Orr spotted a lone enemy aircraft at 15,000 feet heading southwest and started after it; identifying it as a Kate. The enemy pilot saw Orr and dove into the clouds and Orr followed for three minutes while the skilful enemy veteran pilot maneuvered through the clouds to evade Orr. The equally skilful Orr followed the Kate through the clouds and finally, the Kate pilot made a break for the sea and as Orr closed the Kate made a sharp turn. Orr fired high angle deflection shot without observable results and the Kate then dove to wave top altitude along the coast. Orr followed and fired as the dive bomber pancaked but remained on the surface in shallow water as Orr came around and strafed it.

1Lt. Franklin Love, leading Green Flight, saw a single Tony flying west at Love's altitude of 15,000 feet over Karimwe at 10 o'clock and about three miles away. Love chased the Tony that took no evasive action

**Capt. George Orr** (center with 1Lt. Charles McDonald, left, and 1Lt. Pope) shot down a Kate for his fourth and last victory. (AAF)

**1Lt. Marvin Grant** shot down two Kates to give him seven final victories. (AFAA)

except a shallow dive down to 10,000 feet Love fired a two second burst from dead astern and the Tony went out of control and crashed at the north end of Sorendidori Strait.

After these victories the 348FG would not score any more aerial victories until they reached the Philippines: 340FS on 11 December 1944; the 341FS on 7 December, the 342FS on 10 December; and the newly arrived 460FS on 12 November.

**June 1944: 49FG Biak**

The ground echelons of the 49th and 8th Fighter Groups had been dispatched to Biak in early June with the prospect that the Japanese air bases on the island would fall quickly to the Americans. The men of the 49FG were unloaded on 5 June and due to circumstances it was necessary to pack them into a small camp area under poor conditions. On 12 June a Japanese bomber dropped four bombs into the area and 19 men were killed and 29 were injured. These losses delayed the 49er mobilization with many of the air echelon and line crews eventually transported by sea to Mokmer Airdrome on the 15th. However, missions were flown from Hollandia until the ground echelon was reinforced and meanwhile, the P-40 line crews immediately were established at Mokmer under the command of the 308th Air Task Force. For the next two weeks, P-40s and P-38s were shuttled from airdromes in the rear to refit the units preparing to move up to Biak.

**Mid-June 1944: Situation**

When problems were encountered after the invasion of Biak, MacArthur decided another landing was necessary in the northern area to insure that airbases would be available for the future scheduled advance toward the Philippines. About this time Kenney and Whitehead met at Nadzab discussing the plans for the Biak clean up operations and the suitability of capturing Noemfoor in order to secure a base large enough to operate the aircraft of the 5AF and the RAAF, as well as those of the 13AF and the RNZAF, which were scheduled to come under 5AF command on 15 June. MacArthur had set 2 July as the date of the Noemfoor landing and around 1 August for the invasion of Sansapor, on the north coast of the west end of New Guinea, about 200 miles west of Biak. Airdromes were to be constructed at Noemfoor and Sanspor to support the next advance which would be to capture the island of Morotai, the northernmost of the Halmaheras, on 15 September, the same date that the Navy was scheduled to land at Palau.

Noemfoor Island was selected because the Japanese already had some airfields there and its location some 81 miles west of Biak and 45 miles east of Manokwari on the Vogelkop Peninsula of Netherlands New Guinea made it ideal to disrupt any enemy action from the north. The 5th Bomber Command began its attacks on Noemfoor on 20 June and without any enemy air opposition they were able to methodically bomb it while fighter escorts circled unchallenged. The landing was made on the island on the morning of 2 July against minor resistance. This was one of the few times during "island hopping" in the Pacific where enemy troops were bombed to the point where they were literally reeling and a number of prisoners were taken which had not occurred previously.

**15 June 1944: The Far East Air Forces (FEAF) Formed**

Kenney informed Whitehead that on 15 June he would announce the organization of the Far East Air Forces (FEAF), which he would command, in addition to commanding the Allied Air Forces and that Whitehead would be promoted to Major General and take command of the Fifth Air Force from Kenney while Maj.Gen. St. Clair Streett would command the 13AF from his headquarters at Los Negros.

**Mid-June 1944: 8FG**

The ground echelons of the 35th, 36th, and 80th squadrons of the 8FG remained on board LSTs from 12-14 June when they were debarked at Bosnek. After several anxious nights expecting Japanese infiltrators they were ferried to Owi Island just south of Biak on the 18th to prepare for the arrival of their air echelon. Unfortunately, a scrub typhus epidemic broke out among the ground echelons and before it ran its course over 200 men had been stricken, some fatally. The first two squadrons of the 8th Fighter Group flew into Owi on the 21st and 23rd of June and they were joined by the third squadron on 1 July. In addition, a detachment of the 421st Night fighter Squadron arrived along with some P-39 Airacobras of the 82nd Reconnaissance Squadron.

**June and July 1944: 348FG Ground Support**

During June and July 1944 Japanese infantry and airmen were retreating on foot from the south toward Cape D'Urville and Sarmi between Wakde and Biak. The 348FG had developed lethal strafing tactics in which they attacked beaches early in the morning or late in the afternoon. For example, four plane flights of the 340FS would be staggered upward in a string formation. When the leader on the low end of the string sighted enemy troops he would chandelle steeply and the other three P-47s would follow that signal and strafe the area with a deadly pattern of fire that enveloped the hapless enemy. Ironically, the pilots of the 5FC probably killed as many Japanese pilots retreating on the ground as they did on the air.

**14-30 June 1944: 421NFS: Move to Owi Island**

On 11 June the Squadron received orders that its Nadzab ground echelon was to prepare to move to a secret new base. The Squadron's equipment was packed and it and the 126 man ground echelon were transported to Lae and loaded on board the *USS Thomas Nelson*. They sailed at 0300 on the 14th and arrived at Finschhafen at 0840 to join a convoy which arrived at Humboldt Bay, Hollandia on the 17th where they waited for assignment. At the end of the month both the air and ground 421NFS echelons were joined at their new base at Owi Island laying only one half mile across a strait from the much larger Biak Island which was still fiercely defended by Japanese holdouts in caves and the dense jungle. The island was infested with the Scrub Typhus mite and 37 members of the Squadron became infected but eventually recovered. The remedy was to soak all clothing in a solution of DDT, GI soap, and other disinfectants and then hung out to dry. The Japanese continued to send small nightly raids of one to three bombers which caused damage and some casualties. But the biggest casualty was a good night's sleep and the personnel on the island were routed from their cots to take refuge in foxholes blasted out of the coral.

**16 June 1944: 348FG/342FS**

The 342FS sent up 16 Thunderbolts to patrol the Biak area. The Air Controller had plotted a bandit over the end of Biak Island and vectored Green Flight toward it. The Green Flight Leader's radio malfunctioned and 1Lt. Theodore Wood took over. At 1050 Wood saw the Dinah and made a firing pass, getting hits on its fuselage and saw flames flowing from both engines and Wood broke away as the Dinah pulled away in a slight dive. Green #3 man, 1Lt. Robert Martin, followed the Dinah that then leveled off and the fires went out. Martin closed to 250 yards at 8 o'clock and began to fire and continued firing until he was at 20 yards and 6 o'clock. The entire Dinah was burning as it suddenly went down in a spin and crashed into the sea for Martin's second and last victory.

**16 June 1944: Escort to Jefman Island**

The American invasion of the Marianas in June had placed the Japanese between the two pincers of attacks from the Central and Southwest Pacific and stretched their personnel and material resources to their limits and prevented further aerial reinforcement for the 23rd Japanese Air Flotilla. Thus Japanese attacks on Biak lessened as Saipan was invaded between 13-15 June and the enemy's attention was diverted to the Marianas for the time being.

**Jefman Airdrome** under attack. (AAF)

However, the Japanese air complex at Jefman-Samate continued to threaten the Biak area and to facilitate the capture of the strategic islands north of New Guinea MacArthur and Kenney needed to nullify Japanese air strength there, especially on Jefman Island. A maximum effort by B-25s was planned for 16 June against these airfields and had bomb bay fuel tanks installed to allow them to complete their longest mission to date. The B-25s staged into Hollandia and the P-38s of the 8th and 475th Fighter Groups moved up to Wakde early on 16 June for refueling before taking off on the long leg to Jefman.

During the B-25 escort to Jefman and Samate Island Airstrips, northwest of Geelvink Bay, all three squadrons of the 8FG got into action. The 36th and 80th Squadrons took off from the Hollandia area between 0930 and 1000 while the 35th left Nadzab at about 0800 and all squadrons staged out of Wakde at 1000. Rendezvous with the Mitchells was made by all P-38s of the 8FG and 475FG over Waar Island at 1130 and the formation arrived at the target about an hour later. This would be the first mission that the 35FS would score with its newly acquired P-38s. The 5FC P-38s claimed 26 enemy aircraft downed while the bombers (over) claimed another dozen. Additionally, the B-25s destroyed numerous aircraft on the ground and left the airstrips on Jefman Island and the one at Samate on the mainland in ruin.

**16 June 1944: 8FG/80FS/35FS/36FS**

80FS

Capt. Jay Robbins was leading 13 Lightnings of the 80FS that took off from Wakde at 0950 on high cover B-25 escort. They reached the rendezvous at 1130 and arrived at the target at 1255 where Robbins saw some Japanese fighters taking off from Jefman Strip. After the flight dropped their tanks they made wide, sweeping turns in spirals downward toward the Japanese. Robbins' first pass was a head on, short deflection shot into a Ki-51 Sonia reconnaissance bomber. The Sonia flew past Robbins and was lost from sight for a no claim. Robbins then fired several more deflection shots at several Zeros before he set fire to the right wingroot of a Zero that spun in from 200 feet just south of Samate. Robbins called for his flight to regroup for the return home but only one pilot could find him and the two headed for home at 6,000 feet. Robbins turned and saw another Zero heading for Jefman with other 80FS P-38s racing to get onto the Zero's tail. Robbins almost collided with a 432FS P-38 while following the Japanese into a cloud but finally caught it and set fire to its port wing and the Zero crashed into a mountain on Jefman Island. Robbins then turned for home, now a quadruple ace with 20 victories. 2Lt. Ardice Roberts shot some pieces off an Oscar that started smoking for damaged claim.

**Maj. Jay MacDonald** after he shot down two Zeros for his 18th and 19th victories. (AAF)

Capt. Burnell Adams was at 10,000 feet when Robbins called out the enemy and dove with the other flight; Adams' Flight stayed as top cover but seeing no enemy aircraft there descended and made a pass on a Zero which Robbins shot down before Adams could make another pass. Adams climbed back to 2,000 feet where he saw an Oscar below dogfighting with two other P-38s. After Robbins shot down Adams' Zero; Adams had no qualms about poaching and dove and followed the Oscar into a port turn, leaving the first two P-38 attackers behind. Adams fired and hit the Oscar's engine and canopy with a long burst and the enemy's wing caught the water, breaking it off and sending the aircraft cartwheeling. Adams then escorted a 475FG P-38 flying on single engine back to Wakde. Burnell's tour ended several days later and he rotated home with one 6NFS P-70 night fighter victory and six others with the 80th Squadron.

35FS

Maj. Harold McClelland and Maj. Robert Smith flew down from 8FG HQ to lead 16 new Lightnings of 35th Squadron's White and Green Flights, respectively on this mission. They rendezvoused with the second wave of B-25 over Japen Island to provide low cover. Smith flew with Wingman 1Lt. George Slingmeyer (assigned to the 35FS from the 36FS) and Capt. Bennett McCoy and his Wingman, 1Lt. Carl Weaver. Due to bad weather Smith's flight became separated from the Squadron and was accompanied by an additional element of two Lightnings; 1Lt. William Gardner and Wingman, 1Lt. Gail Loveless. The Flight arrived north of Jefman at 1255 at 6,000 feet when Smith heard Capt. Robbins of the 80FG call out the enemy taking off from the airfield. Smith turned the Flight toward Jefman where he saw P-38s in combat with Japanese fighters low on the water just north of the Island. Simultaneously, four Oscars and Zeros descended from 8,000 feet to bounce the P-38s flying just below Green Flight. Smith's #3 and #4 men, McCoy and Weaver, dove to assist a P-38 about to be attacked by two Oscars while Smith led Wingman Slingmeyer into a head on pass on the other enemy fighters. The Wingman of the lead Zero chandelled up and made a head on pass on Smith who fired into its belly. It immediately burst into flames and its pilot bailed out before it crashed and sank for his third victory. Meanwhile Gardner and Loveless had broken off to cover Smith and Slingmeyer and went after the two other diving Oscars. These Oscars outran them and were attacked by another flight. Gardner and Loveless then met two Zeros climbing at 6,000 feet and after unsuccessful head on passes they made two more passes. Gardner's Zero made evasive diving vertical rolls and weaves. After each pass Gardner pulled up waiting for "him to stop messing around." On his third run, the Zero was only 500 feet off the water and Gardner closed, holding his fire, until he was 300 yards away and fired. The Zero was hit and its pilot made a tight turn and caught a wing tip in the water and crashed and his Zero floated briefly before sinking. Loveless was also about to attack Gardner's victim but it hit the water before he could fire. After Smith shot down his Zero he pulled up to the right and sighted a Sonia heading north for Jefman and made four passes at the nimble Japanese plane without success as it made quick turns and barrel rolls to evade. However, with its every turn the Sonia was losing altitude and then flattened out over the ocean near a beach, seemingly trying to crashland. Slingmeyer flew past Smith to get on the tail of the fleeing Sonia and fired a burst that hit its fuselage and it crashed into the water just before it reached the shore for his only victory (Slingmeyer's victory with the 35th was credited to his assigned 36FS unit). As Smith continued north of Sorong where the P-38s were supposed to reform to return to base he saw a lone Oscar with eight P-38s chasing it. Smith joined in and got some hits before it entered a cloud bank for no claim.

White Flight led by Maj. Harold McClelland arrived over Jefman with 1Lt. Richard West leading the second element when his Wingman, 1Lt. Thomas Alsop, lost the fuel supply to his port engine and fell behind and

**1Lt. Richard West** scored his seventh victory. (AFAA)

**1Lt. William Gardner** shot down his fifth enemy aircraft to become an ace. (AAF)

**1Lt. Thomas Alsop** shot down his only enemy aircraft. (AAF)

West dropped back to cover him. Alsop was able to restart his engine but meanwhile, the two pilots had become separated from the Squadron and they entered clouds. When they emerged they saw six P-38s circling near the strip at Jefman and joined them. They saw Japanese fighters attacking the strafing B-25s and West and Alsop dropped their tanks and dove to the attack. West chose the nearest Zero and took a turning 90 degree deflection shot that got hits on its belly but it didn't go down or take any evasive action. As the Zero reversed, Alsop fired a three second burst from behind getting hits from nose to cockpit causing the Zero to crash into the water for his only victory. Another Zero appeared below and West throttled back to lose altitude and closed into firing position from behind. His first burst hit the canopy and fuselage and started a fire in the cockpit but its pilot managed to bail out and West strafed the enemy pilot in his chute "just as the Japanese pilot would have done to him." It was West's seventh victory. West then briefly joined a large P-38 Lufbery but broke away and descended to strafe a small three man enemy sail boat carrying cargo on its deck. West's cannon shells and machine gun bullets set fire to the cargo and persuaded the crew to abandon ship. Later, West joined a 36FS P-38 and the two attacked a lone Zero up the coast and "about 16" P-38s swarmed in. West got in some good shots before having to break off in the face of a head on P-38 attack and another Lightning attack from the side. West and the 36FS pilot then attacked a barge along the coast and he expended his ammunition on the first pass but the 36FS pilot continued the strafing until his ammunition ran out. Cy Homer of the 80FS then dove on the hapless barge to finish the strafing.

36FS

Capt. Orville Erdmann led Blue Flight over Jefman and saw the P-38s below and descended gradually and finally ordered the flight to drop their tanks. As soon as they did Erdmann saw an Oscar on deck with "about 10 P-38s" around it. Nonetheless, Erdmann, and Wingman, 1Lt. Steele Griswold, dove on it on a front quarter pass but was diving too fast and was only able to fire a short burst and missed. Griswold fired from out of range and missed. The two pulled up because of "so many P-38s" and flew east of Jefman where they found a lone Oscar at 500 feet on the deck over a destroyer near Sorong. Erdmann dove and fired a two second 30 degree deflection burst that passed behind it. The Oscar pulled sharply starboard and Erdmann was unable to follow. Griswold again fired from out of range and the Oscar turned into him. Griswold fired from a diving head on pass and got hits and the Oscar half rolled and went into a Split-S, crashing near the destroyer for his first of two victories.

Erdmann's Second Element Leader, 1Lt. Roy Randolph, immediately dove in trail with Erdmann. He fired a 90 degree shot that missed and but continued after it but was unable to turn inside the Oscar and broke away with his wingman still with him. He then saw an Oscar 3,000 feet above and dead ahead and pulled up, firing all the time until he passed it, getting some hits. Randolph made a tight climbing turn to the right and closed on the Oscar's tail but the Oscar suddenly dove and crashed into the water. Since the Oscar was not smoking Randolph presumed that its pilot had been killed and claimed his only victory of the war. "While in the wild confusion of about 10 P-38s against on Oscar" Randolph "got in two or three good shots" and got some hits near the cockpit but the Oscar seemed "to suffer no serious damage. After almost driving all the P-38s wild chasing him, the Oscar escaped by ducking into a large low cloud.

**16 June 1944: 475FG/431FS/432FS/433FS**

On 16 June Jefman was scheduled for attack and the entire 475th was only able to supply 38 P-38s for the early morning flight to Jefman with a stopover at Wakde where they landed to refuel.

431FS

Col. Charles MacDonald led 15 Hades P-38s off Hollandia 0645 but before they reached Wakde at 0715 six Squadron P-38s turned back, including Col. MacDonald who experienced engine trouble. Capt. William O'Brien assumed the lead of the Squadron and led them to Wakde. Once the Squadron landed at Wakde the composition of the four flights had to be modified and the lead of the 431FS was assumed by Maj. Thomas McGuire who led the squadron off Wakde at 0930 with nine remaining fighters. McGuire's Wingman in the Red Flight was rookie pilot, 2Lt. Enrique Provencio and the second element was led by 1Lt. William Gronemeyer with 1Lt. George Veit as his Wingman. After rendezvousing with the B-25s over Roon Island the Squadron flew on to the target. An improvised second flight was formed from the remaining P-38s of Hades Blue and White Flights with Capt. William O'Brien as Flight Leader. Rookie Wingman, 2Lt. Horace Reeves, and veterans Capt. Paul Morriss (the previous second Flight Leader) and 1Lts. Frank Monk and Christopher Herman made up the new Flight. At

**Maj. Thomas McGuire** became a quadruple ace with a Sonia and Oscar victory. (AFAA)

**2Lt. Horace Reeves** scored his first of eight victories. (AFAA)

**Capt. Paul Morriss** became an ace with two victories. (AFAA)

**1Lt. Franklin Monk** became an ace by shooting down an Oscar. (AAF)

1245 the Squadron arrived over the target with the bombers at about 6,000 feet and soon enemy aircraft were called taking off from an airstrip below. McGuire's flight dropped their tanks and followed their leader into a diving attack. McGuire arrived first and made a firing pass at a Ki-51 Sonia and hit an engine which started smoking but in his fervor to be the first to score, McGuire's excess speed caused him to overshoot the target and Gronemeyer chopped his throttles and got on the Sonia's tail. As it turned to starboard, Gronemeyer followed and continued to fire and set its right side on fire and crash into a wooded area on Doom Island for his third victory. There were four or five other Sonias cruising in the area and McGuire chased one down and put it into the water with a 60 degree deflection shot. As the Squadron broke up, McGuire's Wingman Provencio stayed on McGuire's wing during the action and saw some Oscars taking off to meet the B-25s. McGuire led Provencio into a firing pass on an Oscar that started to make a pass on the bombers. The enemy pilot maneuvered through a number of hard turns but McGuire stayed on the Oscar's tail and finally exploded him on a reverse to make him a quadruple ace with 20 victories which still left him eight victories behind Bong. McGuire saw another Oscar on the tail of a P-38 and raced in and took quick shots at it; hitting and driving it away. Provencio followed this damaged Japanese fighter and fired a long burst from 10-15 degrees head on that hit between the engine and cockpit that set it on fire for his first of two victories.

As Gronemeyer pulled up from his Sonia victory he and Wingman Veit had lost McGuire and Provencio and joined two P-38s chasing an Oscar that was shot down by the lead Lightning. Veit had dropped below to make a head on pass at an enemy fighter and his starboard engine cut out momentarily and when Gronemeyer made a sharp diving port turn to cover Veit; he lost him. Veit tried find his Squadron but decided to head home alone. As he headed back Veit saw P-38s chasing a lone enemy fighter near the shore and made a pass. The enemy pilot made a double snap roll to the left and Veit followed firing until he had to pull up. As Veit came around onto the Oscar's tail he saw another P-38 make a pass but losing it when the Oscar pilot made another double snap roll. The Oscar pilot must not have seen Veit who attempted no evasive maneuvers and Viet's burst set its wing on fire but was seen going down just north of Lolobata Airdrome for his only victory. Viet had to break off when his engine cut out again and upon landing he discovered that his engine had been damaged by his own released drop tanks which put his fighter out of service for repairs. After losing Veit, Gronemeyer looked for more P-38s and joined a Lufbery but there was no action and he returned home.

Capt. O'Brien was leading Hades White Flight down in a large spiral and lost contact with McGuire's Red Flight but kept his four wingmen with him. A formation of Oscars appeared below and he dove quickly and made several passes and one of his short bursts was seen by 1Lt. Frank Monk to set an Oscar's engine and cockpit on fire for his third victory. On one of O'Brien's passes he fired a short burst at an Oscar before it maneuvered out of his line of fire. 2Lt. Horace "Bo" Reeves saw the Oscar reverse its course at about 300 feet over the water and turn sharply to the right. Reeves turned right and fired a 90 degree deflection shot for as long as he could hold the lead and saw several small explosions around the wings and cockpit. The Oscar glided into the sea and skipped into the air before settling back into the water. After O'Brien's Oscar crashed, Monk was in a diving port turn and saw two Oscars climbing up at 30 degrees deflection to attack his White Flight Leader. Monk turned sharply into the path of the leading Oscar and fired a short head on burst that hit its engine and cockpit. Monk had to break away to avoid colliding with the flaming enemy fighter which Reeves saw hit the water, confirming Monk's fifth and last victory to become an ace. After the Sonias were shot down, White Flight fifth man, Capt. Morriss, saw an Oscar in a turn to his left and got behind it and fired a long burst that sent into the sea. Morriss rejoined the flight and saw a P-38 firing at a lone Oscar from out of range without doing any damage and broke away.

Morriss went after the Oscar that was in a tight port turn and Morriss dove and fired to get his fifth and last victory of the war to become an ace.

432FS

Twelve P-38s of Clover Squadron were led on this mission by Maj. Meryl Smith of 475FG Headquarters as medium cover for the first group of B-25s attacking Samate and Jefman. The Squadron flew low at 1,500 feet and to starboard of the Mitchells until they were about 10 miles from the target. They then climbed to 7,000 feet and dropped down to be directly above them. Between 20 to 30 Zeros, Oscars, and one fixed gear aircraft that was officially identified as a Val but more probably was a Sonia which were in the area. Smith led his Red Flight down to the attack two enemy aircraft taking off from Jefman, an Oscar and a "Val." Smith fired on the Oscar but overran it badly; getting only a short burst. As Smith passed over the Oscar he encountered the "Val" which made a 30 degree turn to the right and leveled off. Smith fired a close range, 30 degree, shot from astern and started a fire in its port engine nacelle and it was seen to crash two miles from the Jefman Strip for Smith's fifth victory to make him an ace. Smith's #4 man, 1Lt. Robert Hadley, shot down the Oscar that Smith missed . Hadley and his Element Leader, Hedrick, climbed back up to 7,000 feet where they were bounced by two Zeros from 3,000 feet above them and headed 180 degrees. As the first Zero dove from 10 o'clock its pilot tried a 90 degree deflection shot at Hedrick, which put Hadley in position for a 90 degree shot at the Zero. Hadley's gunfire hit the cockpit and the pilot bailed out for Hadley's third and last victory. The second Zero got on Hadley's tail and fired from 50 yards and hit his fighter. Hadley skidded violently back and forth to escape but finally eluded by cutting his throttle and kicking full left rudder. Hadley joined the 431FS for escort to base and saw Thomas McGuire shoot down an enemy fighter while Hedrick joined Capt. Morriss of the 431st and watched him shoot down a Zero with a difficult deflection shot for his second victory of the day to make him an ace.

**Maj. Meryl Smith** became an ace. (AFAA)

433FS

Maj. Warren Lewis was leading 11 Possum Lightnings as left flank top cover for B-25s to the Jefman-Samate area. The Squadron flew over the target area at 8,000 feet while the B-25s were attacking at minimum altitude. As the bombers were finishing their run a lone Tojo was making a rear quarter attack on the bombers. Lewis ordered tanks to be dropped and led a frontal attack on the Tojo but missed. Lewis made anther pass but missed again. Lewis' #4 man, 2Lt. Ethelbert Roberts came in a fired but also missed the Tojo with a long burst. The Oscar broke away to starboard and turned into Roberts and fired tracers that passed just over Robert's right wing. Robert's Element Leader, 1Lt. Howard Stiles, started a pass on the Tojo and overran it. The Tojo turned sharply into Stiles and hit his port engine that began to smoke heavily. Roberts closed to 50 yards and fired from 15 degrees as it began to Split-S, hitting its cockpit and fuselage to finally send it down for his first of two victories. Meanwhile, Lewis started on the tail of an Oscar but broke off when it tried to lure him into the AA fire from enemy warships below. He then chased another Oscar and got some hits for a damaged claim, his last claim of the war. Lewis had seven victories but an unusually high number of probable (five) and damaged (three) claims. 1Lt. Clarence Rieman was leading the second flight and as Lewis was making his pass on the lone Tojo, he saw an Oscar making a pass on the #4 in the third flight. Rieman's ICR states that he turned sharply into the Oscar and overran it but forced it to break off its attack. Rieman followed it as it approached the B-25s and fired as it slow rolled twice and turned left. Rieman closed to 100 yards and fired at 10 degrees deflection. His fire hit the cockpit and it rolled to port and fell into the water north of Doom Island. Rieman's Wingman, 2Lt. Joseph Price, states in his ICR that he followed Rieman down during Rieman's first attack and when Rieman overran the Oscar Price followed up with a burst into its cockpit and it fell off on its left wing and exploded. It seems both pilots received credit for the same Oscar; Rieman's second and last and Price's only victory.

1Lt. Howard Stiles, the 433FS pilot who had survived Black Sunday was last seen low over Jefman Harbor chasing an Oscar and was listed MIA. On this mission several P-38s were damaged. Oliver McAfee, from Headquarters, flying with the Squadron that day, was hit by a Tojo which he overshot in his attack. Robert Hadley of the 432FS landed safely in his P-38 that was damaged by 20 mm fire from enemy aircraft.

During the time over the target enemy AA fire coming from the ground and from warships in the harbor was considered "moderately heavy" and there were reports by several pilots that aerial bombs were dropped on American bomber formations during this mission. After Combat Reports distinguished the enemy interception as "uncoordinated and rarely pressed home with any determination." The Satan's Angels had now scored over 350 confirmed kills had about 50 pilots lost from all causes. But combat operations were beginning to take their toll again during June.

**1Lt. Clarence Rieman** was credited with his second and last victory. (AAF)

**17 June 1944: 475FG**

The 475th returned to Jefman Island on 17 June escorting 38th and 345th Bomb Group B-25s. The 38BG sank or damaged a number of ships in the harbor while the 345BG swept the nearly deserted airfields while some 475FG P-38s got into the action by strafing barges and luggers near Cape Sorong. Japanese AA fire was so light and inaccurate that only one B-25 reported any significant damage. For the next few days 5AF missions were particularly routine for the 475FG consisting of A-20 and B-25 escorts or an occasional PBY rescue cover mission. The P-38s were in more danger just taking off or landing on their own bases.

**17 June 1944:8FG/80FS**

Eleven P-38s took off from Wakde on a B-25 escort and arrived over Jefman at 1345. Capt. Cyril Homer was leading the second flight and saw two Zeros 2,000 feet above which separated going in different directions. Homer chased one toward a thunderhead and fired at 150 yards and got hits and explosions on its fuselage. The enemy pilot went into steep vertical reverses but Homer hit it with a 50 degree defection shot before it entered the cloud. Homer followed and came out of the cloud at 500 feet and saw the enemy leaving and fired a short shot from astern, hitting the fuselage, but then overshot. The Zero (Sonia?) looked like it was attempting to ditch on the water but cartwheeled and exploded 10 miles northwest of Jefman Strip. Homer was unable to photograph this claim due to rainy weather and was officially awarded a probable which would be the 8FG's last claim for five weeks.

**19 June 1944: Battle of the Philippines Sea**

After Adm. Raymond Spruance, C-in-C, Central Pacific Forces, sent a series of carrier raids from Task Force 58 on Saipan, Tinian, Rota, Pagan, and Guam in the Marianas, during which they destroyed approximately 140 aircraft and 13 vessels. A landing was made on Saipan on 15 June. The island was not declared secure until 9 July 1944 as the tenacious Japanese garrison held out until the last man. On the 19 June the Japanese fleet sailed east of the Philippines which was close enough to Spruance's fleet for him to launch his carrier aircraft. The Japanese then turned back west through the channel between Formosa and the Philippines; evidently intending for their aircraft to attack Spruance's Fleet and then continue on to their fields in the Marianas, from which they could conduct further operations or return to the Philippines by way of Yap, Palau, and Mindanao. The Japanese launched 400 aircraft but instead of exploiting these large numbers in a well coordinated mass attack their attacks were characteristically piecemeal and uncoordinated. The Japanese air forces were decimated leaving their fleet without air defense. Spruance then moved west and launched his aircraft and although some of the enemy fleet escaped; the two day battle cost them 428 airplanes, three aircraft carriers, and two tankers; along with three other carriers, a battleship, three cruisers, and three destroyers damaged. Task Force 58 lost 122 aircraft and 72 aircrew, while two carriers and a battleship suffered superficial damage. After this disastrous defeat Premier Hideki Tojo resigned and Gen. Kuniacki Koiso had taken his place. The consequence for MacArthur and Kenney of this great victory was another advance in the Joint Chiefs of Staff schedule for the Philippines invasion.

Although **MacArthur** (left) was **Kenney's** (center) direct superior, Kenney continued to rely on "Hap" Arnold for supplies and personnel, and it led to divided loyalty. (AAF)

**22-25 June 1944: 49FG**

By 20 June, the 49ers were bivouacked two miles east of Mokmer Airfield and on the 22nd Capt. Edward Peck brought in 24 7FS Warhawks but two were damaged during an overly enthusiastic landing display. The next day three more 7FS fighters were out of service; one during a take off accident and two due to mechanical failures. That afternoon 24 Warhawks of Maj. Charles Petersen's Black Sheep landed safely. The Mokmer strip was constructed of freshly crushed coral and was much like concrete runways except that the Warhawk and Lightning Allison engines all would ultimately require complete overhauls due to the abrasion from the fine, wind blown coral dust. Finally on the 25th, Maj. Wallace Jordan flew in 24 Fighting Knights' P-38s to complete the 49er squadron contingent.

**26 June-2 July 1944: 49FG**

Noemfoor was a smaller island 100 miles due west of Biak with a small airstrip and shallow harbor at Karimi Village. The Screamin' Demons and the Black Sheep immediately began a series of tactical sorties there but the Japanese had already abandoned Karimi. On 2 July an U.S. Army infantry regiment made an unopposed landing there and a RAAF P-40 squadron was immediately based at Karimi and the 49ers returned to fly tactical missions over western Biak.

**28 June 1944: Japanese Situation**

On June 28 the Japanese 23rd Air Flotilla headquarters retreated from Sorong on the Vogelkop Peninsula to Ambonia on the island of Ceram and all organized Japanese air strength in New Guinea had been defeated. At this time enemy resistance in New Guinea was reduced to small pockets holed up in caves but the enemy's total destruction required another month's action on the ground.

**30 June 1944: 475FG/431FS/431FS**

The 432FS took off late in the morning on its first dive bombing mission. The target was personnel and supply dumps south of Karimi Airdrome. The mission was a total failure with only four bombs hitting anywhere near the target. 1Lt. Robert Crosswaite of the 431st was listed as MIA but there is no mention as to the cause (enemy AA or mechanical failure?). Charles Lindbergh was along as a civilian observer as he had been sent to the Pacific to scrutinize, criticize, and then fine tune fighter units in the South Pacific. Lindbergh's sojourn in the SWPA will be described in detail later.

**Late June 1944: 5FC Situation**

During the last two weeks of June 1944 the 5FC encountered little air action and their major target was the barge traffic and occasional supply ship that was foolish enough to risk entering into range of 5AF bombers. Noemfoor was to be invaded in early July which would close the entire Geelvink Bay area to the Japanese and this operation would strand thousands of first line Japanese troops.

**June 1944: The Kenney-Arnold Relationship Deteriorates**

Although MacArthur was Kenney's direct superior. Kenney continued to rely on Hap Arnold, the Army Air Forces' CG, for the supplies and personnel he needed. The problem of his divided loyalty between two superiors with very different viewpoints and agendas was a basis of increased tension and conflict for Kenney as the war progressed. Within the limitations of the strategic agenda of the war, Arnold did his best to provide for Kenney's frequent requests and was generally impressed by Kenney's leadership and the ability of his 5AF in the SWPA to produce remarkable results with a minimum of aircraft. By the middle of 1944, several issues caused their relationship to deteriorate. Kenney and Arnold disagreed over such things as rotating officers from the Headquarters in Washington to the theater for combat duty and the low priority given to the Southwest Pacific for spare

The Japanese moved their air forces to **Ambonia**, on Ceram Island, which was heavily bombed.

parts and personnel, but their biggest disagreement was over Kenney's continued requests to obtain the long range B-29 bombers for his theater. Arnold maintained that the Superfortress could best be utilized for the strategic bombing of the Japanese Homeland while Kenney maintained that the B-29s based in Australia could be better used to bomb East Indies oil facilities and severing and other natural resources from that area to Japan.

Arnold grew weary of Kenney's unending lobbying for the B-29. It was Kenney's habit to take his complaints outside the Air Force that provoked Arnold even more. In early 1944, Kenney's contention, which was supported by other officers of MacArthur's command, that Japan could be more quickly defeated by using Adm. Nimitz' Central Pacific forces to support MacArthur's drive to the Philippines. However, Arnold supported a separate Central Pacific advance to capture the Marianas Islands for B-29 attacks on Japan. Kenney maligned this plan, by stating to naval planners that basing the B-29 in the Marianas was a "stunt" that would only produce "nuisance raids." When Arnold heard these negative comments about strategic bombing, made to officers outside of the Air Force, he became incensed. To Arnold and many other officers in the AAF strategic bombing was the means for validating an independent United States Air Force in the post war and Kenney's comments made him appear disloyal to the aims of the future of the Air Force. Near the end of the war Kenney was able to reconcile with Arnold and although Kenney remained loyal to MacArthur, he no longer made divisive statements and closed ranks with his fellow airmen in the post war battle for an independent Air Force.

# 9

# July 1944

## July 1944: Vogelkop and Babo Airdrome

By the end of June, Babo was only Japanese air base remaining on the New Guinea mainland that was any threat. Babo was located in an isolated low lying swampy area on the south central part of the Vogelkop Peninsula on the southern shore of McCluer Gulf at Babo Village. It was built prewar by the Dutch and was the final destination for KLM Airlines route in Dutch New Guinea. During November 1941, a RAAF engineering party assisted by the Dutch upgraded the airstrip for military use. A Japanese Army Detachment landed at Babo on 2 April 1942 and developed the area into a major base used by both Japanese Army and Navy units in the Vogelkop Peninsula, and as a staging point to southern airfields to the south or New Guinea to the east. The Japanese expanded the airfield, building a second hardtop runway with two strips: 4,530 feet and 2,660 feet. Naval troops constructed 15 bomber and 24 fighter revetments with more under construction. During the middle of 1943, the airfield became a regular target for Allied heavy long range bombers and by mid-1944; the base was in range of 5AF medium bombers

**Babo Airdrome.** (AAF)

and strafers and suffered heavy attacks. After the American landing at Biak on 27 May 1944, aircraft from Babo opposed the American landings but suffered heavy losses with the 24th Sentai losing 20 pilots and 40 planes in only 30 days before being withdrawn. The 202nd Kokutai was temporarily withdrawn from Babo for defense of Truk, then returned to Babo in June 1944 and lost 12 aircraft defending Biak and were then disbanded. During American and Australian bombing many Japanese aircraft were destroyed by parafrag bombs. By October 1944 Babo was neutralized from the air and isolated from resupply or rescue, and the surviving Japanese remained at the base until the end of the war.

**July to Mid-August 1944: 418NFS**

In July raids were carried out against air strips at Moemi, Babo, and Sagan. Enemy coastal shipping, barges, small vessels, and a schooner was also targets for the night intruders. On one of these missions around Soembroko Island 1Lt. Richard Day and his crew flying in a B-25 spotted a lugger and after making two bombing and strafing passes, the lugger was left afire and badly listing and sank later. Upon returning to base Day found that his hydraulic system was damaged by enemy AA fire and fluid was rapidly being lost. S/Sgt Lowell Eich and Sgt. Weimar Smith were able to contribute enough "fluid" from urine and coffee to pump the wheels down and lower the flaps so the B-25 could safely land. The Squadron's history reported that: "They particularly recommend coffee with lots of sugar and cream in it so as to increase the viscosity of the hydraulic fluid." A sad addenda to the Squadron History was that one gunner was seriously wounded by flak and died shortly afterwards in the hospital. On another mission a B-25 did not return but the uninjured crew was located and returned to base. In early August further losses occurred as two gunners were killed on one raid and a B-25 was shot down in another with the loss of the entire crew. Their work was dangerous but even with these losses, these night fighters were creating even greater losses on the enemy. On 18 August these missions would suddenly halt as the 418NFS would soon be transitioning to the P-61.

**July to October 1944: 348FG Ground Support**

From July through October the 348FG was chiefly engaged in neutralizing Japanese airbases on the Vogelkop Peninsula, west of Geelvink Bay and attacking the Ambon-Ceram and Halmahera Islands area. Biak, Halmahera, Noemfoor and Morotai were being prepared as staging areas to strike at the Dutch East Indies and for the coming invasion of the Philippines.

**July 1944: 348FG: 460FS Arrives**

In July the 348FG became the only Fighter Group in the Southwest Pacific with four operational squadrons when the 460th Fighter Squadron, "Black Rams," arrived. The 460th was constituted as the 1st Airdrome Squadron on 7 November 1942 and activated on 20 November 1942 at Syracuse, NY, and assigned to the Air Service Command. On 28 December 1942 it was assigned to the Second Air Force and then trained in A-20s with the 16th Bombardment Training Wing stationed at Biggs Field, TX from 2 February to 17 April 1943. On 1 June 1943 it was assigned to the 5th Air Force flying P-47s and attached to the 310th Bombardment Wing on 1 February 1944 and then the 85BW from 16 May to 17 July 1944. It was redesignated as the 460th Fighter Squadron on 14 July 1944 and finally assigned to the 348FG on 23 September 1944.

After being promoted to Major on 20 September 1944, William Dunham of the 342FS was assigned to command the 460th. His first move was to have Capts. George Orr and Robert Sutcliffe and Lts. Willis Cooley, Frank Russo and DeWitt Searles transferred from the 342FS. William Carter, Wallace Harding and Richard Frost were transferred from the 340FS while the 341FS sent Charles Cronk, John Lolos, George Della, Frank Morrison and James Curran to the new squadron. However, the 460th was not ready for combat in the Southwest Pacific as it was rushed from the States as soon as it was formed to meet the recurring requests of theater commanders for increased air strength. While the Squadron's pilots were certainly well trained, there was no unity and organization in the Squadron that only experience would ingrain. Training was started at Nadzab and for once, there were enough aircraft available to conduct at least a basic combat training program.

**July 1944: 475FG to Biak Airfield**

At the end of the first week of July the 475FG began to prepare for its move from Hollandia to Biak Island and on 10 July the first echelon of the group flew to the island. Poor weather delayed the 432FS' arrival at Biak and it flew one of its last missions from Hollandia on 11 July when 12 Clover P-38s escorted A-20s to Kokas. On 12 July 20 transport vessels loaded with ground personnel and equipment set off for Biak. After an uncomfortable voyage the transport anchored at Biak on the 14th to be unloaded. The airstrip on Biak was surrounded by high brush but the strip was hard coral that provided a good runway and ready made hardstands. The sun's reflection off the coral was dazzling and the reflected heat became nearly unbearable by mid day. The Japanese had not been subdued and sporadic gunfire could be heard nearby and the Japanese sent nighttime air raids over Biak. By the end of July the 475FG was joined at Biak's three airfields by a number of B-24 and B-25 units on as well as an Australian P-40 unit and some F-5 photo recon Lightnings.

**2 July 1944: Noemfoor Landings**

Before the combat phase of operations on Biak Island was completed, GHQ, SWPA, had already made plans for the next Allied strategic move. An Alamo Force (Sixth Army) Task Force was to invade and capture Noemfoor Island, less than 100 miles west of Biak and more than 400 miles northwest of Hollandia. Major airfields and minor naval facilities were to be established on Noemfoor for the further support of Allied operations to the west and northwest. Air units on Noemfoor would facilitate fighter escorts for bomber strikes on the Moluccas, maintain the neutralization of enemy airfields on the Vogelkop Peninsula, and prevent the Japanese from reinforcing or raiding Biak Island. Noemfoor was used as a staging area for Japanese troops moving to reinforce Biak which was invaded by the Allies in May 1944. Japanese barges could travel from Manokwari to Noemfoor, about 60 nautical miles during one night, and then to Biak.

Noemfoor was chosen as the Allied Commanders believed that Japanese troops equivalent to less than one battalion would be based there; the Allies were already experiencing a shortage of amphibious vessels and Noemfoor could be seized without large scale operations; it also had the greatest number of useful airfields in the smallest area and; Japanese air defences in western New Guinea were almost negligible. At the end of June, RAAF HQ reported that while the Namber and Kamiri airfields were serviceable, they were barely being used and "a possibly generous" estimate suggested that only 19 Japanese bombers and 37 fighters remained in New Guinea. The original date for the landing was set for 30 June 1944 but it was later advanced to 2 July 1944.

Noemfoor is an oval coral island less than 15 miles in diameter, located at the northern entrance to Geelvink Bay between Manokwari, New Guinea, and Biak Island. The terrain is gently sloping from the coast to coral limestone terraces in the interior, with a maximum elevation of about 670 feet in the west central section. Except for old native clearings along the coastal plain, Noemfoor is covered with a dense rain forest. Overland communications depended upon a native track coursing about two thirds of the way around the perimeter of the island. The island had no sheltered harbors or anchorages and was encircled by a barrier reef and the beaches were considered unsuitable for use by landing craft. The initial landing point was to be opposite the southern portion of Kamiri Airstrip where, according to aerial photographs, a reef extended for 400 yards offshore with

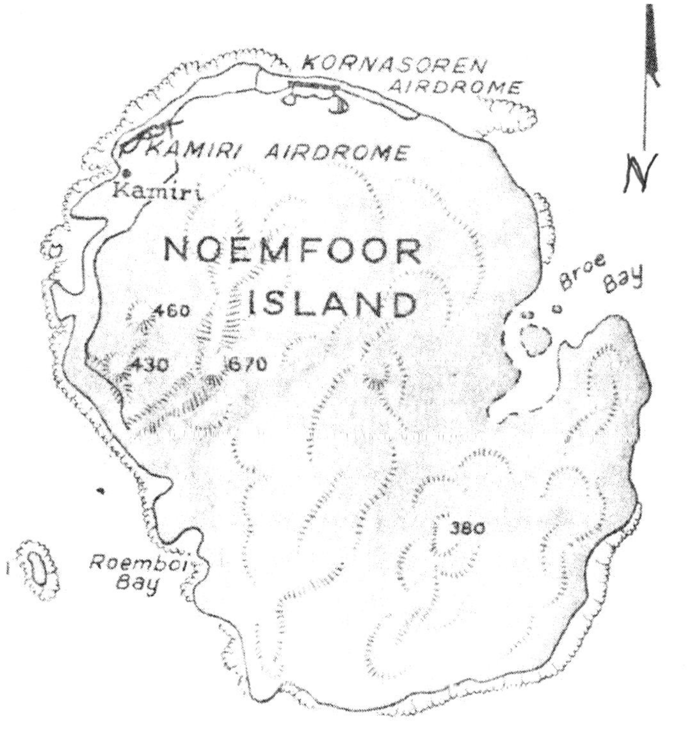


shallow water between it and the shore. Landing conditions were expected to be among the worst yet encountered in the Theater; in addition to the wide reef, the landing was in effect a frontal assault on an airstrip believed to be well defended.

The Island was occupied by Japanese forces in December 1943 and intelligence information estimated that 3,000 Japanese troops occupied Noemfoor, of which 1,600 were combat troops. However, since the enemy base at Manokwari, New Guinea was only 50 miles to the west of Noemfoor, more troops could be easily transported from that area. Intelligence anticipated no Japanese naval resistance was except, perhaps, from submarines. However, a "moderately heavy aerial reaction was to be expected, especially at night," since the Japanese had at least 49 operational airdromes within an 800 mile radius of the island and seven advanced staging fields within a radius of 200 miles. Maximum enemy air strength of 554 aircraft, principally fighters, was expected within a radius of 600 miles of Noemfoor.

Planners considered surprise as crucial to the success of the landing and therefore, the 158th Regimental Combat Team of the 32nd Division staged from Toem, New Guinea, near the Wakde Islands, and moved by convoy close to Biak Island to appear as reinforcements for that island. Then, at nightfall on D minus 1 (1 July) the convoy with supporting elements continued westward for the attack on Noemfoor under an air cover of fighter aircraft from Wakde and Biak. Because of an anticipated heavy enemy opposition, the naval bombardment was doubled from usual and was supplemented by the precision bombing by 17 B-24s dropping 250 pound instantaneous demolition bombs from 0640 to H Hour (0800). The result was an extremely effective neutralization of Japanese defenses and a complete absence of opposition to the landing. At 0800 on D Day, 2 July 1944, 3,000 troops of the 158th Regiment were transported over the reef at landed against dazed and easily defeated defenders. However, one of the enemy prisoners under interrogation said there were 5,000 Japanese combat troops on the island when Allied intelligence estimated not over 1,500. Consequently, the 503rd Parachute Regiment was quickly flown to Hollandia and on the 2 July C-47s dropped 2,424 paratroopers on Kamiri Airdrome. The actual number of Japanese on Noemfoor was only about 1,000 and was never reinforced, although Manokwari was only about 60 miles away. A third airborne drop was then canceled. Kornasoren Airfield/Yebrurro Airfield was secured by 4 July and Namber Airfield came under Allied control without resistance on 6 July. By 7 July the enemy had retreated into the interior of the island and Noemfoor was officially declared secure.

C-47s dropped 2,424 paratroopers of the **503rd Parachute Regiment** on Kamiri Airdrome. (U.S. Army)

**Noemfoor Island Airfields**

There were three partially completed Japanese airstrips, all of which were very near the beach: Kornasoren at the north end of the island; Kamiri, four miles away on the northwest coast; and Namber, nine miles south of Kamiri on the southwest coast. In an attempt to accelerate the completion of these airfields during November 1943, in addition to a 600 man Formosan labor unit, the Japanese had conscripted about 3,000 Javanese men, women, and children for slave labor many of whom died of diease and starvation.

The construction plan for Noemfoor Island was established by GHQ, SWPA, on 17 June 1944 (D minus 15). The plan called for the minimum of port and base facilities essential for handling supplies and equipment for forces on the island; bulk aviation gasoline storage and distribution facilities; and air facilities completed in the shortest possible time for two fighter groups and one half squadron of night fighters and then as early as practicable for a third fighter group, two light bombardment squadrons, and two medium bombardment squadrons. In construction, maximum use was to be made of local labor, materials, buildings, and facilities. Engineer units assigned to the Task Force for combat operations were approximately

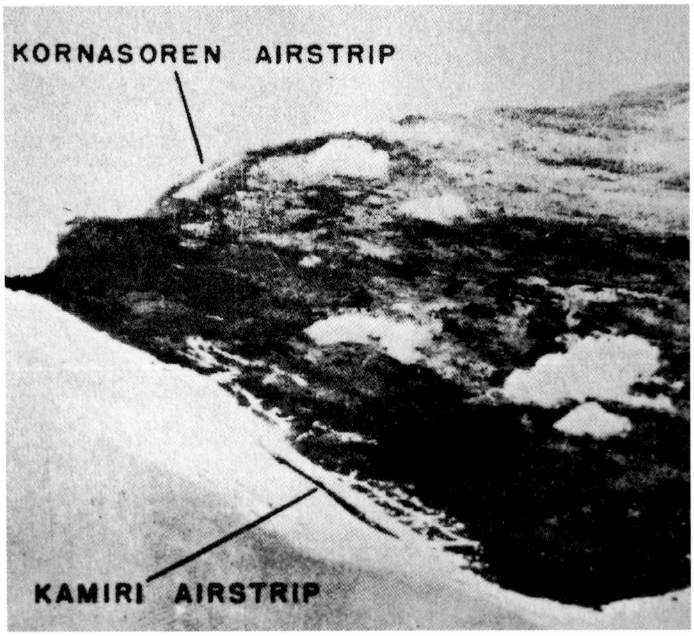


**Noemfoor Airfields**. (AAF)

1,700 men while engineer units assigned for construction were approximately 3,000 troops.

Alamo Force issued construction directives after the landings had started to give the Task Force Engineer more detailed instructions than those given in operations instructions and field orders. The D Day instructions first defined the construction of the bulk petroleum storage and handling facilities. Airdrome construction was considered in a second directive issued on 9 July 1944 (D plus 7) which specified construction of three airfields: two Type D with runways, 6,000x100 feet, and one Type E with a runway, 7,000x100 feet. Initially, a 5,000x100 foot runway was to be usable by D plus 3 and then an additional runway, 6,000x100 feet, was to be usable by D plus 28, while all airfield construction was to be complete by D plus 66. The necessary dispersal areas, operations buildings, dumps, and aviation gasoline facilities were to be built along with the airfields.

The Task Force Engineer and his staff landed with the assault troops and immediately began a reconnaissance and a survey of the Kamiri airstrip. Heavy secondary growth made reconnaissance exceedingly difficult and often the survey teams had to be preceded by heavy bulldozers. An extensive, but unsuccessful, exploration was made to find a better site than that of the Kornasoren airstrip on which only a small amount of Japanese construction had been completed prior to the Allied landing.

Kamiri Airdrome

Immediately after landing on D Day, elements of the 27th Engineer Combat Battalion began to repair the Kamiri airstrip by filling in bomb and naval shell craters, and by dragging the field with lengths of Japanese rails pulled behind trucks. Japanese rollers found on the airstrip were used to consolidate these repairs and by D plus 2 the runway was usable for transports. However, soon a heavy rain made the runway unserviceable and all work was abandoned until better weather. Meanwhile, the 1874th Engineer Aviation Battalion arrived and started work on the permanent improvement of the Kamiri airstrip. A 5,200 foot runway constructed of stabilized white coral sand was built on the approximate line of the old Japanese airstrip and was operational for transport aircraft on 16 July (D plus 14). Two alert areas were completed and a parallel taxiway was usable 10 days later, Kamiri Drome, including a total of 76 hardstands, was completed by 31 August (D plus 60). There was an acute shortage of engineer supplies on Noemfoor Island during the initial construction phase. It was only through use of supplies brought from Aitape by a RAAF works supply unit that even the most urgent construction could begin and with this exception, few supplies were available. As had happened in many previous operations, the lack of spare parts resulted in down time for engineer equipment.

Kornasoren Airstrip

The Japanese airstrip at Kornasoren, on which only a small amount of construction had been completed prior to the Allied landing, was captured on 4 July (D plus 2). The new Allied strip was constructed on the approximate location of the existing enemy airstrip. The engineers

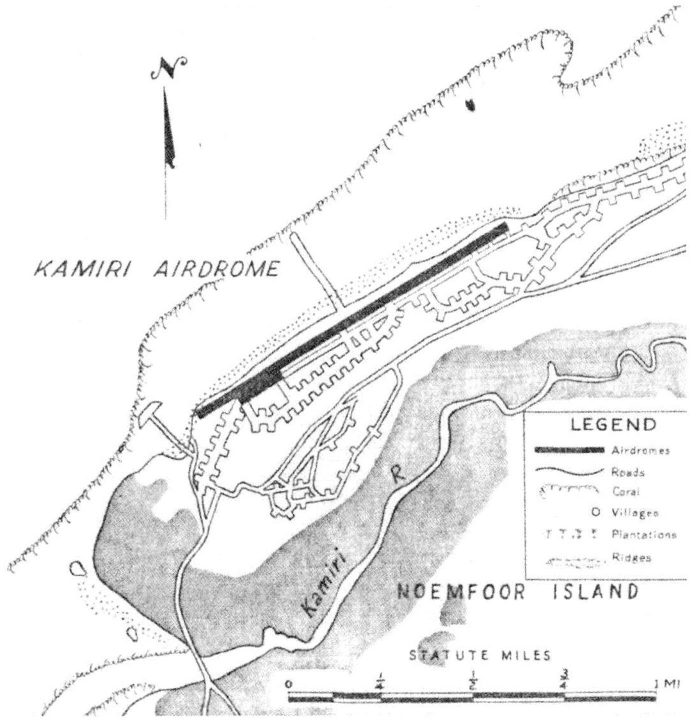


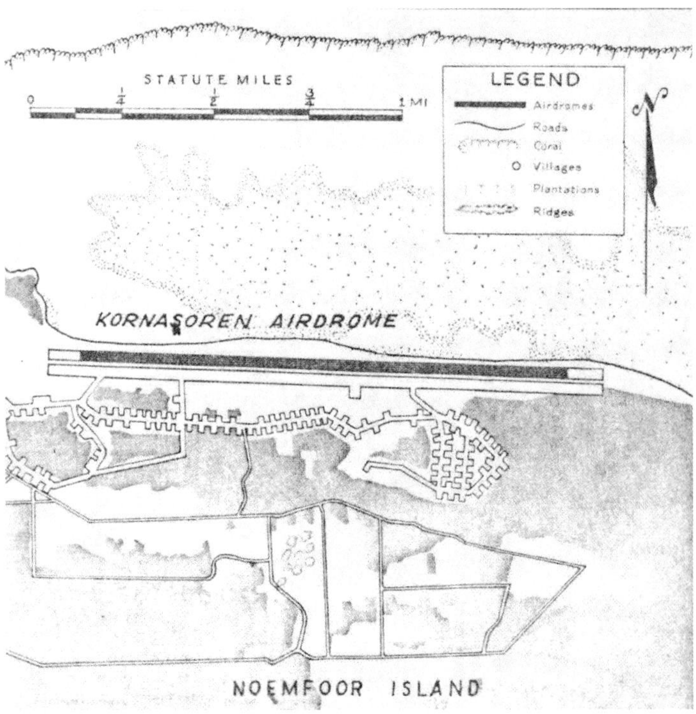

found that it was necessary to clear away heavy jungle and remove 15 inches of loam top soil in order to reach a suitable white coral sand base. Approximately 15 inches of coral were placed on top of this base to from the surface of the runway. The first runway was usable on 25 July (D plus 23) and from this runway fighter aircraft covered the succeeding invasion at Sansapor. Although this runway was completed on 2 August, the second runway was not usable until 1 September (D plus 61). Both were 7,000x100 feet with 500 foot overruns and 50 foot shoulders. The west alert area was completed on 25 July (D plus 23) and the last on 12 August (D plus 41). Because the irregular terrain around Kornasoren Drome required heavy cuts and fills, engineers made slow progress in the construction of the more than 200 dispersal areas required but by early October, all had been completed. At that time, Allied bombers based there made several heavy raids and severely damaged the oil refineries at Balikpapan, Borneo.

Namber Drome

After a shore-to-shore movement from Kamiri, Namber Drome was captured on 6 July (D plus 4). It was improved for fighter and transport use only and included a single, compacted coral runway, 4,400x100 feet. Because the runway could not be lengthened and because the location was inaccessible from the other airdromes, Namber Drome was developed only for emergency use.

Development of Noemfoor Island was never as extensive as had been planned because of the heavy seas and the resulting poor unloading conditions. Nevertheless, occupation of this island had served a strategic role in SWPA operations by protecting the flank of combat forces on Biak during a critical period. During the establishment of the Allied base at Sansapor, adequate support was provided by day and night fighter patrols staged from Noemfoor Island. By the end of 1944, all engineer personnel had been moved to forward areas and in March 1945 plans were made for the abandonment and evacuation of facilities on Noemfoor Island as soon as the equipment still on the island could be sent to more forward bases. On 4 July 1945, after removal of the last equipment and personnel, the island was abandoned.

**7 July 1944: 421NFS: First Victory**

After Owi was attacked by two enemy bombers just before midnight the Owi Fighter Controller scrambled P-61 pilot 1Lt. Owen Wolf and his R/O 2Lt. Byron Allain and gunner S/Sgt. Donald Trabing. Wolf flew at minimum altitude southwest from Owi to avoid friendly AA fire and then climbed to 10,000 feet, south-southwest. Ground Control Intercept (GCI) called a vector but bad weather obscured the P-61's radar scope and no contact could be acquired. Wolf was next vectored on a course parallel to and just ahead of a bogey. R/O Allain directed Wolf to slow up and turn slightly to port so that the bogey would cross the nose of the P-61 if it continued on course. Wolf was now out of GCI range and requested to continue his search with his radar and visually. He flew on for about five minutes on a westerly course with light rain hampering his search. GCI ordered Wolf to return if he made no contact but granted permission to continue his search for a few more minutes when a blip appeared on the radar scope at 0055. The R/O then assumed control in directing the course of the aircraft. He instructed Wolf to turn the Black Widow in a gentle port turn and then to starboard which was intended to place the P-61 one mile behind and below the tail of the enemy aircraft flying at 6,500 feet. Allain told Wolf to throttle back so he wouldn't overshoot. Wolf saw a twin engine bomber with tapered wings and thin fuselage ahead with easily visible exhausts which he identified as either a Sally or Dinah. Once the enemy was in sight Wolf increased his speed slightly and opened fire with all eight guns at 150 yards and scored hits on the starboard engine which caught on fire and part of the fuselage exploded; throwing off pieces which hit the P-61 damaging its lower fuselage and port spinner. Wolf continued to press his attack, firing long bursts with his 20mm cannon and .50 caliber machine guns, causing the enemy to flame and fall in a steep dive. Wolf followed at 400 mph and saw the enemy crash and explode in the water on the southwest side of Japen Island.

**1Lt. Owen Wolf** and his R/O, 2Lt. Byron Allain, and gunner SSgt. Donald Trabing, scored the 421NFS' first victory. (AAF)

**8 July 1944: 49FG/9FS**

Since their arrival at Mokmer the 9FS Flying Knights, flying their favorite Lightnings again, had remained on alert status without seeing any action. On the 8th, they were assigned to a long range sweep to the small satellite base at Facfac Village, 75 miles due west of Babo at the far western end of McCluer Gulf. When the 9FS arrived over Facfac, they found enemy aircraft and Squadron Leader Wallace Jordan ordered two flights to strafe the airdrome and docks. On his strafing run 1Lt. Howard Oglesby's fighter was rocked by an explosion of a warehouse and debris holed his starboard radiator. He feathered the prop and made a single engine flight back to Mokmer.

**14 July 1944: 49FG/9FS**

On 14 July 18 Flying Knight Lightnings under Capt. William Williams used Lindbergh's cruise control technique of increasing the Allison engine's rpms while thinning out the fuel flow to a minimum. The mission was a 1,200 mile roundtrip trip bomber escort to the Boela petroleum complex on Ceram, a large island in the southern Molucca Islands. Over the target the Knights met no enemy interceptors and the Lightnings had enough fuel available to strafe ground targets.

**23 July 1944: 8FG/80FS**

Samate Airstrip was attacked on 23 July and F/O Robert Tate of the 80FS, flying his first mission, was returning home after an uneventful mission and ran out of fuel east of Noemfoor and was killed in the crash.

**26 July 1944: 8FG/36FS**

On 26 July the 36FS dispatched four P-38s on a B-24 escort to Babo and as usual, there was no interception and the bombs exploded on the last four twin engine bombers left on the strip. Other squadrons of the 8th Group also were bored by the lack of opposition.

**27 July 1944: Halmaheras/8FG/475FG**

On 27 July 62 B-24 bombers and 48 B-25 strafers escorted by 52 Lightnings flew the first of a series of attacks to eliminate Halmahera as an air base. At 0945 52 Lightnings from the 8th and 475th Fighter Groups took off from the new base at Owi Island. A few P-38s aborted but the others encountered some scattered clouds and a little rough air on the way to the target, the airstrip on Miti Island. Although pre-strike recon showed that the Japanese had withdrawn some of their aircraft, the attack destroyed 50 enemy aircraft on the ground while the P-38s claimed 15 of the 20-25

Lolobata and Hatetabaco Airdromes, **Halmaheras**. (AAF)

Japanese fighters flown by unskilled and unenthusiastic pilots that intercepted. Two P-38s were lost but both pilots were recovered. The 5BC bombers attacked at 6,000 feet, which gave ample warning for a large scale interception but they could have been low on fuel and it appeared the bombing finished off their fuel dumps.

**27 July 1944: 8FG/80FS/35FS/36FS: Mission to the Halmaheras**

The 35th, 36th, and 80th Fighter Squadrons, led by Maj. Clifton Troxell of the 36FS, approached the target at 1230 when 10 Japanese fighters were sighted below and four others diving from above. However, the Japanese attacks were unenthusiastic and did not close on the bombers or their large escort.

**1Lt. Vernon Jenner** shot down a Lily for his second victory. (AAF)

80FS

Seventeen P-38s took off at 0930 and arrived over the target at 1240 escorting B-24s of the 22BG on Lolobata Airstrip, in the Halmaheras. After the bombers finished their run the Headhunter flights headed home. Two Oscars passed at 1,000 feet under Capt. Cyril Homer's flight in the opposite direction. Homer fired a 45 degree deflection, getting hits on its fuselage and then closed from astern getting cannon hits on its tail section and it was seen spinning down out of control but Homer was not able to confirm this kill. Four Zeros bounced Homer and one got on the tail of his Wingman, 1Lt. William Prideham. Homer frantically scissored and closed head on but his guns did not fire and Homer scissored in again and only one of his guns fired this time and the Oscar broke away toward the sea. Homer than dove on two Oscars to 1,000 feet over the Harbor but overshot and the rear Oscar got on Homer's tail but Homer easily lost this Oscar in a dive. He returned to the dogfight to find an Oscar on the tail of a Lightning whose pilot was using vertical reverses but was unable to shake his pursuer. Homer closed to 200 yards astern and fired a three second burst with only three of his guns working and blew off its canopy and one of its wheels dropped down. The Oscar fell off and crashed in a fiery explosion near a freighter in the harbor for Homer's 14th victory.

1Lt. Vernon Jenner was flying as the Wingman in Capt. Kenneth Ladd's Flight when two Oscars were spotted below but the Flight did not drop their tanks and circled the target area. The Zeros in the target area were scattered low at about 5,000 feet in groups of twos or threes. The P-38s closed slowly on the fast flying Zeros but Jenner finally got a snap shot at one but it got away. He and Ladd then chased a single engine fighter from Lolobata Strip toward the northwest when a Lily came across their flight path. Ladd's windshield had fogged over and he was unable to fire and Jenner closed on its tail and fired and the Lily went down trailing black smoke and hit the water for his second victory.

**1Lt. Allen Hill's** P-38, "Hill's Angels," stands adorned with his seventh victory. (AAF)

**Capt. Cyril Homer** damaged and then shot down an Oscar for his 14th victory. (AAF)

After the bombers made their run, Green Flight Leader, 1Lt. Allen Hill, and Wingman, 1Lt. Howard Sheehan, were at 17,000 feet and saw four enemy fighters below the overcast at 3 o' clock but they were soon dispersed by Blue Flight 80FS. Hill next saw six to eight Oscars on the deck, dropped his tanks and began to dive from 14,000 feet. Hill chose two and began to close on the second and fired his first burst at 800 yards for two seconds but had too much speed and overran and then closed to 100 yards on the leader and fired a three second burst with no apparent results. Sheehan had too much speed to drop his tanks and rejoined Hill on his second pass. Hill led his flight to 6,000 feet and Hill and again dove on the two Oscars at a much lower airspeed. Hill chose the leader and Sheehan the Wingman. Hill fired a two second 90 degree deflection shot that missed entirely. Both Oscars turned away from the Americans, giving them a 30 degree shot. Hill fired a long seven second from 200 to 100 yards which exploded along the wing roots and cockpit, and this Oscar snap rolled out of control and crashed into a hill for his seventh victory. As Hill pulled up the second Oscar reversed his turn and had turned into him. However, Sheehan was on its tail and fired a 30 degree from 500 yards but over led by 20 yards but then got a good deflection shot into its canopy and it began to trail smoke and then made a long sweeping left turn into the trees. Hill's fighter was hit and coolant leaked from the port engine and as Hill was leaving the area two Zeros trailed him for 20 miles before Maj. Clifton Troxell of the 36FS and 1Lt. Robert Damon of the 80FS chased them off and escorted Hill to safety to celebrate his seventh victory.

35FS

Maj. Harold McClelland took off with 16 P-38s on a B-25 escort to Galela Airfield in the Halmahera Islands but several Lightnings turned back. The four flights became three and proceeded at 1,000 feet until they were 10 minutes to the target when they climbed to 8,000 feet. At 1125 they were turning on the south side of the field at 8,000 feet, as the Mitchells were about to make their bombing run. 1Lt. Richard West, McClelland's Second Element Leader spotted three Tonys about 5,000 feet below on the deck at 3 o'clock and peeled off with Wingman, 1Lt. Rolland McMillen, and McClelland and his Wingman, Capt. Lee Everhart, became the second element of the Red Flight and followed West down. The three enemy fighters separated and flew off in different directions. West and McMillen gained high a speed in their dives and quickly drew dead astern of the farthest left Tony while the middle Tony flew straight ahead and the right Tony climbed to the right. McMillen fired first got a few hits but was closing too fast and passed over the Tony. West fired a long burst into its fuselage and cockpit and as he broke away in a tight turn and then reversed West saw the Tony pilot in his parachute to confirm his eighth victory. West saw other P-38s engaging a Tony slightly out to sea and using his altitude advantage dove into the fray. As the Tony rolled West got on its tail and closed but another Lightning whizzed by, firing at West's intended victim. West had to veer away to avoid a collision and then saw that the intruding P-38 missed hitting the Tony. West chandelled to get into position to fire on the Tony but yet another P-38 scored hits on "his" Tony and it went down in a dive into the sea. Meanwhile, Everhart attacked the Tony climbing to the right and fired a 60 degree shot as he was banking and saw his cannon shells hit the cockpit and the doomed fighter rolled over and Split-S'd into the Bay for his sixth and last victory of the war. 1Lt. Lynn Witt and West went after the middle Tony as proceeded straight ahead but Witt closed too fast and overran and West had to break off to avoid a collision. The lead Tony fired and put a hole in the top of Witt's fuel tank. Green Flight, led by Maj. Robert Smith, arrived to come to Witt's rescue but Smith and his Wingman also overshot the wildly banking and skidding enemy fighter. Witt then saw an Oscar ahead and followed it down to Galela airstrip and as it turned left just above the trees on the east side of the strip Witt fired a 45 degree deflection shot that exploded the Oscar that crashed on the south side of the strip. AA fire over the strip hit Witt's prop and he returned safely to base as an ace with his fifth victory.

**1Lt. Richard West** scored his eighth victory. (AFAA)

1Lt. William Gardner was leading Green Flight but his second element aborted and Gardner and Wingman, 1Lt. Arthur Sullivan, joined Maj. Robert Smith and his Wingman, 1Lt. William Dwyer, to complete Smith's undermanned Green Flight. Smith had followed McClelland's Flight into the attack on the three Tonys and saw the lead Tony hit Witt's fighter. Smith fired a snap shot at that Tony that was executing violent skids and banks and missed. Dwyer took a good shot but observed no hits. Gardner then throttled back and closed from dead astern on the skidding Tony; hitting it in the cockpit and it went straight in from 2,000 feet for his sixth victory.

36FS

Seventeen P-38s took off from Owi at 0945 as top cover for a B-24 attack on Miti Island at 1230 to 1255. After the Liberators made their bombing run the Squadron was to seek out enemy fighters. Capt. Everett Van Patten led White Flight with Wingman, 1Lt. John Dunaway and Second Element Leader, 1Lt. William Turner, and his Wingman, 1Lt. Darrel Spurlin, and an add on from 36FS/HQ, Lt.Col. Abe Beck. When they reached the target area at 16,000 feet an enemy fighter was spotted at 600 feet flying east from Lolobata Airdrome. Van Patten and Dunaway dropped their tanks and Van Patten made a stern pass but missed when the Oscar made a tight port turn. Wingman Dunaway made a pass but the Oscar pilot went into a wingover and he also missed. When Van Patten made his second pass the Oscar pilot made a tight starboard turn and as Van Patten fired the enemy pilot went into a vertical reverse to port, finishing with an Immelmann. Van Patten got hits on its tail section with no apparent damage. The Oscar went into a steep climbing port turn and Dunaway then came and fired a no deflection, no lead shot from 70 to only 20 yards and the Oscar stalled out and burst into flames and crashed into the sea. Meanwhile, the second element and Beck dropped their tanks and descended to 7,000 feet over Wasile Bay and remained over the target area where Turner, Spurlin, and Beck were joined in string by five other P-38s from other flights. Turner saw a lone enemy fighter with its wheels down at 7,500 feet which he thought was a Val until it retracted its wheels. He closed from dead astern on the enemy pilot who made no evasive maneuvers and fired a two second burst that started the Oscar smoking from its fuselage and rolled over and crashed for Turner's first of three victories. Lt.Col. Beck, White #5, was flying as #3 wide in the second element and had fired a long range burst at Turner's Oscar and had followed it down as it was in its death throes. Beck pulled out of his dive and sighted another enemy fighter below flying west along the south shore of Wasile Bay. Beck continued his dive and closed quickly and opened fire and the Oscar skipped across the water two or three times.

Capt. Thomas Huff was leading Green Flight and went after a lone Oscar but was beaten to it by Van Patten and Dunaway. Huff's Second Element Leader, 1Lt. William Giroux, and his Wingman, 1Lt. Roy Randolph, pulled up to 6,000 feet and proceeded toward Lolobata Airstrip, where Randolph called two Oscars at 3 o'clock. Randolph peeled off first, made a pass, and pulled up. Giroux dove and closed on the Oscar to 200 yards and fired until he was within 50 yards. The damaged Oscar Split-S'd from 400 feet and crashed into the trees at the end of the strip. Giroux then chased a second Oscar but during the chase two more Oscars were sighted and Giroux engaged one and made five passes on the skilful enemy pilot who would either outturn him so Giroux could not get a lead or try to draw him across the strip into the anti-aircraft fire. Giroux went across the strip once and was lucky to escape the AA fire. Giroux headed for home with his second victory.

**1Lt. William Giroux** claimed his second victory. (AAF)

**1Lt. John Dunaway** scored the first of his seven victories. (AAF)

**27 July 1944: 475FG/432FS/432FS: Mission to the Halmaheras**

431FS

Maj. Thomas McGuire led 19 P-38s off Mokmer Drome at 1000 on a close cover for B-24s on an attack on the Halmaheras and arrived at the target at 1255 at 14,000 feet. The Liberators completed their bombing run over the target without interference and turned for home. At 1300, McGuire saw several enemy fighters on Lolobata Drome and ordered his P-38s to drop their tanks and led them down to make stern attacks on the Oscars. McGuire's Oscar turned sharply and he missed. The air battle then turned into a free for all on the Oscars which were scattered singly or in pairs. McGuire headed for the strip saw an Oscar and fired a deflection shot from ahead and above scoring hits around the cockpit and port wing. McGuire had to pull away to avoid the AA fire around the airstrips. The Oscar was seen to crash in the trees between the two strips by McGuire's element leader, 2Lt. Robert Herman, to confirm his 21st victory.

Capt. Paul Morriss, White (second) Flight Leader, saw two Oscars below, on the deck, and spiraled down at high speed and circled the strip. Morriss made an overhead pass at the Oscar that was headed north and overran as he closed on its tail and the Oscar turned left and Morriss right. Morriss' Wingman, 1Lt. Wilson Ekdahl, followed with a 45 degree pass but missed and broke away. Maj. Harry McAfee, the Second Element Leader, came in too close to get a shot. The #4 man, 1Lt. George Veit, followed, firing from 90 to 10 degrees before having to pull up to avoid a collision. O'Brien saw the Oscar crash into the trees near the Lolobata strip to confirm Viet's only victory.

Green (fourth) Flight Leader, 1Lt. William Gronemeyer, started after an Oscar over the Bay, west of Lolobata Strip. The Oscar made a sharp turn inside him and headed for the strip. Gronemeyer's Wingman, 1Lt. Foch Benevent, used his combat flaps to make a sharp turn and got to within 500 yards behind the Oscar. He began firing at 250 yards and continued firing until it hit the strip to score his only victory. Green #4, 1Lt. John Pietz, followed the Oscar down and strafed the burning Oscar.

**Maj. Thomas McGuire** scored his 21st and last victory until he returned from furlough in October. (AAF)

432FS

Maj. John Loisel led 17 P-38s (one abort) on a medium cover B-24 escort to Lolobata. As they approached the target at 1240 at 21,000 feet Loisel observed that the close cover had dropped down, so he led his Lightnings down closer to the bombers at 14,000 feet. Loisel then saw a lone enemy fighter heading 300 degrees toward Miti Drome on the deck and deciding that the bombers were safe, told White Flight to remain with the bombers, and descended after this apparently easy target without dropping their tanks. Loisel and his Wingman closed on the Zero at high diving speed to 200 yards when the Japanese pilot did a quick starboard turn giving Loisel and then his Wingman only short deflection shots and both Americans missed. Loisel followed and closed and the Japanese pilot made a quick port turn, again giving Loisel and his Wingman only a brief high deflection shots that missed. Loisel and his Wingman both dropped their tanks for more speed and better maneuverability but still made two more unsuccessful passes as the Zero pilot only allowed them brief full deflection shots. Loisel called down White Flight to help box in the skilful enemy pilot. Six P-38s then spent the next five minutes making coordinated and individual attacks on the Zero whose pilot used the fighter's famed maneuverability to its greatest advantage; staying on deck, skidding and slipping left and right and presenting only unsuccessful full deflection shots. Meanwhile, the Zero pilot managed to take some deflection shots at Loisel's P-38 and hit its right wing causing minor damage. Loisel's ICR states: "when it became apparent that we were wasting good ammunition and gas, I called off the fight and headed for Miti Strip" and the Zero pilot escaped. One of the six P-38s blew an intercooler and two P-38s left the area with him, leaving Loisel with three P-38s. Loisel fired at a Zero that turned away and then strafed Miti which already had smoking aircraft on it. After strafing a Sally on the field Loisel and his Wingman were attacked by a Zero and turned into it with coordinated attacks but "to no avail. After chasing this Zero for 20 minutes we gave up with the Zero flying merrily off while we headed for our home base." So during a day when other Squadrons were scoring victories, the 432[nd] flew home empty handed as it had met some very skilled veteran enemy pilots.

2Lt. Leo Blakely of the 432FS crash landed near Cape Waios and was rescued up by a PBY. 1Lt. William Elliott of the 432FS spent the night at Noemfoor after this mission to have a mechanical problem repaired. He took off at 0830 for Biak and at 1100 Elliott radioed that he had only five minutes fuel remaining and was going to ditch. Subsequent searches failed to find him and he was listed as MIA.

**28 July 1944: 49FG/9FS**

When recon discovered enemy aircraft on the airdrome on Ambonia Island, located near the western tip of Ceram, Lt.Col. George Walker, new 49ers CO, decided to join one of the Flying Knights elements for the 1,200 mile round trip escort. Mission leader Maj. Wallace Jordan was not thrilled over Walker's decision to fly but the mission was a milk run as only two Val dive bombers got airborne at 1015 over Elpapoetih Bay at 6,000 feet. Seven Knight Lightnings dove from 10,000 feet and all pilots fired on the unlucky pair. McElroy fired first but missed and then 1Lt. Wade Lewis made a 30 degree deflection shot, getting hits from 100 yards and hitting the wing root, starting a fire but the Val turned inside Lewis and 1Lt. James Haislip fired a deflection shot and it slowly descended into the ocean for his only victory. Wingman 1Lt. William Maddox made six passes on the other Val "and made many hits... And had the Val on fire once but the flames lasted only three seconds...and I expended all my ammunition as a Possum Flight finished it off." However, there are no other (than Haislip) 49[th] Fighter Squadron claims for that day.

**29 July 1944: 8FG/80FS**

The 80FS sent out 14 P-38 to patrol a west bound Allied convoy north of Manokwari. At 1315 1Lt. Allen Hill was leading Blue Flight at 2,000 feet when the convoy reported three bogeys 15 miles to the southwest. Hill led his flight to 13,000 feet when he spotted the bogeys and started to close on

**1Lt. James Haislip** claimed his only victory of the war. (AAF)

them. One bogey disappeared but Hill took off after the other two which Split-S'd to the deck. When Hill's Flight pulled out of their dive after bogeys, now identified a Vals, they were two miles ahead flying at high airspeed. The Val pilots had difficulties in choosing their escape path as the clouds were solid to the tops of the hills. The Japanese pilots chose a narrow valley and as one banked to check on Hill he crashed into the side of the cloud covered ravine. Even though Hill had not fired, he was awarded his eighth confirmed victory; his last with the 80FS (In October, Hill was named the CO of the 36FS and his 9[th] victory in December). The flight then chased the remaining Val through the hills and ravines for 20 minutes but the skilled Japanese pilot outflew the Americans at every turn; using the ravines as escape avenues and the low clouds as cover.

**July-August 1944: 58FG Situation**

During July and August the 58FG remained at Saidor as the war moved further away from them and morale began to wane, especially for the fighter pilots who had been trained for air-to-air combat. During these two months the 58FG continued bombing targets in the Wewak airfield complex. There were an estimated 40,000 Japanese troops trapped in an area bordered on the east by Hansa Bay and on the west by Aitape. The Japanese repeatedly attempted to break through Allied lines and it was the 58[th]'s job to help in their eventual annihilation.

**1Lt. Allen Hill** got his eighth and last victory with the 80FS before being named 36FS CO. (AFAA)

**Middleburg Airdrome.** (AAF)

**July-December 1944: 35FG Drop Tank Problems**
During this period the Group's P-47's were equipped with external wing tanks and had a record of accidents attributed to a deficient release mechanism. The Group lost seven aircraft destroyed and had three pilots with severe burns, as these aircraft crashed with without releasing their tanks. The installation of an electrical release mechanism was so successful that no serious accidents or deaths occurred after its inauguration.

**Late July 1944: Situation**
By the end of July the enemy air activity over New Guinea had ceased except for an occasional night raider over Biak or Noemfoor. Japanese air strength throughout the Netherlands East Indies had diminished to about 150 miscellaneous aircraft spread over a dozen airdromes. In the Halmaheras the Japanese maintained between 175 and 200 aircraft while greatly increasing their air forces in the Philippines. Allied Intelligence was puzzled as to why the Japanese retained this many aircraft in the Halmaheras as they did not use the fields there to attack the crowded 5AF airfields on Owi, Biak, and Wakde. After their unhappy experience at Hollandia the Japanese dispersed their remaining aircraft on Halmaheras at six widely separated fields. On 1 May Allied Intelligence estimated only 50 operational enemy aircraft in all the Philippines but by 25 July that number had increased to 1,400, of which 800 were listed as operational combat types and 600 as training aircraft.

**30 July 1944: Sansapor Invasion**
During the early morning of 30 July 1944, American ground forces landed in the Sansapor area of the Halmaheras Islands against light opposition and the infantry moved inland immediately and took the airfield sites and Sansapor village. Upon the seizure of the airfields at Sansapor it was decided that the fighter units of the 13th Fighter Command would be moved forward as quickly as possible and the 347th Fighter Group and a detachment of the 419th Night fighter Squadron were shuttled into Sansapor by mid-August, and the air echelons flew into the strip of Middleburg Island just off Sansapor later in the month. Brig.Gen. Earl (Diz) Barnes, the head of the 13FC went ashore with the troops as the Air Force Task Commander to supervise the construction of the airdromes and take charge of air operations from Sansapor when that base was established.

Sansapor was the last step in the leapfrogging advance up the coast of New Guinea and now positions were to be consolidated and buildup of men and equipment started for the next operations toward the Philippines. By the end of July 1944 the squadrons of the 13th Fighter Command getting situated at their relatively more plush new bases at Sansapor (Mar Airdrome) and on Middleburg Island Drome (also known as Toem) while the units of the 5th Fighter Command remained at their crowded bases at Biak, Noemfoor, and Owi. While the 5FC slowly began to receive new aircraft and equipment, the personnel continued to live in the same deplorable conditions eating dreadful food consisting of C-rations, canned beef, and dehydrated vegetables which continued to compose the bulk of the menu. Then add bad weather, insects, and tropical diseases to the list of reasons for flagging morale.

**Late July 1944: 49FG**
Lt.Col. Furlo Wagner, who Wurtsmith had named to act as interim 49FG CO, was transferred back to 5FC HQ and 49er Command was delegated to Lt.Col. George Walker who was not a dynamic leader but he was a good administrator. Importantly, he understood that his training was academic and he would be wise to rely on the experience of his senior staff and flight leaders in actual operations. Meanwhile, the Screamin' Demons CO Edward Peck contracted a mild case of Malaria and Deputy CO Capt. Robert Harrison took over temporarily until Peck returned.

**July 1944: 58FG Totals**
During July the 58FG flew 859 combat sorties and dropped 144.5 tons of bombs on enemy targets. While no aerial opposition was encountered the enemy continued to counter with AA fire. The 69FS flew 310 sorties, dropping 49 tons of bombs; the 310FS flew 270 sorties and dropped 45 tons of bombs while the 311th flew 187 combat sorties, dropping 43.5 tons of bombs were dropped, and 245 hits on targets were compiled. The Squadron also flew 292 training sorties.

# 10

# Lindbergh Visits

**Lindbergh Visits the 5th Fighter Command**
**Mid-June to Mid-August 1944**
**June 1944**

After dedicating May and early June to Marine Corsair units, Charles Lindbergh, the famed American trans-Atlantic flier, arrived in the New Guinea. He was greeted by Kenney who introduced him to MacArthur and the three discussed at length the poor performance that the pilots of the 5th Fighter Command were getting from their P-38s. Kenney commented that, "If anyone could fly a little monoplane all the way from New York to Paris and have gas leftover, he ougfht to be able to teach my P-38 pilots how to get more range out of their aircraft." Lindbergh told MacArthur and Kenney that through management of the rpm controls to a lower setting, then coordinating the manifold pressure (throttle) setting to conform to the setting of "Maximum Economy of Operation," and with mixture setting in automatic lean, that no pilot should have any fuel problems. By utilizing this method of cruise control the P-38J should be able to fly 10 hour missions which the pilots certainly would not relish. MacArthur gave Lindbergh his OK and "For the next six weeks he did a superb job."

Lindbergh flew to General Wurtsmith's Headquarters at Nadzab in mid-June. When the straight laced Lindbergh drove along the fighter strip with Gen. Wurtsmith he wrote in his Wartime Diaries: "The cheapness of the emblems and names painted on the bombers and fighters nauseates me at times – mostly naked women or '*Donald Ducks*' and names such as '*Fertile Myrtle*' under a large and badly painted figure of a reclining nude."

His checkout flight in a P-38 was with Col. Robert Morrissey's 49FG during the afternoon of 16 June. During his take off run one of his brakes froze but the veteran flyer compensated with brief pressure on the port throttle and continued to fly for an hour knowing he would have to land with a frozen brake. He blew a tire on contact with the runway and the Lightning swerved to the right. He jammed on the left brake and managed to hold the runway and stopped only 20 feet off to the right side. However, Lindbergh did make rookie mistakes during his tenure with the 5FC. Shortly after take off on one of the missions that Lindbergh flew, the other P-38 pilots jockeyed for position in the formation and looking back over his shoulder, one of them sighted Lindbergh struggling to catch up. Glancing back once more, the pilot noted that Lindbergh had not retracted his landing gear. Radio silence was broken with the caustic comment, "OK, Lindy, that ain't *The Spirit of St. Louis* you're flying. Get your gear up."

Lindbergh was the consummate pilot and could fly any aircraft almost immediately. In early June Lindbergh was visiting another P-38 squadron when 421NFS Capt. William Bradley, who happened to know Lindbergh invited him to try his hand at flying the new P-61 Black Widow. After getting the feel of the large fighter, Lindbergh put it through maneuvers that pushed it to its design limits and then and again tested the aircraft with a feathered prop.

When the "Lone Eagle" arrived he was "nauseated" by the "cheapness" of the aircraft nose art depicting "naked women or Donald Ducks." (AAF)

**26 June 1944: Lindbergh Joins the 475FG**

The first meeting between Col. Charles MacDonald and Charles Lindbergh was inauspicious at best. On 26 June 1944, in the hot, humid mid-afternoon, MacDonald and newly promoted Lt.Col. Meryl Smith were playing checkers in MacDonald's billet. During the game a tall and thin, 40ish, man in a khaki uniform with no insignia came to the door but neither officer heard his name as he introduced himself. MacDonald and Smith resumed their game while the man explained that Gen. Donald "Fighter" Hutchinson, the Third Air Task Force Commander, had assigned him to discuss P-38 combat operations. The checker game continued as MacDonald half heartedly answered the civilian's questions. Finally, these questions seemed to be oddly intelligent and technical and MacDonald then paid more attention and at last it occurred to him that he was talking to the Charles Lindbergh! The subsequent unbroken conversation about the Lightning drew in other pilots, including Thomas McGuire, and continued for hours. For Lindbergh to understand the P-38 in operations it was decided to have him fly one on an operational flight. McGuire was thrilled over meeting the distinguished visitor and agreed to protect a middle aged civilian with no military flying experience by having him fly on his

**McGuire** (right) was thrilled over meeting the distinguished visitor, and agreed to protect a middle aged civilian with no military flying experience by having Lindbergh fly on his own wing. (AAF)

own wing. During a meeting that evening with Hutchison, MacDonald learned that Lindbergh was in the SWPA as a representative of United Aircraft Corporation and had previously visited Marine F4U Corsair units and had made many constructive suggestions. Thus, Lindbergh began a two month stay with the 475[th] which was to be his longest with any air unit in the Pacific. Fortunately, during Lindbergh's visit there was a lull in contact with enemy air units.

**27 June 1944: 475FG**

On 27 June Lindbergh appeared on the flightline for his first combat mission for a 0530 take off to fly with an illustrious flight consisting of MacDonald, Smith, and McGuire but rainy weather delayed the take off until 1030. Although just recently checked out in the P-38 Lindbergh flew in flawless combat formation toward the Japanese airfields at Jefman and Samate. Hoping to draw up enemy aircraft they circled the airfields at 9,000 feet, weaving to avoid accurate AA fire. The flight then continued up northern coast of the Vogelkop Peninsula where they came upon some camouflaged barges and luggers and prepared to strafe them. During Lindbergh's turn he fired three bursts; missing with the first two due to a poorly calibrated gunsight but his third hit the target. As the flight proceeded farther along the coast they encountered more camouflaged barges and luggers that the Japanese had positioned in a bay surrounded by steep mountains, so that they had to be attacked in a sharp bank or steep chandelle up the mountainside after firing. Lindbergh approached his first target, banking only 10 feet over the trees while firing and hitting the lugger. On his second pass he hit the lugger amidships at the waterline and it exploded just as Lindbergh's Lightning passed over at just 30 feet. The flight proceeded up the coast and Lindbergh made several more strafing passes, but his .50s jammed and then ran away and fired until he used all his cannon ammunition.

**Lindbergh** (center) flew with MacDonald (right), Smith (left), and McGuire for his first combat mission. (AAF)

**1 July 1944: 475FG/433FS**

Over the next several days the eager Lindbergh flew every combat mission he could get on and was hoping to meet Japanese fighters in combat. On 1 July he joined MacDonald's 433FS flight as the Second Element Leader, designated on the flight as "Possum Special Three." The mission was to sweep the Geelvink Bay coastline to Nabire and then on to the northwest to strafe the Japanese airstrips up to Sagan. The flight flew low over the trees at 20 to 30 feet to avoid enemy radar without spotting anything on Nabire Strip except wrecks. As they reached the airfields at Sagan they saw parked aircraft and Lindbergh descended for a strafing pass on Otawiri Strip. He strafed a hut but made the rookie mistake of holding his sights on his target so long that he nearly flew into the ground, just clearing the hut. As they flew through profuse Japanese light AA fire the pilots observed that the parked aircraft were wooden mock-ups placed to attract prowling American enemy planes into the AA fire. The four Lightnings returned base at 1708; and after flying for 6:50, Lindbergh, practicing minimum fuel consumption, returned with 210 gallons remaining in his tanks.

**3 July 1944: 475FG/433FS**

On 2 July Noemfoor Island was invaded by American troops and it was hoped that the Japanese Air Forces come up to oppose the landings. Lindbergh again flew with the 433FS but the Possum Squadron patrol was uneventful. The next day Lindbergh flew his first escort mission which was to take B-24s to Jefman Island where it was hoped that Japanese fighters would appear. The mission became routine as no Japanese interceptors appeared. On the return home, MacDonald allowed the 12 Possum Lightnings to strafe the numerous barges that plied every bay and inlet along the Vogelkop Peninsula. One by one the P-38s began to run low on fuel and turned back to base while Lindbergh continued to strafe the barges. When his Wingman turned back Lindbergh inquired about how much fuel he had remaining and was told, "about 175 gallons." Lindbergh instructed him to reduce engine rpms to 1,600, to put his mixture control in auto-lean, and to open his throttle enough to stay in loose formation. When the two pilots landed at Owi Strip, Lindbergh's Wingman was surprised to find that he had 70 gallons remaining but was amazed when Lindbergh had 260 gallons left. The P-38s refueled and returned to Hollandia. Word got around about Lindbergh's fuel saving/range-extending techniques but initially there was concern that the engine manifolds would be damaged and the sparkplugs would foul. After awhile no engine damage occurred but Crew Chiefs found they were continually changing sparkplugs. Pilot Lindbergh's technique of reducing rpm and manifold pressure to increase range was well known but had not been applied to the P-38's powerful Alison V-1710. Meanwhile, Engineer Lindbergh studied and determined the proper settings for maximum engine efficiency. That night Lindbergh lectured the pilots on maximum range and fuel efficiency. The next day the 433FS flew a bomber escort and then strafed barges during 6:40 hour flight in which the pilot with the lowest fuel left reported he had 160 gallons.

### 5-14 July 1944: Lindbergh Grounded

It was not long before 5FC CO, Col. Robert Morrissey heard scuttlebutt that Lindbergh was flying on combat operations with the 475FG and on 5 July Morrissey grounded him. The next day Lindbergh flew to 5AF HQ where he spent several days with Kenney, Morrissey and even MacArthur trying to persuade them that he would ultimately increase the P-38's range to 700 miles as well as the ranges of other fighters in the theater. Lindbergh argued that weather was always an unknown aspect in air navigation over New Guinea and had caused several operational losses. Lindbergh's technique would give 5FC much more latitude in skirting or continuing through adverse weather conditions such as had occurred on Black Sunday. On the 12th he met with Kenney in Brisbane who told Lindbergh that flying as a civilian was prohibited and that if the Japanese captured him, they would cut off his head and that would look bad back in the States! Kenney finally relented and sent the Lone Eagle back to New Guinea as an observer not to fly combat. Before he left he met with MacArthur and Sunderland and impressed them by stating that his technique gave the P-38 much more combat radius. MacArthur said "that would be gift from heaven" and asked if he was ready to go back to New Guinea to instruct pilots there? On 14 July Lindbergh picked up a P-47 at Eagle Farms and filed a non-stop flight plan to Horn Island but was refused as he was informed that the Thunderbolt did not that kind of range. Lindbergh landed at Horn Island with enough fuel to continue to Nadzab with a two hour reserve.

### 20-27 July 1944: 475FG/433FS Lindbergh Back in Combat

On 20 July, Lindbergh was back flying combat waiting for Morrissey at Owi Strip to join MacDonald and Smith on a sweep to the southwestern part of the Vogelkop. MacDonald and Smith strafed several barges and buildings but no other significant action was encountered. Over the next several days circumstances conspired to prevent Lindbergh from flying on an upcoming and promising mission to the Halmaheras. It had been reported that the Japanese had reinforced the area's 150 aircraft. Col. Merian Cooper had ordered Lindbergh not to fly even though he had been cleared by MacArthur, Kenney and Whitehead. On the 24th Lindbergh phoned Wurtsmith who said he would get back to him and the next day Wurtsmith cleared Lindbergh to flight status but the mission was scrubbed. On the 27th Lindbergh joined the 433FS to escort B-25 strafers to the enemy airdromes on the Halmaheras. Although aircraft were seen on the fields the bomber strafers subdued them and the flight was uneventful for the 433rd.

### 28 July 1944: 475FG/433FS Lindbergh's Victory

At 0740 17 433FS P-38s took off with Maj. Warren Lewis leading as Possum Red One with 2Lt. Andrew Anderson as his Wingman; 1Lt. Herbert Cochran flew the element lead with 2Lt. Bert Roberts as Possum Red Four. Col. MacDonald led Possum Blue Flight with Capt. Danforth Miller as his Wingman while Lindbergh was Possum Blue Three with 2Lt. Edward Miller as his Wingman. 433rd's target was the island airstrips on Haroekoe, Liang, and Ambon, all just south of Ceram. Rain squalls and cloud banks threatened to scrub the mission as the clouds gradually began to close in while the P-38s rendezvoused with the 345th Bomb Group B-25s. After awhile the B-25s flying at lower altitudes radioed that they couldn't penetrate the rain and clouds and were heading back. However, the weather improved as the formations approached the enemy bases at Ceram.

The P-38s proceeded to the airstrips on the Ceram west coast and when they showed no sign of enemy activity the flights started back east. The 8FG reported that they had encountered enemy aircraft near Amahai. MacDonald, leading Blue Flight, called Capt. Jack Fisk and his Possum Yellow One to join him on a spur-of-the-moment fighter sweep over the south central Ceram coast which he thought held the possibility of air combat. As the two flights cruised at 13,000 feet over south Ceram, the interior was covered in solid clouds but the southern coast was clearing with just a few clouds at about 4,000 feet. The two Possum flights flew back and forth along the south Ceram coast; watchful for Japanese aircraft.

**Lindbergh** "flying as #3 as an observer" opened fire only when the Sonia opened fire on MacDonald's aircraft. (AAF)

The P-38s encountered some AA over the south central coast near Amahai on Elpapoetih Bay and MacDonald ordered the flights to drop their tanks and split the two flights and he turned toward Ambonia. At the time, two Ki-51 Sonia reconnaissance aircraft were on a search and rescue mission for their own downed aircraft. When spotted by the Americans one Sonia broke away toward the protection of local AA fire and MacDonald took a fleeting high degree deflection shot that and got some hits for no claim. The other Sonia broke into the haze and its pilot skillfully evaded the 9FS pilots until they were running low on fuel and ammunition. Blue Flight came on the scene and MacDonald made the first pass with a full deflection shot which caused it to smoke and forced it into a sharp opposite bank. Lindbergh's Wingman, Capt. Danforth Miller took a quick shot but the Sonia continued to turn in the direction of Lindbergh who fired his guns and got several hits. The enemy continued to turn into Lindbergh who fired again and hit its engine as the two aircraft passed within ten feet of each other when Lindbergh pulled back the wheel. The Sonia fell into a spiral that became a violent spin into the Bay. The kill was reported as a "Sonia type" downed by Lindbergh who was described in MacDonald's ICR as "flying as #3 as an observer" and who opened fire only "when the Sonia banked quickly right and was getting into position for a head on attack on my P-38." (as per Lindbergh's ICR). Lindbergh rejoined Possum Blue Flight and they headed for Mokmer after an eight hour mission.

1Lt. Herbert Cochran's P-38 developed engine trouble while he was trying to from up with the lead element and fell behind Red Flight. His Wingman, 1Lt. Ethelbert Roberts saw him drop behind and thought that he was aborting the mission. Both of Cochran's engines stopped and he crash landed into the sea just off Sorido Village, got into his life raft, and waited for a PBY to rescue him. While he was waiting, a returning B-25 happened to jettison its bomb load right over him, but fortunately, the bombs missed. He then paddled small raft all the way across the Sorido Lagoon and then walked back to camp.

### 1 August 1944: 475FG/Lindbergh Mission

On 1 August 1944 the main mission of the day was scrubbed and Lindbergh, wanting to see more action after his Sonia kill, persuaded MacDonald to fly a four plane fighter sweep to the distant Palaus where Japanese fighter strength was reported to be 150 aircraft. At 0930 MacDonald led Danforth Miller, Meryl Smith, and Lindbergh for Babelthuap in the Palaus. The four Lightnings approached Peleliu at noon and began their sweep and about a half hour later strafed a 400 ton lugger and set it on fire. Just as MacDonald was turning to strafe another Japanese vessel, he noticed two enemy aircraft patrolling at one

**Lindbergh** (left) joined MacDonald's (2nd right) Flight, in which MacDonald shot down a Val and Rufe for his 13th and 14th victories, while Lt.Col. Meryl Smith (2nd right) shot down a Rufe for his sixth victory (Capt. Henry McAfee is on the right). (AAF)

end of the convoy. At the same time Smith called out two Zero Rufe floatplanes at two o'clock high and MacDonald went into a fast, climbing turn to get on the tail of the nearest plane that climbed for the clouds above. As he closed on the floatplane MacDonald fired a three second burst and it burst into flame at the wingroot and a spun toward the sea. The other Rufe dove away to the south and Smith and Lindbergh chased it. Lindbergh radioed that he was going to attack and took a long shot as a second fighter with twin booms appeared; "It's Smith. But he's supposed to be on my wing guarding my tail; he was on my wing a moment ago. Thank God it was a long shot; that I didn't hit him." The two chased it down to the water and Smith got hits that sent it skipping off the water several times and then sinking under the waves. Lindbergh writes: "The temptation was too much. He (Smith) just couldn't resist getting ahead to get that floatplane." While Smith was beating out Lindbergh to shoot down the Rufe another Japanese fighter closed on Smith's tail. MacDonald dove to the rescue and the Hamp got away by pulling up into the clouds. Soon a Japanese Val dive bomber meandered along over the shipping below and MacDonald got on its tail of the enemy and shot it down in flames with a single burst and one of its crew bailed out. With the Japanese now alerted, MacDonald checked his fuel and reassembled the flight once again for an indirect to return home. As they turned a Zero came down through the clouds and onto Smith's tail. Lindbergh tried to turn into the Zero to save Smith but he turned too soon and he became the Zero's target. Lindbergh was too low to dive and the speed of the incoming Zero was too fast for Lindbergh to outrun or out climb it. MacDonald radioed for Lindbergh to break right and MacDonald closed the distance between them. MacDonald fired a quick burst at the Zero which climbed away toward the clouds. Both Smith and Miller took shots at the Zero and Miller got credit for a smoking probable.

After **MacDonald** left for the States Lindbergh flew with the pompous McGuire, who was said to be condescending and disparaging toward Lindbergh because of his fame and civilian status. (AAF)

After they returned to base Col. Morrissey phoned MacDonald saying that he had caused him problems with the 5th Bomber Command as the Fifth Fighter Command HQ had been claiming their fighters could not cover the bombers as far as the Palaus! Kenney gave MacDonald, the most harsh punishment a young combat commander could be given; he was ordered back to the United States on 60 day leave with the invasion of the Philippines impending. Meryl Smith became interim Group Commander but MacDonald was not too upset over this forced furlough as he got to go home and see his baby son for the first time.

**4-12 August 1944: Lindbergh Continues in Combat**

After MacDonald left, Lindbergh moved in with 431FS CO, Thomas McGuire, and continued to fly missions. On 4 August he flew as #3 on an uneventful bomber escort and on the next day as Flight Leader on another B-25 strafer mission but was turned back by bad weather as were the missions of the next three days. Lindbergh would fly his last combat mission on 9 August on a bomber escort to Haroekoe Island, south of Ceram. Heavy clouds prevented the bombers from dropping their bombs and the fighters dropped down through the clouds looking for enemy aircraft and ground targets. As they dove on the airstrip on Ambonia the Lightnings were bracketed by heavy AA fire but they manage not only to avoid it but also from colliding with each other while weaving to safety. As they crossed Haroekoe Strait they saw a large sailing ship that was strafed into a flaming hulk.

**13 August 1944: Lindbergh Grounded for Good**

On the 13th Kenney sent orders that Lindbergh was to be grounded and after visiting each of 348th Fighter Group's Squadrons on Wakde Island on 17 August Lindbergh flew a borrowed P-47 down to Saidor at 1800. After his late arrival he had dinner with Col. Gwen Atkinson and met with 58FG officers. The next day, Lindbergh lectured each of the three Squadrons in turn, stressing long range missions and fuel economy. After completing the afternoon lecture he went fishing with some officers. The next day he flew a 311th Squadron P-47 over the island and then left the Group to proceed to advise the 35FG. Since receiving their P-47s the 35FG conducted many fuel consumption flight tests under varying conditions. In late August Charles Lindbergh arrived at Noemfoor to advise the Group on extending the range of the Thunderbolt. His advice would culminate in the historic Balikpapan missions of 10 and 14 November 1944 when the Group flew 1,700 miles round trip from Noemfoor.

It seems as though most pilots respected Lindbergh and accepted and utilized his range increasing techniques. However, in his wartime diaries he considered them unsophisticated, criticized them for their non-military dress and demeanor, he detested the vulgar nose art on their P-38s, and could not understand their brutal and almost inhuman attitude toward the enemy. There have been various conflicting written and oral accounts of the relationship between McGuire and Lindbergh. Most describe the pompous McGuire as condescending and disparaging because of Lindbergh's civilian status while only a few allege that the repartee between them was mutual and usually friendly. The former is most likely.

# 11

## August 1944

**August 1944: Situation**
The previous calamitous strikes against the Japanese air forces on New Guinea, the Halmahera and Celebes Islands, and Palau caused them to withdraw their remaining aircraft from those areas. On 1 August the Celebes had 329 aircraft but on the 29th reconnaissance counted 164 while during the same period Halmahera declined from 81 to 5; and Palau from 81 to 5.

**August 1944: 35FG Situation**
After being virtually inactive at Gusap waiting to have their new base at Noemfoor to be constructed on the high, undulating ground, covered with brush and small trees. On 7 August, Lt.Col. Edwin Doss led the air echelon on its non-stop 900 mile flight from Nadzab. On the 9th the Group began operations at Noemfoor under the 309th Bomb Wing. It would not be until 18 August before the 41FS led by Capt. Douglas Parsons arrived at Noemfoor from Nadzab.

The 35th's assignment on Noemfoor was to provide air cover over the Sanspor area on the northern Vogelkop Peninsula until the airstrip on Middleburg Island was completed and also to neutralize enemy air installations in Dutch New Guinea and the adjacent islands. On 30 July Sanspor was captured by an amphibious landing and was considered the final strategic step in the New Guinea Campaign that began in August-September 1942 when the Japanese at Milne Bay and the Ioribaiwa Ridge on the Kokoda Track were defeated and from then on retreating. The capture of Noemfoor had effectively bypassed and cut off 15,000 enemy troops at Wewak.

From 9 to 21 August the 39th and 40th Squadrons continually covered the Sansapor area and on the 16th the Group began using the P-47 to test the new glide bombing technique. The first trials were conducted on Mapia Island when the 39th and 40th flew eight sorties dropping 15 250 pound demolition bombs. The results were considered "good" for inexperienced pilots.

After the completion of the Middleburg Island Airstrip the Group began to use glide bombing on enemy airdromes and installations and for the rest of the month the three squadrons routinely glide bombed enemy targets at Jefman, Moemi, Ransiki, Samate, Saowi, Waren, and Utaron. On 23 August the Thunderbolts were loaded with two 250 bombs and the three squadrons set a new record for bomb tonnage dropped at 50 tons. However, on this day, 1Lt. William Richards of the 39FS was shot down by enemy AA fire over the Jefman area.

**August 1944: 348FG**
Operational activity for the group was limited to strafing and glide bombing of troops and supplies east of the Waintoe River and on the southern side of the Sarmi Peninsula. Numerous enemy gas and oil dumps were destroyed and enemy troops on Biak and Noemfoor Islands were harassed and killed. No enemy aircraft were sighted in the air or on the ground and enemy shipping also was absent from the area.

**1 August 1944: 475FG** (see Part 6, Chapter 10: Lindbergh Visits)

**4 August 1944: 475FG/431FS/432FS**
On the same day that MacDonald left for home, the 431st flew a B-24 (90BG) escort mission to Liang Strip with a flight consisting of 15 P-38s. The 9FS of the 49FG was also on the escort positioned approximately five miles from Liang at 17,000 feet while the 432FS was on top cover at 18,000 to 21,000 feet. Capt. William O'Brien led Red Flight with Wingman, 1Lt. Owen Giertsen, who had recently returned to the Group while Maj. Meryl Smith led Blue Flight with 2Lt. James Barnes as his Wingman. The Hades flights made contact with two Japanese fighters over Ceram, north of Liang, at 21,000 feet. O'Brien and Giertsen heard the call of bogeys in the area and O'Brien ordered flight tanks to be dropped but Giertsen had problems with his right tank and fell behind. Giertsen applied full power but still fell slowly behind. Giertsen saw O'Brien make a stern attack but the enemy pilot Split-S'd toward the clouds. O'Brien pulled off to starboard and made a 270 degree climbing turn. Second Element Leader, 1Lt. Enrique Provencio, flew ahead of Giertsen who was now #3 as O'Brien made an abrupt 180 degree turn over Giertsen who racked his fighter around to

**Capt. William O'Brien** rammed an Oscar for his fourth victory but was KIA. (AAF)

catch his leader. Provencio's right engine cut out and his Wingman, 2Lt. Kenneth Hart, tried to catch O'Brien while Giertsen stayed behind with Provencio. Several members of the Squadron saw a large ball of fire and pieces of debris falling. Other witnesses saw O'Brien closing on the tail of an Oscar when the Japanese suddenly pulled up in a tight loop and O'Brien rammed the inverted enemy fighter head on. A few seconds a later parachute opened below the collision and for several days afterwards Hades pilots flew futile search missions for O'Brien who was given posthumous credit for his fourth victory.

**4 August 1944: 49FG/9FS**

For two weeks the 9FS had flown escort for dive bombing Warhawks and search and destroy missions west of Biak and swept all of the known, but empty, southern enemy airdromes. On the 4th the Flying Knights were at 17,000 feet over Liang, north of Ambonia escorting B-24s with the 431FS. Blue Flight Leader, 1Lt. Charles McElroy, and Wingman, 1Lt. Arthur Hufford, saw two Oscars flying at their altitude. The Oscars first turned into the Blue elements but then the higher Oscar turned toward the bombers and dropped an aerial phosphorous bomb which exploded behind the bomber formation without doing any damage. The lead Oscar got on Hufford's tail but McElroy after a brief chase; caught the Oscar and fired a destructive volley to its mid fuselage. The Oscar attempted a chandelle but stalled at the top and exploded in a huge fireball for McElroy's second victory.

**Mid-August 1944: 475FG/432FS**

By 15 August the airstrip on Middleburg Island off the coast of Cape Sansapor became operational. The forthcoming American operations in the Central Pacific caused the Japanese to abandon the area east of the Philippines with the Vogelkop Peninsula virtually in Allied control. Fewer exchanges with Japanese occurred with the weather being a major factor in limiting operations. Between mid-August and the end of the month weather canceled six 432FS missions while five others either were completed to the primary or diverted to secondary targets because of the weather. With the limited aerial activity, Squadron aircraft maintenance was finally on schedule and more P-38s were available for operations and to train newly arrived pilots.

**Early August 1944: 49FG**

During this period 7FS Screamin' Demon and 8FS Black Sheep Warhawks were dive bombing targets within 400 miles of Biak carrying a 300 pound bomb under each wing, plus a 500 pound bomb on the centerline rack. For longer range missions the Warhawks were fitted with a 200 gallon Thunderbolt "Fat Boy" belly tank, which was elliptical in cross section, rather than the standard tear drop Curtiss type. Using Lindberg's technique of lean fuel mixture and high rpms, Ops Exec Capt. Harold Sawyer took off using the main tanks and climbed to 10,000, where he then switched over to the Fat Boy tanks and was able to stay airborne at 200 mph for 4.5 hours which meant that he still had the remainder of his fuselage tanks in reserve which would have provided an addition three hours of flight.

On 8 August, an infantry battalion landed at Sansapor Village on the northwestern most point of the Vogelcop Peninsula. Two days later, engineers were landed at tiny Middleburg Island to build a 5,000 foot strip there and 7FS Warhawks temporarily moved to Middleburg to mop up of Sansapor and soon the 8FS moved up to crowded Middleburg Island with the Demons. After Vogelcop Peninsula's north coast was secured, the Warhawks returned to Mokmer for the final mop up of the stranded Japanese troops on Supiori Island lying just west of Biak. During the last week of August, the P-40s completely destroyed the trapped enemy garrison at Korido Village and when American troops came into the area they were unopposed and found hundreds of dead enemy troops.

**12 August 1944: 421NFS**

During the early morning a routine patrol was being conducted near Owi by P-61 pilot 2Lt. David Pahlka, R/O Ralph Hulsey, and gunner T/Sgt. Harold Cobb when a Red Alert was sounded. GCI vectored the crew toward the enemy at 11,000 feet and Pahlka immediately pursued and closed. R/O Hulsey picked up the enemy bomber and took over the controls when they were four miles from contact. Hulsey maneuvered the aircraft onto the tail but his closing speed was too fast and he overshot. He orbited and again closed his aircraft onto the enemy's tail where the pilot and gunner saw exhausts and were able to make a visual contact, identified as a Helen. The enemy bomber went into violent evasive maneuvers and its tail gunner fired a heavy stream of bullets. Gunner Cobb swung his turret and opened fire at 300 feet down to 50 feet were the pilot fired his 20mm cannon which finished off the Helen which went into a steep dive and crashed into the sea at 0415. The air battle had been in sight of the men at Owi Airbase and they cheered as the bomber crashed. However, as the P-61 came in for a landing base AA fire began to fire on them and they had to turn away. Base Controller then advised them that there were unexploded bombs embedded about half way down the runway and recommended that they were to bail out or land in the nearby water. Pahlka told controller that he would land on the "safe" half of the strip if someone on the ground would shine a light across his touchdown spot. The Black Widow landed safely and the crew was informed of its confirmed victory which was shared by pilot Pahlka and gunner Hulsey.

**17 August 1944: 8FG/80FS/35FS**

The 8FG continued to fly to the Halmaheras throughout August but the weather was more of a problem than the Japanese. The Japanese Army Air Forces in the area was to provide a rearguard action while other air forces were being strengthened along a line to protect the Philippines. So it was not unexpected that these enemy pilots who were to protect positions which were not to be defended against Allied advances would be motivated to fight with any resolve. On the 17th 30 Lightnings of the 80FS and 35FS were to escort five B-24 squadrons on a mission to Haroekoe Airdrome located south of Liang Airdrome on Ambonia Island on 17 August. The Japanese send up 15 enemy fighters to intercept the Americans.

80FS

Capt. Jay Robbins was leading 14 P-38s (one aborted) of Red, White, Blue, and Yellow flights of the 80th Squadron on their take off from Mokmer at 1125. They rendezvoused with the bombers at 1250 over Pinanu Island and arrived over the target at 1420 at 14,000 feet. Robbins saw several Oscars at about 5,000 feet and led Red Flight down first. He then called down the other 80FS flights when he saw that there were about 10 more Oscars flying at 2,000 to 3,000 feet in and out of the clouds below. After dropping their tanks Robbins led his flight down on one Oscar that Split-S'd out of range. Robbins chased another Oscar that made a hesitant turn into Robbins' pass and then turned away. Robbins closed and hit its port wing, engine, and cockpit from close range and the blazing Oscar fell out of control into

**Maj. Jay Robbins** scored his 21st victory and last while flying with the 80FS before he moved up to the 5FC HQ. (AAF)

The 80FS scoreboard after three victories on this day, and would not add to the scoreboard again until November. (AAF)

**2Lt. Kenneth Lloyd** got his only victory of the war when he shot down a Zero near Ambon Island. (AAF)

the ground. Robbins quickly got a few hits on another Oscar that frantically half rolled away. Robbins followed and fired a 90 degree deflection shot that scored numerous hits but it again got away and would later be attacked by 2Lt. Kenneth Lloyd. The victory was Robbins' 21st victory and last while flying with the 80FS before he moved up to the 5FC HQ.

2Lt. Kenneth Lloyd was flying in 1Lt. Louis Schriber's flight as the #4 man and followed him in a dive as he chased a Zero along the coast. After the other three pilots in his flight fired and scored a few hits, Lloyd closed to within 100 yards and fired and got hits on the engine and cockpit and it crashed into the jungle for Lloyd's only victory. After Schriber's P-38 developed supercharger problems he returned to base with the other two flight members and Lloyd joined Capt. Mark Kaspar's flight as the #4 man. Lloyd's Element Leader, 1Lt. William Ravey, dove on a Zero and Lloyd followed him into a narrow valley surrounded by mountains. Lloyd flew around the other side of a mountain to cut off the Zero while Ravey chased it. When Lloyd next saw the Zero it was turning into Ravey who was in very tight turn very close to the ground into the Zero. From 1,000 feet Lloyd saw the predicament and dove on the Zero and fired but saw hits but no apparent damage and he turned up another valley and escaped. When he looked around Lloyd saw that Ravey had crashed.

Immediately upon arriving in the target area 1Lt. John Stanifer saw an Oscar 4,000 feet below and dropped his tanks and fired a three second 20 degree deflection shot and the Oscar began to smoke as it disappeared into a cloud. Stanifer pulled above the cloud and as the enemy fighter emerged Stanifer overran it. Stanifer's Wingman fired a burst just as the Oscar Split-S'd back into the cloud. As the Oscar came out of the clouds Stanifer was waiting and the Oscar passed directly in front of his sights. Stanifer fired a very long burst and got hits from nose to tail. The Oscar entered another cloud but when it emerged it crashed into a hillside just south of Fasa for Stanifer's second and last victory. On his way back to base Stanifer strafed a float plane at the south end of Bogoeala Bay but on a closer look he saw it had been unserviceable for several months and served as a decoy.

35FS

Capt. Charles Rainville was leading the mission of 15 P-38s and Red Flight on a B-25 escort to Liang at 15,000 feet. At 1415 they encountered many Oscars ducking in and out of the clouds at 6,000 feet and dove on them but did not catch them as they retreated into the clouds. Rainville then led Red Flight in a climb to continue its top cover for the B-24s until he led his flight back to base.

1Lt. Kenneth Pool was leading White Flight at 15,000 feet when he sighted eight to ten Oscars at 7,000 feet. He dropped his tanks and made a firing pass at a flight of four and fired and got hits on two; one lost both of its wings and dived into the water. After this pass Pool zoomed up to 12,000 feet and spotted two Oscars going into a Lufbery Circle Pool began a pass on the rear Oscar until he saw Second Element Leader, 1Lt. Lovelace, approach and became the Flight Leader. Pool led the Oscar and got hits along the fuselage and it crashed into the water to give him four total victories. Loveless cut his throttle and dropped his maneuvering flaps to cut his speed and made a high side pass and shattered its elevator and tattooed its fuselage which destroyed the enemy fighter for his only victory.

After White Flight's first pass at the 8 to 10 Oscars, Pool's #4 man, 2Lt. Rolland McMillen, made seven passes but fired only on two as the Oscars would head into the clouds or over the hills to escape. On his first of two firing passes he fired from astern and above a turning Oscar and

**1Lt. Kenneth Pool** shot down two Oscars to put him one shy of becoming an ace. (AFAA)

got telling hits on its tail and fuselage. McMillen continued firing at the Oscar as it went down and got cannon hits from its tail and cockpit, and the Oscar fell off into a dive into the water for his only victory. Pool's Wingman, 2Lt. George Baker, followed his leader down and made an unsuccessful pass on the original eight to ten Oscars and pulled up through the clouds and lost Pool. Baker made another pass on an Oscar and got a few hits near the canopy but it Split-S'd away into the clouds for a damaged claim. Baker noticed that the fuel in his main and port reserve tanks was gone and headed for base. Due to bad weather he could not find his base and headed east and crash landed on Point Monopasimin. Baker slept there over night and was picked up by natives at 0830 the next morning and they rowed him to Ansoes Point but on the way he was picked up by a PBY at 1330 and returned to base about three hours later.

1Lt. William Gardner, leading Blue Flight, followed Pool's White Flight down and chased some Oscars which escaped into the clouds before he could close on them. A Tojo made a 90 degree pass on him but he had the speed advantage and broke away into the clouds. As Gardner was circling above the clouds to rejoin his flight he saw a Sally bomber about five miles out, trying to land on the airstrip in the middle of the battle. He put his P-38 into a high speed dive but was closing too fast, so he decided to open fire somewhat out of range and held the triggers down until he was on the Sally's tail. As he broke upward to the right the Sally was ablaze with flame coming from the wing roots for his seventh victory.

After four victories while returning to base, the P-38s ran into a solid front of rainstorms which caused the formation to disperse. Most of the pilots worked their way through the front but others were forced to land at Noemfoor and returned to base during the next day.

**1Lt. Gail Loveless** (left) claimed his only victory of the war. (AAF)

**26 August 1944: 49FG/8FS**

8FS Ops Exec Harold Sawyer led 15 Warhawks to strafe Utarom Airstrip 70 miles due south of Babo on the southwest New Guinea coast. The P-40s descended through the sporadic cloud cover to find no enemy aircraft present but some AA fire was thrown up and 2Lt. Leighton McCabe was hit and was declared MIA.

**28 August 1944: 475 FG/432FS**

The 432FS flew its last noteworthy mission of August when 16 Clover P-38s, each carrying a 1,000 pound bomb, took off early in the morning, to dive bomb and strafe the Halong seaplane base on Ceram. The P-38s bombed the hangar and barracks area and then strafed and destroyed two barges and damaged another ship. One Lightning bombed a float plane on the water but it was later determined to be a dummy decoy.

**31 August 1944: 49FG**

On 29 August, the 9FS first staged to Middleburg Island and two days later they joined the 80FS in the first escort by American fighters over the Philippines since the disastrous days of early 1942. Maj. Jordan led 15 Lightnings on a 1,100 mile round trip over Buayan Airdrome on southern Mindanao but once there they found the base without enemy aircraft.

**Late August 1944: 13AF P-38s Accompany the 5FC**

In late August, Brig.Gen. Earl Barnes' P-38s from the 13AF had begun to operate from Sansapor and his pilots practiced the Lindbergh technique of extending range. Barnes requested that a few of his P-38s accompany the 5FC from Sansapor on a long range flight to Davao. If they found that during the flight that they were running low on fuel they could turn back to base. As the formation approached the target the 13AF Lightnings were still there and proceeded to shoot down one of the three Japanese interceptors and then raced on to strafe the Davao waterfront and airdrome north of the city. The Fifth's P-38s followed them through the strafing and returned with them to Sansapor but to show their superiority in long range operations, refused to land there and continued on to Biak, even though they had an alternate landing site at Noemfoor, which would have saved them almost 100 miles. They all had enough fuel to reach their home base, although some of their tanks were almost empty by the time they had taxied to their dispersal areas. Thus, began a rivalry.

**Late August 1944: Halmaheras**

By the end of August the enemy airdromes on the Halmaheras had been neutralized. From 7 August on, the enemy sent up no interceptors during 5AF attacks. The heavy bombing attacks on the 9th and 10th destroyed about 35 aircraft on the ground and thereafter they Japanese did not attempt to repair the runways or bring in any more aircraft. On 26 August recon flights sighted only 21 enemy aircraft, scattered on the six airdromes in the Halmaheras and the recon photos determined that most of these were unserviceable.

**Late August 1944: 58FG Moves to Noemfoor**

On 21 August the 310th Squadron was assigned to be the first 58FG Squadron to move to Noemfoor Island from Saidor. On the 23rd, two LSTs arrived at Saidor to transport the main 58FG echelon to Noemfoor under Lt.Col. Jasper Durham, the new 58th Deputy Group Commander. Only the essential equipment necessary to begin combat operations were to be loaded aboard the LSTs while all heavy equipment and non-essential items would be loaded on a coastal freighter which was to arrive soon. About 400 men of the 58th boarded the two LSTs with the officers billeted in the crew's quarters while the enlisted men found refuge between the vehicles and equipment on deck because of the heat and crowded conditions below decks. The LSTs departed Saidor about 1030 on 26 August; leaving a skeleton crew behind at Saidor. After a six hour stop at Hollandia on 28 August to refuel the LSTs arrived at Noemfoor late on 30 August and immediately the men went ashore and began work on the new camp.

# 12

## September 1944

**Situation: SWPA**

By early September 1944 strategists in Washington decided that the European war would be over by 1 November and placed increasing attention to planning for a possible acceleration of the war in the Pacific. MacArthur sent Maj.Gen. Richard Marshall, his Service of Supply Chief, to Washington on 27 August with all the supply and shipping requirements for the following schedule of operations:

| | | |
|---|---|---|
| Morotai Island | 15 September | 1944 |
| Talaud Islands | 15 October | 1944 |
| Sarangani Bay, Mindanao | 15 November | 1944 |
| Leyte | 20 December | 1944 |
| Mindoro | 15 January | 1945 |
| Aparri, Luzon | 31 January | 1945 |
| Lingayen, Luzon | 20 February | 1945 |

Kenney was informed that as soon as the European war was concluded his Far East Air Forces would be augmented by six heavy bombardment groups, one medium group, four fighter groups, and three troop carrier groups.

**September 1944: Rotation Policy**

By September 1944 a number of veteran 475FG pilots were rotated home. From the 433FS Clarence Rieman had the most accrued combat missions with 162 while William Jeakle followed closely with 160 and Stanley Northrup was leaving with 139 missions. Seven victory ace, Vincent Elliott, of the 431FS was credited with 117 missions while squadronmate Charles Samms had returned on 96 missions. Cliff Mann of the 432FS had 121 missions; James Farris, 119; John Michener, 117; and Edward Dickey, 106. The rotation program finally caught up in the Philippines and beginning from the end of 1944 and beginning of 1945 most of the old veterans boarded troopships for home. In the 475FG, John Loisel would be a noteworthy exception as he remained on duty throughout the war and became the 475FG CO in July 1945; probably serving a longer tour in the Pacific than any other fighter pilot.

**September 1944: 348FG**

During the month the Allies landed on Palau and Morotai and while the Group's Thunderbolts did not participate in the landings they did contribute by neutralizing enemy air forces and destroying enemy supply and communications on their surrounding island bases. The Kaoe Airdrome in the Halmahera Group was completely neutralized by 348FG glide bombing Thunderbolts. The airdromes a Langgoer on Kai Island, the Waren Airdrome on New Guinea, Galela in the northwest Halmaheras, and the Amahai and Boela Dromes on Ceram were also heavily attacked. The new 460FS flew its first mission over Rabaul without incident. The Group received enough of the new P-47D 25s to completely equip three squadrons.

**September 1944: 547NFS**

In September 1944, the 5FC received a new night fighter squadron, the 547NFS commanded by Col. William Odell. The 547[th] was based at Oro Bay for their first month where they were relegated to lackluster tasks such

P-61 Black Widow night fighter of the **547NFS**. (AAF)

as loading ammunition and base maintenance. The Squadron was made up of many experienced pilots and R/Os who had previous night fighter and night intruder experience with the RCAF, RAF, and the U.S. 8th and 12th Air Forces. In mid-September, soon after the 547th arrived in 5AF area, Brig. Gen. Paul Wurtsmith met with Col. Odell at his Owi Island HQ and informed him that along with operating as a night fighter unit with the ordinary missions most squadrons performed, the 547th was to be used to back up and reinforce many night fighter efforts in the area. Wurtsmith's decision was based on the need for experienced and combat tested crews found in the 547th. Whenever an inexperienced night fighter unit required support or was performing ineffectually, the 547th would be sent to assist. This assistance would also be given to Gen. Earl Barnes, 13th Fighter Command CO, who also knew of the 547th's capabilities. Thus the 547th had the opportunity to take part in operations at critical times and in a great many places and so the 547th would pioneer the testing and use of advanced equipment, such as the P-38s with APS-4 Radar.

When the 547th's ended its tedious month at Oro Bay, they were sent to Owi Island to relieve the 418NFS and to reinforce the 421NFS. The 418th air echelon transferred to Morotai to join their ground echelon and to operate in the Philippine campaign. Once the Philippines were invaded the 547th was left behind to defend Owi Island and would end the war with a relatively low number of seven victories but they were a pioneering night fighter unit.

**1 September 1944: 49FG**

On 27 August Senior Capt. William Drier extended his tour and was named CO of the 8FS Black Sheep. On 1 September, Drier was notified that all 8FS Warhawks were to be sent to the maintenance pool at Biak by mid-month. All senior 8FS flying officers who were P-38 qualified were assigned Lightnings to fly in permanent mission assignments. All junior pilots who were not on the Warhawk mission roster were to report for P-38 transition training at Mokmer Field. Meanwhile, all of enemy airfields in western New Guinea would continue to be attacked by P-40 fighter bombers. If any Warhawk experienced mechanical failure it was to be written off, even if it could be repaired. The P-38 transition program encountered inevitable problems as several accidents occurred in the rebuilt J model Lightnings, including the loss of two fighters and the death of 2Lt. Walter Clark on the first day. Despite these problems by 15 September the Black Sheep were flying four Lightning patrols over Geelvink Bay.

**1 September 1944: First Bomber Attack on the Philippines**

The first attack on the Philippines since 1942 was to strike Davao on Mindanao. B-24s were scheduled for the mission on 1 September but once they approached to within 50 miles of the target the formation was turned back by poor weather.

**2 September 1944: First 5FC Fighter Escort on the Philippines**

Nine P-38s of the 8FG took off from Owi Island and were joined by like small numbers of P-38s from the 9FS and 432FS to be staged through Middleburg Island. The P-38s were to leave Middleburg by 0845 and arrive over Davao three hours later.

**2 September 1944: 8FG/35FS/36FS**

35FS

Maj. Harold McClelland with Lt.Col. Earl Dunham of the 5FC/HQ as a "guest pilot" departed with five P-38s of the 35FS from Middleburg at 0845 on the B-24 escort to Davao. At 1215 Maj. Robert Smith of 8FG/HQ was flying the #2 position in McClelland's flight north of Matina Drome when he saw a lone Zero pass through an "unaware" P-38 formation and continued on in a shallow dive. Smith rolled over and went after the enemy that made no evasive moves and Smith quickly got onto his tail. Smith fired a good 90 degree burst into the Zero's fuselage and a small fire began in the starboard side of the engine. As other Lightnings came on the scene and the Japanese exited the cockpit and bailed out for Smith's fourth and last victory.

**Maj. Robert Smith** claimed his fourth and last victory. (AAF)

36FS

This mission was to be Capt. Kenneth Ladd's first as the new Commander of the 36FS. Ladd led a flight of four Lightnings to Davao but along the way Capt. Everett Van Patten's fighter experienced an engine fire and Capt. James Moss, was assigned to escort him back to Middleburg; leaving only Ladd and Capt. Kenneth Giroux to continue on. The two pilots circled the target area for 10 minutes before Giroux saw a twin engine plane diving off to port.

1Lt. Robert Crow, McClelland's Second Element Leader, saw an enemy bomber at 5,000 feet and immediately gave chase on the bomber identified as a Lily. Captains Ladd and Giroux joined Crow and the three did a 180. Ladd made the first attack, a head on pass, and got a few hits before he overran the bomber. Giroux then attacked with a 90 degree deflection and fired a short burst knocking off pieces of the cowling before he passed over the Lily that trailed smoke. The Lily went into a shallow dive and Smith and Ladd turned a 360 for a stern attack. Ladd made his attack with no apparent results and pulled away. Smith chopped his throttle and took a long six second burst "that seemed to cover the whole bomber" and he broke off when he on pressed his attack to within 20 yards. Other aircraft made passes on the ill-fated bomber until it crashed into the water. This

**1Lt. Robert Crow** shot down a Lily for his second and last victory. (AAF)

combat, although well documented in both Giroux's ICR and the Squadron Mission Report, was officially credited to 1Lt. Robert Crow who got a shot at the same bomber before it crashed as described in Crow's ICR for his second and last victory.

**2 September 1944: 475FG/432FS**

Generally September 1944 saw the 475FG fly scattered ground attack and escort missions against little air opposition and was to be one of the least active months in the history of the Group. But on 2 September, the 432FS participated in the first escorted bombing mission to the Philippines when it joined a force of B-24s, escorted by P-38s of all three 5FC Groups, in an attack on Davao, Mindanao. Five Clover Squadron Lightnings took off from Middleburg Island and rendezvoused with the bombers over the target where the bombing results were was considered to be excellent with some light, inaccurate flak. The 432FS saw no enemy interceptors two Japanese aircraft fell to other squadrons.

**2 September 1944: 49FG/9FS**

On 2 September, the 9FS Knights flew to Mindanao on a bomber escort and did not meet enemy opposition except for inaccurate flak. Back over to Biak, the Lightnings orbited over the water while the bombers were stacked up in their landing pattern. 1Lt. John McLean's Lightning was making a low offshore turn when its wingtip suddenly hit the water and the fighter smashed into the sea, killing the pilot.

**3 September 1944: 475FG/432FS**

During the long range escort to the Lembah Straits in the Celebes of 3 September, rookie 2Lt. Robert Schuh of the 432FS was hit by AA fire over Lolobata-Miti Island. His Lightning was hit in the starboard boom and vertical stabilizer, damaging the control cables and pulleys and the IFF box self-destructed. However, Schuh was uninjured and was escorted safely back to Biak.

**5-11 September 1944: 49FG**

From 5-11 September, all three 49er Squadrons conducted numerous fighter bomber sorties throughout the Molucca Islands to support Kenney's agenda to finally close the New Guinea Campaign. On the 5th, the 7FS flew to Samate Airdrome on Salawati Island on the western most cape of Vogelcop Peninsula to drop eight 500 pound bombs on the abandoned airfield.

**2-30 September: 8FG**

After Smith's and Crow's victories on the 2nd the 8FG would not file more claims in September as Japanese found that there was a more immedi ate American threat in the Central Pacific and sent fewer and less well trained aircrew south of the Philippines. With no air opposition fighter escorts were unnecessary for bomber missions as far north as southern Mindanao. Thus, the Fifth Air Force could sweep the area north of New Guinea unmolested. The 80FS was assigned to dive bomb Japanese fields in the Halmaheras and other islands. On 5 September the 80FS attacked Galela Drome and on 30 September the squadron attacked Haroekoe. Other missions included rou- tine fighter sweeps intended to keep the 8FG pilots in practice for the coming and more dangerous missions to the Philippines.

P-61 pilot **2Lt. Carl Bjorum** shot down a Sally. (AAF)

**6 September 1944: 49FG/9FS**

On 6 September, four Flying Knight P-38s escorted a PBY which was to rescue a downed bomber crew at Tifore Island, located beyond greater Halmahera Island, 100 miles in the center of the Molucca Sea. The PBY conducted an unsuccessful search and turned back. On the return a lone Zero appeared at 9,000 feet over the west coast of Halmahera near little Lembeh Island. Flight Leader 1Lt. Raymond Swift turned southeast toward the Zero which was at his altitude. The enemy fighter flew into the Knight's path and then climbed up through a chandelle and dropped a pair of aerial phosphorous bombs at them. The white spirals of burning phosphorous completely missed and Swift's Flight that turned after the enemy. After a long chase #4, 1Lt. William Baxter caught up and made a dead-astern attack at 500 feet above the water. Baxter's second and last victory was certified back at Mokmer and the victory put the Knight's into a tie with the 80FS Headhunters as the top-scoring 5FC Squadron.

**6 September 1944; 348FG/340FS**

During September Lindbergh's cruise control lessons extended the range of Group ground strike missions as far as Kaoe Bay in the Halmahera Islands. The 340FS repeatedly broke its own records for long distance missions and on 6 September flew a 1,000 mile mission to Kaoe Bay when 16 P-47s each dropped a 500 pound bombs on the Kaoe Airstrip. Enemy AA fire at Kaoe was heavy and 2Lt. Miles McDougal's P-47 was hit and crashed near the mouth Kaoe Bay. To attain these long distances the pilots were advised to remain at altitude unless he could easily reach a helpful tailwind. The power setting was to be 36 inches of mercury with sufficient rpms to maintain 185 to 190 mph at 200 feet minimum descent until reaching 3,000 to 5,000 feet. To lighten the aircraft on his return from the target, the pilot was to jettison empty drop tanks and fire all ammunition when safe to do so.

**7 September 1944: 421NFS**

At approximately 0250, while on night fighter patrol of Owi-Biak area, pilot 2Lt. Carl Bjorum, his R/O Robert Williams, and his gunner S/Sgt. Henry Bobo were given a vector of 70 degrees toward a bogey 40 miles from Owi at 17,000 feet. Bjorum closed on the bogey and at three miles the R/O picked up a blip on his scope. Bjorum closed to 3,000 feet as the bogey began evasive action, diving to the starboard and to port while making slight changes in altitude. He was unable to catch the enemy plane, however, because his port nacelle became so overheated that it appeared to be on fire and he was forced to throttle back. By the time Bjorum diagnosed the problem, which was that the engine primer switch was fixed in the ON position, most of the bottom section of cowl flaps was burned off but the Widow was flyable.

GCI then informed Bjorum that the bogey had entered the AA barrage of fire from the big guns on Owi Island and was told to break off contact and fly a heading almost directly south of Owi, and to orbit there. After making his second circle GCI vectored the P-61 to 190 degrees and to descend from 17,000 to 15,000 feet. As he closed to three miles, the R/O picked up the bogey again on the scope and took over the interception. The IAS (Indicated Air Speed) was approximately 250 mph and Bjorum was closing too rapidly, and the R/O told him to throttle back about 20 mph. At 800 feet below and 100 feet behind Bjorum gained a visual on the bogey, identified as a Sally, which was then 80 degrees above. Bjorum climbed directly on the enemy's tail and fired a five second burst from both the 20 mm and .50 caliber guns while dead astern level and 250 yards behind with the tracers entering the fuselage. The Sally then went into a steep dive off the port side and Bjorum fired another burst at about a 15 degree deflection and saw the tracers hitting the wings and fuselage and 20 mm shells exploding on the Sally's port wing (both inboard 20 mm cannons failed to fire). The Sally's' tail or dorsal turret fired 7.7 mm machine guns fired at them but the burst was low and to the starboard. The Sally went into a vertical dive into the water at 56 miles from Owi Island, 10 miles south of the center of Japen Island. Bjorum asked GCI to confirm his first (of two) victory and was told that he had had two blips on his scope until the time of interception when one suddenly disappeared and the remaining blip was Bjorum's P-61.

**9 September 1944: 421NFS**

Pilot 2Lt. Carl Bjorum, his R/O Robert Williams, and his gunner S/Sgt. Henry Bobo were scrambled in the early hours just before the sounding of a red alert. As Japanese bombers dropped fragmentation and demolition bombs on the field the GCI vectored Bjorum onto one of the bombers that was coming out of the AA zone. Just as he began his pursuit, Bjorum observed a ball of flame in the distance which was an enemy bomber exploding on impact into the sea. Bjorum had been instructed to stay away from that particular area because 2Lt. David Corts' P-61 was being vectored there.

GCI then picked up a second Japanese aircraft that had left the AA defensive ring around Owi and Bjorum was vectored toward it initially on a heading of 80 degrees and then was instructed into a port turn to 220 degrees. Soon R/O Williams reported a bogey on his scope at a range of five miles but as Bjorum was directly on the bogey's tail, the R/O did not take over the interception until instructed to do so by GCI. Once the R/O took over, the P-61 closed on the enemy bomber at 220 mph in a climb with the bogey 15 degrees above. The R/O then reported that his scope had become clouded, as the Japanese bomber was dropping "window" aluminum strips in an attempt to black out the scope. One blip on his scope, however, continued to show a bright beam, and the R/O directed Bjorum behind the bogey and closed rapidly while flying through the screen of window. The gunner and pilot obtained a visual at 1,500 feet as the bogey went into a gentle diving starboard turn from approximately 15,000 feet. Bjorum turned starboard inside the "Nip" and closed to 200 yards, identifying the enemy aircraft as a Betty. When gunner Bobo opened fire with a burst from his turret .50 caliber machine guns the Betty leveled out and Bjorum fired a three second burst with his 20mm cannon simultaneously with another long burst from the gunner from dead astern. The Betty went into a steep port dive and Bjorum kept on its tail in an almost vertical dive. The gunner and pilot again opened fire with a long burst. In the dive the P-61 had closed to 200 yards at an estimated air speed of 400 mph and when Bjorum pulled out of the dive, he almost blacked out. The Black Widow's diving speed was so high that when Bjorum pulled out at 5,000 feet; its great airspeed easily carried him back to 10,000 feet before he leveled off. At 0310 both Bjorum and Bobo saw a sudden bright flash which was confirmed by Corts and his gunner. After Bjorum came out of the dive he remained in the area and was again called by GCI and began a new vector toward another bogey. As they were catching up to the enemy plane it left GCI coverage from the radar site on Biak Island and he discontinued the chase as they were also low on fuel, and had only 40 gallons left when they landed.

**2Lt. Carl Bjorum** (pilot-center), **2Lt. Robert Williams** (R/O-right), and **S/Sgt. Henry Bobo** (gunner-left) shot down a Dinah. (AAF)

Earlier he had been called off as Corts had been vectored toward a bogey. At the time of the raid Corts was already on patrol, orbiting over Japen Island with his crew: R/O 2Lt. Alexander Berg, and Gunner S/Sgt. Millard Braxton. GCI vectored him to intercept bogeys that had attacked Owi just a short time before. R/O Berg led Corts up behind one of the bogeys, when suddenly the cockpit was lit by tracer fire coming from behind and passing below to the starboard of the P-61. Corts turned into the enemy bomber at his rear which apparently confused the enemy gunner who continued firing forward, where his fire inadvertently scored hits on his own Wingman, which was Cort's intended target. The leading Japanese bomber burst into flames and crashed into the water at 0305. Corts had not fired at either bomber but the victory was officially credited to him by both the 5th Fighter Command and the 5th Air Force but the award was rescinded by headquarters of the Far East Air Forces in March 1945.

**10 September 1944: 475F/433FS**

On another long range mission to the west coast of Halmahera, the Lightning of 2Lt. Wesley Hulett of the 433FS was hit in the right wing by flak but he landed safely in spite of damaged hydraulics.

**11 September 1944: 49FG/9FS**

The 9FS attacked Boela Airdrome again but the airfield was unoccupied again so the garrison buildings and the docks were strafed again. The fighters met light AA fire over the airfield and 2Lt. Henry Frank was hit and both engines stopped and he crash landed on the shore and was last seen running into the jungle. Subsequent air searches were unsuccessful and it was assumed that he was probably captured and executed.

After the mission Maj. Wallace Jordan transferred into the 49ers Group Staff and senior Capt. William Williams was temporarily named as the 9FS Commander. The Squadron sent a number of their old J model P-38s to the 7th and 8th Squadrons for transitional training.

**Strategy: Philippines vs. Formosa:**
***Reno, Musketeer, King, Love, Mike, Victor, Causeway* Plans**

Preparation of detailed Philippine Campaign plans was started at SWPA Headquarters in Brisbane. To transport landing forces across the 650 miles of sea between New Guinea and southernmost Mindanao would be difficult and the expansion of Japanese air forces in progress in the Philippines would further complicate the problem. Even from Morotai it was some 350 miles to Mindanao. On 11 July, after discussing *Reno V* with Maj.Gen. Ennis Whitehead of the Fifth Air Force and Thirteenth Air Force's Maj.Gen. St. Clair Streett, Kenney, now commanding the U.S. Far East Air Forces (FEAF) and the Allied Air Forces, SWPA, informed MacArthur that the first two phases of the plan were not in accord with 5FC air capabilities. Both the projected seizure of Morotai and the subsequent invasion of Mindanao-Leyte were, in his opinion, based on an overly optimistic anticipation of support from Pacific Fleet carriers and the planned establishment of air bases which would not be mutually supporting. Kenney believed that "Carrier units are so restricted in their time over targets and radius of action that they cannot be expected to neutralize and maintain neutralization of enemy strong points and air installations which would be within range of our objective." Direct support by carriers over a beachhead would be inadequate because their aircraft were deficient in strafing and bombardment ability. While the carriers could furnish fighter cover over a beachhead, the presence and strength of enemy air, ground, and naval forces, along with the physical limitations of carriers and their aircraft could not guarantee the continuous maintenance of air cover. Kenney agreed that the proposed invasion of the northern Moluccas could be covered by FEAF heavy bombers from Biak but Japanese air installations threatening Sarangani and Leyte would be outside the range of fighter escorted heavy bombers from either Morotai or Biak. Distances between Sansapor, Morotai, Sarangani, and Leyte were all too great for mutual air support; the Japanese could select any one of these bases and wipe it out before SWPA air units could protect it. To solve this problem Kenney would appropriately space airbases by reducing the scale of the individual invasions so as to move and build an airbase every 20 to 30 days. He expressly recommended that if the capture of Sarangani were to be delayed until November, he would attack the Talaud Islands laying midway between Morotai and Sarangani to support it; that he would establish an intermediate fighter and attack aviation base in the Del Monte area of Mindanao prior to Leyte; and that heavy bombers would be operational at Sarangani in time to support the invasion at Leyte.

Kenney's caution, together with the disclosure that the quantity of assault vessels would be fewer than expected, led to a change of plans. It would be necessary to use the same amphibious equipment for both Sarangani and Leyte invasions, causing the Leyte invasion to follow Sarangani by 35 instead of 20 days as planned in *Reno V*. Since the troops put ashore at Sarangani were to remain there for five weeks, they would require additional air support from a base in the Talaud Islands, which would also permit increased air coverage of Japanese targets in the central Philippines and southern Luzon. On 23 July MacArthur advised the War Department that his revised schedule would have to be: Morotai, 15 September; the Talauds, 15 October; Sarangani 15 November; and Leyte, 20 December.

This schedule, however, was tentative, and it was kept under almost day-to-day study by a series of *Wide Awake* planning conferences which met intermittently in Brisbane between early July and September 1944. These conferences prepared a series of Staff Studies covering the planned invasions. Based on a new set of plans called *Musketeer*, the first of these was issued by SWPA on 10 July. *Musketeer*, unlike the more comprehensive *Reno V*, was concerned solely with operations in the Philippines, and at the launch of the plan it was assumed that Allied forces would be established in the Marianas, Palaus, and northern Moluccas. The plan of campaign was directed at the establishment of air units in the central region of Luzon in four major phases of operations: *King*, *Love*, *Mike*, and *Victor*.

The *King* operations were to initially establish bases in the southern and central Philippines to support subsequent operations. The preliminary phase, *King I*, was to be directed at Sarangani Bay in Mindanao on 15 November 1944; while the main effort, *King II*, would be carried out in December 1944 at Leyte Gulf, where major air, naval, and logistic bases would be established.

The Allied advance was to continue northward with *Operation Love*, which was a succession of campaigns, intended to seize a favorable line of departure and to provide air and naval bases for operations against central Luzon. The main effort of this series, *Love I* (January 1945), was to come in the Bicol provinces of southeastern Luzon. In tandem with *Love I*, *Love II* would establish air bases at Aparri on the northern coast of Luzon in order to cover convoy movements through the Luzon Strait. *Love III* (February 1945),the occupation and development of airfields in southwestern Mindoro, was designed as a subsidiary airborne operation directed at securing bases for supplying convoy cover in the San Bernardino Strait-Sibuyan Sea routes, and for launching airborne and air support operations against central Luzon. *Mike I* would occur at Lingayen Gulf in an full scale invasion tentatively scheduled for 1 April 1945; *Mike II* was scheduled for the same month in the Baler-Atimonan area on the eastern coast of Luzon; a simultaneous diversion, *Mike III*, was projected for the Batangas area of southwestern Luzon; and a supporting operation, *Mike IV*, was scheduled for May to attack the west coast of Luzon in Zambales Province in order to prevent a Japanese retreat into Bataan. Consolidation of Luzon, *Mike V*, was expected to follow these preliminary invasions. The final reduction of Japanese garrisons in bypassed portions of Mindanao and the Visayas would comprise the *Victor* series of operations.

In Washington the JPS which had not been informed of *Musketeer*, thought that early March 1945 was the latest date at which POA could invade Formosa. To allow three months for the preparation of an air base at Leyte and the neutralization of Luzon, it would be essential that Leyte was under control by 1 December. Therefore, on 27 July they questioned both MacArthur and Nimitz as to:

1) The practicability of eliminating the attack on the Palaus and substituting smaller attacks on Woleai, Ulithi, and Yap;
2) whether the Talauds and/or Sarangani Bay could be abandoned in favor of direct movement into northern Mindanao and Leyte; and
3) what specific operations MacArthur envisaged in northern Mindanao.

MacArthur answered the inquiry with a passionate response, asserting his resolute disagreement with the assumption that the chief purpose of his invasion of Philippines was to establish air bases for support of Pacific Ocean Areas (POA) operations against Formosa. With the capture of Luzon, the risky operation against Formosa would be unnecessary. In answer to the JPS's specific questions, he stated that the Palaus were essential, that Sarangani Bay and the Talauds could not be eliminated and that operations in northern Mindanao would follow Leyte as soon as possible so as to liberate the civilian population there.

A conference in Brisbane early in August was arranged between MacArthur and the War Department representatives; Maj.Gen. John Hull, Chief of the Theater Group, OPD; Col. W.L. Ritchie, head of the Southwest Pacific Theater Section; Lt.Gen. Barney Giles, Chief of Air Staff. At the conference MacArthur insisted that the Palaus were required as essential flank protection for entrance to the southern Philippines and that the use of shipping released by canceling the Palaus operation would make it possible to move up the Sarangani landing by about five days but there would still be an interval of seven weeks between the invasions of Sarangani and Leyte. Both MacArthur and Kenney were doubtful that the Luzon bases could be neutralized from Leyte and MacArthur repeated his conviction in the necessity of capturing Luzon and the unfeasibility of the Formosa operation. Both Hull and Giles were tentatively convinced of the correctness of MacArthur's position, although they reserved final judgment until they had conferred with Nimitz and Richardson in Hawaii. After the meeting Giles reported to Arnold that he was nearly convinced by MacArthur's views as: "I realize it is very hard to keep from getting 'localitis' after having talked to MacArthur for five hours (I mean listen)."

The Conference did have some positive immediate results on SWPA plans. Both Giles and Hull were convinced that SWPA should have two new Air Commando Groups (completely airborne P-51 groups with their own transport aircraft) which were being trained in the United States. With the prospect of receiving these Groups, the FEAF Staff prepared a new airborne invasion (*King III*) into the Misamis Occidental Province of western Mindanao. This Province was in an area controlled by Guerrillas, so fighter fields could be readied for covering air operations into the Visayas and southern Luzon. With *King III*, Kenney was agreeable to bypass either the Talaud Islands or Sarangani, preferably the latter. Since MacArthur was confident that Luzon would be invaded instead of Formosa; Col. Ritchie investigated an acceleration of operations after Leyte. The *Musketeer Plan* was revised during the last ten days of August and was issued on 29 August.

Primary objectives in *Musketeer II* to a large extent stayed the same as in the earlier plan, with the significant exception being that Formosa and the China coast were no longer in the *Plan*. The initial *King* operations continued to include a landing at Sarangani Bay on 15 November, with the main effort at Leyte Gulf scheduled for 20 December, but *King III*, the new airborne operation, was included for 8 December. The *Love* series was reduced to two phases: the seizure of Aparri on 31 January 1945 and an airborne invasion of Mindoro on 15 February. The *Mike* operations would begin with the main assault at Lingayen Gulf on 20 February instead of April, and *Mike II*, the supporting operation planned for Dingalan Bay on 5-15 March, would be carried out if needed.

Meanwhile, Nimitz pushed for an explicit directive about Formosa as he had agreed to all SWPA operations projected through Leyte and was prepared to cover them with the Pacific Fleet. On 18 August Nimitz asked Adm. King to have the JCS issue a directive for SWPA operations and his own attack on Formosa and Amoy. Nimitz maintained that carrier attacks and land-based bombardment from Leyte could neutralize Luzon; and, if not, Macarthur could move on Luzon during the *Causeway* operation.

*Causeway* targeted Formosa as the next island in the Pacific in the spring of 1945. Allied occupation of Formosa would enable them to provide support to China as well as establish air bases to bomb mainland Japan. Operation Iceberg was an alternative plan that called for the invasion of the Ryukus, the island chain that included Okinawa. The Ryukus were within medium bomber range of mainland Japan and would provide airfields for both bombers and fighters. Okinawa would provide good anchorage, and the islands would help establish support positions for the invasion of first, Kyushu, and eventually industrial Honshu. The Formosa Plan would be rejected because military planners believed that the island could be neutralized without an invasion. On 5 October 1944, Nimitz advised his command that the plan for Formosa had been deferred and that MacArthur would invade Luzon in December of 1944. Then the Pacific forces were to seize Iwo Jima on 20 January 1945 and positions in the Ryukyus by 1 March 1945.)

Nimitz disclosed that he was having problems reconciling the disparities in the estimates of forces required that were submitted by Lt.Gen. Robert Richardson, who was the administrative commander supervising all the Army's planning, logistical preparation, training, and force deployment efforts as part of the overall U.S. Joint forces island hopping campaign, and Lt.Gen. Simon Buckner, who would command the Army forces. Nimitz recommended a directive for *Causeway* with an objective of 15 February 1945 and King forwarded the message to Marshall with a request for JCS action. Nimitz and his planners hoped both Leyte and Formosa would be tied together in one directive, because they were concerned that MacArthur would plan the Leyte operation in such a way to make Formosa impossible. On 23 August, Nimitz restated his request for a firm directive on Formosa.

Meanwhile the War Department had swayed toward MacArthur's position. Richardson and Lt.Gen. Millard Harmon of the AAF Pacific Ocean Areas (AAFPOA) were in agreement on the *Reno* strategy. On 1 August Richardson had informed Marshall that he and his staff did not believe that Formosa could be supported logistically without Luzon. Richardson also did not believe that the Marianas could by any means support an invasion of the scale of *Causeway*. Marshall was in agreement with the proposed revisions to *Musketeer* which projected an earlier target date for Luzon. On 25 August, in a teletype conference with MacArthur's Chief of Staff, Sutherland, Ritchie urged him to send an official message confirming the new target dates and to immediately send a high level SWPA staff officer to Washington for presentation of *Musketeer II*. Two days later, MacArthur confirmed the new target dates.

On 28 August, R.Adm. Forrest Sherman, Nimitz' chief planner, explained the *Causeway* plan to the JPS. The proposed operations now planned use of three Marine divisions against Amoy, on the south China coast, while two Marine and four Army divisions were to seize the southwestern part of Formosa instead of the whole island as originally had been intended. This change had been made in order to employ a minimum force, but estimated forces were still large. Nimitz estimated that 424,000 men would be needed, Richardson 468,000, and Buckner 566,094. Sherman believed that carrier strikes, together with Kenney's air efforts from Leyte and Seventh Air Force attacks from the Palaus, could keep Japanese air units in the Philippines "pounded down." Sherman considered MacArthur's operational plans up through Leyte to be "necessary and well coordinated."

On 1 September, Sherman urged the JPS of Nimitz' immediate need for a firm directive if the Formosa operation were to start on 1 March which was a period of favorable weather. Marshall stated that an immediate decision would have to favor Luzon considering available resources and he proposed that it would be better to await future developments. Conversely, Adm. King urged at length that a Luzon operation would delay the war against Japan. Adm. William Leah, Chief of Staff to FDR, suggested as a compromise that it might be possible to assemble supplies for either Luzon or Formosa and that immediate attention should be given to the directive for Leyte. The JCS directed the JPS immediately to prepare a directive on that basis. A draft directive submitted the next day proposed to inform MacArthur and Nimitz that a firm decision regarding Luzon or Formosa would be postponed. Meanwhile, MacArthur decided to occupy the Leyte-Surigao area on 20 December and establish air bases to support either a POA attack on Formosa on 1 March 1945 or its own invasion of Luzon on 20 February 1945. The POA was to support the Leyte operation, submit plans for the invasion of Formosa and Amoy, and be prepared for assistance to a Luzon operation.

Of course, Adm. King was not satisfied with this resolution and presented his own draft directive to the JCS. He argued that seizure of Formosa would give psychological and material assistance to China; interdict Japanese sea passage to the Indies; establish air, naval, and logistic bases for an attack on the Japanese Homeland. If the JCS were unable to issue a firm directive for Formosa, King recommended that they direct MacArthur to continue with his operations through the invasion of Leyte and Samar and to develop bases on the former for containment of Japanese forces in the northern Philippines and for support of further SWPA and POA advances. Nimitz would provide fleet cover and support for MacArthur's advances through Leyte and to prepare for a move into Formosa-Amoy on 1 March 1945 if the JCS directed it.

At a meeting of the JCS on 5 September, Marshall noted the considerable change between the original plan to take all of Formosa and the new plan to take only part of that island together with Amoy. Until a clearer picture was available, he could only agree to postpone the decision. Leahy, taking a broad view of the Pacific war, saw three possible courses of action: occupation of the Philippines to include Luzon, occupation of southwestern Formosa and Amoy, or occupation of southern Kyushu. Necessary forces were available only for the first, which also promised the smallest number of casualties; he therefore favored a strategy based on reoccupation of the Philippines, together with an intensive bombardment of Japan by B-29s and the thorough air and naval blockade of the enemy Home Islands. On 8 September, the JCS approved the directive which the JPS had furnished on 2 September, substantially as it had been drafted. MacArthur and Nimitz had won approval of their objectives in the northern Moluccas and the Palaus, and Leyte was scheduled for December. With this action, the JCS had finally evolved a directive for the initial invasion of the Philippines.

**Mid-September 1944: Planning the Philippine's Invasions**

By mid-September GHQ had decided to forego the invasion of Talaud and directly invade Sarangani Bay on 15 October. During Halsey's carrier attacks of 13 September a pilot had been shot down and rescued later that day. On debriefing the pilot reported that he had talked with several Filipinos who told him there were only a few Japanese in the entire Leyte area and that they had very few airplanes. Halsey recommended to Nimitz that both the Talaud and Sarangani Bay Operations and the Navy intention to capture Yap Island be canceled and that the next objective be Leyte. The Joint Chiefs of Staff, who were then attending the Second Quebec Conference, were consulted about the proposed cancellations. Nimitz offered MacArthur the XXIV Army Corps, then loading in Hawaii for the Yap operation, if it would help him invade Leyte at an earlier date. The Joint Chiefs attempted to contact MacArthur but he was on a cruiser off Morotai under radio silence. The Joint Chiefs needed a decision to be made immediately and an as expected no one wished to make such an important decision in MacArthur's name without his knowledge but it had to be done. Kenney contended that the preparations approved for 15 October should now be applied to Leyte, providing the Navy would undertake the air cover until land-based aircraft were in place. Kenney also stated that he thought Halsey's Leyte intelligence was mistaken as his Intelligence estimated that over 35,000 troops on Leyte and many aircraft in the Philippines. However, after USN carrier attacks had destroyed 400 airplanes on the ground and only 50 in the air; Kenney agreed with Halsey that the enemy air threat was not great enough to prevent landing on Leyte. During the morning of the 16th a wire was sent to the Joint Chiefs in MacArthur's name (by Sutherland) stating that if he could have the two infantry divisions of the XXIV Corps, he would make a landing on Leyte on 20 October. Several hours later the Joint Chiefs answered canceling the Talaud and Sarangani Bay Operations and to invade Leyte on 20 October. Kenney informed Whitehead of the change in plans and to immediately send his staff to Hollandia to work with Kenney's staff and GHQ to start planning over again. That morning three of Whitehead's heavy bomber groups successfully attacked Kendari; destroying two thirds of the depot buildings and most of the fuel stored there. Only eight enemy aircraft were sent up but refused to fight. Whitehead wanted to cancel the Balikpapan attacks but Kenney declined saying that they would continue as directed on 1 October or sooner, if the field on Sansapor was ready prior to that date.

On the 17th, MacArthur arrived back at his headquarters and not only approved the cancellation of the Talaud and Sarangani Bay Operations but wanted his Staff and Kenney to explore the option of another landing on the same date at Lingayen Gulf. However, it was explained to him that the forces and shipping available would only adequate for a five division attack, which would allocate two at Leyte and only three for Lingayen where the Japanese could oppose him with at least five. MacArthur deferred saying he "wanted to be in Lingayen by Christmas." He then asked his Staff and Kenney to explore the option of a prior operation in Mindoro and possibly Aparri.

Darwin 9th PS veteran **Maj. Robert McComsey** arrived to assume command of the 7FS Flying Knights. (AAF)

**Mid-September 1944: 348FG: A Fighter Bomber Unit**

Morotai Island was invaded on 15 September the 348th P-47s were assigned to cover the landing convoys. The invasion had no problems from the Japanese in the air and within a few days the Allies opened another base and the Japanese bases in the Halmaheras and Mindanao in the Philippines were now well within striking distance of the Group's Thunderbolts. In September the old P-47D-16 and D-21 models were to be phased out of squadron service and replaced by the newer D-23 model. The main difference in the D-23 compared to the older models was the strengthened bomb shackles to carry heavier bomb loads in the Group's increasing role as a fighter bomber unit. Dive bombing technique was refined as a bombing dive would begin from 14,000 feet, diving at a 70 degree angle for about 7,000 feet, using the gunsight to pinpoint the target.

**10-30 September 1944: 49FG**

On the 10th, temporary 7FS CO Robert Harrison led 12 P-40s on the last P-40 mission for the Screamin' Demons; one final attack on bombed out Samate Airdrome. The next day, William Drier's nine Black Sheep Warhawks flew their last P-40 mission; also hitting Samate. From then on all Warhawks were grounded and turned over to the materials squadron at Mokmer Field. The re-equipping of the two Warhawk Squadrons with P-38s met with large number of aborted flights, equipment and mechanical failures, take off and landing accidents, and predictable fatalities. On 14, 25, and 27 September, respectively, 7FS rookie 2Lt. Douglas Humphrey, 8FS rookie 2Lt. Richard Remer, and 7FS rookie 2Lt. Jay Rogers all vanished during over water training.

By the end of September, 49er CO, Lt.Col. George Walker had lost nearly all of the senior flight leaders. Veterans who had left to attend Command Schools in the States were now returning to the 5th Fighter Command but the majority of these officers were assigned directly to Command HQ or to the Group staff level. For the upcoming Philippines Campaign Walker would have qualified Squadron Leaders and Operations Executives but almost all had no combat experience. Walker implored Wurtsmith to release his Staff Officers to lead his 49ers in their Philippines operations until his junior pilots had gained the necessary experience. Wurtsmith promised Walker that veteran 5FC Staff Officers would be available to the 49ers when the time came.

While the transitioning Demons and Black Sheep coped with the war-weary P-38s at Biak, Capt. William Williams began to send his Flying Knights back to Nadzab to ferry the new P-38 L-l and L-5 models to Mokmer. Darwin 9th PS veteran, Maj. Robert McComsey, arrived to assume command of the Flying Knights as Williams resumed his duty as Deputy CO. Leading 9FS ace Maj. Gerald Johnson had rejoined the 5FC at Hollandia and was appointed as the 49ers Group Ops Exec to aid Walker in the future. The confident Johnson commandeered a P-40 for his personal hack as well as a brand new Lightning and had both painted with 13 "meatball" victory flags. Johnson took on anyone who dared in mock dogfights over Sentani Lake.

Maj. Richard Bong returned to the Pacific for his third combat tour and was named the 5FC "Senior Gunnery Instructor." Although he was not expected to fly in combat, Bong asked Walker to be attached to the 49ers and the Colonel eagerly accepted. Bong immediately commandeered a personal brand-new P-38L-l from Capt. Drier's 8FS.

**15 September 1944: Background: Morotai Invasion**

Kenney had requested that Arnold assign B-29s to the 5BC to bomb the Edelanu and Pandasari refineries on Balikpapan which were producing the greater portion of Japan's aviation fuel. With the rapid increase in enemy airpower in the Philippines during the past two months Kenney felt that the Japanese had not yet been able build up a sufficient reserve of gasoline to accommodate all these aircraft. But these attacks could not be delayed for too long, as even when the Balikpapan refineries and the storage tanks were destroyed, it could be a month or two before the fuel squeeze would be felt in the Philippines. Because the round trip from Biak to Balikpapan and back was about 2,500 miles; Kenney proposed to begin a series of large attacks as soon as the Sansapor airdromes were completed probably during the last week in September. The distance was too great to have the fighters escort the bombers unless an airfield could be constructed at Morotai in time. Meanwhile, in order to reduce the Japanese ability to send up interceptors, Kenney ordered Whitehead's bombers to destroy all the enemy airdromes in the northern Celebes, from Menado to Sabang, and eliminate their large airfield and air depot at Kendari. On the 13th Kenney flew to Owi to check on Whitehead's units there. What he found was: "It was the same old businesslike, dependable, well organized outfit. That trio of Whitehead the commander, Wurtsmith looking after the fighters, and Crabb handling the bombers was hard to beat. The Japs could have given some excellent testimony along that line."

Kenney ordered Maj.Gen. Streett to move his 13AF headquarters and his two heavy bombardment groups to Noemfoor at once. Streett was placed in charge of bombing Balikpapan and Whitehead was to transfer sufficient heavy bomber units required for the job. Streett was complete the detailed planning, make the arrangements for refueling at Sansapor, and fix the dates for the attack. Kenney's "only provisos were that I wanted those two refineries destroyed and I wanted it done as soon as possible."

MacArthur agreed that Balikpapan was a primary target and Kenney inquired about omitting the Talaud operation and advancing directly from Morotai to Sarangani Bay, a month ahead of the present schedule. Kenney and Whitehead discussed the acceleration of the schedule by omitting the Talaud Operation. Kenney maintained that the enemy air force was no longer a threat and, if Balikpapan could be put out of action and the Navy's carriers continued their destruction of enemy aircraft, American air forces would unchallenged "anywhere, anytime...if we were willing to gamble a little to speed up the war and get it over with. If the Navy would give us air cover until we could build an airdrome and get our fighters in place, I would be willing to go to Leyte direct, for in the present state of the Jap air force I believed one of our fighter groups, with adequate radar warning, could lick everything the Nips could throw at us." Kenney ordered Whitehead to have his staff prepare a study, due by the 16th, to exclude the Talaud Operation.

On the 15th the 31st Division and a regiment of the 32nd Division landed at Morotai without opposition and the engineers went to work immediately on airdrome construction. Adm. Kincaid's escort carriers were assigned to provide air cover but it was not needed as the Halmahera airdromes were "nothing but airplane graveyards by this time."

**15 September 1944: Capture of Morotai Island**

In their final westward advance before their attack on the Philippines, MacArthur's SWPA forces made an amphibious landing on Morotai Island in the Moluccas group. Once airfields were established on Morotai, long range aircraft could operate over the Philippines, the Celebes, and Borneo,

**Morotai Invasion.** (U.S. Army)

initially on combat, mapping, and reconnaissance missions and later to provide tactical support and flank protection to subsequent land and naval operations against Japanese strongholds in the Philippines and Borneo.

Morotai is a mountainous island about 45 miles by 35 miles in size, located approximately 300 miles northwest of Cape Sansapor. The entire island except for a narrow coastal strip is covered with dense rain forests, cut by numerous rivers and streams. Although the rivers are steep and swift in their upper reaches they become wide, shallow, and meandering when they cross the coastal plains and swamps. A broad alluvial plain forms the southwest section of the island and was chosen for an Allied base, near the village of Gotalalamo on the Gila Peninsula.

The Alamo Force (Sixth Army) to the *Tradewind* Task Force, consisting of the 31st Division, reinforced by the 126th Regimental Combat Team (32nd Division) was assigned to land on Morotai at 0830 on D Day, 15 September 1944. Unlike many previous operations, the engineers were given sufficient time for planning prior to the landing date at which time tentative locations for the various base facilities had been already been determined. In the initial landings, the LCTs and LSTs grounded from 75 to 100 yards offshore on landing beaches on the west side of the Gila Peninsula which had appeared from aerial photographs to be composed of white coral sand on a gently sloping hard coral rock shelf but actually consisted of an irregular underlying reef covered with a soft, sticky white mud. Disembarking troops and equipment became hopelessly stuck upon leaving landing craft ramps and many important pieces of equipment were bogged down for as long as 10 days and often were damaged in the effort to pull them out. Further beach reconnaissance made during the afternoon of D Day found that a beach was more favorable on the other side of the Gila Peninsula and successful LST landings were made there beginning on D plus 1. By 1500, with the almost complete absence of Japanese resistance, patrols had rapidly advanced to reach their D Day objective nearly three miles inland near Doroeba and survey parties began their appraisal of the proposed drome. On their first night ashore, combat forces were bombed by low flying Japanese aircraft which was to be the first of 60 consecutive nightly raids. There was very little enemy resistance throughout the campaign and before the island was declared secure on 4 October with only 111 casualties, aviation engineers had begun work on two airstrips.

**Morotai Airdromes**

The Japanese began the construction of an airstrip near Doroeba but local natives reported that it had been discontinued because of poor drainage. On 29 July 1944 (D minus 48), GHQ, SWPA, issued a very large scale directive for the Morotai Dromes: immediately following the landing, one 5,000x100 foot airstrip by D plus 25; another 7,000 foot airstrip by D plus 45, and a third 6,000 foot, capable of expansion to 7,000 feet. Bulk petroleum storage and handling facilities were required by D plus 5; docking facilities were to be ready by D plus 20; and supply facilities were to be constructed to support 60,000 air and ground troops. Approximately 7,000 engineer service troops were assigned to Morotai construction.

Proposed Drome No. 2 (later Wama Drome) was sited on a coral ridge that ran approximately parallel to the shore line north of Gotalalamo Village. The site of the abandoned Japanese airstrip southeast of Doroeba Village (Drome No. 1) was found unsuitable for further development since it intersected the approach line of Wama Drome and the rotation of this airstrip parallel to the Wama airstrip was not feasible because the large amount of grading necessary to fill a swamp area would require much more time than that allotted for the completion of the runway. Instead, this Japanese airstrip was cleared and used as a 4,300x100 foot emergency strip. Additional surveys specified a satisfactory site, later named Pitoe Drome, for a bomber runway laid out parallel to Wama Drome.

Wama Drome

Wama Drome was given construction priority. The airdrome was located on a sand ridge with large, difficult to remove, coconut trees and was separated from Pitoe Drome by a landlocked swamp. As soon as the runway had been cleared, the local air commander directed that the alignment be rotated 10 degrees despite there being no objections to the previous alignment. Since large amounts of debris had to be moved; it was not until D plus 8 before construction work would begin. The site was low and to lower the water table, deep drainage ditches were dug and the entire area was stripped of a

**Wama Airdrome** under construction (D+16). (AAF)

thick top layer of humus. The stripping was delayed by heavy rains and an unstable sub-base of fine sand which necessitated a heavy layer of crushed coral for stabilization. Because of the slow production rate of coral, the runway was covered with a nine inch base instead of the normally required 12 inch base. The thinner base allowed the runway to become operable three days early and proved satisfactory with the addition of steel mat.

Wama Drome was used for emergency landings of disabled or out of fuel B-24s after missions over Balikpapan, Borneo, on 30 September and 3 October. Some crash landed on areas under construction but most landed on the old Japanese airstrip near Doroeba and at Wama Drome. Many were able to refuel and return to their bases. On 4 October (D plus 19) the runway at Wama Drome was operable for 5,000 feet and at that time it was requested that the runway be extended an additional 500 feet prior to the next attack on Balikpapan planned for 10 October when fighter aircraft based on Morotai escorted the bombers an attack which extensively damaged the oil refineries and storage tanks in the Balikpapan area. On 11 October (D plus 26), the steel mat runway was 5,500x100 feet, with 500 foot overruns at each end, while 22 heavy bomber hardstands and two alert areas were available. Three days later, Allied bombers, escorted by both P-38s and P-47s from Morotai, made a raid so destructive that Balikpapan was practically eliminated as a factor in the Japanese war effort. Construction continued at Wama Drome until late November when the airdrome was complete with a 6,500 foot runway, 5,500 feet of which were surfaced with steel mat, and 79 hardstands.

5FC Units based at Wama
35FG HQ (27 September 1944 - ?
35FG, 41FS (P-47) Owi 17 October 1944 – 21 January 1945 to Mangaldan

Pitoe (Pitu) Drome
Unlike Wama Drome, the coral terrace location for Pitoe Drome was both high and dry but the construction was to first clear the rain forest and strip the heavy top layer and the silty clay subsoil down to a coral sub-base. This construction required a much larger than normal removal of 339,700 cubic yards of material. Then, after necessary leveling and blasting, cut and fill were brought into approximate balance, coral was added where necessary, and the runway was compacted by rollers. Taxiways and hardstands were built of nine inches of compacted coral. The rate at which coral could be supplied largely limited the progress construction. Suitable coral difficult to locate and pits were frequently opened and operated for a time only to be abandoned as the coral became increasingly hard. Low grade coral containing clay was reserved for heavy fills and for road construction.

Pitoe Drome was designed with two parallel heavy bomber runways, 600 feet apart. After 17 October (D plus 32) the south runway, which was given construction priority, was usable for 7,000 feet with 500 foot overruns at each end and a parallel taxiway and 38 hardstands were also in operation. The north runway was not complete until 11 November (D plus 57). When completed on 24 November (D plus 70), Pitoe Drome consisted of two 8,000x100 foot coral, asphalt-surfaced runways with 500 foot graded overruns and 50 foot shoulders and 174 heavy bomber hardstands.

In addition to the three runways and almost 300 dispersals, approximately 58,000 square feet of taxiway were provided at the two Morotai airdromes. In early 1945, Wama Drome was placed under RAAF control in preparation for the staging of air strikes against Borneo in preparation for subsequent landings there by Australian ground forces. Although Wama Drome was closed soon after initiation of the Borneo operations, Pitoe Drome remained operational for all types of aircraft until deactivation of the base.

The 5FC units based on Pitoe were:

8FG: 19 September 1944 to 20 December 1944
35FG: 27 September 1944 to 20 January 1945
418NFS: 28 September 1944 to 26 December 1944

As expected, the water shortage on Morotai was a serious problem. Initially, the main sources of supply were native wells and water in bomb craters. However, in a short time, all wells were condemned except one in Gotalalamo, which operated for several weeks before salt water was drawn in. Thereafter, this water was suitable only for showers. Well drilling equipment had been brought ashore and promptly put into operation. However, wells were hardly dug before the water in them became saline. On about D plus 5, a stratum of water-bearing ground was located and a successful 26 foot well was drilled in which water rose to within 16 feet of the surface. This well was operated for 14 to 20 hours a day and supplied an average of 75,000 gallons daily. With the establishment of other water points, the supply of fresh water rose to eight gallons per day per man. In the search for reserve water supplies, a number of additional holes were drilled but although water was located, it was either brackish or at too great a depth to be pumped by the centrifugal pumps available.

The invasion of Morotai had provided the Allies with a base halfway between the western tip of New Guinea and Davao Gulf, Mindanao. Within a month after the landings there, Morotai airfields were used by fighter aircraft to support long range missions over Borneo. From this base, MacArthur's forces were in a position to launch the long awaited return to the Philippines, only five weeks after the Morotai landing. Heavy bombers from Pitoe Drome carried out a devastating aerial bombardment of the Leyte prior to the landings there. Then, after providing support to initial operations in the Philippines, Morotai was used by Australian forces to support landing operations on Borneo, which were initiated in May 1945. While on Morotai, Australian construction units prepared a staging area and improved roads and other facilities. With the termination of hostilities in the Pacific, the need for a base on Morotai ceased to exist, and on 7 January 1946 the base was closed.

**19 September 1944: 475FG**
During September the 475FG flew several dive bombing and strafing missions to the Halmaheras and Celebes. They flew a mission to Amoerang Town in the Celebes described in the Squadron's report as "a trigger-happy pilot's dream." The 16 Clover P-38s ravaged the target for 45 minutes, setting two warehouses and half of the town's buildings on fire and then strafing four or five barges along the coast. Also on this date 2Lt. Nathaniel Landen was listed as KIA but was not listed as part of the Halmahera mission and probably crashed on a cross country training flight.

**24 September 1944: 475FG**
2Lt. Walter Weisfus of the 432FS was the other 475FG pilot to be lost during September. Weisfus was on a local afternoon flight in a borrowed 66th Service Squadron P-39 with about one and a half hours fuel. After several hours, Air and Sea began its search over Biak and Owi without result and Weisfus was officially declared missing.

**27 September 1944: 35FG moves to Morotai**
At the beginning of September the 35th Group Headquarters was still on Noemfoor with a detachment on Owi Island. The Group's operations from Noemfoor were in their final stages as its squadrons were pounding enemy installations on Vogelkop, Ceram, and most recently on the Moluccan Islands. On 5 September all three 35th squadrons flew the longest combat mission from Noemfoor when they flew 400 miles to glide bomb the enemy airfield at Koae on Halmahera Island in the Moluccan Island Group. Each P-47 carried one 500 pound bomb and auxiliary wing tanks.

On 15 September the Allies seized Morotai, the northern most island of the Moluccan Group and threatened to cut Japan's sea

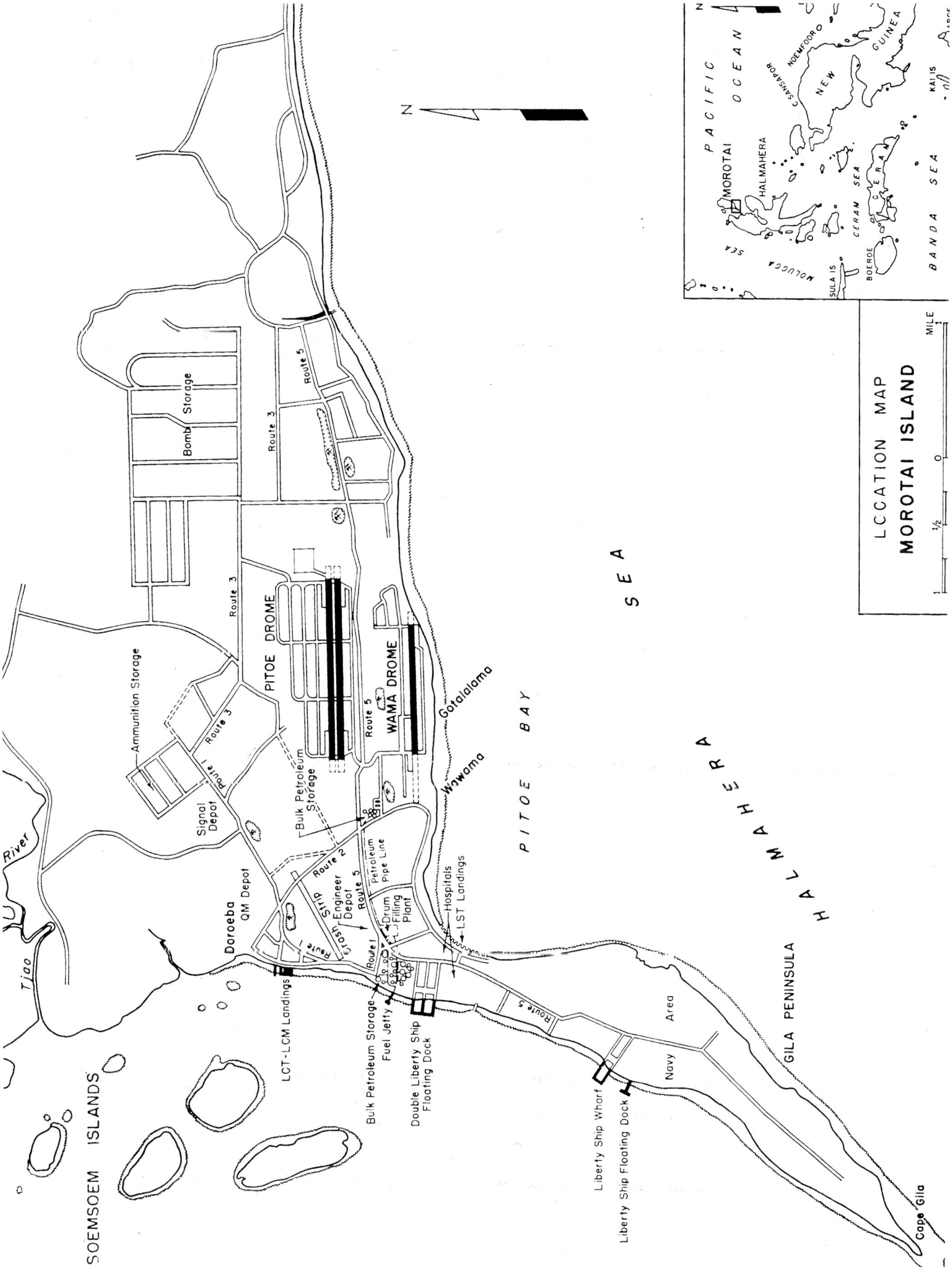
LCCATION MAP
MOROTAI ISLAND
MILE
1
½
0
1
PACIFIC OCEAN
MOROTAI
HALMAHERA
SANSAPOR
NOEMFOOR
NEW GUINEA
MOLUCCA SEA
SULA IS
BOEROE
CERAM SEA
CERAM
BANDA SEA
KAI IS
N
SEA
PITOE BAY
HALMAHERA
GILA PENINSULA
Cape Gila
Navy Area
Route 5
Liberty Ship Wharf
Liberty Ship Floating Dock
Double Liberty Ship Floating Dock
Fuel Jetty
Bulk Petroleum Storage
LCT-LCM Landings
SOEMSOEM ISLANDS
Tjao River
Doroeba
QM Depot
Signal Depot
Ammunition Storage
Route 1
Route 3
Route 2
Crash Strip
Engineer Depot
Drum Filling Plant
Petroleum Pipe Line
Hospitals
LST Landings
Bulk Petroleum Storage
PITOE DROME
WAMA DROME
Wawama
Gotalalama
Bomb Storage

communications with the oil rich Netherlands East Indies. The 35FG detachment on Owi was ordered to Morotai and on 16 September the ground echelons of the 39th and 40th Squadrons boarded the *USAT Andrew E. White* and on the 19th the ground echelons of HQ Squadron and the 41FS boarded the *USAT Stanley Matthews* to join a convoy headed for Morotai and crossed the Equator on the 25th. Meanwhile, the Group air echelon at Noemfoor was closing down operations under the 309BW and preparing to move to Morotai. First it was to move to the vacant base on Owi which was completed on the 21st when the squadrons came under the control of the 5FC. The group flew its last mission from Noemfoor on 13 September when the 41FS flew a glide bombing mission to Koae on Halmahera. After the move to Owi they flew a few glide bomb and patrol missions but were released for training and maintenance. The ground echelon reached Morotai on 27 September; D-Day +12 but because of inadequate docking facilities unloading was slowed as it had to be loaded on barges and landing craft first and then taken to shore. Unloading was slowed further because gasoline tankers were given preference and it was not until 5 October that the ground echelon began unloading and set up a temporary billet in a banana grove which had been the infantry's second line of defense and abandoned only the day before. Finally, ten days later a permanent base was built and occupied in a coconut grove off a main road.

The Owi Detachment joined the ground element at Morotai on 18 October. The air echelon of the 39FS did not arrive at Morotai until the 23rd because it was scheduled to be equipped with the new D-28 model of the P-47 at Owi but this plan did not occur. On 18 October the control of the 35FG was assumed by the 310th Bomb Group but when the 310th left Morotai on 31 October the Group came under the control of the 13th Bomber Command.

**September 1944: The P-38 Model L**

By the end of September the older J-20 model P-38s were completely replaced by the newer L models in the 432FS while all the older J-20s were being transferred to the 433FS which would have to wait until November for their Ls. Opinions on the relative qualities of the P-38L model over the earlier Lightning versions varied but generally most veteran P-38 pilots saw little difference between the J and the L models. A P-38 pilot grew to love his twin engine steed which he felt gave him an inherent advantage over any single engine aircraft. P-38 pilots in the ETO and MTO were more enthusiastic about the high altitude capabilities of the L-model's new dive brakes and the improved ease of maneuver provided by the power assisted aileron controls. They felt that it was somewhat better in climbing and diving. However, Pacific veterans had long adapted to the Lightning's inherent advantages over Japanese fighters: good range, high straight away and climbing speeds, good diving characteristics at lower altitudes, and heavy .50 caliber machine gun and 20mm cannon fire firepower. Lightning pilots were highly disciplined tactically, especially in maintaining formation integrity, which added to the fighter's capabilities.

**Pitoe Airdrome** at the height of its use. (AAF)

# 13

## October 1944

**Early October 1944: 49FG**
During the first week of October, the 49ers were assigned to the Strategic Fighter Wing of the 310th Bomb Wing Air Task Force, commanded by veteran Col. Robert Morrissey, who had a force of nearly 100 Lightnings in three fighter groups. Morrissey immediately planned the next missions which would be the preemptive sorties for the Philippines Campaign. The Flying Knights were tied for the squadron victory lead and the 49ers overall victory total officially stood at 478 and all 49er pilots were looking to increase these totals.

**October 1944: 8FG Dive Bombing Missions**
The 80FS continued their dive bombing missions into October with a strike on 5 October against Geramaon and Ceram (again, Ceram Island was a Japanese base on the way to the oil producing areas of Borneo and the complex of bases in the Celebes). Two days later 35 8FG P-38s flew another escort of B-24s to Zamboanga, located on a peninsula on southwest Mindanao. This mission offered the fighter pilots an opportunity to break the monotony and strafe some ground targets. The 35FS strafed a freighter and a barge, claiming the freighter to be sunk while the 36FS strafed and burned or sank six floatplanes and two other freighters. The 80FS strafed two other vessels and made effective sweeps over San Pogue Airdrome.

**October 1944: 35FG Command Changes**
Maj. Francis Dubisher, Group Deputy CO, was rotated home on 28 September and replaced by Maj. John Young, 40FS CO. Maj. Harris Denton, Group Operations Officer rotated home on 7 October and was replaced by Capt. Robert Yaeger, a former 40FS CO and Deputy Operations Officer.

**1 October 1944: 475FG**
The first Satan's Angels' October mission turned immediately portentous when 1Lt. Charles Joseph, flying one of the 12 433FS P-38s assigned to a dive bombing mission of Fakfak, was killed after his P-38 crashed during take off. The 431FS' assignment for that day was a glide bombing mission to Halong, Ceram and 1Lt. Wilson Ekdahl tried to take off with a drop tank and 1,000 pound bomb when his one of his engines began to misfire. The veteran from the early days in New Guinea landed and returned to the runway for a second try. Just as he became airborne one of his engines quit and he instinctively cut the throttles and retracted the gear and waited to hit the ground in a lethal explosion. Ekdahl's P-38 skidded along the ground before the bomb finally exploded and scattered shrapnel in every direction. After awhile, the ground crew came out from hiding from the cooked off rounds and roaring fire to look for Ekdahl's body. As they were searching Ekdahl called out from behind a pile of coral wanting to know if it was safe to come out!

Six victory ace Capt. **Billy Gresham** was killed in a flying accident. (AFAA)

**2 October 1944: 475FG**
At 1500 six victory ace Capt. Billy Gresham took off from Mokmer on a local flight for a two hour flight to test one of the new P-38Ls. After more than two hours had passed and the Controller was unable to contact Gresham by radio Air and Sea Rescue sent out a search plane. The search spotted a smoking wreck about 10 miles northwest of Borokoe Airdrome on Biak. A search party was sent out the next day and Gresham's body was found in his partially opened parachute.

**7 October 1944: 418NFS**
The air echelon of the 418th had just arrived at Morotai two days earlier but poor weather prevented them from flying. On the 7th P-61 pilot, Maj. Carroll Smith and Radar Operator, 2Lt. Philip Porter, took off on a routine patrol mission over the Morotai area at 0215 and were in the air for 45 minutes at 10,500 feet when they were vectored to 210 degrees toward a possible bogey. After a few minutes the Controller gave a new vector for a definite enemy plot at six miles passing from right to left. R/O Porter took over using his SCR-720 Radar Scope and instructed Smith to begin a steep climbing turn at full throttle using water injection. Upon reaching

**Maj. Carroll Smith** shot down a Dinah over Morotai for his second victory. (AAF)

17,000 feet a visual contact with a Dinah was made at 2,000 feet astern. Smith closed to 300-400 yards and opened fire down to 150 feet and the P-61's 20mm cannon hit the port engine and wings. Smith pulled along side the Dinah and then made a turn to get a deflection shot using his last ammunition from 200 yards. The enemy dove to the right, did a wing over to the left and spun into a tight spiral and was lost from view at 12,000 feet over the water 12 miles south of Morotai. Porter had difficulty seeing the enemy because of all the smoke from the Black Widow's guns. Soon ground AA fire came up and Porter radioed the CCI for further information and was told that the Dinah was no longer on their scope and probably had been shot down. This was Smith's second victory, first in the P-61, since 13 January when he scored in a P-38.

**8 October 1944: 348FG/341FS**

Seven victory ace and 341FS CO, Maj. John Moore, descended through clouds in bad weather over Ceram Island to find his assigned target and was not seen again.

**9 October 1944: 348FG**

The first Japanese raid on the 348th's base at Noemfoor occurred on the night of 8/9 October when a lone Japanese bomber flew over at 0230 and made a south to north pass over Komasoren dropping three phosphorus bombs. The price it paid for destroying the 341st's shower was to be shot down by

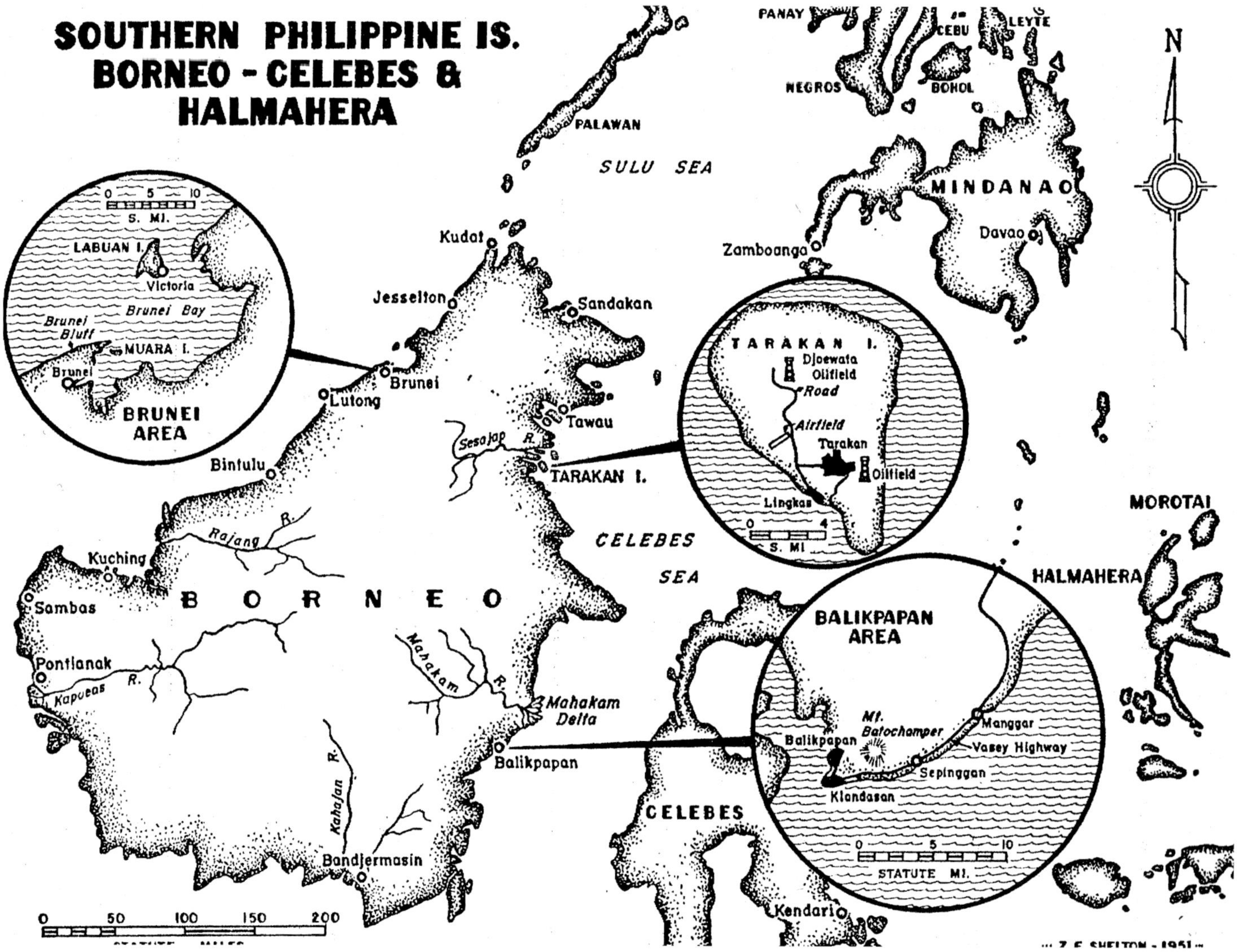

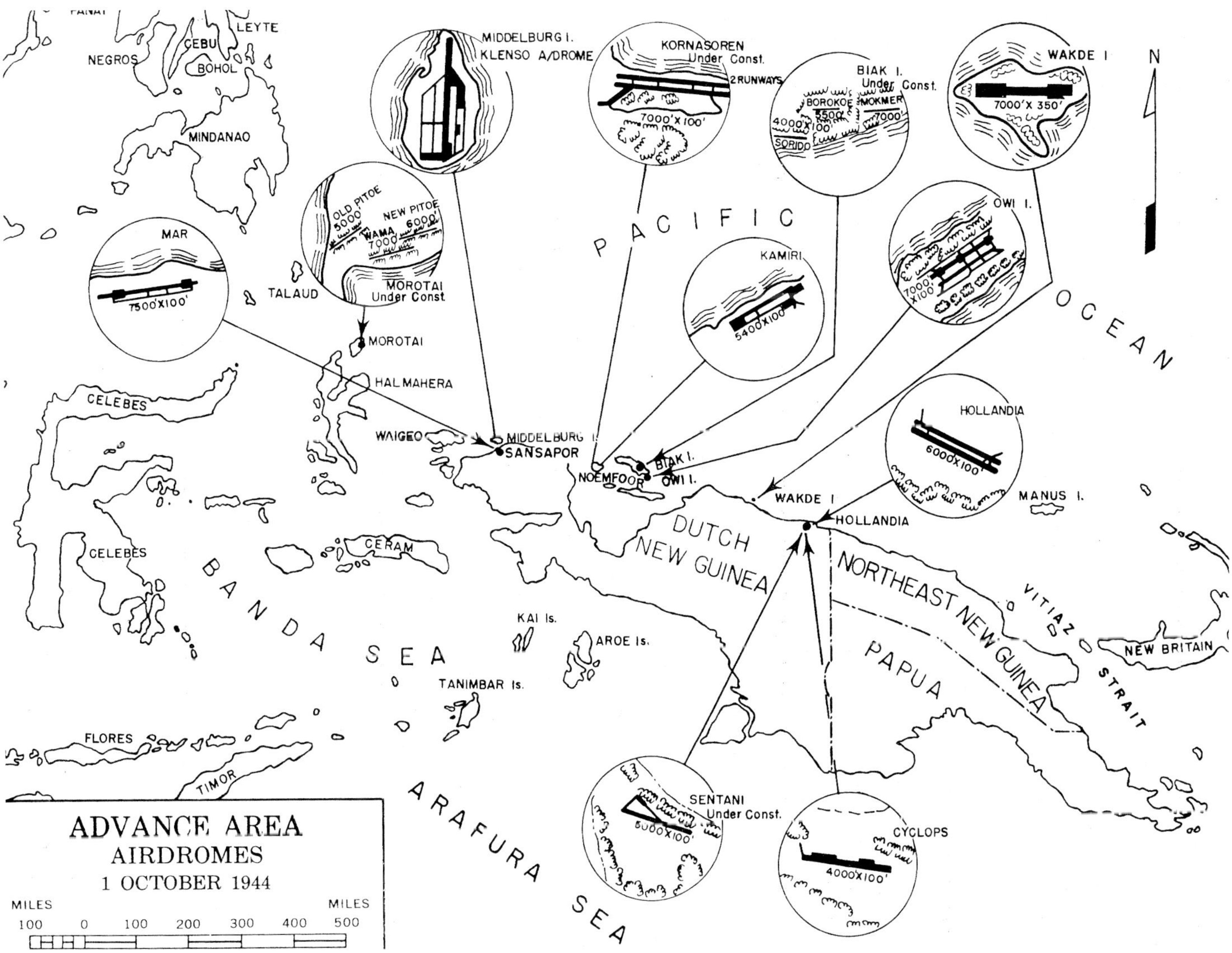


base AA fire. That day the 340FS retaliated when 14 P-47s attacked Boela and Liang Airdromes in the Ambon-Ceram area. Three P-47s dropped 500 pound bombs on Boela and started a fire and the 11 other P-47s cratered Liang strip and its dispersal areas. One P-47 and its pilot, 1Lt. Warren Howland, were missing after the raid. Howland was last seen only 10 miles from base but disappeared without a trace.

### Balikpapan

Since 1942 the Allied air Forces were unable to attack the enemy occupied oil fields and refineries at Balikpapan, Borneo. A few attacks were made by the 380th Bomb Group in 1943 but these were too small to do significant damage to the oil installations there. In summer 1944 Gen. Kenney had requested the loan of two B-29 groups from the 20th Bomber Command to attack the oil facilities at Balikpapan but had been unsuccessful. It was then decided that as soon as possible heavy bombers from the Fifth Air Force and Thirteenth Air Force would fly the long 1,080 nautical mile route from Noemfoor to Balikpapan. Initially the 5th and 307th Heavy Bomber Groups of the Thirteenth Air Force led the way to the Borneo targets unescorted. Although the first mission of 72 B-24s was harassed by enemy fighters it proved that the heavy bombers could reach the target with sufficient fuel to return with good bombing results and minimal losses (four B-24s). However, the second mission 3 October had different results as seven of the 307BG's 20 B-24s were lost. It was determined that future attacks on Balikpapan would require fighter escort. If 5BC B-24s were to attack Balikpapan Kenney decided that the long range cruise control techniques that the P-38 pilots learned would be thoroughly tested. Ground crewmen had determined that a 310 gallon tank could be mounted under one wing of the new model P-47s and P-38s and a 165 gallon tank under the other wing. With this additional fuel these fighters could fly to Balikpapan from Sansapor or Morotai with some fuel to spare.

### Early October 1944: Balikpapan: Planning for Fighter Cover

As early as mid-1943 the massive shipment, refining, and storage of many months supply of oil from the Balikpapan fields on Borneo to Japan was a major concern of Allied strategy. If the Japanese accumulated sufficient oil reserves then the planned future American Naval blockade of the Home Islands would become ineffective. To deal with this potential problem Allied planners decided that strategic bombing of the oil fields was necessary. One unescorted bomber mission from New Guinea in October 1943 produced no palpable results but a year later advances in the SWPA and Charles Lindbergh's input on extending the range of escorting fighters made more concerted attacks on Balikpapan possible.

When Kenney returned to his HQ at Owi he told Wurtsmith to investigate providing fighter cover for Balikpapan from Morotai which was 830 miles away and to be ready in three days. Kenney also wanted to know the distance the P-38s could escort the bombers if the fighters operated

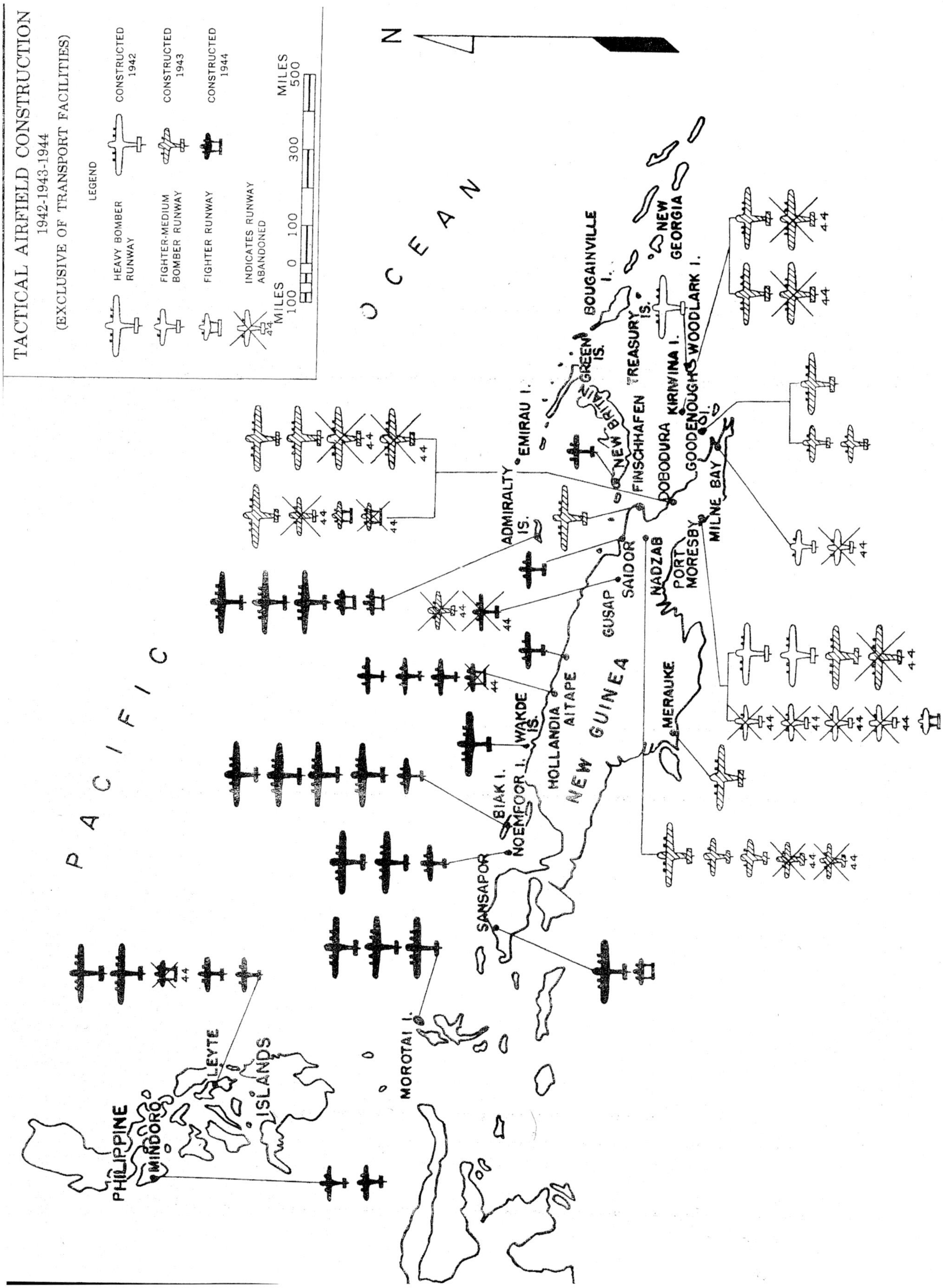
TACTICAL AIRFIELD CONSTRUCTION
1942-1943-1944
(EXCLUSIVE OF TRANSPORT FACILITIES)
LEGEND
HEAVY BOMBER RUNWAY
FIGHTER-MEDIUM BOMBER RUNWAY
FIGHTER RUNWAY
INDICATES RUNWAY ABANDONED
CONSTRUCTED 1942
CONSTRUCTED 1943
CONSTRUCTED 1944
MILES 100 0 100 300 500 MILES
N
PACIFIC OCEAN
NEW GEORGIA
BOUGAINVILLE I.
TREASURY IS.
WOODLARK I.
GREEN IS.
NEW BRITAIN
KIRIWINA I.
GOODENOUGH I.
EMIRAU I.
FINSCHHAFEN
DOBODURA
MILNE BAY
ADMIRALTY IS.
SAIDOR
NADZAB
PORT MORESBY
GUSAP
AITAPE
NEW GUINEA
WAKDE IS.
HOLLANDIA
MERAUKE
BIAK I.
NOEMFOOR I.
SANSAPOR
MOROTAI I.
LEYTE
PHILIPPINE ISLANDS
MINDORO
44

The **Balikpapan** mission was the first test of 5FC long range fighter escort when it escorted 106 heavy bombers. (AAF)

out of Sansapor, which was 1,000 miles from Balikpapan. Previously, the longest fighter mission flown by P-38s operating out of Sansapor was to escort heavy bombers 1,650 miles to Davao and back. Wurtsmith consulted his fighter pilots and 50 would accompany the bombers from Sansapor to Balikpapan and cover them during the bombing. Of course, this meant that they would have only enough fuel to get a third of the way back to base but if Kenney "would just send six or seven rescue Catalinas out to meet them, they would fly as long as they could and then simply parachute down and get picked up by the Cats." Kenney asked Wurtsmith where he found 50 "kids that crazy" and Wurtsmith replied, "If you will let them go, I'll get you 200 in half an hour." Kenney vetoed that scheme.

Later that day Wurtsmith said that as soon as Morotai was operational; fighter support could be furnished by not only P-38s but also by P-47s if the runways were lengthened somewhat and two 300 gallon, droppable, auxiliary fuel tanks were hung on the wings instead of the standard 165 gallon tanks. Kenney instructed Col. Donald "Fighter" Hutchinson, his Air Task Force Commander at Morotai, to add another 500 feet of runway completed by the afternoon of the 9th but he could not complete it until the 11th.

**10 October 1944: Balikpapan**

At 1030 on 10 October was the first test of the 5AF long range fighter escort of 106 heavy bombers to Balikpapan which would involve flying distances longer than any yet flown by an American fighter in the war. The distance from Morotai to the Halmaheras and then to Borneo was 835 miles one way. In planning the mission American fighter aircraft were tested for range and fuel consumption and only the P-47 and P-38 was adequate for the task. The plan of attack for the Balikpapan raid was for the fighters to reach the target before the bombers to draw up the enemy fighters to sweep the area so the bombers had a chance to complete their bombing run unopposed.

The Pandasari Refinery was badly damaged and recon photo interpreters put it "out of action for months" while the lubricating oil refinery was damaged but could be repaired in a month. Three of four large storage tanks were destroyed and 10 out of 38 smaller tanks destroyed. The Japanese sent up 90 fighters and lost 61 while the 5AF lost four bombers (one crew rescued) and one fighter.

**10 October 1944: 35FG/40FS/41FS**

The 35FG sent out 25 P-47s, 11 from the 40FS and 14 from the 41FS. "Our instructions were to work over any Nip fighters we saw in the area…we were told that we definitely were *not* to fly cover for the bombers." The weather was not good at take off and got worse as the mission continued and it appeared for a time that it would be scrubbed.

40FS

The three 40FS flights, totaling 11 fighters, led by Capt. Charles Clark (White Flight), Capt. John Young (Red Flight), and 1Lt. William Strand

**Capt. John Young** shot down two Zeros for two of his three total victories. (AAF)

The **Pandasari Refinery** was badly damaged, and recon photo interpreters considered it "out of action for months." (AAF)

(Blue Flight) took off at 0630 and almost immediately ran into dreadful weather and had to make course alterations to avoid cloud formations adding many more miles to the already lengthy mission. First 40FS Thunderbolts over the target at 1015 were six Red and White Flight P-47s as five aircraft returned early due to the bad weather. 1Lt. Thomas Powell moved up as Young's wingmen and Capt. Linfield Poteet became Clark's wingmen and these two flights then consolidated while Blue Flight was composed of Strand and his Wingman, 1Lt. Hilton Kessel, and arrived last over the target at 1025. The weather over Manggar Strip was much improved and the combined flight circled at 19,000 feet when they saw Japanese fighters taking off below. The pilots were instructed not drop their tanks for combat as the fuel would be needed to get back to base. Also, they did not dive from 19,000 feet on the enemy fighter as they were taking off as that would require too much fuel to climb back and then perhaps climb higher over more bad weather on the way home.

Capt. Clark waited until the Japanese reached 10,000 feet before attacking and then he and Poteet spiraled down in trail and three Oscars in a V were in a right turn when they arrived behind them. Clark closed to 250 yards on the left fighter and then fired a two second burst and hit it just behind the cockpit and it went out control on fire. Poteet also took a quick shot at this Oscar before he and Clark turned into two Oscars heading toward them. Clark hit one for a probable and Poteet took a 90 degree deflection shot as it peeled out in front of him but was unable to hold his lead and broke off to rejoin Clark. The two left the battle, hoping they had enough fuel to get back to base. About ten minutes later they saw a twin engine Nick at 13,000 feet and 2 o'clock low. Clark dove first and fired a port high side pass and Poteet followed with a three second burst from astern before he overran the enemy fighter that was trailing smoke. Poteet followed and got a four second burst just after the enemy pilot made a sharp pull out at 4,000 feet and its left engine started on fire and the Nick spun and crashed into the water for Poteet's only victory.

At this time Young and Powell of White Flight were joined by Blue Flight and dove from 19,000 feet on a formation of five Zeros at 9,000 feet. Young used his diving speed to get under and then zoom up on the last fighter and fired a one second burst and its pilot bailed out as his Zero crashed into the sea. At the end of his pass Young put his Thunderbolt into water injection and zoomed up several thousand feet to get to the other four Zeros. He closed rapidly on the fourth Zero and fired into the wing roots starting a fire that ended in a spiraling crash for his second of two victories. Powell did not fire on his first pass but on the second followed Young who attacked the fourth Zero while Powell pursued on the leader. Powell followed it in a sharp, steep climbing port turn to 150 yards behind the Zero and fired from about 50 degrees and got hits in the cockpit and engine and it snapped over and crashed for his only victory. As he passed over the Zero Powell's engine cowling was hit by one of the falling pieces.

Strand and Kessel joined Blue Flight in the battle by diving out of the sun on four Oscars. Strand fired from dead astern at 250 yards and hit the engine and the pilot bailed out. Strand and Kessel climbed into the sun and attacked five Oscars. Strand fired on the leader's Wingman and closed to 250 yards dead astern and it rolled over and its pilot also bailed out. Kessel closed and also shot down an Oscar. The two Americans climbed into the sun again and picked out four more Oscars and attacked. Three alert Oscars Split-S'd out of the battle but Strand closed on the leader and started firing at 200 yards until it burst into flames and crashed for his third victory of the day to give him four victories. During this pass Kessel became separated from Strand and was never seen again, the only P-47 lost during the mission. The weather on the return was poor and required the tired pilots to navigate round towering rain clouds but all pilots returned safely, arriving around 1430 after eight hour in the air.

41FS

The 41FS sent out 14 P-47s which arrived over Manggar Strip at 20,000 feet at 1025 to conduct a fighter sweep prior to the bombers arriving at Balikpapan. The flights arrived with low fuel reserve due encountering bad weather on the way with most pilots having only enough fuel to make one pass. As they circled the Strip they saw at least a dozen enemy fighters taking off and then 14 more in the air at 3,000 feet and climbing. The American flights descended in a gentle spiral turn to 13,000 feet. There were three Hamps in a string formation trying to cover an Oscar that seemed to be having some problems at 8,000 feet. As Capt. Robert Dorothy led his Blue Flight down two of the Hamps pulled up in a stall turn toward them. The lead Hamp fired ahead from out of range, perhaps to scare the P-47s off. When Dorothy closed to 500 yards at 350 mph and fired a short burst and at 200 yards he hit the Hamp again and it fell off spiraling straight down for his only victory. Dorothy's Wingman, 2Lt. Robert Gustavson, also made a single pass and downed the second Hamp with a long burst and also headed for home as the Hamp plummeted out of control for his only victory. 1Lt. James Scott, Dorothy's Second Element Leader flying at 6,000 feet went after the third Hamp at 8,000 feet in a 90 degree bank. Scott skidded into a 90 degree bank and climbed to 200 yards and fired and despite having only one gun working shot it down for his last of two victories. These victories were the 35th Group's first since 15 March.

**10 October 1944: 49FG/9FS**

The Balikpapen mission was to be challenging and despite the experience gained in the tactical missions being flown by the pilots of the 7th and 8th Squadron in their not so new Lightnings, 49th Group Ops Exec, Maj. Gerald Johnson advised Group CO, Lt.Col. George Walker to select the veteran pilots of the 9th Squadron and from the 49er Headquarters for the mission. On 9 October, 49er CO Walker led 15 Lightnings to the staging base on Morotai, which was the northern most island in the Moluccas. They landed at the crowded airfield and joined the P-47s from the 35FG.

At 0700, the 49er's Lightnings and the 35th's Thunderbolts took off from the Morotai and headed southwest at 10,000 feet for the 850 mile flight to Borneo. The Wingman in Jordan's three ship flight experienced equipment failure and aborted and Element Leader Capt. William Williams became Jordan's Wingman. The remaining 14 P-38s arrived at the Celebes over the Makassar Strait where Walker had his flights begin to climb to rendezvous with the B-24s that had flown a direct course from Biak. At the scheduled rendezvous at 1100, the P-38s and P-47s met the bomber formation near the Borneo coast. The mission check point on the coast line was the river

**Lt.Col. George Walker**, 49FG CO (left), and **Maj. Gerald Johnson**, 49FG XO (right), planned the mission, consisting of selected veteran pilots, including Majors Richard Bong (2nd right) and Wallace Jordan (2nd left). (AAF)

**Manggar Airfrome.** (AAF)

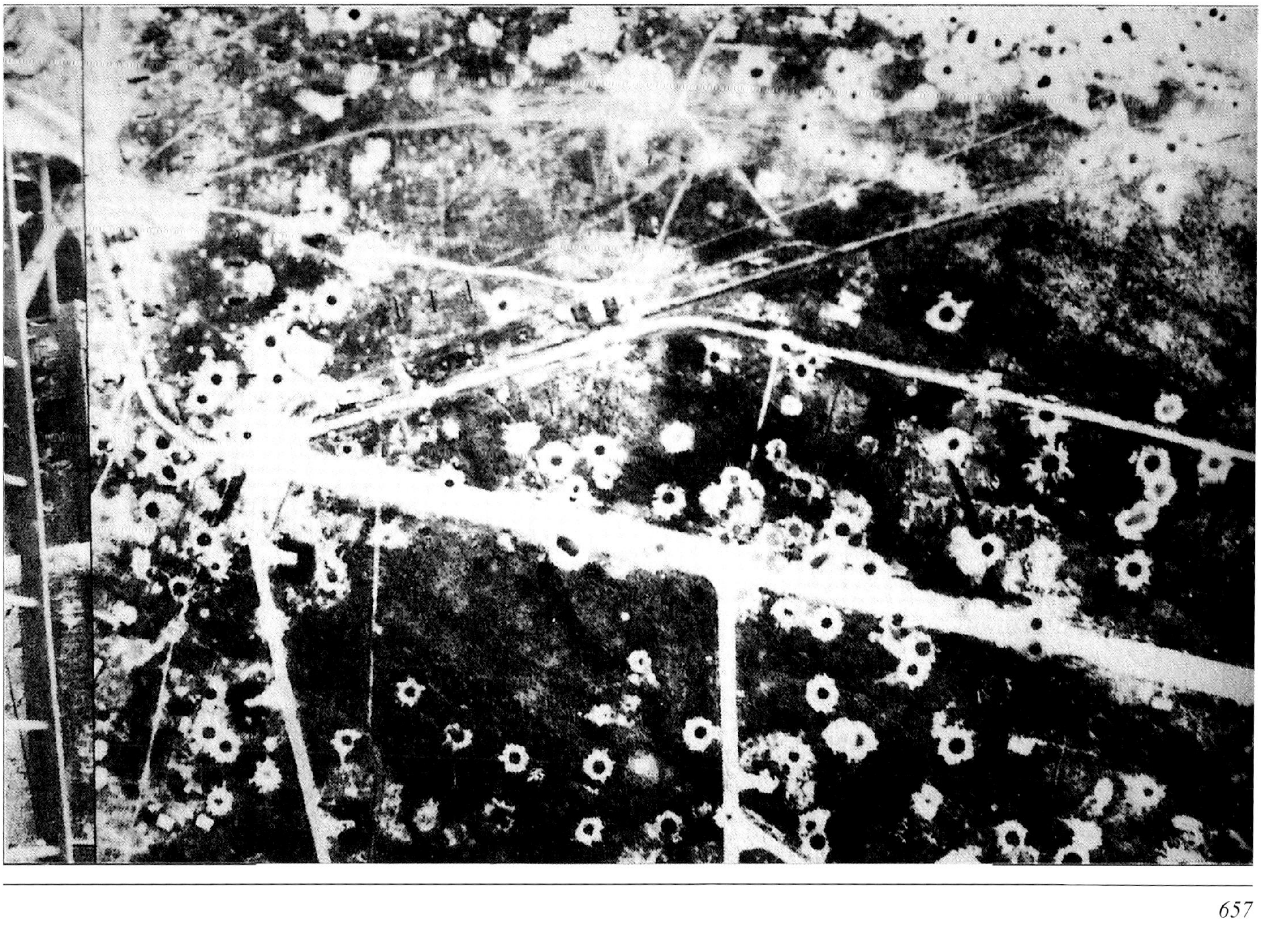

**Maj. Richard Bong** returned from furlough and scored two victories to make him a triple ace. (AAF)

While back in the States **Bong** became engaged to **Marge Vattendahl**, whose picture adorned his Lighting. (AAF)

During the mission (left to right), Majors **Richard Bong** and **Wallace Jordan** and 1Lts. **Edward Howes** and **Warren Curton** all scored victories. (AAF)

delta 10 miles north of the Balikpapen Harbor and the oil refinery. When the formation arrived at the delta, Jordan and Williams' Red Flight flew inland at 15,000 feet to the Manggar Airdrome which based fighters defending the oil field and refinery complex. Over the airdrome Jordan's flight spotted six radial engine enemy fighters at 3,000 to 7,000 feet.

**Maj. Wallace Jordan** shot down two enemy aircraft to become an ace. (AFAA)

**1Lt. Edward Howes'** victory over a Zero was his fourth and last of the war. (AAF)

Lt.Col. Walker's Blue Flight of Wingman, 1Lt. Warren Curton, and Element Leader, Maj. Richard Bong, and Wingman HQ Staff Officer, Capt. Robert Baker. While other Blue Flight pilots were concerned with the single engine interceptors, Bong spotted a lone twin engine aircraft flying below the Lightnings at 5,000 feet. Bong, followed by Baker, snapped into a quick wingover and seconds later, Bong overtook the twin engine Irving for his 29th victory. The Japanese naval pilot bailed out just before his aircraft exploded and Bong and Baker quickly rejoined Walker. Walker then ordered the White Flight to remain in high cover and allowed the 10 Lightnings of the other elements to attack the Oscars which had now turned to intercept.

Though he was the Group CO, Lt.Col. Walker was a combat rookie and fired at any enemy that passed in firing range or not and only damaged one. Wingman Curton tried to protect Walker as the Colonel maneuvered into position but a nimble Oscar lured Curton into a very tight turn that momentarily put him into a high speed stall. Curton recovered quickly and made one more pass with his CO. On the pass Walker attacked a pair of Oscars whose trailing Wingman suddenly

Back at their base at **Biak**, the pilots of the 5FC and 9FS pose after their record-breaking mission. (AAF)

turned from head on and the alert Curton caught the enemy fighter with a destructive burst and its engine was set on fire for his second victory. Blue Element Leader Bong and Wingman Baker attacked the Oscar formation and Bong became America's first 30 victory ace when his victim disintegrated in a ball of fire.

Maj. Jordan had also sighted another solo Irving at 12,000 feet stalking the Liberators. Jordan turned through a Split-S against the sun and unsuspecting Irving pilot was caught in his flaming aircraft as it plunged into the sea. Jordan and Wingman Williams reformed, and joined Walker's Blue Flight. Jordan and Williams' Red Flight attacked the Oscars next and after several skilful maneuvers Jordan shot down an Oscar which rolled over and plunged into the Strait, to make him an ace. However, the Oscars had the numerical and then the tactical advantage and the Lightnings retreated from the battle.

1Lt. Edward Howes' Green Flight had been slightly behind the lead flights and its elements separated during their long turning descent into the battle. Howes overtook a Zeke and approached from beneath at dead astern and then made a quick climb to within point blank range and killed the pilot and the victim snap rolled and dove into the Strait for his fourth and last victory. Howes and Wingman 1Lt. Frederick Helterline then saw a pair of Oscars turn from above and one dropped aerial bombs at the rear flank of the retreating B-24s which detonated well behind their targets. Helterline went into a pursuit curve after the trailing Oscar which quickly rolled away and disappeared into the haze along the coast. Howes and Helterline rejoined and turned toward home.

**12 October 1944: 8FG/35FS**

35FS CO, Capt. Lee Everhart, led five P-38s to dive bomb Mapanger Airdrome on Celebes Island while six other Lightnings would attack nearby Sidate Airdrome after which all the P-38s would strafe Langoan Airdrome on their way home. Everhart's flight approached Mapanger from the northwest and turned south to fly directly down the strip for their bombing run. Everhart dove first from 7,000 feet and dropped his bombs at 3,000 feet and pulled out at around 1,500 feet when his left engine begin to smoke. Everhart pulled up into a starboard turn when his engine burst into flame and the burning P-38 nosed over and went into a vertical dive, disappearing into the overcast at 1,000 feet. Ironically, while circling for their attack the pilots saw previous bomb craters on the runway and that the field was already unusable. Everhart never returned and Capt. Lynn Witt took over command of the 35FS.

**13 October 1944: 475FG/431FS**

2Lt. Donald Patterson was MIA during a training flight from Noemfoor.

**14 October 1944: Return to Balikpapan**

A return attack to Balikpapan was postponed for four days due to poor weather. It was expected that after the first American attack that the Japanese would increase their fighter strength over the target. To deal with this expectation the Thunderbolts of the 35FG would leave 15 minutes ahead of the main force for a pre-attack fighter sweep. At 0645 the next morning 33 P-38s of the 9th and 432nd Squadrons were ready to take off on a round trip of more than 1,000 miles. The 432FS still had enough pilots remaining at Mokmer to form a 16 plane flight for the last B-24 escort to Balikpapan. The Clover P-38s were assigned to escort the 13AF B-24s which were to follow the 5AF bombers that were to be escorted by 9FS Lightnings. Lt.Col. Meryl Smith flew in from Headquarters to lead the escort as Clover Red One while the 9FS escort was led by Maj. Wallace Jordan. Two top 5FC aces were flying together on the escort; Maj. Gerald Johnson (11 victories) of 9FS (coded "Captive") White Flight and Maj. Thomas McGuire (21 victories) who managed to fly on the mission in a borrowed brand new 9FS P-38L since his 431st squadron was being transferred on the *SS Charlotte Cushman*.

The return attack to **Balikpapan** was postponed for four days due to poor weather. It was expected that, after the first American attack, the Japanese would increase their fighter strength over the target. (AAF)

**14 October 1944: 35F/40FS/41FS**

40FS

At 0625 eight P-47s of Red and White Flights took off on an offensive bomber escort over Balikpapan. Red Flight consisted of Leader, Capt. John Young, and wingmen, 1Lt. Philip Thomas and 1Lt. William Strand. (Young's original Wingman aborted the flight soon after take off) while White Flight was composed of Leader, Capt. Alvaro Hunter, and Wingman, 1Lt. Jack Simonini, and Second Element Leader, 1Lt. Henry Wilkes, and Wingman, 1Lt. Daniel Laird. The two flights cruised toward Balikpapan at 7,000 feet and 45 minutes before the target started a climb to 24,000 feet and arrived at 1030 before the B-24s. White flight stationed itself 500 feet above Red Flight and both flights began circling the area using the remaining fuel in their wing tanks. They had not completed a half circle when Young spotted Zeros circling for altitude at 1035. The Zeros broke off and Young then dove on a flight of four Oscars at 18,000 feet. As he approached the last Oscar the entire enemy flight made a sharp turn and he was only able fired a short burst. The Oscar pilot evaded most of Young's bullets by slowing and half rolling but several hit its fuselage as the pilot dove away as a probable. Young then zoomed up to 20,000 feet and saw "about 25 Nips all over the target area." He dove again on another flight of four Oscars and arrived beneath the tail of the last enemy. He fired a two second burst and the Oscar caught fire and fell apart into the sea for his third and final victory (plus two probables and a damaged claim). Young again climbed and found another enemy flight at 18,000 feet and repeated his attack on this last man but the Oscar pilot turned short and rolled out away from the onrushing P-47 at 14,000 feet. Young wanted to maintain altitude to conserve fuel and broke off the combat to head home. Thomas did not fire on the initial pass and became separated from Young. Thomas saw a lone Zero about 1,000 feet below heading out to sea and closed quickly at 300 mph. He fired a long burst into it from 100 yards and had to pull up sharply to avoid the debris from the explosion. Thomas turned and saw Strand who had peeled off from the initial attack diving on two Oscars at 15,000 feet. Strand made a dead astern firing pass at from 250-275 yards on the enemy Wingman which exploded. The Oscar leader then turned across Strand's line of fire and was subjected to a hail of fired which set its engine on fire. The Oscar pilot rolled over and bailed out. Strand climbed to 19,000 feet and made a firing pass in a vertical dive but saw no results and headed home. About ten minutes later he saw a lone Sally bomber but did not dare to attack for fear of using too much fuel. Meanwhile, Thomas saw three Oscars circling to the left at 11 o'clock, slightly below and got into position for a head on pass. As he got into range two Oscars broke off left while the last one made a slight turn to the right. Thomas fired a short burst at this last fighter which slow rolled and Split-S'd away into the ground. Thomas saw a solo Tony at 90 degrees and took a 90 degree deflection shot tearing off pieces. The wounded Tony turned tightly and Split-S'd away as a probable claim to go with Thomas' only victory of the war. Thomas' engine began to run rough and he headed back to base where he landed at 1430 with less than 20 gallons of gasoline and a blown master cylinder in his tough Pratt & Whitney R-2800 engine. Strand had even more problems on his return as his main tank was leaking fuel. As he neared Paloe Bay which was a

**1Lt. William Strand** scored two victories to make him an ace with six of his seven total victories. (AFAA)

**1Lt. Alvaro Hunter** claimed two victories to give him four. (AFAA)

designated rendezvous point with the *Daylight* rescue Catalina he radioed its pilot that he was going to ditch. Strand saw the PBY floating about two miles out to sea and ditched his Thunderbolt next to it and was immediately picked up. Strand's two victories made him an ace with six.

Hunter's White Flight circled at 24,500 feet and also almost immediately saw three Oscars climbing at 20,000 feet and dropped their tanks. The flight dove under them and closed on the left rear Wingman from slightly behind. Hunter held his fire until he was very close and tore pieces off and it exploded as Hunter was pulling up and away. Hunter then led the flight up to 22,000 feet and circled in position to bounce another mixed formation of Oscars and Zeros at 17,000 feet. Duplicating his previous pass, Hunter dove and closed on the left rear Wingman until he was very close and fired, apparently surprising the entire enemy formation. Hunter left enemy Wingman which was enveloped in flames for his fourth victory. As Hunter turned away he saw two more enemy fighters going down. After not firing on the first pass Simonini went after the right Wingman which made a slight right turn before Simonini got dead astern and shot off a large piece from the dorsal fuselage and then hit the cockpit and the Zero went down in flames for his only victory. Hunter didn't see Simonini again and was chased by three Oscars and headed for home; not bothering with an enemy bomber 20 miles away. Simonini also headed for home but was attacked from head on and evaded by diving. The Zero followed in a Split-S and continued to fire; shooting off Simonini's fortunately empty wing tank that hadn't released. He shook his pursuer and returned to base. Meanwhile, Hunter's second element, Wilkes and Laird, both made attacks on their first pass. Wilkes took the lead fighter while Laird took the rear both of which were turning and climbing into them. Wilkes fired a 60 degree head on pass that hit the engine and cockpit and the enemy Split-S'd out of control. Wilkes turned and saw a Zero on the tail of a P-47 with its pilot (Laird) calling for help on the radio. Wilkes dove and got a 30 degree deflection shot from slightly above getting hits. The Japanese pilot started to turn into the attacker but then Split-S'd and Wilkes followed through on his back at 40 degrees and fired hitting the engine, cockpit, and wing roots dooming the Zero for his first two of three victories. Wilkes then went after a Tojo but as he approached he saw that it was another P-47 and dove on two Zeros below him but with two other Zeros on his tail. He fired a 90 degree deflection and may have gotten some hits on a wing but had to break off when tracers whizzed past his cockpit. Wilkes turned on the water injection and headed home. His Wingman, Laird had fired and missed on his first run and then missed again on the second run on the rear Oscar. Wilkes then shot the pursuing Zero off Laird's tail after which Laird rolled over on an Oscar that had just recovered out of a Split-S. The surprised Japanese pilot never saw the P-47 that hit its wing roots and sent into the ground for Laird's first of four victories. Laird pulled up and his fighter started to vibrate and oil flowed over his canopy. As Laird headed for a rendezvous with the *Daylight* rescue PBY another Zero got on his tail and 1Lt. Walter Sweeney of the 41FS chased it away. After Laird safely crash landed on the beach in enemy territory and just moved away when a Lightning came down and strafed the Thunderbolt and set it on fire. Laird waded out into the water and was picked up by *Daylight* PBY in less than 30 minutes.

41FS

The 41FS sent out eight P-47s to Manggar on a fighter sweep prior to the arrival of the B-24s. The Squadron was over the Strip at 1035 at 19,000 feet headed for the refineries at Balikpapan. The P-47 pilots made S-turns over the coast and when they saw 10 enemy fighters at 18,000 feet doing aerobatics at 11 o'clock about two miles away they dropped their tanks. 1Lt. Robert Johnson, Red Flight Leader, led his flight on four Oscars and he attacked the left Oscar that tried to evade by climbing into a stall. Johnson climbed with it and fired at 10 degrees deflection from 200 to 100 yards setting the stalled Oscar into a ball of fire. Johnson then chandelled up to port and leveled off and saw a P-47 trailing smoke over Makassar Strait at 12,000 to 14,000 feet with an Oscar following. Johnson chased the Oscar and closed to 300 yards and started to fire on the surprised enemy pilot who went down in his smoking fighter for Johnson's fourth and last victories. Meanwhile, as Johnson was shooting down his Oscar, 1Lt. James Mugavero, Johnson's Wingman, picked out the rear Oscar and exploded it. Mugavero Split-S'd and then saw another Oscar at 3,000 feet below and made an overhead pass firing until he was on its tail and saw smoke and fire in its wing roots and its canopy flew off and the Oscar spun wildly for Mugavero's first two victories toward becoming an ace. Mugavero looked around and saw that he was still being followed and immediately Split-S'd and dove at 450IAS and when he pulled out at 2,000 feet his pursuer was gone. He ended his dive over Manggar Drome and saw aircraft parked wing tip to wing tip but he decided to head home as "I thought I had done enough for today."

Red Second Element Leader, 1Lt. Walter Sweeney, covered Johnson and Mugavero, and shot an Oscar off Mugavero's tail while his Wingman, 1Lt. Raymond Wiedemeyer, shot an Oscar off Sweeney's tail but the last time Sweeney saw Wiedemeyer his Wingman had a Zero on his tail. Sweeney dove to 8,000 feet and leveled off and saw another P-47 (40FS 1Lt. Darrell Laird) being chased by a Zero, Sweeney got in close and fired a short lethal burst but had to flee from another enemy fighter on his tail. Sweeney's two victories and Wiedemeyer's one were their only victories of the war.

Capt. Frank Fariello, White Flight Leader, and his Wingman, 2Lt. Francis Riedle, attacked the Oscars. Fariello fired at an Oscar at very close range, 75 to 50 yards, and Riedle also got a few hits before the pilot bailed out but the victory was Fariello's only one of the war. Riedle was unable to follow Fariello and saw an Oscar at 15,000 feet shot an Oscar off Johnson's tail for the first of his two victories.

On Johnson's return to base four P-38s came up on him and the leader and then his Wingman began to fire from out of range. Johnson tried to dip his wing to show them his Star and Bar but felt bullets hit his aircraft and saw smoke trail behind his fighter. He ducked into a cloud and lost the Lightnings and radioed two *Daylight* rescue PBYs for a rendezvous. With his engine sputtering badly he decided to bail out but as he left the cockpit his foot caught the seat armor plate. After he stumbled out of the cockpit his left shoulder and right leg hit the tailplane but he managed to pull the rip cord at 800 feet and make a soft landing in the water. His legs got tangled in the chute shroud lines and had to use the knife strapped to his right leg to cut them despite having his left arm and right leg immobilized. His Mae West and raft inflated but the raft was upside down and he had great trouble in righting it with his injuries and then was unable to bail it out. P-38s covering *Daylight* found Johnson and led the PBY to him. While, *Daylight* was rescuing Johnson, 1Lt. William Strand ditched closed by and was also picked up.

**14 October 1944: 49FG/9FS**

When the P-38 pilots arrived the Lightning pilots could see 35FG Thunderbolts in battle with the Japanese defenders from the Manggar Airdrome. After flying to the target in clear weather, the 9FS reached Balikpapan at 1030 the clouds were heavier, 4/10 to 6/10, in which enemy fighters could conceal themselves.

The White Flight was composed of Ops Exec Gerald Johnson in the lead with 9FS Wingman 1Lt. Harold Oglesby, with Maj. Thomas McGuire, Commander of the 431FS as the trailing man (another pilot had left Johnson's flight in route). McGuire had surpassed Lynch's 20 victory total and was one behind Kearby's 22, but only Bong remained alive and had a higher total, and Bong's record total became an obsession for the insufferable McGuire. Johnson was not satisfied with only 11 victories to date, and he and McGuire were high at the front of the strike force; both of the self centered aces left formation for combat, forcing the exasperated Mission Leader Walker and his Green Flight to remain in high cover. Captive White Flight led by Johnson as Captive White One and McGuire as White Two was at 19,000 feet about 15 to 20 miles from the target when 30 to 35 Tojo and Oscar fighters were seen rolling and looping above.

Johnson led McGuire into a left climbing turn to get an altitude advantage. Johnson Spilt-S'd on an Oscar making a dive on the bombers and fired getting hits but overran it and McGuire then throttled back and got dead astern and further damaged the Oscar. McGuire then fired a long burst that set the fuselage on fire and as the fighter plummeted its pilot bailed out. Johnson attacked an Oscar from astern as it was flying across the bomber formation. Johnson saw hits on its wing and fuselage and it smoked and then burst into flames as he passed over it. Johnson then made a starboard diving turn and attacked a Tojo from astern and "rode up its tail" and exploded it before it could drop the phosphorous bombs from under its wings to give Johnson 14 victories. Johnson and McGuire regained altitude and McGuire

**1Lt. Howard Oglesby** claimed his first two of four victories. (AAF)

**Maj. Gerald Johnson** was awarded his 12th and 13th victories. (AFAA)

**1Lt. Edwin Cooper** scored his first of two victories. (AAF)

**Maj. Thomas McGuire** scored a career high four daily victories to give him 24 victories, to put him in second place only behind Bong. (AFAA)

**1Lt. Leslie Nelson** scored the last three of his four victories. (AAF)

**Maj. Wallace Jordan** got a probable and his sixth and last victory. (AFAA)

The **49FG** scored 10 victories over Balikpapan (left to right): 1Lt. Howard Oglesby (2v.), 1Lt. Edwin Cooper (1v.), Capt. William Williams (1v.), Maj. Wallace Jordan (1v.), Maj. Gerald Johnson (2v.), and 1Lt. Leslie Nelson (3v.). (AAF)

peeled off to attack a Hamp, knocking off pieces of its tail and then setting its fuselage on fire. McGuire then made a 20 degree deflection pass on an Oscar that began smoking badly and spun from 15,000 feet but McGuire did not see it crash for a probable. Johnson and McGuire were jumped by enemy fighters and Johnson had a Tojo firing on him from dead astern but was lucky to find a nearby cloud to evade. Johnson and McGuire became separated and Johnson made several full deflection passes without result and then was chased by three Oscars for about five minutes staying just out of range of their gunfire. When they turned back Johnson made a 180 and caught the leader from above with a head on pass and it dove into the smoking for his second victory of the day. McGuire made several ineffective high deflection passes when he saw a Tojo chased by a P-38 (1Lt. Edwin Cooper of the 9FS who was credited with a Tojo on the mission) and Cooper tacked onto McGuire's wing. The two chased a Tojo from about 14,000 feet and followed it down to a cloud at 3,000 feet, firing from astern at 300 to 400 yards. It took McGuire awhile to dive and close on the smoking Tojo. Finally, speeding to 400 mph in a 40 degree dive, McGuire fired again and the Tojo began pouring black smoke as it entered a cloud. The two exited the cloud at 1,500 feet still on the enemy's tail. He fired another burst and the Tojo began to burn and suddenly inverted and McGuire had to make a quick turn to avoid a collision for third victory of the day and his 24th. On his way home Johnson saw a P-47 smoking heavily and headed for the sea with its flaps down. The Thunderbolt pilot made a perfect ditching and despite being low on fuel Johnson led a rescue PBY to the area. Once the pilot was rescued Johnson strafed the still floating P-47 three times before it burned and sunk.

Meanwhile, Oglesby was left behind by Johnson and McGuire and made a pass at an Oscar that Split-S'd away and then joined 1Lt. Leslie Nelson who had just shot down a Zero. Nelson had made a steep turn and roll, firing from 60 to 25 degrees, and exploded the Zero. Oglesby became separated from Nelson when they were attacked by a Zero. Oglesby climbed away and dove into the battle where he saw an Oscar on the tail of a P-38. Oglesby fired a shot in front of the Oscar hoping to scare it off but due to his excess speed he overran but his speed caused the Oscar to run into his gunfire and explode. Oglesby climbed to attack another Oscar which Split-S'd straight down and rolled out and the American followed it in a turn and started firing as it leveled out. He continued firing a long burst until he overran and saw the Oscar slowly roll over and spiral into the water for his first two of four victories. Oglesby continued on with Nelson who saw an Oscar at his altitude in a slight climb. Nelson tried to get a lead in a shallow dive but another P-38 came in a shot it down. Nelson climbed and saw a Zero to his port and began to turn into it as the enemy pilot began to turn into him but broke off up and to port. Nelson broke to the right and fired a two second burst into its canopy and it spiraled down. Nelson followed to finish it off but could not get into firing position but the Zero crashed into the water. Nelson climbed and made a pass at an Oscar but couldn't turn with it. Nelson reduced his speed to let the Oscar loop over him and dove to regain speed but another P-38 was speeding in from behind and Nelson pulled over a bit and let this Lightning "get in the shot and it exploded like a clay pigeon." Deprived of a third victory Nelson climbed with Oglesby and saw another Zero and "gave him a good burst into its cockpit from about 45 degrees." Nelson overran but Oglesby saw it crash and explode for Nelson's fourth and last victory of the war.

Capt. William Williams' Blue Flight also descended during the first pass against the Oscars. All pilots of the element fired but only Williams scored when he got on the tail of an Oscar and fired "quite a few bursts." The Oscar went into two slow rolls and went into a tight spin with large pieces flying off and its pilot bailed out. Williams climbed and saw another Oscar which dove into a cloud and followed it in and out of the clouds and finally fired from 250 yards without result and Williams was low on fuel and ammunition and left for the long flight home with his second of four victories.

As Leader of the Red Flight, Maj. Wallace Jordan and Wingman 1Lt. Edwin Cooper both made a firing pass on Oscar but it was Maj. Jordan who got credit for the victory with a two three second burst from astern for his sixth and last of the war. Jordan became separated in the twisting and turning combat and heavily damaged another Oscar. Cooper joined with White Flight's McGuire and Oglesby for their firing run on the Tojos. Cooper hit a Tojo which disintegrated for his first of two victories. Cooper then stayed with McGuire who had run out of ammo and the two turned for home. Of the other two Red Flight elements, Leader 1Lt. Robert Wood, was unable to jettison one of his tanks and joined the high cover. The Flying Knights climbed to 12,000 feet and made the long journey back to Morotai where they remained over night and the next morning, the pilots flew their fighters back to Mokmer to a welcome by cheering officers and ground crews.

After the mission McGuire reported: "The Japanese pilots seemed eager and experienced, although their attacks were not coordinated. Besides the bunch we fought there was another bunch of 15 to 20 dropping aerial burst bombs from above us and the bombers. I saw two parachutes and about 30 aerial bomb bursts."

After Col. McDonald returned to the 475th Fighter Group he supposedly berated McGuire for flying a mission with the 9FS at time when his squadron was in the process of relocating. To make matters worse, McGuire's three victories were credited to the 9FS. McGuire had become obsessed with becoming the top American fighter ace, especially since Bong had returned to combat and was six victories ahead of him with 30.

**14 October 1944: 475FG/432FS**

The 432FS took off from Biak in the afternoon of the day before and landed at the Morotai staging point. After taking off at 0645 the 16 Clover P-38s had passed the 13AF B-24s at 1015 at 12,000 feet about 45 minutes before reaching Balikpapan. Lt.Col. Meryl Smith was about 10 minutes from the target when he picked up the radio chatter from the dogfight ahead and AA bursts were seen over the target. When they reached the target, the first wave of 5AF B-24s were turning from their bombing run, and they saw the Thunderbolts of the 35FG shooting down Zekes and Oscars over Manggar Airdrome. When the Clover Squadron arrived over Balikpapan, McGuire and the other 9FS' Lightnings were leaving the area. However, there were at least six Zeros and Hamps circling at about 7,000 or 8,000 feet over the shoreline between the airfield and the town. Clover Red Flight (Lt.Col. Meryl Smith) immediately dove to the attack with Clover White (1Lt. Charles Ratajski) following in trail while Clover Blue (Capt. Harry Condon) remained above as top cover. As Lt.Col. Smith's Red Flight dove on the enemy fighters they escaped safely into the clouds. When they exited they kept their distance so the P-38s could not get any good shots and would not press their attacks even when they had the advantage. Smith fired at two enemy fighters without seeing any results but when a Hamp carelessly dove in front of Smith he fired a burst that hit the enemy's engine cowling which began to burst flames for his seventh victory. By 1100 the first wave of bombers were already well on their way back to base and the battle was winding down. Clover Red Flight continued to fend off Japanese interceptors who were attacking the remaining bombers while they were leaving the target area. The P-38 pilots were beginning to become anxious about their fuel supply for the three and a half hour flight back to Morotai. On his way back Smith saw a P-47 that had been accidentally been shot up by a P-38 crash en route to Morotai but fortunately, the Thunderbolt pilot was able to bail out over the water and get into his life raft about eight miles west of Karong Point in the Celebes. Disregarding his fuel situation, Smith called Search and Rescue and circled the area over the downed pilot until the Catalina, *Daylight 12*, was over him.

**Lt.Col. Meryl Smith** shot down a Zero for his seventh victory. (AAF)

**1Lt. Joseph Forster** claimed his fourth victory. (AFAA)

1Lt. Joe Forster and Wingman, 1Lt. Dean Olson, had moved from the second element in Green Flight to White Flight due to repositioning caused by aborts in Green and White Flights early in the mission. White Flight Leader Ratajski made several unsuccessful passes and Forster made two attacks on Zeros without any hits. Then a Zero made a high 6 o'clock attack on White Leader while Forster and Olson were turning. Forster immediately took a long shot to scare off the Zero but it continued to fly on. Another Zero crossed in front of Forster who rolled over and fired a one second burst at 90 degrees and the enemy fighter went down in flames for his fourth victory. As the two were leaving the target area a Zero Split-S'd on Red Leader Smith and then pulled up in a tight loop and turned sharply onto Forster's tail and came quickly into firing position from behind and slightly to port and opened fire. Forster's port engine was hit and exploded and he rolled and then dove the P-38 to starboard. Once again the Lightning's remarkable diving speed saved one of its pilots. Forster's port engine was quickly losing oil pressure and he feathered the engine and then made the long 850 mile flight back to Morotai on a single engine

**14 October 1944: 8FG/36FS: Balikpapan**

The 8FG had not participated in the first Balikpapan mission on the 10 October raid but on the second mission a four plane flight consisted of four imposing 8FG pilots; Lt.Col Abe Beck representing 5FC/HQ; Lt.Col. Earl Dunham, CO of the 8FG; Maj. Jay Robbins, 5FC Deputy Commander who was to represent the 80FS; and Capt. Kenneth Ladd, the new CO of the 36FS. The four took off at 0710 from Morotai to escort the B-24s with fighters from other units. Soon after take off Beck's P-38 had mechanical difficulty and he aborted. The other three flew on without problems through clear weather until Robbins found that he was mysteriously running low on fuel and also turned back. Dunham and Ladd continued and arrived at the

Balikpapan area about 1100 at 14,000 feet and then climbed to 17,000 feet in anticipation of meeting enemy fighters. Four Oscars appeared below and Ladd was the first the dive on the Japanese fighters with Dunham following behind. The Oscars seemed to be oblivious to their attackers and Ladd fired a long burst at one which caught fire and its pilot bailed out. Ladd then got more hits on another Oscar which started smoking; Split-S'd and began gliding in a shallow dive toward shore for Ladd's 12th and last victory. Ladd flew back 30 degrees off Dunham's tail when Dunham noticed an Oscar below and took an 80 degree deflection shot. When he pulled up Ladd was no longer behind him and he circled for a few minutes and gained more altitude. When he reached 19,000 feet he tried to call Ladd on the radio but was unsuccessful and Dunham decided to return home with other P-38s. Ladd didn't return to Morotai or any of the other bases and some of the returning P-38 pilots reported seeing Ladd's P-38 on the tail of a Tojo that was going to crash while a B-24 waist gunner reported seeing a smoking P-38 being attacked by a Tojo. While yet another report told of a P-38 being ditched just west of North Celebes and PBY patrols were alerted to pick up the downed pilot. The popular Ladd was never seen again.

**14 October 1944: Balikpapan: 13th Fighter Command**

The 13th Fighter Command sent out 42 P-38s from Middleburg and Sansapor to escort the mission but due to mechanical problems and lack of fuel, only six Lightnings of the 68th Fighter Squadron reached the target and shot down two with a probable and damaged. After the battle the 13th Air Force P-38s joined the Lightnings of the 5th Air Force and flew as far as Morotai with them where they landed and refueled after which they had to fly the final leg of their 1,873 mile trip back to Middleburg. While the five strikes on the refineries had done extensive damage, there was no permanent, non-repairable destruction and the Japanese quickly had the installations operational. These missions gave the Fifth Air Force and the Thirteenth Air Force a lot of long range experience which would become important in the upcoming Philippine Campaign.

**Lt.Col. Meryl Smith** shot down a Zero for his seventh victory. (AAF)

**24 October 1944: 348FG/342FS**

On 24 October four 342nd Squadron P-47s took off at 1000 for a bombing mission to the Laha Airdrome on the Vogelkop Peninsula. The weather deteriorated during the flight and the four Thunderbolts diverted to Babo Airfield which had been bombed earlier in the day by 14 Thunderbolts of the 342FS. At least one twin engine Japanese bomber was sighted near the south end of the strip and four P-47s were sent to strafe it and any others. At 1045 the P-47s roared over the field and met very light antiaircraft fire and destroyed a Dinah and damaged another Val in a revetment. The four P-47s reformed and turned back for another pass. However, on the pass 1Lt. Malcolm Rand pulled up into a right turn off the strip, when his engine started smoking and his fighter plunged into the ocean and exploded.

**15 31 October 1944: 35FG**

After the two Balikpapan missions on 10 and 14 October the Group's missions for the remainder of the month were relatively subdued but covered long over water distances to such targets as the Visayas in the Central Philippines, the Moluccas, the Sulu Archipelago, the Celebes, and Northeastern Borneo.

**15-31 October 1944:**
**8FG Strafing Missions to Mindanao and Balikpapan**

Once Morotai was secured the 8FG moved onto new strips there on 19 September and Mindanao was now only about 300 miles away and most of the Philippines were in range of the P-38, credited in large part to Lindbergh's fuel economy advice.

On 16 October the 80FS dispatched eight P-38s to northern Mindanao to strafe targets of opportunity on the road between Cagayan and Valencia. When they arrived at 1100 seven P-38s swept the road for about 25 minutes until they encountered a convoy of 50 to 60 trucks and a number of staff cars. The Headhunters strafed the column and destroyed or set fire to about 35 trucks and six of the staff cars. Cagayan Harbor was strafed and three boats were set on fire while a Sally bomber was set on fire on Cagayan Airdrome.

On 17 October the 36FS flew a sweep near Zamboanga, Mindanao looking for targets of opportunity. 2Lt. Gregory Nevans made a strafing pass over shipping targets but his plane hit the water, bounced back into the air, and then crashed killing Nevans.

On 20 October, the day that the Philippines were invaded by the Allies, 12 Lightnings of the 80FS flew to southern Mindanao on another strafing mission on targets of opportunity. They strafed 11 trucks along the Polloc Harbor-Digos Road while eight others between Digos and Davao were set on fire and at least 10 others were damaged but did not burn. A barge in Polloc Harbor was set on fire and a gasoline dump at Manaboan was also strafed.

On 23 October, eight P-38s of the 80FS continued its long range tactical missions with a strafing sweep on the Sayre Highway on Mindanao. The Headhunters destroyed 12 trucks, two tractors, two staff cars, and a steam roller along the highway and then set fire to three vessels off the coast. One large thatched roof building along the road was also destroyed but the pilots avoided attacking possible artillery pieces in the open meadows because civilian carts were nearby.

On the next day four 80FS P-38s escorted a B-25 strike off the north-eastern coast of Borneo near Sandakan which was a shipping fuel supply point for the defending airstrips in the Balikpapan area. The American formation flew through some light AA fire and bombed and strafed more than 20 vessels in the harbor north of Tambisan Island and south of Bahaia Island. The P-38s then strafed the lighthouse near Cape Unsang before rejoining the Mitchells.

On 25 October 12, Lightnings from the 80FS covered a B-24 anti-shipping strike in the Mindanao Sea. The formation arrived over the target area at 0910 and discovered eight warships, two transports, and a naval support vessel. The B-24s badly damaged three of the warships while the 80th strafed a support vessel and set it on fire despite light but accurate AA fire from the vessel. 1Lt. Wilby Calderwood's P-38 was hit by AA fire and crash landed into the sea and sank quickly taking Calderwood with it.

On 30 October 16 Headhunter P-38s arrived at the airdrome at Tambisan Island near Sandakan at 1115 and claimed four more aircraft destroyed on the ground: an Oscar was set on fire at one end of the runway and another at the other end while a Lily and Betty in revetments were destroyed. Buildings on the drome were damaged or destroyed and a ship in the nearby harbor was badly damaged. The lighthouse at Cape Unsang was again strafed as the P-38s left the area. Meanwhile, Capt. Kenneth Giroux was leading 10 Lightnings of the 36FS over the Tambisan Island target at about the same time that the 80FS attacked. Giroux led his P-38s on six aircraft parked on the strip below and destroyed all of them in a quick attack. With ammunition remaining, Giroux wasn't ready to leave and flew to the harbor looking for more targets. Two tankers were seen just off the coast and Giroux led the squadron in low over the water and chose a tanker and started firing at about 300 yards. Just as Giroux passed over the ship it exploded and his speeding P-38 was thrown upward about 50 feet and hit by debris but continued to fly. The tanker was burning and broken in half and rapidly sinking. Giroux flew on with the other P-38s to strafe the second tanker which was left burning. The 35FS was flying further down the coast and attacked another tanker but with a gunboat escort which fended off the attackers with accurate AA fire. Capt. Richard West used his ability as a marksman picked off the gunboat's gun crews on successive strafing passes and the squadron then was safe to attack the now defenseless tanker.

**18 October 1944: 475FG Moves toward the Philippines**

On 5 October portions of the 475FG broke camp and began embarking on the *SS Louis Weule*; followed the next day by the 431FS which boarded the Liberty Ship, the *SS Charlotte Cushman*. Their final destination was secret which, of course, was almost certain to be somewhere in the Philippines. But the question was: Where would somewhere be in MacArthur's initial landings in the Philippines?

On 8 October, the sea echelon of the 475FG sailed from Biak for Wakde Island. About noontime the *Louis Weule* anchored in Maffin Bay to pick up a load of 1,000 pound bombs transported via LCTs from shore which would require four days to load the bombs including the day the air echelon flew the Balikpapan mission. The *Weule* left on 15 October and arrived a few hours later at Humboldt Bay where the invasion fleet loading and assembling to leave on the 18th for Leyte. Early on the morning of the 18th the fleet once again went to sea. On 19 October the convoy crossed the Equator, where the old custom of inducting pollywogs, men who had never crossed the Equator, into King Neptune's Court. These men had their hair cut and bodies painted and then ran throw a harassing gauntlet lined up on the ship's decks. The next day the Captain announced that Leyte was to be invaded within the next few days.

# Part Seven
# The Philippines Campaign

# 1

# Philippines Invasion

### General Background

Clearly violating the principle of unity of command, in March 1942 the Joint Chiefs of Staff established two military commands in the Pacific: the Southwest Pacific Area, headed by Gen. Douglas MacArthur, and the Pacific Ocean Areas, under Adm. Chester Nimitz. However, this division of authority seemed to be a feasible compromise. The Navy objected to MacArthur as overall Commander in the Pacific and although he was the senior officer in the area he was unlikely to subordinate himself to anyone. The large size of the Pacific Theater allowed this division but left no single authority to decide between conflicting plans or to coordinate between the two. MacArthur later wrote: "Of all the faulty decisions of the war, perhaps the most unexplainable one was the failure to unify the command in the Pacific, [which]...resulted in divided effort; the waste, diffusion, and duplication of force; and the consequent extension of the war with added casualties and cost." From a strategic perspective, this divided command had a direct impact on decisions leading up to the invasion of the Philippines.

In two and a half years of battle in the Pacific American forces had advanced in two lines of attack. The American advance in the Central Pacific was led by Nimitz whose forces had island-hopped through the Gilberts, the Marshalls, and the Carolines. The American and Australian advance in the South Pacific was led by MacArthur whose forces had halted the Japanese advance toward Australia and then recaptured the Solomons and New Guinea; isolating the critical Japanese bastion at Rabaul. These victories had positioned American forces at the inner defensive line of the Japanese Empire, and in the summer of 1944 they battled through that barrier to capture the Marianas, the Palaus, and Morotai and were positioned about 300 miles from the southern islands in the Philippine Archipelago. While facing superior American materiel and manpower in these battles, the Japanese continued to be fanatical in their defense and American forces faced the most formidable bastions of the Japanese Empire: the Philippines, Formosa, and Okinawa.

### Strategic Background

Japanese

The Japanese realized earlier that the loss of the Philippines would threaten their access to food and critical raw materials, especially oil, from the East Indies and Southeast Asia, and decided that the defense of the Philippines was to be their most important war effort for 1943-44. In late September 1944, the Japanese Imperial Command consolidated its staff at Manila, Luzon and organized 250,000 troops under Gen. Tomoyuki Yamashita, who had vanquished the British in Malaya and Singapore. These troops were posted throughout the Philippines to augment the 180,000 troops already there but many of Yamashita's troops would be drawn off to reinforce other hard-pressed garrisons. However, the Japanese expectation of transferring stranded reinforcements from the Dutch East Indies and receiving oil from Borneo was no longer viable as Kenney's Far East Air Force and the U.S. Navy had continually denied the Japanese Fleet access through the Molucca Islands. Prior to the invasion of the Philippines the Japanese carrier force had been decimated in the Battle of the Philippine Sea on 19-20 June of the same year. Then, in October, the Battle of Leyte Gulf most of the Japanese surface fleet was destroyed with little to show for its sacrifice but the remainder of the Japanese Navy was ready to commit its battle fleet to fend off the forthcoming Allied invasion.

However, there was optimism at Japanese Imperial Headquarters that had been given false intelligence based on greatly exaggerated reports from naval pilots who claimed destroying 1,200 American aircraft and sinking 11 aircraft carriers. Although senior naval officers doubted these claims, the military establishment in Tokyo accepted them and thought it possible to decisively defeat the Americans wherever they landed in the Philippines if Japan could concentrate forces there. However, Japan's once formidable air forces had been decimated giving America air superiority, period.

American

Once the Marianas had been captured, putting AAF B-29 long range heavy bombers in position to bomb the Japanese Home Islands for the first time, the Joint Chiefs of Staff had to decide on their next objective. As discussed previously, early considerations concerned Formosa and the Philippines as the capture of either would threaten Japanese sea lanes between her naval bases and industries in the Home Islands and the resource rich (especially, oil) occupied areas to the south. Adm. Ernest King, the Chief of Naval Operations, had long objected to landings in the Philippines, and by May 1944 Army Chief of Staff Gen. George C. Marshall and Army Air Force Chief of Staff Gen. Henry Arnold had concurred. Marshall believed that MacArthur's Luzon strategy would require too much time to implement and accomplish and that to directly invade Formosa from the Mariana Islands would be quicker and more feasible. But the influential MacArthur had vowed to return to the Philippines and the Joint Chiefs of Staff issued plans for the preliminary operations against islands to the south of Mindanao which were to be stepping stones to launch the Philippine Campaign then scheduled to be begin with the invasion of Leyte.

Although Luzon was the largest island in the Philippines Archipelago and the Headquarters for Japanese forces in the Philippines; the Joint Chiefs of Staff had determined that it would be necessary for Mindanao and Leyte to be taken as part of the preliminary operations to the liberation of Luzon. On 12 March 1944, the JCS instructed MacArthur to plan the invasion of

Mindanao, the southernmost island of the archipelago, beginning on 15 November. In June MacArthur proposed a two-phase operational plan which included the capture of southern Mindanao on 25 October which was to serve as a staging area for a larger amphibious landing on Leyte three weeks later. Both islands were accessible; Mindanao to the south and Leyte to the east had coastlines conducive for amphibious landings that would allow American forces approaching from either direction to preserve uninterrupted lines of communication from recently secured bases. An amphibious attack directly against Luzon, in the northern Philippines, would face far larger enemy forces and would be more difficult to support. MacArthur's staff estimated Japanese combat strength on Mindanao to be 50,000, with another 50,000 in the Visayas, the central Philippine Islands, which included Leyte, while they estimated that Luzon had 260,000 defenders.

Preparation for the invasion of the Philippines was greatly assisted by *Ultra*, the Allied top secret decryption program used on intercepted Japanese radio traffic. For many months, acting on information from *Ultra*, American submarines and aircraft had been surprising Japanese shipping in the Western Pacific and interfering with shipment of resources from the East Indies. In June 1944 *Ultra* discovered that the Japanese had decided to significantly increase its defenses in the Philippines in order to oppose the expected American advance northward toward the Home Islands. These and ensuing decrypts allowed the Allied High Command to concentrate submarine and air attacks against Japanese shipping routes and flight paths to the Philippines but despite escalating losses, the Japanese buildup in the Philippines continued through the Summer and Fall of 1944.

Thus, it was imperative that the invasion began as soon as possible but the availability of amphibious shipping, fleet fire support, and air support presented major difficulties in moving up the invasion date. Various headquarters conducted logistical studies that gave contradictory answers to whether there was sufficient shipping available in the Pacific to support major landings on both Mindanao and Leyte. On 8 September, unable to fix a timetable for the invasion, the Joint Chiefs of Staff could no longer wait and directed MacArthur and Nimitz to invade the Leyte and Surigao Strait area beginning on 20 December.

The questions of objectives and operational scheduling were finally established by fleet-covering operations in support of the invasion of the Palaus and Morotai. Beginning on 7 September 1944, carrier task forces from Adm. Halsey's Third Fleet attacked Yap and the Palaus, as well as Mindanao and islands in the Central Philippines. Air attacks continued in October against Japanese airfields on Okinawa, Formosa, and Luzon, as well as on enemy shipping in adjacent waters. In addition to about 180 enemy merchant ships, it was estimated that these attacks destroyed more than 500 enemy aircraft in the Philippines and a similar number elsewhere. The success of these aerial attacks convinced planners that a major landing on Mindanao was no longer necessary and that available shipping and logistical strength could now be concentrated on Leyte. Consequently, the Joint Chiefs of Staff directed MacArthur and Nimitz to cancel their intermediate operations and to accelerate their planning to carry out an invasion of Leyte on 20 October.

MacArthur's selection of Leyte Island was both daring and strategically viable as the Japanese expected an attack at Mindanao first as it was both within reach of the Allied airfields north of Vogelkop and required less time to reach by any sizable invasion fleet than Leyte. Leyte Island was also strategically positioned to cut Japanese forces in the Philippines off from each other but only if the Americans could hold the Island against the expected dogged enemy resistance.

### *King II* and Airfield Planning

Once MacArthur drove the Japanese from New Guinea he was ready at last to fulfill his promise to return to the Philippines. The Joint Chiefs of Staff issued plans for the preliminary operations against islands to the south of Mindanao which were to be stepping stones to launch the Philippine Campaign then scheduled to be begin on 15 November with and invasion at Sarangani Bay, Mindanao to be known as the *King I Operation* and then continued by an invasion of Leyte (*King II Operation*) on 20 December. Meanwhile, MacArthur's SWPA forces established heavy bombardment groups in strategic areas to provide air support to Pacific Ocean Areas (POA) forces which were preparing for island hopping operations with the objective of linking the Central Pacific Area (CENPAC) forces (a subdivision of POA) with those of SWPA. The pincers carried out by the coordinated forces of the South Pacific Force (SOPAC) (another subdivision of POA) and SWPA, with supply lines through the New Hebrides and Australia, had advanced steadily northwestward. Operations of CENPAC, with their supply route through the Hawaiian Islands, had moved westward through the Gilberts and Marshalls to the Marianas. Protruding between the combined forces of SOPAC and SWPA and those of CENPAC was the deteriorating but still intimidating enemy bastion at Truk and its supporting island bases in the western Carolines. This salient had been under attack from three sides and the POA was planning operations to neutralize and bypass it by seizing the intermediate stepping stones of Ulithi, Yap, and Palau which would also provide an advanced fleet anchorage essential to the projected invasion of the Philippines. Besides coordinating bombing strikes, SWPA forces had been preparing to further support these POA operations by moving into the Moluccas at Morotai simultaneously with the POA attack on Palau, 480 miles north of Morotai on 15 September.

Near the end of August 1944, Adm. Halsey's Third Fleet began probing operations in the western Carolines and the Philippines. His carrier raids were directed against Yap the Palau Islands, and Mindanao. The 12 September missions against the central Philippines confirmed earlier intelligence concerning the weakness of the Japanese garrisons in the Leyte area. Halsey immediately contacted Nimitz, Commander in Chief, POA (CINCPOA), recommending the cancellation of the operations against Yap, Mindanao, and islands to the south of Mindanao, and advancing the schedule for the attack on Leyte. Nimitz presented these recommendations to the Joint Chiefs of Staff with an offer to place the Third Amphibious Force, which included XXIV Corps then embarking in Hawaii for the Yap invasion, under MacArthur's command for the attack on Leyte. MacArthur informed the Joint Chiefs of Staff that he was already prepared to change his plans to land on Leyte to 20 October instead of 20 December. The JCS promptly issued instructions to both MacArthur and Nimitz to implement the Leyte operation on 20 October and to discard the previously approved intermediate operations.

These changes in strategy by the High Command canceled a substantial portion of previous airdrome planning. The originally scheduled operations on Leyte would have been supported by land-based aircraft from Mindanao until airdromes could be constructed in the Leyte area. The arrival of a specific number of Engineer Aviation and Engineer Construction Battalions, as well as an immense amount of construction supplies, had already been meticulously scheduled. However, this scheduling could not easily be accelerated to meet the new earlier invasion date. Units already committed to other operations could not be relieved and supplies ordered from the United States could not arrive in time. Furthermore, by eliminating these intermediate or stepping stone operations at Ulithi, Yap, and Palau before invading Leyte, SWPA forces would be 800 miles from their nearest fighter base, 1,000 miles beyond their established line of bomber bases, and 1,600 miles in advance of their closest supply base at Hollandia. All air support would necessarily have to be carrier-based until airdromes could be constructed locally.

Therefore, under the circumstances the quick development of 5AF airdromes on Leyte would be of critical importance. But when invasion dates and objectives were changed, there were less than 25 days remaining to submit new requisitions, combat load cargo vessels, and move them to the rendezvous north of New Guinea. The only option was to reroute vessels which were bulk-loaded with base construction materials for the now canceled operations against Sarangani Bay and the islands to the south of Mindanao. However, these vessels carried thousands of tons of items that were not going to be needed initially and would have to be unloaded on the beachheads to get to the totally inadequate tonnages of items that would be really needed such as landing mat, surfacing bitumen, and bridging materials nor could these items be shipped separately in time. The substitution of the XXIV Corps for the XIV Corps further added to the engineer's logistical and manpower problems. XIV Corps, then engaged on Bougainville Island under POA control was not scheduled for Leyte until December so the XXIV Corps scheduled for canceled Yap operation was immediately assigned in its place. Its convoy was loaded for an entirely different type of operation where the importance of the early construction of airdromes was not crucial because it was to be covered by unlimited carrier support and the Japanese had only limited air strength in the Central Pacific. The tactical units and landing craft to be used in the Yap invasion had been given preference over engineer troops, equipment, and building materials since no extensive overland operations were anticipated. Only one naval Seabee Construction Battalion had been included in this first landing of XXIV Corps originally scheduled for Yap. No Engineer Battalions had been allocated and only an insignificant amount of airdrome and construction supplies and totally inadequate motor transport had been loaded. Most worrisome was that the XXIV Corps convoy exceeded by 23 LSTs the total amount of shipping originally scheduled to carry the XIV Corps. This necessitated a reduction of all other shipping allocations to maintain assault echelons within the capabilities of available facilities for unloading on the beaches and resulted in reducing by approximately 50% the number of engineer units planned for the first four decisive days on Leyte. It would be 23 days before turnaround shipping could move additional engineer units forward.

The planning for the logistic support for a tactical force of approximately 250,000 men under this situation, particularly when it was to be conducted during the beginning of the rainy season, was a complex and grave responsibility. Fortunately, by this time, a major change in the previous operating procedure had come into existence, as the Sixth Army was now to be supported by the Army Service Command (ASCOM). This newly created headquarters unit had been organized by United States Army Services of Supply (USASOS) to assume logistical planning while the Army Staff concentrated on the tactical phases. Besides organizing and implementing immediate logistic support to Sixth Army tactical forces, this command was responsible for the preparation and completion of plans for new bases. Under USASOS, ASCOM had been activated in July 1944 and its initial headquarters had been set up in Brisbane, under command of the highly competent Maj.Gen. Hugh Casey temporarily detached from his assignment as Chief Engineer, General Headquarters (GHQ), SWPA. Almost all officers and enlisted men for Headquarters, ASCOM, had been assigned from Headquarters, USASOS. The Headquarters of this new command had been organized into five sections: Administration and Personnel, Intelligence, Construction, Base Development, and Troop Unit. The key personnel for ASCOM's engineer staff had been provided by Headquarters, 5201st Engineer Construction Brigade, which also constituted ASCOM's Construction Command for Leyte. Responsibilities of this construction command included not only engineer construction operations but engineer supply activities as well. Actually, ASCOM was an advanced echelon of USASOS which was to function in the landing area initially under Sixth Army direction, and, while not actually an engineer command, approximately 50% of its manpower consisted of engineer troops. The personnel under this command, once a base was established and turned over to USASOS, could revert to USASOS control without any major disruption and replacements, as had been previously experienced when construction and other service responsibilities had been vested in Sixth Army until USASOS took over responsibility for a base.

Planning for the *King I* (Mindanao) and *King II* (Leyte) operations had been ASCOM's first assignments and its Construction Command had expended substantial time and effort in making preparations for construction troops, equipment, and supplies to meet requirements of these operations as originally planned. Early in September, Headquarters, ASCOM, had moved from Brisbane to Hollandia where, on 15 September, it had been attached to Sixth Army. On the same day the Mindanao Operation had been canceled and the date for Leyte advanced. The following day, Headquarters, Base K, had been established as a separate organization and assigned to ASCOM. By that time base planning had almost been completed and requisitions for all classes of supplies and equipment had been submitted to USASOS for the originally contemplated *King I* and *King II* Operations. A heightened sense of urgency arose when the two month advance in the date for the *King II* Operation necessitated significant additional effort as revisions in original plans and procedures had to be made; material deficiencies caused by the advanced invasion date had to be remedied and the reallocations of personnel, supplies, and equipment had to be made. Plans for the utilization of civilian labor were prepared to offset the now looming shortage of engineer troops. A Civil Affairs unit was organized by ASCOM that was to engage, register, classify, allocate, and pay civilian employees immediately after landings on Leyte. Various conferences were held at ASCOM, USASOS, and Sixth Army headquarters to review all details for the elimination of any possible errors while the ASCOM staff made continual analysis of planned procedures, field orders, and terrain data. The limited aerial photography and available pre-war maps used for the study were inadequate. Until recently Leyte had been beyond the range of land-based photographic aircraft and only 47 photo-mapping missions had been flown during the remainder of September which provided inadequate photography for accurate mapping coverage.

Leyte is a 115 mile long island with a width varying from 15 miles across the center to 43 miles in the north and 32 miles in the south. It is accessible from both the Pacific Ocean and the Visayan Sea and was well situated for construction of air facilities from which strikes could be launched against existing enemy airdromes in both the northern and southern Philippines. Planners designated an amphibious landing approach through the deep Leyte Gulf onto a 30 mile strip of fair to good landing beaches on the north central portion of the east coast. These beaches provided access to the broad and prominent Leyte Valley which was the principal strategic aspect of the island as it was apparently adaptable for rapid development of air and supply bases. This valley extends across the island from Carigara Bay on the north coast to Tacloban and Abuyog on the east coast, and covers 250 square miles of comparatively level, fertile, well-irrigated land covered with rivers and streams. The best roads on the island were in this valley but were not designed for military traffic. Good construction timber was available in all sections of the island and sand and gravel was plentiful in stream beds and along coastal areas bordering Leyte Valley.

The information on existing airfields on Leyte was limited and vague. When the Japanese invaded the Philippines in December 1941, there were two short runways at Tacloban and construction had been started on a second airfield at Ormoc. Subsequent Japanese airfield development was indicated on Allied terrain studies but the locations given were only approximate and status of completion was indefinite. Tacloban was reported as operational; as were airstrips at Buri, San Pablo, Dulag, and in the vicinity of Valencia north of Ormoc. Other sites were indicated at Anibong, Bayug, Mojon, San Andres, Dao, and a seaplane base at Anibong Point were supposedly, but not definitely, scheduled for completion prior to the Leyte invasion.

Airbase construction plans also had to consider the anticipated weather. When the planners advanced in date for the invasion they had to accept the risk of it coinciding with the worst part of the typhoon season, which occurs in the central Philippines during November and is only slightly less intense during October and December. Samar Island somewhat protects Leyte from the northeast monsoons from September through May but those in October through December can strike the east coast of Leyte with torrential rains and high winds that can paralyze road travel and hold up shipping, frequently for weeks at a time. The magnitude of the engineer's problem on Leyte was evident to the planners from the start.

On 21 September 1944 (A Day minus 29) GHQ, SWPA issued operations instructions for the Invasion of Leyte: "Forces of the Southwest Pacific, covered and supported by the Third Fleet, will continue the offensive to reoccupy the Philippines by seizing and occupying objectives in the Leyte and western Samar areas and will establish there in naval, air and logistic facilities for the support of subsequent operations."

The engineer mission for Leyte was enormous in comparison to previous programs, and because of its size construction was classified under four main headings: air facilities; naval facilities; petroleum handling and storage facilities; and other base facilities. The required air facilities included one Type C, two Type D, and one Type E airfields with Type 2 hardstands for 380 aircraft. The initial engineer construction mission, with an A plus 5 goal was for the provision of a 5,000x100 foot runway and undispersed parking for two fighter groups and one squadron of night fighters. The other three airfields were to be ready by A plus 15, A plus 30, and A plus 45, respectively. All these airfields were to be developed into Type D but one was subsequently to be converted to Type E (two 7,000 foot runways) by A plus 60. Each airfield was to be provided with a control tower, a fighter sector headquarters, operations buildings, and alert huts. Also specified were an air depot and a separate glider and fighter assembly plant. A restricted total of four million square feet of aprons, hardstands and connecting taxiways was to be provided. If the Allied Air Forces considered it necessary, an additional Type D airfield and 286 more hardstands were authorized.

The landing beaches were the initial problem which confronted the landing forces on Leyte and affected not only the engineer mission but tactical considerations as well. The contingency had been foreseen during the planning phase, but, unfortunately, engineer advice had not been heeded. The landing beaches selected were in the general area of initial objectives: Tacloban airdrome in the north and the four airdromes inland from Dulag to the south. Despite an accurate hydrographic survey prepared in peacetime, the problems evident in them and pointed out by the engineers was not heeded in the planning phase. The survey indicated that LSTs landing at Tacloban would be stranded anywhere from 100 to 250-350 feet from the beach and both the CG, ASCOM, and the Engineer, Sixth Army, urged that a pontoon causeway be provided but they were on vessels off the Dulag beachhead, 25 miles away.

As a result of the intense preliminary aerial and naval bombardment, the early enemy resistance to the initial landings was insignificant at all beaches except in the vicinity of Tacloban. So when the LSTs became grounded hundreds of feet offshore of Tacloban as predicted, they were vulnerable to enemy artillery and mortar fire. During the long wait for the pontoon causeways to arrive from Dulag, personnel and heavy equipment were hastily transferred from the grounded LSTs into small boats and ferried to shore under enemy fire. Meanwhile, other LSTs were diverted to the end of the Peninsula on which Tacloban airdrome was located in order to beach quickly and unload their cargo which totally upset the unloading plans. The unloading of heavy engineer equipment, which was essential to initial airfield development, was critically delayed as all supplies whatsoever were unloaded there. The Tacloban Airdrome site became completely congested by the thousands of tons of ammunition, supplies, and equipment which were unloaded there. This cargo had to be reloaded on trucks and moved to the appropriate supply dumps on a single, narrow access road leading over the neck of the Peninsula and soon traffic moving inland came almost at a total halt when it encountered the engineer dump trucks moving in the opposite direction from the coral pit to the airdrome.

The principal activities of both the Combat and Service Engineers had to be concentrated on providing initial unloading facilities and establishing the key means of communication from all beachheads. Meanwhile, the Japanese held local air supremacy which could not be overcome until air facilities for land-based fighters were built. The Catch-22 was that the major engineer effort had to be initially concentrated on building the exit roads from the beaches so that supplies could be moved inland to areas less vulnerable to enemy air attack. However, the inland areas for depots and dumps, selected from the inadequate aerial photography available during the planning phase, were limited as swamps and rice paddies actually covered most. Reconnaissance, as permitted by the tactical situation, had been begun immediately by advanced elements of the 5201st Engineer Construction Brigade which had arrived on A Day along with the CG, ASCOM, and part of his staff. However, the Palo area, originally planned for the location of Headquarters, Sixth Army and ASCOM, continued to be in enemy hands. Japanese resistance in the Dulag area did not permit vitally needed reconnaissance there for several days and Samar was not accessible for ground reconnaissance. In the meantime, many units were debarked at unscheduled locations because of the diversion of shipping and had arrived and established themselves at bivouac areas on their own initiative only to be forced to move when other units came ashore. Further reconnaissance revealed that even areas selected for many base and air installations were unsuitable and a general reallocation of areas was required. Conferences were held by the major commands to determine the reallocations necessary but continuous heavy rains made the task of this group extremely difficult since estimates of usable areas had to be revised downward frequently as various sections became inundated or turned into quagmires while each succeeding unloaded ship increased the congestion ashore. The congestion problem was increased by the general shortage of local labor. The widespread looting (up to A plus 5) by many civilians of food stores, homes, and Japanese warehouses, provided them plentiful supplies and left them with little incentive for work. Many local laborers refused to work near the dock area or airstrip due to the enemy bombings in the vicinity of Tacloban as did the lack of transportation to and from work sites and failure to supply a noon meal. Some of these problems were gradually surmounted by recruiting cooperative local officials and priests to urge the locals to work but the number of laborers actually appearing for work remained far below the number registered. However, the most serious delays to construction were by the almost continuous heavy rains which began a few days after the landings. Heavy construction which originally was normally 80% effective each day was reduced to 50% and during particularly heavy rains to 25% effectiveness. Essential supply roads soon became quagmires and engineer troops had to be diverted from other necessary assignments in a maximum effort to keep the roads open. The development of vital airstrips rapidly fell further behind projected schedules when fanatical enemy opposition increased and even required the diversion of additional construction units to combat support. Thus the tactical advantage gained by invading Leyte in October at the beginning of the rainy season was coming close to turning into a serious stalemate but it did permit the subsequent landing on Luzon to be made at the beginning of the dry season. Had Leyte been invaded in mid-December as originally planned, construction might have been accomplished on original target dates without a radical redistribution of engineer effort on the ground but similarly unfavorable weather conditions could have jeopardized the subsequent and more extensive operations on Luzon.

The responsibility for airdrome site selection on Leyte had changed from those followed previously in New Guinea. In each New Guinea operation, the Task Force Engineer selected the airdrome sites with the agreement of the Air Task Force Commander. However, prior to the Philippine

Campaign, Allied Air Forces had insisted upon, complete responsibility for the selection of airdrome sites which was granted by GHQ, SWPA. But field reconnaissance on A Day soon revealed that, of all the sites selected by the AAF, only Tacloban was suitable for construction during the rainy season and that the previous intelligence on the number and condition of Japanese airstrips in the Dulag area had been misleading. Only four airfields: Dulag, San Pablo, Bayug, and Buri were located in the southern area and their condition was very poor. They were built on soft, poorly drained soil and all were completely dependent for access upon the very unsatisfactory and narrow Dulag-Burauen road which also was the main supply route for tactical forces moving west and north.

**Opposing Forces**

Japanese Forces

Leyte is one of the larger islands of the Philippine archipelago, extending 110 miles from north to south and varies from between 15 and 50 miles in width. The sandy beaches and deep water approaches on the east side of the island were suitable for amphibious and resupply operations. The island's interior is covered by a heavily forested north-south mountain range that separated two large coastal plain valleys. The larger of the two, Leyte Valley extends from the northern coast to the long eastern shore and included most of the towns and roads on the island. Highway 1 ran along the east coast for 40 miles and the roads and lowlands extending inland from Highway 1 provided opportunities for tank/infantry operations, as well as for airfield construction. Ormoc Valley, the other lowland valley, is located on the west side of the island, and connected to Leyte Valley by Highway 2. Mountains up to 4,400 feet as well as the jagged outcroppings, ravines, and caves which were typical of volcanic islands offered formidable defensive opportunities to the Japanese. Additionally, the invasion was scheduled during the time of the late year monsoon rains which would inhibit combat troops and pilots, as well as logistical units.

**Gen. Tomoyuki Yamashita** was responsible for the defense of the Philippines. (AFHRC)

The Imperial Japanese Army controlled all forces in the Pacific and Southeast Asia through its Southern Army, which included four area armies, two air armies, and three garrison armies. The 14th Area Army, commanded by Gen. Tomoyuki Yamashita, was responsible for the defense of the Philippines with the responsibility for defense of Mindanao and the Visayas delegated to the 35th Army, commanded by Lt.Gen. Sosaku Suzuki who assigned the 16th Division, under Lt.Gen. Shiro Makino, to defend Leyte. By October Japanese strength in the Philippines, including air and construction units totaled about 432,000 troops, with Makino's 16th Division controlling just over 20,000 soldiers on Leyte.

The 14th Area Army was supported by considerable air and naval forces. Both the 4th Air Army and the 1st Air Fleet were headquartered in the Philippines and could summon reinforcements from task forces in the Malaya and Formosa areas totaling four carriers, seven battleships, two small carriers, 19 cruisers, and 33 destroyers. American intelligence estimated the Japanese had between 100 and 120 operational airfields in the Philippines, with 884 aircraft of all types. The largest of the six airfields on Leyte was at Tacloban, the provincial capital, and could also accommodate medium bombers.

American and Allied Forces

For the invasion of Leyte, American and Allied forces mounted the largest amphibious operation to date in the Pacific. The Joint Chiefs of Staff had designated MacArthur as Supreme Commander of sea, air, and land forces which had been drawn from both the Southwest Pacific and Central Pacific Theaters. Allied naval forces which would transport and land ground forces to Leyte consisted primarily of the U.S. Seventh Fleet made up of 701 ships, including 157 warships, commanded by V.Adm. Thomas Kinkaid.

The U.S. Sixth Army, commanded by Lt.Gen. Walter Krueger, consisting of two corps of two divisions each, would conduct operations ashore for a total of 202,500 ground troops. Maj.Gen. Franklin Sibert's X Corps included the 1st Cavalry Division and the 24th Infantry Division. Maj.Gen. John Hodge's XXIV Corps included the 7th and 96th Infantry Divisions. The Sixth Army reserve would include the 32nd and 77th Infantry Divisions. Of these six divisions, only the 96th Infantry Division had not yet seen combat. The new Sixth Army Service Command (ASCOM), commanded by Maj.Gen. Hugh Casey was responsible for organizing the beachhead, supplying units ashore, and constructing or improving roads and airfields.

During the transport and amphibious phases air support for the Leyte operation would be provided by the Seventh Fleet which included fast carrier Task Force 3, and then would be transferred to Allied Air Forces, commanded by Lt.Gen. George Kenney, when conditions ashore allowed. Air support for more distant coverage would be provided by the four fast carrier task forces of Halsey's Third Fleet, whose operations would remain under overall command of Nimitz. Strikes were flown by these carrier aircraft against the Japanese bases at Formosa where numerous aircraft were destroyed on the ground and in the air.

**Lt.Gen. Walter Krueger** commanded the U.S. Sixth Army, consisting of two corps of two divisions each. (AFHRC)

### Kenney's Relationship with the Navy

In contrast with the usually good rapport he had with Army officers, Kenney's relationship with the Navy was very antagonistic. Throughout the war Kenney mistrusted the Navy's intentions and was particularly suspicious of the Navy's efforts to meddle in air operations. Prior to the war Kenney had few dealings with Naval officers and only had limited knowledge of naval warfare. His attitude was affected by the inter-service rivalries of the time, especially the friction between the Air Corps and the Navy over the mission of coastal defense. During the war he frequently was at odds with a number of Navy officers, especially Adm. Daniel Barbey, an amphibious expert, over the method to conduct air operations during amphibious landings. Barbey, who arrived in Australia in early 1943, made a case for the procedures used by the Navy: standing air patrols over the convoys and landings at dawn to hide the ships under the cover of darkness and to surprise the defending forces. Kenney, alternatively, maintained that standing air patrols were wasteful and inefficient; urging later landing times so that his aircraft could bomb the beaches just before the troops landed. Ultimately, various combinations of the methods were used in operations but the constant squabbling between the services kept the inter-service conflict seething.

During the months following the successful Hollandia Campaign, Kenney and other Allied commanders grew increasingly convinced that the Japanese military had been seriously weakened and no longer presented a viable fighting force. After meeting little resistance on several bombing raids in the Philippines, Halsey suggested eliminating the scheduled invasion of Mindanao in the southern Philippines for an assault on Leyte. Invading Leyte earlier than planned would accelerate the American invasion of Luzon, a move that would completely sever the sea lanes between Japan and their southern resources areas and place American forces in a prime position for invading Japan. Bypassing Mindanao, however, also meant no land-based air support for the invasion of Leyte, forcing MacArthur once again to rely on the aircraft carriers. This time Kenney chose not to voice any criticism about using the carriers without the benefit of land-based aircraft. But once land-based aircraft arrived on Leyte, Kenney's quarrels with Adm. Thomas Kincaid, MacArthur's Naval Commander, prevented the two from combining forces at a time when cooperation was badly needed. While the weight of American material superiority covered many of the problems caused by conflicts between the services, Kenney's combativeness did little to improve inter-service cooperation.

### The Invasion

By the second week in October, 1944, MacArthur's Southwest Pacific Command and Nimitz's Central Pacific Fleets had completed plans for the liberation of the 115,000 square mile Philippine Archipelago which was defended by 230,000 to 250,000 enemy troops commanded by Gen. Yamashita. In the first phase of the liberation the Chiefs of Staff had directed MacArthur to capture Leyte Island that garrisoned 35,000 troops and had at least 20 airfields within range.

The Sixth Army assignment of securing Leyte was to be carried out in three phases. The first phase would begin on 17 October, three days before and some 50 miles east of the landing beaches, with the capture of three islands controlling the eastern approaches to Leyte Gulf. The second phase began on 20 October, "A-Day," when the X and XXIV Corps would land at separate beaches on the east coast of Leyte, the former on the north and the latter 15 miles to the south. As soon as possible, the X Corps would capture the city of Tacloban and its airfield, both just one mile north of the Corps' beachhead, secure the strait between Leyte and Samar Islands, then push through Leyte Valley to the north coast. The XXIV Corps' assignment was to secure the southern end of Leyte Valley for airfield and logistical development. In the third phase, the two Corps would take individual routes through the mountains to drive the Japanese from Ormoc Valley and the west coast of the island, and then establish a base on Samar Island 35 miles north of Tacloban.

During the U.S. Navy air strikes on Formosa and Luzon during the period between the 10th and the 18th October, the carrier pilots claimed the destruction of 655 airborne and 465 aircraft on the ground. During this time fighter aircraft of the 5th and 13th Fighter Commands were bombing, strafing, and escorting bombers of their respective air forces against targets

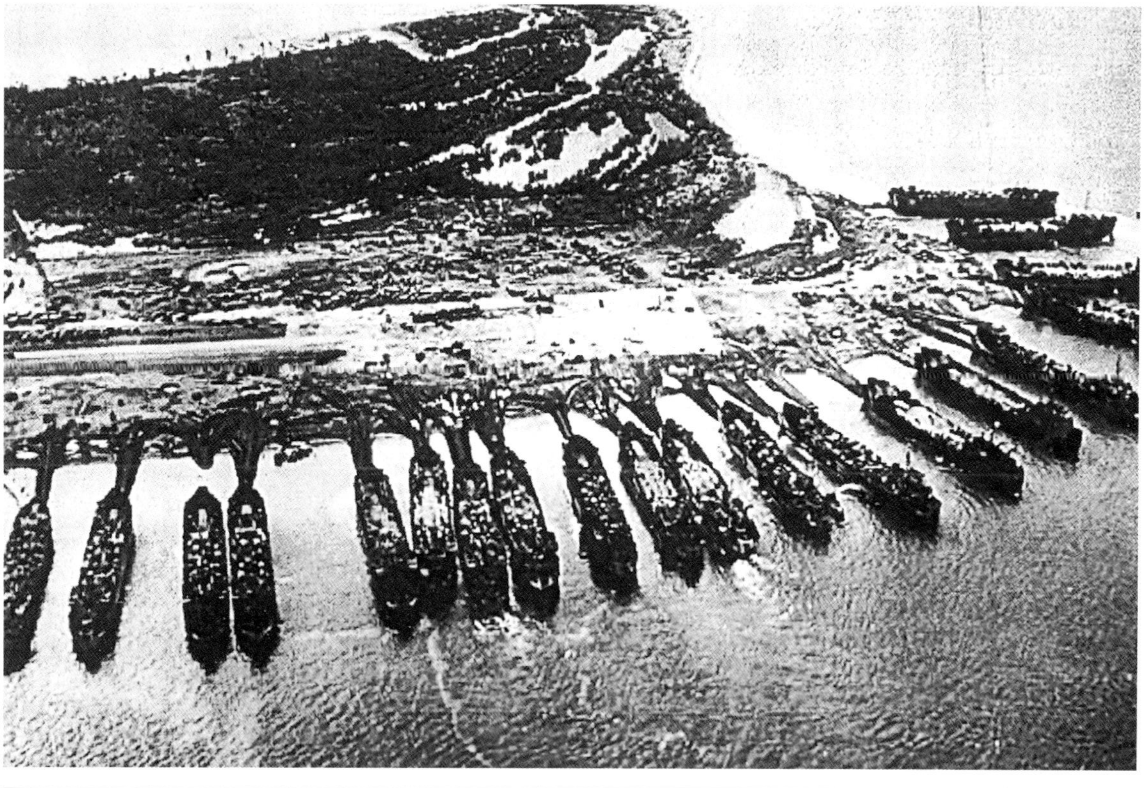

LSTs unloading at **Tacloban** on 20 October (Tacloban Drome was located directly on the landing beach). (AAF)

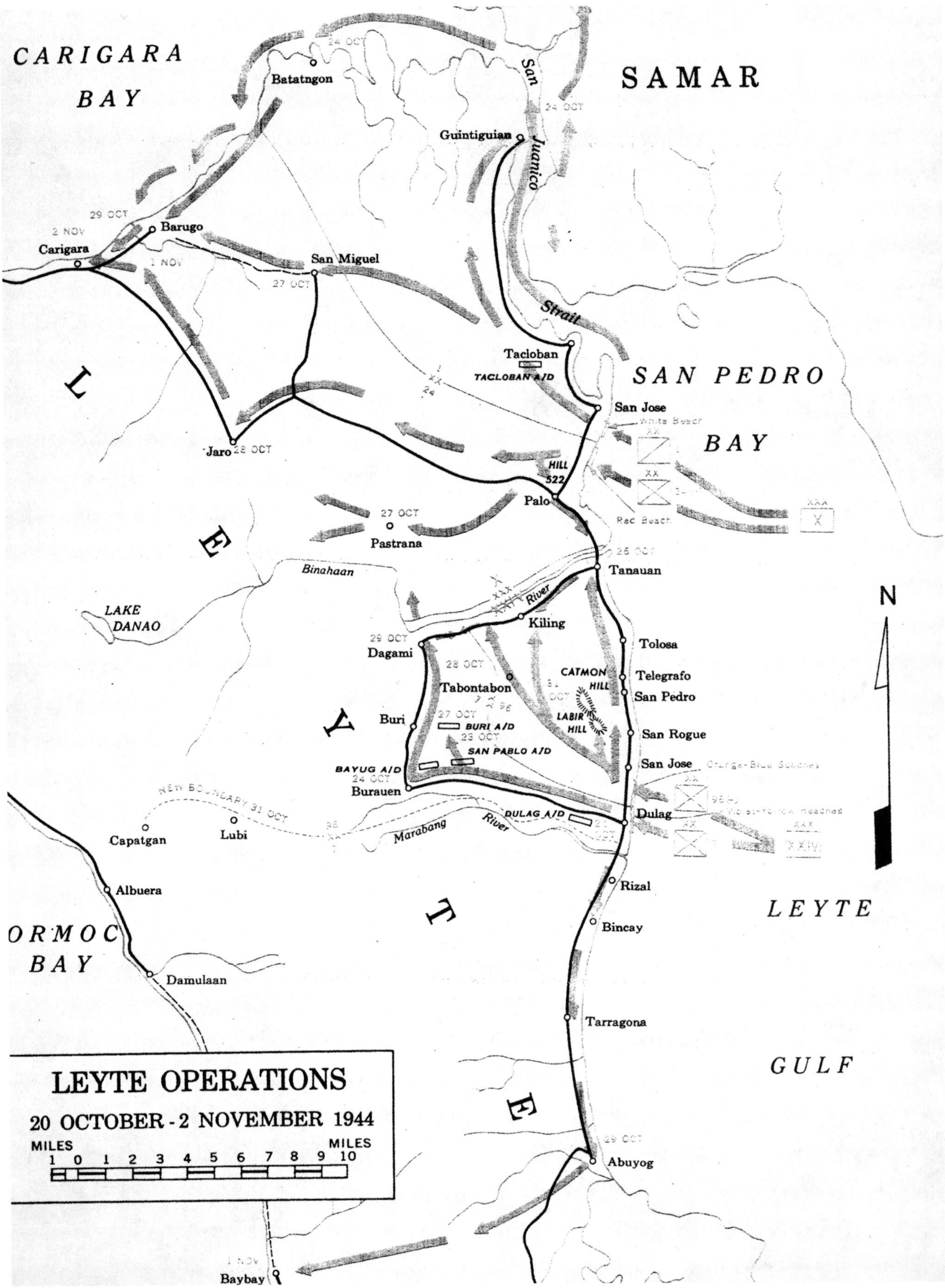

CARIGARA BAY
SAMAR
San Juanico Strait
SAN PEDRO BAY
LEYTE
ORMOC BAY
LEYTE GULF
LAKE DANAO
Binahaan River
Marabang River
Batatngon
Guintiguian
Barugo
Carigara
San Miguel
Tacloban
TACLOBAN A/D
San Jose
Jaro
HILL 522
Palo
Pastrana
Tanauan
Kiling
Dagami
Tolosa
CATMON HILL
Telegrafo
San Pedro
Tabontabon
LABIR HILL
Buri
BURI A/D
SAN PABLO A/D
San Rogue
BAYUG A/D
San Jose
Burauen
DULAG A/D
Dulag
Capatgan
Lubi
Albuera
Rizal
Bincay
Damulaan
Tarragona
Abuyog
Baybay
Red Beach
24 OCT
29 OCT
2 NOV
1 NOV
27 OCT
28 OCT
23 OCT
24 OCT
NEW BOUNDARY 31 OCT
N
LEYTE OPERATIONS
20 OCTOBER - 2 NOVEMBER 1944
MILES
1 0 1 2 3 4 5 6 7 8 9 10
MILES

**MacArthur's** dramatic return to the Philippines through the surf. (U.S. Army)

on Mindanao and Negros Islands. These fighters met little or no opposition, as the enemy did not have the time or the aircraft to rush reinforcements to the Philippines.

On 10 October Halsey's Third Fleet had attacked Luzon's airdromes and harbors while R.Adm. Thomas Kinkaid's Seventh Fleet attacked 600 miles south in the southern Philippines in direct support of the Leyte Campaign. For three days before the invasion carrier aircraft attacked the island of Luzon where Japanese airfields and aircraft there received the majority of the attacks which were intended to reduce the enemy's defensive airpower which the invasion fleet was certain to meet during and shortly after the landings. So after these combined aerial bombardments from Kinkaid's fast escort carriers and Kenney's 5AF heavy bombers, the main USN invasion fleet entered Leyte Gulf from the southeast on the night of 19 October.

Following four hours of heavy naval gunfire on A-Day, 20 October, U.S. Sixth Army forces landed on assigned beaches at 1000 hours. The X Corps advanced across a four mile stretch of beach between Tacloban airfield and the Palo River. Meanwhile, 15 miles to the south, XXIV Corps landed on a three mile beach between San Jose and the Daguitan River. Both Corps found that the swampy terrain was more problematical than the Japanese. Within an hour after the landing, units in most sectors had secured beachheads deep enough to receive heavy vehicles and large amounts of supplies. By 1330 MacArthur made his dramatic entrance through the surf to announce:

> "People of the Philippines, I have returned! By the grace of Almighty God, our forces stand again on Philippine soil."

By the end of A-day, the Sixth Army had moved inland as deep as two miles and controlled Panaon Strait at the southern end of Leyte. In the X Corps sector, the 1st Cavalry Division captured Tacloban airfield, and the 24th Infantry Division had taken the high ground commanding its beachhead. In the XXIV Corps sector, the 96th Infantry Division held the approaches to the highest point in both corps beachheads and the 7th Infantry Division had taken the town of Dulag. The invasion had cost the Americans 49 killed, 192 wounded, and six missing.

Leyte's provincial capitol of Tacloban was located 20 miles north of Dulag on the small coastal inlet of San Pedro Bay on the mouth of the narrow strait that separated Leyte on the west and Samar Island on the east. Immediately to the east of Tacloban was the narrow, two mile long peninsula named Cataisan Point which projected north into San Pedro Harbor and where the Japanese had constructed a primitive runway. An American infantry division immediately captured the abandoned capitol and on the afternoon of the 20th MacArthur returned to the Philippines and restored Sergio Osmeno as President of the Philippines. During the next several days the Sixth Army advanced steadily inland against the Japanese who had put up stubborn resistance in several areas but was unable to coordinate an overall island defense.

The Leyte invasion surprised the Japanese and their naval forces were not situated for immediate retaliation but plans were being prepared for a counterattack. Meanwhile the invasion fleet and beachhead underwent intermittent though brutal air attacks. The Japanese plan was to send a task force centered on their surviving carriers south from Japan in an attempt to lure the main American fleet north then two other forces, without carriers, would attack the invasion fleet in Leyte Gulf.

**October 1944: MacArthur and Kenney Miscalculate at Leyte**

While the Leyte landings on 20 October 1944 went smoothly, the rest of the Campaign required much more time and was considerably more costly in men and material than estimated. Part of the reason was MacArthur's ambition to return to the Philippines as soon as possible and his staff's compliance led them to ignore the possibility of a strong enemy opposition. Another reason was the decision to depend only on aircraft carriers for air cover. The naval aircraft successfully covered the initial landing but after the carriers were pummeled by Japanese naval and air attacks, they required resupply and repair and were forced to leave soon after the invasion which was what Kenney had earlier feared. Meanwhile, the construction of the airfields on Leyte to support 5AF land-based aircraft was more difficult and time consuming than MacArthur anticipated despite the accurate predictions of his aviation engineers.

Kenney and the other air commanders badly planned the air portion of the Leyte invasion. Besides disregarding the concerns of the aviation engineers, they did not identify the key differences in the battle for air superiority between earlier campaigns and in the Philippines. The previous operations in the Central and Southwest Pacific Areas were against relatively small and isolated Japanese-held areas with a limited number of airfields where it was possible to destroy every aircraft there and stop the influx of replacement aircraft. This was not possible in the Philippines as there were a number of airfields scattered throughout the surrounding islands that permitted the Japanese to disperse their aircraft, making it extremely difficult to find and destroy all of them. Also the relatively short distance between Japanese-held Formosa and Luzon allowed the Japanese to fly in large numbers of reinforcement aircraft.

Japanese changed their tactics which further intensified Kenney's problems. In previous operations the Japanese sent out small numbers of aircraft and were mostly unsuccessful in disrupting American operations but during the battle for Leyte the steady flow of reinforcements allowed the Japanese to attack in large formations. In addition, they began lethal Kamikaze attacks which were found to be almost impossible to stop. Problems in building the airfields coupled with miscalculations about the enemy strength and the changes in Japanese tactics forfeited the American advantage of air superiority. The combined effect was the loss of American air superiority to contend with the Japanese ground reinforcements sent to Leyte which slowed the American advance. Although the Japanese air attacks remained Kenney's main priority, his aircraft flew other missions, directed at interrupting enemy reinforcements and directly supporting the movement of American ground forces.

In the forthcoming invasions on Mindoro and Luzon and the planning for the invasion of the Japanese Home Islands, Kenney would spare no effort to make certain that his aircraft were always in position to support the landing, regardless of the planned support from the carriers. In early January 1945, shortly after the Allied landing on Luzon, the Japanese would withdraw their aircraft from the Philippines. So when the threat of Japanese air attacks vanished Japanese ground forces there retreated into

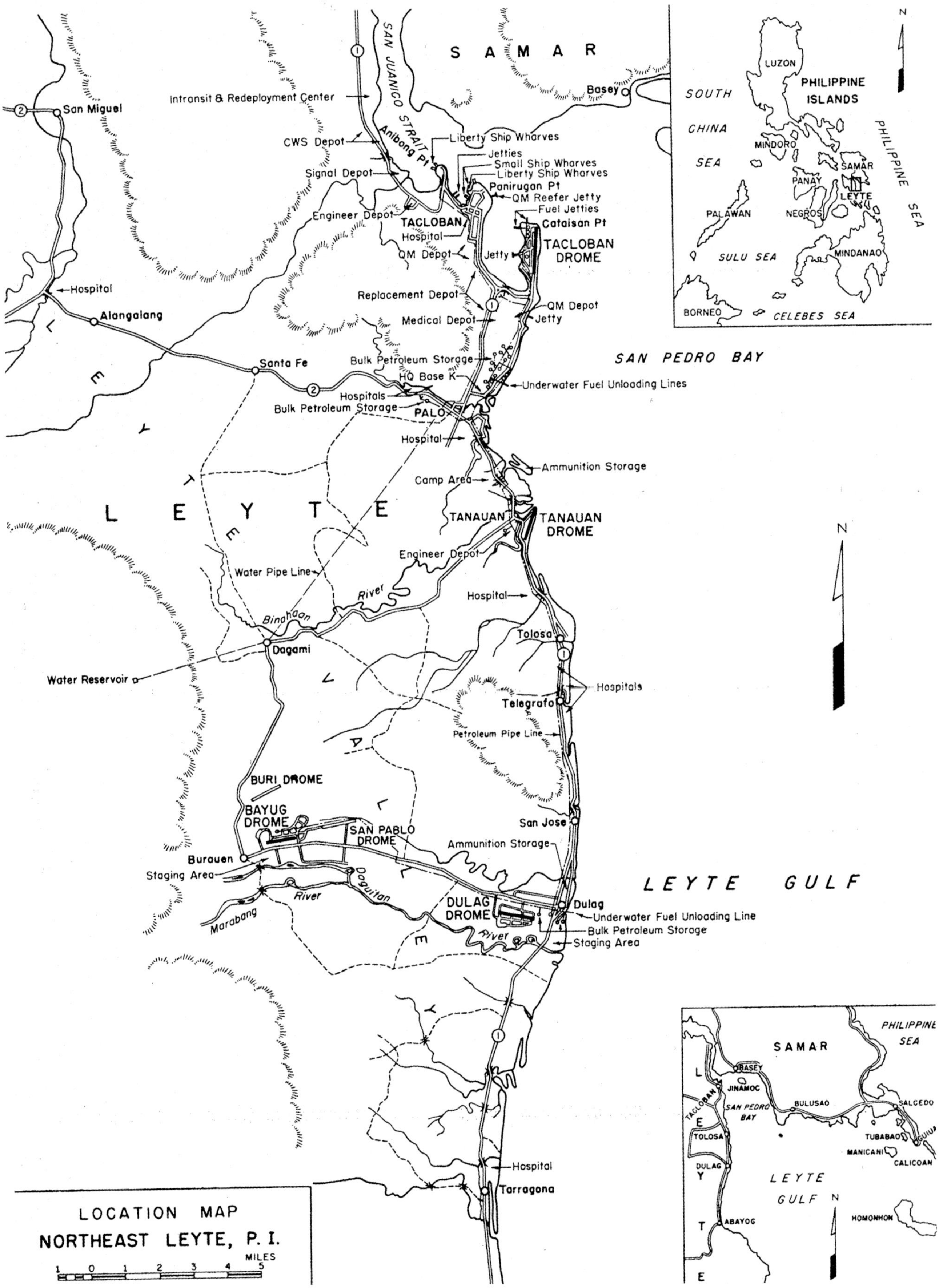

SAMAR
SAN JUANICO STRAIT
Basey
San Miguel
Intransit & Redeployment Center
CWS Depot
Liberty Ship Wharves
Anibong Pt
Jetties
Small Ship Wharves
Liberty Ship Wharves
Signal Depot
Panirugan Pt
QM Reefer Jetty
Fuel Jetties
Engineer Depot
TACLOBAN
Cataisan Pt
Hospital
TACLOBAN DROME
QM Depot
Jetty
Hospital
Replacement Depot
QM Depot
Jetty
Alangalang
Medical Depot
Bulk Petroleum Storage
SAN PEDRO BAY
Santa Fe
HQ Base K
Underwater Fuel Unloading Lines
Hospitals
Bulk Petroleum Storage
PALO
Hospital
Ammunition Storage
Camp Area
L E Y T E
TANAUAN
TANAUAN DROME
LEYTE VALLEY
Engineer Depot
Water Pipe Line
Binahaan River
Hospital
Tolosa
Dagami
Water Reservoir
Hospitals
Telegrafo
Petroleum Pipe Line
BURI DROME
BAYUG DROME
SAN PABLO DROME
San Jose
Ammunition Storage
Burauen
Staging Area
Daguitan River
Marabang River
LEYTE GULF
DULAG DROME
Dulag
Underwater Fuel Unloading Line
Bulk Petroleum Storage
Staging Area
Hospital
Tarragona
LOCATION MAP
NORTHEAST LEYTE, P. I.
MILES
1 0 1 2 3 4 5
N
LUZON
PHILIPPINE ISLANDS
SOUTH CHINA SEA
MINDORO
SAMAR
PANAY
LEYTE
PHILIPPINE SEA
PALAWAN
NEGROS
SULU SEA
MINDANAO
BORNEO
CELEBES SEA
PHILIPPINE SEA
BASEY
JINAMOC
TACLOBAN
SAN PEDRO BAY
BULUSAO
SALCEDO
TOLOSA
TUBABAO
GUIUAN
MANICANI
CALICOAN
DULAG
LEYTE GULF
ABAYOG
HOMONHON

mountain strongholds and had no supply lines that could be cut off. So when Kenney had no enemy aircraft or supply lines to contend with and he could turn his hoard of aircraft loose on missions in direct support of the ground forces.

**24-25 October 1944: The Battle for Leyte Gulf**

The portion of Adm. Takeo Kurita's fleet which had survived the first battle of the Philippines Sea in June had been refitted in Singapore and had left the port 1,500 miles to the west under the codename *Operation SHO-1* to challenge the imminent Allied invasion. A diversionary force of four carriers but equipped with only a small air contingent sailed from Japan into the northern Philippine Sea to circle above Luzon. After these enemy carriers were sighted by submarines off Formosa, Adm. Halsey assumed they were the real threat and sent his entire Third Fleet north to intercept; leaving Adm. Kinkaid's Seventh Fleet off Leyte. Kurita would take advantage of the Halsey's mistake of dividing his superior USN force. As Kurita approached the outer islands of the western Philippines he divided his fleet into two to engage in a pincer attack force. Kurita's warships advanced due east toward the San Bernardino Straits north of Samar Island while V.Adm. Shoji Nishimura turned south through the Sibuyan Sea toward the Surigao Straits which led directly into Leyte Gulf and the American invasion fleet.

Halsey's carriers continued north 700 miles away, leaving Kinkaid's force of smaller warships and fast escort carriers, carrying only 800 aircraft, protecting the troopships and landing beaches, as the only barrier to Kurita on the north flank and Nishimura on the south. On 24 October Kinkaid dispatched his carrier aircraft against Kurita who was moving down the east coast of Samar but the attacks were unsuccessful. That night Nishimura's force survived a fierce naval engagement in the Surigao Straits and in the early morning the two Japanese naval pincers moved into the southern and northern Leyte Gulf and approached the invasion beaches and helpless troopships anchored offshore.

The Americans finally were going to pay for not naming a Supreme Commander over the entire Pacific Theater. MacArthur was responsible for the SWPA and had always played Army vs. Navy politics which now placed the situation in the field in utter confusion. The network of Army and Navy communiqués was hopelessly muddled. Halsey had been duped and had hastily turned north and Central Pacific Commander Nimitz desperately attempted to warn Halsey of the impending calamity at Leyte. Meanwhile, MacArthur's only hope for his beachhead lay with Kinkaid's small carrier air wing and destroyers to turn back the enemy warships that were entering Leyte Gulf and were about to ravage the American Philippines invasion.

On the 25th, Kinkaid's courageous pilots and destroyer escorts saved the day. Nishimura had expected but did not receive adequate JAAF land-based air cover and his southern force was devastated by the USN destroyers which attacked in hit and run flanking assaults in the early morning darkness. At sunrise, Kinkaid's Seventh Fleet Wildcats, Hellcats, and Avengers swarmed over Kurita's battleships so that the Japanese Admiral believed he was being attacked by Halsey's larger carrier force. Only minutes from their planned rendezvous, the demoralized Kurita ordered Nishimura to withdraw and he followed.

Hours after Kurita's retreat back through San Bernardino, the greatest sea battle of the Pacific war ended with Americans devastating *Operation SHO-1*. Halsey hunted down the enemy fleet northeast of Luzon and sunk all of its carriers. Nishimura's southern force was so beleaguered that only one destroyer survived. Kurita's force skulked away into the western seas and evaded Halsey's final pursuit and the Japanese navy would never be a threat again.

During the battle the Japanese introduced a desperate new tactic against shipping as their pilots had deliberately crashed into USN shipping. These pilots had sworn to serve the Emperor in the role of the divine wind called the "Kamikaze" and had had committed suicidal attacks on the carriers *Princeton*, *Santee*, *Suwanee* and *St. Lo*, as well as several Liberty Ships. The *St. Lo* was sunk and the *Princeton* was beached while their aircraft were diverted to Tacloban, which was still under construction. That night, crews finished the remaining 500 feet of sand and coral runway and Tacloban was ready for the arrival of the 49FG.

A Navy FM-2 Wildcat makes an emergency crash landing at **Tacloban** after its escort carrier was sunk. (AAF)

**24 October 1944: 475FG in the Battle of Leyte Gulf:**
The first American troops had established two wide beachheads on Leyte's eastern shore and the 1st Cavalry and 24th Infantry Divisions captured Tacloban Airstrip and the high ground on the northern coast. On 24 October during the Battle of Leyte Gulf, 475FG personnel aboard their ships underwent two Japanese air attacks. The first occurred just as their explosive and gasoline-loaded ships arrived at Tacloban but all bombs missed. The second attack occurred just as the first attack ended. The Japanese missed the 475th ships again but the men saw a Kamikaze crash into a nearby LST turning it into a large fireball. Once the Japanese left, the 475th sea echelon landed at Violet Beach and anchored off Dulag Town where they spent the night on their ships. The Japanese attacked during the night and the 432FS Flight Surgeon, Adjutant and pilot, 2Lt. Edgar Williams were seriously wounded and evacuated. The 475th endured two more air raids during the next day but there were no additional casualties. Only when the USN had gained air superiority over the beaches did the Navy begin to transfer 475FG personnel from the *Louis Weule*.

During the Leyte Invasion, American planners deviated from their policy of assaulting an objective that was in the range of effective land-based airpower but fortunately the invasion of Leyte caught the Japanese by surprise and the initial push into the Philippines was so successful that by 30 October all of northeast Leyte was nominally under American control from Leyte Valley to the hills overlooking the route to the main Japanese base at Ormoc on the western shore.

**Tacloban Airstrip and the Battle of Leyte Gulf**
The Leyte Air Task Force Commander was Col. David Hutchinson who had been nicknamed "Photo Hutch" as the 49ers old CO was Donald "Fighter Hutch" Hutchinson, and now was the new Chief of Staff of the FEAF. Photo Hutch was a zealous planner and then achiever who immediately improved the Cataisan runway to base the fighters needed to defend the area. On the broad, flat plain between Dulag and Barauen there was space for three more airfields which would require some time to be secured by the infantry and then constructed. In the mean time the airstrip at Cataisan would have to serve as Kenney's first airbase in the Philippines.

To put the primitive strip, to be known as Tacloban Airfield, into service, every available truck and man was enlisted to transport the raw coral excavated from a beach several miles away. Five days and nights of continuous labor were required to complete the 3,000 foot runway of mixed coral and sand. Two thousand feet of the runway which was only just the minimum length for a P-38 to take off or land had been covered with Marston mat. The 49th Fighter Air Control Squadron set up there air control station at Palo village six miles to the south.

Japanese aerial reconnaissance and enemy soldiers who remained in the area masquerading as Philippine workers kept the Japanese Command apprised of the American build up at Tacloban. The Japanese attacked the base but these attacks never seriously affected its progress any more than the worsening weather which proceeded the monsoon season.

**26 October 1944: Leyte/Tacloban**
It was crucial that land-based aircraft were available to cover the shipping in the harbor which was loaded with men and supplies waiting to go ashore. During the morning of 24 October 5th Fighter Command ground crewmen began to arrive to prepare the captured airfields but were hampered by the lack of materials and equipment and enemy air raids. On the 26th the Japanese sent 12 air raids, comprising of 150 aircraft. The first one was at 0515 and continued through out the day with four attacks coming without warning. In the face of all these interruptions; by 1500 about 1,000 feet of steel mat had been laid. Kenney was conferring with a Colonel who headed runway construction; using a map of the area spread out on the top of his jeep when about 500 yards away four Japanese fighters began a strafing run. Kenney dropped on the ground behind the jeep as the enemy fighters swept along the runway strafing and dropping bombs. Kenney and the jeep escaped but a truck 10 feet away was set on fire and its driver wounded. Two men were killed in an AA machine gun pit about 50 feet from the General and two Navy planes were set on fire and destroyed and two other men were killed and 10 wounded. Many of the enemy bombs failed to explode or the damage would have been much worse as one of the duds landed in front of a tent in which 30 or 40 Navy flyers were having coffee.

A pre-invasion recon photo showing the primitive condition of enemy-held **Tacloban**. (AAF)

On the 26th, the Japanese sent 12 air raids comprised of 150 aircraft, which were met by intense naval and ground AA fire. (AAF)

A newly arrived P-38 destroyed by Japanese bombs. (AAF)

On the 26th, **Kenney** asked Whitehead to send 34 P-38s from Morotai, as there would be space at Tacloban for that many by noon the next day. (AAF)

A U.S. Army AA gun emplacement on **Tacloban** beach with the invasion fleet in background. (U.S. Army)

By that evening 1,500 feet of steel mat had been laid and Kenney had the engineers working all night to get at least 3,000 feet by noon of the next day as a good P-38 pilot could land on 3,000 feet of runway. Kenney radioed Whitehead to send up 34 P-38s from Morotai as there would be space for that many by noon the next day. Adm. Kincaid's escort carriers left the area on the 27th as they needed to be refueled and many repaired. The Japanese made single plane attacks on the airdrome at intervals all night. While the damage was relatively light; it interfered with the work on the runway and by noon only 2,500 feet of steel mat had been laid. During the final hour before noon, coral was rolled into the sand for another 1,000 feet at the end of the strip so that if the P-38s overran they would have less chance of having an accident. All 34 Lightnings landed safely and were personally greeted by Kenney and MacArthur. Engineers worked obsessively laying steel mat all afternoon and by 1600 had laid another 1,000 feet. For some reason no enemy aircraft appeared marking the longest period without an air attack since the first day of the landings. Radar had been installed that morning and, while it wasn't working very well yet, it gave about 10 minutes warning of an attack. At 1700 five enemy aircraft appeared and were intercepted by the newly arrived Lightnings.

When Kenney returned to Hollandia he told Whitehead to go to Leyte to establish his HQ there and to keep Tacloban supplied with fighters as quickly as space became available. Kenney's HQ was to be established at Colosa, on the Gulf about 12 miles south of Tacloban by 1 December.

**Gen. Hugh Casey and the Army Service Command in the Philippines**

In New Guinea, logistics and construction activities were coordinated by task force engineer staffs but these were often hastily assembled and had not always been able to meet the demands imposed by base development in such a demanding theater of operations. The scale of operations in the Philippines was to be much greater, so for this purpose the Army Service Command (ASCOM) was formed in Brisbane on 23 July 1944. with Casey appointed as its Commander. Although part of USASOS, ASCOM operated under the control of Sixth Army, moving as far forward as combat operations allowed, developed new bases, and operated them until USASOS was ready to take over, at which point the units under ASCOM simply reverted back to USASOS, allowing a seamless transfer of command. For the Battle of Leyte Casey's ASCOM had 43,000 men, of whom 21,000 were engineers. Casey and some members of his staff came ashore on A-Day; the advance echelon of his ASCOM headquarters arrived two days later. Work began immediately on the airfield at Tacloban and soon it was fully occupied with the 100+ aircraft on hand and Dulag could handle another 75 fighters. Work commenced on airfields in central Leyte soon after they were captured but heavy seasonal rains thwarted attempts to develop the airbases there. The roads became rutted quagmires; keeping the engineers busy filling holes to keep traffic moving at all. The 12 mile journey from Tacloban to Dulag took three to four hours in a jeep or a truck. San Pablo was progressing slowly; while the two airdromes located very close to the front to the west at Burauen and Bayug were limited to a group of bombers or a group of strafers. Whitehead had established his advanced headquarters at Burauen only a mile and a half from the front with Wurtsmith running it. Thus, it was decided to construct a new airbase on the coast at Tanauan. While suitable from a construction point of view, there was a 250 foot hill at one end of the runway and the site was already occupied by Sixth Army headquarters. However, the need to get aircraft based on Leyte to stop the Japanese from reinforcing the island was so pressing that Lieutenant General George Kenney was persuaded to accept the site and Lt.Gen. Walter Krueger agreed to move his headquarters.

**Leyte Airfields**

Tacloban

Although the Tacloban runway had not been used by the Japanese for some time; reconnaissance had determined that it could be quickly developed and on A Day, the 46th Engineer Construction Battalion arrived to focus its efforts here. The site was located on a sand spit approximately a mile long and about 300 yards wide and to obtain the specified 6,000 foot length, it was necessary to rotate the center line of the existing runway 10° from its original alignment. Even though construction at Tacloban involved virtually all new construction, the target date for completion to operational standards for one fighter group was set at A plus 5. This pre-established early completion date was deemed difficult but possible and set because air support over Leyte was only provided by carrier-based aircraft until air facilities for land-based aircraft could

**Tacloban**, mid-November 1944. (AAF)

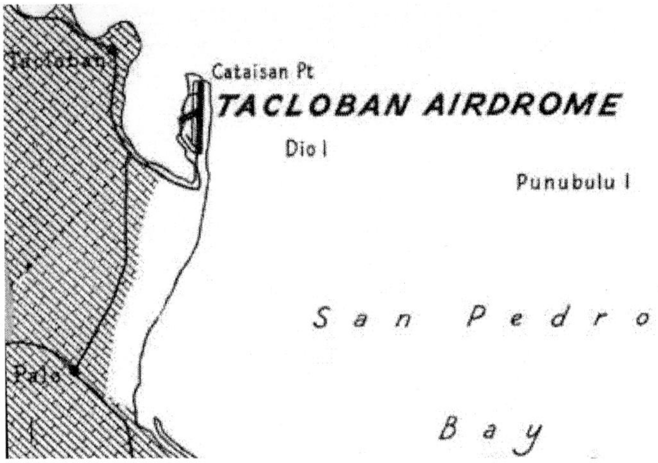


become available. For the first four days after the invasion the Japanese air attacks were moderate and the weather remained comparatively good but then the weather became rainy and the Japanese air attacks increased and were compounded by other inhibiting circumstances. The foremost circumstance was the use of the airdrome area as an unloading area for supplies, equipment, and ammunition which basically stopped all construction. Debarking troops and vehicles came directly on shore at the Drome and swarmed across the construction area and converged on the single access road leading inland. This congestion not only interfered with the filling of bomb craters and rough grading but also seriously delayed the hauling of coral which had to be placed over the existing surface before steel mat could be laid. A coral deposit had been located about two miles from the south end of the runway but dump trucks hauling the coral had to travel almost continually in low gear against an increasing flow of combat equipment and supply truck traffic moving in the opposite direction. By A plus 3 Kenney protested

**Tacloban**, late January 1945. (AAF)

the beaching of landing craft on the edge of the unfinished runway and was demanding the movement of steel mat ashore so the runway could be surfaced and land-based air operations started. The aircraft carriers providing air cover could remain offshore only for a few more days before leaving to refuel and rearm and if land-based fighters were not in place by then to provide air cover, the Japanese would have free rein to cause havoc on the Allied beaches. Fortunately, on A plus 3, the 1881st Engineer Aviation Battalion and the 240th Engineer Construction Battalion arrived to reinforce the 46th Engineers. On A plus 4 Japanese aircraft were attacking the area almost unopposed as Japanese naval forces were approaching Leyte and the Allied carrier-based aircraft, which had been providing air cover on shore, were now urgently supporting the naval battle off shore. Every available soldier and Filipino was pressed into service clearing the airdrome to expedite its completion to get land-based aircraft into the air. Then, the supply of coral from the pit on Cataisan Point was running low and Headquarters, ASCOM, quickly diverted a dredge that was excavating the channel into Tacloban to that of pumping coral fill material directly ashore for grading the airdrome. By that night two barges loaded with steel mat arrived for the final runway surfacing as soon as the six inch coral base was completed. To accelerate runway completion the mat was to be laid from both ends and quarter points of the runway and cut and welded at points of juncture. But by A plus 5, as the engineers were completing the laying the subgrade, suicide attacks by Kamikaze aircraft were taking a heavy toll of supporting carriers which had been continually sending out their aircraft to fly patrols over the fleet and the shipping in Leyte Gulf. Several of the carriers were damaged or sunk and their aircraft were unable to land on them and flew to Tacloban before they ran out of fuel. Tacloban's runway was not completely rolled for landings and about 25 of the first 65 aircraft to land were wrecked and had to be bulldozed off the runway into the sea to prevent additional delays to construction. Meanwhile, the runway surface was hurriedly rolled, and succeeding aircraft which landed were quickly refueled, loaded with bombs and ammunition.

Although the rains started on A plus 5, sufficient steel mat had been laid and limited dispersals were ready for fighters by A plus 6, only one day behind schedule, despite an unequaled combination of obstacles which now included determined enemy air attacks and continuous rain. Extension of the steel mat surfacing and construction of taxiways and hardstands proceeded despite heavy losses for the engineers in both equipment and personnel. Meanwhile carrier-based aircraft were thinly spread trying to cover the entire area. Weather prevented the planned forward movement of P-38s from Morotai to Tacloban until the next day, A plus 7 when 34 P-38s arrived. While these P-38s were only able to provide a limited defense against enemy air attacks and the carriers and their aircraft departed; the Japanese inexplicably switched the emphasis of their air attacks to night actions. Meanwhile, the Japanese began reinforcing their Leyte garrisons through Ormoc Bay on the west coast of Leyte. When a large enemy convoy approached Ormoc Bay on 2 November, only eight P-38s could be spared from base CAP to attack the Japanese transports. 5BC bombers based on Morotai had to stage through Tacloban to engage the convoy. The small numbers of aircraft based at Tacloban were packed too tightly on the facilities developed so far, and the engineer units, aided by more than 1,500 Filipinos, were frantically working around-the-clock under rainy weather and Japanese air attacks. By 9 November (A plus 20), they had completed not only the 6,000 foot, steel mat covered runway but also a 2,000 foot parallel taxiway and a 2,100 foot diagonal taxiway. The runway was extended to 6,900 feet and 92 hardstands were provided by early February 1945. Tacloban was completed by 25 February when the last nine hardstands were completed.

5FC units based at Tacloban were;

**49FG:** 7FS (P-38) from Biak on 24 October 1944 to San Jose on 30 December 1944
**49FG:** 9FS (P-38) from Biak on 24 October 1944 to San Jose on 30 December 1944
**49FG:** 8FS (P-38) from Biak on 25 October 1944 to ?
**71TRG:** Air Echelon (P-40) from Biak on 3 November 1944 to ?
**348FG:** 460FS (P-47) from Noemfoor on 10 November 1944 to Tanauan on 12 December 1944
**348FG:** 340FS (P-47) from Noemfoor on 30 November 1944 to Tanauan on 14 December 1944
**348FG:** 342FS (P-47) from Noemfoor on 1 December 1944 to Tanauan on 16 December 1944
**348FG:** 341FS (P-47) from Noemfoor on ? December 1944 to Tanauan on 12 December 1944

Tacloban became so busy and space was at such a premium that it became SOP that any aircraft that could not be repaired within 24 hours was to be bulldozed into the Bay. During the early morning at the end of November a loaded B-24 started down the Tacloban runway on its take off run when at the same time a C-46 transport started to land from the wrong direction. When the control tower saw that it was obvious that the two aircraft would collide on the runway they fired a red flare. The Liberator was about three feet off the ground its pilot tried to swerve to the left. Many aircraft were parked along the runway but the B-24 pilot managed to miss all of them but hit the C-46 which was loaded with wounded and both aircraft burned completely and over 50 men burned to death.

### Dulag

Although the Dulag airstrip was captured on 21 October (A plus 1), no engineer units were available until the 808th Engineer Aviation Battalion was landed in the vicinity of Dulag during the morning of the 23rd and immediately unloaded and by 1700 was on its way to the airstrip. Dulag was located on the flat flood plain of the Marabang River, 300 yards from, and parallel to, the main Dulag-Burauen road. The existing short airstrip had been leveled by the Japanese and covered with a thin layer of gravel approximately one inch thick. The 808th immediately began preliminary work on the runway, and, by early morning of the 24th, the Battalion put three shifts to work. The following morning, construction equipment had to leave the site as naval aircraft from carriers under attack or sunk were forced to use Dulag and Tacloban for emergency landings. The 808th Engineers spent the day clearing the runways of wrecked aircraft, hauling torpedo bombers out of the swampy area off the end of the short runway, and refueling and rearming aircraft which could still take off. Navy aircraft continued to land and take off throughout the next day under intermittent enemy air raids and the dangerous fall of spent shell fragments from friendly AA guns from ships in the harbor. On 27 October the 821st Engineer Aviation Battalion arrived and work on the airdrome was resumed as the last of the naval aircraft returned to designated carriers. Soon thereafter, the 842nd Engineer Aviation Battalion arrived to augment the 808th and 821st Engineers at Dulag.

The constant rainy weather would soon limit the availability of dry clay for stabilization of the sand base being placed on the runway and it was decided to cover a half inch layer of compacted sand with a thee inch layer of compacted gravel before laying the steel mat. Meanwhile, the road from the runway to the sand and gravel sources continually crumbled under the heavy construction traffic and engineers had to be diverted to surface the road with steel mat. The gravel was of poor quality, being 50% sand, and in the midst of construction, a flash flood flooded the gravel pit; submerging many pieces of equipment and completely washed out the road to it.

**Dulag Airdrome.** (AAF)

**Dulag Beach** and Airdrome ammunition dumps under enemy attack. (AAF)

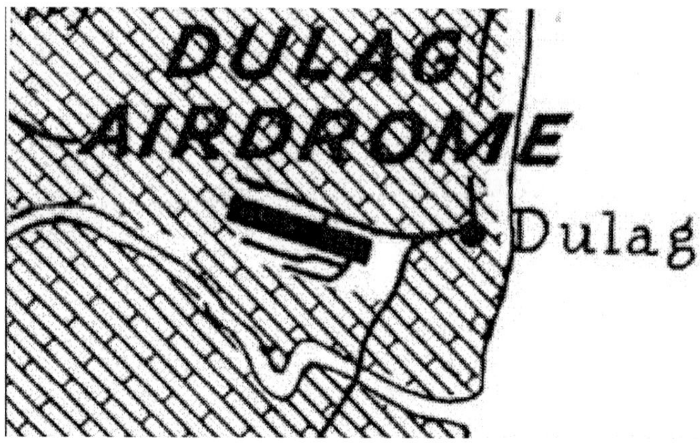


Because of the airdrome's flat terrain, drainage was a problem and required an extensive system of long drainage ditches to the Marabang River.

On 17 November the 821st Engineers at Dulag were laying steel mat around-the-clock in the rain to accelerate the transfer of fighter aircraft from the now over crowded Tacloban. After working all night in a downpour, the Battalion completed steel mat coverage of a 4,100x100 foot section of the runway and 35 Lightnings flew in from Tacloban during the afternoon. Rain and mud not only continued to interfere with airdrome construction but the engineers had to be diverted to maintaining the gravel haul roads but also to improving and widening the main Dulag-Burauen road which was the only way inland and was being destroyed by the heavy military loads continually moving over it. By 9 December the runway had been extended only to 5,000 feet and there was much work was to be completed on the shoulders and drainage. Construction to complete the 6,000x100 foot steel mat runway and 80 hardstands was not finished before the end of February.

5FC units bases at Dulag:

**HQ 475FG:** from Biak on 28 October 1944 to 5 February 1945 to San Jose

**47FG/432FS (P-38):** from Biak on November 2, 1944 - ?

**71TRG/110TRS (ground):** from Biak on 3 November to 25 December 1944 to San Jose

**8FG/35FS & 36FS (ground echelons):** from Morotai on 5 November 1944 to ?

**6PRS/8PRS (F-5):** from Biak on 4 November 1944 to 20 May 1945 to Clark Field

**475FG/431FS (P-38):** from Biak on 9 November 1944 to 28 February1945 to Clark Field

**475/FG/432FS (P-38):** from Biak on 9 November 1944 to 27 February 1945to Clark Field
**475/FG/433FS (P-38):** from Biak on 9 November 1944 to 28 February 1945 to Clark Field
**475FG/433FS (P-38):** from Biak on 13 November 1944 to 5 February 1945 to ?
**6PRG/20CMS (ground):** from Biak on 15 November 1944 to 18 May 1945 to Clark Field
**8FG/80FS (ground):** from Morotai on 15 November 1944 to ?
**8FG/35FS (P-38s):** on 28 November 1944 to ?
**8FG/36FS & 80FS (P-38s):** on 30 November 1944 to ?

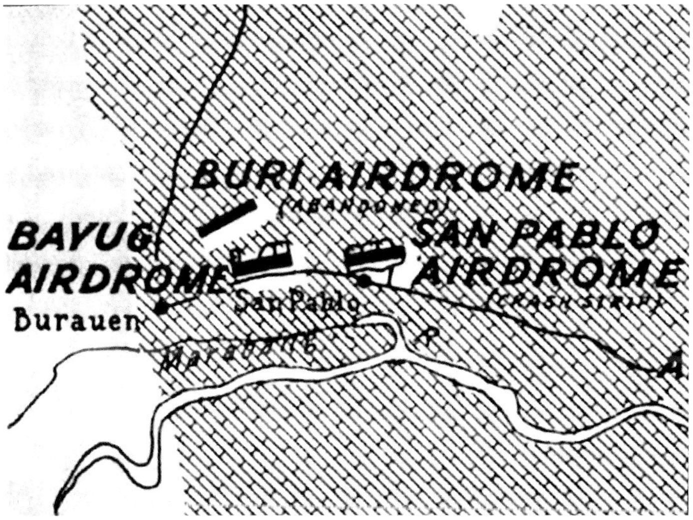


**Burauen Area Airdromes**: Bayug, Buri, and San Pablo.

Bayug

Bayug Airfield was located east of Burauen and to the west of San Pablo Airfield, It was built by the Japanese in 1943 with a single runway and two revetments with the taxiways in a V shape from the main runway. It was captured on 24 October (A plus 4) and was first developed for dry weather operations. After all bomb craters were filled, the airstrip had been put in use by fighters on 3 November 1944 but, once the heavy rains began, the P-38s based there had many accidents. The 1906th Engineer Aviation Battalion and the 61st Naval Construction Battalion worked under the same adverse conditions as those faced at Dulag. Heavy rains and numerous air raids caused long delays and disrupted construction schedules. The runway was covered by a one to five foot layer of surface of silt that became very unstable when wet and it became necessary to cut large dragline ditches to drain the airstrip. Because of the poor subgrade it was thought that the runway, even with a steel mat surface, would not be operational for any reasonable length of time and recommended that it be abandoned. However, Kenney did not agree and the decision was made to complete it by substituting a parallel taxiway and alert areas along the airstrip instead of the two dispersal taxiway loops which had been originally planned but which would have been unfeasible to develop on the poorly drained site. Sufficient steel mat was not available until mid-November and although good construction practice dictated that a suitable base should first be laid, the urgency of the air situation demanded that the mat be laid on graded earth. Even so progress was slow because of wet weather, supply difficulties, the emergency use of the runway by aircraft; the continued heavy maintenance of the access roads which took personnel from Dulag. Further delay was caused by Japanese paratroops that disrupted work at this and two adjacent airstrips for three days. By 22 December, 35 days after start of mat installation, the 4,500 foot long runway was finally completely covered. During January and February 1945, 32 hardstands and the parallel taxiway were

**Bayug Airdrome**. (AAF)

added to complete the airdrome but, owing to the unstable base under the runway as well as the reduced need for air facilities in that area, Bayug was relegated to a reserve airdrome status by the end of May.

5AF units based at Bayug:

**5AF HQ, 5FC, and 5BC:** from 20 November to January 1945;
**308th Bombardment Wing:** from 22 October 1944 to 11 January 1945.
**310th Bombardment Wing:** from 14 November 1944 to 15 December 1944.
**71st Recon Group:** from 5 November 1944 to 5 February 1945.

Buri
The capture of the Buri Airstrip area encountered significant enemy resistance and aircraft, artillery, and tanks had to be engaged before the Japanese were dislodged on 27 October. Despite the heavy fighting the Buri airstrip was left in nearly serviceable condition. By 5 November the runway had been prepared for dry weather use and was being employed by fighter aircraft but its maintenance required a great amount of effort and new construction involved only the addition of an access road and clearing of approach zones. Engineer Construction Battalions, meanwhile, were being diverted to support the X and XXIV Corps to maintain their long overland lines of communication. By late November, it had become obvious that there were an insufficient number of engineer troops available to develop all of the planned airdromes under the trying conditions of heavy rains, poor drainage, and inferior access roads. The strip was built on a flood plain and the engineers could not keep the water off the strip and the P-38s were always getting stuck, and the engineers were continually moving the aircraft around with tractors. The airfield was used by the 431FS/475FG. Finally, Kenney agreed that manpower was being wasted at Buri and work on the project was abandoned on 30 November. Part of the Japanese paratrooper attack on 7 December landed near Buri.

San Pablo
The San Pablo airstrip was captured on 23 October against light enemy opposition and a 5,000x100 foot runway had been rough graded when heavy rains virtually stopped all construction and turned the access roads into quagmires. Further construction was abandoned on 23 November because of the slow progress and the large amount of engineer effort was still required to finish the field. The field was used as an emergency field and by liaison aircraft.

Tanauan
With the slow opening of the Leyte airdromes, the available facilities for local air defense continued to be seriously inadequate especially when they would be needed to provide air support to the approaching Mindoro Campaign. ASCOM continued its reconnaissance and located the one potential airdrome site that could be quickly developed. The site was located at the beach area at Tanauan, approximately midway from Tacloban and Dulag. It had a good sandy surface which drained readily and was considered excellent for all-weather airdrome construction. The north approach of the proposed runway was over water and unlimited. However, Tanauan had one disadvantage that could make it unacceptable to Kenney and Krueger; a 250 foot rocky hill centered on the south approach limited the glide angle at that end to 11 to 1. Initial Fifth Air Force reaction to a one way approach field was at best negative. Also the site was occupied by the Sixth Army HQ which had recently been moved there from Tacloban. Nevertheless, both Kenney and Krueger realized there was an emergency and relented. With the abandonment of San Pablo, two engineer aviation battalions had become available for the Tanauan project. When the Mindoro Campaign was postponed another Engineer Aviation Battalion become temporarily available for 10 days and was assigned to the development of the urgently needed second runway at Tanauan. Construction started as soon as the Sixth Army moved on 28 November. The jungle was cleared and drainage was provided and about four inches of coral was added to the sandy soil to act as a binder. Sheepsfoot and smooth rollers

**Buri Airdrome.** (AAF)

**San Pablo.** (AAF)

**Tanauan Airdrome.** (AAF)

produced a compact surface which was then overlaid with steel matting and the airdrome became operable on 16 December only 18 days after work had begun. Seven days later the runway had been lengthened to 6,000 feet, with a 50 foot coral overrun, a parallel taxiway built, and 22 dispersals. By mid-February Tanauan Drome was complete and no accident was ever reported due to either the rocky hill or the one way approach.

5FC units based on Tanauan were:

**348FG:** 460FS (P-47) from Tacloban on 12 December 1944 to ?
**348FG:** 340FS (P-47) from Tacloban on 14 December 1944 to San Marcelino on 4 February 1945
**348FG:** 341FS (P-47) from Tacloban on 15 December 1944 to ?
**348FG:** 342FS (P-47) from Tacloban on 16 December 1944 to San Marcelino on 4 February 1945

**Mid to Late October 1944: 49FG Move to Tacloban**

After their missions to Balikpapen, the 9FS Flying Knights' Lightnings were refitted and returned veteran Maj. Robert McComsey was welcomed as their new CO. Meanwhile, Capt. William Drier and his 8FS Black Sheep were at Biak as the last of his junior officers transitioned to the rebuilt P-38 J models. The 7FS Screamin' Demons CO, Capt. Edward Peck, was still plagued with Malaria that grounded him from combat and Ops Exec Capt. Robert DeHaven served as acting CO. Meanwhile, back at Hollandia, the ground echelon had boarded the troop ships as early as the 16th, and then had to wait in anchorage aboard the crowded vessels. So, while the 49ers had been designated as the first 5FC Group for the Philippines air mobilization; on the 20th, 49ers' CO Lt.Col. George Walker was still at Mokmer.

Finally, on the 19th, the ground echelon boarded their LST and steamed out of Humboldt Bay, Hollandia, and was joined enroute by the aircrew echelons from Biak who also packed aboard another LST. The 49ers had been informed as to their part in the invasion as the AAF had circulated a packet to every enlisted man describing MacArthur's objective of liberating the Philippines, along with educational material on the customs and language of the island's population. Both 49er ships arrived at the crowded Leyte Gulf beachhead during the night of the 24th and the next morning, in the middle of an air battle, steamed into San Pedro Bay with their priority being to get the airfield operational ASAP.

With their shipboard gunners firing at Japanese aircraft overhead, the LSTs arrived at the seaward shore at Cataisin Point just south of the airfield but the water there was too deep. Engineers and Philippine laborers quickly constructed a makeshift dock of sandbags and planking and as the

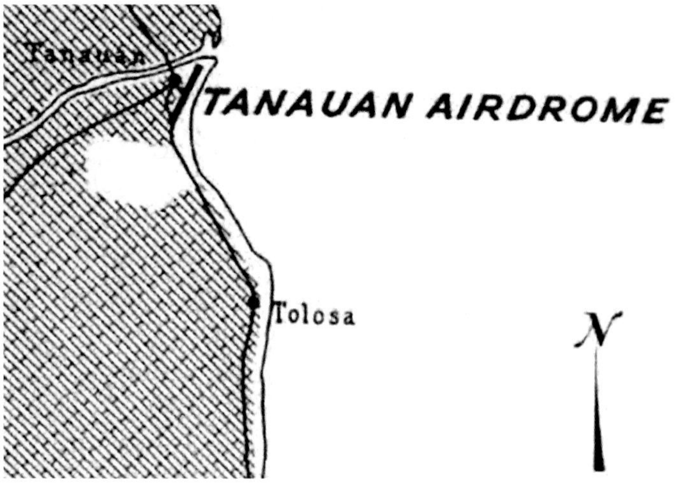


men disembarked, a LST a short distance down the beach was hit and set ablaze by enemy aircraft. While Naval AA gunners fired and infantry gunfire was heard from deep within the forest, the 49ers joined Hutchinson's labor force and reached the airfield by boat and via the single narrow road from the south. An aircraft dispersal area had been graded out on the peninsula's west bank but there was virtually no space remaining for either anti-aircraft gun pits or air raid shelters. The 49ers were at the mercy of any strafing Japanese fighter or dive bomber.

On the 22nd, Walker's 49FG fighters staged to Morotai but the situation at Tacloban forced them to stay at Morotai for another four days. Finally, at 0900 on 27 October Wurtsmith ordered Walker's fighters to leave Morotai for the 700 mile one way trip. The 34 P-38s crossed the open sea, led by a navigation B-25 in the lead and flew over the eastern Mindanao coast by mid morning and then arrived over Tacloban at noon. When Group Leader Walker, Wingman Col. Robert Morrissey, Element Leader Richard Bong and Wingman Gerald Johnson turned left into the southbound approach to Tacloban Walker gave the veteran Morrissey the honor of the first landing by an AAF fighter pilot in the Philippines since 1942. The Flight landed, only to find that 35FS 1Lt. William Gardner had been forced to land there only hours before when his P-38 was hit by friendly AA fire during a morning fighter sweep over the invasion fleet.

The other 30 P-38s landed and were greeted by their ground crews and Gen. Kenney who immediately welcomed his favorite pilot, top ace Dick Bong, who was now supposedly relegated to the non-combat role of "Gunnery Training Officer." Bong told Kenney that he probably would not enter into operations right away but then asked, "Could I just join up with the first patrol to get to know the place?"

**27 October 1944: 49FG**

After arriving and meeting Kenney Col. Morrissey and Maj. Johnson met with MacArthur, and then hurried back to Tacloban Airfield and found that Bong was ready to fly as Kenney had personally given him permission to join the next patrol. Flights of eight Lightnings were to be continuously rotated to patrol over the west bank of the crowded Leyte Gulf while another eight remained in readiness to respond to any alert. After checking in at the Ops tent, the three pilots got themselves assigned to the next 9FS patrol and were airborne at 1600. The three staff officer pilots were designated Green Flight and flew as an attached escort to the other eight Flying Knights whose Lightnings each carried 1,000 pound bombs to drop on enemy fortifications just south of the Dulag Village. While the Knight fighter bombers attacked their targets, Morrissey and Bong turned inland to search for enemy planes.

After bombing their target near Dulag, Mission Leader 1Lt. Robert Wood recalled his Yellow Flight Wingman, 1Lt. Arthur Hufford, Element

**1Lt. William Gardner** (with Gen. Kenney) was the first American pilot to land on the Philippines since 1942, when he was forced to land at Tacloban after his P-38 was hit by friendly AA fire. (AAF)

**Maj. Gerald Johnson** shot down a Val and Oscar to make him a triple ace. (AFAA)

**1Lt. Arthur Hufford** was credited with his only victory in this battle. (AAF)

**1Lt. Bernard Krankowitz** claimed a probable and his only victory. (AAF)

Leader, Bernard Krankowitz, and John Hanisch, and then radioed Flight Leader 1Lt. Harold Olgesby and his three wingmen to regroup over the water. As the eight Knight fighters climbed through the overcast, Wood's aircraft experienced engine problems and he returned to Tacloban, leaving Yellow Element Leader Krankowitz in command. Krankowitz then turned north but separated from Blue Flight in the clouds and ordered Blue Flight to return on their own. After Krankowitz got his Yellow Flight together, rain clouds closed to 8,000 feet as they were about to enter the approach pattern to Tacloban. Krankowitz sighted three Val dive bombers in a V formation passing the Lightnings at their altitude flying in the opposite direction along a shallow valley just south of Tacloban Town. Hufford dove on the right Val and closed to 300 yards and fired a short burst and then closed firing four or five bursts from 200 to 150 yards and set fire to its left wing near the fuselage and it was confirmed by his wingmen for his only victory of the war. Krankowitz immediately turned left for a rear quarter attack on the right Val and as he pulled into firing range on the lead Val, its rear gunner opened fire but the Lightning's .50 calibers killed the gunner immediately and got hits on the wings and fuselage but overran with his only victory. Wingman Hufford simultaneously opened fire on this right element dive bomber and fired when his guns ran away and the Val escaped as a damaged claim. Yellow Flight separated as they broke away from the initial attack but Krankowitz was able to catch the trailing Val element and fired at the #2 man with a two second burst from astern and it trailed black smoke before it disappeared into the overcast for a probable.

Col. Morrissey and illustrious wingmen Majors Bong and Johnson took off from Tacloban at 1600 and patrolled the area at 8,000 to 14,000 feet when at 1720 the Controller called air activity over Tacloban. They were 20 miles northwest of Yellow Flight where they spotted four Oscars at 8,000 feet. Bong turned on one and Morrissey on the other. Morrissey closed from dead astern and fired a 10 degree left deflection and the enemy fighter went straight down in a cloud at about 1,500 feet and Bong and Johnson confirmed Morrissey's second victory. Bong fired a short 90 degree deflection shot at the Oscar but Johnson, following somewhat behind the two, turned on Bong's intended victim from dead astern and quickly destroyed the enemy fighter with a long, fatal burst. Bong then saw another Oscar at 10 o'clock high and gave chase and when he fired he saw "hits all over the airplane" and the Oscar fell off on its right wing and went into the water for his 31st victory. He then chased a second Oscar through rain squalls to Leyte's far northern shore and followed it through several clouds and fired a number of short bursts at it before it disappeared into dark rain clouds over Biliran Island for a damaged claim. Morrissey climbed back to 8,000 feet and saw a Val down on the water and dove and was closing rapidly when he saw Johnson on the same Val at 45 degrees and fired first getting hits and the Val started down toward the water making Johnson a triple ace with 15 victories. The Val's tail gunner was still firing from his doomed dive bomber and Morrissey closed to 30 degrees and killed the stubborn gunner. The two were out of ammo and low on fuel, and landed at Tacloban, believing that they had made the first AAF kills over the Philippines only to learn that Krankowitz had that honor.

**28 October 1944: 49FG/7FS/9FS**

Bong wanted to return to northern Leyte early the next day where he was sure there would be happy hunting but the weather was too bad. During the heavy rains, the Japanese landed a convoy of reinforcements into the large harbor which served the garrison at Ormoc Village on Leyte's west coast. Kenney was informed of these reinforcements but his Lightnings at Tacloban were weathered-in. Kinkaid's escort carriers in the south were able to launch a small sortie which attacked the Ormoc docks in the marginal weather but the Japanese troops landed with minimal interruption.

At 1430, weather recon flights reported improved weather conditions to the north and west and 12 7FS Screamin' Demons reached Ormoc Bay and dropped their heavy ordinance on tiny Masisingi Island south of the garrison and then turned back to patrol over the interior of the mainland. The weather continued to improve and by late afternoon and both the Japanese and Americans were back in the air. Tacloban alerted its standby flights at 1600 and newly promoted Capt. John Haher led his Flight to join the standing patrol. As his flight broke out above the overcast at 15,000 feet, Haher immediately saw an enemy contact 10 miles south of the Tacloban. Haher's Flight consisted of two other wingmen but the outnumbered trio readily chased after six Oscars which approached them at 2,000 feet high. Haher, with wingmen 2Lts. George Spruill and George Rogers, throttled forward and climbed behind the enemy to 27,000 feet without being seen. Haher was about to fire from dead astern when the enemy leader and Wingman both rocked their wings. Haher thought for a moment these aircraft might be U.S. Navy but when the leading four aircraft turned in a climb he sighted of their red wing roundels and he closed on the trailing Oscar and opened fire but the Oscar got away in a Split-S descent. Haher then dove after the escaping Ki-43 and quickly hit the enemy with a heavy burst which set the center fuselage on fire and it plunged into the jungle for his third and last victory. Meanwhile, Spruill and Rogers fired at the next pair of Oscars but the two rookie pilots became targets when the Oscars out turned them. Rogers was able to escape in a high speed dive and Haher arrived just in time to chase the Oscar off Spruill's tail. Haher continued after Spruill's attacker in a turning descent to 15,000 feet, where he fired several bursts without apparent effect. As he reached the western coastline Haher's guns suddenly seized due to the G-forces. Without his rookie wingmen, Haher was in danger if the Oscar turned into him. But suddenly Bong appeared and shot down the Oscar.

Maj. Richard Bong led the expert Captive Yellow Flight of Wingman, Maj. Gerald Johnson, and the second element of Cols. Robert Morrissey and George Walker off Tacloban at 1600 on a Red Alert. Bong believed that the Oscars were based at a strip on Biliran Island and turned north with Morrissey and Walker and the three flew over Biliran at 11,000 feet. Yellow Flight reached the southern most end of Masbate Island where they intercepted a lone Oscar cruising above in the opposite direction at 12 o'clock and saw another P-38 (Capt. John Haher) make an ineffectual pass and Bong chased it. He finally caught it on the west side of Leyte and fired from directly astern. Bong's bullets struck home and the Oscar inverted and started down with Bong following and firing until it caught fire and crashed. Yellow Flight climbed with Walker and Morrissey and circled waiting for Johnson. When Johnson did not appear the three headed toward Masbate Island at 11,000 feet. At 1650 when they reached the west end of the island they saw an Oscar slightly above them. Bong chandelled toward the Oscar pilot dropped its belly tank and started to dive away. As he fled the enemy pilot dropped his bomb which hit the Oscars empennage which broke off sending the Oscar into the water for an easy victory. Yellow Flight climbed back up to 10,000 feet heading toward Masbate Strip when they saw 17 Oscars milling from 3,000 to 7,000 feet at 9 o'clock over the southern end of the island. Morrissey turned back to find help and Bong and Walker "shadowed" the enemy fighters. The Oscars saw the two P-38s and Bong attacked the top Oscars because "he was rolling his wings and trying to warn the others." Bong fired a 45 degree deflection shot that got hits as it Split-S'd away for a damaged. Bong pulled up and fired a 30 degree shot that got some hits for another damaged claim. The whole enemy formation then dropped their tanks and bombs and started after them. Bong dove towards Tacloban and when Bong rejoined Walker he had to shut down his port engine which was overheating from a single bullet hole in his radiator. Bong had scored victories #32 and #33 and added two damaged for the day; nine ahead of McGuire who had 24.

9FS

Also on the 28th, 9FS Red Flight, under 1Lt. Raymond Swift flew another dive bombing mission to Ormoc. After they dropped their bombs, the four Red pilots began a routine patrol over Leyte at 10,000 feet. As they passed over the east coast, they saw US Navy AA bursts and saw a lone Oscar Spilt-S'd swiftly to the west. Swift followed it down to 5,000 feet caught the enemy, fired, and scored a few hits as it briefly disappeared under the broken overcast. Swift pursued west through the overcast using a dead reckoning heading and caught the Oscar again 60 miles beyond Ormoc as it crossed the Ormoc Bay coastline. Swift fired and hit its port wing and fuselage over the west coast of Cebu Island and finally it dropped off on one wing and crashed for his third and last victory after getting his second victory exactly a year before.

After Bong shot down two Japanese fighters Kenney wired Arnold, informing him of the victories by an ace pilot who was supposed to be grounded:

**1Lt. Raymond Swift** got his last of three victories, waiting a year after downing two enemy aircraft. (AAF)

In accordance with my instructions Major Richard Bong is trying to be careful, but the Nips won't do their part. On the twenty-seventh, five hours after arriving at Tacloban, Bong was again forced to defend himself and number thirty-one resulted. On the twenty-eighth, while looking for suitable localities for airdromes in the vicinity of Tacloban, he was assaulted by two more Nips, who became number thirty-two and thirty-three. Unless he was bothered again today this is his latest official score.

(Signed) Kenney

Arnold wired an answer a day or so later:

Major Bong's excuses in matter of shooting down three more Nips noted with happy skepticism by this headquarters. Subject officer judged incorrigible. In Judge Advocate's opinion, he is liable under Articles of War 122 (willful or negligent damage to enemy equipment or personnel).

(Signed) Arnold

Kenney posted copies of both radiograms on the group bulletin board.

**29 October 1944: 49 FG/7FS**

On the morning of the 29th, Leyte was again shrouded by squalls and only seven Screamin' Demons were able to take off at 0610 on a scramble over *Pepsi Cola* Controller's area. Capt. Robert DeHaven's Pinky Red Flight had trouble joining up not only due to the poor weather but also due friendly AA fire in the area and then because DeHaven's radio could not transmit. DeHaven's two wingmen separated in the climb through the overcast and DeHaven flew on alone. Soon he saw four Navy F6F Hellcats above him and climbed so they saw he was friendly and patrolled in their area until 0725. At this time *Pepsi Cola* called bogeys approaching the southern tip of Biliran Island. DeHaven climbed to 17,000 and as he neared Biliran four other Hellcats attacked a flight of Oscars. One was shot down and a second Split-S'd away but the third one escaped toward DeHaven with three Hellcats in pursuit. DeHaven dove under this Oscar and went down after the second Oscar. After catching the frantically fleeing enemy at 5,000 feet and 350 mph over Biliran, DeHaven fired as it went into a slight left turn. The Oscar pilot then rolled left and then rolled right which presented DeHaven with an almost stationary target. Pieces flew off the Oscar and hit DeHaven's P-38's port wing, rudder, prop, and coolant flaps. DeHaven overran the Oscar that rolled over and crashed near the area of the Hellcat's victim. When DeHaven landed he sent 1Lt. Cecil Archer back up over the area to confirm the wreckage and his 11th victory.

Meanwhile, Red Flight led by Capt. Elliot Dent remained together after take off when they broke out of the clouds at 10,000 feet. *Pepsi Cola* Controller vectored Red Flight due west at 16,000 feet. Once over Ormoc Bay, Wingman, 1Lt. Robert Searight, reported that his oxygen gear had malfunctioned causing Dent descend with Searight but as they reached 13,000 feet just over Cebu Island a lone Oscar came out of the clouds from 2,000 feet above and all four Demons climbed toward it and was hit

Publicity photo of the **49FG** celebrating their victories of 27-29 October (L to R): **Lt.Col. George Walker**, 49FG CO **Col. Robert Morrissey**: One victory 10/27: #2 **Maj. Gerald Johnson**, 49FG XO: two victories 10/27: #14-15 **2Lt. Milden Mathre**: His first victory on 10/29 and the 49FG's 500th **Maj. Wallace Jordan**, 9FS CO (temp) **Maj. Richard Bong**: One victory on 10/27 and two victories on 10/28 to give him 33 **Maj. Thomas McGuire**: Did not score and trailed Bong with 24 victories **Capt. Robert DeHaven**: Scored his 11th victory on 10/29

by the first three pilots and it started smoking. Red #4 2Lt. Milden Mathre was closing on the hapless Oscar when Red #3 fired and put three holes in Mathre's wing! Mathre continue to close and took two five second no deflection shots that tore off the Oscar's canopy. As he overran the Oscar he looked over into its cockpit that was "like a blast furnace" for his first victory toward becoming a five victory ace. The two Demon victories that day put the 49er total at 500.

When the 7FS returned they had learned that after they took off, two Oscar strafers caught ground crews in the open, killing one and wounding two others. Also, three Flying Knight P-38s were destroyed and four damaged but replacements from Morotai would soon arrive.

**30 October 1944: 49F/8FS**

At the end of October the 8th Fighter Group continued to be based on Morotai assigned to cut Japanese supply lines to its oil supply in Borneo. On 30 October Capt. William Giroux led the 36th Fighter Squadron against the airfield at Sandakan on the northern end of Borneo. Giroux describes the mission:

> The enemy was using it as a refueling station for the planes they were sending in to reinforce the big oil center of Balikpapan. When we got there we found only six planes on the ground. We knocked them out in a hurry. There were a couple of tankers a little way out in the harbor, so I took my squadron and went in on them. I singled out one and made a run on it. I came in pretty low, just skimming the water. I started shooting at about 300 yards and then pulled up over it. I must have hit a depth charge or some other high explosive because just as I got over the tanker the explosion caught me. I was traveling around 400 miles per hour and it blew me about 50 feet and a lot of debris damaged my plane. After I had passed over I found my plane would still fly and when I looked back the tanker was burning. It had broken in two parts and was starting to go down. I made a couple of passes at the second tanker, and all the rest of the guys got a shot at it. We left it burning badly and listing.

**31 October 1944: 49FG/7FS/9FS**

7FS

The 7FS sent out patrol flights, and during an attack by Vals, and as 1Lt. Robert Searight approached Tacloban, returning with engine trouble, nervous Army AA crews fired on the low flying P-38; it rolled over into a fatal plunge into the Gulf. 2Lt. Francis Hill was the last inbound pilot of Pinky White Flight, and as he was about to land Val dive bombers were coming in at 50 feet to bomb the field. He immediately retracted his landing gear and pulled the nose of his Lightning up to fire at the trailing Val, but the AA batteries which had shot down Searight had begun to fire at him. Hill broke off and turned a short distance inland to avoid the "friendly" flak, then turned to intercept the bombers four miles southwest of Cataisan Peninsula. Flying at 600 feet, he looked down and started shooting at a Val flying at 200 feet and hit its port wing root. The enemy pilot was so low that he sheared off the telephone line and Hill had to pull up to avoid a collision. Hill made a second pass from 30 degrees and hit the Val behind the cockpit, and it exploded 15 feet off the ground for his first victory.

9FS

At 1815 9FS Flying Knight 1Lt. Charles McElroy's four White Flight Lightnings was alerted by the Air Controller of bandits in the area of their landing approach. Five minutes later they saw three Vals in their bombing run one mile from the end of the strip. McElroy ordered tanks to be dropped and firewalled to intercept the Vals but they were too late to prevent them from dropping their bombs. After releasing their bombs the Vals went into a shallow dive and one turned left, one continued straight, and the other turned left. McElroy and Wingman, 1Lt. Noah Williams, chased after the middle Val down to 200 feet altitude. McElroy fired and started the Val smoking but overran. Williams came in and fired from 30 to five degrees and hit the cockpit and the Val then exploded for his first victory. 1Lt. Wade Lewis and Wingman, 2Lt. Ernest Ambort, chased after the left Val and Ambort made a 90 degree turn and fired first at 20 degrees and continued firing from dead astern and the Val exploded only 30 feet away but Ambort flew through the debris living to celebrate his first victory of five.

**2Lt. Ernest Ambort** got his first of five victories. (AFAA)

**31 October 1944: 49FG/7FS**

Flying Knights' new CO, Maj. Robert McComsey, who arrived at Tacloban three days earlier, had just gotten out of his jeep and was caught in an open dispersal area when Val dive bombers dropped their bombs among the parked Lightnings. He was critically wounded and sent back to America and Maj. Wallace Jordan became squadron CO.

**31 October 1944: 49F/8FS Arrives at Tacloban**

8FS CO, Capt. William Drier, was able to land 16 Lightnings on storm-racked Tacloban in the mid-morning of the 31st and finally joined the other two squadrons of the 49th Group. They had flown from Mokmer, staging through Morotai, but had lost three pilots. After they arrived they joined the other 5th FC personnel in losing sleep as they were kept awake during the night by nonstop red alerts as Japanese aircraft seemed to be overhead constantly. Despite the heat, rain, and bombardment, the ground crews kept enough fighters serviced, repaired, and ready each morning.

**31 October 1944: 421NFS: Movement to the Philippines**

On 18 September the Fifth Fighter Command issued an advanced Movement Order for the 418th, 419th, and 421st NFS to prepare for relocation to the Philippines. The 421NFS ground echelon was to join the 489th Fighter Group, a day fighter unit, scheduled to be the first Air Force units to reach the Philippines which ultimately was not to be. The flight echelon, alternatively, would remain in temporary quarters at Owi until they were ordered to fly their Black Widows to their new base at Tacloban.

**1Lt. Noah Williams** claimed his first of two victories. (AAF)

The ground echelon would be moved to Leyte by LST with the loading of equipment to begin on 13 October and the squadron was to break camp at Owi early on the 14th. They boarded the LST bound for Hollandia where it was to join with the convoy early on the morning of the 18th and sailed with 67 other naval vessels towards the Philippines for an uneventful six day trip. However, during the early morning of the 24th, four days after the initial landings, the convoy arrived at Leyte and met a concerted Japanese air attack including Kamikaze units. The 421st NFS personnel watched large dogfights overhead, witnessed bombing and strafing, and saw dozens of aircraft brought down by American AA fire and air patrols. Their LST was blocked by a sandbar 50 yards from the beach and the gap had to be filled by sandbags and bulldozers; all under Japanese air attacks. Once the 421st unloaded they found that their bivouac location was a swampy area infested by mosquitoes, a few enemy infiltrators, and daily enemy air attacks.

On 31 October the first six P-61s flew from Owi to Tacloban and on their first night there were sent out on a night patrol. Almost immediately the 421st's pilots found that one of Tacloban's great dangers was from nervous "friendly" Army and Navy AA gunners as two fighters were holed while in their landing patterns. Consequently, because of this danger, and also because the terrain surrounding Tacloban was unsuitable for night operations, P-61 night patrols would be very limited. Ideally, the GCI Stations and ground radar would detect enemy aircraft and then direct the night fighters on an intercept course to their intended targets. However, at Tacloban the location of the GCI station was so restricted that its radar sweeps were able to cover only a 90 degree area of the horizon which severely limited vectoring night fighters. The Squadron was later assigned to dusk and dawn convoy cover and mission in conjunction with PT Boat operations.

Japanese air raids continued into November and on the 4th the 421st suffered the worst day in its history. At 0745 an air raid on Tacloban occurred after no alarm was given and four low flying Zeros strafed and bombed the American aircraft and living quarters and several bombs exploded near the Squadron's mess and tents catching the men completely by surprise as they were eating breakfast or showering. Six men were killed and a number were hospitalized. Several days later Tacloban would receive the protection of the P-38s of the newly arrived 49FG. In later raids several other 421st personnel were slightly wounded.

Once the squadron's P-61s arrived at Tacloban many were in need of engine replacement. A large number of replacement engines had been shipped to and stored at Finschhafen and Biak. However, these engines had not been protected with a preservative and over 400 had succumbed to rapid corrosion in the humid jungle. The squadron was thus limited to six operational aircraft.

**31 October-November 1944: 35FG Assigned to the 13th Bomber Command**

On 31 October the 35th Fighter Group was assigned to the control of the 13th Bomber Command and the Group's missions from Morotai during late October and November were medium and heavy bomber escort missions which were to neutralize enemy airfield in the Netherlands East Indies area and thus secure the rear of the Philippines Campaign. Through methodical and repetitive attacks against enemy airdromes, oil fields and refineries, supply areas, and any shipping within range of Morotai the NEI was placed into an ever-tightening aerial blockade. Soon the refineries were shut down, any shipping was reduced to nighttime barge traffic, and enemy airdromes no longer had aircraft. Enemy ground units were cut off, not only from the Home Islands, but from each other. All land, sea, and air routes were closed from the NEI. The 35FG performed its duties so successfully that no 13BC formation was turned back from its target due to enemy interception. However, during this period the Japanese conducted concerted night attacks on 35FG bases on Morotai causing considerable damage to aircraft on Pitoe and Wama Airstrips. During the night of 28 November enemy bombs killed four enlisted men.

# 2

## November 1944

**November 1944: Situation**
The Leyte offensive came as a complete surprise to the Japanese High Command at Manila and after the late October monsoon; they finally were able to organize a stronger counter offensive. They withdrew troops from China, Malaya, and Indonesia, to join divisions from the northern Philippines to reinforce Leyte. More JAAF and JNAF units moved into the northern airfields to provide escort over Japanese convoys and to attack the new Allied airfields and beachhead. To counter this these new enemy units; on 31 October, the 8FG moved into the new Bayug Airfield just east of Barauen Village and the 475FG moved to the new airstrip on the coast at Dulag while the three Squadrons of the 49FG were finally together at Tacloban.

**1 November 1944: 49FG: 7FS/8FS/9FS**
Morning Mission: 7FS/9FS
On 1 November at 0940 the 9FS Flying Knights and the 7FS Screamin' Demons were vectored north of Tacloban. Knight's Flight Leader, 1Lt. Howard Oglesby, and Wingman, 2Lt. Cheatham Gupton, dove on two Vals escorted by a single Oscar. Oglesby took care of the escort for his third victory and the Gupton shot down both of the dive bombers for his first to of five victories. Gupton shot down the second Val while cutting off Demon Ops Exec Capt. Robert DeHaven who filed a duplicate claim on the Val and was irritated when the claim was awarded to the rookie Gupton. The sulking DeHaven then attached himself to the very next flight off Tacloban and with total disrespect for the airspace assigned to the Satan's Angels; he shot down a Zero directly over the Dulag strip for his uncontested 12th confirmed victory. After the sortie an equally irritated, 49er Ops Exec, Gerald Johnson met DeHaven on the flight line and ordered him not to fly again that day.

Afternoon Mission: 7FS/8FS
It would not be until late afternoon when the newly arrived Black Sheep finally got their first victory in the Philippines. New 8FS Black Sheep Ops Exec, Capt. Nelson Flack, was leading the last patrol of the day when the Air Controller vectored his Flight across the mainland to Ormoc Bay. The Black Sheep were joined by a Demon Flight led by Capt. Elliot Dent and the eight Lightnings arrived in a spread formation at 10,000 feet over Ormoc at 1700. Flack searched briefly to the west and then spotted a lone Oscar flying below near Duligan Point, a large headland southwest of Ormoc. Flack led the attack down to 3,000 feet, only to encounter a larger mixed formation of Zeros and Oscars that had been hidden by the scattered clouds. Element Leader 1Lt. John Bodak led his Wingman in a brief climb for a more coordinated attack and hit an Oscar with a lethal head on volley causing it to crash in the narrows just west of Gumalae Island for his third and last victory. Flack's elements regrouped and made a second pass, Flack and Wingman 2Lt. Nial Castle each downed a Zero (Flack's third). On the third pass Castle got his second Zero of five victories while Bodak's rookie Wingman 2Lt. Walter Meyer downed an Oscar over Matlang Point for his first of two victories. The combatants descended toward the Japanese ships at anchor and flak bursts erupted nearby and Flack had his Black Sheep to withdraw.

Demon Flight Leader Dent made a diving attack on the same lone Oscar that the Black Sheep abandoned at the onset. As Dent pursued the Oscar into the vicinity of the larger enemy formation below his three wingmen briefly lost him in the clouds. Dent suddenly confronted the larger formation and he decided to fight rather than take a chance on trying to outrun his adversaries. For the next ten minutes, Dent maneuvered through the enemy formation in the uneven fight which descended to the wave tops. Although Dent's Lightning was hit several times, he shot down two Zeros which crashed into the Bay and a third which crashed into a mangrove swamp near Duligan Point to make him an ace with six victories. As Dent was leaving the battle he was forced to make a low pass over enemy ships where his fighter was hit hard by AA fire. Dent bailed and landed safely among the vessels which had shot him down.

Meanwhile overhead, 7FS Element Leader Capt. John Haher covered Wingman 1Lt. Fernly Damstrom whose fighter had a defective starboard

**Capt. Elliott Dent** (shown during an earlier time) shot down three Oscars to make him an ace with six victories, but he was shot down and rescued. (AFAA)

supercharger while 2Lt. Harold Harris attacked a flight of Oscars. The confident Harris attacked the enemy and downed a Ki-43 and damaged another for his first of four victories. The Demons flew back to Tacloban to the east while Dent was last seen drifting in the bay.

Capt. Elliott Dent became separated from his flight that afternoon and described the situation in his ICR:

> "Four Zekes came out of the clouds from the right and I turned into them. Evidently my flight had lost me in the clouds because I never saw them after that. I made a head on pass at the four enemy, firing a burst at the lead ship. The outside man of the flight chandelled to the outside of the formation while the two center men split, 1 going up and the other down. From then on, for at least 15 or 20 minutes, which seemed like forever, my memory is very hazy as to individual passes, but during the entire time, I was either attacking or being attacked. As I would go in for a pass on 1 Zeke I'd see one or two others coming in on me. Firing short bursts, I was able to chase 1 and pull into another before the second one could do any harm. On two occasions, to save myself, I had to split-ess at fairly low altitude, one time pulling out just over the water as my plane buffeted severely. This continued until only one Zeke was left, two of the others had gone down in flames, while the third crashed into a mangrove swamp.
>
> "At about 1,000 to 2,000 feet, as I closed on the fourth Zeke from the stem, he passed over a Japanese destroyer and turned to the left. As I was just ready to fire, I must have been right over the destroyer, because my right engine was shot out by what sounded like machine-gun fire. I was blinded by the smoke and couldn't see even after my canopy was jettisoned. Because of the slipstream, I had a difficult time getting out, being pushed back in the cockpit several times. I finally recovered enough to realize I was going too fast, so I chopped the throttles and succeeded in laboriously forcing my way out. Just after the chute opened, the fourth Zeke made 1 pass at me without scoring any hits. I landed on the water about 1 mile offshore from Tolingon. I seemed to be exhausted, and it was several minutes before I could extricate myself from the parachute harness. This was about 5:50 PM. Luckily, my rubber raft wouldn't work, because I think I would have been picked up by the Japanese had it been visible. Only 1 side of my Mae West would innate. I saw a coconut floating about 10 yards away and swam over to it, placed my head alongside, and hoped the two objects looked alike.
>
> "Within the next five minutes an enemy destroyer came within 200 feet of my position but turned away. A little later, a Sonia, flying about 50 feet off the water, came over me but I was lucky again, it kept going. Still later, another destroyer headed for me and came so close I could make out features of Japanese on the deck, but it turned away. They were heaving stuff, possibly garbage, off the deck of this destroyer.
>
> "I gradually tried to edge my way toward shore, swimming slowly, and just before the sun went down I heard voices, and a few minutes later, I saw two Filipinos in a boat."

The Filipinos took him inland where he would hide for eight days. On the 10th, several different guerilla groups guided Dent north and on the 15th he rendezvoused with a Navy PT boat rescue and at noon, he was welcomed back at Tacloban where his furlough orders were awaiting him and never flew another mission.

**1Lt. James Mugavero** shot down a Kate over Cebu for his third victory. (AFAA)

**1 November 1944: 35FG/41FS**

1Lt. James Mugavero was leading four P-47s of White Flight to cover a Catalina rescue in the Cebu area. After making rendezvous with the PBY at 1020 15 miles south of Cebu City Mugavero saw three Kates in loose formation trailing the Catalina about three miles behind and 100-300 feet off the water. Mugavero and his Wingman, 2Lt. William Haefele were at 6,500 feet just south of Mactan Island. Mugavero went after the #4 Kate and fired at very close range without causing apparent damage and broke away. Haefele skidded to starboard as this Kate turned the same direction and fired a long burst hitting the cockpit and causing an explosion at the right wing root and the doomed Kate quarter rolled into the water below for his only victory. The Kates made a turn toward Cebu Island and Mugavero closed on one from just above and 350 yards astern and fired, closing down to 25 yards getting hits on the fuselage, wing roots, and cockpit. It started to smoke and went into a gentle glide and crashed into Cebu Island for his third victory. Haefele then pulled up and saw White #3 attacking the #2 Kate and he attacked the #3 and fired only short burst that was interrupted by four Zeros that caused Haefele to go into a sharp port climb using water injection. Meanwhile, Mugavero climbed to 3,000 feet and saw two Zeros attacking the Catalina and made a head on pass. He was out of ammunition but the Zeros went into an Immelmann and took off for Cebu. Haefele joined Mugavero and the two left for home.

1Lt. Raby Jeanes was leading the three P-47s of Blue Flight on a *Daylight 21* Catalina rendezvous and escort to Corte Point and then to cover the rescue. The P-47s rendezvoused with the PBY at 0845 and flew to a point 10 miles south of Mactan Island at 0945, where the P-47s assisted the PBY searching for wreckage of a B-24. As Blue Flight approached the Cebu Coast four Zeros in a V at 500-1,000 feet closed on the Catalina. Jeanes was at 2,500 feet and his two wingmen at 3,000 feet to his rear. As Jeanes dove on the Zero, it headed for Cebu Town, where two Zeros pulled up in front of him. The last Zero circled and then dove after the other two toward Lagtan. Jeanes followed the latter Zero to within 200 feet of the ground and fired a short burst out of range and closed to 150 yards and fired a two second burst into the wing root and cockpit. The Zero dipped into the trees just below and exploded. Jeanes chandelled to the right and saw Zeros coming up toward him from Cebu City. Just as he was going to attack he had to break off as another Zero was making a head on pass at him from above. Jeanes pulled up into this Zero and fired a three second burst into its engine and under its wing roots. The Zero turned on its back and crashed into Cebu Town for Jeanes' first two of three victories.

**1 November 1944: 475FG/431FS**

Four flights of 17 P-38s took off from Morotai on a ferry flight to Tacloban led by Maj. Thomas McGuire. When they arrived over Tacloban at 1030 the Air Controller asked McGuire to remain on patrol as there was a Red Alert

**Maj. Thomas McGuire** poses for his 25th victory. (AFAA)

on. McGuire took up patrol at 10,000 feet 10 SW of Tacloban with his Red Flight and White Flight; leaving Blue and Green Flights at 15,000.

At 1115 Hades White Leader called a bogey at 2 o'clock, 1,000 feet high, and after flying 10 miles the Tojo finally saw the approaching Lightnings and turned toward a cloud. McGuire chased after the Tojo and caught it just south of San Pablo. McGuire fired one burst at 300 yards from 45 degrees deflection and got hits and saw an explosion around its cockpit. As he closed from 100 to 50 feet McGuire fired two more bursts that tore the Tojo's tail assembly off for his 25th victory.

**1 November 1944: 8FG/80FS/35FS/36FS**

80FS

The fifteen P-38s of the 80th Squadron were the first to arrive over Carolina Drome on Negros and observed 40 to 50 Japanese aircraft, including Zeros, Oscars, and some bombers parked on the field. Some were crudely camouflaged with branches and painted olive green but were still obvious from the air. The Headhunters strafed and left about 20 enemy aircraft on fire with another six damaged.

1Lt. Robert Damon was leading the second element of the second flight on his pass when he strafed Japanese bombers in their well concealed revetments. He exploded one bomber and damaged the other. As he pulled away he had become separated from his flight but decided to make another pass. However, the Japanese gunners were alerted and put accurate fire into the diving P-38 that hit his port engine. He was unable to feather the engine and it caught on fire which could not be blown out by zooming. Damon headed for the ground at high speed but luckily he received only a small head wound when the P-38 slid to a stop. He jumped out of the flaming fighter and heard people yelling which he thought were Japanese and he ran into the jungle. Soon he was surrounded but was very relieved to find that they were Filipino civilians. They outfitted him in sport shirt so he would be much less obvious to any Japanese and was taken to the house of the local guerilla officer to hide. He was joined two days later by the only survivor of a downed B-24 and during the next weeks they waited for an opportunity to walk out. On 29 November the opportunity finally came when he and four rescued B-24 crewmen were guided on a long difficult march to Couyagan on the west Negros. They waited there until 12 December when the flashes of their mirror distress call was spotted by a flight of Liberators and later that day a PBY picked them up from the beach.

1Lt. Leo New made five strafing passes destroying two enemy aircraft on the ground. After escorting a damaged P-38 and found that he was running low on fuel and turned inland toward home when two single engine enemy fighters attacked him. He turned into them and got solid hits on one but was credited with a probable as he did not see any final results. His fuel tanks had been holed and he had only 60 gallons remaining he was about to bail out when he found Farm Project #2 on northern Mindanao. Not being familiar with the camouflaged layout of the field, New decided on a wheels up landing to reduce the chance of turning over. He released the canopy, destroyed the IFF, and made a successful landing. Almost immediately armed men approached him but, fortunately were Filipino guerillas who got him back to Allied lines.

35FS

Eighteen P-38s: Red (Capt. Lynn Witt), White (Capt. William Gardner), Blue (Capt. Richard West), and Green (1Lt. Kenneth Pool) Flights of the 35FS took off at 0700 on a fighter sweep of the Alicante Airdrome on the northwestern end of Negros Island. At about 1000 the 35FS encountered a number of Japanese aircraft that were taking off and landing. At 1020 the squadron dove from 12,000 feet and surprised some of the Japanese in the traffic pattern.

Blue Flight Leader, Capt. Richard West, led his flight directly over the airfield at high speed and turned to the right where he quickly got behind a Tojo that was just leaving the ground. West fired an accurate 35 degree deflection shot at only a few hundred feet off the ground but the enemy pilot was able to get out of his burning fighter and bail out into the sea off the coast of Negros. West climbed and saw a Tojo attacking White Flight's #4 man from above. West climbed to intercept and the Tojo pilot broke off and climbed almost vertically and at the top of his climb Split-S'd to attack a P-38 below him. West closed and fired a 90 degree deflection shot and the Tojo fell into the sea for his 10th victory to become a double ace. West led his flight back to the airdrome when he saw another Tojo about 1,000 feet above and a mile away. West turned into the enemy pilot and he dove away and West followed at full power and closed very slowly. He fired a short burst at only 30 feet astern and the Tojo streamed smoke and oil which covered his windshield. West was unable to see forward and he called his Element Leader, 1Lt. Paul Callahan, to come in and finish the enemy fighter. Gardner and Wingman Spitler were chasing the Tojo on the tree tops as Callahan closed. After a P-38 in front of him fired and broke away to port, Callahan fired a short burst at 45 degrees and saw the Tojo go down but was unable to "tell whether I had hit him or not." He didn't as Gardner collected his eighth and last victory.

As White Flight Leader, Capt. William Gardner, was about to strafe the field he saw a Dinah and ordered tanks dropped and dove quickly to get onto tail for a 70 degree deflection shot that damaged the Dinah and pulled away. Red Flight Leader, Capt. Lynn Witt, who had seen the

**Capt. Richard West** and crew celebrate his two victories to make him a double ace. (AFAA)

**Capt. William Gardner** writes up his eighth and last victory. (AFAA)

**Capt. Lynn Witt** shot down a Dinah for his sixth and last victory. (AFAA)

Dinah under broken clouds turned and followed to get directly astern of the Dinah and fired a short 70 degree deflection shot from the astern and overhead. Witt's Flight of Wingman Capt. Gladson Turnbull and second element of F/O Robert Hamblin and #4 Robert Odgers managed to only take snap 80-90 degree deflection shots that caused no damage. Before Witt could get into position for a second pass Blue Flight flew in from under the clouds and fired a few ineffective shots before Witt fired a long burst that set its engines on fire and it glided into a crash into the trees for his sixth and last victory credit. Witt's second element also made ineffective passes until they climbed to 5,000 feet where the two spotted a single enemy fighter climbing directly in front of them. Hamblin pulled up in an Immelmann and took a snap shot but could not get a proper lead. The Tojo pilot rolled on his back and climbed to 7,000 feet and rolled out and started into a skidding 30 degree dive. Odgers got on the tail of the Tojo and fired into the cockpit and engine and it immediately caught fire and half rolled from 1,000 feet into the ground and exploded for his only victory. Gardner and led his flight in a climb back up to 7,000 feet where a Tojo bounced his #4 man. Gardner turned toward the Tojo which climbed straight up for about 1,000 feet and then headed down toward him for a head on pass. Just before Gardner turned into the Tojo and was going to fire, it exploded in front of him as West fired a 90 degree shot. Another Tojo was approaching over the water and both West's Red and Gardner's Blue Flights chased after it. West and his flight were in position to attack first and the Tojo was soon surrounded by eight P-38s. The Tojo turned to escape over Panay Island when West opened fire from close in. He hit the enemy's engine but found his windscreen covered with oil which forced him to disengage. West's Wingman, Callahan closed and fired and Gardner then chased the Tojo inland until he caught up and shot it down for his eighth and last victory of the war. West was unable to see forward from his fighter so Gardner stayed on his wing until they reached Morotai and then made a successful simulated landing alongside West's P-38.

Many of the 35$^{th}$'s P-38s made numerous strafing passes (five to seven) on Alicante that left "22 fires burning when we left and many more planes shot to pieces. There were probably, roughly speaking 75-100 planes on the strip and at least half were left in flying condition" (Hamblin). Other 35FS ICRs reported from 20 to 24 burning aircraft on the field along with "quite a few unserviceable aircraft and some dummies." The Japanese had left the field virtually undefended with no AA guns and only one light machine gun firing on the P-38s. The only 8FC casualty on this mission was 2Lt. James Spitler of the 35FS who apparently ran out of gas over the ocean as he was heading to Leyte for emergency refueling.

36FS

Ten P-38s took off from Morotai at 0730 led by 1Lt. Harold Graham to arrive over Bacolod, Negros at 1020 for a fighter sweep, seeking out enemy fighters and then strafe the airfield. At Bacolod they saw Japanese aircraft lined up for an easy strafing attack and as 2Lt. Gerald Lowrey was about to get into position for his strafing attack a Val dive bomber approached Bacolod for a landing and fired a short easy shot and destroyed it for his first and only victory. Lowrey pulled up to join the strafing pattern when he saw an enemy fighter in the pattern and pulled around on it but it broke off and began to climb. Lowrey climbed with it for about a minute when it turned into him. Lowrey fired and the enemy turned to starboard and started to dive and Lowrey was unable to stay with it. 2Lt. Lawrence Hyde had made a strafing pass on the airfield and was pulling up to 1,500 feet when he spotted a Tony at 2,500 feet in a gentle starboard turn and Hyde fired a short 40 degree burst and slid behind it as the enemy pilot leveled out and Split-S'd down but pulled out at a 90 degree turn and headed to the deck. Hyde followed and got on its tail, firing short bursts that finally hit the engine and oil cooler. Oil splattered Hyde's windshield obscuring the result of his fire but Hyde's first of two victories was confirmed by White Flight Leader, 1Lt. John Dunaway who saw it crashing into the mud flat near a wharf on the coast.

During the strafing attack on Bacolod four Vals, three Tonys, and three Helens were destroyed on the ground along with two unidentified aircraft believed to be destroyed. The Squadron landed at Tacloban to refuel before returning to Morotai.

**2 November 1944: 475FG/432FS**

Japanese air attacks seemed to decrease after the P-38s arrived on Leyte, causing the Americans to relax. The 475$^{th}$ Crew Chiefs and other ground crew that had been sent out to service Navy aircraft that were forced down on Tacloban had returned to the 475$^{th}$ by the end of October. While their new base at Dulag was being readied, heavy rain produced thick mud when the 432FS began operations from the Tacloban and Bayug strips. Throughout the first week of November the 432FS flew dawn to dusk patrols over the shipping in Leyte Gulf. The 432FS ground crews arrived at Tacloban just in time to service the squadron's own P-38s that had landed there from Morotai on 2 November and on their arrival they went into combat immediately.

When the 432$^{nd}$ landed at Tacloban at 1230, a furious air battle was beginning nearby. 1Lt. Joseph Forster had just gotten out of his fighter after the long flight from Morotai when the red alert was sounded. At 1315 he was scrambled as the Green Flight Leader with rookie 2Lt. Walter Freeman on his wing. At 12,000 feet Forster tried to get a vector from the Controller

**Bacolod Airdrome**, Los Negros. (AAF)

but Forster's map was not coordinated with the Controller's grid, so he led his flight out to sea where the action seemed to be centered over the Japanese convoy at Ormoc Bay. Finally the Controller directed Forster to fly a heading along the northern tip Ormoc Bay where he came upon an Oscar at 2 o'clock which was at the top of its climb in the front and to the right. The Oscar was turning toward the tail of Forster's #4 man and Forster had to deploy his dive brakes to get into a wingover that was tight enough to head off the Japanese fighter. The Oscar pilot reefed his fighter in a tight turn to close but before he could open fire, Forster had completed his turn and was closing on the Oscar's tail. The Japanese Split-S'd and Forster lost the green camouflaged Oscar that blended into the jungle below. Forster estimated the Oscar's flight path and sighted it again about at 7,000 feet. Forster flew his fighter to its limits and caught his fleeing target at 3,000 feet south of Ponson Island where he shot it down with two short bursts to make him an ace.

**2 November 1944: 8FG/36FS**

Capt. Thomas Huff led 12 Lightnings (one would later abort) from Morotai at 0900 and rendezvoused with 26 B-24s at Tagolo Point at 1125 that were searching for a Japanese convoy over the Mindanao Sea for an anti-shipping sweep. The Mission's Flight Leaders were: Red: Capt. Kenneth Giroux; Blue: Capt. William Turner; and White: 1Lt. Steele Griswold. The bomber formation arrived over the Japanese convoy in Ormoc Bay at 1215 to attack the shipping while the P-38s engaged an estimated 13 Hamps and Oscars.

**1Lt. Joseph Forster** shot down an Oscar to become an ace. (AFAA)

**Capt. William Giroux** shot down three Hamps to become an ace. (AFAA)

The defensive AA fire from the shipping was quite heavy as the bombers approached the ships and during their bombing run.

Capt. Kenneth Giroux saw a Hamp that flew through its own AA fire to make a pass on the bombers and fired a 90 degree deflection shot just as the enemy pilot was about to make a pass and caused it to break away. It was trailing a wisp of smoke and Giroux thought it would crash but flew on instead. Giroux climbed into the sun where he saw this Hamp make another pass on the bombers. He dove and came up under it and fired a short burst from 25 yards that exploded it. As the bombers had completed their bombing run and were returning to base Giroux was joined by 1Lt. Raymond Loh. The two followed the bombers to 25 miles from Camotes Island where they saw a fighter drop a phosphorous bomb on the bomber formation. Giroux closed on this fighter and fired three shots at it; all from deflections of 90 to 40 degrees. The third shot was a short burst from only 100 feet above the water; hitting its wing root and exploding it just above the water. Giroux then saw another Hamp 500 feet to port above him and climbed and turned into the Hamp, which fired a short burst at Giroux. The Hamp pilot executed a wingover, but Loh got on its tail and fired a few shots before it turned and Loh pulled up. Giroux followed with a 40 degree deflection shot which set the Hamp on fire and it crashed near Pacijan Island. The three victories made Giroux the 36FS' first ace.

Blue Flight Leader, 1Lt. William Turner, sighted three enemy aircraft inland from Ormoc Bay. His Second Element went after one while Turner closed and fired on another but missed short. He then closed to 200 yards and fired with a slight deflection and tore off about three feet off the end of its wing and it spun into the ground for his second of three victories. Turner saw a lone enemy fighter entering a large cloud inland from Apale Point. Turner flew to investigate and was joined by White Flight Leader, 1Lt. Steele Griswold who had made several previous ineffective passes and had to fly around the heavy AA coming up from the Japanese convoy. They spotted the Oscar popping in and out of the clouds and waited for it to exit. As the Oscar exited the cloud, Turner made two passes without result and Griswold made four. On his third pass Griswold fired from out of range and saw pieces come off its starboard wing. The Oscar did not enter the clouds this time and flew at an angle to it. On his last pass Griswold fired from astern at 150 to 50 yards that hit its wing and fuselage; tearing out more large pieces. The Oscar entered the clouds and when it exited it was smoking and burning and half rolled into a steep dive into the sea for his second and last victory.

2Lt. Robert Maynard, Capt. Huff's Wingman, followed his Leader into a shallow starboard dive just out of the Japanese AA screen. As they completed a 360 at 10,000 feet they spotted a lone enemy fighter 2,000 feet below to port. Huff overran the enemy and the Oscar turned into Maynard who fired a short burst from out of range. Maynard closed and fired another burst that hit its wing root and it exploded for his first of two victories and the Squadron's sixth victory of the day.

The assessment of Enemy Tactics in the Unit Narrative Combat Report was described as "Displayed very poor tactics. Familiar Split-S maneuvers were ineffective. Enemy had no apparent coordination. Usually sought cloud cover when attacked." The Evaluation of the Enemy was described as: "A poor performance. No set plan for attacking our bombers. No cooperation from other planes when attacked by our P-38s. No successful evasive actions. A generally befuddled enemy." The Evaluation of Own Force stated: "Splendid example of teamwork."

**1Lt. William Huisman** (9FS) scored his last of three victories, as he was killed after landing his damaged P-38. (AAF)

**2 November 1944: 49FG/7FS/8FS/9FS**

First Battle: 8FS/9FS

At 0810 on 2 November, the 49ers were assigned to fly a sweep to remove enemy fighters before the first dive bomber sorties against the newly arrived enemy merchant vessels. The 9FS Flying Knights and 8FS Black Sheep took off from Tacloban and reached their assigned patrol areas north and east of Ormoc Village, respectively. The scattered cumulus clouds over the mountainous interior made it very difficult to hold formation in and in both the Knights and Black Sheep elements there was continual exchange in position with pilots from different elements.

9FS

At 0830, enemy aircraft were seen to the north and minutes later, the Flying Knights Flight of two P-38s flown by 1Lt. William Huisman and Wingman 2Lt. Melvin Hanisch patrolling just east of Ormoc frantically radioed for assistance as they came under attack. While climbing through the clouds in search of their lead elements, the two were attacked by seven Zeros at 6,000 feet. Hanisch called out the attackers but Huisman was late in reacting and in the break away, his fighter was hit by the Zero in its first diving pass. The two pilots separated and Huisman had to fight alone. Despite having damage to his fighter Huisman shot down two of his opponents before his P-38 was more heavily damaged. After Huisman had destroyed two Zekes that day he was about to touch down when another P-38 from the 35th Squadron approached from the rear and its propellers hit Huisman's tail, causing it to slide down the runway into some heavy equipment. The pilot of the other Lightning was killed and a number of men working in the area were injured. TSgt. Howard Harclerode and Sgt. Alfred Robinson of the 9FS braved the flames and exploding ammunition to pull the badly burned Huisman from the aircraft. He was quickly taken to a hospital ship just offshore but despite these heroic efforts Huisman died of his burns that night.

Hanisch was attacked from dead astern and had his starboard supercharger damaged and his port engine set on fire. Hanisch tried to escape at tree top altitude for another 15 miles inland but finally his starboard engine seized and he crash landed in a small open area. The Zero pilot flew over for a final firing pass but missed. Hanisch was able to stop the bleeding from the deep gash in his forehead and was quickly found by Philippine villagers who led him to a Guerilla camp. He was then was taken by boat down the coast and then turned over to 7th Infantry Division on 6 November and then caught a ride in a Piper Cub and reached Tacloban before nightfall.

Mission Leader 1Lt. William Maddox's White Flight took off from Tacloban last and heard the Huisman-Hanisch call for help. Maddox with 2Lts. Ernest Ambort and Alex Datzenko in tight formation sped to the west and then dropped their long range fuel tanks for greater speed. In the meantime, Red Flight Leader 1Lt. James Poston had seen the Zeros attack Huisman and Hanisch but both White and Red Flights could not reach the pair in time. As the White and Red Flights arrived, another flight of Zeros appeared and an even larger dogfight broke out.

White Flight Leader, Maddox, ICR:

> We immediately heard a fight going on over Ormoc. We dropped our tanks and climbed to 15,000 feet. We engaged enemy on diving pass. I hit an Oscar on quarter head on pass and observed cannon and machine gun hits at wing roots and engine. He went

> down smoking and crashed just off the west side of Ormoc and in water and exploded.
>
> Next Oscar was hit from tail and 20-30 degrees deflection. Observed hits on fuselage and cockpit, left wing and aileron. Smoke poured out underside and more pieces came off wing. He spiraled down and crash landed on a small field, went into a ditch and burned. I strafed the Oscar as he was sliding across the field into the ditch. I claim one Oscar destroyed. (These were Maddox' only two victories)
>
> Red Flight Leader, Posten, ICR:
>
> We sighted 12-15 Zekes at around 13,000 feet. While we were at 10,000 feet they dropped their auxiliary tanks and dove down at us. I turned the Flight into them and I fired a short burst to turn them off. Then we tried to climb but they came back and pulled up in front of me. Two of them were together and climbing. I fired a long burst and the closest one started to burn. He turned over and went into the ground; the other one turned away and left....
>
> Another one made a pass at me from above and over shot. He dove straight down and I followed him down firing at him. He never started to burn but crashed into the trees and I climbed back up. My right engine was shot out and my right coolant was gone. I returned to the field and crash landed. (Poston's two Zeros gave him three total victories)

Poston's Wingman, 2Lt. Paul Nahnibida, became separated and joined the fight with the 8FS.

Maddox's Wingman, 2Lt. Ernest Ambort found his right engine running cold after he dropped his tanks. He climbed to 16,000 feet until the engine heated up and lost his Flight. He joined another flight and saw some Tojos on the tail of a Lightning and came in from above and started firing. The enemy pilot went into a number of diving turns which Ambort followed while firing from 10 degrees dead astern. Large pieces started coming off the Tojo and as Ambort continued to fire he hit its engine and Tojo began to spin but Ambort broke off as a Zero got on his tail. Ambort Split-S'd 2,000 feet and got on his attacker's tail and fired from dead astern. The Zero did not burn and made a 180 into Maddox who finished it off. When he returned to altitude Ambort saw a Tojo at 6,000 feet and chased it down to 3,000 feet getting hits on its engine but had to break off to avoid a collision when the Tojo went into an abrupt spin for his second victory. Ambort did not receive a victory for the first Zero as there was no confirmation.

2Lt. Thomas Hamilton the Element Leader of Posten's Red Flight scored two victories as described in his brief ICR account:

> First Nips were sighted at 10,000 feet. We dropped tanks as they turned into us. I tightened my turn coming in at 45 degrees and closing to a tail end shot. The Zeke burst into flames and crashed into a valley. I then continued my turn and was in position for a shot at another Zeke. Again I was on his tail. I fired a long burst, expending my ammunition. The canopy came off and his cockpit was riddled and he went straight down out of control. This plane was observed to crash. (Hamilton's first two of three victories)

8FS

Black Sheep CO Capt. William Drier was flying a standing patrol over Tacloban when he also heard the Huisman-Hanisch call for help. *Gabriel* Air Controller released Drier's flights from base protection and his 12 Lightnings jettisoned their auxiliary fuel tanks and sped due west. Eight 8FS P-38s reached the Ormoc dogfight at the same time the JAAF arrived. Capt. Drier with wingmen 1Lt. Robert Campbell and 2Lt. Wright Boyd made an initial 90 degree diving pass on two Oscars which Split-S'd away and the Element separated but Drier was joined by 2Lt. Paul Nahnibida of the 9FS. They made a front quarter attack on two Oscars that turned to port. Drier fired on one and got hits on the wing roots and engine and the Oscar crashed just inland on the west shore of Ormoc Bay. Nahnibida chased after the other Oscar and shot it down for his only victory. Drier and Nahnibida rejoined and made an unsuccessful passes on several Zeros at 10,000 feet and Nahnibida returned to his 9FS base. Drier then made a diving front quarter attack on two Zeros which were on the tails of two P-38s. Drier's attack drove off the Zeros and Drier followed one and fired a 30 degree deflection shot that knocked off pieces and the Zero spun in. Drier climbed away from a tail attack and as he continued to 12,000 feet, climbing over a mountain he encountered a lone Zero coming over the mountain and fired from below and observed hits in its belly and engine for his third victory of the day and his first three of six.

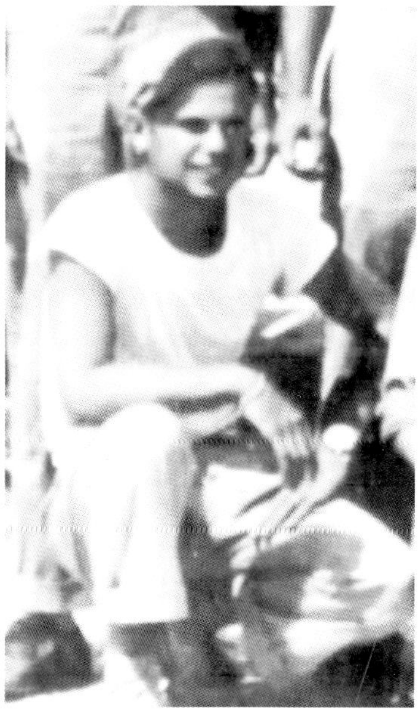

**1Lt. James Poston** (9FS) shot down his second of two enemy aircraft. (AAF)

**2Lt. Ernest Ambort** (9FS) claimed his second victory. (AFAA)

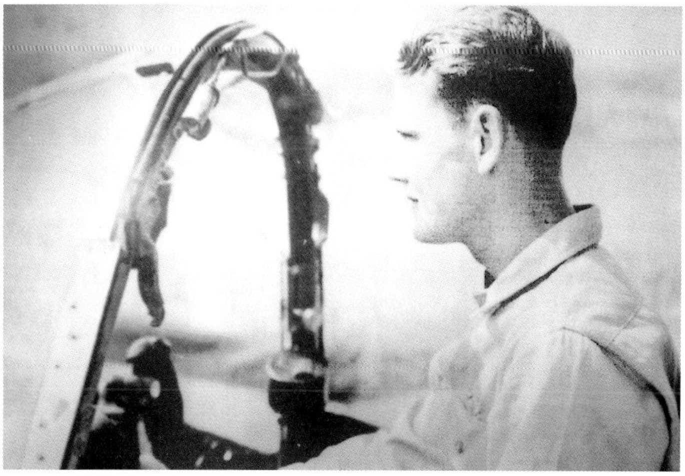

**Capt. William Drier** (8FS) got his first three of six victories. (AFAA)

After separating from Drier's original Flight, 2Lt. Wright Boyd and 1Lt. Robert Campbell of immediately saw three Oscars and made a diving stern pass at them but were cut off by 9FS Lightnings and broke off their attack. They soon saw six Zeros at 7,000 feet which were joined by six more Zeros and made an unsuccessful pass. The two attacked the same Zero, but only made a few hits before they were forced to break off. They flew on to make passes at several more Zeros at 4,000 feet. Boyd made a high side high angle deflection shot and saw pieces fly off the wings and fuselage which was later seen to crash by Campbell. Boyd looked around he saw a Zero closing and firing on him but also saw Campbell make a high side approach firing on it with a 40 degree deflection shot and the Zero rolled right and Spilt-S'ed. Campbell pulled up and rolled into an unexpected overhead pass and his first burst hit the cockpit that inmediately began to burn probably killing the pilot who took no more evasive action. Campbell overran the enemy fighter and had to pull around to finish the now blazing plane off for his first of three victories.

Capt. Nelson Flack was leading Blue Flight at 11,000 feet over Ormoc Bay when he saw three Zeros at 9,000 feet and dove on them. He chose the third Zero and made a 45 degree high astern pass but the Zero turned into him and "kicked bottom rudder and made a good shot impossible." Flack climbed away from his pursuer and seven to ten Zekes milling around at 7,000 to 11,000 feet. Flack made a 90 degree level deflection shot to 50 yards but saw no result. He then saw he had a Zero on his tail, 200 yards behind but saw E.V. May, who had become separated from his flight, come in and shoot it down to save Flack and gain his first victory. Flack flew on and saw a P-38 chased by two Zeros in string. Flack made a high rear quarter pass closing to 75 yards on the first Zero and saw smoke trailing from its fuselage as he passed over the enemy fighter. The Zero spun a few times and hit the ground for Flack's fourth victory.

Second Battle: 7FS

At 0930, 15 7FS Screamin' Demons in four flights left Tacloban for the first dive bomber mission of the day. The Mission Leader was Red Flight Leader Capt. John Haher who flew directly to the north side of Ormoc Village at 12,000 feet where he spotted enemy fighters patrolling overhead at 15,000 feet. He also saw a large freighter anchored near the Ormoc docks and was determined to attack it. Haher ordered his other three flights to remain in high cover to keep the Zeros from attacking his flight which would be diving on the freighter. To gain more speed, Haher led his two wingmen through a turning descent on the target but as he dropped under the broken overcast, the other Demons momentarily lost radio contact. White Flight leader 1Lt. Frederick Dick finally reached Haher and found that they still had not dropped their two 1,000 pound bombs. Dick realized that the remaining P-38s could not remain in high cover while carrying their own 1,000 pounders. Dick ordered the three higher flights to close ranks and they all flew over the enemy held village and salvoed their bombs from 12,000 feet. Meanwhile, Haher and his two wingmen hit the merchant ship and set on fire. Haher regrouped his Demon Flights and then turned back to continue search for the Zeros but they had already left. The Demon flights then separated to search along the entire west coast. Dick's White Flight climbed to 22,000 feet where they soon spotted four dark silhouettes 3,000 feet below, south of the Bay. The enemy fighters were soon identified as the new Mitsubishi Jack and Dick and his wingmen peeled off but overshot and Element Leader 1Lt. Robert Decker was the only pilot to score hits. As the White Flight pulled up into a zoom climb, Decker followed his target but was separated from his wingmen. Suddenly, six Jacks got on his tail and Decker dove to the north and escaped at over 400 mph. Low on fuel, Decker turned toward Tacloban, but saw a lone Jack below also flying north. Decker dove to dead astern and fired a long burst tattooing along the fuselage and shattering the cockpit for his first of four victories.

**Capt. Nelson Flack** (8FS) scored victories during two sorties to become an ace. (AFAA)

Third Battle: 8FS/9FS

At 1030, Black Sheep Ops Exec Capt. Nelson Flack had only seven serviceable fighters available for the next mission and led his flights to Ormoc again. After only 20 minutes two pilots became separated from the flight due to bad weather. 1Lt. E.V. May became Flack's Wingman and were joined by 8FS Deputy CO Capt. Philip Kriechbaum with his wingmen, 1Lts. Marion Felts and Thomas Holstein, who got through the weather. As the five pilots continued through the high clouds at 16,000 feet, they saw enemy ships in the harbor in the far distance. Just then a lone Oscar passed in front of Kriechbaum, Felts, and Holstein and the trio flew after it when four Zeros came onto the scene and crossed their path 2,000 feet below. Flack and May immediately changed their course and turned after the Zeros; a decision which divided their force as the lone Oscar was a decoy for others waiting in ambush. Flack and May dove to 9,000 feet on a 45 degree attack on the four scattered Zeros ahead of them. Flack closed to 300 yards of the third Zero whose pilot turned into Flack disrupting his firing run. Flack then made a high speed climb and saw seven to ten Zeros and Oscars milling around at 7,000 to 11,000 feet. He made a level 90 degree shot closing to 50 yards but saw no results. Flack continued on and found an Oscar following to within 200 yards of his tail. Flack's Wingman, 2Lt. E.V. May, made a pass at the Zero that chandelled right. May turned left and rolled out and lost it. May continued on and ran into several Zeros and had to dive away. As he pulled out, May saw four more Zeros below and had to pull up to get away. As he pulled out of his climb he saw four more Zeros above and went into a dive to escape them. On his dive he ran into the Zeros that were below him flying in the opposite direction. May stopped running and made a dead astern attack that set the Zero on fire for his second victory of the day and his last of the war. Seconds later May's right wing reserve tank was hit by a 20mm shell and his right engine belched a cloud of smoke and stopped and he feathered the prop and went into a dive to escape. On the way down May felt the heat on the right side of the cockpit from his burning aircraft and leveled off at 4,000 feet. He slowed down and opened the canopy and was "sucked out of the cockpit." He waited to pull the rip cord so he wouldn't be strafed and landed in a tree about 75 feet above the ground and was knocked unconscious. When he came to he braced himself while he cut his chute free of the tree. He climbed down and was greeted by U.S. Army Scouts who treated his burned right arm and he was evacuated to a hospital that same day. Meanwhile Flack saw a P-38 with two Zeros in string on its tail and made a high rear quarter attack closing to 75 yards of the first Zero. The wounded Zero turned down to starboard trailing smoke and then spun several times before crashing into the sea for Flack's second victory of the day to make him an ace.

2Lt. Ralph Easterling, F/O Harold Bechtold and 2Lt. William Bechdolt were in a three plane flight that attacked a Zero and while Easterling and William Bechdolt broke away Harold Bechtold continued on to fire a 60 degree deflection shot that blew off pieces of the right wing and aileron and the Zero went into a stalling glide and crashed and burned for his first of two victories. Bechdolt and Easterling made unsuccessful passes at several Zeros when Bechdolt finally got a good long burst into an Oscar that went smoking into the ground for his only victory. Easterling became separated from Bechdolt and fired several good burst from 45 degrees at an Oscar which flew away smoking and was later confirmed for his lone victory.

Capt. Philip Kriechbaum led 1Lt. Marion Felts and 1Lt. Thomas Holstein at 16,000 feet near Ormoc Bay they saw a lone Zero at about a mile below and as they attacked it Split-S'd away each time the Americans closed to fire. As the Zero neared the deck and leveled out Holstein closed and "got a fair shot at it" and it went down toward the water. Instead of going in the enemy pilot was able level out over the "Nip" convoy docked at Ormoc. Holstein dove at 30 degrees and hit the cockpit from 50 yards and it crashed on an island in the Bay. As Holstein made his attack two Zeros got his tail from out of a cloud. In concentrating on their attack the Japanese pilots did not clear their rear, and Felts made a dead astern attack on one and it began smoking and made a spiraling turn, crashing in flames into the shore. The second Zero tried to turn inside Felts but the American followed it straight down, firing until it tried to crashland in the water near the shipping. As Felts pulled up he looked back to find two Zeros on his tail and as he "whipped over" he then saw two more to one side. The Zeros had Felts "boxed in so I tried to outrun them trying every trick I knew, but to no avail." He went into a slight dive to gain speed but when he engaged his superchargers neither would kick in and finally his right engine began to smoke. He attempted to feather the engine but was unsuccessful and called out a May Day over the radio that he was going to bailout. The engine burst into flames and filled the cockpit with smoke. Felts tried to open his canopy but was only able to open the top hatch, and as he stood up he was torn out into the 400 mph slipstream. When he landed Felts found that he had suffered a badly sprained back, a broken arm, and a sprained knee; to make matters worse, he was being fired on by enemy infantry. He managed to hide, and after 13 days he and Flying Knight Robert Hamburger returned to Tacloban.

As Holstein pulled up he saw Felts' predicament and covered him as he parachuted to the ground. Holstein rejoined Kriechbaum and saw his Leader turn into two Oscars at 3,000 feet above Ormoc Bay but then saw three more get behind him. The veteran Kriechbaum had joined the 8FS in August 1943 at Marilinan and had flown over 200 missions but had never encountered an enemy aircraft. While pursuing the lone Oscar he heard Felts' call for help and broke off. As he came into the battle, Felts had already bailed out, and Kriechbaum did see the large flight of Oscars waiting overhead. He tried to rejoin Holstein so the two could fight their way to safety, but three Oscars dove on the helpless American, who was at only 3,000 feet, and his P-38 became enveloped in flames and exploded in a massive fireball five miles northeast of Ormoc village.

Kriechbaum's fighter was on fire by the time Holstein got into range. As Holstein fired on and damaged the nearest Oscar as he saw Kriechbuam's plane fall off on fire and head for the sea. Holstein looked behind and saw three Zeros soon to be joined by two more and zoomed over the Valley at 400 mph. As he circled he saw Felts' chute on the ground but there was no sign of Kriechbaum even though he had time to bail out. As he made another circle of the valley he fired and hit another Oscar but "was too busy to see what happened to him."

Meanwhile, Holstein continued after the decoy Oscar and headed directly over the anchored enemy ships and Ormoc Town followed by an intense AA barrage. He finished off the Oscar and it crashed just northwest of the village. In his pursuit Holstein flew past Felts dangling in his chute and covered Felts until he was safely on the ground. Holstein then climbed away and searched for Kriechbaum was already dead. Soon Holstein was chased by seven Ki-43s but the Lightning soon out distanced the Oscars and Holstein was the last Black Sheep to land at Tacloban.

**1Lt. Ralph Easterling** (8FS) was credited with his lone victory of the war. (AAF)

**1Lt. Harold Oglesby** (9FS) fell short of becoming an ace when he was awarded his fourth and final victory. (AAF)

9FS

9FS Flight Leader 1Lt. Harold Oglesby scrambled a flight of three wingmen off Tacloban. As the Knights neared Ormoc, seven Oscars tried to catch Oglesby's team with decoy trick but Oglesby disrupted the ploy by ignoring the lone Oscar and turning into the other diving Oscars and exploded the lead enemy aircraft; causing the others to withdraw to the safety of the clouds.

Fourth Battle: 7FS

At 1330, 14 Demon Lightnings were back in the air for another sortie. Six Lightnings of Blue and Green flights flew at 12,000 feet carrying a pair of 500 pound bombs to for the docks and shipping at Ormoc. Mission Leader, Capt. DeHaven with his three wingmen and the four pilots in White Flight would provide high cover at 15,000 feet. At 1400, the high cover flights passed over the Bay in order to distract enemy AA batteries and immediately Blue and Green Lightning dive bombers made a direct hit on a merchant vessel. While DeHaven's flights were regrouping over the coast, he spotted a lone radial engine Jack several thousand feet below, headed west. DeHaven with his three wingmen trailing, chased the Jack to the western end of Ormoc Bay.

The radial engined Mitsubishi **J2M Jack**. (AAF)

**Capt. Robert DeHaven** shot down a Jack fighter for his 13th victory. (AFAA)

Among the Japanese reinforcements sent to stop the Americans were several new types of aircraft, including the excellent Jack fighter powered by a large radial engine. While flying top cover for other Lightnings dive bombing shipping at Ormoc Bay, Capt. Robert DeHaven, veteran ace of the 7FS met one of the new Jacks:

> The bogey was about 16,000 feet and even at a distance was easily identified as a new Jack-type fighter, I used full gun trying to reach his altitude and he started climbing, also making a slow right turn. I kept turning in behind him and was gradually catching him in the climb when he decided I was too close, so he started a shallow dive toward Poro Island. At the time, I was at 18,000 feet and directly behind him, so I kept full gun and began to close very slowly, going downhill in about a 20 degree dive. At 15,000 feet I was indicating 400 mph and slowly catching him. He must have been using water injection, for there was a faint trail of dark smoke behind him. About 13,000 I was in range to shoot, so opened fire from dead astern and nearly point-blank range. After the second burst, he started letting out heavy gray smoke, and after the third burst, he came all to pieces. I flew through the wreckage, denting my wings and throwing oil all over my plane. What was left of him crashed on Poro Island.

When DeHaven returned to base his fighter was written off, as it was severely damaged by the debris from his victim. When DeHaven's aircraft was being cannibalized for parts a fragment of a map from the Jack was found.

Blue Flight was assigned to dive bomb enemy shipping in Ormoc Bay and Blue Element Leader, 2Lt. Douglas Hart, lost his Flight Leader in the heavy AA fire. Hart joined Green Flight Leader, 1Lt. Fernly Damstrom, and the two climbed to 14,000 feet and saw two Oscars heading south at about 2,000 to 3,000 above. The Oscars climbed to 19,000 feet where they went into a gentle right bank and then leveled out at 20,000 feet where the two Americans finally closed. Hart slid over and fired a short burst at the second Oscar which immediately burst into flames. Damstrom closed quickly and fired on his Oscar simultaneously and it smoked and quickly caught on fire. As Damstrom overran his Oscar he saw it half roll and go straight in.

After the battles of the day Walker found that seven of his P-38s and some of his most veteran flight leaders had been lost in combat and several more Lightnings were written off during the continuous enemy bombing raids of the past two days. Walker had to shuttle his remaining serviceable fighters to Dulag and Baruaen for safer off duty dispersal while the Tacloban crews tried to put damaged Lightnings back into operations.

**3 November 1944: 49FG: 500 Going on 600**

MacArthur's HQ Press Release:

> 3 November 1944 – Supreme Command HQ, Tacloban, Leyte:
>
> Today the 49th Fighter Group of the Far East Air Force has shot down more than 500 enemy planes since the beginning of the march back to the Philippines. The 49th Fighter Group in the air battles of the Southwest Pacific has set a record for the destruction of enemy aircraft which I believe is unsurpassed by any group in the war. Before coming to the Philippines as our first land-based unit, they were crowding the 500 mark and are now shooting for 600. They are unsurpassed in the air.
>
> Gen. Douglas MacArthur

**3 November 1944: 475FG**

At 1130 2Lt. Arnold Nielson of the 431FS collided with another aircraft from another group during his landing approach to crowded Tacloban Field.

**3 November 1944: 418NFS**

Pilot 1Lt. Harold Whitten and R/O Bunyan Crain took off from Morotai and 0345 and were immediately vectored toward an enemy fighter but Crain's radar set malfunctioned and he replaced a number of fuses to get it working but made no contact. At 0410 Crain got a radar contact at eight miles ahead at 240 degrees. Crain put Whitten directly behind and below but was unable to get a visual and Whitten flew a 360 and Crain gave him a contact at seven miles at 230 degrees. Whitten climbed quickly and got a visual at 200 feet and fired a short burst on a twin engine aircraft which burst into flames. It exploded and Whitten had to pull up to avoid hitting the debris for his only victory.

**4 November 1944: 8FG/36FS**

The 36th sent out 19 P-38s in five flights under Mission Leader, Capt. Kenneth Giroux. Two Lightnings would abort due to fuel problems soon after 0700 take off from Morotai and the remainder of the Squadron would rendezvous with B-24's at 12,000 feet and continue onto another strike against Alicante Airdrome on Negros. The Squadron arrived over the target at 1050 and met a mixed batch of 15 Japanese interceptors that included Zeros, Tonys, and Oscars who were much more aggressive and experienced than those two days before over Ormoc Bay.

Capt. Giroux circled Alicante at 14,000 feet a few times before he saw an enemy fighter taking off from the strip. Giroux dove after it and the enemy pilot ducked into a low cloud but as it exited Giroux was ready

**Capt. William Giroux** scored three victories to give him eight victories. (AFAA)

**1Lt. Harold Graham** shot down two Tonys to give him his first two of three victories. (AAF)

and fired a 90 degree deflection shot but was short on his lead. The enemy pilot rolled out of his turn and started to climb and Giroux followed to 4,000 feet and as he was about to fire the Japanese pilot made a turn but Giroux adjusted and hit its right wing about three feet from its tip. The enemy pilot tightened his turn and Giroux fired a short full deflection shot into the cockpit. As Giroux started to climb he found an Oscar on his tail and made a turn. As the Zero started to fire White Flight Leader, 1Lt. John Dunaway, who had followed Giroux's flight fired a two second burst from 45 to 90 degrees and the Zero crashed into a beach near Alicante for his second victory. Giroux then climbed to 7,000 feet where he saw a Zero fly into a cloud. Giroux stayed below the cloud until it came out and headed for Alicante. Giroux followed and chased it down to the trees and fired and got a few hits on its wing tip which was enough to have its wing hit the tree tops and explode into the trees. Giroux then climbed to 6,000 feet and half way between Alicante and Bacolod Dromes he spotted a lone Oscar. The enemy pilot skillfully evaded with tight turns and by ducking into the clouds. Giroux fired four bursts all from 45 to 90 degrees deflection; getting several hits each time and the Oscar finally crashed south of Alicante. As he started for home Giroux was attacked by two Tonys to port 1,000 feet above. Giroux dove at full throttle through a cloud and escaped with three victories to give him eight.

Green Flight Leader 1Lt. Harold Graham had both wingmen in his flight abort due to fuel problems, which left his Second Element Leader, 1Lt. Steele Griswold, as his Wingman. They arrived over the target at 16,000 feet and circled the area and saw several single engine fighters taking off from Alicante minutes before the bombers were to begin their run. As the B-24s arrived Graham saw a Tony diving on the bombers out of the sun at 18,000 feet. The two turned into the Tony which turned into them and started climbing. Graham closed to 200 yards and fired at 40 degrees deflection and continued to fire until he lost his lead. Griswold came in and fired through 90 degrees before he had to break off. The Tony continued to climb and Graham climbed after it until he was above and behind. The Tony dove to port and Graham got on its tail and fired a two second burst that tore large pieces off its right wing root and tail surfaces and it went down trailing heavy black smoke and crash. Graham and Griswold rejoined and flew toward Alicante where they saw a Tony at 9 o'clock level, circling tightly under two Lightnings. The two dove on the Tony and the Tony turned into them and both Americans fired head on until they both had to break away to the right and left. By the time Graham completed his 180 turn the Tony was firing a 90 degree deflection shot on Griswold's tail. Graham closed and the Tony dove to starboard; he followed, firing a two second burst from 300 yards and knocking pieces from its fuselage and tail. It crashed trailing black smoke into the water near Alicante for his first two of three victories.

2Lt. Gerald Lowrey and his Wingman encountered no enemy fighters and climbed for home when three Tonys attacked from above and one hit Lowrey's starboard engine which began to smoke and then caught fire. Lowrey radioed his Wingman that he was going to bail out and climbed to 1,000 feet and near Pandan Point in Quimaras Strait. He didn't open his chute until he was at 300 feet as one of the Tonys was circling. The Tony pilot strafed Lowrey when he was 50 feet above the water but missed low. Another Tony came in and fired when he was at 20 feet but Lowrey had unbuckled his chute straps and dropped into the water. Four Tonys then made strafing passes on Lowrey when he was in the water but he swan underwater as much as possible to get away from the chute which the Japanese were using as a target. On each pass Lowrey ducked under the water but on one pass he came up too soon and the Tony pilot saw him and tried to push down his nose to fire but came in too low and his prop hit the water and the fighter exploded. The other three Tonys circled for about five minutes and then headed back toward Negros. Ten minutes later one of the Tonys returned and strafed Lowrey's chute and left. A sail boat arrived and picked up the chute and left. Lowrey only had his Mae West which he had not inflated until he was some distance away from the area where he landed. He was swimming about a quarter mile from shore and about a mile and a half from Pandan Point. He swam south to get close to the hills in case he wasn't rescued the next day. Before dusk a single aircraft flew over the Strait at 10-15 minute intervals and that night sail boats seemed to be patrolling the Strait. All night aircraft passed overhead and at daybreak Lowrey saw that they were Lily bombers from Negros. At 1100 the next morning P-38s were searching for him and he opened his sea marker and swam around to spread the dye and also flashed his signaling mirror. The Lightnings missed him on their first pass but spotted him on their next pass. About a half hour later a PBY (*Daylight 21*) picked him up and returned him to Morotai.

**4 November 1944: 49FG/8FS**

A new weather front had moved in but missions continued in the marginal weather. An early morning armed reconnaissance mission over the Visayan Islands had been scheduled to find and attack a merchant convoy trying to reach Ormoc. Before the mission could take off the Japanese attacked Tacloban before dawn and cratered the main runway and the mission was scrubbed until the Marston mat could be repaired but then the weather also closed in. At 0730 Demon Ops Exec Capt. Robert DeHaven and Black Sheep 1Lt. Walter Leaf were on the flight line when the air raid siren sounded and four Oscars suddenly descended through the overcast over the field. DeHaven and Leaf ran to the nearest fighters on the flight line and in seconds, they were taxiing for the take off through enemy tracers and friendly AA. DeHaven sped down the runway, avoiding the torn Marston steel matting and bomb craters. Leaf followed seconds later but DeHaven had already disappeared into the overcast. DeHaven climbed until he reached the cloud top and leveled out in brilliant sun at 15,000 feet and then turned south toward the first vector of Vals attacking Dulag. Leaf never rejoined the speeding Ops Exec and both were alone. Meanwhile, four Lightnings from of 8FS "Raccoon" Flight had followed them into the air.

**Capt. Robert DeHaven** finished his career with 14 total victories. (AFAA)

DeHaven reached Dulag but the Controller already had a confirmed contact from the 8FS Raccoon Flight. DeHaven searched to find if the Vals had been escorted and he saw three dark silhouettes 15 miles to the northwest. He climbed into the sun, to gain another 3,000 foot altitude advantage, and as he neared the north coast he was close enough to identify them as Zeros. The two lead Zeros descended below the cloud deck while the trailing one made an idle turn to the west. DeHaven quickly flew behind the lone unsuspecting Zero and his burst of fire caused an explosion in mid fuselage, the Zero pilot snap rolled to bail out for DeHaven's 14th confirmed victory.

DeHaven continued to patrol for about another hour waiting for another vector which never was radioed. Leaf had intercepted another flight of enemy fighters and his fighter was damaged in the battle and was in final approach to Tacloban when another aircraft forced him out of the pattern. Leaf's P-38 crashed into San Pedro Bay during his attempt at a go around and both plane and pilot vanished. As DeHaven was celebrating his 14th victory Group Ops Exec Gerald Johnson informed DeHaven that his tour was over ten days ago but that the orders had just arrived.

**4 November 1944: 348FG: 460FS First Mission**

The 460FS was fully equipped and trained in time to be chosen as the 348FG's first squadron to land in the Philippines. On 4 November 17 460FS Thunderbolts took off from Morotai and headed for the Philippines led by Squadron CO, Maj. William Dunham. The Squadron landed at Anguar Island and was delayed when it was ordered to cover a B-25 shipping strike on 10 November which was to be its first mission. The B-25s attacked a Japanese reinforcement convoy to Ormoc Bay, Leyte that was attempting to counter the three week old Allied invasion. The aggressive Dunham led his Thunderbolts down on a Japanese destroyer that was defending its convoy with a heavy AA barrage against the American medium bombers. The destroyer was heavily damaged as were several other ships in the badly scattered convoy. The Squadron suffered its first casualty when on the inbound flight to Leyte. As 2Lt. Andrew McLendon straggled three miles behind his squadron some aggressive P-38s pilots who apparently were not familiar with the silhouette of the P-47 or did not expect to see it so soon over the Philippines attacked McLendon and shot him down into the Mindanao Sea and he was listed as KIA.

**5-6 November 1944: 49 FG**

During the afternoon of 4 November, a strong monsoon completely shut down operations at Tacloban and the next day, the heavy rain and fog lifted only long enough in the morning to allow two flights of two fighters to conduct a brief patrol before the weather closed in again at mid-day. Black Sheep 1Lt. George Smerchek totaled his P-38 but was uninjured during a heavy landing on the wet steel mat that caused his fighter to slide and collide with a fuel truck. On the next day the Japanese made an unexpected attack on Tacloban, flying through poor weather they descended through the cloud deck and dropped their bombs on the 7FS flight line, destroying three Lightnings and seriously wounding three men. Also on the 6th at Bayug Airstrip, 7FS 2Lt. Maynard Oehlbeck was waiting in his P-38 on alert standby when a 110 TRS P-40 slid into his Lightning. Oehlbeck suffered a broken leg and the two fighters were written off.

**5 November 1944: 35FG/40FS/41FS**

40FS

The 40Fs sent 16 P-47s on the B-24 escort to Bacolod Airdrome in Los Negros and arrived over the target at 1100. In the air battle 1Lt. Robert Powers, flying as Second Element Leader in Red Flight, was the only pilot to score a victory. Power's Flight Leader had oil covering his windshield and called Powers and his Wingman in to attack a bogey that had passed under their wing. Powers closed to 300 yards from the port quarter and fired bullets into the cockpit and engine of the Oscar that crashed into the sea for his only victory of the war.

41FS

The 41FS sent 13 P-47s on the B-24 escort Bacolod Airdrome in Los Negros and arrived over the target at 1100. 1Lt. James Mugavero was leading two P-47s of White Flight (his second element turned back) and joined with 1Lt. Raby Jeanes' Yellow Flight inbound. At 1130 just after the bombers left the target at 15,000 feet and made a 180, Jeanes was just ahead and above them when a single Hamp Split-S'd through the formation attempting to draw the P-47s with it and leave the formation without cover. After the Hamp left, Mugavero spotted two Tonys at 6 o'clock at 18,000 feet and began to follow when he saw the Tonys dive on the bombers. The Tonys broke off their attack on the bombers when they saw the P-47s in a climbing turn to

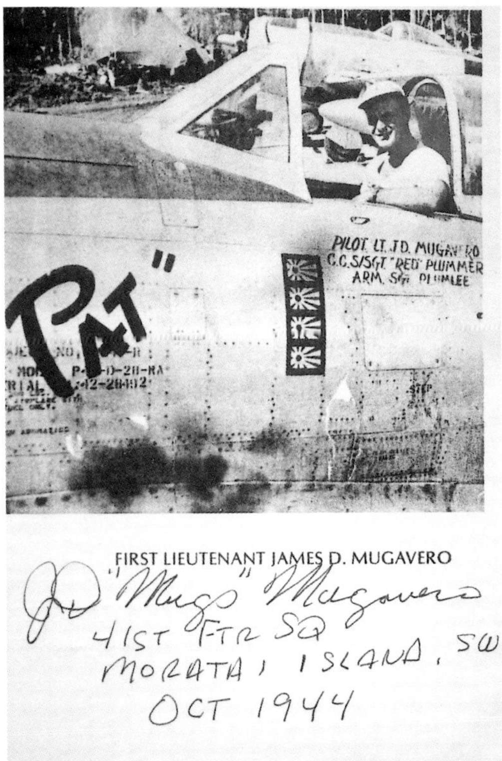


**1Lt. James Mugavero** scored his fourth of six victories. (AFAA)

gain altitude. Jeanes dove and made a wide turn to the left and got on the tail of the #2 Tony that turned off into a steep left dive when Jeanes began to fire. Jeanes fired in a steep dive from 350 yards until he passed over the target getting hits "all over" and seeing the pilot open his canopy. Jeanes chandelled to the left and looked around and saw Tony #1 wingover on his tail. Then saw Mugavero approach this Tony as it was about to stall. Mugavero fired at the top of a wingover at 20-30 degrees deflection for two seconds. The canopy opened and the pilot bailed out of the burning Tony. As the Flight left the area they saw two Japanese parachutes floating down; one for Jeanes' third and last victory and the other for Mugavero's fourth victory.

**Capt. Richard West** got two victories to give him a dozen. (AFAA)

**5-6 November 1944: U.S. Navy Attacks Luzon**

From the 28 October to 4 November the 5FC shot down 350 Japanese aircraft in air combat and destroyed 120 more on the ground. However, the Luzon airfields remained heavily occupied by a continual supply of enemy aircraft streamed in from the north to harass MacArthur's ground and air forces. The small number of 5AF aircraft that had arrived at Leyte could only cover the Tacloban and Leyte Gulf area so Kenney asked MacArthur to request that Halsey's carrier aircraft attack the active enemy airdromes on Luzon; especially the great airdrome at Clark Field outside Manila. Halsey agreed to a maximum effort on Luzon on 5 and 6 November and his aircraft shot down 113 enemy aircraft in aerial combat and destroyed 327 more on the ground. Meanwhile the 5FC destroyed 58 enemy fighters and a bomber in combat over Leyte and Cebu.

**1Lt. Kenneth Pool** (left), with **Langdell** and **West** (right), became an ace. (AFAA)

**6 November 1944: 8FG/35FS/36FS**

At noon on the 6 November 15 Lightnings of the 36th Squadron joined nine from the 35FS in a sweep over Fabrica, Bacolod, and Alicante Airdromes on Negros.

35FS

Capt. Richard West was leading a flight to Fabrica and as he approached Alicante Drome he saw two unidentified aircraft at 13,000 feet and turned after them. After chasing them for 50 miles he saw that they were P-47s and headed back toward Bacolod where he saw a fighter taxiing on the field as if it had just landed. He led his flight up the coast toward Fabrica and over Alicante he saw several apparently serviceable aircraft on the field but continued on. Near Fabrica he saw two trucks heading toward the field and ordered tanks to be dropped. The West dove and attacked the trucks from the rear and hit both, stopping them. On his second pass he destroyed the lead truck. The flight moved on and attacked a "Sugar Charlie" lugger transporting fuel just off the coast and West exploded it with one burst. West's flight was at 500 feet when he heard the 36FS call bandits overhead. The flight climbed at full power to 8,000 feet and saw an Oscar chasing a P-38, both in a vertical dive. As the P-38 dove into a cloud West fired on the Oscar with an overhead 90 degree deflection shot and sent it into the ground. As he circled the area and started to leave he heard the 36FS in a dogfight and turned around and dove through broken clouds at 4,000 feet. West attacked lone fighter with an 80 degree overhead pass, hitting its horizontal stabilizer. West's Wingman, 1Lt. James Beckett, followed with a 30 degree deflection shot hitting its cockpit for his only victory claim of the war. West's Element Leader, 1Lt. Kenneth Pool, spotted a Tony on the deck and closed to 300 yards and fired until it went out of control for his fifth victory. West and Beckett saw another enemy fighter scream directly in front of them chased by three P-38s. West took an easy shot at the Oscar, hitting it squarely with a 75 degree deflection shot while in a 45 degree dive and sent spinning into the ground for West's 12th victory. West flew into a piece of the Oscar's fuselage and it damaged his starboard spinner and engine. Meanwhile, Beckett lost West and then had his engines lose fuel pressure and cut in and out and left the fight.

**1Lt. James Bekett** (right), West's Wingman, claimed his only victory. (AAF)

36FS
Capt. Kenneth Giroux led 14 P-38 from Morotai at 755 for a fighter sweep over Fabrica Airdrome, Negros at 1145 to 1215. The Squadron arrived over Bacolod and saw only one plane taxiing and continued on to Alicante that had about 15 parked aircraft but none took off. They continued on to Fabrica and descended to 4,000; getting ready for a strafing run and saw Capt. West's 35FS strafing a Sugar Charlie in the Bay. The Squadron arrived over the target at 4,000 feet to strafe the field and Green Flight led by 1Lt. Harold Graham was left above to provide top cover. Approximately 15 mixed fighters (Tonys, Oscars, and Zeros) and two Kate bombers would be encountered in the area.

Capt. Giroux and Wingman, 2Lt. Francis Collins, were alerted by Graham of enemy aircraft coming in high. They started to climb and spotted three Oscars (or Zeros) and Giroux fired just as he was on the verge of a stall but missed but Dunaway had gained altitude and closed to shoot it down. Giroux then saw an Oscar on the tail of a P-38 and fired a desperate shot from 1,000 yards and chased it off. Giroux turned around a cloud and saw Dunaway shoot down another Oscar. Giroux climbed to 8,000 feet and heard Dunaway call for help saying he was alone on the west side of the field. Giroux led Wingman Collins and Lt. Morgan Element Leader of Blue Flight and saw two Tonys. Collins went after one and Giroux the other. Giroux fired a two second burst into the cockpit and it burst into flame for his ninth victory. As Giroux rolled away he saw Collins fire an 80 degree deflection shot. The Tony then rolled into a turn into Collins who held his lead and got hits into the wing and cockpit and rolled over and crashed into the ground. Giroux then headed west and saw Dunaway shoot down a Tony.

1Lt. John Dunaway was leading White Flight at 4,000 feet and led his flight down to strafe the airstrip. When the flight descended to about 3,500 feet they saw three enemy fighters (Zeros or Oscars) ready to bounce Giroux's Red Flight. Dunaway climbed toward two Zeros and the first Zero broke off its attack but the enemy Wingman continued the attack on Giroux, who then pulled almost straight up to fire one quick but inaccurate burst at the Zero. Dunaway arrived as the Zero pulled up in a wing over and fired a 30 degree two second burst from only about 150 yards that tore pieces off the enemy fighter that rolled over and crashed in flames into the ground for Dunaway's first victory of the day. The other two enemy fighters tried to get into position for a pass but gave up and dove away to the deck. Wingman 2Lt. Francis Ford dove after it and got on its tail and fired a long burst that started its wing on fire. Ford continued to follow the Oscar and fired again. The Oscar pilot snap rolled into a cloud and saw it come out the other side and crash for Ford's only victory. Dunaway's Element Leader, 2Lt. William Wooddell, broke after an Oscar that was firing at a P-38 and fired tracers that passed in front of it. The Oscar turned to starboard and Dunaway quickly got on the tail of another Zero and followed it down to 3,000 feet shot it down at 200 yards with a no deflection three second burst for his second victory of the combat. Dunaway began climbing again when he saw two Tonys closely chasing two P-38s. Dunaway called the Tonys and one of the P-38s turned into the Tonys casing them to overshoot and the other P-38 snap rolled into a cloud. One of the Tonys had pulled up to make a pass on one of the P-38s and Dunaway closed to 300 yards firing a 45 degree three second burst that started a fire in the cockpit and the Tony went down smoking badly. Dunaway followed it down and watched it crash into the mountains on the east side of the strip for his third victory. Dunaway climbed to gain altitude and saw two Kates flying south of Fabrica. He dove quickly to get onto the tail of one Kate and fired a five second burst from 250 yards to 50 yards knocking off the entire tail assembly of the bomber which went into five or six snap rolls into the ground five miles south of Fabrica for his fourth victory of the day and give him six victories to make him the second and final fighter ace of the 36FS. Wooddell became separated from his flight and joined Green Flight Leader Graham and the two broke under the clouds after a call from Dunaway to come down south of

**1Lt. John Dunaway** shot down two Zeros, a Tony to become an ace with six victories. (AFAA)

The Negros Islands Airdromes were subject to strafing attacks. (AFAA)

the strip. As they exited the clouds Graham went after a Hamp on the right and Wooddell saw another closing on Graham from 9 o'clock and called it to Graham who turned into it. The Hamp fired a short deflection shot at Graham and Wooddell fired a short deflection shot at the Hamp that gotten on Graham's tail again. As Wooddell was closing on the Hamp, another P-38 fired a short ahead of it from 90 degrees and the Hamp turned to port. Wooddell fired from 150 yards and it exploded causing Wooddell to veer to avoid the debris. This was Wooddell's first of two victories.

**6 November 1944: 35FG/39FS/40FS/41FS**

39FS

At 1040 15 P-47s of the 39FS were patrolling over the Negros Islands at 14,000 feet and Red Flight Leader, 1Lt. Richard Rose, with Wingman Avant and Element Leader Steele were the first to call out the Oscars and Red Flight went after them with the other three 39FS Flights to remain as top cover. The two unaware Oscars were flying at 11 o'clock low and Rose ordered wing tanks to be dropped and Rose led the attack getting hits on Oscar's right wing and fuselage (for a probable claim). Avant had followed too close and was unable to fire at the first Oscar; meanwhile, the second Oscar made a 360 and got on the American's tails. Rose and Avant outclimbed this Oscar and headed home.

Blue Flight led by 1Lt. William Rogers with Wingmen 2Lt. Paul Foster and 1Lt. Maurice Boland spotted a single Oscar flying at 9 o'clock level. When the enemy pilot spotted the approaching Thunderbolts he made several climbing turns and Blue Flight dropped their tanks and took off after it. At 18,000 feet the Japanese pilot turned to make a head on pass but broke away as Rogers fired a deflection shot. Foster, despite having one of his tanks still attached, fired a deflection shot as the Japanese pilot rolled out into a 60 degree dive. Foster followed and fired from astern getting hits in the Oscar's wings. The two pilots continued their dive with Foster firing intermittently. At 4,000 feet and 450 mph IAS Foster pulled out but the Oscar stayed into its dive and crashed into the sea for Foster's only victory. Meanwhile, Rogers climbed after a second Oscar and maneuvered behind it at 23,000 feet and fired out of range, observing some hits, and then followed the Oscar into a dive. At about 10,000 feet Roger's fighter began to shutter violently as the wing controls were fouled by a gas line that did not detach with the wing tank. Rogers was finally able to pull out of the dive at 5,000 feet with a probable claim.

**2Lt. Paul Foster** got his only victory of the war. (AAF)

1Lt. Carl Rymer, White Flight Leader, with Second Element Leader, Perkins and Wingman Aycock (Rymer's Wingman aborted the mission) were patrolling at 14,000 feet when they spotted a single Oscar flying under some clouds below. Rymer, who wasn't able to jettison one wing tank, led the Flight after the Oscar around a mountain side and just as he got into firing range the Oscar pilot did a half roll and partial Split-S and then came out just below tree level with another half roll, causing Rymer to overfly. As Rymer came around for another pass he saw Perkins and Aycock making unsuccessful passes as the Oscar pilot executed more adept evasive maneuvers. Rymer came in from dead astern and "popped the stick" to stay with the evading Oscar but as Rymer fired his fighter skidded due the balky wing tank and he missed. Perkins came in for another pass at 30 degrees and got hits between the cockpit and tail but then overflew the Oscar whose pilot pulled up and fired on Perkins. Aycock then attacked head on but did not fire as the Oscar turned away. Rymer closed for his third pass as the Oscar pilot was breaking away from his attack on Perkins. The enemy pilot rolled and Split-S'd but Rymer was ready for this repeat maneuver and the Oscar flew into Rymer's fire and crashed, flaming, into the ground for Rymer's only victory.

Yellow Fight, led by 1Lt. Marcus Trout, saw a single Oscar diving from 12 o'clock and Trout and Wingman Crawford maneuvered behind it as it passed through and got some hits on it. Element Leader 2Lt. Ernest Johnson came in on a 45 degree diving turn to cut off the Oscar. The Oscar pilot rolled away from his pursuers but Johnson rolled with the Oscar and found himself at very close range at the end of the roll and fired seeing the Oscar go down in flames for his first of two victories.

40FS

The 40FS flew 13 P-47s on a fighter sweep to Fabrica Drome and arrived at 1040 at 18,000 feet when Blue Flight Leader, Capt. Jack Marvin called out a bogie below and then saw two more and Red Flight dove after them. Blue Flight followed Red Flight down but stayed above as top cover and then returned to 14,000 feet to patrol. After circling once Marvin saw a bogie approaching from 2 o'clock high and pulled up level to the Hamp. The enemy pilot turned left and Marvin with his Wingman, 2Lt. Jack Finegan, following slightly in trail and tried to circle to gain an advantage on the Hamp but the battle became a stand off. Marvin then engaged his water injection and dropped his nose to go into a tighter turn and gained 500 feet on the Hamp. The enemy pilot went into a vertical reverse and Split-S'd giving Red Element, 1Lt. Jack Powers, a firing pass which caused the Hamp to Split-S again. This maneuver put the Hamp at 250 yards, 40 degree deflection, straight and level to Marvin who fired and the Hamp plunged straight down into the clouds. After being credited with a probable and damaged on 4 March 1944, this was Marvin's only victory of the war.

Yellow Flight Leader, 1Lt. Henry Wilkes soon saw another bogie at 3 o'clock and 6,000 feet below and led his Flight after it. When Wilkes closed and was ready to fire he heard a radio call, "Are you sure they're Nips?" Wilkes pulled up slightly to the right and saw the red roundels and dropped down and closed quickly and began firing at 100 yards. Wilkes saw hits on the wing roots and fuselage before he had to pull up violently to avoid a collision. Wilkes' Wingman, 2Lt. Ira Weaver closed on the Hamp from 250 to 50 yards and got hits on its canopy and fuselage but the wounded Hamp would not catch fire and rolled over slowly and disappeared into the clouds to give Weaver a probable claim. Wilkes pulled up to 14,000 feet and saw another bandit at 9 o'clock low. As Wilkes dove the Hamp turned into him and then a Wilkes began to fire the enemy pilot Split-S'd. Wiles followed him at 40 degrees, flying and firing inverted, scoring hits on its cockpit, wing roots, and fuselage. This Hamp started smoking and spun straight down, out of control, its pilot apparently dead. After claiming two victories on 24 October this would be Wilkes third and last victory of the war.

41FS

Maj. Douglas Parsons led 10 (three aborts) P-47s to provide cover for 24 B-24s on a bombing mission to Caroline Airdrome in the Negros Islands. After rendezvousing with the Liberators over Guimara Islands at 1003 the mission continued with the bombers at 12,500 feet and the 41FS above at 15,000 feet. At 1015 a bogie was called in and the Squadron dropped their wing tanks.

Parson's Red Flight was responsible to fend off enemy fighters attacking the bombers and turned 360 to get slightly ahead of the bomber formation. Parsons "closed very easily using water injection" on an attacking Oscar but fired low on his first burst and missed. Parsons pulled up slightly and his bullets entered the Oscars' fuselage. The Oscar Split-S'd away to the left toward its base on Cebu with a slight trail of smoke for a probable claim. Parsons returned to the bombers and encountered a Tony that had just passed through the formation. Using water injection again, Parsons closed and led the Tony which was in a gentle turn. Parson's first burst passed under its wing but he raised his nose and increased his deflection and got hits into the cockpit. Parsons overflew the stricken Tony but his Wingman confirmed the victory. Parsons climbed back above the bombers, down sun at 16,000 feet and soon saw a Tojo dive from the right to make a pass on straggling bombers. The Tojo pilot seemed to be so intent on making a good pass that Parsons was able to close without being noticed and got a long burst that exploded the fuel tank behind the enemy pilot's head but the pilot miraculously was able to bail out. These two victories were Parson's third and last of the war. Parson's Element Leader, 2Lt. Vernon Brown, watched as Parsons and his Wingman attacked. He saw two enemy fighters make a pass on the bombers and then pull up behind him. Brown turned into the closest Tony and came into firing range and fired a three to four second burst into the wings and fuselage and the Tony plunged into the ground. As Brown was recovering from this combat another Tony came at him head on and the two began to fire at each other. Brown had to pull up at the last second, as it appeared that the Japanese pilot wanted to ram him. During the skirmish another Tony got on his tail at 8,000 feet and Brown had to go into a full throttle, water injection, screaming dive to escape, pulling out at 1,500 feet with his only victory of the war.

White Flight, led by F/O Milton Rowell, was flying top cover for Blue and Yellow Flights that were flying close cover for the B-24s. Shortly after rendezvousing with the bombers, Rowell called out four Oscars at 3 o'clock high and dropped tanks and climbed for altitude. As he was watching the four Oscars below, he saw six Tonys at 6 o'clock low and then four more at 11 o'clock low. Two Oscars started to make a pass on the B-24s and Rowell made an overhead pass without seeing any results. He pulled back up over the bombers and as they began their bombing run he saw a Tony 6,000 feet below. As there were no other enemy fighters in the area, Rowell dove and began shooting at 10 degrees to dead astern and got hits in the engine and cockpit. As he continued to fire there was an explosion and the Tony fell off on one wing and headed toward the sea for his second and last victory.

Blue Flight Leader, 1Lt. John Saunders, saw two Oscars at 12 o'clock and 3,000 feet above as the bomber approached Caroline Drome at 14,000 feet. Both Oscars headed toward Blue Flight but broke off in different directions before they were in range. Saunders went after the lead Oscar and his Wingman took on the Oscar #2. The lead Oscar pilot Split-S'd and rolled straight down and Saunders followed and fired a "good" burst into the cockpit, killing the pilot. Saunders led the Flight back up to the bombers that were finishing their bombing run and heading out to sea. As they closed they saw two Oscars attacking tail end bombers in the formation. Saunders led the Flight down and engaged the #1 Oscar while his #4 followed the second Oscar. Saunders' Oscar performed the same evasive maneuvers as his previous victim, a Split-S and downward roll, and with the same results, fatal hits into its canopy as it began to smoke and spin away. (These were Saunders only victories of the war). Meanwhile, Blue #4, 2Lt. William Greenart's #2 Oscar did a half Split-S and half wing over and Greenart fired from 70 degrees, raking the Oscar engine to tail and then head straight down and explode as it hit the water for his only victory of the war.

**6 November 1944: 418NSF**

1Lt. William Ross and R/O, 2Lt. Raymond Duethman, took off at 0300 to relieve another P-61 on a routine patrol over Morotai at 8,000 feet. At 0328 a Red Alert was sounded and Morotai was blacked out and Ross received several vectors but made no contacts as Ross saw bomb explosions and heavy AA fire at Morotai. While making a hard port turn toward another vector the canopy over the pilot was blown off and hit Ross and he suffered a four inch gash, causing him to lose consciousness momentarily. He righted the damaged P-61 that vibrated severely at high speeds, as the canopy had struck the horizontal stablilizer. At 0400 Ross received another vector at 190 degrees at full speed at five miles. At four and a half miles and 10,000 feet, Duethman made a radar contact and put Ross in visual contact at 1,200 feet on a Betty bomber. Ross closed to 1,000 feet somewhat below and fired two bursts at no deflection with his four 20mm cannons and the bombers exploded and crashed in the mountains of the Halmahera Island for Ross' only victory.

**1Lt. Edwin Cooper** was credited with a probable and his second and last victory. (AAF)

**7 November 1944: 49FG/9FS**

The monsoon lifted on the 7th and the effect of Halsey's carrier raids were already evident as the Japanese only sent flights of two or three aircraft at a time. The Flying Knights first morning patrol over the Dulag Drome area claimed the only victories of the day just west of Buri over Ormoc Bay.

Red Flight Leader 1Lt. Edwin Cooper led four P-38s off Buri Strip at 0630 and patrolled until 0730 when they saw AA fire north of Dulag and bogies called in strafing Dulag. No plot was called and Cooper flew west to intercept the enemy fighters on their way home. Cooper's Wingman, 2Lt. James Hovik, saw a bogie at 6 o'clock high and Cooper turned and pulled up into the enemy, fired but then stalled out. The two Americans continued circling as did the Japanese above them. Hovik saw an Oscar make a 360 degree turn that put it on his tail and fire on him from out of range. This Oscar then went into a shallow dive toward Cooper who pulled up into the Oscar and fired but the Oscar headed away, unharmed, in a shallow dive. Because Cooper had been climbing his airspeed was down to 130, and he used water injection to close within 50 to 100 yards dead astern and fired again, with this three second burst resulting in many hits in the cockpit, wings, and fuselage. The Oscar rolled over and went straight down (but its pilot was able to bail out) for his second and last victory. Cooper turned a 360 and saw four more Oscars attacking P-40s from above. Cooper turned into one of the Oscars and fired at 40 degrees deflection, knocking off small pieces and causing it to trail a slight smoke plume for a probable. As the two headed back to base they saw a P-40 and an Oscar engaged below and Cooper and Hovik joined the fight. After making two or three unsuccessful passes which the Oscar pilot deflected by turning into them, another P-38 came on the scene. This P-38 made a head on pass on the Oscar which put it diving into Hovik's sights. Hovik led the Oscar and fired a short burst which passed behind it. Hovik adjusted his lead and fired a long burst into its cockpit. The Oscar rolled over and just before it hit the water it burst into flames for Hovik's only victory.

The 7FS flew a morning strike to Ormoc and rookie 2Lt. Hubert Manes got caught in a runway snafu and took off late. Manes decided to search for his flight alone and was attacked by an Oscar which shot out his right engine but he eluded the attacker and turned for Tacloban. As he neared the base his damaged Allison burst into flame and he bailed out west of Tacloban and was immediately rescued by the Filipino Guerillas and returned to base that night.

**7 November 1944: 71TRS/110TRS**

The 110[th] Tactical Recon Squadron of the 71[st] Tac Recon Group had its first combat of the war downing four Oscars over Ormac Bay at 0715; one each by Capt. Rubel Archuleta, 1Lt. George Marman, and 2Lts. Harry Johnson and Martin Regan.

**6-7 November 1944: 475FG/432FS**

On 6 November 24 sorties were flown by Clover Squadron with operations starting at 0600 when four P-38s took off and ended at 1730 when the last four landed at Bayug. Finally, at 0600 on 7 November, the Japanese sent a surprise attack over Bayug and the American AA batteries mistook the Japanese fighters for P-40s and did not fire. Several antipersonnel bombs damaged three of the 432FS' P-38s. A simultaneous raid to Dulag caused heavy damage to the new construction there. Despite the weather and enemy air raids air patrols continued, as 24 sorties had been flown that day and six more on the next day in the face of a solid weather front.

**7 November 1944: 35FG: Change in Command**

35FG CO, Maj. Richard Cella, was ordered back to the Command and General Staff School at Fort Leavenworth, KS and was succeeded by Capt. Leroy Grosshuesch who would lead the Squadron until July 1945 when he was briefly replaced and then would command the Squadron during the Occupation until April 1948.

**8 November 1944: 475FG**

Capt. Joseph Forster took off at 0615 with 2Lt. Lakin Parlett on his wing to cover an LCI off Patcan Island in very poor weather. As the two P-38s were just turning after taking off when they saw AA bursts over Dulag. Forster approached the AA bursts and then saw its target, an Oscar flying due west and approaching San Pablo Strip #2. Forster radioed for the AA to stop but they didn't and Forster had to wait until the Oscar flew clear of the AA fire. He then dove to attack from 2,000 feet, using his war emergency power. Forster closed into within range over the Catmon Mountains and fired and the Japanese fighter began taking hits just before it evaded into the clouds. Forster followed the Oscar in and out of the clouds, firing available 10 to 30 degree deflection shots. When the Oscar emerged the third time he fired a long burst until the Oscar entered the clouds again. The next time he saw the Oscar it rolled out of the clouds trailing flames with the pilot bailing giving Forster his sixth victory.

**9 November 1944: Japanese Convoy Attacked**

On the 9[th] the Japanese made another attempt to reinforce their ground forces on Leyte by sending a convoy south from Manila. The convoy was sighted late on the afternoon of the 9[th] near Ormoc. B-25s, P-38s, and P-40s were immediately sent up before the enemy troops could be landed under the cover of darkness. The American pilots ferociously attacked the convoy and although none of the ships was sunk, many troops were killed, and much equipment was destroyed before darkness fell.

49FG/7FS

The Flying Knights flew eight bomb-carrying P-38s over Ormoc to strike a convoy which had just arrived in the early morning. The mission caused some damage but rookie 2Lt. Donald Kanoff was hit by the convoy AA batteries and his flaming P-38 crashed in into the sea among the enemy ships.

**9 November 1944: 547NFS Arrives**

The 547NFS's "Special Detachment" arrived on 9 November and immediately went into action testing the feasibility of a P-38 night fighter modification. The Squadron's crews had received some training in Australia after which they returned to the 547NFS on Owi for further training. After completing their training, they conducted intruder missions over backwater Japanese installations in the Dutch East Indies. But Headquarters wanted them to get into combat and moved the detachment to Leyte. They flew dusk and dawn intruder missions over Japanese airdromes 100 to 150 miles away in the Cebu, Negros, and lower Luzon areas. These nuisance missions were supposed to hamper the enemy from taking off from his airfields in order to attack Allied fields at night. It was found that when the Japanese detected night fighters in the vicinity of their airfields, it caused them to go on a red alert, which prevented the enemy from launching strikes against the Allies. A typical 547NSF mission was for the patrol to remain in the area until it was determined that daylight would meet the incoming enemy if a take off was ordered and would place the enemy bombers in the path of Allied fighters. Then the intruders would fly to airdromes closer to their own base and repeat the procedure. Because of the Lightning's speed this system was easily realized, enabling them to arrive over the airdrome well in time to signal a red alert before the enemy bombers were allowed to take off. From the time the 547[th]'s P-38s morning or dusk patrols were initiated, Tacloban enjoyed quiet nights. When the 418[th] moved on to San Jose on Mindoro the LST which carried most of their ground service equipment was hit by Japanese Kamikaze and sunk. To help out in this emergency, the 547NFS was sent to San Jose in late December.

**1Lt. Joseph Forster** claimed his sixth victory while defending Dulag Drome. (AFAA)

The Japanese sent a convoy from Manila to reinforce their position at **Ormoc**, which was heavily attacked by the 5AF. (AAF)

After nearly three months of operations, the 547th's Special Detachment found that the added fuel of the external tanks made the P-61 a very good long range night fighter. They also found that besides being a good R/O trainer, the APS-4 equipped B-25 was a very good night intruder. However, they had a low opinion of the P-38 as a night fighter; and felt it was better suited for intruder operations and for dawn and dusk missions where there was a possibility of daylight air combat. They also determined that in order for pilots to carry out successful intruder missions they required additional navigation training.

**10 November 1944: 475FG/432FS/431FS**

432FS Morning

At 0815 12 Lightnings in three flights: Red: Col. Charles MacDonald with 2Lt. Calvin Anderson and Second Element Leader, 1Lt. Dean Olson and Wingman, 2Lt. Grady Laseter; White: 1Lt. Perry Dahl and Wingman, 2Lt. Henry Toll and Second Element Leader, Capt. Richard Kiick and Wingman, 2Lt. Donald Willis; Blue: 1Lt. Charles Ratajski and Wingman, 2Lt. Albert McKenzie and Second Element Leader; 2Lt. Roger Palmer and Wingman, 2Lt. Robert Schuh. The Squadron was scrambled by the Air Controller who plotted enemy aircraft over Ormoc Bay. Col. Charles MacDonald led the scramble to 10,000 feet and arrived over the enemy shipping in Ormoc Bay at 0915. He spotted a lone Oscar followed by three other unidentified aircraft flying in and out of the rain and clouds. MacDonald immediately chased the Oscar until it vanished into the clouds again. Once he emerged from the clouds, MacDonald regrouped and saw the Oscar leaving the cloud at 2 o'clock. MacDonald closed to about 200 yards behind and fired a 30 degree deflection shot that hit the Oscar's wing roots and started it on fire and then closed with several more telling bursts and the Japanese pilot bailed out. The Japanese destroyers in the Bay were throwing up moderate to heavy AA fire and with his fuel running low MacDonald turned the formation over to 1Lt. Perry Dahl and White Flight and returned to base with Wingman Anderson. Meanwhile, MacDonald's #3, 1Lt. Dean Olson, fired at the Oscar from out of range and got no hits. He then saw another Tony below flying at 90 degrees to him and dove and fired at 90 degrees and missed. The Tony pilot seemed oblivious to Olson's attack and continued on course. Olson closed from astern and fired a long burst that hit its belly from the coolant scoop forward. The Tony burst into flame and was seen to crash by Ratajski for Olson's only victory of the war.

Now in command of Clover Squadron, Dahl followed a Zero and fired a few short bursts before it entered the clouds. Not wanting to lose Clover formation in the clouds Dahl broke off his attack Dahl flew back into the open and circled with the Squadron intact. Because of the surrounding clouds the Squadron was in an unsafe situation as they could be bounced at any time and position by the Japanese. Dahl decided that the best defense was to keep up speed and to weave, always keeping the tail end of the formation in sight. Soon 12 (to 16) enemy aircraft were seen approaching level from the west, flying in and out of the clouds and overcast. The overcast was beginning to clear over areas of Ormoc Bay and Dahl ordered his P-38s to power climb into the area of better visibility above where they circled in the open sky at 9,000 feet, northwest of Ponson Island and waited. Within a few minutes the enemy fighters, now identified as Tonys emerged from the overcast at 9 o'clock. Dahl's P-38s had a 500 foot altitude advantage

**1Lt. Perry Dahl** shot down his seventh enemy aircraft before he was rammed mid-air, but he was able to bail out. (AFAA)

**2Lt. Grady Laseter** was KIA when his P-38 rammed Dahl. (AAF)

**Capt. Richard Kiick** scored his only two victories of the war. He would later become the CO of the 421NFS. (AAF)

**1Lt. Dean Olson** shot down a Tony for his only victory. (AAF)

**2Lt. Henry Toll** scored two of his three total victories. (AAF)

and dove out of the sun and surprised the Tonys which separated into ones or twos and generally Split-S'd or turned away to port. Dahl went after the leader and fired a 45 degree deflection shot from above getting hits in the engine and cockpit before it went out of control and crashed below for his seventh victory. Dahl's Wingman, 2Lt. Henry Toll, saw a Tony directly ahead and closed from three quarters front and fired at 200 yards, corrected, and fired again getting numerous hits on the wing roots and cockpit area. The Tony snapped up and went into a flat spin. Toll followed and could see the Tony pilot slumped over and Capt. Kiick confirmed the kill. Toll dropped down into the P-38 string and while banking in a circle and saw another Tony ahead and closed to 250 yards and fired a 30 degree deflection shot that hit the rear part of his engine cowling. The engine began to smoke s the Tony dove at 45 degrees toward Ponson Island for Toll's second victory of the day and 2/3rds of his career victories. Dahl's Second Element Leader, Capt. Richard Kiick fired at a Tony that Split-S'd in front of him and hit the engine. This Tony caught fire immediately and spun into Ormoc Bay. Kiick came upon another Tony that was about 400 yards ahead and turning 60 degrees to port. His fire hit the rear of its cowling and lower fuselage and the Tony started to smoke and was seen to be on fire by Lt. Olson as it hit the Bay for Kiick's only two victories of the war. Kiick's Wingman 2Lt. Donald Willis saw a Tony firing on Dahl's tail and getting solid hits for a probable but diverted the Tony from its attack on Dahl. Willis then was dumbfounded when he saw Dahl's P-38 colliding with another Lightning (2Lt. Grady Laseter) and the two fighters plummeting toward the ground. As Willis rejoined the string his P-38 was hit from behind in both wings, the cockpit, both wheel well doors, punctured the starboard tire, and the starboard boom. As the Tony overshot, Willis fired and tore off its wing at the root and it exploded just before it crashed for his only victory. Willis was escorted home by Ratajski and landed safely on one engine.

1Lt. Charles Ratajski was leading Clover Blue Flight and when he spotted the 12 Tonys he led his flight in a 180 degree turn to port and made a 6 o'clock high pass on the scattered Tonys. Ratajski watched as a number of Tonys were shot down by the leading Red and White Flights. He then made two climbing passes at Tonys, observing that he "didn't have any trouble climbing with the Tonys... and I could close on them at 175mph." However, both Tonys did steep wingovers at the top of their climbs and Ratajski missed both shots at them. Ratajski watched Willis shoot down his Tony and saw another Tony ahead and somewhat above in a shallow climb going away. Ratajski closed and fired a three second burst that hit its engine in front of the wing. A fire started and the Tony dove into the Bay for his third victory. Ratajski then escorted Willis back to base. Ratajski's Wingman, 2Lt. Albert McKenzie, dutifully followed his Leader and reported firing no shots at the Tonys. Ratajski's Second Element of 2Lt. Roger Palmer and 2Lt. Robert Schuh saw a Tony at 3 o'clock about to wingover on the P-38 formation. Schuh fired at 40 degree deflection, hitting the coolant radiator and fuselage and Palmer saw it go down for Schuh's only victory. Palmer made four passes on Tonys, hitting one in the wing root and coolant radiator and saw white smoke emerge from the radiator. He made another pass on this Tony but lost sight of it as it Spilt-S'ed away for no claim. Schuh also got a good shot at a Tony but also lost it for no claim.

During the battle two P-38s were seen to collide in midair and after the Squadron landed it was determined that the two Lightnings were Dahl's and 2Lt. Grady Laseter's. However, Ratajski reported that he had seen a parachute descending below the collision. After Dahl had shot down his Tony he broke to the left with Willis following close behind. For some reason, perhaps mechanical problems or combat damage, Laseter turned and headed directly at Dahl and chopped off the P-38's left wing and tail booms. Dahl's P-38 was on fire and he was badly burned on the neck and shoulder while leaving the cockpit to bail out. He landed near four Japanese destroyers and one opened light machine gun fire on him and as he inflated his life raft a bullet grazed his head and Dahl decided to play possum, clinging to the raft as the destroyer came close by to investigate. Suddenly, the destroyer sped away with its AA batteries opening fire on attacking B-25s. After the destroyer and B-25s left, a lone Tony began circling Dahl's raft and made one strafing run before it left. After the Mitchells left the area the destroyers returned but did not find Dahl. By sunset the wind had blown Dahl in toward shore and he saw canoes coming toward him. After nine hours in the water, Dahl did not want to be picked up by the Japanese and paddled toward the beach and hid into the trees. Soon Filipino civilians found and hid him, fed him, and treated his wounds. The next morning he was led to Santa Cruz where he was sent by boat to Matlang. He was then taken to the 3rd Battalion of the 96th Infantry Regiment Aid Station where he remained until 3 December and was joined by several other downed airmen, including 1Lt. Leroy Ross of the 433FS who was downed on 24 November. On 7 December arrangements were made to have Dahl and the others picked up on 10 December but they had to walk back to Matlang for the rendezvous. After being flown back to Tacloban in the PBY Dahl flew back to Dulag in a L-5 and walked in; surprising his squadron mates that he was still alive.

432FS Afternoon

Later that day the 432nd sent out eight P-38s in two Special Flights, #1 and #2, under 1Lt, John Hannan, to cover B-24s to Ormoc Bay and Ormoc Township. Special #1 was led by Hannan with Wingman, 1Lt. Laurence LeBaron and Second Element Leader, 2Lt. Lakin Parlett and Wingman, 2Lt. Lawrence Roberts; while Special #2 was led by 1Lt. Joseph Forster and Wingman, 2Lt. Walter Freeman and Second Element, 2Lt. Harrold Owens and Wingman, 2Lt. Robert Kimball (who lost Special #2 and moved to #5 in Special #1). The Squadron rendezvoused with the bombers east of Tacloban and flew up the Luzon west coast to the target. They were at 20,000 feet when they saw four Tonys below at 14,000 feet. Hannan led the dive and the Tonys broke up into four elements. Hanna made several unsuccessful passes but Wingman LeBaron fired at an element Wingman from five degrees below and got hits on its tail but lost contact. LeBaron made a head on pass from five to 10 degrees below on a lone Tony and got numerous hits on its engine and wing root and saw it crash in flames for his first of four victories. Hannan's #4, 2Lt. Lawrence Roberts, had a Tony make a head on pass at him and Roberts fired a long burst that exploded the Tony which came so close that Roberts had to pull up to avoid being rammed and barely escaped with his first of three victories. Forster made several passes with Special #2 Flight but two of the four Tonys were shot down by Special #1 and the other two escaped after LeBaron made his head on pass. The 432nd continued its B-24 escort without further enemy contact.

**1Lt. Laurence LeBaron** was credited with his first of four victories. (AAF)

431FS Afternoon

Seven P-38s in Red and White flights took off from Tacloban at 1330 to escort P-38s on a dive bombing mission on an enemy convoy. When they arrived 20 minutes later the dive bombers were early and had left. At 1440, while patrolling at 14,000 feet an Oscar was spotted coming through the clouds. McGuire ordered White Flight to stay up and cover his Red Flight of four P-38s. McGuire caught up with the Oscar and fired two short burst from dead astern at 50 feet above the water, hitting it around the cockpit. After the second burst it crashed into sea. McGuire's victory was a milestone as he, too, now had surpassed Capt. Eddie Rickenbacker's WW-1 standard of 26 victories. Meanwhile, Bong had scored his 34th victory that day and McGuire remained his usual eight behind.

**Maj. Thomas McGuire** claimed victory #26, which tied him with Rickenbacker's WWI record. (AAF)

**10 November 1944: 8FG/80FS/36FS**

80FS

The 80FS officially moved to Dulag on Leyte on 15 November but continued to operate from Morotai (Owi) until 30 November. On 10 November the Headhunters would finally break the scoring hiatus that had continued since 17 August. Three flights (Red, White, and Blue) with 12 Lightnings of the 80FS Lightnings were led by Capt. Cyril Homer, on his last mission before becoming 36FS Commander. They took off took off 1030 with a stop at Leyte at 1400 to cover three squadrons of 13th Fighter Command P-38s which were to dive bomb an enemy convoy in Camotes Bay. Six Japanese warships were spotted 15 miles offshore at 1415 and were identified as four transports, three destroyers, and a smaller vessel (gunboat?). The 13AF P-38s dropped their bombs on the convoy northwest of Palompon with "moderate accuracy" and lost one Lightning to AA fire from the warships, which was characterized as "light and inaccurate." At 1430 while circling and weaving at 11,000 feet Homer saw two

**Capt. Cyril Homer** became a triple ace. (AFAA)

**Maj. Richard Bong**, the center of war correspondents' attention, attached himself to the 7FS and scored his last victory with them (#34) to remain eight ahead of McGuire, who got #26 that day. (AAF)

Oscars fly into a cloud south of the Japanese convoy and then saw three more Oscars above the same cloud. He called White Flight to attack the upper three while he descended after the other two with Wingman, 1Lt. William Coleman and 2Lts. Hugh Hatfield and Robert Peters following him. The four pilots caught the Japanese fighters that dove to 7,000 feet and then pulled out at a 40 degree angle. Homer fired at the rear Oscar from 200 yards astern. The surprised enemy pilot quickly looped and then rolled his fighter but Homer remained on his tail and closed to 50 yards and fired again and had to avoid the debris from his disintegrating 15th and last victim of the war to make him a triple ace. Simultaneously, Coleman, Hatfield, and Peters were chasing the other Oscar. Coleman and Hatfield fired at the Oscar getting some hits but it was Peters who finished it off with a 90 degree deflection shot in a right turn from 100 yards. Peters' gunfire hit the wing root and canopy and the Oscar's wing hit the water and it blew up and Peters had to avoid the debris to collect his only victory. Homer remained in the area looking to increase his score but would score no more as he continued to lead 36FS into the spring of 1945 when he was rotated home. White and Blue Flights returned to Morotai but Red Flight had to land at Tacloban and remain overnight as there was no fuel available until the next morning.

36FS

Capt. Thomas Huff led 18 P-38s assigned to cover 13AF/18FG P-38s that were to dive bomb enemy shipping in the straits of Ormoc Bay in the northern Camotes Sea. Huff led his Red Flight over the target at 1350 at 18,000 feet. Just as the first 18FG Lightning was about to make its bombing run two Oscars were spotted 2,000 feet above headed in the opposite direction. Huff ordered tanks to be dropped and turned after them. The Oscars turned to port and began a pass on Huff's flight from 10 o'clock. Huff turned into them and started after the first Oscar but it was out of range and protected by the other one. Huff called his Element Leader, 2Lt. Wayne Donker, to attack the first while he attacked the second on a head on pass. Huff banked left as did the Oscar pilot. Huff then reversed his bank and fired a one second 30 degree deflection shot that set the enemy fighter on fire at the wing roots and tail and its pilot bailed out for Huff's second and last victory.

**10 November 1944: 49FG/9FS/7FS**

9FS: Bong's Last Mission with the 9FS

On 10 November, Richard Bong approached acting Flying Knights CO, Maj. Wallace Jordan, to ask permission to fly freelance on the morning mission. Jordan agreed and bumped the scheduled Flight Leader to lead the sortie himself. At 0730, Jordan and Wingman 2Lt. Ismael Corley, Element Leader 1Lt. Thomas Hamilton and Wingman 1Lt. James Hovik took off to escort a flight of 110TRS P-40s on an armed reconnaissance of Ormoc Harbor. Bong joined the flight as the trailing fifth man.

The 110TRS reached Ormoc with their potent escort of nine 49ers cruising above the clouds at 15,000 feet. As the P-40s descended on their objective and disappeared into the cloud base, five Oscars appeared between the Lightnings and Warhawks. Bong indicated his intention to attack the trailing Ki-43 and all five 9FS Lightnings dropped their auxiliary fuel tanks and dove after Bong. Bong's first target escaped and he then climbed back up through the clouds and quickly sighted another Oscar. Bong fired a short deadly burst that set the enemy on fire and checked out the crash site of his 34th victory and returned to base with his flight. Rookie Corley fired at a fleeing Oscar which also crashed in flames, leaving him only 33 victories behind Bong but Corley would claim no more victories.

7FS

Capt. Edward Peck's 7FS was also scheduled for escort duty on the same mission and the CO would lead a flight. Col. Morrissey asked to fly attached, so Ops Exec DeHaven gave the Colonel the element lead position. 2Lt. George Rogers was to be Peck's Wingman and 2Lt. Albert Meschino was to tail Morrissey. The Demons also joined in the attack on the Oscars over the Bay but none reached a position to make a firing pass. After the Demon Flight regrouped south of Ormoc Harbor, Morrissey took over the lead in pursuit of the Oscars which were seen fleeing west. The Demons flew to Cebu Island's northern Cape and after orbiting there Morrissey spotted one of the Oscars. All four Lightning pilots flew head on passes against the lone Ki-43 pilot who boldly fought for ten terrifying minutes before Morrissey hit him with a rear quarter deflection shot that allowed Peck to finish him off for his second victory of the war. As the Oscar' pilot was descending in his parachute Morrissey tried to snare billowing chute but overran it and then he fired a wild burst at the enemy pilot but missed.

**10 November 1944: 421NFS**

1Lt. Albert Lockhard and his Black Widow crew R/O 2Lt. Stuart Thornton, and gunner S/Sgt. Joseph Mazur scored the squadron's first double kill, when they shot down two Tony fighters while flying a cover patrol near Ormac Bay. The patrol was providing protection to PT Boats in the Surigao Straight and

**1Lt. Albert Lockard** (left with Capt. Paul Zimmer, 421NFS CO) shot down two Tonys for his only victories of the war. (AAF)

had been divided into two sections: one P-61 to the north and the other to the south, near Leyte. About a half hour before the PT Boats released the patrol the other Black Widow flown by 1Lt. Rollo Forrester developed a problem and left for Tacloban. Once the boats were in open water, Lockhard turned toward Tacloban, over Kikilo, gunner Mazur, spotted two aircraft crossing from left to right at about 11 o'clock, about 100 feet off the water. At first the crew thought that these aircraft were P-51 Mustangs but soon as they drew closer it became apparent that they were Japanese. Lockhard radioed the sighting to Tacloban Controller and requested that day fighters be dispatched to intercept the incoming fighters. He was asked to repeat the message and then was asked to repeat it again when his transmission had been cut off by another aircraft. The frustrated Lockhard began a 270 degree turn and pursued the enemy fighters. When Mazur activated the turret one of the actuator motors burned out and the turret locked in the vertical position. Nonetheless, Lockhard continued closing on the two Tonys that were flying almost in trail. He fired a short burst at the trailing fighter and hit the port wing root and fuselage and the enemy rolled over to port and dove straight into the Valley just west of Kikilo. The leading fighter continued flying on a straight flight and Lockhard closed and fired a long burst, getting numerous hits over the wings and fuselage and the stricken enemy crashed into the same valley as his Wingman. Lockhard circled and strafed both of the burning wrecks.

Lockhard would have another victory a few days later that would be unconfirmed. 1Lt. Dorrie Jones and Lockhard were on a patrol over Ormac Bay with two other 421st NFS pilots. At the end of the patrol, about 40 to 50 miles from base, Jones ordered the flight to head for home. Lockhard radioed that he was pursuing another Japanese fighter (later identified as a Zero) and was heard to say: "I've got this bastard!" Lockhard was just above and behind the Japanese fighter, that was desperately trying to dive away, when he fired. Lockhard stayed on the Zero's tail and watched as the Japanese pilot crashed into a hillside as he tried to evade the P-61. The 5th Fighter Command, however, refused to credit him for the downed fighter as there were no witnesses.

**11 November 1944: 49FG/7FS (Bong's Final 7FS Mission)**

Lt.Col. George Walker, 49er CO, joined Bong and Morrissey on the next 7FS mission being led by Capt. John Haher who soon found his lead position usurped by Group Ops Exec, Maj. Gerald Johnson. 1Lt. William Minto was assigned as the fifth man and the Flight took off at noon to escort a C-47 transport flying east for an airdrop at Homonhon Island. The 100 mile round trip covering the C-47s only took 30 minutes and was without incident as the Dakotas dropped their supplies to Allied troops on the Island.

Once the Lightnings returned to Tacloban, Johnson led the "Pinky Special" on a sweep of Ormoc Bay. At 1230, the five pilots arrived over the hulks of the latest enemy supply convoy from Manila that had been battered by Kinkaid's carrier aircraft only a short time earlier. Ground Control alerted the Flight of bogies flying along the coast of Ormac Bay and Johnson led the Flight up to 13,000 feet and saw a few lingering Navy bombers leaving the area. As they passed over the Zeros, the enemy pilots turned into them to get on their tails. Johnson made a 20 degree left rear deflection pass and closed dead astern and the enemy fighter exploded. Johnson flew through the sheet of flame. Johnson climbed after another Zero that was about to attack six USN TBF Avenger torpedo bombers. Johnson fired and but had to break away as it began to smoke and lost sight of it. Johnson came upon another Zeke along the Ormoc coast and fired and its cockpit filled with flames and it rolled off to the right and "burned al the way down" for his second victory of the day (#s 17 and 18).

After the two aces downed their victims Morrissey hit a Zero that was a damaged claim. Once back at Tacloban U.S. Navy sent Bong and Johnson an invitation to dinner on the destroyer, *USS San Pedro Bay*; their first real meal in over two months.

9FS

At 1330, 1Lt. Frederick Dick's flight of Wingman 2Lt. Harold Harris, Element Leader 1Lt. Fernley Damstrom and Wingman 2Lt. Kenneth Markham took off on patrol and were immediately vectored back toward Ormoc. They arrived over the target at 10,500 feet, where Dick saw two Tojos and climbed to the attack but the swift enemy fighters escaped to the west. Dick regained altitude and searched further west in order to cut off the enemy's escape route to Cebu. Over Ponson Island, Dick saw three more Tojos at 7,000 feet over the island's coast. Dick dove on the unsuspecting Tojo leader but was diving too fast and overshot. He then dove from astern on another Tony and his cannon shells tore off its right wing and it spun into the water for Dick's third victory. Harris had followed Dick during his attack on the three Tojos and attacked the right Wingman and started firing from dead astern and closed rapidly getting more hits and it exploded after Harris passed by and crashed into the water. Dick and Harris broke off and zoom-climbed to regain altitude for another pass and saw two Tonys which split ranks and Dick and Harris followed the one going to the deck and Dick got into position for a tail shot. When he squeezed the trigger nothing happened as he was out of ammunition. Soon the second element arrived and Damstrom and Markham made passes on the beleaguered Tojo. After "two or three" passes Harris got dead astern and fired at 20 yards and finally sent the Tojo down for his second victory of the day and his second and third of four. Meanwhile, Damstrom saw a phosphorous bomb dropped by a Tony explode in mid-air as his Wingman Markham slid under him after a

**1Lt. Frederick Dick** and his crew after his third victory. (AAF)

Gunsight camera film still of **Bong's** Zero victory. (AAF)

Bong's ICR:

7TH FIGHTER SQUADRON, 49TH FIGHTER GROUP ARMY AIR FORCES APO 72

12 November 1944

INDIVIDUAL COMBAT REPORT OF MAJOR RICHARD I. BONG.

A) Mission No. 439 7th Fitron 5 P-38's 11 Nov. 1944.

B) Escort C-47 to Hemenhon Island.

C) Time of attack: 1235. Altitude: 10,000 feet.

D) I was element leader of Pinky Special and took off from Tacloban at 1045 to escort a C-47 on a dropping mission to Hemenhon Island. After completing our mission, we proceeded to Ormoc Bay to see what the Navy had done. The controller called us and said that there were some bogies south of Ormoc, so we climbed to 13,000 feet and sighted several Navy planes on the way. At 1230, we sighted 7 Zekes at 13,000 feet about to make an attack on 6 Navy TBFs. We dropped our tanks and turned to attack. In the ensuing engagement, I shot at 3 Zekes and got 2 of them smoking without being able to observe them crash. I saw Major Johnson, the flight leader, shoot down his first one in flames and saw where four planes had crashed in the water. We landed at base at 1300.

In later discussions, it was found out that both of the enemy I had started smoking had crashed. I claim 2 Zekes definite as witnessed by Major Gerald R. Johnson.

Major R.I.Bong

Air Corps.

Majors **Bong** (left) and **Johnson** flew in a "Special Flight", and each scored two victories (Bong #35-36 and Johnson #17-18). (AFAA)

Tojo heading west. The Tojo started weaving and Markham pulled up past it and the enemy pilot banked right and dove slightly toward Damstrom. Damstrom fired a 45 degree deflection shot that started the Tojo smoking and as he followed it he saw it catch on fire and crash into the water for his second victory.

Dick regrouped his flights and all landed safely and the air battle of 11 November closed for the 49ers. The only loss occurred when Demon 2Lt. Hubert Manes, was returning to base from a late day patrol in a badly damaged Lightning and had to bail out west of the airfield where he was quickly recovered.

**11 November 1944: 475FG/432FS**

Early Mission

At 0845 1Lt. John Hannan led eight P-38s off San Pablo #2 on a scramble and were vectored 25 miles NW of Damulan at 15,000 feet. The 432nd was joined by The "Pinky Special" Flight that included 475th CO, Col. Robert Morrissey, super aces, Richard Bong and Gerald Johnson of the 5FC/HQ, and Lt.Col. George Walker, 49er CO. At this point Hannan, like 7FS Flight Leader, Capt. John Haher, relinquished his mission lead and took over White Flight.

The original vector and others were unproductive but while tracking two bogeys between Palompon Town and Cebu Hannan spotted a bogey at 10 o'clock low and initiated a pass after informing the Morrissey. Hannan closed on the stern of an Oscar which Split-S'd. Hannan rolled with it but had too much speed to follow through. Just as Hannan rolled to an upright position the Oscar pilot turned to Hannan's right. Hannan banked right and chopped his throttles and as the enemy pilot pulled up Hannan had a 20 degree tail shot. He closed to 300 yards and fired. The Oscar rolled and dove and its pilot bailed out before his fighter exploded for Hannan's second and last victory.

Noon Mission

At midday Col. Charles MacDonald led six P-38s on a scramble over Ormoc Bay. Two P-38s aborted due to mechanical problems while the other four continued the mission. At 1245 at 12,000 feet, three aircraft were seen at 500 feet above at 11 o'clock. The Americans climbed, but so did the Japanese fighters, now identified as Jacks. MacDonald turned into them and the lead Jack fired on MacDonald's #4, 2Lt. Noles, who snap rolled while the Jack Split-S'd away. The other two Jacks were closing in on #2, 2Lt. Leo Blakely, and McDonald and Element Leader 1Lt. George Beatty closed on them. MacDonald got on the tail of the last Jack and fired a long burst that tore off parts of the wing and canopy. The Jack went straight in and crashed. Beatty closed from dead astern on the remaining Jack and fired from 100 yards and hit its wings and fuselage. The Jack pilot turned to port and Beatty followed and fired again and the Jack nosed over, caught fire, and plunged into the Bay. The Flight was down to 7,500 feet when MacDonald saw another Jack and closed from dead astern to 50 feet and blasted its wings and fuselage for his 16th victory. When the Jack went down MacDonald's windshield was spattered with oil. Meanwhile, another Jack was making a pass on #2 Blakely, who rolled violently and the Jack overshot and Split-S'd away. Two more Jacks arrived overhead and one made a pass at MacDonald from high astern but turned off without firing. Beatty closed on this Jack's tail and fired and saw some hits as its pilot turned sharply left. Beatty let this Jack escape as there was another directly ahead and slightly higher. Beatty closed and opened fire and saw hits as the Jack pilot banked to port but Beatty held his lead and saw cannon hits in its cockpit and bullet hits on its wings and port wing root. The enemy pilot did a slow Split-S and Beatty followed until the Jack rolled out of control into the Bay for his second victory of the day and of three total. Beatty then led MacDonald back to base for a safe landing.

**1Lt. George Beatty** assessed the new enemy Jack fighter. (AFHRC)

In Beatty's ICR he discusses the new Jacks:

> I would class them with the Tony. They weren't very fast and we could turn with them, using dive flaps. Their maneuvers were mainly Split-S's and sharp banks to the left, most of their maneuvers were to the left. They seem to have self-sealing fuel tanks as they don't blow up as Nip airplanes usually do when they are hit. I hit one with a short burst that would ordinarily set fire to an older model Nip fighter. They were easy to outmaneuver as far as getting the advantage for firing.

**12 November 1944: Kenney Attacked**

At 0500 Kenney was suddenly awakened by an explosion outside his bedroom which tore off the shutters and gravel shattered the window. Fortunately, the bomb was delayed fused so it penetrated about 10 feet into the ground before exploding causing minor damage.

**Col. Charles MacDonald** was credited with two victories, numbers 15 and 16. (AFAA)

**Capt. Frederick Champlin** shot down two enemy aircraft to make him an ace with six victories. (AFAA)

**Maj. Thomas McGuire** (receiving an award from Gen. Wurtsmith) led a Special Flight and got his 26[th] victory to tie Rickenbacker's standard, and moved to six victories behind Bong. (AAF)

**431FS** Victors (L-R): Capt. William O'Brien (did not score), Capt. Robert Cline (one victory), and Capt. Frederick Champlin (two victories). (AAF)

**Capt. Robert Cline** shot down his last of two enemy aircraft. (AAF)

**12 November 1944: 475FG/431FS/432FS**

431FS

Morning Mission

Capt. Fredric Champlin led four Red Flight P-38s from Buri Strip at 0630 to patrol over a convoy in Leyte Gulf. During their two hour patrol they were given continuous plots to the south and east. After the last plot they returned to the convoy at 9,000 feet and saw three bandits approaching at their altitude. As they turned into the bandits they were identified as a Lily escorted by two Oscars. Champlin then turned into the Oscars, which had gotten astern of his flight but had left the Lily alone. Champlin turned on the Lily and closed and fired a short 45 degree burst that sent the enemy bomber into the sea for his fifth victory. Champlin then saw the Oscars closing on his #4 man and Champlin made a 180 to make a head on pass on them. When Champlin was almost in range, the two Oscars Split-S'd away. Champlin dove on the first and his second burst hit it in its belly and it burst into flames into the sea. Its pilot bailed out but his chute did not open before he hit the water. The remaining Oscar flew wide and to starboard and Red #4, 2Lt. James Moreing; rolled over as it Split-S'd and chased it down. Moreing fired as the Oscar pulled up and hit its canopy for his first of three victories.

Mid-Afternoon

At 1445 Capt. Robert Herman led four Blue Flight P-38s from Buri to cover "Powder Base." After 2 ½ hours of patrolling Herman was given permission to return to Buri when a plot was called in. Herman led his flight to 14,000 feet where they saw a Hamp below. Herman's Second Element Leader, 1Lt. John Tilley, overran the Hamp before it disappeared into a cloud after which the flight returned to Buri.

Late Afternoon

At 1630 Maj. Thomas McGuire led four P-38s of Special Red Flight on a patrol of the Dulag area and at 1700 an enemy "recco" was spotted heading west and they chased after it but it headed into a cloud and disappeared. As Red Flight headed back toward Dulag at 12,500 feet they sighted four Jack fighters escorting a Lily bomber at 10,000 feet at 10 o'clock, 2,000 feet below. The Jacks immediately split into elements, one to the left and one to the right. McGuire and his Wingman, Col. William Hudnall, started down after the enemy fighters, splitting to the left while Capt. Robert Cline and Maj. Jack Rittmayer flew after the right hand pair. The Jacks climbed to meet McGuire and his Wingman in a head on pass. McGuire's fired a short burst with no observable results as they passed and then used his dive flaps to turn inside one of the Jacks which he set on fire with two or three bursts in deflection. The Jack began to burn slowly and crashed into the hills in the northern part of the Cebu Peninsula. McGuire then drove a Jack off Hudnall's tail with a deflection shot but saw no damage. A Jack then made a high side pass and McGuire turned into it but was unable to get it into his sights. The Jack broke off and got on Rittmayer's tail but Hudnall, half rolled with the Jack firing throughout his pass and scored hits on it from front to rear; causing it to dive and crash into the ground for his only victory of the war. Cline saw a Jack to port and below him and dove after it. The enemy pilot turned into Cline who rolled and fired a deflection shot when the Jack came into range. The Jack turned under Cline who lost sight of it but McGuire saw it belly into the ground in a cloud of dust. McGuire caught up with the last Jack as it attempted to escape and attacked from dead astern tearing the Jack's tail assembly completely off, whereupon it crashed and exploded for his 28th victory; to put him six behind Bong.

Early Evening

1Lts. Kenneth Hart and Louis DeMontier were scrambled at 1750 and climbed immediately to 16,000 feet over Dulag Harbor. They saw AA burst from Allied ships in the Harbor firing at an enemy aircraft and saw it silhouetted against the clouds. The ICR's of both pilots describe solid hits on the Oscar but it was credited as a probable for Hart.

432FS

First Mission: Noon

Capt. Elliott Summer took off at 1230 with three P-38s to patrol the Dulag area. When they didn't find any enemy fighters over Dulag, Summer led them inland and found two bogies at 1330 flying in tight formation at 8,000 feet. Summer dove quickly from 10,000 feet and when he closed to 50 yards behind them, he recognized them as Zeros and snapped a shot at the leader and the Zero exploded immediately. Summer was so close that he flew through the debris and fire. When his P-38 emerged from the explosion its entire right wing was singed black and his bulletproof windshield was shattered from a piece of the debris. The second Zero Split-S'd into the clouds below and Second Element Leader, 2Lt. Harrold Owen, followed and closed to 50 yards and opened fire getting hit in its cockpit. The enemy pilot did a steep wingover and Owen was closing so fast that he was unable to fire more shots at it. The smoking Zero turned down as Owen pulled up and escaped for a damaged claim. White Flight swung around and found two more planes over Tacloban Bay. Summer again did not recognize the planes until he was very close and one was on its dive bombing run. Summer had to switch his attack to its Wingman and fired a short burst from 100 yards. The Zero smoked badly and burst into flames before it disappeared into the clouds below for his second victory of the day and his ninth victory.

Late Afternoon Mission

Capt. Henry Condon led four P-38s from San Pablo #2 at 1500 but aborted and 2Lt. Calvin Anderson assumed command of the flight. The Air Controller vectored bogeys coming in from the southwest and soon Anderson saw three Oscars at 10 o'clock about 2,000 feet above their altitude of 8,000 feet. Anderson made a pass at the last Oscar as it dove on the shipping off Dulag. Anderson fired a three second burst at 100 yards and pieces of its canopy and nacelle flew off and the Oscar went into a vertical dive and crashed off Dulag. Soon #4 man, 2Lt. Lawrence Roberts, was low on fuel and returned to base leaving Anderson and his Wingman, 2Lt. Robert Schuh to patrol. A few minutes later a Hamp was seen at 11 o'clock high, flying south. Anderson climbed to 12,000 feet but was seen by the Hamp which dove to make a pass at him. Anderson pulled a lead on the Hamp and got a few hits on its canopy and fuselage. The Hamp continued its Split-S under Anderson who followed through and when the Hamp pilot pulled out Anderson was still behind him and fired at 100 yards. The Japanese fighter caught on fire and broke to starboard and exploded for Anderson's only two victories of the war.

Last Mission

After flying in the first 432nd mission of the day and damaging a Zero, 2Lt. Harrold Owen led a three plane flight in a local scramble. As the flight was flying at 12,000 feet 12 enemy fighters were seen flying west through AA fire at 12,000 feet. The Japanese were in two plane elements in no particular formation. Owen attacked one of the two plane elements and one Zero turned away and one turned into Owen who fired a short 15 degree burst that hit its engine. Owens' Wingman, 2Lt. Albert McKenzie, confirmed the Owens' first of four victories. Owen's guns jammed and McKenzie and #3, Larson made a few passes at the other Zeros before darkness ended the combat.

**12 November 1944: 348FG/460FS First Victory**

The 460FS sent 16 P-47s on a glide bombing mission to Linao where they bombed and strafed several buildings in the area, one of which exploded, and then strafed a seaplane which was destroyed. They saw 17 barges and a minelayer near a beach on Ormoc Bay and attacked and destroyed three of the barges and several others were damaged. The 460FS pilots also saw their first flying enemy aircraft when they observed two unidentified planes at 10,000 feet over the north coast of Leyte.

**2Lt. Calvin Anderson** was credited with his only two career victories. (AAF)

**Capt. Richard Frost** registered the first victory for the 460FS, his second of three with the 348FG. (AAF)

Later that day the 460th bombed targets at Ormoc and flew an uneventful fighter sweep to Negros Island. Capt. Richard Frost, originally from the 340FS, was leading a flight of P-47s patrolling the Tacloban area at 9,000 feet when a single Hamp was sighted about a 1,000 feet below flying across the area. Frost turned to dive on the enemy fighter which reacted with back and forth moderate turns, maintaining its course while watching the attacking Americans. On his first pass, the impatient Frost overshot the Hamp which belatedly attempted a ragged Split-S maneuver. Frost maneuvered behind the Hamp and fired a 30 degree deflection shot which hit the Japanese fighter in the wings and fuselage. The Hamp's left wing caught fire and it hit into the water off San Jose for the 460th's first aerial victory and Frost's second of three (he scored his first victory with the 340FS on 27 December 1943).

**November 1944: Mindoro and Luzon Operations Postponed**

On the ground at Leyte, the Japanese were driven across the island into a beachhead area extending from Ormoc in the north to Baybay to the south. The Japanese had urgently tried to reinforce Leyte but most of the attempts were thwarted. Allied air and naval power destroyed Japanese shipping in Luzon's harbors and their convoys were caught either en route or in coves and inlets where they were hiding during the day. The relentless bombing and strafing took a heavy toll on enemy equipment and troops on land but nonetheless, the persistent resistance of the Japanese on the west side of Leyte caused the postponement of the landing at Mindoro to 15 December and the larger landing at Lingayen Gulf on the main island of Luzon was postponed to 9 January 1945. Kenney did not have enough airfields on Leyte to utilize his Far East Air Forces and even after Mindoro was captured its airfields would have to be restored to operate the bombers, strafers, and fighters necessary to support him over Luzon until enough aircraft could be moved there. The GHQ Staff was to assign aircraft from Kincaid's small carrier force but these carriers did not have the endurance or provisions for more than a few days of air support. In addition, if Kamikaze attacks sunk or badly damaged these carriers or they were forced to withdraw altogether; then the invasion forces faced possible disaster. MacArthur agreed and gave Kenney enough shipping to move the equipment for two heavy bombardment groups, a strafing group, and several fighter groups into Mindoro, with sufficient engineers to build airdromes quickly soon after the invasion. Fortunately, this was to be Luzon's dry season for the next four or five months, so that airfields could be rapidly constructed.

**13 November 1944: 418NFS**

1Lt. Harold Whittern and 2Lt. Bunyan Crain took off from Morotai at 0345 and reached their orbit area when they were vectored to a bandit. Their AI Radar was out and Crain had to replace the fuses to have it function. At 0400 they made an AI contact at eight miles on a 240 degree heading. Whittern closed to 400 feet above and dead ahead but was unable to get a visual and turned 360 and was again vectored toward the enemy flying at 230 degrees and at seven miles. Whittern close quickly and got a visual at 200 feet. Whittern climbed slightly and fired a short burst and the twin engine bomber burst into flames and exploded on Whittern's second burst and he had to turn quickly to avoid a collision to live through his only victory.

**13-21 November 1944: 475FG/432FS**

During this time heavy rainfall jeopardized each take off and landing on the airstrips on Leyte. The steel matting became covered and slick with mud and caused numerous accidents. The 432nd Squadron was grounded by the mud on Bayug Airstrip from 13-21 November. The bivouac areas were called "swamps" and were almost unlivable, only the loathed "Ten in One" rations were available, and any bathing was done from helmets filled with rainwater. Strict blackouts were in effect as every night enemy aircraft flew over and the men lost sleep leaving their tent to take shelter in rain-filled trenches.

**14 November 1944: 49FG/8FS**

While on base patrol three 8FS P-38s were between Tacloban and Dulag when they were bounced from the north by two Zeros. On the first firing pass 2Lt. Irwin Dames' port engine was hit and he immediately feathered the burning engine and left for the safety of friendly Tacloban AA defenses. Flight Leader 1Lt. George Smerchek and Wingman 2Lt. Walter Hickok turned to fight but the obviously veteran Zero pilots easily bested Hickok and damaged his hydraulics. Smerchek and Hickok also escaped to Tacloban's flak corridor and the three American pilots landed safely. Minutes later, one the earlier Zeros attacked the two ship Black Sheep Flight of 2Lt. George Reed and Wingman 2Lt. Robert Goodwin. Goodwin spotted a Zero at 12 o'clock high that barrel-rolled down on the two Americans who peeled away as the Zero came out of his dive. Reed fired and hit the Zero which turned away to the right but flew directly into Goodwin's gunfire and went down in flames into the jungle for Goodwin's first of two victories.

**14 November 1944: 8FG/35FS/36FS**

35FS

The 35th Fighter Squadron, led by Capt. Richard West, was heading an escort of 26 B-24s to Alicante at midday when calls from the 36FS reported that they were engaged by several Japanese fighters north of the tip of Negros Island. When the 35th arrived no enemy fighters were found and West led his flight back to Alicante. West's Flight was low on fuel by this time and turned back to base but found a single Oscar about 1,000 feet above and a mile away. West ordered tanks dropped and climbed parallel to the enemy. The Oscar pilot turned right but saw that West was cutting him off and reversed his turn and climbed. The veteran enemy pilot turned toward West for a head on pass. But, as the Oscar rolled out the turn he came in range and West fired a short burst of cannon shells that hit the cockpit and fuselage. The Oscar spun out of control, trailing smoke for 14,000 feet down and crashed about eight miles east of Alicante for West's 13th victory.

After West attacked the Oscar the Squadron broke formation, and 2Lt. John Grillet was joined by 2Lt. James McLain. The two were flying through cloud masses slightly above and behind the rest of the squadron when two Hamps attacked McLain. The Hamps passed under them and began to turn and the Lightnings turned with them. The Hamps completed their turns before McLain and Grillet began to fire on them, but McLain pulled his fighter through to meet the attack. The Hamps passed under them again and made a steep starboard turn which put the Hamps in front of Grillet who fired from slightly out of range. Grillet followed, trying to close, but at intervals the enemy pilot would dip his wing violently as if to make a sharp break but remained on course. Grillet finally was able to close and get hits on the fuselage and it dove, smoking heavily, into the clouds for his only victory.

1Lt. Kenneth Pool, leading White Flight, had followed West's Red Flight after the Oscar but after West shot it down Pool saw single engine bogeys at 9 o'clock and gave chase. Upon catching them he found that they were P-47s and returned to base. Pool's ICR suggested: "When operating in an area such as we were, P-47s cause much disturbance which could be easily avoided by using only P-47s."

36FS

Fifteen P-38s under Maj. Jay Robbins took off from Wama Strip at 0845 as a roving top cover for two groups of B-24s attacking Alicante Airdrome, Negros. During the approach five Lightnings aborted reducing the mission to 11 fighters. Upon reaching the target at 1215 at 15,000 feet the four flights formed in string led by Capt. James Moss' Red Flight. Moss' Flight was over Alicante at 17,000 feet when they spotted seven Zeros at 9-10,000 feet below and dove on them but were seen and the Zeros separated. Moss and Wingman, 2Lt. Francis Collins, dove after one that was in a diving turn to port. Moss fired a short burst that went behind the Zero. The Zero pilot saw

Moss' tracers and went into a series of S turns. Moss closed to 300 yards and fired a two second burst from 10 degrees deflection getting hits on the fuselage and wing root. The Zero trailed smoke, rolled over, and crashed for his first of four victories. 2Lt. Wayne Donker, Red Flight Second Element Leader, closed astern of a Zero from 30 to 10 degrees opening fire at 200 yards; knocking off pieces and starting a fire in its in engine and cockpit. Donker then chased another Zero but could not close as he was to drop one of his tanks. He fired from 500 yards as the Zero was heading for a cloud. Donker fired his last shots from 350 yards getting some hits as it entered the cloud. Donker's Wingman, 2Lt. John Dale, confirmed Donker's first of two victories.

1Lt. John Dunaway's Flight followed Moss' flight down on three Zeros which broke away and headed for the deck. Dunaway chose the left Zero and caught it at 7,000 feet where the enemy pilot slow rolled. Dunaway fired a two second burst from 150 yards just as the Zero was on its back, tearing off large pieces and starting an engine fire. The Zero crashed five miles from Alicante. Dunaway saw a Zero 1,000 feet above and chased it toward the deck and caught it at 2,000 feet where the Zero pilot went into violent skids. Dunaway fired five bursts tearing off large pieces; one of which hit his fighter. The Zero disappeared into a cloud and Dunaway's ICR claims that his Wingman, 2Lt. Walter Payne observed the Zero to crash. However, Payne's IRC merely states that: "He (Dunaway) got hits on the second and the Nip pulled up into the clouds." The IRC of Dunaway's #4 man, 2Lt. Joseph Paul, stated: "...(Dunaway) shot one down in flames but registered only hits on the other which rolled into a cloud." Dunaway was not given credit for this second victory and ended the war with seven victories. After watching Dunaway shoot down his Zero, 2Lt. Henry Patterson, Dunaway's White Flight Wingman, pulled out below the overcast and started to climb when he spotted a lone Zero about 600 yards in front of him. Patterson followed the Zero and closed, firing from 90 to 30 degrees and got hits in the cockpit. The Zero made a 360 degree diving turn heading inland and crashed

Maj. Jay Robbins of the 8FG/HQ flew with the 36th that day leading Blue Flight. By November 1944 Robbins had been in combat for two years, rising from Second Lieutenant to Major and Deputy Group Commander and was by far the highest-scoring pilot in the 8FG with 21 victories and was scheduled to leave in the next few weeks after 29 months in combat. At 1215 the Squadron was at about 16,000 feet when a Zero followed by three Oscars was sighted below at 8,000 feet, apparently descending for a landing. Robbins quickly dropped tanks and led his flight in a dive and the enemy fighters separated into two elements of two; sending two to the left and two to the right. Robbins followed the two that broke to the right and chopped his throttle completely but as he came almost into firing range the enemy element Wingman turned to the right but the veteran Robbins suspected that this was a planned maneuver that would allow the enemy Leader to make a tight turn and get on his tail. To make the enemy pilots think their ruse had worked Robbins started to turn with the enemy Wingman but calling his own Wingman, 1Lt. Raymond Loh, to attack the enemy Wingman. Robbins then went into a shallow dive under and outside the enemy Leader's gradual right turn. Opening up his throttles Robbins closed to 150 yards and fired with his first burst knocking pieces off its rudder and port wing. Robbin's second burst blew off its canopy which barely missed his Lightning. The Zero pilot attempted to bail out but his chute hit the Zero's tail and failed to open and both the pilot and fighter fell into the sea for Robbin's 22nd and last victory of the war to make him the second-ranking AAF fighter ace on active duty in the Pacific.

**Maj. Jay Robbins** scored his 22nd and last victory. (AFAA)

**1Lt. John Dunaway** scored his seventh and last victory. (AFAA)

Maj. Robbins describes his last of 22 victories in an interview:

The assignment for Agate (36FS) was roving top cover for two groups of B-24s, which were to strike Alicante Airdrome, Negros Island. After approximately an hour, five Agate planes had 'snaffued,' reducing the squadron to 11 P-38s and Blue Flight to 3 planes.

Headed north at 16,000 feet over Alicante we sighted one Zeke and three Oscars at 8,000 feet at 10 o'clock position. They probably had just finished a patrol or had been warned that we were in the vicinity and were attempting to land before we sighted them. As we started our dive we were sighted, and the enemy separated into two elements of two planes each. This prearranged teamwork took one element to the right and one to the left. I followed the two that broke to the right. With my throttle completely chopped, I came almost within firing range when the Wingman in the element made a moderately sharp turn to the right. I believe this was a planned maneuver, the leader expecting me to follow the Wingman, thus putting him in position for a tight turn onto my tail. So that he might think his ruse had worked, I deceptively started to turn after the Wingman, calling at the same time to my Wingman and telling him to take the enemy Wingman. Then I made a shallow dive and went underneath and to the outside of the enemy leader's gradual right turn. Giving my plane the throttle, I drove up to within 150 feet before opening fire. My maneuver made the enemy flight leader lose me, and he continued his turn without further evasive action. My first burst knocked pieces out of his rudder and left wing, and my second burst hit the canopy, which blew off, barely missing my plane. Black smoke and flames came from the left side of the plane. The pilot attempted to bail out. His chute hit the tail of his plane and either ripped or failed to open, as both the pilot and plane fell to the ground several miles northeast of Alicante Airdrome.

It is my opinion that the Japanese fighter pilot has a very well-defined blind spot when you come in low and behind him. In the destruction of my last nine enemy planes, I used this approach on six of them, and in each case I was able to approach to an extremely close range without detection and without encountering the evasive half roll that detection usually brings.

**15 November 1944: 348FG Moves to the Philippines**

After the 460FS moved to the Philippines the rest of the 348th began preparations for the move to Leyte at the end of the first week of November. Thirty enlisted men and thirty officers of the 341FS remained behind with the aircraft while the rest of the personnel boarded LST 569 bound for Dulag, Leyte. They landed on 15 November and unloaded vehicles and equipment in torrents of rain and deep, sticky mud and then with great effort they began to set up camp near Burauen. The LST transporting the 342FS broke down on the first day a returned to Biak and boarded another LST. Within a few days they caught up to the convoy and landed on schedule in the soaking rain.

Most of the 348FG personnel moved to Tacloban strip #2 by the end of the November and waited for their fighters due around the first of December. One of the last formation s to take off for Tacloban from Morotai; was a 28 plane formation of the 342FS led by Maj. William Banks while Captains Robert Knapp, David Eastham, Charles Whistler and George Davis each led the flights. The last leg of the formation took off at 0945 but near the northern part of Mindanao the weather deteriorated and the formation was forced to divert to the northwest. The P-47s crossed Mindanao and tried to find a route through Bohol Island and the Camotes Sea to the west coast of Leyte. They had no success and with fuel running low and no good route to Leyte, Knapp asked Major Banks for permission to return to Morotai and permission was granted and Whistler, Eastham, and Davis followed Knapp with of their flights.

In the flights that decided to head for Leyte, 2Lt. Charles Hartman led one of the first flights to run short of fuel. His flight crossed the south end of Bohol and flew on the deck up the coast of Cebu, then out below Camotes Island to the west coast of Leyte. They crossed Leyte south of Baybay and continued to follow the east coast. Somewhere southeast of Bugho Point the P-47s began to run out of fuel and Lt. Rumpf went down and who picked up by a native boat after his P-47 almost sank immediately. A few minutes later Hartman's Thunderbolt's fuel was almost gone and he began searching for a landing area. His engine cut out once and he switched to auxiliary gas which lasted long enough for a single gentle turn before the engine stopped again. Hartman opened his canopy, leveled the fighter, dropped flaps, cut switches and waited for the crashlanding. Hartman touched the tail down first as was taught for a water crashlanding. The tail bounced twice and the nose then came down into the water, completely stopping the P-47. Hartman quickly unbuckled his parachute, inflated the Mae West around his neck and dove over the side and was rescued within a few minutes by a launch. In the group that headed back for Morotai, Lieutenants Samuel Kilgore, Douglas Matthews, and Albert Newman ran low on gas and were never seen again. On 2 December the 342FS lost three pilots in a single non-combat flight; more than they had on any one combat mission.

**Capt. Richard West** scored a victory the day before, and then closed his career by shooting down an Oscar to give him 14 total victories. (AFAA)

**Capt. James Moss** claimed his second of four victories. (AAF)

**15 November 1944: 8FG/35FS/36FS**

35FS

Nine P-38s led by Capt. William Gardner covered B-24s to La Carlota Airdrome on Negros Island. Capt. Richard West led a flight in the formation but by the time he reached the rendezvous point his second element returned to base with engine trouble and the P-38s and bombers had continued on to the target. Nonetheless, West and his Wingman, 2Lt. Arthur Schell, continued on to Negros to find the bombers but were unsuccessful and rejoined the rest of the 35FS formation just before noon. About 20 minutes later six Oscars appeared at 11 o'clock and West and Schell immediately engaged them but two of the Oscars got on Schell's tail. West dropped his flaps to turn sharply into a head on pass at them. One of the Oscars went into a quick dive while the other pulled up into a climb. West followed the one in the climb until it turned and climbed almost vertically almost into a stall. West fired a 90 degree deflection shot that the devastated the Oscar that disintegrated as it fell into the clouds for his 14th and last victory of the war. West and Schell continued on to strafe a Japanese "Sugar Charlie" lugger anchored on the coast near Alicante. West's guns jammed during a strafing and the two pilots, exhausted after five hours of flying, headed for Morotai. As they neared the southern tip of Cebu, Schell found that he did not have enough fuel to reach Morotai and the two diverted for Tacloban on Leyte. Now running dangerously low on fuel, the two pilots reached Leyte and found it to be heavily socked in at the coast by a large weather front. West and Schell then decided to head for Guerilla-held Tagola Point on Mindanao about 40 minutes away. When they reached the Point they descended and saw a rice paddy near the town of Dapitan where they could make a belly landing. Schell safely crash landed his Lightning on a dry section of the field and West then slid his fighter down, landing not far from Schell. The two were quickly surrounded by hundreds of Filipino civilians who led the Americans to Dapitan. Later, two Guerilla officers arrived and took the Americans to a radio station where other Americans were held.

The next morning they traveled by foot and horseback to Dipolog were they were joined by two survivors of a downed B-24. Meanwhile, the radio station had contacted Headquarters and arrangements were made to send a PBY to pick up the downed airmen at Dipolog. West and Schell spent the next few days at leisure and were picked up on 28 November and flown back to Morotai.

36FS
Eight P-38s took off at 0850 and were to rendezvoused with the B-24s over Tagolo Point at 1120 and were over La Carlotta Airdrome from 1205 to 1245 on a roving escort. However, the rendezvoused was not made and the 36th flew on to the target area. Capt. William Giroux was leading White Flight and was unable to contact the bombers and proceeded to the northern end of Negros. While flying between Alicante and Fabrica at 14,000 feet the Squadron was about to descend when the 35FS called out bogeys approaching at about 4,000 to 6,000 feet high. Giroux made a 180 turn and climbed which put him into the lead. As Giroux climbed toward the seven Oscars the 35FS hit them and the Japanese fighters split up into pairs but only two Oscars peeled off to meet them. Giroux turned into one and Capt. Moss into the other. Giroux fired at one in a head on pass but the Oscar turned just as he fired. Giroux pulled up and half rolled and got on the tail of another "Nip." He fired from 200 yards and saw fire and smoke "roll out its side." Giroux pulled up and joined two P-38s that were flying above him. Meanwhile, Moss and his Oscar came together in a head on pass but while still out of range the Japanese pilot turned to starboard which gave Moss a short 10 degree deflection shot which hit its port wing root and then catch on fire and crash for his first of four victories. Giroux continued on and saw a Tojo 1,500 feet directly below and at first mistook it for a P-47 and closed to see its red roundels but by that time the Tojo pilot was able to duck into the clouds. Giroux returned to base as a double ace with 10 final victories for the war.

**15 November 1944: 49FG/9FS**

On the 15th the Japanese used a dense storm front to sneak in another reinforcement convoy into Ormoc Bay. The early afternoon 9FS mission to Ormoc was unable to penetrate the front on its return and Flight Leader, 1Lt Charles McElroy, became separated from his wingmen and ran out of gas and safely bellied in on the beach near Barugo on the north coast where he was soon rescued by the Filipinos and returned to base the next day. Meanwhile, Wingmen Datzenko, Hanisch, and Hovik flew beyond Cabalian Bay and when their fuel ran out they searched for a place to crash land. Hanisch, who had survived a crash landing earlier in the year, safely landed first in a rice paddy and waved for Datzenko and Hovik to come down. They also safely bellied in and the next day Filipino escorted them to the coast where they were rescued by a PBY and dropped off at Tacloban.

**16 November 1944: 421NFS**

On 16 November 1Lt. Owen Wolf led flight of four P-61s on a 0900 morning daylight patrol west of Dulag and south of Ormac Bay. Wolf's flight consisted of 1Lt. Dorrie Jones, 1Lt. Frank Mott, and 2Lt. Lloyd Partridge. The P-61s were patrolling at 12,000 feet when they were surprised to see a number of Zeros at 11,000. The Japanese fighters were all carrying bombs (droptanks?), which they jettisoned, and then they split into two flights. In the dogfight that followed, the P-61s were joined by several P-38s. During the battle the experienced and aggressive Japanese pilots used slow rolls, Split-S's, and quick dives. Jones fired a volley and a Zero burst into flames and dove straight into the ground. Soon Jones chased another Zero which went into a tight turn at about 350 mph which caused Jones' P-61 to lose its entire rear gondola. Jones was able to complete his turn and fire at three more Zekes, which all out turned the crippled P-61 and escaped. Jones' aircraft was buffeting violently when the controls locked and the aircraft dove to 1,500 feet with its elevator jammed in the nose up position. Jones had to wrap his arms around the control wheel and brace his knees up against the control panel to keep the large fighter from looping. The crew was preparing to ditch but Jones dropped the flaps and regain control and flew safely back to Tacloban. During the same combat 1Lt. Owen Wolf, 2Lt. Lloyd Partridge, and 1Lt. Frank Mott each scored hits on other Zeros which would be listed as damaged since none was not observed to crash.

**1Lt. Dorrie Jones** scored his only victory, but would become the 421NFS CO in June 1945. (AAF)

**16 November 1944: 348FG/460FS Arrives at Tacloban**

460FS CO, Maj. William Dunham, used his influence and the new Squadron was chosen as the 348th Fighter Group's first squadron to go the Philippines as its ground echelon at Nadzab was ready to be transferred north by ships available in their immediate area. On 23 October his ground echelon boarded LSTs and headed for Leyte while the Squadron's pilots left Noemfoor on 4 November, However, the pilots were detained on Morotai for six days by bad weather before arriving at Tacloban on 10 November (enroute 2Lt. Adrian McClendon was mistakenly shot down by friendly P-38s as he straggled far behind the main formation). On their trip from Morotai the Group had escorted B-25s to a Japanese convoy attempting to reinforce its garrison at Ormoc Bay. Maj. Dunham led his Thunderbolts on strafing attacks on enemy destroyers that diverted enemy AA fire from the low-flying Mitchells. The air echelon continued its attacks throughout the month during which it sunk 50,000 tons of enemy shipping: including nine large vessels, freighters, and transport. It destroyed one floatplane on the ground and 10 in the air. With the 110th Recon Squadron and the overwrought 49FG, the 460th was one of three units which represented the total U.S. airpower in the Philippines. By the end of the month it was flying over half of the missions that took off and landed at Tacloban; despite poor weather and receiving no new aircraft or spare parts during the period. During the month 2Lt. Perry Tubre of the squadron was KIA on the 30th.

Meanwhile, on 7 November the remainder of the Group left Noemfoor in three LSTs and arrived at Dulag on the 16th followed by 33 officers who arrived separately two days later. The pilots of the three squadrons waited on Noemfoor for the development of new strips on Leyte.

**16 November 1944: 49FG/9FS**

1Lt. Warren Curton's four Lightnings were on the last Flying Knight mission of the day and were just about to land after an hour and half patrol of the east coast when the air controller alerted them of contacts approaching Dulag from the west. Curton searched the skies and saw 10 aircraft descending out of the sun. Curton turned into the oncoming aircraft that held the advantage of diving out of the sun but Curton held his fire until he confirmed that were hostile. Five Oscars zoomed by and then pulled up to get on the P-38's tails. Curton went into a tight diving turn on the trailing Oscar and fired from 60-70 degrees deflection but the enemy pilot broke away in a desperate Split-S. Curton followed and closed to 200 yards and got some hits but "my guns were definitely firing inaccurate." The Oscar pilot made a steep turn towards the clouds but closed to 100-150 yards dead astern a fired a deadly five second burst and then followed him through two clouds, firing all the time. As the Oscar entered the third cloud it exploded in a ball of fire for Curton's third victory. Wingman 2Lt. Jack Lewis took a long range shot at an Oscar who had tried to get on Curton's tail and got no hits and chased it off. Lewis followed another Oscar as it was about to strafe Bayug Airfield and fired a long burst from 100 yards and it burst into flames and crashed. Lewis climbed and joined Fowler at 8,000 feet when they saw five Oscars heading toward Ormoc; one at 9,000 feet, two at 5,000 feet and two on the deck. Lewis dove on one of the lower Oscars and fired another long burst from about 200 yards and saw no hits but no apparent damage. Lewis had to pull up to avoid a collision but when he looked back he saw flames from the cockpit and wing root and Gupton would confirm Lewis' second and only two victories of the war.

The second flight of five Oscars attempted to follow the first five in cutting off the lead P-38s but overshot Curton's trailing Element Leader 1Lt. Cheatum Gupton and Wingman 2Lt. Warren Fowler. Both pilots Split-S'd and caught the enemy fighters just as they bottomed out of their dives and were spreading out to bomb the Tacloban Airfield. Gupton and Fowler pulled out of their dives at 450 mph and closed to 200 to 100 yards behind the Oscars. Gupton shot down his first target at only 1,000 feet above the jungle, and its landing gear dropped and it rolled over, crashing into the ground just west of the Bayug runway. In his turn Gupton observed another Oscar 500 yards to his right at 2 o'clock and turned after it. The enemy pilot made several evasive turns but then headed for some clouds. Gupton opened fire at 150 to 200 yards and the dove to the right and exploded into the ground for Gupton's second victory of the day to give him four total. After Gupton's first victory Fowler fired a short burst at an Oscar and observed an explosive cannon shells hitting the cockpit and wings. The Oscar peeled off to port and descended and did not catch fire until it hit the ground. Fowler then saw an Oscar at 5 o'clock low, turning into him and Fowler closed quickly to 150 yards and fired two bursts that started the Oscar smoking. When it turned up it burst into flame and crashed into a hillside near Ormoc Bay for his only two victories. The adrenalin-driven Curton found that his guns had jammed but nonetheless, he closed directly on the tail of an Oscar and harassed the enemy pilot all the way to Ormoc before AA fire caused him to break off his futile chase. Curton and his three wingmen returned safely to Tacloban with seven victories.

**16-23 November 1944: 8FG/35FS' Last Missions from Morotai**

On November the 35FS flew a fighter sweep to Tarakan where they found a large freighter which after many passes was left smoking. On November 23 four P-38s were to cover a C-47 on a flight to Leyte. This mission was the last for the squadron from Wama Airdrome on Morotai before the move to Dulag and was very likely the last mission from Morotai for the entire 8FG.

**17-18 November 1944: 49FG**

The weather cleared on the 17th and enemy dive bombers avoided 49ers patrols and bombed Tacloban again. Early the next morning, another Japanese attack set fire to the supply dump on the Cataisan beach causing the 49ers to temporarily move to Bayug while the fires were being extinguished.

**18 November 1944: 418NFS**

On 18 November at 0235 Maj. Carroll Smith of the 418NFS shot down a Betty and claimed another as a probable west of Morotai, NEI. At 0715 1Lt. Edward Glascock (8FS) downed a Zeke in the Dulag area and then chased and downed a Frank near Kanipa.

**18 November 1944: 421NFS**

Two P-61s, piloted by Second Lieutenants Thomas Malone and Chester Craft, were flying mission to protect returning PT boats from a night patrol west of La Paz near San Agustin. They were flying at 7,000 feet with a flight of four P-38s above them. A flight of four Oscars was spotted approaching from 9 o'clock but the P-61s quickly swung around to their 6 o'clock position. The Japanese fighters made a firing pass at the P-38s, hitting one that crashed. Three of the four Oscars continued their attack, heading for the P-61s at the lower altitude. Malone took evasive action and then turned to chase the Japanese aircraft. Craft was unable to follow Malone and the three Oscars got on his tail but dove below the P-61 surprisingly without firing but then the fourth went after Craft. 2Lt. Ralph Moore, Craft's R/O, had saw the incoming enemy aircraft and took over the .50 caliber turret and managed to hit the Oscar's engine. The crippled fighter went into a steep vertical dive, trailing smoke behind the cockpit. Although a P-38 pilot witnessed the Oscar going down he did not see it crash and the 5FC eventually listed it as "probable." Of the four Oscars that attacked the American planes, the one single fighter pressing the attack on Craft to around 300 yards failed to fire his guns. Malone pursued a few of the fighters but did not make contact and both pilots returned to base.

**18 November 1944: 475FG/431FS**

1Lt. Wilson Ekdahl led four P-38s from Tacloban at 0630 on a local patrol. While patrolling at 10,000 feet the Controller requested that Ekdahl break up his flight into two elements to patrol at 4,000 and 14,000 feet. Ekdahl and Wingman, "guest pilot" Maj. George Dewey were at 14,000 feet at 0725 when they spotted three Oscars flying north in a V-formation south of Tacloban. Ekdahl rolled on the Oscar that began a gentle dive toward the American strip and fired from 400 yards to 100 feet, causing it to smoke heavily and crash into the water off Tacloban for his first of two victories. Two Oscars got on Maj. Dewey's tail and the second element of 2Lt. James Moreing and Wingman, 2Lt. Jack Olson, chased it away. Dewey rejoined Ekdahl who sighted an Oscar who was maneuvering to make a stern attack. The Oscar saw the Lightnings and turned into clouds at 5,000 feet. Ekdahl followed and continued to fire until he ran out of ammunition. Dewey was in position to fire and opened up at 100 yards and saw pieces fly off and a fire envelop its starboard wing and then dive out of control for Dewey's only victory. Meanwhile, 2Lts. Moreing and Olson were flying at 4,000 feet and saw two Oscars 1,000 feet above and chandelled up astern of them. As Moreing closed on one Oscar, its pilot skidded violently but Moreing was able to hit its port wing root and it went into a steep dive, enveloped in flames for his second victory. As the second element circled another P-38 with two Oscar about to attack it tried to join them. Moreing used his dive brakes to turn around to make a head on pass that caused the two enemy pilots to break off their attack.

**1Lt. Wilson Ekdahl** scored his first of two victories. (AAF)

**18 November 1944: 348FG/460FS**

The 460FS continued bombing and strafing missions until 18 November when Maj. Dunham was leading an early morning patrol of four P-47s

**Capt. William Dunham** became a double ace. (AFAA)

over the Buri area when two unidentified enemy fighters were seen attacking a P-61 Black Widow night fighter (421NFS?). The P-47s chased the enemy fighters away but they disappeared into cloud. Five minutes later two Japanese Zeros bounced the four P-47s and Dunham turned his flight into the attack. The bold Japanese pilots lost their nerve and quickly turned west toward Cebu. Dunham closed to within 30 yards and fired until the Zero crashed into the water west of the Camotes Islands for his 10th victory which made him the only other pilot in the 348th besides Kearby to become a double ace. Dunham's Wingman fired at the other Zero but lost it when it dove vertically to 2,000 feet. 2Lt. William Thompson, leading the second element, was trying to follow Dunham when he saw a Tony flying below at about 2,500 feet. Thompson and his wingman dove to attack the Tony from astern and Thompson fired one long burst and the Tony began to trail white smoke before it rolled over and crashed into the sea about 100 yards off the coast of Cebu for his only victory of the war.

**18 November 1944: 49FG/8FS**

On the 0700 morning patrol 1Lt. Edward Glascock was patrolling with rookie 2Lt. Gerald Triplehorn who had arrived at the Squadron only three days earlier. The Tacloban Air Controller immediately vectored them south toward Dulag and after a quarter hour above the heavy overcast, Glascock spotted a single Zero just west of Bayug Airfield and made a single pass. The duo continued their patrol and 30 minutes later were vectored north of Tacloban to intercept a southbound enemy flight. Glascock and Triplehorn climbed to 15,000 feet and turned north where they soon met four new JAAF Nakajima Type IV fighters designated as the Ki-84 and code-named Frank which was a more heavily armed, higher powered version of the Ki-44. Glascock immediately engaged the new fighters and quickly found that these fighters were superior to previous enemy fighters, and was hard-pressed to finally gain the advantage over one for his second and third and last career victories. However, the rookie Triplehorn was completely overwhelmed and was killed as he turned back to Tacloban.

**18 November 1944: 49FG/9FS**

Four P-38s of the 9FS led by 1Lt. Leslie Nelson took off at 1405 for a late afternoon patrol over Ormoc Bay. After patrolling for two hours at 10,000 feet a lone Zero was observed flying about 3,000 feet above them. Nelson led the Flight in a fast 180 degree climb but the Zero went into a shallow dive and Nelson and his Wingman followed and fired getting some hits as the Zero headed for the deck. Second Element Leader, 1Lt. Thomas Hamilton, was covering the first element and got a chance to fire when Nelson had to pull up about 500 feet off the water. The busy Zero pilot did not see Hamilton who closed to 100 yards and fired a short lethal burst into the wing root that sent the Zero crashing into the beach. When the Flight reformed at 7,000 feet they saw two P-38's engaging a Zero and joined in the fight. Nelson fired a good tail shot that knocked off pieces for a damaged claim. After downing two Zeros on 2 November this was Hamilton's third and last victory.

**8 to 18 November 1944: 58 FG Move to Leyte**

On 8 November 1944, 58FG CO, Col. Gwen Atkinson, was informed that his Group was to be moved immediately from Noemfoor to the Philippines. Navy transports, the *USS Sheriden* and the *USS Mercury*, were already at Noemfoor and by the morning of 10 November all men and equipment were on board but the loaded vessels remained at anchor off Noemfoor until 14 November. On 13 November, a few of the pilots who were originally scheduled to fly the planes, or be flown, up to the Philippines boarded the transport ships. By 0800 on 18 November, the convoy was nearing the Leyte landing beaches when suddenly, three Japanese planes were attacking the convoy and the escorting destroyers were firing. One transport was hit and several Japanese aircraft were destroyed or damaged by AA fire.

**19 November 1944: 475FG/433FS**

The 433rd sent out three flights of four P-38s, an hour apart, during the afternoon to patrol the Dulag area and all encountered enemy aircraft. 1Lt. William Richmond led the 1345 flight and while at 9,000 feet over Ormoc Bay the Air Controller vectored the flight toward two groups of enemy fighters approaching from 230 and 240 degrees. At 1530 Richmond's #4

The **8FS/49FG** met the newly arrived JAAF Nakajima fighters designated as the Ki-84 Frank. (AFHRC)

called out bogeys which were identified as three Lilys, four or five Vals, escorted by three Oscars. The Lilys turned away and circled below and the Vals were lost from sight. As Richmond was about to dive on the Vals the Oscars attacked his #4 man. Richmond was able to get behind an Oscar by using his dive flaps but as he fired the Oscar pilot Split-S'd away into the clouds after receiving some hits on the center of its fuselage. All but Richmond's #4 man rejoined the flight but his #3 was having engine problems and the outnumbered Richmond decided to head home.

1Lt. Leroy Ross led the 1450 flight which was uneventful until about 1640 when the Controller reported possible bogeys to the SW. Ross led the flight in string at 9,000 feet and spotted two bandits at about 2 o'clock heading east toward Salacot Point. One bandit turned into Ross and the other disappeared into a cloud. As Ross closed, the enemy fighter turned to starboard which prevented Ross from getting a shot but his Wingman, 2Lt. Samuel Morrison, came in for a 90 degree deflection shot as it was diving but missed. Ross' Second Element Leader, 2Lt. Pierre Schoener, dropped his dive flaps and went into a Split-S and got on its tail and closed to 100 yards and fired 30 rounds of 20mm cannon shells which exploded into its cockpit and port wing root. Schoener's Wingman, 2Lt. Wesley Hulett, confirmed Schoener's only victory and Ross' flight finished its patrol and returned to base.

1Lt. Calvin Wire led the 1550 flight toward Molly to support Richmond's Flight which reported that it was in combat. Wire was unable to find Richmond and patrolled the west coast of Leyte and at 1615 sighted eight single engine fighters headed south with six flying at Wire's altitude of 14,000 feet and two about 1,000 feet behind and below. Wire's flight approached at 5 o'clock and the rear two Oscars saw them and went into 45 degree dives straight ahead. Seconds later one of the six saw Wire and waggled its wings to alert the others. Four Oscars climbed steeply with the extreme one left going into a gradual level turn and the extreme right one going into a slight starboard turn. Wire followed the latter and opened fire at 200 yards. The enemy pilot rolled over and Split-S'd and Wire used his dive flaps to follow and closed to 100 yards and fired a long burst and it dove straight into the water. As his flight continued its patrol and at 1615 Wire observed a lone bogey headed north at the same altitude. Wire immediately got on its tail but the enemy pilot saw Wire closing at 200 yards and climbed straight up, trying to reach the overcast. Wire followed and fired at 50 yards and his cannons destroyed its engine and cockpit and it exploded on the ground south of Baybay for his seventh and last victory.

**Capt. Calvin Wire** shot down two Oscars for his 6th and 7th victories. (AFAA)

**19 November 1944: 348FG/460FS**

The 460FS sent up four P-47s on a local patrol when 1Lt. George Della saw a Hamp flying above him at 19,000 feet. Della pulled almost straight up and made a head on pass and fired a long burst; hitting the engine and port wing. As the Hamp flew under Della's wing the American Split-S'd and he and his Wingman watched the Hamp crash into the water between Cebu and the Comotes Islands for Dell's second victory.

Another four plane 460FS Flight was scrambled to 18,000 feet south of Ormoc Bay The Flight saw a Hamp flying about a 1,000 feet above and went into a steep climb when the Japanese pilot suddenly turned into them giving 2Lt. Paul McGuire a chance to fire hitting the Hamp's port wing and engine. McGuire watched as his only victim of the war crash into the sea also between Cebu and the Comotes.

**21 November 1944: 35FG/39FS/40FS**

39FS

Capt. Leroy Grosshuesch was leading 16 P-47s at 10,000 feet and stacked up to 15,000 feet on area cover over Bacolod Airdrome on the Negros Island. After covering the area for about 10 minutes, Grosshuesch took two flights down below the clouds because of the poor visibility at their altitude. At 5,000 feet they sighted a Zero that had just took off and was heading towards the sea at 1,000 feet. Grosshuesch started down but was unable to get a proper lead and didn't fire. Grosshuesch's Wingman, 2Lt. Ervin Pratt, however, was able to get a 60 degree deflection shot that hit the cockpit and the burning fighter nosed over and crashed and exploded into a small wooded area southwest of Bacolod Strip. Grosshuesch led the Flight along the coast and headed south, and made no contacts and returned to Bacolod 10 minutes later. Grosshuesch then headed west toward the largest strip at about 1,200 to 1,500 feet with two flights stacked up and acting as top cover. He spotted a Dinah heading east at about 300 feet toward the northeastern-most strip on Bacolod Airdrome. The American closed to 300 yards and fired a two second burst and observed numerous hits in the cockpit area of the plane. At 200 yards, he fired another two second burst again observing hits in the cockpit area when it was about 50 feet over the end of the strip. The enemy pilot lost control and crashed on the side of the strip, nosed up twice, and slid to approximately 25 yards away from the east side of the strip. Grosshuesch came back and strafed but was unable to start a fire to cap off his first of eight victories. But his Wingman, Lt. Graber, shot three men running away from the plane.

**1Lt. Leroy Grossheusch** scored the first of his eight victories. (AFAA)

40FS

The 40FS sent out 16 P-47s to escort B-24s as close cover to Bacolod Strip and arrived over the target at 1045. At 1120 Red Flight Leader, Capt. William Strand, was about to leave the target when a bandit was called on the deck. Strand dove and sighted it flying directly over the Strip but it went under a cloud at 500 feet out over the Bay. Strand picked it up again as it came out of the cloud with its wheels down as if to make a landing. Strand started firing out of range from 90 degrees down to 200 yards and 70 degrees tattooing the entire fuselage and the Jill crashed into the water for Strand's seventh and last victory. On his way back base Strand experienced engine problems and had to make and emergency landing at Tacloban.

**22 November 1944: 8FG/36FS**

One of the 36FS' last missions from Morotai was a patrol looking for enemy shipping. At 0940 1Lt. John Dunaway led Lieutenants Thompson and Collins over Kaoe Bay, north of Miti Island in the Halmaheras. Collins saw a barge hiding among a small group of islands just north of Miti and he led the way to the barge through some rain squalls. When the three Lightnings got under the clouds Dunaway's fighter banked too close to the water and caught a wing tip and cartwheeled and exploded. A crash boat was sent out to find the seven victory ace but found only two floating oxygen tanks.

**22 November 1944: 475FG/432FS**

Col. Charles MacDonald was leading four Lightnings on a patrol of the Dulag area when they were vectored west by the Air Controller. At 1730, while flying at 11,000 feet the flight spotted four bogies due west about 4,000 feet above. MacDonald led the flight in a climb but lost the bogies in the sun. He turned the flight back toward the coast and found three more bogies just under a cloud layer at 9,000 feet. MacDonald closed from the rear at 30 degrees high on the Hamps and attacked the Leader who got away from the high scoring ace. Capt. Paul Lucas went after the Wingman and fired from close in, 30 degrees above and got hits around the canopy but overran and pulled up. Lucas' Wingman, 2Lt. Robert Kimball, continued to follow the Hamp in diving port turn and fired a burst from out of range but then closed to 100 yards and scored hits over the entire fuselage from 30 degrees deflection and the Hamp rolled over into the sea for Kimball's first of three victories. Lucas then dove on the third Hamp that pulled up sharply left from his pass. Lucas followed in a dive and closed to 200 yards but fired with too much lead and hit its outer wing panel and it turned tightly right to escape into a cloud; depriving Lucas of his first victory since 21 August 1943.

**23 November 1944: 35FG/41FS**

The 41FS sent 13 P-47s on a midday sweep over Negros Island. Capt. Morgan Beamer was leading a flight at 20,000 feet when he saw a lone Zero approaching at 1 o'clock at the same altitude. Beamer made a level frontal approach and as he began to fire the Zero rolled and dove. Beamer dropped his tanks and fired short burst and the enemy pilot went into three different Split-Ss and pulled out at 12,000 feet with Beamer still 300 yards on his tail. Beamer closed to 100 yards and got hits on the right side of the engine, fuselage, and wing root. The Zero began to wobble and fell off and was seen to crash by Beamer's Wingman for Beamer's only victory.

**Late November 1944: Bong and McGuire**

On 10 November, both Bong and McGuire had shot down an Oscar. For McGuire it finally meant that he went into the select group of American fighter aces who claimed 26 or more aerial victories which was the "Rickenbacker Standard" as America's World War I Ace-of-Aces. For Bong it was an added margin to insure that he would always be the American top ranking ace. By the end of November Bong had moved from his old 49th Fighter Group to the 475th Group. Gen. Kenney maintained that he kept the two aces together because "they wanted to fly together" but, of course, the public relations aspect was priceless. In truth, McGuire was frustrated by Bong's consistent eight victory lead he held over him. McGuire was difficult and irritating, at best, and goaded Bong ruthlessly. Finally, the mild mannered Bong had enough and abruptly moved from the billet he shared with McGuire.

By the end of November, the irascible **McGuire** (right) had intensified his rivalry with the mild-mannered Bong. (AAF)

**24 November 1944: Situation**

The Japanese High Command was concerned that Allied aircraft based at Barauen, Tacloban, and Dulag would interdict their crucial lines of communication between the Japanese Home Islands and the oil-rich Netherlands East Indies. Gen. Suzuki, commanding the 35th Army on Leyte, was to open an offensive to capture Barauen and to destroy the facilities at Dulag and Tacloban; code-named the *WA Operation*.

As a further concern; with the impending arrival of better weather, the Japanese High Command correctly deduced that the Allies would make another amphibious landing at Ormoc. To meet the invaders they frantically attempted to reinforce their weakened Leyte garrison on 23 November. Kenney immediately attacked Ormoc and during grand air battle of the 24th, the bulk of the enemy reinforcements were attacked on the open water under a clearing weather front. For the next three days, Kinkaid's carrier aircraft and Kenney's tactical groups decimated thousands of enemy troops trapped on the transports.

**24 November 1944: 348FG/460FS**

The 460FS sent out 15 Thunderbolts at 0915 for a bombing mission on the airdrome on Masbate Island where they bombed the runway and adjacent buildings and then strafed other installations. When returning from the mission enemy shipping was seen in the Port Cataingan area and eight more P-47s were dispatched on a skip-bombing mission. At 0215 two P-47s attacked a large freighter in northern Port Cataingan and scored four direct hits and the freighter was left listing. Another freighter was hit in the stern by a bomb and the Japanese beached it to keep it from sinking. A third vessel, thought to be a barge, was hit by another bomb and then all three ships were then strafed by the P-47s after they had dropped their bombs.

**1Lt. George Della** scored his fourth victory. (AFAA)

As the Thunderbolts were returning from Port Cataingan, 1Lt. George Della and 2Lt. Edgar Stoudt took off on a patrol of Nagaha Bay. They patrolled for half an hour at

15,000 feet when Della saw a flight of 475FG P-38s below at 8,000 feet in combat with four Jacks (?). Della and Stoudt immediately dove into that battle and Stoudt shot down one of the Jacks with his initial burst while Della missed with a deflection shot. Della then chased the escaping Jack which went into a port turn and Della overshot. He pulled up into a zoom climb to gain altitude and dove on the enemy fighter's tail again. Della fired one more short burst and the Jack slow rolled into a vertical dive and burst into flame before it crashed on the south coast of Pacijan Island for his third victory. The remaining Jack headed for Cebu but Della and Stoudt were short of fuel and reluctantly left the Jack to the P-38s.

**24 November 1944: 475FG/431FS/432FS/433FS**

431FS

0700 Patrol

Four P-38s of Daddy Red Flight took off from Dulag at 0700 to patrol over shipping in Leyte Gulf. (The 431st had changed its call sign from Hades to Daddy) The Flight was led by 1Lt. John Pietz with 2Lt. James Barnes as his Wingman, and a second element of 2Lt. Robert Koeck and his Wingman, 2Lt. Erling Varland. Pietz's A Radio Channel was out and Wingman Barnes had to relay messages from the Controller. At 0800 the Controller relayed a plot of 15 bogies at 14,000 feet approximately 20 miles from Tacloban. Pietz led the flight to 21,000 feet to gain the altitude advantage on the enemy fighters milling below. Pietz dove on one but overran and #3 Koeck came in from below and behind and pulled up, firing several bursts that started it smoking and then roll over into the ground in flames. On Pietz's next pass on an Oscar the enemy pilot turned into him and broke off and lost his second element and he and Wingman Barnes spotted two Oscars at 2 o'clock high and six more at 6 o'clock high and the two waited for the enemy to commit. Finally they Split-S'd and one got on the tail of a P-38 (Koeck?) and Pietz used his dive flaps to get a 10 degree deflection shot tearing off three feet of its port wing and it inverted into a spin. Pietz climbed to 10,000 feet where he saw a Lightning chasing an enemy fighter but the Lightning pilot broke off when the Oscar dove into a cloud. Pietz saw a hole in the clouds and went through it to try to find the Oscar below. He was unable to do so but when he climbed through a small break in the clouds he found himself right on the Oscar's tail. Pietz fired and saw pieces fly off its fuselage and then burn and go spinning down into the ground south of Carigara for his second victory of the day. Pietz and Barnes then sighted two Tonys in a slight dive away from them and gave chase. One Tony turned into them for a head on pass while the other made a shallow dive in the same direction. Pietz dove directly behind the latter but overshot and Barnes got a head on shot that hit its fuselage before to break to the right in a steep dive, putting it directly astern of Barnes' guns. Barnes fired and it began to smoke but Barnes broke off, thinking the Tony was finished but watched as it leveled off and began to fly away. Barnes made a 30 degree deflection shot and scored hits on its wing root and cockpit and this time the Tony was finished for Barnes first of two career victories. Pietz then attacked the other Tony and got off three shots before he ran out of ammunition. After Koeck downed his Oscar he and Wingman Varland climbed and circled when Koeck saw another Oscar ahead and made a pass at it but it broke away. At this point Koeck lost Varland and circled around looking for him but saw an Oscar chasing a Lightning and dove to its rescue. When the P-38 broke away the Oscar was dead astern and Koeck fired and it burst into flames, rolled, and exploded. Koeck broke away in a climb when he saw another Oscar at 9 o'clock and turned into it and when he squeezer the trigger he found he was out of ammunition and his potential third victim of the day (and war). Varland was lost without a trace.

0755 Patrol

1Lt. Kenneth Hart led four P-38s of Daddy White Flight off Dulag at 0755 on a scramble over the base. Hart's flight consisted of Wingman, F/O Edward O'Neill and the second element of 2Lt. Harold Gray and his Wingman, 2Lt. Alvin Neal. Hart's radio was out so he immediately climbed to have the altitude advantage and when they got to 7,000 feet they saw a dogfight at 12-14,000 feet and climbed to 18,000 feet but on the way up the second element snafued and returned to base. As Hart and O'Neill approached the fight four Tonys suddenly appeared, flying in the opposite direction and Hart dove on them as they turned to port. Hart used his dive flaps and easily held his lead and began firing at 35 degrees deflection. The Tony's engine flamed and its pilot bailed out near Mt. Cabungangan for his second victory of the day. As Hart broke to starboard he saw a Tony headed west and slightly below. Hart dove and fired, hitting its tail and wing and then fired again setting it on fire and this pilot also bailed out. Hart then saw a Tony on O'Neill's tail and made a sharp 180 and fired a short burst head on that persuaded the Tony pilot to break off. Hart then saw an Oscar on a P-38's tail and as he was about ready to attack he saw Koeck shoot it down.

1105 Patrol

1Lt. John Pietz was again a Flight Leader when he led Daddy Red Flight off at 1105 to relieve Daddy Blue Flight from its shipping patrol over Leyte Gulf. As the flight was climbing at 3,000 feet Pietz's Wingman, 2Lt. James Barnes, spotted a bogie but lost it when it entered a cloud. The flight continued to climb and at 4,000 feet Barnes saw a Kate at 1 o'clock high ready to dive into its attack on the shipping in Dulag Harbor. Pietz climbed toward the Kate and when it was directly over the shipping it made a 180 degree turn toward Daddy Red and rolled over in a dive toward the shipping in the Harbor. Pietz inverted his Lightning and dropped his dive and combat flaps and pulled out directly astern of the Kate in a 40 to 50 degree dive. He opened fire and got hits on its fuselage and port wing which caught fire at the root and peeled off pieces. The determined Kate pilot pulled out of the dive and passed under Pietz and crashed into the waterline of a ship below. The Kate rear gunner had continued to fire at Pietz's Lightning and got a hit on his starboard wing and shot out its hydraulic system and Barnes escorted him back to base with his third victory of the day and third, so far.

1345 Patrol

At 1345 Daddy Blue Flight Leader, 1Lt. Richard Roark, and Wingman, Lt. Thomas Oxford, were sent to relieve Pietz's Daddy Red Flight to patrol over Dulag shipping at 10,000 feet. During the first hour of their patrol the Controller sent them on several vectors all of which proved negative. At 1435 the Controller dispatched them toward a bogie six miles to the north, heading at 240 degrees. They immediately headed NW to place themselves between the bogie and the Controller. A few minutes later the Controller called bandits over the Harbor shipping and Roark turned south and dove through overcast in the area where he saw AA fire over the shipping and searched to find the bogie flying in line of the AA bursts. After making several descending S-turns at 7,000 feet Oxford called the bogie but Roark could not spot it and called for Oxford to make the attack. Oxford went into a steep dive and arrived at 90 degrees and came around to 45 degrees; firing a deflection shot and carrying it 25 degrees, hitting the left fuselage and cockpit. Oxford fired another shot from 15 to 0 degrees and knocked off some large pieces. As the Kate flew on Oxford fired a short burst as the Kate gradually turned to port and Oxford fired another burst as it exploded for Oxford's first of three victories.

1545 Patrol

At 1545 Lt.Col. Meryl Smith led three P-38s on Bannon Special Flight consisting of wingmen, 1Lt. Kenneth Hart and 1Lt. Pietz on Hart's wing. After patrolling for about an hour Smith returned to base with hydraulic problems and after escorting Smith down and watching him pump his wheels down the two plane patrol resumed. As Hart and Pietz were about to return to base they heard a call from another P-38 flight about an enemy float plane NW of Tacloban. They turned toward Tacloban but ran into heavy "friendly" AA fire and turned away from it and ran into a Jake heading west toward a small rain squall where they lost it and then saw it again but they were flying too fast to have a good shot. As they repositioned themselves both Hart and Pietz got good hits before the Jake entered another cloud. As they flew into the cloud it became a bright red as though the Jake was on fire. However, as the Jake exited the cloud the rear cockpit occupant was holding a lighted flare; hoping that the Americans would believe his plane was on fire. Hart came in with a 35 to 20 degree deflection shot and knocked off pieces of its tail. One of the Jake's occupants bailed out for Hart's third victory of the day.

**1Lt. John Pietz** claimed the first three of six victories. (AFAA)

432FS

0635 Patrol

Capt. Paul Lucas led four Red Flight P-38s off Dulag at 0635 on a local patrol. At 0750 the Air Controller called out 15 to 25 bogies to the 433FS flying N/NW of Tacloban. Lucas ordered a fast climb to the indicated area but two P-38s aborted due to engine problems; leaving Lucas and 2Lt. Lawrence Roberts. They continued to 23,000 feet about 20 miles NW of Tacloban where they saw four bogies above. Since the enemy had the altitude advantage the two P-38 pilots climbed parallel to the bogies which were identified as Tonys. The enemy pilots went into a Lufbery Circle and Lucas attacked the last Tony which took no evasive action until Lucas fired from 50 yards and hit its engine. The enemy pilot tried to Split-S but dove into the ground. Lucas then pulled up on the third Tony and took a quick shot that slightly damaged the Tony. Lucas pulled up and saw another Tony passing 90 degrees under him and about 1,000 feet lower. Lucas dove from 30 degrees and fired at 10-20 degrees deflection and got hits on its canopy and engine as the enemy pilot tried to pull up but turned slowly to starboard and plunged into the ground. These two victories made Lucas an ace. Roberts had followed Lucas through his two victories and the two then saw a mixture of 16 Japanese fighters. Roberts dropped back to go after a Hamp and fired from 500 yards and from 30 to 0 degrees deflection. As Roberts closed on the Hamp he chopped his throttles and lowered his flaps and fired three bursts into its wing root and fuselage that started the Hamp smoking. Its pilot went into a glide and bailed out. Roberts looked around and found four enemy fighters on his tail and he Split-S'd into a cloud to escape with his second victory. Lightnings of the 433FS were also in the area and Lucas saw 1Lt. Leroy Ross shoot down a Jack and Ross reciprocated by confirming Robert's victory. One 433FS pilot chased a Hamp which turned and made a head on at Lucas and nearly rammed his port wing. At this time Lucas had only one gun firing and Roberts was almost out of ammunition and the two returned to base.

**2Lt. James Barnes** got his first victory of two. (AAF)

0845 Patrol

1Lt. George Beatty led four White Flight Lightnings on a 0845 to 1125 patrol of the Dulag area at 12,000 feet. Beatty spotted a bogie at 13,000 feet just off the east coast of Dulag which began a steep dive on the Allied shipping in Dulag Bay. Beatty raced after it and got into position for a 90 degree deflection shot. Beatty rolled to lessen his deflection and opened fire at 30 degrees but had to break away when he saw he was too close to the water for no claim. Beatty then made a pass at a Nate that turned into him and fired from 1,000 yards until it passed under him. When he banked sharply Beatty saw two P-38s of the 431FS after the Nate. 1Lt. John Pietz opened fire from dead astern at 300 to 50 yards and it crashed near a Liberty ship in Dulag Harbor for his third victory of the day. White was low on fuel and landed at 1125.

**1Lt. Kenneth Hart** scored his first three victories of eight. (AFAA)

1045 Patrol

1Lt. Calvin Anderson led four P-38s on a patrol of the Dulag area with 2Lt. Robert Koles flying his wing and 2Lt. Robert Kimball flying the Second

Element alone until his Wingman caught up with the flight. At 1115 at 11,000 feet Koles spotted a Kate at 11 o'clock low and called it out. Anderson didn't see it and Kimball went after it and closed to 50 yards directly astern and fired a short burst. The Kate immediately burst into flames and dove straight into the water for Kimball's second victory. The flight saw no other enemy aircraft on the patrol and returned to base.

433FS
Early Morning Flight
At 0645, 1Lt. Leroy Ross led Wingman, 2Lt. John Berry, Second Element Leader, 2Lt. Pierre Schoener, and #4, 2Lt. Carl Redding, on a patrol over Albuera on the western Leyte coast at 14,000 feet. At about 0800, 20 to 30 enemy aircraft were seen in a stacked formation at 13,000 to 18,000 feet heading east. As his flight was headed south Ross turned starboard to gain an altitude advantage and to initiate an attack from astern. Ross selected two fighters in the rear and to the side of the formation but as he closed to fire his guns malfunctioned and the enemy ducked into the clouds before the rest of the flight could fire. Ross climbed for a second pass but lost his second element in the maneuver. Ross saw two Tonys high in the rear of the formation and as the Tonys turned to port Ross fired a 30 degree deflection shot at one and observed hits in its right wing root and engine and it was seen to go down west of Tacloban by Capt. Paul Lucas of the 432FS. After his second victory of the day Ross again attacked the Tonys followed by his Wingman Berry who followed about 100 yards behind. A Tony fired on Berry head on from 2 o'clock high and Berry started firing at 300 yards and shot pieces off its right wing root that just missed his canopy and dented his right wing. Berry continued firing until the Tony banked only 30 yards in front of him and rolled over sideways on its back and crashed. After diving away from two Tonys that were on their tails, Ross and Berry were still in their dives when they saw four Tonys SW of Tacloban at 8,000 feet and closed from 50 degrees astern. Berry fired at the third Tony in the string from 400 yards at 40 degrees and missed. He fired again and got a few hits before the Tony disappeared for no claim. Ross and Berry then chased the other three Tonys which broke away. The second element of Schoener and Redding lost sight of Ross and Berry in the sun and were unable to contact them by radio. The two climbed to 15,000 feet over the assigned patrol area and sighted a lone enemy aircraft flying west and dove on its tail. Schoener fired from 300 yards as the Zero pilot dove to port into the thin overcast and Schoener followed. He fired again as the Zero headed into the overcast again where Schoener lost sight of it. Redding took a 60-70 degree shot at it but did not see any results but followed and fired and started it on fired and it rolled on it back and its pilot bailed out into Ormoc Bay for Redding's first of two victories.

Early Afternoon Flight
1Lt. Morton Ryerson led a four plane patrol at 10,000 feet over Albuera when at about 1445 the Controller called Bogies approaching from the west and at the same time Ryerson's second element called bogies at 4 o'clock. Ryerson continued in a wide right climbing spiral and called for IDs but none was made. Ryerson and his Wingman, Morrell, continued climbing until he saw bogies at 9 o'clock and saw his second element go into an attack several thousand feet below on three or four enemy fighters. Ryerson dove on a Tony that was attempting to get on the tails of his second element. This Tony dove away and Ryerson then followed a second Zero and fired from 60 degrees and followed it into a turn and then Split-S'd. Ryerson rolled with the Zero but overran it and had to roll out. He then fired on a Jack getting several hits but lost sight of it. He saw another Jack at 1 o'clock and dived slightly and fired two bursts from 30 to 0 degrees and got hits in its cockpit and engine, and oil spattered his windshield. The Jack winged over and was seen to crash by element Leader F/O Richardson. Ryerson saw another enemy aircraft to starboard and each pilot made a head on pass with neither hitting the other and both broke away. As Ryerson made his turn he ran into a Jack closing on him from 90 to 60 degrees. He rolled left and received some hits as he tightened his turn. As Ryerson skidded downward and to the right and saw another P-38 attack his pursuer and scared it away. Ryerson's fighter had received hits in its left wing and coolant radiator and he went into a high speed climb and then feathered the engine and headed home.

Ryerson's second element of Leader, F/O Richardson and Wingman, 2Lt. John Berry separated from their Flight Leader when Richardson saw six enemy aircraft at 9 o'clock south of Ponson Island and led Berry after them. Richardson came down to their altitude and fired at 90 degrees at the first three. Richardson has just begun to fire when the other three started to fire on him. Berry was 300 yards away and fired on these three enemy fighters, but the first two turned sharply into him. As he looked around to escape, Berry saw four more enemy fighters on his tail and as he climbed away, his pursuers stayed with him. He pushed his throttles to war emergency and climbed at 190 mph and two of his pursuers broke off at 10,500 feet but the other two continued to fire from 400 yards. The third one broke off at 11,500 feet and the last at 13,000 feet. Ryerson and Morrell rejoined the flight to fight the 10 Jacks. Berry saw two Jacks at 9,000 feet heading back toward Ponson Island to rejoin their flight. Berry circled over them and dove straight down on the lead Jack and began firing at 400 yards hitting its engine and cockpit. Berry had to turn away to shake a Jack off his tail but Ryerson saw Berry's victim crash into the water off Ponson for second victory of the day and his career.

Late Afternoon Flight
1Lt. Leroy Ross led a flight that was scrambled at 1448 and proceed to an air battle in progress over Ormoc Bay. Soon after they had taken off and reached 9,000 feet they spotted four enemy aircraft headed NW at 5,000 feet three miles south of Poro Island and Ross put his flight into a string formation. Ross scored hits on a Jack while his Wingman, 2Lt. Edward Edesberg, followed and fired at it. Pieces came off the Jack and some hit Edesberg's fighter but he continued firing until the Jack exploded for his only victory. A Jack got on the tail of Ross' #4 man but a P-47 came in and chased after it. Ross followed the Thunderbolt chasing the Jack and when the P-47 broke away Ross quickly closed and fired shots into its port wing which set it on fire and it crashed into the sea for his second victory of the day. Ross reformed with his Second Element Leader, 2Lt. Wesley Hulett, and his Hulett's Wingman, and climbed to 2,000 feet, where they saw a Jack flying on deck. Ross dove and fired a short burst before he ran out of ammunition and broke away while the second element continued its pursuit.

While Ross was waiting for his second element, another Jack dove out of the sun and shot out both Ross' engines and dove away. Ross recalled his flight saying he was out of ammunition and his fighter badly damaged. Edesberg, who was also out of ammunition and the second element, began to escort Ross home. Ross soon feathered his right engine and the left was smoking badly and he was forced to ditch a mile south of Cabgan Island. As his flight was circling they saw him standing on his wing with a number of native boats surrounding him.

**24 November 1944: 49FG/7FS/8FS/9FS**
The senior staff situation for Capt. William Drier's 9FS was becoming desperate until Capt. Robert Aschenbrener and 1Lt. Sammie Pierce returned from Stateside Command School. Aschenbrener was assigned as the new Ops Exec and Pierce as the Ops Deputy while Flack became the new Deputy CO to replace MIA Philip Kriechbaum.

Although the Ki-61 was considered superior to the P-40 upon its introduction; P-38s piloted by accomplished pilots such as Drier and Aschenbrenner took their toll on the Tonys over the Philippines (AFF).

**Capt. William Drier** was credited with three victories to give him six to become an ace. (AFAA)

**Capt. Robert Aschenbrenner** shot down four enemy aircraft to make him an ace with seven victories. (AFAA)

8FS

Drier and Aschenbrener teamed up as wingmen and joined two other Black Sheep on the first morning patrol north of Ormoc. After 30 minutes the Tacloban Controllers vectored Drier's flight to 20,000 feet and 40 miles west of Tacloban. As they flew over the Carigara coast, Aschenbrener saw aircraft below. The trailing element was assigned to fly top cover while the two veterans dove on the Tony formation. Aschenbrener attacked a straggling Tony first at 8,000 feet, where his first burst ripped off its tail section and one third of its right wing. The duo climbed to regroup but on the way up, Drier called out five Lily bombers escorted by about a dozen Zeros overhead at about 13-14,000 feet. The two climbed wide and then saw 25-30 more bandits at 18,000 feet. They followed and made contact with four Zeros in formation flying parallel to the Ormoc coast at 15,000 feet. Drier followed one to 20 degrees and fired and hit one which dove in flames and crashed inland. Meanwhile, Aschenbrener went after one of the Zeros that broke away and sent it into the water between Jaro and Patong Islands. Drier tried to rejoin Aschenbrener who was below making a pass on an Oscar that fell off on a starboard dive to escape but Aschenbrener set it on fire but watched as its pilot bailed out. Drier made a stern pass on a Tony which began to smoke and then caught on fire and crashed for his second victory of the day. Aschenbrener then took on the remaining Tony but found that only one of his guns was working. He closed to 50 yards and fired the one gun; the Tony burst into flames and it crashed into the Bay for his fourth victory of the day to make him a seven victory ace. Drier made a head on diving, head on pass at another Tony, getting some hits. The enemy pilot then rolled with Drier following in a Split-S that put Drier at 30 degrees astern. Drier's burst caused the Tony to smoke, then flame, and finally crash to become as ace with three daily victories that gave him his sixth and final victories of the war.

7FS

Morning Flight

Pinky Red Flight Leader 1Lt. James O'Neil and wingmen 2Lts. Oliver Atchison, James Franks, and Hubert Manes took off from Tacloban at 0645 and climbed to 10,000 feet. At 0745 *Austaire* Controller called a bandit at 7,000 feet a few miles west of Tacloban. O'Neil immediately saw a lone below the overcast at 6.500 feet. O'Neil scored several hits on his first pass as the enemy pilot dove right. O'Neil followed and made a second pass that caused the Zero to catch fire and explode into the ground. *Austaire* Controller radioed new plots on bandits approaching at 20,000 feet from the north and west. O'Neil saw several bandits about 20 miles SW of Tacloban and took his Flight down but cut off by other P-38s and Red Flight climbed to 20,000 feet when they saw two groups of bandits; one group of four or six at 10,000 feet and another four at their altitude. O'Neil watched as other P-38s (Drier's Flight) dove on the lower bandits and then the top four bandits dove on these P-38s. O'Neil then led his Flight into the swirling fray. O'Neil took several deflection shots without results and then got a few hits on a Tony before it escaped into the clouds for a damaged claim. He got astern of a Tony and closed very fast and fired until he overran through pieces coming off the stricken Tony, As he overran the Tony, O'Neil looked back and saw a "Nip" diving from behind and turned into it and fired but found that he had only one gun working but the short burst set the Tony on fire and its pilot bailed out for O'Neil's second victory of the day and his third and final victory. O'Neil's ICR states: I made one pass at the Nip in the chute but I don't think I hit him." O'Neil's Flight tried to reform but Element Leader 2Lt. James Franks and rookie 2Lt. Oliver Atchison became separated. As they climbed through the overcast where they saw two bogies below at 12 o'clock and dove. Franks closed, unseen, on the Leader and "observes him burst into flames" for his first of two career victories. Atchison closed, also unseen, to 100 yards of the Wingman and fired, hitting the cockpit and wing root, and it fell off and crashed into the water for his first of two career victories.

Afternoon Flight

Later that afternoon 1Lt. James O'Neil led the same three morning flight members on their second patrol. As the flight passed directly over Tacloban, the air controller vectored a single contact approaching from the northeast. They climbed to 13,000 feet which placed them in ideal position to attack. Atchison, who was again in the customary rookie tail end position, attacked first in turning descent on the target and fired a poor deflection shot that was followed by firing passes by the two lead elements who both overshot the target. 2Lt. Hubert Manes, who was the only pilot not to score in the morning's air battles, made a full turn that positioned him directly behind the Zero and he got his only victory when the fighter crashed into San Pedro Bay.

Late Afternoon Flight

The good weather continued into late day; necessitating a standing patrol with Pinky White Flight taking off at 1655. At 1820, Flight Leader 1Lt. Robert Decker and wingmen 2Lts. Harold Harris and Nicolas Zuniga of the 7FS were approaching Tacloban at 9,000 feet. As they entered their landing pattern, the air controller called a pair of intruders from the north at 2,000 feet low. Visibility was poor in the twilight but after a starboard turn, the enemy aircraft identified as small two-man Glen floatplanes, were spotted. Decker descended into firing range as one of the enemy aircraft disappeared but he closed to 200 yards hitting the engine, He turned around and on his second attack from even closer in he set the fuselage on fire with the flames quickly enveloping the starboard wing for his second victory

9FS

At 0830, seven P-38s were scrambled from Tacloban on a local patrol. 9FS Element Leader F/O Henry Hammett was joined by newcomer Capt. John Petrovic, and the pair became separated from the other element after their late take off and then couldn't find the other element while breaking through the overcast. While on their patrol they were vectored toward a JNAF Dinah that was heading southwest away from Tacloban. To catch the speedy twin-engine recon bomber they dropped their auxiliary tanks and full throttled into a climbing 30 minute chase to 25,000 feet over Cebu Island's North Cape where they finally caught up. Hammett closed directly astern and his first burst hit the Dinah's right engine and then jinked to port and damaged the other engine. The stricken enemy bomber descended in a flat spin when its right fuel tank exploded and after its burning starboard wing broke away it plummeted into the clouds for Hammett's first of three victories.

**Capt. Alvaro Hunter** shot down his fifth and last enemy aircraft to become an ace. (AAF)

**24 November 1944: 35FG**

39FS

On the 24$^{th}$ 16 P-47s of the 39FS were assigned to cover B-24s to Alicante Airdrome on the northeast tip of Negros Island at 13,000 feet. At 1210 two enemy fighters were called by Blue Flight Leader, 1Lt. William Rogers at 4 o'clock high ready to dive on them. The flight dropped tanks and went into a firewall dive to escape and soon outdistanced them. Rogers then led them into a climb back to catch them and turned into them at 90 degrees to their course. Rogers took a 90 degree deflection shot from 400 to 150 yards but saw no hits. The enemy Wingman chandelled sharply to the right while the leader Split-S'd right. Rogers and his Wingman, 2Lt. Joseph Doody, followed the chandelling Wingman and Rogers fired at 50 yards tearing pieces out of the right wing root and hitting the fuselage forward of the cockpit and then a wing tank blew off. As the wounded Zero passed under Roger's wing Doody came in and fired and the Zero's internal fuel exploded. Meanwhile, 1Lt. Maurice Boland was leading Green Flight at 16,000 feet and after leaving the target spotted two Tonys turning toward their flight from 2 o'clock. Boland turned into the Tonys and fired a short burst from 10 degrees head on, hitting the engine and cockpit. The Tony went straight down and crashed for Boland's only victory.

40FS

The 40FS dispatched 12 P-47s on a close cover B-24 escort to Alicante Airdrome on the north end of Negros Island. Capt Alvaro Hunter, leading Red Flight, arrived over the target at 1215 at 14,000 feet where they spotted two Oscars and a Zero in the distance 1,000 feet above and preparing to get into position to attack the Liberators. Hunter was unable to drop one of his wing tanks but maneuvered his flight behind the Oscars but was seen. The lead Oscar Split-S'd while the enemy Wingman pulled sharply down and Hunter took a quick shot at the Wingman but missed due to the unbalancing caused by the wing tank. The enemy Wingman came around and got on the tail of Hunter's #4 man but misjudged the P-47s lower speed and his distance behind it. This allowed the #3 second Element Leader, 1Lt. Graydon Franklin, to kick over behind him. The Zero pilot saw him and rolled over and started to Split-S but Franklin also rolled and fired a three second burst from 30 degrees deflection on his back and exploded it into a violent spin into the water for his only victory. Red Flight regrouped and continued their escort and Hunter finally dumped his faulty wing tank just before approaching two more enemy fighters above them. Once again the lead Oscar Split-S'd while the Wingman pulled sharply down to get on the P-47's tails and again he misjudged and Hunter was able to get behind it and fired a deadly two second burst for his fifth victory to make him an ace. Meanwhile, Hunter's #4 man, 2Lt. Warren Wycoff, was one of the P-47s to have the Oscar Wingman get on his tail but Franklin kicked over behind the attacker who responded by rolling over and starting a Split-S. Franklin rolled with the Oscar and fired a three second burst, inverted, from 30 degrees deflection and the Oscar exploded for Franklin's only victory. Wycoff had another Oscar dive on him from 2 o'clock high and turned into him but the Oscar pilot turned to port giving Wycoff an opportunity for a tail shot. But the enemy pilot went into a vertical bank giving him a 70 to 90 degree deflection shot which scored hits as the Oscar Split-S'd away and was seen to hit the water. Red Flight regrouped and saw an Oscar at 3 o'clock high and started to climb after it but as soon as they reached its altitude it Split-S'd away and the flight headed for home. As they were flying over Alicante Strip they spotted an Oscar at 3 o'clock level, heading in the opposite direction and went after him. Franklin and Wycoff, chased it down and both fired from 250 yards, getting hits. The Oscar immediately rolled over in a slow Split-S, giving Wycoff a perfect belly shot which sent it crashing west of the Strip for his second victory of the day and war.

1Lt. Robert Steffy was leading Blue Flight and five minutes after their arrival saw two Oscars and a Zero climbing over Panay. Hunter's Red Flight went after the Oscars while Steffy chased the Zero whose pilot, realizing it couldn't get to the bombers Split-S'd to the deck. As it leveled off Steffy made a stern pass at 200 yards but the Zero pilot evaded with a steep port turn but Steffy's Wingman, 2Lt. Ellis Baker, was in good position and fired a two second, 35 degree shot that sent the Zero spiraling down in flames. Steffy regrouped his flight and rejoined the bombers at 8,500 feet to escort them out of the area. On the way they spotted and Oscar over Soledad flying 180 degrees away from them. Steffy wheeled around as the Oscar made a gentle right turn allowing the American to close and fire from 150 to 50 yards. The Oscar's left gear dropped and pieces flew off the canopy and tail and fire broke out from the engine as the fighter crashed. Blue Flight continued and saw yet another enemy fighter on the deck but as they were preparing to attack three P-47s dove on Blue Flight but luckily identified them before any damage was done.

**24 November 1944: 348FG/460FS**

Fifteen 460FS' P-47s took off at 0915 for a bombing mission on the airdrome on Masbate Island and bombed the runway and adjacent buildings and then strafed other installations. When returning from the mission, enemy shipping was seen in the Port Cataingan area and eight more P-47s were dispatched on a skip-bombing mission. At 0215 two P-47s attacked a large freighter in northern Port Cataingan and scored four direct hits and the freighter was left listing. Another freighter was hit in the stern by a bomb and the Japanese beached it to avoid its sinking. A third vessel, thought to be a barge, was hit by another bomb and all three ships were then strafed by the P-47s after they had dropped their bombs.

As the Thunderbolts were returning from Port Cataingan, 1Lt. George Della and 2Lt. Edgar Stoudt took off on a patrol of Nagaha Bay. They patrolled for half an hour at 15,000 feet when Della saw a flight of 475FG P-38s below at 8,000 feet in combat with four Jacks (?). Della and Stoudt immediately dove into that battle and Stoudt shot down one of the Jacks with his initial burst while Della missed with a deflection shot. Della then chased the escaping Jack which went into a port turn and Della overshot. He pulled up into a zoom climb to gain altitude and dove on the enemy fighter's tail again. Della fired one more short burst and the Jack slow rolled into a vertical dive and burst into flame before it crashed on the south coast of Pacijan Island. The remaining Jack headed for Cebu but Della and Stoudt were short of fuel and reluctantly left the Jack to the P-38s; Della with his third victory and Stoudt with his only victory of the war.

**24 November 1944: 8FG/80FS**

1Lt. Vernon Jenner took off at 1830 flying a P-38J of the 421NFS climbed to 24,000 feet and patrolled over the Morotai airfield on a searchlight mission waiting for Japanese intruder aircraft. At 2045 the Controller called a plot flying in from the south at 21,000 feet. Jenner continued to fly at 24,000 feet to maintain a 3,000 foot altitude advantage. Jenner saw some AA bursts and then saw the bandit in the searchlight beam and went into a dive and closed but the enemy pilot went into a 180 degree right turn at 19,000 feet. Jenner fired a single burst as the enemy, identified as a Dinah, completed its turn. There was a bright flash that almost blinded Jenner but when his night vision returned he was only 50 yards behind the Dinah whose gunner was firing very ineffectively at Jenner who fired a long burst and almost rammed the Dinah. The Dinah flew away but the Controller reported that it was seen falling into the sea. The Controller then vectored Jenner to 25,000 feet but then sent him down to 14,000 feet where another enemy aircraft was approaching the field. Jenner went into a very high speed dive and overran the target. Jenner made a 360 and after five miles found the target again in the searchlights and fired a short burst at 150 yards. There was another bright flash and Jenner and the searchlights lost it. Jenner got another plot at 14,000 feet approaching the field from the east. Once Jenner was over the field the Controller determined the bandit was above and behind him. Jenner asked that the searchlights be turned on and when they were Jenner was in their beam and took evasive action and asked that they be turned out. The Controller radioed that the two aircraft were so close together that they could not be separated on the radar. Jenner climbed north but the enemy turned south and Jenner lost it. After 20 more minutes he ran low on oxygen and landed with a second victory over a Nick that was confirmed by a 421NFS pilot who was also on patrol with the 229th Searchlight Battalion. It was Jenner's fourth and last victory of the war and the last of the V Fighter Command's 47 victories for the day.

After two victories ten days before, **1Lt. Cheatum Gupton** became an ace when he shot down an Oscar. (AFAA)

**25-28 November 1944: 348FG/460FS**

Between 25-28 November the 460FS flew missions on enemy airdromes, coastal shipping, and escort cover while other bombing and strafing missions were also flown with varying results.

On 25 November the 460th returned to Port Cataingan to finish off any enemy ships still afloat after the previous day's mission and attacked the beached freighter which exploded. Later, four P-47s bombed Bitoon Harbor and eight others attacked Valencia and San Jose Airdromes. One Betty bomber was claimed on the ground at San Jose but the strafing P-47 was damaged by flying rocks from its own gunfire. Later in the afternoon four other P-47s patrolled Valencia and called in strikes until low fuel forced them to return to base. Yet another flight of four Thunderbolts returned to bomb shipping in Bitoon Harbor before returning to base just before dusk.

**26 November 1944: 49FG/7FS/9FS**

Throughout the remainder of the Leyte Campaign the 49FG would fly almost daily missions with out any casualties to enemy aircraft or AA fire while continuing to inflict irreplaceable losses of aircraft and crews on the enemy.

7FS

Four P-38s of 1Lt. Cecil Archer's Pinky Red Flight took off at 1000 and were to patrol until 1230. They patrolled at 10,000 feet over the Tacloban area for an hour when *Austaire* Controller asked Pinky to climb to 19,000 feet as they had a plot approaching at that altitude. The Flight patrolled for half hour at that altitude when *Austaire* called that bogies were now over the base. Archer and his Wingman, 2Lt. Oliver Atchison, saw two Zeros below and 12 o'clock, 20 miles away. Archer took the Leader and Atchison took the Wingman. Archer fired and smoke began to trail behind the Zero and he fired again as the Zero headed into a cloud. Archer's Element Leader, 2Lt. William Fernandez, and his Wingman, 2Lt. Kenneth Markham, saw the Zero leave the cloud now on fire to confirm Archer's only victory of the war. Meanwhile, Atchison closed, unseen, on the enemy Wingman and fired a dead astern shot from within 100 yards for his only victory which was confirmed by Markham

9FS

At 1230 1Lt. Cheatum Gupton's 9FS patrol of four "Beware" P-38s was vectored 10 miles northwest of the Tacloban and at 1300 they encountered three Oscars flying east at 11,000 feet. One Oscar separated from the other two and headed for the American airstrip. Gupton chased after the two Oscars and wasn't seen and opened fired at 150 yards at 30 degrees deflection and an explosion (oxygen tank?) tore off the Oscar's tail section but the enemy pilot was able to bail out for Gupton's fifth and last victory to become an ace.

**26 November 1944: 35FG/39FS/40FS**

39FS

The Squadron sent 16 P-47s on a B-24 escort mission to La Carlota Airdrome in the Los Negros. 1Lt. Kenneth Dunn was leading White Flight at 13,000 feet when they were bounced from the rear by two Tonys south of the Airdrome. The enemy was spotted only 600 yards away and Dunn's Wingman and Element Leader Split-S'd to the right and the Tonys followed them. Dunn firewalled and put his fighter into a skid to clear his tail and went into a sweeping Split-S and fired at the Tonys from far out of range to scare them off the P-47's tails. As one Tony was closing on Dunn's Wingman it turned into Dunn while the other also broke off its attack and headed for a cloud. Dunn made a quick vertical reverse that put him in position to close and fire a climbing deflection shot at the Tony. When he was at 300 yards he fired a one second, 40 degree shot that caused black smoke to trail back along the fuselage. The Tony rolled out enough to allow Dunn to cut his throttle and fire a two second, 20 degree burst from 250 yards that exploded into the cockpit. The Tony continued ahead and Dunn cut his throttle and fired another two second burst into its tail that finished it for his first of two victories.

40FS

The 40FS dispatched 12 P-47s on a fighter sweep over Los Negros and arrived before the bombers. After flying over the area for 15 minutes at 13,000 feet, two bandits were spotted at 1 o'clock high at 14,000 feet. Wingman, 1Lt. Jack Gautreaux, called them out to his Flight Leader who lost them from view when they dove away. Gautreaux dove after them and one went into a cloud at 7,000 feet while the other made a diving port turn but Gautreaux had trouble catching it and then realized he hadn't jettisoned his wing and belly tanks. Once he dumped them he closed and started firing at 20 degrees deflection until his gunsight malfunctioned. He continued to fire and got hits that hit the wing and exploded inside the cockpit for his only victory.

**26 November 1944: Japanese Commandos Attack Barauen Airfields**

On 17 November, the U.S. Army 7th Division carried out a series of attacks on strong enemy positions in the steep hills west of Barauen, nine miles west of the airdrome and bivouac site. These attacks were successful and by the next day the enemy had retreated several miles into the hills but it was necessary to relieve the beleaguered 7th Division after the attack and elements of the 11th Airborne were transferred into the perimeter on 20 November. By 22 November the Japanese began to move to recapture or destroy the major airfields at Tacloban and Dulag. Construction had begun on three new airfields west of Dulag: San Pablo, seven miles west of Dulag; Bayug, eight miles west; and Buri, nine miles west and north. These three fields were in the vicinity of Barauen, defended by the 11th Airborne. The Japanese planned an initial airborne attack on the three airfields around Barauen to disrupt American forces and to destroy aircraft and installations. The Japanese would then follow this attack with three more nights of parachute drops in the area that would be coordinated with attacks by their ground forces to retake the three airfields. Simultaneously, the airfields at Tacloban and Dulag would be subjected to air strong attacks.

Gen. Suzuki, commanding the 35th Army on Leyte, was to open an offensive to capture Barauen and to destroy the facilities at Dulag and Tacloban; code-named the *WA Operation*. In support of the *WA* offensive the Japanese had flown almost 100 sorties on the morning of 24 November; attacking airfields, anchorages, and shipping in Leyte Gulf. Halsey's carrier group endured frenzied attacks from the Kamikazes but with four carriers hit and damaged, Halsey was forced to temporarily withdraw from the battle area. Kenney had just arrived at Tacloban on the 24th when 40 Japanese aircraft appeared for their second attack of the day. Although the Japanese destroyed six aircraft on the ground and damaged another five, the raid was costly to the Japanese as Thunderbolts of the 348FG shot down 33 enemy aircraft losing three while AA gunners claimed another eight. Three 5FC fighters were lost in combat. The Japanese air offensive continued for four days while the 5AF attacked the convoys attempting to supply Ormoc, on the west coast of Leyte, only 27 miles due west of Dulag.

On 26 November, to initiate the *WA* offensive, four Japanese transport planes took off from Lipa and headed to Leyte. On board were teams of demolition specialists, armed with explosives to destroy American aircraft and airfield installations at the airfield complex in the vicinity of Barauen. However, only one of these transports reached their target and attempted to land at Buri. As it attempted to land AA ripped into the transport and it crashed, killing all on board. The other three transports could not locate their target and chose to crashland in the water just south of Dulag. American units in the area thought the crashing aircraft were friendly and began rescue operations but came under fire. In the counter attack, two of the transports were destroyed but at least 30 fully equipped men with demolitions did get ashore but all were hunted down and killed before they did any real damage. A document was found on a body in the crash at Buri which described the upcoming enemy offensive and the plans for an attack by paratroopers. The next day the Fighter Groups were placed on a general alert and all personnel were to be armed at all times.

**27 November 1944: 475FG/431FS/432FS**

431FS

1Lt. Louis DuMontier led four P-38s of White Flight from Dulag at 1135 to cover shipping east of Dulag. While they were climbing they observed AA fire from the ships west of the convoy and P-38s chasing two bogies at 10,000 feet but lost them as they headed into the clouds. DuMontier then saw two more bogies headed east but did not pursue them as there were three more bogies above and took evasive action. But the bogies were found to be P-47s and DuMontier then headed toward the area that he previously saw the two bogies. As he climbed over a cloud at 8,000 feet he saw two bogies and went into a fast shallow dive and caught them just before reaching Ormoc Bay. As the Flight closed, the bogies dove into the clouds but one broke into a clearing and DuMontier fired from 500 yards and got hits behind the cockpit that started it smoking and then trailed a sheet of flame as it dove toward the ground. DuMontier dropped his dive flaps and gave the Jack a final burst and it inverted and spiraled into the ground for his first of three victories.

432FS

0815 Patrol

Capt. Paul Lucas led four White Flight P-38s at 0815 on a patrol of the Dulag. 2Lt. Robert Koles left the flight early with a blown engine and 2Lt. Lakin Parlett moved up to the #3 position behind Lucas' Wingman, Capt. Richard Kiick. The mission was uneventful until 1055 when the flight was letting down to land from 15,000 feet about 10 miles from base. Seven Zeros attacked from 13,000 feet and Lucas put his flight into a tight Lufbery and climbed toward the Zeros which were also circling. Lucas attacked the last Zero but broke off when he saw Lt. Parlett with three Zeros on his tail. Lucas turned sharply inside and tried to drive the Zeros off and chased after the last one. He closed to 50 yards and fired setting it on fire. The flames spread from the back of the cockpit to the wing tanks with a violent explosion but somehow its pilot managed to bail out. The victory made Lucas an ace. While Lucas was chasing the Zeros on Parlett's tail, Parlett saw two Zeros in position for a 90 degree deflection shot and pulled in tight and fired a long burst and shot one down for his only victory. When he looked around, Parlett saw he still had two Zeros on his tail and Split-S'd away. In the combat Parlett's fighter had been hit by three 20mm shells and numerous bullets. There was a large hole in his starboard wing flap and smaller holes in his elevator and stabilizer. Parlett was able to trim the damaged controls and landed safely despite a flat tire.

**Capt. Paul Lucas** scored two victories to become an ace. (AFAA)

1050 Patrol

2Lt. George Beatty led four Red Flight P-38s off Dulag Strip at 1050 with 2Lt. Robert Schuh as his Wingman, 2Lt. Henry Toll and his Element Leader and, F/O Laurence Dowler as his #4. At 1130 two Zeros and a Jill were seen flying NW at 9,000 feet. Beatty maneuvered the flight into attack position with Beatty and Schuh taking the Jill and the Second Element one Zero. Beatty dove on the Jill and fired a 45 degree deflection shot from 150 yards and got hits on its cockpit and nacelle. The Jill banked sharply left but Beatty followed and overran it. Schuh then took an 80 degree deflection shot at the Jill but was unable to keep turning with the Jill, or Beatty and lost the Flight. Meanwhile, Beatty had to swing around quickly and fired a low deflection shot getting many hits on the cockpit and wing roots. The Jill burst into flames and while Beatty followed the flamed died out and the Jill glided toward the shipping in Tacloban Harbor and crashed into the water for Beatty's third and last victory of the war.

Meanwhile, Toll and Dowler saw a lone bogie at 3 o'clock, slightly low and descended to investigate. Toll turned 180 toward it and ID'd it as a Zero and opened fire at 700 yards at 30 degrees deflection getting hits on its wing roots and cockpit. Toll found himself to be overtaking the target too quickly and had to skid side to side, taking short bursts, most of which hit the Zero. As Toll overtook the wounded Zero he saw it descending into a cloud at 2,000 feet. Dowler reported that he saw the Zero crash to confirm Toll's third and last victory. Toll encountered hydraulic trouble and returned to base. After Dowler saw Toll's Zero crash, he saw another Zero about 2,000 yards away and turned into it. Dowler fired and thought that he had gotten several hits before it went into the clouds. Dowler followed and when they were in a clearing Dowler got some more hits from dead astern at 300 yards. The Zero began a dive toward the shipping in the harbor and Dowler continued to follow; firing on it until it crashed into the water. Dowler then saw another bogie headed north about 4,000 yards to the east and 200 yards slightly below. As Dowler closed to 400 yards after it, the enemy pilot pulled up into a cloud. Dowler dropped combat flaps and dive brakes and followed the enemy into the cloud on the same course. As they exited the cloud, Dowler saw the Zero only 100 feet below to starboard. Dowler dropped his nose and fired into its wing and the Zero pilot Split-S'd, giving another P-38 a below a short burst as the Zero turned toward the clouds. Dowler followed and fired a 60 degree deflection from 200 yards that hit the Zero as it inverted into the clouds head down at 30 degrees. Schuh confirmed Dowler's second of four career victories. (Note: Not all sources credit Dowler with this second victory, *i.e.* Olynyk). With no more enemy aircraft in the area red Flight returned to base.

**28 November 1944: 475FG/432FS/433FS**

432FS

Col. Charles MacDonald led a patrol of four P-38s from Tacloban at 0630 on a shipping patrol over Leyte Gulf. MacDonald had 2Lt. Jack Shelton on his wing and 2Lt. Calvin Anderson and Wingman 1Lt. Austen Morris as his Second Element. After an hour of patrolling the Air Controller called bogies over Ormoc at 17-18,000 feet. As they climbed and reached 14,000 feet off Apalo Point, Ormoc Bay, two Zeros dove on them. MacDonald turned into one and fired head on but missed. As the dogfight intensified; Morris described it as "like a free for all with single P-38s after one Nip from all angles." MacDonald closed and fired a 30 degree deflection shot astern of a Zero. Its pilot began to climb and MacDonald hit the Zero again. A parachute opened while the Japanese pilot was still in his fighter and pulled him out. The victory was MacDonald's 17th.

433FS

1Lt. William Richmond led five Red Flight P-38s off Tacloban at 1545 to cover bombers attacking a Japanese convoy heading for Ormoc Bay. At 1615, while flying at 11,000 feet, he spotted four enemy fighters about five miles off Carmasa Island at 2 o'clock and 2,000 feet below. As Red Flight dove on them at 4 o'clock, the first enemy element sped ahead of its second element at full throttle and made a steep starboard turn which caused Richmond to break off his attack. Richmond then climbed away as the second two Oscars came in from behind. Richmond's Second Element Leader made a steep pass at the first two Oscars without result and Richmond called him to rejoin but his guns had jammed and he and the second element Wingman returned to base. Richmond and Richards made a pass at the second Oscar but broke off when they flew into the clouds. They then circled behind a group of American bombers and climbed to 15,000 feet above two other flights of P-38s and headed toward the Japanese convoy which could not be seen under the overcast. Once over the area that he assumed that the bombers were attacking the enemy convoy, Richmond dropped to 8,000 feet and spotted a lone Oscar above, flying just below the overcast. Richmond climbed above the overcast to get the altitude advantage for an attack but only got glimpses of the Oscar below and finally lost sight of it. Several minutes later this Oscar again appeared out of the overcast at 2 o'clock and 1,000 feet above. Richmond went into a gentle dive to 150 yards astern and fired a long burst and it fell to port in flames and spun into the water off Apale Point at the entrance to Ormoc Bay for Richmond's only victory claim of the war.

**Maj. John Davis**, former 40FS CO and 49FG Ops Deputy, was flying Bong's P-38 when it crashed. (AAF)

**28 November 1944: 49FG/7FS**

For the next several days the Japanese did not return to Tacloban where they had lost several aircraft. The 49ers returned to Ormoc's north coast on a mid afternoon weather reconnaissance and search to the for the next expected reinforcement convoy. Black Sheep Ops Exec Aschenbrener came upon three Tonys patrolling through the cloud deck at 5,000 feet. The enemy fighters quickly dove into the clouds and Aschenbrener searched over the area until one of the Tonys re-emerged. Before it could disappear again, Aschenbrener quickly dove behind the target and fired from dead astern at 300 yards and it caught fire, rolled over, and fell in an inverted dive into the clouds for Aschenbrener's eighth victory.

Later, P-38 #42 stalled on take off and became a blazing wreck. Number 42 was Bong's aircraft and word quickly spread that Bong had died. Kenney's staff called to confirm the report but the downed fighter had been flown by Ops Deputy Maj. John Davis.

**28 November 1944: 418 NFS**

Capt. Carroll Smith took off at 0230 in a P-38J for a searchlight cooperation patrol and climbed to 25,000 feet. At 0406 a Red Alert was called and enemy fighters were reported at 22,000 feet about 25 miles away. Smith remained at 25,000 feet until the lights picked up a "Nip" on a northerly course at about 16-18,000 feet. The Controller released Smith but as he closed the searchlights had just lost the enemy. However, Smith made one pass at the enemy which was flying at 350-400 mph and opened fire at 14,000 feet at 300 yards at 500 IAS. Smith's burst hit the enemy's wing but he observed no serious damage and was credited with a probable. Smith recovered from his high speed dive at 12,000 feet where he was directed to quickly climb as another Nip was in the area. Smith made a steep 180 climb which dropped his speed from 500 to 150 mph. Smith saw another enemy in the lights flying west and was cleared to attack. He opened fire at 16,000 feet at 300 yards and tore pieces off the tail and fuselage. He fired a second burst at 150 yards and saw hits on the wing roots. A third long burst hit the wing roots; exploding the Betty for his third victory.

**2Lt. Robert Pew** shot down a Zero for his only victory of the war. (AAF)

**1Lt. Owen Wolf** (left) with 1Lt. Dorrie Jones claimed his second of 2½ victories. (AAF)

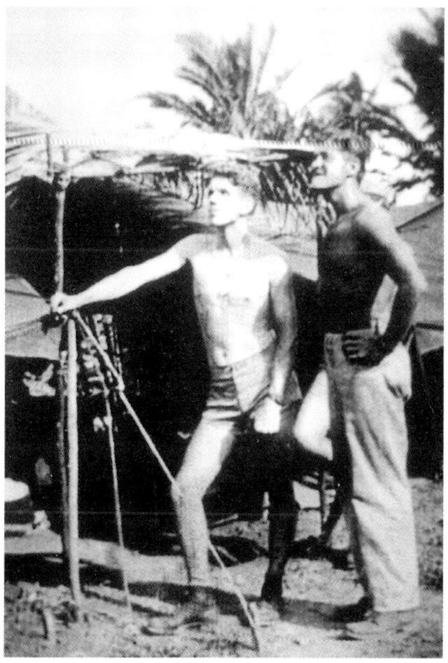

**1Lt. Wade Lewis** was credited with his only victory. (AAF)

**28 November 1944: 421NFS**

On 28 November 1Lt. Owen Wolf was leading four P-61s of "D" Flight on a PT Boat escort mission covering them from Panaon Straight to Baybay. The flight consisted of pilots Wolf, 2Lt. Robert Pew, 1Lt. Hoke Smith and 2Lt. Carl Bjorum. At 1735, Wolf's Flight was flying at 1,000 feet looking for a bogey as directed by GCI when they got a call from GCI of bogeys at about 1 o'clock high at about five or six miles. Wolf initially saw two or three fighters above at some distance away flying in and out of the cumulus clouds. There was a formation of six Zeros and a Hamp flying in trail formation at about 7,500 feet at about the 10 o'clock position from the P-61s. When they saw the Americans they immediately went into a steep climb, perhaps, mistaking them for twin-boomed P-38s. The P-61s also went into a steep climb after them. They soon out climbed the enemy until the Zeros were only about 300 feet above, turning from port to starboard. At this steep climb angle no American pilot was able to get a shot with the 20 mm cannons except Wolf's fighter. Wolf's crew for the mission was R/O 2Lt. Byron Allain and gunner S/Sgt. Emil Weishar who destroyed the Hamp with his turret .50 calibers using an adept deflection shot placing his tracers into the fighter's cockpit, causing it to catch fire, explode, and crash into the ground. The other enemy fighters came around to make a slight diving passes which put them in range of turret gunner Weishar who shot down a second Zero as did 2Lt. Robert Pew's turret gunner, S/Sgt. Ralph McDaniel, who destroyed another Zero making this diving pass. 2Lt. Carl Bjorum's P 61 met the diving Zeros, and he waited for his R/O, 2Lt. Robert Williams, in the turret to begin firing, but fortunately the other three Black Widow turrets were firing and shot down two Zeros while the other broke off (Bjorum later found that the turret circuit breakers had not been reset after their last servicing).

The remaining Japanese fighters then went into turning climbs and attacked the P-61s from the 6 o'clock position. One came in on 1Lt. Hoke Smith's tail, and 2Lt. Robert Bremer, the R/O, noted that the guns in the enemy's port wing were not working. This may have saved the Black Widow, as Bremer also noticed tracers from the right wing firing past his gondola and took over control of the turret from the gunner, Sgt. James Pilling. Bremer put a steady burst into the Zeke, destroyed the attacking enemy fighter while the remaining fighters turned and fled. Shortly after the enemy had broken away, Pew reported that he had lost an engine and had feathered it and Wolf called the flight to return to base; completing the Squadron's best day of the war with four of its 13 total victories.

**29 November 1944: 49FG/9FS**

Flight Leader 1Lt. Wade Lewis led eight Lightnings of White Flight on a sunrise vector to Ormoc. Once over the target at 15,000 feet, no enemy aircraft came up and Lewis took his flight further north. But as they turned away from Ormoc, two Zeros came out of the overcast and made an ineffectual rear quarter attack. The AAF flight turned aggressively into the attack and Lewis closed to within 100 yards and destroyed one. Element Leader 1Lt. Warren Curton cut off the enemy Wingman who tried to out turn into Lewis who put slugs into the Zero's engine and the enemy pilot bailed out. As Lewis and Curton climbed back to safety they were bounced by nine diving Tonys. The two Americans turned into the Japanese breaking up their attack and then made several high speed passes from head on, each hitting a Tony with deflection shots but were credited with a damaged (Lewis) and probable (Curton) to go with Lewis' only victory and Curton's fourth.

**29 November 1944: 348FG/460FS**

On 29 November 16 460FS Thunderbolts took off at 0815 to attack a convoy north of the Camotes Islands. One Thunderbolt had problems and its pilot aborted his take off and landed in the water. The P-47s continued at 6,500 feet toward their target, and the formation was just completing its bomb run at 0920 when 2Lt. Thomas Sheets saw a lone Oscar behind and to the left. Sheets jettisoned his remaining bomb and climbed in the direction of the Japanese fighter. The Oscar saw Sheets coming toward him and started to dive away to the west. Sheets' P-47 could out dive an Oscar anytime, anywhere and drew into range and fired several short bursts. Sheets saw hits over the enemy plane which went into a steep dive to crash and explode in the water east of Cebu for Sheet's first of three victories. 2Lt. Robert Smith and 1Lt. Lynn Parson strafed a destroyer and Smith's fighter either hit the destroyer masts or was shot down by AA fire and crashed and he was killed.

**30 November 1944: 49FG/8FS**

While the Japanese were reforming to meet the invasion 8FS Red Flight Leader, 1Lt. Thomas Holstein, led four P-38s on an early morning search mission over the Comotes Island. The Controller called bogies in the vicinity of Ormoc Bay and they headed that way at 10,000 feet when Holstein's Wingman called a bogey at 7 o'clock. Holstein identified the bogey as a Dinah and turned after it and caught the speedy Dinah at 11,000 feet and fired at 10 degrees deflection; setting its left wing on fire for his second and last victory (plus three damaged claims).

**30 November 1944: 348FG/460FS**

At 1450 16 P-47s of the 460FS took off to bomb shipping at Port Carmen on the east coast of Cebu and half an hour later, flying at 13,000 feet, the P-47s started on their routine bombing runs. The P-47s were surprised when six Oscars dove through the third flight and shot down 2Lt. Perry Tubre who crashed into the sea with his P-47. All P-47s jettisoned their bombs and reacted quickly and split into elements and flights. 1Lt. DeWitt Searles was leading the first flight and turned to climb after the Oscars above and ahead. For some reason the Oscar pilots did not vary their course and even when Searles reached their altitude they only attempted a shallow dive to port. Searles followed on the lead Oscar's tail and fired a 45 degree deflection shot, getting many hits on the canopy and fuselage. Searles watched while the Oscar dove vertically trailing smoke and flames, disappearing into a cumulus layer at 3,000 feet. After the initial attack, 2Lt. Samuel Denmark, flying in the last flight, lost the Oscars in the clouds but saw another Oscar at 3 o'clock (right) and 500 feet below. Denmark and the Oscar were headed in the same southerly direction and Denmark was able to close to within 100 yards. The two were only about 200 feet above the water when the P-47 opened fire and pieces of cowling ripped off and it rolled over and crashed into Bohol Strait. All the other Oscars disappeared from the area and the P-47s returned to base. It was the first time since its arrival on Leyte that the Japanese prevented the 460FS from completing a bombing mission. 2Lt. Perry Tobre was reported as KIA.

By the end of November the 460FS' 10 victories since they arrived had almost equaled the entire total of the other three 348FG squadrons for the past six months. However, on 30 November the 340$^{th}$ and 341$^{st}$ Squadrons landed on Tacloban and would end the 460$^{th}$'s monopoly in the Philippines.

**Late November 1944: Situation**

As a consequence of the air battles fought during November, Fifth Air Force fighters based in the Philippines enjoyed a decided supremacy over the hard-pressed Japanese. The 49$^{th}$ Fighter Group had converted to the P-38 and had a total of well over 500 aerial victories by the middle of the month. The 80FS of the 8FG had taken the lead as high-scoring squadron in SWPA with over 200 victories until the 9FS regained the honors for good later in November.

During November the Americans were established on Leyte and the Japanese were persevering to make one more desperate stand. The pilots of the Fifth Fighter Command had scored momentous victories over the Japanese air forces over Leyte; greatly aided by the ground crews men that kept the fighters flying despite untold hardships. The Leyte airfields were problematic as of the five strips on the island, only Dulag and Tacloban were entirely operational. Bayug was a fair-weather fighter base but at the end of November a short steel plank surface was installed there. Both San Pablo and Buri airdromes had to be abandoned when the rainy season began.

During the night of 28 November another Japanese convoy came down from Manila covered by poor weather but the reinforcements were attacked and two of the ships were sunk by USN torpedo boats. However, supplies and men were unloaded at Ormoc from several ships before they came under attack from P-40s and P-47s the next day. Although their forces were not built up to the required strength, the Japanese were determined to begin their scheduled offensive to defeat American forces on Leyte.

# 3

# December 1944

**December 1944: Situation**

MacArthur's next major operation was scheduled for 5 December with a landing at San Jose on Mindoro Island, 150 miles due south of Manila. Once Mindoro was secured, airfields were to be promptly established to provide air cover and support for the landings on Luzon in early January. However, the slow development of the air strips on Leyte meant that there would a lack of air support for the Mindoro operation. Construction of the three air fields near Barauen had encountered so many problems that work on them was reduced and only light liaison and communications aircraft were using the Barauen fields at this critical time. Instead, a concerted effort was made to construct a new all-weather field on the beach at Tanauan, 11 miles north of Dulag. The engineer units that were to go to Mindoro were diverted for several days to assist in the construction effort at Tanauan. On 1 December Gen. Krueger, Commander of U.S. forces on Leyte, received a welcome reprieve that would delay the Mindoro landings for 10 days, until 15 December.

Meanwhile, the Japanese continued their strong night attacks on the Leyte beachhead with could not be countered by AAF night fighters which were unable to close on the enemy raiders because their speeds were about equal. On 3 December, a Marine night fighter squadron, flying F6Fs, were brought into Tacloban from the Solomons. The next day five more Marine fighter squadrons arrived equipped with their imposing new F4U Corsairs

**December 1944**

**Japanese Fighter Units in the Philippines**

After their retreat from New Guinea the Japanese air forces had been decimated and the Japanese desperately needed to reorganize their air defenses to confront the American invasion of the Philippines. They quickly re-equipped and remanned three Oscar units, the 1st, 11th, and 22nd Sentais which were integrated into the 2nd Hiko Shidan which would take part in most of the combat in the Philippines through December, 1944.

The 1st Sentai also appeared over the Philippines after it had converted to Ki-84 Frank fighters in the spring of 1944 and deployed 20 fighters there by the end of October. The Sentai's pilots had little flying time in their new fighter at Clark Field and by November the Sentai was down to only three operational fighters. When replacement fighters arrived at the Sentai they were flown by scarcely trained pilots who were easy prey for the veteran American fighter units.

The 11th Sentai took heavy losses just before it was deployed to Luzon at the time of the Leyte Invasion and by the first of November it was almost completely annihilated and was withdrawn to reconstitute. Because of the shortage of pilots, poorly trained reservist pilots were employed to face overpowering American air power which would support the invasion of Leyte and Mindoro. After escorting suicide planes on the 20 December attack on the American invasion convoy for the remainder of the year the 11th was engaged in many night attacks on Mindoro with steady losses and finally in January the 11th was withdrawn to Formosa.

**New U.S. Fighter Units in the Philippines**

421NFS

December 1944 changed the Squadron's history as MacArthur was displeased with the dawn and dusk protection afforded by his night fighters. The 421NFS and its P-61s experienced problems which encouraged the Japanese continue their night bombing attacks. The principal reasons for poor night fighter support included: the GCI station's limited search range; the lack of spare parts; poor operating conditions; and the limited number of P-61s available to the 421NFS. The 421NFS record for November documented that it had shot down seven Japanese aircraft, along with three damaged and a probable which was much better than the other night fighter squadrons in the Southwest Pacific during the month: the 6 NFS had one kill; the 418th had three; and the 419th none. MacArthur maintained that the P-61s were not able to contend with the Oscar and newer version Zero fighters that the Japanese employed over the Philippines. When MacArthur approached Nimitz the 421NFS record in their battles with Oscars and other Japanese fighters was at 11 kills and 0 losses and seemingly were recently coming into their own. An argument made by one Naval Liaison to MacArthur was that the Hellcat had a longer range, higher speed, and folding wings that could save valuable space on the crowded Tacloban strip. Although the Hellcats did have a slightly longer range (1,085 vs. 1,010 miles with internal tanks only) and slightly higher top speed (376 vs. 366 mph) than the P-61s, the patrol and base protection missions that they would fly at night would not require this features. Also, the F6F-5N/E night fighter version of the Hellcat did not have folding wings. As for folding wings, this particular model of the Hellcat did not have this ability. The upshot of the argument made by the 421st and most of the other night fighter squadrons was that the experience of the RAF and Luftwaffe night fighters over Europe was wholly lost to the upper echelon leadership in the SWPA who had the "day fighter mentality" and had little or no actual understanding of the deployment and utilization of night fighter forces.

VMF(N)-541, the "Bateyes," was scheduled to arrive at Tacloban on 3 December for a period of two weeks, while the 421NFS would send a detachment of its aircraft to Peleliu for some air operations and "R&R" for the same amount of time but the actual time was nearly six weeks. The Japanese on Peleliu fought to the death and had been buried in mass

The P-61s of the **421NFS** experienced problems while at Tacloban and were replaced by Marine VMF(N)-541 Hellcats. (AAF)

graves and the island had a foul odor and millions of flies. Thousands and thousands of land crabs were scuttling everywhere at night and sand flea bites caused the men to button their collars and tie off their shirt and pant cuffs. Air operations consisted of flying regular alerts against an enemy that was long gone and occasional test flights.

Conversely, while at Tacloban VMF(N)-541 was credited with 924 combat hours, 22 enemy aircraft shot down, and 5 more destroyed on the ground. When the Marine Night Squadron left Tacloban MacArthur earnestly informed Nimitz that they had performed "magnificently" and honored them with the only AAF Distinguished Unit Citation awarded to a non-AAF unit during World War II. Although VMF(N)-541's accomplishments were admirable; none of their kills were made under radar control and were dawn and dusk missions, not night time, so MacArthur's wish for night protection was unfulfilled as Japanese aircraft, in fact, continued to bomb Tacloban at night with VMF(N)-541 there or not. On 11 January VMF(N)-541 returned to Peleliu and the 421st NFS returned to Tacloban.

348FG

The pilots of the three squadrons had waited on Noemfoor for the development of new strips on Leyte. On 1 December the 342FS arrived from Morotai and lost five fighters and three pilots in brutal weather but, nonetheless, flew its first mission the next day. The 340th was ready for its first mission on the 11th and the 341st on the 7th. In order of prevalence the Group flew routing patrol missions, shipping coverage, attacks on airdromes (Visayan, Southeastern Luzon, and Clark Field), ground support, air combat, and attacks on enemy shipping.

3rd Air Commando Group

A new Group, the 3rd Air Commando, arrived at Dulag on 1 December from the U.S. equipped with new P-51s. The Group also included two Liaison Squadrons and one Troop Carrier Squadron which remained at Nadzab.

71TRG/82TRS

The Squadron flew its first P-51 mission in the Pacific and destroyed three barges. Squadron leader, Capt. William Shomo, taxied into the back of a truck on landing but escaped unhurt.

**December 1944: Air Operations**

**1 December 1944: 475FG**

Popular 11 victory ace, Capt. Francis Lent, was killed in a flying accident when he crashed into the ocean off Lae while flying a F-6D.

**2 December 1944: 475FG/431FS**

At 1600 1Lt. Enrique Provencio led four Lightnings (Wingman, 2Lt. James Barnes, and second element of 1Lt. Kenneth Hart and Wingman, 2Lt. Harold Gray) of Green Flight on a local patrol. At 1705 while patrolling at 6,000 feet the flight saw a bogie headed west at 3,000 feet. Provencio chased after the Val which swung 180 degrees, attempting a head on pass on him. Provencio fired at it from about 15 degrees head on but missed. He made a large starboard circle and the Val crossed in front of him with Hart's P-38 closing on its tail. Provencio followed and saw Hart get "excellent" hits on the Val's tail before breaking off to the right. Provencio broke off to the left which put him dead astern of the Val. The Val pilot went into evasive action and its rear gunner fired as Provencio closed. As Provencio fired Hart cut in and fired and hit its fuselage and gunner and the Val nosed over at 2,000 feet in an inverted loop and crashed and exploded on its back near the shore about 20 miles south of Ormoc for Hart's fourth victory.

**2-5 December 1944: Situation**

Except for 1Lt. Kenneth Hart's Val victory on the 2nd; no other enemy contacts were encountered until the 5th as the Japanese opened their final defense of their stranded Leyte garrison. During the morning of 5 December, the USN Seventh Fleet assault ships moved out of the huge fog bank that shrouded the Surigao Straits and then turned north into the open sea for

Popular 11 victory ace **Capt. Francis Lent** was killed in a flying accident. (AAF)

the assault on Ormoc Bay. Throughout the morning, the USAAF and USN aircraft flew over the convoy as it entered the Camote Sea.

**5 December 1944: 475FG/431FS/433FS**

431FS

1Lt. John Tilley led four P-38s of Daddy Special Flight at 1650 to patrol over shipping in Surigao Strait. The Flight consisted of Tilley, his Wingman, 2Lt. Mortimer Olster, and the second element 1Lt. John Ballard and Wingman, 2Lt. Douglas Thropp. The Controller sent them to the convoy which was supposed to be under attack but when they arrived there were no enemy fighters but the Controller told them that the bandits were headed west back home and Tilley headed west at high speed to cut them off before they reached their base. He then turned east sweeping over their probable course and was just east of Cebu Town when Ballard saw a lone bandit above them at 2,000 feet headed west. Tilley led the flight into steep climb ing turn toward the Oscar but the enemy pilot saw them and firewalled and tried to out climb them. Tilley firewalled his fighter and closed but as he got within range the Oscar peeled down to port and Tilley followed about one third of the way down getting some hits from 60 degrees dead astern. The skilled veteran Japanese pilot zigzagged up a dead end canyon in the mountains west of Cebu Town; trying to "auger in" the Americans by pulling up at the last minute. The Special Flight was unable to get any good shots but finally Olster made a quarter attack from the rear and the Oscar rolled over and crashed into a hillside for his only victory.

433FS

1Lt. John Purdy led four Lightnings off at 1620 for a patrol of the Albuers-Plaridel area. At 1700, Purdy's Wingman, 2Lt. Clifford Ettien, called out a single bogie at 8 o'clock near the deck heading toward Cebu at 8,000 feet. The Flight chased the bogie but lost it at the Cebu coast. After turning 360 at 8,000 feet over Cebu Town they saw six Vals heading toward Cebu and allowed them to pass and lose altitude. Purdy made a pass on a lone Val flying at 500 feet and fired a long burst into its engine which smoked momentarily and the Val exploded. Purdy immediately fired a short burst on a second Val from 250 yards behind and 40 degrees deflection and it rolled over and crashed into the ground. Purdy fired 90 degrees on a third Val but saw not hits and had to break off when eight to ten Oscars appeared overhead. Purdy decided to head back to base but his #4 man called enemy fighters starting a pass at 6 o'clock. Purdy turned his flight 180 degrees in a string formation and made a head on pass at the lead enemy fighter and after only a short burst at him, the Japanese leader turned away. Purdy again tried to lead his flight back to base and again his #4 called another enemy attack from 6 o'clock. Purdy again turned 180 into it and the Japanese again broke away; this time without Purdy having to fire a shot. Purdy was not attacked on his third attempt to return home with two victories; his first since mid-May.

**1Lt. John Purdy** was credited with victories #2 and 3. (AFAA)

**5 December 1944: 49FG/9FS**

Morning Mission

At 1100, 9FS 1Lt. Charles McElroy and his Blue Flight wingmen F/O Henry Hammett and 2Lt. Ernest Ambort arrived over the leading destroyers on the convoy's port flank and relieved 1Lt. Warren Curton's patrolling White Flight. Only minutes after White Flight departed, a bomb exploded near the bow of one of the American ships and McElroy saw a Val hurrying west at wave top level. The Blue Wingmen dropped their belly tanks and peeled off after the escaping Val in a curving port dive when McElroy saw seven Vals in a sprawling formation descending out of the clouds over the Leyte coast. The P-38's immediately turned and dove from 7,000 to 3,500 feet into the descending enemy dive bombers and opened fire. McElroy broke hard starboard and fired head on through the Val formation. He hit a Val that began to glide toward the sea trailing smoke and McElroy followed the victim until it crashed.

Wingmen F/O Hammett and 2Lt. Ambort separated from McElroy when they pursued their own Vals. Ambort took one that was about to start its bomb run and attacked high from 90 degrees, firing a short burst and the Val exploded in front of Ambort who flew safely through the flames and debris. Ambort lost McElroy and joined Hammett who had chased the third Val that was closing in on a destroyer in the convoy's left flank. He shot it down from dead astern at 150 yards with a necessarily quick burst as he had to pull up so as not to hit the water. Hammett's victim aimed his flaming fighter at a destroyer and hit its bow. Hammett and Ambort climbed to search to the south for the separated McElroy but Ambort saw two unsuspecting bomb-carrying Oscars flying west at 3 o'clock high over the coast. The two Flying Knights turned under enemy and climbed up behind them at point blank range. Ambort fired a long burst into the enemy Leaders canopy and wing, knocking the aileron off before he could drop his bombs. Hammett fired at the other Oscar from dead astern into its cockpit and the Oscar started on fire and Ambort radioed Hammett to stop

**2Lt. Ernest Ambort** shot down a Val and Oscar to give him four victories. (AFAA)

**1Lt. Charles McElroy** shot down a Val for his third victory. (AAF)

**1Lt. John Curton** became an ace over Ormoc Bay. (AAF)

and "save his ammo." The triumphant wingmen located McElroy and the regrouped Blue Flight returned to base; McElroy with his fourth and last victory; Ambort with his two victories to make him an ace; and Hammett with his two victories which were his second and third and last.

Afternoon Mission
At 1600, 1Lt. Warren Curton's White Flight returned for its second convoy patrol of the day. During their patrol at 4,000 feet on the north flank of the convoy, the coastal fog extended farther over the ocean and limited visibility. When White Flight was notified of approaching aircraft, visibility was nil. Hoping for better visibility, Curton lead his flight in a circling orbit down to 1,000 feet, where he finally saw a Hamp speeding west directly over the USN ships which were firing a heavy AA barrage. Curton attacked but the Hamp escaped in the undercast before White Flight was in firing range. During their continued search White Flight became strung out and tail end 2Lt. Troy Smith was attacked from behind by a lone Zero. Smith broke away and Curton turned back toward the Zero which also broke off. The Japanese pilot tried to escape into a cloud bank over Duligan Point but the Lightning pilot easily caught up and the wounded Zero dove and aimed his fighter at a pair of PT boats in the bay. Curton fired a desperate long burst at the flaming Kamikaze, which finally missed the boats by only 50 yards. The victory was Curton's fifth and last to make him an ace.

**6 December 1944: *WA Operation***
The Japanese scheduled *WA Operation* D-Day for the early evening of 6 December but the 33rd Japanese Division, occupying the hills west of Barauen, prematurely attacked on the morning of the 6th which only placed U.S. forces on alert. The Japanese 3rd Parachute Regiment of the 2nd Parachute Brigade, at Angeles and Lipa Airdromes on Luzon, were ready to board transport aircraft for their scheduled airdrop on Leyte. However, the Japanese had so few transport aircraft that only one regiment at a time could be sent on the mission and the other two regiments had to be scheduled to make their drops on the next two nights. At about 1540 39 twin-engine Topsy transports left Angeles Field on Luzon loaded with paratroopers to be dropped on Leyte aircraft. To avoid detection they flew over the Visayas, passed around the southern tip of Leyte, and then flew north over Leyte Gulf. At sunset they turned inland near Dulag to follow a river that led to Barauen. To cover the parachute drop, about 36 enemy fighters and bombers attacked, bombing, and strafing the airfields causing light damage except at San Pablo, where a liaison plane was destroyed and the fuel dump set afire. As the enemy transports approached the drop zone, flying at 750 feet, and four were shot down by AA fire. Most of the paratroops were supposed to land on Buri Airdrome at 1840, with smaller groups assigned to capture Bayug and San Pablo Fields. In the confusion of the attack, caused by the darkness and heavy AA fire, most of the troops landed on San Pablo. Only about 60 paratroopers landed on Buri, including their Commander, while none landed on Bayug. Also, small contingents were to land at Dulag and Tacloban, and destroy aircraft, fuel and bomb dumps, and then dig in until killed; denying their use through 7 December. The paratroops were initially successful as they burned a dozen liaison planes and the fuel supply at San Pablo and took possession of the Strip at Buri, adjacent to Gen. Whitehead's 5th Air Force Headquarters. They were able to hold San Pablo until about noon on 8 December by which time Sixth Army troops had killed half of them and drove the rest west, where they joined with paratroops and a small group of infantry who had broken through to join them from the hills. The 463 paratroopers in the attack were virtually annihilated by 12 December and order was restored around Barauen.

A Japanese Tabby transport aircraft, which looked similar to the American C-47, slipped into Tacloban's traffic pattern in an attempt to land. It was reported that an English speaking Japanese pilot called for permission to land on the airstrip using a call sign of one of the P-38 units stationed there. The ruse failed and AA fire opened up on the enemy transport which swerved and skidded onto the beach parallel to the landing strip. It plowed between a PBY and a P-61 before hitting a grader and exploded. Two 421NFS enlisted men were hiding in a small slit trench when the plane exploded and a gasoline fire engulfed them. Both men ran into the ocean to extinguish their flaming clothing and were hospitalized with badly burned bodies. The transport had carried Japanese Marines, who intended to land and attack the field, but none survived the crash.

5th Air Force Headquarters was cut off for five days and Gen. Whitehead was trapped there until 10 December, when the Japanese infantry made a final attempt to link up with the paratroops east and north of Whitehead's HQ. They were repulsed but some of the fighting took place in the 5AF Headquarters area where HQ personnel killed 23 enemy soldiers but had two HQ defenders killed and seven wounded while some of the Headquarters buildings and tents were set on fire and destroyed.

At this time the 348th Group's P-47s were operating from Tacloban while the majority of its personnel were based inland near Burauen when 300 Japanese paratroopers landed less than a quarter mile away and cut the only road to the camp. For several days the camp was isolated and foxhole bound by the paratroopers to the east and the enemy patrols to the west. Two sentries of the 341FS were killed by an enemy patrol but the camp defense prevented a breakthrough.

While little damage was done, the enemy paratrooper's greatest achievement was to cause some anxiety and more alert sentries around the airfields for the next few nights. The enemy paratroopers were finally overwhelmed by infantry and tanks after three days fighting.

**6 December 1944: 475FG/431FS/432FS/433FS**
433FS
1Lt. Morton Ryerson with Wingman, 2Lt. George Gabik, Second Element Leader, 1Lt. Albert Coburn, and Wingman, 2Lt. Wesley Hulett, took off on an early morning cover for Allied shipping in the Surigao Strait. At 0845 the Possum flight was patrolling at 15,000 feet off Ponson Island and saw at least seven Jacks flying at 8,000 feet. Ryerson maneuvered his flight so it could make a slightly high dead astern attack. Ryerson made a pass on the second of three trailing Jacks. He surprised the enemy pilot who pulled up into Gabik's path. Gabik fired a long burst into its port wing and cockpit and it started to trail heavy black smoke which coated most of Gabik's windshield before it crashed for his only victory. Gabik rejoined Ryerson

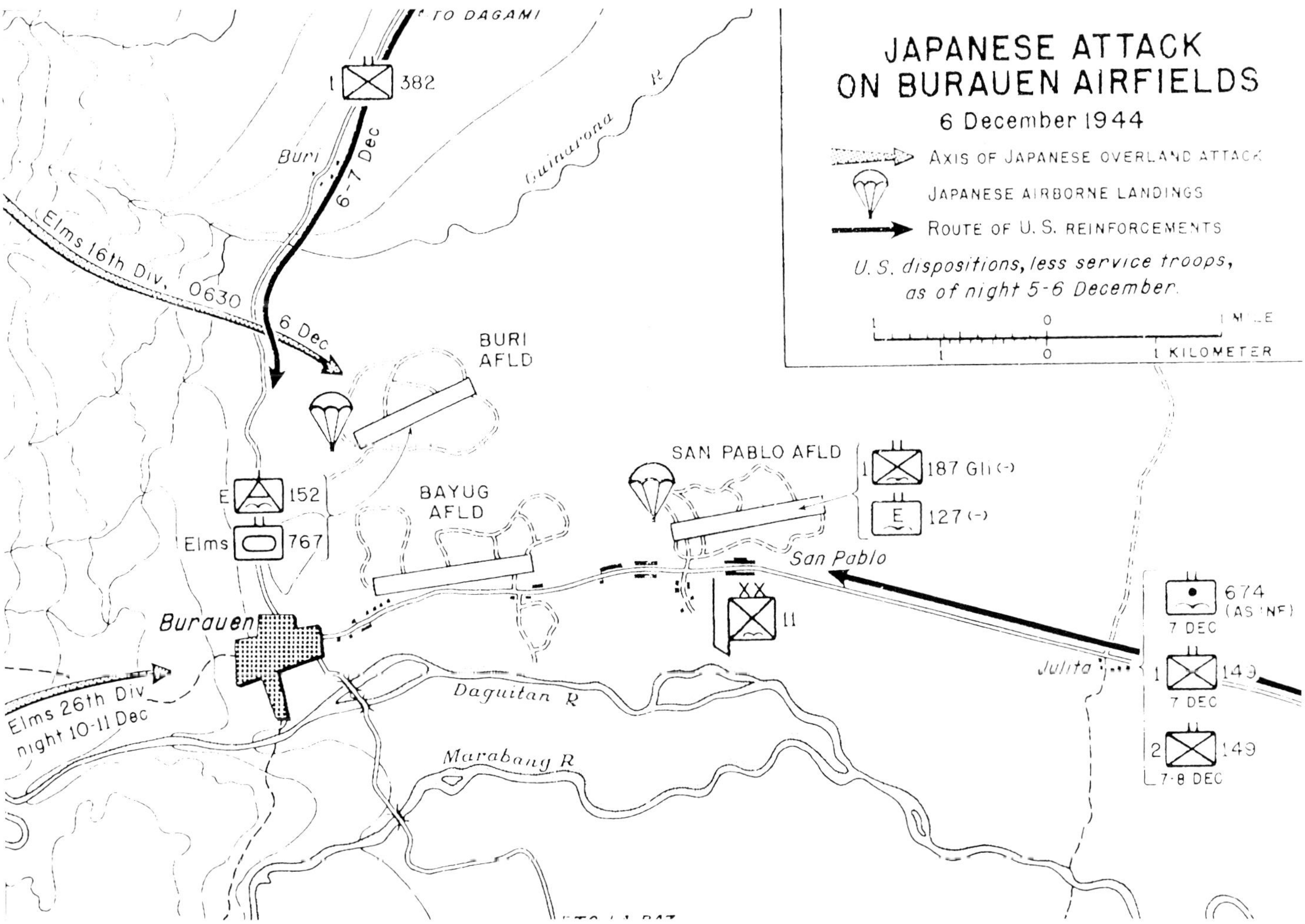


just as he was making a firing pass on another Jack; getting numerous hits on its fuselage but the Jack flew away as the two broke off for a probable claim for Ryerson. Due to his obscured windshield Gabik lost Ryerson and he tried to find his flight but ended up with an enemy fighter on his tail and took evasive action but was saved by another P-38 that chased it off his tail. This enemy fighter broke to port and pulled up head on into the path of Hulett who nosed over as the Jack turned into him. Hulett fired a long burst and the Jack caught fire but the enemy pilot made a desperate attempt to ram Hulett before diving into the water for Hulett's first victory. A Jack made a deflection shot at Gabik but had another P-38 on its tail and broke away. Gabik pulled up sharply to get a head on pass on his former pursuing Jack which was being overcome by the P-38 and Gabik had to avoid colliding with the Jack. Gabik joined Coburn who was making a pass on the Jack that had been on Hulett's tail. Coburn nosed over and took a 30 degree deflection shot getting hits on its cockpit and fuselage. Coburn continued to pursue and fired at 10 degrees from such close range that he had to pull up violently to avoid a collision. Coburn then made a climbing port turn and opened fire at 300 yards making hits on its wings, engine, and cockpit. Pieces flew off the Jack that began to burn as it broke off toward the ground. He did not see its demise, as he saw a Jack trying to get on the tail of a P-38 directly in front and below him. Coburn increased his speed and then had to chop his throttles to avoid overrunning and opened fire on the unsuspecting Jack from 200 yards. The enemy pilot then responded with a steep dive for the deck but hit the water for Coburn's second victory of the day and only two of the war. Coburn was so low that he had to use his dive flaps to pull out just in time. Gabik had lost Coburn through his fouled windshield and radioed that he needed escort and Coburn and Ryerson appeared at his side and the three climbed to 15,000 feet where they continued the patrol before returning to base. Ryerson had conversed with Coburn and Gabik several times as they approached home with no indication of any problems before Ryerson crashed fatally three miles south of the field.

432FS

Escort

Eight 432nd P-38s of Red and White Flights were assigned to an escort for P-47s dive bombing the Talsiay area of the Negros Island. When the Clover flights arrived over the target at 1340 three enemy fighters were spotted. White Flight chased them under the clouds and lost them. 1Lt. Charles Ratajski's Blue Flight remained at 12,000 feet and about 10 minutes later a Jack was seen at 3 o'clock, slightly below. Ratajski made a pass as the Jack started to dive away. Ratajski closed to 200 yards and fired but then closed to 40-50 yards and fired again hitting the cockpit area and fuselage; tearing off pieces. Ratajski followed it as it descended smoking toward the water. He broke off and Element Leader Capt. Richard Kiick dove and fired "quite a few long bursts" that started it on fire. #4, F/O Laurence Dowler followed the doomed Jack and witnessed it to crash. Ratajski was awarded his fourth and last victory.

Patrol: Search & Rescue

Seven Clover P-38s, Red and Special Flights, led by 1Lt. George Beatty took off from Dulag at 1315 and headed for the southern end of Negros Island to

Veteran **Capt. William Gronemeyer** fell short of becoming an ace when he scored his fourth and last victory. (AAF)

**2Lt. Chester Parshall** claimed his only victory of the war. (AAF)

escort a PBY to Dipolong. The Lightnings circled the area for "quite some time" without contacting the Catalina. As the 432nd turned toward home at 1630 they spotted a Nick crossing their path at the southern tip of Cebu at 11 o'clock. The Beatty turned after the twin engine enemy fighter but began to fire from too far out of range as the Nick was headed for the safety of a distant cloud layer. The Nick accelerated and went into the clouds but soon reappeared and as Beatty closed the Nick's tail gunner fired and Beatty took a long burst getting hits and the tail gunner no longer fired. Beatty's ICR claims that his tracers "were spiraling" and that he broke off his attack and called his Wingman, 2Lt. Austin Morris. Morris ICR states that he began to overtake Beatty but made two or three more turns so that his Leader could get in several more shots at the Nick. "After holding off for awhile" (*e.g.* while Beatty missed) Morris then began shooting and fired from 10-15 degrees but missed and shortened his lead and began to get hits on its right engine and fuselage. Morris' next volley was fired from the left and hit the Nick's left nacelle and it snapped to port and spun into the ocean near Cebu Town for his only victory.

431FS

Capt. William Gronemeyer led four P-38s of White Flight from Dulag at 1300 to patrol shipping at Dinagat Sound which were vulnerable to Lily Kamikaze bombers that were flying on suicide missions on Navy ships that were sweeping the Surigao Straits for mines to insure the safe passage of an invasion convoy carrying the 77th Infantry Division that evening. White Flight consisted of Gronemeyer, his Wingman, 2Lt. Chester Parshall, and the second element of 1Lt. Christopher Herman and his Wingman, 2Lt. Harold Gray. They took up their patrol position at 7,000 feet over the convoy. The Controller called a Lily and gave a vector but White arrived too late as the Lily attacked and damaged a ship. As the Lily passed over the ship the Flight went after it. Gronemeyer fired at 250 yards and set its port engine on fire and the Lily was seen to crash for his fourth and last victory. The Flight returned to its patrol and was vectored and Herman called another bogie at 1 o'clock low and Gronemeyer turned to attack but the Lily pilot saw him and turned 180 degrees, jettisoned his bombs and tried to escape. Gronemeyer firewalled his Lightning and started after the Lily. As the Flight got farther away from the convoy, Gronemeyer sent Herman and Gray back to cover the convoy. Gronemeyer and Parshall continued after the Lily that had a 50 mile head start and finally caught up with it. Gronemeyer started to fire at the evading Lily and pieces fell off its port engine. Gronemeyer continued to fire as the Lily evaded and when he closed to finish it off he was only able to fire a few rounds before he ran out of ammunition. Parshall fired and got hits on the Lily's canopy and its pilot climbed to clear a hill as Parshall began to fire again and it banked to port and Parshall fired a long burst and its left engine flamed and the Lily hit the ground and exploded for Parshall's only victory. The task force left Leyte Gulf in the late evening of 6 December for Ormoc Bay on the northwestern coast of Leyte.

**6 December 1944: 348FG/460FS**

Eight P-47s of the 460FS took off at 0815 on a bombing mission to the Carolinas Airdrome in the Negros but they couldn't find this airdrome and bombed another which was thought to be Silay. At 0940, while flying at 15,000, feet F/O Howard Minnick, Element Leader of the Lead Flight, saw a Dinah approaching from the east at 10,000 feet. Minnick made a 180 degree diving turn but once he got into range astern of the Dinah, it went into a shallow, high speed turn. Minnick's .50s hit the right engine, setting it on fire and then hit the left engine which also caught fire. The Dinah went into a tight spiral and exploded about 2,000 above the ground for Minnick's first of two victories.

**6 December 1944: 35FG**

The 40FS sent out 16 P-47s to precede B-25s on a fighter sweep of the Cagayan, Del Monte, and Jacol Airdromes on Mindanao; an area which had not seen action since the first days of the war. Red Leader, Capt. William Strand, arrived over Del Monte at 1035 and 20 minutes later they were about to leave the area when a bogey was spotted flying on the deck. As Strand approached he saw the bogey was a torpedo carrying Jill. Strand made three level passes but the Jill was difficult to hit as it flew so close to the water. Finally, on his third pass he hit the tail gunner. Strand's Wingman, 2Lt. William Colsh, came up and also made a pass before Strand was able to finish the Jill off with a shallow dive and 30 degree shot for his first of four victories.

**6 December 1944: 49FG/7FS**

At dawn Capt. John Haher with wingmen 2Lt. William Thompson, element leader 1Lt. James Jarrell and Wingman 2Lt. Oliver Atchison were on a 7FS convoy patrol at 6,000 feet off Dinagat Island over the eastern Surigao Strait. They were alerted to a lone aircraft approaching from the north and spotted a Dinah at 12,000 feet and five miles away. The flight dropped their auxiliary tanks and raced toward the Dinah which they expected to withdraw. Instead, the Dinah dove toward the convoy trailed by Haher, who firewalled to 400 mph at 1,000 feet above the water. As he closed to maximum firing range he began to fire and continued to point blank, getting numerous hits but the Dinah kept flying. When Haher ran out of ammunition Jarrell and Atchison took over. Atchison fired and overran but Jarrell finally hit the port engine which began to smoke. Before Thompson could engage, the wounded Dinah slowly dipped to starboard until the wingtip hit a wave and it cart wheeled into a dramatic explosion to give Jarrell the first of his four victories.

**6 December 1944: 419NFS**

Pilot 1Lt. Robert Winslow, R/O F/O A.A. Grotzinger, and gunner Sgt. M.W. Ridenour encountered a Betty 15 north of Kaoe Airdrome. Winslow was credited with a probable at 0400.

**7 December 1944: Situation: Ormoc Landings**

Naval Plans

Once Navy was informed that the Ormoc invasion was to take place; the Mindoro operation was postponed and the shipping reserved for the Mindoro was allocated to the Ormoc force. R.Adm. Arthur Struble was given command of Task Group 78.3, which was to transport and land the 77th Division, and its supplies and equipment in the Ormoc Bay area and support the landing by naval gunfire by six destroyers. Struble divided his task group into six units with the landing to be made by five assault waves between the Baod and Bagonbon Rivers. The northern half of the beach was called *White I* and the southern half *White II*.

Air Plans

The Fifth Air Force would provide both day and night air cover for the passage of the assault convoy to the target, for the landings, and for the return convoy. It was estimated that on 5 December, for the voyage to the target, 17 night fighter sorties and 72 day fighter sorties would be required. Protection would also be furnished by the bombers, and 46 aircraft would be available on call for strikes against enemy installations and targets of opportunity, as well as for special missions.

On the day of the landings, the air support would be accelerated. There would be 19 night fighter sorties and 96 day fighter sorties; 10 flights of 40 bombers to cover the beachhead; six flights of 24 bombers to cover the return of the assault convoy; and 11 night fighters to cover the LST and main assault convoys, the beachhead, and the return convoy. Also available would be 16 bombers for interception or additional cover for the beachhead and convoy; 24 P-47s for interception, ground support, and attacks against enemy shipping or targets of opportunity; 16 P-40s for ground strikes; and 34 F4Us for cover or interception.

**Ormoc** Landings. (U.S. Army)

**6 December 1944: Landings at Ormoc Bay**

The Landings

The 77th Division continued to assemble its troops on Tarragona Beach, on the east coast of Leyte, and during the night of 5 December the loading of supplies and equipment on the landing ships started but the loading was slowed by frequent air alerts. The convoy would be unable to remain in the landing area more than two hours and consequently there was no attempt to load bulk supplies, as they would take too long to unload. Thus, all supplies and equipment (highest priority to ammunition, water, and rations) to support the initial assault had to be loaded on the vehicles that could be brought ashore upon debarkation.

On the 6th, MacArthur's amphibious force held off 50 miles south of Ormoc Bay making its final preparations for the landing scheduled for the following morning. Kinkaid's destroyers paraded up and down the coast lobbing volleys all along the western shoreline to deny the Japanese any hope of the actually preventing the landing while Kenney's tactical dive bombers hammered shore installations and the enemy headquarters further north.

On the 6th, MacArthur's amphibious force held off fifty miles south of Ormoc Bay making its final preparations for the landing scheduled for the following morning. Kinkaid's destroyers paraded up and down the coast lobbing volleys all along the western shoreline to deny the Japanese any hope of the actually preventing the landing while Kenney's tactical dive bombers hammered shore installations and the enemy headquarters further north.

About 0700 on 6 December the assault shipping rendezvoused off Tarragona and Rizal Beaches and one hour later the assault troops began to board the vessels. The loading was completed at 1200 and the convoy assembled offshore from Dulag to await the arrival of the twelve escorting destroyers. On the third anniversary of Pearl Harbor the 77th Division landed four miles south of Ormoc town. Their landing coincided with the beginning of the northward advance of the 7th Infantry Division which had driven to the west coast of Leyte in the vicinity of Damulaan. The 7th was to link up with the 77th and close all but the extreme northwestern area of Leyte to the enemy for areas of reinforcement. However, the Japanese had chosen that day to land troops on San Isidro Bay, 18 miles north of Ormoc. Marine Corps F4U Corsairs, which had just arrived at Tacloban, attacked convoy and sunk several ships but 4,000 enemy troops were landed. The U.S. landing force rapidly joined the infantry advancing from the east which divided Japanese forces in the Leyte highlands.

The Japanese had held their depleted air forces in reserve to repel the anticipated invasion and once unleashed they would participate in what was to be its largest air commitment of the Leyte Campaign. The Japanese reacted with particularly savage air battles throughout the day and the fighters of the Fifth Air Force claimed 66 Japanese aircraft, many determined Kamikazes, for the loss of a single but important pilot.

**7 December 1944: 475FG/431FS/432FS/433FS**
432FS
Mission #1
1Lt. Joseph Forster was leading four P-38s on Clover Squadron's first mission of the day, a patrol over the Allied convoy in Ormoc Bay. At 0750 while flying at 11,000 feet Forster saw a twin engine bomber at 8,000 feet headed east. Forster "firewalled" his fighter toward a speedy Dinah that saw him and raced for clouds that covered Catmon Mountain. "After several miles at speeds over 400 mph" Forster caught it at 400 yards and fired a two second burst before it entered the cloud. Forster spotted the Dinah again as it exited the cloud and fired a three second burst before it entered another cloud. The Dinah was much easier to spot as it exited this cloud as its port engine was trailing black smoke. The two adversaries were only a few hundred feet over the mountain tops when Forster got one last no deflection shot before the Dinah entered the clouds. Forster never saw this Dinah again and claimed probable west of Dulag Strip at 0800.

Mission #2
Capt. Elliott Summer was leading six P-38s of Blue Flight on a convoy cover patrol from 0815 to 1025 at 10,000 feet. At 0940 10 to 12 enemy single engine bombers, "possibly Kates," were seen heading south over land about 30 miles from Ormoc. After Summer notified the Air Controller of the enemy bombers; he led his Flight down on them. Immediately, two Oscars dove from the overcast and Summer turned into them and by reefing in he was able to out turn the Oscars and shoot the #2 Oscar down with a 30 degree deflection shot that hit its wing roots and it burst into flames and crashed straight into the ground to make Summer's a double ace with his 10th and last victory.

Mission #3
At 1015 the third Clover patrol mission over Ormoc Bay took off with eight P-38s in two flights: Red Flight led by 1Lt. Joseph Forster and White Flight led by 1Lt. John Hannan. Forster's Flight was assigned to patrol over Ponson Island and at 1045 Forster reported seeing a Japanese fighter crash into the bridge of a USN cruiser. Half hour later Forster saw two Zeros on the deck south of Ponson and dove after them. One Zero was chased by another P-38 flight and Forster went after the other. Forster made three passes from 30 to 0 degrees deflection astern and observed hits on its wings and fuselage, The enemy pilot was able to keep control of his fighter and as Forster about to make his fourth pass another P-38 swooped in a knocked off a piece of its elevator with a cannon burst. Forster was closing very quickly and had to chop his throttles to avoid a collision. Forster's ICR states: "The canopy was open and I could see the enemy pilot very clearly. For a few seconds we stared at each other at point blank range. He was wearing a sun tan helmet and green goggles." Finally, Forster slowed down enough to fire a long cannon burst into its fuselage and wing roots. Forster continued to patrol and saw a Dinah on deck headed west just off the east coast of Ponson. Forster dove on the Dinah from the rear and as he closed another P-38 dove in from ahead and began to shoot. However, his machine gun bursts were erratic, probably because he had burned the barrels. Forster chased the Dinah that had dropped its left wheel and firing from 50 to 25 yards, blowing up its port engine and the Dinah skidded in for a belly landing. Oil from the Dinah's engine covered Forster' windshield and he had to be led back to Dulag for a safe landing by his Wingman, 2Lt. Lawrence Roberts, who had his guns jam early in the combat and dutifully stayed with his Leader throughout the mission. During this patrol Forster had scored his 7th and 8th victories.

1Lt. John Hannan, White Flight Leader, reported that there was "confusion from too many Controllers" and that they searched too many vectors without result. After completing one vector search Hannah was orbiting when he saw the shiny silhouettes and dove at them but soon the silhouettes were identified as P-38s. Hannan decided that they would follow them "for want of something better to do...and surely they were chasing something." Hannan saw a dark plane approach the convoy and since there was a crippled P-47 reported in the area he wanted to make positive ID. Hannan radioed that

**Capt. Elliott Summer** shot down an Oscar for his last victory to become a double ace. (AFAA)

**2Lt. Robert Kimball** (right, with Joseph Forster) shot down his third and last enemy fighter. (AAF)

**1Lt. Joseph Forster** was credited with two victories and a probable to give him eight victories. (AFAA)

**Col. Charles MacDonald's** crew applying three victory symbols to make their leader a quadruple ace with 20 victories. (AFAA)

**Lt.Col. Meryl Smith** shot down two Jacks to give him eight total victories. (AFAA)

**2Lt. Leo Blakely** scored his only victory of the war. (AAF)

any Thunderbolt in the area waggle its wings. At about 500 yards the black Jack saw Hannan and Split-S'd away and was too fast and Hannan could not follow. Hannan's Second Element was waiting low for this move and as the Japanese pilot half-rolled and pulled out to turn and shoot at Hannan. 2Lt. Robert Kimball, the #4 man, was in the perfect position to take an astern shot and fired but saw no hits. Kimball closed and started firing again at 200 yards to dead astern at 30 degrees deflection. Kimball overran and broke off and watched as the Jack roll over and then burst into flames as it hit the Bay for his third and last victory. The P-38s continued patrolling until just after noontime and returned to Dulag to refuel and rearm.

On this mission, Col. Charles MacDonald, 475FG Commanding Officer, and Lt.Col. Meryl Smith, 475FG Deputy Commanding Officer, took off with Smith as the Wingman. They were intending to join with Clover White Flight but encountered three Jacks which were milling around at 3,000 feet. MacDonald and Smith were at 8,000 feet and immediately dove on them. Smith attacked at 6 o'clock level and shot one down with a short burst and it crashed and exploded into the sea. MacDonald attacked the bomb-carrying Japanese Leader from astern and set on fire with a short burst for his 18th victory. A few minutes later MacDonald and the third Jack got into a wild dogfight "in which neither of us could afford to break off." Smith dove on this Jack which went into an immediate sharp turn and Smith followed it around to get a long burst that disintegrated the enemy fighter for his ninth victory.

Mission #4

Capt. Harry Condon was leading seven P-38s at 7,000 feet west of Allied shipping in Ormoc Bay when, at 1430, they saw five enemy aircraft two miles west of Ponson Island at 12,000 feet. Condon led a high speed climb and as he was ready to attack another flight of P-38s flew through the enemy formation without firing. Since these P-38s did not fire, Condon began to think that the"enemy" could be P-47s but as he closed Condon definitely identified them as enemy. Just as he was to fire another flight of P-38s swooped in a shot down two and dispersed the others. Condon then saw three aircraft, possible Kates, below, heading toward Cebu, but they ducked into cloud cover to escape. Condon then saw a lone Dinah below, heading 180 to it. When the Dinah pilot spotted Condon he turned 180 and headed toward his Cebu sanctuary. Condon went into a high speed dive and "being very eager to make the kill, I made the error of starting to fire at maximum range, which resulted in burned out guns before I could get enough hits to knock the enemy plane down." Condon's Wingman, 1Lt. Albert McKenzie, then closed and fired a long burst and the Dinah exploded for his only victory.

Mission #5

At 1430 MacDonald led another four plane patrol with 2Lt. Leo Blakely as his Wingman and with Lt.Col. Meryl Smith leading the Second Element. They were patrolling the shipping off western Leyte at 6 to 7,000 feet when a number of Jacks bounced them from 6 o'clock. They began a pass at Blakely but MacDonald turned into the attack and two Jacks immediately broke away. MacDonald hit one from 50 degrees to stern and set it on fire. MacDonald then pulled straight up into another Jack that was on the tail of the Flight's #4 P-38. MacDonald "Immelmanned out" behind it and shot off its entire tail section. A Jack then made another pass at the Flight's #4 man but a P-38 from another Squadron intercepted it and shot it down. MacDonald then attacked a Zero at 1 or 2 o'clock and closed until it was almost in range but it then disappeared into a cloud. MacDonald and Blakely followed and MacDonald took several shots but the Zero pilot pulled straight up, rolled over and out of the cloud. MacDonald continued to pursue the skilful enemy pilot who maneuvered out of the veteran American ace's firing passes. Finally, the Zero pilot turned inside MacDonald and Blakely got a stern shot on it scoring hits on its tail. The enemy pilot turned to the right and Blakely hit its fuselage and then reversed his turn and went into a gentle dive. Blakely closed to 100 feet and fired into its wing roots and started fire and the Zero went into a steep dive into the water for his only victory. Sometime during the fight Smith's fighter was damaged in an attack by two Jacks and his P-38 was last seen heading away from the protection of his flight toward Ponson Island with the enemy fighters still after him. Paradoxically, the only 475FG loss in the intense air battle was the venerable nine victory ace and leader.

Last Mission
Six P-38s in two flights of three Lightnings; Clover Red and Clover White; took off at 1420 to cover shipping off the west coast of Leyte. Clover White Flight Leader had radio problems and Clover Red Leader, 1Lt. John Hannan, took the lead of both flights. They had to fly south at 17,000 feet to get over the weather covering the coastal mountains. Once at Ormoc Bay patrols were set up at 5,000 feet and soon the Air Controller called in a vector for an enemy fighter approaching the shipping. By the time White and Red Flights arrived the AA fire from the ships had downed the reported enemy. The patrol was resumed and a few more vectors were investigated without result. Weather was moving in from the north and the patrol was ordered to descend below the clouds and at 3,500 feet the Squadron found themselves flying in and out of rain squalls. The Controller called out another bogie that was seen coming out of a cloud with a P-38 on its tail. The two were flying through AA fire and the bogie was hit and went into a spin into the Gulf. The overcast dipped to 1,000 feet, and after 15 minutes the Controller called more bogies but gave no direction. Hannan saw six bogies, identified as Jacks, flying in and out of the clouds only a half mile away at 2 o'clock, parallel and toward the convoy. The last Jack turned into Hannan but then dove away as Hannan took a quick shot at it and got a few hits. The Jack pilot turned a 360 and Hannan turned into him again but the Jack pilot fired a 90 degree deflection shot at Hannan and missed. Wingman Roberts was in position for a 30 degree deflection shot and fired from 200 yards and shut down the Jack's engine. Roberts then closed to 100 yards and fired at 10 degrees and set the fuselage on fire. The Jack was only 100 feet above the water when its pilot tried to bail out but his chute did not open. The remainder of the patrol was uneventful and the Squadron returned to base at 1700.

**McGuire's** Lightning with its triple ace victory scoreboard. (AAF)

Both leading 5FC pilots scored two victories: **McGuire** for #s 29-30 and **Bong** for #s 37-38, thus keeping McGuire his usual eight behind. (AAF)

431FS
1040 Flight
Maj. Thomas McGuire started the day with 29 confirmed victories to his credit and was trailing Bong by seven. McGuire and Maj. Jack Rittmayer took off from Dulag at 1040 on a two man patrol over Ormoc and the convoy area. They patrolled the area for an hour at 10,000 to 13,000 feet, investigating plots but saw no enemy fighters. At 1140 the Controller called them down to investigate a dogfight to the west. When they arrived they saw an Oscar in the clouds and another battling four P-38s. This Oscar temporarily got away from its pursuers and McGuire rolled on it with an overhead pass, shooting from dead astern, getting several hits. The Oscar pulled up into the clouds and started burning. McGuire fired as the Oscar entered the cloud. Rittmayer followed and held his course in the cloud and when the Oscar exited Rittmayer fired a burst and saw it hit the water. Rittmayer's ICR emphatically states: "This Oscar was Major McGuire's kill!"

1430 Flight: McGuire/Bong
McGuire led four Daddy Green P-38s flown by Rittmayer as his Wingman and Maj. Richard Bong as Daddy Green Three and 1Lt. Floyd Fulkerson as his Wingman. The mission was a convoy patrol south of Ormoc but the weather was so bad that the four P-38s were stationed northwest of the convoy at 4,000 feet. Bong was the first to call out the enemy when he sighted a Sally bomber at 1505. McGuire describes the combat:

> As I did not see the enemy, he (Bong) took us into the rear of the Sally and shot her down in flames on the northeastern tip of Bohol Island. We then resumed patrol northwest of the convoy, and at 1540 I sighted a Kate north of the convoy and led our flight in to the attack. The anti-aircraft from our convoy was heavy, so I took 1 good burst at the Kate, getting some hits, then broke away to avoid the A/A. Major Rittmayer, my Wingman, followed through the A/A, and as a result of his attack, the Kate went into a spin and crashed into the water. We resumed patrol, and at 1610 I sighted 5 Tojos flying in from the north and just under the overcast at approximately 2,500 feet. We started for them just as the convoy opened their defensive fire. I felt it was necessary to break up the Tojo's attack so, despite the A/A barrage, I led the flight in. I singled out the Tojo to the left, fired from astern, and the Tojo crashed to the rear of the convoy. Maj. Rittmayer made a rear attack on a Tojo, which flew down one lane of shipping. That Tojo crashed into the bay. I made a pass at one but lost him in a turn, directly over an LST, at low altitude, and Lieutenant Fulkerson latched him, causing the Tojo to explode near the shipping. As there were no more Japanese around, I climbed up to the left and to the north of the convoy. At this time I saw a Tojo crash into the water after Maj. Bong hit him on a head on pass. Lieutenant Fulkerson then joined me, and we resumed patrol.

Bong's description of this significant confrontation between the two great aces was:

I sighted a Sally low on the water, at 12 o'clock, and gave chase. Closing to 1,000 feet I set the left engine on fire and she crashed on Bohol Island at 1510. We returned to patrol the convoy and sighted one Kate among the AA bursts. Major Rittmayer shot him down out of control from astern and amid the AA fire at 1540. We again resumed patrol at 3,000 feet over the NW corner of the convoy and sighted five Tojos, at 2 o'clock level, coming toward us. We attacked from 30 degrees deflection from dead astern but I did not like the idea of driving into the AA so I turned left and met the tail end man head on and observed several hits on his engine. I observed Major McGuire shoot one Tojo down, just astern of the convoy and Lieutenant Fulkerson shot one down that exploded just before it contacted with the water. The Tojo that I had hit from head on spiraled down with a dead engine and crashed just to the rear of the convoy. I then observed Major Rittmayer attacking a Tojo from astern and the Tojo started smoking and made a 360 degree turn and ended up right in front of me. I took a shot at him but he was already finished and he crashed in the water at 1630. We were ordered to go up and cover a destroyer which had been previously hit. We arrived just as it and its escorts were firing at a single Nip airplane. We gave chase but another flight of 431st P-38s beat us to him.

Daddy White Flight came into the action and stole the victory away. Now it was 30 victories for McGuire but the eight victory gap remained with Bong still in the lead with 38. The descriptions of this combat, not only by McGuire and Bong, but also by Rittmayer and Fulkerson reveal McGuire's willingness to fly into AA fire to get a victory while Bong was unwilling to do so. Rittmayer was the top scorer for day with three victories which were his first of the war. After shooting down the Kate early in the combat Rittmayer "singled out one Tojo and followed him down, firing from dead astern and as he dived between a line of LSTs. I made hits and the Tojo went straight into the water. I then sighted another Tojo who was closing in on me from behind and level. I turned sharply to my left and the Tojo stopped firing and immediately made a 180 degree turn as I turned into him. This maneuver of his parked me directly on his tail. I closed in firing from directly astern and continued firing until his speed fell off and the Tojo went out of control. The Tojo went into a shallow and crashed into the water."

1600 White Flight
Capt. Frederick Champlin was leading Daddy White with 2Lt. Thomas Martin as his Wingman and 1Lt. Enrique Provencio flying as Daddy White Three with 1Lt. Kenneth Hart as his Wingman. The Flight took off at 1600 to patrol over the convoy SW of Leyte in the Camotes Sea. Almost immediately Champlin was vectored to a plot north of the convoy and flew in that direction for 10 minutes but saw no enemy aircraft. White Flight continued its patrol and after completing a 180 degree turn saw a lone bandit flying NW at 8,000 feet. Champlin closed and fired into its engine which burst into flames and the enemy pilot rolled his doomed fighter on its back and parachuted to safety (Champlin's seventh victory). Champlin took his flight to resume its patrol and was given another plot but was unable to see the enemy. However, his second element did see it and Provencio and Hart dove after it. Hart had the position advantage and fired from 0 to 30 degrees deflection from astern and observed flames in its engine and the Oscar rolled over and went into the sea east of Olango Island. At this time Hart had joined Champlin's Wingman Martin while Provencio joined Champlin. White Flight reformed and continued its patrol and another plot was called NW of the convoy. Two bandits were seen at 12 o'clock high and Champlin began to climb and saw the last one break to the left and as he closed he saw it was a Corsair that had broken away from its attack.

**1Lt. William Ekdahl** (being decorated by Gen. Wurtsmith) was credited with his last of two victories. (AAF)

**Capt. Frederick Champlin** celebrating his seventh victory. (AFAA)

**2Lt. Douglas Thropp** had his only victory over Cebu. (AAF)

Champlin continued his climb to 10,000 feet after the enemy fighter but could not close quickly enough as his engine could not pull enough power. Provencio closed on the Zero and shot it down for his second and last victory. Meanwhile, Hart and Martin saw an Oscar at 6,000 feet and chased it down to the deck where it broke to the right. Hart fired a 30 to 60 degree deflection shot, scoring hits on its engine and cockpit for his second victory of the day to make him an ace with six.

1515 PBY Escort Flight

1Lt. Wilson Ekdahl led four P-38s over Dulag at 1515 on a PBY search mission to the water north and northwest of Leyte Island. His flight was composed of 2Lt. Howard Max on his wing and a second element of 2Lt. Harold Madison and his Wingman, 2Lt. Douglas Thropp as his Wingman. The flight remained with the Catalina for an hour while it searched and then continued to fly along the Cebu east coast after it left. While flying west Ekdahl sighted two Hamps flying east at the same altitude of 9,000 feet. He made a 90 degree turn and closed to 100 feet but saw no hits and as he broke away. Max followed and fired, also with no results. Madison then closed and fired but the charmed Hamp escaped. Ekdahl turned right and again closed astern and then moved to the Hamp's left while Max closed on its right. The Hamp turned into Max who fired without observable results and then it turned into Ekdahl who fired a long burst at 200 yards and it finally Split-S'd into the water for Ekdahl's second and last victory. The flight climbed back to 6,000 feet, heading north and saw two more Hamps heading west at 10,000 feet. Ekdahl turned into them and climbed to their altitude and closed astern and fired at 300 yards. One Hamp turned to port and Ekdahl closed on it to 100 feet but it pulled up and away. The other three flight members took turns making passes and missed. Ekdahl returned to get dead astern and fired from 60 degrees but missed again. Thropp closed to 200 yards and fired from 45 to 10 degrees astern and the Hamp finally rolled over into the sea for his only victory.

433FS

Capt. Chase Brenizer led four P-38s of Red Flight from Dulag at 1630 to cover Allied shipping in the Baybay area. The flight was below the overcast at 2,500 feet near Albuera when flight Second Element Leader, 1Lt. Glenn Maxwell, called out a bogey at 6 o'clock. Brenizer turned to starboard and saw an enemy fighter that had just dropped bombs on landing craft and was climbing toward the overcast out to sea. Brenizer climbed slowly toward the enemy and once at its altitude fired a 70 degree deflection shot and got some hits on its tail. Brenizer then pulled up and over on his back and fired a slight deflection shot at close range that hit its wing root. As Brenizer turned away his Wingman, 2Lt. Samuel Morrison, came in and fired from 30 degrees low and astern and hit its fuel tanks and then followed around and fired a no deflection shot from astern that set on fire and it started spinning with pieces coming off its of its right wing falling off. Its pilot managed to bail out at 1,500 feet but Morrison had the first of three total victories. At 1730 while the Flight was patrolling over shipping 30 miles south, the Controller called in several bogies and was joined by two other P-38 flights in the search. At 1745 a single bogie was called 15 miles NW at 5,000 feet and Brenizer observed AA bursts in the direction of Tugas Point. Brenizer led the flight from 4,000 to 6,000 feet toward Tugas and saw a twin engine aircraft at 7,000 feet. Brenizer climbed slightly above it and when he was a mile and a half away the enemy pilot saw the P-38 and made a slight diving turn toward Bohol Island. Brenizer opened fire at 400 yards and got hits on the Helen's wings and there was no return fire from its gun positions. He then closed and fired a long burst at 30 degrees and got hits on its port engine and fuselage, setting its port inboard fuel tanks on fire. Brenizer closed to 100 yards and fired a long burst at no deflection into its fuselage and engines. Brenizer pulled up sharply to port in a tight loop and got in another long burst hitting the starboard engine and the center of the fuselage and the Helen was nearly engulfed in flames. Brenizer almost dove into the water on this pass and as he pulled up for another pass he saw the Helen skip off the water and then settle with Morrison taking a few last shots at it. Brenizer left the sinking Helen with his third and last victory. The 475$^{th}$ had claimed 26 victories on 7 December to surpass 450 confirmed victories since it had begun operations in August 1943.

**7 December 1944: 49FG/7FS/8FS/9FS**

Mission #1/7FS

At 0730, Flying Knight Flight Leader 1Lt. Charles McElroy, Wingman 2Lt. James Hovik, Element Leader F/O Henry Hammett and Wingman 2Lt. Rentchler were vectored in uncertain weather to the northern end of Leyte. Although they saw no enemy aircraft they did verify the next Japanese reinforcement convoy of seven troop ships and four destroyer escorts. The flight continued to shadow the enemy convoy for almost an hour before seeing four Oscars flying overhead. As the flight climbed, Hovik's fighter lost power in one engine and aborted the mission. The remaining three Knights continued after the Oscars and as they closed at 17,000 feet the Oscars turned to counter attack. McElroy fired a quick head on burst and the Oscar trailed heavy smoke but was not confirmed as a kill. Rentchler didn't to rejoin with McElroy and Hammett and the pair continued their patrol with sufficient fuel and ammunition but the enemy fighters were gone.

Mission #2/7FS

At 0830, 7FS Blue Flight Leader 1Lt. Fernly Damstrom with wingmen 2Lts. Ralph Watson and William Fernandez were vectored to the west coast but were unable to find the enemy in the haze, so they turned back toward Ormoc Village. As they approached the village at 11,000 feet, they saw U.S. Navy ships firing at a lone Nick flying at about 6,000 feet below above the cloud layer. Damstrom jettisoned his empty tanks and followed, losing sight of it several times. Damstrom finally closed and his first burst started its right engine on fire and he fired again and got hit on its wing roots and the Nick blazed and fell into the overcast. After the flight regrouped Watson had to abort due to "ear trouble" and Damstrom and Fernandez continued the Blue Flight patrol. The duo eventually joined four Lightnings of Pinky Green and at 0950 *Valentine* Controller radioed a vector and Damstrom and Fernandez descended to investigate while Pinky Green flew high cover. After a few minutes the two began to climb back and saw bogies over the Peninsula at 12,000 feet. While they were climbing toward these bogies, they saw two Oscars making a pass on USN destroyers with a flight of Lightnings)Pinky Black) shooting them down. Having lost Pinky Green, Damstrom and Fernandez then headed south and saw six "possible Nicks" at 4,000 feet, headed east, at 11 o'clock low in a V of Vs formation. The two Americans closed and fired. Damstrom fired on the left Wingman of the first V and got hits on his right engine and wing and pulled up and returned after Fernandez overran it. Damstrom hit the right wing which caught on fire and the Nick crashed in the water just north of Poro Island for his second kill of the mission

Mission #3/7FS

The two Oscars seen by Damstrom were the victims of the "Pinky Black Special" of the 7FS. Knowing the Japanese would assign every available aircraft to stop the Ormoc landings, 49FG staff officer Col. Robert Morrissey had attached himself to the 7FS as a Flight Leader hoping to add three more victories to become an ace Group CO Lt.Col. George Walker, who had not yet scored a victory, and Group Ops Exec Maj. Gerald Johnson also joined leaving 2Lt. Harold Harris as the "designated Wingman" and only true Screamin' Demon in the quartet. Morrissey led the Pinky Black Special from Tacloban at 0830 and they climbed to 12,000 feet when they reached the Duligan Peninsula. Morrissey and Johnson searched until 1000 when they began their pursuit of the formation of six Nicks which would be

**Lt.Col. Gerald Johnson** would have the best day of his career with four victories to give him 21. (AFAA)

**Lt.Col. George Walker**, 49CO, scored his only victory. (AAF)

**Col. Robert Morrissey** got his third and last victory. (AAF)

engaged by Damstrom's Blue Flight. While descending toward the Nicks, the Pinky Blacks met a closer flight of three Oscars in high escort to six Helen bombers flying at 13,000 feet down the coast. Morrissey quickly turned toward the Oscars and fired a badly aimed burst which missed the agile Oscars.

Element Leader Walker arrived and turned toward the Oscars while Wingman Harris flew wide to cover him. The inexperienced 49er CO sped into the combat and overran the targets. (Johnson's ICR: The Oscars turned into him (Morrissey) and he was unable to get a good shot"). Ops Exec Johnson simply reports the combat in which he scored his 18th, 19th, 20th, and victories:

> I closed on the last Oscar and shot him down in flames. I then went down after the other two and then followed them into a climb. As they turned sharply to the right and I had good deflection shots and was able to get both of them.

Walker's ICR states: "My Wingman (Johnson) shot down all three enemy planes in 45 seconds."

The Flight reformed and continued patrolling at 12,000 feet and immediately set off after the six Helens flying in a V of Vs at 8,000 feet. Walker quickly got into firing position dead astern of the next Helen and was surprised when there was no return fire from its tail gunner and easily hit the Helen and Walker finally got his first and only victory of the war. However, the Helen pilot tried to aim his doomed bomber toward the USN destroyers below and barely over flew one before crashing into the water nearby. Morrissey and Wingman, Harris finally caught the bombers as they descended near Duligan Point. He opened fire on the right most Helen and made a good firing pass and shot out an engine for his third and last victory. Wingman Harris closed in on the last Helen of the first V and fired and started its right engine smoking and the Helen began to spiral right and crashed, hitting the water just in front of a destroyer. This was Harris' fourth and last victory. The remaining three Helens continued toward the destroyers.

Johnson fired on the left Wingman of the left V of three remaining Helens and it began smoking and left the formation. Johnson then made a front quarter pass on it over Duligan Point and it went down in flames and plunged into sea just offshore from Tilagen Village for his 21st victory. The last two Helens frantically escaped into the clouds to the north.

Mission #4/8FS/7FS
8FS
1Lt. Robert Campbell was patrolling over the convoy at 5,000 feet when his Flight encountered six Oscars flying at 12,000 feet over Duligan Point and started a high speed climb toward them. As they reached 8,000 feet, the Oscars dove on them and Campbell led his Flight into the clouds and radioed the position of the attacking Zeros. When they exited the clouds the six Oscars were being engaged by another Flight of P-38s. Campbell made "approximately 12 passes…but the Nips would half roll as soon as I would fire, which provided target for a very short time." Finally, on one 45 degree high side pass, Campbell fired down to 10 degrees and the Oscar began to smoke and went into a vertical dive; crashing into the sea. Campbell immediately saw another bogie against a cloud and took off after it; but his Wingman did not hear his call and Campbell met the Sally bomber alone. He fired a three second burst on the unaware bomber from dead astern and then the pilot became aware and went into a tight 180 degree turn into a cloud. Campbell followed and was above and to the right of the Sally when it exited. Campbell then made "approximately 10 successive passes' on the Sally as its pilot maneuvered in and out of the clouds. Finally, on a climbing

**1Lt. Milden Mathre** was awarded victories #2 and 3. (AFAA)

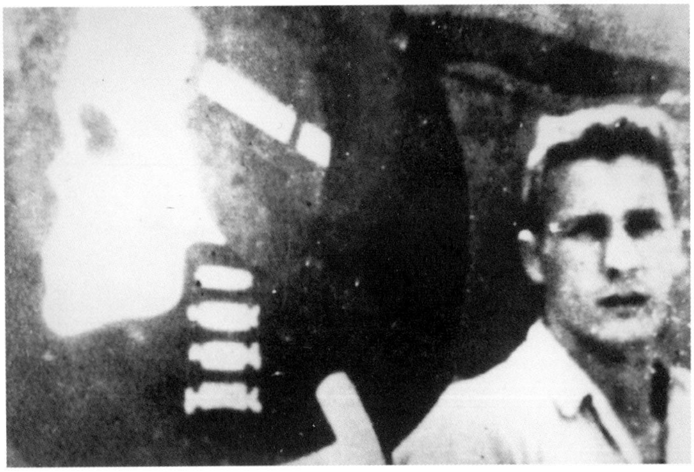

**1Lt. Joel Paris** got his first P-38 victory after scoring three in the P-40. (AFAA)

50 degree deflection Campbell sent the Sally spinning 5,000 feet where it pulled out just above the water. Campbell had followed the bomber and fired a dead astern volley which finally sent it into a hillside for his second victory of the day and his third and last of his career.

7FS

7FS 1Lt. Joel Paris led Pinky Red Flight off at 1015 to patrol the Ormoc landings. Paris' element was flying 4,000 feet and 2Lt. Milden Mathre was leading his second element at 8,000 feet when Controller *Chatterbox* called bogies at 13,000 feet. Paris ordered his Flight to climb and at 10,000 feet he saw six Oscars attack his second element. Mathre and his Wingman dove from 10,000 feet to 7,000 feet and pulled out and climbed back up to rejoin Paris. On the way up Mathre took snap shots at several "Nips" without result. At 4,000 feet he saw an Oscar at about 1,000 feet and dove on it but was cut off by four or five other P-38s but the Oscar was flown by "a good pilot and could out turn us" but Mathre finally got some hits and followed and fired a second burst into "a huge flame" and fell into the sea. Mathre rejoined Paris as he was chasing a Nick with several other P-38s and Mathre remained above the fight to cover his Leader. Finally, the Nick pilot maneuvered enough and the Lightnings broke away out of ammunition. Mathre then closed behind the Nick and hit its right engine and it crash landed in the water but sank in seconds and Mathre left for home with his second and third victories. During the fight the Nick's rear gunner put three 7.7 bullets into Paris' right engine destroying the coolant system and magnetos. Paris feathered the engine returned to base safely.

Mission #5/7FS/9FS

9FS

The air battles continued into the afternoon for the 49ers. At 1400 Flying Knights, 1Lt. Charles McElroy led Pinky Green Flight with Wingmen, 2Lt. Ernest Ambort and 2Lt. Wilford were flying top cover for Pinky Red until *Chatterbox* Controller separated them.

Ambort called bogies at 9 o'clock, 3,000 feet high, turning toward them. The three Lightnings began to climb and the bogies, identified as Zeros passed over only 500 feet above and dropped their tanks, trying to hit the American fighters (Ambort's ICR). The Zeros turned on the Lightnings at 6 o'clock and McElroy called for a dive. Ambort's plane was hit and he Split-S'd away and rolled out and pulled up into a head on passinto eight bogies firing on McElroy. Ambort fired on the Leader and hit the cockpit and the enemy pilot pulled up exposing its belly to Ambort who saw flames spurting from its cowling and wing roots. Ambort rolled out with his second victory of the day and his fifth to make him an ace. He then dove on another Zero and chased it maneuvering behind into three vertical rolls and two Split-Ss, firing all the time to no avail as the Zero escaped. Ambort was attacked by another Zero and ducked into a cloud and rejoined his Flight.

After McElroy dove from the Zeros he turned into them making several unsuccessful deflection passes. Another flight of P-38s arrived and the "Nips scattered everywhere for cloud cover in an attempt to get home." McElroy spotted an Oscar diving away and got astern and set it on fire and it exploded for his fourth and last victory.

7FS

In the same dogfight, Demon *Pinky Blue* Flight Leader, 1Lt. Fernly Damstrom, led four P-38s covering the convoy at 6,000 feet. At 1420 Element Leader, 1Lt. James Harris, called bogies at 11 o'clock high which were intercepted after a five mile chase north of Ponson Island at 10,000 feet. The bogies (Zeros) were being attacked by another flight of Lightnings but Damstrom saw three other bogies "playing around" over the Peninsula at 13,500 feet. Damstrom and his Wingman, dove on the Zeros as they were maneuvering to attack some P-38s. Damstrom sped to the attack on the second last Zero and got hits on its right wing root and the Zero pilot "racked

**1Lt. Fernley Damstrom** also became an ace. (AFAA)

**2Lt. Ernest Ambort** became an ace by shooting down a Zero. (AFAA)

**1Lt. Charles McElroy** claimed an Oscar for his fourth and last victory. (AAF)

it to the right to follow his Leader" but Damstrom fired into its right wing which burst into flames and Split-S'd into the ocean for his third victory of the day to become an ace.

Mission #6/9FS/8FS
At 1520, 9FS veteran Capt. Willis Treadway and wingmen 1Lt. Cheatham Gupton and 2Lt. Troy Smith were flying in Beware White Flight on a dive bombing mission to Ormoc when the Tacloban Air Controller directed the Flight to drop their bombs and then proceed on a vector toward Zeros approaching the beachhead. After dropping their bombs on the enemy Ormoc garrison from 9,000 feet (Smith's ICR: "which were not accurate"), they climbed directly over the USN invasion task force at 13,000 feet where Treadway spotted eight Zeros flying in loose formation 4,000 feet below. Treadway guided his Wingmen into a position in the sun over the Japanese right flank. The Zeros were so intent on attacking the American fleet, that the Lightnings were able to move in, dead astern, without being detected.

Treadway waited until he got within 150-200 yards before shooting and a fire broke out in its right wing root and Treadway "gave it a little more lead" and it exploded for his second and last victory. Smith fired at 15 degrees deflection as the Zero started to turn left and then straightened out as Smith fired again. Smith fired from directly astern and didn't miss and the Zero exploded directly in front of him for his only victory. Gupton firewalled to overtake the Zeros out ahead but then the Zeros entered into near vertical dive and Gupton saw one of the Allied ships (LST?) explode from the impact of one of the Kamikazes.

8FS
8FS Ops Exec, Capt. Nelson Flack, and wingmen 1Lt. Walter Meyer and 2Lt. Harold Strom arrived over Ormoc Bay at 1430 and Flack immediately called a bogie and climbed to attack the Dinah which went into a shallow, climbing chandelle. Flack and Strom fired but the Dinah disappeared into the clouds smoking slightly and Strom was credited with damaged claim. The three Black Sheep then joined Treadway's 9FS trio of Gupton and Smith. When they returned to their patrol area the Flight saw dive bombing Tonys which also escaped into the clouds. The Blacksheep watched Treadway shoot down his Zero when Flack called a Zero on the deck. The Flight dove on it and Flack and Strom overran as the enemy pilot turned sharply. Meyer got behind and above and opened fire getting hits from "nose to tail" but the Zero Kamikaze which was able to crash into a small freighter which was stopped when the Flight left for home. Meyer's pyrrhic victory was his second and last.

Mission #7/9FS
As the day was ending, 9FS Green Flight Leader McElroy was hoping for an alert that would send him into combat for the third time and give him a chance for his fifth victory to make him an ace. At 1630, he led his flight on a patrol that unsuccessfully searched for an hour and half before they turned back to Tacloban. Just as they turned the Air Controller vectored a lone contact and McElroy made a fast climbing turn toward Ormoc Bay. At 7,000 feet McElroy saw a lone Lily whose skilful pilot evaded McElroy until he exhausted his ammo in riddling the bomber which would not go down. The other three pilot of the Flight also fired at the Lily until 1Lt. Noah Williams closed in and hit the bomber's engines, setting its fuel tanks on fire and it finally exploded. When McElroy returned to base he confirmed Williams' second and last victory.

Final Mission #8/7FS
7FS Screamin' Demons Mission Leader, 1Lt. Joel Paris, with wingmen 2Lts. Perry White and Milden Mathre to form Pinky White Flight were joined by Pinky Green Flight led by Capt. John Haher and Wingman 2Lt. Kenneth Markham for a last patrol at 1630 over the invasion fleet. They arrived at

**1Lt. Walter Meyer** also scored his second and last victory, but his Kamikaze victim hit a small freighter. (AAF)

**Capt. Willis Treadway** had his second and final victory. (AAF)

their assigned station at 15,000 feet and after 45 minutes six Oscars were spotted and the five Lightnings attacked though the supposed safety of the Navy's flak corridor but nonetheless nervous fleet AA gunners forced them to break off the attack. The Demons retreated back to 14,000 feet and 15 minutes later Haher called out a lone Nick racing east toward the fleet at 4,000 feet but Paris could not see it. The enemy pilot saw the Lightnings and 180'ed for home. Haher then rolled onto to a steep dive and easily caught the Nick from dead astern, killing the rear gunner and destroying the port engine. Haher's windshield was covered with enemy engine oil and he called for Paris to dispatch the Nick. Paris closed into point blank range and shot out the right engine and his windshield too became covered with oil but the Nick fell into the sea 10 miles from Cebu City. The victory credited to Paris (his fourth) and Haher and Paris had to return to base because of the oil on their windshields.

Element Leader Mathre and the other two wingmen finished the patrol over Ormoc Bay at 4,000 feet where Markham saw a second Nick flying southwest along the leading edge of long, low cloud front and dove to 1,000 feet closing to nearly dead astern. Mathre dove at the unsuspecting enemy bomber first but closed too fast and fired an inaccurate burst and had to break away to avoid a collision. Markham made a large circle and got astern fired and demolished the cockpit and then exploded the right engine. The final Demon flight of the day circled the invasion fleet one last time and landed at Tacloban at 1800.

**7 December 1944: 348FG/460FS/340FS**
460FS
Morning Mission
Sixteen 460th Fighter Squadron P-47s took off in four flights to escort a bombing mission against an enemy convoy headed for Leyte's west coast. At 0950 at 18,000 feet over Jaro, Leyte they spotted a dogfight over Ormoc and the P-47s split into flights and elements to cover each other; the first flight formed cover at 10,000 feet while the other flight attacked a formation of nine Sally bombers flying at 5,000 feet starting their bomb run on an American destroyer in Ormoc Bay near Ponson Island.

Element Leader, 2Lt. Thomas Sheets, of the fourth flight and his Wingman, F/O William Aswell, were flying over Jaro we they saw nine Sally bombers flying in three plane Vs at 5,000 feet between Ponson Island and Calunangan Point, making a bombing run on a USN cruiser and destroyer.

Aswell and his Leader each attacked a Sally. Aswell's first short burst missed and he adjusted his aim and hit the Sally's turret and continued to fire until the Sally caught fire and crashed north of Ponson Island for his only victory. Sheets fired a burst from astern that put his Sally crashing near Aswell's victim. The rest of the Sally formation turned right and Sheets made a 270 degree turn to get on the tail of one and fired and got hits. He had to break off when a P-38 dove into his line of fire causing Sheets to break contact and the Lightning pilot proceeded to shoot this Sally down. About 15 other P-38s came into the area and crowded Sheets out so that he was unable to make another attack and had to settle for his second victory.

The third flight, was flying west over the Camotes Islands, when they spotted a Nick below at 3,000 feet. Wingman 2Lt. George Grace followed his second element Leader in a dive and when the Leader overshot Grace took a long burst from astern and set both its engines on fire and it crashed in the water north of Poro Island for his only victory. A third element engaged seven Zeros flying between Palompom and Valencia at 10,000 feet but none were hit and three managed to drop bombs.

Afternoon Mission

During the afternoon mission Maj. William Dunham, 460FS CO, led 10 P-47s (one would abort with engine problems) off at 1345 on a fighter sweep over San Isidro Bay. While flying over Arevalo Bay at 18,000 feet they spotted 13 Zeros flying in four plane flights northeast at 12,000 feet over the north end of Cebu. Dunham and his Wingman, F/O John Smith, led the flight down in a line abreast attack. These Zeros jettisoned their aerial phosphorous bombs and Dunham attacked the Zero Leader from astern and fired a short burst and the enemy pilot bailed out. Dunham then turned to port and attacked another Zero at six o'clock as it was pursuing a P-47 from another flight. He shot it down and watched it crash into the water off the north tip of Cebu Island for his second victory of the day. Fifteen minutes later Dunham had picked up 1Lt. Gerald Economoff as a Wingman and was circling the target area at 14,000 feet waiting for his P-47 formation to reassemble when four Oscars were sighted above at 16,000 feet flying south over the San Isidro area. Dunham chased the four Japanese but when he closed, one of the Oscars apparently saw him and broke down to the right while the others continued straight ahead. Dunham continued after these three and concentrated on the right hand Oscar and fired a single burst that caused this fighter to burn fiercely and crash into the water off Palompon. Dunham then turned left and sent yet another enemy fighter into the water north of the Camotes and these four victories increased his total to 14. F/O John Smith, Dunham's original Wingman had followed Dunham into the 13 Zeros but in the pandemonium, did not fire on a Zero. On the second pass Smith attacked the Zero on the right from 6 o'clock and his bullets tore pieces out of the cowling and wings and it went into a vertical dive into the water for his first of two victories. At 1400 2Lt. Boris Popov, the Wingman of the Second Element Leader of the first flight, only covered his Leader as they dove on the Zeros and did not take a shot. The Zero formation scattered and three other P-47s joined Popov and his Leader. A Zero was seen heading west on the deck and Popov followed the others in the flight in their attacks. Popov got astern of a Zero and fired from 150 yards and the Zero crashed in the Camotes Sea for Popov's only victory.

**Maj. William Dunham**, 460FS CO, had a career day with four victories, bringing his total to 14. (AAF)

**1Lt. Frank Russo** got his last two of three victories. (AAF)

1Lt. Gerald Economoff was an Element Leader in the third flight, and also saw the 13 Zeros and closed on one, giving it a short burst and then followed it in a port turn, firing and setting it on fire and a 10 degree deflection shot caused it to explode. Fifteen minutes later Economoff then joined Dunham as his Wingman and fired a short burst at the left Oscar from astern and fire broke out at its starboard wing. The enemy pilot broke right. Economoff fired another deflection shot hit around the canopy and the Oscar spun in for his first two of three victories.

1Lt. Frank Russo was the Flight Leader of the fourth flight and led his Flight onto the right side of the 13 Zeros. He closed on one from dead astern and fired a devastating volley that started a fire, caused its landing gear to deploy, and finally its engine fell off. When Russo broke away he saw a Sally below at 8,000 feet and its pilot immediately turned toward San Isidro for the protection of the AA fire put up by the Japanese convoy there. Russo fired one long burst and the Sally's right engine and wing caught fire and it crashed into the water for third and last victories. F/O Gerald Minnick was the Wingman of the Element Leader of the fourth flight which attacked the last Zero flight. Minnick closed and got hits on the engine and cockpit and the Zero caught fire and went into a tight spiral and crashed off the north tip of Cebu Island for his second victory in two days but his last.

341FS

At 1445 the 341FS was conducting a glide bombing mission on the same Japanese convoy approaching Leyte. Capt. William Foulis was leading White Flight back from the mission about an hour later when he spotted a Dinah coming in from the northwest about 1,000 feet above. Foulis led his Flight in a climbing pursuit but the Dinah attempted to outrun them but Foulis caught it and fired from about 50 yards away and slightly above. Just as the bomber started to turn to the right Foulis fired a one second burst and both engines immediately burst into flames and the Dinah made a diving turn and crashed into the water for his second victory in a year of operations.

The 348th had scored 14 victories to score in double figures for the first time since 11 March. The Group had 16 aces by the beginning of December and their total of kills was over 250.

Convoy Attacks: 341FS/342FS

Throughout the day the 341FS and 342FS and Marine Corsairs attacked an enemy convoy of four transports and an escorting destroyer in San Isidro Bay on the northeast coast of Leyte. The 348FG P-47s carried 1,000 pound GP bombs with a 4-5 second delay fuse to skip bomb the convoy. At 1030 341FS Thunderbolts scored two near misses and a possible underwater hit on the first transport which began to smoke. Four bombs exploded near the second transport while a bomb fell "in the vicinity" of the third transport and the fourth suffered two direct hits and possible other hits. The destroyer and transports were strafed after the bombing runs. Three P-47s were damaged by AA fire, one severely. At 1510 the 342FS returned to San Isidro Bay to attack the convoy. One transport was hit repeatedly and burned ferociously and finally turned over. Two other transports received numerous direct hits and near misses and were last seen burning. The transport that was heavily damaged in the morning raid was not attacked. All three vessels were heavily strafed during the attack. One P-47 was severely damaged and another moderately by AA fire. At 1720 the 341FS returned for the Group's final attack on the convoy. It only attacked the fourth undamaged transport and hit it with four bombs setting it on fire.

**8-9 December 1944: Situation**

After losing 66 aircraft on the 7th the Japanese made feeble, sporadic attacks over the next two days as MacArthur consolidated the Ormoc beachhead. The Baruaen highlands were secured the next day and Ormoc Village was captured on 9 December. The Ormoc garrison numbering 15,000 Imperial soldiers and sailors retreated into the northern mountains where they were pursued and eventually exterminated.

**8 December 1944: 348FG: Japanese Ground Attack**

Cpls. Daniel Murello and Milton Sova of the 341FS were standing guard duty during the night of 7/8 December and were ambushed and killed by a 15 man Japanese patrol. The airfields in the area were occasionally harassed by enemy infiltrators and additional sentries had to be employed. The body of a Japanese infiltrator was dragged out in the open and a number of men got their pistols out and shot the dead enemy soldier. When asked why they did that the answer was: "When I get home I want to say I killed a Jap."

2Lt. Cletus Thomas of the 341FS was listed as MIA during a mission over north central Leyte.

**9 December 1944: 418NFS**

2Lt. Bertram Tompkins and F/O Vincent Wertin were on a regular night patrol over Morotai from 0130 to 0330 when the controller called a red alert at 0245. Fifteen minutes later two vectors were given by the GCI Controller, but they could not be intercepted due to ground scatter on their radar scope. Almost immediately the GCI called out another vector and this time it was contacted by R/O Wertin at seven miles and he gave Tompkins the elevation and range readings which brought him to visual contact at 3,500 feet. Tompkins saw two exhaust flames which he mistook for a twin engine bomber but as he closed to 100 feet he saw the twin floats on a single place seaplane. The enemy pilot made a sharp right turn and lost the P-61. Tompkins retarded the throttle and Split-S'd directly under the enemy and chandelled back to 13,000 feet. Meanwhile, Wertin called the GCI for another vector but before the GCI could reply Thompkins' climb had positioned Wertin to make a contact at 13,000 feet. This time the P-61 closed more slowly and Tompkins made another visual contact at 3,000 feet. Wertin kept calling out the range and Tompkins fired for three to five seconds at 800 feet with his cannon shells starting a fire in the right wing root. The enemy seaplane slow rolled on its back and Tompkins put another burst into its belly and at 0315 exploded in the water near Wana Airstrip, Morotai for his first of three victories.

**10 December 1944: 348FG/460FS/341FS/342FS**

**460FS**

0700 Flight

Capt. Lynn Parsons led four P-47s off at 0700 on a patrol of the Ormoc area. While approaching the patrol area at 10,000 feet they were vectored to 2,000 feet to investigate a bogie. At 0820 while flying at 2,000 feet south over Ormoc they spotted a lone Sally flying west at 2,500 feet. Parsons immediately went into a 90 degree turn in pursuit, closed quickly, and fired a long burst from astern at 45 degrees deflection. He got hits along the nose and fuselage and the port began to smoke as the bomber crashed in the Bay two miles from Oro Town for his only victory.

**Capt. Lynn Parsons** scored his only victory of the war. (AAF)

1145 Flight

1Lt. James Curran was the Flight Leader of a four plane flight leaving at 1100 for a patrol of the Ormoc area. The flight was orbiting Ormoc at 12,000 feet when they saw two Tonys flying northwest over Cuartro Island at the same altitude. The flight pursued the Tonys which did not deviate from course and Curran arrived at the 6 o'clock astern position on the left Tony and fired three long bursts and then broke off. Curran's Wingman then got some hits on the Tony before breaking off and Curran attacked again firing while closing to 50 yards, putting many bullets into the wings and fuselage and it crashed in flames into the sea off the Camotes Islands for his only victory.

The Element Leader on this flight was 2Lt. Edward Demeter who chased the right Tony northwest toward Cebu and closed, taking several dead astern and stern deflection shots which did not stop the evading Tony. The frustrated Demeter took one last pass from astern getting hits on the wings and fuselage and the Tony crashed into the ground on the tip of Cebu Island. Demeter was attacked by a Tony from above and the American went into a skid to the right and the Tony overshot and then broke left. Demeter chased the Tony toward the Negros and closed and fired all his ammunition and the Tony flew off in a shallow high speed dive trailing smoke to give Demeter a damaged claim to go with his only victory.

1505 Flight

Four P-47s of the 460FS took off at 1505 on a patrol of the Ormoc area. While flying north at 10,000 feet on their patrol south of Baybay they saw three Sallys flying east at 5,000 feet. The flight immediately dove to attack but the Sallys turned to the southwest and tried to escape into the clouds. The Flight Leader, Capt. Richard Frost, and his Wingman went after the Sally on the right and the Element Leader and his Wingman attacked the two on the left.

**Capt. Richard Frost** shot down a Sally for his third and last victory. (AAF)

Frost's first volley was low and he then corrected and got numerous hits on the fuselage and engines, and the Sally burst into flames and crashed near Catarman Point for his last of three victories.

2Lt. Robert Smith, the Second Element Leader, and his Wingman, 2Lt. Samuel Denmark, went after the left two Sallys, which disappeared in a cloud; when the two Americans emerged they were separated. Smith closed on one and fired at 200 yards and hit the canopy and wings and it crashed near Catarman Point. Denmark took on the other Sally and closed fast from astern and fired a long burst that tore out pieces from the canopy and fuselage and crashed near Smith's victim.

**341FS**

16 P-47s of the 341FS took off at 1100 to strafe and glide bomb Lamonon, near Apale Point, Ormoc Bay, and on the return encountered enemy fighters flying at 5,000 feet. 2Lt. John Mastilock, Wingman to Lt. Lins in the Yellow Fight, on his return at 5,000 feet saw a lone Tony 1,000 feet below and dove with his flight, then soon found himself on the Tony's tail. He fired a three second burst from 300 yards with no observable results and closed again. He fired from 250 yards and saw numerous hits all over the Tony which headed for the clouds using evasive maneuvers. Mastilock held his fire and just before the Tony entered

clouds he fired and got hits on its engine. He lost sight of it in the clouds but squadronmates saw the crippled Tony leaving the clouds with its engine on fire and heading in a vertical dive for Mastilock's only victory.

Capt. Robert Ducharme, Blue Flight Leader, and 2Lt. Robert Morris, Element Leader of Blue Flight, were retuning from their bombing and strafing runs when they saw a Tony and Zero about five miles apart flying at 5,000 feet heading north just above the overcast. Ducharme was credited with Tony damaged while Morris was credited with a Zero probable.

2Lt. Craddock, then followed the Air Controller's report of 12 more bogies at 5,000 feet but these were not found. The Air Controller then reported eight bogies nearing Dulag and when Ragsdale and Craddock arrived through the clouds over Dulag they spotted a lone bogie at flying dead ahead and level. Ragsdale wasn't sure if it was a bogie or friendly until it made a sharp head on turn and he identified it as a Zero. Ragsdale opened fire from 20 degrees head on and hit its cockpit and center fuselage and as he looked around Ragsdale saw it burst into flame and crash for his only victory.

**342FS**

At 0940 1Lt. William Wallace was leading a four plane 342FS flight on a patrol from Baybay to Green Beach to cover USN LCMs on the beachhead. While patrolling the Ormoc Air Controller gave Wallace a vector to a bogie at 9,000 feet, 10 miles out heading for Ormoc. Wallace led his flight at full throttle and climbed to 15,000 feet and saw a twin engine Dinah at his altitude. The Dinah saw the Americans and began a gentle diving turn. Wallace closed to 300 yards and began to fire until 50 yards and both engine caught fire and the fuselage began to smoke. The Dinah went into a vertical dive and crashed about a half mile from the LCMs for his second and last victory.

At 1430 1Lt. George Davis led four P-47s of the 342FS on another patrol from Baybay to Green Beach to cover USN LCMs on the beachhead. After patrolling for 1:15 at 10,000 feet they were jumped by four Tonys from high astern and Davis turned his flight into them just as they fired at his second element. The Tonys passed through and broke away and then made a pass at Davis' element and the two American elements separated. Davis followed a Tony through some rolls and Split-S's firing some short bursts but was never able to gain enough deflection so Davis broke away as the Tony entered a cloud at 7,000 feet. Two more Tonys diving from 14,000 feet continued to make passes but broke off in a climb to head for Negros Island followed by Davis. Davis climbed to 15,000 feet and after about five minutes he closed the several mile lead they had on him. As Davis came up behind them over Cebu they made several gentle turns and began to climb. Davis closed to dead astern and blew up one Tony and had to swerve to avoid the wreckage. The other Tony dived and Davis followed him almost to Negros, where the Tony ran for a cloud, but Davis fired from 250-300 yards, getting good hits before it entered the clouds just before Davis turned around for home with a probable claim, losing his bid for his fifth victory. As he looked back he saw a parachute under the cloud (his report particularly notes that he did not fire at it).

**1Lt. George Davis** (left, with 1Lt. Michael Dikovitsky) claimed two Tonys to move him closer to becoming an ace with four victories. (AFAA)

**1Lt. John Purdy** claimed two Oscars to become an ace. (AFAA)

Capt. Charles Whistler led four 342FS Thunderbolts on another late afternoon patrol to cover USN LCMs on the beachhead. While on patrol 1Lt. Truman Ragsdale, Second Element Leader, spotted three enemy twin engine aircraft at 9 o'clock low and led the dive on them. Just as they were going to close, four other P-47s came in and shot down one of them (460FS Denmark's twin engine Sally?). The other two bogies broke off and headed for the clouds and Ragsdale climbed above the cloud to watch for them to emerge. One, identified as a Nick, came out from directly below but saw Ragsdale and went back into the cloud. Ragsdale and his Wingman,

**11 December 1944: 49FG/8FG and 475FG**

After the 348FG shot down 11 enemy aircraft southwest of the invasion fleet at Ormoc Bay on the 10th, no enemy contacts were made on the northern side of the island. Fifth Fighter Command HQ decided, instead of waiting for the enemy over Ormoc it would send the 49ers Black Sheep and the 475th's Satan's Angels for a sweep of two larger islands of Negros and Panay to the west of Cebu. Panay, the most westerly island, had airstrips on its northern coast at the villages of Cadiz and Pilar while the north shore of Negros included airstrips at Fabrica and Silay. USN and AAF aerial reconnaissance had revealed a considerable number of aircraft of all types on all four fields and at 0600 Lightnings from the two Fighter Groups left Tacloban to attack the Panay/Negros airfield complex.

**11 December 1944: 475FG/433FS/432FS/431FS**

433FS

Early Morning Mission

At 0745 1Lt. Jack Purdy led a flight of four Possum P-38s on a PBY escort to Ormoc Bay with 2Lt. Carl Redding as his Wingman and a second element of 2Lt. Joseph Miller and his Wingman, 2Lt. Wesley Hulett. The flight rendezvoused with a PBY over Tacloban at 0810 and was to proceed west of the Ormoc Peninsula. The flight was uneventful until 20 miles north of Cebu where they spotted 11 or 12 vessels which at first they assumed were friendly. A few minutes later they saw several groups of bogies through the clouds heading east which was part of the enemy convoy's air cover. Miller then called out four to six enemy aircraft at 12,000 feet north of the convoy and Purdy ordered the PBY to head back. Purdy led his flight in a climb to gain an altitude advantage and when they reached 20,000 feet they circled down to 12,000 feet where they saw the enemy convoy again with the 20-30 aircraft circling it from 7,000 feet to the deck. Purdy made his first attack on an Oscar from 6 o'clock at 7,000 feet and fired a short burst as it turned right. The Oscar started smoking and Split-S'd toward the deck for a damaged claim. Purdy started a second pass from 6 o'clock at 6,000 feet and as the enemy pilot Split-S'd Purdy fired a short burst from 80 degrees deflection from 200 yards and the Oscar crashed seven miles from Bantayan Island. The flight made several more ineffective passes on the Oscars before Hulett came in from above and began firing from 60 to 30 degrees deflection getting numerous hits that sent one gliding into the water for his second and last victory. Meanwhile Miller descended on an Oscar from the right and fired from 70 to 0 degrees and this Oscar crashed about 15 miles from Bantayan for his only victory. Purdy then saw two Oscars closing on his second element from 8 o'clock and dove on them. The lead Oscar broke away before Purdy could get in range but the second Oscar continued on and Purdy closed to 50 yards and fired from 10 degrees and saw numerous hits and cashed into the sea five miles from Bantayan and his second victory of the day made him an ace. Purdy began another pass on an Oscar which Split-S'd away and Redding scored hits behind the cockpit but Redding did not see it crash as he had to pull up and away before his victim hit the water but Purdy confirmed the victory. On their way back to base the flight ran into poor weather and were forced to detour around the southern tip of Leyte where Purdy ran out of gas and crash landed his fighter on Cabugan Grande Island. Miller then led the flight safely back to base. Purdy was picked up by a Catalina at 1440 and returned back to base by L-5 the next morning.

Mid Day Mission
Possum Blue Flight led by 1Lt. William Richmond took off at 1245 on a scramble to patrol the south of the northwest tip of Leyte. At 1300 the flight reached 15,000 feet and Richmond saw four bogies at 10 o'clock at 3,000 feet. Richmond made a diving 180 diving turn on the Zeros at 6 o'clock. The first two went into a cloud and Blue Flight went after the rear two. Richmond's Wingman got hits around the engine and wings of one Zero before it Split-S'd into clouds. 2Lt. Samuel Morrison, the #3 man, went after the other Zero that went into a violent diving turn and Morrison blacked out as he tried to follow. Two Zeros then closed on the #4 man and Richmond turned into them and drove them off into the clouds. As Richmond broke off and circled he saw another Zero break out of the clouds at 9 o'clock and he then chased it getting some hits on its wings before it went back into the clouds. Morrison anticipated that the Zero would pop back out of the clouds and when it did it was firing on the tail of one of the flight's Lightnings. Morrison was ready and fired from very close range, hitting the Zero's port wing, working his fire toward its cockpit. On his second pass he fired from directly astern from 150 yards and it burst into flames, inverted, and then exploded off the northwest coast of the Ormoc Peninsula. Capt. Paul Lucas of the 432FS confirmed Morrison's second victory.

432FS
Capt. Paul Lucas led four P-38s of Clover Red Flight on a scramble at 1230 NW of Tacloban at 18,000 feet. Richmond's Possum Blue Flight had just attacked four Zeros and split them into two elements. One Zero fired on a P-38 and pulled up directly below Lucas and then dove away. Lucas dove 2,000 feet and fired a direct tail shot at 50 yards into its fuselage and engine which caught fire. The Zero rolled on its back into a cloud layer for a probable.

431FS
1Lt. John Tilley led four P-38s of Daddy Special Flight from Dulag at 1600 and were patrolling over the convoy for 30 minutes at 18,000 feet when they saw a plane go down below them. Tilley went down to investigate the fight and saw P-47s of the 348FG engaged by three or four Zeros. A Zero flew directly in front of Tilley who got on its tail and fired from 200 yards dead astern; getting numerous hits. The Zero pilot turned and Tilley turned with him, keeping his lead and getting many more strikes that turned his fighter into a sheet of flame for his third victory and the last of the 475th's 19 victories for the day.

**1Lt. John Tilley** shot down a Zero for his third victory. (AFAA)

**Capt. Robert Aschenbrenner** claimed his ninth victory. (AFAA)

**11 December 1944: 49FG/8FS/7FS**
8FS: Morning Mission
Capt. Robert Aschenbrener and wingmen 2Lts. Harold Strom, George Reed, and 2Lt. Francis Hill took off at 0615 for a fighter sweep over northern Cebu and to search for an enemy convoy. They located the convoy two hours later and shadowed it for a half hour when the Japanese air cover arrived. The 25-30 Zeros, Tojos, and Oscars were stacked from 28,000 through 10,000 feet at four different levels northeast of Panay.

Aschenbrener led his Flight to 24,000 feet and attacked five Zeros and Tojos from astern and he fired at Zero which began to trail smoke after a few hits and dove vertically for a damaged claim. Aschenbrener then fired on a Tojo which dropped a landing gear after being hit and went into a 45 degree dive at high speed for no claim. When Aschenbrener followed his canopy began to break up and he could not follow. During the attack on the 25-30 enemy fighters Element Leader Reed fired on a Zero that Split-S'd and fired a long burst at 90 degrees and it went straight down for his only victory of the war. The Flight engaged eight enemy fighters but made no claims. Aschenbrener then saw a lone fighter near the water with its landing gear down (he believed it to be the same Tojo he attacked previously). Aschenbrener and Strom fired a few more bursts but Aschenbrener's last burst blew off its aileron and finally got his ninth victory when the Tojo exploded. Strom's fighter was damaged by the debris as he flew over. About 30 miles from base Strom's right engine's prop ran away and he decreased its rpms but the engine ran rougher and then blew up. Strom feathered the engine and slid back his canopy and prepared to bailout but the fire went out and he was able to land safely.

7FS
While the Black Sheep returned to Tacloban, four 7FS Pinky Red Flight P-38s were directed to patrol over the convoy in Ormoc Bay. Flight Leader 2Lt. James Keck and Wingmen 2Lts. Louis Denkovic, William Thompson, and rookie James McCrary arrived over their patrol area at 1015 but Keck had to abort due to engine problems and Denkovic assumed the Lead. At 1030 as the flight had just turned north at 16,000 feet to get over less dense cloud cover when McCrary spotted a lone bogie at their level and the Flight

prepared to attack when three more Zeros appeared overhead at 5 o'clock. The Flight then took off after this Nip who pulled up and made a very sharp 180 and shot out Denkovic's right engine. The outnumbered and damaged Flight went into a shallow diving escape, escorting Denkovic to safety. As Denkovic dove away the engine fire went out and he radioed his wingmen that he would head back to base on his good engine and that they should head back and Thompson and McCrary resumed their patrol. They sighted "two Nips level at 11,000 feet" and climbed to 13,000 feet and attacked them from astern. The enemy Leader saw them first and winged over to the left and Thompson went into a 1/3 turn and fired at 90 degrees deflection for a probable. Meanwhile, McCrary fired a telling four second burst on the enemy Wingman bailed out for McCrary's only victory.

On his way back to base Denkovic's other engine overheated and he shut it down and glided until it cooled off. He then restarted it before he reached Tacloban, only to find his landing gear would not lower completely. His only alternative then was to ditch off Tacloban but the damaged Lightning dropped off on its dead port engine, dragged its right wingtip in the water and cartwheeled to a stop where it sank to the bottom but did not completely submerge. Denkovic had his legs pinned under the collapsed instrument panel and was on the verge of drowning as the rescue team frantically tried to free him before the tide came in. Rescuers had to hold his head above the water until the Flight Surgeon arrived to consider amputating his legs to free him. Finally he was freed with a six foot steel lever that pried the panel up enough for the rescuers to pull him out of the cockpit. After a time in the hospital Denkovic would fly again.

8FS: Second and Third Afternoon Missions

After the Black Sheep's first morning sweep to Cebu, Capt. Robert Aschenbrener led the same four elements on a second unsuccessful mid-day sweep off the west coast. After they landed in mid-afternoon, the Lightnings were refueled and Aschenbrener led another sortie at 1600. This third sortie was to be an escort for a Navy Catalina PBY search flight off northern Cebu. George Reed of the previous sorties had mechanical problems and was replaced by 1Lt. Harold Bechdolt and joined Aschenbrener and wingmen 2Lt. Harold Strom and 2Lt. Francis Hill. The Black Sheep rendezvoused with the Catalina but as reached Ormoc Bay five Zeros were seen off Taglaurgon and two attacked the PBY. Aschenbrener dove and cut off the first attacker and hit him with two long bursts forcing Zero so low that it actually skipped off the water back into the air. Aschenbrener's long burst had overheated his guns ("one was so hot that it began to corkscrew") and Wingman Hill's first burst punctured its wing tank, and then his second burst set it on fire and it exploded into the ground for his second victory. With Bechdolt's starboard engine out and Aschenbrener without working guns, the four pilots of Mascot Red Flight flew back to base.

**11 December 1944: 348FG/340FS/342FS/460FS**

340FS

On 10 December the P-47s of the 340FS arrived at Tacloban from Morotai. One pilot was reported to have bailed out enroute but was probably picked up by a Catalina since no report of a 348FG fatality was submitted. The 340FS scored its first victories in the Philippines on 11 December during a cover mission over the Ormoc beachhead. 1Lt. Michael Dikovitsky was leading four P-47s of White Flight when he saw four Zeros scattered northwest of Ormoc Bay. He led his Wingman, 2Lt. Charles Murray, in a dive on the two closest enemy fighters. Dikovitsky's eight .50s hit the tail of his Zero and on his second pass his bullets tore the empennage completely off the fuselage. Murray followed his Zero who tried to evade with two or three barrel rolls but Murray got into range and fired and hit it in the center fuselage and wing roots. Murray continued after the wounded Zero but had to pull up sharply to avoid colliding with a Marine Corps Corsair. As he looked around Murray saw his Zero trailing smoke and explode in the sea for his only victory.

342FS

The next combats took place in the late afternoon. To prevent enemy planes flying down from the north, Majors William Banks and Walter Benz of the 342FS planned a fighter sweep over the enemy air bases on Cebu which would be most liable to be used to stage aircraft to protect their shipping and to attack the American supply vessels.

Early Afternoon

At 1215 Maj. William Banks, 348FG CO, took off on a two plane sweep to the northern Cebu area and arrived at 14,000 feet over an enemy convoy southeast of Carnasa Island of the northwest tip of Leyte. They saw three Zeros in a V at 12,000 feet headed south. Banks made a diving turn to come astern but the Zero turned into them and they only had 90 degree deflection shots as an option. Banks fired a short burst at the #3 fighter and it burst into flames from the cockpit and wing roots. The flames died out but the Zero rolled over and crashed into the sea in a gentle dive for Bank's seventh victory. The lead Zero turned into Banks but his Wingman drove it off into the clouds after scoring hits.

**Maj. Walter Benz** became an ace with his Oscar shoot down. (AFAA)

**1Lt. Michael Dikovitsky** (2nd left with crew) came closer to becoming an ace with his fourth victory. (AFAA)

Mid Afternoon
At 1455 Maj. Walter Benz led two P-47s, with 1Lt. Gerald Sheely as his Wingman, on a sweep on northwest Leyte. Half way between Leyte and northern Cebu at 18,000 feet the two sighted an Oscar (?) at 19,000 feet and climbed toward it. The enemy Split-S'd into a dive and Benz fired from dead astern as he chased after it. At 8,000 feet Benz fired a last long burst that sent the Oscar into the sea for his sixth victory. The two then flew to Cebu and saw seven more Oscars (?) in two flights and attacked out of the sun. Wingman Sheely fired at the #3 from dead astern at 300 to 50 yards and it began smoking at the wing roots and rolled over and dove into the sea for his only victory. Flying on they attacked three more Oscars (?), but Benz' guns jammed on his first pass, Sheely was nearly out of ammunition, and they were outnumbered, so the two retreated toward base.

Late Afternoon
At 1500 eight P-47s of the 342FS took off in two flights to rendezvous with P-40s and F4Us and then cover their bombing attack on a Japanese convoy off the northern tip of Cebu Island. After reaching their orbiting area at 15,000 feet they saw four or five Zeros at 9 o'clock and at 8-9,000 feet. Capt. Robert La Bounty was leading the second flight when he saw the Zeros and circled and made a diving turn at the second Zero. The enemy pilot made a sharp port turn and La Bounty fired a short 90 degree deflection shot and pulled up to the left and circled finding that he had lost the others in his flight. He flew over Cebu and again contacted enemy aircraft and made two or three passes on them as he found he could easily maintain the altitude and speed advantage on them. La Bounty flew after them, west over Cebu, by keeping the sun at his back. By now there were eight Zeros in a large Lufbery Circle at 3,000 feet. As La Bounty was about to make another pass he saw another P-47 at 10,000. La Bounty made a left frontal pass at 5-10 degrees deflection hitting the cockpit and wing and as the wounded Zero passed under his wing La Bounty saw it crash near the northern end of Cebu. As La Bounty climbed two Zeros attacked him but missed, and then another P-47 joined him and the two climbed into the sun to track the Zeros, which were no longer in their Lufbery, but milling around at 3,000 feet. La Bounty made a pass firing two long bursts at a trailing Zero which began to smoke heavily and crash. Three Zeros then turned and fired at La Bounty as he passed through but again his fighter was unscathed because La Bounty reported that "they used very small or no lead at all." 1Lt. William Overbey was an Element Leader on this mission and dove to the attack but Overbey was not seen again.

460FS
Eight P-47s of the 460FS took off at 1115 from Tacloban to cover a shipping strike northwest of Leyte. The Squadron approached the target from the southeast at 14,000 feet when they spotted two Zeros at 12,000 feet circling over the convoy just south of Carnasa Island. The first Thunderbolt flight dove and the Zeros immediately headed for cloud cover and escaped. A lone Zero was seen by the second element of the second flight which dove to the attack and missed and this Zero also escaped into the clouds. 2Lt. Robert Smith, the Flight Leader of the second flight, was flying north at 9,000 feet over Carnasa Island when he saw two Zeros at 8,000 feet also flying north. Smith immediately made a 180 degree diving turn and closed from 45 degrees astern to within 150 yards and fired a long burst at one that Split-S'd. Smith followed part way through, continuing to fire; knocking off large pieces of the canopy and crash just south of Carnessa Island for his second victory in two days. The second Zero escaped.

**12 December 1944: Bong Receives the Medal of Honor**
Gen. George Kenney recommended Maj. Richard Bong for the Medal of Honor for reaching his 36th victory of the war with his two victories on 7 December. For the ceremony at Tacloban on 12 December, Bong's previous P-38 #42 was borrowed and adorned with 36 Japanese victory flags. The always immaculate MacArthur, flanked by Kenney and Whitehead, made the presentation in a light drizzle to Bong who was dressed in wrinkled khakis.

**MacArthur** congratulates Bong, who is wearing the Medal of Honor. (AAF)

**Maj. Richard Bong** was awarded the Medal of Honor at Tacloban on 12 December 1944 by MacArthur (behind MacArthur are Kenney and Whitehead). (AAF)

**Maj. Richard Bong** in his official Medal of Honor portrait. (AAF)

An honor guard consisting of pilots from his former 9th Fighter Squadron was present as were hundreds of airmen and soldiers along with MacArthur's usual retinue of newsmen and photographers. After walking on water during his return to the Philippines; MacArthur was almost as theatrical when he put his prepared speech in his pocket and went on extemporaneously. He placed his hands on Bong's shoulders saying: "Major Richard Ira Bong, who has ruled the air from New Guinea and the Philippines. I now induct you into the society of the bravest of the brave; the wearers of the Congressional Medal of Honor of the United States." MacArthur slipped the Medal over Bong's head, shook hands, and exchanged salutes. After the ceremony #42 was returned to the 49FG which was in dire need of any serviceable fighter.

After America's top ace endured the newsmen and photographers for the day, he requested to be returned to the mission schedule and the Bong-McGuire scoring race continued at Bong 36 and McGuire 28. However, Bong had indicated to Kenney that he would like to return to the States by 15 December to attend his fiancée's college graduation.

**12 December 1944: 475FG/431FS/432FS**

431FS

1510 Patrol

1Lt. Herman led 1Lt. Owen Giertsen and 2Lt. Alvin Neal off Dulag at 1510 on a shipping patrol over Surigao Strait. While on patrol they heard another P-38 flight call out bogeys and soon saw that flight engaging enemy fighters about 2,000 feet below. When an enemy fighter, identified as a Zero, pulled up to their altitude Herman fired and got hits and broke away after the Zero looped. Neal then pulled up behind the Zero and fired at 20 degrees dead astern sending the Zero into the water three miles off the southern tip of Leyte for his only victory.

1535 Patrol

1Lts. Horace Reeves and James Moreing took off at 1535 on a shipping patrol over Leyte Gulf and soon the Controller sent them to check out a plot at 5,000 feet over the Surigao Strait. The Controller then gave another plot five miles west of the convoy and sighted two single engine fighters climbing quickly away from 6,000 feet. The P-38s climbed after them and as they closed to within 1,000 feet they saw one rock his wings vigorously as if it were a friendly aircraft. As they climbed and closed to 500 yards the bogeys were identified as Zeros and one broke off, and Reeves and Moreing went after the one on the right. Reeves closed to 300 yards and was about to open fire when the Zero rolled and Split-S'd. Reeves rolled with it and fired a deflection shot getting hits on its fuselage and wing roots. Reeves did not follow the Zero all the way down but broke away wide and came back around on its tail as the Zero closed out its Split-S. As Reeves and Moreing closed on the Zero again, its pilot turned slowly away and both Americans scored hits but the enemy pilot quickly rolled into another Split-S. Reeves broke away wide again and came around on the Zero and just as he was about to open fire the slow rolled to starboard and then made a sharp turn to starboard but Reeves stayed with the maneuver. Reeves fired a 90 degree deflection shot at 50 yards and hit its wing roots but the Zero continued to fly without catching fire. As Reeves broke away, Moreing came in from dead astern and the skilled Japanese pilot slow rolled, reversed his turn, and again Split-S'd away. Reeves came around on its tail as it climbed and got in range and opened fire. The Zero pilot skidded to the left and down and Reeves rolled with him and fired but the Zero skidded under Reeves line of fire. A P-38 from another flight came in and got hits on its canopy but the Zero pilot Split-S'd again and pulled up just above the water. Reeves came in for another deflection shot and got more hits on the Zeros' wing roots. As Reeves made a 360 he saw another P-38 make a deflection shot without getting any hits. Reeves then made his sixth and final pass on the stubborn Zero and fired a 45 degree deflection shot that hit its fuselage and canopy and as Reeves closed he saw a fire in the cockpit and watched as the "cleverest of all Nip fighter pilots I have ever encountered" crashed into the mountains.

432FS

After the mission, 1Lt. Robert Schuh of the 432FS was trying to land when the nosewheel of his P-38 became stuck in the up position. He had no option other than wheels up crashlanding which he walked away from unhurt but his P-38 was transferred as a total loss to the 479th Service Squadron.

**12 December 1944: 49FG/7FS**

At 1400, Mission Leader 1Lt. James O'Neil led Demon Flights on an armed reconnaissance on the enemy convoy sighted in the Visayan Sea the day before. As the Demons flew over Leyte's west coast at 10,000 feet White Flight, led by 1Lt. Joel Paris, spotted a single Betty bomber in the distance. The four White Flight P-38s dove on the bomber with Paris with his Wingman 1Lt. George Rogers attacking from the right while White Element Leader 1Lt. William Bauer attacked from the right. Paris fired first shutting down the bomber's port engine and destroyed its cockpit and canopy. The bomber crash landed on the water just offshore and Paris and Rogers made two strafing runs on the still floating bomber which then caught fire and Paris confirmed his fifth victory.

O'Neil regrouped his flights and continued patrolling the Visayan Sea and when they returned to the area of their first contact at 1615 at 13,000 feet, 1Lt. Warren Greczyn's Blue Flight met two bogies cruising over the water off Campopo Bay at 2 o'clock. Greczyn and Wingman, former 35 FG veteran ace, Capt. Richard Suehr, turned a 180 and identified the bogies as "Japs" and one Betty turned into them and the two dropped their tanks and made another 180 as did the Betty pilot but Greczyn got astern and fired and exploded its wing fuel tank and it crashed onto a coral reef in shallow water off Campopo beach. Greczyn and Suehr strafed the wreck and saw four crew running to shore and killed two and then Greczyn "sprayed the bushes just as the remaining two entered and I doubt if they got far."

**1Lt. Joel Paris** shot down a Betty bomber to become an ace. (AFAA)

Meanwhile, White Element Leader 1Lt. Robert Decker made a head on pass on the second Betty and chased it to he deck where the Betty pilot turned to port and Decker made a 60 degree firing pass and exploded its port engine and crashed into the trees near the beach for Decker's third victory. Decker watched as Greczyn strafed his Betty and Decker thought "I better make sure no one got out of mine" and went back but saw it burning furiously.

**13 December 1944: 475FG/431FS**

1610 MacDonald Patrol

Col. Charles MacDonald led four Lightnings off at 1610 to patrol a convoy in the western Mindanao area but as they arrived over the patrol area MacDonald could not contact the Controller. They patrolled for 30-45 minutes before they contacted the Controller and as they reached their designated patrol area they saw a Sally coming in over the overcast at 10,000 feet. MacDonald called the Controller and asked him to hold the

**Maj. Thomas McGuire**, with a victory over a jack narrowed his race with Bong by one; Bong 38/ McGuire 31. (AAF)

**Col. Charles MacDonald** shot down a Sally for his 21st victory. (AFAA)

AA fire over the convoy, as he thought he could get at the Sally before it attacked the shipping. Nonetheless, the AA fire immediately opened fire as the Sally dove and its rear gunner opened fire on MacDonald. The Colonel opened fire with a short burst from 1,000 feet and hit the bomber's mid fuselage and stopped the fire from the rear gunner. At 500 feet he shot out its port engine and the Sally crashed near a cruiser below for his 21st victory.

1635 McGuire Patrol
Maj. Thomas McGuire, eager to increase his score, led fighter sweep of two P-38s with Wingman, 1Lt. Harold Madison over Negros Island and Cebu Island. While flying over Tanza Airdrome, Negros, at 14,000 feet they saw a fuel truck on the runway and about 25 aircraft lined up on the side of the strip as if preparing to take off. The two flew over the other strips and found that they were not in service. As they returned to Tanza they saw dust on the runway and dove from 14,000 feet. McGuire went after a Jack that was on the deck and got hits from 60 degrees deflection but the Jack turned inside McGuire who then went after an Oscar but was unable to get off a shot. McGuire turned on another Jack and took a 60 degree shot as it was taking off but saw no results. McGuire resumed his attack on the first Jack from 90 degrees full deflection and got hits into its cockpit and it was witnessed to crash by his Wingman. McGuire led Madison from the area as the Japanese fighters were now airborne and had the numerical and altitude advantage. With his 31st victory the ace race between Bong and McGuire had narrowed by one; Bong 38/ McGuire 31.

**13 December 1933: 35FG/40FS**
During a B-24 escort to Carolina Airdrome on Negros Island, 1Lt. Ira Weaver's P-47 was bounced by two enemy fighters at 1200 that destroyed his rudder and aileron trim, locking it in the full left position and destroyed all left aileron control. The Thunderbolt went out of control momentarily and dropped 2,000 feet. Weaver regained control and dropped his tanks and turned toward Cebu where rescue PBY *Playmate 41* was stationed. The P-47 vibrated badly, its left aileron was fluttering, its wingtips oscillated a foot and a half and the entire aircraft drifted 5 degrees on either side of any heading taken. Weaver needed both hands to hold enough right stick to stay to the right and both feet to hold right rudder. Two Hamps came in from right and above and made 15 passes at Weaver, who turned into them each time, and they scored only a few hits before they ran out of ammunition and left. Weaver decided that he could make it to Dipolog and crash landed on a beach there at 1315. He found 20 holes in his rugged fighter, three by 20mm cannon shells that did most of the damage to his tail section and tail controls. A Catalina arrived an hour later and returned Weaver to Morotai where he had a piece of shrapnel removed from his shoulder.

**14 December 1944: 475FG/433FS**
Four P-38s took off at 0935 led by 1Lt. John Purdy to patrol the Negros Islands where, while flying at 8,000 feet they encountered a Tojo flying 3,000 feet. Purdy made a pass but missed and as the enemy pilot began a port turn, 2Lt. Clifford Ettien, the #2 man, fired a 30 degree deflection shot and got hits on its port wing and engine. The Tojo caught fire and went into a spin but its pilot bailed out for Ettien's only victory.

**14 December 1944: 348FG/340FS/341FS/460FS**
340FS
The 340FS commanded by Capt. Meade Brown had just transferred to Tanauan Airdrome on Leyte when they were assigned their first mission from their new strip. Brown led his ten P-47s off at 0930 on a dive bombing and strafing sweep to the Negros' airdromes at Talisay and Silay. They arrived over the target at 1115 to 1140 where they saw approximately 12 twin engine bombers and 20 fighters parked on the field. The 16 Thunderbolts dropped 32 500 pound GP bombs and strafed the field; leaving an undetermined number destroyed or damaged. Capt. Brown then led a four plane patrol when Brown saw a P-38 chasing a Tony. The Tony dove into a cloud, losing the Lightning, but Brown picked it up on the other side and dove on him from 8,000 to 2,000 feet and made a stern attack, firing a two second burst that exploded the starboard wing root. The Tony rolled and crashed north of the Negros Airstrip but Brown was credited with any claim as there were no witnesses.

The Thunderbolts quickly returned to base where they were refueled and loaded with 500 pound bombs. The 340th returned to Silay to bomb the field accounting for six twin-engine bombers and four fighters while four bomb hits in the center of the runway rendered it temporarily unserviceable. Three strafing passes were made following the bombing and an additional five bombers and five fighters were destroyed.

341FS
At 0930 16 P-47s of the 341FS took off to bomb and strafe the La Carlota Airdrome on Los Negros Island at 1015 where they sighted seven parked enemy aircraft which were bombed with unobserved results. 2Lt. Andrew Mix was the Element Leader of Blue Flight and was returning home at 10,000 feet when he saw a single bogie flying north at 5,000 feet about 10 miles east of Cebu. Mix and his Flight Leader went down to investigate and found the bogie to be a Zeke. Mix covered his Leader as he attacked but the Zero broke off sharply toward a cloud and Mix followed it down to 2,000 feet and fired when he saw it in the clouds and got a stern shot at 100 yards and the Zero did a Split-S and exploded five miles from Tagamacan for his first of two victories. Two P-47s collided in mid-air but were able to return to base safely with 2Lt. August Svancarey crashing on landing but receiving only minor injuries.

460FS
Early Morning
At 0550 Capt. William Dunham led four 460FS Thunderbolts on a sweep over Los Negros to recce the airdromes and to intercept any enemy aircraft there. They were flying at 2,000 feet over Talisay when they saw two Sallys at 500 feet. Dunham and his Wingman, 1Lt. Dewitt Searles, dove and Dunham attacked the lead Sally with a 15 degree stern deflection shot and the Sally burned and crashed in the bay off Talisay to make him a triple ace with 15 victories. Searles hit his Sally heavily and went into a steep dive and crashed south of Bagasay for his second victory.

Later Morning
The 460th sent out another four plane fighter sweep over Los Negros later that morning. 1Lt. Wallace Harding was the Element Leader of the second element flying at 14,000 feet over the Salay Strip when he saw a lone Tony flying an the deck. Harding dove immediately and as he closed the Tony took evasive action. Harding initially attacked from astern and then followed the Tony through 90 and then 180 degrees of his turn before he had to break away after scoring many hits on the fuselage and wing roots. Hardings' Wingman made a pass on the Tony but did not make any hits. Harding came around and closed from astern but the Tony turned sharply left and flew into Hardings' fire and was hit in the canopy and engine but the Tony continued flying on. Harding turned into a head on pass and got hits on the cowling and although the Tony started to smoke it flew on. Harding pulled up and closed on its stern one more time but the severely damaged Tony pilot tried to evade as Harding fired from dead astern and turned as Harding's bullets ripped the fuselage from the cockpit aft. The Tony went into a gentle turn into a cloud and finally crashed near Alicante for a hard-earned first victory of three.

**14 December 1944: 35FG/40FS/41FS**
40FS
During December the 35th Fighter Group continued to provide bomber escort for the 13th Bomber Command attacking installations and airdromes on the Negros, Cebu, Panay, Palewan, Mindanao, the Celebes, and Moluccas. The highlight of the month for the Group occurred on 14 December when 11 40FS P-47s intercepted an unescorted Japanese bomber formation consisting of 13 Helens and a Sally armed with bombs and torpedoes headed toward the USN Task Force. The Thunderbolts had just sighted the bomber force when 10 Navy F4Fs from a carrier in the task force also came in the area. The Thunderbolt Commander, 1Lt. Robert Steffy, checked in with them and the Navy flew top cover while the Air Force pilots attacked the bombers. In the ensuing battle near Soledad at 0940 the 40th slaughtered all of them. The battle was a rewarding victory for the 40th which had not seen any air action over Leyte since they transferred to the Philippines with their Thunderbolts in mid-November.

**Maj. William Dunham** became a triple ace when he shot down a Sally. (AFAA)

At 0940 1Lt. Robert Steffy was leading 11 P-47s and the Red Flight on a fighter sweep over Negros and was alerted to enemy fighters by P-38s of the 433FS that arrived 10 minutes earlier. Steffy saw three bogies at 9 o'clock on the deck just south of Soledad. Steffy sent his Red second element, Leader 1Lt. James Meeks and #4, 2Lt. Warren Wycoff, down while he and Wingman, 1Lt. Ellis Baker, followed and covered them. As they approached they saw 14 well camouflaged bombers, 13 Helens and one Sally bomber in three plane Vs in a string. Meeks and Wycoff closed on the rear Helen element but overshot as they were so well camouflaged. Meeks then closed on the rear Helen at 250 yards dead astern with a long burst that knocked out the rear gunner, stitched the fuselage, right engine, and cockpit and it fell off to the left. Meeks moved over to the lead Helen while Wycoff took the third bomber. Meeks gave his bomber a long burst that set on fire. Meeks came around for a second pass and closed to 150 yards and a short burst exploded its right engine. 2Lt. Warren Wycoff, separated from Meeks and Wycoff turned to starboard and fired a long burst on a Helen's tail and it tried to make a crash landing inland but crashed and exploded. Meanwhile, Steffy and Baker followed Red second element and attacked the outside bombers of the second flight. Steffy fired on one from dead astern and it started smoking and crashed into the sea in a shallow dive. The other bombers turned right and headed along the coast and Steffy pulled up and fired a short burst on a stern pass that hit the starboard wing and engine sending it into the ocean. Wingman Baker attacked the inside bomber and fired from dead astern setting both engines on fire and sent it down in flames. Baker pulled up in a gentle right turn and as he rolled out he found himself on the port wing of another Helen. The Helen made a right turn which helped Baker to slip behind the bomber to fire several bursts that hit the tail turret and fuselage, and both engines. The bomber exploded in mid air and the debris caused slight damage to Baker's fighter. Steffy continued along the coast and made another stern attack but was out of ammunition but continued with the flight and saw Red #4, 2Lt. Warren Wycoff. Wycoff had been flying along the coast and saw three Helens but by the time he could get into range they were all shot down. He closed on a fourth which was flying just over the water and fired a close in tail shot into the cockpit and the bomber nosed into the water. A lone Helen was outrunning the rest so Steffy made a high side pass on it, heading directly toward its cockpit and then pulled up sharply and the nervous Japanese pilot jerked his stick and crashed into the ground to give Steffy his third victory of the day and last of the war, leaving him one short of becoming an ace.

JAAF Nakajima **Ki-49 Helen** eight place twin engine bomber. (AFHRC)

**2Lt. Ellis Baker** shot down two Helen bombers for victories #2 and #3. (AAF)

Blue Flight followed Steffy's Red Flight on the Helens and Blue Leader, 1Lt. Roger Howe, and Wingman, 2Lt. William Colsh, made their pass on a Helen getting hits but causing no apparent damage. Second Element Leader, 2Lt. Harold Vaughn fired two five second bursts at 40 degrees deflection and closed to 75 yards dead astern getting hits in the port engine, wing roots, and cockpit. As Vaughn closed again, the Helen went into a 45 degree dive and exploded into the water. As Vaughn and Howe proceeded up the coast Howe fired on a Helen flying along the deck with its flaps down and shot it down about 500 feet off shore in shallow water. Some of its crew escaped and were strafed in the water by White Flight. The enemy turret gunner remained at his gun and fired at the strafers. The three Blue pilots became separated and as Colsh continued along the coast he saw Baker to his left shooting at a bomber from astern getting numerous hits that caused it to explode just before it hit the water. Colsh flew further along the coast and saw another bomber and closed, getting hits on the fuselage and both engines and it nosed into the water, momentarily skidding and then exploding. As Colsh flew over the wreckage he saw another Helen and fired a short then long burst and it too nosed into the water and exploded. Colsh was out of ammunition and turned toward home.

During the initial attack called out by Red Flight, White Flight composed of 1Lt. Anthony Faikus and Wingman, 2Lt. Ralph Bryner, and Second Element Leader, 1Lt. Ralph Hartley and Wingman, 2Lt. Robert Haigh remained above for top cover. Once White Flight entered the battle, Hartley was unable to make his pass because he had to avoid another P-47 making a pass and he broke off but his Wingman, 2Lt. Robert Haigh, chased a Sally that was skimming just above the waves 500 feet off shore. Haigh fired a long 30 degree burst from dead astern that raked the Sally from rear turret forward silencing the turret gunner who had been putting out intense but inaccurate fire. The bomber settled on the water and was strafed by Faikus and Bryner who saw two crewmen escape from the rear of the bomber which sank quickly.

The pilots stated that "the Japanese pilots seemed confused and gave each other no mutual gun support." The P-47 flights broke off in individual attacks on the bombers. After their fighters were out of ammunition four of the P-47 pilots made numerous passes on the bombers to draw the top turret fire away from the Thunderbolt that were still armed and firing. 1Lt. Robert Steffy shot down three Helens (his fourth and last victories); double Helen victories were claimed by 1Lt. James Meeks (his only two victories) and 2Lts. Ellis Baker (for his third victory), William Colsh (for his third victory), and Warren Wycoff (for his fourth and final victories). 1Lt. Roger Howe (his only victory) and 2Lt. Harold Vaughn (his only victory) got single Helens and 2Lt. Robert Haigh (his only victory) downed the Sally.

41FS

The 41FS sent 11 P-47s on a mid-morning B-24 escort on Fabrica Airdrome. 2Lt. Francis Riedle was leading Yellow Flight and after rendezvous with the bombers spotted lone bogie southeast of Pamplona at 14,000 feet and 10 o'clock level. As Riedle approached he identified the bogie as an Oscar and fired a 70 degree deflection shot at 200 yards but observed no hits. The Oscar pilot Split-S'd and Riedle followed and fired long bursts that tore pieces off the right wing root. Riedle was out of ammunition and climbed away and saw the Oscar was seen to go into an uncontrolled spin and crash for his second and last victory.

**15 December 1944: Mindoro Invasion**

Before Luzon could be dealt with, MacArthur would need a base of operations closer to Luzon than Leyte and chose the island of Mindoro just to the south of Luzon. Mindoro is approximately half the size of New Jersey and virtually covered by mountains with a few narrow plains along the coast. Mindoro was minimally defended and airfields could be built to supplement the inadequate fields recently constructed on Leyte. Possible landing areas in the northeastern area were considered best but continuous stormy weather and the airfield's proximity to the remnants of Japanese air power on Luzon discounted that area. As an alternative, planners chose a beachhead on the southwest corner of the island in order to capture airfield sites near San Jose and Mangarin Bay, Mindoro's best anchorage. Once secured this area would provide a base for an amphibious invasion fleet directed on Luzon and allow land-based American aircraft to intensify attacks against the Japanese on Luzon.

The 7 December landings at Ormoc and the subsequent eradication of the enemy Army and Navy on Leyte gave MacArthur another opportunity to advance his Philippine's agenda. Allied intelligence had confirmed that heavy air raids and Guerilla activity on southern Mindoro had rendered the Island's garrisons virtually defenseless so MacArthur decided to move 375 miles north of Leyte and invade Mindoro on 15 December.

To relieve the overextended 308BW at Tacloban, which included the beleaguered 49th and 475th Fighter Groups, Kenney called up a new tactical unit designated as the 310th Bomb wing under the command of Col. C.T. Murtha waiting in New Guinea. Meanwhile, the Tacloban strategic groups would stand in reserve until the airfields near San Jose were captured and readied; tentatively for the third week of December. As part of Murtha's 310BW staff for Mindoro, Kenney appointed able veteran Col. Robert Morrissey of 5FC as special liaison in planning the Mindoro air defense aboard the *USS Nashville*. The appointment suited his career agenda as a successful leadership stint on Mindoro would lead to an assured promotion; perhaps to becoming the first fighter pilot since Wurtsmith to be promoted to General. Kenney also appointed Col. Bruce Hill as the Task Force Commander. The 8FG with its newer model Lightnings was assigned as the first 5FC Group to provide Mindoro air cover while the P-47s of the 58FG would provide tactical support for the invasion. The air wings of the USN escort carriers were to add to the air cover, including Hellcat night fighters to provide protection after dark.

The infantry attack on Mindoro was to be directed by the Sixth Army's Lt.Gen. Walter Krueger who assigned Maj.Gen. Roscoe Woodruff, commander of the 24th Infantry Division, for the mission. Although the landing forces were relatively small, naval support was substantial, consisting of six escort carriers, three battleships, six cruisers, and many small warships providing direct support. Several days preceding the landing of American ground forces on Mindoro on 15 December Fifth Air Force and the Thirteenth Air Force fighters attacked all Japanese bases in the area from which counter strikes could be flown against the USN task force moving north.

The main threat to the amphibious assault vessels and supporting warships came from Japanese land-based Kamikaze suicide planes. During the final stages of the Leyte Campaign the Japanese first used the Kamikaze as a desperate measure. The invasion convoy sailed on 12 December from Leyte Gulf but was soon spotted by the Japanese and attacked from the air. At 1430 on 13 December one enemy aircraft managed to get through the convoy defenses and crashed into the cruiser USS *Nashville*, causing 275 casualties and putting the cruiser out of action. Among those killed were Col. Bruce Hill, Chief of Staff of the Mindoro Task Force and the Communications Officer of the Naval Attack Force. Col. John Murtha, commanding the 310th Bomb Wing was wounded and died later. Brig.Gen. William Dunckel, commanding the invasion forces, was painfully burned but refused to step down from his command and he and his staff moved to the destroyer *Dashiell*. R.Adm. Arthur Struble, the Naval Attack Force Commander, had to transfer his flag from the *Nashville* to the destroyer *Dashiell*.

As the Mindoro invasion force was heading north into the narrow straits off Siquijor Island, protected by a large force of Army and Navy fighters; unknown to them they were only minutes by air from the surviving Kamikaze units based at Fabrica Airdrome on the nearby Negros Island. Just after 1500 general quarters sounded the Kamikaze attack and one ran the gauntlet of AA fire and air cover to crash the *Nashville*. The bomb collapsed Morrissey's cabin and shattered his right leg. Surgeons saved his life and then leg but Morrissey's military career was finished. Later on board the *Nashville*, the bodies of Colonels Murtha and Bruce Hill were recovered. Other invasion ships were hit in the Kamikaze attack and 75 members of the 58FG ground echelon were killed when their troop carrier was hit. In the attack Kenney

The **Mindoro** invasion force was unopposed. (U.S. Army)

The **Mindoro** bound convoy came under Kamikaze attack. (USN)

had lost a future Fighter Command leader, a Wing Commander, a Task Force Commander, and nearly all of a fighter group ground echelon.

Beginning 14 December, Adm. Halsey's Task Force 58 attacked enemy air installations on Luzon and claimed 270 enemy planes destroyed and six ships sunk for the loss of 27 Navy planes. However, an unpredicted strong typhoon damaged Halsey's Fleet causing him to withdraw to Ulithi for extensive repairs. Meanwhile aircraft based on the invasion convoy's escort carriers claimed 34 enemy aircraft destroyed and struck air fields within range. Also, the discovery of this invasion convoy by the Japanese signified another invasion and marked the end of the Japanese attempt to resupply and hold Leyte and thus they effectively abandoned their 35th Army which was to defend the island.

The Mindoro invasion, coded *U-Day*, began at 0730 on 15 December against virtually no Japanese resistance, as only about 1,000 Japanese troops were on the large island. Enemy air attacks had increased as the convoy approached the beaches and one destroyer and two LSTs were hit and had to be abandoned but the Japanese lost 23 aircraft to AA fire. P-38s and Navy F4Us covered the beachhead during *U-Day* and shot down eight enemy aircraft. The two LSTs sunk carried all the equipment of the 8th Fighter Group and the 418th Night Fighter Squadron however, the 25 remaining LSTs in the convoy were quickly unloaded on *U-Day* and all returned to Leyte without damage. The 19th and the 503rd Parachute, Regimental Combat Teams (RCT), landed on the beach and quickly advanced inland as the Japanese defenders left when the naval bombardment began. Gen. Dunckel was ashore by 1030 and the 19th RCT had pushed eight miles inland and the 503rd RCT captured San Jose by noon. By the end of the first day, Army engineers were constructing airfields for the invasion of Luzon with the first completed in five days and a second was ready in 13 days. These airfields would provide American aircraft more direct support for the planned Luzon beachhead, the ability to attack Kamikaze airfields before they could take off, and to harass Japanese shipping traveling between Luzon, Formosa, and southern Japan.

Just after the RCTs moved inland the engineers began surveying for the fighter strip and by mid-afternoon the 3rd Airdrome Construction Battalion of the RAAF and the 1874th Engineer Aviation Battalion was ready to begin construction of the strip while other engineer units began construction on roads, dumps, and similar facilities. The first 5,750 foot strip, named for Col. Bruce Hill killed on the cruiser *Nashville* on 13 December, was operational by 20 December with enough dispersal areas for one fighter group. The San Jose all-weather strip, with a 7,000 foot runway, parallel taxiway, 35 hardstands and a cargo unloading area was ready by 27 December. Elmore Field was located just west of the sugar mill at San Jose. It was ready for emergency use by 23 December and was operational by the 26th by the 82nd Reconnaissance Squadron. It's two clay and gravel 6,000 foot strips could only be used in good weather. Two more strips, "C" and "D" strips were under construction.

After the invasion convoy left, the Kamikazes and conventional Japanese air forces continued to attack the resupply convoys throughout the remainder of December claiming five LSTs and five Liberty ships badly damaged or sunk. The Japanese conducted over a 100 sorties over the beachhead on 16 December and then until the end of the month, another 400 sorties were flown. During this period the enemy lost 55 aircraft in air-to-air combat and 48 to AA fire.

Gen. Walter Krueger, Commander of the Sixth Army, on the Mindoro Operation:

> The risk taken in launching the Mindoro attack was considerable, but it was a calculated one, fully justified by the strategical and tactical results. It gave us a base from which the Fifth Air Force could launch strong air attacks in support of the Luzon operation and in protecting the sea lanes leading to Luzon from the south. It also deceived the enemy to some extent as to where we would make our initial descent on Luzon.

MacArthur's Mindoro Campaign had been bold and fraught with risk. The JCS had advised MacArthur that the operation was "too daring in scope, too risky in execution" and, as usual, did not give much regard to the opinions of the Pentagon. Adm. Kincaid, commanding the Seventh Fleet, warned of the danger of running the Fleet and convoys through the Surigao Strait and the Sulu Sea. MacArthur was convinced that Gen. Yamashita would not fight for Mindoro as he had for Leyte but would save his forces for the impending fight for the Luzon and Manila. The result was that the Sixth Army had suffered only 70 men killed or missing in the Mindoro Campaign and 180 men wounded. The huge gamble moved the 5th Fighter Command 300 miles from Leyte to Mindoro and within easy access of the many enemy air fields in the Manila area.

**Mindoro Airfields**

The 19th and 503rd RCTs began landing at 0730 on 15 December and by late afternoon had posted a final beachhead line lying seven miles inland. Troops secured the San Jose airstrip, a prewar emergency landing field roughly five miles inland, against no opposition. Beach conditions were almost ideal, and an observer from the 2nd Engineer Special Brigade, watching the unloading, was prompted to report that the "operation was really just a maneuver" for shore party units.

Since expansion of the San Jose strip was not feasible, engineers quickly began surveys for a better site and soon found one about three miles south of the field. By mid-afternoon the 1874th Engineer Aviation Battalion and No. 3 Airdrome Construction Squadron (RAAF) had begun work on the new site, ultimately called Hill Drome. The field was ready as scheduled on 20 December, on which day Fifth Air Force P-38s and P-61 night fighters began arriving; P-47s reached the field from Leyte three days later. Meanwhile, engineers began work on another strip called Elmore Field, about two miles northwest of Hill Drome. This second field was ready for limited use on 23 December and for continuous dry-weather operations on the 28th, a week ahead of schedule.

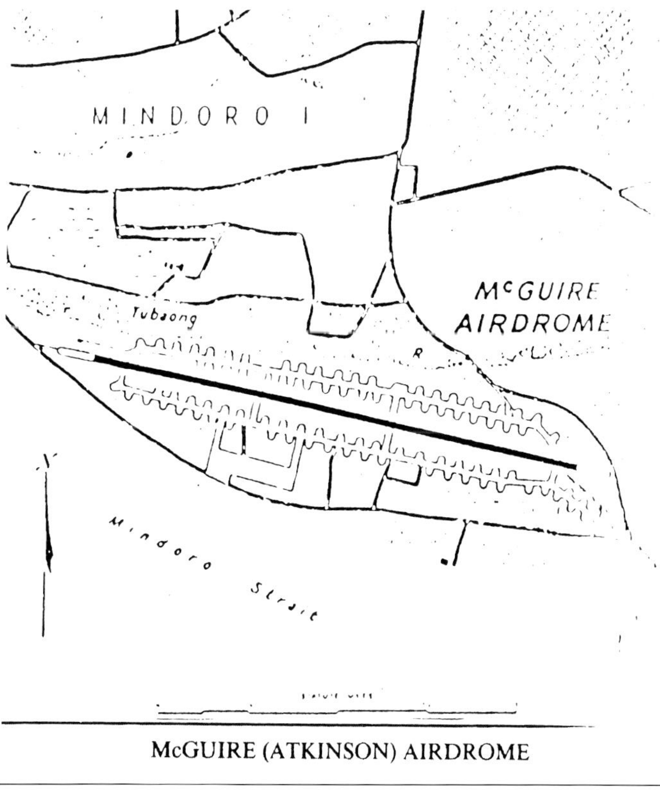


McGUIRE (ATKINSON) AIRDROME

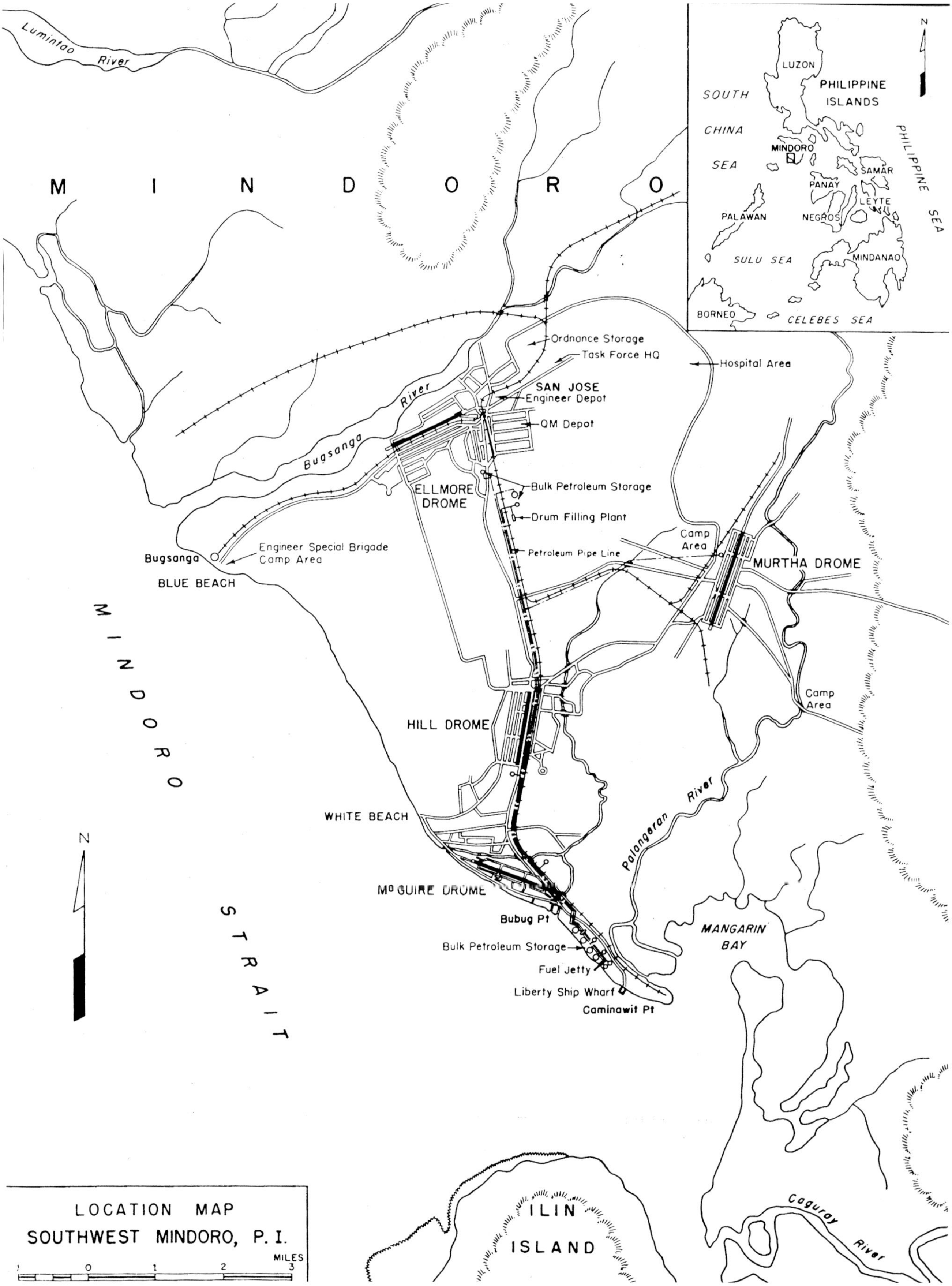
Lumintao River
M I N D O R O
LUZON
PHILIPPINE ISLANDS
SOUTH CHINA SEA
MINDORO
SAMAR
PANAY
LEYTE
PHILIPPINE SEA
PALAWAN
NEGROS
SULU SEA
MINDANAO
BORNEO
CELEBES SEA
Ordnance Storage
Task Force HQ
Hospital Area
SAN JOSE
Engineer Depot
QM Depot
Bugsanga River
Bulk Petroleum Storage
ELLMORE DROME
Drum Filling Plant
Camp Area
Petroleum Pipe Line
MURTHA DROME
Bugsanga
Engineer Special Brigade Camp Area
BLUE BEACH
MINDORO STRAIT
HILL DROME
Camp Area
Palangeran River
WHITE BEACH
McGUIRE DROME
Bubug Pt
MANGARIN BAY
Bulk Petroleum Storage
Fuel Jetty
Liberty Ship Wharf
Caminawit Pt
LOCATION MAP
SOUTHWEST MINDORO, P. I.
MILES
1 0 1 2 3
ILIN ISLAND
Caguray River

The first runway was barely operational in time to be of use in helping to turn back new Japanese counterattacks. On or about 20 December the Japanese Naval Air Service in the Philippines, which had executed the majority of the attacks against Mindoro so far, was reinforced by around 50 aircraft flown in from Formosa, bringing its operational strength to about 75 planes at bases within easy range of Mindoro. With this force, augmented by a few Japanese Army Air Force aircraft, the Japanese renewed air attacks on 21 December, 15 the day before ships of an Allied resupply convoy were scheduled to reach Mindoro. About 20 Kamikazes attacked the convoy, so damaging two LST's that they later had to be abandoned, and inflicting lesser damage on two destroyers and a Liberty ship. The Japanese lost seven aircraft planes in Kamikaze attacks and three others to shipboard AA fire.

Murtha Field
Single runway of 7,000 x 100 feet PSP surfaced
5FC Units based at:
8FG/36FS (P-38)

Hill/Hammer Field
Unpaved single runway 5,750 x 100 feet surfaced with packed earth. Dust during dry periods and mud during rains; caused a move to Murtha Airfield after completion.
5FC Units based at:

71TRG, 82TRS (F6D) 1 January 1945 Morotai via Tacloban to Lingayen

**Murtha Field**. (AAF)

**San Jose (McGuire) Field**. (AAF)

San Jose/Elmore/Atkinson/McGuire Field
A pre-war field used by the Japanese and improved as a single runway parallel to the coast. 7,000 x 100 feet, gravel and asphalt surfaced.

After Atkinson returned later in January the new field on Mindoro was renamed McGuire Field. Gen. Hap Arnold ordered Kenney to refrain from the hurried naming of air bases for the departed.

5FC Units based at:

8FG: 35FS, 36FS, 80FS (P-38) Morotai Dec 20, 1944 - ?
58FG: 311FS San Roque Dec 21, 1944 - ?
71TRG: 17RS Biak Dec 23, 1944 - ?
71TRG: 110TRS (P-40) ? Nov 3 - Dec 25, 1944 to San Jose
310BW: 418NFS (P-61) Morotai Dec 26 - ?, 1944
71TRG: 82TRS (F-6 & P-40) Dec 29, 44 - Jan 17, 45 Lingayen
49FG: 8FS (P-38) Tacloban Jan 2, 1945 - Feb 27, 1945 Lingayen
6PRG: 25PRS (F-5) Jan 3, 1945 - ?
71TRG: 110TRS (P-40) Tacloban Jan 4 - 22, 1945 - Lingayen
86FW: 547NFS (P-38 & P-61) Owi Jan 5 - 16 1945 Lingayen
71TRG: 17RS (B-25) Tacloban Dec 7, 1945 - ? San Jose

**15 December 1944: 8FG Moves to Mindoro via Leyte**

The 8FG ground echelon left Morotai on 5 November and joined a convoy headed to Leyte two days later. During the voyage a determined Japanese torpedo bomber released its torpedo that just missed the *USS Almaak*, carrying the 35FS ground echelon, and the cargo attack ship immediately behind and then a destroyer that maneuvered out of the torpedo's path. On 14 November the 35FS' equipment was unloaded, or better dumped, in darkness, where ever there was space available. The next morning the ground echelon found it's supplies and equipment scattered everywhere along the beach with the incoming tide ruining much of it. When the ground echelons sorted out their equipment they waited in camps on the beach for the LSTs to arrive. The tedious wait continued until noon on 12 December when the 35th boarded *LST 738* to be transported to the Mindoro invasion scheduled for 15 December. The ships left Tacloban Harbor and joined the convoy three hours later and for the rest of the voyage the crews would worry about Japanese Kamikaze suicide aircraft. The next afternoon a Japanese suicide plane slipped under the warning net and crashed on the cruiser *Nashville* with devastating results. On 15 December the convoy reached the Mindoro beaches and the 8FG personnel were scheduled to go ashore with the third wave. At about 0900 Japanese torpedo bombers broke through the CAP screen and one dropped its torpedo and then crashed into *LST 738* amidships. The LST listed with flames and smoke spreading over its torn hull. For all the chaos and damage, casualties were very minimal with only Aircraft Mechanic, Pvt. Baltazar Rubio killed and several other 8FG personnel suffering burns which required hospitalization.

The attack on the ground echelon of the 80FS was described:

> On the morning of the fifteenth, D-Day, fireworks broke loose. *LST 738* was out five miles from shore, while our task force started shelling Mindoro. At about 0845 hours the enemy began coming over. No one had a clear idea of how many Japanese planes there were because of all the excitement going on.
>
> *LST 738* became the target for a Japanese plane, which approached it from the starboard side. It was thought that the plane would make its pass and then zoom up. However, the enemy was a member of Radio Tokyo's boasted Kamikaze Special Attack Corps of Suicide Pilots. He dove his plane directly at the ship and crashed into it amidships. Fires broke out on deck among the trucks, and the abandon-ship order was given about 30 minutes after the ship had been hit. A destroyer pulled alongside and attempted to put out the fire with its hoses, the water system of the LST having been damaged. Lines and ladders were lowered for the men to go over the side. Most of the men left the ship in an orderly manner; however, some men jumped over the side and others left by climbing down the anchor chain. There were PT boats, LSTs, and destroyers nearby to pick up survivors, who were brought to shore in a couple of hours and taken to the 310th Bomb Wing on Mindoro. Later it was learned that 13 enlisted men were hospitalized aboard the hospital ship *USS Brooks*, while 12 officers and enlisted men returned to Leyte on a destroyer. The men who had been brought ashore slept in the fields that night, as all equipment had gone down with the ship. A couple of days later they moved in with the 307th Airdrome Squadron, where they were supplied with a change of clothes, cigarettes, and other odds and ends.

After learning of *LST 738's* ordeal, the second 8FG echelon left Morotai for Mindoro on *LST 911* on 20 December. The next day first enemy planes appeared over the convoy and were mistaken for the American escort and two enemy fighters zoomed through the convoy before any AA guns could be fired. Japanese attacked in force in the afternoon when 23 enemy aircraft attacked and although many were claimed to be shot down were all claimed shot down two LSTs were destroyed and another ship damaged. The second echelon landed safely at Mindoro on 22 December.

The apprehensive third echelon left Leyte for Mindoro on 26 December on *LST 916*. The first Japanese attack hit the convoy even before it even left the harbor but the convoy was protected by heavy AA fire that drove the Japanese off. Attack alerts continued into the next morning when five Japanese raiders were first sighted and exploded an ammunition ship which sank with all aboard. *LST 916* was anchored immediately behind the doomed ammunition ship but escaped damage. This attack was followed by waves of aircraft throughout the day and into that night which were driven off before causing any damage. The planning for the ensuing convoys to Mindoro had included more AA fire and large numbers of P-38, P-47, and F4U escorts. During the morning of 28 December a lone Japanese plane appeared and was dispatched. Then late in the day about 20 to 30 Japanese raiders arrived and damaged another LST before they were driven off but anti-aircraft fire continued through the night. By the time the convoy arrived at Mindoro during the morning of the 29th more than 40 Japanese aircraft had been shot down by fighters, AA fire, or suicide dives. The third echelon moved directly to their new base at Hill Field where they found that night alerts were numerous and the men spent many hours in their slit trenches.

35FS Lightnings on **Hill Field**. (AAF)

**17-22 December 1944: 58FG Moves to Mindoro**

Loading of the 58th Fighter Group began on schedule on 17 December into three LSTs and on the freighter *SS John Clayton*. The personnel of Headquarters and the Group's three Squadrons were sent to the ships and loading was completed on the 18th and these ships joined the resupply convoy of six large freighters and 17 LSTs. The convoy was covered by 11 new Fletcher Class destroyers and a separate Escort Carrier Group when it sailed south out of Leyte Gulf, and then west into the Mindanao Sea, north through the Sulu Sea then into the Mindoro Strait arriving at Mangarin Bay off San Jose, Mindoro on 22 December. The convoy was attacked enroute by approximately 20 suicide aircraft at various times; sinking two LSTs and seriously damaging a Liberty ship. The P-38s of the 49FG were forced to cover the convoy by flying their extreme range and only shot down one of the enemy attackers but had to face the danger from the convoy's trigger-happy AA gunners who shot down many of the Japanese attackers but, unfortunately, the crashes of their suicide aircraft claimed the others. The 58th began to unload on the morning of the 22nd amid Red Alerts but the enemy attackers were dispatched by P-38 cover. The 58th camp was located about two miles north of Hill Field and about two miles from the San Jose Strip (later Elmore Field). The 311FS left Noemfoor with 22 P-47s on the 23rd with an intermediate refueling stop at Morotai before landing at Hill Field. The Squadron suffered the loss of two aircraft on the soft newly graded strip. The 69FS flew into Mindoro on Christmas Day and also lost two fighters while landing and a few hours later the 311th lost another P-47 which ran off the runway after a patrol.

The new Hill Airstrip, named in honor of the late Task Force Commander, Col. Bruce Hill, immediately began operations to receive AAF squadrons. The 5,700 foot sand and gravel runway was adequate, despite the intermittent rains. Elmore Strip, a short distance to the north, would be completed by 23 December to alleviate the congestion at Hill. Col. J.A. Wilson, the new replacement Commander of the 310BW, sent 8FG Lightnings and 418NFS Black Widows to Hill Field on 20 December and they were operational by the end of the day.

**15 December 1944: Mindoro Invasion Air Operations**

475FG/431FS

Maj. Thomas McGuire led four P-38s of Daddy Special from Dulag at 0630 with Maj. Richard Bong as his Second Element Leader. The Flight arrived over Negros Island at 0700 and circled over the airdromes on the northern and eastern side of the Island for an hour. Bong led his Element to Panubulon Island where Wingman, 1Lt. Floyd Fulkerson, called out a lone bandit below. They turned 360 but lost the bandit and then turned to the 60 degree heading that the enemy was flying. Bong saw the Oscar at 3 o'clock low at 7,000 feet and dove on it. He closed and fired a short burst from 90 to 60 degrees and saw a hit on its starboard wing before he overshot. Bong made a 360 turn to port and closed to 1,000 feet and opened fire from 50 degrees and scored hits that caused it to turn descend to the right. Bong closed from astern and finished the Oscar off for his 39th victory to put him the usual eight victories ahead of McGuire. As Bong and Fulkerson rejoined McGuire they strafed Tanza Airdrome and Fulkerson lost his canopy and was escorted back to base by Bong.

**348FG/342FS/341FS**

342FS

At 0715 December Maj. Walter Benz led 14 P-47s in four flights on a patrol over the Mindoro beachhead. At 0900 while on patrol at 12,000 over Semirara Islands they saw a single enemy fighter at 10,000 feet. Benz led his three plane flight down and took a 40 degree deflection shot and saw hits on its cockpit. The Zero continued on and Benz took another 15 degree shot that ripped off pieces and started a fire as the Zero crashed into the ocean for his seventh victory.

341FS

1Lt. David Mumper was the Leader of a three plane flight and while they were patrolling 10 miles off the beach at 7,000 feet they saw two enemy fighters about 9,000 feet high. Mumper dropped only one of his wing tanks and saw a Zero Split-S, so Mumper turned toward it and it leveled off, only to go into another Split-S. Mumper fired, missing with the first burst, but then hit him with a 30 degree deflection shot that set it on fire for his first of two victories. Mumper and his flight continued their patrol and saw another lone Zero diving toward he deck. Mumper dove first but was too far out of range to fire and while he was chasing him, Mumper's two Wingmen having no wing tanks and the speed advantage roared past him. 2Lt. Roy McCord who had joined Mumper's flight from the 342FS during the battle, started firing from underneath Mumper and when the Zero turned McCord got a fatal deflection shot for his only victory.

49FG/7FS

At 0730, newly appointed Demon Ops Exec Capt. John Haher took off with seven P-38s as part of a large fighter sweep against Los Negros Airdrome outside San Jose, which was Mindoro's provincial capitol located on the southern most coast of Mindoro. After flying an hour the Lightnings were over the invasion fleet, and immediately, the 475 FG contacted an enemy force over Seminara Island 10 miles south of the Mindoro mainland.

The 7FS approached Mindoro with Haher's Pinky Red Flight (Wingman, 2Lt. Milden Mathre; Element Leader, 1Lt. James Jarrell; and Wingman, 2Lt. George Spruill) at 9,000 feet and 1Lt. Fernley Damstrom's trailing Pinky White Flight (Wingman, 2Lt. William Thompson; Element Leader, 2Lt. Nicanor Zuniga; and #4 2Lt. Oliver Atchison) in high cover at 15,000. At 0915, Red Flight elements spotted a flight of seven Zeros above and to their left. The eight Demon pilots jettisoned their tanks and Red Flight zoomed into a climbing port turn. White Flight circled to the starboard behind the enemy fighters which also dropped their tanks and now the obviously inexperienced enemy pilots were caught between the two Demon flights. Two tried to escape west and Haher's Red Flight went after them while Damstrom's White Flight chased the other five which continued to climb left.

Haher's Flight chased after the two Zeros whose pilots Split-S'd away as the Lightnings were gaining on them. Haher and Wingman Mathre took the #2 man while Jarrell and Wingman, Spruill went after the Leader. Haher and Mathre chased their Zero to the deck where Haher fired and the Zeros Split-S'd and flew straight at Mathre who fired from out of range and missed. When the Zero turned to port Mathre fired a 30-40 degree deflection shot and got hits "all along the fuselage" sending it into the water without catching fire or smoking for Mathre's fourth victory. Jarrell made eight passes on his Zero and scored hits on three of the passes as the enemy pilot "took very good evasive action, leaving me only 90 degree deflection shots, except for one 30 degree shot which I scored hits on his fuselage and started him smoking." On his next pass from the front quarter, Haher started a fire in its cockpit and the Zero exploded in the water for Haher's second victory.

Damstrom attacked the third Zero in the second element and shot at it as it was trying to turn inside the P-38 and got a few hits. Damstrom closed on the Zero from 90 degrees getting a few more hits but then Damstrom pulled up sharply to the left and took a 60 degree shot at another Zero which had turned into the Americans. The Zero caught fire and lost altitude, finally going into a spin into the water. Zuniga and Atchison saw a Zero climbing on a head on pass and Zuniga broke left in a steep chandelle, while Atchison turned into the Zero and fired from slightly below from 300 yards and hit its engine, wing root, and cockpit. Instead of turning away, the Zero pilot tried to ram the P-38 and Atchison broke sharply under the Zero, which missed him by only 50 feet. The Zero was smoking and dropped on its right wing and exploded into the water for Atchison's second and last victory. At 0930 the Controller sent Damstrom's Flight to cover the convoy sailing west of Panay. At 1015 the convoy's Controller vectored Damstrom toward a Zero that was located at 500 feet and 10 miles away. Damstrom and Wingman, 2Lt. William Thompson dove from 10,000 feet while the second element covered them. Damstrom closed astern and fired and got hits first on its left wing and then on its right wing root which started a fire. As pieces came off, the Zero inverted and crashed into the water for his second victory of the day and his seventh.

**17 December 1944: 35FG/41FS**

At 1220 12 Thunderbolts of the 41FS arrived over Tarakan, North Borneo to strafe the airdrome there that was expected to hold aircraft staging from southern Borneo to Mindoro. If no aircraft were on the field then they were to strafe the drome or the nearby oil installations. 1Lt. Richard DeBaugh was leading White Flight at 14,000 feet and circled there to cover Red and Yellow Flights while they strafed the field which had aircraft on it. While circling he saw two Oscars flying at 500 feet at 2 o'clock and as he dropped his tanks the enemy fighters turned north and as DeBaugh closed at 1,000 feet above the water, an Oscar turned into him and but passed under him without noticeable hits. The Oscar fired at DeBaugh's #2 man but leveled off toward his #3 man, 1Lt. Charles McKiearnan. Both pilots fired but the machine guns of two enemy aircraft were no match for the P-47's eight .50s that scored hits on the wing roots and the Oscar went down in flames and was credited as McKiearnan's only victory. Meanwhile, DeBaugh went down to strafe and burned a Hamp and Oscar. After his third pass and turning into the fourth at 500 feet, the #2 man called out a bandit at 3 o'clock high. DeBaugh put his fighter into water injection and climbed toward the Oscar that saw him and turned and DeBaugh was unable to shoot. The Oscar pilot turned left and DeBaugh turned hard right to get a 45 degree deflection shot. At 250 yards he fired a one second burst; hitting the fuselage. When he got on its tail after the deflection shot he fired a three second burst and pieces came off the wing root and the Oscar descended and exploded at 500 feet for DeBaugh's only victory.

**17 December 1944: 475FG/431FS/433FS**

431FS

Maj. Richard Bong led four P-38s of Daddy Special from Dulag at 1450 on a fighter sweep of the Mindoro beachhead. His flight consisted of Wingman, Maj. Jack Rittmayer and Second Element Leader, 1Lt. Floyd Fulkerson, and his Wingman, 1Lt. Owen Giertsen. The flight arrived over

**Maj. Richard Bong** poses after claiming his 40th and last victory, which would make him America's all-time ace-of-aces. (AAF)

Mindoro at 9,000 feet at 1605 and at 1615 the Controller called that the beachhead was being strafed. At the same time Bong spotted two bogeys at 12 o'clock high and he dropped his tanks and elected to climb after the bogeys, identified as Oscars. The enemy pilots turned 180 and headed north and Bong and Rittmayer chased after them at 9,000 feet. The Oscar pilots made no effort to turn into the Americans but chose to try to escape. After a five minute stern chase Bong closed on the Leader, who dove right and separated from his Wingman. Bong fired and the Oscar disintegrated and caught fire before it plunged into the ground 20 miles from San Jose for his milestone 40th victory. Rittmayer chased the Oscar Wingman and fired at close range, knocking off pieces of its rudder and wings. The Oscar wobbled violently, lost speed, and fell off into a shallow dive, apparently out of control. Rittmayer dove after it and at 6,000 feet the enemy pulled out and regained control where Rittmayer fired from slight deflection and got solid hits into its fuselage and right wing root. The Oscar still continued to fly on and Rittmayer closed and fired until the Oscar became a solid sheet of flames for his fourth and last victory.

Bong's ICR for the combat:

> I took off from Dulag Strip at 1450 as leader of Daddy Special Flight on a fighter sweep to Mindoro beachhead. We climbed to 9,000 feet on course and arrived over Mindoro at 1605. I contacted the controller and started to patrol.
>
> At 1615 the controller said that the friendly beachhead was being strafed. At the same time I sighted two bogeys at 12 o'clock high. As friendly flights were down to take care of the strafers I dropped tanks and started climbing for altitude.
>
> The Oscars made a 180° turn and headed straight north. We gave chase and I closed on the leader, who had dived to the right separating from the other e/a, and shot him down at 1625 from an altitude of 9,000 feet. The Oscar disintegrated and then caught fire and dived straight down and crashed about 20 miles north of San Jose.
>
> I then watched Major Rittmayer, my wingman, shoot down the other Oscar. We reformed formation and patrolled over San Jose until 5:15 and returned to home base, landing at 1830. Lieutenant Fulkerson saw the Oscar crash and will confirm it.

Fulkerson's ICR reported that he had seen Bong "close in on the Oscar from dead astern and fire a short burst which brought pieces from the Oscar. The Oscar turned right and with another burst from Major Bong, did a half-roll, trailing fire, and crashed in the jungle."

When Kenney heard of Bong's 40th victory he issued an order for Bong to fly his plane to Tacloban and fly no further combat and return to the United States as soon as possible. Bong wanted to reach 50 victories but Kenney would not hear of this.

Later some pilots of McGuire's Squadron criticized Bong's tactics during this mission as did the Squadron Intelligence Officer who wrote: "Though the flight was successful in the destruction of both of the e/a, good flying technique was neglected when the leading flight separated, thus forcing the second element to separate to protect them." The 475FG History states: "those pilots seemed more interested in running up their individual scores than protecting themselves and flight members and following our standard operating procedures." "Those pilots" meaning Bong and Rittmayer.

433FS

Thirteen Possum Lightnings took off at 1355 and reached their patrol area at 6-8,000 feet over the Mindoro beachhead at 1500. The patrol continued until 1615 when Red Flight called out four bogies at 3,000 feet headed west.

**1Lt. John Purdy** shot down two Zeros to give him his seventh and last victories. (AFAA)

**Capt. William Grady** (right, with 1Lt. Clarence Rieman) claimed his fourth of four victories. (AAF)

At 1625 1Lt. John Purdy's Blue #4 man, 2Lt. Robert Morrell, called out two Zeros at 9,000 feet heading NE about four miles from Magaran. The Zeros turned toward Blue Flight and since the enemy had the altitude advantage, Purdy turned away momentarily which led the Zeros to return to their original heading. Purdy then chased after the Zeros and caught them about eight miles east of Tombonac. The two Zeros were now in line abreast and Purdy closed from 6 o'clock on the one on the right and fired a short burst into its fuselage and canopy and the Zero rolled over and crashed into the mountains below. Purdy then turned toward the other Zero and fired a 10 degree deflection shot into its right wing and engine and it burst into flames, its pilot bailed out and also crashed into the mountains for Purdy's seventh and last victory of the war.

Red Flight Leader, Capt. William Grady, saw four Jacks flying west at 2 o'clock at 3,000 feet over San Jose Strip with the first three flying about a half mile ahead of the fourth. Grady made a 180 degree turn and closed slightly behind the last Jack to 200 yards. Just as Grady was about to fire his gunsight malfunctioned but he was able to fire a long burst that hit the Jack's port wing root and canopy which blew off and the Jack fell off on its wing and plunged straight into the water four miles from Ambulong Island for Grady's fourth and last victory.

**18 December 1944: 475FG/433FS**

Capt. Jack Fisk led seven P-38s, four from his Blue Flight and three from Green Flight (Green Flight Leader aborted), to cover the beachhead over southern Mindoro Island. As the 433rd neared the patrol area the Controller urged Fisk to hurry as there were enemy aircraft overhead and that he would have friendly AA fire stopped while the Lightnings fought the enemy fighters. As Fisk neared the beachhead at 10,000 feet, flying west he spotted a single bandit 2,000 feet below flying north. Fisk attacked the Jack out of the sun firing a short burst from 150 yards and the 20mm shells ripped into its cockpit and tore off pieces of its fuselage and starboard wing. The Jack Split-S'd as Fisk pulled away and crashed into a mountain slope south of Hagdanan. Almost immediately Blue Flight saw eight more enemy aircraft at 12,000 feet apparently heading after Green Flight. Blue Flight was at 7,000 feet flying south and Fisk led them in a climbing turn to 12,000 feet and came in on their rear. As they closed four of the leading Zeros dove for the deck; two to the left and two to the right. Fisk chose the right two; one of which broke left toward a cloud and the other continued straight ahead and Fisk pursued it. He closed to 200 yards when the Zero made a starboard vertical turn and he rolled with it and got a two second burst that got solid hits on its cockpit, wings, and fuselage for Fisk's second victory of the day to make him an ace with six victories.

After the Green Flight Leader aborted the Second Element Leader, 2Lt. Samuel Morrison, took over with 2Lts. Joseph Sperling and George Gabik continuing with the flight. After Fisk claimed his first victim, Morrison led Green Flight after two bandits but as they climbed they were attacked by a Tony and Jack from head on above at 45 degrees.

Gabik turned into the Tony head on and got hits that started it smoking heavily for a probable claim. At the same time, a Zero pulled up in front of Morrison who fired from 30 to 20 degrees deflection as the Zero stalled out at the top of its climb. Morrison's fire devastated the Zero, blowing off its entire tail section and a large chunk from its wing. Morrison last saw it spiraling down, smoking heavily and only claimed it as a probable. Morrison's ICR describes the "action in the following moments as hectic." Two Oscars made an overhead pass from the rear but missed entirely. Morrison then spotted another Oscar heading north at 6,000 feet and closed to 250-300 yards level and fired from 30 degrees and got scattered hits on

**Capt. Jack Fisk** (left with 1Lt. Clarence Rieman) shot down two enemy fighters to make him an ace with six victories. (AFAA)

its fuselage and cockpit. Morrison then "administered the *coup de grace*" and it went straight down in flames. As Morrison was making has attack on his Zero, another Zero pulled up in front of Sperling who pulled a lead on it and fired from 40-60 degrees getting hits on it. Sperling was unable to see the results as his low speed caused his fighter to be severely buffeted and its right wing to drop and he had to fight to drop his nose and follow to the right to recover. Suddenly, Sterling heard a warning on his radio that an enemy fighter was on his tail and then heard two loud explosions behind him. He had not yet gained enough speed to make any significant evasive maneuvers and his fighter buffeted and stalled and headed straight down. Sperling again had to fight to recover and finally pulled up into a cloud and then stayed just under the cloud base, turning several times to clear himself. When he started to fly west he saw two Zeros above and ducked back into the clouds. Sperling accessed the damage to his fighter and found two four inch holes in his port engine cowling, numerous jagged holes in his port wing and a one inch hole in his forward fuel tank. Morrison was recalling his Flights but Sperling was unable to respond as his radio transmitter was damaged. Sperling saw some P-38s above and climbed to join them but his port engine started to run rough and overheat and then his generator became inoperable. Sperling was able to make momentary radio contact with Capt. Fisk, informing him that he was heading home and broke away from the P-38 flight he had joined. Sperling's engine began to smoke heavily and overheat off the gauges and decided that it was "poor policy" to continue back to base alone and turned back to bail out over friendly shipping. On his first attempt to bail out his chute pack caught the side of the cockpit and after a few more unsuccessful attempts to bail out he decided to ditch. Fearing friendly AA fire from the shipping, Sperling lost altitude and ditched "nicely" out of AA range. The fighter sank almost immediately and he was unable to inflate his life raft but after 30 minutes in the water he was picked up by a PT boat where he spent the night before returning to base the next day where he learned that his only victory of the war had been confirmed by 310BW personnel on the ground.

2Lt. Lynn Peck was the leader of the third flight and was patrolling at 15,000 feet over Mangaria Bay when they were bounced by five Zeros from 1,000 feet above. The flight dropped their tanks and dove to escape and then turned into the attack. Peck had evaded two separate attacks by a two plane element by diving to 6,000 feet. As he was climbing to join another P-47 flight he saw five Zeros, two flying far behind him and three flying 500 feet below at 8,000 feet and about a mile ahead. Peck suspected that these were the same Zeros that had originally attacked him. He closed quickly on the right Zero and fired from 250 yards but had to pull up rapidly to escape a collision with his victim which was a sheet of flame. The other Zeros turned to attack Peck and he evaded and then turned on the left Zero and fired but missed. Peck turned and then made a head on pass but missed again only to have the Zero follow but soon gave up and Peck returned to base with his only victory of the war.

**18 December 1944: 49FG/9FS**

In the late day patrol of the beachhead, Ops Exec Capt. William Williams spread 11 Flying Knights in a formation between 5,000 to 7,500 feet in a due south heading. Williams sighted a lone Dinah speeding away toward Panay and after a brief chase the veteran pilot descended below the bomber's flight path and closed to within 200 yards where he climbed to fire a quick burst setting the starboard engine on fire and then hit the port engine and saw his fourth and last victim of the war crash into the water, 10 miles south of the beachhead.

**Capt. William Williams** shot down a Dinah for his fourth and last victory. (AAF)

**18 December 1944: 348FG/460FS**

460FS

At 1015 the 460th sent of three flights of three P-47s to cover the beachhead at Mindoro. At 1100 1Lt. Gerald Economoff was leading the third flight and flying west at 14,000 feet toward the patrol area when they saw a lone Judy at 12,000 feet. Economoff and his Wingman dropped their tanks and dove on the Judy that went into a diving 90 degree turn and the two Americans chased it for 10 to 15 minutes across the Jintotole Channel before Economoff closed into range from dead astern and slightly below. Economoff pulled up and fired from 250 yards and knocked pieces off the fuselage and wing roots and spun twice and exploded for Economoff's third and last victory after his two on 7 December. The two P-40s had to return to base as they used too much fuel to complete the assigned patrol.

1Lt. Dewitt Searles was the leader of the first flight and was patrolling over the beachhead at 13,000 feet when he saw a Sally approaching at 12,000 feet. Searles and his Wingman dropped their tanks and dove to port but before they got into range the Sally turned sharply to port and only gave Searles a difficult 90 degree deflection shot. Searles called his flight to swing wide so if he missed they would be in position for a head on pass. However, Searles aim was good and the Sally started to burn and spiraled into the sea. After Searles' third and last victory, his Flight continued to patrol and was attacked by five Zeros (?) from 15,000 and the flight went into a dive and then zoomed up and lost them.

**1Lt. DeWitt Searles** finished his career shooting down a Sally for his third victory. (AAF)

**20 December 1944: 8FG/36FS**

Capt. Allen Hill led 14 Lightnings off from Tacloban at 0845 to rendezvous with 14 C-47 transports at 3,000 feet that had just taken off from Tacloban and escort them to Mindoro. At about 1100 the formation arrived over San Jose on Mindoro and the Lightnings circled at 3,000 feet while the transports landed and unloaded at Hill Field from between 1130 and 1215. While the Lightnings were circling and the transports were beginning to take off 20 mixed fighters (Zeros, Hamps, Oscars, and Nicks) came in to attack at 10,000 feet and 6 o'clock.

Capt. Hill and Wingman, 2Lt. Robert Maynard, of White Flight spotted a lone Oscar at 6,000 feet and climbed to attack for a 30 degree deflection shot but the enemy pilot Split-S'd away before Hill could close in and escaped. They then saw eight more Oscars ready to attack them from 2,000 feet above and behind and dove away to safety from this disadvantageous situation. They climbed to 15,000 feet and saw a lone Oscar about 2,000 feet below and dove to 100 yards where Maynard fired two three second bursts; scoring hits on its cockpit and fuselage. The Oscar fell and started to burn and Hill claimed his first victory with the 36FS and his last of nine total victories. About 10 minutes later, while flying at 11 o'clock level, they sighted another Oscar with its landing gear down. Hill attacked and overran it and pulled up. Maynard attacked and Hill covered him while he fired two bursts that sent the Oscar down for his second and last victory.

**Capt. Allen Hill** shot down an Oscar and claimed his ninth and last victim. (AFAA)

**2Lt. Francis Ford** was fortunate to walk away from a belly landing. (AAF)

Yellow Flight led by 1Lt. Harold Graham was the high scorers of the day for the 36FS with three victories, one each by Graham, his Second Element Leader, 1Lt. William Turner, and Turner's Wingman, 2Lt. Charles Finnell. Graham spotted bandits at 6 o'clock and climbed away from them to gain altitude to make his attack while Turner and Finnell broke off after another. Turner and Wingman Finnell chased their Oscar down to tree top level and each pilot fired, Turner got no hits with his burst but Finnell dropped his flaps and fired a long head on deflection shot and tore its wing off for his only victory. Graham then saw a Nick flying on the deck coming inland from the sea. Graham dove from 2,000 feet and fired a 30 degree deflection burst long that hit the Nick's port engine and wing. Finnell fired but Graham made a second pass by lowering his flaps and fired from 150 to 10 yards, tattooing the Nick's fuselage; killing the tail gunner who had put a hole in Graham's wing. The Nick hit the water just off San Augustin and cartwheeled for Graham's third and last victory.

Blue Flight Leader, 2Lt. Bion Morgan, and Wingman, 2Lt. Kenneth Creighton, were bounced by Oscars from above. Morgan turned into two and followed one down, closing to within 200 yards before firing from dead astern. The Oscar burst into flames and fell off into a dive into the water. The two then met a Hamp and chased it for 15 minutes and got some hits before it escaped. They then chased an Oscar and closed to 250 yards and just as Morgan was about to fire; the enemy pilot Split-S'd in front of Creighton who fired and hit the hydraulic system as its wheel dropped but Creighton's engine began to cut out and the two returned to Leyte; Morgan with his only victory and Creighton with a damaged claim. Morgan's Blue Second Element of Leader, 2Lt. James Maucher, and #4 man, 2Lt. Gerald Lowrey, broke off and began to climb after a flight of enemy fighters at 10 o'clock and 2,000 feet above. They were unable to get into position to attack and were attacked themselves. Lowrey was hit from behind and several bullets penetrated his fighter which began to lose coolant and fuel and soon he was forced to feather his starboard engine but was able to land safely but severely damaged his fighter his fighter.

Red Flight Leader, Capt. Robert Anderson, and Wingman, 2Lt. Francis Ford, turned in to the Japanese attack. Anderson went after one but his P-38 was hit and Anderson returned to base where he crashed and burned upon landing and was severely injured. Ford's Lightning was also hit by a Hamps that fired shells into his port wing tip, shattered part of his aileron, hit the port engine that began to throw coolant and lose gasoline. Ford attached to Capt. Hill but was attacked again with his starboard engine and boom hit and also destroying its prop. Ford headed back to base and was about to land when his running engine began to quit and his gear would not come down, but he made a successful belly landing.

**20 December 1944: 348FG/342FS**

Maj. Walter Benz led 12 342FS Thunderbolts on a 1005 mission over the Mindoro beachhead and the newly captured San Jose Airdrome. Once over the area the Air Controller assigned White Flight (second) to cover the beachhead at 5,000 feet and the Red and Blue Flights (first and third) to cover the airdrome at 10,000 feet. Benz was leading Red and Blue Flights to 10,000 feet when he saw 20 Zeros above him with two of their flights already in a steep dive out of the sun for a stern pass. Benz ordered his Flights to drop their tanks and go into a port dive to escape but the Zeros hit Benz #3 (Whistler) and #4 (Patc) fighters. Three Zeros passed to Benz' left but he could only fire a short burst as other P-47s were closely pursuing them He then saw another Zero with a bomb diving on the airstrip and chased it, firing from 60 degrees astern and then from directly astern as it turned left to escape; the Zero smoked and crashed. Benz pulled up and saw 1Lt. George Davis, Element Leader of his third (Blue) flight turn into the Zeros and pull up and fire three burst at 20 degrees deflection and scored hits in the cockpit and it crashed into the water. Davis then made passes at two Zeros from dead astern but when he got into firing range another Zero made a head on pass at him hitting his engine and prop and also his port wing and blew out the tire and oxygen cylinder. Benz followed Davis after two other Zeros but Davis broke off saying he had been hit and Benz accompanied him back to base. However, a Zero attacked Benz from astern but missed and Davis broke away but was unable to see through his oil covered windshield to shoot. The enemy pilot broke away in a climb and Benz followed and fired from dead astern getting telling hits for his eighth and last victory of the war. The enemy pilot bailed out but his parachute caught on the burning tail assembly. Benz rejoined Davis whose canopy and fuselage were covered with oil and the two landed safely. Davis' victory made him the Group's 17th ace.

Capt. Charles Whistler was flying as Benz #3 man with 2Lt. John Pate as his Wingman in the Red Flight. They were jumped by four Zeros and Whistler made a head on pass at two Zeros and took a 20 degree deflection shoot at rear one which began to smoke, broke to port and went into fatal dive, crashing three miles from the airstrip. The Whistler was surprised by an explosion in the port wing that tore off the ammunition box door and disrupted the air foil forcing him to land at the San Jose strip below. The damage was partially repaired and he flew back to base the next day. Meanwhile, one of the Zeros overran Pate while trying to shoot at his Element Leader (Whistler) and pulled sharply to the left. Pate fired a 10 degree deflection at minimum range getting hits that sent him into a shallow dive and crash in flames for his only victory. As Pate broke away he felt his fighter being hit "all over and saw a big hole appear in my wing." Pate dove

**Maj. Walter Benz** shot down two Zeros to end his tour with eight victories. (AAF)

**1Lt. George Davis** became an ace when he shot down a Zero. (AFAA)

**Capt. David Eastman** claimed his only victory of the war. (AAF)

to 3,000 feet and circled San Jose strip letting down to 1,000 feet. He made one approach but found he had no flaps and his gear would not descend so he climbed to 1,200 feet and bailed out over the beach about a mile from the strip. He landed safely only wrenching a knee and shoulder.

Capt. David Eastham was leading four P-47s of Benz' third (Blue) flight over the airstrip and evaded when Zeros attacked and he lost his Flight. Eastham saw a lone Zero being chased by a P-47 and joined the chase and when the other P-47 overshot Eastham placed a four second volley into the Zero which smoked and crashed. The other P-47 rejoined Eastham and the two flew back to the beachhead where four more Zeros attacked them from above and behind. The two Americans turned into them and the Zeros fled toward the clouds. Eastham took a short 50 degree deflection shot at the #4 man and got hits on the fuselage, causing its pilot to bail out for his second victory of the day and his only two of the war. 2Lt. Richard Watrous was the #2 man (Eastham's Wingman) and tried to release his wing tank that did not drop and he lost his flight and joined another flight of P-38s. The Lightnings dove on enemy fighter flying on the deck and pulled up. Watrous started down but lost the well-camouflaged enemy fighter in background of the jungle foliage. As he turned he saw a lone Dinah with P-38s but the Lightning pilots missed and broke off giving Watrous his chance. He slipped behind and quickly closed and fired at 300 yards and 20 degrees deflection and then fired again at 150 yards and lastly at 100 yards. Its port engine streamed smoke and the Dinah yawed sharply to port and headed for a flat area for a crashlanding. Its wing hit a river bank and flipped over and exploded and Watrous rejoined some P-47s and returned home with his only victory of the war.

**Capt. Robert Knapp** shot down two Zeros and claimed another probable to make him an ace with these last victories. (AFAA)

Capt. Robert Knapp was leading the second (White) flight toward the beachhead when the Zeros attacked the other two flights. One Zero had pulled up out of the fight and Knapp and his Wingman, 2Lt. William Krueger, chased it to 2,000 feet where Knapp fired a two second burst and it crashed about five miles from the San Jose strip. Knapp then saw another Zero at 12,000 feet and climbed and pursued him for 10 miles and fired a short burst from dead astern and it crashed about a mile inland for his fifth victory to become an ace. Shortly afterward Knapp saw a Zero shooting at four P-38s. Knapp fired a short burst but overran and Krueger fired a two second burst that hit the cockpit and the Zero fell off on one wing and crashed in flames for his only victory. The two continued on and saw another brave Zero pilot attacking six P-38s at 5,000 feet. Knapp dove and fired a two second deflection shot around the canopy but the two had to pull up sharply to avoid the P-38s and lost track of the stricken Zero and Knapp was awarded a probable to go with the victory that made him an ace.

**20 December 1944: 49FG/7FS**

Morning Mission

Col. George Walker's 49FG continued to fly cover for the fleet at anchor, as well as to patrol over the sea routes through the southern islands. Flight Leader, 1Lt. Joel Paris and his wingmen, 2Lts. Milden Mathre and James Jarrell, took off at 0930 from Tacloban on a 7FS VIP escort mission to Mindoro. The three pilots rendezvoused at 8,000 feet over a USN PBY Catalina carrying AAF officers who were to attend a staff conference at Mindoro. The flight progressed without incident until noon when the four aircraft approached the beachhead at which time Paris was notified that Navy radar had detected enemy aircraft in the immediate area. Immediately, AA bursts appeared over San Jose Airdrome and Paris ordered the Catalina to land at sea and simultaneously sent Wingman Jarrell up to 13,000 feet for high cover. No sooner had the PBY safely landed and Jarrell had climbed to high cover than a lone Zero was seen between Jarrell's and Paris' respective altitudes. The Zero, apparently hit by San Jose AA, was trailing a whisp of smoke as it sped off to the north with Jarrell immediately diving and firing on the crippled Zero. As Paris confirmed Jarrell's victory a second Zero creped out of the clouds behind Paris and opened fire. Paris turned violently into his attacker just as an explosive round hit the cross bar in his canopy frame directly above his head; causing a six inch hole in Paris' canopy. The raging slip stream sucked his leather helmet and goggles off his head but the attached radio wires saved the helmet and Paris pulled it back over his head and dove out of danger. After leveling out at 8,000 feet, Paris jettisoned his tanks and radioed his wingmen. Jarrell, in high cover, warned Paris and Wingman Mathre of two more Zeros closing in behind them. Upon hearing the warning, the pair sped up in a starboard turning climb in which Paris became separated and Jarrell dove and after a brief chase, he closed in and blew off the canopy of his second victim of the mission which crashed into the Bay for his fourth and last victory. Meanwhile, Paris climbed and finally closed behind one of the Zeros which was preparing to attack the Catalina ferrying the VIPs which was taxiing toward the safety afforded by nearby Navy gunboats. Paris fired and set the Zero on fire and after its pilot bailed out it crashed on Manadi Island, lying just off shore from the beachhead. As the enemy pilot descended in his parachute, Mathre made a firing pass on him but missed and the pilot was captured by the Navy when he landed in the Bay. Soon, another patrol flight arrived in relief and Paris' Flight regrouped and returned to Tacloban where Paris received the Silver Star for saving the VIPs.

**1Lt. Fernley Damstrom** claimed his eighth and last victory. (AFAA)

Because the Navy was caught up in the Typhoon northeast of Luzon, it was urgent that the AAF attack the Japanese air forces in the north. The 308BW at Tacloban was assigned to attack the enemy aircraft based at Lipa Airdrome on south central Luzon that had been detected by aerial reconnaissance. The mission plan was for a flight of 7FS Lightnings to glide bomb the airdrome with single 1,000 pound bombs and then climb to fly high cover for the 35FG P-47s which would then dive bomb the airdrome after which both Groups were to strafe the aircraft on the airdrome.

Afternoon Mission

At 1415 the fighter bomber flights took off for their two hour, straight line course for Lipa. Demon Flight Leader, 1Lt. Fernley Damstrom, and his three wingmen arrived over Lipa at 16,000 feet accompanied by four 35FG Thunderbolts flying below. However, the target was entirely covered by thick clouds and the Thunderbolt Flight Leader diverted south for the secondary target on Masbate Island. On their arrival at the alternate target they found it to also be obscured and after a lengthy radio discussion about fuel consumption and the P-47 Mission Leader decided that all elements, including Damstrom's Flight, were to pattern bomb the target from their present altitudes. So, eight 1,000 pound bombs were dropped indiscriminately from over 12,000 feet. The Thunderbolts which were running low on fuel immediately left for Tacloban but Damstrom's Flight still had ample fuel and continued to patrol. As the Flight arrived over northern Leyte, they received a vector to a radar contact located far to the east. One Demon decided he did not have enough fuel and returned to Tacloban but rookies, 2Lt. William Thompson and 1Lt. Harold Harris stayed with Damstrom who turned toward Samar Island. The Flight searched for 20 minutes and was running low on fuel when two Oscars approached at 18,000 feet, flying south, and parallel to the Samar coast. The Demons turned up sun but the JAAF pilots saw them and snap rolled into Split-S escape dives in different directions. Damstrom and Harris followed the lead Oscar, while Thompson broke after the other. Thompson pursued his Ki-43 down to the sea and hit it with a short burst but it reached the safety of the clouds and disappeared. Meanwhile, Damstrom and Harris chased their frantically maneuvering target and got off several snap shots that hit it. Finally, at 1,000 feet, Damstrom closed and shot off pieces of its rear fuselage and the stricken Ki-43, made one last hard port bank and then drifted out to sea, catching on fire and going into an inverted roll into the water for his eight victory. Down to just a few gallons of gasoline on their return to Tacloban in the early evening, the flight had to dodge searchlights and friendly flak to land safely.

**21 December 1944: 8FG/80FS/35FS/36FS**

80FS

After transferring their aircraft to the 49[th] Fighter Group at Dulag on Leyte, the pilots of the 80[th] waited two months to be reequipped with new P-38Ls. The Squadron arrived on Mindoro on 20 December at their new base at Hill Field. Late next afternoon (1625) Capt. Paul Murphey led 10 P-38s on a local patrol to relieve another 80FS flight. After half an hour the Air Controller vectored the first Japanese fighter heading north at 7,000 feet and Murphey led Blue Flight in a climb at full throttle. As Murphey approached the Zero he throttled back and fired two bursts at the Zero. Its canopy blew off and it rolled over and spun in to make him and ace. As Murphey continued his patrol the Controller called two bogies over White Beach at 3,000 feet but as they approached they saw five or six more Zeros heading above them at 5,000 feet flying in the opposite direction. Murphey turned into them and the enemy pilots responded likewise. Murphey took a deflection shot and hit one that smoked a little before it hit the water for his sixth victory. Murphey flew around for a short time before he took another "very good" burst at an Oscar but did not see the result (a probable), as Murphey saw a Zero on his Wingman's tail and turned into it, but it flew away with some slight damage. 1Lt. Bud Fletcher was Murphey's Second Element Leader with 2Lt. Richard Souhrada as his Wingman. As Murphey was climbing toward his last victory Fletcher and Souhrada were attacked from behind by two Oscars and they broke away into a dive to lose the Oscars. They zoomed back to close on their former pursuers and Fletcher made a head on pass with only one gun firing and got hits on its engine as he flew over the top. Souhrada then followed and opened fire at 250 to about 100 yards on its tail and got a long burst knocking off pieces around the engine and fuselage. The Oscar then rolled and started down and Souhrada followed and gave it another burst as it crashed into the sea for his only victory. Fletcher saw another Oscar climbing up sun and chased after it. As it broke down and away he took a three second burst at 30 degrees getting hits along its fuselage and it rolled straight down toward the water. Fletcher then spotted another Oscar and 500 feet below and made a diving 15-30 degree pass and got hits on its tail but then lost it into a cloud. Although Fletcher's ICR made two damage claims he was not officially credited with either.

1Lt. Russell Roth was leading Murphey's second Green flight and dove under Murphey's Flight's first attack in case the Zero Split-S'd away but they didn't. When the Squadron met the next batch of Zeros Roth climbed after them and found that there were 12 or 13 of them. Roth fired on one getting hits on its fuselage and right wing but it flew into a cloud before Roth could determine any result. Roth chandelled up and started after three Zeros that turned into them and two got on the tail of Roth's Wingman, F/O Campbell, who fired but got no hits. Roth's element leader 1Lt. Nicolas Zinni had fired at one Oscar during a head on pass but neither he nor the Oscar got any hits. When Zinni spotted the Oscar on Campbell's tail he fired and got hits as it on the Oscar that broke off in a tight turn dove into a cloud. Zinni followed and as they left the cloud Zinni had closed considerably on it. The Oscar pilot then climbed toward another cloud but Zinni put a long burst into it and the Oscar became enveloped in flames. As his doomed fighter spiraled into the ground the pilot bailed out at about 1,000 feet and Zinni's first of two victories was assured. Roth and Campbell followed two more Oscars but they Split-S'd away. They continued to follow these Oscars and fired but got no hits as the enemy pilots again Spilt-S'ed away and on each of the next three Roth/Campbell passes they again evaded with the tried-and-not always true Split-S maneuver. Roth and Campbell followed the Oscars pilots up the coast unseen and Roth closed to 100 yards and fired. The Oscar exploded and spewed oil over Roth's windshield obscuring his forward vision. Campbell made ten passes and scored a few hits on the second Oscar but his guns were not bore sighted "and (he) could not hit anything." The skilful Oscar pilot continually turned inside Campbell's Lightning and Split-S'd on the tree tops and finally escaped into a cloud.

35FS

At 1630 Capt. Fred Boerman was leading White Flight on a local patrol over San Jose Airfield and was about to land when a bandit was called heading northwest. Boerman began to climb and spotted the enemy at 6,000 feet and 11 o'clock and gave chase at full boost and maximum rpm. Boerman gained slowly and identified the Jack which was headed for a large cloud. Boerman hastily fired a long burst from 1,000 yards before the Jack entered the cloud and got hits on its right wing. Boerman did not see the Jack crash but later his first of two victories was confirmed by an observer on the ground.

36FS

During the morning seven 36FS P-38s of Red Flight led by 1Lt. Steele Griswold and White Flight led by 2Lt. Wayne Donker took off at 0815 were to circle at 10,000 feet from 0915 to 1100 over the convoy that was transporting their second echelon. As soon as they reached the patrol area they spotted four Oscars at 7,000 feet that were on their way to attack the convoy. The Squadron divided into pairs and dove 3,000 feet out of the sun to surprise the enemy planes over Panay Island.

White Leader Donker was the first down on the Oscars, followed by Wingman Taylor. Donker dove on the last Oscar but overran it because he could not identify it as an enemy until he passed it. The Oscar then went into a dive to the right and Taylor fired at short burst and the Oscar which rolled away in a Split-S. Red #3, 2Lt. Charles Peck, followed it down 3,000 feet when the Oscar pilot turned about five degrees head on into Peck who started firing from 100 to 75 yards from a slight lead as the Oscar crossed in front of Peck from point blank range. The Oscar went into a slow spin and exploded 300 yards from shore for Peck's only victory. Donker closed on the Lead Oscar which took evasive action and came around on Peck's tail but firing out of range. Peck crossed in front of Donker, giving him a good

**Lt.Col. Emmett Davis**. **Maj. Jay Robbins**, and **Generals Whitehead** and **Wurtsmith** (L-R) celebrate the 80FS passing the 200th victory mark on 21 December. (AAF)

**Capt. Paul Murphy** had a good day with two victories to give him six and added a probable and a damaged claim. (AFAA)

**1Lt. Russell Roth** claimed his second and last victory. (AAF)

deflection shot from 40 to 90 degrees at the following Oscar; getting hits on its engine and fuselage. Donker continued his pursuit and took a few snap shots and then a head on pass that hit the fuselage, wing root, and engine and the Oscar spun in dropping large pieces until it crashed on the Panay coast to give his second and last victory. Griswold went after an Oscar that Split-S'd in a shallow dive and soon was in firing range but found that his guns malfunctioned. 2Lt. William Wooddell then closed and opened fire at 400 feet and only 200 feet above the ground. Hits were scored around the cockpit and fire quickly broke out around the cockpit and port wing and the Oscar crashed about a mile off shore for his second and last victory. After the combat the Squadron continued their patrol until 1100.

80FS
At 1630, just before the 80FS was preparing to take off for its patrol, eight P-38s of the 35FS were strung out in their landing approach. Capt. Fred Boerman was leading White Flight at 2,500 feet in the landing pattern when a bandit heading northwest was called out. He and Wingman, 1Lt. George Lynch, climbed steeply after the enemy fighter, identified as a Jack, as it was about to escape into a cloud bank. Boerman saw that he would not reach the Jack in time and fired a desperate 300 yard shot and saw hits in the starboard wing and the enemy fighter rolled over and headed down as a probable. Lt.Col. Abe Beck of 8FG/HQ was flying with the 35th that day and saw the smoking Jack come out of the bottom of the cloud and crash to confirm Boerman's second victory in two days but also his last.

**21 December 1944: 49FG/8FS**
Seven Black Sheep left Tacloban at 1500 and flew north to their patrol station at 4,000 feet above the USN invasion fleet at Mindoro. The flight was vectored several times but could not contact the attackers flying just over the waves where the dazzle from the setting sun on the water was blinding and made identification nearly impossible. Finally at 1730, Flight Leader Robert Aschenbrener saw a Zero that had just evaded a flight of Navy Hellcats and had climbed slightly above the Black Sheep formation. Aschenbrener and Wingman 2Lt. Francis Hill climbed into a dead astern firing attack and closed in on the unsuspecting enemy pilot. The Black Sheep ace fired at 100 yards hitting his quarry with a single burst which tore off its canopy and hit the engine. The burning Zero rolled over and dropped into the sea where Hill confirmed Aschenbrener's tenth and last victory of the war.

**Capt. Robert Aschenbrenner's** last victory made him a double ace. (AFAA)

**22 December 1944: 348FG/340FS/342FS/341FS**
By late December there were enough 5FC fighters available to provide escort for 5BC B-24s to attack targets on Luzon with these missions beginning on 22 December. Their first target was the northern suburbs of Manila and Clark Field near Manila which had special strategic and symbolic meaning for Americans. It had been the key American air base in the Philippines and the scene of one of the greatest humiliations for American airpower when virtually the entire Far East Air Force was caught on the ground and destroyed in the first days of the war. Now Clark was the main enemy airbase for launching enemy air raids on Leyte and Mindoro. The 348FG was to have the honor of the meeting the Japanese first in combat over Clark Field after returning to the Philippines. Between 0730 and 0815 48 P-47s from three squadrons of the 348FG took off to escort 36 B-24s (called "Mikes" in the report) that were to bomb Clark Field.

340FS
At 0730 the 340FS sent off 16 P-47s to escort the B-24s to Clark Field. On the way back home at 9,500 feet, 1Lt. Lyle Dowsett, the Flight Leader of Blue Flight, saw a lone Oscar directly ahead and 1,000 feet higher. Dowsett started to climb to catch the Oscar that was about to attack one of the last of B-24 formation. Dowsett did not catch the Oscar until he had finished his pass and fired a five second burst that set it on fire and a short second short burst caused the pilot to bail out for Dowsett's fourth and last victory.

**1Lt. Michael Dikovitsky** became an ace when he shot down a Zero over Clark Field. (AAF)

1Lt. Michael Dikovitsky, the Second Element Leader of White Flight, was flying at 12,000 feet and after the bombers had made their bombing run he saw a lone single engine aircraft (Zero) at 4 o'clock high when it immediately started a dive on the P-47s. Dikovitsky called his Flight Leader 1Lt. Mahoney to dive hard to port and Dikovitsky did the same in order to get in position to make a head on pass which intimidated the Zero pilot who broke away in a climbing turn. Dikovitsky used his water injection to increase his speed while his Wingman turned wide to cut off the Zero and the second element remained overhead as protective cover. Dikovitsky tried to turn inside the Zero and fired a brief burst, getting some hits, but could not hold his firing lead. The Zero pilot went into a stall to evade but Dikovitsky stayed with him and fired getting more hits but the Zero continued flying. The enemy pilot did a wing over when Dikovitsky was only 30 yards behind. This time his bullets shattered the canopy and the Zero burst in to flames and crashed for Dikovitsky's fifth victory to make him an ace.

**1Lt. Lyle Dowsett** shot down a Zero for his fourth and last victory. (AAF)

1Lt. Robert McNaulty was the Flight Leader of Green Flight when his Flight was attacked by and Oscar and two Zeros at 12,000. McNaulty's Wingman, F/O Harry Mansfield, called out a Zero diving away at 2 o'clock and turning inside McNaulty. Mansfield got on the Zero's tail and fired a long burst from 400 yards and then fired at 200 yards setting it on fire for his only victory. Mansfield rejoined McNaulty and the two climbed back up the ongoing air battle. During their climb an Oscar dove from 4 o'clock and McNaulty turned into it. The Oscar turned away sharply to the right and McNaulty got a 90 degree deflection shot which slightly overshot. McNaulty adjusted his lead and the Oscar flew into his bullets getting hits on the Oscar's wings, fuselage, and engine. The enemy's engine started smoking and it went into a slow diving turn. McNaulty did a wingover and got astern for another firing pass that tore pieces off the Oscar which dented McNaulty's wing. The Oscar Split-S'd and pulled out on the deck glided for a large open field without power. The pilot attempted to turn left and McNaulty fired a short burst but only two of his guns were firing when the Oscar crashed for McNaulty's only victory.

342FS
At 0800 16 P-47s of the 342 FS took off under Maj. Walter Benz to rendezvous with the bombers and their flight to the target was unopposed. At 16,000 feet over the target Benz called out a Tony and dove on it and overshot and 2Lt. Bert Lee, the #4 man in the second flight, closed on it but only took a fleeting shot at it as it Split-S'd away. Benz and Lee headed away south from Clark where they saw two Zeros with wing tanks making a left climbing turn. The Americans fell in trail with the Zeros and sped toward them and as they closed one Zero Split-S'd out of combat. Lee half rolled and then rolled while Benz dove in a port turn, fired, but was unable to hold his lead as the Zero pilot made a sharp turn. Lee then Split-S'd to starboard and closed for a dead astern attack starting the Zero on fire causing the pilot to bail out for his first of two victories.

341FS
At 0815 15 P-47s in four flights took off to escort the B-24s to Clark Field. Yellow Flight was composed of Flight Leader, Capt. Brasseur and his Wingman 1Lt. David Mumper and Capt. Gerald Excell, as the Second Element Leader. The Flight was flying at 19,000 feet, 20 miles southeast of Clark Field at 1025 when they spotted a single seat fighter at about 21,000 feet. The Zero turned on Excell from the stern but he was able to evade and Brasseur took a 60 degree frontal deflection shot while Excell continued a diving turn with the Zero and fired. Mumper then came in on the enemy's tail and fired a long burst from 200 yards and the Zero finally caught fire and spun in about 10 miles from Clark Field for Mumper's second and last of two victories.

**Capt. Fred Boerman** (left with CC) got his second of two victories. (AAF)

Capt. William Foulis, Blue Flight Leader, and Wingman, 1Lt. James Morris, were flying at 19,000 feet five miles from Clark Field when he saw two Tonys 2,000 feet overhead and climbed to meet them. The Tonys separated with one diving to port and Foulis' Flight pursued it. The Tony pilot made a very tight port turn using his flaps and Foulis followed, firing through one third of the turn. When Foulis broke off the Tony was able to get behind him but Foulis' Second Element Leader, Capt. Louis Reker, got behind the Tony and fired at 250 yards getting hits on the port wing root and flames erupted from the cockpit and wing root and the pilot bailed out for Reker's first of two victories. The Flight reassembled at 16,000 feet and saw a single Tony at the same altitude. The Tony pilot saw the P-47s and went into a dive and Foulis followed firing at 200 yards. The Tony momentarily leveled off at 10,000 feet and then Split-S'd to 5,000 feet where it again leveled off and Split-S's again and finally succumbed to Foulis' fire and crashed seven miles from Clark. A short time later Blue Flight rejoined and was flying at 14,000 feet when #4 man, 1Lt. Andrew Mix, saw a lone Zero approaching at the same altitude and turned into it. The Zero pilot attempted to out run the Thunderbolt but Mix got a stern shot at 300 yards and the Zero dove as Mix continued to close getting numerous hits, the canopy and large pieces flew back at Mix. The Zero went into a slow roll and crashed at the base of Mt. Arayat and Mix had his second and last victory.

**22 December 1944: 8FG/35FS/80FS**
35FS
At 0725, 10 new P-38s led by Lt.Col. Earl Dunham took off on a local patrol over Hill Field. At 0900 bogies were sighted 50 miles from the strip over the water. The eight Zeros approached Hill at about 1,000 feet above the patrolling Lightnings and the enemy Leader split his formation into three groups of four, one, and three planes. Dunham immediately responded by splitting his flight into two elements to attack the Japanese formation. Dunham quickly dove 1,000 feet and got slightly under and directly onto the tail of the lead Zero and fired at 200 yards and shot it down for his only victory of the war. But the second Zero escaped Dunham by diving away but flew right into the path of Capt. Fred Boerman who shot it down with a long deflection burst for his second victory in two days but his last. Boerman's Wingman, 2Lt. Arthur Schell, saw a bogie about 1,000 feet above and off his port wing. The bogie began a diving turn toward the last man in a 36FS flight and as the enemy pilot broke off; Schell got on its tail and fired from directly astern. Schell got some hits and the Zero went into a very steep diving turn and Schell got a good 30 degree deflection shot into the cockpit and the Zero crashed and exploded and Schell had his only victory.

Flight Leader, 1Lt. Thomas Flood, saw three Hamps 1,000 feet above, with one below the other two. Flood and his Wingman chased the upper two Hamps and as they closed the Hamps saw them and the Leader broke off to the left. Flood followed and fired getting numerous hits and the Hamp snap rolled into the sea for Flood's only victory. 1Lt. George Lynch, leading Flood's second element, and his Wingman went after the lower Hamp. After pursuing it for a short time the Hamp turned into Lynch and Lynch fired; starting its engine smoking. Lynch pulled up and around and fired a 20 degree deflection shot into its cockpit. The Hamp made two spirals before it hit the water. Lynch made another pass on a Hamp and starting it smoking. Lynch followed it 3,000 feet until it crashed for his only two victories of the war. These victories would be the last for the 35FS until 14 August 1945.

80FS
Capt. Louis Schriber was leading a formation of 14 Headhunter Lightnings that took off at 0645 on a routine patrol over Hill Field and vicinity. The flights patrolled until 0900 when he saw two enemy fighters on the deck. He lost sight of one but went after the other, identified as a Hamp. Schriber fired a short burst from 20 degrees and crashed in flames into the ground for his fourth victory.

1Lt. Howard Sheehan led Green Flight with 1Lt. William Coleman as his Wingman, 1Lt. Nicolas Zinni as his Second Element Leader and 2Lt. Lawrence Henkes as the #4 man. At 0855 the Air Controller called three plots and Sheehan headed Green Flight in a climb toward the southern plot at 8,000 feet. As he reached 10,000 feet he saw bogie at 15,000 feet but it soon disappeared. When they reached 14,000 feet four Oscars approached from 180 degrees and 3,000 feet above. One broke off and made a pass at Green Flight's rear. Sheehan and Coleman turned into the attack but could not make the turn and broke off. Second Element Zinni and Henkes closed with Zinni, firing from 400 yards, and the Oscar's wheels dropped and it caught fire for his second victory in two days, but also his last. Another Oscar then made a pass on Zinni from 8 o'clock and Wingman Henkes fired a short burst from 30 degrees that set this Oscar on fire and it crashed south of the strip for his only victory.

**Capt. Louis Schriber** moved closer to becoming an ace with his fourth victory. (AFAA)

**22 December 1944: 49FG/8FS**

On 22 December, Aschenbrener's 8FS flight flew to Hill Air Field for a sortie and at 10,000 feet over Seminara Island on their final approach to Hill they were diverted to a vector in their flight path. Aschenbrener immediately dove after a solo Tony cruising at 4,000 feet over the eastern coast of the island but his closing speed was much too fast to shoot accurately. Wingman, 1Lt Francis Hill, was in the ideal position to catch the Ki-61 as it escaped from Aschenbrener and Hill fired a burst into its cockpit and set its engine on fire and it fell into shallow offshore water for Hill's third victory.

**23-26 December 1944: Manila-Clark Field Attacks**

Kenney had the combined forces of the 308BW at Tacloban and the 310BW at Hill available to attack the Japanese air force complex around Manila. Manila was only 160 miles from Hill, a distance which allowed every fighter type in the 310BW to easily reach targets there; even the war-weary P-40 Warhawks of the reconnaissance squadrons would join in the tactical attacks on the Philippines' capitol. However, the Tacloban fighter pilots would have to fly 800 miles round trip to well-defended Clark airdrome, which was the principle staging air depot of the Japanese Luzon defense.

**23 December 1944: 475FG/432FS**

2Lt. Austin Morris of the 432nd Squadron was returning from a B-24 escort on 23 December when his nosewheel collapsed on landing at Dulag but he escaped injury.

**23 December 1944: 348FG/341FS**

On 23 December Clark Field was given a respite from 5th Bomber Command B-24s and their escorts from the 348FG. That day saw five P-47s of the 341st Squadron make a fire bomb raid on Palombon. It was also the first recorded use of Napalm by a 5th Fighter Command unit.

**23 December 1944: 49FG/9FS**

All three squadrons of the 49FG made the first escort to Manila on 23 December. The Flying Knights escorted the B-24s to the Grace Park Airdrome directly north of Manila. Both Maj. Wallace Jordan and Capt. Edward Howes of the 49er's HQ Staff flew attached to the 9 FS and both fired at enemy fighters which did not seem to be eager to get too close to the formidable American formation.

**23 December 1944: 58FG Move to Mindoro**

During the morning of 23 December the 311FS was the first 58FG squadron to leave for their new base on Mindoro Island in the Philippines. The 69FS departed the next day and the 310th followed on 26 December. As transport aircraft became available the 58th's Thunderbolts were followed by the extra pilots and the ground crews that had remained behind at Noemfoor to service the aircraft.

**24 December 1944: 348FG/HQ/340FS/341FS/342FS/460FS**

Once again the 348th was escorting B-24s to Clark Field and the Japanese were obligated to either defend the base in the air or lose their remaining aircraft on the ground just as the Japanese had done to the Americans in the first days of the war. The 348FG would send up 66 Thunderbolts to escort B-24s over Clark Airfield and have their best day of the war with 34 victories, one probable, and one damaged.

*Special Flight*

Maj. William Banks of the 348th HQ and Wingman Capt. Gerald Excell from the 460FS took off at 0800 and arrived at 1015, 25 minutes ahead of the main formation, to radio positions and altitudes of enemy interceptors to the remainder of the escort. Banks and Excell immediately sighted two Zeros and four other unidentified enemy aircraft flying at 18,000 feet northeast from Floridablanca. The two Thunderbolts immediately dropped their wing tanks and climbed to 25,000 feet to gain the altitude advantage and position themselves behind the enemy. Banks led the dive in a line astern attack but the Zeros saw the two P-47s and made 180 degree turn and made a line abreast attack into Banks. In the head on combat Banks fired at the right Zero and hit its right wing and fuselage behind the engine and it began to tumble and then spiraled to crash 20 miles north of Floridablanca. Banks and Excell then made climbing turn and saw two more Zeros 1,500 feet below and ahead of them and descended. As they closed line astern on the Zeros from above as the enemy pilots made a quick level left turn but Banks hit the #2 Zero in the canopy and rear fuselage and it Split-S'd, trailing smoke but leveled off and disappeared into a cloud for a damaged claim. The other Zero continued to turn and Excell fired a deflection shot from 10 o'clock high and this Zero crashed near Floridablanca. Banks had lost Excell in the combat and while circling he saw the main 348th formation about 40 miles away and radioed the number, position, and altitude of the enemy. Banks then saw another P-47, 1,000 feet below, on the tail of a Zero, firing a long deflection shot but the Zero turned sharply inside of the Thunderbolt's fire. Banks came in and made a 30 degree deflection shot from the rear. Smoke and pieces of the cockpit flew back toward Banks' fighter before the Zero

**Maj. William Banks** scored his ninth and last victory shooting down a Zero. (AAF)

crashed 15 miles from Floridablanca. After Excell lost Banks in the combat he continued to circle the area until he saw a P-47 in the distance and as he approached he saw it was Banks and the two returned to base. The two victories were Banks' eighth and ninth and last of the war.

340FS

The 340FS dispatched 16 P-47s at 0830 and arrived over the target at 1045. At 1045 Capt. Meade Brown was leading the 340th's Red Flight just west of Clark Field at 16,500 feet when four Zeros and Oscars attacked. The first Zero dropped a phosphorus bomb on Red Flight and the bomb exploded at the same altitude but too far to the right. Brown chased the Oscar down and took a 20 degree deflection shot from the rear at point blank range and the Zero exploded for his fifth victory to become an ace. Brown attacked another Zero with a good vertical deflection shot but did not see any hits. When he reviewed his gun camera film he saw streamers of smoke in front of the cockpit and Banks certified Brown's sixth and last victory of the war.

**Capt. Meade Brown** shot down two Zeros, giving him six total victories. (AFAA)

1Lt. Jack Quinlan was leading the second element of Red Flight and after the phosphorous bomb exploded and Brown had gone after the first of the four Zeros, Quinlan turned into the other three. Quinlan made a head on attack on what he identified an Oscar and saw solid hits and smoke around its engine cowling. The other two Japanese fighters were attacking Quinlan's Wingman, forcing the two Thunderbolts into a hard starboard turn and were able to dive to safety. At 5,000 feet Quinlan found a single Tony turning towards him at 4 o'clock level and closed to 100 yards and hit it with a 60 degree deflection shot tat caused the pilot to bail out for two of his four victories.

As 2Lt. Francis Hall flew into the battle he saw an Oscar diving into an attack from 4 o'clock and went into a violent dive and pulled out to safety at 8,000 feet. As soon as he leveled out he saw a Zero at 9 o'clock, turning into him and he took a 90 degree deflection shot from above. Hall lost the Zero as it passed under him but picked it up again diving away into a narrow valley. He chased after it and made a tail on firing pass at 650 yards and saw hits on its tail and fuselage despite having some of his guns malfunction. Hall climbed over the Zero to gain altitude and made another pass astern and hit the fuselage. Hall had to pull violently away to avoid a collision with his smoking victim which would be his only victory.

1Lt. Noble Jones was the Element Leader of Blue Flight and saw a single Zero at 9,000 and led the Flight into an attack. When the Zero pilot saw the P-47s he made a climbing right turn but Jones got behind him and scored hits on the fuselage and wing root. The enemy pilot went onto a sharp left bank but Jones continued to fire and got further hits on the on the cockpit. The Zero fell smoking heavily and crashed for Jones' last of three victories. 2Lt. John Doenges, Jones' Wingman in Blue Flight, saw a lone Zero in a slow climb at 9,000 feet and his Element Leader shot it down. Doenges then saw an Oscar climb toward him and he lowered the nose of his fighter and fired as the Oscar pulled out of his climb and started a port turn and Doenges saw hits on its fuselage and wing. The Oscar reversed his turn and began to climb to starboard and Doenges closed and fired at 25-30 yards. The enemy's canopy was shattered and its engine began to smoke and it fell off on one wing. Doenges continued to fire and it rolled over in flames while its pilot unsuccessfully tried to bail out for his first and only victory.

341FS

The 341FS sent out 16 P-47s at 0815 in four flights. At 1110 about 10 miles from Clark Field 15 enemy fighters were approaching Blue Flight from the west at 16,000 feet. Capt. William Foulis was leading Blue Flight and would become the 348th's high scorer of the day. He immediately ordered his flight to drop their tanks and climbed above an Oscar and hit it with a single 30 degree deflection shot and saw smoke and pieces come from his first target. He then made a head on attack at another Oscar and saw hits over the engine and trailing smoke as the two opponents passed. Several minutes later Foulis got a turning 10 degree deflection shot that doomed another Oscar. A minute later he made a head on pass and saw an Oscar pass by with smoke pouring from its engine. Five minutes later he dove on another Oscar from the rear and his bullets struck the wings and fuselage and the enemy fighter burned and was confirmed by 1Lt. William Anahu of the 342FS who had just escaped a close call from an attacking Oscar. For the day Foulis claimed three victories and a probable to make him an ace with his sixth and last victories of the war. Foulis' Wingman, 2Lt. Ollie Miller, separated from his Leader when he saw an Oscar approaching below him and made a 70-90 degree pass at it and continued to fire as it passed under his nose trailing smoke. Miller climbed to rejoin Foulis when he saw another Oscar at 12 o'clock and started to fire at 300 yards until the enemy fighter passed only 50 feet over him with its engine on fire and Miller then saw the enemy pilot bail out for

**Capt. William Foulis** had a great day, scoring three victories (and a probable) to make him an ace with six. (AFAA)

**2Lt. William Schlegel** shot down two Tojos for his only career victories. (AAF)

Miller's second victory of the day and last for the war. Capt. Louis Rekers, the Second Element Leader of Blue Flight, and his Wingman 2Lt. James Mullen broke left to meet a Zero that was diving head on into him. Rekers fired head on and got hits in its wing roots and the Zero fell off smoking and finally crashed in flames for Rekers' second and last victory. Mullen followed Rekers and fired a very long 30 degree deflection burst from 200 yard at a Zero that was on his Leader's tail. The Zero Split-S'd and crashed into the sea for Mullens' only victory.

At 1100 Capt. Reine was leading his Red Flight at 14,000 feet when they encountered 20 mixed Japanese fighters scattered from 9,000 to 16,000 feet, 15 miles northwest of Clark and dropped their tanks and climbed for altitude. Second Element Leader, 1Lt. Robert Redner, made a pass at a Zero but had to break off when a Tojo attacked him from 130 degrees but when Redner turned into it the Tojo pilot quickly broke left and down, exposing him to Redner's stern attack from 250 yards that exploded the Tojo. Redner lost his Wingman and circled, looking for another circling over Clark at 11,000 feet. Redner was running low on fuel and looking for another partner to return to base with. He saw another P-47 whose pilot radioed him to slow down so he could join up. As Redner throttled back he saw a Zero closing in on his tail, but the other P-47 caught up and fired at the Zero but missed. Redner pulled up above the Zero and dived. The Zero evaded right and then left, but Redner persisted and fired three bursts from 250 yards, getting hits, but the Zero didn't catch fire. Redner continued firing and finally the Zero lost control and spiraled into the sea. As he was concentrating on this combat another Zero got on his tail and he escaped in a climb to 11,000 feet to join two P-47s and flew back to base with his only two victories of the war.

2Lt. William Schlegel was the Wingman to White Flight Leader, Capt. Brasseur, when they saw an estimated 50 enemy fighters approaching in pairs from 15,000 to 16,000 feet. Brasseur and Schlegel were attacked by a Tony which got on the Wingman's tail. Schlegel rolled over and out dove on his attacker but when he pulled up and saw a Tojo closing but, unaccountably, reversed his turn and Split-S'd away. Schlegel pushed over and got on the enemy's tail and fired a four second burst that started a fire and the pilot to bail out. Schlegel broke away and climbed to 10,000 feet where he met and attacked another Tojo from 90 degrees and slightly above. The Tojo made a sharp 30 degree turn and then a wingover to the left but the Thunderbolt pilot followed and fired from 200 yards astern and fire erupted from its wing root and pieces came off the fuselage and tail; followed by an explosion for Schlegel's only two victories.

342FS

The 342FS sent 16 P-47s from Tanauan at 0745 as close cover for the B-24's left flank. At 1045 the Squadron approached Clark at 15,000 feet and just before the bombers made their run 1Lt. George Davis saw two Zeros attack the B-24 formation from about 1,000 feet above and dropped aerial phosphorous bombs. Davis had lost his Wingman who had a leaking belly tank and aborted and he joined 2Lt. Clark Kooper, the Second Element Leader of Red Flight and his Wingman, 1Lt. William Anahu. Davis and Kooper each went after a Zero, following them down about 5,000 feet. Kooper's Zero turned directly into him and he fired point blank getting hits that caused its pilot to bail out for his first of two victories. Anahu took on took on Zero that Davis missed and closed for a stern attack, firing three bursts while closing from 350 yards to dead astern and then saw the pilot bail out. The three then rejoined the bombers and continued their escort. Anahu saw an Oscar diving on a P-47 and fired a 90 degree deflection shot ahead of the Oscar, The diving Oscar turned into Anahu and the P-47 pilot turned sharply into the Oscar and scored a few hits from 30 degrees deflection. The Oscar made a quick port turn and Anahu fired from 45 degrees and finished off his foe for his second victory of the day and his last of the war. During

**1Lt. George Davis** claimed his seventh and final victory in the Pacific. (AFAA)

**Maj. George Davis** scored 14 more victories in Korea, and was one of only seven pilots to become an ace in both WWII and Korea. He was awarded the Medal of Honor posthumously for gallantry in Korea. (AAF)

the combat an Oscar got on Anahu's tail and he tried a few evasive turns and then the heavy Thunderbolt's tried and true steep dive escape but could not shake the talented Japanese pilot. Davis saw Anahu's fighter under attack and dove to the rescue and fired to drive off the Zero but it turned head on into him. Davis fired three short bursts from full 90 degrees deflection and it caught fire and crashed into the mountains northwest of Clark Field. Davis then climbed to return to cover the bombers and saw another Zero approaching the bombers from above. Davis climbed to prevent the attack and closed from astern and fired at 200 yards, no deflection, and it started on fire and spun into the ground for his second victory of the day and his seventh and final victory in the Pacific. Davis then scored 14 more during the Korean War flying F-86 jet fighters for the 4th Fighter Group of the 5th Air Force. On his last mission over Korea, flown on 2 February 1952, he and his Wingman took on 12 MiG-15s and he destroyed two but was shot down and killed. For this action became the second, although former, 348FG pilot to win the Medal of Honor (*e.g.* Kearby). Davis also was only of only seven pilots to become an ace in both WWII and Korea.

460FS
At 0830 16 (plus two from the Banks/Excell Special Fight) Thunderbolts of the 460FS took off for their B-24 escort duties and arrived over Clark ant 1015 at 20,000 feet. They patrolled for 45 minutes when they saw 15 Zeros in two plane flights and one three ship flight milling at 17,000 to 19,000 feet.

1Lt. George Della, Leader of the third flight ordered his flight to drop their tanks but his Wingman, 2Lt. Floyd Stone, was unable to drop one of his wing tanks (which dropped off on its own on the flight home). Della's flight would begin the first of four passes on four different two plane enemy flights at 1100. The first pass was unsuccessful as the Zeros Split-S'd away before the P-47s could get into position. On the second pass the Della got a full deflection shot on the enemy Wingman which burned and crashed north of Clark. On the third pass Della shot down the Wingman of another enemy flight with a low angle deflection from astern, hitting the cockpit. On the fourth pass the two Zeros were at 10 o'clock slightly below and climbing to attack. Della and Stone both fired head on and missed and the enemy leader Split-S'd away but his Wingman did not follow. Stone fired a 40 degree deflection at the Wingman and continued to fire short burst to 15 degree deflection and the Zero rolled over, smoking heavily, and crashed northwest of Clark. The two victories would make Della an ace while Stone scored his only victory of the war.

2Lt. Robert Smith was the Leader of the fourth flight and saw a lone Zero flying south at 19,000 feet about 25 miles north of Clark. Smith led his flight west up to 22,000 feet where they dropped their tanks but by this time the Zero had disappeared. Another lone Zero was seen at 19,000 feet heading south and the P-47s made a 90 degree diving port turn to get on its tail. The Zero turned 180 degrees in a dive and Smith followed and fired from 300 yards getting hits on its wings and fuselage and caused its right landing gear to drop. The Zero went into an uncontrolled flaming spin and crashed 20 miles north of Clark. Smith led his flight back up to 12,000 feet where they were attacked by a Zero from behind. Smith and his Wingman went into a vertical dive while the second element turned into the enemy. Just as Smith and his Wingman pulled out of their dive and pulled up they were attacked by another Zero at 6,000 feet. Smith pulled up and left while his Wingman went down and right. Smith came in behind the Zero that was attacking his Wingman and fired a desperate 90 degree shot from out of range hoping to scare the enemy away. It turned away to the right and Smith fired from dead astern and the enemy crashed 30 miles northeast of Clark. Before Smith could rejoin his Wingman they both were attacked and had to dive away. Smith was so low on fuel that he had to land at Mindoro to refuel and returned home with his third, fourth and final victories of the war.

1Lt. Wallace Harding was the Flight Leader of the first flight saw the original 15 Zeros from 20,000 feet and picked out three Zeros in a V formation 2,000 feet below. Harding dove and the enemy Leader and his right Wingman immediately Split-S'd into the clouds. Harding closed on the left Wingman and fired from 200 to 50 yards astern, and it went into a spiral and crashed 10 miles from Clark. At 1130 Harding was flying at 13,000 feet north of Clark when he saw a Zero flying 1,000 yards ahead of him at same level and in a gentle easterly dive. Harding moved in astern but another P-47 cut in front of him and started to fire but the Zero turned to the right and the too eager Thunderbolt overran. Harding then slipped in behind the Zero and fired at 200 yards and the Zero exploded to claim his final two of three victories and of the last of the 348th's 34 victories.

The 34 victories were the 348th's highest single day total for the war; Meade Brown, George Della and William Foulis became the last aces of the 348th; and the Group was awarded which its second Distinguished Unit Citation for this performance this day. 2Lt. Kenneth Saunders was the 460th's only casualty when his P-47 was attacked on the way back to base by a lone enemy fighter and crashed into the water and no parachute was seen. The 341FS lost two pilots; 1Lt. James Morris and 2Lt. August Svancarek (who had collided with another P-47 and crash landed on the base runway on 14 December). 1Lt. Gerald Sheely of the 342FS was uninjured after his P-47 bellied in with damage from enemy fire.

The glory days of the 348th were over and after scoring 300 victories the 348th's squadrons would claim only 20 victories more during the remainder of the war. The 340FS would not score until August when it got eight victories (76 total); the 341FS would claim two more (70 total) in mid March; the 342FS five more (123 total) with three in March and two in August; and the 460FS got five more (51 total) in August. During 1945 the 348FG would make its contribution by flying important and dangerous ground support missions.

**1Lt. George Della** became an ace by shooting down two Zeros. (AFAA)

**1Lt. Wallace Harding** shot down two Zeros to give him three total victories. (AAF)

**25 December 1944: Prelude**
By the middle of December the Japanese position in the Luzon airfields temporarily gave them the advantage of attacking American sea and air targets with little opposition. The first air raids on Clark Field of any significance began on 22 December. Nonetheless, Fifth and Thirteenth Air Force B-24s were hindered by the crowded conditions on the Tacloban Airdrome and were forced to fly missions on alternate days. On 24 December the P-47s of the 348FG escorted the bombers and scored a hefty 34 victory claims. So it was apparent that the pilots of the 5FC were about to add a large number of victory symbols to their aircraft as the Japanese were clearly committed to heavy resistance to protect the Clark Field complex. After their huge losses on the 24th the Japanese sent the last of their reserves from the northern most Luzon airfields into the Clark airdrome complex that covered a 25 mile wide valley. On the next day, Christmas, 1944, the Lightning Groups of the 308BW struck Clark Field again and the greatest air battle of the Philippine's Campaign would take place.

**25 December 1944: 475FG/431FS/432FS/433FS**
On Christmas morning, the 475FG was scheduled to escort heavy bombers over Mabalacat, a field on the northern part of the Clark Complex. Col. Charles MacDonald was the mission leader, flying at the head of three P-38s of Clover Squadron. Of course, Maj. Thomas McGuire was particularly eager to add to his victory total over Clark. Despite being the Mission Leader, MacDonald's flight followed McGuire into the Mabalacat target area by a few minutes. At the end of Christmas Day the 475th Fighter Group had scored 28 victories so there certainly was a reason to celebrate that night.

431FS

Although Capt. Robert Cline had taken over as 431FS CO from McGuire in early December, McGuire led 15 Lightnings of the Squadron when it took off from Dulag at 0755 on a top cover B-24 escort Mabalacat Airdrome. The P-38s rendezvoused with the Liberators at 0910 over the southwest tip of Masbate Island. The 431st would have their last great day of the war scoring 17 victories. The Flights consisted of:

Red: McGuire and Wingman, 2Lt. Alvin Neal; Second Element Leader 1Lt. Enrique Provencio and Wingman, 2Lt. Robert Koeck

Blue: Capt. Fredric Champlin and Wingman, 2Lt. Harold Gray; Second Element Leader 1Lt. Louis DuMontier and Wingman, 2Lt. James Moreing

White: 1Lt. Floyd Fulkerson and Wingman, Maj. George Dewey; Second Element Leader 1Lt. John Ballard and Wingman, 2Lt. Thomas Oxford

Green: 1Lt. John Tilley and Wingman, 2Lt. Thomas Martin; Second Element Leader, 1Lt. John Pietz (3 plane flight)

(Note: There are discrepancies in the make up of the flights, especially in McGuire's ICR and careful analysis of all available 13 IRCs (two pilots did not return) has resulted in the above flight compositions.)

When McGuire's formation arrived over the target area at 21,000 feet at 1035 the first 20 Japanese fighters, mostly Zeros, were spotted with an altitude advantage of 5,000 feet to the rear of the P-38s. The enemy pilots flew coordinated attacks from 2 and 8 o'clock and after they made their passes McGuire turned to port after the Zeros attacking from 8 o'clock and sent Champlin's Blue Flight after the 2 o'clock attackers. The attacking Zeros dove through Red Flight and Champlin flying below put his Blue Flight in string to meet them. Two Zeros got into position to attack Blue #4, Moreing from astern and McGuire immediately went into an Immelmann and fired a expert deflection shot that hit the enemy's wing roots and the Zero burst into flames and exploded for victory number 32, putting him seven behind the inactive Bong. McGuire made a head on pass at another Zero that disappeared after the two planes sped past each other. McGuire's ICR claims he was returning to protect the bombers when he "happened to notice" two more Zeros below and dove after them. McGuire fired and knocked pieces off the Zero which began to smoke and then started to smoke before it crashed near the town of Mexico for victory # 33. Remarkably, Wingman, 2Lt. Alvin Neal followed McGuire through his attack and confirmed the victory. McGuire then took his flight to 15,000 feet, flying behind the bombers, when he saw four P-38s dive after two Zeros just as three more Zeros dove out of the overcast to get on the tails of these four P-38s. Despite two more Zeros diving on his own flight from 7 o'clock high, McGuire "felt it necessary" to go after the three Zeros closing on the other P-38 flight. McGuire fired from dead astern with a 60 degree

**2Lt. Alvin Neal** got his second of two total victories. (AAF)

**1Lt. Louis DuMontier** got his last two of three total victories. (AAF)

**Maj. Thomas McGuire** scored victories # 32, 33, and 34 to move him within six of Bong. (AAF)

**1Lt. John Pietz** shot down two Jacks to become an ace. (AFAA)

**1Lt. John Tilley** moved within one victory of becoming an ace. (AFAA)

**Capt. Frederic Champlin** got his eighth victory. (AFAA)

**2Lt. Harold Gray** claimed his only victory of the war. (AAF)

deflection shot and hit one of the Zeros that trailed smoke as it went down to crash near the town of La Paz. Victory # 34 was witnessed by Maj. George Dewey of Group HQ. The two remaining Zeros broke from their attack on the P-38s and looped around to the rear of McGuire's Flight but he broke and lost them. Another pair of Zeros came down from above and behind and McGuire easily outdistanced them in a starboard turn. He then saw two more Zeros which separated and McGuire attacked the one on the left and got a good burst before it passed under him. McGuire went after another Zero but when he fired from slight deflection only one of his machine guns fired and this Zero got on Dewey's tail. McGuire swung around to make another pass on this Zero but now his good gun would not fire and the Zero continued its attack on Dewey. McGuire made another pass temporarily scaring off the Zero that then turned into Dewey again. McGuire "told my Wingman Lt. Neal to go and get him." Neal fired from 60 to 20 degrees deflection and the Zero trailed smoke and was seen to crash near Santa Rosa for his second of two victories. The 475FG history comments that McGuire turned in early that night, "eager to make the most of the good hunting while it lasted." However, sometime during this combat McGuire's second element of Provencio and Koeck, was shot down. There is no mention of Provencio's demise in any of the ICRs. Koeck was last seen by Oxford and Fulkerson being attacked by a lone Jack that leveled out of its dive and hit Koeck's fighter and sent it down in a shallow dive with one engine smoking badly toward Clark Field. Fulkerson was unable to get a shot on the pursuing enemy fighter as Koeck took no evasive action and radioed for him to bail out. There was no answer and Fulkerson last saw Koeck entering the overcast, seemingly in control of his fighter. As this Jack broke away from its attack on Koeck, Ballard attacked it from astern and shot it down. Ballard then joined a circle of P-38s but his older J-15 model Lightning was unable to keep up and he and Wingman Oxford started after another Jack. Ballard fired from 20 degrees astern and then pulled up and Oxford then fired a long burst from 1,000 feet and the Jack pilot went into a climb but Oxford continued firing until its pilot bailed out. Then Oxford saw a Zero that McGuire had engaged pass under McGuire's fighter and come into his sight. Oxford fired a long burst and this Zero went for his last two of three victories.

Fulkerson joined Red Flight and circled the area when a Zero Split-S'd on the flight and Fulkerson fired from 90 degrees and scared it off. Two more Jacks made a high overhead pass on the flight and one overran and Fulkerson pulled up on the second and after a non-deflection burst sent the Jack down in flames. Fulkerson lost Wingman Dewey and saw a lone Jack and followed it to the deck and fired a short non-deflection shot and the Jack rolled over and burst into flames into the sea for his fourth and last victory of the war. After chasing a Tojo for a short time Fulkerson left for home in a slight dive but looked back and saw a Jack on his tail. Fulkerson skidded and rolled violently but the Jack pilot got hits that holed the P-38's coolant system and the escaping Prestone stream appeared to be smoke. When the Jack broke off. Fulkerson feathered his left engine but then the temperature on his right engine soared and Fulkerson restarted his left engine. He realized that he had to either bail out or crash land and immediately looked for a field on which to crash land. He found one with a 20 degree slope with trees on both sides. He landed the Lightning straight in, skidding 200 feet, before coming to a stop. Fulkerson quickly escaped from his burning fighter and was rescued by friendly Filipinos.

After the initial enemy pass, Capt. Champlin's Blue Flight spotted a lone Oscar below and Champlin closed on the Oscar that was in a shallow port dive. He fired a short burst from 30 degrees as the Oscar swung under and to port of Champlin whose speed was so great that by the time he completed his 360 the Oscar was coming head on to him. Champlin opened fire and the Oscar rolled over on its back and dove straight in for his eighth victory. The flight then saw a Jack flying south and closed on it and Champlin opened fired but the Jack snap rolled away. Wingman Gray rolled with the Jack and fired from 90 degrees deflection at very close range and then followed with a 70 degree shot that hit its canopy and saw the Jack crash out of control near Arayat Airdrome. Another Jack was spotted directly below and it tried to lure Blue Flight across the airdrome's AA fire. The Lightnings broke off and were attacked from directly astern by two more Jacks and Gray's left engine was hit but he was able to escape by going into a shallow dive to the deck and finally outdistance his pursuers after a long chase. Meanwhile, Blue Flight element Leader DuMontier lost Champlin when he avoided a collision with another P-38 and continued on with Wingman Moreing. DuMontier followed a Zero through a Split-S and fired from 40 to 20 degrees deflection and watched it roll to port and crash into the low hills near Clark Field . The two Americans then climbed to 12,000 feet and saw five enemy aircraft above them which dropped aerial bombs on them. DuMontier and Moreing became separated and DuMontier joined two other P-38 and make six or seven passes that were ineffective because the enemy pilots always turned into them which gave the P-38 pilots only snap shots, a favored American tactic. The Americans did not dive on these enemy fighters because there always were more enemy fighters above. DuMontier's Wingman, Moreing then fired at a Zero coming in from 2 o'clock and got hits on its belly and Moreing saw it crash and explode NE of Clark Field for his third and last victory. As they were climbing, three unaware enemy fighters dove in front of DuMontier who sped forward and fired a 30 degree deflection shot from below and saw hits on its tail section. The Zero broke away and DuMontier was unable to follow but Champlin saw it explode for his second victory of the day and his last of three total.

Tilley's Green Flight was attacked by 30 to 50 bandits with a 10,000 foot altitude advantage and boosted full throttle in a climb to escape and then circled back on them. Wingman Pietz stayed back with Wingman Martin who was having engine problems and could not keep up with Tilley who joined Champlin's Flight. Tilley "milled around" in a dogfight with Blue Flight and "after getting snap shots and getting shot at" he rejoined Pietz. While escorting Martin, Pietz and Martin were attacked by four Jacks from 2 o'clock high and Pietz took a snap shot as they Split-S'd away and at this point Pietz lost Martin. Martin had turned onto a Jack's tail that was in a steep turn at 15,000 feet and got hits on its wing and it flipped over and dove straight down for his first of three victories. As Pietz began to climb he met Tilley and the two saw a Jack and dove after it. It rolled over and Pietz went after it and shot it down with a 90 degree deflection shot. After losing Pietz, Tilley joined other P-38s circling Clark Field at 10,000 feet. A Jack attacked from below and starboard and Tilley turned into it and fired but the enemy pilot turned right and Tilley turned sharply left and got on its tail. But before Tilley could fire again the enemy pilot made a sharp diving port turn and Tilley followed him through and fired a 70 to 35 degree deflection shot getting hits on its canopy for his fourth victory. During his firing run Tilley became inverted in a 60 degree dive and had to roll right side and pulled out at 2,000 feet. After Pietz lost Tilley he heard Fulkerson call that he was in distress and flew over Clark Field where he was attacked by six Jacks and immediately called for help and went on the defensive firing deflection shots while evading their passes. Pietz got hits on the wing root of one from 60 degrees and got astern and shot it down for his fifth victory to become an ace.

432FS

Capt. Henry Condon led 16 P-38s on the B-24 escort to Mabalacat Airdrome and adjacent installations. Clover arrived over Mabalacat at 19,000 feet and climbed to 25,000 feet to have an altitude advantage on any enemy aircraft coming out from under the clouds. There were many "turn arounds" on this mission and vacated slots had to be filled by members of other flights. Condon heard chatter on the radio indicating combat and Condon ordered tanks to be dropped and turned south and

**Col. Charles MacDonald** (left, with Gen. Wurtsmith) shot down three fighters and claimed a probable for 24 victories. (AFAA)

**1Lt. Joseph Forster** was credited with his ninth and last victory. (AFAA)

**Capt. Henry Condon** shot down two Zeros over Mabalacat Airdrome to become an ace. (AFAA)

immediately saw four Zeros emerge from the clouds. Condon and Wingman, 2Lt. Lewey Noblitt, turned 180 and came up on the tail of the last two Zeros but the enemy formation had seen the P-38s and pulled up to port. Condon closed and fired a 30 degree deflection shot from 300 yards and got hits on its canopy, port wing root, and engine. The Zero rolled over and its pilot bailed out at 18,000 feet.

Condon's Wingman, Noblitt, followed Condon down on the two Zeros and took the one on the left and dropped his nose and fired some shots that hit the Zero but passed over it before he could observe any results. Condon and Noblitt then saw two more Zeros and Condon again took the one on the right and Noblitt took the one on the left. Condon fired and got some hits before his target Split-S'd away to the right. Noblitt's target also Split-S'd away but to the left and he dropped his nose and fired a long burst that hit the engine and cockpit. The Zero spun into an explosion when it hit the ground for Noblitt's only victory. After Condon and Noblitt shot down their aircraft Condon's Second Element Leader, 1Lt. Harrold Owen, followed Condon and Noblitt who saw a Zero at 10,000 feet and chased it to the deck. Condon and Noblitt pulled up and Owens closed to 300 yards and fired three short bursts, getting hits on the fuselage and wing roots. The Zero pulled up from 100 foot altitude and rolled into the ground. Owens then pulled up behind Condon and Noblitt who were closing on a Zero on the deck. When Condon and Noblitt broke off Owens continued the pursuit of the speeding Zero. Owens was able to close slowly and when he went to fire Owen discovered his gunsight was out and closed to 200 feet and fired low. He closed and fired a short burst that hit the wing roots and fuselage, and the Zerio rolled over at 100 feet and exploded into the ground for his second victory of the day and two of four total. After escorting the bombers safely out of the area Condon descended to 12,000 feet and headed back toward Mabalacat where he saw another Zero at 7,000 feet. Condon dove and fired a short burst at 90 degrees deflection and the Zero was seen to crash by 2Lt. William Savale to make Condon an ace.

Col. Charles MacDonald led three P-38s into the battle and encountered 15 to 20 Jacks and Zeros at 14,000 feet north of Mabalacat. MacDonald's pilots were able to split the Japanese formations by using the P-38's superior speed and by constantly turning into their attacks without suffering any losses. The dogfights descended down to 5,000 to 7,000 feet and forced the Japanese pilots to take most of their passes from head on to the front quarter where they had to face the P-38s heavy .50 machine guns and 20mm cannon. MacDonald took many deflection shots with unobservable results, including a Jack that was hit and seemed to fall out of control for a probable. MacDonald then got a stern shot on a Jack from 50 yards, causing it to burst into flames and fall to the ground shedding pieces. MacDonald's #3 man, Capt. Miller, left for home with engine trouble and Joseph Forster took his place. MacDonald closed on a Jack carrying a phosphorous bomb and fired a three second burst that set the Jack completely on fire. As MacDonald passed over his victim the bomb exploded to decimate the fighter. He spotted two Zeros above diving through the overcast headed west and MacDonald climbed at full throttle. The oblivious Zeros flew over and MacDonald chandelled to starboard and got behind them, a little low. He chased them south of Clark Field where he fired a long burst on the Wingman who bailed out. MacDonald went after the element leader who pulled around in a tight turn and MacDonald used his dive flaps to get his firing lead. However, his turn pulled too many G's and all his guns stopped. As MacDonald turned toward home his fighter was bombarded by enemy AA fire from Clark and adjoining fields. As he was weaving through the AA fire he saw that his #3 man, was missing. As MacDonald and his Wingman, 2Lt. John Murphy, continued on they saw a P-38 being attacked by a Zero from astern. MacDonald instructed his Wingman to do the shooting while he made a head on pass at the Zero which broke off its attack. In his ICR MacDonald reported the enemy pilots to be "aggressive and extremely clever at aerobatics." The three victories gave MacDonald 24.

Forster had begun the mission as Clover White Three with Capt. Richard Kimball on his wing. In the initial attack Forster fired a short burst at 90 degrees deflection at a Zero that slid off into a dive, began to trail smoke, and then break into flames and crash fro his ninth and last victory. Meanwhile, Jacks had positioned themselves above to attack and one dove on Kimball and two more on the White Flight Leader. Forster closed quickly on the two attacking White Flight Leader and fired two or three quick bursts at them which was enough to make them break off their attack. A Jack then made a diving pass at Forster who "kicked the controls all over the cockpit, losing several thousand feet in altitudes" to get away. After Forster joined MacDonald he saw the Colonel shoot down his third victim, Forster chased an Oscar and made a 90 to 30 degree deflection pass and "observed hits but no serious damage." Forster's final pass was head on at an Oscar that fired first. As Forster pulled the trigger only one gun fired and the Oscar came straight at him and just missed ramming his port wing.

433FS
Possum Squadron sent out 14 P-38s on a low level sweep over Mabalacat Airdrome/Dasol Bay. While flying at 3,000 feet near Mabalacat Airdrome at 1122 a single Zero dove on Blue Flight from 6 o'clock. As it passed through Blue Flight in a shallow turn it passed in front of Red Flight and then chandelled up to the left and leveled out. Red #3, 1Lt. Glenn Maxwell, opened fire from about 350 yards but saw no hits and then closed to 200 yards at 6 o'clock and this time got hits on its canopy and wings. The Zero turned to port, close to the deck and Maxwell closed to only 25 yards and got hits that set the Zero on fire and it half rolled into the ground for the Squadron's only victory of the day and Maxwell's only victory of the war.

**25 December 1944: 49F/7FS/8FS/9FS**
The 49er Mission Leader was Capt. William Williams, who led the Group and his 9th Squadron off Tacloban at 0800 headed for Masbate Island, which was their rendezvous point with the Liberators that were headed to bomb Mabalacat Drome. 1Lt. Joel Paris was the 7FS Screamin' Demon Flight Leader and led his 12 wingmen on their take off from Tacloban 10 minutes after William's Knights, also headed for Masbate. Capt. William Drier was scheduled to lead his 8FS Black Sheep Squadron but immediately after take off his Lightning lost an engine. Drier radioed Tacloban where Capt. Aschenbrener was waiting in reserve caught up with his 14 wingmen to take over the 8FS lead. The Black Sheep had been designated as the last squadron to take off from Tacloban as Allied Intelligence anticipated that the Japanese would launch every fighter available to intercept the attack and be most vulnerable after the raid as they landed to rearm and refuel. The Black Sheep and several elements of the Satan's Angels were assigned to wait in high cover east of the target and when the last of the Liberators left, these Lightnings were to ambush the enemy fighters in their landing pattern. The 49er formation had the Flying Knights in the lead at 13,000 feet; the Screamin' Demons to the left and slightly higher; and the Black Sheep at 14,000 feet some distance to the rear. As per plan, at 0900, the 49er's 38 Lightnings rendezvoused with the large Liberator formation over Masbate and assumed their position on the Liberator's port side across the formation from the 42 Lightnings of Col. Charles MacDonald's 475FG.

The large formation flew along the spine of mountains on the southern Luzon mainland, directly to the target. At 1030, the lead B-24 turned west over the broad central Luzon plain to begin its bomb run for Clark under high, thin cirrus clouds and brilliant sunshine which afforded excellent visibility. Immediately, the bomber crews called out sightings of many single-engine enemy fighters approaching. The air battle began in earnest directly over Clark Field at 1035 with the 431st Squadron of the 475FG engaging and 10 minutes later the 49ers swept over Mabalacat Airstrip on the eastern edge of the Clark complex. Elements of the 7th and 9th Squadrons fired simultaneously at the horde of enemy fighters sweeping in at 13,000 feet.

9FS
Mission Leader and Red Flight Leader, Capt. William Williams, was leading 10 Knight P-38s in close port cover of four B-24 Squadrons when they approached the target at 1045 at 13,000 feet when White Flight Leader, 1Lt. Albert Lewelling called out three Tojos approaching from 10 o'clock level. Williams led Red Flight into the attack but only Lewelling's Flight would make any victory claims.

Lewelling's White followed Red Flight into the attack and as the P-38s closed the Tojos broke away putting Lewelling in "excellent position" to turn directly behind the enemy #3 man. As Lewelling followed his Tojo, Williams called for all Knights to return to protect the bombers. As Lewelling was about to return, the last Tojo in the flight leveled out and slowed to release a phosphorous bomb which gave Lewelling an opportunity to close rapidly from dead astern and fire a short burst that sent it rolling over on its back and explode as Lewelling passed over it for his fourth and last victory. Lewelling rejoined the bombers an as he was weaving back and forth over the bomber formation another P-38 flight passed through and Lewelling got mixed into that flight thinking it was his Red Flight. As he was trying to find Red Flight he saw a Tojo making an attack on the #3 man of another squadron and the #4 man firing on the Tojo. As the Tojo broke away it flew into Lewelling's sights and he hit the wing root, starting a fire as it passed under his wing. As Lewelling turned to finish off the Tojo it was heading straight down and crashed in an explosion for his second victory of the day and his last of four total. Lewelling continued on after several single enemy fighters in the area but every time "I started after them…someone always beat me to them." 2Lt. Troy Smith was Lewelling's Wingman and followed him through his first Tojo victory and rejoined the bomber formation with him at 11,000 feet where they spotted "Nips a little below." White again followed Lewelling as he shot down his second Tojo but then lost him. He saw a Tojo diving on a P-38 and came in astern and fired at 10 degrees deflection and "it seemed to explode and smoke came out." Smith continued firing and the Tojo rolled, smoking badly when Smith lost it for only a probable claim. The P-38 he saved was that of 1Lt. Noah Williams who would limp home on one engine. Lewelling's second element Leader, 1Lt. Noah Williams, was in the dogfight and had a Tojo shoot out his left supercharger and he Split-S'd to the deck, followed by the Tojo that Smith shot at. Lewelling's #4 man, 2Lt. Dan Holladay, turned into a Tojo that had finished making a pass at the bomber formation and fired at 60 degrees deflection. The Tojo pilot dropped his flaps and began a sharp climbing turn to the right as Holliday's gunfire registered on the enemy fighter's wings and fuselage, knocking off pieces. Holliday stalled out but was seen to spin in flames and crash for his only victory.

7FS
Meanwhile, Demon Mission Leader Paris climbed from Tacloban at 0810 to 13,500 feet about 1,000 feet above the bombers with his three flights:

Red: #1) Paris, #2) 2Lt. Dewey Renick, #3) 1Lt. James Franks, #4) 1Lt. Joseph McHenry
Blue: #1) 1Lt. James Jarrell, #2) 2Lt. Ralph Watkins #3) 2Lt. Albert Meschino, #4) 2Lt. William Thompson
White: #1) 1Lt. William Minto, #2) 2Lt. Robert Klemmedson, #3) 1Lt. Robert Decker, #4) 2Lt. Kenneth Markham

Upon their arrival at the target area at 1045 they were bounced by 15-20 Zeros coming down from 18-20,000 feet to attack the bombers. Paris led his Squadron above the bombers as the Zeros Split-S'd through the formation

**1Lt. Lewis Lewelling** got his final two of four victories. (AFAA)

**1Lt. Joel Paris** claimed his seventh victory. (AFAA)

dropping aerial phosphorus bombs. Paris fired on one which exploded for his seventh victory. Paris' Element Leader 1Lt. Franks fired snap shots at an enemy element which were in a tight left turn. The enemy wingman pulled inside Franks but the American was able to fire a 30 degree deflection shot at the leader which exploded as Franks crossed over the top of it for his second and last victory. After a few turns the Zeros cut Franks off from his flight and he dove from 12,000 to 4,000 and escaped. As Franks climbed back to 8,500 feet when he was attacked and had his port coolant and left supercharger shot out. Franks was forced to dive away again but his Wingman, 1Lt. Joseph McHenry came in and fired immediately from 50 to 30 degrees and the enemy fighter slowly inverted and McHenry followed in a 45 degree dive and fired again and the Zero burst into flames as it went in fast spins that were ended as it crashed into the sea for his only victory. McHenry had another chance for a victory but ran out of ammunition.

Blue Flight Leader, 1Lt. Jarrell immediately became separated from his Flight and Wingman, and his ICR described six firing passes with hits scored on two but finally had to break away from combat when he was attacked by three Zeros and head for home. Jarrell's Wingman, 2Lt. Ralph Watson's ICR has him standing off from the battle but the Blue Second Element of Leader 2Lt. Albert Meschino and Wingman 2Lt. William Thompson got into the thick of the battle after they became separated and were "too busy to join up afterward." After a series of evasive maneuvers the two got away from the "Nips" and were about to attack when three more Zeros "latched onto them out of the sun." As the first passed through Meschino "hooked onto him" while Thompson skidded to the left and wide of Meschino so he could turn into them. The second Zero came in on Meschino's tail and Thompson pulled up into it. The Zero pilot pulled up into a high chandelle which became a loop. Thompson followed, using his dive brakes, and fired and set it on fire for his only victory. Meschino continued his pursuit of the first Zero and made a 45 degree steep side pass and fired causing a small explosion in the port wing. As the Zero began a tight diving turn, Meschino made another pass that put him on his back as he completed it. The Zero inverted and its pilot bailed out. Five minutes later Meschino saw P-38s engaging a Zero and he joined in. As he approached the fight the Zero turned into him and was greeted by a five second burst that made a few hits. Meschino followed the Zero down getting more hits until all but one of his guns stopped firing. Other P-38s came in and finished the Zero. Meschino headed for home but his flight was interrupted when he saw a Lightning being chased by two Zeros. As he climbed to help the P-38 was attacked by a second Zero and it rolled over and headed down on its back trailed by the two Zeros. Meschino fired with his only gun to distract the Zeros but had to break off when more Zeros appeared overhead. After Meschino shot down his Zero he shook off an attacking Zero and joined Jarrell and flew back to base. This was Meschino's first of two total victories.

White Flight Leader 1Lt. William Minto ordered his Flight to drop their tanks when the enemy fighters dove from 18,000 feet. Minto made three ineffective firing passes that were evaded by the experienced enemy pilots. Minto then saw a single Zero maneuvering on the tail of a P-38 and got behind and "rode on the Zekes' tail" and fired until he had to pull up to avoid a collision with the disintegrating Zeke for his only victory. Minto's Wingman, 2Lt. Robert Klemmadson, following a Zero down on his first pass; firing from 30 to 0 degrees for his only victory. After finishing this firing run the #2 Zero fired a few small caliber 7.7mm bullets into his fuselage but no damage was done and he landed safely. As the Zeros passed through White Flight, White #3, 1Lt. Robert Decker dropped his nose 20 degrees and fired a short burst that hit the engine and right side of the cockpit and watched as the pilot bailed out for his fourth and final victory.

8FS

As planned, Aschenbrener's Black Sheep and several of the 475th's 431st and 432nd Squadron elements swept inland as the B-24s headed back to base. Aschenbrener's Blue Flight foursome spiraled just above Banban Village located between the Mabalacat and Clark bases. As Intelligence predicted, the enemy fighters began to descend to rearm and refuel. Aschenbrener and Wingman 2Lt Arthur Terry descended directly over Mabalacat where Aschenbrener spotted a lone Zero and went into a 400 mph dive to 500 feet above the field. The Zero pilot saw him approaching and evaded. Aschenbrener made a wide turn and got inside the Zeros and fired a short deflection burst with the damaged Mitsubishi turning away again. Aschenbrener's second attack led directly over the northern perimeter of Mabalacat where the now alerted airdrome AA gunners hit Aschenbrener's P-38. Shrapnel cut into his legs and gashed his forehead and knocked out his port engine which he feathered. Then his starboard engine began to trail smoke and stopped and Aschenbrener prepared for a crash landing. Aschenbrener's Wingman Terry flew through the AA barrage and his fighter shuttered as it was hit but everything seemed functional and Terry fired to hit the Zero which pulled up and over Terry. Blue Element Leader 2Lt. James Atkinson, flying immediately behind Terry, swept in and finished off the Zero which crashed on the airfield. The Blue Flight Elements then began to strafe the field's gun emplacements and parked aircraft, setting a Dinah and two Oscars on fire. As they climbed away Blue #4, F/O Harold Bechtold, saw a lone Oscar fly across his line of flight and followed it down to the deck and caught up to it 500 feet over the edge of Bam Bam Drome and fired at 30 degrees hitting the Oscar that climbed slowly and then crashed near the Drome for his second and last victory.

1Lt. Edward Glascock led Green Flight at 10,000 feet over Baler Bay when an Oscar flew directly over the Flight at about 500 feet and flew out and then turned back into the Americans. Glascock made a steep turn into the Oscar which then broke down and away. Green Element Leader, 1Lt. John Bodak, made the first attack as the Oscar Split-S'd and as Bodak broke away 2Lt. Robert Goodwin followed the Oscar down for about 1,000 feet and fired from dead astern and claimed his second and last victory.

Aschenbrener crash landed against a hard-packed rice paddy jetty, 10 miles southeast of the airdrome. Aschenbrener was in severe pain with a severe back strain and two cracked vertebrae and two bruised spinal discs. As an electrical fire broke out in the gun bay, Aschenbrener painfully crawled to safety as a small band of Huk tribesmen arrived. The tribesmen carried Aschenbrener on a caribou to their small village and then to a village of the Huk Bala Hop guerillas where he rested for a week. A few days later, he was joined by a Navy Hellcat pilot, an Avenger bomber pilot and his gunner. The guerrillas took the flyers to a small railroad where they traveled aboard a small handcart across central Luzon to the Lingayen coast, 60 miles away. For two weeks, they moved to one small camp to another and eventually met with the Volunteer Guards and reached the hills only a short distance from the north coast where they would have to wait until the Japanese were off the main roads and the trail to the coast was clear. Once at Lingayen, Aschenbrener was flown back to Hill Field after 27 days.

**25 December 1944: 547NFS**

Pilot Capt. Robert Blackman and R/O 1Lt. Jean Harper took off at 1830 to fly a local patrol over the San Jose, Mindoro area when they were vectored by the GCI to a bandit headed northwest on an evasive course. Harper made an AI contact at 9,000 feet and six miles and gradually decreased range until Blackman made a visual at 500 feet as the bandit crossed hard port to starboard. Blackman turned hard to port and fired a short deflection shot hitting the left fuselage and nacelle. Blackman had to pull up sharply to avoid a collision as the enemy dove into the water at 1930 for the squadron's first victory.

**26 December 1944: 475FG/431FS/433FS**

The past few days had taken their toll of the Japanese air defenses in the Clark Field area, greatly curtailing both the number and aggressiveness of the interceptors. Some American combat reports for the Christmas Day mission mentioned that the Japanese seemed almost certainly intent on ramming. On the 26th the Japanese were expected to be as determined but not nearly so plentiful.

431FS

After his three victories the day before over Clark Field which put him only five behind Bong, McGuire was eager to repeat the good hunting in the Clark area. He led the Squadron and Daddy Red Flight while Capt. Fred Champlin led Daddy White Flight and 1Lt. John Tilley led the rear two man Daddy Blue Flight with 1Lt. Horace Reeves flying as his Wingman. The 10 P-38s took off at 0810 and rendezvoused with the B-24s over Masbate Island at 0900. The Liberators arrived over the target at 1030 and made their bombing run without incident while the P-38s covered them at 16,000 feet, somewhat above and to the starboard. As the bombers turned

**Maj. Thomas McGuire** shot down four enemy aircraft to give him 10 for December and 38 overall, putting him only two behind the inactive Bong. (AAF)

away McGuire saw five Zeros descending from out of the overcast on the rear of the formation.

McGuire described his combat:

> The bombers had completed their run and were heading away from the target when, at 1035, I sighted 1 enemy aircraft at 8 o'clock high. There were about five Zekes coming down on the tail of the bomber formation from above, out of the overcast. We were about 2,000 feet above and behind the bombers. As I started down, I saw two enemy aircraft heading south below us. As I started my attack, the first Zeke had finished his pass and the second was driving up the last bomber flight's tail. This was at about 13,000 feet. As the enemy was pressing his attack, and I could see no return fire from the bomber, I opened fire from 45 degrees deflection from about 350 to 400 yards range, getting hits right in the cockpit. The Zeke started to burn, but as he was still on the B-24's tail, by then about 50 yards behind it, I closed to within 100 feet, firing another burst. The Zeke rolled over and burst into flames. Captain Weaver, my Wingman, saw the Zeke burst into flames and explode.
>
> I shot at the third Zeke in the string, shooting in about 70 degrees deflection, but observed no results. Turning to the left and down, I shot two bursts into another Zeke at about 60 degrees deflection. The enemy plane started burning, and Captain Weaver saw him crash in flames.
>
> About three more had come, so I turned on 1, shooting a burst from 30 degrees deflection, then another good burst from about 45 degrees deflection and got hits around the cockpit. The enemy started down and crashed in a dry stream. Lieutenant Herman, my element leader, who had broken off to clear himself from another Japanese, saw him crash, going down from 5,000 feet.
>
> I was then by myself, as my Wingman had lost me on that pass. I saw another Zeke heading down, so I turned on it and caught it at about 1,500 feet. I fired two bursts from about 40 to 60 degrees deflection, getting hits around and behind the wing roots, and the Zeke started burning, then crashed near the dry stream. Lieutenant Herman saw the Zeke burn and crash.
>
> As I was on the deck, I started climbing, and at about 6,000 feet I saw an enemy aircraft diving down quite a distance in front of me. The enemy plane pulled up, so I gave chase, but another flight came down from above to attack him. As the Japanese started for the clouds, it was hit and burst into flames just before reaching the clouds. I saw Lieutenant Pierce, leader of the 8th Fighter Squadron flight, destroy this aircraft.

1Lt. Christopher Herman who was leading McGuire's second element, also lost his Wingman trying to follow the wild flying McGuire but managed to confirm these victories while shaking Zeros off his own tail. Herman continued on to see McGuire chase a Zero into a dive and then to make another expert deflection shot to send his victim burning and crashing near the same dry stream for victory number #4 for the day and #38 total. The zealous, adrenalin-driven McGuire saw a Tojo in the distance which promised to make him an instant, Ace-in-a-Day. He raced after the Japanese fighter which was climbing for the safety of the overcast before McGuire and other diving P-38s caught the same Tojo. 1Lt. Sammy Pierce of the 8FS was also in the area when McGuire started after the Tojo and watched McGuire and the other P-38s miss one firing pass after another as the Tojo pilot skillfully evaded the overly eager Lightning pilots. Just as the Tojo was about to reach the clouds, Pierce went into a dive and fired one accurate burst and sent the fighter down in flames. The fuming McGuire cursed the intruder who stole his victory over his radio but Pierce flew

**Capt. Frederic Champlin** was credited with his ninth and last victory near Clark Field. (AFAA)

**1Lt. John Tilley's** P-38 has his fifth victory applied. (AFAA)

home also scoring four victories for the day to become an ace with seven victories. (See 26 December 1944: 49FG)

For time being McGuire would have to be satisfied with 38 victories which put him only two behind the grounded Bong. Meanwhile, Herman broke out of the combat after he almost collided with another P-38. He saw a Zero turning inside him below and reversed his turn and lost the Zero and also his Wingman. Herman joined 1Lt. John Tilley's Blue Flight which had watched McGuire shoot down the incoming Zeros. Tilley spotted four Zeros flying over the mountains to the west of Clark and sped toward them. The Zeros saw Blue Flight and went into a tight Lufbery at 12,000 feet. Tilley and Reeves remained near the top of the enemy Lufbery. One Zero broke out of the Circle, but instead of continuing to follow the other Zeros in the Lufbery, most of Tilley's Flight followed after a lone Zero that was skimming the tops of the clouds over the mountains. Tilley had to use full war emergency power to catch the speeding Zero. After two minutes chase Tilley finally fired at 2,000 feet at 250 yards astern getting hits on its fuselage and tail. The Zero pilot made no evasive turns and Tilley fired from 10 degrees at 200 yards and got more hit on its fuselage and starboard wing. The Zero still did not go down and Tilley closed to 100 yards and fired from dead astern; observing numerous hits on its port wing which caught fire. Tilley closed to 50 yards and fired and the Zero finally exploded into a ball of fire to make Tilley an ace with five victories. One pilot who didn't follow Tilley was his Wingman Reeves who saw a Zero making a too wide turn in the Lufbery and dove and fired a 30 degree deflection shot at 200 feet getting hits which sent it down in flames for his third victory. Champlin's White Flight had remained over the initial combat and made several ineffective passes. When there were no more enemy aircraft in the area Champlin led his Flight home, but spotted a lone enemy fighter at 6 o'clock high. Champlin turned 180 and climbed, but the enemy pilot saw him and dove for the clouds. Before the Zero reached the clouds Champlin fired a 20 degree deflection and it burst into flames and crashed into the hills near Clark Field for his ninth and last victory.

433FS

Capt. Jack Fisk was leading two flights of 433FS P-38s covering B-24s over Clark at 13,000 feet when he saw McGuire's flight engaging the Zeros about 1,000 feet above. Fisk led his Possum Red and White Flights into the battle but Fisk's port engine cut out and once he restarted the engine White Flight #3 called out an attack from 7 o'clock from the rear. Fisk turned 180 degrees head on into a Tojo which broke away into a diving vertical banking turn that gave Fisk a 70 degree deflection shot at 250 yards, getting some effective hits around the cockpit and the Tojo dove straight down and crashed just southeast of Clark. Fisk's seventh and last victory ending the 475$^{th}$'s scoring for the year. The Group had confirmed 99 kills in December and their wartime total now was 522 after devastating the enemy opposition over Clark.

**Capt. Jack Fisk** was credited with his seventh and last victory. (AFAA)

**26 December 1944: 49FG/8FS**

While McGuire would shoot down two Zekes over Clark three veteran Black Sheep: Flight Leader 1Lt. Thomas Holstein, Wingman 2Lt. Nial Castle and Deputy Ops Exec 1Lt. Sammy Pierce would account for seven of the 14 day's victories claimed in only 15 minutes of combat.

Blue Flight Leader Holstein called an enemy formation of seven interceptors which had suddenly broke out of the clouds three miles south of Clark. Mission Leader William Drier did not answer Holstein's call and although Red Flight under Capt. Nelson Flack did respond; it was only in time to make one firing pass. Holstein's rookie Wingman, 2Lt. David Wicks had problems jettisoning his tanks and was unable to rejoin the flight. Blue Element Leader Castle took the Wingman position followed by Pierce in his old K-model Lightning. Pierce had joined the flight only after their original #4 had aborted earlier in the mission.

The approaching Zeros were in a formation of two Vs of three with a single trailing element but as they closed to within firing range they suddenly separated. Two elements attempted to cut off Holstein but Pierce, trailing slightly above, immediately dove and turned head on into the Zeros.

Pierce had been flying as the #4 man in 1Lt. Thomas Holsteins' five man flight at 16,000 feet when bogies were called in and the flight dropped their tanks. Pierce turned up into three Zeros that were trying to get on Holstein's and his #2 and #3 tails. The middle "Nip" turned and met Pierce head on and did not break off until Piece was sure he would be rammed. When the Zero pilot dropped his nose to fire, Pierce fired and hit its engine, starting a fire and have pieces come off as the Zero passed under him. Nearby, Holstein chased another Zero and sent it down in flames. Pierce then felt a "bad jar that felt like ack ack" and caused his right wing to rise up and he tried to rejoin his flight and saw the debris from his victim floating down. Pierce then saw four Tojos following Holstein's Flight below and rolled over as a Tojo was about to fire on the #3 P-38. Pierce's cannon and machine guns hit the Tojo which turned belly up and gave Pierce a no deflection, broadside shot and the Tojo went into an inverted spin, trailing smoke. Pierce again lost his flight and saw five "Nips' diving on the bomber formation and dove. But as he arrived above the Zeros he saw ace McGuire shoot down two Zeros, one of which collided with the tail of a B-24 and then seconds later he saw Black Sheep Nial Castle destroy another that tried to Split-S away. Castle was now within one victory of becoming an ace. Pierce finally got into firing range of the remaining three Zeros and he went after the #2 man that "pulled a rolling turn back under him" and Pierce followed with a half turn but was unable to get a shot and Pierce pulled around after the #1 man who was being pursued by other P-38s that were still out of range. Pierce gave this Zero a short burst from high astern that caused it to smoke. Pierce fired a second burst that missed but his next burst sent the Zero down in flames. Again Pierce tried to rejoin other P-38s but was bounced at 10,000 feet by three more Zeros and went into a shallow full power dive and then a high speed climb and lost them. Pierce now had the altitude and speed advantage and dove on the two Zeros that still were below. One half rolled away and Pierce attacked the other and fired a 15 degree burst from high astern and hit and smoked its engine. In the meantime, the #2 Zero had gotten behind Pierce and was firing on him from high astern but a 431FS P-38 chased the Zero away with a head on pass. Pierce continued after the #1 Zero into the overcast that topped the nearby mountains but fired on it when it emerged. Its wing roots were hit and the enemy fighter began to smoke and disappeared into the clouds. Pierce then climbed to 6,000 feet and saw eight or ten P-38s chasing a lone Nip at 2,000 feet below. As Pierce approached he saw two P-38s fire and miss and overrun it and then he cut off the other Lightnings "that were out of range" and fired a very long burst from 20 degrees deflection high and started it on fire. As Pierce released his triggers the over heated guns continued to fire until their ammunition was expended. Pierce's ICR then states: "I then pulled up and went with Major McGuire as his Wingman." When Pierce landed, his damaged nose wheel collapsed, and he found pieces of enemy fuselage imbedded in his port engine radiator, and two large holes in his fuselage; the cost for his four victories of the day's combat, which made him an ace with seven final victories.

**1Lt. Sammy Pierce** got four victories and a probable to make him a seven victory ace. (AFAA)

There is a story (not substantiated by either pilot's ICRs) that Pierce's fourth victim was desperately trying to outrun a formation of eight Satan's Angels, led by McGuire who had already claimed four victims to give him 38. Just as McGuire was about to claim a certain fifth kill Pierce dove and overtook the fleeing Zero and set its center fuselage on fire, within view of the livid McGuire who shouted into his microphone for the pilot who had just shot down his Zero to identify himself. Pierce, with his distinctive Carolinian drawl answered, "This ere's Raccoon Blue numba-fo'ah, Majah." McGuire replied, "Pierce, you little bastard. Is that you?" After a brief silence McGuire added, "Nice shot!"

### 26 December 1944: Japanese Mindoro Task Force

Despite the determined Japanese defense of Mindoro, the Island was lost and placed American forces very close to the southern shore of Luzon which made the Japanese defense against invasion very difficult. The utter failure of the Japanese air forces against the Americans on Mindoro also was of great concern to the Japanese. So during the last two weeks of December desperate circumstances forced the Japanese into a risky countermove to attack the American beachhead off San Jose and shell their positions and equipment on the Mindoro perimeter.

When the American forces landed on Mindoro on 15 December the Japanese High Command began to formulate plans to seriously disrupt the operation. Adm. Soemu Toyoda, of the Japanese Chief of Staff, ordered R.Adm. Susumu Kimura, commanding in the South China Sea, to prepare a task force to strike at shipping offshore at Mindoro, and then shell the beachhead installations. This task force, made up of the heavy cruiser *Ashigara* (identified as a battleship), the light cruiser *Oyodo*, and six destroyers, sailed from Cape St. Jacques (Saigon) at 0900 hours on 24 December. Adm. Toyoda had ordered the new 27,000 ton carrier *Unryu* to join the task force, but as she steamed south to join the task force, she was intercepted in the Formosa Strait by the USN Submarine *Redfish* which attacked in daylight and put two quick torpedo hits into the carrier which was vital to the attack. After the completion of the attack on Mindoro the fleet was to send the three small destroyers (they were also converted to act as minesweepers for the larger units) to Manila for refueling. The remainder of the task force would retire as quickly as possible to Camranh Bay.

No sooner had the Japanese task force sailed when its presence was reported by USN submarines. Forewarned by these sightings, Brig.Gen. William Dunckel, commanding on Mindoro, dispersed his supplies inland and the Navy Commander ordered all shipping to leave Mindoro and take refuge behind Ilin Island. SWPA search patterns were extended to the coast of Indo-China. At 1600 hours on 26 December a PB4Y search Catalina reported what it believed to be a battleship, heavy cruiser, and six destroyers 100 miles west of Mindoro, speeding toward the Allied position at 28 knots. It was ascertained that the nearest comparable Allied task force, consisting of four cruisers and nine destroyers, could not close with the enemy before 1430 hours on 27 December. The only Navy vessels near the beachhead were a score of motor torpedo boats under Lt.Cdr. N. Burt Davis, who also had to protect the merchant ships and LSTs present.

Meanwhile, Col. Jack Wilson, CO of the 310th Bomb Wing, and in command of the 5th Air Force units on Mindoro, alerted all air units, and directed as many planes as possible to be armed with bombs and the others prepared for strafing. But Wilson was informed that all bombs were still on the coast of Mindoro after being unloaded and the Japanese naval forces would arrive before they could be delivered. Nonetheless, it would have been very dangerous for fighters to take off at night on the short, soft, and bumpy air strips and so it was decided to send the fighters out without the bombs. Because low level attacks on enemy destroyers were so dangerous Squadron Commanders were reluctant to order their men on such a mission, but the pilots volunteered without hesitation.

The Navy had no warships available to stop the enemy task force so a small force of Air Force aircraft and Navy PT boats was assembled. The AAF force was made up of P-38s of the 8th Fighter Group, P-47s of the 58th Fighter Group, whose prior combat had been restricted to ground support operations, P-40s of the 110th Tactical Reconnaissance Squadron, and B-25s of the 17th Bomb Squadron. All available aircraft were to make the attack and 44 P-38s, 28 P-47s, 20 P-40s, and 13 B-25s would attack the enemy ships. The attacks on the ships were to be made from different heights and directions to confuse the enemy gunners. The American aircraft were to turn on their navigation lights during their attacks on to avoid collisions. It was found during the actual attacks that the Japanese were reluctant to use searchlights to find their attackers for fear that they would reveal their location.

**26 December 1944: 8FG/35FS/36FS/80FS**

After their nine victories in 22 December the 8FG did not take part in the large and successful air battles of 24 and 25 December when 34 and 46 Japanese aircraft were destroyed. However, on the 26th they would be awarded the Distinguished Unit Citation (DUC) for an action in which they did not destroy one aircraft in the air.

35FS

At 1830 Capt. Lynn Witt was informed of the Japanese naval force and told to have all available 35FS aircraft on alert and armed with 500 pound GP bombs and to have his pilots on readiness. The fighters had landed at 1845 from a previous mission and had to be serviced and there was no time to arm them with bombs. The lack of refueling facilities at the field also hampered orderly organization for taxiing to the line. Half an hour later Witt was ordered to have all his pilots on the line and they were in the Operations Room by nightfall and ordered to take off. Since there were no bombs the 35th was ordered to strafe the enemy ships; paying particular attention to the destroyers which were now only 20 miles from the field.

The taxiing and take off was conducted under an enemy bombing and strafing attack and at 2045 Witt took off and was followed by 14 other P-38s in a scattered formation. An hour later the Squadron arrived over the enemy convoy that was firing at other aircraft. The night was clear and the enemy ships were easily seen in the distance by their concentration of AA fire and then by the wakes of the maneuvering destroyers and then their silhouettes. The pilots would make their passes towards the shoreline as from that direction the moon would make the enemy ships stand out more clearly. Also the pilots realized that their machine gun fire would temporally blind them and used the shoreline as a reference point to pick out the end of their strafing runs. After their first passes the pilots of the flights usually became separated. The 35th's Lightnings continued their strafing but the darkness prevented them from accurately accessing the damage. The AA fire seemed to be mostly from machine gun fire with a much lesser concentration of explosive shells fired from dedicated AA cannon. "The Japs never knew where to shoot. We were all over the place." (1Lt. Robert Hamblin)

Witt was first to attack and closed on a destroyer from 4,000 feet firing with his machine guns and cannons and a large explosion occurred as he passed. It seems that a torpedo from a USN PT Boat exploded just as he passed over the target and caused the sinking.

1Lt. Robert Bowerman describes the action:

> The initial pass was started in my flight with (1Lt. James) McLain on my wing. After the first pass we were entirely separated. I then pulled out and circled, picking out my first target, a destroyer. It was very hard to see, but as I closed in, guns opened up on me, so I returned fire and noticed hits all along the deck. I came in from 500 to 200 feet and closed to 200 yards and then broke off and went up, getting set for another pass... Another ship was then burning so I went down for a run on it. I made several other passes on destroyers and one on the battleship. I believe I silenced some gun positions on the battleship... The ack-ack over this force was moderate to heavy but fairly inaccurate. Most of my passes were made at about 350 mph and around 300 feet altitude, coming in from bow to stern at a front quarter attack on the ship.

36FS

At about 1830 Capt. Kenneth Giroux led 18 Lightnings of the 36FS to the southeast quadrant of ocean off Mindoro where the enemy naval force was expected to be found. The clouds obscured the moon, making for a very dark night and Giroux almost passed over the enemy heavy cruiser *Ashigara* at 500 feet before he realized that it was there. When the 36FS discovered at least three of the enemy ships they strafed them through their AA fire for about 45 minutes until the 36FS was recalled so that the dive bombers could come in to attack. When Giroux and his unit were heading back to Leyte he discovered that the coolant shutters on his starboard engine were jammed closed and within minutes the engine would seize. Giroux flew toward the coast near San Jose and parachuted into the sea within swimming distance of shore and was rescued and returned to Mindoro. 2Lt. Wayne Donker also had to bail out and be rescued.

80FS

At 2130 Capt. Paul Murphey led 11 Lightnings of the 80FS to attack the convoy. Four of the P-38s were carrying some of the few 500 or 1,000 pound bombs available for fighter use on Mindoro. When the 80th found the Japanese ships about 20 minutes later the clouds finally dispersed and the moonlight showed the pandemonium of zigzagging wakes, AA fire, and the burning wreckage of a motionless destroyer and another ship on fire that was moving frantically to escape. The 80th scored four near misses with their 500 pound bombs and strafed the Japanese vessels until they ran out of ammunition.

The attack of the 80th Squadron was described:

> The evening of the 26th of December was one that will long be remembered. At 1900 that evening a meeting of all squadron personnel was held, and we were informed that a Japanese task force was approaching Mindoro. Plans for evacuating the camp and taking to the hills were laid down. Engineering, armament, and ordnance men were sent to the line to bomb up and prepare the planes for an aerial attack on the task force. All available planes on both strips were sent into the air: P-38s, P-47s, B-25s, P-61s, and P-40s. Our ships took off at 2120 hours. From camp the flashes of explosions and patterns of tracers could be seen. Only four of our planes were bombed up, two of them secured four near misses on two enemy destroyers. Two of our pilots were forced to bail out that night. Lieutenant Kenneth Lloyd had completed five or six passes on a destroyer when his left wing either hit the water or was hit by flak. The left wing was curled up at a 45 degree angle and the prop was bent back over the engine. Lieutenant Lloyd managed to get 2,000 feet of altitude and get back to the field. He bailed out rather than risk a single-engine belly landing in the dark; he was picked up and brought back to camp uninjured.

Lieutenant Orland Harris underwent a harrowing experience that night, one that was almost unbelievable. He came in to strafe a destroyer from the side when he received a jolt that threw his head up against the gun sight, stunning him momentarily. On recovering from the shock, he became aware that his left engine was on fire and his plane below the superstructure of the destroyer, which he had evidently hit on his pass. He pulled back on the stick trying to gain altitude. Because of blood running into his eyes from the cut on his forehead and the dizziness he felt, he had no idea of his altitude until he heard a voice in his earphones saying, His right engine is on fire, but he's high enough to bail out. Lieutenant Harris figured they were talking about him, so he trimmed up his ship and bailed out. That's when his worries began; he landed in the middle of the Japanese task force. After disengaging himself from his chute, he swam away from the destroyer nearby, taking his rubber raft with him. When he turned on the valve to complete the inflation of the raft, the hiss it made was so clear and loud that he had to shut it off until the ship was out of earshot. He finally got the raft inflated and was about to get into it when he saw another destroyer coming straight at him. This time he believed he was done for, but ducked down behind the raft and waited. Again the ship went right past him, so close that its wake carried him along for several yards. He finally got into the raft and paddled toward shore, not making much headway, as the ocean was very rough. He was picked up by a friendly barge early next morning after 12 hours in the water.

At about 2030 hours that night the Japanese warships started shelling both strips on the island. Bright star shells, which lit up the entire area, were used to illuminate the targets. Some of the men took off for the hills when the shelling became too much for them. The shelling lasted about 30 minutes and did not accomplish its main objective, which was to render the strips unserviceable. The convoy withdrew under fierce attack by our planes after three destroyers were sunk and the cruiser damaged. (These claims were greatly overestimated.) All friendly planes took off with wing lights on and kept them on while in the area to keep from having A/A thrown up at them. Some Japanese planes sneaked in with their lights on and strafed the strip, destroying 1 and damaging 4 of our planes in revetment areas. Nine planes of the 80th that participated in the attack on the task force landed at Leyte at 2400 hours that night; seven of them took off the following morning to return to base."

The dangerous mission took its toll on the 8FG. 1Lt. James McLain had his canopy blown off by machine fire but was unhurt and landed safely at Tacloban. After five passes, 2Lt. Robert Hamblin received two small holes in his tail from expended AA fire. 2Lt. Orland Harris' strafing P-38 hit the superstructure of one of the ships and he bailed out. 2Lt. Francis Lloyd's P-38 was damaged by AA fire but he nursed it over the beach where he bailed out. The next morning 1Lt. Russell Roth was flying back from Leyte and was forced to bail out into the sea 10 miles south of Mindoro and was rescued by a PT boat. Three P-38 pilots were reported missing in action: 2Lt. John Grillet of the 35FS and 2Lts. Wayne Donker and Samuel Ford of the 36FS. Donker was later rescued but Ford, who he walked away from his burning fighter on 20 December, was later listed as KIA.

**Col. Gwen Atkinson** was the CO of the 58FS and led the fateful mission, flying with the 311FS. (AAF)

**Maj. Milton Self** was the CO of the 69FS and would be KIA in the battle. (AAF)

**Maj. Harry Odren** (left) was the CO of the 311FS and **Capt. Donald Jander** led a 311 Flight. (AAF)

**26 December 1944: 58FG: Greatest Day of the War**

Once the Japanese Task Force was discovered, Col. Jasper Durham, 58FG Deputy Group Commander established a ground perimeter around the camp in case the Japanese landed infantry. He also ordered food, supplies, and ammunition loaded on some trucks and others to stand by to evacuate personnel to the interior.

Without a coordinated plan of attack, all 32 available Thunderbolts of the 58FG were ready to take off at approximately 1800. The mission was to be led by 58FG CO, Col. Gwen Atkinson, who was to fly with the 311FS with 1Lt. Arthur Marston on his wing. Maj. Odren led the remainder of the 311th, which consisted of Capts. Stephen Benner, Frank Ellis, and Donald Jander; 1Lts. Horace Borden, Joseph Borunda, Kenneth Crepeau, Raymond Evans, Oliver Foster, Max Itzkowitz, Lynwood Johnson, and James O'Leary; and 2Lts. Joseph Benson and Joseph McDonald. Maj. Milton Self led the 69FS, which included Capts. George Bosenbark and Arthur Jackson; 1Lts. Donald Bridgeford, Hubert Emrich, Robert Foulkes, John Linton, Robert Lewis, Chester Majka, Charles Martin, and Jack Nacht and 2Lts. Stuart Campbell, Blaine Ellenberger, Joseph Girard, and Charles Gregg.

As the pilots headed for the field a red alert was sounded indicating Japanese aircraft were approaching. The first 311th fighters quickly taxied out and took off at 2015, rendezvoused, and headed up the coast. The enemy planes arrived at dusk and began bombing and strafing the strip and revetment areas and continued intermittently until dawn and the 58FG fighters had to take off between attacks. The soft taxiways and runways caused the fighters to bog down and had to be pulled out. Although the field was subjected to enemy strafing and bombing, T/5 Everett Huffman worked for 45 minutes until he towed nine planes to the strip for take off. When two P-47s crashed and burned while trying to take off from the soft runway and blocked the strip and Huffman then commandeered a bulldozer and pushed the burning planes off the runway. Maj. Self's 69FS was not able to take off until 2130 due to the confusion. First, 1Lt. Linton's Thunderbolt hit a hole and veered off the runway into a rice paddy but he was uninjured but delayed further take offs. It was not until 2300 hours that the 14th fighter of the 69FS left but then 1Lt. Charles Martin aborted because of mechanical trouble.

The first flights haphazardly rejoined over the field and proceeded toward the last reported position of the enemy fleet. Fortunately, ceiling and visibility were unlimited along the west coast of Mindoro except for a thin layer with a base between 7,000 and 10,000 feet. At about 2100 phosphorescent wakes were seen on the water and soon the ships causing the wakes were seen running southeast approximately parallel with the Apo Reefs. Darkness made close formation flying impossible and individual fighters would have attack following the ship's wakes and open fire when within range, strafing the vessels from stern to bow.

When first spotted the Japanese Task Force was moving southeast in three columns in line astern, with the "battleship" (the heavy cruiser *Ashigara*) and the other cruiser in the center column. Once under attack these capital ships held course while the accompanying destroyers started quick "S" turns. Most pilots turned 270 degrees to begin their initial attack from 10,000 feet, diving north to south; stern to bow, but subsequent attacks were made from all directions. On their strafing runs most pilots descended at 350 to 400 mph, passing over the enemy ships at 50 to 100 feet and then stayed on the deck, skidding violently to avoid AA fire until out of range. Once safe they switched on wing lights to avoid collisions and climbed, turned off their lights, and continued their attacks. The first attacks converged on the cruisers but their AA fire drove them to divert their subsequent attacks on the destroyers. The destroyer AA defenses were mainly medium AA gun fire bursting at about 10,000 feet and the lighter AA gun fire at about 5,000 feet. Some heavy caliber AA fire was reported in the 5,000 to 10,000 foot range, using high explosive shells with short fuses. The Japanese gunners could not see the attacking American planes and would wait until the Thunderbolts opened fire with their tracers to open fire. While their fire was vigorous it was inaccurate and no fighters that returned to base were damaged by AA fire. No searchlights were used by the task force. Japanese aircraft appeared in the area throughout the night and one attacked a P-47, damaging its vertical stabilizer. The American pilot skidded and chopped his throttle, and attacked the enemy plane, but overran and lost it in the darkness.

Original briefings had specified that, after the attack, the planes were to proceed about 275 miles to land at Tacloban, Leyte, so that, if the Japanese shelled the strip at Mindoro, the planes would be safe. After leaving the battle Atkinson, Odren, Ellis, Itzkowitz, Powell, Evans, MacDonald, Lewis, Jackson, Bosenbark and Campbell proceeded to Leyte and landed without mishap. Jander, O'Leary, Marston and Gregg, doubtful of having enough fuel to fly to Leyte landed back at Mindoro. Jander decided then to try to go on to Leyte but changed his mind after take off and returned to Mindoro. Lynwood Johnson landed at Mindoro, attempted to take on some fuel and then proceeded safely to Tacloban. Foster and Crepeau landed at Mindoro, attempted to refuel, then took off and headed for Leyte. Bad weather made navigation difficult and, after searching in vain for Tacloban, they landed at a small strip at Valencia, near Ormoc, on Leyte. Capt. George Bosenbark and 2Lt. Stuart Campbell had taken off with the mission but never got a chance to attack because they met damaged aircraft that requested escort back to Leyte where the pilots were instructed to land because the Mindoro strips might be unserviceable as a result of the expected naval bombardment.

The battle was best described by Col. Atkinson the Official Group History:

After a brief search we found the task force fifteen miles up the coast and five miles offshore. The ships were dark blobs on the water marked by phosphorescent wakes. I knew we could do no formation fighting in the darkness. Our best chance lay in each man fighting his own fight, going in on the ships from all angles. There was grave danger of our ramming into each other, so I ordered that all passes be made from west to east, so we could all be going in the same direction. Too, this would silhouette the ships against what light there was.

At this time I saw, or thought I saw, a battleship, two heavy cruisers and five destroyers below. Official reports say there was no battleship, but one heavy cruiser, a light cruiser and six destroyers. I believe official reports. But I saw a battleship from where I sat in the dark sky that night.

Picking a ship, I went down for a first pass. As I opened fire I was spotted by my tracers there had been no time to remove them as we usually do for night fighting and every ship opened up on me. It was as if a volcano had erupted to blast open the night. With fire like that turned up on us I didn't expect any of us to come out of that fight.

There were bombers and fighters of other outfits up there with us that night. But I saw none of them. I saw none of my own planes. I was alone. Every pilot was alone. I kept diving, strafing, pulling up and climbing to dive again. I made passes from stern to bow and from abeam. I held my fire until I could see the superstructure of a ship so that I could do all the damage possible. I strafed all the ships, taking them one by one. The big baby may not have been a battleship but it was long enough and wide enough and had enough firepower for a battleship. Passing over it was like passing too close over a blast furnace. Other planes, Nip planes and ours were flitting shadows all over the sky.

How did I feel? I didn't feel! I wasn't a man. I was part of a fighter plane and I don't remember thinking of anything in particular. I guess you just fly and fight by instinct and the habits developed by experience when the action is this hot.

I made nine strafing passes in all before my ammunition gave out. The last gun to run dry was the outboard gun of my right wing. During my last strafing pass it was the only gun firing, and it was putt-putting like a toy rifle. I missed the buck of my plane that comes when all guns cut loose. I felt as if I were fighting with a BB gun.

I kept my eye on my gas gauges. After the fourth or fifth pass I called our Ground Controller and told him we had just enough gas left to get to Leyte Island. We had been ordered to land on Leyte, in case the Japs managed to get ashore at Mindoro and capture our airstrip. The controller just answered "Attack the target." So I forgot the gas gauges and kept strafing until that last gun put-putted out. Then I headed for Leyte. I could see two ships of the task force burning.

As I sped away tracer bullets suddenly streaked in front of me. Another stream of them passed on the left. I was being fired on by Nip planes that had been covering the task force. But the Nip lost me, and I kept my nose headed toward Leyte.

Leyte was 300 miles away. The weather was bad. I had enough gas left for about two hours of flying. After an hour and 40 minutes of flying on instruments through thick weather, I came over the island, but was a long way from safe. The weather was thick at 1,000 feet and thick at 11,000 feet. I tried both levels. There was little hope of finding the airfield in that muck and I had only about twenty minutes of gas left. There was little fear of having to jump and perhaps spending days or weeks in the jungle-not after what I had just survived.

My savior was the Ground Controller at the Leyte airstrip. He was good. He took me over; his instructions flew my plane for me until suddenly I saw the flattened beam of a searchlight filtering through that soup sky.

Then like magic, a hole appeared in the murk. Through it I saw the most beautiful sight I shall ever see, the green lights that bordered the air strip. I had just gas enough for four minutes flying time when I set the plane down. On checking I found that I had squeezed 2 hours and 22 minutes out of what I thought would carry me two hours.

We lost five pilots in the hell that was thrown at us that night. That's a lot of good men. Others landed all over the Philippines, and it was days before we got back together again. One was seriously wounded, another was hit and had to bail out. He was rescued by Filipino guerrillas. Others ran out of gas and jumped.

Our pilots fought better than a good fight, they took all the Japs could give. Some of our pilots, despite the possibility that they may be delivering themselves to the Japs, landed back at Mindoro for more gas. They had to siphon it out of wrecked planes. One landed after the task force had been whipped and was crawling home and called from his plane to ask if any bombs had been brought up.

We all feel that something more than luck was with us that night-call it what you will. And we all know that the finest feeling in the world is just to be alive.

The next best thing is to know that the job you set out to do was done, damned well done. The Japs never landed a man on Mindoro that night. Their shelling was brief and inaccurate.

Final reports of the battle showed both of the heavy ships badly damaged, two of the destroyers sunk, and a third damaged. A captured Jap naval petty officer has said that the shelling was so poor because all range finders and automatic aiming devices for the ships guns had been shot out.

Fighter pilots of the 58th didn't do all of that. Maybe we did very little of it. But we helped, and we are proud of that. That's what we are over here for.

Although the 5AF had badly damaged Japanese naval force, it bombarded the Mindoro beaches from about 2240 until 0100 hours on the 27 December. The Japs began shelling with hundreds of star shells to light the sky and then fired star shells mixed with high explosive shells. However, the shelling was very ineffective causing no casualties and very minimal damage and the airstrips weren't hit. One Liberty ship which had not taken shelter behind Ilin Island was sunk. Throughout the night enemy aircraft harassed the San Jose area but without any effect. At 0130, 27 December 1944, a message was received from 310BW HQ that the enemy striking force was withdrawing.

**1Lt. Charles Gregg** was the only 69FS pilot to return to base. (AAF)

**1Lt. Joseph Borunda** was one of four 58FG pilots to crash on take off. (AAF)

The loss was heavy for the 58th and the following is a list of those pilots and planes lost during the night action off Mindoro on 26 and 27 December 1944. Missing in action from the 311th were Capt. Steven Benner, 1Lts. Leroy Borden and 2Lt. Joe Benson. Missing in action from the 69FS was: Maj. Milton Self; 1Lts. Donald Bridgeford, Herbert Emrich, Robert Foulkes, Chester Majka and Jack Natch, and 2Lts. Blaine Ettenberger and Joseph Girard. 1Lts. Joseph Borunda and John Linton crashed on take off but were uninjured while the P-47s flown by 1Lts. Kenneth Crepeau and Oliver Foster were damaged by a B-25 making an emergency landing at Valencia, Leyte.

At daylight on the next morning the 5276th Rescue Composite Group began the search for the missing pilots and airmen and Maj. Milton Self and 1Lt. Chester Majka were located on 27 December. Self's plane had been damaged by AA fire during the attack and as he arrived over Mindoro, he joined with Capt. Bosenbark and they headed for Leyte where they were joined by another P-47. While over Leyte Gulf the three became separated and finally Self's Thunderbolt ran out of fuel and he bailed out. Self had difficulties getting out of his aircraft which was falling in an inverted spin. Upon landing in the water he became entangled in the shroud lines of his parachute and nearly drowned before he was able to free himself. He was able to get into his life raft and fired his pistol and was able to attract the attention of one of the many naval vessels in the Gulf and was immediately picked up. 1Lt. Chester Majka's fighter was badly damaged by AA fire and was forced to bail out when his engine quit. When he tried to bail out his aircraft his leg was broken when it struck the aircraft. When he landed on the ground near the city of Ormoc he broke his ankle and three ribs. When American soldiers found him the next morning he was in severe pain.

For their part in the battle against the enemy task force the 58th Fighter Group was awarded a Distinguished Unit Citation, which read:

> Flying P-47s, the 58th Fighter Group strafed a Japanese naval task force attempting to strike the newly established American base on Mindoro Island. When an enemy air attack made it impossible to load the planes with bombs, the pilots were given the option of refusing the mission but all volunteered although a strafing mission on naval vessels was almost suicidal. By their mast high strafing attacks they set several destroyers and a cruiser afire and killed many of the Japanese crewmen. Due to lack of fuel several pilots were forced to ditch their planes at sea. 26 December 1944.

Sixth Army CO, Brig.Gen. William Dunckel's, appraisal of the 58FG's night action off Mindoro on the 26th: "The action of our Air Units on that night will stand forever as one of the most gallant deeds to be established in the traditions of American fighting men."

**26 December 1944: 5FC Toll**

The 5AF sent 107 aircraft into combat; including 30 Thunderbolts of the 58FG (two planes crashed on take off); 44 Lightnings from the 8FG (Nine from the 80FS, 15 from the 35FS, and 18 from the 36FS); while the 71st Reconnaissance Group attacked with 13 B-25s of the 82nd Squadron and 20 P-40s of the 110th Squadron. The 418th Night Fighter Squadron maintained patrols over the battle and Mindoro and was credited with two enemy aircraft destroyed. Of the 107 aircraft sent into combat 26 were lost: three B-25s, seven P-38s, 10 P-47s, and six P-40s for an exorbitant casualty rate of 25%. Despite the losses the AAF did accomplished their mission as the task force broke off the engagement and retreated into the darkness. The personnel and aircraft loss to the 8th and 58th Fighter Groups has been previously tabulated above.

**1Lt. Idon Hodge** shot down two Sally bombers for two of his three total victories. (AAF)

As the Americans began their air attack, PT-223 torpedoed the new destroyer *Kiyoshimo*, which later sank when attacked from the air. Although no enemy vessels were destroyed by aircraft; the fighters and bombers did extensive damage to the enemy warships by destroying main and AA batteries; killing a large number of deck and gun crews. The American aircraft were to attack under unfamiliar blackout conditions but most had to turn on navigation lights to keep from colliding with each other which made them excellent targets for anti-aircraft fire. The Japanese force did not land and their warships could only mount a dismal 45 minute barrage that sunk only a single American vessel, a Liberty ship that had not taken refuge behind Urn Island as directed.

The next afternoon the 80FS sent two P-38s out to find the Japanese convoy which was 200 miles southwest of Mindoro and now consisted of five ships of the original eight with some trailing smoke and oil slicks. The broken convoy would be harassed by air and naval forces all the way back to Indo-China. This was the last attack by Japanese naval surface forces that would threaten the Philippines, and thereafter only enemy aircraft and occasional submarines would obstruct the invasion. Following this battle the AAF fighter and bomber strength on Mindoro was built up as quickly as possible. The primary limitation of operations from the bases there became the shortage of fuel and bombs that resulted from the loss of tankers and supply ships to enemy Kamikaze attacks; a situation that would not be resolved until shortly before the invasion of Luzon on 9 January.

**27 December 1944: 35FG/39FS**

After their huge losses on Christmas Japanese fighter action subsided considerably over the next several days for the 5FC. On the 27th the 39FS flew four P-47s led by Idon Hodge on a fighter sweep and heckling mission to the Halmaheras. While flying at 10,000 feet at 1730 they spotted two Sallys flying at 500 feet on the deck near the Djailolo Airdrome. Once the Americans started their dive one of Sallys began to lag behind as their formation turned to the left. Hodge dove the second and third Sallys and fired a 70 degree burst at the lead bomber getting a few hits. As he adjusted his lead the Sally went into a gentle turn just over the end of the strip and sustained more hits on a two second slight deflection shot and the bomber began to burn vigorously at the wing root and crashed near the Strip.

As Hodge was about to turn toward the second Sally when it was fired on by another P-47 and Hodge broke away. This P-47 was that of Element Leader, 1Lt. Edgar Beam, who made a pass and missed and was followed by #4 man, 2Lt. Carl Worley, who took a 60 degree five second burst that hit the cockpit and exploded on the wing root and this Sally exploded and burned when it hit the ground for his only victory. Worley circled after the remaining Sally and fired a long burst from 200 yards getting some hits before breaking off. Hodge's Wingman, 2Lt. Leo Barkus followed Worley's attack made the next pass and also saw some hits before he broke off. Hodge fired just after Bartkus left and fired from 150 to 50 yards dead astern just over the trees. Hodge saw hits on the fuselage and as he pulled up to avoid hitting the trees he saw the Sally catch its port wing on the trees and tear it off the wing outboard of the engine and crashed about a mile or two from the strip.

**Late December 1944: 475FG**

With the end of the year came a mass of rotations home. 433FS pilots rotated home included Robert Tomberg, Herbert Cochran, Robert Anderson, Joseph Price, and Donald Weimer.

**Late December 1944: 49FG Moves to Mindoro**

After the great Christmas air victories Kenney moved the ground echelons of the 49FG moved from Tacloban to the advanced bases on Mindoro. After many delays, on 1300 on 26 December, the 7th and 8th Fighter Squadrons boarded one LST and the 9th another and sailed by that night. The squadron personnel had no

Aces of the **431FS** in late December: (L-R) Champlin (9v), McGuire (38v), Cline (2v), and Monk (5v). (AAF)

regrets over leaving Tacloban which was as bad as any of the bases they had flown from in New Guinea. It had the same rain and mud, mosquitoes and Malaria, insufficient and poor food, a chronic shortage of potable water, and the same damp tents and cots. The new bases on Mindoro were rumored to be no better.

On the 27th as the convoy turned north into the waters northwest of Panay, adequate friendly air cover for the approach to Mindoro was lacking and the sightings of enemy aircraft increased throughout the day; followed by more General Quarters alarms sounded throughout that night. At 1030, as the convoy entered Mangarin Bay, only ten miles from the beach, they found themselves under a powerful air raid as three Kamikazes crashed into ships in the convoy. As they lay at anchor just offshore, there were many more alerts during that afternoon but CAP and shipboard AA gunners kept the enemy planes at bay until the 29th when the Japanese slipped through the Mindoro air defense in the mid-morning marginal weather. A Kamikaze pilot got through to the LST carrying the 9th Squadron and HQ personnel but heavy AA fire diverted its course and the damaged Kamikaze glanced off the bow of the LST, causing only minor damage. Despite continuing air raids, at noon on 30 December, the two LSTs finally dropped their ramps on the Mindoro beachhead and the exhausted squadron ground personnel went onshore to be transported to Hill Airfield. When they arrived they found that Hill had received little damage as the Japanese had concentrated on the beachhead shipping and better; it was a high and dry field.

**27 December 1944-7 January 1945: Kenney Grounds McGuire**

McGuire was known in the theater as "Eight behind McGuire" because he always seemed to be eight victories behind Bong. But Kenney had sent Bong back to the States and now, after his four victories on the 26th, McGuire had an opportunity to catch and pass his rival. However, Kenney had other plans as Bong was on his way to America as the leading American fighter ace of World War II. Kenney was concerned that if McGuire remained in combat Bong would be second when he arrived for the planned celebrations, so McGuire was grounded until after the first of the year.

Bong had raised his score to 40 confirmed aerial victories by 17 December and Kenney finally ordered him out of combat and was also on his way home by the end of the month as the leading American fighter ace of all time. McGuire, who resented Bong, was determined to take his title away at any cost as time was running short as he was feeling the effects of combat fatigue and Malaria.

On 27 December the score in the Bong-McGuire scoring duel stood at 40 Bong to 38 McGuire. On that day Kenney sent for McGuire. Kenney describes the meeting with McGuire:

> I told McGuire that I was taking him off flying as he looked tired to me. Tommy protested, 'General, I never felt better in my life. Besides I'm only two behind and…'
>
> "That's just it," I said. "You're tired and you won't be rested enough to fly again until I hear that Bong has arrived back in the United States and been greeted as the top scoring ace of the war. As soon as I get that news, you can go back to work. If I let you go out today you're liable to knock off another three Nips and spoil Dick's whole party."
>
> Tommy laughed but he didn't want to spoil anything for Dick, so it was okay. He'd relax, take it easy, get a lot of sleep for a few days, and then he hoped the Japs wouldn't run out on us for a while yet. By the way, when was Bong going home?
>
> "As soon as I can get him over here and loaded on a plane bound for the United States," I replied.
>
> Bong came back from Mindoro the 29th. The weather had held him up the day before. I had a seat assigned to him on a plane bound for San Francisco that night. He packed up his stuff, I gave him a letter to General Arnold which gave him a courier's status with high priority for air travel, and said goodbye. He left at midnight.
>
> On the afternoon of the 6th I got word that Bong had arrived back home and the newspapers had acclaimed him as the top scoring ace of the war. I sent for Tommy McGuire to have dinner with me that evening. After the meal, I told him that I believed he was now sufficiently rested and could go back to work shooting down Nips. I begged him, however, to take it easy and not try to get all the Jap airplanes left, in his first combat. If he would just play a hit-and-run game and get them one at a time he would live through the war but if he started pressing or got careless his luck might run out. I didn't want to have to write a letter back to his parents.
>
> Tommy assured me that he would be careful. He said that the next morning he and Major Rittmayer, a visiting P-38 pilot from the Thirteenth Air Force, who had four to his credit, were planning to take along a couple of youngsters, who had just arrived in the squadron, for a sweep over the Jap airdromes on Cebu and Negros to see if they could stir up something. We said goodnight. On the morning of the 7th McGuire and Rittmayer and the two new lads took off on the mission as scheduled.

**27-28 December 1944: 418NFS**

Ritchie/Wertin

Black Widow pilot, 1Lt. Malcolm Ritchie and R/O F/O Vincent Wertin left Mindoro at 1815 (27 December evening) for a local patrol over their base. After patrolling for two hours off the Mindoro coast CGI Controller vectored Ritchie toward a bogey approaching from the south. At 2038 Wertin picked up the bogey at four and a half miles and as Ritchie closed the Tony began evasive action. Wertin was able to continue radar contact as the Tony made hard turns and led Tompkins down to 10,500 feet. Ritchie got a visual at 2,500 feet from its tail and closed to 100 yards astern. Ritchie fired a short burst but was blinded by his tracers and when he next saw the Tony it was "five feet" from its tail. He throttled back and pulled up hard to miss a collision. The Tony pilot turned hard to port and Ritchie countered with a hard right and hard left turn to get on its tail. He fired a short burst and set the enemy fighter on fire with hits on its wing roots. He followed it down and fired a second burst that exploded the Tony which crashed near Ambulong Island.

Tompkins/Wertin

Pilot 2Lt. Bertram Tompkins and radar operator. F/O Vincent Wertin took off at 2330 (27 December late evening) for a local patrol and shot down two Tonys just after midnight (at 0010 and 0022) west of the Mindoro Coast. Tompkins describes the skirmishes:

> Approximately one and a half hours after becoming airborne the GCI controller vectored me onto a bogey approaching from the northwest. F/O Wertin made radar contact with bogey at 0010 at a distance of six miles and altitude of 10,000 feet on heading of 280 degrees. He directed me to 2,000 feet directly behind and below the bogey and I obtained a visual and identified it as a Tony. I closed to 150 feet and fired one short burst. The Tony exploded and fell burning into the water approximately 20 miles west of base. No evasive action was used by enemy aircraft.
>
> Immediately GCI vectored me onto second bogey, which was 20 miles southeast of me. F/O Wertin made radar contact at six miles and directed me to 3,000 feet, directly behind and slightly below the bogey, where I got a visual. I closed to 300 feet and fired 1 burst, and enemy aircraft exploded and fell to

the water burning. Kill was made approximately five miles west of Mindoro coast. E/A was identified as a Tony. Violent evasive action was used.

Sorbo/Kerstetter
1Lt. Albert Sorbo and R/O 2Lt. George Kerstetter claimed a probable Betty at 2145 over the base.

**29 December 1944: 8FG**
80FS
Early Morning Mission
At 0700 1Lt. C.B. Ray was leading five P-38s over Hill Field but upon take off 1Lt. Lloyd Johnson's P-38 had an engine cut out and the veteran of 68 missions was killed when his fighter crashed into the water. The Controller called in a bogie at 14,000 feet and 20 miles out. Ray climbed south in a shallow turn and at 14,000 feet he spotted the bogie, which he identified as a Dinah reconnaissance aircraft. The Dinah dove about 1,000 feet into a small cloud and when the Dinah dived from the cloud Ray chased the Dinah at full throttle and caught it at 10,000 feet about five miles north of Hammer Strip near San Jose. The Japanese pilot was apparently unaware of Ray as he took no evasive action when Ray opened fire from 200 yards and hit the starboard engine which started on fire. Ray followed the Dinah down and fired another long burst and it burst into flames just before it spun into the ground for his fourth victory (nearly a year after his first).

**1Lt. C.B. Ray** shot down a Dinah during a morning sortie, and then became an ace in the late afternoon by downing a Zero for his fifth and last victory. (AFAA)

Afternoon Mission
8FG convoy patrols continued throughout the day and at 1435 12 P-38s took off to patrol over the convoy. While patrolling at 11,000 feet Ray sighted a lone bogie on the deck five miles north of the convoy. As he dove his windshield clouded and he could not see to fire and a 36FS pilot (2Lt. Kenneth Creighton?) came in and downed the Kate. Ray climbed back to 3,000 feet north of the convoy with his Wingman where they spotted the two bogies that the Controller called. Ray climbed into the enemy fighters, identified as Zeros, that pulled into a thin layer of clouds at 5,500 feet. Ray fired a short burst at the rear Zero at 250 yards and it began to smoke. Ray was eager to finish off the wounded enemy and dove for 1,000 feet at high speed, firing intermittent short bursts without much apparent damage. On his second pass at 1,000 feet Ray hit the Zero as it tried to Split-S but crashed into the sea for his victory to become an ace. During this combat a Zero got on Ray's tail at 1,500 yards and Ray headed for a cloud 3,000 feet off the Panay Coast. The Zero continued to follow Ray for 10-15 minutes while firing from out of range before finally giving up the chase.

36FS
Eleven P-38s under Mission Leader, Capt. James Moss, took off from Mindoro at 1445 to patrol above the Mindoro convoy at 8,000 feet. The Squadron had been flying since early morning with little rest between patrols and had been in the air for three hours when they saw 15 mixed enemy aircraft (Sonia, Val, Helen, and Kate) at 9 o'clock, 6,000 feet above. Suddenly the enemy formation began frantic evasive action and Red Flight Element Leader; 2Lt. Gerald Lowrey called out two bogies at 2 o'clock and both were in position to get behind for a firing pass. Moss chased a Sonia and made a 30 degree bank and fired a three second burst from 250 yards and its port wing root and fuselage burst into flames and it crashed into the sea for his got his third victory. Moss' Element Leader, Lowrey fired on the other "Val" and saw pieces fly off and trail smoke. Lowrey's Wingman, F/O Walter Miller, fired at it from 35 degrees and got hits on its port wing root and cockpit and it rolled over and plummeted into the water. The IRCs of both pilots differ here as Lowrey's IRC describes his damage as pieces flying off and trailing smoke, ready to crash but since Miller got in the last shots he was credited with the victory. Moss and Miller had difficulty deciding whether they had shot down Sonias or Vals but the official records then credited Moss was with a Sonia and Miller with a Val!

Capt. Allen Hill, leading Blue Flight, saw two Kates separating after diving on the convoy. Hill went after the one heading northeast and chased it to the deck and fired but only got a few hits. Hill's Wingman, 2Lt. Kenneth Creighton, followed and fired a long burst and it crash landed into the water and its two crewmen crawled out into the water. After watching Creighton shoot down his Kate, Blue Flight flew to the west side of the convoy at 4,000 feet. Soon a Helen was seen heading away from the convoy and Hill fired getting some hits on its right engine before he broke away. Hill's Wingman, Creighton was out of ammunition and Element Leader, 2Lt. Lawrence Hyde, closed from 500 feet behind just above the water and fired a short burst into its canopy and it plunged directly into the water. Hyde's IRC states that he believed that he hit the pilot who slumped over the controls and caused it to crash.

**29 December 1944: 71TRG**
At 1615 the 110RS ran into a formation of Hamps and three were shot down by 1Lt. John Evans and 2Lts. Daniel Brattoli and Roy Rule.

**29-30 December 1944: 418 NFS**
At 1745 three P-61s, Major Carroll Smith, 2Lt. Bertram Tompkins, and 1Lt. Malcolm Ritchie took off to cover a resupply convoy southeast of Mindoro. A few minutes after take off Tompkins' aircraft developed prop trouble and returned to base. Smith and Ritchie patrolled over the convoy until 1900 when the GCI vectored an approaching bogie at six miles.

Smith/Porter (29 December)
At 1900 while patrolling at 7,000 feet 15 miles southwest of the convoy the convoy Controller vectored Smith toward a bogie which Porter immediately obtained a head on AI contact at 8,000 feet. Porter directed Smith to a visual on an Irving 5,000 feet away. Smith made a climbing 180 degree turn at full throttle to get behind the enemy which dove for cloud cover about 4,000 feet below. Smith followed the Irving into the cloud and Porter tracked it through the cloud and, afraid to lose it as it exited the cloud Smith fired at 1,000 feet and scored numerous hits before the Irving entered more clouds. The Irving gunner had fired five or six bursts that came close before entering more clouds. When the Irving broke out of the clouds it was only 500-600 feet away at 500 feet altitude in a diving turn. Smith closed into more fire from the bomber's tail gunner but he hit the Irving's wing roots and it burst into flames and crashed into the water and was confirmed by the destroyers below. In the combat Ritchie lost Smith and Smith ordered him to return to base. A few minutes later Smith and Porter were again patrolling when Porter made an AI radar contact about eight miles southeast of the convoy

**JNAF Nakajima J1Ni Irving** 2-3 place recon/night fighter. (AFHRC)

**Maj. Carroll Smith** (left), with **R/O 1Lt. Philip Porter**, shot down two Irving night fighters before midnight to make him an ace. (AFAA)

heading at 180 degrees and at 500 feet altitude. Porter directed Smith to 1,800 feet behind the bogey which Smith identified as another Irving. Smith made a front quarter attack; opening fire at 600 feet and continuing to 100 feet, getting many hits around the canopy and the Irving cart wheeled into the water. Smith completed his patrol at 2020 with two more victories for the day to make him an ace.

**Maj. Carroll Smith** shot down a Rufe and Frank in the early morning to give him his seventh and last victory to make him the top-scoring Pacific night ace. (AFAA)

Ellings/Burman (30 December)
2Lt. George Ellings and R/O Milton Burman took off at 0110 (30 December) to fly a routine patrol between 0100 and 0330 of the Mindoro area. At 0215 the GCI informed them of a bogey at 330 degrees and the pilot pursued it for three minutes before Burman made AI contact at a range of 9,000 feet and at an altitude of 8,000 feet. Burman directed a hard turn to port, then to starboard, and as they got to about 4,000 feet of the enemy Burman asked for a speed reduction to prevent overshooting. Ellings got a visual on a single Rufe at 2,000 feet dead head and 15 degrees above and closed to 300 feet and fired and closed more and fired another burst. The Rufe caught fire and inverted and plunged into the overcast between Ilin Island and Mindoro for Ellings only victory.

**2Lt. George Ellings** and **R/O Milton Burman** shot down a Rufe for their only victory. (AAF)

Smith/Porter (30 December)
At 0511 Maj. Carroll Smith and R/O Philip Porter took off on a patrol of the Mindoro area. They patrolled until 0545 when the GCI vectored them to a bogey. Porter picked it up at three miles and instructed Smith to descend from 6,000 to 500 feet. Smith slowly closed at 160 mph for eight to ten minutes at 300 to 500 feet as the GCI and Porter kept Smith in contact. Smith finally made a visual on a Rufe that was trying to dive and Smith fired a short burst from 100 feet that sent the enemy in flames into the water off the Mindoro coast.

Smith and Porter continued their patrol at 3,000 feet and just before 0700 the GCI called another contact at 8,000 feet and six miles and Porter made an almost immediate AI contact. Five minutes later Smith was able to make a visual contact of a "Frank" at 5,000 feet. Both aircraft were flying on the same course with the enemy above, straight and level at 200 mph. Smith closed slowly from behind and underneath as Porter called down the range to150 feet. Smith was running low on ammunition and closed to 75 feet for a sure kill. When they returned to base they learned that Smith had used only 400 rounds of ammunition. Porter stated in his ICR: "The Major is pretty keen on the trigger." These two victories gave Smith seven to make him the highest scoring night fighter ace in the Pacific.

**30 December: 419NFS**
Pilot Capt. Richard Stewart was credited with a Betty that he downed 400 yards off Cape Opmarai at 0034.

**30 December 1944: 8FG/36FS/80FS**
36FS
Capt. Allen Hill was leading 12 Lightnings during the 1230-1600 afternoon local patrol and was accompanied by such veteran pilots as Kenneth Giroux, Harold Graham, James Moss, and William Turner. As the Squadron was about to be relieved and was landing when the tower radioed them of bandits to the south. At 1545 five Oscar Kamikazes rushed in from 1,500 feet and 12 o'clock just as Capt. James Moss was leading Hill's Blue Flight down and saw an Oscar at 11 o'clock heading for a Liberty ship. Moss with Wingman, 2Lt. Robert Maynard, slightly behind, got on its tail and fired until the Kamikaze exploded in flames and bounced off the sea 50 yards from its target but remained airborne long enough to crash into the waterline. Another Kamikaze crashed into a destroyer while the other three were shot down by AA fire or crashed and missed their target. The AA fire in the area had been heavy and accurate and Moss had flown into it. Despite the unique twin boom silhouette of his P-38. U.S. Navy gunners continued to fire and Moss' port engine was hit and burning and he pulled up to 1,000 feet and jumped but his chute did not open. Maynard's IRC honors his leader: "Capt. Moss's shooting undoubtedly caused the enemy plane to miss its target in its intended dive." Moss sadly lost his life while claiming his fourth and the 36th Fighter Squadron's 94th and final victory of the war (plus 19 probable and 11 damaged claims).

**Capt. Louis Schriber** had a mixed bag of claims, with one victory (his fifth and last) and a probable (his sixth) and damaged. (AFAA)

80FS
Capt. Louis Schriber was leading a formation of 11 P-38s at 1530 on a local patrol of the San Jose Valley when his fighter had a mechanical problem and he returned to Hill Field and commandeered another fighter rejoined the patrol, flying with 1Lt. John Stanifer's flight. At 1730 they were patrolling north of Hammer Strip when four enemy fighters were seen flying low over the foothills. Stanifer did not see them and Schriber quickly rolled over and got behind the tail end Zero and fired long bursts and the fighter broke in two and crashed near a river bed. Schriber closed on the next Zero and fired and it began to smoke, but it climbed over a small rise for a probable. Schriber then pulled to starboard behind the lead Zero and got hits on its right wing, but this Zero began to turn on Schriber, who was in the middle of the Japanese formation and retreated with a damage claim. Schriber's victory was his fifth and last to make him an ace, but it was also the 213th and last victory for the 80FS Headhunters in the war (plus 57 probables and 31 damaged claims).

**31 December 1944: 475FG/431FS**
2Lt. Clifford Eltien was on a C-47 escort to Mindanao when he developed mechanical problems near Masbate late in the afternoon. He was seen to bail out too late to survive.

**December 1944: 58FG Summary**
During December the 58th Fighter Group flew 254 combat sorties; had no bombs to drop; and fired 40,000 rounds of .50 caliber ammunition, almost all on the night of 26 December. The Group flew 253 training sorties from Noemfoor Island before they left for Mindoro. The 58th had lost or had damaged 24 aircraft during the month and had six men missing in action and was down to a roster of 38 pilots. The 69FS flew only 12 combat missions during December, the small number due to being short of aircraft upon leaving Noemfoor, the loss or damage to five planes while on Morotai, the loss of two aircraft upon landing at Mindoro, and the final losses of nine planes on the night of 26/27 December. The 310FS flew 86 combat sorties in December, all in the last four days of the month. The 311th flew 133 sorties during the month expending 20,000 rounds ammunition, all on the 26 December night mission.

# 4

# January 1945

**January 1945: Situation**

At the turn of the New Year, 1945, the Allies were successful in all theaters of the war. In Europe the Russian advances into Germany and the Allied counterattacks after the Battle of the Bulge would lead to a victory in Europe four more months later. In the Pacific, MacArthur's forces had secured the islands of Leyte and Mindoro in the Philippines; Halsey's Task Force 38 was attacking the Japanese Home Islands and Formosa; while the Central Pacific Forces were preparing to invade Iwo Jima in February. The invasion of Mindoro had two immediate objectives. The first was to provide a sizeable airbase from which Far East Air Forces aircraft could cover the attack upon the main Philippine island of Luzon and the convoy routes supplying this operation. The second was to deceive the enemy as to where the invasion of Luzon would take place.

Gen. Tomoyuki Yamashita, commanding Japanese forces in the Philippines, had elected to conduct his defense of the Philippines on Leyte and committed nearly all his forces to that end. This commitment was based on the knowledge that strong Allied air bases on Leyte would eventually sever the crucial supply line carrying the main source of oil from the islands of the East Indies to Japan. Confronted with the overwhelming strength of the Allies on Leyte and the more recent successful occupation of Mindoro, Yamashita recognized that he had lost the Philippines. Consequently, he abandoned his forces on Leyte and began buttressing his defenses of Luzon to provide a delaying action in the Philippines much as MacArthur had accomplished in early 1942. Yamashita and his staff several options to consider to where the Luzon invasion might take place: either Lingayen Gulf on Luzon's west coast; in the Batangas Province south of Manila; or on the northern coast in the vicinity of Aparri. Also, rumors intentionally placed in the U.S. media suggested that Luzon would be by-passed and Formosa would be the next major objective. Besides the uncertainty of where there was that of when as their intelligence concluded that any invasion could not take place before late in January or early February. Actually, American forces were already loading the invasion convoys and the Navy Attack Force left Leyte Gulf on New Year's Day.

Consequently, Yamashita had to stretch his forces to cover all possibilities. Although he had 90,000 frontline soldiers, 25,000 air force personnel, and 20,000 sailors; this large force was sprawled over hundreds of miles, hindered by a totally inadequate transportation network suffering from serious shortage of fuel. Yamashita faced this untenable position and chose to begin moving essential supplies into fortress-like positions in the Baguio area and into the mountains north and east of Manila. Due to the transportation challenges he was mostly unsuccessful and by the end of 1944 he had succeeded in storing only about 10,000 tons of critical supplies in those areas. Additionally, there were only about 50 first line fighters and 20 bombers, crewed by experienced crews, available on Luzon. The balance of the enemy air forces was either obsolete or manned by less experienced personnel. While these forces were numerous on paper; many aircraft were out of service due to a lack of spare parts resulting from an almost non-existent supply system, or from a lack of even simple repairs, due to the previous abandonment of skilled mechanics on New Guinea and other South Pacific islands. After the American capture of Clark, Nichols, and Neilson air bases it was revealed that over 1,500 enemy aircraft based there had been destroyed, damaged, or captured.

Therefore, due to these circumstances, the Japanese defense of Luzon would depend mainly upon the new and highly successful Kamikaze aircraft operating from Luzon and Formosa (and high speed PT-type boats, armed with high explosives). The advantage in implementing suicide tactics, which were compatible with the Japanese character, was that all types of aircraft could be utilized, including obsolete types and trainers that could be piloted by inexperienced pilots and crews. By the first week of 1945 the remaining enemy air force on Luzon totaled only 70 operable fighters and bombers which Yamashita had committed to Kamikaze attacks on Allied shipping rather than have them shot down in droves by the vast number of Allied aircraft. To prepare for the Kamikaze attacks Japanese pilots from remote satellite fields in the north evaded the ubiquitous American air patrols and continued to stage into the Clark Field. During initial stages of the Lingayen invasion the Kamikazes became a major concern to Kinkaid's Seventh Fleet. To stop the suicide attacks Kinkaid and Halsey combined their carrier forces with Kenney's 5AF in the largest coordinated air operation of the Pacific Theater to that time.

Composing the Far East Air Forces, the 13th Air Force was stationed on Morotai while the 5th Air Force was at Leyte but was preparing to move to Mindoro in January. The 13th Bomber Command would remain on Morotai until war's end while the 13th Fighter Command moved to Leyte by 10 January and would later move to Puerto Princessa on Palawan, where they would attack targets in the East Indies, Singapore, and the Malay Peninsula until the end of the war.

Kenney was anxious about his fighter forces, particularly his single engine fighter types. The long-promised P-51 Mustang had failed to appear and only 95 had been received by the end of 1944. Old P-40s were still in use by two reconnaissance squadrons. The number of P-47s, now equipping the 35th, 58th and 348th Fighter Groups, had been reduced to 257 by the end of the year as compared to 429 at the end of August. Kenney ordered the Service Command to reclaim as many old Thunderbolts as possible from second line status (*e.g.* the fighter school at Nadzab) and in the first weeks of January they managed to salvage only 17, requiring 4,000 man hours each. The P-38 units, the 8th, 49th and 475th Fighter Groups, were manned at only three quarters strength. The 8th Fighter Group, the only complete P-38 outfit on Mindoro at year end, was short 17 P-38s (and were to lose another 15 more on the night of 2/3 January to enemy attacks).

The mission of the 310th Bomb Wing, which commanded all air units on Mindoro, was to blockade the coast of Luzon from Vigan to Batangas from 23 through 31 December and then, as the Lingayen invasion forces departed Leyte on 1 January, to furnish air cover along the sea routes and to attack points in southern Luzon to further deceive the enemy as to where the main invasion would develop. Forces available on Mindoro at the start of 1945 were:

- 8th Fighter Group (P-38s): arrived on 20 December.
- 49th Fighter Group (P-38s): the 7FS and 9FS had arrived on 30 December while the 8FS would arrive in the first week of January.
- 58th Fighter Group (P-47s): all three squadrons were operational.
- 418th Night Fighter Squadron (P-61s).
- 82nd and 110th Tactical Reconnaissance Squadrons (P-40s but beginning a changeover to F-6 Mustangs).
- 17th Reconnaissance Squadron (Bomb) (B-25s).
- 3rd Attack Group (A-20s): HQ and men had arrived but there was no space for their aircraft until another strip became operational.
- 417th Bomb Group (A-20s) had arrived on 22 December.

Other supporting forces, based on Leyte and Angaur, continued to make regular strikes on Luzon from those locations.

In addition to the shortage of aircraft, there were also shortages of fuel, ammunition, bombs, and even rations. This situation became so critical that the 310th BW issued orders to curtail all flying after 30 December. However, this order was immediately countermanded by Kenney and a determined effort was made to correct the supply situation initiating a C-46 and C-47 airlift on 3 January that delivered 600 barrels of fuel a day. On 5 January the fuel shortage situation was soon permanently corrected by diverting a Navy tanker from the Lingayen convoy to Mindoro to pump 10,000 barrels of gas. This, plus the 600 barrels per day that the troop carrier planes were bringing in daily, eliminated the need to conserve fuel. Bombs and ammunition continued in short supply, as the transport ship carrying munitions in the Second Resupply Convoy had been hit by a Kamikaze on 28 December and was completely destroyed in the huge explosion. It was not until 4 January that another ship carrying the urgently needed bombs and ammunition arrived at Mindoro, but this second ship was immediately attacked by a Kamikaze and was hit, resulting in another stunning explosion off San Jose.

The Luzon Attack Force sortied from Leyte on 1 January, led by Adm. Thomas Kincaid commanding aboard the amphibious force command ship, *Wasatch* with Gen. Walter Krueger, 6th Army Commander, also on board. Following this lead force were two main amphibious groups, the beaching group and the big transport group. The Bombardment Group, consisting of battleships, heavy cruisers, and destroyers was commanded by Adm. Jesse Oldendorf, who would command at Lingayen Gulf until Kincaid arrived. In addition to the above there were three more battle groups: the covering group of light cruisers and destroyers, the escort carriers and the minesweeping force. These naval forces totaled six battleships, six cruisers, 49 destroyers, 12 escort carriers, 11 gunboats and 64 minesweepers.

Enemy suicide attacks began just as soon as the Allied forces began their passage through the Sulu Sea and major damage began on 4 January when the carrier *Ommaney Bay* was sunk. The next day the cruiser *Louisville*, the *HMAS Australia*, the carrier *Manila Bay* and a destroyer all were hit, but not sunk. On 6 January the battleship *New Mexico* was hit and its Captain and Lt.Gen. Herbert Lumsden, Churchill's liaison officer serving with MacArthur's headquarters were killed.

**January 1945: 5FC Situation**

**35FG**

As December closed the Group began preparing for another ground and air echelon movement to Luzon at Lingayen Gulf four days after the initial landings. In the meantime, the majority of the missions flown by the Group from Morotai between 1-13 January were no longer bomber escorts as there was no longer any possibility of enemy air interception. The new dive bombing and strafing missions were directed northward to Silay, Telissy, Sidato, Bacolod, Cotabato Airdromes in the Southern Philippines and westward to Mapanget, Celebes, and Tarankan (Borneo). The Group continued perfecting and operating close support sorties. The Group also defended the Morotai area and covered rescue Catalinas.

After the initial invasion convoy another convoy with the advanced echelons of the 35FG on board was headed to Luzon from Morotai on the Group's longest voyage to a new base during the war. For the movement the Group was divided into three components: Advanced Ground Echelon (ground personnel, equipment, and supplies), Air Echelon (pilots and minimal operational ground personnel), and Rear Ground Echelon (non-essential personnel, equipment, and supplies to arrive later). The Ground Echelon boarded their LST on 31 December 1944, rendezvoused with other ships on

**35FG/41FS Thunderbolts** at Mangaldan, Leyte. (AAF)

5 January 1945, crossed the Equator, and neared the Philippines where they were subjected to two air attacks. Finally, on the 13th the convoy reached Lingayen Gulf where they anchored to await unloading but ammunition, fuel, food, and infantry supplies had priority. On the 15th the Ground Echelon LST landed on Lingayen Beach and they established a temporary camp in buildings west of the airstrip. The Air Echelon arrived on the 18th but the second LST did not land until the 20th but near Mangaldan were they had to set up a temporary camp in a rice paddy. The next day the group at Lingayen joined the one at Mangaldan to select a permanent base, also at rice paddy, on the Mangaldan-Dagupan Road, adjacent to the Mangaldan Airstrip (Honey). The base was built by local labor using native bamboo. The new base was located in the first civilized area that the Group had seen in two and a half years since its time in Australia and morale rose.

348FG

During January the four 348FG Squadrons each flew an average of 92 combat missions with these missions allocated so that each squadron would fly a proportionate share of missions in each category (i.e. convoy cover, local patrols, etc.). Convoy cover was the main mission (33%) of the Group followed by armed reconnaissance (21%) over the Visayan Mindanao airdromes and those on southeastern Luzon. Local patrol (14%), escort of transport planes (9%), including the newly introduced Curtiss C-46 Commando and weather recon (6%) were the next prevalent missions while bombing took up only (4%). The 341st was transitioning from the P-47 to the P-51 during the month and much of its activity was restricted to local patrols and check out flights. Its first mission in the Mustang was on 6 January. During the invasion at Lingayen the 348FG's main task was to get the Allied convoy safely through Visayan area to Mindoro area where other AAF units took over the escort. The character of the Group's accomplishments changed drastically during the month as only one enemy fighter was shot down. One lugger and four barges sunk and six small vessels damaged for two of their aircraft lost and seven with major damage. 2Lts. Paul McMath and Randall Tuttle were killed during enemy action. The Group flew its last missions from Tanauan Strip at the end of the month and the ground echelon boarded ships and headed for their next base at San Marcelino while the rear air echelon continued to operate from Tanauan.

The 348FG received its first Mustangs during the month and would equip its squadrons one-by-one. The 341FS flew the Group's first mission on the 6th. The transition and training period for each squadron was planned for 20 to 30 days during which time there was to be no operational demands other than orientation and training. But only a week after the P-51s were delivered, the 341FS received operational orders putting the Mustangs into combat with the pilots barely checked out. This problem would be further increased by a sudden and almost complete turnover of veteran pilots headed home and rookie pilots were being trained by equally inexperienced flight leaders. Also at this time when all the new Mustangs were required for combat there was a lack of spare parts available leaving an inadequate number of fighters on hand for training. Despite these problems the 341st was able to fulfill its operational requirements and although it lost no pilots; five Mustangs were written off and one was severely damaged. The 340FS would begin P-51 operations on 10 February and by the end of March the 348FG had transitioned from its Thunderbolts to the Mustang.

421NFS

January began with Capt. William Bradley, relinquishing command to Capt. Paul Zimmer who, in turn, was rotated home and left the squadron on the 15th, when 1Lt. Dorrie Jones took over command but only for five days until Capt. Richard Kiick became the new Commander on the 20th. Kiick had flown P-38s with the 432nd Fighter Squadron and shot down two Tony fighters on 10 November 1944, and had flown over fifty missions. So Kiick, a 24 year old day fighter pilot who was not a night fighter pilot and had not been trained with a crew to fly night missions took over command of the 421NSF and would prove to be an able leader and would remain in command until 15 December 1945.

**Capt. Richard Kiick** assumed command of the 421NFS. (AAF)

**348FG/341FS Mustangs** replaced the Squadron's Thunderbolts. (AAF)

49FG

As 49er ground crews were making themselves at home on Mindoro, the Group's air echelons at Tacloban made final preparations for the move to there. Meanwhile, their escort missions to Manila and Mindoro continued and the older P-38s were beginning to show the inevitable attrition; particularly the Black Sheep Lightnings. 49er CO had promised 8FS CO Capt. William Drier that new fighters were earmarked for his squadron and that they would be the first to deploy to Hill Airfield. Since the loss of Col. Morrissey on the *Nashville* on 13 December, ace Gerald Johnson was promoted to Lieutenant Colonel and took over Morrissey's responsibilities as 5FC Coordinator. Maj. Wallace Jordan became the 49er's Ops Exec and Capt. William Williams resumed his post as CO of the Flying Knights.

**Capt. William Williams** resumed his post as CO of the 9FS. (AAF)

At the turn of the year, the 7FS and 9FS had only about 10 to 12 P-38s in service and 20 to 25 pilots each on their flight rosters. Only the 8FS was equipped to fly the arduous schedule of early missions and four Black Sheep pilots were transferred to the Flying Knights.

475FG

The 475FG had experienced a shortage of P-38s since the end of December and even the high-ranking ace Thomas McGuire had to wait for a new P-38 when his *PUDGY IV* was removed from operations. Because of this shortage the 475FG was only able to send up formations of a single flight of four during most of January 1945. While these small formations limited the chances for and success in aerial combat, they were appropriate for operations like convoy patrol and ground attack which were becoming increasingly important in the northward advance on toward Manila and the Cagay Valley. Part of the 475th's shortage of P-38s was due to having some of its aircraft being transferred to the 8th and 49th Fighter Groups which had been short changed while the Satan's Angels received their P-38 allotment.

3rd Air Commandos (3ACG)

Lt.Col. John Alison, a seven victory Flying Tiger ace, successfully formed the First Air Commando Group (1ACG) and Combat Cargo Groups (CCG) in support of Gen. Orde Wingate's Chindits. In March 1944, Alison was recalled to Washington by Gen, Arnold for a report on the 1ACG and advice on what to do with the two new ACGs being formed. Alison replied that one ACG should be sent to the CBI but the other Group could be sent to the Pacific theater for use in the Philippines invasion. Arnold sent Alison to Australia to persuade Kenney to utilize an Air Commando Group.

In late June, Alison met with Kenney and presented him with a letter from Arnold's Deputy Commander, Lt. Gen. Barney Giles, describing the Air Commandos. In the letter Giles wrote: "the broad field which exists for operations, involving the movement by air of large ground forces (airborne and ground infantry) and the maintenance and supply of these forces for an extended period from the air. The Air Forces will not be able to play their full part in major campaigns until they are able to move and supply troops without dependence on surface transportation." While the new ACGs and CCGs being formed were perfect to fulfill this mission; Arnold believed that the Philippines rather than the CBI would be better to utilize the "bold and imaginative employment needed… We are willing to go a long way on this project provided the expenditure is justified." Kenney was always disposed to receive more men and aircraft for his chronically shorthanded Fifth Air Force and on 5 July 1943 he replied to Giles: "It did not require any argument from you or Alison to sell us on this idea… My immediate reaction is to ask you to send all or any of these units as soon as possible... These types of operations are right down our alley. The organization, the equipment, the method of employment, and, in fact, the whole idea fits in perfectly with the tools, necessities and experience of this theater."

Kenney requested that if the Air Commando and Combat Cargo units could reach him not later than October, they would be employed in an "eye-opener" of a tactical role at the forthcoming assault of Sarangani Bay on Mindanao. Kenney wanted both Alison and Lt.Col. Philip Cochran, co-founder of the 1ACG, to command his new ACG units as in his 5 July reply he stated that "These two men are cracker-jacks and I will need them to operate these expeditions… I think it is vital that we switch to airborne operations and air supply. Boats are alright in their place but the Navy fights a different war and the Air Force here would like nothing better than to rely solely on air transportation." Although Kenney did not get Cochran, Alison assisted formulating plans for the use of the Air Commando and particularly Combat Cargo units during the invasion of the Philippines. Thus, though the 3rd ACG would be active in MacArthur's SWPA command, it would be in an entirely different manner than that of the 1st ACG in Burma.

The 3ACG, the last Air Commando Group of World War II, was activated at Lakeland AAF on 1 May 1944 with Maj. Klem Kalberer as the Acting Group Commander until arrival of former Flying Tiger, Col. Arvid Olson. The 3ACG was organized similarly to the 2ACG composed of two fighter squadrons with 25 P-51s each, a TCS with 16 C-47s and 32 gliders assigned, three liaison squadrons of 32 L-5s and four UC-64s each, four Airdrome Squadrons (ADS), and a medical dispensary. At the time of its activation, the 3ACG consisted of only the 3rd Fighter Reconnaissance Squadron, the 4th Fighter Reconnaissance Squadron (both of which were soon redesignated Fighter Squadrons), the 334th and the 335th ADS. Many of the Group's original cadre of fighter pilots came from the 2ACG's 1st Fighter Squadron, to which they been reassigned from the 23rd Tactical Reconnaissance Squadron, the 97th Tactical Reconnaissance Squadrons, the 76th Tactical Reconnaissance Group, which had all been disbanded in April. Many of these fliers, though, were soon transferred again and replaced by veteran fighter pilots. Since no aircraft were yet assigned to the 3ACG's fighter squadrons, most of the already trained fighter pilots were granted leave in May while the personnel in the ADSs, underwent the usual intensive training required by newly organized units. Over the next several months the remainder of the Group's units were activated. Olson assumed command of the Group in June and his staff was comprised of eight victory P-40 CBI Ace Lt.Col. Elmer Richardson as Ops Officer and Kalberer as Executive Officer. The 3rd Fighter-Recon Squadron (3rd Fighter Squadron, Commando) was commanded by 19.75 ETO ace, Col. Walker Mahurin, while the 2nd Fighter-Recon Squadron (2nd Fighter Squadron, Commando) was commanded by Maj. Steven Wilkerson who was assisted by 1Lt. Louis Curdes, an eight plane ace in Europe. Mahurin had served with the 56FG in the ETO before being forced to bail out and evade. Since he had intimate information on the French Resistance who aided his return to England, he was grounded. While giving unbearable War Bond sales pitches back in the Stated Mahurin used his old friendship with Alison to return to combat as the CO of the 3ACG's 3ACG. When the 3ACG's fighter squadrons finally received their fighters, they were an assortment of war-weary P-40s and P-51B/Cs. In mid-August 3ACG HQ and the fighter squadrons and their ADSs moved from Lakeland to Alachua AAF outside of Gainesville, FL to begin a series of important exercises involving the entire Group. During its Preparation for Overseas Movement (POM) inspections the plans and timing on how to use the 3ACG were experiencing drastic changes. For months the Joint Chiefs of Staff (JCS) had been pondering whether the next advance across the Pacific should be directed at the Philippines (Luzon), at Formosa and the China coast, or at both targets. MacArthur argued for the Philippines, while Admiral King, the Chief of Naval Operations and Commander of the

USN, wanted Formosa. The squabbling over the strategy for the forthcoming Pacific operations continued for the next few months. Finally, in early September, the JCS approved MacArthur's plan for landings at Sarangani Bay, Luzon, for 15 September with further advances in the Philippines were set for 20 December, with the landings on Leyte in the Surigao area. Whether Luzon or Formosa would follow was left unspecified.

When Alison returned to the SWPA, he was placed in charge of planning an airborne assault on Mindanao using gliders from both the 3ACG and other troop carrier units. However, these plans were abandoned in mid-September when Adm. William Halsey, thinking that the Japanese were weak in the Philippines, recommended canceling the Peleliu and Morotai operations and, instead, strike directly at Leyte. But it was too late to call off the Peleliu and Morotai landings, but a drastic decision was made to invade the Philippines at Leyte on 20 October rather than at Mindanao on 15 November. The Air Commandos would have had problems to have been available by 15 November and therefore the 20 October date was impossible.

Following the POM inspections, most of the Group proceeded to Drew Field, Tampa to begin processing for the overseas movement. The 3ACG's air echelons were the first to deploy as fighter pilots were flown by transports to Nadzab, where they received their new P-51D Mustangs and also some replacement pilots. Most of these replacements had been in the SWPA for several months and had been ferrying P-40s and while none had any Mustang experience but their checkout was easy with few glitches.

Meanwhile, back in the U.S., the Ground Echelon stayed briefly at Camp Stoneman, north of Oakland, and during the afternoon of 6 November boarded the transport *USS General M.L. Hersey* for a 24 day voyage with brief stops at Guadalcanal, Finschhafen and Hollandia; it arrived off Leyte near the village of Palo on the 30th. With no fanfare, the men of the 3ACG spent the next few weeks in a tent camp in heavy rains on the crowded beach before being directed a move a few miles down the beach to San Roque. Conditions were only slightly better there as the Group's equipment, including cots, had begun to arrive. The Group was just getting established when, on December 10, a fire started in the dump adjacent to the Group's camp. Little firefighting equipment was available and the fire was allowed to burn itself out and sadly, much of the Group's personal equipment and possessions were lost in the fire.

**Maj. Steven Wilkerson** was the CO of the 2FS. (AAF)

Meanwhile, the Group's fighter pilots were transitioning to their new P-51Ds back in New Guinea, and they would soon arrive on Leyte. The Air Commandos were officially assigned to the 5th Fighter Command on 13 December, and five days later they were further assigned to the 86th Fighter Wing. Several days after Olson's arrival at Leyte the Group moved several miles north of San Roque, near Tanauan, where an airfield paralleling the coast had been under construction since 21 November and had just opened to traffic on 16 December. The field had a 5,300 foot PSP runway, another 3,500 feet of taxiways, and 10 hardstands. Further construction lasting into January lengthened the strip another 700 feet and added more taxiways and another 43 hardstands. Tanauan, however, had an obstruction at its south end where a 300 foot hill rose directly south which limited approaches from that direction leaving an over water approach from the north which ultimately caused no problems. Much construction remained to make the base a fully functioning facility and much of December was involved to do so. On 7 January 1945, the 16 P-51Ds arrived over Tanauan following their long flight from Biak Island and formed four flights of four and buzzed the airstrip before making sharp breaks into their flashy landing pattern.

**Lt.Col. John Alison**, a seven victory Flying Tiger ace, successfully formed the First Air Commando Group. (AAF)

**Lt.Col. Philip Cochran**, co-founder of the 1ACG and the inspiration behind characters in the "Terry and the Pirates" and "Steve Canyon" cartoon series by Milton Caniff. (AAF)

**Col. Arvid Olson** was the first CO of the 3ACG. (AAF)

**Col. Walker Mahurin**, a 19.75 victory ETO ace, was the CO of the 3FS. (AAF)

**January 1945: 5FC Operations**
**1 January 1945: 49FG/7FS/8FS**
To begin the New Year the 49ers took off from Tacloban for a raid on the Clark Field complex on Luzon. The pilots met marginal weather on the way and by the time they reached the target area it was overcast and the Lightnings from all units on high cover were spread out all over at 16,000 feet.

7FS
Eleven P-38s of the 7FS took off from Tacloban at 0815 led by Demon CO Capt. Edward Peck who aborted early and passed the lead to Senior Flight Leader 1Lt. Joel Paris. At 1050, an aerial phosphorous bomb exploded over the northern flank of the Liberator formation, followed by the sighting of the first flight of five Zeros from Clark Field at 14,000 feet and 11 o'clock low. The five enemy fighters were surrounded by Lightnings and went into a Lufbery Circle that the Demons were unable to break up. Paris began another Circle inside their Circle but flying in the opposite direction. Paris took two snap shots one of which knocked the aileron off one which broke up the Japanese Lufbery and they all Spilt-S'd under the clouds. The Demons regrouped and continued patrol. Five minutes later, a second flight of 15 Zeros approached at 16,000 feet and at 2 o'clock high. Paris again led the attack as the Zeros scattered and overtook one and in a long, slow turn, he fired from a 90 degree deflection and downed his eighth victim that burst into flames. Red Flight Element Leader 2Lt. Milden Mathre saw two Zeros chandelle to the left and then one turned and fired head on at Mathre who fired back and saw hits on the engine and cowl. The Zero flew under Mathre inverted and when he looked back he saw a parachute to become an ace with his fifth and final victory.

8FS
Meanwhile, on the other side of the formation Capt. Drier's 12 Black Sheep strained to keep up their close cover escort position on the bombers. Once the Liberators salvoed their bombs and left for home, the four P-38s of the Black Sheep White Flight climbed to escape a cloud front. One pilot separated and joined another flight but White Flight leader 2Lt. Irwin Dames, Element Leader 2Lt. Francis Hill and rookie Wingman 2Lt. Eldon Brezier remained together on reaching 16,000 feet. Once there at 1050, four Oscars were sighted south of Clark and Dames led the attack, diving to 10,000 feet, where he closed in on the trailing #4 Oscar. Dames fired as the Oscar was about to Split-S and saw a wisp of smoke as the enemy plane passed behind him. Dames' only victory was confirmed by Hill. The three Black Sheep regrouped to rejoin the bombers when Hill called out two more Zeros through the clouds, flying at 12 o'clock low and headed in their direction. Hill rolled over, dropping down behind the trailing enemy element and fired dead astern causing the enemy pilot to immediately bail out, for Hill's fourth and last victory.

AAF bomber formations were well on their way south headed toward home when Black Sheep 2Lt. Nial Castle and Wingman 2Lt. Wallace Hickok passed over a twin-engine Nick at 8,000 feet headed back for Clark Field, using the clouds for cover. Castle turned about and pursued into a lower rear quarter attack and pulled to within a 100 yards, then climbed and opened fire at 20 degrees from below and astern shot out the enemy's starboard engine. The stricken Nick dropped off on its flaming wing and cartwheeled across the countryside. Nial Castle had scored his fifth and final victory.

Return
As the American formations withdrew the weather worsened. The Demon Flights intended to fly down Luzon's east coast for Tacloban but several of its elements were separated as the clouds closed in over this southern route. Other elements drifted west and decided to head for Mindoro. Veteran Capt. Richard Suehr was leading White Flight whose two trailing wingmen

Veteran **1Lt. Joel Paris** shot down his eighth enemy aircraft. (AFAA)

**2Lt. Milden Mathre** claimed his fifth and final victory to become an ace. (AFAA)

had already separated from the flight during the fight. Rookie Wingman 2Lt. Ralph Watson stayed in close formation with Suehr at 13,000 feet and the two were some of the last elements to leave the target Suehr chose the southern route for Tacloban and the two became even further removed from the main force and after 35 minutes, Suehr and Watson became completely enveloped in clouds. Suehr led Watson east to be certain that they were over Lamon Bay before they descended to the deck to find a safer course under the weather front. However, the cloud ceiling was down to the sea and when Suehr tried to turn back, his port wingtip dragged through the waves and his P-38 cartwheeled and quickly sank. Watson orbited four times over the area but saw nothing and recorded the site as five miles off tiny Coringo Island and flew for 30 minutes on instruments before he broke into clear skies at 14,000 feet over San Miguel Bay, 100 miles southeast of Lamon Bay. Watson landed at 1330 and reported Suehr's loss.

**2-7 January 1945**
The 49ers continued to fly missions despite poor weather conditions. The Demons and Knights escorted the B-24s across entire central Luzon. They flew as far as Lingayen Bay, a prominent 20 mile wide Gulf on the east coast which was MacArthur's the next objective but no enemy aircraft appeared.

By 3 January, Drier's Black Sheep had been re-equipped with the new L-model Lightnings and flew into Hill Airfield. Drier's unit was reassigned to the strategic operations in Col. Wilson's 310BW and continued flying non-stop missions. Hill Airfield, which they found to be a great improvement. The bivouac had complete pre-fabricated mess kitchens and laundries and tents with wooden floors and individual electric generators.

By the end of the first week in January, the Flying Knights and Screamin' Demons moved to San Jose airdrome complex with the Demons situated at Elmore Strip and the Knights at Murtha.

**1 January 1945: 475FG/431FS/432FS/433FS**

After a brief respite in combat at the end of December the 475FG returned to attack the Clark area with 15 P-38s from all three squadrons taking off by 0830. Col. MacDonald was again the Group Leader and the Lead of Clover's five P-38s with Maj. Campbell Wilson as the Lead of the three fighters of Possum Red Flight and Capt. Christopher Herman the Daddy Flight. The 475th rendezvoused with the B-24s at 0945 and reached at 18,000 feet but descended to 14,000 feet over the target area which was just under the overcast.

431FS & 432SFS

MacDonald sighted a lone recon Dinah approaching from the northwest at 12,000 feet and dove head on toward the bomber which went into a slight dive and turned away. MacDonald was able to fire only a very short burst at about 40 degree deflection and when he turned to take a stern shot MacDonald saw the Dinah rolling over into a vertical dive in flames and then disintegrate on the way down. When MacDonald searched for other enemy aircraft, he saw that they were all engaged by other P-38s. MacDonald spotted a camouflaged Tojo at 4,000 feet flying west and made a diving stern attack on it, firing a series of short bursts that sent it down several miles east of Clark Field. MacDonald's 26th victory placed him as one of the elite American fighter pilots who matched Eddie Rickenbacker's WW-1 total.

Capt. Paul Lucas was Leading Clover White flight and lost MacDonald after he shot down the Tojo when MacDonald's Flight slipped under a cloud layer. Three Zeros passed overhead perpendicular to Clover White's flight path and Lucas split his flight into elements and was joined by #2 2Lt. Douglas Thropp and #3 Capt. Christopher Herman of the 431FS in the pursuit of two Zeros. Lucas got on the tail of the Zero Wingman and closed to within 50 yards, getting hits that dropped its wheel and hit its port wing root and fuselage; soon the flaming victim crashed. Lucas chased after the now alerted Zero Leader who took off in a high speed climb. Lucas and his Wingman made eight passes at this very experienced enemy pilot who used every aerobatic maneuver to escape, including pulling up and back in an Immelmann and then firing while on his back. Lucas ICR reported, "After wasting 10 or 15 minutes on this Nip we broke off."

Shortly after Lucas shot down his Zero, Herman was joined by 2Lt. Edward Edesberg of the 433FS and another P-38 from the 49FG. They saw a Zero several thousand feet above and climbed parallel to it and at 12,000 feet it broke off in a shallow dive. Herman closed to 200 yards and fired at 20 degrees above and to port and saw hits from its engine to tail. The Zero half rolled to the right and its pilot bailed out for Herman's only victory of the war and the 431st's only victory of the day.

433FS

The 433FS took part in the main battle of the day when Capt. Campbell Wilson led three Red Flight P-38s and 1Lt. Ethelbert Roberts led five White Flight P-38s on a B-24 escort to Clark Field. As the Possum Flights approached Clark Roberts' Flight had three mechanical aborts leaving him only with Wingman, 2Lt. John O'Neill. At 1100 Wilson was flying at 19,000 feet with Wingman, 2Lt. Edward Edesberg, and third man, 2Lt. Jerome Hammond, and spotted a large formation of 15 Jacks flying 4,000 feet, below, heading west nearing Clark. The formation let down in spirals to attack a flight of five Jacks from 6 o'clock. Wilson fired two quick bursts that missed, and his greater diving speed caused him to overrun. As he pulled up after turning a 360 he was alone over and astern of four Jacks.

**1Lt. Christopher Herman** (right) was awarded his only victory of the war.

**Capt. Paul Lucas** got his sixth and final victory. (AAF)

**Col. Charles MacDonald** (right with Gen. Wurtsmith) shot a Tony and Dinah for his 25th and 26th victory. (AAF)

He attacked a Wingman from 500 to 100 yards with short bursts and as it passed under him, Wilson saw it smoke and then its pilot bailed out. Wilson then joined a loose flight of P-38s and continued with them for 10 minutes and fired on a Jack getting hits on its wings and fuselage before it Split-S'd away under control for a damaged claim. At 1125 Wilson was circling at 10,000 feet to reform his flight 15 miles east of Manila when a twin engine enemy aircraft (Lily or Nick?) emerged from the clouds slightly above Wilson heading north. Wilson chandelled and got on its tail and fired two long bursts into its starboard engine that began to smoke. Wilson checked to see if it had a belly gun and then fired a third long burst from underneath and the aircraft exploded and burned furiously as it fell to the ground north of the Laguna de Bay east of Manila but the two victories left him one short of becoming an ace. When Wilson dove on the Jacks Edesberg fired several bursts on one that peeled off to the right and missed. The Jack broke off and was astern on Hammond who fired a 30 degree to 15 degree deflection shot while closing; scoring hits on its wings and cockpit causing its pilot to bail out for his only victory.

After the initial attack on the five Jacks, Roberts and O'Neill became separated from Red Flight and dove through the overcast at 19,000 feet and sighted a Tony 4,000 feet below. Both White Flight pilots made an unsuccessful attack on the Tony but immediately, the two saw a Jack 2,000 feet below being pursued by two P-38s. The Jack made a starboard diving turn that put it in front of Roberts who fired a 30 to 0 degree deflection shot from 200 yards to 50 yards and got hits on its engine cowling, right wing root, and fuselage. The Jack turned away trailing heavy smoke and Roberts closed for another pass and fired a decreasing deflection shot from 250 to 50 yards and it burst into flames and crashed five miles from Clark Field for his second and last victory.

**2 January 1945: 475FG/432FS**

The popular Capt. Henry Condon, who had assumed command of the 432FG, took the lead of 11 Clover P-38s to cover B-25s on a strike to Porac and Floridablanca Airdromes early in the morning of 2 January. The Clovers rendezvoused with the bombers over Bilrran Island but they lost contact in the overcast and Condon continued to lead his P-38s to the target area. A few miles north of Manila Condon found a train transporting Japanese soldiers and he led his Clover Squadron P-38s down on a strafing pass. Condon's bullets perforated the locomotive's steam boiler on his first pass but as he pulled around for a second pass on the stopped train, Condon's fighter began smoking. Condon tried to get out of the cockpit but before he could escape, his mortally wounded fighter quickly dropped and exploded into a field north of the highway running through the village of Began.

Five victory ace **Capt. Henry Condon**, CO of the 432FS, was KIA on a B-25 escort. (AFAA)

**January 1945: 8FG**

2 January: 80FS

After the Luzon landings the 8FG conducted fighter sweeps to support Gen. Krueger's Sixth Army. On 2 January at 1415 the 80FS sent 13 Lightnings to participate in the invasion at Lingayen Gulf. Four of the P-38s were armed with bombs to dive bomb shipping and while the other nine were to escort A-20s to the same area. On take off 2Lt. Richard Souhrada's heavily loaded P-38 had problems on take off. He jettisoned his bomb load but was killed in the crash. After searching for two hours the 80th contacted Japanese shipping in Lingayen Gulf off San Fernando Point. The three remaining bomb-carrying P-38s braved intense antiaircraft fire and reported leaving two ships burning after their attack. The A-20's bombs hit a large transport that was left sinking and started fires on two other vessels.

3 January: 35FS: Mahoney KIA

On 3 January, the 35FS was assigned to a strafing mission to Puerta Princesca on Palawan Island. Col. Grant Mahoney of 5FC/HQ, a hero from the CBI Campaign, took over the mission lead from 1Lt. George Lynch who then flew as his Wingman. When they arrived there was a floatplane in the harbor near the airfield. Lynch warned Mahoney that the floatplane was either a dummy or decoy for enemy AA batteries. But Mahoney decided to attack and soon gun flashes appeared and Lynch dove to strafe them but Mahoney's fighter was hit and crashed into the ground; and Mahoney was KIA.

11 January: 36FS

On 11 January 1Lt. Kenneth Creighton of the 36FS was killed when his P-38 crashed on take off from Mindoro. That same day 2Lt. Edward Taylor of the 36FS was strafing Clark Field on Luzon when his P-38 was probably hit by AA fire and he was killed in the crash.

18 January: 80FS

At 0845 on 18 January 13 Headhunter P-38s flew to northern Luzon and approached their assigned targets: an enemy fighter strip near the town of Bamban, a three-span bridge in the Vigan area, and various military buildings and vehicles in the area. When the 80th arrived at Bamban, one of Clark Field's auxiliary runways, there were seven or eight single-engine aircraft on the strip. When the Headhunters left the area the Bamban Strip aircraft were strafed on the ground and the town was burning with some explosions; one span of the Vigan Bridge was collapsed; and eight vehicles were strafed and one was on fire.

21 January

Three days later sixteen P-38s escorted B-24s to Taiwan with good weather all the way to the target but heavy AA fire came up over Clark Field on the way to the target and damaged one P-38. The mission went well and the bombers hit the target.

22 January

The next day nine P-38s were scheduled to escort another B-24 mission but did not make the rendezvous so the Squadron circled the Reito Airdrome waiting for the Liberators. Fifteen Japanese aircraft were on the revetments below but heavy and accurate flak and mission orders prevented the Headhunters from attacking this tempting target and turn for home.

26 January: 80FS

On 26 January the Headhunters escorted a C-47 transport formation that landed at Lingayen and then later in the day they patrolled over a convoy heading into the Gulf.

27 January: 80FS

On 27 January, the 80FS carried Napalm for the first time on a bombing mission to the Cavite, Luzon area. Four P-38s dropped eight of these fire bombs on Japanese defensive positions in a creek at the head of Pagapas Bay. The results of the attack were unobserved except that fires were started. On this date 2Lt. Robert McIlvride of the 36FS had just recovered from scrub typhus and could have been sent home but insisted on flying more missions. On his first take off his engine cut out and he rolled over and died in the crash.

28 January: 36FS

On 28 January 1Lt. Robert Edmonds of 5FG Group Operations was flying with his old squadron, the 36FS, on a sweep to the Cagayan area on Luzon. In a low level strafing attack his wing tip hit a tree and his fighter crashed and exploded immediately. Ground support missions and take off accidents were claiming more pilots than Japanese pilots ever had.

**2 January 1945: 110TRG**

On 2 January 2Lts. John Burrud and Robert Fenske of the 82RS/110TRG shot down a Dinah and Tojo, respectively for the day's only action.

**3 January 1945: 58FG**

In the history of the 58th Fighter Group, 3 January was considered its second most important day; second only to the night action of 26 December 1944. During this day the large American naval armada en route to Lingayen Gulf on Luzon came into range of the enemy Kamikazes based on Luzon. Far East Air Forces intelligence determined that the Kamikazes in the Philippines were based on the Clark Field air complex and on the air fields around Manila. For the day, the three squadrons of the 58FG were to be active: the 69th was to escort a heavy bomber attack on the Clark airfields; the 310th was to conduct a succession of small fighter sweeps over the Manila-Clark Field area and maintain an airborne patrol over that area during most of the day; and the 311th was to maintain a maximum all day alert for whatever missions that would be required.

The first mission that morning at 0700 was a two plane 310th fighter sweep to the Clark Field area by Maj. Edward Roddy with 1Lt. Crystal Andress on his wing. Roddy was quickly followed by Col. Gwen Atkinson, leading his two plane 311th mission with Wingman 2Lt. Roy Kindred. These two flights were intended to find "airborne targets of opportunity in the Manila area." At 0720, three aircraft of the 310th took off on another fighter sweep. At 0830 the 16 Thunderbolts of the 69FS were dispatched on an escort mission to cover the B-24s to Clark Field. Because of the relatively heavy Japanese air opposition encountered on the previous day, the 311FS, scheduled for ground alert, were to assist in covering the bombers while in the Manila area.

At 0915, Roddy and Andress arrived in the Clark Field area first at 18,000 to 20,000 feet and circled and saw a large number of aircraft lined up on the grass strip. The two pilots dropped their tanks, and dove through the AA bursts and then the tracers of smaller caliber guns. They strafed on

**2Lt. John Burrud** scored his only victory of the war. (AAF)

deck at full throttle and set several aircraft on fire and then remained on deck until they cleared the intense AA fire.

After take off Col. Atkinson and Kindred headed for Clark Field but were diverted by the Mindoro Controller to a reported bogey approaching the ships in Mindoro Harbor. After unsuccessfully searching the Harbor area, the two again headed for Clark Field and arrived there shortly after 0915 hours and made radio contact with Roddy requesting the position of the 310th flight. They saw the column of smoke rising from Clark Field and then the enemy fighters lined up near the end of Clark Strip Number 4. They strafed the line of Japanese fighters from west to east and when they left all were on fire. Atkinson and Kindred continued on the deck toward another line of camouflaged enemy planes just east of the airstrip. As Atkinson passed over the end of the strip he observed a twin-engined Dinah that had just become airborne flying north at 50 feet. Atkinson banked in an abrupt 180 degree turn to close on the Dinah but was hit by AA fire but continued to close on the Dinah which did not try to evade. He opened fire at 300-400 feet from directly astern, putting a short first burst into the port engine, then a short burst into the other engine, tearing off parts of the cowling and engine, and finally one into the cockpit area. The Dinah burst into flames and crashed about a mile and a half from the strip and Atkinson finally claimed a victory

**Col. Gwen Atkinson** was credited with a well-deserved victory, but was shot down and reported KIA. (AAF)

**2Lt. David Batey** scored his only victory. (AAF)

**2Lt. John Shriver** also scored his only victory. (AAF)

**Capt. Frank Ellis** led the 311FS flight and scored his only victory of the war. (AAF)

JNAF **Aichi E13A Jake** two place recon floatplane. (AFHRC)

**1Lt. Albert Sorbo** (left) and **R/O 2Lt. George Kerstetter** shot down two Jake floatplanes. (AAF)

but his last. After the combat Atkinson discovered that his feet were hot from a fire in the cockpit and he then turned northeast, pulled up, and bailed out close to the ground. His parachute opened just before he hit the ground and less than 300 feet from where his fighter crashed.

Roddy had been searching for an enemy plane he had seen preparing to take off when Atkinson called telling Roddy that his fighter was on fire. Roddy responded that he would try to join him. Andress then called out a P-47 in a vertical bank which crashed and burned in a fireball off the end of the airstrip. Roddy never was able to contact or see Atkinson or his Wingman, Kindred again during the combat. Roddy and Andress both had aircraft damaged by the concentrated AA fire and had to return to Mindoro without searching for the 58FG CO. At debriefing they reported that Col. Atkinson had been killed in action and Kindred who had not returned was officially listed as MIA. Kindred's body was eventually recovered by advancing American troops and was returned to Mindoro where he was given a military funeral on 18 March 1945. The 58th Fighter Group was credited with destroying somewhere between 11 and 17 enemy aircraft destroyed on the ground plus the one enemy plane shot down.

Meanwhile both the 69th and the 311th missions, covering the B-24s, approached their target and while there was no enemy fighter interception there was heavy AA fire which downed one of the B-24s. The third 310FS fighter sweep of four aircraft, which had departed at 0900, had to report that they had sighted an enemy ship off the north coast of Calatagen Island. Upon arriving in the Clark Field area a short time later they reported seeing four twin-engine enemy bombers on a dirt strip and another 20 single-engine fighters on a dirt strip just north of Clark Field. For some reason the 310th did not attack these grounded aircraft on this sweep or any of their other sweeps during the day. On their last sweep at 1435, Clark was closed in by thunderstorms and the mission detoured over Manila, where they encountered AA fire from Neilson Field and returned to Mindoro via Manila Bat, landing at 1900.

After Atkinson and Kindred failed to return, the 311th quickly initiated a search mission departing Mindoro it 1430. Capt. Frank Ellis led the flight, with 2Lt. David Batey on his wing while 2Lt. Joseph Benson led the second element, with 2Lt. John Shriver in the number four position. The weather over Luzon had deteriorated as the day progressed but Ellis led his flight through the weather at about 5,000 feet and arrived in the Clark Field area at 1515. The flight descended through a thin layer of clouds to 3,000 feet and immediately spotted two Zeros which escaped into the cloud cover. Then Ellis noticed two more enemy aircraft far below, flying south at about 500 feet toward Clark Field, which was about five miles away. As Ellis' Flight was headed on a northwesterly course when he spotted enemy he had to make a steep diving port turn which put him on the tail of the leading Zero. He fired a very short burst which started a fire in the starboard wing root and the enemy plane rolled slowly to port and hit the ground and exploded for the Squadron's first victory. Ellis then turned sharply right after the other Zero which was headed directly toward Clark. He fired a few short bursts but had to break away. Batey, Ellis' Wingman, closed on this Zero and started firing at about 300 yards and pressed home his attack, scoring hits that caused it to burn. He had to break away to avoid hitting it and the ground.

During this action the two 311FS elements became separated. Shriver, flying wing to Benson, observed a Hamp flying south, about 100 feet lower and to port. The enemy attempted to escape by climbing into the overcast at about 3,000 feet but Shriver followed him through the thin cloud cover and almost immediately they broke into the clear. The enemy pilot made a sharp starboard turn but Shriver stayed with him closed in and fired a burst at 100 yards and scored numerous hits that caused the right landing gear to drop. The enemy pilot leveled out and went into a shallow diving turn away but Shriver again closed on his tail and fired at only 30 yards. The Hamp immediately burst into flames and crashed.

**3 January 1945: 348FG/460FG**

The only aerial victory scored by the 348FG during January 1945 occurred when eight P-47s of the 460FS were on convoy cover and reconnaissance over Negros Island. The Squadron reached their patrol assignment northeast of the convoy when the Controller vectored them to investigate a plot southwest of the convoy. F/O John Smith sighted a Zero at about 5,000 feet above and climbed and scored on the engine and canopy. The Zero pilot had tried to evade and his fiery fighter glided into the water about 40 miles north of the convoy for Smith's second and last victory.

**4 January 1945: 418NFS**

1Lt. Albert Sorbo and R/O 2Lt. George Kerstetter took off from San Jose at 0050 for a local patrol over Mindoro. Once there the Controller placed them on a routine vector for "a couple of hours" at 5,000 feet until they were vectored to a bogey. Kerstetter directed Sorbo to descend to 3,000 feet and got an AI contact at three miles. Kerstetter put Sorbo within 1,500 feet and 15 degrees above where he got a visual. Sorbo closed to within 200 feet where he fired a short burst into the left wing root that caused the Jake to explode and crash just north of Ilin Island at 0330.

At 0405 the Controller again called a bogey vector and Kerstetter got a head on AI contact at eight miles with the help of the Controller. The closing range decreased quickly as the P-61 descended to 6,000 feet and turned to starboard slightly at a range of 3,000 feet. The P-61 turned hard to port at 5,000 feet but the range increased to 10,000 feet and 10 degrees below. They descended further to 3,000 feet but the range further increased to 15,000 feet and five degrees above. Kerstetter slowly guided Sorbo to within 1,500 feet and 20 degrees above where he got a visual on another Jake. Sorbo fired shots into the wing root and the Jake which burst into flames and quickly crashed into the water about 60 miles from San Jose for the team's second victory.

**4 January 1945: 58FG/311FS/310FS**

At 0730 1Lt. Kenneth Crepeau, accompanied by Lieutenants John Horning, Glenn Alexander, and David Batey led a 311FS flight to patrol Mindoro Strait and furnish cover for the Minesweeper Force, clearing the way. Naval Controllers vectored Crepeau's flight toward a bogey over Semirara Island, where, at 1035, they sighted a Judy flying at about 500 feet. Crepeau immediately pursued the Judy which was at 11 o'clock, almost dead ahead. Crepeau closed and fired from astern and observed hits as the enemy pilot made a sharp 180 degree turn to port. Each of the other pilots in the flight dove on the slow moving Judy but their higher speed limited them to short passes but with observed hits. Crepeau slowed after his attack and got behind the Judy which made a feint to the right and then dove in a sharp port turn. Crepeau closed in to 50 yards and fired and the enemy became engulfed in flames, hit the water, and exploded. Either the enemy pilot or his observer parachuted when the plane was only about 100 feet above the water. Crepeau and his flight immediately returned to base.

**1Lt. Kenneth Crepeau** shot down a Judy for his only victory. (AAF)

At 1312, the 310FS was assigned to a full strength mission of 16 P-47s (one would return to base early with mechanical problems) to cover the Navy Bombardment Force (second in line after the Minesweeper Force) as it proceeded through Kayo Pass East. Maj. Howard Tuman with 2Lt. Fred Shipley as his Wingman and Capt. Charles Roach leading the second element broke up into flights as the Convoy Controller held the patrols at 15,000 feet even though there was considerable activity at sea level. The 310th was to be relieved at 1600 but no relief appeared and the 310th was requested to remain on patrol even though the pilots would become perilously low on fuel. Another hour passed and the Squadron had reached the point of maximum fuel endurance when the Controller vectored them to 270 degrees on a search for bogies. After flying approximately 15 miles 2Lt. Shipley, #2 two in Tuman's flight dropped down to 12,000 feet where he spotted four bogies off in the far distance at 12 o'clock, approaching head on. As soon as these aircraft were spotted and before they could be identified, three broke away, turning 180 degrees. The remaining aircraft, now identified as a Hamp, evidently did not see Tuman's flight until he passed under them. When he did see the four Americans above him, the enemy pilot also turned 180 degrees to attempt to escape. Tuman led his flight through a 360 degree turn which put him on the tail of the enemy. Because Shipley had been the pilot who first spotted the enemy plane, Tuman allowed him to make the first pass. Meanwhile, Tuman and the other pilots had spread out during the action in order that the enemy plane would not escape. Shipley closed quickly and began firing at about 200 yards. The enemy pilot then made a Split-S, recovering at 6,000 feet with Shipley continuing after him. The enemy pilot then proceeded straight and level until his plane burst into flame, did a wingover, and crashed into the sea approximately two miles north of the Cuyo Island group for his only victory.

Meanwhile, back at Mindoro, the 69FS was on a local patrol mission led by the Squadron Commander. Maj. Milton Self when they were alerted to an approaching unidentified aircraft. At 1745, Self was flying on a northeast heading when he spotted a Sonia flying at 3,000 feet two miles north of San Jose Harbor. Self immediately turned into the enemy plane and fired one short 90 degree deflection shot but before he could press a second attack the enemy entered an area where it was drawing heavy AA fire from all the ships in the harbor. Self continued to pursue and fire at the enemy while his Thunderbolt was damaged by friendly AA fire. The enemy aircraft was a Kamikaze that crashed into a newly arrived ammunition ship that disappeared in an enormous explosion. Self found his fighter was smoking and prepared to bail out when the smoke stopped. After he landed he saw a two foot hole in the bottom of the fuselage and the fighter was scrapped. The Captain of the Navy ship that hit Self sent him a case of beer and a bottle of brandy and in reply Self told him that he would do it again the next day.

Almost out of fuel, the 310th began to straggle back to San Jose. At 1754, 1Lt. Francis Peugeot ran out of gas and crashed landed his P-47 in an open field about one mile north of San Jose Strip. Peugeot was slightly injured in the crash but his fighter was a total loss. When the rest of the Squadron arrived they were delayed as the local P-61 night fighters were being scrambled for the Red Alert caused by the Kamikaze that crashed the ammunition ship. 2Lt Shipley landed a few minutes later and hit in an excavation at the beginning of the runway and nosed up in the soft dirt on the end of the runway. A tow truck was immediately dispatched to clear Shipley's fighter from the runway. While waiting for the runway to be cleared, veteran Capt. Russell Harris ran out of fuel and attempted to make a dead stick landing. Without power, Harris was not able to clear the tow truck and towed fighter and crashed into them, exploded, and burned. Harris was thrown from the wreckage by the explosion but was fatally injured and died an hour later. Maj. Tuman was very critical of the lack sufficient cover for the convoy and of lack of relief for the 310th at the scheduled time which resulted the loss of three P-47s and the death of Capt. Harris while the lack of fighter cover had caused unnecessary damage to the task force.

**4 January 1945: 475FG/431FS**

Four flights of 431FS P-38s took off from San Jose, Mindoro at 1015 on a B-25 escort to Floridablanca Airdrome, Luzon. 1Lt. Horace Reeves was leading the fourth Squadron flight and was heading inland at 1150 over the west coast of Luzon at 8,000 feet when he saw an enemy aircraft at 3 o'clock level. After calling it to the Squadron Leader, Reeves closed on the Zero as it crossed over the convoy at 3,500 feet. When the enemy pilot leveled out Reeves fired a long burst but did not see any results and the Zero rolled into a vertical turn to port. Reeves fired from 200 yards and got numerous hits from its engine to tail. The Zero rolled with flames along its fuselage and engine left side and crashed into the water for the 475th's only victory for the day and Reeve's fourth.

**5 January 1945: 418NFS**

At 1700, pilot 1Lt. Albert Sorbo and R/O 2Lt. Kerstetter took off from San Jose with seven other P-61s to patrol over an Allied convoy. Upon reaching the convoy at 1820 they were immediately vectored to a routine patrol by the Air Controller. After 40 minutes they were vectored to a bogey plot moving from north to west and made an AI contact at six and a half miles dead ahead and 10 degrees below. The P-61 was flying at 10,000 feet and dropped to 6,000 feet and closing. Kerstetter put Sorbo within two miles

**1Lt. Horace Reeves** and crew celebrate his fourth victory. (AFAA)

where the pilot was able to make a visual. Sorbo fired at 300 yards and hit the right side and set it on fire. The bogey, identified as a Val, exploded and Sorbo had to swerve to avoid it and the two scored their third victory in two days for their third and final victories that placed them as the second highest NFS team in the 5FC.

**5 January 1945: 58FG**
As the 311FS was returning from a 12 plane combat patrol mission at 0945, 2Lt. Harold Evanski was landing when a dump truck crossed the runway immediately in front of him. His Thunderbolt crashed into the truck and was destroyed and he suffered a serious back injury and other injuries to his face and head.

**5-7 January 1945: Situation**
Bad weather over Luzon and throughout the Philippines prevented a heavy bomber mission on the Clark Field complex and as a result 50 to 60 enemy Kamikaze aircraft were able to attack the Lingayen convoy which was spread out from the Sulu Sea to the west coast of Luzon. Two cruisers, the *Louisville* and *HMAS Australia*, were crashed off Subic Bay while the carrier *Manila Bay*, another carrier, and three destroyers were also crashed by the suicide planes. While the advance echelon of minesweepers cleared the Gulf of enemy mines Halsey's Third Fleet, consisting of three task forces, were refueling at sea in preparation for assuming responsibility to provide the air cover for the landings at Lingayen Gulf on the next day.

On the $6^{th}$ the Minesweeper Force and the Bombardment Group were exposed to the Kamikaze attacks despite the continuous cover by the Navy planes of the Escort Carrier Task Force, the enemy pilots managed to break through and crash 16 vessels. While most of suicide crashes were absorbed by the minesweepers; the battleships *New Mexico* and *California*, cruisers *Louisville* and *HMAS Australia* (both for a second time), the cruiser *Columbia* and the destroyers *Walke*, *Barton*, and *Sumner* were also hit.

Halsey's Task Force 38 was scheduled to attack enemy air fields on northern Luzon all throughout the day but bad weather and solid overcast over most of northern Luzon prevented the execution of this attack. Halsey then decided to maintain continuous air patrols over Lingayen Gulf and when MacArthur insisted, he sent fighter sweeps as far south as Manila Bay. The carrier pilots claimed 18 aircraft shot down and another 19 destroyed on the ground.

Intelligence sources could not identify the location of the Kamikaze bases. The USN thought they were operating from various northern Luzon airfields and FEAF maintained that the Clark Field area was the principal base (unknown at the time the FEAF's assumption was correct). Believing in their assumption the FEAF sent 22 B-24s of the $22^{nd}$ Bomb Group to Clark Field and 54 B-24s of the $5^{th}$ and $307^{th}$ Bomb Groups to Nichols and Neilson Fields on the $6^{th}$. Nonetheless, neither Halsey nor the FEAF were able to stop the Kamikaze attacks. The major loss was when a suicide plane crashed the battleship *New Mexico* and killed Herbert Lumsden of the British Royal Marines who was Churchill's representative to MacArthur.

On 7 January, in order to ease the pressure on shipping in or approaching Lingayen Gulf, Task Force 38 attacked all known Kamikaze airfields on northern Luzon; claiming 75 more Japanese aircraft destroyed on the ground. The Navy coordinated their attack with the largest SWPA mission in the war to date. The $345^{th}$ and $312^{th}$ Bomb Groups flew into Mindoro from Leyte and refueled and then joined the $417^{th}$ Bomb Group on Mindoro covered by easily identifiable P-38s from Mindoro. Then 132 B-25s and A-20s flew to Clark Field and attacked at low level; strafing and dropping 7,836 parafrag bombs. Meanwhile, B-24s bombed Grace Park, Nichols and Neilson Fields in the area around Manila. Nonetheless, Kamikazes attacked and sunk the minesweepers *Hovey* and *Palmer*. After these 7 January attacks that destroyed the remnants of the Japanese air forces on Luzon the air war in the Philippines was sporadic.

**7 January 1945: 58FG/310FS**
Due to the presence of the two different carrier groups off Luzon and to prevent a mistake that would involve Navy and Army pilots attacking each other, the $58^{th}$ Fighter Group was only to patrol over and south of Mindoro. On the $7^{th}$, the $58^{th}$ continued to patrol the local area and to cover the convoys as they passed through the Mindoro Strait. At 0717, Maj. Howard Tuman led two flights of the $310^{th}$ on a patrol over the San Fabian Attack Force, which was passing through the Strait on the way to Lingayen Gulf. In excellent weather with unlimited visibility the Squadron climbed to their assigned altitude of 8,000 feet and separated into flights and patrolled over the convoy which was passing through the Apo East Pass.

**1Lt. Joseph Dugan** shot down a Sally for his only victory of the war. (AAF)

About five miles south of Tubile Point, on Mindoro, Tuman's flight saw a lone Sally twin-engined bomber at six o'clock at about 6,000 feet, headed north toward the convoy. Tuman turned 180 degrees and began a stern chase. The bomber's crew detected the attacking P-47s and, as Tuman closed in, began a diving turn to the left. Tuman chased the bomber for three miles and closed in to 200 yards and began firing with many bullets hitting around the cockpit and the wing roots. Tuman continued to fire as he closed in to point blank range and as he pulled up over the bomber he saw smoke surging from the bomber's port engine. Tuman's Wingman, 1Lt. Joseph Dugan, began to fire from 400 yards and after a short burst, he closed to 200 yards and fired a long burst. The Sally burst into flames and crashed into the sea a mile west of Tubile Point at 0845. Tuman's flight continued their patrol until 1030 and returned to Mindoro at 1059. The second flight continued to cover the convoy and returned to San Jose at 1204.

**7 January 1945: 49FG**

On this day the 49FG had one of the more successful missions in a while when P-38s from the 49FG covered a massive raid by 132 A-20s and B-25s against Clark Field in which nearly 8,000 parafrag bombs were dropped on the airfield. No enemy fighters challenged the escort, although half a dozen Hamps attempted to hit a B-25 formation with phosphorus bombs. After this destructive mission even Kamikaze attacks against American shipping was almost nonexistent. When American troops went ashore on the morning of January 9 at Lingayen Gulf, there was practically no enemy air opposition.

**7 January 1945: 348FG/341FS/342FS/460FS**

During January 1945 the 348FG suffered 14 operational accidents; six occurred in the 341FS, four in the 340FS, two in the 342FS, and two in the 460FS. Eight fighters were totaled while the six others received major but repairable damage. There were six take off accidents, four landing, and four others from assorted causes. During the late afternoon on 7 January 1945, 342FS pilot 1Lt. Wallace Montague was part of a flight of four P-47s on a convoy cover mission over Negros. After an uneventful mission the flight headed home at 1800 and Montague began to smell gas fumes in the cockpit. At 1845, over San Pedro Bay, the fumes had become much worse when a cylinder blew out of the cowling and the engine burst into flame. While he was flying a half mile away from a beach at 2,000 feet Montague applied full throttle in a futile effort to extinguish the flames and decided to bail out before his fighter exploded. Montague bailed out and plunged into the water at full velocity, either because he lost too much altitude before bailing out or because his parachute failed to open. Montague was astonished to surface still alive and was rescued shortly afterward with only a few bruises and possible internal injuries. During January and February the Group lost nine pilots during ground attack missions:

**1Lt. Wallace Montague** of the 342FS was credited with no victories and survived a bloodcurdling bailout. (AAF)

- 8 January: 2Lt. Randall Tuttle (460FS) MIA during a strafing attack at Mactan Island.
- 9 January: Lt. Charles Erickson (341FS) MIA on a strafing mission.
- 12 January: Lt. Paul McMath (460FS) KIA from AA fire over Luzon, Central Valley.
- 26 January: Lt. David McMahon (460FS) Injured on take off and died 29 January.
- 29 January: Lt. Ralph Prouty (341FS) MIA on a convoy cover mission.
- 1 February: 1Lt. William Anahu (342FS, Asst. Ops Officer) KIA on a landing accident after convoy cover.
- 2 February: 1Lt. Herbert Peterson (340FS) was listed as MIA while on convoy cover.
- 20 February: Lt. Earl Loucks (342FS) crashed while making an emergency landing when his P-47 overturned in the water and he drowned.
- 21 February: Lt. Earl Mix (341FS) was listed as MIA during a ground attack mission.

**7 January 1945: 475FG Death of McGuire**

The Japanese decided to withdraw into the interior of Luzon as the Cagayan Valley northeast of Manila was ideal for Japanese defense. The defense of the Valley would require only limited Japanese forces which could live off the land and retreat grudgingly to hold off an American advance through the narrow Balete pass. Although there were some operational enemy air units on Negros and a few other islands, Japanese airpower had been decimated by the time Luzon was invaded and the prospect of major aerial engagements there seemed to evaporate which would drive McGuire to become even more reckless in his quest to become the American Ace-of-Aces.

The following account is a compendium of eyewitness accounts, particularly from Capt. Edwin Weaver's and 2Lt. Douglas Thropp's ICRs and the two Japanese accounts. The evening before the mission McGuire was standing around talking with seven of eight pilots including Maj. Jack Rittmayer and Capt. Edward Weaver who were to fly Daddy Special One Flight the next day and (of course) the topic of the conversation was how to get McGuire three victories the next day. A heavy bomber escort to the Negros Island was scheduled for the 7[th] and McGuire had decided to fly a fighter sweep Fabrica Airdrome on Negros to draw enemy fighters up to intercept. Most of the air combat in the Philippines had moved north to Luzon but the Japanese continued to operate a few fields in the Negros. Although the few enemy missions flown from these fields were considered no more than nuisances, McGuire thought he could get the Japanese to send up interceptors. 2Lt. Douglas Thropp entered the conclave and McGuire asked him if he would like to join the distinguished Daddy Special Flight. At 0620 four plane fighter sweep to took off at five second intervals and climbed to 10,000 feet in clear weather. McGuire was flying in Capt. Fred Champlin's P-38L, *Eileen Ann* (#44-24845) as *PUDGY V* for reasons not clear was unavailable. McGuire's Crew Chief, Frank Kish, has stated in Charles Martin's *The Last Great Ace* that the gaudy 38 Japanese Rising Sun victory symbols painted on *PUDGY V's* nose would make McGuire's Lightning a particular target, so McGuire decided to fly Champlin's P-38, which was a spare that day. It seems unlikely that other reports stating that the 475FG was experiencing a shortage of fighters and maintenance men at the time and McGuire's P-38L-1, *PUDGY V*, was waiting to be serviced are accurate. McGuire always demanded the best Crew Chiefs and had priority on maintenance and new/spare parts (after Col. MacDonald).

For the mission Weaver was Daddy Special Two while Rittmayer led the second element with Thropp as his Wingman. The four silver and red P-38s took off at five second intervals, each carrying two underwing 160 gallon auxiliary fuel tanks. They leveled off at 10,000 feet and headed toward Fabrica, 40 minutes west of Dulag. They flew over a solid undercast at 6,000 feet but Rittmayer was having some engine problems and the second element was two miles behind McGuire and Weaver. McGuire ordered Thropp and Rittmayer to change positions with Rittmayer trailing as #4 about 1,000 feet behind. Also, sometime early in the flight McGuire specifically instructed the flight not to drop their tanks until ordered so as not to decrease the "hunting" range of the mission. Gradually they broke out below the clouds at 1,700 feet about 10 miles north of Fabrica Airstrip and circled the Airstrip for five minutes without seeing any opposition. The impatient McGuire headed for the airstrips on western Negros at 1,400 feet where Weaver spotted a bogie climbing at 500 feet directly below and about 1,000 yards ahead. The bogie was actually an Oscar flown by W/O Akira Sugimoto of the 54th Sentai who had been flying in search of an American supply convoy headed for Mindoro or Lingayen Gulf. The weather had been so poor that Sugimoto headed back after a long and frustrating flight. Weaver and Thropp hesitated in initiating an attack so as not to deprive McGuire of his kill. As soon as the bogie passed under McGuire's wing he made a diving turn to port to trap the bogie and again called for his flight to hold onto their tanks. Thropp did not identify the Japanese fighter as anything but a bogie in his ICR while Weaver identifies it as a "Zeke" in his ICR (Allied pilots often misidentified Zeros and Oscars in their ICRs). Thropp started to follow McGuire but the Oscar pilot turned left to get on Thropp's tail (who was now the number three P-38 after switching positions with Rittmayer). Thropp skidded and jinked his Lightning to avoid Sugimoto's fire and Rittmayer raced in, firing from 80 to 90 degrees deflection but overran to the outside. The Oscar was known for its great maneuverability and Sugimoto pulled up, kicked left rudder, rolled hard to port and reversed his course and found himself behind Weaver and McGuire. The two Lightnings were maintaining a level turn in close formation with Weaver on McGuire's starboard (outside) wing after just completing a 270 degree turn to port and were starting to head into their original westerly direction. The Oscar was in an accelerating dive across the circle, pulling lead towards them when Weaver called that the Zeke was on his own tail. Weaver tightened his own turn until he was inside and a little below McGuire as was the Oscar. Sugimoto continued to close and McGuire ordered the flight to keep its drop tanks even as the Oscar was out turning the P-38s. The tanks were nearly full and further hampered the maneuverability of the Lightnings. Within a moment that mistake would be deadly as Weaver saw McGuire increase his turn "tremendously" to get a lead on the Oscar. McGuire's Lightning shuttered on the verge of a stall and instead of backing off the tight turn McGuire continued and the last Weaver saw of McGuire was when his P-38:

**Maj. Thomas McGuire's** (right) death-defying effort to surpass Bong's 40 victories ended two short when McGuire was KIA. (AAF)

> snap-rolled to the left and slipped in an inverted position with the nose down about 30 degree. Because of the attitude of my plane, I then lost sight of him momentarily. The Zeke broke off his attack just before Major McGuire's crash and climbed to the north. A second later I saw the explosion and fire of his crash. It is my opinion that the enemy did not at any time change his attack from me to my leader. I believe his crash was caused by his violent attempt to thwart my attacker, although it is possible that the Major was hit by ground fire, which had now begun. (Note: There was no AA fire reported and the nearest possible ground fire was three miles away and witnesses on the ground stated that they did not hear any ground troops firing on McGuire before he crashed.)

Thropp's ICR indicates that McGuire was shot down by Sugimoto: "I turned back toward the flight and saw the flight leader and his Wingman in a tight left turn with a Zeke to the rear and turning with them." Because McGuire was only 1,000 feet above the jungle he had no chance to recover control with the heavy tanks still in place.

At this time Sugimoto either saw his opportunity to escape or was driven off by Thropp who had come around in the circle at 6 o'clock and was able to fire a three second burst at the Oscar before it entered the overcast. The damaged Japanese fighter raced off to the north where Sugimoto made a forced landing. After landing Sugimoto was either immediately shot dead by Filipino partisans or died of wounds from Thropp's guns. Meanwhile, Sgt. Mizonori Fukuda flying a Frank of the 71st Sentai was landing at Manapla Strip on Negros when he noticed a dogfight to the north and raced toward it. Fukuda arrived just about the time McGuire crashed and Sugimoto escaped into the clouds. While the three remaining P-38s were still in confusion, Fukuda dove out of the clouds at 10 o'clock from the left head on and got hits on Thropp's port engine and starboard boom. Weaver pulled his nose up and fired a 30 degree deflection shot and then followed Rittmayer in a 180 degree right turn, finally dropping their tanks, to pursue the Zero (Frank). Fukuda swung around and attacked from 10 o'clock high and fired a 90 degree deflection shot that sent Rittmayer crashing to his death less than two miles from Pinanamaan Town. Weaver, in the third position, pulled up to the right and fired a 30 degree shot that damaged the Frank which crash landed back at Manalpa with 23 bullet holes and was a complete write off. Thropp, with a damaged port engine attempted to join Weaver who pulled away from him and headed north and Thropp then started home.

The news of McGuire's MIA was not released until 17 January and McGuire's widow, Marilynn ("Pudgy"), also received notice from Gen. Kenney in a personal letter on that day (better than hearing the news on the radio). On 8 May 1946 a posthumous award of the Medal of Honor was made by Gen. George Kenney to McGuire's widow at City Hall, Patterson, NJ, for his outstanding actions over the Philippines during late December. Kenney and Charles Lindberg also attended the funeral. Marilynn returned to San Antonio and remarried six months later. On 17 September 1949, Fort Dix Army Air Field at Wrightstown, NJ, was renamed McGuire Air Force Base. McGuire's charred body was removed from the crash and secretly buried by Filipino farmers. When the Japanese arrived a few hours later the farmers refused to divulge the burial site. After the war McGuire's body was returned to the U.S. and was interred at Arlington National Cemetery.

**8 January 1945: 71TRG/82TRS**

Using newly issued armor-piercing and incendiary .50 cal. ammunition the Squadron destroyed 40 box cars and four grounded aircraft along with 300 enemy troops and many trucks on Luzon, near Lingayen Gulf. During the landing procedure Lt. Franklin landed his Mustang and was clearing down the strip when Lt. Malone landed and was given faulty directions from the tower air control truck and accelerated and ran into and over Franklin's fighter. Both aircraft caught fire and only Malone escaped.

**8 January 1945: 3ACG/3FS**

The 3FS received orders for their first missions the following day; two flights were sent to bomb and strafe the enemy airfields at Surigao and Del Monte on Mindanao, while the remainder of the Squadron flew patrol missions. The morning mission to the airfields was uneventful while the afternoon mission put the Japanese airfields out of action temporarily and two enemy planes were destroyed on the ground. However, the later mission was costly as 1Lt. Earl Thibodeau and 2Lt. William Tudor pulled up from their strafing runs, they collided and crashed. It was Thibodeau's first combat mission but Tudor was a veteran of 50 missions in the Mediterranean. During the next several weeks the 3FS Fighter Squadron, flew missions everywhere over the Philippines although poor weather hindered operations. The 3FS would be joined by the 4FS on 16 January.

**8 January 1945: 418NFS**

Due to the destructive bombing attack on the enemy at Clark Field on the 7th there was an absence of enemy resistance as on the 8th. 2Lt. James McQueen and R/O Hugh Gordon took off at 0345 and arrived in the patrol area at 0500. Fifteen minutes later, the GCI vectored them toward a bogey southeast at an unknown altitude. Gordon picked up the AI contact at two miles and closed with a beam approach and followed it through some "easygoing" evasive maneuvers. However, the enemy was too low and the P-61 was closing too fast. McQueen throttled back, closed the cowl flaps and dropped the flaps to stay behind him. McQueen got the bogie ID'd as a Jake at 100 feet and tried to pull up in back of him but the Jake turned under the Black Widow and opened fire with its flexible gun. McQueen again tried to get behind the wily Japanese pilot who again turned under the American night fighter and escaped at 500 feet. McQueen climbed to 3,000 feet and was vectored back toward the convoy. At 0530 the GCI vectored them to 90 degrees to meet bogeys heading directly at the convoy and then sent a vector of 270 degrees which was to put them on the tail of the bogey at 8,000 feet. The bogey turned out to be four fighters flying together and due to the accurate CGI vector. McQueen closed to 1,000 feet for a visual. However, the GCI quickly ordered the P-61s away as it was entering an AA fire zone. McQueen told the GCI that he was going in and closed to 1,500 feet and fired a long burst on the enemy aircraft on the left and then fired another long burst on the second without seeing any damage. As the first bomber dove off to port in a tight diving turn, McQueen fired a second burst in full deflection and saw it hit the water. The first bomber was also seen to go into the water 205 miles from San Jose for the only 5FC victories of the day and McQueen's only two of the war.

**9 January 1945: Luzon Landings**

To defend Luzon, Gen. Tomoyuki Yamashita, headquartered in Manila, recognized that he would receive only minimal outside support from the Japanese Navy and Air Forces which had been largely destroyed in the previous months. Furthermore, Yamashita's 260,000 defenders on Luzon were lacking in artillery, transport, armor, and modern equipment and would be unable face the well-equipped American Army units in open warfare. To counter these limitations Yamashita decided to fight a delaying action in order to continue the already lost battle for as long as possible. MacArthur, during his 1941-42 defense of the Philippines, considered Manila, the central Luzon plains, and the Bataan Peninsula critical because of their harbors and airfields. Yamashita, however, planned to withdraw the bulk of his forces from these areas into three widely separated remote mountain redoubts to conduct a long battle of attrition.

The largest of these groups, the *Shobu Group,* was under the direct command of Yamashita and was positioned in northern Luzon with about 152,000 troops. A much smaller force, *Kembu Group,* with approximately 30,000 troops, occupied the Clark Air Field complex as well as the Bataan Peninsula and Corridor. The third major force, *Shimbu Group,* consisted of some 80,000 soldiers occupied the southern sections of Luzon, an area that included the island's long Bicol Peninsula as well as the mountains immediately east of Manila which controlled the vital reservoirs that provided most of the capitol area's water supply.

MacArthur intended to land at Lingayen Gulf, an area of sheltered beaches on the northwestern coast of Luzon which would position his troops near to the main roads and railways on the island, all of which traversed the central plains south to Manila, which was his main objective. Also, by landing that far north of the capitol, MacArthur gave his large force maneuvering room after the beachhead was secure for a southern drive to the Filipino capitol. Once this central core and Manila Bay were captured MacArthur's forces would control Luzon and any further coordinated defense by the Japanese would be extremely difficult. Ultimately ten American divisions and five independent regiments would be in combat on Luzon, making it the largest campaign of the Pacific War

American forces returned to **Luzon**, at Lingayen Gulf, and established their beachheads without difficulty. (U.S. Army)

and would engage more American troops than were used in North Africa, Italy, or Southern France.

At 0700 on "S-Day," 9 January, under ideal weather a devastating pre-invasion naval bombardment of the coast of the Lingayen Gulf began and was followed at 0930 by about 68,000 men under General Walter Krueger of the U.S. Sixth Army landing at meeting no opposition. A-20s of the 417BG and the B-25s of the 345BG were to support the infantry but were not needed and soon were sent on strikes on enemy communications. Kamikaze attacks continued throughout the day and four ships were crashed but not sunk. Navy pilots claimed 17 enemy planes destroyed in their area which was north of a line extending from Hermana Mayor Island to Camiling. MacArthur made his famous "I shall return" wade ashore that afternoon and visited all four Division command posts. That night the Japanese launched their newest from of Kamikaze attack, sending 70 small, fast boats armed with depth charges against the fleet. The attack was somewhat successful sinking two LCIs and damaging four LSTs.

A total of 203,608 were eventually landed over the next few days, as the assault forces quickly captured the coastal towns and secured the 20 mile beachhead stretching from Sual, Lingayen and Dagupan (XIV Corps) to the west, and San Fabian (I Corps) in to the east. While the I Corps, commanded by Lt.Gen. Innis Swift protected the beachhead's flanks; Lt.Gen. Oscar Griswold's XIV Corps prepared to drive south, first to Clark Field and then to Manila. Once the Manila area had been secured Swift's I Corps was to advance north and east to capture the vital road junctions leading from the coast into the mountains of northern Luzon.

Despite their success in driving out the Japanese Army stationed at Lingayen, the Ameicans suffered relatively heavy losses, particularly to their convoys, due to Kamikaze suicide attacks. From 4 to 12 January a total of 24 ships were sunk and 67 damaged by Kamikaze planes, including the battleships USS Mississippi and *USS Colorado* (accidentally hit by friendly fire), heavy cruiser *HMAS Austr*alia, light cruiser *USS Columbia*, and destroyers *USS Long* and the *USS Hovey*. Following the landings, the Lingayen Gulf was turned into a vast supply depot for the rest of the war to support the American assault on Manila.

**9 January 1945: 475FG**

Capt. Vincent Elliot took command of the 432FS after Condon's death and led Clover Squadron from Dulag at 0815 on a skip bombing mission on a bridge north of Manila. When the four P-38s, each carrying a single 1,000 pound bomb, approached the bridge they found that it had already been heavily damaged by B-25s and A-20s, and chose an alternate bridge where they dropped three bombs that did no damage whatsoever while the fourth was jettisoned by accident.

**9 January 1945: 419NFS**

Pilot 1Lt. Ralph LeVitt, R/O 2Lt. Frederick Kahn, and gunner SSgt. John Graham encountered a Betty southwest of Pitoe Island and LeVitt was credited with the victory at 0250.

**9 January 1945: 547NFS**

On the 9th the 547NFS sent up four night fighters, three P-61s and a P-38 piloted by 1Lt. Roy Oakes to cover a convoy. Soon the GCI recalled a P-61 piloted Capt. Edwin Annis and Oakes' P-38 to cover the beachhead. Just south of Lingayen Oaks sighted a Hamp at one half mile flying at 1,500 feet turned to port for his firing run. Oakes passed over Annis' P-61 and went into a slight dive and came up behind the enemy for a short stern shot and then passed over the Hamp. Annis then made a pass, firing three bursts on the enemy's tail at 900 to 600 feet. The two pilots were credited with one of the few shared victories when they each fired at a Hamp at 1900 between Umanday and Aguillar at 1900.

**Capt. William Shomo** scored his first victory, the only 5FC victory of the day. (AFAA)

**10 January 1945: 71TRG/82TRS**

At 0915 after coming from an on deck photo run on Tuguegarao Airstrip Capt. William Shomo saw a Val bomber approaching the Field and pulled up to 700 feet and shot it down south of the Field for the day's only victory for the 5th Fighter Command.

**10 January 1945: 58FG**

The division in the air command system over Luzon would prove to be problem. In addition to the air missions of the Carrier Task Force, Halsey's Task Force 38 was attacking targets of opportunity across northern Luzon, occasionally reaching as far south as Manila Bay. Direct air support for shipping in Lingayen Gulf and for Army ground units advancing southward into Luzon was provided by Task Force 77.4, Because of the rapid deployment and advance of the Army units the carrier operational zone had been extended twice by 10 January. Before and during the invasion of Luzon at Lingayen Gulf, the 58th Fighter Group was assigned patrol and convoy cover missions but afterward escort and intruder missions were added to their schedule.

Morning Missions

During the morning the 310FS flew one of its most successful strafing missions thus far when they sent a fighter sweep along the roads in the Balete Pass area of central Luzon. Four trucks and six personnel carriers were destroyed; five enemy staff cars were strafed; and a railroad boxcar was demolished. The 311FS sent an intruder mission to Lubang Island, where they strafed three enemy aircraft which were believed to be unserviceable. They also destroyed a truck on the air strip and more trucks on other parts of the island.

Afternoon Missions

At 1307 eight P-47s of the 310FS led by Capt. Donald Booty, took off on an intruder mission seeking targets of opportunity over Luzon in the Gapan to Cabanatuan to San Jose area. Booty's flight consisted of his Wingman, 2Lt. Paul McKay; 1Lt. Joseph Dugan leading the second element with 2Lt. Fred Shipley as his Wingman. Booty's radio became inoperative and he signaled for Dugan to assume the lead while he dropped back to become the Element Leader. At 1440 while flying at 1,500 feet they encountered a flight of Navy FM2 Wildcats over the village of Munoz, eight miles west of San Jose. The Thunderbolt pilots attempted to signal and show their identity but the Navy pilots attacked, later explaining that they identified the P-47s as radial engine Tojos. In the combat that followed Booty saw tracers hit his fighter and immediately skidded violently to port and executed a wing over, pulling out on the deck. He turned toward home and found that his hydraulic system was inoperative but made a safe landing.

Shipley and Dugan rocked their wings and shouted over their radios but the Wildcats attacked them at 1,200 feet. The lead Wildcat went after Dugan and fired at 100 yards and hit the P-47 in the cockpit area but no one in the flight observed what happened to Dugan after he had been hit and when he failed to return to base he was listed as MIA. Meanwhile, Shipley racked his fighter out of the Navy pilot's line of fire. The Navy pilot was then joined by another pilot of his flight and both chased the Army pilot. Shipley gave the fighter full power and tried to radio his identity and meanwhile rocked his wings violently. The Navy pilots then climbed away. Filipino guerrillas saw Dugan bail out of his burning fighter and reported that his parachute did not open properly and he was dead when they reached him. The Filipinos gave him a funeral and buried him where the Japanese would not find the body. They saved his clothing and his pistol which they later turned over to advancing American troops. After U.S. forces secured the area, Dugan's body was exhumed and given a military burial.

**Maj.Gen. St. Clair Streett.** (AAF)

**10 January 1945: Change in Command**

A change in the overall Air Force command in the SWPA occurred on 10 January. General Arnold had requested that the ailing 13th Air Force Commander, Maj.Gen. St. Clair Streett (who commanded at Saidor in the Spring of 1944), be returned to the States. Lt.Gen. Paul Wurtsmith, long time commander of 5th Fighter Command, was promoted to command the 13th Air Force. Gen. Arnold then returned Lt.Gen. Frederick Smith to the Far East, to assume command of the 5th Fighter Command.

**Lt.Gen. Paul Wurtsmith.** (AAF)

**11 January 1945: 71TRG/82TRS**

At 0935 2Lt. Maurice Lambert of the 82TRS was on recon when he shot down a Sally over Balete Pass, Luzon.

**Lt.Gen. Frederick Smith.** (AAF)

Shomo Medal of Honor Mission

At 1010, Capt. William Shomo and Wingman, 2Lt. Paul Lipscomb, were flying a photo and strafing mission to Aparri and Laoag Airdromes in northern Luzon. Due to patchy clouds they were flying at only 500 feet when just south of Baguio Shomo spotted a Betty bomber, one Tojo, and eleven Tonys above and to the right. It seems that the Japanese either didn't see the climbing Mustangs or thought they were more Tonys coming up to join them as at a distance the new AAF in-line engine fighter resembled the enemy fighter. The two Mustang pilots climbed and turned a 180 degree reversal to get in behind the enemy formation, flying a two ship formation stacked down. As Shomo and Lipscomb completed their climbing turn to 2,500 feet they engaged the enemy. Shomo and Lipscomb were to the right when Shomo opened fire on the last Tony element on the enemy formation's left flank. Shomo and Lipscomb fired and exploded two of these fighters that seemed to be confused over employing any type of tactic to respond to the aggressive Americans. The two 82TRS pilots then moved up to position themselves behind the second flight as Shomo shot down the leader of this formation and Lipscomb opened fire on the Wingman; and both Tonys exploded. As Shomo and Lipscomb turned right to get into position behind the fighters flying to the right of the bomber, they closed in on the leader and Wingman of the first element to the left of the bomber. Lipscomb opened fire on the Wingman and it exploded in mid-air for his third victory of the day. The leader of the first element on the left broke down to port Shomo on the leader and shot it down. Shomo and Lipscomb were to the left and behind the Betty and Lipscomb made a pass on it but observed no damage. Shomo dove below the Betty and put a burst into its belly and it went into a gentle dive; attempting to crash land with two Tonys following it down. Lipscomb then broke down to port in the general direction of the Leader of the first Tony element on the left, who had just made his break. Due to the clouds he could not locate him and made a 180 degree turn back toward Shomo who was climbing to the left. With four victories Shomo encountered a Tojo in the climbing turn that started to fire at Shomo from below at about 60 degrees deflection. Shomo tightened his climbing

**Capt. William Shomo** shot down six Japanese aircraft in one mission. (AFAA)

**Lipscomb** (left) and **Shomo** (right) are congratulated by Gen. Whitehead. (AAF)

Shomo's Wingman, **2Lt. Paul Lipscomb**, scored three victories on the same mission. (AFAA)

**Gen. Ennis Whitehead** (left) presents Capt. William Shomo his Medal of Honor.

turn and the Tojo skidded behind him broke off and disappeared in to the low clouds in flames. By this time, Shomo was headed in the original direction of the running fight and saw his Betty crash into a field and burst into flames. Flying south at 800 feet, Shomo then spotted two Tonys in element formation, close to where the bomber crashed. Shomo pursued and closed astern on the lead Tony and fired a burst into him and it exploded and disintegrated. The other Tony broke to the right and dove steeply to 300 feet. As Shomo closed on this Tony's tail, he leveled out and closed to point blank range and fired a burst that hit its engine which started streaming black smoke. As Shomo overran this Tony he veered off above and to starboard and snapped a photo just before the Tony struck the ground and burst into flames for his seventh victory of the day. The remaining three Tonys turned and fled into the clouds. For his destruction of seven enemy aircraft in just less than 15 minutes Gen. Kenney immediately promoted Shomo to Major and recommended him for the Congressional Medal of Honor that was approved on 7 April 1945. Over the next three weeks there was a lack of enemy targets as the air war over Luzon was virtually over.

**11 January 1945: 58FG/69FS**

The 69FS launched an eight plane strafing mission along the west coast of Luzon from San Marcelino to Lipay where they located and destroyed 11 trucks and three rail freight cars loaded with enemy personnel. The pilots then strafed San Marcelino Airdrome and destroyed two camouflaged aircraft and a large fuel supply dump. They also found and strafed two enemy aircraft at Zablam strip. A later 69FS patrol of four aircraft went to Lingayen Gulf and found and strafed a number of cars and trucks; then they strafed two enemy aircraft on Lija Airdrome; and finally found a taxiing fighter on the strip at Zablam. As they came in to strafe the enemy plane its pilot stopped and abandoned his plane and ran away.

**11 January 1945: 348FG**

During January the 348th was again relegated to ground support missions. On 11 January 1945 14 P-47s attacked Paridel Bridge, 30 miles west of Manila where a convoy of 33 enemy trucks was discovered on the highway south of Paridel. The Thunderbolts destroyed 25 trucks and a large number of troops were killed and wounded and four light tanks were attacked and one exploded. More extensive damage was prevented because of the concern for the large numbers of civilians on the highways.

**13 January 1945: 58FG/69FS**

Air-to-air combat over Luzon virtually ceased and the 58FG continued normal patrol and convoy cover missions and the ever popular fighter sweep or intruder mission. For the first time in the war in SWPA pilots were operating over civilized territory which offered a multitude of likely targets; trucks, automobiles, railroad rolling stock and, on occasion, enemy personnel. Except for an occasional encounter with a stray enemy plane, 5AF pilots would find no more Kamikazes in the Philippines, as the Kamikazes now had to fly down from Formosa.

The 69th Fighter Squadron had one of these last chance encounters with the enemy plane on 13 January. At 1555, 14 aircraft departed Mindoro to strafe targets of opportunity across southern Luzon. Once over Luzon they met an overcast ceiling at 6,000 feet, with visibility restricted by haze. Early in the mission the pilots strafed a staff car and five trucks, all of which were destroyed. The mission climbed back to 4,500 feet and 15 miles east of Balara Airdrome, 2Lt. George Samis, Wingman to 1Lt. Howard Wells, spotted an unidentified aircraft flying south just under the overcast at about 5,500 feet. Suddenly, another aircraft, which turned out to be a twin-engine Nick fighter, attacked Wells and Samis from 9 o'clock in a dive. Wells turned into the attack by making a sharp climbing 270 degree turn to port. Fortunately, the enemy pilot did not follow up his initial advantage and immediately broke away in a climbing turn to starboard which allowed Wells to immediately close on the enemy pilot who was headed for the safety of the overcast. Wells closed to within 200 yards and fired a long burst as the Nick entered the thin cloud layer. Wells flew on through the cloud layer and when momentarily breaking into the clear he fired two more long bursts and saw his hit tracers hit the fuselage and suddenly the Nick rolled over into a steep dive in a trail of smoke and Wells followed it down and saw it to crash and explode for the 69th's first victory since 17 December 1943. All 69th pilots returned safely to San Jose at 1815.

**13 January 1945: 475FG**

During the second and third week of January, weather and the shortage of P-38s hindered operations but sorties against ground targets were conducted whenever possible. On 13 January to cover a convoy off the island of Panay the 431st and 432nd Squadrons could only supply two P-38s each to make up a complete flight of four fighters.

**13 January 1945: 3ACG: 3FS**

The 3FS had its best day so far during a reconnaissance of southeast Luzon when its pilots discovered a concentration of enemy troops and vehicles attempting to cross a river using a cable-drawn ferry. The Mustangs flew repeated strafing runs that destroyed the ferry and caused several trucks to disintegrate in huge explosions, and leveled a village at the ferry site. The Squadron then continued flying up and down the road strafing trucks along the way until an estimated 12 to 15 trucks had been destroyed and an undetermined number had been damaged. When they flew over the Bulan Airdrome on the way home they destroyed a Zero found in a revetment.

**14 January 1945: 58FG/311FS/69FS**

311FS

The 15 Thunderbolts of the 311FS were released from their A-20 bomber escort to Tuguegarao and dropped down to the deck to strafe targets of opportunity on the way home. Their first target was two camouflaged barges with about two dozen soldiers on each barge in the Cagayan River near the town of Bayo. Next they found three foliage-covered trucks and a staff car parked on the main highway about a mile west of San Felice. One truck was set on fire and the other vehicles were riddled by the strafing. A few minutes later, at 1215, the third flight of the formation led by 1Lt. Raymond Evans was flying at 800 feet, when a twin-engine Nick was spotted flying southeast at only 500 feet near the barrio of Santa Maria. The Nick was approaching head on at 11 o'clock, at about 200 miles per hour and Evans waited until it was at approximately 9 o'clock and then turned quickly onto the Nick's tail. The apparently unaware enemy pilot took no evasive action as Evans closed in and began to fire at about 500 yards, first hitting the port engine which burst into flames. After being hit the Nick pilot began a slow diving turn to port while Evans fired until the enemy plane continued to fly into the ground and exploded for Evan's only victory.

The Squadron then turned toward home but at about 1245 they sighted a convoy of 25 to 30 trucks on the main highway leading out of San Jose. The Squadron had already been in the air for three hours and was low on gas and ammunition; so this tempting target was spared.

69FS

Later that afternoon the 69FS was on an eight plane mission to attack Silay Airdrome on Negros Island. Capt. George Bosenbark was leading the mission with 2Lt. James Bilodeau as his Wingman. Bosenbark saw several enemy aircraft parked in a revetment area. Although the planes appeared to be unserviceable, both pilots went down to strafe them. As Bosenbark made the initial strafing both their fighters were hit by AA and small arms fire. Bosenbark's P-47 was not critically hit but Bilodeau's Thunderbolt was seen to be smoking as he pulled up from his strafing run and then burst into flames. Bilodeau bailed out at about 400 and other pilots saw him land in a field about two miles northwest of the airstrip. Bilodeau was not seen to move after he hit the ground and was reported as MIA.

**14 January 1945: 3ACG/3FS**

During the morning 10 Mustangs led by Maj. Walker Mahurin escorted B-25s in a strike on the town of Aparri. After the B-25s bombed the town, the P-51s strafed the nearby airfield destroying a Tony, a Betty, a Nick, and one other unidentified aircraft. Also a pair of camouflaged luggers that were hidden in a nearby cove was also heavily strafed. As the P-51s returned south down the Cagayan Valley, they saw a pair of unaware twin-engine enemy bombers, flying about 5,000 feet below. Capt. Charles Adams, the 3FS Operations Officer, and his Wingman dove on the nearest bomber, which was identified as a Sally. The enemy pilot sped up without taking any evasive action as Adams closed to almost pointblank range and sent it crashing into the hills for the Squadron's first victory and Adam's only victory. Meanwhile, Mahurin chased after the second bomber, which was a fast Dinah bomber. The Dinah pilot had been alerted and immediately reversed course and tried to speed away. Mahurin dropped his wing tanks but it took ten minutes for him to get close enough to begin firing. After a few short bursts the Dinah rolled slowly onto its back and crashed." ETO ace with Maj. Walker Mahurin with 21 victories got his only Pacific victory (he would score 3.5 victories during the Korean War).

**1Lt. Raymond Evans** shot down a Nick for his only victory. (AAF)

**Maj. Walker Mahurin** was credited with 19¾ victories in the ETO and added a Dinah in the Pacific, and then 3½ during the Korean War. (AFAA)

**Mid-January 1945: Airfield Situation at Lingayen**

US Army engineers landed at Lingayen Gulf with the infantry to begin construction of airfields and facilities but poor weather and heavy seas prevented them from landing heavy equipment and steel runway mat ashore during first three days. During this time every effort was made to making the established enemy airfield behind the beach operational. Craters were filled with beach sand and then covered with palm and bamboo branches and then 5,000 feet of PSP was laid over this base and then the entire surface was coated with asphalt. This strip, named Lingayen, was ready on 16 January, for regular troop carrier service and P-61 night fighters. The next day the P-38s of the 18th Fighter Group of the 13th Air Force and some P-40s and P-51s of the 82nd Reconnaissance Group arrived. On 17 January the Far East Air Forces and the 308th Bomb Wing would assume responsibility for air cover of the beachhead and for ground support of the advancing ground units; relieving the Navy carrier and battleship task forces.

The engineers also started construction of a new airfield at Dagupan but after six days it was abandoned in favor of a more suitable site at Mangaldan. To accelerate its construction another engineer battalion was assigned and it was ready by 22 January to receive the 35th Fighter Group and the 3rd Air Commando Group. Mangaldan was constructed of only compacted earth and sprayed with oil to prevent dust and was greatly affected by rain which delayed arrival of two Marine Corsairs Air Groups and the 38th Bomb Group. Navy PB4Y search aircraft were to be based there but the field would not support their weight.

As the Navy left Lingayen Gulf, their intelligence estimated that "no more than 10" enemy aircraft remained in flying condition on Luzon. Adm. Shigeru Fukudome, the Japanese Navy Commander on Luzon escaped from Manila to Singapore during the night of 15 January by flying boat; abandoning the Philippines.

It was found that the kunai grass fields surrounding the Lingayen airstrips harbored Scrub typhus, which is the milder form of typhus transmitted to humans by the bite of the rat flea and distinct from epidemic typhus, as it is not transmitted from person to person. To counter this health threat rigorous measures were instituted. The grass was cut and burned. Each man was required to treat his socks and trouser legs in a solution that was called "typhus juice," and all personnel were given typhus booster injections. An extermination program was established against the numerous rats that carried the fleas and contests with prizes were devised to rid the camp areas of the rats and many imaginative ways were tried in this pursuit. In mid-January the 310FS was particularly hard hit with Scrub Typhus as 13 of its men were hospitalized and one had died.

Gen. Casey and the Lingayen Landings

Casey had intended to come ashore on the first day of the landing at Lingayen Gulf but was delayed a day because the destroyer he was traveling on had to escort a crippled transport. Despite enormous difficulties ASCOM was able to finish numerous projects on time and some ahead of schedule. On 13 February 1945, ASCOM was transferred to USASOS and redesignated the Luzon Base Section (LUBSEC). Casey then resumed his post as Chief Engineer, GHQ SWPA. As the Chief Engineer, General Headquarters, Allied Forces, Southwest Pacific Area (GHQ, SWPA), by the end of the war, Casey controlled an engineer force of over 275,000 officers and men.

After the war Casey hoped to become Chief of Engineers when Lt.Gen. Raymond Wheeler retired in 1948 but President Truman passed him over in favor of the Missouri River Division Engineer, Maj.Gen. Lewis Pick (of course, Truman was from Missouri). Instead, Casey remained in Japan as MacArthur's Chief Engineer where he was instrumental in rebuilding the devastated enemy country. Casey retired on 31 December 1949 and then worked for Schenley Industries from 1951 until 1964. Casey died on 30 August 1981 at the age of 83.

**Mid-January 1945: Luzon Air Situation**

By the first half of January the 5AF claimed to have destroyed 79 locomotives, 466 rail cars, 468 trucks, and 66 automobiles on Luzon which virtually paralyzed Japanese communications and allowed the rapid advance of U.S. forces toward Manila.

**14 January 1945: 58FG: Atkinson Alive**

On 14 January the 58th Fighter Group received the news that Col. Gwen Atkinson was alive and with Guerrillas on Luzon. In Atkinson's absence, Lt.Col. Jasper Durham had assumed command of the 58FG and Maj. Edward Roddy was temporarily named as Deputy Commander. Capt. Donald Jander moved up from the 311FS to Headquarters as Assistant Operations Officer on 12 January.

Atkinson had parachuted into a plowed field only about 200 feet from where his P-47 crashed. A Filipino farmer with a young boy 8 to 10 years old was nearby and Atkinson asked the boy, who spoke some English, where the Japs were. The boy pointed toward Clark Field and Atkinson headed in the opposite direction without his shoes as all Filipinos were barefooted and he didn't want to be followed. After keeping up a fast pace for about a mile he had to stop as he had pulled a muscle in his left rib cage from the jolt of his parachute opening. For the next six or seven days he painfully moved toward Mount Arayat on the central plains of Luzon, traveling from village to village until the Japanese apparently abandoned the chase. Atkinson had to rest for a day, as he was unable to get up by himself after lying down. On the seventh or eighth day he met the crew of a Navy dive bomber who had bailed out and they met a Guerrilla unit who, unfortunately, were the Communist Hukbalahaps (Huks) who were loyal to the side that paid the most. They met their Leader who agreed to allow lead them into the USAFFE Guerrilla area (the officially recognized Guerrilla forces in the Philippines). The night they were to leave they were approached by a Filipino who identified himself as a USAFFE Guerrilla sent to the Huks as a spy and told them the Huks could not be trusted. Atkinson overpowered the Huk guide and forced him to conduct them across the Japanese patrolled area. Along the way Atkinson picked up 28 other downed flyers including a four year escapee from the Bataan Death March and headed 110 miles toward USAFFE Guerrilla Headquarters near the Sierra Madre Mountains on the east coast of Luzon. There was a flat area at the foot of the mountain behind the Headquarters village measuring about 800 feet long and 100 feet wide. The men, aided by the Guerrillas, cleared an airstrip and sent a message and liaison aircraft were sent in and rescued all the downed flyers.

It was AAF policy was that an escapee was not to remain in a theater where he had escaped with the help of the local inhabitants. Atkinson was

After being shot down on 3 January, the 58FG received word that **Col. Gwen Atkinson** was alive and with Guerrillas on Luzon. (AAF)

allowed to remain if he did not to fly outside gliding distance of the airdrome he took off from. To hide his escape he was listed as MIA until 11 months after the end of the war. Atkinson returned to Mindoro by the end of January and resumed command of the 58th Fighter Group. During this time Lt.Col. Jasper Durham had contracted typhus and was hospitalized.

The heavy bomber field then under construction on Mindoro had been named Atkinson Field in honor of Col. Gwen Atkinson, the 58th Fighter Group Commander, who had been listed as killed in action at Clark Field on 3 January. After Atkinson returned later in January the new field on Mindoro was renamed McGuire Field after the actually KIA Maj. Thomas McGuire. Gen. Hap Arnold then ordered Kenney to refrain from the hurried naming of air bases for the departed.

**15 January 1945: 475FG/432FS**

Aerial reconnaissance discovered 15 operational enemy single engine fighters on repaired runways at Silay Airstrip on the northwest coast of Negros. Capt. Paul Lucas, a 432FS veteran from the early New Guinea Campaign, was leading a patrol of six P-38s on a convoy patrol during the morning near Negros. After the patrol was completed, he decided to strafe Silay but during a strafing pass, his Lightning was hit by light AA and machine gun fire and he was forced to crashland with both his engines on fire. His wounded fighter bounced about 50 feet on impact onto a field on the west bank of the Malisbog River. The belly tank burst into flames and the tail broke off. Pilots of his flight saw Filipinos waving white handkerchiefs and running toward Lucas who was slumped in the cockpit of his wrecked P-38 and the seven victory ace was listed as KIA.

**16 January 1945: 49FG Last 7FS Philippine's Victory**

Although the Kamikaze threat from distant Okinawa and Formosa continued to be a source of concern, the frequency of their attacks was considerably reduced and in the following days enemy air contacts became more infrequent. Escort missions in poor weather continued for two weeks and without any enemy air opposition they became so tedious that the 49ers turned to strafing coastal and road targets.

During the afternoon of the 16th the four Lightnings of the 7FS was on a routine PBY Catalina VIP escort to Lingayen. The PBY flew near the water while the Demons were at 8,000 feet but as they reached their destination the Catalina pilot cancelled the flight due to the deteriorating weather. The Demon flight then turned back to Mindoro and climbed to 16,000 feet. When the flight was just west of Manila Bay the Flight Leader decided to look for better weather at a lower altitude and the two lead P-38s descended through the clouds. Soon they radioed the two trailing elements, 2Lts. Albert Meschino and Hugh Manes, to maintain their position above the thick overcast. Both pilots were veterans familiar with flying in the Philippines' weather and after they circled for 30 minutes they decided to proceed to Mindoro; sure that they would find a break in the clouds to the south. As they approached Balayan Bay on the north side of to the straits separating Luzon and Mindoro they confirmed their position through a clearing in the clouds before crossing to Mindoro. As they were about to cross they spotted a single aircraft headed south about five miles away and both pilots chased after it. Meschino arrived first and identified the bogey as a Jake floatplane. He flew past the unaware Japanese pilot cruising at 200 feet above the sea to make a head on attack. Just as Meschino closed to point blank range the Jake pilot slid off into a flat turn, but Meschino was too close to miss and Meschino had his second and last victory. When Meschino and Manes regrouped the weather had closed in and completely covered the coastline. In hopes of finding better weather the two climbed to 12,000 feet but to no avail. They headed south for another hour and half but still could not find an opening and finally, low fuel and with darkness approaching they were forced to descend through the overcast. Once through, they found themselves over the west coast of Negros Island which was 160 miles beyond their destination on Mindoro. Manes, who had bailed out of a damaged P-38 in November, chose a belly landing in shallow water, instead while Meschino bailed out. The two met on the beach and were retrieved by the Negros natives and two weeks later a Navy PBY rescued them. When they rejoined the Squadron on 31 January, and Meschino learned he had scored the Demon's 178th and last victory of the war (with 19 probables and 24 damaged).

**16 January 1945: 3ACG/3FS**

After the 4FS joined the Group on the 16th; both of the Squadrons were busy for the next few weeks strafing and bombing locomotives and rolling stock, trucks, and other vehicles. Four 3FS Mustangs attacked the Clark Field complex that afternoon and caught a cluster of unsuspecting enemy aircraft on the ground at Angeles South, which was located a few miles southeast of the main Clark complex. Four Tojos were lined up at the end of the runway with their pilots apparently concentrating on checking their engine magnetos prior to take off. 1Lt. Glenn Larimore dropped a 500 pound bomb that scored a direct hit exploding one of the Tojos. The blast set off an explosion in an adjacent fighter, which, in turn, set the remaining two fighters on fire. The Air Commandos destroyed five more enemy fighters and damaged three more in their attack.

The same day, another 3FS flight flew a barge sweep of Iloilo Bay on Negros Island. Although no barges were found, several aircraft were discovered camouflaged on an airstrip. Capt. Charles Adams set one on fire but enemy 20mm AA fire hit his Mustang and he had to bail out over the sea. As his flight circled over head, friendly natives rescued Adams and took him to a nearby island. An OA-10A, the AAF version of the Navy's PBY-3 Catalina, picked up Adams the following day and returned him to Leyte.

**17 January 1945: 58FG**

On the 17th the 69FS sent sixteen P-47s Thunderbolts to cover the A-20s on a shipping strike along the northern coast of Luzon. After finishing their escort, the pilots searched for targets of opportunity. Over Salomague Harbor they saw one large vessel and five heavily camouflaged smaller boats all flying Japanese flags. The strafing attack sunk all five of the smaller boats and left the larger one burning. On the homeward bound leg 2Lt. Arthur Cain suddenly bailed out at 1,000 feet without apparent reason and his plane crashed a half mile offshore from Vigan Point. Cain's parachute opened but he was seen to hit his aircraft before it sank. The Flight's pilots circled as long as possible but saw no signs of life in the oil slick.

**18 January 1945: 58FG/311FS**

On 18 January the 311FS dispatched 16 Thunderbolts on a full squadron fighter sweep over the north coast of Luzon. Despite thunderstorms, cloud cover, and poor visibility the Squadron descended to the deck where they spotted a staff car on a highway and strafed and destroyed it. Then 2Lt. Roger Carroll spotted a single Nick, closed on its tail, and got numerous hits as he pressed his attack. The Nick pilot made a sharp dive into the clouds and disappeared; denying Carroll of a victory as no one observed the crash. Veteran 1Lt. James O'Leary radioed that his oil pressure was dropping and that he was returning to Mindoro and was accompanied by his Wingman, 2Lt. William Shwab. Somewhere between Bagabag and Lingayen the two pilots became separated by bad weather. While they were still in radio contact and Shwab heard O'Leary say that he was going to bail out. Shwab never saw O'Leary's P-47 nor did he see any sign of a parachute. Subsequent searches failed to find him and he was listed as KIA.

**18 January 1945: 3ACG/4FS**

With the increases strafing attacks the decimated Japanese Air Forces turned to hiding their remaining parked aircraft and few enemy planes were caught in the open. Capt. Ray Lahmeyer of the 4FS led a late afternoon sweep on Del Monte Airfield on Mindanao to find the Japanese bomber that had been flying nocturnal nuisance raids over their base. As the Flight arrived over Del Monte the sun was on the horizon and dusk was beginning to fall. When Lahmeyer neared the field he saw a flickering and then spotted a Betty with its engines running. He went into a tight turn and as he fired on the bomber he could see several Japanese running away before the bomber exploded; finally giving the Squadron a good night's sleep.

**17-30 January 1945: 3ACG**

The Air Commandos' sojourn on Leyte was quite short as the ground personnel boarded *LST 919* for the trip to Lingayen Gulf, Luzon. It was not until midnight 30 January that the LST beaches near San Fabian on the northern end of the landing beaches where the Air Commandos unloaded the following morning and proceeded by road convoy to Calasiao (liaison units) and Mangaldan (3FS and 4FS).

As *LST 919* sailed toward Lingayen Gulf, the two fighter squadrons remained behind temporarily which continued flying missions until they, too moved to Luzon. During a fighter sweep of Mindanao on 20 January, 2Lt. William Isgrigg pressed his attack on a truck too low and snagged a tree and his fighter cartwheeled and exploded.

On the 23rd, the 3FS' final mission from Tanauan was notable as it targeted Baguio, Yamashita's luxurious Fourteenth Area Army Headquarters in the hills northeast of Lingayen Gulf. Sixteen ACG Mustangs, each carrying two 1,000 pound bombs, followed a B-24 raid and shortly after the Liberators pulled off the target, the P-51s rushed in to dive bomb Camp John Hay. Their accurate bombing scored direct hits on the administration building, the message center, the quartermaster stores, a barracks, and the plush staff officer's quarters. Following this mission, the 3FS returned to Tanauan, refueled, then flew to their new base at Mangaldan, code named *Honey Strip*. Three days later, the 4FS also moved to the new field.

**19 January 1945: 5AF Situation**

Fifth Air Force pilots had become so eager in their interdiction of enemy communications that they were beginning to interfere with the rapid advance of the Army ground forces. The Army was moving so quickly that there were several instances of aircraft attacking friendly troops causing Gen. Krueger to request a new system, whereby the bomb line was established at least 24 hours in advance of expected troop positions. On 19 January Krueger requested that the concentrated air attacks be immediately curtailed and from then on, no bridges were to be bombed unless such an attack was requested. He also restricted all attacks against railroad equipment with the exceptions of trains actually in motion.

**19 January 1945: 49FG/9FS Last 9FS and 49FG Victory in the Philippines**

After a morning attack against the abandoned enemy satellite airstrip at Guagua Village; during the mid-day fighter sweep to Luzon's northwestern cape, the 9FS Red Flight finally encountered a flying target. The flight was flying at minimum altitude under low rain clouds just off shore of Banqui Bay when they saw a single twin-engine P1Y, Frances, flying just over the water. Once it was seen, the speedy Frances broke for the safety of the squall line but rookie 2Lts. Troy Smith and John Forgey quickly overtook the enemy. Forgey fired first, followed by Smith, but the Frances continued flying until Forgey finished it off for his only victory and the Flying Knight's last victory as well that for the 49ers in the Philippines.

**19 January 1945: 49FG and Hong Kong**

While on Mindoro the 49ers received new pilots and ground crews in advance for their move to Luzon. By the end of January, all three 49er squadrons were re-equipped with late model P-38s, which gave the Group four full flights per Squadron. With this increase in fighter strength, Kenney expanded operations beyond the Philippines. The 86th Fighter Wing was moved up from Biak to operate against the Japanese north and west of Luzon.

The Japanese air units based in China presented a threat and 5FC Coordinator Lt.Col. Gerald Johnson developed a daring plan to sweep enemy airfields on the south coast of Hong Kong with the long dangerous flight path protected by rescue submarines and PBYs. On the morning of 19 January, Johnson led 16 P-38s from each squadron from Hill Airfield. But only a quarter hour into the mission, weather reconnaissance reported the route was weathered in and the 49ers were diverted back to the Luzon coast to attack their secondary targets. Subsequently, the China operation was postponed until the landings on Luzon were completed.

**17-20 January 1945: Luzon Ground and Naval Situation**

On 17 January, Kruger's Sixth Army began to advance south in two columns from Lingayen and Japanese resistance intensified as the Americans closed in on Clark Field. In somewhat marginal weather, the 49ers provided close support to aid Kruger for the next three days; three sorties per day for each squadron. The 49ers, aided by P-47 dive bombers, destroyed highways and their traffic, rail lines and rolling stock, and obliterated so many bridges that Kruger requested that they leave his infantry, "a bridge or two on the road to Manila."

On 19 January, a second American landing was made 60 miles north of Manila at San Antonio on the west coast. These divisions on the Japanese flank immediately advanced inland over a pass through the coastal hills to link up with Kruger splitting Yamashita's western forces. For the next two weeks, the Americans drove the surviving enemy forces into the caves of the west coast range or into a hasty retreat into the east coast forests. By the first week in February, Kruger's left flank forces advanced across the interior, cutting off the route to the Cagayan Valley in the north.

From 17-19 January 1945, Halsey's Third Fleet, including Task Force 38, again struck Formosa and the China coastal targets and three days later departed the China Sea and supported the Luzon invasion. By this time Halsey had lost 201 aircraft, 167 pilots and crewmen, and had had 205 men killed on board his ships that had been hit by the Kamikaze pilots.

**23 January 1945: 58FG**

The 311FS' last mission of the day was a three plane fighter sweep over central Luzon departed at 1315 and arrived in the area they intended to strafe at 1420. 1Lt. Howard, Davis, from 58FG HQ led the flight and strafed and burned a truck parked under trees southwest of Loobac. They encountered accurate, moderate, medium and light AA fire and Davis' fighter was hit by AA fire on his first pass. Davis headed his burning aircraft south toward Laguna de Bay to attempt to ditch. When Davis released his wing tanks; one failed to release. As he crash landed in the water his P-47 cartwheeled and came to a stop underwater. The pilots circled the crash but no sign of Davis was seen and he was officially listed as MIA and presumed KIA.

Later that day, at 1800, Lt.Col. Jasper Durham, acting Group CO, was leading an eight plane 310FS mission and was returning to base. The runway was very muddy and slippery and after he touched down he passed up the first off ramp because of his high speed and the condition of the runway. He stopped on the overrun of the runway but could not unlock the tail wheel and could not taxi off to the side of the runway overrun. 1Lt. Cutler Webster was next to land and he also passed up the taxi ramp and continued to the end of the strip. Unaware that Durham's fighter was still on the runway, Webster collided with Durham. Neither pilot was injured but both Thunderbolts were extensively damaged and sent to the service squadron for repair or salvage.

**20 January 1945: 71TRG**

1Lt. Robert McAlpin of the 82RS downed an Oscar near San Nicholas.

**22 January 1945: 475FG/432FS/431FS**

During an unsuccessful return mission to Silay on 17 January four 1,000 pound bombs had been released but all failed to explode for an unknown reason. The most successful bombing mission flown by the 432FS during January was an attack on the airstrip near the resort town of Baguio, north of Lingayen. Four P-38s, three armed with a single 2,000 pound bomb and the fourth with a 1,000 pound bomb took off at 1045 and arrived over the target at 1330. The three 2,000 pound bombs exploded the middle of the strip while the fourth exploded just off the west end of the runway. The 431st also bombed the strip that day and all their bombs fell within the target area; making the Baguio Strip unusable for air operations in opposing the expanding Lingayen landings.

**22 January-8 February 1945: 421NFS: Move to San Marcelino**

On 22 January the 5FC ordered the ground echelon and one flight of P-61s of the 421st NFS to move to Luzon. The remainder of the flight echelon was to stay at Tacloban with a necessary number of maintenance personnel. During the morning of the 24th a LST, with nine officers and 145 enlisted men aboard, joined a convoy and arrived at Mindoro on the 25th where it remained for several days before resuming the voyage. The ship sailed for Luzon on 2 February arriving at Subic Bay the following day. Unloading of the LST was completed the same day and the Squadron moved inland about 12 miles into its new area at the San Marcelino Airstrip. Even with the relocation of a part of the Squadron, flying would continue at both Tacloban and at San Marcelino. After the tense and active period the Squadron went through at Tacloban, the 421st NFS was disappointed to find Japanese activity over the new area was negligible but the uninterrupted nights of sleep were welcome. This new camp was a decided improvement over the jungles of New Guinea and the swamplands of Tacloban and Filipino labor was again contracted to help construct buildings. A well was dug and water was made available for showers and other facilities. On 8 February, six of the 421st NFS P-61s arrived at San Marcelino from Tacloban and flight operations were established and for the remainder of February the squadron would operate from both bases.

**22-31 January 1945: 35FG**

During this initial period, 22-26 January, the Group's operations were committed entirely to escort and local patrol without any enemy air reaction. From the 26th the Group was assigned to the support of ground operations. On that date all three squadrons strafed (15,480 rounds) and dive bombed (11 tons of GP bombs) San Nicholas Town and the enemy airdrome at Tuguegarao in 45 Thunderbolt sorties.

**21-23 January 1945: 49FG to Formosa and Luzon Tactical Missions**

In mid January, aerial reconnaissance of the Formosa airdromes estimated that there were approximately 600 mixed aircraft primarily based on the fields on the island's west side. Again the 49ers's Operations Coordinator, Lt.Col. Gerald Johnson devised another detailed plan to attack the Formosan Dromes. On 21 January, the 86FW implemented a 1,400 mile round trip sweep to Choso Airdrome, one of the major enemy air bases in southern Formosa but neither the 49th or 8th Fighter Groups found any enemy aircraft. No enemy aircraft appeared during their raids on Takao Airdrome on the 22nd and 23rd. For the remainder of the Philippines' Campaign the 49er Lightnings were to continue their twofold assignment of flying escort to distant Formosa and tactical missions against Luzon. After five continuous days of close aerial support; on the 26 January Kruger's army captured the decimated Clark Field.

**24 January 1945: 475FG/433FS Last Victory**

During January the 433FS had been employed on PBY escort, courier missions, and convoy patrol duties. During one of those convoy patrols on 24 January the last Possum Squadron aerial combat and victory was recorded. 1Lt. Leroy Ross took off at 1515 leading a flight of four P-38s over a convoy south of Sequijor Island, east of Negros. The Convoy Controller requested that Ross split his flight and he and his Wingman, Lt. Lowman, patrolled at 11,000 feet while his element patrolled at 3,000 feet. Once at these altitudes the Controller called Ross to investigate unidentified aircraft to the east. Several minutes later Ross saw two bogies ahead and approached them at 6 o'clock and about 100 feet above and dove on the Zeros and fired on the one on the right from 120 yards level and exploded its wing and belly tanks and it descended with its pilot bailing out. Lowman fired on the left turning Zero and took a 60 degree deflection shot that did no damage. Ross then dropped his belly tank to chase another Zero and took a 90 degree deflection shot as it passed over the parachuting enemy pilot Ross had just shot down. The Zero Split-S'd away without any apparent damage and Ross turned away, as he had lost his Wingman. Ross' victory was his third and last, and also the last and 121st victory of the war for the 433FS with 23 probables and 12 damaged.

**24 January 1945: 421NFS**

The remaining flight echelon at Tacloban continued patrols and on the 24th 1Lt. Owen Wolf downed his fourth confirmed enemy aircraft for the Squadron's 13th victory. Wolf and his regular crew; R/O Lt. Byron Allain and gunner S/Sgt. Donald Trabing, were on patrol over the Ormac Bay area, in the vicinity of Natagog. Wolf was flying at 10,000 feet when the GCI gave vectors on a bogie heading west of Ormac toward Burauen. Wolf turned 180 degrees turn to fly a heading of 90 degrees. R/O Allain saw a blip on his scope and took over the interception but the bogie disappeared. At 2030 Wolf was given a starboard turn by the GCI and Allain again made radar contact with the bogie and instructed Wolf to climb to 12,000 feet at approximately 250 mph, giving the P-61 a 20 mph closing advantage on the bogie. At about 1,500 feet gunner Trabing sighted the bogie, identified as Zeke off the port side. The Japanese pilot seemed to be surprised as he took no evasive action. Wolf throttled back and made a gentle turn, closing to 1,000 feet, to a point where the pilot and gunner opened fire simultaneously with the 20 mm and .50 caliber machine guns. Tracers and high explosive ammunition hit the fuselage, wings, and engine cowling of the Zeke which Split-S'd into the overcast, bursting into flames, and crashing in the hills near the 5th Fighter Command at Barauen. Another bogie contact was made later that evening but communications problems between the P-61 and GCI caused Wolf to lose any chance he may have had for contact and to become one of the few night fighter aces.

**25 January 1945: 58FG/311FS**

In the afternoon of 25 January four P-47s of the 311FS dropped Napalm on an enemy defensive position near Loobac, Luzon. This mission was considered one of the most effective to date while using the new Napalm tanks. A large ammunition dump received direct hits and the Napalm fires caused a huge explosion, sending smoke and flame up to 1,500 feet. Four Napalm tanks were dropped on gun positions, completely covering them in flames. One Thunderbolt was so badly damaged by AA fire that it was written off as a complete loss after it landed safely.

**26 January 1945: 71TRG**

On the 26th 2Lt. William Johnson of the 110RS shot down an Oscar north of Manila.

**27 January 1945: 49FG/7FS**

With no enemy aircraft in the air over Luzon, tactical missions continued and on the 27th as the 7FS flew along the western coast from Lingayen to Laoag Airdrome, 150 miles north. Laoag was once a main satellite airfield from Formosa to Clark Field for the Leyte Campaign but now was abandoned and the JAAF aircrews stranded there were still able to send up an effective light caliber AA fire. The 7FS attack set several buildings on fire but the squadron lost 2Lt. Epke Ives who crashed 200 yards from the enemy airstrip.

**27 January 1945: 475FG/432FS/433FS**

Throughout the end of January and the beginning of February the shortage of P-38s continued in the 475FG. Only two or four plane flights could be mounted due to the lack of aircraft and missions were usually transport escort or routine patrols, while other units on Mindoro Island were assigned to the more demanding operations. Maj. John Loisel, flying in Col. MacDonald's P-38 *Putt-Putt Maru*, led a flight of four 432FS P-38s on an early morning convoy patrol south of Leyte. The mission was uneventful and the Clover flight headed back to Dulag to land at 1045. Loisel landed on Dulag #1 and stopped at the end of the rain-soaked and congested runway. He turned "his" P-38 in the direction of the incoming flight to direct them down. As he waited, one of his Clover P-38s piloted by 2Lt. Arnold Larsen came straight at him, somewhat too fast and too flat. Under the best of circumstances the runway was only adequate for a normal landing so Arnold's Lightning skidded into Loisel's parked fighter. Neither pilot was injured but both P-38s were sent off for repair. 2Lt. John Berry of the 433FS also collided with a 432FS P-38 that day on the same rainy strip and both aircraft were taken out of service which further depleted the number of serviceable 475th P-38s.

**28-29 January 1945: 3ACG/4FS**

For the 3ACG fighter pilots, the move to Mangaldan had meant that their major role would be flying close support missions for the infantry. Manila had been the major objective in the invasion of Luzon and the drive toward the capital was on a relatively narrow front leaving both Sixth Army flanks exposed as the infantry advanced south. The Air Commandos were needed to protect the Sixth Army's flanks until it turned back north to assault Yamashita's stronghold. On 28 January the 4FS initiated flank protection when they attacked possible enemy positions northeast of Manila. From that time on, until even after the Campaign was officially declared as over, the 3ACG continued providing close air support to the infantry. Two more ground support missions were flown the following day and the late morning mission was particularly successful. Sixteen 4FS Mustangs attacked several villages east of Plaridel that were thought to be sheltering the enemy. All of the Air Commando 500 pound bombs, except for a few near misses, landed on target.

**1Lt. Leroy Grosshuesch** shot down two biplanes over Formosa to give him three victories. (AAF)

**29 January 1945: 475FG**

The Group lost two pilots on this day; 1Lt. Robert Patterson of the 431FS and F/O Charles Nacke of the 432FS. Patterson was listed as MIA but no other details were given. Nacke was MIA as his fighter exploded northwest of Dulag for unknown reasons and he biked out unsuccessfully.

**29 January 1945: 71TRG/110RS (Last P-40 Victory in the Pacific)**

On the 29th 2Lt. Robert Hammond of the 110RS shot down a Zeke at 0910 near the Mamrarang Mountains for the last known P-40 victory in the Pacific. Hammond was flying southeast at 9,000 feet as the Wingman of a two plane recon. While trying to find a hole in the clouds they spotted a lone Zero at 3 o'clock flying east at 10,000 feet. The enemy pilot went into a shallow dive and the two P-40s followed in line astern for four or five minutes. Hammond was closing too fast and was forced to pull up to the left to lose come speed. Hammond's Flight Leader closed from dead astern and opened fire from 500 yards and held it until only 20 yards; hitting the wings and fuselage before he broke off up and right in front of the Zero. Hammond came in from above and astern and fired a burst that missed just below the tail. He then pulled slightly up and fired; exploding the left side of the enemy's engine in a ball of flames. Hammond followed the stricken Zero down and observed it to crash and explode.

**Late January 1945: Formosa, Indochina, and North to Victory**

Missions against industrial installations on Formosa were initiated by Fifth Air Force bombers via night attacks in early January 1945. By the end of that month the bombers were attacking by day escorted by P-47s and P-38s of the 5th Fighter Command.

**30 January 1945: 35FG/40FS/39FS over Formosa**

40FS

The Squadron sent out nine P-47s on a sweep to Formosa. At 0930 while flying near Okayama at 9,000 feet #4 man in Red Flight, 1Lt. Ellis Baker, spotted a Zero at 2,000 feet below. He made a high side pass from dead astern firing a long burst at 75 yards that exploded it in mid air. The enemy pilot may have been unaware of Baker as he took no evasive action. Baker's fourth victory was the first for the 5FC over Formosa and the Squadron's only victory for January.

39FS

The 39FS had not made a claim since 27 December and 1Lt. Leroy Grosshuesch led eight P-47s on a long range fighter sweep to Formosa, hoping to see some air action. After patrolling over Taichu at 10,000 feet for 45 minutes, Second Element Leader, 1Lt. Eugene Haws, spotted a twin engine bomber about at 3 o'clock low. Haws and his #2 dove first and Grosshuesch and Wingman, 2Lt. Ervin Pratt followed; leaving the second element of White Flight as top cover. Haws lost the Sally in a cloud but Grosshuesch saw one of several obsolete biplanes flying slowly at 9 o'clock at 2,000 feet. Grosshuesch and Pratt dove but both had too much diving speed. Grosshuesch overran after firing a short burst, getting a few hits, as did Pratt after firing a short burst. Grosshuesch controlled his speed on the second dive and got numerous fatal hits. The two climbed to 3,000 feet where they saw another biplane of the same type and Grosshuesch clobbered it from the rear for his second and third victories. 1Lt. Idon Hodge and Wingman 2Lt. Charles Posey, White Flight lead element, also dove on the biplanes and attacked two. Hodge overshot and Posey got a short burst at 90 degrees deflection getting hits on the tail which caused it to go out of control and crash.

After dispatching the biplanes the Squadron regrouped and flew on to Shinchiku Airdrome where two flights of three and four Zeros were encountered. The eight P-47s closed from astern at 2,000 feet. Hodge and Posey fired first with both of their targets set on fire and crashing. Haws chased a Zero and got hits in the cockpit, then followed it in a sharp right and then left turn and finally fired another volley that sent it exploding into the ground for his only victory. As Hodge and Posey climbed over Shinchiku A/D Posey saw a Tony on the deck heading for the airdrome. Posey immediately dove and fired a continuous burst but was forced to break away in the face of heavy AA fire. Hodge saw the Tony crash but also informed Posey that his tail assembly had been hit and the two headed back to base where they landed safely. Posey had had a great day but these would be his only three victories of the war and Hodge claimed his third and last victory. Meanwhile, 2Lt. Eli Tueche had joined Grosshuesch's Wingman 2Lt. Ervin Pratt saw two Zeros flying east at 2,000 feet; Tueche took the left one and Pratt the right, but as Pratt fired the two enemy fighters broke in opposite directions. Tueche turned with his target and started to fire but the Zero turned sharply below and under him. Tueche put his nose straight down and the Zero flew through his line of fire scoring hits on its fuselage from nose to tail. Tueche turned sharply to port and saw his Zero crash and explode and Pratt's cartwheel only 50 feet away. When he pulled up Tueche saw a P-47 chasing another Zero and then break off, apparently out of ammunition. Tueche closed in and fired from 500 yards on the weaving Zero and saw his bullets falling short. He ceased firing until he closed to 300 yards getting god hits on its tail. The Zero pilot skidded his fighter to the right, trying to get under its P-47 attacker but Tueche fired and got hits on its cockpit. The Zero wobbled and then skidded into a vertical bank just above the trees. Tueche thought he saw another aircraft to his left and banked after it but found that "it was just a tree" and when he turned back to his right he had lost the wounded Zero which was credited as a probable. After the Zeros separated Pratt chased the right Zero which went into a roll and continued and crashed near Tueche's victim. Pratt pulled up to the right from this combat and saw a Zero five miles above to the west. Pratt dove from 3,000 feet straight down on its tail as it began a shallow port turn. Pratt fired until he ran out of ammunition and the Zero caught on fire and was seen to crash by Tueche. Pratt was credited with his second victory and probable while Tueche was credited with his only victory.

**30 January 1945: 58FG/69FS**

During the end of January 1945 the 58th Fighter Group had taken part in an assortment of missions in support of the operations around Subic Bay along with a few worthy fighter sweeps to the Batangas Province to keep the Japanese forces there occupied and stymied as to future American plans for the area. This month of ground support, escort, and interdiction was taking its toll on the Group's pilots and aircraft as illustrated by the 69FS' missions on 30 January. At 0617 four P-47s of the 69FS took off from San Jose on a sweep over Batangas Province. Over Batangas they descended to the deck to search for targets of opportunity. 2Lt. John Swift was leading one element, with Wingman 2Lt. Alexander Gregory. They were flying along the highway northeast from Batangas City and as they passed the small barrio of Rosario, Swift was seen to make a sharp turn and climb to about 400 feet and then slowly nosed over and crashed straight into the ground. No AA fire was observed and it was speculated that Swift had suffered a fatal wound from small arms fire. At 1250 that day, 2Lt. Blaine Ellenberger was returning to San Jose from another 69FS mission to Luzon and ran out of gas, probably due to a fuel leakage from small arms fire, and made a belly landing along the coastline. Ellenberger was uninjured but his fighter was a total loss. He had just returned from being a MIA from the battle with the enemy task force on 26 December. During another mission, the 69FS was returning from convoy cover and as they were landing at 1345, 1Lt. Wallace Hart slowed down and stopped before he cleared the end of the runway and 2Lt. Robert Hansen did not see that Hart had stopped and the two planes collided. Neither pilot was injured but the aircraft were damaged.

**31 January 1945: Third Luzon Landing**

On 31 January, in order to cut off the Japanese escape route to the south, MacArthur's third amphibious landing in the Luzon Campaign took place on the wide peninsula south of Manila Bay at Nasugbu Village. The infantry quickly advanced inland and until it met heavy resistance just east of the village.

**31 January 1945: 49FG**

The 49FG was part of the third Luzon invasion air cover and their Lightnings sortied at sunrise carrying two 1,000 pound bombs 130 miles to the beachhead. Once a pilot dropped his ton of bombs on the village he strafed the highway leading to the beachhead. Black Sheep Flight Leader 1Lt.

**1Lt. James Mugavero** shot down two enemy fighters to become an ace with six victories. (AFAA)

Thomas Holstein and Wingman 1Lt. Francis Hill were making their third strafing run on enemy troops trapped on the road through nominal ground fire when Hill was either hit by gunfire, or he misjudged his altitude as his Lightning crashed and exploded into the surrounding forest.

**31 January 1945: 35FG/39FS/40FS**

39FS

On 31 January eight P-47s of the 39FS escorted B-25 on a late afternoon search for three enemy destroyers south of Formosa. Red Flight, led by 1Lt. Hussa, was flying top cover for the Mitchells at 12,000 feet. Just after they sighted the enemy destroyers; enemy fighters were called in head on and 1,000 feet below. As the enemy fighters passed under Hussa he dove on the formation and broke it up. Hussa dove after one while 2Lt. Albert Wiget dove on the other. Wiget fired at 300 yards and got hits on the wing roots and cockpit and Wiget broke away but the victory was confirmed. Wiget then climbed and saw a lone Zero heading back to base. He closed and fired two long bursts that set the enemy fighter on fire and its pilot bailed out for Wiget's second victory of the day and his last. 1Lt. Marcus Trout was leading the White Flight at 12,000 feet and followed Red Flight into the attack. Trout saw a Zero on the tail of a P-47 and watched as it turned and headed toward his White Flight. Trout was unable to turn tight enough to make a head on pass into the attacker and as the Zero passed by Trout pulled into a tight wingover and got on the Zero's tail. Trout had to chase the Zero 4,000 feet to get into range and opened fire at 300 yards and fired a four second burst and saw hits on both wing roots and cockpit (Lt. Aycock, the #4 man confirmed Trout's first of two victories).

41FS

The 41FS sent out one flight of P-47s on this mission to Formosa and #2 man, 1Lt. James Mugavero spotted five enemy fighters coming toward his flight at 11 o'clock high. Mugavero used water injection to get behind the Hamps but found that every enemy fighter had a P-47 on its tail. Finally he saw a Hamp Split-S away but was unable to follow so he climbed to gain altitude until the Hamp leveled out. Mugavero went into a high speed dive and fired a four second burst from 400 to 100 yards that blew off the wing and canopy. As Mugavero pulled up he saw an Oscar chasing a P-47 in a tight turn and closed from 90 degrees and fired at 400 yards to dead astern at 100 yards and its pilot bailed out just before his fighter exploded. The two victories made Mugavero and ace with six victories. Capt. Homer Dellinger, the Second Element Leader, lost his Wingman as he dropped his tanks and circled at 9,000 feet until he saw a Hamp pursuing a P-47 at 5,000 feet. Dellinger approached and saw the Hamp go after another P-47 and closed

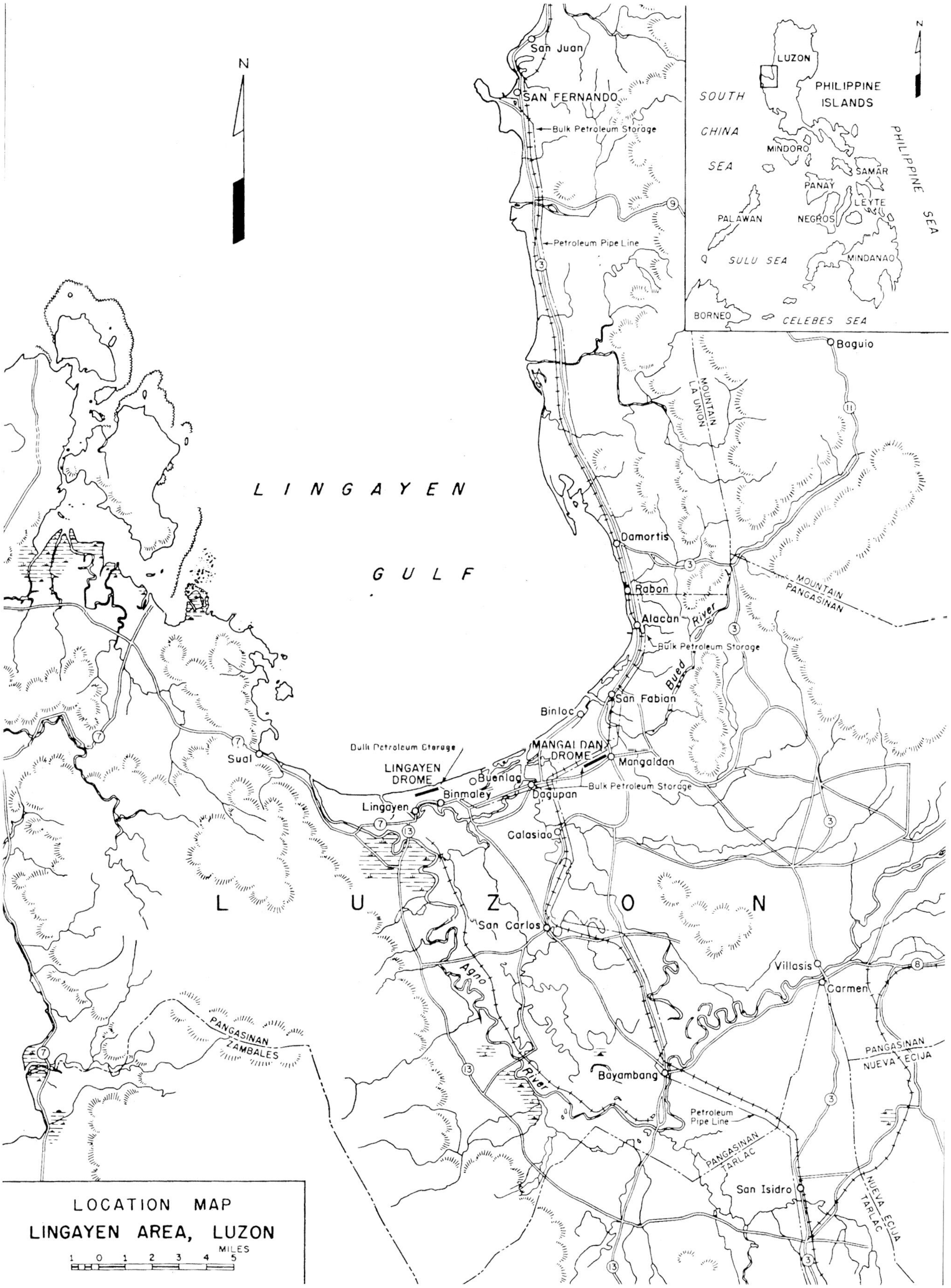


LOCATION MAP
LINGAYEN AREA, LUZON

astern the Hamp getting hits on the engine cowling, cockpit, and tail. The Hamp spiraled in flames but its pilot was able to bail out. DeBaugh's and Dellinger's only career victories would be the last of 97 victories (and 10 probable and two damaged) for the 41FS during the war.

**January 1945: 58FG Monthly Summary**

During January the 58FG shot down eight enemy aircraft in aerial combat and probably destroyed another 20 or 30 on the ground. The Group claimed to have destroyed 67 trucks, three fuel trucks, six personnel carriers, two half-tracks, a tank, three locomotives, 46 boxcars, and at least 21 vessels of all types. They flew 1,420 combat sorties and dropped 61 tons of bombs and 10,440 gallons of Napalm. The month was costly as Capt. Harris and Lieutenants Kindred and Swift had been killed in action. Another seven pilots, Lieutenants Dugan, Bilodeau, Cain, O'Leary, Courington, Fish, and Davis, were missing in action. Four more pilots received injuries in aircraft accidents and 34 Thunderbolts had been lost or damaged in combat or in various accidents, not including many others that had received minor damage from AA fire and were repaired. Corp. Joseph Hruska died from scrub typhus and several other men had to be evacuated to the rear areas or sent home to the States for various illnesses.

**Late January 1945: Situation**

Ground

US Army units on Luzon continued to advance and overran the Clark Field complex on 27 January and captured the former major U.S. Army post of Fort Stotsenburg on the 28th. A landing at Subic Bay was to be made on the enemy's left flank rear on 29 January which was to prevent the Japanese from retreating into the Bataan Peninsula, as MacArthur had done in 1942. The invasion was to be supported by Fifth Air Force fighters and bombers between 21 and 28 January when they dropped 175 tons of bombs on the former American fortress on Grande Island at the mouth of Subic Bay. No air opposition was encountered as the 38th Infantry Division landed at San Antonio, north of Subic Bay on 29 January and quickly drove the enemy from Olongapo. Meanwhile, Guerrilla forces captured the former American air field on the Bay at San Marcelino. On 30 January the USN began clearing the Subic Bay facilities for use.

Air

The few Japanese aircraft reinforcements that were sent down to Luzon were quickly dealt with and the 5FC pilots had to settle for ground support and strafing of enemy ground targets and installations. As the infantry advanced eastward and southward, airstrips were immediately constructed in order to move aircraft forward. By 17 January the P-38s of the 18FG of the 13AF and the P-40s and P-51s of the 82RS were stationed at Lingayen Airstrip. The veteran 35FG and the new 3rd Air Commandos equipped with P-51s of the Fifth Air Force arrived at Mangaldan Airstrip on 22 January.

**Lingayen Area Airfields**

Lingayen

Lingayen Airfield, built prior to the war by the American and Philippine Army, was located at Lingayen Town, parallel to the beach running roughly east to west along Lingayen Gulf. The Japanese occupied the field when they landed at Lingayen Gulf in December 1941 and used it extensively in 1944 for both JAAF and JNAF aircraft arriving from Formosa and Japan as American forces approached Luzon.

The field was liberated on the first day of the American landings at Lingayen Gulf on 9 January 1945. The airfield was repaired and improved by the 836th Engineer Aviation Battalion, and Filipino labor and completed in late February and was immediately operational by fighter and tactical reconnaissance squadrons, and was able to fly B-25 and larger aircraft. It included a runway on the beach built using

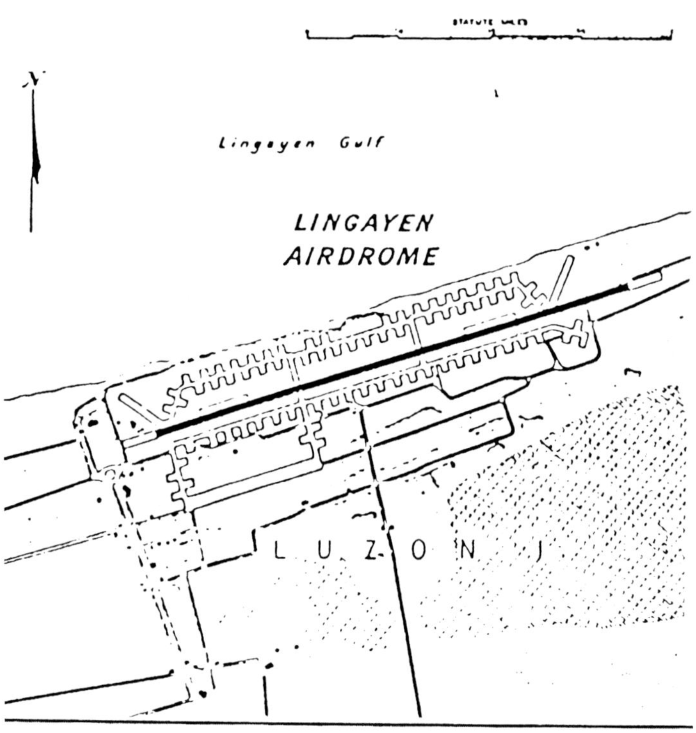


LINGAYEN AIRDROME

woven palm fronds with PSP over it to from the runway surface. It was used as an emergency field for damaged aircraft returning from strikes against Formosa that were damaged or did not have enough fuel to reach Clark Field.

5FC Units Based At Lingayen:

547NFS: (P-38, P-61) San Jose 16 January to 13 August 1945 Ie Shima
71TRG: 82TRS (F-6, P-40) San Jose Jan 17-20, 45 - ?
71TRG: 110TRS (P-40) San Jose 22 January to 28 July 1945 Okinawa
49FG: 7FS (P-38) San Jose 25 February to 16 August1945 Okinawa
49FG: 8FS (P-38) San Jose 27 February to 16 August 1945 Okinawa
49FG: 9FS (P-38) San Jose 26 February to 16 August 1945 Okinawa
35FG: 41FS (P-51) Mangaldan 16-19 April to 20 April 1945 Clark*
35FG: HQ Morotai/Mangaldan to 19 April 1945 Clark
35FG: 39FS (P-47) Mangaldan 10 April to 21 April 1945 Clark
475FG: HQ, 431FS (P-38) Clark 19 April to 8 August 1945 Ie Shima
475FG: 432FS (P-38) Clark 19 April to 8 August 1945 Ie Shima
475FG: 433FS (P-38) Clark 19 April to 8 August 1945 Ie Shima
475FG: HQ Clark 20 April 8 Aug 1945 Ie Shima
(*Stationed briefly at Lingayen but because the Squadron's P-51s had problems with the PSP upon taking off from the field it was transferred to Clark Field)

Lingayen was not only MacArthur's HQ but was a mega base compared to the previous primitive coral airstrips. The runways were longer and the revetment parking had poured concrete in areas. The bivouac area was a well-supplied military camp with fully outfitted quarters, even for the enlisted men. Unlike the informal bases in New Guinea, Biak, and the early Philippines regulation uniforms were to be worn and the men were subject to routine inspections of their quarters (as per MacArthur).

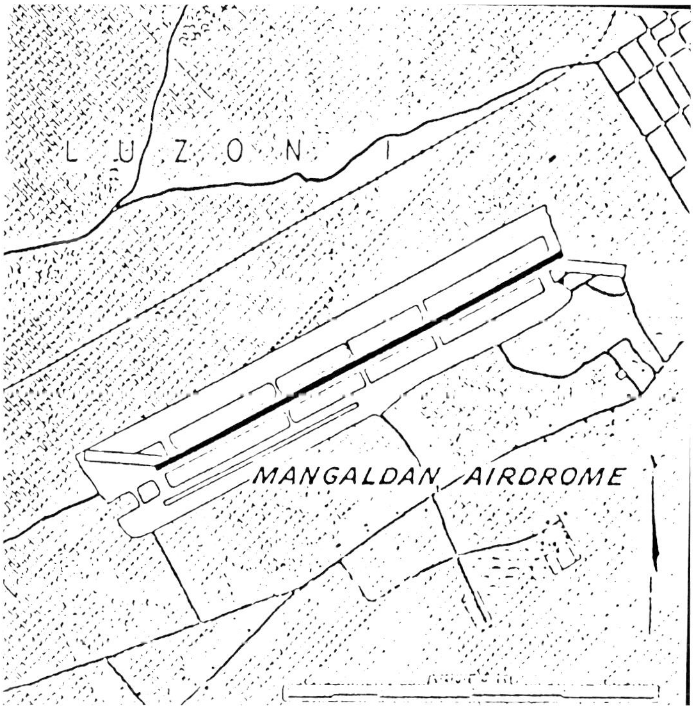


**Mangaldan**

Mangaldan (code named "Honey") was constructed after the American liberation in early January 1945 north of Mangaldan near Lingayen Gulf, to the east of Dagupan. Two parallel runways were built, running east to west parallel and south of the road running through Mangaldan. It based both USAAF and USMC aircraft.

Units Based At Mangaldan:

5FC Units based at Mangaldan:
35FG: HQ Morotai 20 January 1945 to ?
35FG, 39FS (P-47, P-51) Morotai 22 January to 10 April 1945 Lingayen
HQ 3Air Commando Group 26 January to 30 April 1945 Laoag
3ACG: 3FS & 4FS (P-51) Leyte 26 January to 15 April 1945 Laong
35FG: 41FS (P-47, P-51) Wama 21 January to 16 April 1945 Lingayen
35FG: 40FS (P-47, P-51) from Wama January 45 to ?
58FG: HQ from San Jose 5 April 1945 to ?
58FG: 310FS (P-47) from San Jose 6 April to 18 April 1945 Porac
58FG: 311FS (P-47) from San Jose 7 April to 17 April 1945 Porac
58FG: 68FS (P-47) from San Jose 7 April 7 to 17April 1945 Porac

# 5

# February 1945

**February 1945: Situation: Philippines**

Southern Philippines and the NEI

In early February 1945, with the mammoth ground battle continuing on Luzon and with no specific directive from the Joint Chiefs of Staff for any operations after Luzon, MacArthur considered the recapture of the other islands in the Archipelago. Several factors shaped MacArthur's plans for the liberation of these islands with the principal being prestige, both his and that of America. MacArthur believed that his promise return to the Philippines meant all of the Philippines, not just Leyte and Luzon. The fulfillment of his pledge would erase the humiliation of the surrender of 1942 which he felt tarnished American honor. Undoubtedly, MacArthur assumed that a succession of victories in the Philippines would advance the likelihood of being chosen to command the projected invasion of Japan. Two further factors influenced MacArthur's plans. Militarily, these southern islands, with their cities, ports, and airfields, could be used to support future operations as their capture would allow Allied aircraft to more efficiently interdict the line of communications from the Netherlands East Indies through the South China Sea to Japan and, also, would support planned amphibious landings in the Netherlands East Indies. The northern Philippines were also a logical staging area for the enormous numbers of men and quantities of equipment which would be required for the invasion of Japan. So, without JCS directives to the contrary and without an urgent need for either the Seventh Fleet or the Eighth Army outside his area, MacArthur proceeded with his plans for the southern Philippines.

MacArthur's major commands in the Philippines included Lt.Gen. Walter Krueger's Sixth Army, fighting on Luzon, and Lt.Gen. Eichelberger's Eighth Army, part of which was supporting Krueger on Luzon with the remainder in temporary reserve for the invasion of the Southern Philippines. The Southern Philippines covered a vast area of 240,000 square miles consisting of Mindanao, the second largest island in the Philippines, and other major islands lying between Mindanao and Luzon including Bohol, Cebu, Negros, and Panay, which were collectively known as the Visayas. Opposing the Eighth Army was the Japanese 35th Army composed of 30,000 trained combat troops spread over the larger ports and towns in the area with emphasis on Cebu City and Davao City, and Zamboanga Peninsula on Mindanao. Many of the smaller Japanese garrisons would be by-passed. So on 6 February 1945, three days after units of Krueger's Sixth Army entered Manila, MacArthur issued the first order for operations in the southern Philippines, code-named *Victor* with Adm. Kincaid's Seventh Fleet and Brig.Gen. Wurtsmith 13th Fighter Command to be the assault force to support the U.S. 8th Army in its actions in the southern Philippine. The 13FC would met virtually no air opposition and play a major role in ground support.

Luzon

Meanwhile, the Japanese forces in southeastern Luzon threatened to join with the troops defending Manila so on 31 January, the 511th Airborne Infantry Regiment was sent on a reconnaissance-in-force to prevent this by landing at Nasugbu in an operation known as *M-6 Beachhead*. If enemy resistance was light, the 511th Parachute Infantry Regiment was to be dropped ahead of the ground troops to secure Tagaytay Ridge in Batangas Province to prevent the enemy from holding that strong position and would then clear the area west of Leguna de Bay and cut Luzon into two parts. Early on the morning of 3 February 48 C-47s of the 317th Troop Carrier Squadron departed Mindoro with the first contingent of the 511th Paratroopers which jumped over Tagaytay at 0800. The C-47s returned directly to Mindoro and the second wave boarded, but on this drop many of the paratroops landed outside the drop zones over a six mile stretch of highway, but the mistaken widespread drop may have actually contributed to the rapid advance of the Division. On this day the troop carriers were covered by a P-38 escort while A-20s of the 3BG and 417BG and the P-47s of the 58FG attacked the old Japanese airfields at Lipa and Kalingatan. By the end of the day American ground forces had entered the north outskirts of Manila and the 11th Airborne prepared to move forward from the shores of Leguna de Bay to turn northward and approach Manila from the south, cutting highways and rail lines south of the city. The final drop of the 11th paratroopers occurred on the morning of 4 February and three hours after this last drop the 11th Airborne captured the highway junction and had prepared to drive on to Manila.

Air

Effective 1 February 1945, the Far East Air Forces directed that the 5AF would become responsible for Luzon while the 13th Fighter Command, now based on Leyte, was given responsibility for the remainder of the Philippine Islands and the Netherlands East Indies. The 13th Fighter Command would then hand over their command to 13AF Headquarters as soon as 13AF arrived from New Guinea.

Meanwhile, the 5th Fighter Command was to continue to fly air combat and increased ground support missions from the northern Philippines where Yamashita would conduct a tenacious defense. These ground support missions saw the increased use of Napalm. Tanks ranging from 75-to-165-gallon capacity were filled with the mixture of Napalm gel and gasoline and dropped on enemy installations on the island. Although gasoline alone had been used at times against enemy troops in dug-in positions, the Napalm proved to be much more effective, as the flames lasted much longer and penetrated deeply.

**February 1945: Situation: Formosa**

Formosa, called Japan's "natural aircraft carrier," had 24 main airdromes, 18 located on the western coastal plain, plus 20+ satellite fields. The only important strategic targets were the sugar refineries which produced alcohol-based synthetic fuel, hydroelectric plants, railway centers and traffic and airdromes. The Chiefs of Staff had originally planned to invade Formosa after Luzon was secured. Formosa was part of the Japanese Home Islands and was a logical base for future B-29 operations but the successes in the Central Pacific and the Philippines significantly advanced the final plan to invade Japan Home Land, projected for October 1945. Despite the initial Allied setback during the great Japanese summer 1944 offensive the situation stabilized there by the end of the year. Operating from their new bases in the Marianas Islands 20th Air Force B-29s subjected the Japanese mainland to ever increasing attacks in October. The JCS thus concluded an air campaign by the China-based 14AF, along with Halsey's carriers and the FEAF in the northern Philippines, would neutralize remaining Japanese forces in China and prevent their organized retreat to Formosa. Nimitz' capture of Iwo Jima on 19 February placed U.S. air forces only 800 miles from the Japanese mainland and would put an end to the plans to invade Formosa.

By early February the assault phase of the liberation of Luzon was completed but the exhausting job of advancing against dug-in Japanese positions situated throughout Luzon would require seven more months of grueling fighting and the 5FC fighters were mainly confined to bombing and strafing missions. The only missions where they would engage in air-to-air combat would come on the missions to Formosa and French Indochina, escorting the bombers that continued to cut the enemy's supply lines from the south.

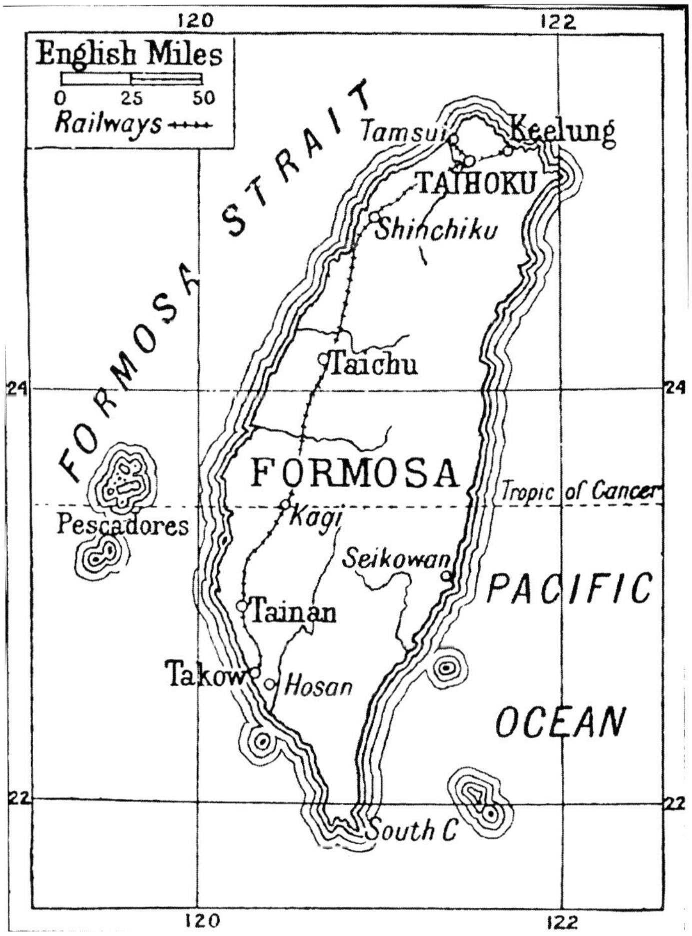


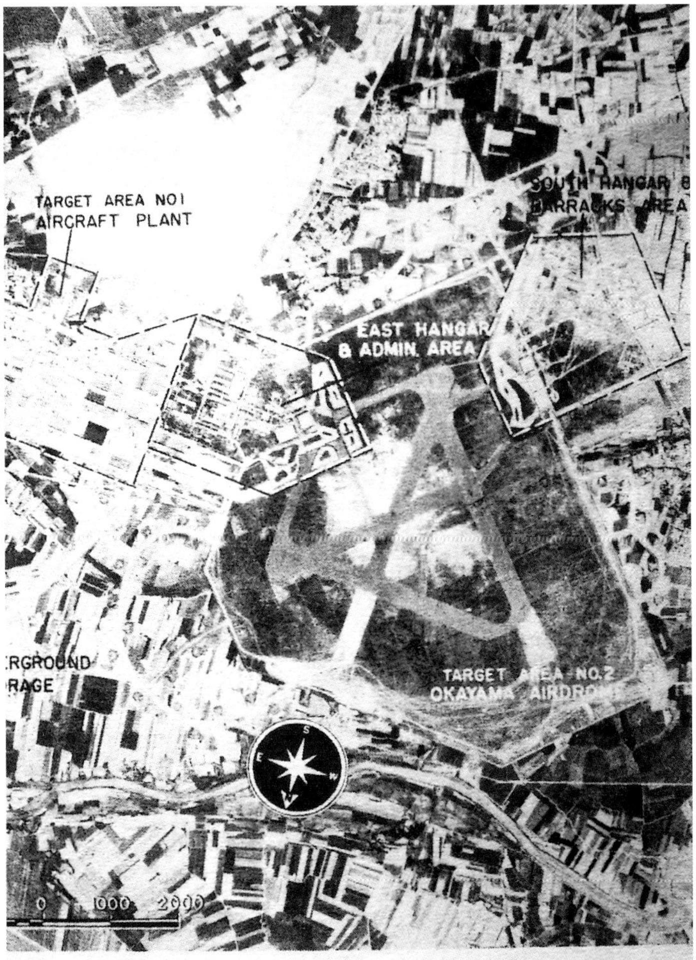


Airfield at Okayama, Formosa.

**Okayama Airfield** was one of 24 well developed airfields on Formosa; called Japan's "natural aircraft carrier." (AAF)

**February 1945: 49FG**

As of 1 February Kenney transferred the tactical 308BW from Tacloban to Hill Airfield while the strategic 310BW moved to the new advanced Lingayen airstrips. The 49th Fighter Group was restored to the 308BW but would continue operating within the strategic 86FW at Hill. Meanwhile, the 49FG continued their ground support missions on the Japanese troops retreating deeper into the Philippine interior or their sweeps on the airdromes on the west coast of Formosa. 49FG operations in Formosa expanded in February, but during 10 weeks of attacking the heavily defended airdromes, the 49ers could claim only a single aerial victory. But also despite numerous strategic missions to Formosa combined with tactical missions over Luzon, the 49ers suffered minimal losses.

**1-4 February 1945: 58FG**

During first days of February the 58FG was to provide the air cover and support for the convoy and the 511th Airborne Infantry Regiment beachhead at Nasugbu. The Group's area of responsibility was to cover the entire southern part of Luzon and continue northward to include the Manila area. On the first two days of the operation each of the three squadrons of the 58FG sent four P-47s each on long fighter sweeps up the Cagayan Valley to Eschague and Aparri. 311FS pilots strafed and destroyed seven barges about three miles north of Massiping on the Cagayan River and a refueling truck on the northern end of Eschague Airdrome. 69th pilots strafed and burned a staff car and a large van loaded with supplies between Cordon and Santiago and also destroyed an unserviceable twin-engine bomber on Eschague Strip. Later, during a late afternoon fighter sweep to Aparri, 310FS pilots strafed two trucks loaded with supplies on the highway about ten miles south of Aparri. 2Lt. Norman Gillmore flew into some trees during his strafing run but managed to return to San Jose to land uninjured but his fighter received major damage. Upon landing 2Lt. Ross Mathis' P-47 suddenly caught fire, probably from a gasoline leak caused by small arms fire during the mission. Mathis stopped the plane and escaped but the Thunderbolt was destroyed. Misfortune continued to plague the 310th that day. Upon take off at 1346, on a two plane sortie to cover transports to Leyte, 1Lt. Richard Colette hit a Marine F4U Corsair that had stalled on the far end of the runway. Colette was able to become airborne and land safely but his P-47 was sent to the service squadron for repair or disposal. On 2 February, A-20s of the 3BG and 417BG and 58FG Thunderbolts wiped out enemy defenses along Route 17 in advance of the invading 11th Airborne units that were heading toward Tagaytay Ridge. For their work, Gen. Eichelberger sent his congratulations stating that the only thing delaying his advance was that "the route was uphill all the way."

**1 February 1945: 3ACG**

Air recon located a large destroyer and a destroyer escort, heading south in the Luzon Strait between Formosa and Luzon. During the afternoon the 3ACG sent 22 Mustangs, from both fighter squadrons, loaded with 500 pound bombs and found the ships just before 1800. The fighters scored two direct hits and five near misses on the larger vessel and two hits on the smaller one. Fires broke out on both ships but the enemy's damage control quickly extinguished the flames despite strafing runs made after the bombing attacks. The Japanese deck AA gunners hit several Mustangs and two fighters crashed on the way home but both pilots were recovered. Post war Japanese records showed the "destroyer" was actually the *Landing Ship T.115*, which eventually sank, and the "destroyer escort" was a submarine chaser which escaped, though damaged.

**1 February 1945: 49FG**

On 1 February 2Lt. John Forgey, who had claimed the last 49er victory over Luzon 10 days before, was hit by ground fire and his damaged aircraft stalled and fatally crashed in his approach to Hill Airfield.

**4-13 February 1945: 8FG**

Enemy aircraft still based to the east and south of Mindoro were worrisome to MacArthur and Kenney even though this threat was minimal. But there were so many operational aircraft and equipment dispersed on the Mindoro airfields that dawn to dusk local air patrols were scheduled. In addition, the 8FG was scheduled to fly routine close air support during February. During January and February the strafing and dive bombing missions of three 8FG squadrons claimed more than 50 Japanese aircraft destroyed on the ground, and destroyed or damaged about 100 trucks, several ships, enemy positions, and several ammunition and fuel dumps

4-8 February

The enemy airfields on Negros were also worrisome and on 4 February the 36FS attacked Japanese aircraft at the Fabrica Airdrome and claimed a bomber and four Oscars. However, AA fire hit 2Lt. Bion Morgan's P-38 and while he was able to bail out; his parachute failed to open and he fell to his death. Another sweep by the entire group on 6 February destroyed a supply depot in northern Luzon and the next day five more enemy aircraft were destroyed on the ground. On the 8th, the 80th strafed Legaspi Airdrome and destroyed a Lily, a Tojo and two Zeros on the ground.

13 February

On 13 February 2Lts. Thurman McWhorter and Robert Hamlin were part of 12 P-38s of the 36FS returning from a routine mission. While on a left hand formation roll, McWhorter was #11 in the string formation and turned to the right by mistake. Hamblin was directly behind him and when McWhorter lost speed to let him catch up there was a collision and large explosion, killing both pilots instantly.

**5 February 1945: Situation**

Even though Manila had been declared an Open City, the Japanese tenaciously defended the city which is said to have suffered the most extensive damage up to that time; second only to Warsaw which the Germans purposely raised virtually to the ground. After Manila was secured in the remnants of Japanese forces retreated into the northern mountains of Luzon; into the Zambales Mountains between Subic Bay and Lingayen Gulf (from which they could harass the Clark Field area); into the mountains in the Leguna de Bay area; and other small units and individuals attempted to escape in the Bataan Peninsula.

On 5 February MacArthur issued a directive that outlined these objectives:

1) To clear Bataan and Manila Bay and open that port to shipping.
2) To clear Leguna de Bay and the Bicol Peninsula in order to open up Batangas Bay to shipping.
3) To clear the northwest coast of Luzon above Lingayen for airfield development.
4) To drive into the mountains and contain or destroy enemy units to the north and east of the central plain and around Leguna de Bay.
5) To prepare for operations in the Cagayan Valley.

**5-8 February 1945: 58FG**

The MacArthur directive would affect the 58th Fighter Group for the next several weeks. Besides its continuing support for the advance on Manila from Batangas Province, the 58th would now also cover a newly planned amphibious assault near Mariveles, at the tip of the Bataan Peninsula, on 15 February and would attack and support an airborne assault on Corregidor on 16 February. Kenney planned that the 5th Air Force would pulverize Corregidor before the paratroops attempted to take the island fortress. Supported by the attacks by the 58FG in the Nichols Field area on 6 and 7 February, the 11th Airborne Infantry captured Nichols Field on 8 February. All three 58FG squadrons continued to maintain two plane patrols along the transport aircraft route over Panay and Negros Islands to cover the C-46s and C-47s supplying the 11th Airborne with fuel and beginning the buildup for the coming attack on Corregidor Island

**7 February 1945: 3ACG: Formosa**

Formosa provided the Japanese with numerous airfields and several harbors with excellent anchorages for naval units and merchant vessels. The two 3ACG fighter squadrons flew fighter sweeps and anti-shipping strikes and escorted bombers. The large island was heavily defended by AA and four Air Commando pilots would be lost to the flak and four more would be shot down but recovered.

On 7 February the Air Commandos flew their first mission to Formosa when the 3ACG's two fighter squadrons escorted B-25s on a shipping strike off the Island's

**Capt. Louis Curdes** shot down a Dinah for his only Pacific victory after scoring eight victories in the MTO with the 82FG. (AAF)

southwest coast. No enemy aircraft were sent up to intercept and the Mustangs searched for targets of opportunity. The Mitchells and fighters combined to sink a small submarine in Takao Harbor and then damaged several merchant vessels. The Takao Airfield was strafed where 15 new Frank fighters were seen and several aircraft were claimed damaged and a number of vehicles were destroyed. As 2Lts. Clifford Huntington and Marvin Menter made their runs on the airfield, AA fire hit their Mustangs. Huntington's Mustang suffered a shell hit that burst directly under his seat, tearing open a large hole and disabling his landing gear. Menter's fighter showed only minor damage to one wing but on the way back to the rendezvous point, he radioed Huntington that his oil pressure was dropping and that he was going to bail out about 17 miles offshore. Menter jumped and was seen climbing into his life raft in very choppy water. A Catalina could not reach him before dark and a search the next morning did not find any trace of the downed pilot. 1Lt. Louis Curdes, of the 4FS spotted a twin-engine Dinah at about his own altitude about 30 miles from Formosa. As soon as Curdes approached, the enemy pilot saw him and suddenly dove for the deck at full throttle. It took Curdes several minutes to chase down the speedy Dinah before he closed to open fire and sent the bomber down in flames for his only Pacific victory after scoring eight flying P-38s with the 82FG over the MTO.

**8 February 1945: 3ACG/3FS and 4FS**

Fighters from both 3ACG Squadrons were to escort B-25s on a shipping strike to Formosa but poor weather forced the cancellation of the mission and all aircraft returned to Luzon to attack secondary targets. The 12 P-51s of the 4FS strafed enemy installations on the Philippine island of Fuga on their way home. Meanwhile, some Mustangs of the 3FS encountered a Sally also heading for Luzon. A flight led by 1Lt. Glenn Lairmore had been late in taking off and never joined the rest of the Squadron and when he received the weather recall Lairmore led his flight back toward Mangaldan. Soon an enemy bomber was sighted ahead making a slow climb toward an overcast layer at about 900 feet. After dropping their wing tanks, Lairmore and his Wingman slowly overtook the Sally and closed on each side of the bomber and Lairmore made a 20 degree deflection shot from 200 yards shattering the cockpit and setting an engine on fire. The bomber burst into flames, nosed over, and went into the sea for his only victory although he was be credited with two Zero probables on 8 April.

**1Lt. Glenn Lairmore** shot a Sally for his only victory, but would be credited with two probables in April. (AAF)

**8 February 1945: 475FG**

In early February a few 475FG contingents moved to Mindoro and billeted with the 8th Fighter Group at Elmore Field which would be one of the worst billets used by the Group. It was located between San Jose and Bugsanga on the southwest end of the island, in the middle of a sun-baked, treeless, brown plain whose dust covered everything.

The 475FG flew missions to search for enemy convoys, sweep the Cagayan Valley where the Japanese were slowly retreating in the face of overwhelming American pressure, and dive bombing those enemy positions that withdrew too slowly. MacArthur had prevented the Japanese from repeating of his defense of the Bataan Peninsula by making a landing there, thus mandating the Japanese to make a secondary retreat toward Manila.

On 8 February, Capt. Perry Dahl led four weathered P-38s, each carrying a 500 pound bomb and a belly tank, on a dive bombing mission to Meriveles on the Bataan Peninsula. After they successfully bombed their initial target at 1000, Dahl led his flight down to strafe Mariveles barracks and a jetty at Cochinos Point. On the same day nine group pilots flew back to Hawaii to pick up brand new P-38s while other new fighters were being flown up from Biak to bring the 475FG nearly up to full operational strength.

**10 February 1945: 3ACG/3FS and 4FS**

During the morning 1Lt. Louis Curdes led a flight on a search mission for missing pilots along Formosa's west coast where they encountered a lone Dinah. The enemy pilot made little effort to evade and 2Lt. Robert Scalley fired a 20 degree deflection shot that set the bomber's starboard engine on fire; while his second pass set the other engine aflame, and the Dinah crashed into the water for his only victory. Curdes continued the search for the missing fliers, and had no success and he decided to split his flight to cover a wider area. Curdes and his Wingman flew off one way, while Scalley and Wingman 2Lt. Robert LaCroix explored Bataan Island, one of a string of smaller islands between Luzon and Formosa. As they neared Bataan another Dinah was seen and LaCroix fired a few bursts that sent it down also for his only victory. The two saw several aircraft, including some apparently new Tonys, parked on Bataan's airstrip, and Scalley and LaCroix went down to strafe them. Three of the Tonys were claimed destroyed but accurate AA fire hit LaCroix's fighter sending hot coolant and smoke into his cockpit. In his effort to get out of the cockpit LaCroix had forgotten to roll in enough trim, so when he rolled over to drop out of his fighter, he became wedged between the seat back's armor plate and the rear of his cockpit. Just as the ocean was coming up fast, he made a desperate shove on his control stick and popped out and away from the doomed fighter. He splashed into the water and scrambled out of his chute and inflated his life raft. After all this frenzy LaCroix found that there was a bullet hole in his ankle and the Japanese on Bataan were firing at him. Scalley had called for help and Curdes and his Wingman proceeded to strafe the Japanese guns while Scalley watched over LaCroix. As the Mustangs were finishing their strafing passes, a C-47 suddenly appeared en route to Clark Field from Leyte. The C-47s had been flying in clear weather until reaching the south end of Manila Bay when clouds then began building and the transport pilots were soon flying on instruments and had become lost shortly before noon. Turning east, they slowly descended until they spotted some small islands with an airstrip on one of the islands. Not realizing that the Japanese held the island the transport pilots decided to land before running out of gas and lowered their landing gear in preparation to land. Curdes noticed the C-47 approaching the airfield and tried to contact it but received no reply. Curdes was unsure that the C-47 was American as the Japanese had the Tabby which was a licensed DC-3. Curdes fired a warning shot across the transport's nose and the American pilot made a sharp port turn but then headed back toward the island again. Curdes next made a head on firing pass, striking the C-47's right engine while a second pass from the rear knocked out the transport's other engine. The C-47 pilot made an amazingly smooth ditching about 300 yards offshore, and all 12 occupants on board, including two nurses, scrambled into three rafts. As soon as they got into the rafts, the Americans were fired on by the Japanese but the enemy's gunfire was inaccurate and the crew stayed well away from the island throughout the remainder of the day. Curdes circled the survivors for about an hour before he and the other Air Commandos headed back to Mangaldan. Air-Sea Rescue was notified of the C-47's ditching but because of approaching nightfall; it was not until the next day before they could arrive.

**Capt. Louis Curdes** poses with his unusual scoreboard. (AFAA)

**2Lt. Robert Scalley** tallied his only victory of the war when he shot down a Dinah. (AAF)

**1Lt. Robert LaCroix** also shot down a Dinah for his only victory. (AAF)

In the meantime, the 39TCS crew and passengers put up sails on the rafts and, by paddling and wind power, were able to get six miles away from Bataan. Rough seas churned up in the morning and the survivors decided the water near the island would be calmer. A short time later they pulled LaCroix from the water and he explained what had happened. Just a few minutes later a Catalina landed and recovered everyone. A short investigation followed, and Curdes was absolved of any blame. Actually, his quick thinking and accurate shooting prevented a disaster, and he was rewarded with a Distinguished Flying Cross. His Mustang soon was painted with a new American flag victory symbol to go with the German, Italian, and Japanese victory flags. Curdes had a varied career during WWII as he was sent to the MTO and flew with the 82FG; first in North Africa. He scored his first victories by downing three Me-109s on 29 April 1943 and then became an ace with a double victory on 19 May. On 24 June he shot down an Italian Mc202 and finished his MTO tour by shooting down two Me-109s on 27 August. Curdes is one of a few Allied pilots to score victories over all three Axis Powers. Curdes remained in the post war Air Force and retired as a Lt. Colonel in 1963.

**10 February 1945: 35FG/39FS**

On 10 February 1Lt. Leroy Grosshuesch took off with eight P-47s on a sweep on Formosa. Soon three Thunderbolts had to turn back with mechanical problems which forced Grosshuesch to consolidate the mission into a five plane flight, stacking up the last three fighters for better protection. They arrived over the target at 1430 at 8,000 feet and after patrolling for a half hour a plane was seen taking off from Kobi Airdrome but as the flight dove they lost it. While they dove about 25 training biplanes were called in and each Thunderbolt pilot chose a target and began their attack passes in what would become a swirling, but unequal, dogfight. Grosshuesch dove and fired quickly getting a few hits but had too much speed and had pull up over it. Another biplane then flew in front of him and Grosshuesch fired and hit the engine and cockpit and the trainer plunged into the ground. Grosshuesch attacked another trainer and observed some hits in the cockpit but it flew past without result. Another trainer was heading toward the strip and Grosshuesch got on its tail and fired a short burst and the fragile trainer nosed over and crashed about 12 miles from a safe landing. 2Lt. Winfield Langhorst made several initial passes on the trainers that were ineffective and when another flight of trainers was spotted at 3 o'clock he saw a lone Zero flying in the opposite divrection and parallel at 4 o'clock. Langhorst maneuvered until he got on its tail and fired three short bursts while closing getting hits on the tail assembly, wings, and fuselage. Langhorst continued to follow and saw the enemy pilot trying to bail out but the Zero nosed down and crashed for Langhorst's first of two career victories. 1Lt. Edgar Beam chose his trainer which was flying on the deck and fired a half second burst at 250 yards at 30 degrees. Hits were seen on the engine and cockpit and it dove directly into the ground from its low altitude. Next Beam made a pass on two other trainers and fired on both from 90 degrees and although hits were seen on both, they kept on flying and one landed on the strip and the other on an open area a mile north of the field and Beam was credited with a damaged for each. Beam then saw another trainer about 15 miles north of the airdrome and closed on it at 90 degrees and fired a short burst. The trainer exploded and two chutes fell out of the wreckage, but when 2Lt. Robert Rohrs passed by he saw that there were no pilots in them. Beam did all his scoring in one mission, finishing the war with two victories and two damaged. Rohrs fired a short burst on trainer and some hits around its cockpit and pulled up and saw another trainer approaching the airdrome. He got on its tail and fired a three second burst and hit its cockpit and it crashed and burned. 2Lt. Charles Covey was closing so fast on the slow trainer that he only had time to fire a quick burst at 60 degrees deflection and didn't see any hits at that high speed. Covey turned to starboard and fired as it

**1Lt. Leroy Grosshuesch** celebrates becoming an ace with six victories when he shot down three Willow biplane trainers. (AFAA)

Yokosuka **K5Y Willow** trainer.

turned 90 degrees but again he was closing so quickly that he had time for a half second burst which was enough to start the trainer on fire and crash. Covey followed Grosshuesch and saw a trainer about a mile north of the airdrome and closed from dead astern at 150 yards. The one second burst hit the cockpit and wing root and it was seen to crash about a mile and a half from the field. Covey turned west and saw a trainer and a small plane and closed on the trainer and fired a short burst from 200 yards and hit its cockpit and engine but did not see it crash and claimed a probable.

Seven trainers, identified as JNAF Kugisho K5Y Willows were shot down. One was listed as a probable and two were damaged. Grosshuesch reformed the flight and headed for Taichu Airdrome looking for more enemy aircraft. They arrived at 1540 at 8,000 feet and Lt. Covey called out two bandits approximately 10 miles northwest from the field. The bandits were a Zero and Dinah. Covey and Langhorst went after the Zero and Beam and Grosshuesch covered Lt. Rohrs who was out of ammunition and came along for protection. Covey went after the Zero that saw him and turned to run but Covey closed and opened fired from dead astern and got hits on its engine and then fired at 150 yards getting hits on the engine and cockpit. The Zero went out of control and then into a gentle glide and crashed and exploded near a railroad track close to the airdrome. After Covey shot down the Zero, he and Langhorst went after the Dinah. Covey fired first and got hits on the fuselage and the left engine started to smoke but he ran out of ammunition and broke away. Langhorst was next and he fired from dead astern and observed hits on the fuselage and port engine and he broke away. Beam got into firing range and got a few more hits from dead astern on the engine and a fire and heavy smoke poured started before he broke away. The Dinah went into a shallow dive toward the deck and the flames died out. Grosshuesch then made a pass and fired two good bursts at 20 degrees at 300 yards and observed hits. He then closed between 100 to 50 yards and fired causing the Dinah to finally nose down and explode. The three victories made Grosshuesch an ace with six victories. Beam's three victories and Covey's two (and a probable) and Rohr's one were their only claims during the war.

Grosshuesch reformed the flight again and headed for Kato Airdrome where Rohrs called in three Zeros on the deck and as the flight turned after them they encountered at least 17 Zeros and a Tony. Outnumbered, low on fuel and ammunition Grosshuesch ordered the flight to return to base. Surprisingly, only four of the Zeros chased after the P-47s which went into a high speed climb to escape.

**9-10 February 1945: 58FG**

On 9 February the rear echelon of the 58FG that had remained at Leyte since late November arrived on Mindoro and the Group was finally together for the first time in nearly seven months (a rear echelon had remained at Saidor until the move to the Philippines). The move meant that the work schedule would be less and Group personnel would have more free time.

The next day 69FS 2Lt. James Bilodeau, who had been missing after he bailed out over Silay Airdrome on Negros on 14 January, returned to the Squadron. After he had escaped from his burning plane near the enemy airdrome he limped on a sprained knee for cover into a nearby ravine where a Filipino boy hid him and ran away; saying he would be back. Bilodeau's hiding place was approached by Japanese with dogs but they left before nightfall. The Filipino boy returned and led him to a village about ten miles west of Silay. The difficult trip further injured his knee but after a night's rest he walked 15 miles to Guerrilla headquarters in the mountains. For the next 16 days he was led over 100 miles before reaching the southwest coast in friendly territory. A rescue aircraft was to meet at Linaon, a small village 30 miles down the coast. After traveling by boat and horse, he arrived at Linaon two days later and then waited six more days before a PBY Catalina flying boat arrived to fly him out.

**11 February 1945: 348FG/340FS**

On 11 February the 340FS was patrolling off the Bataan Peninsula and sighted four Japanese barges heading for Manila and destroyed them in a strafing attack. 1Lt. David Standiford was forced to ditch during the attack and when he got into his life raft he found that he was perilously close to the barge survivors he strafed. Six Japanese began to swim toward Standiford but were strafed and killed by his flight. While waiting for rescue Standiford sighted another dozen barges. After his Catalina rescue, he led another P-47 flight to attack these barges which were about to deliver supplies and reinforcements to Bataan. Another 30 barges on their way to Bataan were destroyed during the day.

**13 February 1945: 35FG/39FS**

On the 13th 11 P-47s in three flights were sent on a mid afternoon B-25 escort to northern Formosa under Capt. William Rogers who led White Flight. After the Mitchells left the P-47 conducted a fighter sweep at 7,000 feet and at 1345 sighted an enemy formation consisting of one twin engine Sally bomber that appeared to be leading nine Franks. The enemy formation was flying among two separate solid overcast areas and continued on course at 7,000 feet. Rogers ordered that the tanks to be released and dove into the attack.

Rogers, followed by his Wingman, 2Lt. Samuel Teese, dove on the last Frank on the left but it pulled up sharply and Rogers could not follow and turned to the right to attack another. He closed to 200 yards and started firing continuously at a slight deflection until at 20 yards the enemy fighter exploded and disintegrated, covering the left side of Roger's fighter with oil. Another apparently unaware Frank passed directly in front of Rogers and flew into a stream of .50s that sent it trailing smoke into the overcast where Rogers lost sight of it for a probable claim. Rogers then saw another lone Frank to the starboard and got on its tail and opened fire to 75 yards. Hits were seen on the tail and wings and a fire broke out in its wing roots and it landing gear dropped. The Frank was seen to crash into the mountains for his only two victories and probable. Teese then intercepted a Frank while flying parallel to Rogers and fired a 40 degree shot at close range but the enemy pilot turned inside Teese. Rogers tried a snap 90 degree deflection as the Frank passed in front of him but found that he was out of ammunition. The Frank continued down trailing smoke and just before it entered the overcast its pilot bailed out for Teese's only victory.

**Capt. William Rogers** shot down two Franks and claimed a probable for his only two victories. (AAF)

Meanwhile, 1Lt. Ernest Johnson and his Wingman Lt. Aycock made a quick climb after the first Frank that Rogers could not follow to prevent it from diving on the other P-47s. Johnson opened fire at 300 yards and got hit on the wing, from tip to root. The Frank went into a turn and Aycock fired a short burst as the enemy pilot leveled out. Johnson opened fire for the second time from 200 yards with hits on the cockpit and engine. Large pieces flew off and it began to stream smoke. Johnson then fired from 150 yards getting more hits in the engine and port wing root and the Frank burst into flames and headed for a cloud. Johnson followed it into the cloud and when it emerged was burning from engine to tail and headed for a mountain for his second and last victory.

1Lt. Marcus Trout was leading Blue Flight was flying at 7,500 feet, slightly above and to the right of the enemy formation which was approaching head on. Trout led his flight down and got on the tail of a Frank and fired a four second volley at 300 yards from dead astern and got hits on the cockpit and wing roots. The enemy pilot Split-S'd to the right but burst into flames in the right wing root and spun and then exploded. Trout then pulled up slightly to port and opened fire on another Frank at 400 yards and got hits on the wing and fuselage but had to break off when his engine began to cut out and was credited with a damaged claim to go with second and last victory.

1Lt. Kenneth Dunn was leading Green Flight and led his flight inside Roger's flight on the initial attack. Dunn attacked the third Frank in the initial enemy formation but saw that Rogers was attacking the same fighter. Dunn pulled up over Rogers and Teese and closed on the Frank on the Sally's wing and opened fire at 300 yards with a one second burst which was low. Dunn closed to 200 yards and opened fire again getting hits on the tail and starting a fire. Dunn fired again at 50 yards and hit the wing root and the pilot bailed out for his second victory. When the 39th broke off combat only the lead Sally and one Frank escaped into the overcast.

Assessment of the Frank

Capt. William Rogers of the 39FS/35FG stated in his ICR of 13 February: "The whole action occurred along a straight course with apparently inexperienced enemy pilots taking either ineffectual evasive action or none at all. They either didn't know we were there or mistook us for friendly planes since I every case they continued a straight course until each one was picked off one by one. They were reluctant to go down into the clouds below because of the mountain crests rising up to the top of the overcast. The performance of these new type fighters (Franks) seemed excellent in the cases where it was used. (Its) speed…was equal at least to the P-47s. Construction must be more rugged than the older type Japanese fighters because al planes destroyed and probably destroyed took a great deal more punishment before burning or blowing up."

JAAF Nakajima **Ki-84 Frank** fighter/fighter bomber. (AFHRC)

**13 February 1945: 475FG/432FS/431FS**

By mid-February the 475th had finally received enough P-38s to from a formation of 16 fighters to escort B-24s and B-25s over a Japanese convoy along the South China Sea Coast. Col. MacDonald once again led the 475FG escort mission and headed a five plane flight from the 432FS from Elmore Field at 0730. The bombing of the convoy was fruitless because the heavy Liberator bombers had to salvo their bomb loads through a heavy undercast while the low-flying Mitchells were warded off by the intense AA fire from the enemy warships in the convoy and headed back to base at 1145. Ten minutes later a single enemy Topsy transport plane was sighted headed for Hong Kong at 10,000 feet. MacDonald closed on this easy undefended target and fired several bursts from 40 to 0 degrees deflection to dead astern. His volley hit the starboard engine and knocking off large pieces and the Topsy went into a spin, burning furiously, and crashed into the water. MacDonald reported that a few passengers were seen trying to escape the inferno by jumping out without parachutes. The easy victory was MacDonald's 27th and last which made him the third highest 5FC scorer. MacDonald returned to the States in May and served in a number of Command and Staff assignments and retired from the Air Force as a Colonel in 1961.

431FS

Lt. Arthur Schmidt was listed as MIA on this mission.

**14-16 February 1945: 58FG: Bataan and Corregidor**

To begin the softening-up process on Bataan and Corregidor, all three 58FG squadrons were sent to dive bomb those locations over the next three days. The 58FG flew a large number of uneventful sorties patrolling, bombing, and strafing over a wide area extending from Legaspi on the southeast to Manila and Subic Bay on the north.

Large air attacks were conducted on Corregidor and the smaller adjacent Caballo Island on 14 and 15 February in anticipation of the paratroop drop scheduled for 16 February. On the 14th the 58FG dropped 73 tons of bombs on Corregidor which was the greatest tonnage the Group had ever carried in one day. The 311FS dropped 29.75 tons which was the greatest tonnage ever dropped on a target by 58th squadron in a day. The 311th had sent out 16 Thunderbolts carrying two 1,000 pound bombs under the wings and a 500 pound bomb under the fuselage. Their target was the east tunnel entrance and 1Lt. Kenneth Crepeau, placed at least one of his 1,000 bombs directly into the tunnel entrance and exploded an ammo dump inside. The next day the 58FG directed their efforts against the small fortified island of Caballo and the caves on Corregidor. On 16 February, the 5AF saturated the Corregidor defenses with 3,000 tons of bombs per square mile in advance of the paratroop attack at 0830 marking the heaviest air attack in the history of the SWPA. The drop was a success with the AA being suppressed and no troop carriers were lost and of a total of 2,022 men dropped, 12 paratroopers had been killed and 267 wounded or injured. The resistance on Corregidor continued until 27 February as American intelligence had estimated that Corregidor was defended only by about 850 enemy troops but actually there were about 6,000, all of whom were killed except for 19 prisoners. Total American losses for the entire operation were 209 killed, 725 wounded, and 19 missing. By 1 March 1945 Manila Bay was opened and the first shipping entered the famous harbor.

**16-28 February 1945: 5FC**

During the last half of February 5FC missions were mainly routine with a few exceptions as the main effort of the Far East Air Forces was to support ground operations for Gen. Krueger's Sixth Army. The 5AF averaged over 200 sorties per day and the 5FC sent an average of over 100 missions per day to support Gen. Eichelbeger's Campaign in southeastern Luzon.

**Col. Charles MacDonald** had an easy victory when he shot down a Topsy transport for his 27th and last victory. (AAF)

**17 February 1945: 49FG/7FS**

On 17 February 1Lt. Leo Fairbanks of the 7FS was half way back to base from a raid on Formosa when his Lightning lost power and crashed near Itbayat Island and he was KIA.

**19 February 1945: 49FG/9FS**

On 19 February a flight of 9FS Lightnings was investigating the alleged basing of Japanese aircraft on Silay Airdrome on Negros Island when AA fired fatal hits on the fighters of 2Lts. John Kinsman and Harold Thorson.

**19 February 1945: 547NFS**

Pilot 1Lt. Arthur Bourque and R/O 2Lt. Bonnie Rucks took off from Lingayen at 1855 to patrol the Rosario area of central Luzon and an hour and a half later were vectored to a bogey flying 50-60 miles south. After five minutes GCI lost the vector but put Bourque on another which was a Betty. Bourque closed to the starboard but encountered return fire from the tail gunner and fell astern for a shot. He fired two or three bursts without result but on the fourth burst exploded the left fuel tank and the enemy fell in flames and blew up upon hitting the ground.

**1Lt. Arthur Bourque** shot down two Bettys for his only victories. (AAF)

After this victory Bourque was vectored to a bogey at 30 degrees by one GCI and by another GCI to one at 20 degrees. At 2135 he made a visual on another Betty at 11,000 feet near Beleti Pass. He fired three or four bursts at the enemy which took violent evasive action to escape. He fired two more bursts and saw hits that caused the enemy's left engine caught fire and the bomber rolled over into the overcast for Bourque's second victory of the day and his last of the war.

**Mid-February 1945: 418NFS**

Capt. William Sellers of the 547NFS transferred to the 418th as CO when Squadron CO, Maj. Carroll Smith, left on furlough to the US.

**18-20 February 1945: 58FG Command Changes**

On 18 February, Maj. Joseph Klemovich, who had moved to a desk job with the 86th Fighter Wing at Saidor, rejoined the 58th and was appointed CO of the 311FS. Klemovich had led the 311th on the first combat mission by the 58FG at Dobodura on 2 February 1944; then commanded the 310FS for a short time; and finally served as Group Operations Officer for more than a year before going to the 86FW. Maj. Harry Odren, the long time Commander of the 311FS, was promoted to Group Operations Officer, replacing Maj. Edward Roddy, who became Deputy Group Commander. Maj. Roddy replaced Lt.Col. Jasper Durham, who was medically air evacuated back to the U.S. suffering with a "tropical fever."

Between 18 and 20 February the 58FG sent eight pilots to Sydney, Australia, on leave. These were to be the last R&R leaves to that popular city as the war had long since left Australia behind. There was an acute shortage of aircraft in the Far East available to make the 8,000 mile round trip to Sydney. As a result the pilots there on leave were stranded in Sydney for long periods of time. In 1944 this situation would have been welcomed but now it was not, because all administrative processes, including finance, had been transferred north. Thus the pilots on these last leaves were cut off without pay or transportation and were finally dependant on the American Red Cross for support before they could find transportation back to the Philippines.

**Maj. Joseph Klemovich** rejoined the 58FG as the CO of the 311FS. (AAF)

**18-25 February 1945: 3ACG/3FS and 4FS**

While the Air Commandos regularly visited Formosa they also continued to lend steady ground support for the infantry at Baguio, Antipolo, Balete Pass, and the Villa Verde Trail. Although ground support in the Philippines was greatly appreciated by the infantry it was not a favorite of the pilots as the results of their efforts were seldom seen through the dense growth. Results from missions to Formosa were more definite as buildings, shipping, locomotives, vehicles, and aircraft could be seen and they were on fire and destroyed by explosions. However, the flak encountered over Formosa was far more lethal than that met over Luzon.

On 18 February six 3ACG Mustangs swept over rail yards on Formosa's east coast and destroyed nine locomotives, a railway station, a water tower, a railway crane, and a streetcar while another 11 locomotives, many boxcars, and several warehouses were damaged.

On 22 February, 16 Mustangs of the 4FS bombed and strafed the Philippine village of Angin. Ground fire was heavy and accurate and as one pilot made his low level strafing run, his aircraft was hit and smashed into the ground, killing him instantly.

On 25 February 16 P-51s of the 3FS swept Formosa's east coast and strafed a radar station and several gun emplacements at Garan Bi on the island's southern end. Enemy AA gunners sent up an intense and accurate barrage that shot down two fighters and damaged three others. F/O Sylvester Everhart flew his seriously damaged aircraft only about one half mile offshore before he bailed out. The circling Squadron pilots saw him struggle to get loose from his parachute shrouds and then saw that his raft did not inflate and they finally lost him from sight in the rough seas. When the Air-Sea Rescue Catalina landed to pick him up, they only found a glove and a piece of life raft. Meanwhile, 1Lt. Scott Alexander managed to get his damaged fighter out 30 miles to sea before bailed out. As he exited, first, his foot caught under his seat and he frantically jerked it loose and then, as he fell free, his leg struck the horizontal stabilizer, breaking it. Alexander hit the water in intense pain and inflated his Mae West but his life raft also failed to inflate. However, the ASR Catalina soon picked Alexander up. Upon their return to Mangaldan, one of the three damaged 3FS Mustangs crashed on landing but the pilot escaped injury. The day was to be one of the worst in 3ACG history.

**21-28 February 1945: 348FG/340FS/341FS**

During January and February the 348th Fighter Group traded its Thunderbolts for longer range Mustangs which were ideal on the missions to escort B-25s on shipping sweeps to Formosa and southern China. Some of these missions were 1,400 to 1,600 miles long and kept the pilots in the cramped cockpits of their P-51s for as long as eight hours. The 341FS began flying P-51 operations on 6 January the 340FS flew its first on 10 February.

The main problem the pilots encountered on these missions during February was the weather. During the month the 341FS flew eight and he 340FS three of these long range missions but on four of these missions the pilots were unable to reach the target due to poor weather and of nine anti-shipping missions scheduled for the 348FG, four were aborted due to weather fronts that were encountered en route.

On 21 and 22 February the 340FS received 26 more P-51s and more long range missions were now possible. On the 23rd, 12 340FS Mustangs escorted B-25s along the Indo China coast on an eight hour shipping strike. This mission was followed on the 25th by a similar long range mission to Indo China and to the same area on 26 February. The next day another dozen 340th Mustangs escorted B-25s to Hong Kong where three Ki-84 Franks were sighted and pursued but lost in a heavy overcast. On 28 February the 340FS returned to ground attack missions with two Napalm strikes on the Fort Stotsenburg area. These missions had been successful and the pilots of the 340FS felt a growing confidence in their new P-51 Mustangs.

During February the Group flew about equal numbers of bombing/strafing (147) and local patrols (132) and half that number of convoy cover (69) with 18 PBY and B-25 escorts. The primary objective of the Group's operations was in west central Luzon to prevent the Japanese from retreating into the Bataan Peninsula where they could make a prolonged last stand much as MacArthur did in 1942. The infantry was to first cut across the neck of Bataan from Subic Bay along the Olongapo-Dinalupihan Road. Next the infantry was to divide Bataan in two at the center by securing the Bagac-Pilar Road and then occupy the Bataan's east coast road between Hermosa and Pilar. The final phase of the plan was to be a drive from Pilar and Mariveles, where a landing was to be made on the 15th, and then meet near Cabcaban.

**Mid-Frebruary: 348FG**

In this plan the 348FG was to play a major part in destroying enemy resistance along the road network around Bataan by flying missions against enemy troop concentrations, supply and ammo dumps, road junctions, artillery positions and barge hideouts. The Group was so successful in interdicting the road net that the Japanese resorted to using barges to escape from Manila to the east coast by barge. During eight missions flown by the 340FS from 11-14 February the Squadron sunk 31 30 foot barges, 21 49 foot barges, 12 motor launches while the other three squadrons claimed seven more launches. Over 2,000 Japanese troops were killed. The Group also supported the Corregidor landing on the 16th when they flew 34 missions against enemy troops and installations near Botolan, killing an estimated 700 enemy troops. Wing tank Napalm bombs were used by the Group during the month during ground support missions on west central Luzon, Bataan Peninsula, and Corregidor.

During the month seven aircraft were lost and six sustained major damage in operational accidents with the 342FS losing 1Lt. William Anahu and 2Lt. Earl Louks killed and 1Lt. Andrew Mix (341FS) and 2Lt. Herbert Peterson (340FS) missing. No pilots were lost on combat.

**22 February 1945: 475FG/433FS**

A runaway C-47 transport crashed into the 433rd parking area and killed three Crew Chiefs.

**22 February 1945: 58FG**

2Lt. Elroy Marion, a rookie pilot assigned to the 311FS earlier in the month, was scheduled for a local training flight on the morning of 22 February. As he took off from Elmore Strip, his propeller ran out of control and he managed to make a 180 degree turn and then attempted to make a wheels down landing headed east on the runway. In turning back, he was unable to line up with the runway and crashed head on into a gasoline truck and trailer opposite the Elmore Field control tower. Upon hitting the fuel truck his Thunderbolt exploded and crashed into two P-38s parked nearby and a third P-38 also caught fire and was destroyed. Five enlisted men of the 433FS were working on the P-38s when the crash occurred and three were killed and two were injured.

**23 February 1945: 58FG/69FS/311FS**

On 23 February the 69th and the 311th Squadrons flew a special 550 mile, six hour round trip, bombing mission that 58FG HQ later described as the "best bomb mission of the month." Sixteen fighters, eight from each squadron, were dispatched on a very long range mission to northern Borneo. This was to be the longest mission since the so-called "fanny busters" flown from Noemfoor Island to the East Indies in October 1944. The mission departed at 0730 for the Jesselton area of northwestern Borneo. On the way they encountered and penetrated a broken line of clouds 15 miles wide and extending from 5,000 to 7,000 feet high, extending from Balabac Strait northeast over the Sulu Sea to the Cuyo Islands. Once in clear weather again, they passed east of Palawan, which was covered with broken clouds. A 311th pilot developed mechanical problems and was accompanied by another fighter back to Mindoro. The Group arrived off Borneo at 1000 and found the target area clear, with 6/10 cloud cover. The runway at Jesselton appeared to be unserviceable, with bomb craters holing it from end to end and no signs of attempted repair. A barracks area midway between the Airdrome and the buildings and installations in the town looked to be undamaged with many buildings appearing to be new. The barracks area appeared to be the most worthwhile target and several bombs fell in the barracks area and on the radio station close by. Another bomb hit in the center of a large building in town, causing an explosion and damaging adjoining buildings. A boat house south of town and 300 feet railroad track were also destroyed.

**25 February 1945: 475FG/431FS**

The 431FS would score some of its last aerial victories of the war over the coast of French Indo China (now Vietnam) during one of the PB4Y Privateer long range "Snooper" missions and strafing missions in that area. The 431st sent up 12 Lightnings under Capt; John Tilley at 0725 from Elmore Field and five minutes later rendezvoused with a pathfinder B-25 over the beach south of Elmore. The P-38s never made contact with the PB4Y they were supposed to cover but strafed Japanese shipping in Cam Rahn Bay and destroyed one ore lugger and damaged three other ships. They also came upon a seaplane base with several Zero Rufe floatplanes anchored on the water. The flight went down and destroyed four of the Rufes and damaged another. Two Rufes arrived over their base and foolishly decided to attack the Lightnings. White Flight under, 1Lt. James Barnes was flying cover at 2,000 feet and saw the Rufes coming from 3 o'clock low. Barnes made an overhead pass on one but missed the slow flying floatplane. Barnes turned on its tail but Second Element Leader, 1Lt.Thomas Martin, slid outside the Rufe's turn. The enemy pilot turned his agile Rufe inside Martin and made a head on pass. Martin dropped his dive flaps and hit the Rufe with his cannon but the Japanese pilot turned to ram Martin who had to climb quickly to avoid the brave enemy pilot. The "Nip rolled over and made a beautiful splash in the Bay" for Martin's second victory. Barnes saw another Rufe on the tail of Red Flight #4 and turned and fired on the Rufe from astern and hit its port wing. The enemy pilot skidded to escape but Barnes continued his pursuit and its engine started on fire and its pilot bailed out for his last of two victories. After the air battle the Flight strafed six anchored Rufes and destroyed three.

**25 February 1945: 35FG/39FS**

Capt. Leroy Grosshuesch was leading a flight of four P-47s on a late evening sweep over Formosa and on their arrival they found that the east coast was closed in and climbed over the mountains to the west coast. At 1830 they saw two Dinahs in the Chikunan area flying at 7,000 feet, 500 feet above the P-47s. As soon as the P-47s dropped their wing tanks the Dinahs scattered and went into evasive action. Grosshuesch went after the lead Dinah while his element leader, 1Lt. Idon Hodge, pursued the other fast enemy bomber. Grosshuesch fired two bursts from 300 yards at 30 degree deflection but the apparently veteran Japanese pilot evaded both. Grosshuesch

**1Lt. James Barnes** shot down a Rufe floatplane for his second and last victory. (AAF)

**1Lt. Leroy Grosshuesch** shot down his third career Dinah for his seventh victory. (AAF)

closed to 150 yards where it would be more difficult for the enemy pilot to evade. He fired a two second burst at 10 degree deflection that hit the fuselage and right wing. The enemy pilot flew through the overcast with his right engine on fire and Grosshuesch followed the smoke and flames. When the Dinah broke into a clearing in the sky Grosshuesch fired a quick half second burst from dead astern at 100 yards and started a fire in the left engine. A crewman attempted to jump from the burning Dinah but his chute did not open. The Dinah then nosed over and dove 4,000 feet directly into the ground with a huge explosion. The return flight was made at night and despite poor weather with cloud and rain at 1,000 feet and a 20-25 mph crosswind, successful landings were made at 2130.

**25 February 1945: 35FG/40FS**

The 40FS would score its only victories in February during a late afternoon four plane sweep to Formosa consisting Flight Leader, Capt. Daniel Cherry and his Wingman, 2Lt. Louis Bush and Second Element Leader, Capt. Darrell Laird and his Wingman, 1Lt. Ralph Hartley. While flying over Formosa for a half hour the flight was over Hogan at 1745 when the flight spotted a large number of enemy aircraft in the vicinity flying north and 1,000 feet above.. There were nine aircraft, identified as Franks, flying in one four plane formation with three more above and then two more above that. Cherry and Bush turned toward the top five while Laird and Hartley took on the lower formation of four. Cherry and Bush began their attack but were bounced by five Franks coming out of the sun and had to dive for their lives and lost each other but pulled out with no pursuers. Cherry climbed back up to attack the four Franks but was again bounced and had to dive violently away from three Franks. Meanwhile, Laird quickly got onto the tail of the enemy #4 man and set it on fire. As he and Hartley turned from the attack there were four Franks to their rear firing on them from out of range. The two Americans pushed over sharply and rolled into a Split-S and immediately rolled back out and lost the Franks at 800 feet. The two climbed back but Hartley began to use his water injection to head back to base and Laird ordered him to stay with him that he could rejoin him. As Hartley was turning five more Franks appeared at 3 o'clock to him. Hartley turned right and came in from above and passed through the enemy formation and was chased by them. Laird climbed and dove on the last Frank from dead astern at very close range and had to pull up sharply to avoid its explosion. Laird moved to starboard and went after the furthest Frank ahead and downed it and easily escaped to head home without Hartley who did not return. Laird's three victories gave him four which would leave him one shy of becoming an ace during the war. 1Lt. Ralph Hartley did not return to base.

**Late February 1945: 58FG**

Preparing for invasion on 28 February, an all-out attack by the 5FC on the Puerto Princessa defenses occurred on 26 February. The 347th Fighter Group (13FC) attacked first with Napalm; A-20s of the 3rd and 47th Bomb Groups from Mindoro next came; followed by 36 13FC P-38s with more Napalm. The three 58th Fighter Group squadrons then hit an industrial area.

Three officers and 19 enlisted men of the 58FG were flown from Mindoro to San Marcelino on Luzon and ordered to report to the Commander, 348FG for special instructions. The 348FG was in the process of exchanging their Thunderbolts for new P-51 Mustangs. This 58FG contingent was to work with the new Mustangs on the conjecture that the 58FG would be the next Group to transition from the Thunderbolt to the Mustang. However, Kenney finally decided that the 58th would continue with their P-47s and the upshot was that the 58th contingent would then accept and prepare some of the 348th's Thunderbolts for transfer to the 58th.

**28 February 1945: 547NFS**

Pilot 1Lt. Kenneth Schrieber and R/O 2Lt. Bonnie Rucks were flying over the Cagayan Valley looking for enemy vehicle movement. When they approached Gamu Airstrip they saw red lights and flood lights on the strip and flew a 360 around the strip at 3,000 feet and five miles away but continued on their original patrol over the Cagayan Valley. After continuing their road search south for a short time they decided to turn back toward Gamu where R/O Rucks who was using his AI set to plot the terrain saw a fast moving blip on his scope and soon "guest" observer, Col. Robert Johnson spotted its landing lights and rudder light. Schrieber made a port turn and closed on the rudder light to five miles astern and closed at full throttle. Schrieber realized that he was closing too fast and cut the throttles and got a visual at 2,000 feet. The configuration was that of a DC-2 or -3 codenamed Tess. As he closed to 225 feet behind and 30 feet below Schreiber fired and exploded the right fuel tank and tore away the right wing for his only victory. Schreiber had to pull up sharply to avoid the debris and when the P-61 landed there was a six inch den in the port wing leading edge from hitting the Tess' vertical tail assembly and also dents in its tail assembly.

**February 1945: 58FG**

During February the 58FG flew 1,095 combat sorties; 417 escort and patrol, 118 fighter sweeps, 374 bombing, 120 ground support, and 66 miscellaneous. The Group dropped 1,320 gallons of the new Napalm weapon; 386.75 tons of bombs were dropped; and 86,471 rounds of ammunition expended. During this period all squadrons were short of aircraft, never more than about 75% of the normal allotment.

**February 1945: 35FG**

In February the Group was under the operational control of the 308th Bomb Wing and flew 1,367 sorties; flying on all but four days of the month; the 10th, 13th, 25th, and 27th.

The Group had settled in at its base at Mangaldan and maintained its role of maintaining fighter air supremacy over Luzon employing not only an active defense but also offensive sweeps over Formosa which the Group History described as "Attack to Defend." During the month the Group was also concerned with support and escort mission over northwest Luzon and a secondary responsibility of long range missions to Formosa. Over northwest Luzon their mission was dive bombing and strafing attacks on enemy airdromes, supply and bivouac areas, and defensive positions in the Cagayan Valley, Baguio-Balete Pass, and San Fernando area. The Group's fighters were prohibited from attacking targets of opportunity outside the Cagayan Valley because of the American and Filipino Guerrilla forces operating in western and southern Luzon.

A large proportion of the Group's escort and cover sorties involved transport aircraft which dropped supplies, arms, and ammunition to isolated friendly groups. Their other escort missions included covering PBY Catalina rescue aircraft orbiting at Ambil Island, North Island, Pretus Reef, and Mabudis Island. PT boats and convoys operating along Luzon's west coast were covered from Lingayen Gulf as far north as Cape Bojeander.

As the month progressed the basic land objectives on Luzon had been achieved and U.S. air power was directed toward Formosa. Weather permitting the Group flew cover for bombers attacking shipping, harbor installations, railways, industry, and airdromes mainly at Tainan, Meito, Toko, Koshun, Choshu, Kagi, and Takao. Although Intelligence estimated that there were a large number of Japanese aircraft on Formosa they were seldom encountered anything but heavy, accurate AA fire defending the enemy airdromes.

Newly arrived ETO combat veteran **Capt. John Petrovich** became the 9FS CO. (AAF)

**February-March 1945: 49FG: Command Changes**

During the third week in February, the 49FG again made changes in their squadron commands. Capt. Edward Peck, who had served the longest in command of the 7FS was promoted to Major and assigned as 49FG Ops Executive. Capt. Robert Aschenbrener, recovering from his back injury relinquished his 8FS command. 9FS CO William Williams was furloughed back to the States and newly arrived ETO combat veteran, Capt. John Petrovich, became the Flying Knights' CO.

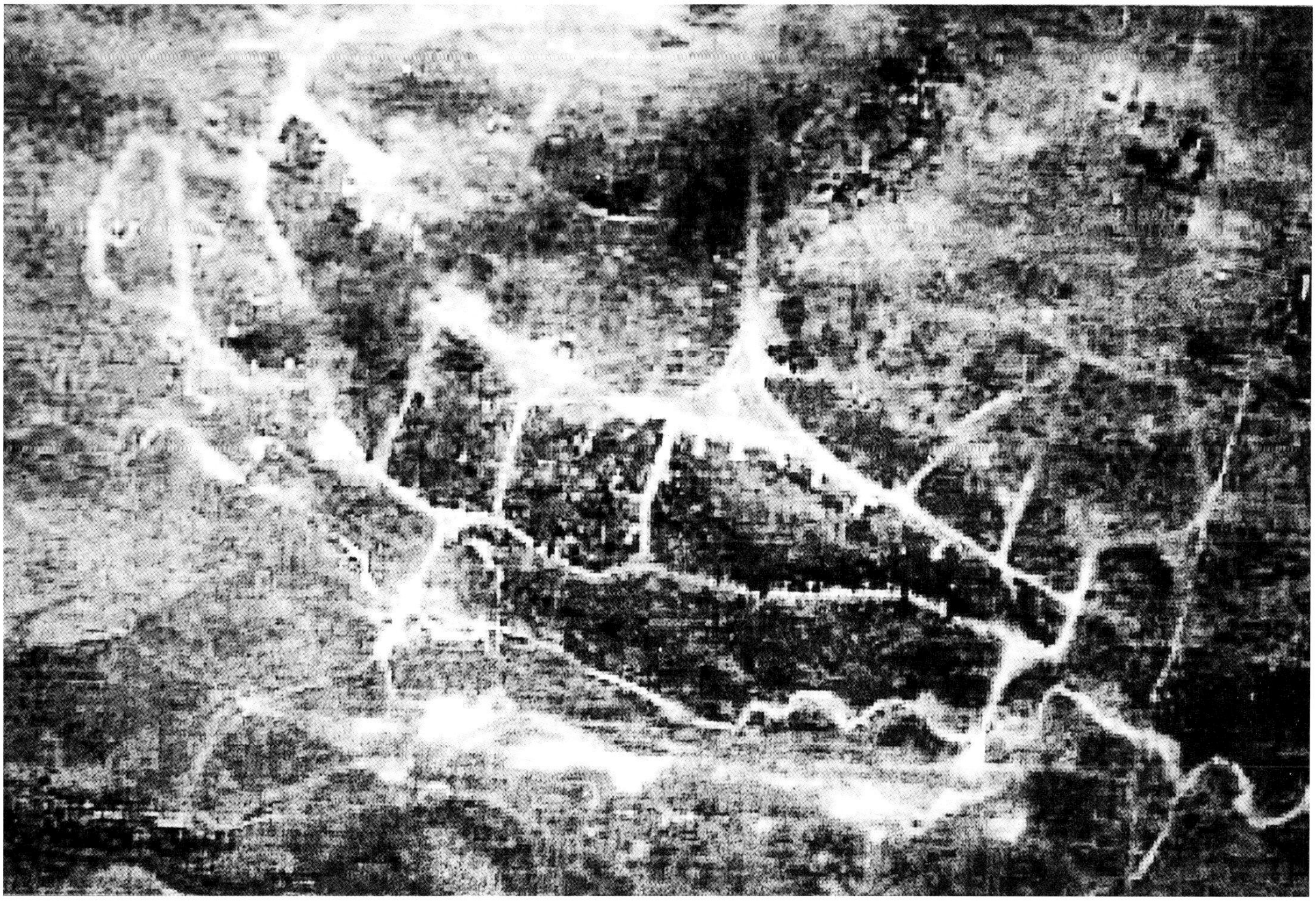

**Clark Airfield** immediately after its capture. (AAF)

AIR FORCE BASES
LUZON-MINDORO
AIRFIELDS
PRINCIPAL HIGHWAYS
STATUTE MILES
L U Z O N
M I N D O R O
PACIFIC OCEAN
SOUTH CHINA SEA
Lingayen Gulf
Solano
Baguio
Bayombong
Bani
Santa Fe
MANGALDAN
LINGAYEN
Camiling
Paniqui
Tarlac
Sangitan
Gapan
Bamban
CLARK
PORAC
SAN MARCELINO
FLORIDABLANCA
POLILLO ISLANDS
Manila
Manila Bay
NIELSON
NICHOLS
Laguna de Bay
CORREGIDOR I.
LAMON BAY
ALABAT I.
LUBANG ISLANDS
Balayan
Lucena
Batangas
TAYABAS BAY
RAGAY GULF
MARICABAN I.
VERDE I.
Calapan
MARINDUQUE ISLAND
ELMORE
MURTHA
HILL
McGUIRE
CALAMIAN GROUP
N
S
E
W

**Clark Airfield** as a fully-developed facility. (AAF)

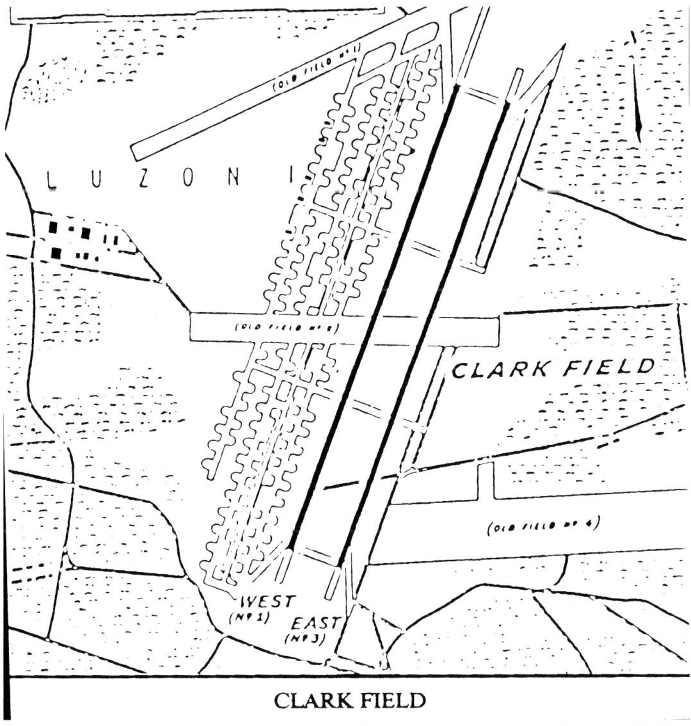


CLARK FIELD

**Manila Area Airfields**

Clark

During 1917 construction began outside Fort Stotsenberg on a half mile long earth runway, hangars, and other support facilities. Construction was completed in 1919 and improvements continued until 1941 when war loomed and it was expanded to eight main airfields: Clark 1, 2, 3, 4, 5, 6, Clark North, Clark East. Other airfields in the surrounding area included five strips at Angeles, two at Mabalacat, and one to the north at Bambam.

Runway #1 was the first runway built at Clark Field and was a single grass runway and served as the main runway until the start of the war when it was sealed as an all-weather runway.

Runway #2 was a single runway located to the south and parallel to Runway #1. Runway #4 was located to the south.

Runway #3 was a single runway located to the northeast of Fort Stotsenberg.

Runway #4 was a single runway located to the south and parallel to #1 and #2 runways.

Runway #5 was a smaller single runway located to the southeast of Runway #4.

Runway #6 (Clark North) was a smaller single runway located to the west and parallel to Runway #3, to the north of Fort Stotsenberg.

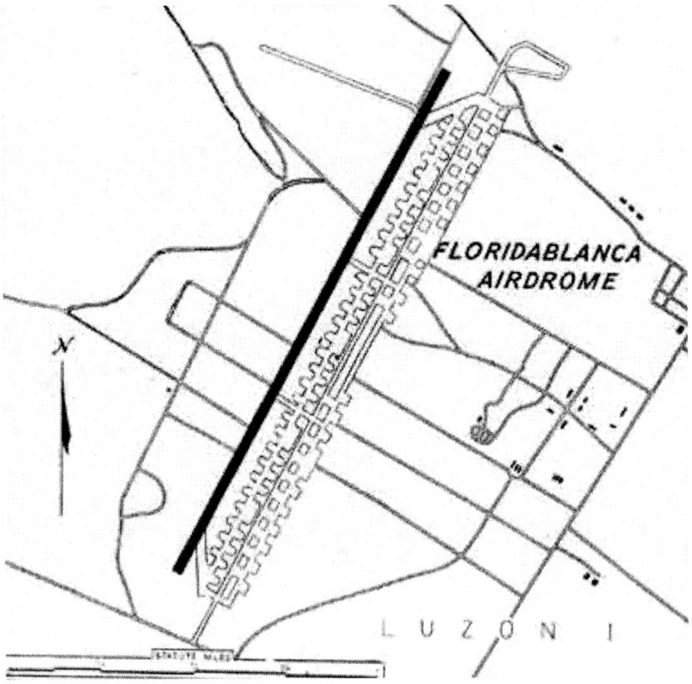


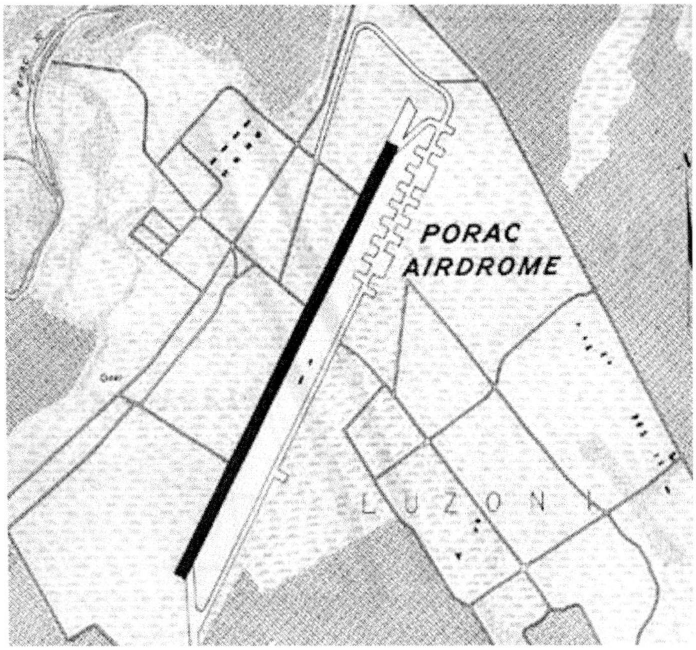


The first American air raid against Japanese occurred on 24 December 1944. The battle for its liberation began on 24 January 1945 by the U.S. Army 40th Division advancing along the hills to the north of Clark Field area and 37th Division advancing from Bambam to Mabalacat, Dau, Angeles and across the Clark Field base. The battle lasted until 31 January and the enemy retreated to the Zambales Mountains.

5FC Units based at Clark Field:

475FG, 432FS (P-38s) from Dulag 27 February 27 to 20 April 1945 Lingayen
475FG, 431FS, 433FS (P-38s) from Dulag 28 February to 20 April 1945 Lingayen
5th Fighter Command from Mindoro March 1945 to 1 August 1945 to Okinawa
5th Air Force HQ from Mindoro 2 April 1945 to 31 July 1945 to Okinawa
35FG HQ from Lingayen 3 April 3 to 28 June 1945 to Okinawa
35FG, 41FS (P-51s) from Lingayen 20 April to 30 June 1945 to Yontan
35FG, 39FS (P-47, P-51s) from Lingayen 21 April to 30 June 1945
421NFS (P-38s, P-61s) from San Marcelino 26 April 1945 to ?

Floridablanca

Floridablanca was located about 10 miles south of Clark Field and 5 miles west of San Fernando near Porac. Floridablanca was built prior WWII, as an American base for B-17s and was used sparingly by the Japanese after the fall of the Philippines.

After the Americans liberated the Field they enlarged and improved it as a base for AAF heavy bombers.

5FC units based at Floridablanca:

348FG HQ San Marcelino 15 May 1945 to 9 July 1945 to Ie Shima
348FG 340FS (P-47, P-51) San Marcelino15 May 1945 to 12 July 1945
348FG 342FS (P-47, P-51) San Marcelino 15 May to 12 July 1945
348FG 460FS (P-47, P-51) San Marcelino 15 May to 12 July 1945

San Marcelino

The ground echelon of the 348FG was lying off San Marcelino waiting for the infantry to secure the area while their air echelon remained back at Tanauan. The 38th Infantry had landed near San Antonio unopposed and quickly captured San Marcelino Strip which was located due west of Clark Field and the naval base and large harbor at Subic Bay. The ground echelon landed on the 4th and the air echelon flew in C-46s over the next three days. The San Marcelino Strip was a pre-war emergency strip that the Japanese had developed into a base that could accommodate 500 aircraft. However, before retreating they destroyed all installations and grounded aircraft there. U.S. engineers immediately lengthened the runway and surfaced it with hard clay to 6,000 feet and established temporary operations buildings so that by the 5th the 340FS was flying local patrols and by the next day and days thereafter ground support missions were flown to the Zigzag Pass area where U.S. troops were being held up by stiff enemy resistance.

5FC Units Based at San Marcelino:

348FG: HQ, 340FS (P-47s) Tanauan 4 February 1945 to ?
348FG: 342FS & 460FS (P-47s) Tanauan 6 February1945 to ?
348FG: 341FS (P-47s) Tanauan 7 February 1945 to ?
421NFS Tacloban 8 February to 26 April 1945 Clark Field

Porac

Porac was a single runway built prior to the war located to the southwest of Porac and east of the Porac River. It had a taxiway parallel to the runway with dispersal area near the northern end of the strip. It was used by the Japanese until the American liberation in early 1945 when the AAF improved the field.

5FC Units Based at Porac:

58FG: 69FS (P-47) Mangaldan 17 April to 8 July 1945 to Okinawa
58FG: 311 FS (P-47) Mangaldan 17 April to 8 July 1945 to Okinawa
58FG: 310FS (P-47) Mangaldan 18 April to 9 July 1945 to Okinawa
58FG: HQ (P-47) Mangaldan 18 April to 9 July 1945 to Okinawa
58FG: 201st Mexican Fighter Squadron

# 6

# March 1945

**March 1945: Situation**

By the beginning of March 1945 Krueger's U.S. Sixth Army had defeated the Japanese everywhere and so that it could no longer threaten Luzon's central plains. The Sixth Army had captured Manila after a brutal battle and then gained control of Bataan and captured Corregidor, opening Manila Bay's North Channel and then captured Ternate, a key position on the South Channel. Preparations were ongoing to capture the other islands and strategic points to clear the South Channel which would completely open Manila Bay. In this drive thousands of POWs and civilians imprisoned by the Japanese had been liberated. The Army had isolated and was clearing the Zambales Mountains west of Fort Stotsenberg while operations had commenced to drive the enemy from the Antipolo-Montalban-Ipo Dam sector northeast of Manila and in the mountains of north Luzon-Baguio-Villa Verde Trail-Balete Pass, and open the way into the Cagayan Valley area. A drive was also begun to clear Batangas Province which would clear Balayan and Batangas Bays for Allied shipping. Sixth Army had suffered 3,480 men killed, 13,164 wounded, and 211 missing to date. Its only major objective was to clear the San Bernardino Strait east of Luzon (the Legaspi area). However, to mop up all Japanese forces on Luzon would prove to be a difficult undertaking and would only end with the surrender of Japan.

The Japanese forces were separated into three isolated groups that could not support one another: one in the mountains of West Luzon, a second in the mountains of North Luzon, and units in the Ipo Dam area and South Luzon. In the North Gen. Yamashita was in direct command of forces defending the Baguio-Balete Pass-Cagayan Valley sectors but movement in these northern mountains was especially limited because of inadequate roads, by Guerrilla pressure, and, principally, by the 5AF.

**Early March 1945: 5FC Command Changes**

In an assignment that had been long anticipated, during the first week of March Maj.Gen. Paul Wurtsmith handed over his Fifth Fighter Command to the popular Brig.Gen. Frederick Smith, Kenney's former Chief of Staff. Wurtsmith was awarded his second star and effective 1 March Maj.Gen. Wurtsmith took command of the 13AF. 49FG veteran Donald "Fighter Hutch" Hutchinson became the only other 5FC officer in the war years to receive congressional approval for the rank of General. Gen. Hutchinson was Kenney's personal choice for his new Chief of Staff for the Far East Air Force.

**March 1945: 35FG Receives the P-51**

The most important event for the 35FG during March was the transition from the P-47 to the P-51 Mustang. The P-47 had made its first appearance in November 1943 slowly replacing the obsolete P-39s of the 40th and 41st Fighter Squadrons at Nadzab. At the time the 39FS was flying their beloved P-38s on the long range Rabaul mission out of Port Moresby. But by late November it too began transitioning to the Thunderbolt and when the 39FS moved to Nadzab in mid-December it was fully equipped with the P-47. By the end of January the last P-39 was left behind at Nadzab as the Group moved to Gusap.

The first D-model Mustangs appeared on 1 March and unlike the Thunderbolt it was enthusiastically received by Group pilots. Transition training began immediately and by the end of the month all three Squadrons were checked out in the type. The first operations occurred on 12 March when four sorties were flown by the 40FS on a local patrol over the Lingayen Gulf. On the next day 40th Mustangs flew their first offensive mission when they flew eight sorties on sweeps over the Cagayen Valley strafing trucks on the Gatteran Highway. The first long range, over water mission occurred on the 14th when two 40FS P-51s escorted a PBY to North Reef. The first dive bombing mission was carried out on the 18th when eight 40FS Mustangs bombed enemy concentrations southeast of Baguio. The first mission to Formosa was on the 25th when two flights of 40FS P-51s covered B-25s on a locomotive sweep over the southwestern section.

**Maj.Gen. Paul Wurtsmith** (left) handed over his Fifth Fighter Command to the popular **Brig.Gen. Frederick Smith**, Kenney's former Chief of Staff, and Wurtsmith took command of the 13AF. (Both AAF)

The **58FG** specialized in close support and interdiction missions throughout the war, scoring only 13 aerial victories. (AAF)

**35FG P-51s** at Clark Field. (AAF)

**March 1945: 58FG Close Support Missions**

The procedure for conducting close support missions was to thoroughly brief the pilots on the ground situation in the area, terrain features, enemy dispositions, AA positions, and the location of friendly forces. Once the flight arrived at the predesignated orbiting point the Flight Leader contacted the Support Air Party (SAP) of the ground forces to receive instructions for the attack. Usually the target was marked either white phosphorous smoke shell or by an L-5 light aircraft dropping colored parachutes. Ideal weather conditions and faultless coordination with the Ground Controller were essential. If poor visibility of the target caused any uncertainty as to the location of friendly forces or if there was poor communication with the Ground Controller; the flight would be diverted to a secondary target.

**March 1945: 3ACG**

Group CO, Arvid Olson reorganized the Group and made a number of personnel changes promoting individuals while others left for assignments elsewhere. In addition to forming a Light Planes Section, Olson merged the other ADSs with their respective flying squadrons. The 3rd Fighter Squadron and the 334th ADS became the 3rd Fighter Section while the 4th Fighter Squadron and the 335th ADS were combined into the 4th Fighter Section, and the 318th TCS and the 343rd ADS became the Troop Carrier Section. Among the most noteworthy personnel moves were the transfers of Group Operations Officer Elmer Richardson to the 308th Bombardment Wing, where he replaced John Alison as Wing Operations Officer when Alison moved up to the Fifth Air Force with Walker Mahurin becoming the new Group Operations Officer and being replaced as 3rd Fighter Section Commander by Capt. Charles Adams.

The 3ACG had previously pioneered simultaneous two ship take offs and now that Mangaldan became a crowded field basing not only the Air Commandos but also the Marine Aircraft Group 24, the Marine Aircraft Group 32, the AAF 38th and 312th Bomb Groups making the standard one aircraft at a time take offs extremely time consuming. Mangaldan's runway was 100 feet wide, which Air Commando CO Olson decided was more than wide enough for four ship take offs. Mangaldan was operated by a Marine Colonel who somewhat reluctantly granted permission to try the four ship take offs but was soon convinced that the ACG's take offs were the most efficient way of conducting operations and the other groups on the field followed as did other units throughout the Philippines that also adopted the procedure.

During the month nearly 95% of the 3ACG's missions were close air support as the front lines were not far from their base at Mangaldan. The Villa Verde Trail ran from San Nicolas only about 25 miles from Mangaldan to the village of Santa Fe on Route 5 north of Balete Pass. The trail traversed some of the roughest terrain on Luzon, affording the Japanese strong defensive positions. On 1 March, 16 Mustangs P-51s placed their 500 pound bombs accurately on target and started a large grass fire whose smoke could be seen from Mangaldan. In March the Air Commandos Fighter sections flew several uneventful missions to the China coast.

**1 March 1945: 35FG First Use of Napalm**

Thirteen P-47s of the 39FS dropped 24 165 gallon fire bombs on enemy positions at San Fernando Point, Luzon, to support ground operations.

**1-3 March 1945: 58FG**

By the beginning of March the 58th Fighter Group had been settled at San Jose area of Mindoro for several weeks and the Japanese air attacks had concluded with the invasion of Luzon on 9 January. U.S. troops had to be constantly supported by sea convoys and aerial resupply and consequently, the main task of the 58FG in early March was the daily patrolling of these air and sea routes. There were only a few remaining enemy aircraft scattered in hiding places throughout the Philippines but the 58FG had only one encounter with an airborne enemy aircraft during the month.

After the first three days of March the 58th began to support the Sixth Army primarily in the southern Luzon region; from Batangas to Legaspi. Mainly, these missions were to keep the enemy from moving troops and to harass him by attacking supply dumps, fuel dumps, and tactical objectives like pill boxes, gun positions and bivouac areas.

**2 March 1945: 8FG**

In March the 8FG continued its arduous schedule of transport escort and ground support missions. Although these missions were routine there were three losses in the Group and all were unconventional deaths. The first occurred on 2 March when the 36FS sent six P-38s to patrol the C-47 flight paths around Negros, Cebu and Panay. The utter boredom of the patrol encouraged two pilots to buzz Tuburan Strip on northeast Cebu and for some unknown reason, 1Lt. Howard Damon's Lightning fell off, crashed, and exploded on the strip.

**2 March 1945: 3ACG**

On 2 March the Air Commandos had a close call. Shortly before 0100 a red alert was sounded but was followed by an all clear a few minutes later and everyone settled back to sleep. Then, about two hours later, without warning, four enemy bombers swept in over the field, dropping fragmentation and demolition bombs on the camp areas and on the taxiway. An ammunition dump was exploded and one Marine SBD was destroyed, another was damaged, four men were killed, and 78 more men were wounded, none Air Commandos. The bombs did only minor damage to the taxiway and Mangaldan's runway was undamaged, allowing all units to fly their planned schedules for the coming day. The Air Commandos sent 32 Mustangs, 16 from each section, to escort B-24s to Formosa. The Japanese did not send up interceptors the P-51 strafed rail lines and installations.

**Early March 1945: 58FG**

The 58FG spent the first five days of the month protecting convoy and air routes and in flying ground support missions in southern Luzon. Enemy personnel and supplies were the assigned targets in support of the Legaspi Task Force. Many of the strike results were being reported by the controllers as "excellent."

**4 March 1945: 35FG**

Dive bombing was the principal operation during the month against targets on Luzon and Formosa. The Luzon targets were troop concentrations, supply areas, and enemy defenses while the main target on Formosa was the hydro electric plant at Takao. However, on 4 March the 35FG was assigned on a major effort on the Tuguegarao Airdrome in Luzon's Cagayan Valley. The 39FS sent up 30 P-47s armed with two 1,000 pound GP bombs each and the 41FS sent up 29 P-47s carrying 58 1,000 pound bombs and completely cratered the runway. 2Lt. John Warner of the 41FS was MIA.

**5 March 1945: 475FG/432FS**

In their first mission from the Clark Complex, eight Clover P-38s were scheduled for a afternoon fighter sweep to Formosa (one would snafu) under Capt. Perry Dahl. Two thirds up the Formosa coast Dahl put his Squadron into string and began a strafing run on a fleet of fishing boats but soon Dahl terminated the attack when he thought that the ships might be civilian junks. As he pulled up from his strafing run Dahl saw an unidentified twin engine aircraft at two miles ahead at 1,500 feet above heading

**Capt. Perry Dahl** (center) being congratulated on shooting down a Sally bomber for his eighth victory. (AFAA)

inland north. Dahl did a sharp wingover and identified the bogie as a Sally bomber. As Dahl closed on its tail, the Japanese pilot dove toward the sea at high speed. Just as the Sally began a turn Dahl fired a short burst that started a fire in its starboard engine. Dahl continued to close and fired two more bursts into the Sally's fuselage and tail assembly. The bomber crash landed on the beach and Dahl saw five survivors fleeing from the burning wreckage, confirming Dahl's eighth victory.

**2-6 March 1945: 49FG**

After the 49ers moved to Lingayen their mission schedule increased with a determined effort to end the enemy resistance in the eastern hills and Formosa. The P-38s soon began carrying 1,000 pound bombs as far as Formosa, particularly concentrating on Kosh Airdrome on the southern cape and rail yards at Bozan, on the west coast. These missions were very successful as the 49ers contributed to the total destruction of the rail system and the enemy air fields where 100's of aircraft were destroyed on the ground. Air reconnaissance reported that the estimated count of 600 enemy aircraft in late January had been nearly halved by mid-March. During these missions the 49ers missions lost only two aircraft which crashed after returning to Lingayen on 5 March. 2Lts. James White and William Minto were both hit ground fire at Bozan and while their aircraft were written off they both survived.

**6 March 1945: 58FG/311FS**

Filipino Guerrillas reported that the Japanese had been flying a daily Tess transport aircraft from Del Monte Airdrome on Mindanao which took off at about 1700 and landed at about 1900 at Silay Airdrome on Negros. It was supposed that it refueled there and continued on to Yamashita's headquarters on northern Luzon, carrying critical supplies, important personnel, and urgent dispatches. To engage the enemy transport the 311FS began dispatching a patrol of two P-47s to the Negros area in the late afternoons during the last days of February and continued into March. On 6 March 1Lt. Lynwood Johnson and 2Lt. Russell Doose departed Mindoro at 1635 and arrived at their assigned patrol area at 1730 at about 4,000 feet, in scattered cumulus clouds which extended from 3,000 to 10,000 feet. They patrolled for the next hour and a half when they saw an unidentified aircraft approaching Silay Airdrome. The bandit was on a southeast course and about five miles southeast of Silay at about 5,000 feet and Johnson immediately climbed to the altitude of the oncoming aircraft which was identified as a twin-engine Tess transport. The enemy pilot sighted the two Thunderbolts and immediately began a steep dive toward the water and in the direction of Silay. The Americans made a diving starboard turn which them on the tail of the Tess. Doose did not reduce his speed and made the first firing pass but could only get in a short burst before he completely overshot. Johnson throttled back to about 140 mph, the speed of the transport, and swung around on its tail at an altitude of only 25 feet and was able to fire two accurate bursts. The Tess crashed in a huge explosion into a wooded area just south of the Airdrome. The victory was the sixth and last for the 311FS during the war.

**1Lt. Lynwood Johnson** shot down a Tess transport for his only victory and the 311FS' sixth and last victory. (AAF)

**6 March 1945: Situation**

Early on 6 March, the Sixth Army began an offensive to capture the Batangas Province and thus open Balayan and Batangas Bays to Allied shipping. The 11th Airborne began its advance with an attack on the southern Shimbu Line. The 6th Infantry and the 1st Cavalry advanced into the mountains and encountered heavy enemy concentrations in the Ipo Dam-Antipolo line. Enemy defenses there consisted chiefly of intricate cave positions, which were relatively well stocked with food, equipment, and weapons of all varieties. These positions slowed the American advance and the SOP was to suppress these positions with air and ground bombardment so that demolition teams could approach and seal of the cave entrances. Between 8 and 11 March, 450 fighter attacks were concentrated on the Antipolo area and the 1st Cavalry, reinforced by the 43rd Division, captured Antipolo town on 12 March.

**6 March 1945: 49FG/7FS/8FS**

The 49ers had spent many weeks flying fighter sweeps over Luzon and Formosa without encountering any enemy fighters but they finally found the Japanese Air Force on the large island of Hainan, far to the west over the South China Sea. Hainan was occupied by a large enemy garrison which included the heavily defended Samah Airdrome on the southern coast. The JNAF aircraft on Samah threatened Allied shipping in the South China Sea and on 6 March a large formation of B-25 strafers was sent there with the 7FS assigned to escort the Mitchell formation and 8FS assigned to cover the strafers' withdrawal.

**Capt. Frederick Dick** (left with **Capt. Richard Ganchan**) shot down two Zeros to become an ace. (AFAA)

**Capt. Joel Paris** got his ninth and last victory as the 7FS finished combat with 178 victories. (AAF)

7FS
At 0845, the 7FS Demons left Lingayen in close support to the three groups of B-25s and 45 minutes later the 8FS Black Sheep followed. After a long flight, the main strike force approached the Hainan coastline at 1300 and turned inland west of the Samah. Although the Lightnings were directly over the low flying Mitchells, the haze restricted visual contact with the leading strafers which were nearly five miles ahead.

The escorts were led by veteran Capt. Frederick Dick with his three Red Flight wingmen at 4,000 feet at the front of the formation. As the Mitchell's descended to the deck across the west perimeter of the airdrome, two Zeros closed in the hazy sky at a slightly below the Lightnings. Red Flight jettisoned their tanks and dove on the Zeros. Dick scored the first kill of the mission five miles northwest of Samah when the lead Zero broke to starboard and was shattered by Dick's first volley but its pilot bailed out. Directly, Red Element Leader 1Lt. William Bauer and Wingman 2Lt. Dewey Renick opened fire on the trailing Zero which had broken off in the opposite direction. Bauer executed a high speed starboard turn which took his fighter out of range but Renick stayed with the Zero to get a long burst flaming the enemy's engine and it's pilot also bailed out to give him his only victory of the war. Meanwhile, Dick hit his second victim in a head on pass for his fifth and final victory of the war to become an ace.

Closely trailing Red Flight at 6,000 feet higher was Green Flight, led by newcomer Capt. Dwight Henderson, followed by his Wingman Capt. Richard Ganchan, attached from 5FC, and veteran Wingman 1Lt. William Fernandez. As they passed the scene of Green Flight's kills Henderson sighted two more Zeros closing heading west at 8,000 feet. As Henderson closed in to within 100 yards the Zero entered into a starboard turn but the American followed and fired shattering the enemy's canopy and it plunged into the side of a hill just north of the airfield and exploded for his only victory. After Green Flight regrouped but AA fire from the airfield and destroyers offshore was too intense and they broke off their second attack on Samah and headed home.

**2Lt. George Spruill** shot down a Zero for his only career victory and the last of 178 victories scored by the 7FS. (AAF)

Meanwhile, Capt. Joel Paris' Blue Flight of rookie Wingman 2Lt. Ralph Oxford, veteran 2Lt. George Spruill, and tail-end 2Lt. Albert Meschino remained at 8,000 feet. As they heard of Dick's Red Flight first combat they were escorting the third wave of Mitchell strafers, ten miles from the airdrome which had been heavily damaged by the preceding Mitchells. Oxford and Spruill both fell behind briefly with hung up belly tanks. Spruill rocked his fighter but the tanks did not separate so he decided to continue on with them still attached. Oxford was able to shake his tanks but then a lone Zero suddenly closed in directly behind him. Oxford radioed his predicament and all three Blue Flight veterans turned to help the rookie. Oxford tried to break away as Paris flew under Oxford to pass directly under his attacker. Paris' maneuver gave his fighter enough speed to begin a zooming climb that put him into point blank range under the Zero. Paris opened fire and ripped away the enemy's engine cowling which would crash on the north side of Samah for Paris' ninth and final victory. The veteran Meschino got trapped in a wild turning fight against three other Zeros and as he shot one of them down another shot out his port supercharger. Meschino used his experience to regain control and left for home. At the same time, Blue Element Leader Spruill saw a descending Zero and as it came within range, Spruill, still carrying his belly tanks, snap rolled to port in a high angle wingover, placing him above his unsuspecting target. Spruill quickly dove and fired a perpendicular deflection that hit the Zero's canopy and engine and the stricken fighter exploded, near the end of the Samah runway. It was Spruill's only career victory, and would eventually be confirmed as the Screamin' Demons' 178th aerial victory of the war and its last (along with 19 probables and 24 damaged).

8FS
The day's combat ended for the 49ers, long after the Mitchells had departed the target and far out to sea. The Black Sheep cover flight for the returning B-25s was orbiting 20 miles east of the target when a Navy PBM rescue amphibian radioed that it was flying closer to Samah to check on a damaged Mitchell. The haze made visual contact impossible and soon the PBM was no longer in radio contact. The Black Sheep pilots decided to remain in the area until their fuel supply still allowed them to return to base. They climbed to 5,000 feet and five minutes later met a lone Zero heading for Hainan. 2Lt. Jack Page chased the Zero and finally closed in behind and shot it down with its pilot bailing out for Page's only victory.

**9 March 1945: 547NFS**
At 1940 2Lt. Francis Raidt was flying a P-38J on a bombing run Tuguegarao Airdrome at 3,000 feet. Raidt noticed flashing white lights near the right side of the strip and closed, cutting back the throttles, and prepared to fire on the aircraft he identified as a Tess or Topsy transport. Amazingly, the enemy pilot turned his landing lights on and made his landing approach. Flying at 500 feet, Raidt opened fire at 3,000 to 5,000 feet, head on, and no deflection. He fired three bursts to within 100 feet and the enemy pulled up briefly and then exploded as he passed over. After his only victory of the war, Raidt saw another enemy aircraft parked on the field and strafed and bombed it without seeing any results.

**March 1945: The P-51 in the Pacific: 348FG**
Although the Mustang was revered in the ETO and was arguably the best AAF fighter of WWII; like its P-38 and P-47 predecessors the P-51 also did not win easy initial acceptance. Both the P-38 and the P-47 had proven themselves over many months of combat. First the twin engine P-38 proved itself to be able to fight with their nimble Japanese adversaries and on long range missions there was the safety factor provided by its second engine. The 348FG pilots were disappointed when they turned in their P-40s for the huge P-47 instead of the proven P-38. In time the P-47 became renowned for its ability to sustain heavy battle damage and its eight .50 caliber guns were especially devastating to the lightly constructed Japanese aircraft. Thunderbolt pilots had learned to use the tremendous dive and roll rate of the P-47 to impressive advantage. The newly arrived pilots who were trained only on the P-51 were passionate about it. Even though the P-51 was considered to be easy for veteran pilots to transition to; veteran P-47 pilots had problems breaking the well-established habits they had learned in the P-47. The 460FS transitioned to the P-51 during March on Mokmer Strip, Biak and later in the month Capt. Wallace Harding led 17 transitioned 460th pilots to Morotai and flew to the Philippines around March 21.

**11 March 1945: 421NFS**
Two days later, gunner TSgt. Brady Swinney flying with 2Lt. Carl Remington of the 421NFS shot down a Betty at 0626 for the 421st's 13th and last victory of the war (plus one probable and three damaged claims).

The **348FG** transitioned to the P-51. (AAF)

**11 March 1945: 348FG/342FS: First P-51 Victory**
The first air victory of 1945 for the 342FS occurred when flying their first long range mission since converting to the P-51. Four P-51s took off at 0740 and approached Poulo-Canton Island off the Indo China coast at 1105 on a mission to cover a rescue PBY. The flight was flying at 1,000 feet and 75 miles from the rendezvous when a lone Betty bomber on an anti-submarine patrol was seen on the deck, three miles away, heading out to sea. The Betty was alerted and turned back toward the coast and the Flight Leader closed and knocked out the rear gunner. The Betty broke away and #2 man, 2Lt. Bert Lee, closed and fired fatal hits that killed the pilot and the bomber exploded in the ocean for Lee's second and last victory.

**11 March 1945: 421NFS: Last Victory of the War**
Early on the morning of 11 March, 2Lt. Carl Remington, on patrol southwest of Lingayen Gulf with his R/O, F/O William Boze, and gunner, T/Sgt. Brady Swinney. GCI vectored Remington toward a bogie and the Radar Observer got a blip on his scope. The Japanese released window to obscure the radar but Boze was able to keep contact and closed on the enemy bomber. Once within range Swinney fired his turret .50s on the Japanese bomber, identified as a Betty which burst into flames, went into a steep dive, and crashed into the ocean at 0625 that morning for the squadron's 13th and last victory of the war. The squadron's official total would remain unchanged at 13 as 1Lt. David Corts' "victory" on 9 September 1944 in which one Japanese bomber shot down another trying to shoot down Corts, who was between the two, was disallowed. The unit also claimed one probable and one three damaged.

**13 March 1945: 35FG First Use of Delayed Action Bombs**
The Group hit Tuguegarao Airdrome with 22 1,000 pound delayed action bombs which were set to explode from one to 72 hours later.

**13 March 1945: 348FG/342FS**
The 342FS sent 12 Mustangs on a fighter sweep off the coast of China to Samah Airdrome on Hainan Island but as they neared their target one Mustang aborted and returned to base. 2Lt. Robert Dow and Element Leader, 1Lt. Clark Kooper, were in the last element and got separated as the Flight Leader made a mistaken turn into the clouds and signaled his formation to abort the mission as they were running low on fuel. While at 12,000 feet Kooper spotted a Japanese transport with its wheels down making a landing approach on Samah. Dow followed Kooper in a steep dive as they raced to catch the transport while it was still in the air so they could claim it as an aerial victory. As they were half way in their dive they saw seven fighters above at 10,000 feet and broke off the attack and climbed toward the menacing fighters. As the Americans reached 10,000 they made head on passes at the Franks and three broke to the right and the other two to the left. Dow and Kooper broke left and out turned the group of three but the other two Franks slipped in behind and every pilot broke into an individual dogfight. One of the Franks overshot Dow and pulled up at "no miss" range and Dow fired at the Frank's belly and engine and started a fire and the Frank burned until it crashed into the water. Two more Franks got on Dow's tail and his Mustang easily turned inside one of the Franks while Kooper diverted and then shot at the other which went into an uncontrolled crash. The two American's broke off from the other three threatening Franks. As they headed to base Dow saw smoke trailing from Kooper's engine which quit about 20 miles southeast of Hainan Island and where he bailed out and inflated his raft. Dow circled long enough to radio his position before turning to base almost three hours away with a dangerously low fuel supply. Kooper was never found and Dow would also became a casualty three months later when he was killed in a take off accident on another mission.

**14-15 March 1945: 8FG/80FS**
Highway 21 was one of the main rail and road routes in southeastern Luzon, as this strategic road connected the Batangas area with towns around Laguna Bay just southeast of Manila. The fighting in the region made the Highway of vital tactical importance to the Japanese and its capture would strangle their effort in the area. So, after the fall of Manila in mid March the fighter squadrons of the 5FC were assigned to attack the Highway.

On 14 March the 80FS sent up four P-38s at 0800 to bomb and strafe targets in Lipa Town north of Batangas. The P-38s followed a smoke marker into Santo Tomas which had just been bombed by A-20s and dropped eight

**2Lt. Carl Remington** of the 421NFS tallied the Squadron's 13th and last victory, plus one probable and three damaged. (AAF)

1,000 pound bombs which disrupted the Japanese and paved the way for American infantry to move in. Later that day eight Headhunter P-38s carrying two 1,000 pound bombs each were dispatched to bomb San Pablo, northeast of Lipa. A spotter plane radioed that an enemy bivouac area was located in the southern part of San Pablo near the cemetery. P-47s had bombed the town earlier with Napalm that almost completely covered the area and just before the 80FS arrived, a A-20s bombed San Pablo and the town was virtually obliterated but the bivouac survived. The 80th dropped 12 bombs which exploded within 200 yards of the Japanese bivouac. Another pair of P-38s strafed Highway 21 between the villages of Pililla and Kapalong; hitting a parked bus and truck and further down the Highway a truck and a bulldozer were hit, but did not burn and finally, two more trucks were strafed but did not burn. Because all these vehicles were parked in the open and none caught fire Intelligence concluded that the Japanese were short of gasoline.

In the morning of 15 March two P-38s took off to continue the strafing attacks on Highway 21. A steamroller and camouflaged truck were strafed and the town of Pangsanjan, near the eastern tip of Laguna de Bay, was observed to be completely burned out. Later that afternoon two more P-38s took off for a long range sweep of the Legaspi-Lucena area. They flew over the target area for about a half hour without finding anything worth strafing and decided to make a low level pass over Naga Airstrip, northwest of the far southern end of Luzon, near Legaspi. Two unserviceable Oscars were parked in the revetment area and when they encountered heavy Japanese small arms fire they left the area. When the P-38s landed the ground crew discovered bullet holes in the cowlings of both fighters! One final strafing mission was sent to Highway 21 late in the afternoon. Two P-38s came upon two trucks parked on a bend of the highway near the town of Pililla. They dropped two 260 pound bombs that missed and then bombed and missed another truck on a nearby bridge. The pilots then methodically strafed them and destroyed them.

For the remainder of March the 8FG carried out their customary sweeps, convoy and C-47 cover, local patrol, and ground support missions. Manila had been captured and both Clark and Nichols Fields would soon be available for service and the 8FG would soon be able to sweep beyond the Philippines toward Formosa and even southern Japan. However, for the 8FG and the other 5FC Groups the end of March marked a further deterioration in air action as there no longer would be any grand air battles and even ground support missions would become so routine s to become monotonous.

**15 March 1945: 49FG/8FS Last Victory**

From 10 to 14 March the 49ers continued to patrol along the China coast from Hong Kong to the Formosa Straits. On the 15th veteran Capt. William Drier led four Black Sheep in escort of a Navy PB4Y flying boat on a rescue mission to the western Formosa Straits. The P-38s were at 10,000 feet, 35 miles south of the rendezvous at tiny Namoa Island, when one of Drier's wingmen spotted in a lone Tojo which suddenly appeared out of the clouds 2,000 feet below and behind the Black Sheep flight, heading toward China. Drier and rookie Wingman 2Lt. James Ward dove into a Split-S to attack with the other three elements holding in high cover. As they descended through a full turn, another trailing Tojo Wingman broke directly into Drier's flight path. Drier's snap shot at the lead Tojo tore some pieces from its rear fuselage. As the wounded lead Tojo rolled away to safety, Drier quickly fired on the trailing Ki-44 which immediately broke down and away only to fly directly in front of Ward, who opened fire from dead astern and the enemy Wingman briefly pulled out of his dive then rolled over and plunged into the sea for Ward's only victory. After this combat the Black Sheep would never engage another enemy aircraft and would end the war with 207 victories (with 23 probables and 17 damaged claims).

**15 March 1945: 348FG/341FS Last Victory**

Two flights of 10 341FS P-51s took off at 0750 and flew a fighter sweep to Kai Tak Airdrome near Hong Kong and arrived after a long flight at 1115 at 10,000 feet. Blue Flight Leader, 1Lt. Ruben Moskalof, and Wingman, 2Lt. Albert Spielvogel, were flying at 9,000 feet when the saw a Jack at 4,000 feet and dropped their tanks and dove to attack. Moskalof closed and banked to 300 yards astern and began to fire at 10 degrees deflection getting hits on the wing roots. The Jack Split-S'd in flames into the ground five miles east of Kai Tah for Moskalof's only victory of the war. Moskaloff saw another Jack in the Kai Tah landing pattern but was out of range and position and took a desperate and unsuccessful shot and overran the Jack as it landed and Moskaloff fled the area as AA fire was bracketing him. Moskalof's Second Element Wingman 2Lt. Albert Gould, saw a Tojo flying in the 10 o'clock position at 7,000 feet. He and his Element Leader dropped their wing tanks and went into a diving attack. Gould made an astern attack and got hits on the fuselage and wing roots and the enemy fighter exploded causing the wing to sheer off but somehow the pilot managed to bail out also for Gould's only victory which would mark the last of 70 total for the war for the 341st (plus seven probables and two damaged claims).

Although the 348th would not score any more aerial victories it would participate in the much more dangerous ground support and attacks on enemy transport and airfields. During the last three weeks of March the Group would lose eight pilots:

8 March: Lt. Robert Redner (341FS)
12 March: Lt. Clark Kooper (342FS)
15 March; 2Lt. Roy Martin (340FS)
18 March: 2Lt. Robert McPeak (342FS)
20 March: Lt. Ferdinand Peterson (342FS)
22 March: Lt. Richard Garst (341FS)
26 March: F/O James Clements (342FS)
30 March: F/O Samuel Macken (340FS)

**2Lt. Albert Gould** claimed a Tojo as the 341FS scored the last of 70 total victories. (AAF)

**Maj. Edward Roddy**, who scored eight victories with the 342FS/348FG, took over the command of the 58FG from Col. Gwen Atkinson. (AAF)

**15 March 1945: 475FG/432FS**

475FG operations during the mid March typically consisted of C-47 cover missions, patrols, and an occasional escort to the China coast. On 15 March, the 475th began ground support missions for American troops advancing along the coast north of Luzon and into the Cagayan Valley. That day the 432FS sent a dozen P-38s to bomb the resort town of Baguio, just to the northeast of Lingayen Gulf where the pilots placed 17 of the 22 bombs near the primary target. Later, another mission was flown to the same target by the same 12 P-38s; this time the bombs were dropped on Japanese bivouacs and a radio station with one building destroyed and the radio station partially destroyed by a direct hit. Although some accurate light and medium AA fire was met but only 2Lt. Lawrence Roberts' fighter took a hit from a single bullet.

**15 March 1945: 35FG/41FS**

Veteran 1Lt. Raby Jeanes of the 41FS was KIA during a dive bombing mission on Takao, Formosa.

**Mid-March 1945: 3ACG: Mindanao Campaign**

By February the 3ACG had proven itself and Kenney's staff requested that the Air Commandos and another fighter squadron be sent south for use in the Mindanao Campaign which started on 10 March. Fifth Air Force Commander, Maj.Gen. Ennis Whitehead, staunchly opposed this idea because the highly trained Air Commandos and their long-ranged P-51s were needed for use against Formosa. Instead of using the Air Commandos in the Mindanao Campaign, Whitehead thought that the short-ranged Marine SBDs which were also based at Mangaldan and Marine F4U Corsairs would be a better choice. Whitehead prevailed and the Air Commandos did not move and the Marines were sent south.

**Mid-March 1945: 58FG Command Changes**

On 12 March, Maj. Edward Roddy assumed Group Command from Col. Gwen Atkinson who had been in command of the 58FG since December 1942. Atkinson had conducted operational training on the Thunderbolt and had moved the 58th overseas in November 1943 and was now being advanced to a new position in the 5FC. Roddy had arrived in the SWPA in June 1943 with the 342FS of Col. Neel Kearby's 348FG where he had scored eight confirmed victories during the air fighting over New Britain in late 1943. He had transferred to the 58FG as Operations Officer and had recently become Deputy Group Commander. Maj. Odren, who had just moved up to be Group Operations Officer in mid February, replaced Roddy as Deputy Group Commander.

Maj. Milton Self, 58FG Commanding Officer, was transferred to a new assignment as Commander of the Combat Replacement Training Group at Nadzab, New Guinea. Self arrived at the 69FS as Operations Officer in February 1943. When Capt. Stuke and the other pilots went to Africa on the *USS Ranger*, he became the 69FS CO for 25 months. He led the 69th through operational training in the U.S. and then in combat for a year and a half. Self led his squadron at every opportunity and, despite his administrative duties; he had logged more combat hours than any of his pilots. Capt. George Bosenbark, 69FS Operations Officer assumed temporary command but several days later Maj. Thomas Winburn was assigned as Squadron CO. Winburn was returning to the Pacific for a second tour after spending 22 months with the 35th Fighter Group as a new pilot and by the end of his tour he was commanding the 40FS and had been credited with two aerial victories during his first tour.

**Mid-March 1945: 58FG**

By mid-March the 310FS flew 258 sorties supporting the army in and around Batangas. Ground Controllers with the infantry reported that these missions achieved excellent results. The 69FS flew 246 sorties, carrying 216 tons of bombs, claiming 87% were delivered into the target areas. The 311FS missions ranged from the strategic bombing of supplies, fuel dump, and warehouses in towns behind enemy lines to pill-boxes, gun positions and bivouac areas in very close support of the infantry. The Ground Controllers were so satisfied with the results they often called for the pilots to deliver their attack within 200 yards of their position.

**Mid-March 1945: Situation**

Gen. Kenney arrived in Washington on 14 March to coordinate the plans for the use of air power during the remainder of the Pacific war. He met with Gen. Marshall on 17 March and told him that, in his opinion, Japan was defeated as not only had enemy air power been destroyed but also most of Japan's navy and merchant marine. He reported that although a large number of aircraft remained in Japan; they had been neutralized because of a lack of gasoline and were effectively cut off on the Home Islands.

**17 March 1945: 3ACG/4FS**

On 17 March the 4th Fighter Section, led by Capt. Raymond Lahmeyer, was on a close support mission, dive bombing enemy positions. Normally when bombing, the Mustang pilots dropped down from about 10,000 feet in a steep dive which gave them plenty of altitude to pull up. But that day there was a cloud deck at 6,000 feet which would cause them to come in lower and flatter. As Lahmeyer pulled up after dropping his bombs, he felt a thump and heard a popping noise and then saw smoke and flames flowing over his wing. He pushed his canopy open, rolled his fighter over and dropped out just as the Mustang exploded. After he landed in his parachute, Lahmeyer ran to the top of a hill to get his bearings where he found Army personnel from an artillery unit. He was escorted back to their base, given a beer, and sent on to Division Headquarters where he boarded an L-6 and was back at Mangaldan in an hour.

**17 March 1945: 5AF Ground Support Results**

Although 5FC pilots were unable to observe the results of their bombing and strafing sorties due to the heavily wooden ravines and mountains; Lt.Gen. Walter Krueger, CO of the Sixth Army sent the following letter to Gen. Ennis Whitehead of the 5AF:

> "I would appreciate announcing to all ranks of your command my gratitude for their fine cooperation and effective results obtained in the support being rendered by units of the Fifth Air Force to the Sixth Army during the vital Luzon Campaign. It is superb and is assisting materially in taking out objectives and holding our battle casualties to a minimum." (Letter 17 March 1945)

**18-21 March 1945: 421NFS**

Because enemy air activity was nil, at San Marcelino there had been only two alerts throughout the month; ground support was added to the Squadron's usual night patrols and alerts. Both Squadron Detachments carried out extensive strafing in support of ground troops throughout the month. The San Marcelino Detachment commenced missions over the lines west of Fort Stotsenberg and the Tacloban detachment attacked Cebu Island.

On 18 March Lts. Robert Pew and David Youker were briefed by Squadron CO, Maj. Richard Kiick, and Intelligence Officer, Lt. Isadore Nachman for a special mission. An urgent radio message had been received from Cebu that the Japanese were advancing on an important airstrip on the island. Youker was to lead a flight from Tacloban to Cebu early the next morning to pick up Col. Gushing, a Guerilla officer who would direct the P-61s on a low level strafing attack on the target which was a Japanese Headquarters. Rather than selecting day fighters for this mission, P-61s were selected because of their heavy firepower and because of their capability of landing on and taking off from the short landing strip at Cebu. Just after sunrise the flight landed at Cebu and was welcomed with a huge breakfast, including fresh eggs and fried chicken. After breakfast Youker boarded his Black Widow and with Col. Gushing seated directly behind him, he and Pew prepared to take off from this very short runway. Before starting the take off run, they taxied to the extreme end of the strip, applied full power to both engines with the brakes applied and half flaps. Youker and Pew became airborne with extra runway. To find the airstrip the Guerilla Colonel had a crude map that was on such a large scale that it was useless from the air at a speed of 250 mph. To make matters worse the Colonel became airsick and threw up but after awhile he finally composed himself. He found the target area and Youker circled, using the airstrip as a reference to orient the Colonel, who was then able to direct the pilots to several enemy barracks nearby the airstrip. The P-61s strafed the area at high speed on the deck and made several runs, encountering ground fire from small arms and machine guns which were ineffective in firing at the speeding strafers. Youker returned the Colonel to the Guerilla Strip on Cebu and then returned to Tacloban. The Guerillas radioed that the mission had been successful but they Japanese remained and they wanted another attack. On the 21st, Youker and Pew returned and while Youker picked up the Colonel, Pew flew cover. The two then strafed the target again but on the return to drop off the Colonel, the .50 caliber guns on Youker's fighter became so hot they involuntarily fired every few seconds and had to be aimed straight up so as not to endanger anyone on the ground. The following day, the Colonel reported that the enemy had retreated and the airstrip was out of danger.

**19 March 1945: 421NFS: Moves to Clark Field**

On 19 March the Fifth Air Force instructed the 421NFS to begin a move to Clark Field. The Tacloban detachment was to move first by LST on the 23rd. However, on the 19th an officer and two enlisted men left San Marcelino to establish a camp at the new area. On the 24th Capt. Dorrie Jones led the entire Tacloban Detachment to Clark with the Detachment at San Marcelino standing by to move to Clark. Tacloban was then transferred to the Filipinos. The Squadron's 11 P-61s were now divided between San Marcelino and Clark Field. With four new aircraft assigned, both the Clark and San Marcelino Detachments continued routine operations, though the decreased enemy activity reduced their scale.

**21 March 1945: 35FG/39FS/40FS**

The 40FS flew eight P-47s to the China Coast to escort B-25s on an anti-shipping raid. Four 39FS P-47s escorted a rescue Catalina on this mission.

**21 March 1945: 58FG/69FS/310FS/311FS**

The 58FG dispatched a full complement of 48 aircraft mission on Naga City that was the outstanding mission of the month for the Group. Each squadron sent off 16 Thunderbolts, armed with Napalm, incendiary, and fragmentation bombs intended to destroy the important rail and highway junction 50 miles northwest of Legaspi, prior to U.S. landings on the east coast of southern Luzon intended to open the San Bernardino Strait. A 58FG pilot was stationed over Naga to coordinate the attack; to oversee that each flight arriving over the target was assured sufficient time to drop their bombs and clear the target before the other flights made their bombing runs. Since he was in control, radio chatter would also be kept to a minimum. The 5FC Chief of Staff was to observe the mission while on board a B-25 which circled the area while the raid was in process. The pilots reported that warehouses were set on fire, an ammunition dump was hit resulting in a large explosion and fire, numerous buildings set afire, a radio tower destroyed, and many other large fires in the center of town spread to engulf a large portion of the city.

**22 March 1945: 8FG**

On 22 March 2Lt. Robert Crandall had just taken off for a patrol when he had mechanical problems and turned back to base. While he was landing, he overshot the field and crashed beyond the end of the runway where his fighter burst into flames. The crash truck arrived at the burning wreckage in time to save the pilot but the fire equipment malfunctioned and Crandall perished in the flames.

**23 March 1945: 348FG/341FS**

The 341FS flew escort for B-25s to Vlin Harbor, Hainan Island. 1Lt. Wilfred Joyal's fighter developed an oil leak and he was forced to bail out off the southern tip of Hainan and was picked up by a submarine and eventually returned to San Marcelino.

**24 March 1945: 5AF**

5AF Headquarters and Fighter and Bomber Commands moved to old Fort Stotsenberg, just west of the Clark Field complex. Far East Air Forces Headquarters would eventually move into old Fort William McKinley, just outside Manila, but this move would not be completed until April, after General Headquarters (MacArthur) had been established in downtown Manila on 12 April 1945.

**24 March 1945: 8FG/36FS**

On 24 March a Navy SBD Dauntless had been forced down on the enemy airdrome at San Jose de Buenavista on Panay and the 36FS was ordered to strafe and destroy it before the Japanese could salvage anything from it. The two P-38s arrived over the airstrip and could not locate the Navy dive bomber. However, there were five Japanese aircraft parked along the strip and to break the monotony the two passed over the strip when an enemy AA gun opened fire. The pilots then decided to strafe the enemy gun position and when 1Lt. Wladyslaw Sokolowski led the attack he suffered a direct hit and died in a fiery crash.

**Capt. Perry Dahl** (pictured at his 1978 Air Force retirement) shot down a Hamp for his ninth and last victory. (AFAA)

**25 March 1945: 35FG/39FS: Last P-47 Victory**

On 25 March Capt. Leroy Grosshuesch left Mangalden at 1555 with four P-47s on a late sweep over Formosa with 2Lt. Ervine Pratt as his Wingman and 1Lt. Edgar Beam as his Element Leader. The weather was generally bad over the east coast and the Flight crossed the mountains where they found some clear areas in the vicinity of Takao. Pratt spotted a lone Zero coming in from the west over Lamtun on the west coast at 11 o'clock at the same altitude (6,000 feet). Beam and his Wingman turned into the enemy while Grosshuesch and Pratt maneuvered to cut off the Zero. Grosshuesch opened fire and got a few hits and the Zero descended into Pratt's line of flight. Pratt firewalled with water injection and closed to fire at 300 yards at 40-50 degrees deflection and then closed to 150 yards dead astern and fired getting hits on the cockpit and fuselage and starting a fire in the engine nacelle. The Zero fell off on its left wing and exploded into some warehouses in Lamtun Town setting about half a dozen on fire. This was Pratt's third and last victory and the victory was the last Thunderbolt victory for the 35FG.

**28 March 1945: 475FG/431FS/432FS/433FS/HQ**

During late March more missions were being flown to the Asian mainland, as well as Formosa and the southern periphery of the Japanese Home Islands. After a few days of intensive dive bombing missions northeast of Lingayen, in the general area of the Ipo Dam, the 475th flew one of its most important missions to French Indo-China. At 0800 eight P-38s of the 431FS led by Maj. Robert Cline (who aborted and 1Lt. Kenneth Hart took over), seven of the 432FS led by Capt. Perry Dahl, and four of the 433FS led Maj. John Loisel, who also led the entire mission, took off on a B-25 escort mission.

432FS

Capt. Perry Dahl led his Squadron of eight P-38s (and Blue Flight) on an escort of B-25s to the French Indo-China Coast (Vietnam) to attack an armed enemy convoy. A B-25 pathfinder was to lead the Lightnings to their rendezvous with the B-25s in the Ben-Goi area. The exact location of the convoy was unknown and the Mitchell pathfinder returned to base before the B-25s arrived. Dahl searched for the convoy for 45 minutes and located it at 1130. The convoy consisted of 11 ships including two light cruisers and four destroyers or destroyer escorts. Due to the sea haze, Dahl led the Squadron down to 7,000 feet to maintain visual contact with the enemy ships but this altitude also put them within range of light but accurate enemy AA fire. Dahl alerted the incoming B-25s of the convoy's location just as Clover Red Flight sighted several enemy aircraft on the deck but did not observe 20 more above. Red flight dove on two enemy stragglers below. Dahl with Blue Flight tried to warn Red Flight by radio of the 20 enemy above but the frequency was jammed. The Japanese fighters began to attack Red Flight from above in two plane elements spaced 1,500 feet apart in a loose box formation which was stacked from the deck to 18,000 feet. Dahl and his flight climbed to meet them and the enemy fighters broke and zoomed back up. Dahl's climb put his Lightning on the verge of stall and he lowered the nose of his P-38 to gain speed and then pulled up into the next two diving fighters to deflect their attack from Red Flight. Soon, Dahl noticed a Hamp initiating an attack on the Red #4 man whom Dahl had been protecting. 1Lt. Richard Kimball dove after the Hamp but his guns jammed, so his Wingman 2Lt. George Wacker, pulled inside Kimball, fired a short burst from 1,000 feet at 60 degrees, getting hits on its wings causing the Hamp to break off in a violent roll to the right and Split-S away. Wacker followed and closed to 300 yards and fired again; hitting its canopy and setting it on fire for his only victory. The Japanese fighters continued to dive on the flight of P-38s below and Dahl maneuvered constantly to fend them off. During the battle Dahl brought a Hamp down with a 60 degree deflection shot for his ninth and last victory. The battle continued for 20 minutes and flight used so much of their fuel that they were forced to break off the combat and return to base. F/O DeWeese of Blue Flight ran low on fuel and was forced to bail out 40 miles west of Cabra Island, 1Lt. Leo Blakely radioed DeWeese's position and since his fuel consumption had not been high he circled him for as long as possible. He saw DeWeese struggle with his life raft, which did not seem to want to open. Blakely circled but the PBM rescue plane did not appear, and Blakely had to return to base. Blakely refueled at Mindoro and went back to search for DeWeese until dark and landed back after 10 hours in the air. The PBM also could not find the downed pilot.

475FG/HQ and 433FS

Maj. John Loisel of 475FG/HQ led four P-38s and part of 20 P-38s and at 1125 while circling the convoy at 6,500 feet north of Tre Island, Loisel saw 12 unidentified enemy aircraft loitering from 18,000 feet to the deck. Loisel dropped his tanks and began a diving turn and got on the tail of two Franks. One Frank turned sharply to port as Loisel fired a sighting burst while the other Frank continued to fly straight in a slight climb. Loisel closed and scored good hits on its fuselage and right wing and it crashed

**Maj. John Loisel** claimed his 11th and last victory of his long WWII service. (AFAA)

near the enemy convoy for his 11th and last victory. A few minutes later Loisel saw his #4, 2Lt. Wesley Hulett, being chased by an enemy fighter which was chased off by a Lightning from another flight. Hulett radioed that he had an engine out and there was an enemy fighter on his tail. Loisel dove and chased it off with a short burst but lost sight of the P-38. Hulett radioed that both of his engines were now out and Loisel instructed him to glide east and he would send a rescue Catalina. Hulett was never seen again.

**2Lt. Thomas Martin** shot down a Hamp for his third and final victory. (AAF)

431FS

Capt. Robert Cline led eight P-38s of Banyan (new call sign) Yellow and Green Flights from Clark Field #1 at 0800 but an hour later Cline had to return to base and 1Lt. Kenneth Hart took over the mission and Green Flight with 1Lt. Thomas Martin as his Wingman and 1Lt. Horace Reeves as his #3. They reached the target area at 1155 at 11,000 feet. About 10 minutes later they made their first passes at two bandits getting hits without seeing any results. These Hamps Split-S'd away and were followed by Yellow Flight. Green Flight was then bounced by three Hamps at 7 o'clock high and Hart and his Wingman Martin quickly shot one down each. Martin turned into the Hamp and fired into its cockpit an engine and closed and fired a few more short bursts and it rolled over and crashed into the base of the mountains with a parachute descending nearby. Hart then fired a long burst from 30 to 0 degrees and the pilot bailed out as it burst into flames. Hart got on a Hamp's tail and he fired as the enemy pilot skidded and rolled. Hart's burst hit its cockpit and the pilot also bailed out. Hart, Martin, and Reeves rejoined at 3,000 feet and climbed to 8,000 feet over the Bay and were about to return home when they were jumped by four more Hamps. Hart and Martin broke left and started around on them while Reeves went into a violent roll and Split-S'd and lost his attacker. As Reeves attempted to rejoin Hart and Martin he saw Hart climbing after one of them but also saw one climbing on Martin's tail and closed and fired on the P-38. Reeves closed on the attacker who Split-S'd after Martin who was diving away. Reeves fired a desperate snap shot and hit the Hamp's cockpit and it dove straight into the water and exploded. Reeves then saw a second attacker and heading for the clouds over the mountains to the west of the Bay. Hart was leading the chase and fired at very long range before it entered the clouds but without success. Reeves dove under the clouds hoping to meet the Hamp in a head on pass in case it Split-S'd and came out below the clouds while Hart remained above them. Reeves "latched onto the Nip as he came out below." The Hamp was 500 feet below the clouds and Reeves rolled to starboard and got on its tail and fired at 200 yards and fired a long burst that scored hits but the Hamp continued to fly. He then closed to 50 yards and fired again and the Hamp flew on. Reeves fired again and finally started a fire and it crashed into the Bay. Hart's and Reeves' two victories gave each pilot eight total for the war. Meanwhile, 1Lt. John Pietz was leading the second element of Yellow Flight with 2Lt. James Barnes as his Wingman when two bogies were called in at their level. They chased the two Japanese fighters to the deck where they identified them as Tojos. After making numerous passes in a turning dogfight Pietz was able to close on the tail of a Tojo and fired to gain his sixth victory and the 11th of the day for the 475FG.

**1Lt. John Pietz** shot down a Tojo for his sixth and last victory. (AFAA)

**1Lt. Horace Reeves** had a big day, shooting down four Hamps to give him eight total victories. (AFAA)

**1Lt. Kenneth Hart** shot down two Hamps to give him eight total victories. (AFAA)

**29 March 1945: 475FG/431FS/432FS: Final Victories**

Ten P-38s of the 431st and 432nd Squadrons took off at 0710 for another B-25 anti-shipping mission to French Indo-China with 1Lt. Laurence LeBaron from Group Headquarters leading the mission. The Lightnings rendezvoused over Capones Island with their B-25 pathfinder which would lead them on a four-hour flight to the target. One 431FS and one 432FS P-38 returned early and since the 432nd would be in the target area later than the 431st, 2Lt. John O'Rourke of the 431FS volunteered to fill in the vacant 432FS position.

432FS
1Lt. Harrold Owen led Green Flight with 2Lt. Lawrence Dowler as his Wingman and with O'Rourke as the new #4 man. About 1130, as the flight was nearing the target area, LeBaron called out 11 Zeros at 1 o'clock level at 4,000 feet. Green Flight made a climbing turn to the right and came down at 6 o'clock on the Zero's tails. LeBaron immediately chose one of two stragglers and hit it in the fuselage and wing root from 200 yards at 30 degrees deflection. The Zero began to burn and glided into the water. Meanwhile, Owen fired on other straggler with a four second burst that hit it in the wing roots and cockpit and it fell off to the right. Owen started to follow it but his port engine supercharger malfunctioned and he broke off (Dowler would confirm Owen's fourth and last victory). As Owen continued his right turn he faced two more Zeros in a head on pass as they were closing on LeBaron. The two Zero split up and broke off their attack on LeBaron. At this time, LeBaron closed rapidly on another Zero and fired from 150 yards getting numerous hits on its wings, fuselage, and tail and it began to smoke and LeBaron overran it and the Zero was not seen to crash. After he overran the Zero, LeBaron pulled up and fired from 100 yards astern and tore off pieces from the trailing edge of its wing and it immediately plunged into the water. As LeBaron shot down his second Zero O'Rourke came in and shot down a Zero for his only victory. When LeBaron's element rejoined Owens' element, the remaining Zeros slipped in behind them. Owens crossed over and broke up their attack with a head on pass. A Zero then made a head on pass on Dowler from above. Dowler pulled up and turned into the Zero. The Zero pilot fired at 400 yards but Dowler held off firing until 300 yards and the Zero passed over Dowler and crashed into the trees a half mile inland. LeBaron made several more passes and got a few hits when he saw a Zero heading inland. He chased it as the enemy pilot reversed his turns in several clouds and apparently thought he lost LeBaron and straightened out, heading south. LeBaron came up from below and directly astern and fired a long burst from 150 yards. The Zero began to disintegrate and smoke heavily and crashed in a small clearing for his third victory of the battle and his fourth and last victory. Dowler saw another Zero heading in the opposite direction 2,000 feet above him and suddenly it swung onto Dowler's tail. Dowler turned into it and scored a few hits but his speed was low and he put his Lightning into a dive to gain speed. The Zero pilot again got onto Dowler's tail and Dowler responded by climbing in a steep spiral to the right. When the Zero stalled out Dowler stall turn down on it and fired and causing the Zero to start smoking badly. Dowler closed to 200 yards and fired a long burst that caused a large fire that Dowler had to pull up to avoid. The enemy pilot managed to bail out but his parachute seemed to be on fire as his body crashed into the ground and Dowler had his second victory of the day and his third and last victory. Owen feathered his engine and was escorted 850 miles back to Clark Field. After flying for eight and a half hours he found that his hydraulic system had been shot out and he had to hand pump his gear down to land safely with four career victories. These seven victories were the last for the 432nd and 475th and for the next five months the Satan's Angels would conduct important, but not glamorous, ground support and patrol missions. The 431st had claimed 221 victories and 14 probables and seven and a half damaged; the 432nd claimed 167 victories, 21 probables and 14 damaged; while the 433rd had claimed 121 victories, 23 probables, and 12 damaged for the war.

**29 March 1945: 3ACG**
On 29 March the Air Commandos attacked enemy troops along the Villa Verde Trail. As the two 3ACG P-51s pulled out of their runs, they collided but both pilots parachuted safely and were picked up later by friendly troops.

**1Lt. Laurence LeBaron** shot down three Zeros, falling short of becoming an ace with four total victories. (AAF)

**2Lt. John O'Rourke** shot down a Zero and damaged another for his only victory of the war. (AAF)

As March ended the monsoon season was approaching and the rains would make Mangaldan, with its high water table, unsuitable for operations and so the Fifth Air Force Headquarters planned a major move not only for the Air Commandos but for all units based at Mangaldan.

**March 1945: 58FG**
The 58FG established several new records during March. A total of 1,360 sorties were flown, during which the Group dropped 702.5 tons of bombs and 144 Napalm tanks (over 100 tons) and fired 330,439 rounds of ammunition. The 310th Fighter Squadron established a new record for the Squadron by delivering over 220 tons of explosives. The 69th carried 216 tons while the 311th dropped 721 bombs of varying description totaling 194 tons. The 311th dropped half of the Group's Napalm and used 135,168 rounds of the ammunition. 1Lt. Lynwood Johnson of the 311FS also shot down one of the few enemy planes remaining in the Philippines.

**Late March 1945: 49FG**
During the second half of MacArthur's March offensive, Kruger's Infantry closed in on the more remote enemy strong points in the mountains just east of the Lingayen. All three 49er Squadrons participated in aerial attacks which concentrated on the Balete Pass and the Villa Verde Trail area

where the enemy was mounting a tenacious resistance. For two weeks, 49er Lightnings would often fly three tactical sorties per day to the highlands facing small arms fire but suffering relatively small losses. On the 25th, the Black Sheep bombed the Villa Verde highway and 1Lt. John Lang's port engine was hit and he bailed out from his burning fighter 15 miles from Lingayen and no trace of the pilot was found. Two days later rookie 2Lt. Dewey Renick was killed instantly by intense ground fire from Japanese fortifications he was strafing.

**Late March 1945: 8FG Command Changes**

From the mid-December 1944 Mindoro landings until Clark Field was secured in the second or third week of March 1945; the 8FG operated directly under the control of the 5FC. Subsequently the Group was assigned to the 310th Bomb Wing for operational control. The Group found that working directly for the 5FC had some definite advantages as it assigned to the choice missions and had a direct pipeline to Group Command; many of whom were former Group members. The transfer to the 310BW eliminated these advantages.

**March 1945: 348FG**

During March the Group continued to operate from San Marcelino on Luzon under the 309BW for tactical operations and under the 85BW for administrative purposes. Once Corregidor was captured and the Bataan Campaign was nearly completed the 348th was assigned to attack Caballo, a small island just southeast of Corregidor, the Fort Stotsenburg area, and the Yamashita Line located in the rugged Rizal Province which was established after the Japanese retreated from Manila.

During March the Group flew 620 missions of which 36% were ground support, 28% local patrols, 15% Manila patrols, and 13% convoy patrols. Eight bombing and strafing missions were flown to the Fort Stotsenburg area in the first week of the month and killed nearly 600 troops and were instrumental in securing the area. Strikes in the Santa Maria Valley caused over 300 enemy casualties and materially aided Guerilla forces there in securing that area. Caballo Island was hit by 95 missions dropping standard bombs and Napalm causing the Japanese to try to evacuate the ravaged island on 3 March. The Group flew 14 missions to the Indo-China and China Coast, covering B-25s and encountering enemy air opposition, destroying five aircraft. On 3 March the 342FS had entirely converted to the P-51 and on the 24th the 460FS became the last squadron began flying its P-51s operationally on a long range mission to Indo-China. At the end of the month the ground support missions to Caballo Island, Corregidor, and Fort Stotsenburg were completed but neutralizing enemy positions in the Rizal Province, east of Manila had only started.

The group lost 13 aircraft due to operational accidents while 14 more incurred major damaged. The 340th and 342nd each had two fatalities due to operational accidents and the 340th had one and the 341st two missing to operational accidents. The only loss due to enemy actions was 1Lt. Clark Kooper of the 342FS.

**Late March 1945: Situation**

The Villa Verde Trail, the Balete Pass, and the Baguio area were areas vital to Yamashita's defense of northern Luzon. Highway 5 led almost due north and entered the mountains winding through the Balete Pass before reaching the southern end of the Cagayan Valley at Santa Fe. The Villa Verde Trail connected the central plain of Luzon with Santa Fe. The Trail entered the mountains northeast of San Nicholas (Pangasinan Province) and progressed northeast and east through very rough terrain, passing the town of Salasac and entered into the Cagayan Valley at Imugam, about four miles west of Santa Fe. The area around Baguio, the pre-war summer capitol of the Philippines, was very important because the Japanese had constructed a new road across the northern mountains via Kayapa and Pingkian, connecting with Highway 5 about 25 miles northeast of Santa Fe at the town of Bambang. This Highway allowed access to the rear of the enemy stronghold north of the Balete Pass, in the Santa Fe area. Yamashita was now able to transfer men and supplies to either front to respond to attacks. Balete Pass-Santa Fe was consequently the crucial position in the enemy defenses of northern Luzon. To control the Pass would provide access to the entire Cagayan Valley and to gain control the U.S. Sixth Army would have to secure control of all three approaches: Baguio, the Villa Verde Trail, and Balete Pass.

To accomplish this and open the south end of the Cagayan Valley, the 25th Infantry Division was to move north along Highway 5 to meet the Japanese at Balete Pass; the 32nd Infantry Division holding the center was to advance along the Villa Verde Trail; while the 33rd Infantry Division was to drive north along Highway 11 and capture Baguio. An element of the 33rd Division had advanced north on Highway 3 along the west coast of Luzon in March and joined up with a Filipino Guerrilla Force at San Fernando. The 37th Infantry was to be introduced into the fighting at San Fernando and were to advance eastward toward Baguio. On 1 April the Sixth Army began its campaign with the 25th Division beginning a double envelopment of the Balete Pass while the 32nd started fighting at San Fernando on the west coast and drove east toward Baguio. The 33rd attacked the Japanese in the mountains on two sides, south of Baguio. On 27 April the 37th Division captured Baguio and the old American fort, Camp John Hay. The Japanese defenses then buckled around Baguio and they fled eastward toward Santa Fe and contact was lost with the enemy east and north of Baguio. The Americans captured large stocks of ammunition, supplies and equipment in the area and turned over to the Guerrilla forces. By 29 April the 37th advanced northward from Baguio along the mountain highway to Bontoc and had captured La Trinidad. The retreating enemy was constantly harassed by the 5th Air Force which continually bombed and strafed them as they escaped toward their mountain stronghold at Bontoc.

To the east, in the Balete Pass and Villa Verde Trail sectors, the 25th and 32nd Divisions met persistent enemy forces that had to be routed out of every one of their prepared defensive positions. The U.S. advance along Highway 5 through the Balete Pass was much better than the Villa Verde Trail. Despite damage by overuse, landslides, and rain heavy artillery could be moved up the Highway to be used at point blank range to fire directly into the enemy caves and pill boxes. Meanwhile, the Villa Verde Trail had experienced so much damage in the fighting that hauling these heavier guns there was impossible. The advance was slow, but by 20 April the 32nd Infantry had advanced and secured the controlling terrain at the Salasac Pass, which was about three miles west of the town of Imugan, which was about five miles west of the vital junction at the city of Santa Fe.

After being supported by very heavy air action on 30 April the 25th Division advanced along the ridges overlooking the Balete Pass and by 5 May had captured the heights surrounding the Pass. The Japanese reacted by transferring units from the Villa Verde Trail defenses to stop the advance of the 25th Division which then opened the way for the 32nd Division which bypassed the remaining enemy strong points on the Trail and captured Imugan and by 8 May had advanced on Santa Fe from the west. After heavy air and artillery bombardment on 13 May the 25th Division overwhelmed the Japanese defending the Balete Pass and pushed north toward Santa Fe. The Japanese defenses began to disintegrate everywhere and by 25 May Santa Fe was completely surrounded. After intense air attacks on 26 May the 25th Division drove through the city and advanced along the highway into the Cagayan Valley. After 100 days of continuous fighting the 32nd Division captured Imugan and joined with the 25th Division to conclude this part of the campaign. The Japanese forces that managed to retreat into their mountain strongholds would succeed in holding out until the end of the war. The ground fighting on the island of Luzon was very costly for the Sixth Army which had 8,140 killed, 157 missing and 29,557 wounded on Luzon. The Japanese killed and missing were 180,860 (triple the 56,655 killed on Leyte) with untold wounded and missing.

# 7

# April 1945

**April 1945: Situation Philippines**

On 31 March Kenney returned from his trip to Washington as a four-star General. In addition to the 5th and 13th Air Forces, he would eventually add elements of the 7th Air Force to his command. On 15 April Kenney was notified that the FEAF would acquire three P-47 Groups, three more B-24 Groups (two of which had already been operating under FEAF), one B-25 Group and one Group equipped with the new Douglas A-26 Invader attack bombers.

Gen. Yamashita's XIV Area Army was forced into a deliberate fighting retreat up the Balete Pass into the Cagayan Valley and by the end of April Yamashita would be driven out of his plush Baguio Headquarters with its swimming pools, golf courses, and comfortable accommodations. A series of ground operations carried out in the central Philippines during March had gained control of Panay, Cebu, Bohol, Negros, Palawan and had established the 8th Army, now under the command of Gen. Robert Eichelberger, on Mindanao. The Filipino Guerrillas were becoming stronger, better equipped, and better organized each day, and were putting immense pressure on the remaining enemy forces trapped on the various islands and were participating in the mop up operations. Once the Japanese were eliminated from an area the Filipinos began to reorganize and rebuild their country. So with the lack of any effective Japanese air opposition the 5FC found itself with an increased ground support role in April.

**April 1945 Situation Formosa and Okinawa**

April 1945 was one of the worst months for the Japanese war effort. On Easter Sunday, 1 April 1945, after the 5AF had cleared the way the previous day, the 158th Regimental Combat Team landed on the beaches at Legaspi. They encountered little resistance as the enemy had abandoned their defenses to escape the heavy aerial bombardments. By the end of the day the 158th had captured the port, town, and air field.

On this same day the 10th Army, under Gen. Simon Buckner, landed on Okinawa, the beginning of a vicious 82 day battle to capture that first piece of Japanese Homeland. The invasion force consisted of 100,000 troops, thousands of ships, three U.S. Navy Task Forces and one British Royal Navy Task Force. Okinawa's capture would expose the Home Islands of Kyushu and Honshu to devastating attacks by the long range AAF heavy bombers and be the base for the invasion of the Japanese main Homeland Island of Kyushu. Six days later, the mighty battleship *Yamato* was lost in a futile operation against U.S. naval vessels off Okinawa and on that day fighter-escorted B-29s began to attack the Home Islands.

The U.S. attack on Okinawa came as a complete surprise to the Japanese. Partly due to the powerful U.S. air attacks on the Formosan airdromes in March, the Japanese High Command rationalized that MacArthur would certainly land his forces there, probably somewhere on the Island's southern coast. In anticipation, the Japanese marshaled their air units to Formosa's northern airfields and to those on Okinawa in hopes of engaging the American Fleet in a decisive sea battle in the northern Philippines Sea. The Kamikazes were to inflict such severe losses on the USN invasion fleet and disrupt the Formosa invasion that the Americans would be compelled into cease fire negotiations and that peace might follow.

The unexpected and very powerful invasion of Okinawa ended any Japanese plans for Formosa. The completely disorientated Japanese High Command sacrificed wave after wave of Kamikaze pilots against the huge USN task force lying off Okinawa. Although the damage inflicted on Nimitz' Advanced Task Force at the beachhead was substantial; America's inexhaustible reserves in men and material were far beyond Japan's desperate, pitiful defense. Within a week, the U.S. Navy and Marine Corps fighters had annihilated entire enemy air units in what was to be the last major counter offensive of the enemy air force.

During the Okinawa Campaign the FEAF based at Lingayen was relegated to the strategic support of Nimitz' western flank. The 49FG continued to fly interdictions against the west coast of Formosa plus escorting the many anti-shipping attacks by the medium bombers in the Formosa Straits. The 5FC also flew numerous escorts for the USN and AAF rescue flights.

**April 1945: Situation and the Introduction of the Aerial Rocket**

In April the 5FC returned once more to flying tactical sorties against the remnants of the Japanese Army on Luzon. By mid April U.S. infantry had reached the north coast and began to advance east rapidly against Gen. Yamashita's troops frantically retreating toward Aparri Village on the mouth of the Cagayan River. Likewise, the 5FC flew concerted attacks in the central highlands, approximately on a line running from Balete Pass, up through the Villa Verde Road crossing, and into the Bagiuo Hills, referred to as "The Yamashita Line." Close air support allowed the U.S. Sixth Army to break out through the highlands and then advance into the southern end of the Cagayan Valley. By the end of April, the Japanese retreated to fortified enclaves hidden in the ravines and caves of the steep, forested hills. Sorties to eradicate these indistinguishable targets required pin point accuracy and a new weapon, the aerial rocket was introduced.

While on leave in Hawaii 8FS pilots picked up eight late L-model Lightnings and ferried them to Lingayen by way of the Pacific Ferry Route

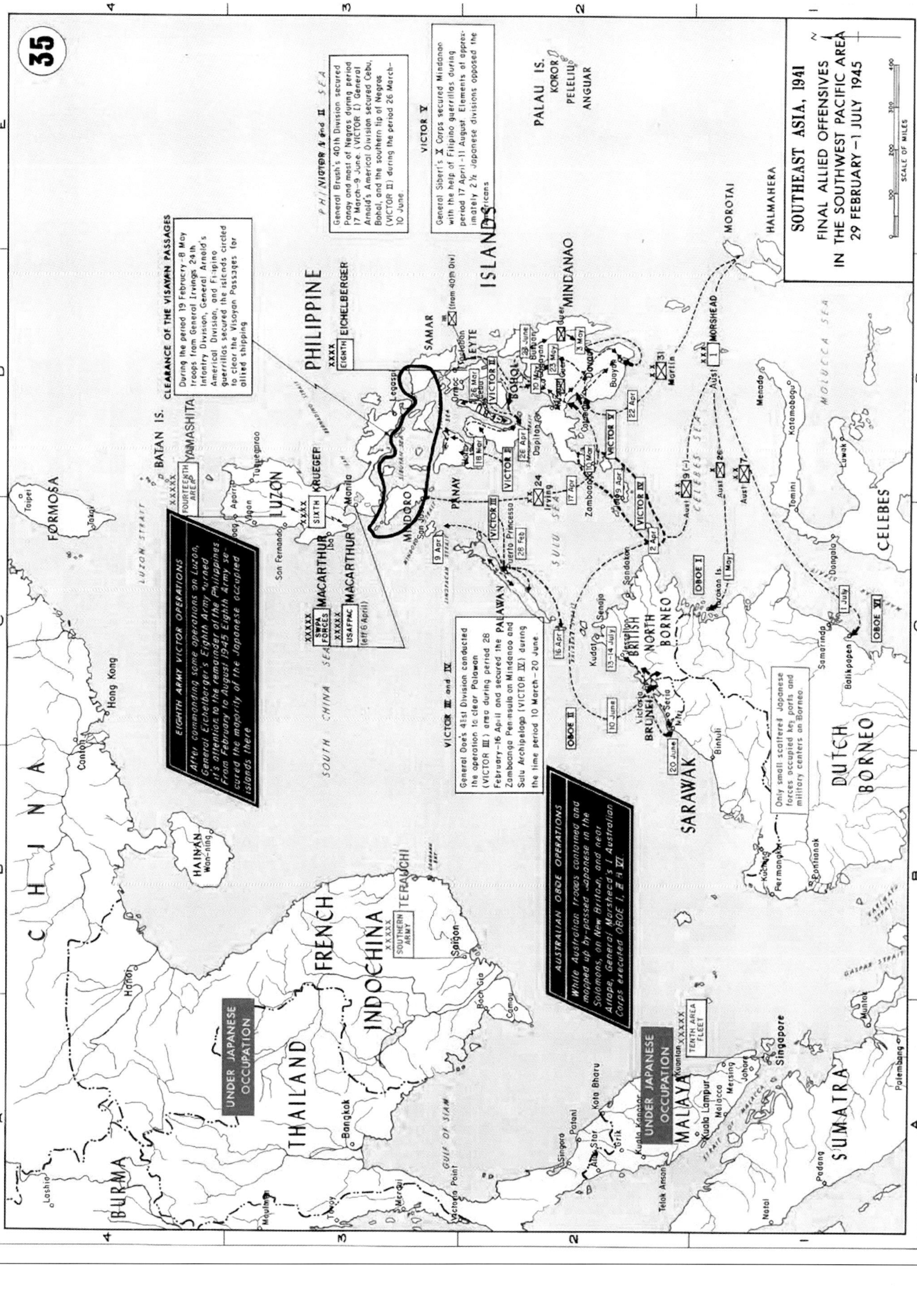
35
SOUTHEAST ASIA, 1941
FINAL ALLIED OFFENSIVES
IN THE SOUTHWEST PACIFIC AREA
29 FEBRUARY – 1 JULY 1945
SCALE OF MILES
CLEARANCE OF THE VISAYAN PASSAGES
During the period 19 February–8 May troops from General Irving's 24th Infantry Division, General Arnold's Americal Division, and Filipino guerrillas secured the islands circled to clear the Visayan Passages for allied shipping
VICTOR I and II
General Brush's 40th Division secured Panay and most of Negros during period 17 March–9 June. (VICTOR I) General Arnold's Americal Division secured Cebu, Bohol, and the southern tip of Negros (VICTOR II) during the period 26 March–10 June.
VICTOR V
General Sibert's X Corps secured Mindanao with the help of Filipino guerrillas during period 17 April–11 August. Elements of approximately 2½ Japanese divisions opposed the Americans.
EIGHTH ARMY VICTOR OPERATIONS
After commanding some operations on Luzon, General Eichelberger's Eighth Army turned its attention to the remainder of the Philippines. From February to August 1945 Eighth Army secured the majority of the Japanese occupied islands there
VICTOR III and IV
General Doe's 41st Division conducted the operation to clear Palawan (VICTOR III) area during period 28 February–16 April and secured the Zamboanga Peninsula on Mindanao and Sulu Archipelago (VICTOR IV) during the time period 10 March–20 June.
AUSTRALIAN OBOE OPERATIONS
While Australian troops contained and mopped up by-passed Japanese in the Solomons, on New Britain, and near Aitape, General Morshead's I Australian Corps executed OBOE I, II & VI.
Only small scattered Japanese forces occupied key ports and military centers on Borneo.
UNDER JAPANESE OCCUPATION
UNDER JAPANESE OCCUPATION
PHILIPPINE ISLANDS
LUZON
MINDORO
SAMAR
LEYTE
BOHOL
MINDANAO
PANAY
PALAWAN
FORMOSA
CHINA
FRENCH INDOCHINA
THAILAND
BURMA
MALAYA
SUMATRA
BRITISH NORTH BORNEO
SARAWAK
DUTCH BORNEO
CELEBES
HALMAHERA
MOROTAI
PALAU IS.
HAINAN
SOUTH CHINA SEA
SULU SEA
CELEBES SEA
MOLUCCA SEA
FOURTEENTH AREA ARMY
YAMASHITA
SIXTH KRUEGER
EIGHTH EICHELBERGER
SWPA FORCES MACARTHUR
USAFPAC MACARTHUR
SOUTHERN ARMY TERAUCHI
TENTH AREA FLEET
MORSHEAD
OBOE I
OBOE II
OBOE VI
VICTOR I
VICTOR II
VICTOR III
VICTOR IV
VICTOR V

The **P-47N Thunderbolt** was a superlative fighter bomber which could carry varied armament. (AAF)

A Japanese coastal transport under rocket attack. (AAF)

via Wake and Guam Islands. These P-38s were equipped with detachable, underwing racks, each of which could mount five 60 pound high velocity rockets. The V-shaped racks hung down nearly two feet from the underwing surface and were compared to an inverted Christmas tree (and called that). The 20mm cannon ammunition was not carried when the 600+ pounds of racks and rockets were fitted. The rockets were only used on a few operational sorties in late April and during May and were found to be very effective. The weapons were aimed through the standard fighter gunsight and were most effective at ranges of up to 500 yards. The engulfing fire of Napalm was considered to be tactically more effective against hidden emplacements, while the firepower of rocket projectiles were considered to be better suited for larger targets such as enemy shipping, particularly when the Lightnings would be attacking ports in Japan's Inland Sea later in 1945.

**3 April 1945: 8FG**

On 3 April eight 35FS Lightnings took off from Luzon and used Lingayen to refuel and then flew their escort of B-24s to Hong Kong for the first time. The escorts met no interceptors and the B-24s destroyed a warehouse and sank three ships in the harbor without loss to the bombers or escorts.

Local missions took their toll on the 8FG in April. On 3 April, Capt. Richard Johnson had navigation problems on a local mission and ran out of fuel and crashed off Mindoro. That same day, 1Lt. Harold Manning was killed taking off on a strafing and bombing mission when the tail fin of one of the bombs he was carrying fell off and armed the bomb. Then one engine failed and Manning decided to ditch and not knowing one bomb was armed, he routinely jettisoned the bombs and his plane was demolished by the explosion.

**April 1945: 35FG**

In April the Group flew a decreased number of sorties due to two reasons. First, a heavy rain storm on the 4th closed their strip Mangaldan for the next eight days. Mangaldan had been considered as a temporary strip, fair-weather strip since its inception on 20 January. On 10 April, when it was almost fully equipped with the Mustang, the Group began its move to a new base at Lingayen which was covered by PSP and was well-drained to be serviceable during heavy rains. The new base was pleasant, located in a coconut grove lying along the beach just west of Lingayen Town. The first billets were tents and a the construction of permanent buildings was initiated, However, the construction was halted suddenly on the 17th as the airstrip was closed to the P-51 as there was a recurring strong crosswind and the coral runway was considered too rough. On the 19th the Group was then ordered to the Clark Field Complex, near Fort Stotsenburg. The base had formerly been occupied by the 475FG which had moved to the 35th's old base at Lingayen. The move was completed in only two days as they Groups moved into each other's completed bases. The new base was highly developed and very comfortable and needed little improvement.

The Group engaged in aerial combat only once during the month and primarily conducted dive bombing missions in direct support of Luzon infantry operations during the month. Its dive bombing sorties were instrumental in aiding the advances by the U.S. Sixth Army in its operations in the rugged terrain of the Balete Pass. The Group lost two men in combat during the month. 2Lt, John Rosewicz of he 40FS was MIA after he was last seen bailing out after being hit by AA fire on the 13th during a B-25 escort mission to Shaka, Formosa. Capt. James Scott of the 41FS was killed on 3 April when his P-51 developed engine trouble on take off. Scott tried to turn around and land but bounced as he crabbed and crashed and exploded. The popular veteran Scott had been credited with two victories.

**1-8 April 1945: 475FG**

During April through June 1945 the 475FG flew its heaviest mission schedule of the war but the 475FG was relegated to less prestigious ground support missions over the Philippines, rather than the glamorous fighter-versus-fighter combat that had been the reason for the Group being activated in mid-1943. From the beginning of April the number of ground attack missions flown by the 475th increased until that type of mission became prevalent and because of the short distances flown to the target area; it often flew two or three missions a day against the enemy positions around Baguio, the Balete Pass, and also the Ipo Dam area along with an occasional escort or strike against the Asian mainland. It would have good success in its ground support role using a combination of general purpose and Napalm bomb loads against Japanese positions, billets, and bridges. Attacking railroad targets was relished by the pilots with locomotives being especially gratifying, as a spectacular spout of steam would rush up for hundreds of feet when bullets and cannon shells struck the engine's boiler.

On 1 April the 432FS escorted a PBM Mariner that was patrolling offshore of Formosa. On 2 April five 432FS P-38s were loaded with 1,000lb general purpose bombs and four armed with Napalm flew an impressive Napalm attack mission on the Villa Verde trail, west of Santa Fe. The mission started large fires in the target area which caused a U.S. forward air controller to comment that the Group's bombing was the "best (he) had ever witnessed."

On 2 April Lt. Laverne Busch was flying with the 433FS in a flight led by 1Lt. William Richmond on a mission to Clark Field. On route to the target his Napalm bomb hung up and he bailed out. He landed with multiple fractures and in severe shock and died three days later.

On 8 April eight 433FS Lightnings were escorting B-24s to bomb an airfield on Formosa and after circling the area for 15 minutes they saw a locomotive and five freight cars on the main north-south track near Taichu and systematically strafed and destroyed it.

During the first week of April Japanese positions defended by diehard fanatics rather than organized troops in both the northern Kembu and southern Shimbu areas were methodically and gradually being weakened by the FEAF, with small formations of bomb-carrying 475FG P-38s. Perhaps the most threatening Japanese positions of all during this period were those defending the Ipo Dam area.

**April 1945: 3ACG**

The capture of Gabu placed the 3ACG closer to Formosa and the Chinese mainland. In late March officers representing each of the 3ACG Sections flew to Gabu to survey bivouac and operations areas. The airstrip needed to be rehabilitated and the Group's aviation engineer unit arrived in C-47s to begin work. While the earth at Gabu was more suitable for airfield construction than that at Mangaldan, dust was a problem, and a 5,100-foot asphalt and gravel runway, a parallel taxiway, and extensive hardstands needed to be built. It was imperative that the Gabu runways and facilities be completed as Mangaldan would be useless when the rainy season began. Runway construction proceeded quickly, and in early April the 3ACG began moving all of its units and their equipment (except for the liaison squadrons). The C-47s of the 318th TCS was responsible for the move which was completed after 12 days. During this time there was only one problem which could have been disastrous. A C-47 was taking off from Mangaldan when its right engine quit and the sudden loss of power caused the transport to swerve and its wing to catch the ground. The transport crashed and burst into flames but quick action by ground crews saved all aboard, mainly pilots from the 4th Fighter Section. Group Headquarters was established in San Nicolas, a small town about six miles from the Gabu field. The Headquarters offices were on the ground floor of a school while students continued to attend classes on the second floor.

While Gabu was being prepared, missions continued to be flown from Mangaldan. The transfer of operations from Gabu progressed so seamlessly that when the 3rd Fighter Section moved, 16 of its Mustangs were armed with bombs and ammunition at Mangaldan, flew a raid on Baguio, then landed at their new field and then the following day they escorted B-24s to Formosa. The 3ACG continued to fly fighter sweeps to Formosa with missions on 1 April, 22 April, and 26 April being particularly fruitful as Group Mustangs destroyed 23 trucks, eight locomotives, and numerous facilities. On 2 April, 12 Mustangs of the 3rd Fighter Section escorted B-24s on a shipping strike to Hong Kong. Shortly after their rendezvous with the bombers near the target, two Zeros were spotted, which were the first enemy aircraft seen in the air in three months The enemy pilots began a head on pass on the P-51s, which were flying in three flights in trail. The first Air Commando flight dove away, leaving the second flight to face the enemy pilots who had switched their attention to the second flight led by 1Lt. Glenn Lairmore. Both opponents closed and fired before one of the Zeros broke off its attack but the other enemy pilot turned quickly and got on 2Lt. Joseph Singletary's tail. Singletary had been unable to drop his external tanks and was now in an exposed position. When the Zeros roared past, 2Lt. Barrett Wagner broke left, and put his Mustang behind Singletary's pursuer who tried to dive away. Wagner closed quickly and began firing as the two aircraft dove through 3,000 feet getting hits on the enemy's fuselage and wing root. Wagner expected the Zero pilot to pull out and stayed high and watched as the Zeke pilot belatedly realized how close he was to the water, banking slightly and then making a last sharp turn, catching his wing in the water and suddenly disintegrating giving Wagner his only victory. Meanwhile, Lairmore reformed the other pilots in his flight at 12,000 feet, where he saw two more Zeros heading away from him. Just as he began to chase after them, they turned back in a head on pass. Lairmore began firing at about 600 yards and saw pieces of one of the Zero's cowling tear off and it rolled over and spiraled downward for a probable. Lairmore then noticed that his Wingman was missing and began a search and sighted the other Zero below making a pass on a flight of Mustangs. He dove on the enemy, opening fire at 800 yards and continuing until he was just 25 yards away before the Zero rolled over on its back, spinning earthward. The Zero's spin continued from 8,000 feet until Lairmore lost sight of it in the haze and smoke at 1,000 feet for another probable.

**2Lt. Barrett Wagner** shot down a Zero over Hong Kong for his only victory of the war. (AAF)

Except for an uneventful trip to Hong Kong on 13 April and a few more lackluster missions to Formosa, the Air Commando Fighter Sections spent the remainder of their stay at Gabu flying close support missions for the 32nd Infantry Division that was advancing slowly over very difficult terrain along the Villa Verde Trail. Often, the infantry was only a matter of just yards from enemy positions which was considered too close for air support. However, Group CO, Arvid Olson was confident his fighter pilots could make such close in strikes and by the end of the Campaign the 32nd's CO, Maj.Gen. William Gill wrote a letter of commendation to Olson stating:

> The close support strikes accomplished by the men of your command have been most gratifying to me. These attacks have materially aided the advance of the 32nd Infantry Division troops along the Villa Verde Trail and other fields of battle in northern Luzon... The bombings have been precise and accurate; their strafing runs have been to my mind perfection itself. ... It is my belief that this is the first time that pilots of the supporting air arm have visited die forward ground units in the combat zone to view the terrain and study the tactical situation in the area they are to be employed. To my knowledge it is the first time that such action has been undertaken by the pilots own volition. The daring and aggressiveness displayed by the Third Air Commando Group is indeed gratifying to myself and the men of my command. I am proud to say I have had them as a supporting arm to my offensive in the northern Luzon campaign.

**April 1945: 421NFS**

During April many of the original members of the Squadron transferred including Captains Elston, Jones, Roady, Robbins, and Townsend; Lieutenants Bjorum, Blanchard, Crawford, Forrester, and Oiley; and Sergeant/gunners Banosi, DeHaven, Swinney, Recs, and Weishar.

The move of the San Marcelino Detachment to Clark was completed 26 April and for the first time since January the 421st was together. A training program was initiated for all the aircrews to give them additional training in strafing technique, night fighting operations, formation flying, and instrument flying. With the lack of any enemy opposition it was felt that continual training would keep the crews in a constant state of readiness. The concern about night fighter operations and how the P-61s were being used in combat was broached again to the 5FC by Squadron CO Maj. Richard Kiick who protested that the P-61 was rarely provided with opportunities to make use of the tremendous firepower but again, nothing came of his protest. The mission of the Squadron for April had chiefly been night patrols; with Squadron records showing that a number of bogies had been run contacted, only to be identified as American and no enemy aircraft were encountered. On 12 April the 421st NFS engaged in its first P-61 bombing mission. At 1500 Capt. Beverly Bowers dropped two 500 pound bombs in support of infantry action north of the town of Infanta but no results were observed.

**April 1945: Japanese Remain Dangerous**

Although the Philippines were secured, the Japanese left behind some hazards that could be fatal. The Japanese had poisoned some of the local liquor before leaving and a large number of men died and some became blinded. Headquarters actually erected a large billboard showing statistics of how many had died but unfortunately, even with the warnings many continued to drink. Also, small pockets of Japanese remained in the local hills and snipers were a constant danger. Another hazard was land mines and booby traps rigged in buildings and former Japanese equipment.

**1 April 1945: 348FG**

After months of relative inactivity in air combat and as payback for their yeoman work in their ground support role over the northern Philippines; the 348FG thought it would be involved in the invasion of Okinawa at the beginning of April. Unfortunately, the Group was already committed to moving to Floridablanca when Okinawa was invaded on 1 April and consequently the 348th had to continue the mop-up war on Northern Luzon during April and May.

During these operations the Group lost six pilots:

2 April: Lt. George Goddard (342FS)
11 April: 1Lt. Charles Nickell (342FS)
11 April: 1Lt. Walter Abraham (460FS)
? April: 1Lt. Truman Ragsdale (342FS)
? April: 2Lt. Robert Wolffe (341FS)
27 April: 1Lt. Richard McAfee (341FS)

**2 April 1945: 49FG: Last 9FS Victory**

For the Flying Knights' mission along the southern China coast Lt.Col. Gerald Johnson was joined by his old friend from Dobodura Maj. James Watkins, who recently rejoined the 49ers as their Group Deputy CO. Johnson flew the lead in the 16 fighter escort for B-24s sent against Hong Kong's airdromes; one of several long range airfield suppression strikes in support of the Okinawa Campaign. The flight took off from Lingayen at 1005 and arrived at the target at 1300 as the Liberators were bombing the docks and the JNAF airdrome. The Lightnings orbited over the city at 14,000 feet for 40 minutes, when Johnson finally spotted two Tojos northwest at about 10 miles at 8,000-10,000 feet. The two aces rolled to the attack before their wingmen, 2Lt. Rudolph Bellan (Johnson) and 2Lt. Walter Koby (Watkins) and closed as the enemy interceptors tried to escape.

Johnson made a dead astern attack on one of the Tojos that tore holes in the left wing root and fuselage. Johnson returned for a second pass from 20 degrees deflection and got hits on the engine and fuselage area. The Tojo went into a spin and crashed into a dry river bed about 10 miles north of Hong Kong for Johnson's the 22nd and last victory of his magnificent career. Johnson's illustrious Wingman, Capt. James Watkins, attacked the second Tojo from the rear and fired a long burst until the enemy pilot Split-S'd away to 3,000 feet and continued its descent "right into mother earth's bosom."

When their wingmen arrived two Oscars were seen under the Flying Knights formation and the excited young Lieutenants broke formation in a wild pursuit of the targets. 2Lt. Bellan fired a deflection shot at the lead Oscar and got some hits but it broke away and flew directly in front of 2Lt. Walter Koby fired about five three bursts from 10 to 20 degrees deflection

By April 1945, the **49FG** was led by a nucleus of veteran pilots: Standing (L-R): Capt. George Laven (3v), Lt.Col. Gerald Johnson (22v), and Capt. Clayton Tice (2v). Kneeling (L-R): Capt. Robert DeHaven (14v), Maj. Wallace Jordon (6v), and Capt. James Watkins (12v). (AAF)

**Lt.Col. Gerald Johnson's** scoreboard was always one to three victories ahead of his official total. Here he poses with his last victory #23, which was officially #22. (AAF)

The **49FG** Scoreboard shows a final victory tally of 273, which conflicted with the official total of 254 victories, 63 probables, and 20 damaged. (AAF)

Like Lt.Col. Johnson, **Capt. James Watkins'** scoreboard did not reflect his official total of 11 victories. (AFAA)

**Capt. Anthony Faikus** claimed his only victory while flying this P-51. (AAF)

while closing down to 100 yards and 2,000 feet. The stricken enemy fighter continued its descent and crashed into a hillside north of Hong Kong. Koby's only career victory was also victory #254, and the last victory of 9FS, the highest scoring fighter squadron in the Pacific. The 9FS also claimed 63 probables and 20 damaged.

**3 April 1945: 35FG/40FS**

From 1-18 April the 35th Fighter Group was under the operational control of the 308BW but after it moved to Clark it was assigned to the 5FC. Transition from the P-47 to Mustang was completed by the 19th but only the Mustang saw combat only once during the month.

On 3 April eight 40FS' Mustangs took off at 1215 from Mangalden to provide cover for 12 B-25s (Sugars) on a sweep to Luzon's west coast. At 1500 the 40th was flying west at 4,000 feet when three enemy aircraft, identified as a Nick leading two Zeros, were sighted flying southwest at 4,500 feet in a V. 40FS' Red Flight led by Capt. Anthony Faikus were at 5,500 feet when the enemy spotted them and echeloned to the right with the two Zeros on the right and the Nick on the left. One of the Zeros then made a gentle port turn while the other Zero flew straight ahead. Faikus, made a pass from directly above and slightly astern of a Zero to his right and as he closed to about 200 yards, the Zero made a 90 degree left turn and Faikus got off a quick one second burst, getting hits on the fuselage and canopy. The enemy pilot Split S'ed and when he straightened out Faikus fired a three second burst exploding the Zero but its pilot was able to bail out. Faikus dove on the second Zero that had remained in the area but this Zero suddenly pulled up and Faikus made an ineffective head on pass and he had to settle for only one career victory.

At the same time 2Lt. William Colsh, Red Element Leader, was flying in the opposite direction from Faikus and turned left on Faikus' Zero and turned ("the P-51 as easily as the Zero") and made a head on pass firing a one second burst head on from only 50 yards. The Zero never fired and burst into flames and crashed into the ground and Colsh left combat one victory from becoming an ace. 2Lt. Irving Pine, Colsh' Wingman made a pass on the Nick from 90 degrees deflection, firing a two second burst that hit the cockpit and set the Japanese bomber on fire for his only victory. The 35FG would have no more claims until early July when it was the first 5FC Group to get into action from Yanton Okinawa.

**5-7 April 1945: 58FG**

Between 5-7 April the 58th Group Headquarters and most of the personnel of the three squadrons were flown up to Lingayen or to Mangaldan Airdrome. Mangaldan, located about 12 miles east of Lingayen along the Gulf coast, was designated as the future home of the 58FG. Mangaldan was temporarily unusable at this time due to heavy rains which had made a bog out of the dirt runways. The Mangaldan Strip was developed because the air base begun at Dagupan after the invasion in early January had to be abandoned when its site was found to be unsuitable. The Mangaldan taxiways and long and wide strip had been completed very quickly of only compacted earth, sprayed with oil to prevent dust and to aid in drainage. When dry, Mangaldan appeared to be a splendid coral runway, much like that on Noemfoor but it was plagued with dust and when it rained it became a quagmire. Operations began from Mangaldan on 10 April but the rains soon returned and by 16 April the aircraft had to be liberated from the mud and were returned to the Lingayen Airstrip. The 69th and the 311th Squadrons began operations from Lingayen the day after their arrival.

The 58FG flew as many as 40 missions per day from Lingayen with some of the pilots flying two missions per day. The targets were usually enemy gun positions, caves, supply areas, and motor pools. The pilots could not readily access results of their attacks due to the trees and undergrowth but the forward controllers with the infantry reported mostly excellent results. These Ground Controllers stationed with the front line troops directed the pilots after their arrival at his location. The standard procedure was for the Ground Controller to mark the target with a white phosphorous shell to direct the pilots to bomb that particular area.

**10 April 1945: 49FG**

Popular eight victory ace and newly appointed 7FS Ops Exec, Capt. Fernley Damstrom and a Wingman F/O Sylvan Sisson flew to the Laoag Airstrip to assess the field's potential as an advanced staging base and also to place the 49ers on the flight path of an irritating enemy intruder that harassed the

Lingayen base nightly for the past week. The two were assigned to stay at Laoag and intercept the intruder but after several days it did not appear. On the 10th the two Demons left Laoag but on take off one of Damstrom's engines seized and his fighter snap rolled and crashed into the beach, killing him instantly.

**17-23 April 1945: 58FG/69FS/310FS**

On 17 April, the 69th and the 310th Squadrons and the remaining P-47s of the 311th left for Porac Airstrip. After they left the men and equipment were taken to the rail terminal at Dagupan for transportation to the northeast station to Porac. After delivering the men and equipment to the railroad terminal at Dagupan for a slow and uncomfortable 70 mile overnight rail trip to Porac. The next morning the 58FG set up a temporary camp and operations resumed on 19 April. After their arrival at Porac almost all missions flown during the remainder of the month were directed to ground support of the Army along the Villa Verde Trail and in Balete Pass and during the last two days of the month the target area was expanded to include the Baguio area. The first week or two of operations at Porac was carried out without revetments and aircraft were parked in a grassy field. Movement of trucks and aircraft on the comparatively soft ground soon filled it with ruts that were quite a nuisance and were hazardous to moving aircraft.

While at Porac a number of Japanese soldiers had infiltrated the area and the men of the 58FG established an outer perimeter around the camp and set up guard posts in the revetment areas to protect the aircraft. On 23 April the officers and men of the 58th, accompanied by Guerrillas, carried out large patrols in a heavily enemy infiltrated area three miles south of Porac and at least a dozen or more enemy soldiers were killed.

**18-25 April 1945: 8FG**

On 18 April, the 475FG received orders to move to Lingayen the next day. The order was an unpopular one the crews would have to leave the relative comforts of the Clark Fields for the crude airstrip and temporary structures at Lingayen beach. The reason for the transfer was that the more fragile P-51Mustangs of the 35FG could not operate from the rough Lingayen strip whereas the more rugged P-38s, with their tricycle landing gear, were more proficient on the demanding Lingayen runway. Lingayen's billets were again tents and the facilities were basic and while the base was located near a stunning white beach there was little shade and the sun was brutal. However, an advantage of Lingayen as their new base was that it shortened the flying time to the tactical objectives around Baguio.

During this transition to their new base the 475th saw an interruption in combat operations but by 19 April the 475th had effectively replaced the 35th there. On 19 April Lt. Reed Pietscher of the 432FS was flying on the Group's fourth dive bombing mission of the day and was seen to crash into the side of a mountain near Minuli, Luzon. His fighter was seen to have AA damage to its belly from enemy fire from Route #5. Three days later the Group flew multiple sorties against ground targets around Baguio until that entire area fell to two American Army Divisions on 26 April. Elsewhere, the Japanese were establishing a defensive line along transport routes into the Cagayan Valley, which gave the FEAF's fighter and dive bomber units a multitude of moving and fixed targets to attack. The move to Lingayen placed the 475FG in an improved position from which to attack long-range targets on Formosa and mainland Southeast Asia. And even though ground support missions would continue, pilots soon came to appreciate the possibilities offered by this more strategic location.

**25-30 April 1945: 8FG**

By the end of the month missions to the Indo-China mainland became more numerous.

On 25 April the 8th sent a number of 35FS and 80FS Lightnings to escort B-24s to the Saigon area in an uneventful mission.

The next day 8FG P-38s, including eight from the 80FS led by Capt. Larry Henkes, escorted the B-24s to Saigon again. Five Japanese fighters were called out but no one engaged and the four month hiatus in aerial combat continued.

On the 26th 2Lt. William White of the 35FS was on a Catalina cover mission when one of his engines seized and the other overheated. He bailed out off the coast of Indo-China and saw a sailboat displaying a Japanese flag which headed off when American planes appeared. One of the planes was the Catalina he had been escorting which landed and picked him up.

On 28 April five P-38s of the 80FS led by Capt. Nicolas Zinni swept Saigon at 1145 at minimum altitude. They found a subchaser and a camouflaged freighter on the Saigon River and the P-38s strafed the enemy vessels. Further down the River they saw barges spread out over 300 yards and strafed them before they returned to base.

By the end of April the Japanese fighting in southeast Luzon were divided into the Shimbu and Fuji Forces. One dogged group of the Fuji Force had rooted itself in caves and pillboxes on a hill directly in the path of the advance of the 511th Parachute Infantry. Artillery had been ineffective and an air strike was called in for 0800 on 29 April. After withdrawing about 400 yards for safety 16 8FG Lightnings, each carrying Napalm bombs, attacked the Japanese positions and scored four direct hits killing 320 Japanese and disabling their guns. The surviving Japanese were so disoriented that they offered little organized resistance to the American attack.

**Maj. George Laven** shot down an Emily flying boat off the Formosa coast. (AAF)

**26 April 1945: 49FG: Last Victory?**

The weather on the morning of the 26th was marginal at best but the new and aggressive 49FG Exec Maj. George Laven took off at 1000 on a freelance sortie to the chemical factory at Shinen, Formosa with a single Wingman, Maj. Campbell Wilson of the 475FG. When these two Staff Officers reached the Formosa coast, it was clouded in and they descended under the overcast at Bozan and flew north for 50 miles at 3,000 feet. Just before they reached Shinen at noon they flew under the 300 foot ceiling and both pilots glide bombed the plant with their 1,000 pound bombs. As Laven was about to begin strafing the collapsed buildings at he spotted a locomotive, three miles west and blew up the steam engine in his first pass and then flew on deck to hunt more rail targets. He strafed a second engine 15 miles north of the Shinen and then headed back to base with Wilson. When he reached the coast he saw an enemy fighter, tailing what he thought was an American PBY amphibian in the mist over Kato Village. This was the opportunity that Laven had sought for two years; the chance to become an ace (officially or not). Laven soon closed into firing range from dead astern and saw that both aircraft were Japanese. The Val climbed into the overcast and vanished as he approached but the other was a four-engine JNAF Emily amphibian which continued on its parallel course to the coast. Laven descended under the path of the enemy and closed, pulling up within point blank range and fired. The huge bomber immediately crashed in flames on the beach at Kato, scattering flaming debris over the village, setting fire to some buildings. Laven quickly then flew back to circle Choso Airdrome eager to waylay the Val but it never reappeared and he returned to base to claim that he was now an ace. The abrasive Laven had claimed three previous (officially unaccredited) victories in addition to his one official credited victory during the Alaskan Campaign from September 1942 to February 1943 and painted his P-38 with four victories during his stint with 49HQ.

The controversy began as soon Laven returned to base when his sergeant Crew Chief, whom he had alienated, read Laven's combat report and then mockingly painted a PBY victory silhouette on Laven's P-38's cowling scoreboard. After the war an Air Force inspection team surveyed the wreckage at Kato Village and eventually it was confirmed as an Emliy. However, the Air Force offered a qualification for only two of his three disputed Alaskan claims as "official kills scored, but unconfirmed," so Laven was officially credited with four victories. Over the next 50 years, George Laven obstinately continued his claim to ace status by scoring the last aerial victory for the 49FG in World War Two.

**26 April 1945: 8FG/432FS**

On 26 April two American Divisions had broken through into Baguio but the Japanese were digging in all along the route that led into the Cagayan Valley and 5FC fighter bombers were assigned to neutralize these enemy positions. The next day the 8FG demonstrated an example of the devastating effects of the ground support role. Capt. Laurence LeBaron flew in from Group HQ to fly the afternoon mission with the 432FS He led 12 P-38s off at 1400 to dive bomb enemy troops and supplies around the town of Ipil. LeBaron led the first of the three flights which set fire to a gasoline dump that engulfed a large part of the town in flames. The second flight, led by 1Lt. Henry Toll, destroyed two other fuel dumps south of the town while 1Lt. Robert Schuh led the third flight west of town and demolished a series of buildings and underground shelters. The three flights then strafed entire area, concentrating on fortified pillboxes. The 432[nd] Lightning fighter bombers withdrew and had virtually destroyed anything of use to the Japanese. The 475FG ended April with another series of missions against Formosa in which their P-38s covered B-25s and B-24s and went down on the deck to strafe truck convoys, airdromes, factories, and barracks

**27 April 1945: 58FG**

After the capture of Baguio by the 37[th] Division on 27 April, nearly the entire strength of the 58FG was sent up to disrupt the enemy retreat toward their mountain stronghold around Bontoc. The U.S. Sixth Army wanted landslides created to block the Baguio-Bontoc Highway to prevent reinforcements and supplies from reaching the retreating enemy and to trap as many as possible in the Baguio area. The precision low level bombing by 58[th] pilots resulted in several landslides at strategic locations along the route. In this type of close support pilots typically could not identify their targets and instead aimed their bombs at the white smoke shells used as markers by the infantry. Maj.Gen. Charles Mullins, CO of the 25[th] Division sent this praise to the 58[th] after he personally observed an attack in the Balete Pass:

> The Commanding General of this Headquarters wishes to commend very highly all the pilots...for their excellent work this morning. (They) moved in on them very fast and the targets were difficult and in very close support. I wish to commend them also in the patience and efforts in striking this area. Thank you very much.

**April 1945: 348FG**

During April the Group flew fewer missions than in previous months with 85% being ground support missions. However, the preponderance of support missions led to a record monthly tonnage of bombs being dropped for any fighter group thus far in the Pacific along with almost 1.9 million rounds of .50 caliber ammunition being fired during strafing. The Japanese had retreated from Manila into the rugged area along the Markina and Angat Rivers in the Rizal Province. Here they were able to set up strong defensive positions in caves and intricate trench networks in the river gorges and Angelo Mountains. The battle was slow and costly and in order to keep casualties down the Group was called on for air support by the XI Corps. The area of attack was generally divided into three areas: the Marikina-Wawa sector, the Ipo Dam area, and the Siniloan-Real area. Much of the success of these missions was due the coordination of the fighter bombers with the ground forces through the 309BW ground liaison officer and the 348[th]'s liaison officer. There were no enemy air interceptions but losses to enemy ground fire was high. The 342FS had one fatality (1Lt. Charles Michell); the 460FS had a fatality (1Lt. Walter Abraham); and the 341FS had a MIA (2Lt. Richard McAffe). Six fighters were a total loss and four received major damage from ground fire. Operational accidents also took their toll with one fatality (1Lt. Truman Ragsdale). Five fighters were declared a total loss and seven suffered major damage.

**April 1945: 58FG**

The 58[th] Group flew 1,691 sorties in April: 629 for the 311FS, 586 for the 69FS, and 476 for the 310FS. The largest number of sorties was to Balete Pass, followed in order by Villa Verde Trail, Baguio, Highway 5 north of Santa Fe, and enemy bases in the Cagayan Valley. Another 105 miscellaneous missions were flown, including local patrols, weather reconnaissance, scramble, search and covering air transport routes (while at Mindoro). A total of 1,375 tons of bombs were dropped: 480 tons by the 69FS, 471 tons by the 311FS, and 424 tons by the 310FS. An additional 164 Napalm tanks were also dropped. The 58[th] expended 244,440 rounds of ammunition in strafing during the month.

**April 1945: 8FG**

During April the 8FG would fly numerous dive bombing missions and other ground support operations but in diminishing numbers over the next months and would cease by July. The 35FS would fly 57 missions in April while the 36FS flew 48 and in May both Squadrons would fly 44 missions and then the 35[th] flew 40 in June and only 10 in July. Most of the missions were local patrol, rescue plane cover, or occasional ground support utilizing between two and eight fighters.

# 8

## May 1945

**May 1945: Situation: Ipo Dam**

By the last week in April, Kruger's infantry had surrounded Yamashita's troops in the hill country 20 miles north of Manila. A stronghold of 4,700 determined enemy troops had fortified their position at Ipo Dam at the head waters of the Ipo and Angat Rivers. The reservoir was one of Manila's main fresh water sources and by contaminating the water or blowing up the earthen Ipo Dam the Japanese could easily cause hardship on the population of the newly captured capitol city. MacArthur prioritized the capture of the dam and reservoir.

In April Generals Walter Krueger and Charles Hall, Commander of XI Corps, prepared plans to capture the Ipo Dam. On 7 April the 169th Regimental Combat Team (RCT) conducted a reconnaissance in force of that area in order to determine the enemy positions and strength. They had encountered strong resistance about five miles southeast of the Dam on the right and about four miles west, along the Metropolitan Road, and then withdrew. On 19 April, MacArthur ordered that XI Corps to immediately proceed to seize the Ipo Dam. On 1 May XI Corps transferred Gen. Leonard Wing's 43rd Division to that area, with orders to begin an offensive on 7 May to capture the Ipo Dam and the Marikina River watershed area.

The Japanese concentrated their defenses to meet the expected American attack along the Metropolitan Road. Gen. Hall, XI Corps CO, correctly anticipated the enemy defenses and planned his main attack where the Japanese had weakened their positions and planned his secondary attack to be along the Metropolitan Road to keep the enemy engaged and to prevent the movement of their troops to meet the main attack. Filipino Guerrillas, attached to the 43rd Division, were divided into a North Force and a South Force. The North Force was to turn the enemy flank on the north while the South Force was to move far to the south and launch an attack toward the Ipo Dam from the southeast.

The Air Plan for the Ipo Dam was to drop 250,000 gallons of Napalm on the enemy positions and force the enemy soldiers from their caves and strong points. The Napalm attacks were immediately followed up by 5BC medium bombers that dropped fragmentation bombs to kill the exposed enemy soldiers. Finally 5BC heavy bombers were to accurate drop demolition bombs on key defensive positions.

Although Napalm had long been used as a tactical weapon in the Philippines, the tactical missions over Luzon brought about increased use in the first week of March by P-38s and P-47s. The fire bombs were simply a 150 gallon drop tank fitted with a standard bomb tailfin and an impact detonator to ignite the jellied gasoline inside. The targets north and east of newly captured Manila were continuously attacked with Napalm.

On 3 May, FEAF fighter bombers from Lingayen were assigned to mount the largest maximum effort in the Philippines Campaign to eliminate the enemy in the southern highlands Five enemy strong points, each consisting of three million square yards were targeted and more than 270 Lightnings, Thunderbolts, and Mustangs armed with Napalm and high explosives flew saturation attacks for four consecutive days which reached from Ipo Village through the foothills for 45 miles southeast to Santa Maria Village. Initially, the fighters were closely spaced in their attack but the smoke from the first wave obscured the target for following waves. To overcome the problem the Napalm runs were from downwind with each successive wave dropping its bombs on the near side of the Napalm bursts from the wave which preceded it; following each other at 10 to 15 second intervals. A-20s or B-25s then followed the fighter bombers dropping parafrags and strafing. The 5FC confirmed that it could send up a fighter force large enough to completely blanket a large area with Napalm sufficient to crack the most fanatic defense. The 5FC reported, "From the first, the saturation strikes were so successful that target areas had to be changed daily to keep ahead of our advancing infantry." American Intelligence estimated that these missions killed over 2,000 enemy defenders and shattered enemy morale.

With the offensive scheduled to begin on the morning of 7 May, Gen. Hall decided to send the 103rd Infantry Regiment to conduct a surprise night attack on 6 May. The Japanese were totally unprepared and the 103rd broke through and advanced about five miles during the night and by sunrise was within two and a half miles of the Dam. The attack of the 172nd Infantry Division along the Metropolitan Road the next morning met the expected heavy resistance but managed to drive slowly ahead. By 12 May the 43rd Division controlled an arc west and southwest of Ipo Dam. The Filipino North Force, with heavy 5FC air support, had moved to within two miles north of the Dam. On 13-14 May the weather worsened and the rains made the roads completely impassable so that supplies could not be moved to the front. Air drops had to be hastily organized to carry some supplies forward while over 1,000 Filipino "cargadores" were engaged to haul supplies on their backs on a three day walk to the front. The evacuation of the wounded was a major problem as some were at least 20 hours from the nearest hospital. The American infantry continued its slow advance and by 16 May all units were within 300 to 500 yards of the Dam.

The first massed Napalm attack on Ipo had been so successful that on the 17th Gen. Smith of 5 FC sent a force of twice the size, 680 fighters, to Ipo. Flights orbited over the foothills as the preceding units attacked and when their turn came the fighters aligned in line abreast formation with eight elements wingtip to wingtip, turning into an ascending formation separated at 300 yard intervals. At 800 feet above the hills, the pilots flew toward the smoke boiling up from the five square mile target area. As they arrived over the target, the fighter bombers were buffeted by rising thermals

**Napalm** was used far more often in the Pacific than in the European or Mediterranean Theaters. The photo shows a Philippine coastal village under Napalm attack. (AAF)

from the fires. As they passed over the release point the flight jettisoned their bombs in unison; flight after flight, the conflagration was fed. The 45 minute air strike, in which 70,000 gallons of Napalm were dropped onto enemy positions around the Dam, cleared the path for a concentrated attack which captured the Dam intact. For the next two days, the Japanese troops in the highlands were attacked and with the depletion of their ranks due to starvation and disease, the Allies were able to secure the entire shoreline of Luguna De Bay with light casualties. Ipo Dam was also later (17 May) captured intact without opposition. The Japanese had prepared the Dam for destruction but the enemy unit guarding it was killed before they could detonate the explosive charges.

After the 17th the Japanese were again forced to rely on dug-in positions around the hills and forests surrounding Ipo. Between 17 and 21 May the 475th, 58th and 348th Fighter Groups made concentrated attacks on the Wawa Dams area, using the much-feared Napalm to devastating effect especially against heavily Japanese fortified positions. The results of the series of strikes on the Ipo-Wawa Dams area were described as excellent and when the 43rd Division was able to easily sweep through the valley and then captured the Wawa Dams intact. By 21 May all organized enemy opposition had ended except to mop up the remaining small pockets of resistance in the area. By 10 June elements of XI Corps had reached Infanta on the east coast of Luzon but some Japanese defenders fled deeper into the mountains and would continue to hold out until the end of the war.

Gen. Kenney's Report on the 5th Air Force involvement in the Ipo Dam Campaign:

> On the 14th I invited Whitehead to my house in Manila to have dinner and spend the night. After one of Sergeant Raymond's best meals, Whitey and I walked out around the swimming pool, which was empty, as the water for that section of Manila came from the Ipo Dam which the Japs held in spite of Krueger's efforts to dislodge them from the hills on each side. I told Whitehead that I wanted water in the pool so that I could invite him down for a swim before dinner sometime and suggested that he get in touch with Krueger and offer to put a couple of hundred planeloads of Napalm on the Jap positions and burn them out. I thought if the job was done on a big scale the Nips would not have time to blow up the dam and Krueger's troops could then turn the water on, Manila's water problem would be solved, and we could go swimming.
>
> Four days later a deluge of radiograms poured into the office from the Commander of the 43rd Division, General Wing, the commander of the 11th Corps, General Hall, from Krueger, and from MacArthur. They spoke of "magnificent preparation," "masterful execution of a difficult and complex mission," "outstanding support," and "fine coordination" for the job we had done. I passed them all along to Whitehead.
>
> Following a continuous drenching of the Jap hill positions on each side of the Ipo Dam with over 200 fighters, each carrying over 300 gallons of Napalm, the troops of the 43rd Division had taken the whole position with negligible losses. Twenty-one hundred dead Japs had been buried when our troops finished counting. The dam had been mined for demolition but the Nips evidently did not get a chance to blow it up and our troops turned on the water.
>
> I suddenly remembered that I had left the valves open in the swimming pool. I called the house and was informed by the sergeant there that the whole place was flooded with water a foot deep all over the lawn but that he had dived into the pool and shut the valve and he thought it would soon drain off. It did drain off fairly well and evaporation took care of the excess, but for three days the place threatened to become a mud hole. I never did dare tell Krueger what impelled me to hurry up his attack on the Ipo Dam.

**475FG** Lightnings dropping Napalm tanks (see right P-38). (AAF)

After the first three days of strikes in the Ipo area, mainly with Napalm, a series of teletype messages from XI Corps were received by Fifth Fighter Command Groups:

> Our troops closely followed strikes and overran all target areas with a bare minimum of friendly casualties. Conservatively estimated at least 650 Nips killed by air action with other casualties caused by Nips running from fire and burning areas and being caught by combined frag bombs, artillery fire, and mortar fire. All areas hit had previously held up our attack, causing friendly casualties to mount. At least five large gas dumps of unestimated gallonage were destroyed, an estimated 68 vehicles including staff cars and trucks were destroyed along with food, supplies, and ammo. Many positions were overrun in which guns and ammo, still serviceable, were found abandoned by the enemy in his flight to safety. In addition approximately 75-100 caves were sealed by bombs, three of which were known to have contained Nips and guns. Since our last strike enemy resistance has been negligible as our forces continue to move forward. A request was made and granted for an air evaluation team to go in the area for more definite and detailed count.

A second message read:

> 43rd Division has counted over 2,100 Nips dead in their area. 38th Division area: following closely behind our Napalm strikes the troops captured, with negligible resistance, areas struck. Targets included areas which the troops had been attacking 5-7 days meeting stiff resistance with little advancing. All target areas hit have been consolidated to date. The division stated they had counted 600-700 Nips dead in their area killed by air action and artillery, with ammo, gas, food supplies in flames for one half hour after strikes.

**May 1945: 35FG**

Throughout May the Group continued its primary tactical mission of providing air support for ground forces on Luzon. After five months on the Island the Sixth Army's campaign there had developed into a series of mopping up operations in central and northern Luzon. The 35th's dive bombing supported the infantry on two fronts: at the Ipo Dam, northeast of Manila and at the Belete Pass which was the southern approach to the Cagayan Valley, leading to Aparri in the north. The Group operated from Clark Field which was in range of both fronts which allowed two 16 P-51 missions per squadron per day.

During the month the Group lost two pilots. On 25 May, 1Lt. Daniel Devins of the 41FS was on dive bombing mission near Santa Fe when his fighter was seen in spin on fire and then exploding into a mountain side. On 16 May, Maj. John Young, Group Operations Officer, was standing near his jeep at the edge of the runway at Clark Field when a Mustang veered off the runway and hit vehicles there and its Napalm tank fell off and ignited. Young suffered severe burns and was hospitalized and died 12 days later of burn-related pneumonia.

**May 1945: 348FG**

Since San Marcelino was not an all-weather field plans were being made to move the Group to Floridablanca before the rainy season started. The advanced echelon from Group HQ left on 1 May to establish the new base and the last mission from San Marcelino was flown on the 13th. Most of the Group's personnel arrived at Floridablanca by the 15th and operations were begun on the 17th. The Floridablanca base was considered the best of any so far in the war. After the move the Group was no longer under the control of the 309BW and was transferred to the 5FC.

During the month only 250 offensive missions were carried out as compared to 622 the month before and of these, 87% were ground support. Despite the large number of missions flown by the 5FC over northern Luzon the previous month the Japanese continued their heavy resistance, particularly in the Ipo Dam area. On the 17th and 18th the Group participated in a concentrated attack on the area with other units, dropping 16,000 gallons of Napalm that caused heavy casualties in the thousands and the loss of 65 vehicles.

No enemy fighters were engaged during the month and only one fighter bomber suffered major damage. However, 2Lt. Leonard Hovick and 1Lt. Wayne Randolph of the 340FS were listed as MIA when they collided in mid-air over central Luzon and1Lt. Gerald Economoff's fighter (460FS) disintegrated in mid-air east of Manila. Eight other aircraft were a total loss and five received major damage in operational accidents.

**May 1945: 421NFS**

During May the Squadron continued its training program for the aircrews but was somewhat hindered by the lack of aircraft. The Squadron began May with 10 aircraft and 24 pilots and crews and by the end of the month the Squadron had lost two more aircraft so then the Squadron almost three crews per plane. Even so, the Squadron's training program improved the crew's performance in standard interception missions and it also gave the crews practice in radar bombing in which they realized excellent results. The P-61 did not have a bombsight since it was never intended to be used as a bomber and bomb shackles had to be placed on the aircraft's wings to haul a load of two 500 pound bombs to harass the enemy. but was never intended for precision bombing. Radar bombing was a system of bombing developed by P-61 pilots on a system derived from the combination of the distance to a target, the altitude, and airspeed; basing it on a triangular pattern, using the radar to determine the distance from the ground.

**May 1945: 58FG**

During this first week of May the 58FG continued its support of the infantry divisions of I Corps in the Balete Pass, Villa Verde Trail, and Baguio areas. Poor weather, or a lack of a suitable target, diverted these missions up the Cagayan Valley, where one of the principal targets was the city of Tuguegarao (the largest city in the Valley) and the air installations there.

Porac Airbase was to be modified during May into an all-weather base so that the 311FS would become inactive beginning 5 May, followed by the 69FS on 7 May. The 310FS was selected to keep the 58FG operational by moving their aircraft 18 miles away to Strip #7 in the Clark Field complex on 4 May. Between 7 and 16 May the runway and taxiways at Porac were permanently resurfaced. With two of its three squadrons inactive for the next two weeks the 58th Fighter Group continued its administrative work and

**58FG** Thunderbolts attacking targets in the Cagayan Valley. (AAF)

to prepare for the orientation and transition training of its newly assigned 201st Mexican Squadron. Meanwhile, on 8 May, Group Commander, Maj. Edward Roddy, was promoted to Lieutenant Colonel.

**May 1945: 3ACG**

The 3ACG underwent a change in administrative control when it was removed from under the 86th Fighter Wing and assigned directly to Fifth Fighter Command on 16 May. Less than two weeks later its longtime association with the 308th Bombardment Wing was ended when it was placed under the operational control of the 309th Bombardment Wing. These changes made no difference in the Group's every day operations in which the numerous close support mission for the infantry remained a high priority but missions to Formosa also continued to be flown.

During May the inherent dangers involved in close support cost the 3ACG. On 1 May, during a fighter sweep by the 4th Fighter Section along the east coast of Formosa 2Lt. Robert McNeill was attacking a bus and lost perspective and crashed into the bus, careened into a telegraph pole, and his fighter was then enveloped in a fireball. On 11 May 1Lt. Kenneth Ogden was seriously injured during an attack on a truck convoy near Okayama, Formosa. As he and Louis Curdes zoomed past the convoy they had been strafing, an enemy shell tore through Ogden's cockpit and ripped into his leg. Despite the intense pain, Ogden nursed his plane back to Gabu and a safe landing. On 19 May, 30 Air Commando Mustangs attacked the Heito Airdrome on Formosa where 1Lt. Durward Fortier had to bail out of his fighter because of a coolant leak and landed in the water a few miles southwest of the small island of Ryukyu Sho. He was picked up by a rescue submarine within 30 minutes but because the submarine remained on its rescue station, it took two weeks before Fortier was put ashore. On 30 May during a fighter sweep along Formosa's west coast 2Lt. Joseph Bulack and his element leader had great success in locomotive busting near Hokuwan. The two then made two passes on a bus but during a turn out to sea the element leader lost sight of Bulack, who was never seen again despite an extensive search. The next day was even more costly, when the 4th Fighter Section sent 16 Mustangs on another fighter sweep of Formosa. Although the Air Commandos destroyed nine trucks and five locomotives and damaged several more vehicles; they encountered light but very accurate enemy ground fire. Four P-51s of A Flight flew safely up the island's eastern shore at low level but almost as soon as they turned inland to head back south, Japanese small arms fire erupted and 1Lt. Fergus Mead's P-51 was hit only a few hundred feet above the ground and Mead had no chance to bail out before he crashed. The remaining A Flight pilots continued south and were about to turn out to sea when F/O Bernard Moncrief felt heat on the right floor of his cockpit which soon filled with smoke. Moncrief immediately released his canopy and hauled back his stick in a desperate attempt to gain altitude. As he tried to climb out of his cockpit, his parachute caught on something. His fighter then stalled and he was suddenly flying through the air. Moncrief blacked out and did not remember pulling his ripcord but his chute opened and he quickly hit the ground with a thump and was dragged for a distance before he was finally able to slip from his chute. He suffered a dislocated shoulder, a wrenched left leg, and huge blisters on his right leg that were probably caused by leaking hot coolant. Soon a large band of Japanese soldiers and civilians appeared and he was taken prisoner. In the prison camp his wounds were treated only superficially, his shoulder remained dislocated, while his burns festered. Moncrief weighed 135 pounds when he was shot down and when he was liberated he when he was liberated just two and a half months later, he weighed only 89 pounds due to the lack of food and medical treatment.

**May 1945: 58FG**

Once the construction at Porac was completed it was just in time for the 69th and the 311th to be take part in the largest Napalm attack of the war to date. The 45 minute attack around the Ipo Dam on 17 May featured a maximum effort by the five 5th Air Force fighter groups and cleared the way for the capture of the Dam intact that same day. The 310th sent 19 aircraft into this attack and was successful in placing all their Napalm tanks into the target area with excellent coverage. The 311th sent 31 sorties to the attack on 17 and 18 May, which burned out large areas around the Dam and the Squadron's pilots reported seeing U.S. infantry advance after the bombing. On 19 and 20 May the 58FG was again diverted to the Baleen Pass area and then reverted to Napalm attacks clearing areas of enemy resistance in the Ipo Dam area again. Beginning on 25 May the attacks of the 58FG were again concentrated on the northern fronts, from Baguio to Balete Pass, on Highway 5 and in the Highway 11 area.

Two important changes in 58FG Squadron Commanders were made before the end of May. To replace Maj. Thomas Winburn, who had been hospitalized almost since the day of his arrival in the 69FS, Capt. Stanley Andrews was assigned to the 58FG to assume command of the 69FS. The other change occurred in the 311FS where veteran 58FG pilot, Maj. Joseph Klemovich, handed over his command to rotate to the States. Except for several months in Wing Headquarters in New Guinea, Klemovich had served in some capacity in the 58FG since late 1942. He was replaced as Commander by Capt. Steven Benner who had joined the 311FS as a new Second Lieutenant just graduated from West Point in February 1943. He had logged over 450 combat hours and a total of 1,200 hours with the 311th Squadron and had

The **201FS** Mexican Squadron was assigned to the 58FG in May. (AAF)

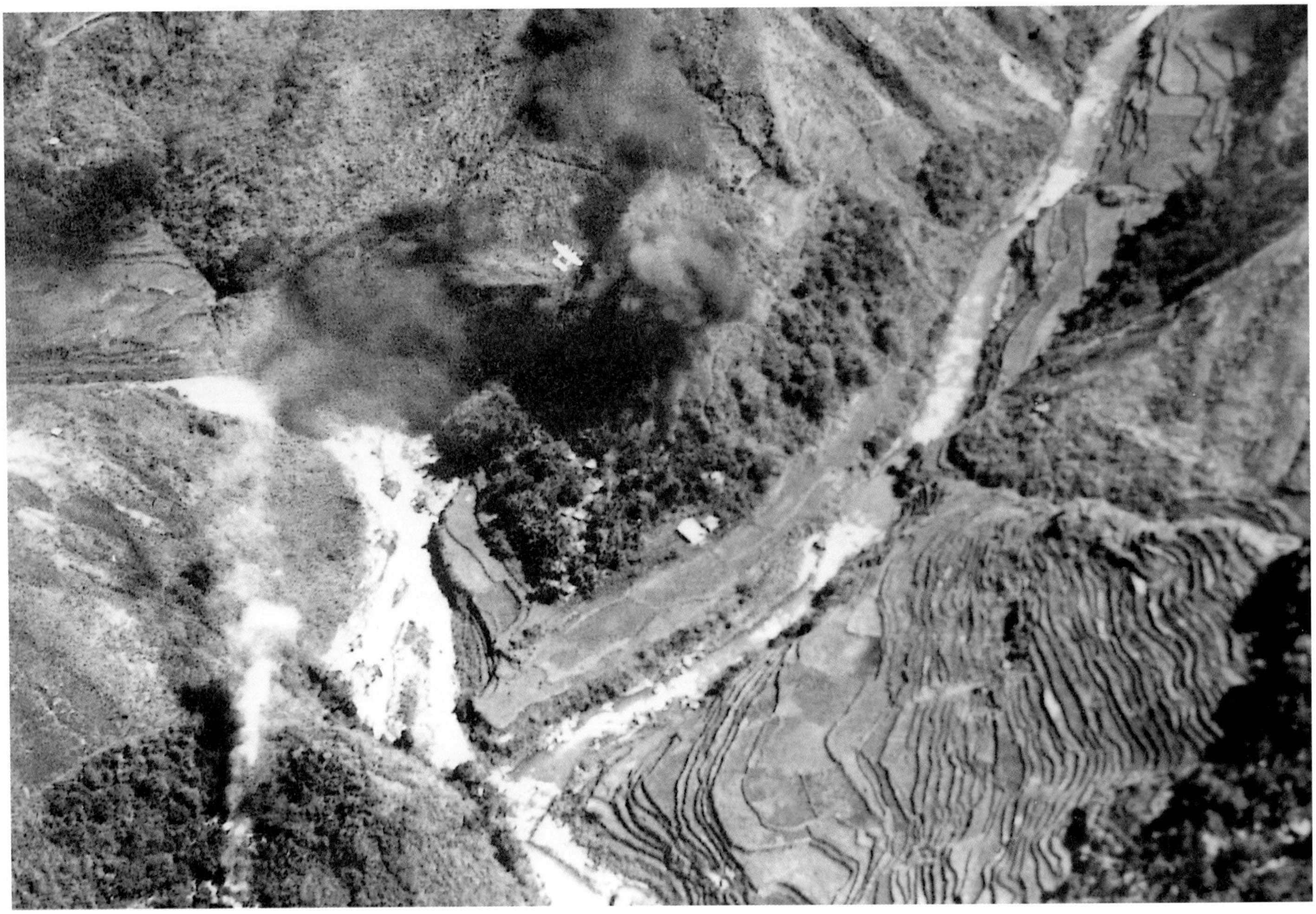

Lightnings from the **475FG** attack targets in the Cordillera Central Mountains. (AAF)

participated in all the most dangerous missions. He had been a flight leader in the first big engagement over Wewak on 11 April 1944. He had ditched in enemy waters west of New Guinea in October 1944 and had eventually been rescued. Two months later he participated in the night action off Mindoro, could not return to base, crash landed off Cebu and spent two weeks on that island evading the enemy forces before being rescued. He was awarded a DFC for this night action off Mindoro. Benner's West Point classmate, Capt. Arthur Marston, who had been with the 311[th] since May 1943, moved up to be 311[th] Operations Officer, replacing Benner.

**May 1945: 58FG/201FS (Mexican)**

After Mexico entered the war on the Allied side, the Escuadrón Aéreo de Pelea 201 (201[st] Air Fighter Squadron) was formed from 300 volunteers including 30 pilots. When the Squadron arrived in the US, in July 1944, Col. P.A. Antonio Cardenas Rodriguez was the Commander of the Mexican Expeditionary Force (FAEM). The enlisted volunteers were sent to different parts of country to be trained by specialty (*e.g.* armorers, mechanics, radiomen, *etc.*) required to from a fighter squadron that was to be equipped with the Republic P-47 Thunderbolt fighter bomber. The pilots received advanced training at various stations in Texas and received their wings on 20 February 1945. Later the pilots and specialists would be reunited at Pocatello AAFB, Idaho. But due to the harsh weather conditions there, the training was moved Texas, in November 1944 where the Squadron completed its training on 23 February 1945. Capt. Radamés Gaxiola Andradethe was named as the Squadron CO.

The Squadron, calling itself the "Aztec Eagles" began training in the Texas on 24 July 1944 with The Squadron arrived in Manila on 1 May 1945 and Kenney assigned it to the 58[th] Fighter Group at Porac Airfield initially for combat training in the Thunderbolt and then for combat operations as its fourth fighter squadron.

As Porac reopened and the 58[th]'s Squadrons arrived; aircraft became available from the other three squadrons for training the newly assigned 201[st] Mexican Fighter Squadron. As usual, with a group of new pilots training in an unfamiliar aircraft, accidents were certain to occur. The three American Squadrons were billeted away from the Mexican Squadron and had little contact with them on the ground. The Mexican Squadron then received 25 new model bubble canopy, P-47D-30-RA fighters which were elaborately marked with the insignia of both the USAAF and Mexican Air Force and had their various controls and systems color coded. The pilots and crews of the 58FG were jealous of the preferences given to the Mexicans in supplying the best of the planes and equipment. The long standing practice was that newer aircraft were assigned to the more important combat rolls and the older aircraft were used by the newer pilots for orientation and training flights. However, the 201[st] was given the new D-30 bubble canopy version of the Thunderbolt through the Lend Lease program; while the three American Squadrons continued using old D-15 versions, some of which had now been in combat for well over a year, with hundreds of hours logged.

Beginning in June 1945, the Mexican Squadron initially flew missions with the 310FS, often twice daily, and would fly more than 90 combat missions, totaling more than 1,900 hours of flight time. They participated in the Allied bombing of Luzon and Formosa. Among the missions flown by the squadron was 53 ground support missions flown in support of the U.S. 25th Infantry Division together with the Philippine Commonwealth Army soldiers and recognized guerrilla units in its break out into the Cagayan Valley on Luzon between 4 June and 4 July 1945, 37 training missions flown from 14-21 July 1945 (including missions of transporting new aircraft from Biak Island, New Guinea), four fighter sweeps over Formosa on 6-9 July 1945, and a dive bombing mission against the port of Karenko, Formosa, on 8 August. The Squadron flew 96 combat missions which included 785 offensive sorties and six defensive sorties. The Squadron made no air-to-air claims. It dropped 957 1,000 pound and 500 500 pound bombs and expended almost 167,000 rounds of ammunition. One P-47 was lost in combat while five more were damaged. Mexico, along with Brazil, were the only two Latin American nations to have Air Forces fighting with the Allies.

During their tour in the Philippines, five pilots died (one was shot down, one crashed, and three ran out of fuel and died at sea), and three others died in accidents during training. When the 201FS deployed, no provision for replacement pilots had been made and the pilot losses in the Philippines reduced its effectiveness. Mexican replacement pilots were rushed through familiarization training in the United States and two more pilots died in flight accidents in Florida. When the 58FS left the Philippines for Okinawa on 10 July, the 201FS stayed behind because of personnel losses, lack of replacements, and the short range of the P-47 on missions flown from Okinawa to Formosa. They flew their last combat mission as a full squadron on 26 August, escorting a convoy north of the Philippines. The 201st Fighter Squadron was commended by General MacArthur and in September 1945 was assigned to the 13AF. The Mexican Expeditionary Air Force was returned to Mexico in November 1945 as the only Mexicans ever to fight in a foreign war but was disbanded soon after. However, Escuadrón 201 is still an active duty squadron today staationed near Cozumel.

**May 1945: 58FG**

During May the 58th Fighter Group flew 1,062 sorties, of which the 69FS recorded 326, the 310FS 401, and the 311FS 335. The Group dropped 957 bombs, all 1,000-pounders: the 69FS dropped 286, the 310FS dropped 338, and the 311FS dropped 333. Napalm was the main ordnance carried with a total of 1,070 165 gallon tanks used: 350 dropped by the 69FS, 410 by the 310FS, and 310 by the 311FS (in spite of both the 69th and 311th being out of operations for about 10 days during the month).

**3 May 1945: 475FG**

On 3 May 433FS P-38s were conducting a dive-bombing mission to the Bontoc area of the Cordillera Central Mountains when the aircraft of formation Leader 1Lt. Jerome Hammond was hit by AA fire setting one of his engines on fire. Hammond made a successful crash landing and escaped from his fighter before it was engulfed by flames and exploded. For three days the burned Hammond successfully evaded Japanese patrols and also his fellow P-38 pilots when they dive bombed a nearby target. He was found by friendly Filipino partisans and then taken to an Allied camp, where he received food, clothes. and treatment for his burns. By 19 May the Filipinos had conducted Hammond back to Lingayen where he rejoined his Squadron and was rotated back home in July.

**4 May 1945: 49FG/7FS**

A flight of 7FS Screamin' Demons had returned from their mission but congested air traffic delayed the landings. While reforming to land, the pilots of the flight challenged each other to mock dogfights and soon P-38s were in a "rat-race" around the field. Below, a large crowd was watching the Lightnings sweeping down from 3,000 feet to make high speed runs right over the runway. Veteran 1Lts. Louis Denkovic and George Rogers came down over the west end of the field and their fighters collided and disintegrated in a fiery explosion.

**May/June 1945: 8FG/Command Changes**

Maj. Cyril Homer rotated home after serving as 80FS CO since 4 October 1944 and Maj. Joseph Johnson became the 80FS Headhunter CO. Johnson's command was sadly short as he was lost on an armed reconnaissance mission on 29 May when his P-38 lost a wing and crashed into the side of a mountain. Maj. Robert Hochuli replaced Johnson. Veteran and six victory ace Lynn Witt who joined the 35FS in March 1943 and had risen from Lieutenant to Major took the command of the 35FS in October 1944 until the end of May 1945. Witt was replaced by Capt. Donald Leighton, who had flown P-38s with the 1FG in North Africa.

During June the 8FG was again to be placed under the direct control of the 5FC with the 310th Bomb Wing as an intermediary. One other change in the 8FG occurred on 16 June when Col. Earl Dunham relinquished command after leading the 8FG through the difficult transition period from New Guinea to the Philippines. Col. Emmett Davis resumed command of the unit and would continue through the end of the war.

**Mid-May 1945: 348FG: Move to Floridablanca**

During mid May 1945 the 348FG made an unhurried move from San Marcelino across the Cabusilian Mountain foothills to Floridablanca which was part of the Clark Field complex. Its runways were being lengthened to accommodate the new Consolidated B-32 Dominator heavy bombers which the Group's Mustang pilots appreciated as they were heavily armed.

While at Floridablanca several 348FG Ordnance personnel were arrested for operating a brothel using GI tents and cots. There was nothing in Army regulations concerning this situation when Court Martial charges were levied. When the perpetrators came to trial they were charged with misuse of government property!

**7-8 May 1945: Germany Surrenders**

On 7 May Hitler's successor, Grand Admiral Karl Dönitz, met Allied Supreme Commander, Gen. Dwight Eisenhower and other Allied officers outside of Rheims, France and signed the instrument of surrender and the next day German officers signed an armistice with the Soviet Union. On 8 May Britain's Prime Minister, Winston Churchill and new U.S. President, Harry Truman declared V-E Day, Victory in Europe to cheering Crowds that packed London's Piccadilly Circus and New York's Times Square.

**May 1945: Situation: Okinawa**

After the Allied victory in Europe, the 5th Fighter Command Fighter Groups began to be transition to new aircraft. The 35FG received P-51s in Spring 1945 while the majority of the P-38 units received the latest model of their aircraft. Following the capture of Okinawa in the Ryukyus in June 1945, the largest airfield construction program in the Pacific began in preparation for the forthcoming invasion of the Japanese Home Islands. Gen. Ennis Whitehead hoped to rush Fifth Air Force fighter units there as possible and before VJ-Day four Fighter Groups and two Night Fighter Squadrons were to be operating from the Ryukyus. The 35th Fighter Group was to be based on Yontan and the 58th from Kadena, while the 348th and the 8th Groups were to be stationed on Ie Shima.

**16-30 May 1945: 5FC Philippines**

The first massed Napalm attack on Ipo had been so successful that on the 16th Gen. Smith of 5 FC sent a force of twice the size, 680 fighters, to Ipo. Flights orbited over the foothills as the preceding units attacked and when their turn came the fighters aligned in line abreast formation with eight elements wingtip to wingtip, turning into an ascending formation separated at 300 yard intervals. At 800 feet above the hills, the pilots flew toward the smoke boiling up from the five square mile target area. As they arrived over the target, the fighter bombers were buffeted by rising thermals from the fires. As they passed over the release point the flight jettisoned their bombs in unison; flight after flight, the conflagration was fed. For the next two days, the Japanese troops in the highlands were attacked and with the depletion of their ranks due to starvation and disease, the Allies were able to secure the entire shoreline of Luguna De Bay with light casualties. Ipo Dam was also captured intact without opposition.

From 18 May until the end of the month the next target for the fire-bombing 5FC fighter bombers was Yamashita's north-central line of defense and the remaining enemy forces in the interior of Luzon. Although the rains reduced the effectiveness of the Napalm, these raids contained the enemy Cagayan strongholds so that Clark Field could be repaired and returned to operational status. Originally plans called for the Clark Field Complex to be ready for the B-29s of new 20AF but the capture of Okinawa superseded that plan. By the third week in May, the 308BW tactical units moved into Clark and Nichols Airfields. By the first week of June, Yamashita's forces were driven from Aparri and his strongholds still intact in the hills flanking the Cagayan Valley were completely surrounded

35FS CO, veteran **Maj. Lynn Witt**, who had served with the 35FS for 27 months, left for home. (AAF)

**March/April/May 1945: 348FG**

During March through May the 348FG flew ground attack missions: 118 in March, 180 in April, and just over 30 in May. Their principal target was the roads the Japanese used to reorganize for a final stand in the Cagayan Valley at the end of May 1945. Other targets were in the Ipo Dam area and the area of Corregidor Island and Fort Drum, a fortified battleship-shaped artificial island blocking Manila Bay. During April 1945, for the first time during the war, a fighter group, the 348th, dropped more bombs in a month than any heavy bomber group. According to a press release:

**Capt. Wilbert Arthur** was shot down and became the only 49FG POW to survive captivity. (AAF)

> The Group's Mustangs dropped 2,091 tons of bombs of which 2,068 were checked off as direct hits on pin point targets…and has been credited with the destruction of 10,000 Japanese by bombing and strafing… Flying as many as 200 sorties a day, the Mustang pilots fired nearly 200,000 rounds of .50 caliber ammunition… they struck every conceivable target: caves, entrenchments, gun emplacements, troops, vehicles, factories, warehouses, bares, shipping, and anything else that was Jap…with the loss of a single plane and that one was rescued…the 348th first established its reputation as a 'Go Down and Blast'em' scourge of Jap shipping, it ran up a record total during the Leyte Campaign and, during one three week period this, its pilots sank one tenth of the Jap shipping credited to the entire Fifth Air Force.

**Capt. Donald Leighton** took over command of the 35FS from veteran Lynn Witt. (AAF)

**30 May 1945: 475FG/431FS**

The 431FS flew an uneventful low level mission to Taiwan but Lt. Millard Sherman's P-38 hit an obstacle (tower or tree) three miles from Sank Yaku town and he was listed KIA.

**31 May 1945: 49FG**

On 31 May, Deputy CO Maj. James Watkins led 12 Flying Knights to the airdrome at Tainan, Formosa. The Knights destroyed two aircraft and several vehicles at Tainan and when they regrouped Capt. Wilbur Arthur, a 9FS veteran who had just returned from a furlough in the States, reported that his fighter had heavily damaged by AA fire. Arthur bailed out and his flight saw him land and then stagger a few steps and was last seen crawling for cover. Arthur was captured and with an untreated broken ankle suffered through the bleak working conditions in a labor camp on northern Formosa. He later evacuated to the prison camp at Atsugi Airdrome on Honshu Island in the Japanese Homeland.

That same day Black Sheep 1Lt. James Atkinson was strafing a vehicle convoy along the coast road when his P-38 was hit flying low over the burning trucks when his Lightning suddenly dropped its wing and cartwheeled in a flaming crash.

Fifteen victory ace **Maj. Cyril Homer** rotated home after serving as 80FS Co for nine months. (AFAA)

# 9

## June 1945

**Early June 1945: Philippines**

By the beginning of June the Americans advance into the Cagayan Valley forced Yamashita to move his headquarters closer to the Bontoc area. The 32nd Infantry Division had broken through the Salasac Pass and joined the 25th Division north of the Balete Pass. Although Yamashita had planned to counterattack; he was stymied by the Americans' steady advance into the Valley and by the 28 June landing of American paratroops in the north near Aparri who then were driving south. On 10 June the converging American and Filipino ground forces reached Bambang at the eastern base of the formidable Baguio-Bambang-Bontoc defensive triangle. The American 6th, 32nd, and 33rd Divisions were advancing north to Bontoc through difficult mountain terrain while the 37th Division was rapidly moving into the Cagayan Valley. The Japanese attempted to live off the land, forming into small Guerilla units with the limited objective of slowing the American advance but Luzon was quickly becoming secured and by the middle of the month the 5FC missions were generally being reduced for lack of specific targets.

**Early June 1945: Formosa**

Intelligence thought that the Kamikazes would shift their operations from Formosa to southern Japan but reconnaissance flights in late May discovered many Kamikazes were still staging into northern Formosa to strike the Okinawa convoys. Nimitz insisted that Kenney's 5AF heavy bombers repeat their reduction of the Formosa airdromes and the 5FC supported the effort with more tactical strikes on the southern airdromes and railroads.

**Early June 1945: 58FG**

Early June was an operational carry-over of the May operations as the 58FG continued to strike selected targets in both the Ipo Dam area and along the Northern Front. The 25th and 32nd Divisions had overrun the Santa Fe area north of the Balete Pass by the end of May and were swiftly advancing up the Cagayan Valley. Missions on the Northern Front could no longer be described as close ground support but were in fact armed reconnaissance, as the infantry was advancing so rapidly that close support could not be carried out safely on many occasions. 58FG Thunderbolts flew several miles ahead of U.S. Infantry forward positions, attacking enemy caves, pill boxes, bridges, gun positions, armor concentrations, and strafing all buildings and transportation along the roads.

During the first two days of June the efforts of the 58FG were directed to pockets of resistance in the Ipo Dam, Wawa and the Marikina Watershed areas. The 69FS sent four missions to Marikina, carrying general purpose bombs and Napalm. Enemy supply points and dug-in positions were hit at the specific direction of the Ground Controllers. The 311FS sent 63 sorties over the same area. One mission dropped 24 Napalm tanks on a troop concentration in a ravine and hillside, burning it out. Fragmentation bombs, 1,000 pound bombs, and strafing brought "excellent" reports from the SAP controllers, who directed the pilots to these specific targets. Operations continued to wind down after 10 June as the 311FS flew only 28 sorties for the remainder of the month, with the exception of a special mission of eight sorties on 23 June.

The new 201st Mexican Fighter Squadron had trained in their Thunderbolts but with several accidents. Beginning on 4 June one of their pilots was inserted into each 58FG flight for their first combat missions. After each pilot had flown a few combat missions with the three Group Squadrons, the 201FS flew its first of 31 missions with the 58FG as a squadron on 7 June. They attacked targets in the Infanta area on the east coast of Luzon and placed 13 of their 1,000 pound bombs in the target area.

**June 1945: 348FG**

The Group continued to operate from Floridablanca under the 5FC. Lt.Col. William Banks became Group Commander on 6 June taking over from veteran Col. Richard Rowland and Maj. William Dunham became Deputy Group Commander. During June only 168 missions were flown as on the 18th operations were suspended in preparation for a move. Again the majority of the missions were ground support (77%) directed first northeast of Manila in support of the XI Corps' mopping up operations. The next ground support operations were flown in support of the I Corps in northern Luzon where Japanese troops were holding out in the Belete Pass area against U.S. troops advancing toward the Cagayan Valley. There was no enemy air opposition and no aircraft lost in combat but seven suffered major damage in operational accidents.

**June 1945: 35FG**

The Group again continued providing air support for infantry attacking Belete Pass which was the southern entrance to the Cagayen Valley. The Japanese had tenaciously held the pass for many weeks and the Sixth Army was slowly advancing with heavy casualties toward Santa Fe and Bone South which blocked the southern approaches from the Pass into the broad Cagayen Valley. The Group's air support played an important part in the breaking the Japanese hold there and the infantry moved toward Tuguegarao, the location of the largest airfield in central Luzon and Aparri the northern most city on Luzon whose capture would mark the end of the Luzon Campaign except for the remote mountains where remnants of the Japanese army retreated to hide and be hunted down by Filipino guerilla

**Lt.Col. William Banks** took over command of the 348FG from **Col. Richard Rowland**. (both AFAA)

forces. The Group flew 38 missions to Formosa without encountering air opposition. Two pilots were killed in June. 2Lt. Herbert Smith of the 40FS was killed on the 3rd when his fighter collided on the Clark Field runway after a mission. On 10 June 2Lt. Hulen Leinweber of the 40FS was shot down by ground fire while attacking a truck convoy.

On 24 June the Group was released from its tactical assignments on Luzon to prepare to move to Okinawa. The Group was packed and ready for the longest airborne move in its history, staging through Laoag for refueling, and then continuing its 1,000 mile flight to Yonton Field. A temporary camp was established at Machinato Airdrome, located about five miles from Okinawa's Capitol, Naha. Soon a permanent site was selected a mile north and by 2 July the entire air echelon was ready to be the first FEAF units to operate against Japan.

**June 1945: 49FG**

In the June buildup at Linuyan, two of the 49ers squadrons initiated new commanders. Robert Aschenbrener turned the 7FS over to Capt. Clay Isaacson, a veteran from the European theater. After recovering from a back injury, Aschenbrener was promoted to Major and moved to the 308BW Staff along with 8FS CO William Drier. The command of the 8FS was assumed by another ETO veteran, Capt. Mark Vinzant. Meanwhile, at the 49er HQ, returning Flying Knights veteran, Capt. Edward Howes, was assigned as special liaison to Fighter Command. Ace Robert DeHaven returned to the 7FS Demons' staff and by the first week of June, the 49FG squadrons were staffed by experienced veterans at all major positions for their move to Okinawa.

The 49th Fighter Group continued its missions to Formosa into the summer of 1945 carrying out new fighter bomber tactics. On 23 June the 9th Fighter Squadron joined other units of the Group in the first Napalm attack on Formosa. The town of Mato was left in flames by waves of four to eight fighters which saturated the area with Napalm bombs. Col. Clayton Tice led the 49th Group to Formosa on 17 July 1945, on an experimental bridge-busting mission using dive, skip, and glide bombing techniques against the Soton Railroad Bridge, using four-to-five second delay fuses on 1,000 pound demolition bombs. The 9FS Squadron attacked first and

Thunderbolts of the **35FG** at Clark Airfield, from which they attacked ground targets in northern Luzon. (AAF)

Maj. **William Drier** left command of the 8FS to Capt. Mark Vinzant. (AAF)

**Capt. Clay Issacson** took over the 7FS from Capt. Robert Aschenbrener. (AAF)

**2Lt. Harlen Hoyt** (left, with **2lt. George Spruill**) crashed into a fatal fireball; he became the 35th and last 49FG pilot to die in the Philippines. (AAF)

neutralized the target by destroying anti-aircraft installations with fragmentation bombs after which other P-38s were able to try the new bombing techniques without interference.

The 49ers flew more than 1,500 sorties from Lingayen during June on targets on Luzon which became operational training sorties for the newcomers, as well as the proving grounds for new weapons and delivery techniques. Eventually, these sorties no longer bombed Cagayan Valley with heavy ordinance but dropped surrender leaflets. However, on a milk-run strafing attack on the central Cagayan Valley, 7FS 2Lt. Harlen Hoyt's P-38 inexplicably crashed into a fatal fireball and Hoyt became the 35th and last 49FG pilot to die in the Philippines.

**June 1945: Gabu Airfield**

Gabu Airfield became even busier in June than it had been as its location as the northernmost field on Luzon meant that it was a sanctuary for damaged aircraft returning from Formosa. During June 37 aircraft carrying 209 personnel made emergency landings at Gabu. However, Gabu saw its greatest activity as a staging field for aircraft moving to Okinawa in preparation of the invasion of the Japanese Home Islands. Large quantities of gas, oil, spare parts, and all other types of supplies were flown in to meet the demand, and a transient camp was swiftly built to handle all the personnel also on the move. In all 253 aircraft staged through Gabu in June, and even more followed in July.

**June 1945: 3ACG**

Air Commando pilots had not seen an enemy aircraft since the Hong Kong mission of 3 April and were impatient to move up to Okinawa to get into air combat but were relegated to Gabu's backwaters. MacArthur declared the Luzon Campaign over on 1 July even though the Japanese remained active in the Cagayan Valley, where Yamashita had assembled the remnants of his forces on Luzon. During June the Air Commando Fighter Sections flew numerous missions in support of the infantry closing in on Yamashita. The Air Commandos suffered the loss of five pilots in June but not due to enemy action. Capt. Charles Adams was leading a ground support mission near Mankayan on 5 June and decided to continue on with the attack when clouds began to gather in the target area. Adams told his flight to watch as he would make a glide-bombing attack rather than dive-bombing. Adams made his pass but apparently realized the clouds were lower than he thought and he suddenly dropped his bombs and began a sharp pull up. His Mustang stalled and whipped into a violent spin from which he could not recover and smashed into a mountainside, killing him instantly. Sadly, orders promoting Adams to Major had arrived at Gabu while he was on this mission and an enthusiastic crowd was awaiting his return to pin on his Oak Leaves. Adams was one of the most well liked pilots in the group and his promotion to Commander of the 3rd Fighter Squadron when Mahurin moved up to Group Operations Officer was a popular choice. Capt. Thomas Williams took Adams' place as 3FS CO.

During June the Japanese were retreating toward the interior and into the Cagayan Valley, and targets for the Air Commandos became sparse and their fighters often returned to base with their bombs. Missions to Formosa continued to be flown regularly, although many of these were just to cover rescue submarines and Catalinas or to escort B-24s bombing the island. Nevertheless, ACG fighter sweeps continued to have a devastating effect on the enemy. In June alone Air Commando fighters destroyed five locomotives and 52 box cars, 25 trucks, 10 bridges, and numerous buildings and other structures. But the Japanese defenses continued to take their toll on the 3ACG. On 26 June, as eight 4th Fighter Section Mustangs made a sweep on Formosa, clouds began to build over the mountains and the fliers turned to head for home. Capt. John Bleecker, 1Lt. John Tillou, and 2Lt. Raymond Wingo were last seen entering the clouds and were not seen again as the three evidently had flown into a mountainside as they attempted to maintain formation. On 29 June rookie 2Lt.

Paul Krikoroff was killed while ferrying a P-51 from Tacloban to Gabu as his plane crashed into San Pablo Bay just after taking off.

**June 1945: 421NFS**

At the beginning of June the squadron saw very little activity outside the routine patrols and was looking forward to a move and receiving some new aircraft as there were only seven well-worn Black Widows left in the Squadron inventory. Many new air crews had arrived and Capt. Owen Wolf was the only original 421st NFS pilot left in the Squadron. The training program continued in the Squadron, with excellent results despite very few aircraft available as two were transferred to a service squadron, leaving only five for the Squadron use. Two red alerts without action were called due to Japanese reconnaissance over Manila on two different mornings but without interception. The night snooper missions over Cagayan Valley were in conjunction with a breakthrough of U.S. ground troops into the last enemy stronghold on Luzon. The P-61s flew missions with the intent to disrupt any possible enemy night air evacuations and also to observe enemy troop activities. The Squadron pilots also continued to strafe and bomb throughout the area and met minimal AA fire over the targets and no planes were hit. The Annual General Inspection by the 5AF finally resulted in a realization by HQ that the 421st was in dire need of aircraft and vehicles and they were promised all new P-61s before their next move which was imminent. Within a week most of the equipment had been moved to a debarkation point, all of the buildings dismantled, the equipment packed, and a fleet of new trucks and jeeps joined arrived.

**Capt. John Bleeker** and two Flight members were killed when they flew into clouds and crashed into a mountain side. (AAF)

**June 1945: 348FG**

June 1945 was another month of relative air inaction as the 348FG but a bright spot was an alert for a move to the Okinawa area late in the month. The missions became very routine during the final drive to the northern Luzon port of Aparri. By the end of June there were only isolated pockets of desperate and starving Japanese troops in remote areas of Luzon. Day after day flights were given detailed briefings and then flew in close cooperation with the Ground Controller and then obliterated ground support targets allowing the infantry to advance, often days ahead of schedule. During June the 348FG was awarded its two Distinguished Unit Awards. About 20 June, all operations for the 348FG in the Philippines ceased as Gen. Yamashita's forces in the Philippines were isolated and ravaged by American infantry, air power, and disease. The Philippines Campaign was concluded and there was literally nothing for the tactical air forces to attack.

During the month the Group lost three pilots during ground attack operations:

1 June: 2Lt. Charles Dilts (340FS) crashed as he was unable to pull out during a bomb run in the Bontoc area.

8 June: 1Lt. Robert Dow (342FS) crashed into a road grader during take off;

10 June: 1Lt. Floyd Stone (460FS) collided with the wing and then prop of 2Lt. James Hamilton's aircraft in a mid-air collision over San Julian, Luzon. Hamilton bailed out safely but Stone was listed as MIA.

**June 1945: 475FG**

With the rapidly collapsing resistance in the south Philippines, the 475FG was delegated to missions in northern Luzon as well to the Asian coast. On 3 June the 432FS flew two missions to the Balete Pass area obtaining excellent results. On the first mission, eight P-38s took off at 0900 to bomb enemy concentrations northwest of Balete Pass after which they made 24 strafing passes in which 10 to 12 warehouse buildings were set on fire on the east bank of the Pambang River. Seven P-38s took off at 1030 on the second mission to bomb and strafe enemy positions in a forest five miles southeast of the Balete Pass; again the controller was "well pleased with the results." The 432FS' bombing of the Balete Pass continued intermittently along with long range strikes through 6 June.

On 13 June, 475FG was occupied with reducing the numbers of the Japanese Army and depriving it of food and armament in a general attack on the Camalaniugan area, located just south of Aparri on the north Luzon coast. The stunned enemy was relentlessly crushed by strafing and 1,000 pound bombs. After this success of this mission; on 18 June the 475FG began its first long range Napalm missions attacking Kari, a town in the southwestern part of Formosa (Taiwan). The Napalm left the entire town in flames but these low-level missions were costly as the Group lost several pilots to small arms fire.

After MacArthur declared Luzon secured on 26 June the Japanese were left with little more than several large pockets of resistance and the 475th flew fewer and fewer missions against fewer and fewer target; sometimes flying one mission a day that took off in the afternoon and returned less than an hour later.

By June 1945 there was the end of all organized Japanese in northern Luzon, and with enemy forces in the south having been all but defeated, there was little for the FEAF's tactical units to do except for sorties against occasional targets in the Aparri region of northern Luzon. By the middle of the month the Philippines were secured and only occasional mopping up missions were being flown. On 18 June the 475th would begin long range Napalm missions with a strike on Kari, in southwestern Formosa.

On 20 June 1945 the 475FG finally officially received its three Distinguished Unit Citations at Lingayen. The first DUC had been awarded to the unit in August 1943 following its impressive debut into battle over Wewak on 17-21 August when its pilots not only protected escorted bombers and also claimed many Japanese aircraft shot down. The second citation followed the Group's combat over Oro Bay on 15 and 17 October 1943 while the third was awarded after the prolonged air battles over the Philippines in the initial stages of the invasion occurring between 25 October and 25 December 1944.

**13 June 1945: 419NFS**

Pilot 1Lt. Harold Michels, R/O F/O Verna Morgan, and gunner Sgt. John Snyder encountered a Nick south of Brooketon, Brunei Bay and Michels was credited with the 419NFS' sixth and last victory (plus one probable) of the war.

**18 June 1945: 547NFS**
At 2110 Pilot 1Lt. Roy Oakes, R/O 1Lt. Ralph Jacqmin, and gunner SSgt. Ralph Knight were flying over Kaputsua Airstrip, Formosa when they saw a Tess approaching them from 90 degrees port and low with its recognition lights onto the field also had its runway lights on. As Oakes approached the Tess went into a sharp starboard turn which put it head on into the P-61 which passed over the enemy transport. Oakes made a 180 degree port turn which placed him two miles and 1,000 feet behind the enemy. The Tess crossed the field at 700 feet and Oakes closed to 330 yards and opened fire with a single long burst that hit the starboard wing and engine. The transport exploded into the ground for the Squadron's seventh and last victory of the war.

**1Lt. Roy Oaks** shot down a Tess transport for the 547NFS' seventh and last victory of the war. (AAF)

**18 June 1945: 475FG**
The low level missions to Taiwan took their toll on 18 June when the 432[nd] lost two pilots on the same mission to small arms fire. Lt. Alvin Roth's P-38 was hit in the right wing tank and he was only partially out of his cockpit to bail out when the fighter crashed into the water. Lt. Edward Carley was also killed when he was unable to bail out successfully at a low altitude. The bodies of neither pilot where never found. Three days later Lt. Herbert Finney crashed and was killed on take off on a flight to Taiwan.

**21 June 1945: 547NFS**
While on a local patrol, pilot 1Lt. Arthur Shepard, R/O 1Lt. Arvid Shulenberger and gunner MSgt. Donald Meech claimed a Tojo destroyed and another probable between 2215 and 2255 60 miles northwest of Lingayen.

**22 June 1945: 547NFS**
Just after midnight Capt. William Dames, R/O 2Lt. Eugene D'Andres, and gunner Sgt. Raymond Ryder flying a local patrol claimed a Rufe flying 60 miles southwest of Lingayen.

**24 June 1945: 547NFS**
Pilot Capt. James Bradford, R/O 1Lt. Lawrence Lunt, and gunner MSgt. Reno Sukow claimed a Betty at 2140 flying 20 miles from Point Charlie.

In addition to local patrols the 547[th] began to fly missions to Formosa and the Chinese mainland either to fly cover for Army B-24s or Navy PB4Y Privateers or harassment missions armed with 1,000 pound bombs. Fourteen cover missions were flown in 22 days and six contacts were made with enemy fighters which were driven off before making contact with the bombers. The intruder bombing missions were not particularly destructive but lived up to their harassment undertaking.

**Mid-Late June 1945: 58FG**
On 16 June, Group CO, Col. Edward Roddy, announced an imminent move from the Philippines to Okinawa in the Ryukyus and all Squadrons were released from operations for next 10 days to prepare for the move. The camp was dismantled sent by truck to be loaded on LSTs docked at Subic Bay by the 18[th]. But the move was postponed until the 24[th] and the Group had to live in tents without electricity until then.

Although the regular 58FG squadrons were not operational during this period; the 201[st] Mexican Squadron continued operations through 25 June. After this time they separated from the 58FG and continued to operate independently in the Philippines. The only combat missions during this period flown by regular 58FG squadrons was a special mission flown by all three squadrons on successive days beginning 22 June. This mission, in addition to attacking a valuable target, was to investigate gas and oil consumption and fuel reserves of the Thunderbolt. Each Squadron sent out eight fighters on successive days loaded with two 1,000 pound bombs. Each mission was intended to be the last combat mission to be flown by each Squadron from the Philippines. On 22 June, the first squadron to fly was the 310FS on their 837[th] mission of the war. On 23 June the 311FS completed their 857[th] and last mission while on 24 June, the 69FS completed their 898[th] mission. The target was Basco Airdrome a major base between Luzon and the Ryukyus. Basco Airdrome was located on Batan Island, 150 miles off Aparri on the north coast of Luzon and was an 800 mile round trip from Porac. These three missions were uneventful and the results of the bombing were judged to be "excellent," with many hits on the runways and revetment areas. The important results of the gasoline and oil consumption tests conducted on these flights proved satisfactory and reached the conclusion that such flights could be made and still maintain a sufficient fuel reserve.

On the morning of 26 June the LSTs had arrived and all personnel of the water echelon, under Lt.Col. Harry Odren, Deputy Group Commander, were to depart Porac and embark for the voyage to Okinawa. Each Squadron was allotted to one LST but some officers and men from 58[th] Headquarters waited for a fourth LST, which was to be the Command vessel of the convoy. Lt.Col. Edward Roddy and all of the pilots remained at Porac, along with a minimum number of ground personnel to service the aircraft for training flights and for the eventual flight north.

432FS CO **Maj. Elliott Summer** relinquished command to Maj. Dean Dutrack due to illness. (AAF)

Except for the missions to Batan Island starting on 23 June, the 58th Fighter Group had been operational for only 16 days of June, flying 633 sorties: 220 by the 69FS, 193 by the 310FS, and 220 by the 311FS. The Squadrons had dropped 429 tons of bombs: 118 tons by the 69FS, 169 tons by the 310FS, and 142 tons by the 311FS. The Group dropped 222 (165 gallon) Napalm tanks: 82 by the 69FS, 54 by the 310FS, and 86 by the 311FS. These figures do not include the 201st Mexican Squadron, which was part of the Group until 26 June 1945.

**June-July 1945: 475FG: Command Changes**

Maj. Elliot Summer, CO of the 432FS was hospitalized with appendicitis and was succeeded by Maj. Dean Dutrack on 5 July. On 23 June, Maj. Robert Cline handed over command of the 431FS to Maj. John Vogel who passed it on to Maj. Edwin Weaver on 16 July. Capt. Calvin Wire rotated home from the 433FS in May and Capt. James Wilson took over until July when Capt. William Haning took over. (Note: Maj. Edwin Weaver had scored two victories and two probables over the Luftwaffe while flying a P-40 with the 57FG over North Africa.)

**Capt. Calvin Wire** rotated home from command of the 433FS. (AFAA)

ETO Veteran **Maj. Edwin Weaver** became 431GS CO. (AAF)

431FS CO **Maj. Robert Cline** rotated home. (AAF)

# Part Eight
## Okinawa to V-J Day

# 1

## July 1945

**July 1945: Situation: Okinawa**

The invasion of Okinawa, under the command of Adm. Nimitz, began on 1 April 1945 and would continue for 61 days before the organized Japanese resistance was broken. Marine Corps F4U Corsairs were operating from makeshift airfields by 7 April to provide ground support and to ward off Kamikaze attacks. By 16 April onsite Navy Commanders concluded that the development of permanent air bases on Okinawa would be so delayed that they decided to invade the small island of Ie Shima off the west coast of Okinawa which already had three Japanese air strips. By 30 April the Navy called in the 7th Air Force's 301st Fighter Wing to support the 2nd Marine Fighter Wing, composed of the 14th, 22nd, 31st, and 33rd Marine Groups. The 7th Air Force had been attached to the Navy and Marine forces for virtually the entire Pacific war. The first Air Force combat unit, the 318th Fighter Group, equipped with Thunderbolts also arrived at this time.

By 1 May the first serviceable all-weather airfield was completed at Kadena and was followed by the opening of a second field on Ie Shima about 10 days later. A short time later the all-weather field at Yontan opened. On 16 May MacArthur and Nimitz met to discuss the enormous build up expected to cover the invasion of Japan proper. They agreed to base 51 air groups on Okinawa to be stationed on 20 different airfields: 11 of these airfields would be allotted to the Far East Air Forces, six to XX Bomber Command B-29s, and the Navy and Marines would operate from the last three. This proposal initiated the largest aviation engineering project ever; employing 80,000 engineering personnel at its peak, creating 25 miles of paved runways, and hardstands and taxiways that were the equivalent of 400 miles of standard two lane highway. In late May the project was almost stopped by storms and torrential rains and it was not until 15 June before construction returned to maximum effort. However, the stormy weather set back construction enough to delay the planned movement of Far East Air Forces units to the island.

7AF Arrives

7th Air Force operations from Okinawa began on 17 May when the 318th Fighter Group began flying night fighter sweeps over Kyushu air fields composed of two Thunderbolts each. The 318th continued to harass the Japanese air bases until relieved by P-61s of the 548th Night Fighter Squadron on 16 June. On 7 June the 318th Fighter Group began dispatching day fighter sweeps to Kyushu where they met with determined opposition, the first and the last of the Okinawa campaign. By 13 June, they had encountered 244 enemy interceptors, claiming 48 destroyed in aerial combat, while losing only three of their P-47s. The 7th Air Force added the Thunderbolt-equipped 413th Fighter Group on 19 May but it did not become operational until 21 June.

The 7AF brought up its third P-47 fighter group, the 507FG, which began operations on 1 July. The 7AF also brought up three bomb groups: the 41st Bomb Group (B-25s) operated from Kadena, and the 11th and 494th Bomb Groups (both B-24s) were based on Yontan Field. The 494BG had arrived from Palau, where they had been operating under FEAF control for several months. The 319th Bomb Group, the final 7AF bomb group to arrive, moved from Italy to the States, where they were equipped with the new Douglas A-26, and then to Okinawa where it flew its first mission on 16 July.

**July 1945: The FEAF Arrives on Okinawa**

Gen. Donald "Fighter" Hutchinson arrived in Okinawa on 14 June, to command the 308th Bomb Wing, the first 5th Air Force unit in the build up of air forces for the invasion of the Japanese Homeland. By 2 July Hutchinson had moved the 35th Fighter Group equipped with its 75 new P-51s to Yontan where they launched a fighter sweep over Kyushu on the next day. The build up was so rapid that Adm. Nimitz was not aware that the 5th Air Force was operating within his command until they had flown a second fighter sweep. Even though these early sweeps by the 35FG were successful, Gen. Whitehead determined that it was not feasible to continue to move aircraft into Okinawa without enough ground crews to maintain them as only the pilots, aircraft, and a few crewmen arrived with the 35th. Whitehead then ordered that aircraft movement and the pilots and crews were to remain in the Philippines until their ground echelons were in place on Okinawa to receive them. The 58th Fighter Group, assigned to be the third tactical fighter unit to move to Okinawa had to wait almost a month at Porac while their ground echelon arrived and became established on Okinawa.

The next 5th Air Force unit to arrive was the 348th Mustang Group but it would not fly operations until the new Machinate Air Base was ready to accept aircraft. The 348th P-51s were sent to Ie Shima Island, 10 miles away. The 348th ground echelon arrived on 9 July and the group flew its first combat mission on 14 July. The 58th Fighter Group was also scheduled to fly from Machinate but had to use Kadena and another facility at Bolo.

Fifth Air Force B-24s of the 22nd, 43rd, 90th, and 380th Bomb Groups had arrived by late July but their ground echelons were delayed in the convoys and did not arrive until early August. By the end of July the 38th and 345th Bomb Groups (B-25s) arrived.

The final 5AF units, the 8th Fighter Group (P-38s), 475th Fighter Group (P-38s), and the 3rd Bomb Group (A-20s) did not arrive until 6 to 8 August. The 49th Fighter Group (P-38s) did not arrive before the end of the war. The one-of-a-kind 386th Bomb Squadron (Very Heavy) flying its B-32 Dominators arrived in early August.

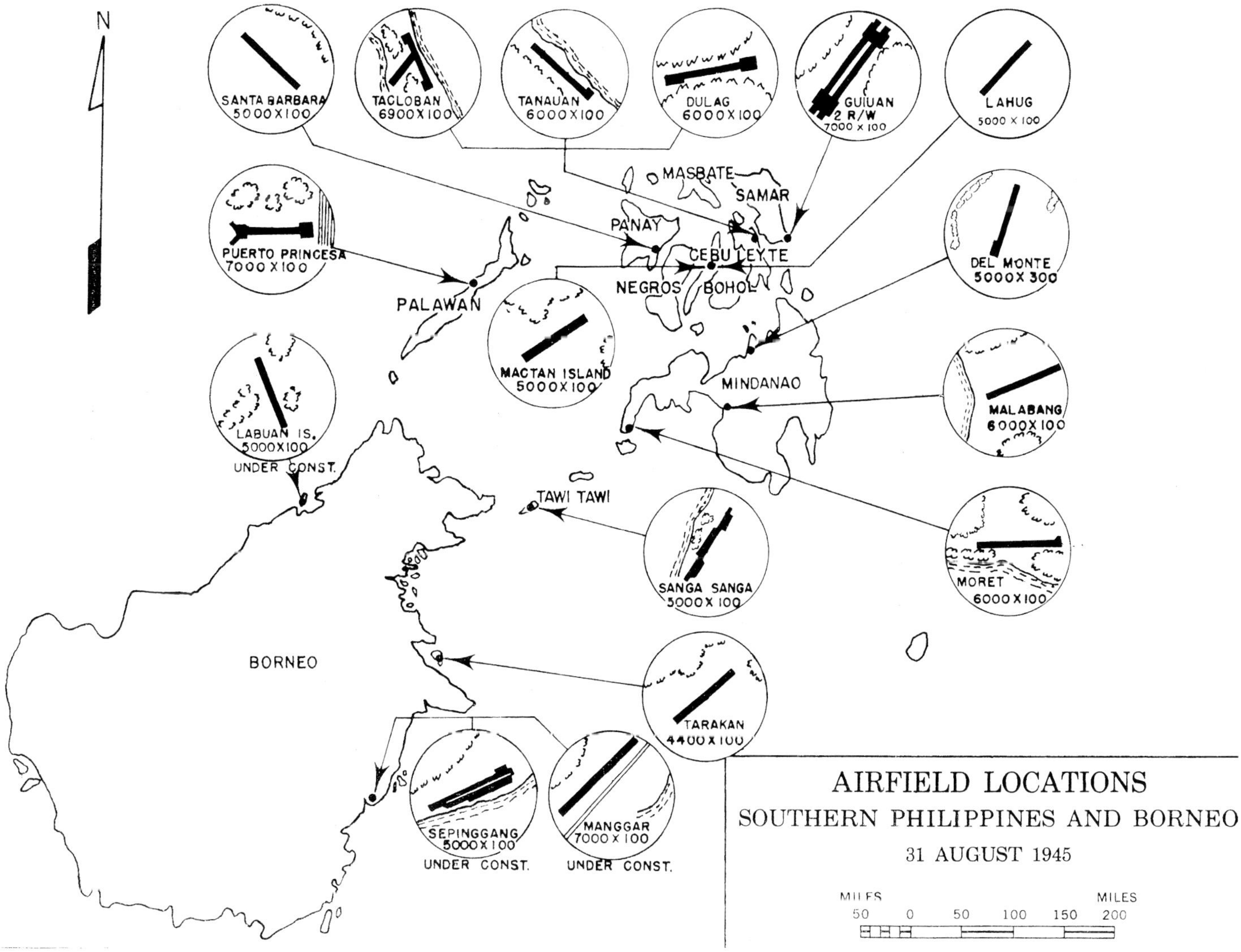

AIRFIELD LOCATIONS
SOUTHERN PHILIPPINES AND BORNEO
31 AUGUST 1945

**2 July 1945: The Last Enemy Air Action Over Okinawa**

The last enemy attempt at an organized interception occurred on 2 July, when 12 enemy fighters appeared to face 47 Thunderbolts of the 318th Fighter Group escorting five B-24 reconnaissance aircraft over Kyushu. However, the enemy fighters declined to press their attack. During this time entire 5th Fighter Command managed to destroy only 32 enemy aircraft in air to air combat, while losing only one fighter. The 7th Air Force registered 51 victories during May, 52 in June, 12 in July, and 39 in August. The last actual enemy interception occurred after the 14 August truce when four B-32s were intercepted by 15 enemy fighters while on reconnaissance flights over Tokyo on 17 August and again on 18 August, The B-32 gunners claimed three of the interceptors destroyed without a loss.

**July 1945: 35FG**

On 2 July the Group had completed its move from Clark Field, Luzon to Okinawa. While it was awaiting the completion of its strip at Machinato, the Group flew out Yonton and had to travel 16 miles from their billets at Machinato to Yonton. It flew the first FEAF mission to the Japanese Home Island on the 3rd when a mass formation of 48 Mustangs flew a sweep over Kyushu, southern Japan. Just after midnight on the 4th the men were awakened by gunfire which continued steadily for an hour and a half as the Japanese were attempting to reach their lines on the southern end of the island. A lone Japanese soldier was challenged by a sentry near the 41FS billet but escaped toward the ocean to join other enemy soldiers. The men of the 40th and 41st Squadrons chased down three of the escaping enemy and killed them.

During the month the 35FG lost four pilots. On 10 July F/O Elmer Ziegler of the 40FS developed engine trouble over south Kyushu and bailed out. His flight dropped a life raft but the weather closed, making rescue unfeasible and he was listed as MIA when searches the next day failed to find him. On 22 July 1Lt. Miles Burlingame of the 41FS ran low on fuel and turned back while dive bombing enemy shipping near Shanghi and did not return to base. On 27 July 2Lt. William Lambert of the 40FS was killed in a mid-air collision during a routine training flight over Okinawa. On 28 July Capt. Steward Smith of the 40FS was killed by AA fire during a dive bombing mission over Sasebo Harbor.

**July 1945: 348FG: Move to Okinawa**

Even though the 348FG had been expecting the move to Okinawa, finally on 29 June orders were issued for an immediate move there. The 342FS dismantled its camp and loaded equipment aboard vehicles to transport it down to Subic Bay. About noon the Squadron was loaded aboard *LST 651* and was ready to leave by nightfall. The 340FS was loaded aboard *LST 660* while some of its excess personnel and equipment were put on the 460FS' LST. By 4 July a convoy of 20+ LSTs and four destroyers was ready to

**348FG** Mustangs over Okinawa. (AAF)

**Ie Shima Airfield**. (AAF)

embark from Subic Bay. Due to transportation problems the enlisted men of the 341FS and Group HQ and the air echelon remained at Floridablanca until the 13th when their convoy left Subic Bay. After being turned back three times by typhoon weather they finally arrived at Ie Shima on 24 July.

After hearing rumors of the fanatic Japanese opposition and the Kamikaze attacks on and over Okinawa; the men of the 348th were apprehensive about their move to Ie Shima. But at least the pilots were given an opportunity for air combat over Okinawa and the Japanese Home Islands. On 9 July the men of the 348FG landed on Ie Shima which was found to be "six square miles of mud, coral and monotony...some 200 feet above the ocean...(and was) singularly uninviting when we looked at it." As had become customary, rain made its usual appearance during the unloading of equipment and personnel. Again there was the urgency of unloading and then dispersing the tempting men, supplies, and equipment before the Japanese could mount an air attack. Every man landed with a blanket and shelter half but by the afternoon of the next day the Squadrons camps were constructed. The P-51s arrived on 12 July and the air echelon transported in C-46s arrived soon afterward. Operations and alert buildings were immediately built but the first mission schedule for the next day was aborted when more than 20 P-51s encountered bad weather on a fighter sweep to Kyushu.

With many of the 348FG veterans finally rotating home the younger pilots found themselves as the ranking officers in the momentarily understaffed Squadrons. The four airfields on Ie Shima made traffic in the area a real problem for even the most the experienced pilots. Flights and Squadrons had to take off from the crowded strips, two at a time, and then return in a tight formation to get the scores of aircraft out of the traffic pattern in the shortest possible time.

The Group's first mission was flown on the 15th when the 341FS covered PBY south of Kyushu. During the month only 76 missions were flown with 65 flown against targets on the Japanese Homeland and 11 against targets in the Shanghai area. Of the 65 missions 30 were covering rescue aircraft and only 18 were offensive missions: sweeps (6), bombing (6) and anti-shipping (5). Of the 11 Shanghai missions five were rescue aircraft escort and six were anti-shipping. 1Lt. Bernard Kane of the 460FS was killed by ground fire in combat and 1Lt. Merle Miller of the 340FS was killed by AA fire over Kanoya Airdrome and two aircraft were destroyed and four received major damage in an operational accidents.

**July 1945: 421NFS**

In July the Squadron lost three more aircraft in accidents but soon the 421st received 11 new P-61s from depot, fulfilling the promise made by 5th Fighter Command for new aircraft and the 421st finished the month with 13 aircraft in inventory and the Squadron was ready for its move from Clark to Ie Shima. The ground echelon was loaded on a LST and left Subic Bay on 13 July and joined the convoy which left for Okinawa on the 16th. The voyage was extended for two extra days when a typhoon forced the convoy to remain close to Luzon until the storm moved north. On the 23rd the convoy dropped anchor at Ie Shima. While the 421NFS ground echelon was on the way to Ie Shima, the flight echelon still continued to fly patrols from Clark. On 5 August at 1500 the 13 Black Widows of the 421NFS, led by Maj. Richard Kiick finally arrived at Ie Shima and the first missions took place on the 8th.

**July 1945: 475FG**

Entering July, Japanese aircraft had disappeared from the skies and very few military targets still existed except for a few ground support objectives and so the rivalry between the 49th and 475th Fighter Groups also calmed. Both Groups had scored their 500th aerial victory during the Leyte campaign but now it was too late for the 475FG to top the 49FG's record score of well over 600 aerial victories. Nonetheless, the two Groups continued trying to top each other on ground missions after there were no more Japanese planes in the skies. The 475FG claimed 30 Japanese aircraft destroyed on the ground during February and March 1945, 10 locomotives destroyed on Formosa during April, and also innumerable Japanese soldiers killed and vehicles or equipment destroyed during their ground support missions. However, in preparation for the move to the Ryukyus, both the 49th and 475th Fighter Groups were relieved of combat duty on 23 July.

In July 1945, after almost two years of nearly continuous combat, there was now a lack of targets which gave the 475FG's stressed pilots and ground crews some respite. There was enough time to take a break to have Brig.Gen. Frederick Smith present 151 decorations to the 75 pilots in the last medal presentation conducted by the 475FG in wartime.

**21 July 1945: 475FG Flies its Last Missions and Moves to Okinawa**

On 21 July the 475FG Squadrons flew their last mission: 431FS and 432FS flew their last missions in World War II, both firebombing and Napalm mission while the 433FS flew convoy cover over the Luzon Straits for its final mission. On 26 July the men of the three Squadrons and Headquarters climbed into trucks that headed for Lingayen Gulf.

**July 1945: 58FG Moves to Okinawa**

On 1 July the 58th Fighter Group's entire water echelon was still at anchor in Subic Bay waiting for the convoy to form for the journey to Okinawa and three more days passed before the Command LST arrived and loaded the Headquarters detachment. The entire convoy consisted of 23 LSTs, two Corvettes, and two Destroyer-Escorts. After an uneventful voyage the convoy entered Naga Bay, Okinawa, during the afternoon of 9 July and remained on board overnight and began unloading early the next morning. By this time the Japanese had been subdued on the island.

As the time approached for the 58FG pilots and aircraft remaining at Porac to prepare to move Okinawa, they were delayed by heavy rains which gave the few overworked ground crews more time to prepare their P-47s for the trip. The 311FS was alerted to fly to Okinawa on 25 July but weather postponed the flight until 26 July. On 26 July the 310FS was first to take off and landed at Kadena strip in a heavy rain storm. The 311FS departed next and flew north and had gotten is far as the north coast of Luzon when heavy weather once more caused the flight to be cancelled and the pilots were diverted to Laoag on the far northwestern tip of Luzon. The Laoag Strip was slow and short and there was great concern as to whether the heavily loaded P-47s, carrying two full external wing tanks and a belly tank, could successfully take off. It was decided to empty the belly tank and remove it from each fighter and the next day every plane made a safe take off and landed safely at Kadena, Okinawa in the afternoon. The 69FS also flew up to Okinawa on the 27th without a problem. The remaining ground personnel had been flown up on 25 July on C-46 transports.

The major depot for new aircraft arriving from the States was still back at Biak Island, New Guinea where newly arrived aircraft were assembled to be flown north to the war. Some of the 58FG pilots had missed the movement to Okinawa because they had been sent on a ferry trip to Biak to pick up their new fighters and fly them to Okinawa via stopovers in the Philippines.

Combat missions for the 58th Fighter Group began on 28 July when the Group dispatched 48 aircraft, 16 from each Squadron, to escort B-24s 630 miles to Kure Navy Base on the main island of Honshu. The 58th flew only 194 sorties during July. The 311FS flew eight sorties from Porac to the Bataan Islands, dropping eight tons of bombs, the only bombs dropped by the Group during the month. In addition to the Porac sorties, the 311FS added another 62 sorties from Kadena while the 69FS flew 60 and the 310FS flew 64.

**July 1945: 3ACG**

11 July 1945: 3ACG

During July 3ACG fighter pilots continued flying to Formosa mostly to cover Air-Sea Rescue Catalinas and lifeguard submarines but hoping to see enemy aircraft in the air. Their perseverance was rewarded at last on 11 July. That morning, four 3rd Fighter Section Mustangs were assigned to cover a Catalina and submarine operating off Formosa's northwestern coast near Shinchiku. The first hour of the mission was another boring exercise, circling over the rescue team but then 1Lt. Herbert French spotted a bogey at his 10 o'clock and out to sea. French and his Wingman, 2Lt. George Mooney, were flying high cover, while the Flight Leader and his Wingman were the low cover. The Flight Leader told French and Mooney to intercept while the other Mustangs continued to cover the rescue team. The two immediately took off toward the bogie heading toward Formosa at about 8,000 feet. As they closed on the plane, it suddenly reversed course and dove for the water. The Americans dropped their belly tanks, pushed their throttles forward and began to chase the plane, which they identified as a Kate and it took them over 15 minutes to catch it. French and Mooney closed to both sides of the enemy plane to prevent it from breaking one way or the other. The desperate enemy pilot tried a bank to the right but Mooney was ready and fired a burst into its wing root and soon pieces flew off the plane and orange flame streaked back as it headed for the sea. Suddenly, a wing ripped off and the Kate began to tumble wildly and then leveled off only feet above the water. Its pilot tried to bail out but his parachute did not open and he and his plane smashed into the water almost simultaneously. Mooney's victory was the last of the 3ACG's eight total aerial victories (plus two probables) in the war.

**12 July 1945: 3ACG**

On 12 July, the 3rd Fighter Section pilots were escorting a B-24 when its pilot reported that the crew would soon have to leave their bomber after it had been hit by flak over Formosa. The sea was very rough, however, and the Catalina could not land so the fighter pilots located the lifeguard submarine and guided it back toward the still flying but stricken bomber. Instead of dropping his men close to the submarine, though, the B-24 pilot scattered them across 15 miles of choppy seas. The four fighter pilots circled low over the B-24 crewmen and dropped sea markers to keep track of them. 2Lt. Charles House spotted one man floundering in the water without a life raft and decided that the only way to save him was to drop his own dinghy, which was attached to the seat part of his parachute. He trimmed his plane for a slight climbing turn so that it would continue to circle over the downed flier. He next unfastened all of his parachute straps and seat belt and pushed his feet against the rudder pedals, raising himself off his seat. House struggled to pull the dinghy from its pack in his fighter's cramped cockpit but finally succeeded. He descended to only a few feet over the bomber crewman and dropped the dinghy. House circled and watched as the man inflated the dinghy, climbed in, and waved. The sub eventually picked up the sodden airman.

**Mid-July 1945: 3ACG Moves to Okinawa**

In mid-July, the Group received orders to move to Ie Shima and an advanced party of personnel from all the ground echelons was directed to move by boat and set up camp there. While this group was preparing to leave, new orders instructed the air echelon to leave first. This group was made up of mainly mechanics, not pilots or aircraft and so when they arrived on Ie Shima, they had nothing to work on. The 3ACG's own 318th TCS conducted the move, making one day, 12 hour or more, round trips between Laoag and Ie Shima. Despite frequent storms the crews continued flying day and night, not only moving the Group forward, but also continuing to drop supplies to Philippine Guerilla units and American troops in the mountains of Luzon.

**July 1945: Rotation Policy**

Unlike MacArthur who never considered sparing troops from combat, Kenney had gone out of his way to protect his aircrew, believing that they could only be kept proficient with morale high in combat if tour limits were scrupulously maintained. In practice, this meant that a fighter pilot in the 5AF could typically expect to be eligible for rotation after about 300 hours in combat or about 15 months on tour, unless he accepted a position of advanced responsibility such as Operations Officer or Squadron Commander.

Eleven victory ace **John Loisel** rose through the ranks from 2Lt., and was finally made Commander of the 475FG as a Lt.Col. (AFAA)

Veteran, 27 victory ace, and 475FG CO Col. **Charles MacDonald** rotated home in July 1945. (AFAA)

After Luzon was secured on June 26, MacArthur approved the new "points rotation system" for a general rotation back home for all FEAF personnel In the previous rotation system, the men with most time in the theater were scheduled to be sent home on an intermittent basis. If adverse combat conditions prevented releasing troops for rotation they could be trapped in that place for the duration. After Germany surrendered, reducing manpower requirements, and with many new troops being trained in America; there would be many replacements readily available. So once a man accumulated at least 85 points under the new system, he would automatically be rotated home. After the implementation of the new policy, units were sending dozens of men home while before then the average was no more than four or five a month.

475FG veteran aces Perry Dahl and Joseph Forster had both joined the 432FS in late October 1943 and remained in-theatre until mid-1945. Dahl's only break from combat during this time came in November-December 1944, when he evaded capture in the Philippines for a month after being forced down following a mid-air collision! Dahl extended his combat service to 21 months when he accepted posting as 432FS' Ops Officer and then rotated home in late June. Forster had spent several months in the U.S. in early 1945 attending a gunnery class but returned to the Philippines by July. 2Lt. John Loisel joined the 475FG at its formation in July 1943 after being given a six-month extension to his tour following nine months in combat with the 36th FS/8th FG. Loisel then progressed through the ranks within the 475FG, being Operations Officer and then CO of the 432FS in 1943-44, after which he became Group Operations Officer when Maj. McGuire was killed in January 1945. By then he was an 11 victory ace and was finally made Commander of the 475FG as a Lt. Colonel when veteran CO Col. MacDonald was sent home in July 1945. Both Loisel and MacDonald remained in the post war Air Force. MacDonald retired as a Colonel in July 1961 after serving in various staff and command positions while Loisel retired in January 1970 as a Colonel.

Gung-Ho veteran enlisted man, MSgt. Clay Cockerill, joined the 475th in Australia in July 1943 and remained with the Group until he was rotated home two years later. Not wanting to rotate home Cockerill was successful in delaying rotation until he came under the provisions of the men over 40 years old regulation.

**July 1945: 8FG Moves to Okinawa**

By the end of June the Cagayan Valley was secured and all serious resistance ended on Luzon which left the 8FG without targets until the prospective move to the new base on Okinawa was accomplished. The ground echelon began to aboard four LSTs on 23 July while the air echelon remained on Mindoro until the beginning of August when they would be the only 5FC Lightnings to operate from Ie Shima. The LSTs left in the late afternoon on the 24th and stopped at Subic Bay on Luzon on 25 July. On the next day they joined a large convoy that sailed through the South China and by the end of July the convoy was off Okinawa and unloaded. The 8FG ground echelon to set up installations for the imminent arrival of its P-38s. Meanwhile, the 8th's air echelon continued on station for any final mission required of them in the Philippines. The 80FS flew eight missions during July and then on 5 August, the Headhunters flew to Ie Shima, leaving the Mindoro in the backwater of the war.

**July 1945: Fifth Fighter Combat Air Action from Okinawa**
**3 July 1945: 35FG/39FS**

On 3 July the 35FG conducted the first offensive mission by any FEAF tactical unit over Japan when 48 P-51s led by Maj. Richard Cella (HQ) flew a fighter sweep over Sesebo on the Home Island of Kyushu, Japan. The 39FS would be the only 35FG Squadron to see aerial combat. Sixteen P-51s of the 39FS were on a sweep at 10,000 feet when at 1315 Blue Flight led by Capt. Robert Mittelstadt; saw a number of bogies flying line abreast on the deck. Mittelstadt led Wingman Lt. Kammeyer and Element Leader 1Lt. Winfield Langhorst after the two easy targets, identified as Rufe floatplanes, without dropping their tanks. Mittelstadt fired on the one on the left and began to fired out of range and held the trigger down while closing; hitting the tail, fuselage and cockpit. The Rufe rolled over in flames to the right and went into the water upside down. Wingman, Kammeyer went after the one on the right which broke immediately away and fired without seeing any damage. Kammeyer then followed Mittelstadt who continued to pursue his Rufe in a long right turn. Meanwhile, Langhorst and his Wingman, Lt. Cook had gotten into position to fire a deflection shot at maximum range and got hits on the fuselage and the enemy pilot flattened his turn giving Langhorst a smaller and closer deflection shot which set the Rufe's tail section on fire and it rolled over a crashed in a brilliant fireball. The Rufes were Langhorst's second of two victories and Mittelstadt's first two of three.

**5 July 1945: 35FG/40FS**

On 5 July 13 Mustangs of the 40th Squadron, led by Capt. Henry Rettinger, flew a sweep over Kyushu. At 1245 they were just south of Sesebo Harbor at 8,000 feet in right echelon when they intercepted four Georges. Rettinger led his Red flight down and closed to about 150 yards and opened fire on the enemy #4 man getting hits on its tail. He made another pass getting more hits and the George broke left and down and Rettinger followed and fired a three second burst that finally caused the enemy to roll over and plummet into the water. Meanwhile the three other enemy fighters rolled and were about to make a pass at Rettinger who only then dropped his wing tanks. He turned sharply and climbed as a George crossed in front, moving to the right and down. Rettinger followed in a sharp right turn and fired a four second 60 to 15 degree deflection shot that hit the engine, canopy, and tail and it began to head for the water for his only two victories. The other two Georges separated and were engaged by 1Lts. John Ebert (#3 man) and Irving Pine (#4 man) who each got credited with probables as they were forced to break off by other attacks before they could determine the fates of their Georges.

Green Flight Leader 1Lt. Ellis Baker went after one of the Georges from the Red Flight attack that broke away under Green Flight. Baker Split-S'd and closed to 200 yards and fired a two second burst from 25 degrees observing fuselage. After the enemy pilot made a few inadequate evasive moves Baker fired again and got more hits and the George plunged into the water. Baker climbed to 7,000 feet where he saw another enemy fighter heading toward a cloud bank and followed it in and found it on the other side. He closed to 150 yards and opened fire; the enemy fighter began to smoke and its pilot bailed out. Baker's two victories would give him six for the war and make him an ace. The four victories would be the 110th and last victories of the war (plus 32 probable and nine damage claims) for the 40FS.

**11 July 1945: 3ACG**

At 1030 2Lt. George Mooney of the 3ACG shot down a Kate near Kumamoto Airstrip for that unit's last victory of five victories (and two probables) during the war.

**1Lt. Ellis Baker** shot down two George fighters to become a six victory ace. (AFAA)

JNAF **Kawanishi N1K2 George**. (AFHRC)

**15 July 1945: 35FG**

At 1115 Capt. Robert Mittelstadt leading eight Mustangs to cover a USN submarine 30 miles off the Kyushu coast. After an hour they were released from this duty to continue on a fighter sweep on western Kyushu. While circling in train at 10,000 feet a pilot in the flight saw a lone bogie at 6 o'clock low that had just taken of from the Kumamo Strip below. Mittelstadt rolled out of a starboard turn and spotted the bogie at 10 o'clock low two miles from the strip and dropping his tanks, began a steep dive. Because of his steep angle of attack Mittelstadt had to completely close his throttle to reduce the excess speed. He approached the bogie, identified as a George, from 6 o'clock and opened fire at 350 yards, holding the trigger down until he had to pull quickly away to avoid a collision. The George rolled over on fire and dove inverted into the ground for Mittelstadt's third and last victory.

Mittelstadt's victory would be the last victories by the 5th Fighter Command for the month as the Japanese were hoarding their fighter aircraft to counter the expected Allied invasion. 5FC fighter missions were then directed to the strafing of transportation, industrial targets, shipping and locomotive busting.

**Capt. Robert Mittelstadt** shot down a George for his third and last victory. (AAF)

**16 July 1945: 348FG: First Mission to the Home Islands**

On 16 July 348th fighters flew their first mission over the Home Islands When fifteen P-51s of the 340FS, carrying one wing fuel tank and a 500 pound bomb, escorted B-25s to Miyakojono on central Kyushu. While the Mitchells bombed their target the P-51s dive bombed a nearby strategic bridge, scoring two direct hits.

**17 July 1945: 35FG/40FS**

Capt. Grayton Franklin of the 40FS led his flight to attack an anchored 10,000 ton enemy cargo ship in Zaki Bay off Amami-Shima. The flight scored five direct hits with 500 pound bombs and left the ship to burn furiously. Franklin returned with his flight later that day and scored seven more hits which sunk the ship.

**18 July 1945: 348FG/342FS: First Tactical Mission over Japan**

On 18 July, 16 P-51s of the 342FS made the Group's tactical debut over Japan with a strike again in the Miyakojono area on central Kyushu. The 16 Mustangs dropped 30 500 pound bombs on worker's quarters at a factory in Miyakojono. On the way back from the mission Lt. Fred Babcock ran out of gas and had to bail out into the sea and was picked up two hours later by a PBM flying boat.

**27 July to Mid-August 1945: 475FG Moves to Okinawa**

Personnel from the 431FS were loaded aboard *LST 793*, the 432FS boarded *LST 752* and the 433FS embarked in *LST 1014*. All three vessels left Lingayen Gulf during the morning of 27 July, and they reached the naval base in Subic Bay, in the Philippines, the next day. By 1 August the Group was sailing again, with the HQ aboard *LST 752* and other elements of the 431FS aboard cramped LSMs which accompanied the convoy. On 6 August the Group arrived in convoy off Okinawa, unaware that the *Little Boy* Atomic Bomb had been dropped on Hiroshima. They remained in Yonobura Harbor, awaiting orders to disembark at Ie Shima six days later.

Capt Elliott Summer had been appointed as interim Commander of the 432FS until 28 July 1945, when he was rotated home and Maj. Dean Dutrack assumed command of the unit just as it began its move to Ie Shima. Maj. Edward Weaver, who had been part of the fateful Daddy Special flight on 7 January over Negros Island, was in command of the 431FS at the end of the war while the 433FS was led by veteran group pilot Capt. William Haning during the July-August 1945 period.

During the last two months of operations, a time when few missions involved no more than two flights of P-38s, the 475FG dropped more than 1,400 tons of high explosives and 1600+ gallons of Napalm. The 475FG pilots bombed and strafed tattered but determined Japanese troops who prevented the final clearing of the Philippines.

**21 July 1945: 475FG: Final Combats**

Combat operations had not entirely stopped in July as the Group occasionally attacked exhausted but stubborn pockets of enemy resistance mainly located in the extreme northern area of Luzon. But by late July even these missions had diminished, and the 49th and 475th Fighter Groups were relieved from combat on the 23 July in preparation for their move to the Japanese Home Island's bases during the impending occupation. Two days earlier, the 475th's three squadrons had flown their last combat missions of the war. The 431FS would flew final mission #1-1008, the 432FS would send eight P-38s on a fire-bombing attack northwest of Kiangan for their final mission #2-907 and the 433FS would fly a convoy cover patrol for their final mission #3-1047. All subsequent 475FG sorties from Lingayen over the next five days would be either training or operational administrative flights. Even these missions concluded on 26 July when the group began preparing for movement closer to Japan itself.

The last two 475th fatalities of the war were sustained in early July. On 8 July Lt. Charles Zarling was on a local flight and was seen diving steeply into Lingayen Gulf. Three days later Capt. George Smith was flying as #3 in a four plane training flight with the 431FS and he half rolled into the water. There was speculation that he suffered from vertigo after the flight left a cloud.

**22 July 1945: 348FG**

Three of the Group's four squadrons attacked shipping in the Hwangpoo River, near Shanghai and sunk six small patrol vessels and made a direct hit on a large tanker and damaged four other small vessels.

**28 July 1945: 35FG**

The 35FG conducted the first 5AF mission to Korea when two anchored Emily Flying Boats were destroyed on the water near Chinnai.

**27 July 1945: 35FG**

Col. Harney Estes was named the CO of the 35FG taking over from Lt.Col. Edwin Doss.

**27 July 1945: 348FG: First Heavy Bomber Escort to Japan**

On 25 and 26 July high wind and the threat of severe weather discontinued operations but on the 27th the Group was assigned to its first escort of heavy bombers over Japan when B-24s struck at railroad marshaling yards at Kagoshima, Kyushu.

**28 July 1945: 348FG: First Medium Bomber Escort to Japan**
Eight P-51s of the 340FS and six from the 341FS provided cover for B-25s and dive bombed shipping in Japan's Inland Sea.

**29 July 1945: 547NFS**
Pilot 1Lt. Robert Bertram, R/O George Fairweather, and gunner Cpl. James Tew claimed a Betty at 0230 flying 30 miles west of Point Zebra,

**30 July 1945: 35FG**
A flight of four 39FS Mustangs led by Maj. Benjamin Widman demolished an enemy destroyer escort and severely damaged another at Mushoszu. Korea.

**30-31 July 1945: 348F**
On 30 July the 340FS concluded its July operations with a six plane sweep to Honshu. On the last day of the month 348FG P-51s dive bombed positions on the northern coast of Kyushu. The 342FS almost saw air combat when 12 to 16 Franks jumped the tail end P-51 and forced it away from the rest of the formation. The Mustang pilot was able to dive away to safety but his squadronmates were upset that he did not lead the Franks into range.

**15-26 July 1945: 348FG Casualties**
On 15 July Lt. Merle Miller crashed on take off for a PBM escort mission. On the 25th 2Lt. Burton Bennett (341FS) was MIA on his first mission and the next day 1Lt. Bernard Kane (460FS) was on a B-25/B-26 escort on Kanoya Airdrome, Japan when his fighter's wing was shot off by enemy AA fire. These were the only three deaths for the month for the 348FG.

**Late July 1945: 49FG**
Lt.Col. Clayton Tice took over command of the 49ers from Gerald Johnson on 15 July. By the last week in July Tice received the dispersal orders for the 49ers ground echelon to move south to Manila for sea transport to Okinawa while the air echelon was to prepare for air transportation from Lingayen.

**Lt.Col. Clayton Tice** took over command of the 49ers from Col. Gerald Johnson. (AAF)

Meanwhile, the 86th Wing was given permission to commandeer any surplus P-38s anywhere remotely within its realm. So a contingent of senior 49er pilots was sent by air transport 1,300 miles to ferry Lightnings from Kunming in western China. These new P-38s required additional long range equipment for the long ferry flights back to Lingayen, requiring two weeks, which left 49er pilots marooned while a rebellion was being fought by the local war lords. On their way back to Lingayen 1Lt. James White misjudged his altitude in the haze and was lost and crashed into the sea. The remainder of the China-Lingayen ferry flights was immediately canceled and three 7FS pilots were still there when the war ended. Tice and the 49ers became impatient as the days went by and they remained at Lingayen and their hope to enter combat and have the 49ers score a record 1,000 victories as a Group.

# 2

# August 1945

**August 1945: Situation**
After the Japanese formed the Peoples Volunteer Corps which made all men from 15 to 60 and women from 17 to 40 responsible to defend the Homeland; Col. Harry Cunningham, 5th Air Force A-2, stated in an official intelligence review on 21 July that stated:

> The entire population of Japan is a proper military target… There are no civilians in Japan. We are making war and making it in the all-out fashion which saves American lives, shortens the agony which war is and seeks to bring about an enduring peace. We intend to seek out and destroy the enemy wherever he or she is, in the greatest possible numbers, in the shortest possible time.

**Early August 1945: 58FG**
During the first five days of August, the 58FG began its operations out of Kadena flying a variety of missions, including aerial combat, escorting bombers, attacks on merchant and naval vessels, dive bombing railroad and highway bridges, attacks on railway facilities and equipment, burning targets of opportunity with Napalm, and even skip and dive bombing aircraft carriers. Air operations flown from Okinawa were difficult because of the exceptionally heavy air traffic. Traffic at Kadena became so heavy that the 58FG temporarily moved to the strip at Point Bolo on 6 August and continued operating from there until the new field at Machinate was completed on 15 August.

**August 1945: 3ACG**
August began with the Air Commandos scattered from the Philippines to Okinawa and Ie Shima. Most of the ground personnel had already moved north or were en route. The fighter pilots remained at Laoag and flew infrequently as their last support mission was flown on 25 July but they particularly enjoyed being fed well and catching up on their sleep. The A-Bombs dropped on Hiroshima and Nagasaki would end the war for the Air Commandos but they did witness some history in the making on 19 August when a pair of Bettys, painted an overall white and carrying large green crosses on their wings and fuselages, landed down on Ie Shima carrying a surrender delegation to meet MacArthur for preliminary negotiations. The envoys transferred to a C-54 for the final leg to Manila while their crews stayed behind to tend their planes and be observed by curious onlookers on the island.

**1 August 1945: 58FG**
Reconnaissance reported that a 9,000 ton freighter was anchored at Nagasaki Harbor and the 58FG sent out 40 Thunderbolts armed with a 500 pound bomb each. However, 14 fighters of the 69FS returned early due to bad weather. Lt.Col. Edward Roddy, leading the 311FS, continued on and his four plane flight was the first to attack, skip bombing the freighter, putting two bombs into the hull, near the stern. 1Lt. Paul Hartz, led the remaining 12 planes, following closely with dive bombing runs. Hartz's pilots scored three direct hits topside and many near misses alongside the ship; encountering heavy AA fire from both the freighter and from shore batteries. As the 311FS left the area, the freighter's stern was burning intensely, with smoke rising to 2,000 feet. By the time the 14 aircraft of the 310FS arrived to attack, the freighter had sunk and they were forced to find alternate targets. Seven pilots attacked a factory building on the extreme tip of Nezumi Shima in Nagasaki Harbor. Two bombs fell directly on the buildings and the other five fell in the general area. Results were not observed because heavy anti-aircraft fire caused the pilots to exit the area. The remaining seven aircraft bombed a group of buildings on the southeast side of Takaboko Shima.

**1 August 1945: 348FG/460FS**
At 0905 on 1 August, Lt.Col. William Dunham, CO of the 460FS took off to lead a four plane sweep on Kyushu at 16,000 feet. The Flight consisted of Dunham's Wingman, 1Lt. Thomas Sheets, Second Element Leader, Maj. Edward Popek of the 342FS, and his Wingman, Capt. William Rumpf. At 1015 Dunham and his flight were flying at 16,800 feet when they sighted a formation of B-24s heading over Take Shima Island off the coast of Kyushu that were being attacked by 16 to 20 Franks and Georges scattered from 9,000 to 15,000 feet. The enemy fighters were making single and coordinated attacks on the B-24s with a flight protecting overhead at 13,000 feet. Dunham led the flight into a dive from 12,000 feet with no plan of attack except to get at the enemy fighters before they could inflict more damage on the Liberators. The Franks were so involved with the B-24s that they were surprised by the attacking Mustangs. At 7,000 feet Dunham made a stern attack on a Frank and got hits on the nacelle and fuselage and the enemy pilot Split-S'd away. But Dunham cut the Frank off before the pulled through the dive and fired into the canopy and killed the pilot. When Dunham broke away another Frank was on his tail but his fast new Mustang easily outdistanced it. As soon as the Mustangs arrived the Franks fled toward some clouds. Sheets followed Dunham closely and also surprised his Frank at 7,000 feet and fired from 500 yards to 300 yards dead astern where he put a long burst into the enemy's fuselage and wing roots and it trailed smoke as it crashed into the water off Take Shima. Sheets climbed and then dove on another Frank flying at 12,000 feet and followed it in a shallow dive and fired two bursts into the wing roots and cockpit but the wounded Frank flew into a cloud for a damaged claim to

**Lt.Col. William Dunham** shot down a Frank to finish the war with 16 victories. (AFAA)

**Maj. Edward Popek** (left) and **Maj. Walter Benz** pose by the 342FS scoreboard after the squadron's last victory. The pictured victory total is 176, which is 53 more than the official total. (AAF)

**Maj. Edward Popek** downed two Franks to end the war with seven victories. Popek's victory was the 342nd's last of 123 for the war. (AFAA)

add to his third and final victory. Popek attacked a Frank making a pass at a B-24 but the enemy pilot saw Popek and pulled sharply away to escape. Popek went after another Frank that went into a tight turn but as it straightened out Popek fired but the enemy pilot went into a steep right turn. But Popek's bullets had hit the Frank's cockpit and it plunged into the sea smoking with its landing gear down. Popek saw a Mustang chasing a Frank and another Frank chasing the Mustang. Popek drove the frank off the Mustang's tail and joined the Mustang pilot who was Sheets. The two American pilots then dove on another Frank at 10,000 feet. Every time they fired the Japanese pilot went into a sharp port turn and finally after five passes, scoring some hits and mostly misses. Popek finally fired a long burst 55 degree deflection shot into the cockpit at 2,000 feet and the Frank fell into the water for his second victory of the battle and his seventh and last of the war.

At this time in the war nearly all 5th Fighter Command pilots were replacements for veterans who had long since rotated back to the Zone of Interior. However, a few old timers remained such as Lt.Col. William Dunham, who led a flight of four 348th Group P-51s over Kyushu that morning and shot down a Frank for his 16th victory dating back to 11 October 1943. Popek's victory was the 342FS' last of 123 for the war (plus nine probables and one damaged claim).

**2 August 1945: 35FG/39FS**

Capt. Leroy Grosshuesch led four P-51s on a sweep to Korea which required a 0415 take off in total darkness and threatening weather. Because of the bad weather the 39th was unable to find their target and went on deck, under 3,000 feet, to search for enemy shipping and low flying aircraft. They strafed two wooden boats outside Iki Shima Harbor and set them on fire and then strafed another docked boat inside the Harbor. At 0630 they spotted two destroyers and strafed them into the face of "the worst ack ack so far encountered" from both the destroyers and shore batteries. The strafing continued until an explosion that "might be called 'Houdini.' First it (the destroyer) was there and then a piece that wasn't large enough to make a large splash." The 39th continued on to strafe a two story radio building using the remainder of their ammunition.

**5-9 August 1945: 8FG/80FS/36FS Arrives on Okinawa**

The 80th Fighter Squadron P-38s arrived on Ie Shima on 5 August and 36th Fighter Squadron followed them on the next day by aircraft while the 35th did not arrive until the 9th. Although both Atomic Bombs had been dropped the war continued and MacArthur, Kenney, and the Far East Air Force prepared to conduct both strategic and tactical bombing missions against the Home Islands. The 8FG was designated to patrol, dive bombing and fighter sweep missions.

**6 August 1945: Atomic Bomb Dropped on Hiroshima**

Hiroshima was the primary target of the first nuclear bombing mission with Kokura and Nagasaki being alternative targets. A 393rd Bombardment Squadron B-29, the *Enola Gay*, piloted and commanded by 509th Composite Group Commander Col. Paul Tibbets, took off from North Field on Tinian. After about six hours flight time the *Enola Gay* dropped the "Little Boy" uranium A-bomb that delivered a blast equivalent to about 13 kilotons of TNT, resulting in a radius of total destruction about one mile and fires across 4.4 square miles. Americans estimated that 4.7 square miles (12 km$^2$) of the city were destroyed. Japanese officials determined that and another 6–7% damaged. Between 70,000-80,000 people, or about 30% of the population of Hiroshima were killed immediately and another 70,000 injured, and 70% of Hiroshima's buildings were destroyed.

**6 August 1945: Death of America's Ace-of-Aces**

On the same day that the Atomic Bomb was dropped on Hiroshima the pilots of the 5th Fighter Command received the tragic news that America's Ace-of-Aces, Maj. Dick Bong, had been killed in the crash of a P-80 jet fighter plane at Burbank, California. After Kenney had removed Bong from combat to safety, Bong was assigned to the 412th Fighter Group which was conducting tests and engaging in experimental work with America's first jet fighter aircraft; the Bell P-59A and Lockheed's P-80A-1-LO Shooting Star.

During a routine flight, as Bong's jet rolled down the runway and became airborne; white smoke emitted from its tail pipe followed by an explosion. The P-80 continued to fly at a reduced rate of climb and Bong turned right using his take off momentum. He jettisoned his canopy at 200

**Maj. Richard Bong** was testing the XP-80 Shooting Star when he was killed. (AAF)

The **Van Nuys** Bong crash scene. (AAF)

to 400 feet and one observer saw him step out of the cockpit to bail out but then get back in just before the aircraft rolled and crashed into the ground and disintegrated about a mile and a half from the runway when the fuel exploded. Happy speculation says Bong got back into the cockpit in order to save the mass of residences under his flight path by directing his stricken aircraft to a vacant utility right of way. The plane then lost flying speed and stalled out and crashed at the edge of the vacant area. The AAF crash investigation determined that the engine flamed out due to lack of fuel but failed to determine why.

**6 August 1945: 348FG/340FS/460FS**

340FS

At 0740 on 6 August 1945 the 340FS dispatched eight P-51 in two flights on a cover flight for two PBY rescue planes (*Playmate 46* and *Jukebox 36*). Red Flight was led by 1Lt. Clifford McMillin and White was led by 1Lt. Charles McDonald. Seven Mustangs (one aborted with electrical problems) were a half hour early on their rendezvous with the Catalinas and circled north of Honshu between the Chosen Strait off North Korea in the Sea of Japan and the East China Sea. As McMillin led his Red Flight over Saishu Airdrome he saw four straggling Japanese aircraft at 1,500 feet just offshore which presented a predicament for McMillin. If his flights dropped their tanks, they might not have enough fuel to rendezvous with the PBYs or if they did not, then the tanks would be a hindrance in combat. McMillin decided that the altitude and surprise advantages prevailed over those gained by dropping the tanks and he led his seven fighters to attack the unsuspecting enemy. McMillin led the attack from the rear and attacked the lead Zero from 5 o'clock high at high speed. His volley passed over the Zero's starboard wing tip but McMillin closed to 90 yards and got numerous hits and had to pull up sharply to avoid a collision. The Zero's wing surface tore off and fire enveloped the fuselage before it exploded for his only victory. Somehow the pilot bailed out but his chute opened just as he entered the water. McMillin immediately attacked a second Zero and fired a 30 degree deflection but the Zero turned into him and McMillin was unable to hold the lead. The Zero then turned into McMillin's Wingman and the two pilots fired at each other but neither got any hits. McDonald descended to 5,000 feet and then dove and fired a 50 degree deflection shot from astern tearing pieces off the canopy, wing root, and fuselage. The Zero rolled over and exploded into the ground. McDonald then climbed to gain altitude and saw a Zero flying parallel to the coast with McMillin firing on it. The Zero turned into McMillin's flight and made a head on pass at McMillin's Wingman and both fired. The Zero passed through and headed up the coast toward McDonald at 1,000 feet. As the enemy pilot approached McDonald's right wing, the American turned sharply inside the Zero and fired a short 90 degree burst, getting fatal hits from nose to tail for his second victory of the day and only two of the war. 2Lt. Carleton Ambler, White Flight Second Element

**1Lt. Clifford McMillin** claimed his only victory of the war. (AAF)

Leader, and his Wingman saw a Zero escape from the formation and head away out to sea on the deck. Ambler closed to 75 yards and opened fire getting many hits and this Zero trailed smoke as it crashed into the sea for his only victory and the 340FS' 76th and last victory of the war (and five probable and no damaged). Because they kept their tanks the Mustangs were able to meet the PBYs and cover them in a search for the crew of a downed American bomber on the seven hour mission.

460FS

While returning from a mission 1Lt. Richard Miller's fighter developed a coolant tank leak. Miller was seen to bail out and get into his life raft but was not found in subsequent searches and was listed as MIA.

**7 August 1945: 418NFS**

At about 1940 five P-61s took off from Kadena on Okinawa for an all night air patrol over the Japanese airdromes at Kumamoto on Kyushu with the task to keep the enemy aircraft on the ground by strafing and destroy any aircraft that became airborne. Pilot 2Lt. Curtis Griffitts and R/O Myron Bigler were flying without a turret gunner which had been removed to lighten the big fighter and increase its maneuverability and speed. They flew to the Kyushu coast at 8,000 feet and began flying with reference to the ground until they approached the target area. Once over the target they saw that two fields had their runway lights on and the surrounding area was not blacked out. They saw two planes taxiing on the runway as if they had just landed and another plane at 1,000 feet on its downwind landing leg with all its navigation lights on and wheels down. Griffitts ordered the R/O to turn off his AI set and turned on all his gun switches and headed over the field at 1,500 feet directly toward the landing plane. Griffitts saw that his overtaking speed was too great which would mean a large degree deflection shot and turned 270 degrees to port and let down to 1,000 feet at reduced speed. At 2330 he came in directly astern and identified the bogie as a Betty and fired a short burst from 5,000 feet and exploded it and had to turn away sharply to avoid a collision. After victory Griffiths strafed the field at 500 to 1,000 feet. The R/O turned his set on again but made no contacts. They flew south ay 2,000 feet and found another field with many lights but as they descended the lights went off and spent another 1:15 patrolling without result before returning to base. Griffitts' only victory was the squadron's 20th and last victory of the war (plus three probable claims).

**7 August 1945: 475FG**

The first air raid alert heard by the 475FG since 5 March in the Philippines was sounded in the early morning and two more air raids later that day caused more anxiety, especially after the news of the Hiroshima Atomic Bombing had increased the anticipation that the war might be coming to a sudden end. Between August 1943 and the end of March 1945, the 475FG's 552 aerial victories had cost it 80 P-38s lost in combat and 75 pilots killed in action. 1Lt William Hasty of the 433FS, who had been downed in June 1944 and captured on the Vogelkop Peninsula, became the only 475th prisoner of war to be repatriated after VJ-Day.

**8 August 1945: 58FG/69FS**

On this day 16 Thunderbolts of the 69FS took off at 0730 to escort B-24s to Usa on eastern Shikoku. The 69FS rendezvoused with the bombers over the northern tip of Tangea Shima at 0910 but one fighter suffered mechanical problems prior to rendezvous and was escorted safely back to base by another. The remaining 14 escorts positioned themselves over the B-24s at 12,000 feet in relatively clear skies. At 1035, 20 minutes from the target, the Liberators were preparing to begin their bomb run, when two Zeros were sighted dead ahead at 12 o'clock, making a diving pass at the bomber formation. 1Lt. Robert Hansen was leading the #3 flight, flying at 12,500 feet, and paralleling the bombers, when the enemy fighters were observed having passed through the bomber formation. Hansen immediately led his flight into a 180 degree turn and the Zeros pulled up in an Immelmann turn and faced Hansen head on. Hansen fired a short burst as the Zeros began a port turn. His Wingman, 2Lt. Terye Rasmussen, also attacked; firing a short burst and then a long burst which hit the engine and cockpit area. The enemy's engine began to smoke and then burst into flame and the Zero glided south in a shallow diving turn for his only victory. Rasmussen followed Hansen through a 180 degree turn, which brought the two Thunderbolts out of the turn onto the tail of the other Zero. Hansen fired two long bursts into the enemy fighter which immediately burst into flames and dove into the sea also for his only victory. These were the fourth and fifth and last victories for the 69FS and only the 13th and last of war for the ground support oriented 58FG. The 69FS rejoined the bombers and escorted them to Usa on their bomb run when they saw a single enemy fighter passing over at high altitude which dropped a phosphorous bomb, aimed at the bombers, but which exploded harmlessly about 1,500 feet above the B-24 formation. On their way back to base the 69th descended to sea level and strafed the towns of Koseda and Ambo on the island of Yaku Jima starting fires. All 14 fighters returned safely to Okinawa at 1400.

**8 August 1945: 348FG/460FS/340FS**

460FS

On 8 August four P-51s of the 460FS took off at 0815 on a B-25 and B-26 escort mission to Tsuiki Airdrome, Kyushu, Japan at 10,000 feet. Flight Leader, 1Lt. Reid Tait was at 14,000 feet and saw a lone Jack at 15,000 feet at 3 o'clock above the bomber formation. When the Mustang flight attacked, the Jack started to dive away to the right and Tait followed to 5,000 feet, closing rapidly and fired at 300 yards tearing off pieces of the right wing and tail. Tait broke upward and the enemy pilot dove to the right, trailing smoke. Tait reversed and turned with the Jack getting more hits. The Jack Split-S'd at 1,500-2,000 feet but was unable to pull out and crashed four miles south of Tsuiki at 1010 for Tait's only victory. Capt. George Elvey, leader of Tait's second element, and his Wingman followed the Flight Leader and his Wingman in a climb to regain altitude. When they arrived they saw a lone Zero breaking away from its attack on B-25s and getting ready to make his second pass. Elvey and his Wingman closed from 7,000 feet and Elvey fired at 300 yards low and then pulled up and fired a long bust at 200 yards and the Zeke caught fire and crashed into hills for his only victory.

340FS

Capt. Jack Quinlan led four P-51s on a B-25 escort mission to Tsuiki Airdrome, with the Squadron covering the Mitchells at 10,000 feet and proceeding up the center of Kyushu. At 1120 about 10-15 miles from the target Quinlan spotted two Zeros carrying belly tanks flying parallel to their formation at 12,000 feet on the other side of the B-25 formation and 500 feet below. Quinlan and his Wingman turned toward the Zeros which then turned away from the bombers. Quinlan chose the lead Zero and began to fire at 60 degrees and continued firing until he turned inside at 270 degrees getting hits on the cowling, knocking off small pieces. The Zero began to smoke and went into a wingover and as Quinlan followed it down through thin overcast and saw it crash about 10-15 miles from Tsuiki.

Meanwhile, Quinlan's Wingman, 1Lt. David Standiford, dove on the second Zero at 60 degrees hitting the wing and fuselage and it went into a wingover and headed for the deck; catching fire along the wing roots before crashing. Immediately, after their two victims crashed, Standiford saw a "Nip plane" (later identified as a Frank) diving for the deck. Before Standiford caught the Frank both were on the deck and the American closed from astern and the Frank erupted into flames on the second burst for

Standiford's only two victories. At this time Quinlan was at 7,000 feet and four Zeros flashed past him in string towards Standiford. Quinlan chased the tail end Zero which pulled up into a level left turn. Quinlan fired a 30 degree deflection shot that started the Zero smoking and then it went into a dive, crashing about 1,000 yards from the Airdrome for his fourth and last victories. These four victories were the last of the 340FS' 76 total for the war (plus five probables).

**8 August 1945: 547NFS**

Pilot 1Lt. Thomas Schultz, R/O F/O Player Hill, and gunner SSgt. Benjamin Boscardin scores the last of the 547th's eight total victories when they downed a Betty at 0243 100 miles north of Point Zebra.

**9 August 1945: Nagasaki A-Bomb**

On the morning of 9, the B-29 Superfortress *Bockscar*, flown by the crew of 393rd Squadron Commander Maj. Sweeney, carried the Plutonium-based nuclear bomb code-named "Fat Man," with Kokura as the primary target and Nagasaki the secondary target but Kokura was socked in and Nagasaki became the unfortunate target. The mission plan for this second nuclear attack was nearly identical to that of the Hiroshima mission. The air explosion was two miles northwest of the planned hypocenter and the blast was confined to the Urakami Valley and a major portion of the city was protected by the intervening hills. The resulting explosion had a blast yield equivalent to 21 kilotons of TNT and the casualty estimates for immediate deaths ranged from 40,000 to 75,000 and total deaths by the end of 1945 may have reached 80,000.

348FG

During the morning of 9 August, 348FG CO Col. William Banks and Maj. Walter Benz were leading a sweep to the Fukuoka when a message was received restricting all aircraft from flying within 45 miles of Nagasaki which was similar to a message had been received on the day of the Hiroshima atomic bombing. The 348FG's sweep area was exactly 45 miles east of Nagasaki at 20,000 feet when the message was received at 1100. The Group's Mustangs were flying in beautiful weather with unlimited visibility and at 1100 saw a brilliant flash of light followed by a huge column of smoke rapidly expanding upward and the valleys and ground below filling with rolling gray smoke. The Mustangs circled warily around the growing mushroom cloud and after a few minutes the flight headed toward home.

**Capt. Leroy Grosshuesch** got his eighth and last victory of the war. (AFAA)

35FG

The 35FG continued to fly sweeps, bomber escort, dive bombing, strafing, and PBY cover as it had the previous months on Okinawa. On the 6th the Group heard the news of the Hiroshima A-Bomb and on the 9th a 35FG flight had actually observed the Nagasaki A-Bomb explosion from a long distance and waited for the war to end.

**10 August 1945: 8FG/35FS/80FS**

On 10 August, 16 Lightnings of the 35FS took off from Ie Shima on a Napalm attack on Kumamoto on Kyushu. When they reached the target they started large fires in the town with an effective spread of the fire bombs. Fifteen P-38s of the 80FS followed and arrived over the same target at 1118 but was unable to bomb accurately due to the heavy smoke from previous attacks. The 80th looked for a secondary target and bombed a cluster of wooden huts about four miles northeast of Kumamoto which were set afire as was most of the nearby combustible material. Several P-38s flew on the deck and strafed two warehouse buildings on the outskirts of the town. Five more 35FS P-38s were sent out later in the day to glide bomb Miyasaki Airdrome on southern Kyushu but weather caused them to abort the mission.

**11 August 1945: 71TRG/110TRS**

After the second Atomic Bomb was dropped on Nagasaki and while the Japanese military hierarchy considered the surrender ultimatum conditions, aerial operations against the Home Islands were suspended. During the suspension of active operations, the 71st TRG flew reconnaissance missions and on 11 August F/O Frank Mulcahy of the 110TRS shot down a Zeke over Kyushu.

**11 August 1945: 8FG/80FS**

The 45 Lightnings of the 80FS arrived over Kyushu at 1000 to bomb bridges in the Sashiki area. The Squadron was to skip bomb the Owan Bridge and 15 of its bombs caused destruction as one bomb hit a section of railroad tracks 100 yards north of the bridge, six bombs hit the Owan river spans, and eight other bombs hit houses in a 300 foot area around the bridge and on the banks of the river. One warehouse about 300 yards west of the bridge was strafed and set on fire. Six small luggers and five small launches were strafed by the 80th as they left the area.

**11 August 1945: 348FG/460FS**

Capt. George Elvey and 1Lt. Wilbur Frable were involved in a mid-air collision and were the last 348FG casualties of the war.

**12 August 1945: 71TRG/82TRS Last Victory**

1Lt. Samuel Sanders shot down an Oscar near Yokanichi while on a recon sortie. Sander's victory was the 18th and last of the war for the 82TRS.

**12 August 1945: 35FG: 39FS and 35FG Last Victory**

Maj. Richard Cella and Capt. Leroy Grosshuesch led eight P-51s of the 39FS, on targets of opportunity over Kyushu and Honshu. At 0815, while flying at 5,000 feet the flight spotted four well camouflaged Franks at 11 o'clock climbing about 20 miles from Bofu Airdrome flying at the same altitude. The Franks went into a climb and the P-51s climbed after them to 9,000 feet and gained a 500 foot altitude advantage in a dense haze. Maj. Cella, on one of his infrequent combat flights, initiated the fight when he led a steep diving turn to the right to get astern of the Franks. Grosshuesch followed, staying above to cover Cella, but the enemy pilots Split-S'd and Cella's flight lost their firing advantage and then lost sight of the Franks due to their evasive maneuvers, their camouflage, and the haze. Meanwhile, Grosshuesch spotted one of the Franks heading north to escape and followed him at full throttle as the Frank pilot evaded using deft, violent evasive maneuvers. Grosshuesch closed to 150 yards and fired two bursts that scored hits while the Frank was in a very steep dive and pulled out at only 500 feet. Grosshuesch then fired into the cockpit area with a one second burst at 50 yards into the cockpit and its wheels dropped. The Frank did a wingover and Grosshuesch almost collided with the enemy fighter and had to snap roll at 400 mph and was lucky to regain control. It was Grosshuesch's eighth and last victory of the war; the Squadron's 178th and last victory of the war (plus 49 probable and 66 damaged claims); also was the 35FG's last victory of the war.

**12 August 1945: 348FG/460FS Last 348FG Victory**

The last aerial victory credited to the 348FG was claimed by 1Lt. Kermit Allen of the 460FS Squadron on 12 August 1945. Allen was the Element Leader of White Flight; part of a 10 plane sweep of northwest Kyushu that took off at 0600. Once over the target area Allen was covering his Flight Leader and Wingman while they were strafing shipping. Allen and his Wingman saw a lone George in a climbing turn at the same altitude. After the George leveled off, it started a gentle dive and Allen had closed and fired a short burst from dead astern and hit its lower fuselage and belly tank which exploded and flew off. The George Split-S'd spewing black smoke and pulled out and Allen made a tight port turn using his flaps and turned inside to fire a three second burst into the cockpit. The George snap rolled, recovered momentarily and the plunged into the ground for Allen's only victory and the Squadron's 51[st] and final victory of the war. It had no probables and only one damaged claim.

**1Lt. Dwight Hollister** poses on the day of his only victory as part of the last air combat of the war. (AAF)

**12 August 1945: 8FG/36FS**

Maj. Harold Graham, 36FS Commander led the 12 August mission on one of the Owan bridges. 1Lt. Charles Wade, who had just returned to the Squadron after leaving it for a tour as a B-24 pilot, found that his target bridge was obscured by near misses from the previous bombs. Wade still had his 1,000 pound bomb and asked for another pass, even though the AA was alerted. He accurately dropped his bomb for the only direct hit of the mission but then made another run over the target fire to confirm the results.

**14 August 1945: 71TRG/110TRS**

The 110TRS entered combat at 0939 when it intercepted a formation of Oscars near Fukuaka Airfield. Maj. George Noland shot down two and claimed another as a probable. 1Lts. Philip Koykka, Cyril O'Neill, and Herman Johnson each shot down one Oscar. These victories were the 20[th] and last of the war for the Squadron (plus two probables and one damaged claim).

**Maj. George Noland** shot down two Oscars and claimed another as a probable. (AAF)

**14 August 1945: 8FG/35FS: Last Aerial Combat**

One reason that the 8FG was not experiencing fighter opposition during the first months of 1945 was that the Japanese decided to concentrate on intercepting the B-29s that were devastating their cities on the northern part of the Home Islands. The only American forces consistently engaging the Japanese were 7AF fighters and 20AF B-29s along with USN carrier-borne aircraft. By mid-August the Nakajima Ki-84, code named Frank, was considered the fastest and most effective JAAF fighters and was used by the veteran 47[th] Sentai since February. In July this unit had suffered heavy losses of leaders and pilots and was now reduced to flying with inexperienced pilots.

Six P-38s of the 35FS had scheduled an early morning mission to cover a flight of rescue planes and another rescue cover mission was scheduled to take off by 0940. For this later mission only seven relatively inexperienced pilots were available: Mission and Flight Leader, Capt. Raymond Meyer, and Element Leader, Capt. William Moore with Lieutenants Collins, Hollister, Keiffer, Owens, and Stevens. All these pilots had come into the 35[th] between the end of 1944 and May 1945 and although they had considerable combat time on ground attack missions; none had any experience in air-to-air combat. After take off Collins and Owens aborted due to mechanical troubles and Meyer was now leading only four other P-38s. At 1215 the flight arrived to relieve fighters covering Catalinas, *Playmate 47* and *Jukebox 25*, in the Inland Sea at 13,000 feet. 1Lt. Dwight Hollister called a formation of six Franks at 18,000 and 20,000 feet, which had the advantage of surprise, the sun, and altitude. But the other Lightnings were unaware that they were under attack until the Japanese began firing at them as Hollister's microphone button malfunctioned. Hollister turned into the enemy #5 man and fired hitting it from propeller to tail and started a small fire. The Frank rolled over on its back while Hollister made a hard starboard turn and climbed 1,000 feet to get on the Frank's tail. The Frank tried to roll but was hit by a long burst and fell into the sea in a flat spin into the water. Hollister and 2Lt. Duane Kieffer got behind a Frank but he hurried ahead to dive in front of the enemy which placed him in range of the Frank's guns which hit Kieffer's port engine and the P-38 rolled over at 4,000 feet and fell in a flat spin. Moore reported seeing Kieffer jettison his canopy and try to get out but the Lightning hit the water first.

When the Franks surprised them, Meyer first broke to the right with Wingman 2Lt. George Stevens, and then reversed to the left as the enemy fighters passed over and turned back. Meyer turned into one and fired a quick head on burst without result. Meyer and the Frank made another head on pass at each other and Meyer fired at 350 yards and scored hits in its engine and cockpit which sent it into a flaming 10,000 foot spiral into the sea. Wingman Stevens had been following Meyer throughout the combat when he saw another Frank directly below. The Frank had been coming off the top of a loop and Stevens dove on the enemy fighter in a head on pass. He fired and hit Frank's engine and it rolled away but Stevens hit it with another burst that caught the Frank in its belly and smoke and flame began to trail back as the Frank plummeted toward the water.

Capt. Billy Moore broke into a Frank head on and as the two closed; neither was in firing position and passed each other. As the Frank pulled up in a steep climb Moore followed and first a short burst without getting any hits and lost it as it went into a steep dive. Moore then sighted another Frank making a pass at a P-38 and dove to attack it from the rear and got hits from astern. The Frank Split-S'd at 9,000 feet and Moore followed to 3,000 feet where it leveled off where Moore fired a sustained burst tearing pieces off its starboard wing and starting a fire. The flames extinguished and the Frank pilot made a series of turns but Moore hit it with short bursts and closed to fire into its cockpit and engine with a 10 degree stern shot that sent it rolling over into the sea.

As Moore was chasing his Frank another Frank attacked Meyer and he turned into it and fired several deflection shots before it Split-S'd away. Meyer saw another Frank on the tail of a P-38 and dove from 7,000 feet and caught the Frank and caused it to break off its attack. As the Frank turned to the right in a shallow climb Meyer fired and hit its cockpit and fuselage and it fell in a violent spin into the sea. A Catalina called a bogie over the mountains and Meyer flew in to attack but overran and broke off the attack. Regaining altitude Meyer saw a lone Frank and closed and fired from 300 to 30 yards getting hits on its wings before his guns "burned out" for a damaged claim.

The 35FS formation returned to Ie Shima with the last fighter combat and victories of the war with Meyers scoring his only two victories; Hollister and Moore, scoring their only victories and Steven's only victory was the last for the 5FC and the Squadron's 125th victory (with eight probables and 11 damaged) of the war.

The final victories had not been without loss. 2Lt. Duane Keiffer had been flying on Moore's wing while they were chasing a Frank along the coast. Keiffer fired a long burst at the enemy, overshot, and pulled up in a climb. Ignoring the Frank on his tail, the Japanese pilot straightened out long enough to put a burst into Keiffer's right engine, setting it on fire. Keiffer jettisoned his canopy but his fighter spun into the sea before he could bail out for the last 5th Fighter Command KIA of the war.

**14 August 1945: 348FG/340FS/341FS: Last Combat Missions**

340FS

Combat operations continued after 12 August and the last recorded combat mission of the 348FG was carried out by 15 Mustangs of the 340FS when they flew an anti-shipping sweep by 15 P-51s to northern Kyushu and south Honshu. At midday the Mustangs fired rockets and strafed two luggers and a sailboat and one of the luggers was left smoking while the other had its stern blown off by a rocket while the sailboat was sunk. A patrol boat was then attacked and left burning after it was strafed. Two barges that were converted into AA vessels, each carrying a number of 20mm AA guns, were also attacked and disabled. Eight small luggers were then attacked near the coast of Kura Shima and the 340th ended combat for the Group by strafing a small fishing boat. By the end of the day as cease fire order was issued.

341FS: Last Bombs Dropped and Shots Fired in WWII

Also on 14 August Lieutenant Joseph Ozier led a flight of 12 Mustangs of the 341FS to bomb shipping off the southwestern coast of Kyushu but the pilots were ordered not to bomb or strafe shore installations in anticipation of Japan's surrender. But it seems shipping targets were not off limits as during his bombing run on coastal shipping Ozier's bomb did not release, so he and his flight orbited while the other fighters attacked. Ozier then attacked and dropped his bomb and two pilots of his flight bombed and then strafed the shipping as they pulled away from the target the 341FS was to be credited with dropping the last bombs and firing the last shots in World War II.

**Mid-August 1945: 58FG**

During the offensive operations in the first half of August the 58FG flew 482 sorties: 155 by the 69FS, 189 by the 310FS, and 158 by the 311FS. The Group dropped 166 Napalm tanks, 215 tons of bombs and fired 144,657 rounds of ammunition. Napalm delivered by the three squadrons was about equal, the 310FS dropped the most tons of bombs, and the 69FS and the 311FS did most of the strafing. The 69FS had two confirmed air-to-air victories. All the 58FG aircraft moved to Machinate by 15 August and the entire Group was not operational until 25 August, except the training missions for the newer pilots. On 25 August flights over Japan were renewed, for patrols, surveillance and to assist rescue aircraft. Three final missions flown on 1 September were surveillance, pending the formal surrender of the Japanese on the battleship Missouri on 2 September.

**15-30 August 1945: 8FG/Last Missions**

On 15 August eight Mustangs of the 35FS took off early the next morning to escort rescue aircraft patrols covering the Navy air strikes that day but they returned home without incident and later that morning the Japanese accepted the surrender terms. The last two weeks of August was an anticlimax of routine missions. 36FS missions included two cover flights over destroyers northeast of Okinawa on 25 August and a sweep by seven P-38s led by Capt. Robert Locke over airfields and shipping on Honshu on 28 August, a B-17 cover over Seoul, Korea and Kyushu on 29 August, another destroyer cover on the 30th and a reconnaissance on the last day of the month. On August 29 the 35FS flew its last mission of the war when four of its P-38s flew a patrol and cover for rescue planes.

**Capt. Clay Tice** and **F/O Douglas Hall** were the first American fliers to land on the Japanese Homeland. (AAF)

**16 August 1945: 49FG/7FS: First AAF Pilot to Land in Japan**

At 0800, 49th Fighter Group Leader Capt. Clay Tice personally led seven 7FS Screamin' Demons in an armed surveillance of Kyushu and the south shore of greater Honshu Island on a 6:45 hour, 1,300 mile round trip mission. Half way through the long flight F/O Douglas Hall reported that his aircraft experienced fuel transfer problems and it was apparent that Hall did not have enough fuel to reach Okinawa. As the P-38s passed near Nittagahara Airfield, Tice turned the mission over to Capt. Kopeck and he and radioed that he and Hall would land at the airfield and be met there by a B-17 tanker. Tice led the way and circled the untouched airdrome and they both rolled to a stop a bearded old man slowly peddled past on a bicycle and after a while a man in a uniform in the lead of a small platoon of boys came by holding up white handkerchiefs. Using hand gestures Tice motioned that his airplane needed fuel and the boys ran off and returned with soldiers driving a fuel truck. Tice feared that their gasoline might not be high enough in octane and chose to wait for the B-17 tanker and once it arrived, Tice had the Japanese hand pump fuel into the Lightnings. Tice and Hall took off from Nittagahara and returned to Okinawa. Supreme Allied Commander, Gen. Douglas MacArthur was furious and wanted the two pilots who had dared to land in Japan first to be apprehended and held for court martial but somehow these communiqués disappeared in 49er radio rooms.

**19-20 August 1945: The Japanese Surrender Flight**

The Japanese accepted the unconditional surrender being offered by the United States, and the details were worked out for Peace Emissaries to fly into Ie Shima and onto Manila to formalize the surrender. Lt.Gen. Torashiro Kawabe, Deputy Chief of the Army General Staff, would lead the delegation of 14 officers with two interpreters and translators sent by Emperor Hirohito by transport aircraft. At sunrise on the 19th the delegation met at Haneda Airport near Tokyo Bay where they boarded a Tabby transport, a Japanese version of the Douglas C-47, which was painted white and marked with green crosses as per an American directive. The Japanese took off at 0611 and landed at Kisarazu Airfield on the East Side of Tokyo Bay 14 minutes later. The delegates were divided into two groups of eight each and loaded into two waiting Betty bombers which were also painted white and marked with green crosses. Both bombers were airborne by 0710, heading for Ie Shima. As they approached the southern tip of Kyushu at 1115, an escort of P-38s from the 8th and 49th Fighter Groups and B-25s from the 345th Bomb Group were to escort the two Bettys from Kyushu to Ie Shima. The escort was led by Lt.Col. Emmett Davis, 5FC Commander, and consisted of 19 Lightnings flown by veterans Maj. Harold Graham, Col. John Pitchford, Maj. Orin Bixby, Maj. Robert Harriger and Capt. Robert Locke. Two flights from the 8FS flew top cover over the field while the Japanese Betty pilots executed poor, bouncing landings. At 1240, the first of the two Bettys landed on the coral airstrip at Ie Shima. As the door of the Betty opened, Gen. Kawabe stepped out of the aircraft followed by his officers by rank. The second Betty was parked immediately behind the first and its passengers also got out. The Japanese delegates were met by a small group of Americans led by Gen. Frederick Smith, Commander of 5th Fighter Command, and his staff. The walkway was lined with the tallest MPs in the Army who towered over the Japanese delegates. The Japanese were led to a waiting C-54 transport aircraft that would be taking them all to Manila. The aircraft landed at Manila's Nichols Field at 1800 that evening where the Japanese were received correctly, but coolly by MacArthur's Chief of Intelligence, Maj.Gen. Charles Willoughby. The Japanese were taken to Rosario Manor in Manila where they were served a turkey dinner. At 2100 the Japanese delegates were taken to the City Hall conference room to meet with the American delegates. Lt.Gen. Richard Sutherland, MacArthur's Chief of Staff, led the American delegation at these talks that continued until the 20th. The Americans set down all the directives and demands concerning the arrival of the first Americans in Japan beginning on the 28th with the harbor facilities at Yokohama and the airfield at Atsugi to be used for the first staging bases well as the surrender ceremony aboard the battleship *USS Missouri*, plus the subsequent reception of the occupation forces was then determined.

The White Japanese Betty carrying the Japanese surrender delegation lands at Ie Shima. (AAF)

The Japanese surrender delegation transfers to a C-47 for transfer to Manila. (AAF)

Once the conferences were completed the Japanese were taken back to Nichols Field and boarded the waiting C-54 and then were taken back to Ie Shima. At Ie Shima it was learned that one of the Bettys had mechanical problems and could not be repaired until the following morning. The whole delegation could not board a single Betty, so the group and the documents were divided so that if one aircraft should have trouble, all would not be lost. The first Betty left Ie Shima at 1840 with a group headed by Lieutenant Takeuchi, who carried the conference documents. The P-38s and B-25s were again called upon to escort the Betty out from Ie Shima but they discontinued their escort, as it was becoming dark. Two 421NFS P-61s, piloted by Lts. Gerald Parker and Robert Savaria, took over the escort from the P-38s and B-25s. Two other P-61s were used as spares but both were turned back 100 miles north of Ie Shima. Lts. Parker and Savaria stayed with the Japanese until they were approximately 15 miles off the southern tip of Kyushu, at which time they headed back to base, landing at 2220.

The first Betty did not return to Tokyo as planned as just before midnight the Japanese delegation was given the command to prepare for a crash landing. The plane safely ditched in the surf along a wide beach near Hamamatsu, about 130 miles short of Tokyo. It was thought, due to the complication of language with the Americans at Ie Shima, that the fuel tanks in the Betty were not completely filled. The delegation then walked to nearby Hamamatsu Air Base where a transport was sent at 0330 to pick them up and take them to Tokyo. The second Betty left Ie Shima the next day after repairs had been completed and had an uneventful flight back to Kisarazu. The Japanese government accepted the surrender documents and the terms would be carried out formally on the *USS Missouri* anchored in Tokyo Bay with MacArthur presiding on 2 September 1945.

**Gen. Frederick Smith** greets Japanese Lt.Gen. Torashiro Kawabe. (AAF)

### The End in the Pacific

From the catastrophic first battles in the Philippines and Java in 1941 the 5[th] Fighter Command units in the South and Southwest Pacific fought their way back through New Guinea to the Philippines and then took the fight to the Japanese Home Islands. As interceptors they had shot down over 3,000 enemy aircraft in the air while as fighter bombers they had destroyed many hundreds more aircraft on the ground and incalculable quantities of equipment, many hundreds of installations, and had killed tens of thousands of enemy troops; all accomplished with a relatively minimum loss of equipment and personnel.

**MacArthur** presides over the formal Japanese surrender on board the USS *Missouri* on 2 September 1945. (AFHRC)

# Profiles

[1.] **Republic P-47 D-4** (?) **RA THUNDERBOLT** s.n. unknown of A/C **"white 85"** of the **9 FS** "Flying Knights" / **49 FG** flown by 2Lt. W.S. Huisman at Gusap airfield in north-central New Guinea in early '44. The lieutenant scored his first aerial victory with "white 85" over Wewak on 15 March. It was also the last of only eight victims claimed by the scoring-leader Knights in six months of flying Republic's rotund "JUG." On 2 November, Huisman would gain a second victory minutes before his fatal crash landing at Tacloban in his battle damaged P-38.

[2.] **Lockheed P-38 J-10-LO LIGHTNING** s.n. 42-67580 **"yellow S - *CORKY III*"** flown by **80 FS** "Headhunters" / **8 FG** Lt. Cornelius M. "Corky" Smith at Nadzab/Finschafen, New Guinea, in late '43. Issued to the ace lieutenant in December, he racked up four more confirmed victories aboard ***Corky III***, including two ZEKEs over Wewak on 18 January '44. Promoted to captain, he continued in the Headhunters' execution of Imperial opponents to become a double-ace in the fourth and last sweep of the JAAF HQ at Hollandia on 12 April.

[3.] **Curtiss P-40 N-20 WARHAWK** s.n. 43-23194 A/C **"black 34"** of the **82 TRS / 71 TRG** at Mokmer airfield, Biak Island, in mid-'44. This "clean" duralumin WARHAWK represents the 5 FC in its transition to a fully dedicated long range offensive. It is a surplus P-40 resulting from the 8 FS reequipping at the time with P-38s. Retaining the black and yellow tactical livery of the "Blacksheep," A/C **"black 34"** was adopted by the resilient 82nd recon outfit, which persevered with "hand-me-down" WARHAWKs and AIRACOBRAs throughout the New Guinea campaign.

[4.] **Lockheed P-38 J-15-LO LIGHTNING** s.n. 42-104380 of **5th FC "A/C pool"** at Nadzab Airfield, New Guinea. Lockheed **#4380** bears distinction for first being the mount of 5 FC Gunnery Instructor **Major R.I. Bong** when he shot down three opponents over Hollandia on 12 April, setting the all-American record at 28 confirmed over the previous tally of 26 achieved in November '42 by U.S. Marines aviator Joe Foss in the Solomons campaign. By month's end, Bong furloughed home and **#4380** was passed on to the redoubtable **Col. R.L. Morrissey** as his liaison A/C for his task force command duties. In its final role as of late June, **#4380** was issued to the legendary "*lone eagle*" aviator, **Charles Lindbergh**, as one of his flying lecterns to demonstrate the techniques of long-range flight.

[5.] **Lockheed P-38 J-10 (?) LIGHTNING** s.n. unknown of **A/C #101** flown by **"Satins Angels" 475 FG** staff officer Maj. Meryl Smith in the long range sweeps of mid-'44 over the Celebes Islands that ultimately reached hotly contested Balikpapen, Borneo. His garish LIGHTNING bears a nose-tip shamrock and green trimmings as homage to the 432 FS "Clover" ground crews who serviced the fighter in June '44. Promoted to lieutenant colonel and new Operations Exec, he was flying with the Satins' CO MacDonald in the great dogfight of 7 December '44 when he scored the last two of his nine confirmed victories before he in turn was killed in action.

[6.] **Nakajima Ki-44 II-Otsu SHOKI (*demon*)** s.n. unknown for this A/C of the **3rd Chutai** (sqn) / **87th Sentai** in mid-'44. The upgraded cousin of the nimble "OSCAR" was the **Ki-44 SHOKI (demon)**, named **TOJO**, which debuted over China in late '42. The speedster was powered by the 1500 hp Nakajima Ha-109 engine, and the ***Otsu*** (modified) model armed with four 12.7 mm machine guns was rightly assessed a viable bomber-killer warranted for the defense of the oil refinery at Palembang, Sumatra. By March '44, Imperial losses in western New Guinea affected the **Sentai's** mobilization 1800 miles eastward for the ill fated defense of Biak. By late August, they retreated 800 miles back to Manggar airfield, just north of Balikpapen's sprawling oil refinery, only to be savaged on 10 and 14 October in the massive air strikes of 5th and 13th AF heavy bombers escorted by a swarm of 5th FC P-38s and P-47s. Ironically, the **87th Sentai** graphics on the tail surface of their **TOJO** fighters symbolized a ***kamikaze*** (divine wind) driving a ***tsunami*** (tidal wave); two ominous elements of nature that mystically empowered the warriors of the Empire. In late October '44, as the invasion of Leyte began, the "*divine wind and wave*" had already carried off the war-torn **Sentai** in its final retreat for the home islands.

[7.] **Lockheed P-38 L-1-LO LIGHTNING** s.n. 44-23951 **A/C "black 81"** of the **9 FS** "Flying Knights" **49 FG** flown by Capt. W.F. "*Wewak Willie*" Williams at besieged Tacloban, November '44. Crimson colors of the **9 FS** adorn **Black 81** flown by Ops Exec Williams just days prior to the Leyte landings. As the senior flight leader, "*Wewak Willie*" had likely fired the first rounds in the 3 June '44 air raid on Babo, and as the new Ops Exec, he had been at the forefront of the Balikpapen escort missions in October. Veterans years later mused that "Willie was a little crazy, but he was a consummate leader," who inherited the **Flying Knights** command in the midst of the Leyte battle. Above the Allied convoy off Mindoro Island on 18 December, Williams added his fourth and last confirmed kill to the Flying Knights' tally of 254 victories that topped all FC squadrons in the SW Pacific.

[8.] **Lockheed P-38 J-15-LO LIGHTNING** s.n. 42-103921 A/C **"yellow 3 – hearts royal flush"** of the **35 FS** "Black Panthers" / **8 FG**, flown by their scoring leader Dick West. Quiet by nature and totally disciplined in aerial combat, West was the sole P-40 ace of the Panthers with six confirmed. When they took up the P-38 in June '44, Capt. West knocked down victim number 7 over Jefman airfield, N. Guinea, and victim number 8 in July over Halmahera Island. Twelve weeks of tactical sorties passed until the aerial duels reignited over embattled Leyte on 1 November. In just four separate encounters in two week's time, West chalked up seven more victories, all be it one victim was not confirmed in that hectic first day over Negro Island. He never disputed being a "qualified" triple-ace. Pilots of West's caliber had nothing to prove.

[9.] **Republic P-47 D-28-RA THUNDERBOLT** s.n. 42-28488 A/C "**red 51** – ***The NEW KID***" of the **40 FS / 35 FG** based at Biak and staging through Morotai airfield, north of Halmahera Island. Though a bit circumspect, this colorful **THUNDERBOLT "red 51"** is very likely the mount of Capt. J.R. Young, flown in the epic escorts to Balikpapen on 10 and 14 October '44. Employing the "Lindbergh technique" of high prop rpm's and lean fuel flow, plus the use of standard Lockheed 175-gallon wing tanks, the "JUG" was able to make the grueling 1700-mile round trip. As an old *AIRACOBRA-man* rejuvenated as a **THUNDERBOLT** flight leader, Young jokingly called himself "*the NEW KID*," but his flight leader skills were a serious matter. Two ZEKE pilots on the first mission and two OSCAR pilots on the second learned of *the NEW KID's* lethal methods the hard way. His **40 FS** brethren would account for another thirty defenders.

**[10.] Lockheed P-38 J-15-LO LIGHTNING** s.n. 42-104372 A/C "**black 4** – ***PENNY II***" of the **36 FS** "Flying Fiends" / **8 FG**, flown by Lt. H.B. "Hal" Graham. After two lean years of 5 FC veterans vying for the coveted P-38, former "Headhunter" Capt. Ken Ladd was at last given command of the 36 FS "Flying Fiends" to induct them into the LIGHTNING wing operations at Mokmer airfield, on Biak. Ladd was MIA on the 14 October Balikpapen mission, but the "Fiends" held up the missing CO's legacy with flight leaders of Hal Graham's prowess. Promoted to captain, he was in the forefront of the advance to Dulag airfield in the Leyte offensive. "**Black 4 -** ***PENNY II***" is very likely the **LIGHTNING** that carried him to victory over a pair of TONYs in the 1 November melee. He counted one last aerial victory on 20 December, but leadership was his greater achievement. In June '45, Major Graham took charge of the "Flying Fiends" for the greater test that thankfully would never come.

[11.] **Lockheed P-38 L-1 LO LIGHTNING** s.n. 44-24116 A/C "**black 6** – ***FRAN***" of the **7 FS** "Screamin" Demons" / **49FG**, flown by 2Lt. H.W. "Hal" Harris at Tacloban. Replacement P-40 pilot Harris arrived at Hollandia in July '44, with scant opportunity to show his inherent pilot skill. But three months later, when the "Demons" were summoned to Tacloban, "little Hal," in his big Lockheed "**back 6 -** ***FRAN***" named for the girl back home, quickly displayed his true stature. In the 1 November shootout, "***FRAN***" brought her man upon two OSCAR intruders who mortally suffered his marksmanship. Ten days later, two TOJO raiders fell victim to his gunnery skills. Recognized as a "hot hand" in the Tacloban camp, VIP flight leaders routinely sought out "***FRAN***'s wingman." On the third anniversary of the Pearl Harbor tragedy, ***FRAN*** and Hal flew as element "Pinky Special No.4" to 5 FC colonels Bob Morrissey, Gerry Johnson, and George Walker. Of the seven kills they posted collectively at day's end, Pinky 4's claim of a JAAF HELEN bomber destroyed was confirmed as his fourth and final score. The **49ers** legend tells of Harris shadowing out-going 5 FC CO M.Gen. Wurtsmith in a farewell aerial survey of the Leyte complex in late November. "Demons" CO Ed Peck purportedly warned "hot-hand" Harris, "If the General doesn"t make it back…you don"t either." Harris and Wurtsmith both survived the aerial survey and the war.

[12.] Mitsubishi **J2M3 Model 21 RAIDEN** (*thunderbolt*) s.n. uncertain of **A/C 381-188** of the **602 Hikotai** (squadron) / **381st Kokutai** (air group) at Kendari airdrome on Celebes Island. Coupled with the JAAF on the western flank of the Pacific war, the JNAF **381st Ku** was sorely challenged to hold the southern front sea lanes and airdromes of the Celebes and Molucca Seas. In late '43, the land-based **602 Hikotai** took up the long awaited replacement of the ZERO-sen, the upgraded **J2M3 Raiden** codenamed "**JACK**" by the Allies. When its relatively small 14-cylinder Kasei Model 23 engine performed well, it could yield nearly 1600 Hp and sprint at 360 Mph. Its stocky airframe bolstered good maneuverability with a nimble climb rate, and armed with a pair of 20 mm cannons in each wing, it was a formidable bomber-killer. But in the end, it was far too few in number to survive against the waves of opposing USAAF and U.S. Navy fighters.

[13.] **Lockheed P-38 L-5 LO LIGHTNING** s.n. unknown for A/C "**black B – *the Criss Cross Queen***" of the **80 FS "Headhunters" / 8 FG**, flown by Capt. J.K. "Jack" Stanifer at Hill airfield, on Mindoro Is., late December '44. Stanifer got his first aerial kill on the 31 March '44 sweep of Hollandia airdrome. As an element leader on 17 August over remote Ambon Island, he claimed the aerial kill that captured the 5 FC squadron victory lead. Just three weeks later, the rival 9 FS "Flying Knights" recaptured the lead to fuel the victory race ever higher. But ten lean weeks would lapse before the **80th** was called to Dulag airfield, where a scant five aerial kills were claimed by the end of November. Despite being sent in late December as "the first team" to hotly contested Hill airfield on Mindoro, only a dozen Imperial raiders were hunted down by month's end. On 30 December '44, newly promoted Capt. Stanifer in his boldly striped "***Criss Cross QUEEN***" led the **Headhunters'** last scoring sortie, where a lone ZEKE was claimed by ace Capt. Schriber. Mission leader "*Cap'n Jack*" never fired the ***QUEEN's*** guns.

[14.] **Lockheed P-38 L-5 (?)-LO LIGHTNING** s.n. unknown for A/C **"yellow 52"** of the **8 FS** "Blacksheep" / **49 FG**, flown by Capt. R.W. (*Asch*) Aschebrener at Tacloban airfield in November '44. Returned veteran Aschenbrener recalled his first P-38 L-model was passed down from a 13 AF unit via the service squadron at Biak. Tagged as the Ops Exec, *Asch* opted to supervise the glut of Blacksheep rookies "from the cockpit of **yellow 52**." With three P-40 kills of record, his subsequent five aerial kills in two sorties aboard the old stager proved his merit. Though trusty "**yellow 52**" was abruptly written off in an enemy air raid before any victory flags were displayed on its hull, two more claims in a new Lockheed tied Asch with former CO double-ace E.A. Harris as the Blacksheep's best. His combat career would end on Christmas '44,which climaxed in an epic 27-day evasion across the interior of occupied Luzon.

15. **Lockheed P-38 L-1 LIGHTNING** s.n. 44-25656 A/C "**red 112 – *KIM IV***" of the **431 FS** "Satin"s Angels" / **475 FG**, assigned to 2Lt. H.W. Gray, Jr. at Dulag airfield in late December '44. The archives cite **A/C "red 112** – Eileen-Anne" being first assigned to ace Capt. Champlain, and she got at least four of his five victories over Leyte. On 25 December over Clark Field, rookie Hal Gray scored his sole aerial kill on the same mission Champlain scored his ninth and final kill with "Eileen-Anne." His combat tour now officially over, the Captain passed "**red 112**" on to Gray, who immediately renamed her "***KIM IV***" and had her totally refit. Combat attrition of A/C left a surfeit of pilots procuring any P-38 for a given mission, and on 7 January of the New Year, Satin's very own tormented Ops Exec, Tommy "*the Terror*" McGuire, abducted pristine "***KIM IV***" for the next sortie in his hell-bent quest to overtake Bong's victory record. The saga of the failed venture over bypassed Negro Island and ***KIM's*** searing blast on the jungle floor has become legend. In the days that

followed, the old timers at Tacloban and Dulag quietly agreed the irritable Major "*just stayed in the game too long*." Hal Gray soberly took up a new Lockheed and flew safely onward till the armistice.

[16.] **Kawanishi N1K1-J Model 11 Type C "SHIDEN"** (*lightning*) **A/C 341A-66** of the **Shishi** (*lion*) **341 Kokutai / 701 Hikotai** formed in late '43 and deployed to the Philippines in late '44. Headquartered on Formosa, the diversified **Shishi 341st Kokutai** operated from several airfields against the advancing American fleet, as well as the China-based Allied heavy bomber raids. In mid '44, the **Shishi** force had taken on several of the much anticipated **N1K1-J SHIDEN** fighter highly transformed from its float plane origins, which the Allies code named "**GEORGE**." It boasted 370 mph top speed, four 20 mm cannons, and a pair of cowling mounted 7 mm machine guns, all of which were negated by an unreliable 1800 hp Homare 21 engine, a limited range, and weak landing gear components. Those not shot out of the Pacific skies were squandered in the horrific honor of *tiatari* (body crashing) that appalled Allied sailors and veteran Imperial flyers alike. **SHIDEN "66,"** with its designator letter **"A,"** denoted the **701 Hikotai** commanded by one Lt Shirane in close support to the expendable "T" (*tiatari*) Special Attack Force. At Shirane's demise in late November, Lt Iwashita next led the self destruction until the **Shishi Ku** was erased. On 4 January '45, twelve **GEORGE** reinforcements slipped into shattered Clark Field, only to have eight of them torched by a pair of marauding P-47 strafers. Three days later, Iwashita staged his four survivor **Shiden** to rustic Tuguegarao strip for their venerable *tiatari* against the vast American fleet entering Linguyan Gulf.

[17.] **Northop P-61A-5 BLACK WIDOW** s.n. 42-5516 of the **421 NFS** attributed to the flight team of pilot Lt. O.W. Wolf, R/O 2Lt. B.N. Allain and gunner SSgt. E.K. Weishar. The **421st** introduced the big night fighter to the SW Pacific in mid-'44 over western New Guinea, where lieutenants Wolf and Allain, with SSgt. D.H. Trabling, scored the first of the squadron's thirteen accredited aerial kills. Trabling was replaced by Weishar, and the new trio hunted down four more victims, making Wolf and Allain the sole "ace" pilot/radar operator team of all the night fighter squadrons in the P.I. campaign. Not only were the air crews' victory claims rarely confirmed, there is disparity as to the actual aircraft used on a given mission. **BLACK WIDOW s.n. 25516**, shown here with four victory flags displayed, can not be confirmed for any hunting successes.

[18.] **North American P-51D-15-NA MUSTANG** s.n. 44-14873 **A/C #73** of the **82 TFS / 71 TFG** assigned to **2Lt. P.M. "Lippy" Lipscomb** at Hill airfield, Mindoro Island, in January '45. The photo archives suggest the two MUSTANGs in this story were actual D-type fighters field modified with the tri-camera fuselage fittings of a recon F-6. CO Capt. Shomo, in his weathered reccie **MUSTANG #66**, gunned down an errant VAL over Tuguegarao the morning of 6 January for his first victory, and a first for the touted **MUSTANG** in the SW Pacific, as well. Primed for another encounter, the Captain tagged rookie 2Lt. "Lippy" Lipscomb in his dusky **MUSTANG #73** as wingman for the legendary armed recon of 11 January '45, when a formation of eleven TONY pilots failed to recognize the newcomer P-51's planform. The results of the ensuing onslaught would be photographed by the Captain, who gunned down six TONYs and the BETTY bomber-transport they escorted. Three more TONY victims were similarly recorded for the Lieutenant's part. Shomo was promoted to Major, and would be the last fighter pilot in the war extant to receive the CMH. Restricted to an administrative role, he still flew to VIP functions in a highly decorated liaison P-51D while "Lippy" soldiered on. Neither of them would ever see another airborne enemy plane.

[19.] **North American P-51K-10-NT MUSTANG** s.n. 44-12089 **A/C "yellow R"** of unknown pilot in the **4 ACS / 3 ACG**, spring '45. In December '44, Col. Arvid Olson began diverting his 3rd Air Commando Group fighter-bombers, transports, and liaison light A/C forward to Hill airfield and satellite strips on Mindoro Island. No longer constrained to the short range, obsolete AIRACOBRA and WARHAWK relics, the superior MUSTANG would lead the way across Luzon, from Hill field and Linguyan onward to the white coral runways of Ie Shima. Olson's expanded tactical sweeps by his red-nosed 3rd Squadron and blue-nosed 4th Squadron fighter-bombers inevitably reached Formosa, Kyushu, and distant Korea's southern coast. Every target, from the rare airborne defender to the air-dromes, the railways, the coastal sea lanes, and troop bivouacs of the collapsing Empire was shattered by the free-lancing Commandos.

[20.] **North American P-51 K-10-NT** s.n. 44-12581 **A/C "white 70 – *Rollicking Rogue*"** of the **342 FS / 348 FG**, flown by CO Major E.S. Popek at Okinawa August '45. A cadre lieutenant from the first days of "Kearby's Thunderbolts" in '43, Popek had reached ace status in June '44 with the trusted P-47 over New Guinea. Furloughed Stateside during the P.I. invasion, he returned in early '45 and was given command of his old **342nd "White Eagle" FS**, currently refitting with the MUSTANG. Despite the Imperial defenders hoarding their last serviceable aircraft for their ultimate test, *"Rollicking Rogue"* Popek outmaneuvered two FRANK interceptors over southern Kyushu on 1 August for the "White Eagles'" last aerial victories. On 8 August, two days after Hiroshima was obliterated, MUSTANGs of the brethren 341 FS claimed four final victims in closing for the Group overall, just two victories shy of the 300 mark.

[21.] **Nakajima Ki-84a - Kai** (*modified*) Type 4 **HAYATE** (*storm gale*) s.n. unknown of **A/C "white 63"** in the **71st Sentai / Chutai** uncertain as attributed to pilot Sergeant Mizonori Fukuda, Negro Island, P.I. late '44. Nakajima's offering to the struggling JAAF was the dynamic **HAYATE**, code named "**Frank**," which literally "stormed" upon the USAAF when first encountered in mid '44 over China. Armed with a 20 mm cannon in each wing and a pair of 12.7 mm machine guns mounted over its 1800 Hp Homare Ha-45 engine, a well-kept **FRANK** was equal to the Allies' best. Anticipating the Allied venture into the Philippines, at least six **HAYATE** *sentais* were deployed to several satellite airstrips throughout the islands. But **FRANK's** promise soon faded in the October whirlwind of U.S. Navy Hellcats and USAAF bomber groups that swept across central Luzon and Formosa. By late December the **HAYATE** units had been crushed, and only veterans the likes of Sgt. Fukuda would sortie alone, or with a single wingman, in support of the "special attack units" dedicated to *tiatari.* This profile is a viable rendering of "**FRANK white 63**" bearing the Sentai's graphic "71" on its weathered tail surface. On 7 January, Sgt. Fukuda would intervene for an OSCAR pilot dueling with three P-38s within the haze just above the jungle. It is highly unlikely he knew the Ki-43 pilot, nor would he have known their opponents were "Satins Angels" led by Major McGuire. Undeterred, he shot down McGuire's able wingman, Maj. Rittmayer, before he withdrew in his damaged **HYATE** that would never fly again.

[22.] **Republic P-47D-28-RA THUNDERBOLT** s.n. 42-29046 **A/C #40** pilot unknown for **310 FS / 58 FG** at Linguyan airdrome, Luzon Island, early '45. Consigned as a Stateside advanced training unit since early '43, CO Col. G.G. Atkinson finally got his eager **THUNDERBOLT** pilots to the fight in New Guinea in early '44. After ten months of rear action tactical sorties from Dobodura to the Celebes Islands and Halmahera, the "**JUG**" pilots advanced to the front at embattled Tacloban in mid-November. Atkinson's journeymen fully proved their metal on 25 December, when a late-day signal alerted all to the Imperial naval destroyers bearing down on the new Mindoro Island beachhead. Afforded no time to arm with heavy ordinance, the determined P-47 pilots with "*eight .50's*" firepower alone, swept down to a point-blank strafing so fierce that the enemy ships withdrew in total disarray; an endeavor worthy of the resultant Distinguished Unit Citation. In the last eight months, long ranging "**JUGs**" the likes of **#40** from the **310 FS** scoured the enemy from the P.I., and flying from Ie Shima, they turned their point-blank assault on Kyushu.

[23.] **North American F-6K-15-NT MUSTANG** s.n. 44-12833 **A/C #16 "*We Three*"** of CO Maj. G.K. Noland **110 TFS** "Musketeers"/ **71 TFG** / Ie Shima airfield August '45. Since mid-'43, 5 FC's **71st recon group** flew an eclectic issue of A/C to "*wreck and record*" the enemy's eighteen months of retreat from New Guinea, the Celebes, and Halmahera. In the P.I., the **110 TFS** "Musketeers" would be one of the first arrivals at Tacloban and immediately displayed what an incensed photo-fighter pilot could inflict upon an airborne opponent. From 7 November '44 to the last days of January '45, thirteen different "Musketeers" accounted for 14 aerial kills; all with the vintage P-40N WARHAWK. Seven months later, when they moved up to Ie Shima under Maj. Roland's command, he demonstrated what his **F-6K #16 "*We Three*"** equipped with its phenomenal K-14 gun sight could exact in a dogfight. Two of his three OSCAR victims were confirmed and five more were accredited to his wingmen after their encounter over northwest Kyushu on 8 August. They were the last MUSTANG aerial kills for the 5 FC.

[24.] **Lockheed P-38L-20 (?) LO** s.n. unknown for A/C **"yellow 8"** of the **35 FS** "Black Panthers" / **8 FG** at Ie Shima airdrome, August '45. It began in May '42, with 5 FC's fledgling **35th** "Black Panthers" **Pursuit Squadron** venturing off to an inauspicious defense of Port Moresby. Barely three years later, a "Black Panther" sortie of five novice P-38 pilots would set off on 14 August from Ie Shima to escort a PBY rescue mission to northwest Kyushu. Just past noon, "Panther leader" Capt. R.F. Meyers, Jr., in his **"yellow 8,"** had his rookie wingmen orbiting at 14,000 feet above the PBY, searching down on the deck, when six FRANKs of the 47th Sentai attacked from overhead. In the next five minutes, Meyers would account for two of five FRANKs to be claimed in the exchange for the loss of Lt. D.L. Keiffer. Ironically, the *sentai* pilots were as untried as the Panthers and boldly declared all the American P-38s were shot down in honor of their wingmen lost in service to the Emperor. So ended the last aerial contest for the "Black Panther" Squadron of the 8 FG and the 5th Fighter Command.

## *Other Books by William Wolf*

---

*Death Rattlers: Marine Squadron VMF-323 over Okinawa*

*Victory Roll: The American Fighter Pilot and Aircraft in World War II*

*American Fighter-Bombers in World War II: USAAF Jabos in the MTO and ETO*

*13th Fighter Command in World War II: Air Combat over Guadalcanal and the Solomons*

*Boeing B-29 Superfortress: The Ultimate Look: from Drawing Board to VJ-Day*

*Consolidated B-32 Dominator: The Ultimate Look: from Drawing Board to Scrapyard.*

*Douglas B-18 Bolo: The Ultimate Look: from Drawing Board to U-Boat Hunter*

*North American B-25 Mitchell: The Ultimate Look: from Drawing Board to Flying Arsenal*

*U.S. Aerial Armament in World War II The Ultimate Look:*

*Vol.1: Guns, Ammunition, and Turrets*

*Vol.2: Bombs, Bombsights, and Bombing*

*Vol.3: Air-Launched Rockets, Guided Missles and Secret Weapons*

*The Fifth Fighter Command in World War II: Volume I: Pearl Harbor to the Reduction of Rabaul*